AA Lifestyle Guides in association with
Millennium & Copthorne Hotels

KU-410-221

WIN one of 20
Fabulous 'Weekends Away' for two
in 5 Free Prize Draws

see overleaf for terms & conditions

Enjoy a break with a difference with Millennium & Copthorne Hotels. Choose from any one of the 17 exclusive 4-star hotels around the UK, offering the highest standard of accommodation, food and leisure facilities.
The recipe for a perfect weekend away.

MILLENNIUM
HOTELS AND RESORTS

For more information on Millennium & Copthorne Hotels, call 0845 30 20001, quoting "AA Lifestyle Guides".

HOW TO ENTER

Just complete (in capitals please) and send off this card or alternatively, send your name and address on a stamped postcard to the address overleaf (no purchase required). Entries are limited to one per household and to residents of the UK and Republic of Ireland over the age of 18. This card will require a stamp if posted in the Republic of Ireland. **Closing date 6 September 2002.**

MR/MRS/MISS/MS/OTHER, PLEASE STATE:

NAME:

ADDRESS:

POSTCODE:

TEL. NOS: E-MAIL:

Are you an AA Member?   Yes/No

Have you bought this or any other AA Lifestyle Guide before?   Yes/No

If yes, please indicate the year of the last edition you bought:

AA Hotel Guide	____	AA Caravan & Camping (Europe) ____
AA Bed and Breakfast Guide	____	AA Britain Guide ____
AA Restaurant Guide	____	AA Days Out Guide ____
AA Pub Guide	____	Other, please state _____
AA Caravan & Camping (Britain & Ireland)	____	

If you do not wish to receive further information or special offers from AA Publishing please tick the box ☐

CCEU02

Terms and Conditions

1. Four winners will be drawn from each of the five prize draws to take place on 04 January, 08 March, 03 May, 05 July and 06 September 2002.

2. Closing date for receipt of entries is midday on the relevant draw date. Final close date for receipt of entries is 06 September 2002.

3. Entries received after any draw date other than the final one will go forward into the next available draw. Each entry will only be entered in one draw. Only one entry per household accepted.

4. Winners will be notified by post within 14 days of the relevant draw date.

5. Prizes must be booked within 3 months of the relevant draw date. Prizes are not transferable and there is no cash alternative.

6. This prize cannot be used in conjunction with any other discount, promotion or special offer.

7. Each prize consists of two nights' accommodation and full traditional breakfast for two adults sharing a standard twin/double room in a UK Millennium or Copthorne Hotel. Supplements may be charged for feature or family rooms. All accommodation is subject to availability.

8. Millennium & Copthorne Hotels provide all hotel accommodation, services and facilities and the AA is not party to your agreement with Millennium & Copthorne Hotels in this regard.

9. No purchase required

10. The prize draw is open to anyone resident in the UK or the Republic of Ireland over the age of 18, other than employees of the Automobile Association or Millennium & Copthorne Hotels, their subsidiary companies or their families or agents.

11. For a list of winners, please send a stamped, self addressed envelope to AA Lifestyle Guide Winners 2002, AA Publishing, Fanum House (4), Basingstoke, Hants, RG21 4EA.

12. If this card is posted in the Republic of Ireland, it must have an appropriate stamp.

13. Once a prize weekend has been booked, cancellation will invalidate the prize.

BUSINESS REPLY SERVICE
Licence No BZ 343

PLEASE NOTE: Requires a stamp if posted in Republic of Ireland

AA Lifestyle Guide 2002 Prize Draw

AA PUBLISHING
FANUM HOUSE (4)
BASING VIEW
BASINGSTOKE
HANTS RG21 4EA

AA

caravan
AND camping
EUROPE

AA Lifestyle Guides

This edition published January 2002
© Automobile Association Developments Ltd 2002
Automobile Association Developments Ltd retains the copyright in the current edition © 2002 and in all
subsequent editions, reprints and amendments to editions

Mapping is produced by the Cartographic Department of Automobile Association Developments Ltd from the
Automaps database using electronic and computer technology.
Maps © Automobile Association Developments Ltd 2001

The directory is compiled by AA Information and Hotel Departments
and generated from the AA's establishment database

The contents of this publication are believed correct at the time of printing. Nevertheless,
the publishers cannot be held responsible for any errors or omissions or for changes in the details given in this
guide, or for the consequences of any reliance on the information provided by the same.
We have tried to ensure accuracy in this guide but things do change and we should be grateful if readers would
advise us of any inaccuracies they may encounter.

Filmset by Avonset, 11 Kelso Place, Bath BA1 3AU
Printed and bound in Italy by Rotolito, Lombarda SpA

Advertisement Sales: advertisingsales@theAA.com
Editorial: lifestyleguides@theAA.com

A CIP catalogue record for this book is available from the British Library
ISBN 0 7495 3218 1
Published by AA Publishing, a trading name of
Automobile Association Developments Limited, whose registered office is
Millstream, Maidenhead Road, Windsor, Berkshire, SL4 5GD.
Registered number 1878835

CONTENTS

HOW TO USE THIS GUIDE

Each country in this guide is divided into regions, so that you can easily find all the sites in your chosen holiday area. Within the regions, place names are listed in alphabetical order, and details of site locations can be found on the country maps at the back of this book. If you need overnight stops on the way to your destination, the country maps should help you find something in the right place. Please remember that these maps are for town location purposes only and not for finding your way around. For route planning and use on the road, you should have a road atlas, such as the AA Big Road Atlas of Europe. Individual atlases of France, Germany and Italy are also available in the series.

ADVANCE BOOKING

Despite the carefree nature of a camping or caravanning holiday, it is best to book well in advance for peak holiday seasons, or for your first and last stop close to a ferry crossing point. However, we do find that some sites will not accept reservations. Although the AA cannot undertake to find sites or make reservations for you, we do include in this guide specimen booking letters in English, French, German, Italian and Spanish.

Please note that, although it is not common practice, some campsites may regard your deposit as a booking fee which is not deductible from the final account.

ON ARRIVAL

Look over the site if possible before you decide to stay. The information for any publication must be collected some time in advance, and ownership and standards may well have changed since our research was done. Even where standards are of the expected quality, the site may be very crowded and you may prefer to look elsewhere for more space and less noise. The descriptions in our guide are very brief, and are compiled from brochures provided by the sites. They are given only as a very loose guide.

When you look over a site, consider the following:

- Pleasant general situation, clean and tidy with plenty of refuse bins, site fenced and guarded.
- Sufficient and clean lavatories, washing facilities and showers with hot water. Well defined roads on site, preferably lit at night.
- Pitches should not be cramped.
- If you have a tent, make sure the surface is suitable for pegs; if you have a caravan, make sure the ground is firm enough.
- In hot weather there should be suitable shade, and if the weather is damp the ground should appear well drained.
- A good supply of safe drinking water.
- If you need the following facilities, confirm that they exist on the site: electric point for razors, Camping Gaz, a well stocked shop, laundry facilities, restaurant serving reasonably priced food, ice for sale.

Although most of the sites in this guide have been selected for the high standards they maintain, we have included, at the request of AA members, a number of sites along touring routes and others near the Channel ports which are suitable for overnight stops. These transit sites tend to become crowded at the height of the season, but provide the necessary amenities.

If you require information on additional sites, lists are free from most national tourist offices. In the introductions for each country we give details of local organisations which either publish a camping guide or provide more detailed information.

CAMPSITE ENTRIES

In order to update our information we send out questionnaires each year to every campsite. Inevitably a number of the questionnaires are not returned to us in time for publication, and where this is the case the campsite name is printed in italics. Most of the sites listed here take both tents and caravans unless otherwise stated.

PRICES

Prices are given in local currencies and are detailed per night, per adult, car, caravan and tent. Most prices will be in Euros, which will make things a lot simpler for those travelling to more than one country. We do not give charges relating to children, as these vary, but generally a 50 per cent reduction is made for children aged 3-14. To determine the cost of one night, simply add up the prices that apply to your party.

Some campsites do have different ways of structuring their prices. Whatever the variations may be, these should be reflected in the entry. Exceptions are:

pp Campsite charges per person. The charge for the vehicle and caravan/tent is included in the price for each person. For a party of four people, multiply the **pp** price by four for the total cost per night.

pitch This is the price per pitch, regardless of whether it is a caravan or a tent. Where the word pitch follows the 'A' for adult price, you should multiply the 'A' price by the number of adults in the party, then add the pitch price to that total to obtain the cost per night for your party.

OPENING TIMES

Dates shown are inclusive of opening dates. If the site is open all year, then 'All year' is written in the entry. All information was correct at the time of going to press, but we recommend you check with the site before arriving. Changes in opening times often occur because of demand and/or weather. Sometimes only restricted facilities are available between October and April.

COMPLAINTS

If you have any complaint about a site, do discuss the problem with the site proprietor immediately so that the matter can be dealt with promptly. If a personal approach fails, inform the AA when you return home. We regret, however, that the AA cannot act as intermediary in any dispute, or attempt to gain refunds or compensation. Your comments, however, help us to prepare new editions. Please use the Readers' Report forms at the back of the guide.

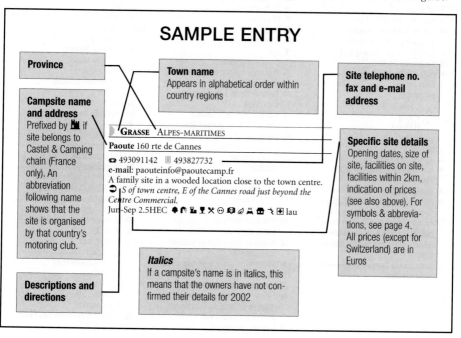

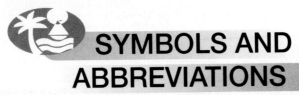

SYMBOLS AND ABBREVIATIONS

For a more detailed explanation refer to How to use this Guide (see contents page).

● ENGLISH ●

* adult
* car
* pp per person
* caravan or motor caravan — charge per night
* tent
* telephone
* HEC 1 hectare (equals approx 2 acres)
* grass
* sand
* stone
* little shade
* partly shaded
* mainly shaded
* shower
* shop
* cafe/restaurant
* bar
* no dogs
* electric points for razors
* electric points for caravans
* Camping Gaz International
* gas other than Camping Gaz
* bungalows for hire
* caravans for hire
* tents for hire
* swimming:
  * L lake
  * P pool
  * R river
  * S sea
* parking by tents permitted
* compulsory separate car park
* facilities not on site, but within 2km
* first-aid facilities
* site belongs to 'Castels & Camping Caravanning' chain (France only)
* CM camping municipal, parque municipal de campismo, or parque de la camara municipal (local authority site)
* KC Kommunens Campingplads (local authority site)
* lau laundry
* pitch pitch charge per night for car with tent or caravan (there is usually a charge per adult in addition to this)
* Cont. Entry continued overleaf

Entries in italics indicate that particulars have not been confirmed by management.

Pour plus amples informations veuillez vous referer a How to use this Guide (voir la table de matières).

● FRANCAIS ●

* Adulte
* Voiture
* pp par personne
* Caravane ou camping car — tarif pour une nuit
* Tente
* Telephone
* 1 hectare (correspond a environ
* HEC 2 acres (mesures imperiales))
* Gazon
* Sable
* Pierres
* Peu ombrage
* En partie ombrage
* Surtout ombrage
* Douches
* Magasin
* Cafe/restaurant
* Bar
* Chiens non admis
* Prises de courant pour rasoirs electriques
* Branchements electriques pour caravanes
* Camping Gaz International
* Gaz autre que Camping Gaz
* Bungalows à louer
* Caravanes à louer
* Tentes à louer
* Natation:
  * L Lac
  * P Piscine
  * R Rivère
  * S Mer
* Stationnement voiture près des tentes autorisé
* Utilisation des parkings voitures obligatoire
* Amenities pas sur le terrain, mais au plus, a 2km
* Poste de premiers-secours
* Terrain fait partie de la chaine 'Castels & Camping Caravanning' (en France seulement)
* CM Camping municipal

* KC Kommunens Campingplads (camping municipal)
* lau Blanchisserie
* pitch Tarif d'un emplacement pour une nuit pour voiture avec tente ou caravane (en general s'ajoute un tarif par adulte)
* Cont. Suite au verso

Une insertion imprime en italiques indique que la direction de l'etablissement n'a pas confirme les precisions.

Fur weitere Angaben beziehen Sie sich auf How to use this Guide (siehe Inhaltsverzeichnis).

● DEUTSCH ●

* Erwachsene (r)
* Auto
* pp Pro person
* Caravan bzw. Campingbus — Preis pro nacht
* Zelt
* Telefon
* HEC 1 Hektar (ca 2 acres)
* Grasboden
* Sandgelande
* Steiniges Gelande
* Wenig Schatten
* Teilschattig
* Grosstenteilsschattig
* Dusche
* Laden
* Imbiss/Restaurant
* Bar
* Hundeverbot
* Stromanschlusse fur Rasierapparate
* Stromanschlusse fur Caravans
* Camping Gaz International
* Gas ausser Camping Gaz International
* Mietbungalows
* Mietcaravans
* Mietzelte
* Schwimmen
  * L See
  * P Schwimmbad
  * R Fluss
  * S Meer
* Abstellen des PKWs neben dem Zelt gestattet
* Separates Abstellen des PKWs obligatorisch

◆ Einrichtungen nicht an Ort und Stelle aber nicht weiter als 2 Kilometer entfernt
⊞ Unfallstation
🏠 Platz gehort der 'Castels & Camping Caravanning' (nur Frankreich)
CM Stadischer Campingplatz
KC Kommunens Campingplads (stadischer Campingplatz)
lau Wascherei
pitch Stellplatzpreis pro Nacht fur Auto mit Zelt bzw. Caravan (normaler weise eine zusatzliche Berechnung pro Erwachsener)
Cont. siehe umseitig

Eine kursiv gedruckte Eintragung zeigt an, dass die entsprechenden Angaben nicht von der Direktion bestatigt worden sind.

Per una spiegazione piu dettagliata, consultare la sezione How to use this Guide (vedi indice).

● ITALIANO ●

🚶 Adulto ⎤
🚗 Vettura ⎟
pp a persona ⎬ Prezzo per notte
🚐 Roulotte o ⎟
   camper ⎦
🔺 Tenda
☎ Telefono
HEC 1 ettaro (pari a 2 acri circa)
▥▥▥ Erba
∴∴∴ Sabbia
◈ Pietra
🌿 Poca ombra
🌤 Ombreggiato in parte
🌳 Ombreggiato in gran parte
🚿 Doccia
🛒 Negozio
✕ Caffe ristorante
🍷 Bar
🐕 Proibito ai cani
⊙ Prese elettriche rasoi
🔌 Prese elettriche roulotte
⊘ Camping Gaz Internatioal
⚑ Altri tipi di gas che non siano il Camping Gaz
🏠 Alffittansi bungalows
🚐 Affittansi roulotte
🔺 Affittansi tende
🏊 Nuoto
   L Lago
   P Piscina
   R Fiume
   S Mare
🅿 E permesso parcheggiare vicino alle tende

🅿 E obbligatorio parcheggiare nel posteggio apposito
◆ Le attrezzature non sono nel campeggio, bensi in un raggio di 2km
⊞ Proto soccorso
🏠 If campeggio appartienne alla catena 'Castels & Camping Caravanning' (per la Francia solamente)
CM Camping municipal (campeggio municipale)
KC Kommunens Campingplads (Campeggio municipale)
lau Lavanderia
pitch Prezzo pe notte di un posto macchina e tenda o roulotte (di solito ciascun adulto paga un extra oltre al posto macchina)
Cont. La lista delle voci continua a tergo

Le voci in corsivo stanno a indicare che i particolari non sono stati confermati dalla Direzione.

Para una explicacion mas detallada, consultese la section How to use this Guide (vease el indice de materias).

● ESPANOL ●

🚶 Adulto ⎤
🚗 Automovil ⎟
pp Por persona ⎬ Precio por
🚐 Rulota o ⎟ noche
   coche-rulota ⎦
🔺 Tienda
☎ Telefono
HEC 1 hectarea (igual a 2 acres aproximadamente)
▥▥▥ Hierba
∴∴∴ Arena
◈ Piedra
🌿 Poca sombra
🌤 Sombreado en parte
🌳 Sombreado en su mayor parte
🚿 Ducha
🛒 Almacen
✕ Cafe/restaurante
🍷 Bar
🐕 Se prohiben los perros
⊙ Tomas de corriente para maquinillas electricas
🔌 Tomas de corriente para rulotas
⊘ Camping Gaz International
⚑ Otros tipos de gas que no sean el Gaz International
🏠 Se alquilan bungalows
🚐 Se alquiln rulotas
🔺 Se alquin tiendas
🏊 Natacion:

L Lago
P Piscina
R Rio
S Mar
🅿 Se permite estacionar el coche junto a las tiendas
🅿 Prohibido estacionarse fuera del aparacamiento
◆ Los servicios no estan en el camping, sino en un radio de 2km
⊞ Puesto de socorro
🏠 Este camping pertenece al grupo 'Castle & Camping Caravanning' (para Francia solamente)
CM Camping municipal
KC Kommunens Campingplads (camping municipal)
lau Lavanderia
pitch Precio por noche de un puesto para coche y tienda o rulota (cada adulto pagara un suplemento ademas del precio susodicho)
Cont. La lista de simbolos continua a la vuelta

Los articulos en bastardilla indican que los detalles no han sido confirmados por la Direccion.

7

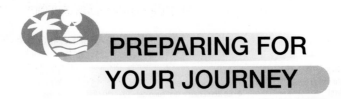

PREPARING FOR YOUR JOURNEY

PLEASE READ THIS SECTION BEFORE YOU SET OFF ON YOUR JOURNEY, EVEN IF YOU ARE AN EXPERIENCED TRAVELLER, AND ALSO READ THE FOLLOWING SECTION ON MOTORING INFORMATION, AND THE APPROPRIATE COUNTRY INTRODUCTIONS.

Before setting off on your Continental holiday, there are certain preparations you should make and some regulations you should know about. Experienced campers and caravanners will, of course, be familiar with most of this, but we hope it will be a useful chapter for newcomers.

PREPARING YOUR CARAVAN

Your caravan should of course be regularly serviced, but the following tips could be useful, especially for the first trip after winter storage.

Just before your trip give the caravan a good airing. If you have a water pump fitted, check the flow and, after sterilising the system, flush with clean water to get rid of any staleness. Make sure that there are no leaks and replace any doubtful washers. Examine all potential leak spots, especially around window rubbers, rear light clusters and roof lights, applying sealing compound as necessary. Test all window, cupboard and locker catches to make sure that they shut firmly. Outside, clean rain gutters and make sure down-spouts and window channel drainpipes are clear.

BRAKES

Check that the caravan braking mechanism is correctly adjusted. If it has a breakaway safety mechanism, the cable between car and caravan must be firmly anchored so that the trailer brakes act immediately if the two part company.

LIGHTS

Make sure that all the lights are working - rear lights, stop lights, number-plate lights, rear fog guard lamps and flashers (check that the flasher rate is correct: 60-120 times a minute).

TYRES

Both tyres on the caravan should be of the same size and type. Make sure that the tread depth is well above the legal minimum (see Continental ABC) and that there is no uneven wear. Look also for cuts and for cracks that might have developed during the winter. Replace any suspect tyres and any tyres over five years old, irrespective of the amount of tread remaining. Remember, caravan tyres rarely wear out but do deteriorate with age.

PREPARING YOUR TENT

Some weeks before your holiday, choose a fine day, spread the tent on the lawn or some other space so that you can make a close inspection of all potential stress points: where guylines attach, where the ground sheet meets tent walls, and where the frame poles come into contact with fabric. The fabric of the tent can be damaged by branches or sharp objects and by mildew if it has not been stored correctly. Additionally, it can lose its proofing through long exposure to the weather, as a result of being splashed by cooking fat or by washing-up water containing detergent. If your tent is damaged in this way, consult a specialist camping supplier. Patch kits of different colours and materials are available, as are proofing preparations and sprays.

PREPARING YOUR CAMPING EQUIPMENT

Use this camping equipment check list when you are planning what to take:

- Air mattress and pump, or camp beds
- All-purpose knife
- Bucket
- Camp stove and fuel
- Clothes-line and pegs
- Cutlery, including cooking utensils
- Dishcloths, scouring pad, and tea towels
- First-aid kit
- Folding chairs or stools
- Folding table

- Food containers
- Ground sheet
- Icebox (portable)
- Kettle
- Mallet
- Matches
- Plastic bags or bags for litter
- Plates, cups and saucers, or mugs
- Rope
- Saucepans, frying pan
- Sleeping bags
- Small brush (useful when camping on sand)
- Teapot
- Tent, poles, tent pegs (spares), sand pegs and discs
- Tent-tidy (for scissors, string, needles, thread, etc.)
- Tin-opener, bottle-opener, and corkscrew
- Torch and batteries
- Washing powder
- Washing-up bowl and washing-up liquid
- Water and milk containers
- Water-purifying tablets
- Windshield

HOW TO ENSURE GOOD ROAD HANDLING

Before you load all your luggage and equipment into the caravan, check on the weight restrictions that apply to it and to the towing vehicle. The laden weight of the caravan should always be less than, and ideally no more than 85 per cent of the kerbside weight of the towing vehicle.

The kerbside weight is defined as: the weight of the vehicle plus fuel and other necessary liquids (e.g. water, oil, brake fluid, etc.) but with no passengers and no load other than normal tools and equipment.

The weight of the caravan is normally specified in the purchase literature, and usually refers to the weight 'ex works' or 'mass in running order (MIRO)'. This can be misleading because it is normally based on the standard model and may not take into account any fitted extras; one way to be certain is to take the caravan to your local public weighbridge. Once you have the accurate unladen weight, subtract that from the manufacturer's recommended gross weight, ('maximum technically permissable weight' - MTPW) and the figure you arrive at will be the amount of equipment you can safely load into the caravan. Remember that, ideally,

the gross weight of the caravan should not exceed 85 per cent of the kerbside weight of your car as given in the manufacturer's handbook. If in doubt, return the caravan to the weighbridge once fully loaded.

Loading can greatly affect the stability of the car-caravan combination on the road. Keep as much weight as possible near the trailer axle, and store heavy equipment on the caravan floor. Never store heavy items at the rear of the caravan in an attempt to counterbalance an excessive nose weight - this causes instability and can be very dangerous. Keep the roof lockers free of luggage if possible and ensure lockers, drawers and cupboards are securely closed so there are no loose items that could roll about.

After loading, check that the caravan, when coupled to the car, is level with the ground, or slightly nose down. If the nose is up, this can be corrected by a hitch height adjuster, available from caravan manufacturers or dealers. An adapter plate can be used to lower the tow-ball mounting, but it does put extra pressure on the bracket.

Check that the nose weight of the trailer complies with the car manufacturer's recommendations. As a guide, the nose weight should be heavier than the rear by about 40-50kg (90-119lbs). Check the nose weight of the laden caravan with bathroom scales and blocks of wood or a spring balance. A twin-axle trailer must be weighed when the coupling is at the exact towing height. Obtaining the ideal weight and weight distribution of the car-trailer combination helps prevent pitching and snaking. Pitching can also be prevented by stiffening the towing car's rear suspension - either fit a supplementary rubber or air spring unit to the rear spring, or use heavier duty shock absorbers, (more expensive) but always ensure first that the car's front and rear shock absorbers are in good condition.

Excessive pitching and/or bad weight distribution can lead to snaking as the vertical movement sways the caravan sideways. This can be particularly dangerous, since the first instinct is to steer against the movement, which only makes matters worse. The best course is to steer straight and gently decelerate. Stabilisers are available, but it is far better to cure the cause. When choosing a car with which you intend to tow a caravan or trailer, remember that the amount of overhang - the distance between the car's rear axle and the towing ball - has an effect on the handling. The greater the overhang the more difficult handling will be.

A FEW FINAL CHECKS

- corner steadies are fully wound up and the brace is handy for when you arrive on site;
- windows, vents and doors are firmly shut;
- any fires or flames are extinguished and the tap on the gas cylinder is turned off;
- the coupling is firmly in position and the breakaway cable is attached;
- the over-run brake is working correctly;
- both car mirrors give good visibility ;
- all the car and caravan lights are working;
- the safety catch on the hitch is on;
- the jockey wheel is raised and secured, the handbrake is released, and the fire extinguishers are operational and close at hand.

Much of the art of towing comes with experience, but many of the problems can be eliminated by being aware:

- Know your car well before attempting to tow.
- Stop before you get tired.
- Plan to use roads suitable for towing.
- Have the appropriate mirrors and use them.
- If traffic builds up behind you, pull up safely and let it pass.
- Keep a safe stopping distance between you and the vehicle in front.
- Switch on your headlights whenever visibility becomes poor.
- Make good use of the gears on hills.
- Allow plenty of time when overtaking or pulling across a main road.
- Never stop on narrow roads, bends, crests of hills, or anywhere that could be dangerous
- In case of breakdown or accident, use hazard flashers and warning triangle(s).

OFF-ROAD HANDLING

On site you may encounter difficult ground. Try to avoid pitches liable to be waterlogged; sand that will not take the force of a driving wheel;

and stone and shingle that provide no grip.

If you have to drive over difficult ground, keep moving slowly with a very light throttle. If you stop, do not accelerate hard or the wheels will spin and dig in. Move gently backwards and forwards to get out of a dip. If the driving wheels do dig in, put brushwood or sacks in front of and behind the wheels. To move the trailer manually, pull sideways on the drawbar and then work the trailer forwards by chocking alternate wheels.

CAMPING FUELS

(This information is intended as a guide only. Full safety regulations and legal information should be obtained from the suppliers or manu-facturers of your equipment.)

Gas in cylinders or bottles, as used in caravans, is mainly of two types, butane and propane. Both are kept as liquid under pressure and become a combustible gas once the pressure is released. They are available on the Continent, but propane is more widely distributed in countries with low winter temperatures. Propane has a higher pressure than butane. See also the paragraph on Branded Gases, below.

CARRIAGE OF GAS BY CAR FERRIES

Vehicles carrying unsealed cylinders of liquefied petroleum gas (LPG) must report at both United Kingdom and European ports for a leakage test at least 30 minutes before the published reporting time. A maximum of three Home Office approved cylinders, not exceeding 35lb net weight each, or up to 12 small expendable cartridges, sealed and packed in an outer container, are allowed for each caravan. Cylinders should be securely fixed in or on the caravan as intended by the caravan manufacturer.

New users of LPG particularly should follow safety instructions and experienced people sometimes need reminding of the safety rules:

- change cylinders with care
- provide fresh air for safe combustion
- don't improvise or tamper with equipment
- have regular maintenance carried out by qualified engineers

GAS SAFETY RULES

1 Always use the right type and length of hose for connections If in doubt, ask the dealer's advice.

2 Replace worn hose. Never try repairs.

3 When fitting the hose, where applicable use worm-drive clips and ensure they are tight.

4 Always use a spanner when fitting connections - finger tightness is not enough. Before fitting a regulator or other screwed connection to a butane cylinder, always ensure that the sealing washer is there and in good condition. When fitting to switch-on or clip-on valves, refer to the manufacturer's or supplier's instructions.

5 Check for leaks by applying soapy water. Any leaks will be shown by bubbles.

6 *Never* check for leaks with a naked flame.

7 Always keep containers away from excessive heat or naked flames.

8 When starting, open container valve slowly.

9 If the container is not to be used for a while close the valve, remove the pressure regulator and replace the valve cover if fitted.

10 When changing a cartridge or container, keep away from any naked light, flame or source of ignition. Ensure good ventilation. With cartridge appliances, check that the sealing washer, usually housed in the appliance inlet connection, is in position and in good condition. Make sure that the valve on the container, where fitted, and the tap on the regulator are fully closed. Never try to change a pierceable cartridge (such as the Camping Gaz type) until you are sure all the gas has been expended. You can usually hear any gas remaining by gently shaking.

11 Once the pressure regulators are set they should not be tampered with. Adjustments or repairs should be left to a dealer.

12 Containers must always stand upright, valves uppermost, whether in use or not. Carry them upright, but not by the valve.

13 Whether full or empty, never store the containers below ground or near drains, as all these gases are heavier than air and will collect at the lowest point in the event of a leak.

14 Good ventilation is essential where gas burning appliances are used. Un-flued appliances must not be installed in sleeping areas. Only room-sealed appliances should be installed in bath or shower rooms.

15 When moving, turn off all appliances and cylinder valves.

16 Do not sleep in a room where gas cylinders are in use.

17 Permanent storage must always be outdoors.

18 When fitting cylinders, always check that the cylinder valve is fully closed in a clockwise direction before removing the valve-sealing cap or plug.

Camping: Single-burner picnic set or double-burner camp stove with 4.5kg butane cylinder

Motor Caravan: Two-burner hotplate or two-burner hotplate grill with 4.5kg butane cylinder

Caravan: Two-burner hotplate or small cooker, with 4.5kg butane cylinder with screw-on connections or 15kg butane cylinder or 7kg butane cylinder which will both accept the switch-on regulator. Take two 4.5kg or two 7kg.

If you follow the instructions a 4.5kg cylinder will last a month on either single or double-burner units.

If you cannot take enough Calor Gas cylinders in your outfit, you are advised to buy a Camping Gaz connecting tap before leaving this country.

PARAFFIN

Paraffin (petrole or kerosene) is not easily obtainable in country districts in Europe and you are advised to get supplies on arrival in large towns. Methylated spirit (alcoöl à brûler) is easier to get.

SAFETY

• Always make sure you have the right size and type of gas cartridge for the appliance.

• Never put a cartridge in a cartridge holder unless the upper part of the appliance has been unscrewed and completely removed.

• A cartridge with gas in it must never be removed from an appliance nor must the upper part of the appliance be unscrewed.

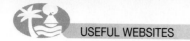

ONLINE RESOURCES

Here are a selection of useful websites that may offer relevant
information to campers, caravanners and travellers generally. These addresses are provided for
information only, and The AA cannot be held responsible for the content of these websites.

Camping:

www.calorgas.co.uk - Official site of Calor Gas

www.lpga.co.uk - Offical site of LP Gas, suppliers of Liquid Petroleum Gas

www.caravanclub.co.uk - Site of Britain's major caravan club.

www.gear-zone.co.uk - Major suppliers of camping gear

Official UK Government Sites:

www.fco.gov.uk/travel: Site of the Foreign and Commonwealth Office. Travellers'
rights, 'Know Before You Go' info on topical issues, and what to do if things go wrong.

www.hmce.gov.uk: Official HM Customs & Excise website

www.passport.gov.uk - Passport Agency Website

www.defra.gov.uk - Official Pet Travel Site of DEFRA

European Union Issues / The Euro etc:

europa.eu.int/euro - Official site of the Euro currency

europa.eu.int - Official site of the European Union On-Line

Tourist sites:

Austria: www.austria-tourism.at - Official Site of the Austrian National Tourist Office

Belgium: www.belgium-tourism.net - Official Site of the OPT (Office for the
Promotion of Tourism in Walloon + Brussels)

www.visitflanders.com - Official Site of Toerisme Vlaanderen (Tourism Flanders)

France: www.franceguide.com -
Official Site of the French Government Tourist Board/Maison de la France

Germany: www.germany-tourism.de -
Official Site of the German National Tourist Board

Italy: www.enit.it - Official Site of the Italian State Tourism Board

Luxembourg: www.luxembourg.co.uk -
Official Site of London's Luxembourg Tourist Office

Netherlands: www.holland.com/uk - Official Site of Netherlands Board of Tourism

Portugal: www.portugal.org/tourism + www.portugalinsite.pt - Official tourist sites

Spain: www.okspain.org - Official Site of the Tourist Office of Spain

Andorra: www.turisme.ad - Official Site of the Ministry of Tourism and Culture

Switzerland: www.myswitzerland.com - Official Site of Switzerland Tourism

CONTINENTAL ABC MOTORING
AND GENERAL INFORMATION

This ABC provides a general background of motoring regulations and general information, and is designed to be read in combination with the relevant country introductions.

Motoring laws on the Continent should cause little difficulty to British motorists, but drivers should take more care and extend greater courtesy than they would normally do at home, and bear in mind the essentials of good motoring - avoiding any action likely to obstruct traffic, endanger persons or cause damage to property.

Road signs are mainly the familiar international ones, but in every country there are exceptions; watch especially for signs showing crossings and speed limits. Probably the most unfamiliar aspect of motoring abroad to British motorists is the rule giving priority to traffic coming from the right, and unless this priority is varied by signs, it must be strictly observed.

A tourist driving abroad should always carry a current passport, a full valid national driving licence (even when an International Driving Permit is held), the vehicle registration document and certificate of motor insurance. The proper international distinguishing sign should be displayed on the rear of the vehicle and any caravan or trailer. The appropriate papers must be carried at all times. The practice of spot checks on foreign cars is widespread; to avoid inconvenience or a police fine, be sure that your papers are in order and that the international distinguishing sign is of the approved standard design.

Make sure that you have clear all-round vision. See that your seat belts are securely mounted and undamaged, and remember that in most Continental countries their use is compulsory. If you carry skis remember that their tips should point to the rear. You must be sure that your vehicle complies with the regulations concerning dimensions for all the countries you intend to pass through (see below and relevant country introductions). This is particularly necessary if you are towing

a trailer of any sort.

Mechanical repairs and replacement parts can be very expensive abroad and many breakdowns occur because the vehicle has not been properly prepared before the journey, which may involve many miles of hard driving over unfamiliar roads.

We recommend a major service by a franchised dealer before you go abroad. You should also carry out your own general check for any audible or visible defects.

It is not practicable to provide a complete check list, but consult the ABC below under the following headings:

Automatic gearboxes
Automatic transmission fluid
Brakes
Cold-weather touring
Direction indicators
Electrical
Engine and mechanical
Lights
Spares
Tyres
Warm-climate touring

Also consult your manufacturer's handbook. AA members can arrange a thorough check of their car by one of the AA's experienced engineers who will submit a written report, complete with a list of repairs required. There is a fee for this service. For more information or, if you wish to book an inspection, please telephone 0845 7500610.

A

ACCIDENTS

The country introductions give telephone numbers for the fire, police and ambulance services. International regulations are similar to those in the UK; the following action is usually required or advisable:

If you are involved in an accident you must stop. A warning triangle should be placed on the road at a suitable distance to warn following traffic of the obstruction. The use of hazard warning lights in no way affects the regulations governing the use of warning triangles. Get medical assistance for anyone injured in the accident. If the accident necessitates calling the police, leave the vehicle in the position in which it came to rest. If it seriously obstructs other traffic, mark the position of the vehicle on the road and get the details confirmed by independent witnesses before moving it.

The accident must be reported to the police in the following circumstances: if it is required by law, if the accident has caused death or bodily injury, or if an unoccupied vehicle or property has been damaged and there is no one present to represent the interests of the party suffering damage.

Be sure to notify your insurance company (by letter if possible), within 24 hours of the accident (see the conditions of your policy). If a third party is injured, contact your insurers for advice or, if you have a Green Card, notify the company or bureau given on the back of your Green Card; this company or bureau will deal with any compensation claim from the injured party. AA policy holders should refer to 'AA Policy Holders Driving Abroad' statement.

Make sure that all essential particulars are noted, especially details concerning third parties, and co-operate with police or other officials taking on-the-spot notes by supplying your name, address or other personal details as required. It is also a good idea to take photographs of the scene. Try to get good shots of other vehicles involved, their registration plates and any background which might help later enquiries. This record may be useful when completing the insurance company's accident form.

AUTOMATIC GEARBOXES

The fluid in an automatic gearbox does more work when it has to cope with the extra weight of a caravan. It becomes hotter and thinner, so there is more slip and more heat generated in the gearbox. Many manufacturers recommend the fitting of a gearbox oil cooler. Check with the manufacturer about what is suitable for your car.

AUTOMATIC TRANSMISSION FLUID

Automatic transmission fluid is not always readily available, especially in some of the more remote areas of Western Europe, so carry an emergency supply.

B

BBC WORLD SERVICE

The international radio arm of the BBC. It broadcasts in 43 languages, including a 24-hour-a-day English Service. World news is on the hour every hour and there are regular bulletins of British news.

If you want to listen to World Service when you are abroad, write for information and a free programme guide to: BBC World Service, Audience Relations, Bush House, London WC2B 4PH. Remember to state the country or countries you are visiting.

A monthly magazine, BBC On Air, provides details of all World Service programmes and frequencies, with background information about features and personalities. It costs £20.00 for an annual subscription. If you would like to receive details, please write to 'On Air', at the above address or browse their website at www.bbc.co.uk/worldservice/onair

If you are buying a new radio to listen to the BBC abroad, the World Service recommends that you choose a digitally tuned radio because it makes finding frequencies easier.

Make sure your short-wave set can receive some of the key European frequencies such as 9410 and 12095 kHz.

World Service programmes can also be heard on the Internet at:

www.bbc.co.uk/worldservice

BOATS

EU citizens may use their boats throughout the year in all EU countries provided VAT has been paid. However, the boats of non-EU citizens are still subject to temporary importation formalities.

All boats taken abroad by road should be registered in the UK, except for very small craft to be used close inshore in France. In France such craft are exempt from registration and the dividing line falls approximately between a Laser dinghy (which should be registered) and a Topper (which need not be); however, to avoid any confusion, registration is recommended. See also Identification Plate.

Registration is carried out by the Small Ships Register at the RSS. Currently the fee is £10 and provides registration for five years. The original Certificate of Registration is required - a photocopy is not acceptable. Application forms for Small Ships Registration, accompanied by notes on the purpose of the Register and eligibility for registration, are available from:

The Small Ships Register, PO Box 165, Cardiff CF14 5FU, telephone 029 2076 8205. Application forms are also available from some yacht/boat clubs, marinas and shipyards.

Of the countries in this guide, an International Certificate of Competence (ICC) and/or Coastal Skipper Certificate is required or recommended for Belgium, France, Germany, Italy, the Netherlands, Portugal and Spain. For further information, contact the Royal Yachting Association, RYA House, Romsey Road, Eastleigh, Hampshire SO50 9YA. telephone 023 8062 7461

The UN agreement covering the ICC has been changed. Those renewing out-of-date certificates and wanting 'inland waters' endorsement must take a test on CEVNI rules. A rules booklet is obtainable from the RYA cost £5.99 including postage.

On 16 June 1998 the Recreational Craft Directive came fully into force. This requires the CE mark on new boats, but has no retrospective effect. Proof of use in EU waters before this date may become a useful document when visiting other EU countries.

Of the countries in this guide, third party insurance is compulsory for boats in Italy, Spain and Switzerland, and advisable elsewhere. A translation of the insurance certificate into the appropriate language is usually required.

BRAKES

Car brakes must always be in peak condition. Check both the level in the brake fluid reservoir and the thickness of the brake lining/pad material. The brake fluid should be completely changed according to the manufacturer's instructions. It is always advisable to change the brake fluid before starting a Continental holiday, particularly if the journey includes travelling through a hilly or mountainous area.

BREAKDOWN

If your car breaks down, try to move it to the side of the road, or to a position where it will obstruct the traffic flow as little as possible. Place a warning triangle at the appropriate distance on the road behind the obstruction. Bear in mind road conditions and, if near or on a bend, the triangle should be placed where it is clearly visible to following traffic. If the car is fitted with hazard warning lights these may only be effective on straight roads, and will have no effect at bends or rises in the road. If the fault is electrical, the lights may not operate, which is why they cannot take the place of a triangle.

Motorists are advised to take out AA Five Star Europe, the overseas motoring emergency service. You can purchase breakdown assistance benefits, and personal travel insurance. It is available to all motorists, but AA members recieve 10% off standard non-member prices for breakdown assistance.

For further information and/or brochures call: 0800 444500
(Republic of Ireland 01 617 9988).

NOTE: AA Personal Members with Options 200 - 400 have the free benefit of 72-hour European Breakdown cover in specified European countries.

Of the countries dealt with in this guide, cover is available in: Belgium, France, Germany, Luxembourg and the Netherlands for any number of trips of up to 72 hours. You must, however, register before each trip by phoning the AA on 0800 731 70 72.

BRITISH EMBASSIES/CONSULATES
(SEE ALSO COUNTRY INTRODUCTIONS)

In most Continental countries there is usually more than one British Consulate. The functions and office hours of Vice-Consulates and Honorary Consuls can be more restricted than those of full Consulates.

Consulates (and consular sections of the embassy) are ready to help British travellers overseas, but there are limits to what they can do. A consulate cannot pay your hotel, medical or any other bills, nor will they do the work of travel agents, information bureaux or police. Any loss or theft should first be reported to the local police, not the consulate, and a statement obtained confirming the loss or theft. If you still need help, such as an emergency passport or guidance on how to transfer funds, contact the consulate. See respective country introductions for addresses and locations of British Embassies and British Consulates.

For up-to-date travel advice see:
www.fco.gov.uk

C

CAMPING CARD INTERNATIONAL

A Camping Card International (CCI) is valid for 12 months from the date of issue. It may be purchased from the AA by anyone over 18 who is a personal member of the AA and/or a purchaser of AA Five Star Europe.*
(To obtain an application form, call the AA Information Centre on 0870 5500 600)

Recognised at most campsites in Europe, the camping card is essential in some cases and you will not be allowed to camp without it. At certain campsites a reduction to the advertised charge may be allowed on presentation of the camping card.

The camping card provides third-party insurance cover for up to 11 people camping away from home or staying in rented accommodation or at a hotel. Although the card is valid for 12 months, expiry of your AA membership invalidates the insurance coverage. Each card purchased is accompanied by a summary of the third-party insurance cover, conditions of use and details of the campers' code. A CCI Information and Discount booklet will also be provided.

On arrival at the campsite, report to the campsite manager who will tell you where you may pitch your tent or caravan. You may be asked to pay in advance, or alternatively, to give into charge the camping card for the length of your stay. Some campsite managers may also insist upon the retention of all passports.
*AA Five Star Europe provides temporary AA personal membership for the period of cover.

CARAVAN AND LUGGAGE TRAILERS

Take a list of contents, especially if any valuable or unusual equipment is being carried, as this may be required at a frontier. A towed vehicle should be readily identifiable by a plate in an accessible position showing the name of the maker of the vehicle and the production or serial number. See **Identification plate** and also **Principal mountain passes**.

CHANNEL TUNNEL
(SEE EUROTUUNEL)

CLAIMS AGAINST THIRD PARTIES

The law and levels of damages in foreign countries are different to our own. Some types of claim present difficulties, the most common relating to recovery of car hire charges. Rarely are they fully recoverable, and in some countries they may be drastically reduced or not recoverable at all. General damages for pain and suffering will often be considerably less than awards made in the UK.

The negotiation of claims against foreign insurers is extremely protracted and translation of documents slows the process. A delay of three months between sending a letter and getting a reply is not uncommon.

Legal costs and expenses are not recoverable in many Continental countries. The AA's overseas motoring emergency packages, such as Five Star Europe, include a discretionary service in certain matters arising abroad requiring legal assistance. This includes the pursuit of uninsured loss claims against third parties arising from an accident involving the insured vehicle. Policy holders should seek assistance from the AA.

COLD-WEATHER TOURING

If you are planning a winter tour, make sure that the strength of your antifreeze mixture is correct for low temperatures.

If travelling through snow-bound regions, it is important to remember that for many resorts and passes the authorities insist on wheel chains and/or winter tyres. However, chains should only be used when compulsory or necessary; prolonged use on hard surfaces may damage both the vehicle and the chains.

In fair weather, wheel chains are only necessary on the higher passes, but (as a rough guide) in severe weather you will probably need them at altitudes exceeding 610 metres (2000ft). Signposts usually indicate if wheelchains are compulsory.

Wheel or snow chains fit over the driving wheels to enable them to grip on snow or icy surfaces. Full-length chains which fit tightly round a tyre are the most satisfactory, but they must be fitted correctly. Check that they do not foul your vehicle bodywork; if your vehicle has front-wheel drive put the steering on full lock while checking. It is essential that you also check the vehicle's handbook for the manufacturer's recommendations. On some vehicles there is insufficient clearance between the tyre and bodywork and wheel chains cannot be used. Wheel or snow chains may be purchased from the AA's Dover and Eurotunnel shops. To check that the required size of chain is in stock, telephone Dover on 01304 208122. Winter or snow tyres are tyres with rugged treads which provide extra grip on snow and ice. Some are designed to take spikes or studs which require specialist fitting and removal limiting their use. In practice, although regulations exist, spikes or studs are seldom used in countries such as Austria and Switzerland. A vehicle equipped with winter tyres without spikes or studs may be used in all conditions. However, the use of winter tyres

does not remove the need to carry chains; such tyres are generally more effective, reducing the need to fit chains. If you travel regularly to Alpine regions it may be worth considering a set of winter tyres. Contact your local tyre dealer for more information.

NOTE: The above guidelines do not apply where extreme winter conditions prevail. For extreme conditions it is doubtful whether the cost of preparing a car normally used in the UK would be justified for a short period. However, the AA's Technical Advice Department can advise on specific enquiries.

COMPULSORY EQUIPMENT

All countries have differing regulations as to how vehicles circulating on their roads should be equipped, but generally domestic laws are not enforced on visiting foreigners. However, where a country considers aspects of safety or other factors are involved, they will impose some regulations on visitors and these will be mentioned in the country introductions.

CRASH (SAFETY) HELMETS

All countries in this guide require visiting motorcyclists and their passengers to wear crash or safety helmets.

CREDIT AND CHARGE CARDS

See under Payment Cards.

CURRENCY
(SEE ALSO COUNTRY SECTIONS)

There is no limit to the amount of sterling notes you may take abroad. However, it is recommended that you don't rely exclusively on any one payment method. A combination of a payment card, traveller's cheques and a small amount of local currency is suggested as the most practical arrangement.

Euro banknotes and coins were introduced on 1 January 2002 in the 12 countries of the Euro area* to replace national currencies. The banknotes have denominations of EUR 5, 10, 20, 50, 100, 200 and 500; the coins EUR 1 and 2 and cents 1, 2, 5, 10, 20 and 50. Most old currencies may still be exchanged after the changeover period according to the national arrangements in force.

*The 12 are Austria, Belgium, France,

Germany, Italy, Luxembourg, Netherlands, Portugal, Spain (included in this guide) plus Finland, Greece and the Republic of Ireland.

CUSTOMS REGULATIONS FOR CONTINENTAL COUNTRIES

Travelling Within The EU

People travelling within the EU are free to take not only personal belongings but a motor vehicle, boat, caravan or trailer across the internal frontiers without being subject to Customs formalities. EU countries are: Austria, Belgium, Denmark, Finland, France, Germany, Greece, Republic of Ireland, Italy, Luxembourg, Netherlands, Portugal, Spain (but not the Canaries), Sweden, UK (but not the Channel Islands). Gibraltar is part of the EU, but Customs allowances for outside the EU apply. When you return to the UK, use the blue exit reserved for EU travellers. You do not have to pay any tax or duty in the UK on goods you have bought in other EU countries for your own use, but you may be breaking the law if you sell alcohol or tobacco you have bought. If you are caught you face imprisonment, and/or confiscation of the goods and the vehicle in which they were transported. To help protect people in the UK, Customs carry out checks on some EU travellers to look for prohibited or restricted goods, including drugs, indecent or obscene material, firearms, ammunition, unlicensed animals and endangered species. This means they may ask you about your baggage. The law sets out guidelines for the amount of alcohol and tobacco you can bring into the UK. If you bring in more, you must be able to satisfy the Customs Officer that the goods are for your own use. If you cannot, the goods may be taken from you, and your vehicle may also be seized. The guidelines are; 800 cigarettes, 400 cigarellos, 200 cigars, 1kg smoking tobacco, 10 litres spirits, 20 litres fortified wine, 90 litres wine, 110 litres beer. **People under 17 are not allowed to bring in alcohol or tobacco.**

Travelling to the UK from outside the EU

When you enter the UK from a non-EU country, or from an EU country having travelled through a non-EU country, you must pass through Customs. If you have any goods over the allowance, or if you are not sure what to declare you must use the Red Channel or the phone provided at the Red Point. If you do not declare items on which you should pay duty you are breaking the law and Customs may prosecute you. Customs allowances for travellers from outside the EU are:

Tobacco: 200 cigarettes or 100 cigarillos or 50 cigars or 200gms tobacco

Wines & Spirits: 2 litres still table wine and 1 litre of spirits or strong liqueurs over 22% volume or 2 litres fortified wine, sparkling wine or other liqueurs.

Perfume: 60cc/ml of perfume and 250cc/ml of toilet water.

Other goods: £145 worth of all other goods including gifts and souvenirs.

All dutiable articles must be declared when you enter the UK from a non-EU country. Articles not properly declared may be forfeit, and if they are hidden in a vehicle that vehicle may also be forfeit. Customs Officers are legally entitled to examine your baggage and you are responsible for unpacking and repacking it. If you require further information, Customs Notice 1 "A Customs Guide for Travellers entering the UK" is available at UK points of entry and exit or by phoning 0845 010 9000. Additionally, information may be obtained from the HM Customs & Excise website at: **www.hmce.gov.uk**

Travelling outside the EU

If, when leaving the UK, you take any items bought in the UK which are high value or look very new it is a good idea to carry the retailers' receipts with you as foreign Customs may wish to confirm where the goods were obtained. Bona fide visitors to non-EU countries may generally assume that they may temporarily import personal articles duty free, providing the following conditions are met:

- that the articles are for personal use, and are not to be sold or otherwise disposed of;
- that they may be considered as being in use, and in keeping with the personal status of the importer;
- that they are taken out when the importer leaves the country;

- that the goods stay for no more than 6 months in any 12 month period, whichever is the earlier.

All dutiable articles must be declared when you enter a country, or you will be liable to penalties. If you will be taking a large number of personal effects with you, it would be wise to prepare an inventory to present to the Customs authorities on entry. Customs officers may withhold concessions at any time and ask travellers to deposit enough money to cover possible duty, especially on portable items of apparent high value such as television sets, radios, cassette recorders, portable computers, musical instruments, etc., all of which must be declared. Any deposit paid (for which a receipt must be obtained) is likely to be high: it is recoverable on leaving the country and exporting the item but only at the entry point at which it was paid. Alternatively the Customs may enter the item in the traveller's passport; if this happens it is important to get the entry cancelled when the item is exported. Duty and tax-free allowances may not apply if travellers enter the country more than once a month, or are under 17 years of age (other ages may apply in some countries). Residents of the Channel Islands and the Isle of Man do not benefit from EU allowances because of their fiscal policies.

A temporarily imported motor vehicle, boat, caravan, or any other type of trailer is subject to strict control on entering a country, attracting Customs duty and a variety of taxes: much depends upon the circumstances and the period of the import, and also upon the status of the importer. Non-residents entering a country with a private vehicle for holiday or recreational purposes who intend to export the vehicle within a short period enjoy special privileges, and minimal formalities in the interests of tourism.

A temporarily imported vehicle, etc., should not:
- be left in the country after the importer has left;
- be put at the disposal of a resident of the country;
- be retained in the country longer than the permitted period; or

- be lent, sold, hired, given away, exchanged or otherwise disposed of.

Generally, people entering a country with a motor vehicle to stay for a period of more than six months (see also Visa), or who intend to take up residence, employment, any commercial activity or who intend to dispose of the vehicle should seek advice concerning their position well in advance of their departure. The AA Information Centre can give advice to members; for assistance, telephone 0870 5500 600.

Additionally the importation of certain goods into the UK is prohibited or restricted.

CYCLE CARRIERS

If you intend taking your bicycles on a rear-mounted cycle rack, make sure that they do not obstruct rear lights and/or number plate, or you risk an on-the-spot fine. The AA recommends roof-mounted racks.

D

DIMENSIONS AND WEIGHT RESTRICTIONS

For an ordinary private car, a height limit of 4 metres and a width limit of 2.50 metres are generally imposed. However, see country introductions for full details. Apart from a laden-weight limit imposed on commercial vehicles, every vehicle has an individual weight limit. See Overloading and also Major road and rail tunnels as some dimensions are restricted by the shape of the tunnels.

DIRECTION INDICATORS

All direction indicators should be working at between 60 and 120 flashes per minute. Most standard car-flasher units will be overloaded by the extra lamps of a caravan or trailer, and a special heavy duty unit or relay device should be fitted.

DRINKING AND DRIVING

There is only one safe rule - if you drink, don't drive. Laws are strict and the penalties severe.

DRIVING LICENCE AND INTERNATIONAL DRIVING PERMIT

You should always carry your national driving licence with you even when you hold an International Driving Permit. A driving licence issued in the UK or Republic of Ireland is generally acceptable, subject to the minimum age requirements of the country concerned, but see also individual country introductions. If you wish to drive a hired or borrowed car in the country you are visiting, make local enquiries. If your licence is due to expire before your return, renew it in good time prior to your departure. The Driver and Vehicle Licensing Agency (in Northern Ireland, Driver and Vehicle Licensing Northern Ireland, DVLNI) will accept an application two months before the expiry of your old licence; in the Republic of Ireland, one month before expiry.

An International Driving Permit (IDP) is an internationally recognised document which enables the holder to drive for a limited period in countries where their national licences are not recognised (see Italy and Spain country introductions under Driving Licence). The permit, for which a statutory charge is made, is issued by the AA to an applicant who holds a valid full British driving licence and who is over 18. For advice on the procedure to follow for personal or postal applications, or to obtain an application form, call the AA Information Centre on 0870 5500 600. (Republic of Ireland 01 617 9988.)

E

ELECTRICAL

General: The public electricity supply in Europe is predominantly 220 volts (50 cycles) AC (alternating current), but can be as low as 110 volts. In some isolated areas, low voltage DC (direct current) is provided. Continental circular two-pin plugs and screw-type bulbs are usually the rule. Check for correct polarity when using a mains hook-up on a touring caravan.

Electrical adapters (not voltage transformers) which can be used in Continental power sockets, shaver points and light bulb sockets are available in the UK from electrical retailers.

Vehicle: Check that all connections are sound, and wiring is in good condition. If problems arise with the charging system, you must consult a qualified auto-electrician.

EMERGENCY MESSAGES TO TOURISTS

In emergencies, the AA will assist in the passing on of messages to tourists whenever possible. Members wishing to use this service should telephone the AA Information Centre on 0870 5500 600.

The AA can arrange for messages to be published in overseas editions of the Daily Mail, and in an extreme emergency (death or serious illness of next-of-kin) undertake to pass on messages to the appropriate authorities so that they can be broadcast on overseas radio networks. Obviously the AA cannot guarantee that messages will be broadcast, nor can the AA or the Daily Mail accept any responsibility for the authenticity of messages.

If you have any reason to expect a message from home, it is best to contact the tourist office or the motoring club of the country in which you are staying. They will be able to advise you on appropriate radio frequencies, and at what time messages are normally broadcast. Before you leave home, make sure your relatives understand what to do if an emergency occurs.

Emergency 'SOS' messages about dangerous illness of a close relative may be broadcast on BBC Radio 4's long wave transmitters on 1515m/198Hz at 06.59 and 17.59hrs BST. These should be arranged through the local police or hospital authorities.

ENGINE AND MECHANICAL

Consult your vehicle handbook for servicing intervals. Unless the engine oil has been changed recently, drain and refill it with fresh oil and fit a new filter. Deal with any leaks.

Brands and grades of engine oil familiar to the British motorist are usually available in Western Europe, but may be difficult to find in remote country areas. When available, they will be much more expensive than in the UK and are generally packed in 2-litre cans (3.5 pints). Motorists are strongly advised to carry a sufficient supply of oil.

If you suspect that there is anything wrong with the engine - even if it seems insignificant - it should be dealt with immediately. And do not neglect such common-sense precautions as checking all drive belts and under bonnet levels.

Any obvious mechanical defects should be attended to at once. A car that has covered many miles will have absorbed a certain amount of dirt into the fuel system, and as breakdowns are often caused by dirt, it is essential that all filters (fuel and air) should be cleaned or renewed.

The cooling system should be checked for leaks and the proportion of anti-freeze, and any perished hoses or suspect parts replaced.

Owners should seriously reconsider towing a caravan with a car that has already given appreciable service. Hard driving on motorways and in mountainous country puts an extra strain on ageing parts, and items such as a burnt-out clutch can be very expensive.

EUROTUNNEL

Eurotunnel provides fast, frequent, reliable travel between Folkestone and Coquelle/Calais for cars, motorcycles, bicycles, campervans and cars with caravans or trailers. Vehicles powered by LPG cannot use Eurotunnel

Eurotunnel operates 24 hours a day, 365 days a year, with up to four departures an hour at peak times. Up-to-date travel information is available on freephone 08000 969 992. The journey takes 35 minutes from platform to platform, and is just over one hour from the M20 in Kent to the A16 in France. To get to the Eurotunnel Terminal in Kent take the M20 and leave it at junction 11A, which is signposted to the Channel Tunnel, and arrive directly at check-in.

Bookings can be made via the Internet on the Eurotunnel website at: www.eurotunnel.co.uk or you can call the Eurotunnel Call Centre on 08705 35 35 35. Prices are charged per vehicle rather than the number of passengers. It is possible to buy your reservation on arrival at Eurotunnel, however you will be accepted on a standby

basis and possibly subject to delay until there is an available space.

Passengers stay with their vehicles for the journey, although they can get out of them to walk about or use toilet facilities. Visual display panels, multi-lingual staff and an onboard radio station keep passengers informed during the journey.

Passengers clear both UK and French frontier controls before boarding the Eurotunnel Shuttle so there are no delays on arrival in France.

F

FERRY CROSSINGS

Before making ferry bookings, remember that the shortest sea crossing from a southern port to the Continent is not always the best choice; consider the roads and ease of travel from your home to a British port (an eastern British port might be easier if you are starting from the north of the country). Similarly consider the roads and travel from the Continental port to your final destination. Motorail services may be worth considering to save time.

FIRE EXTINGUISHER

It is a wise precaution to take a fire extinguisher when motoring abroad. AA fire extinguishers may be purchased from the AA's Dover Shop (Eastern Docks Terminal) or, if travelling via Eurotunnel, the AA's Folkestone shop (Eurotunnel Passenger Terminal).

FIRST-AID KIT

It is a wise precaution (compulsory in Austria) to carry a first-aid kit when motoring abroad. An AA First-Aid Kit or an AA Motoring Abroad Kit, which includes a first-aid kit, can be purchased from the AA's Dover Shop (Eastern Docks Terminal) or, if travelling via Eurotunnel, the AA's Folkestone shop (Eurotunnel Passenger Terminal). See also 'Motoring Abroad Kit'.

FOODSTUFFS (SEE ALSO COUNTRY INTRODUCTIONS)

Countries do have regulations governing the types and quantities of foodstuffs which may be imported. Although they are usually not strictly applied, visitors should know that they exist and only take reasonable quantities of food with them. See the country introductions for any specific regulations.

Tinned, frozen and dehydrated foods are useful for camping. It is best to take only as much as you need until you can shop locally. Good value for money will be found in supermarkets or in the open markets in towns.

NOTE: The importation of food products of animal origin (meat, meat products not heat treated, milk and dairy products) into any country **may** be prohibited due to the risk of foot and mouth disease.

H

HORN

In built-up areas, the general rule is that you should not use it unless safety demands it: in many large towns and resorts, and in areas indicated by the international sign (a horn inside a red circle, crossed through) use of the horn is totally banned.

I

IDENTIFICATION PLATE

If a boat trailer, caravan or trailer is taken abroad, it must have a unique chassis number for identification purposes. If yours does not have a number, you can buy an identification plate from the AA. Boats registered on the Small Ships Register (see Boats) have a unique number which must be permanently displayed on the boat.

INSURANCE, INCLUDING CARAVAN INSURANCE

See under Motor Insurance

INTERNATIONAL DISTINGUISHING SIGN

An international distinguishing sign of the approved pattern, and size (oval with black letters on a white background; GB at least 6.9in by 4.5in), must be displayed on a vertical surface at the rear of your vehicle (and

caravan or trailer if you are towing one). These signs indicate the country of registration of the vehicle. On the Continent, fines are imposed for failing to display a distinguishing sign, or for not displaying the correct distinguishing sign. See also Police Fines.

UK registration plates displaying the GB Euro-symbol (Euro-Plates) became a legal option from 21 March 2001, but must comply with the new British standard (BS AU 145d). These plates make display of a conventional sticker unnecessary when circulating within the EU. The use of a GB sticker is advisable outside the EU, even when displayed alongside a Euro-Plate, as the authorities in some countries still expect to see a conventional sticker.

A GB sign, or an AA Motoring Abroad Kit which includes one, may be purchased from the AA's Dover shop (Eastern Docks Terminal) or, if travelling via Eurotunnel, the AA's Folkestone shop (Eurotunnel Passenger Terminal).

L

LEVEL CROSSINGS

Almost all level crossings are indicated by international signs. Most guarded ones are the lifting barrier type, maybe with bells or flashing lights to warn of a train's approach.

LIGHTS (SEE ALSO COUNTRY INTRODUCTIONS)

For driving abroad headlights should be altered so that the dipped beam does not dazzle oncoming drivers. This can easily be done for most vehicles by using headlamp beam converters. However, don't forget to remove them as soon as you return to the UK. Remember to have the lamps set to compensate for the load being carried.

Dipped headlights should also be used in fog, snowfall, heavy rain and in a tunnel, irrespective of its length and lighting. Police may wait at the end of a tunnel to check. Headlight flashing is used only to signal approach or as an overtaking signal at night. In other circumstances, it is taken as a sign of irritation, and may lead to misunderstandings.

Of the countries covered by the guide it is recommended (compulsory in Andorra and Spain) to carry a spare bulb kit. This will not avoid a fine if you are travelling with faulty lights, but being able to replace a bulb on the spot may avoid the cost and inconvenience of a garage call-out. On some cars it is inadvisable or indeed impossible for anyone other than a qualified technician to change a headlamp bulb or lamp unit (eg. High intensity discharge (HID) lamps), and carrying spare bulbs is not an option. However, it is recommended that spare bulbs are carried for any lights which may be easily and/or safely replaced.

AA Headlamp Beam Converters and/or AA Bulb Kits or an AA Motoring Abroad Kit, which includes converters and bulbs, may be purchased from the AA's Dover shop (Eastern Docks Terminal) or, if travelling via Eurotunnel, the AA's Folkestone shop (Eurotunnel Passenger Terminal). See also 'Motoring Abroad Kit'.

LUGGAGE OR ROOF RACKS

Only use equipment suitable for your vehicle, i.e., approved by the vehicle manufacturer. Distribute the load evenly, taking care not to exceed the vehicle manufacturer's roof rack load limit. A roof rack laden with luggage increases fuel consumption, so remember this when calculating mileage per gallon, and it also reduces stability, especially when cornering.

M

MEDICAL TREATMENT

Travellers who normally take certain medicines should ensure they have a sufficient supply since they may be very difficult to get abroad.

Those with certain medical conditions (diabetes or coronary artery diseases, for example) should get a letter from their doctor giving treatment details. Some Continental doctors will understand a letter written in English, but it is better to have it translated into the language of the country you intend to visit. The AA cannot make translations.

Travellers who, for legitimate health reasons, carry drugs (see also Customs regulations for the United Kingdom) or appliances (e.g., a hypodermic syringe), may have difficulty with Customs or other authorities. They should carry translations which describe their special condition and appropriate treatment in the language of the country they intend to visit to present to Customs. Similarly, people with special dietary requirements may find translations helpful in hotels and restaurants.

The National Health Service is available in the UK only, and medical expenses incurred overseas cannot be reimbursed by the UK Government. There are reciprocal health agreements with most of the countries in this guide, but you should not rely exclusively on these arrangements, as the cover provided under the respective national schemes is not always comprehensive. (For instance, the cost of bringing a person back to the UK in the event of illness or death is never covered). The full costs of medical care must be paid in Andorra and Switzerland. Therefore, you are strongly advised to take out adequate insurance cover before leaving the UK, such as the AA's Personal Travel Insurance.

Urgent medical treatment in the event of an accident or unforeseen illness is available for most visitors at reduced costs, from the health care schemes of those countries with whom the UK has health-care arrangements. Details are in the Department of Health booklet T6 which also gives advice about precautions and vaccinations. Free copies are available from main offices or by ringing the Health Literature Line on 0800 555 777, free of charge. In some of these countries, visitors can obtain urgently needed treatment by showing their UK passport, but in some an NHS medical card must be shown, and in most European Economic Area countries a certificate of entitlement (E111) is necessary. The E111 can be obtained at the post office on completion of the forms in booklet 'Health Advice for Travellers' (T6). The E111 must be stamped and signed by the post office clerk to be valid. Residents of the Republic of Ireland must apply to their Regional Health Board.

MINIBUS

A minibus constructed and equipped to carry 10 or more persons (including the driver) and used outside the UK is subject to the regulations governing international bus and coach journeys, including controls on drivers' hours. Such vehicles must weigh no more than 3.5 tonnes (gross vehicle weight) or 4.25 tonnes including any specialist equipment for the carriage of disabled passengers. The vehicle must be fitted with a tachograph (except for journeys between UK and Republic of Ireland) and carry documentation to show the type of journey being made. The documentation requirements are determined by whether the vehicle is owned or hired and countries to be visited, as follows:

a Outside EU (except Norway and Switzerland)- ASOR waybills for closed door tours (round trips carrying same group of passengers) and model control document. For other kinds of tours or journeys to countries outside the EU, contact:

> The Dept for Transport, Local Government
>   and the Regions,
> Road Haulage Division,
> Zone 2/22,
> Great Minster House,
> 76 Marsham Street,
> London SW1P 4DR,
> phone 020 7944 2766 for advice.

b Inside EU - own account certificate (owned vehicle); (new type) EU passenger waybills (hired vehicle).

For vehicles registered and driven by holders of licences issued in UK (England, Scotland, Wales and Northern Ireland), contact:

a Confederation of Passenger Transport UK, Imperial House, 15-19 Kingsway, London WC2B 6UN, phone 020 7240 3131 for model control document and waybills.

b Department for Transport, Local Government and the Regions, International Road Freight Office, Eastgate House, Kings Manor, Newcastle-upon-Tyne, NE1 6PB, phone 0191 201 4090 for own account certificate.

A person of 21 years or over and holding a car driving licence with D1 restricted entitlement (i.e. not for hire or reward) may drive a minibus with up to 16 passenger seats abroad, provided it is not a hire or reward operation. See Section 1 (5) of the Public Passenger Vehicles Act 1981 for a definition of 'hire or reward'. As a result of subsequent court rulings, that definition has been further refined to encompass situations in which there is payment:

- of cash or kind
- whether paid directly or indirectly
- whether paid by the passenger or someone else on their behalf
- even when paid in the course of an arrangement which is a business activity or an activity which has a 'business-like' nature (i.e. is rather more than a social arrangement).

The effect of this is that most trips abroad by school or scout troops or similar organisations, running a minibus, could very likely be classed by the courts as 'hire or reward' operations for which full D1 driving licence entitlement and a Community Operators Licence are needed. In general, where an organisation is operating a minibus in the UK under a Section 19 'small bus' permit (as issued by the Traffic Area Offices) then this would almost certainly be regarded by the Courts as 'hire or reward'. Traffic Area Offices can advise on obtaining a Community Operators Licence. Drivers involved in such operations are, therefore, advised to obtain a full D1 licence before taking the minibus abroad. To do this they will need to pass a separate driving test for minibus at their local driving test centre. Drivers or organisers are also advised in any event to check the position with their insurance company.

For vehicles registered in the Republic of Ireland, contact the Department of Transport, Road Haulage Section, Setanta Centre, South Frederick Street, Dublin 2 for details about tachographs, and the Government Publications Sales Office, Molesworth Street, Dublin 2 for information on documentation.

MIRRORS

When driving or towing on the right, it is essential to have clear all-round vision. Ideally, external rear-view mirrors should be fitted to both sides of your vehicle, but certainly on the left, to allow for driving on the right.

When towing a caravan it is essential to fit mirror accessories for better rear vision. These include clip-on extensions, arms to extend wing mirrors, and long-arm wing or door mirrors. The longer the mirror arm, the more rigid its mounting has to be. Some have supporting legs or extra brackets to minimise vibration. A mirror mounted on the door pillar gives a wide field of vision because it is close to the driver, but it is at a greater angle to the forward line of sight. Convex mirrors give an even wider field of vision, but practice is needed in judging distance due to the diminished image.

MOTOR INSURANCE

When driving abroad you must carry your certificate of motor insurance with you at all times. Third-party is the minimum legal requirement in most countries. Therefore, before taking a motor vehicle, caravan or trailer abroad, contact your motor insurer or broker to notify them of your intentions and ask their advice. Some insurers will extend your UK or Republic of Ireland motor policy to apply in the countries you plan to visit free of charge, others may charge an additional premium. It is most important to know the level of cover you will actually have and what documents you will need to prove it.

Of the countries covered by this guide, a Green Card is compulsory in Andorra. This document is issued by your motor insurer and provides instantly recognisable proof of insurance. The Green Card must be signed on receipt as it will not be accepted without the signature of the insured.

Motorists can obtain advice through AA Insurance Services for all types of insurance. Several special schemes have been arranged with leading insurers. More information is available from: AA Insurance Services Ltd, PO Box 2AA, Newcastle upon Tyne NE99 2AA.

Finally, do check to make sure that you are covered against damage in transit (e.g. on the ferry) when the vehicle is not being driven.

MOTORING ABROAD KIT

An AA Motoring Abroad Kit has all the essential motoring accessories you require for the countries covered by this guide. Available from the AA's Dover shop (Eastern Docks Terminal) or, if travelling via Eurotunnel, the AA's Folkestone shop (Eurotunnel Passenger Terminal); the kit comprises a nylon holdall with bulb kit, first-aid kit, GB sticker, headlamp beam converters and warning triangle.

O

OFF-SITE CAMPING

Off-site camping may contravene local regulations. You are strongly advised never to camp by the roadside and in isolated areas.

ORANGE/BLUE BADGE SCHEME FOR DRIVERS AND PASSENGERS WITH DISABILITIES

Some European countries which operate national schemes of parking concessions for disabled people have reciprocal arrangements whereby visitors with disabilities get the same concessions by displaying their national badge. In some countries responsibility for the concessions rests with individual local authorities and in some cases they may not be generally available. You will have to ask locally.

As in the UK, these arrangements apply only to badge-holders themselves, and the concessions are not for the benefit of able-bodied companions. Wrongful display of the badge may incur whatever local penalties are imposed.

On 1 April 2000, a standard *blue* parking badge for disabled people was introduced throughout Europe. In the UK the new Blue Badge will be phased in over a 3-year period, as existing Orange Badges come up for renewal. Orange Badges will continue to be recognised in all EU countries. To obtain a copy of the booklet giving details of these reciprocal arrangements, phone the AA on 0800 262050.

OVERLOADING

This can create risks, and in most countries the offence can involve on-the-spot fines (see Police fines). You would also be made to reduce the load to an acceptable level before being allowed to continue your journey.

The maximum loaded weight, and its distribution between front and rear axles, is decided by the vehicle manufacturer, and if your owner's handbook does not give these facts, contact the manufacturer direct. There is a public weighbridge in all districts, and when the car is fully loaded (including driver and passengers) use this to check that the vehicle is within the limits.

Load your vehicle carefully so that no lights, reflectors, or number plates are masked, and the driver's view is not impaired. All luggage loaded on a roof-rack must be tightly secured, and should not exceed the manufacturer's recommended maximum limit. Any projections beyond the front, rear, or sides of a vehicle, that may not be noticed by other drivers, must be clearly marked. Limits apply to projections and may vary from country to country.

OVERTAKING

When overtaking on roads with two lanes or more in each direction, signal in good time, and also signal your return to the inside lane. Do not remain in any other lane. Failure to comply with this regulation, particularly in France, will incur an on-the-spot fine (immediate deposit in France) - see Police fines.

Always overtake on the left and use your horn to warn the driver (except where the use of a horn is banned). Do check the vehicles behind before overtaking. Do not overtake at level crossings, intersections, the crest of a hill or pedestrian crossings. When being overtaken, keep to the right and reduce speed if necessary.

P

PARKING

Parking is a problem everywhere in Europe, and the police are strict with offenders. Heavy fines are imposed and unaccompanied offending cars can be towed away. Heavy charges are imposed for the recovery of impounded vehicles. Find out about local parking regulations and make sure you understand all related signs. Always park on the right-hand side of the road or at an authorised place. If possible, park off the main carriageway, but not in cycle or bus lanes.

PASSENGERS

In many countries outside the UK, it is an offence to carry more passengers in a vehicle than the vehicle is constructed to seat, and some have regulations as to how the passengers should be seated. For information about regulations applied to visiting foreigners, see country introductions. Special regulations (see Minibus) apply to passenger-carrying vehicles constructed and equipped to carry more than 10 passengers, including the driver.

PASSPORTS

Each person must hold, or be named on, a valid passport. Always carry your passport and, as an extra precaution, a separate note of the number, date and place of issue. The only type of passport now is the standard 10-year one.

Standard UK passports are issued to British Nationals, i.e. British Citizens, British Dependent Territories Citizens, British Overseas Citizens, British Nationals (Overseas), British Subjects, and British Protected Persons. A standard UK passport is valid for travel to all countries in the world - but you must check whether a visa is also required. From 5 October 1998 it has been necessary for all children to have their own passports; children entered on the existing passport of a parent before 5 October 1998 may remain until the passport expires or until they reach 16. All passports issued to children under the age of 16 years are for 5 years only. After 5 years a new application must be made.

Full information and application forms are available, on the UK mainland, from main Post Offices, Worldchoice Travel Agents, or from one of the Passport Offices in Belfast, Durham, Glasgow, Liverpool, London, Newport (Gwent) and Peterborough. Alternatively, an application form pack may be obtained by calling the application form request hotline 0901 4700 110 or faxing 0901 4700 120. Application for a standard passport should be made to the appropriate area Passport Office. Allow 10 working days for the processing of your application.

For further information, visit the UK Passport Agency website at:

www.passport.gov.uk

or call the UKPA 24-hour helpline

0870 521 0410

Irish citizens who require an Irish Passport, and who are resident either in the Dublin metropolitan area or in Northern Ireland should apply to the Passport Office, Dublin; if, however, they are resident elsewhere in the Irish Republic, they should apply through the nearest Garda Station or Post Office. Irish citizens resident in Britain should apply to the Irish Embassy in London.

PAYMENT CARDS

Credit and debit cards are as convenient to use abroad as they are at home. Their use is subject to the conditions set out by the issuing bank which, on request, will provide full information. Establishments display the symbols of cards that they accept. However, it is recommended that you don't rely exclusively on any one payment method. A combination of traveller's cheques, a payment card and a small amount of local currency is suggested as the most practical arrangement.

PETROL/DIESEL

You will find familiar brands and comparable grades of petrol along the main routes in most countries. However, remember that leaded petrol is no longer generally available in northern European countries. If a lead-replacement petrol (LRP) is not on sale, an anti-wear additive may be bought from a filling station shop; this should be used in accordance with the instructions if your car

requires this protection. The sale of leaded petrol continues in some southern European countries, but not in Italy, Portugal and Spain.

You will normally have to buy a minimum of 5 litres (just over a gallon) but it is wise to keep the tank topped up, particularly in more remote areas. When calculating mileage per gallon, don't forget that the extra weight of a caravan or roof rack increases petrol consumption. It is best to use a locking filler cap. Some garages may close between 12.00hrs and 15.00hrs, but petrol is generally available, with 24-hour service on motorways. Prices for petrol on motorways will normally be higher than elsewhere. Make sure you know the fuel requirement of the vehicle before you go (LRP, unleaded premium, unleaded super or diesel) and whether or not the car has an exhaust catalyst. Catalyst-equipped petrol cars will usually have a small fuel filler neck, to prevent the use of the larger sized nozzle dispensing LRP. If in doubt, check with a franchised dealer, or with the AA.

Some countries are supplying 97 octane unleaded petrol either in addition to, or instead of, 95 octane. The name may be 'super plus' or 'premium' but look for the octane rating 97. You should be careful to use the recommended type of fuel, particularly if your car has a catalytic converter, and the octane rating should be the same or higher. In some countries, a low (92) octane petrol will be on sale. If you accidentally fill the tank of a catalyst-equipped car with LRP, it will do no harm; simply go back to normal petrol at the next fill. If your car requires LRP and you fill with unleaded, avoid hard use of the engine until about half the tank is used, then fill with an additised lead-substitute petrol or dose the fuel with an anti-wear additive.

Diesel fuel is generally known as 'diesel' or 'gas-oil'. Although readily available it is probably more inconvenient to run out of diesel, and it is wise to keep the tank topped up. If more than about a gallon of petrol is put into the tank of a diesel car (or vice versa) you must drain the tank and refill with the correct fuel before the engine is started.

NOTE: **Importing fuel.** While you may wish to carry a reserve supply of fuel in a can, remember that all operators (ferry, motorail etc.) will either forbid the carriage of fuel in spare cans or insist that spare cans must be empty. In Luxembourg motorists are forbidden to carry petrol in cans in the vehicle. If your vehicle has LPG or a dual fuel system, check also with rail, ferry and tunnel operators.

PET TRAVEL SCHEME

For information about taking cats and dogs out of the UK contact the Pets Helpline on 0870 2411710 or visit the Department for Environment, Food & Rural Affairs (DEFRA) website at:

www.defra.gov.uk/animalh/quarantine

DEFRA can also give information on bringing animals into the UK from other countries.

POLICE FINES

Some countries impose on-the-spot fines for minor traffic offences. Others (e.g. France) impose an immediate deposit, and subsequently levy a fine which may be the same as, or greater or lesser than, this sum. Fines are normally paid in cash in the local currency, either to the police or at a local post office against a ticket issued by the police. The amount can exceed the equivalent of £1000 for the most serious offences. The reason for the fines is to penalise, and to keep minor motoring offences out of the courts.

Disputing the fine usually leads to a court appearance, delays and expense. If the fine is not paid, legal proceedings will usually follow. Some countries immobilise vehicles until a fine is paid, and may sell it to pay the penalty.

Once paid, a fine cannot be recovered, but a receipt should always be obtained as proof of payment.

POLLUTION

Pollution of seawater at certain Continental coastal resorts, including the Mediterranean, may still represent a health hazard, although the general situation is improving. Countries of the European Union publish detailed information on the quality of their bathing beaches, including maps, which are available from national authorities and the European

Union. In many (though not all) popular resorts where the water quality may present risk, signs (generally small) are erected which forbid bathing:

FRENCH

No bathing	Défense de se baigner
Bathing prohibited	Il est défendu de se baigner

ITALIAN

No bathing	Vietato bagnarsi
Bathing prohibited	Evietato bagnarsi

SPANISH

No bathing	Prohibido bañarse
Bathing prohibited	Se prohibe bañarse

POSTE RESTANTE

If you are uncertain of having a precise address, you can be contacted through the local poste restante. Before leaving the UK notify family or friends of your approximate whereabouts abroad at given times. If you expect mail, call with your passport at the main post office of the town where you are staying. To ensure that the arrival of correspondence will coincide with your stay, your correspondent should check with the post office before posting, as delivery times differ throughout Europe. It is important that the recipient's name be written in full: Mr John Smith, Poste Restante, Sintra, Portugal. Do not use 'Esq'.

The Italian equivalent of 'Poste Restante' is 'Fermo in Posta' plus the name of the town or village and the province or region. The Spanish equivalent is 'Lista de Correos'. Correspondence will be lodged at the main post office, and you will need proof of identity (e.g. a passport) to collect it.

PRIORITY INCLUDING ROUND-ABOUTS

(See also country introductions)

The general rule is to give way to traffic entering a junction from the right, but this is sometimes varied at roundabouts (see below). Road signs indicate priority or loss of priority, and tourists must be sure that they understand such signs.

Great care should be taken at intersections, and tourists should never rely on being ceded the right of way, particularly in small towns and villages where local, often slow moving, traffic - farm tractors etc., will assume right of way regardless of oncoming traffic. Always give way to public services and military vehicles, blind and disabled people, funerals and marching columns. Vehicles such as buses and coaches will expect, and should be allowed, priority.

Generally, priority at roundabouts is given to vehicles entering the roundabout unless signposted to the contrary (see France). This is a reversal of the UK and Republic of Ireland rule, and particular care should be exercised when circulating in an anti-clockwise direction on a roundabout. It is advisable to keep to the outside lane if possible, to make your exit easier.

R

RADIO TELEPHONE/CITIZENS' BAND RADIOS, TRANSMITTERS AND DETECTION DEVICES

Many countries control the temporary importation and use of radio telephones and radio transmitters. If your vehicle contains such equipment, whether fitted or portable, approach the AA for guidance before departure.

The use or even possession of devices, whether inside or outside vehicles, to detect police radar speed traps is illegal in most countries. Penalties are severe, including confiscation of the equipment, payment of an immediate deposit to serve as collateral against any fine subsequently levied, and/or a driving ban. Finally, if the case is viewed sufficiently seriously, confiscation of vehicle and even imprisonment may result.

REGISTRATION DOCUMENT

You must take the registration document with you. The document should be in your name and kept with you. If you do not have a registration document, apply to a DVLA Local Office (in Northern Ireland, Vehicle Licensing; Republic of Ireland, Motor Tax) for a temporary certificate of registration (V379) to cover the period away. The address of your nearest DVLA Local Office is in the local

telephone directory or in leaflet V100, available from post offices. You should apply well in advance of your journey, as it may take up to two weeks to issue the document if you are not already recorded as the vehicle keeper. Proof of identity (e.g. driving licence) and proof of ownership (e.g. bill of sale), should be produced for the DVLA Local Office.

If you plan to use a borrowed vehicle, the V5 must be accompanied by a letter of authority to use the vehicle from the registered keeper. If you plan to use a hired or leased vehicle, the V5 will not normally be available and you will need a Vehicle on Hire Certificate (VE103A). Generally the hiring/leasing operator or company transport manager will provide the certificate, but individual users may apply direct if necessary. For advice on the procedure to follow for personal or postal applications or for an application form, call the AA Information Centre on 0870 5500 600.

ROAD SIGNS

Most road signs throughout Europe conform to international standards and most will be familiar. Watch for road markings - do not cross a solid white or yellow line marked on the road centre. In Belgium there are three official languages, and signs will be in Dutch, French or German, see Belgian country information under Roads for further information. In the Basque and Catalonian areas of Spain local and national place names appear on signposts, see the country introduction for Spain for further information.

RULE OF THE ROAD

In all countries in this guide, drive on the right and overtake on the left.

S

SEAT BELTS

All countries in this guide require wearing of seat belts.

SPARES

The spares you should carry depend on the vehicle and how long you are likely to be away. Useful items include a pair of windscreen wiper blades, spare fuses, bulbs (see 'Lights') and a torch.

Remember that when ordering spare parts for dispatch abroad, you must be able to identify them clearly - by the manufacturer's part numbers if known. Always quote your engine and vehicle identification (VIN).

SPEED LIMITS

It is important to observe speed limits at all times. Remember that it can be an offence to travel so slowly as to obstruct traffic flow without good reason. Offenders may be fined, and driving licences confiscated on the spot, causing great inconvenience and possible expense.

The standard legal limits are given in the appropriate country introductions for private cars, for motor cycles and for car-caravan-trailer combinations, but these may be varied by road signs, and where such signs are displayed the lower limit applies. At certain times, limits may also be temporarily varied, so watch out for the appropriate signs.

TOLLS

Tolls are payable on most motorways in France, Italy, Portugal, Spain and on sections in Austria. Over long distances, the toll charges can be quite considerable. Compare the cost against time and convenience (e.g., overnight stops), particularly as some of the all-purpose roads are often fast.

Always have some local currency ready to pay the tolls, as travellers cheques etc. are not acceptable at toll booths. Credit cards are accepted at toll booths in France and Spain. In Austria and Switzerland authorities levy a tax for use of motorway networks. See under Motorway tax in the respective country introduction for further information.

TOURIST INFORMATION

National tourist offices are well equipped to deal with enquiries relating to their countries.

They are particularly useful for information on current events, tourist attractions, car hire, equipment hire and specific activities such as skin-diving, gliding, horse-riding, etc. The offices in London (see country introductions for addresses) are helpful, but the local offices overseas merit a visit when you arrive at your destination for information not available elsewhere.

TRAFFIC LIGHTS

In principal cities and towns, traffic lights operate in a way similar to those in the United Kingdom, although they are sometimes suspended over the roadway. The density of the light may be so poor that lights could be missed - especially those overhead. There is usually only one set on the right-hand side of the road some distance before the road junction, and if you stop too close to the corner the lights will not be visible. Look out for 'filter' lights enabling you to turn right at a junction against the main lights. If you wish to go straight ahead, do not enter a lane leading to 'filter' lights or you may obstruct traffic trying to turn right.

TRAMS

Trams take priority over other vehicles. Always give way to passengers boarding and alighting. Never position a vehicle so that it impedes the free passage of a tram. Trams must be overtaken on the right, except in one-way streets.

TRAVELLERS CHEQUES

We recommend that you take travellers cheques. Local currency cheques can often be used like cash. Sterling cheques may be changed for local currency notes at banks. Your bank will be able to recommend currency travellers cheques for the countries your are visiting. However, it is recommended that you don't rely exclusively on any one payment method. A combination of a payment card, travellers' cheques and a small amount of local currency is suggested as the most practical arrangement.

TYRES

Inspect your tyres carefully: if you notice uneven wear, scuffed treads, or damaged walls, get expert advice on whether the tyres are suitable for further use.

The regulations in the UK governing tyres requires a minimum tread depth of 1.6mm over the central three-quarters of the tyre around the whole circumference. Most western European countries have similar or stricter requirements. However, the AA recommends at least 3mm across the whole of the tyre, as they can wear quickly when down to 3mm. If your tyres are likely to be more worn than this before you get back, replace them before you leave.

Check the car handbook for recommended tyre pressures. Different tyre pressures will be recommended for a fully loaded car travelling at motorway speeds. Remember pressures can only be checked accurately when the tyres are cold, and don't forget the spare wheel.

If towing a caravan find out the recommended tyre pressures from the caravan manufacturer. These will vary with the type and size of tyre. For winter or snow tyres see Cold-weather touring.

V

VEHICLE LICENCE

When taking a vehicle out of the UK for a temporary visit remember that the vehicle licence (tax disc) needs to be valid on your return*. If it will expire while you are abroad, you can apply for a new one up to 42 days in advance of the expiry date on your present disc. Apply in writing to either a Post Office that deals with postal applications (if a vehicle registration document is enclosed) or to a DVLA Local Office. You should explain why you want it in advance, and ask for it to be posted to you before you leave, or to your address abroad. However, your application form must always be completed with your UK address.

To find out which post office in your area offers this service, you should contact Post Office Customer Services Unit listed in your local telephone directory.

Residents of Northern Ireland must apply to Driver and Vehicle Licensing Northern Ireland, Vehicle Licensing Division, County Hall, Castlerock Road, Coleraine BT51 3TA. Residents of the Republic of Ireland should contact their Local Motor Tax Office

*Agreement within the EU provides for the temporary use of foreign-registered vehicles within the member states. A vehicle which is properly registered and taxed in its home country should not be subject to the domestic taxation and registration laws of the host country during a temporary stay.

VISA

EU citizens travelling within the EU do not require visas. A visa is not normally required by United Kingdom and Republic of Ireland passport holders when visiting non-EU countries within Western Europe for periods of three months or less. However, if you hold a passport of any other nationality, a UK passport not issued in this country, or if you are in any doubt at all, check with the embassies or consulates of the countries you intend to visit.

VISITORS' REGISTRATION

In most countries registration formalities are to be undertaken by visitors spending up to three months. However, this formality is usually satisfied by completing a card or certificate when booking into a hotel, campsite or other accommodation. If you are staying with friends or relatives it is usually the responsibility of the host to seek advice from the police within 24 hours of the arrival of guests.

If you intend visiting a country for longer than three months and/or the circumstances are not as described above, then you should make the appropriate enquiries before your departure from the UK.

W

WARM-CLIMATE TOURING

In hot weather and at high altitude, excessive heat in the engine compartment can cause problems. If towing a caravan, consult the manufacturers of your vehicle about the limitations of the cooling system, and the operating temperature of the gearbox fluid for automatics (see Automatic gearboxes).

WARNING TRIANGLES
HAZARD WARNING LIGHTS

The use of a warning triangle is compulsory in most Continental countries. It should be placed on the road behind a stopped vehicle to warn traffic approaching from the rear. The triangle should be used when a vehicle has stopped for any reason - not just breakdowns. It should be clearly visible from up to 100m (109yds) by day and night, about 60cm (2ft) from the edge of the road, but not in such a position as to be a danger to oncoming traffic. It should be set up about 30m (33yds) behind the obstruction, but this distance should be increased to 100m (109yds) on motorways. A warning triangle is not required for two-wheeled vehicles.

An AA Warning Triangle, or an AA Motoring Abroad Kit, which includes a warning triangle, may be purchased from the AA's Dover shop (Eastern Docks Terminal) or, if travelling via Eurotunnel, the AA's Folkestone shop (Eurotunnel Passenger Terminal). See also 'Motoring Abroad Kit'.

Although four flashing indicators are allowed in the countries covered by this guide, they do not affect the regulations governing warning triangles. Generally, hazard warning lights should not be used in place of a triangle, although they may complement it. See the country introductions for France, Netherlands and Switzerland. See also Breakdown.

WEATHER AND TRAFFIC
INFORMATION

The AA is one of Europe's largest traffic and travel information providers offering detailed and accurate reports for the whole of the UK. **Call 09003 401 100 (or '401 100'* from your mobile phone)** for a range of valuable traffic and travel services which include

- The latest traffic information for your local area or any other region of the UK
- A traffic report on a specific UK motorway or 'A' road
- Local and national 5-day weather forecasts

For weather reports on crossing the Channel and northern France, call 09003 401 361, whilst Continental Roadwatch on 09003 401 904 provides information on traffic conditions to and from ferry ports, ferry news and details of major European events. A world-wide, city-by-city six-day weather forecast is also available on 09003 411 212.

For other weather information for the UK and the Continent (but not road conditions) please contact:

The Met. Office
Enquiries Officer
London Road
Bracknell
Berkshire RG12 2SZ

or telephone 0845 300 0300 at any time.
* Calls to 09003 numbers are charged at 60p per minute at all times. Availablity and prices for mobile calls to 401 100 can vary - see your Service Provider for details.

WHEEL OR SNOW CHAINS

See Cold-weather touring.

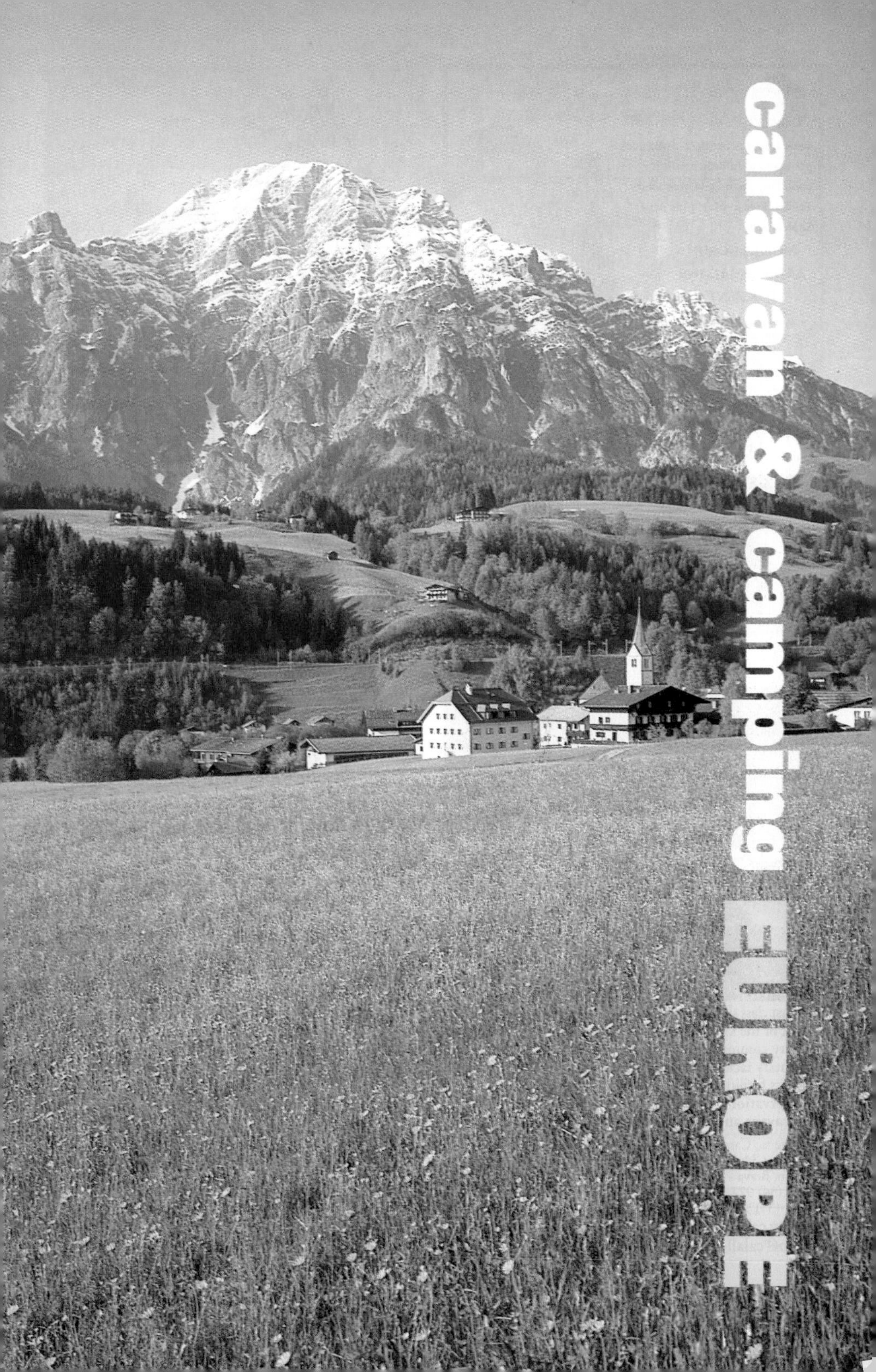
caravan & camping EUROPE

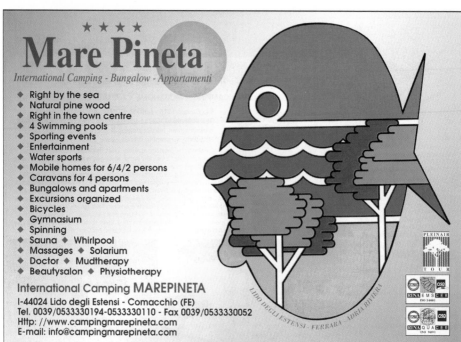

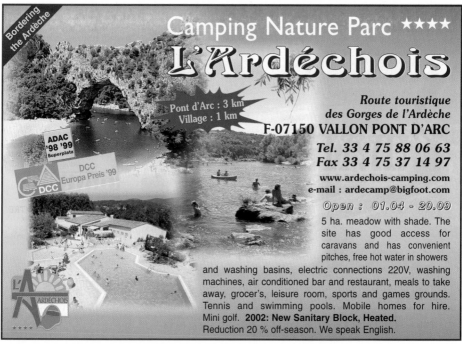

LISBOΛCAMPING
AND BUNGALOWS

No other city has its lungs as close to its heart as Lisbon

900 hectares of green just a stone's throw away from the city centre.

800 camping accommodation units

170 equipped lots

A forest site - totally refurbished and open all the year round.

Swimming pool, restaurant, outdoor cafés, 2 multi-purpose sport centres, mini golf, shopping area, and games rooms.

70 bungalows

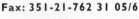

Swimming pool

For further information please contact us at:
Estrada da Circunvalação
1400 - 061 - LISBOA
Tel: 351-21-762 31 00
Fax: 351-21-762 31 05/6

Turismo de Lisboa

Portugal

A list of useful on-line
resources can be found on
page 12 of this guide

The list includes: National
Tourist Sites, Official British
Government Sites concerned
specifically with foreign travel,
Info on the Euro, and useful
caravan and camping resources.

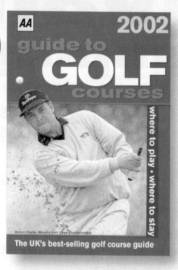

It is best not to attempt to cross mountain passes at night, and daily schedules should make allowances for the comparatively slow speeds inevitable in mountainous areas.

Gravel surfaces (such as dirt and stone chips) vary considerably; they are dusty when dry, slippery when wet. Where known to exist, this type of surface has been noted. Road repairs can be carried out only during the summer, and may interrupt traffic. Precipitous road sides are rarely, if ever, totally unguarded; on the older roads, stone pillars are placed at close intervals. Gradient figures take the mean figure on hairpin bends, and may be steeper on the inside of the curves, particularly on the older roads.

CONVERSION TABLE GRADIENTS

All steep hill signs show the grade in percentage terms. The following conversion table may be used as a guide:

30%=1 in 3	14%=1 in 7
25%=1 in 4	12%=1 in 8
20%=1 in 5	11%=1 in 9
16%=1 in 6	10%=1 in 10

Before attempting late evening or early morning journeys across frontier passes, check the times of opening of the frontier controls. A number close at night; for example the Timmelsjoch border is closed between 20.00 and 07.00hrs and throughout the winter.

Always engage a low gear before either ascending or descending steep gradients, and keep well to the right-hand side of the road and avoid cutting corners. Avoid excessive use of brakes. If the engine overheats, pull off the road, making sure that you do not cause an obstruction, leave the engine idling, and put the heater controls (including the fan) into the maximum heat position. Under no circumstances should you remove the radiator cap until the engine has cooled down. Do not fill the coolant system of a hot engine with cold water.

Always engage a lower gear before taking a hairpin bend, give priority to vehicles ascending and remember that as your altitude increases, so your engine power decreases. Always give

priority to postal coaches travelling in either direction. Their route is usually signposted.

CARAVANS

Passes suitable for caravans are indicated in the table on the following pages. Those shown to be negotiable by caravans are best used only by experienced drivers in cars with ample power; the rest are probably best avoided. A correct power-to-load ratio is always essential.

CONDITIONS IN WINTER

Winter conditions are given in italics in the last column. UO means usually open, although a severe fall of snow may temporarily obstruct the road for 24 to 48 hours, and wheel chains are often necessary; OC means occasionally closed, UC, usually closed, between the dates stated. Dates for opening and closing the passes are approximate only. Warning notices are usually posted at the foot of a pass if it is closed, or if chains or snow tyres should or must be used.

Wheel chains may be needed early and late in the season, and between short spells (a few hours) of obstruction. At these times, conditions are usually more difficult for caravans.

In fair weather, wheel chains or snow tyres are only necessary on the higher passes, but in severe weather you will probably need to use them (as a rough guide) at altitudes exceeding 610 metres (2000ft).

Pass and height	From To	Distances from summit and max gradient	Min width of road	Conditions (see previous page for key to abbreviations)
*Albula 2312 metres (7585ft) Switzerland	Tiefencastel 851 metres (2792ft) La Punt 1687 metres (5535ft)	30km 1 in 10 18.6 miles 9km 1 in 10 5.6 miles	3.5 metres 11ft 6in	UC Nov - early Jun. An inferior alternative to the Julier; tar and gravel, fine scenery. Alternative rail tunnel.
Allos 2250 metres (7382ft) France	Barcelonnette 1132 metres (3714ft) Colmars 1235 metres (4052ft)	20km 1 in 10 12.4 miles 24km 1 in 12 14.9 miles	4.0 metres 13ft 1n	UC Early Nov - early Jun. Very winding, narrow mostly unguarded but not difficult otherwise; passing bays on southern slope, poor surface (maximum width vehicles 1.8 metres, 5ft 11in).
Aprica 1176 metres (3858ft) Italy	Tresenda 375 metres(1230ft) Edolo 699 metres (2293ft)	14km 1 in 11 8.7 miles 15km 1 in 16 9.3 miles	4.0 metres 13ft 1in	UO Fine scenery, good surface, well graded; suitable for caravans.
Aravis 1498 metres (4915ft) France	La Clusaz 1040 metres (3412ft) Flumet 917 metres (3009ft)	8km 1 in 11 5.0 miles 12km 1 in 11 7.4 miles	4.0 metres 13ft 1in	OC Dec - Mar. Outstanding scenery, and a fairly easy road.
Arlberg 1802 metres (5912ft) Austria	Bludenz 581 metres (1905ft) Landeck 816 metres (2677ft)	35km 1 in 8 21.7 miles 32km 1 in 7.5 20 miles	6 metres 19ft 8in	OC Dec - Apr. Modern road; short, steep stretch from west easing towards the summit; heavy traffic; parallel toll road tunnel. Suitable for caravans; using tunnel (see chapter on Major Road and Rail Tunnels). Pass road closed to vehicles towing trailers.
Aubisque 1710 metres (5610ft) France	Eaux Bonnes 750 metres (2461ft) Argelés-Gazost 463 metres (1519ft)	12km 1 in 10 7 miles 30km 1 in 10 19 miles	3.5 metres 11ft 6in	UC Mid Oct - Jun. A very winding road; continuous but easy ascent; the descent incorporates the Col de Soulor (1450 metres, 4757ft); 8km (5 miles) of very narrow, rough unguarded road, with a steep drop.
Ballon d'Alsace 1178 metres (3865ft) France	Giromagny 476metres (1562ft) St-Maurice-sur-Moselle 549 metres (1801ft)	17km 1 in 9 10.6 miles 9km 1 in 9 5.6 miles	4.0 metres 13ft 1in	OC Dec - Mar. A fairly straightforward ascent and descent, but numerous bends; negotiable by caravans.
Bayard 1248 metres (4094ft) France	Chauffayer 911 metres (2989ft) Gap 733 metres (2405ft)	18km 1 in 12 11.2 miles 8km 1 in 7 5.0 miles	6 metres 19ft 8in	UO Part of the Route Napoléon. Fairly easy, steepest on the southern side with several hairpin bends; negotiable by caravans from north to south.
*Bernina 2330 metres (7644ft) Switzerland	Pontresina 1805 metres (5922ft) Poschiavo 1019 metres (3343ft)	15.5km 1 in 10 10.5 miles 18.5km 1 in 8 11.5 miles	5 metres 16ft 5in	OC Dec - Mar. A good road on both sides; negotiable by caravans.
Bonaigua 2072 metres (6797ft) Spain	Viella 974 metres (3195ft) Esterri d'Aneu 957 metres (3140ft)	23km 1 in 12 14 miles 23km 1 in 12 14 miles	4.3 metres 14ft 1in	UC Nov - Apr. A sinuous and narrow road with many hairpin bends and some precipitous drops; the alternative route to Lleida (Lérida) through the Viella tunnel is open in winter.
Bracco 613 metres (2011ft) Italy	Riva Trigoso 43 metres (141ft) Borghetto di Vara 104metres (341ft)	15km 1 in 7 9.3 miles 18km 1 in 7 11.2 miles	5 metres 16ft 5in	UO A two-lane road with continuous bends; passing usually difficult; negotiable by caravans; alternative toll motorway available.
Brenner 1374 metres (4508ft) Austria - Italy	Innsbruck 574 metres (1883ft) Vipiteno 948 metres (3110ft)	36km 1 in 12 22miles 15km 1 in 7 9.3 miles	6 metres 19ft 8in	UO Parallel toll motorway open; heavy traffic; suitable for caravans using toll motorway. Pass road closed to vehicles towing trailers.
+Brünig 1007 metres (3304ft) Switzerland	Brienzwiler Station 575 metres (1886ft) Giswil 485 metres (1591ft)	6km 1 in 12 3.7 miles 13km 1 in 12 8.1 miles	6 metres 19ft 8in	UO An easy but winding road, heavy traffic at weekends; suitable for caravans.

* Permitted maximum width of vehicles 7ft 6in   + Permitted maximum width of vehicles 8ft 2.5in   ++ Maximum length of vehicle 30ft

Pass and height	From To	Distances from summit and max gradient	Min width of road	Conditions (see page 51 for key to abbreviations)
Bussang 721 metres (2365ft) France	Thann 340 metres (1115ft) St Maurice-sur-Moselle 549 metres (1801ft)	24km 1 in 14 15 miles 8km 1 in 14 5.0 miles	4 metres 13ft 1in	UO A very easy road over the Vosges; beautiful scenery; suitable for caravans.
Cabre 1180 metres (3871ft) France	Luc-en-Diois 580 metres (1903ft) Aspres sur Buëch 764 metres (2507ft)	24km 1 in 11 15 miles 17km 1 in 14 10.6 miles	5.5 metres 18ft	UO An easy pleasant road; suitable for caravans.
Campolongo 1875 metres (6152ft) Italy	Corvara in Badia 1568 metres (5144ft) Arabba 1602 metres (5256ft)	6km 1 in 8 3.7 miles 4km 1 in 8 2.5 miles	5 metres 16ft 5in	OC Dec - Mar. A winding but easy ascent; long level stretch on summit followed by easy descent; good surface; suitable for caravans.
Cayolle 2326 metres (7631ft) France	Barcelonnette 1132 metres (3714ft) Guillaumes 819 metres (2687ft)	30km 1 in 10 19 miles 33km 1 in 10 20.5 miles	4 metres 13ft 1in	UC early Nov - early Jun. Narrow and winding road with hairpin bends; poor surface and broken edges; steep drops. Long stretches of single-track road with passing places.
Costalunga (Karer) 1753 metres (5751ft) Italy	Cardano 282 metres (925ft) Pozza 1290 metres (4232ft)	24km 1 in 6 14.9 miles 11km 1 in 8 7 miles	5 metres 16ft 5in	OC Dec - Apr. A good well-engineered road but mostly winding; caravans prohibited.
Croix 1778 metres (5833ft) Switzerland	Villars-sur-Ollon 1253 metres (4111ft) Les Diablerets 1155 metres (3789ft)	8km 1 in 7.5 5.0 miles 9km 1 in 11 5.6 miles	3.5 metres 11ft 6in	UC Nov - May. A narrow and winding route but extremely picturesque.
Croix-Haute 1179 metres (3868ft) France	Monestier-de-Clermont 832 metres (2730ft) Aspres-sur-Buëch 764 metres (2507ft)	34km 1 in 14 21 miles 29km 1 in 14 18 miles	5.5 metres 18ft	UO Well engineered; several hairpin bends on the north side; suitable for caravans.
Envalira 2407 metres (7897ft) Andorra	Pas de la Casa 2091 metres (6860ft) Andorra 1029 metres (3376ft)	5km 1 in 10 3.1 miles 25km 1 in 8 16 miles	6 metres 19ft 8in	OC Nov - Apr. A good road with wide bends on ascent and descent; fine views; negotiable by caravans (maximum height vehicles 3.5 metres, 11ft 6in on northern approach near L'Hospitalet).
Falzárego 2117 metres (6945ft) Italy	Cortina d'Ampezzo 1224 metres (4016ft) Andraz 1428 metres (4685ft)	17km 1 in 12 10.6 miles 9km 1 in 12 5.6 miles	5 metres 16ft 5in	OC Dec - Apr. Well engineered bitumen surface; many hairpin bends on both sides; negotiable by caravans.
Faucille 1323 metres (4341ft) France	Gex 628 metres (2060ft) Morez 702 metres (2303ft)	11km 1 in 10 6.8 miles 27km 1 in 12 17miles	5 metres 16ft 5in	UO Fairly wide, winding road across the Jura mountains; negotiable by caravans, but it is probably better to follow La Cure-St-Cergue-Nyon.
Fern 1209 metres (3967ft) Austria	Nassereith 843 metres (2766ft) Lermoos 995 metres (3264ft)	10km 1 in 10 6 miles 10km 1 in 10 6 miles	6 metres 19ft 8in	UO An easy pass, but slippery when wet; heavy traffic at summer weekends; suitable for caravans.
Flexen 1784 metres (5853ft) Austria	Lech 1447 metres (4747ft) Rauzalpe (near Arlberg Pass) 1628 metres (5341ft)	6.5km 1 in 10 4 miles 3.5km 1 in 10 2.2 miles	5.5 metres 18ft	UO The magnificent 'Flexenstrasse', a well engineered mountain road with tunnels and galleries. The road from Lech to Warth, north of the pass, is usually closed between November and April due to danger of avalanches.

* Permitted maximum width of vehicles 7ft 6in + Permitted maximum width of vehicles 8ft 2.5in ++ Maximum length of vehicle 30ft

Pass and height	From To	Distances from summit and max gradient	Min width of road	Conditions (see page 51 for key to abbreviations)
*Flüela 2383 metres (7818ft) Switzerland	Davos-Dorf 1563 metres (5128ft) Susch 1438 metres (4718ft)	14km 1 in 10 9 miles 14km 1 in 8 9 miles	5metres 16ft 5in	OC Nov - May. Easy ascent from Davos; some acute hairpin bends on the eastern side; bitumen surface; negotiable by caravans.
+Forclaz 1527 metres (5010ft) Switzerland France	Martigny 476 metres (1562ft) Argentière 1253 metres (4111ft)	13km 1 in 12 8.1 miles 19km 1 in 12 11.8 miles	5 metres 16ft 5in	UO Forclaz; OC Montets Dec - early Apr. A good road over the pass and to the frontier; in France, narrow and rough over Col des Montets (1461 metres, 4793ft); negotiable by caravans.
Foscagno 2291 metres (7516ft) Italy	Bormio 1225 metres (4019ft) Livigno 1816 metres (5958ft)	24km 1 in 8 14.9 miles 14km 1 in 8 8.7 miles	3.3 metres 10ft 10in	OC Nov - May. Narrow and winding through lonely mountains, generally poor surface. Long winding ascent with many blind bends; not always well guarded. The descent includes winding rise and fall over the Passo d'Eira (2200 metres, 7218ft).
Fugazze 1159 metres (3802ft) Italy	Rovereto 201 metres (660ft) Valli del Pasubio 350 metres (1148ft)	27km 1 in 7 16.4 miles 12km 1 in 7 7.4 miles	3.5 metres 11ft 6in	UO Very winding with some narrow sections, particularly on northern side. The many blind bends and several hairpin bends call for extra care.
*Furka 2431 metres (7976ft) Switzerland	Gletsch 1757 metres (5764ft) Realp 1538 metres (5046ft)	10km 1 in 9 6.2 miles 13km 1 in 10 8.1 miles	4 metres 13ft 1in	UC Oct - Jun. A well graded road, with narrow sections and several sharp hairpin bends on both ascent and descent. Fine views of the Rhône glacier. Alternative rail tunnel available.
Galibier 2645 metres (8678ft) France	Lautaret Pass 2058 metres (6752ft) St-Michel-de-Maurienne 712 metres (2336ft)	7km 1 in 9 4.4 miles 34km 1 in 8 21.1 miles	3 metres 9ft 10in	UC Oct - Jun. Mainly wide, well surfaced but unguarded. Ten hairpin bends on descent then 5km (3.1 miles) narrow and rough. Rise over the Col du Télégraphe (1600 metres, 5249ft), then 11 more hairpin bends. (The tunnel under the Galibier summit is closed.)
Gardena (Grödner-Joch) 2121 metres (6959ft) Italy	Val Gardena 1862 metres (6109ft) Corvara in Badia 1568 metres (5144ft)	6km 1 in 8 3.7 miles 10km 1 in 8 6.2 miles	5 metres 16ft 5in	OC Dec - Jun. A well engineered road, very winding on descent.
Gavia 2621 metres (8599ft) Italy	Bormio 1225 metres (4019ft) Ponte di Legno 1258 metres (4127ft)	25km 1 in 5.5 15.5 miles 18km 1 in 5.5 11 miles	3 metres 9ft 10in	UC Oct - Jul. Steep and narrow, but with frequent passing bays; many hairpin bends and a gravel surface; not for the faint-hearted; extra care necessary. (Maximum width for vehicles 1.8 metres, 5ft 11in.)
Gerlos 1628 metres (5341ft) Austria	Zell am Ziller 575 metres (1886ft) Wald 885 metres (2904ft)	29km 1 in 12 18 miles 15km 1 in 11 9.3 miles	4 metres 13ft 1in	UO Hairpin ascent out of Zell to modern toll road; the old, steep, narrow, and winding route with passing bays and 1-in-7 gradient is not recommended, but is negotiable with care; caravans prohibited.
+Grand St Bernard 2473 metres (8114ft) Switzerland - Italy	Martigny 476 metres (1562ft) Aosta 583 metres (1913ft)	46km 1 in 9 29 miles 34km 1 in 9 21 miles	4 metres 13ft 1in	UC Oct - Jun. Modern road to entrance of road tunnel (usually open; see chapter on Major Road and Rail Tunnels) then narrow over summit to frontier; also good surface in Italy; suitable for caravans using tunnel. Pass road closed to vehicles towing trailers.
*Grimsel 2164 metres (7100ft) Switzerland	Innerkirchen 630 metres (2067ft) Gletsch 1757 metres (5764ft)	26km 1 in 10 16.1 miles 6km 1 in 10 3.7 miles	5 metres 16ft 5in	UC mid Oct - late Jun. A fairly easy road, but heavy traffic weekends. A long winding ascent, finally hairpin bends; then a terraced descent (six hairpins) into the Rhône valley. Negotiable by caravans.
Grossglockner 2503 metres (8212ft) Austria	Bruck an der Glocknerstrasse 755 metres (2477ft) Heiligenblut 1301 metres (4268ft)	34km 1 in 8 21 miles 15m 1 in 8 9.3 miles	5.5 metres 18ft	UC late Oct - early May. Numerous well engineered hairpin bends; moderate but very long ascent, toll road; very fine scenery; heavy tourist traffic; negotiable preferably from south to north, by caravans. Road closed at night, 22.00 to 05.00 hrs.

* Permitted maximum width of vehicles 7ft 6in   + Permitted maximum width of vehicles 8ft 2.5in   ++ Maximum length of vehicle 30ft

Pass and height	From To	Distances from summit and max gradient	Min width of road	Conditions (see page 51 for key to abbreviations)
Hochtannberg 1679 metres (5509ft) Austria	Schröcken 1269 metres(4163ft) Warth (near Lech) 1500 metres (4921ft)	5.5km 1 in 7 3.4 miles 4.5km 1 in 11 2.8 miles	4 metres 13ft 1in	OC Jan - Mar. A reconstructed modern road.
Ibañeta (Roncesvalles) 1057 metres (3468ft) France - Spain	St-Jean-Pied-de-Port 163 metres (535ft) Pamplona 415 metres (1362ft)	27km 1 in 10 17 miles 49km 1 in 10 30 miles	4 metres 13ft 1in	UO A slow and winding, scenic route; negotiable by caravans.
Iseran 2770 metres (9088ft) France	Bourg-St-Maurice 840 metres (2756ft) Lanslebourg 1399 metres (4590ft)	47km 1 in 12 29 miles 33km 1 in 9 20.5 miles	4 metres 13ft 1in	UC Mid Oct - late Jun. The second highest pass in the Alps. Well graded with reasonable bends, average surface; several unlit tunnels on northern approach.
Izoard 2360 metres (7743ft) France	Guillestre 1000 metres (3281ft) Briançon 1321 metres (4334ft)	32km 1 in 8 20 miles 22km 1 in 8 14 miles	5 metres 16ft 5in	UC Late Oct - mid Jun. A winding and sometimes narrow road with many hairpin bends. Care is required at several unlit tunnels near Guillestre.
*Jaun 1509 metres (4951ft) Switzerland	Broc 718 metres (2356ft) Reidenbach 845 metres (2772ft)	25km 1 in 10 15.5 miles 8km 1 in 10 5 miles	4 metres 13ft 1in	UO A modernised but generally narrow road; some poor sections on ascent, and several hairpin bends on descent; negotiable by caravans.
+Julier 2284 metres (7493ft) Switzerland	Tiefencastel 851 metres (2792ft) Silvaplana 1815 metres (5955ft)	35km 1 in 10 22miles 7km 1 in 7.5 4.4 miles	4 metres 13ft 1in	UO Well engineered road, approached from Chur by Lenzerheide Pass (1549 metres, 5082ft); negotiable by caravans, preferably from north to south.
Katschberg 1641 metres (5384ft) Austria	Spittal 554 metres (1818ft) St Michael 1068 metres (3504ft)	37km 1 in 5 23 miles 6km 1 in 6 3.7 miles	6 metres 19ft 8in	UO Steep though not particularly difficult, parallel toll motorway, including tunnel available; negotiable by light caravans, using tunnel (see chapter on Major Road and Rail Tunnels, Tauern Autobahn)
*Klausen 1948 metres (6391ft) Switzerland	Altdorf 458 metres (1503ft) Linthal 662 metres (2172ft)	25km 1 in 10 15.5 miles 23km 1 in 11 14.3 miles	5 metres 16ft 5in	UC Late Oct - early Jun. Narrow and winding in places, but generally easy, in spite of a number of sharp bends; no through route for caravans as they are prohibited from using the road between Unterschächen and Linthal.
Larche (della Maddalena) 1994 metres (6542ft) France - Italy	La Condamine-Châtelard 1308 metres (4291ft) Vinadio 910 metres (2986ft)	19km 1 in 12 11.8 miles 32km 1 in 12 19.8 miles	3.5 metres 11ft 6in	OC Dec - Mar. An easy, well graded road; narrow ascent, wider on descent; suitable for caravans.
Lautaret 2058 metres (6752ft) France	Le Bourg-d'Oisans 719 metres (2359ft) Briançon 1321 metres (4334ft)	38km 1 in 8 23.6 miles 28km 1 in 10 17.4 miles	4 metres 13ft 1in	OC Dec - Mar. Modern, evenly graded, but winding, and unguarded in places; very fine scenery; suitable for caravans.
Loibl (Ljubelj) 1067 metres (3500ft) Austria - Slovenia	Unterloibl 518 metres (1699ft) Kranj 385 metres (1263ft)	10km 1 in 5.5 6.2 miles 26km 1 in 8 16miles	6 metres 19ft 8in	UO Steep rise and fall over Little Loibl pass to tunnel (1.6km, 1 mile long) under summit. The old road over the summit is closed to through traffic.
*Lukmanier (Lucomagno) 1916 metres (6286ft) Switzerland	Olivone 893 metres (2930ft) Disentis 1133 metres (3717ft)	20km 1 in 11 12 miles 20km 1 in 11 12 miles	5 metres 16ft 5in	UC early Nov - late May. Rebuilt, modern road; suitable for caravans.

* Permitted maximum width of vehicles 7ft 6in   + Permitted maximum width of vehicles 8ft 2.5in   ++ Maximum length of vehicle 30f

PRINCIPAL MOUNTAIN PASSES

Pass and height	From To	Distances from summit and max gradient	Min width of road	Conditions (see page 51 for key to abbreviations)
+Maloja 1815 metres (5955ft) Switzerland	Silvaplana 1815 metres (5955ft) Chiavenna 333 metres (1093ft)	11km level 6.8 miles 32km 1 in 11 19.8 miles	4 metres 13ft 1in	UO Escarpment facing south; fairly easy, but many hairpin bends on descent; negotiable by caravans, possibly difficult on ascent.
Mauria 1298 metres (4258ft) Italy	Lozzo Cadore 753 metres (2470ft) Ampezzo 560 metres (1837ft)	13km 1 in 14 8 miles 31km 1 in 14 19.2 miles	5 metres 16ft 5in	UO A well designed road with easy, winding ascent and descent; suitable for caravans.
Mendola 1363 metres (4472ft) Italy	Appiano (Eppan) 411 metres (1348ft) Sarnonico 978 metres (3208ft)	15km 1 in 8 9.3 miles 9km 1 in 10 6 miles	5 metres 16ft 5in	UO A fairly straightforward but winding road, well guarded; suitable for caravans.
Mont Cenis 2083 metres (6834ft) France - Italy	Lanslebourg 1399 metres (4590ft) Susa 503 metres (1650ft)	11km 1 in 10 6.8 miles 28km 1 in 8 17.4 miles	5 metres 16ft 5in	UC Nov - May. Approach by industrial valley. An easy highway, but with poor surface in places; suitable for caravans. Alternative Fréjus road tunnel (see chapter on Major Road and Rail Tunnels).
Monte Croce di Comélico (Kreuzberg) 1636 metres (5368ft) Italy	San Candido 1174metres (3852ft) Santo Stefano di Cadore 908 metres (2979ft)	15km 1 in 12 9.3 miles 21km 1 in 12 13miles	5 metres 16ft 5in	UO A winding road with moderate gradients, beautiful scenery; suitable for caravans.
Montgenèvre 1850m (6070ft) France - Italy	Briançon 1321 metres (4334ft) Cesana Torinese 1344 metres (4409ft)	12km 1 in 14 7.4 miles 8km 1 in 11 5miles	5 metres 16ft 5in	UO An easy, modern road; suitable for caravans.
Monte Giovo (Jaufen) 2094 metres (6870ft) Italy	Merano 324 metres (1063ft) Vipiteno 948 metres (3110ft)	40km 1 in 8 24.8 miles 19km 1 in 11 11.8 miles	4 metres 13ft 1in	UC Nov - May. Many well engineered hairpin bends; caravans prohibited.
Montets (see Forclaz)				
Morgins 1369 metres (4491ft) France - Switzerland	Abondance 930 metres (3051ft) Monthey 424 metres (1391ft)	14km 1 in 11 8.7 miles 15km 1 in 7 9.3 miles	4 metres 13ft 1in	UO A lesser used route through pleasant, forested countryside crossing the French-Swiss border.
*Mosses 1445m (4740ft) Switzerland	Aigle 417 metres (1368ft) Château d'Oex 958 metres (3143ft)	16km 1 in 12 10 miles 15km 1 in 12 9.3 miles	4 metres 13ft 1in	UO A modern road; suitable for caravans.
Nassfeld (Pramollo) 1530m (5020ft) Austria - Italy	Tröpolach 601 metres (1972ft) Pontebba 568 metres (1864ft)	10km 1 in 5 6.2 miles 10km 1 in 10 6.2 miles	4 metres 13ft 1in	OC Late Nov - Mar. The winding descent in Italy has been improved.
*Nufenen (Novena) 2478 metres (8130ft) Switzerland	Ulrichen 1346 metres (4416ft) Airolo 1142 metres (3747ft)	13km 1 in 10 8.1 miles 24km 1 in 10 14.9 miles	4.0 metres 13ft 1in	UC Mid Oct - mid Jun. The approach roads are narrow, with tight bends, but the road over the pass is good; negotiable by caravans.
*Oberalp 2044 metres (6706ft) Switzerland	Andermatt 1447 metres (4747ft) Disentis 1133 metres (3717ft)	10km 1 in 10 6.2 miles 21km 1 in 10 13miles	5 metres 16ft 5in	UC Nov - late May. A widened road with a modern surface; many hairpin bends, but long level stretch on summit; negotiable by caravans. Alternative rail tunnel for winter (see chapter on Major Road and Rail Tunnels).

* Permitted maximum width of vehicles 7ft 6in   + Permitted maximum width of vehicles 8ft 2.5in   ++ Maximum length of vehicle 30ft

PRINCIPAL MOUNTAIN PASSES

Pass and height	From To	Distances from summit and max gradient	Min width of road	Conditions (see page 51 for key to abbreviations)
*Ofen (Fuorn) 2149 metres (7051ft) Switzerland	Zernez 1474 metres (4836ft) Santa Maria im Münstertal 1375 metres (4511ft)	22km 1 in 10 13.6 miles 14km 1 in 8 8.7 miles	4 metres 13ft 1in	UO Good, fairly easy road through the Swiss National Park; negotiable by caravans.
Petit St Bernard 2188 metres (7178ft) France - Italy	Bourg-St-Maurice 840 metres (2756ft) Pré St-Didier 1000 metres (3281ft)	30km 1 in 16 19 miles 23km 1 in 12 14.3 miles	5 metres 16ft 5in	UC Mid Oct - Jun. Outstanding scenery; a fairly easy approach, but poor surface and unguarded broken edges near the summit; good on the descent in Italy; negotiable by light caravans.
Peyresourde 1563 metres (5128ft) France	Arreau 704 metres (2310ft) Luchon 630 metres (2067ft)	18km 1 in 10 11.2 miles 14km 1 in 10 8.7 miles	4 metres 13ft 1in	UO Somewhat narrow with several hairpin bends, though not difficult.
*Pillon 1546 metres (5072ft) Switzerland	Le Sépey 974 metres (3196ft) Gsteig 1184 metres (3885ft)	15km 1 in 11 9 miles 7km 1 in 11 4.4 miles	4 metres 13ft 1in	OC Jan - Feb. A comparatively easy modern road; suitable for caravans.
Plöcken (Monte Croce-Carnico) 1362 metres (4468ft) Austria - Italy	Kötschach 706 metres (2316ft) Paluzza 600 metres (1968ft)	16km 1 in 7 10 miles 16km 1 in 14 10 miles	5 metres 16ft 5in	OC Dec - Apr. A modern road with long, reconstructed sections; heavy traffic at summer weekends; delay likely at the frontier; negotiable by caravans, best used only by experienced drivers in cars with ample power.
Pordoi 2239 metres (7346ft) Italy	Arabba 1602 metres (5256ft) Canazei 1465 metres (4806ft)	9km 1 in 10 5.6 miles 12km 1 in 10 7.4 miles	5 metres 16ft 5in	OC Dec - Apr. An excellent modern road with numerous hairpin bends; negotiable by caravans.
Port 1249 metres (4098ft) France	Tarascon 474 metres (1555ft) Massat 650 metres (2133ft)	18km 1 in 10 11.2 miles 12km 1 in 10 7.4 miles	4 metres 13ft 1in	OC Nov - Mar. A fairly easy road, but narrow on some bends; negotiable by caravans.
Portet-d'Aspet 1069 metres (3507ft) France	Audressein 508 metres (1667ft) Fronsac 472 metres (1548ft)	18km 1 in 7 11.2 miles 29km 1 in 7 18miles	3.5 metres 11ft 6in	UO Approached from the west by the easy Col des Ares (797 metres, 2615ft) and Col de Buret (599 metres, 1965ft); well engineered road, but calls for particular care on hairpin bends; rather narrow.
Pötschen 982 metres (3222ft) Austria	Bad Ischl 469 metres (1539ft) Bad Aussee 659 metres (2162ft)	19km 1 in 11 11.8 miles 9 km 1 in 11 5.6 miles	7 metres 23ft	UO A modern road; suitable for caravans.
Pourtalet 1792 metres (5879ft) France - Spain	Eaux-Chaudes 656 metres (2152ft) Biescas 860 metres (2822ft)	23km 1 in 10 14.3 miles 32km 1 in 10 20 miles	3.5 metres 11ft 6in	UC late Oct - early Jun. A fairly easy, unguarded road, but narrow in places.
Puymorens 1915 metres (6283ft) France	Ax-les-Thermes 720 metres (2362ft) Bourg-Madame 1130 metres (3707ft)	28km 1 in 10 17.4 miles 27km 1 in 10 16.8 miles	5.5 metres 18ft	OC Nov - Apr. A generally easy, modern tarmac road, but narrow, winding and with a poor surface in places; not suitable for night driving; suitable for caravans (max height vehicles 3.5 metres, 11ft 6in). Parallel toll road tunnel available.
Quillane 1714 metres (5623ft) France	Quillan 291 metres (955ft) Mont-Louis 1600 metres (5249ft)	63km 1 in 12 39.1 miles 6 km 1 in 12 3.5 miles	5 metres 16ft 5in	OC Nov - Mar. An easy, straightforward ascent and descent; suitable for caravans.

* Permitted maximum width of vehicles 7ft 6in   + Permitted maximum width of vehicles 8ft 2.5in   ++ Maximum length of vehicle 30ft

Pass and height	From To	Distances from summit and max gradient	Min width of road	Conditions (see page 51 for key to abbreviations)
Radstädter-Tauern 1738 metres (5702ft) Austria	Radstadt 862 metres (2828ft) Mauterndorf 1122 metres (3681ft)	21km 1 in 6 13.0 miles 17km 1 in 7 10.6 miles	5 metres 16ft 5in	OC Jan - Mar. Northern ascent steep, but not difficult otherwise; parallel toll motorway including tunnel; negotiable by light caravans, using tunnel (see chapter on Major Road and Rail Tunnels).
Résia (Reschen) 1504 metres (4934ft) Italy - Austria	Spondigna 885 metres (2903ft) Pfunds 970 metres (3182ft)	29km 1 in 10 18 miles 21km 1 in 10 13miles	6 metres 19ft 8in	UO A good, straightforward alternative to the Brenner Pass; suitable for caravans.
Restefond (La Bonette) 2802 metres (9193ft) France	Jausiers (near Barcelonnette) 1220 metres (4003ft) St-Etienne-de-Tinée 1144 metres (3753ft)	23km 1 in 8 14.3 miles 27km 1 in 6 16.8 miles	3 metres 9ft 10in	UC Oct - Jun. The highest pass in the Alps, completed in 1962. Narrow, rough, unguarded ascent with many blind bends, and nine hairpins. Descent easier, winding with 12 hairpin bends. Not for the faint-hearted; extra care required.
Rolle 1970 metres (6463ft) Italy	Predazzo 1018 metres (3340ft) Mezzano 637 metres (2090ft)	21km 1 in 11 13.0 miles 27km 1 in 14 17 miles	5 metres 16ft 5in	OC Dec - Mar. A well engineered road with many hairpin bends on both sides; very beautiful scenery; good surface; negotiable by caravans.
Rombo (see Timmelsjoch)				
Routes des Crêtes 1283 metres (4210ft) France	St-Dié 343 metres (1125ft) Cernay 296 metres (971ft)	- 1 in 8 - 1 in 8	4 metres 13ft 1in	UC Nov - Apr. A renowned scenic route crossing seven ridges, with the highest point at 'Hôtel du Grand Ballon'.
+St Gotthard (San Gottardo) 2108 metres (6916ft) Switzerland	Göschenen 1106 metres (3629ft) Airolo 1142 metres (3747ft)	18km 1 in 10 11miles 15km 1 in 10 9.3 miles	6 metres 19ft 8in	UC Mid Oct - early Jun. Modern, fairly easy two to three-lane road. Heavy traffic; negotiable by caravans. Alternative road tunnel (see chapter on Major Road and Rail Tunnels).
***San Bernardino** 2066 metres (6778ft) Switzerland	Mesocco 790 metres (2592ft) Hinterrhein 1620 metres (5315ft)	21km 1 in 10 13miles 9.5km 1 in 10 5.9 miles	4 metres 13ft 1in	UC Oct - late Jun. Easy, modern roads on northern and southern approaches to tunnel(see chapter on Major Road and Rail Tunnels). Narrow and winding over summit, via tunnel suitable for caravans.
Schlucht 1139 metres (3737ft) France	Gérardmer 665 metres (2182ft) Munster 381 metres (1250ft)	15km 1 in 14 9.3 miles 18km 1 in 14 11miles	5 metres 16ft 5in	UO An extremely picturesque route crossing the Vosges mountains, with easy, wide bends on the descent; suitable for caravans.
Seeberg (Jezersko) 1218 metres (3996ft) Austria - Slovenia	Eisenkappel 555 metres (1821ft) Kranj 385 metres (1263ft)	14km 1 in 8 8.7 miles 33km 1 in 10 20.5 miles	5 metres 16ft 5in	UO An alternative to the steeper Loibl and Wurzen passes; moderate climb with winding, hairpin ascent and descent.
Sella 2240 metres (7349ft) Italy	Plan 1606 metres (5269ft) Canazei 1465 metres (4806ft)	9km 1 in 9 5.6 miles 12km 1 in 9 7 miles	5 metres 16ft 5in	OC Dec - Jun. A finely engineered, winding road; exceptional views of the Dolomites.
Semmering 985 metres (3232ft) Austria	Mürzzuschlag im Mürztal 672 metres (2205ft) Gloggnitz 457 metres (1499ft)	14km 1 in 16 8.7 miles 17km 1 in 16 10.6 miles	6 metres 19ft 8in	UO A fine, well engineered highway; suitable for caravans.
Sestriere 2033 metres (6670ft) Italy	Cesana Torinese 1344 metres (4409ft) Pinerolo 376 metres (1234ft)	12km 1 in 10 7.4 miles 55km 1 in 10 34.2 miles	6 metres 19ft 8in	UO Mostly bitumen surface; negotiable by caravans.

* Permitted maximum width of vehicles 7ft 6in   + Permitted maximum width of vehicles 8ft 2.5in   ++ Maximum length of vehicle 30ft

Pass and height	From To	Distances from summit and max gradient	Min width of road	Conditions (see page 51 for key to abbreviations)
Silvretta (Bielerhöhe) 2032 metres (6666ft) Austria	Partenen 1051 metres (3448ft) Galtür 1584 metres (5197ft)	16km 1 in 9 9.9 miles 10km 1 in 9 6.2 miles	5 metres 16ft 5in	UC Late Oct - early Jun. For the most part reconstructed; 32 easy hairpin bends on western ascent; eastern side more straightforward. Toll road; caravans prohibited.
+Simplon 2005 metres (6578ft) Switzerland - Italy	Brig 681 metres (2234ft) Domodóssola 280 metres (919ft)	22km 1 in 9 13.6 miles 41km 1 in 11 25.5 miles	7 metres 23ft	OC Nov - Apr. An easy, reconstructed modern road, but 13 miles long, continuous ascent to summit; suitable for caravans.
Somport 1632 metres (5354ft) France - Spain	Bedous 416 metres (1365ft) Jaca 820 metres (2690ft)	31km 1 in 10 19.2 miles 32km 1 in 10 20miles	3.5 metres 11ft 6in	UO A favoured, old-established route; generally easy, but in parts narrow and unguarded; fairly well surfaced road; suitable for caravans.
*Splügen 2113 metres (6932ft) Switzerland - Italy	Splügen 1457 metres (4780ft) Chiavenna 330 metres (1083ft)	9km 1 in 9 5.6 miles 30km 1 in 7.5 18.6 miles	3.5 metres 11ft 6in	UC Nov - Jun. Mostly narrow and winding, with many hairpin bends, and not well guarded; care is also required at many tunnels and galleries (max height vehicles 9ft 2in).
++Stelvio 2757 metres (9045ft) Italy	Bormio 1225 metres (4019ft) Spondigna 885 metres (2903ft)	22km 1 in 8 13.6 miles 28km 1 in 8 12.9 miles	4 metres 13ft 1in	UC Oct - late Jun. the third highest pass in the Alps; the number of acute hairpin bends, all well engineered, is exceptional - from 40 to 50 on either side; the surface is good, the traffic heavy. Hairpin bends are too acute for long vehicles.
+Susten 2224 metres (7297ft) Switzerland	Innertkirchen 630 metres (2067ft) Wassen 916 metres (3005ft)	28km 1 in 11 12.9 miles 19km 1 in 11 11.8 miles	6 metres 19ft 8in	UC Nov - Jun. A very scenic and well guarded mountain road; easy gradients and turns; heavy traffic at weekends; caravans prohibited.
Tenda (Tende) 1321 metres (4334ft) Italy - France	Borgo S Dalmazzo 641 metres (2103ft) La Giandola 308 metres (1010ft)	24km 1 in 11 14.9 miles 29km 1 in 11 18miles	6 metres 19ft 8in	UO Well guarded, modern road with several hairpin bends; road tunnel at summit; suitable for caravans; but prohibited during the winter.
+Thurn 1274 metres (4180ft) Austria	Kitzbühel 762 metres (2500ft) Mittersill 789 metres (2588ft)	19km 1 in 12 11.8 miles 10km 1 in 16 6.2 miles	5 metres 16ft 5in	UO A good road with narrow stretches; northern approach rebuilt; suitable for caravans.
Timmelsjoch (Rombo) 2509 metres (8232ft) Austria - Italy	Obergurgl 1910 metres (6266ft) Moso 1007 metres (3304ft)	14km 1 in 7 8.7 miles 23km 1 in 8 14miles	3.5 metres 11ft 6in	UC mid Oct - late Jun. Pass open to private cars (without trailers) only as some tunnels on the Italian side are too narrow for larger vehicles; toll road. Border closed at night 20.00 -07.00 hrs.
Tonale 1883 metres (6178ft) Italy	Edolo 699 metres (2293ft) Dimaro 766 metres (2513ft)	30km 1 in 12 18.6 miles 27km 1 in 10 16.7 miles	5 metres 16ft 5in	UO A relatively easy road; suitable for caravans.
Toses (Tosas) 1800 metres (5906ft) Spain	Puigcerdá 1152 metres (3780ft) Ribes de Freser 920 metres (3018ft)	26km 1 in 10 16miles 25km 1 in 10 15.5 miles	5 metres 16ft 5in	UO Now a fairly straightforward, but continuously winding, two-lane road with many sharp bends; negotiable by caravans.
Tourmalet 2114 metres (6936ft) France	Luz 711 metres (2333ft) Ste-Marie-de-Campan 857 metres (2812ft)	18km 1 in 8 11miles 17km 1 in 8 10.6 miles	4 metres 13ft 1in	UC Oct - mid Jun. The highest of the French Pyrenean routes; the approaches are good, though winding and exacting over summit; sufficiently guarded.
Tre Croci 1809 metres (5935ft) Italy	Cortina d'Ampezzo 1224 metres (4016ft) Auronzo di Cadore 864 metres (2835ft).	7km 1 in 9 4.4 miles 26 km 1 in 9 16 miles	6 metres 19ft 8in	OC Dec - Mar. An easy pass; very fine scenery; suitable for caravans.

* Permitted maximum width of vehicles 7ft 6in   + Permitted maximum width of vehicles 8ft 2.5in   ++ Maximum length of vehicle 30ft

Pass and height	From To	Distances from summit and max gradient	Min width of road	Conditions (see page 51 for key to abbreviations)
Turracher Höhe 1763 metres (5784ft) Austria	Predlitz 922 metres (3024ft) Ebene-Reichenau 1062 metres (3484ft)	20km 1 in 5.5 12.4 miles 8km 1 in 4.5 5miles	4 metres 13ft 1in	UO Formerly one of the steepest mountain roads in Austria; now much improved. A steep, fairly straightforward ascent is followed by a very steep descent; good surface and mainly two-lane width; fine scenery.
*Umbrail 2501 metres (8205ft) Switzerland - Italy	Santa Maria im Münstertal 1375 metres (4511ft) Bormio 1225 metres (4019ft)	14km 1 in 11 9 miles 19km 1 in 11 11.8 miles	4.3 metres 14ft 1in	UC Early Nov - early Jun. Highest of the Swiss passes; narrow; mostly gravel surfaced with 34 hairpin bends, but not too difficult.
Vars 2109 metres (6919ft) France	St-Paul-sur-Ubaye 1470 metres (4823ft) Guillestre 1000 metres (3281ft)	8km 1 in 10 5miles 20km 1 in 10 12.4 miles	5 metres 16ft 5in	OC Dec - Mar. Easy winding ascent with seven hairpin bends; gradual winding descent with another seven hairpin bends; good surface; negotiable by caravans.
Wurzen (Koren) 1073 metres (3520ft) Austria - Slovenia	Riegersdorf 541 metres (1775ft) Kranjska Gora 810 metres (2657ft)	7km 1 in 5.5 4.5miles 6km 1 in 5.5 3.5 miles	4 metres 13ft 1in	UO A steep two-lane road, which otherwise is not particularly difficult; heavy traffic at summer weekends; delay likely at the frontier; caravans prohibited.
Zirler Berg 1009 metres (3310ft) Austria	Seefeld 1180 metres (3871ft) Zirl 622 metres (2041ft)	6km 1 in 7 3.5 miles 5km 1 in 6 3.1 miles	7 metres 23ft	UO An escarpment facing south, part of the route from Garmisch to Innsbruck; a good, modern road, but heavy tourist traffic and a long steep descent, with one hairpin bend, into the Inn Valley. Steepest section from the hairpin bend down to Zirl; caravans prohibited northbound.

* Permitted maximum width of vehicles 7ft 6in   + Permitted maximum width of vehicles 8ft 2.5in   ++ Maximum length of vehicle 30ft

KEY TO REGIONS

The country directories, with the exception of Andorra and Luxembourg, are divided into regions, each introduced by a brief description, to help you to plan your touring holidays. Below is a list of the regional headings used in each country directory, followed by a list of the departments, districts or administrative areas that may be included within each region. See also the country maps at the end of the book.

ROME - Frosinone, Latina, Roma, Rieti, Viterbo
SOUTH - Avellino, Bari, Benevento, Brindisi, Caserta, Catanzaro, Cosenza, Foggia, Lecce, Matera, Napoli, Potenza, Reggio di Calabria, Salerno, Taranto
SARDINIA - Cagliari, Nuoro, Oristano, Sassari
SICILY - Agrigento, Caltanissetta, Catania, Enna, Messina, Palermo, Ragusa, Siracusa, Trapani

NETHERLANDS

NORTH - Ameland, Drenthe, Friesland, Groningen
CENTRAL - Flevoland, Gelderland, Noord-Holland, Overijssel, Utrecht
SOUTH - Limburg, Noord-Brabant, Zeeland, Zuid-Holland

PORTUGAL

SOUTH - Algarve, Baixo-Alentejo
NORTH - Costa Verde, Douro Litoral, Minho, Tras os Montes, Alto Douro
CENTRAL - Alto Alentejo, Beira Alta, Beira Baixo, Beira Litoral, Costa de Prata, Estremadura, Ribatejo

SPAIN

NORTH EAST COAST - Barcelona, Girona
CENTRAL - Albacete, Avila, Badajoz, Cáceres, Ciudad Real, Cuenca, Guadalajara, Madrid, Salamanca, Segovia, Soria, Teruel, Toledo
SOUTH EAST COAST - Alicante, Castellón, Tarragona, Valencia
NORTH COAST - Asturias, Cantabria, Guipúzcoa, La Coruña, Lugo, Vizcaya
NORTH EAST - Alava, Burgos, Huesca, Lleida, La Rioja, Navarra, Zaragoza
NORTH WEST - Léon, Logrono Orense, Palencia, Pontevedra, Valladolid, Zamora
SOUTH - Almeria, Cádiz, Cordoba, Granada, Huelva, Jaén, Málaga, Murcia, Sevilla
ISLANDS - Ibiza, Mallorca Menorca

SWITZERLAND

NORTH - Aargau, Basel, Solothurn
NORTH EAST - Appenzell, Liechtenstein, St Gallen, Schaffhausen, Thurgau, Zürich
NORTH WEST/CENTRAL - Bern, Jura, Luzern, Neuchâtel, Nidwalden, Obwalden, Schwyz, Uri, Zug
EAST - Glarus, Graubünden
SOUTH - Ticino
SOUTH WEST - Fribourg, Genève, Valais, Vaud

AUSTRIA

Austria is a land of chalet villages, beautiful cities and majestic mountains. It is bordered by eight countries: the Czech Republic, Germany, Hungary, Italy, Liechtenstein, Switzerland, Slovakia and Slovenia.

FACTS AND FIGURES
Area: 83,858 sq km (32,378 sq miles)
Population: 8,131,111 (2000 est)
Capital: Wien (Vienna)
Language: German
IDD Code: 43. To dial the UK, dial 00 44
Currency: Euro
Local time: GMT + 1 (Summer GMT + 2)
Emergency services: Police 133; Fire 122; Ambulance 144. Or dial 112 & request service you require.
Banks: 08.00-12.30, 13.30-15.00 (extended to 17.30 Thu)
Shops: Mon-Fri 08.00-18.00; Sat 08.00-12.30
Average daily temperatures:
Jan -1°C   Mar 3°C
May 15°C   Jul 20°C
Sep 16°C   Nov 5°C
Tourist information:
Austrian National Tourist Office
UK PO Box 2363 London W1A 2QB
Tel (020) 7629 0461
USA 500 Fifth Avenue Suite 800, New York NY 10110
Tel (212) 944 6880
Camping card: recommended; some reductions on site fees
Tourist info website:
www.austria-tourism.at

The scenery is predominantly Alpine, an inspiring mix of mountains, lakes and pine forests. The splendour of the mountains can be seen in the imposing Dachstein region of upper Austria and the massive Tyrolean peaks. The lakes of Burgenland and Salzkammergut, the River Danube, the forests and woods of Styria and the world-famous city of Wien (Vienna) are outstanding features of this majestic landscape.

Most of the country enjoys a moderate climate during the summer, although eastern areas are sometimes very hot. The heaviest rainfall occurs in midsummer. The language of Austria is German, and English is not widely spoken. The Austrians pride themselves on their informal and easy-going nature, a nature summed up by the word "gemütlich", one of those words that defies adequate translation.

Austria offers a variety of outdoor activities to suit everyone and there are numerous campsites throughout the country. Most are open from May to September, although a number remain open all year.

Off-site camping or caravanning is generally prohibited. In areas with no campsites contact local police to find out whether an overnight stay is possible. If permission is granted, no camping activity must be seen from outside, eg chairs, awnings etc. Open fires are generally prohibited in woodland areas. Campers not on an official site, eg private property, staying in Austria for more than three days should report to the police as soon as possible, and also inform them of subsequent changes of location. Within Wien (Vienna) and Tirol (Tyrol) any form of off-site camping or caravanning is prohibited.

HOW TO GET THERE

Apart from the crossing via the Channel Tunnel, the usual Continental Channel ports for this journey are Calais or Oostende (Ostend). From Calais drive through eastern France to Strasbourg, then via Karlsruhe and Stuttgart, crossing into Austria at Füssen for **Innsbruck and the Tirol**, and beyond München (Munich) for **Salzburg and central Austria**.

From Ostend, drive through Belgium to Aachen, then via Köln (Cologne), Frankfurt, Nürnberg and München (Munich).

As an alternative, you could cross to Dieppe, Le Havre, Caen (Ouistreham) or Cherbourg and drive through northern France via **Strasbourg** and **Stuttgart**, or via **Basel** and northern Switzerland. But see 'Motorway tax' in this and the Swiss section.

Distance
From the Continental Channel ports, Salzburg is about 1140km (708 miles) and Vienna is about 1310km (814 miles), and you will probably need one overnight stop on the way.

Car sleeper trains

Summer services are available from **Denderleeuw** (Belgium) to Salzburg and Villach and from 's-**Hertogenbosch** (Netherlands) to Innsbruck and Villach.

MOTORING AND
GENERAL INFORMATION

The information given here is specific to Austria. It **must** be read in conjunction with the ABC at the front of the book, which covers those regulations which are common to many countries.

Air pollution alarm

Restrictions on the circulation of tourist vehicles may apply at certain times in those areas where the level of air pollution exceeds certain limits. However, these restrictions do not apply to tourists using non-polluting vehicles, i.e. bicycles cars fitted with a catalytic converter system or low-pollution vehicles, i.e. all diesel-engines vehicles put on the road after 1 January 1990. Drivers of exempt vehicles must purchase a permit from the ÖAMTC and display a white test plaque on the windscreen in the event of a pollution alarm.

British Embassy/Consulates*

The British Embassy is located at 1030 Wien, Jaurèsgasse 12 ☎ (01) 716130; consular section, Jaurèsgasse 10 ☎(01) 71613 5151. There are British Consulates with Honorary Consuls, in Bregenz, Graz, Innsbruck and Salzburg.

Children in cars

Children under 12 and 1.5 metres in height are not permitted to travel as front or rear seat passengers unless using a suitable restraint system - see 'Passengers' and 'Seat Belts' in the Continental ABC section.

Currency

With the introduction of the Euro, the **Austrian Schilling (ATS)** ceased to be legal tender from 28 February 2002. However, ATS coins and notes may still be exchanged at local banks until 30 June 2002 (not confirmed) and at the Austrian Central Bank (**Oesterreichische Nationalbank**) for an unlimited period.

Dimension and weight restrictions*

Private **cars** and towed **trailers** or **caravans** are restricted to the following dimensions - height, 4 metres; width 2.55 metres; length, 12 metres. The maximum permitted overall length of vehicle/trailer or caravan combination is 18.75 metres.

Trailers without brakes may weigh up to 750kg and may have a total weight of up to 50% of the towing vehicles.

Driving licence*

A valid UK or Republic of Ireland licence is acceptable in Austria. However, those licences which do not incorporate a photograph will not be recognised unless accompanied by photographic proof of identity, eg. a passport. The minimum age at which a visitor may use a temporarily imported motorcycle (exceeding 50cc) or car is 18 years.

First-aid kit*

In Austria all vehicles (including motorcycles) must be equipped with a first-aid kit by law and visitors are expected to comply. This item will not be checked at the frontier, but motorists can be stopped at the scene of an accident and their first-aid kit demanded; if this is not forthcoming the police may take action.

Foodstuffs*

If the imported foodstuffs are for personal use, there are no limits when travelling between EU countries. Visitors entering Austria from outside the EU may personally import 1kg of meat, all animal products (eg eggs, milk, honey) and all animal based products (eg milk products, sausages, fish and all sea animal products), 1kg of conserves made from meat or animal products as above, and 250g of caviar. Coffee (500g), coffee extract (200g), tea (100g), and tea extract (40g) are free of customs duties, but visitors under 15 cannot import coffee.

Lights*

It is compulsory for motorcyclists to use dipped headlights during the day.

Motoring club

The Österreichischer Automobil-, Motorrad- und Touring Club (ÖAMTC) which has its headquarters at 1010 Wien, Schubertring 1-3 ☎ (01)71199-0, has offices at the major frontier crossings, and is represented in most towns either directly or through provincial motoring clubs. The offices are usually open between 09.00 to 18.00hrs weekdays, 09.00 to 12.00hrs on Saturdays and are closed on Sundays and public holidays.

Motorway tax

All vehicles using Austrian motorways must display a motorway tax sticker (vignette). Stickers may be purchased at the frontier and from ÖAMTC offices, post offices and some petrol stations for periods of 10 days, 2 months or 1 year. The cost of a 10-day sticker for vehicles up to 3.5 tonnes in weight, with or without a trailer is EUR 7.63.

Petrol

(See the ABC under 'Petrol/Diesel)

Roads

The motorist crossing into Austria from any frontier enters a network of well-engineered roads.

The main traffic artery runs from Bregenz in the west to Wien (Vienna) in the east, via the Arlberg Tunnel (Toll: see *Major Road and Rail Tunnels*), Innsbruck, Salzburg, and Linz. Most of the major alpine roads are excellent, and a comprehensive tour can be made through the Tirol, Salzkammergut and Carinthia without difficulty. Service stations are fairly frequent, even on mountain roads.

In July and August, several roads across the frontier become congested. The main points are on the Lindau-Bregenz road; at the Brenner Pass (possible alternative - the Résia (Reschen) Pass); at Kufstein; on the München (Munich)-Salzburg *Autobahn* and on the Villach-Tarvisio road. Additionally, because of increasing traffic from Germany, Klingenbach and Nickelsdorf on the Austro/Hungarian border are very busy. For details of mountain passes consult the Contents page.

Austria has over 1000 miles of motorway (*autobahn*) with additional tolls payable on the Brenner, Karawanken Tunnel, Tauern, Pyhrn

(Gleinalm and Bosruck Tunnels). Triangles marked on motorway posts indicate the nearest emergency telephone (every 2km). A flashing orange/yellow light at the top of telephone posts indicates danger ahead.

Speed limits*

Car / Motorcycle
Built-up areas 50kph (31mph)
Other roads 100kph (62mph)
Motorways 130kph (80mph)
Car towing caravan not exceeding 750kg (1,650lb)†
Built-up areas 50kph (31mph)
Other roads 100kph (62mph)
Motorways 100kph (62mph)
Car towing caravan exceeding 750kg (1,650lb)†
Built-up areas 50kph (31mph)
Other roads 80kph (49mph)
Motorways 100kph (62mph)
† If the total weight of the two vehicles exceeds 3,500kg the following speed limits apply:
Built-up areas 50kph (31mph)
Other roads 60kph (37mph)
Motorways 70kph (43mph)

Notes

i. *To tow a caravan/trailer, the weight of any caravan/trailer equipped with over-run brakes must not exceed the maximum weight of towing vehicle.*
ii. *Driving licence must show entitlement to drive this kind of combination.*

Warning triangle*
The use of a warning triangle is compulsory outside built-up areas in the event of an accident or breakdown. The triangle must be placed 50 metres (55yds) behind the vehicle on ordinary roads and 100 metres (109yds) on motorways to warn following traffic of any obstruction; it must be visible at a distance of 50 metres (55yds).

* Additional information will be found in the Continental ABC at the front of the book.

The town centre of Schwaz is chiefly commercial, but contains a few Gothic buildings of interest. The town's chief attraction, the Silberbergwerk is to the east of the town centre on the Husslstrasse. The Silberbergwerk ("Silver Mine") tour begins with a short train ride into the mine, and continues with a 60-minute walking tour.

CARINTHIA

Carinthia has a diverse heritage, having previously been the home of the Celts, the Romans, the Slavs, and the Bavarians, each leaving behind a fascinating sample of their culture. However, one attraction stands out especially, the hilltop fortress of Hochosterwitz.

Hochosterwitz is 20 kilometres north-east of Carinthia's largest town, Klagenfurt, from where there is a regular train service to the fortress' closest village, Launsdorf. The fortress itself is the perfect fairy-tale castle, and is believed to have been the inspiration for the castle in the Disney classic, *Snow White & The Seven Dwarfs*.

The building dates from 1571 and was designed to repel the threat of Turkish invaders. As a defensive measure, Hochosterwitz was very effective and its gates appeared to be impregnable to opposing armies. Six of the fourteen gates into the fortress sport a bust of one of the von Khevenhüller family, who were responsible for the building, and incidentally still own the fortress to this day.

STYRIA

Styria is the industrial backbone of Austria, and home to Graz, the nation's second city with a population of some 250,000 people. Some 40,000 of these are students, which makes the city an ideal place for bars, nightclubs and restaurants. The city also plays host to a large annual story-telling festival.

Twenty kilometres north of Graz is the village of Stübing (served by eight trains each day). Twenty minutes' walk from Stübing station, lying in a picturesque alpine valley is the Österreichisches Freilichtmuseum (Austrian Open-air Museum). Open from April to October, it stretches for over two kilometres and features full-size examples of traditional Austrian architecture from Burgenland to Voralberg. At weekends volunteers demonstrate traditional crafts such as baking and textiles. On the last

Sculptured fountain at the Kaiservilla, summer residence of Emperor Francis Joseph I in the small spa town of Bad Ischl

TOURIST INFORMATION

TYROL

This is true Austrian mountain country; the region is home to Grossglockner, Austria's highest mountain standing 3,797 metres above sea level, which is served by the country's highest mountain pass. Innsbruck is the Tyrol's provincial centre and one of Austria's most beautiful cities. Its wealth came from the Tyrol's silver deposits, which financed such works of art as its famous Goldenes Dachl, an ornate palace built by Maximilian I around 1500. None of the mines are productive today, but a handful have remained open as 'show mines'. The town is also famous for having twice hosted the Winter Olympics (1964 & 1976).

The summit of the Zugspitze towers over the tiny Tirolean village of Ehrwald,

Sunday of September there is also an Erlebnistag or Activity Day with traditional food and dancing.

UPPER AUSTRIA
The River Danube flows gracefully through Upper Austria and gives the area much of its picturesque charm. The river reaches the height of its powers in the winding valley of the Wachau region which is very popular for bike touring; the north bank has a specially constructed cycle path (the 380km long Donauradweg).

The jewel in the crown of the Wachau's north bank is the walled town of Durnstein, famed for the striking ice-blue and white baroque tower of its Stiftskirche. At the castle

here Richard I of England (the Lionheart) was held for ransom by Duke Leopold V of Babenburg after returning from the Crusades in1193. Thanks to Swedish attack in 1645 only ruins now remain, commanding excellent views over the town.

LOWER AUSTRIA
Lower Austria contains the Burgenland region which has historically been an area of nationalist struggle between Austria and Hungary, but today is one of the most peaceful and attractive regions of Central Europe.

One of the Burgenland's most interesting places is Eisenstadt which was home to the composer, Josef Haydn, who was born in nearby Rohrau in 1732. For many years, Haydn lived in the

The village of Dollach high up in the Molltal, north of Lienz

land of mountains and valleys in the authentic alpine tradition.

Like the Tyrol, Voralberg is famed for its winter sports and breathtaking summer views. One of its most beautiful locations is the awe-inspiring Hochtannberg Pass which stands over 1,679 metres above sea level, with the majestic Lechtaler Alps in the background.

The Hochtannberg Pass was originally settled in the 14th century by Swiss immigrants from the Valais canton, which has given the region a truly unique character. Worth exploring are the small villages of Schröcken, which lie at the entrance to the pass, and Unterboden, further east along the pass.

VIENNA

Vienna is synonymous with the operatic world, having been home to some of the world's great composers. The city stages an opera and classical music festival every year which begins in May and finishes in early June. There is also a Mozart festival just before Christmas to add some warm cheer to Vienna's cold winters. Mozart spent many years in the city, and died there in 1791. He was buried a pauper, and the location of his unmarked grave has never been satisfactorily found, although a monument stands in the St Marxer Friedhof.

Vienna's most famous landmark is the 13th-century St Stephen's Cathedral (Stephansdom), renowned for its famous steep roof, lined with green, yellow, black, and white tiles in bold geometric designs. The North Tower co ntains a lift which opens out onto a wonderful view of Vienna and a close-up view of the Cathedral's famous bell, Die Pummerin. The bell was cast in 1711 from cannons captured from the Turkish army in 1683; its military background came back to haunt it in World War II when the North Tower was hit and Die Pummerin plummeted from the tower into the nave.

The other attractions of St Stephen's Cathedral include the Riesentor (Giant's Door) on the north-west façade, and the impressive tomb of Emperor Friedrich III who died in 1470. The Cathedral catacombs can also be viewed, and just to confirm that nowhere in Vienna lacks an operatic link, Mozart celebrated his marriage here in 1782.

Schloss Esterhàzy, a gigantic medieval fortress with impressive late baroque and neo-classical additions. There are guided tours most weekdays, and the Schloss stages numerous concerts throughout the year.

Other attractions in Eisenstadt include the Haydnhaus, which is open daily, and the Haydn Mausoleum in the hilltop Bergkirche, which is open between April and October.

VORALBERG

The Voralberg region lies in the extreme west of the country towards the Swiss border, and is a

● ● ● ● ● ●● TIROL ●● ● ● ● ●

Magnificent lofty peaks, crystal-clear mountain lakes, peaceful forests and tranquil valleys characterise this area of Austria. The high mountain regions, reaching altitudes of over 10,000ft (4,000 metres), are accessible by mountain road passes and dozens of cable-cars and chair lifts. For the climbing and walking enthusiast this is a wonderland of opportunity. The Tirol has a long architectural heritage; even the trim little provincial towns and villages have dignified burgher houses with impressive façades; there are mosaics on public buildings and private houses, and medieval castles and castle ruins command some of the finest settings in the Tirol. The cheerful hospitality of the region is renowned, and folk festivals, dancing and yodelling are colourful local traditions. Innsbruck, the capital of the region, still boasts its medieval old town, with handsome houses facing narrow, irregular streets. Highlights here include the Golden Roof (Goldenes Dachl), with its gilded copper tiles; the Cathedral (Dom), with its imposing west front and rich interior; and the fascinating and extensive displays in the Museum of Folk Art (Tiroler Volkskunstmuseum).

....

❱ ASCHAU TIROL

Aufenfeld Distelberg 1 ☎ 05282 2916 ▤ 05282 291611
e-mail: camping.fiegl@tirol.com
A well equipped family site on level meadowland backed by thickly wooded slopes.
➲ *Signposted from the Aschau road.*
All year 12HEC ⅏ 🏕️🄿🛠️🍴✕⊙🅿🅰🚿🏪🛒⚡ LP 🏧 lau ➧
⚡R 🔁 Prices: 🛏️4.40-6.50 🚗1.50-1.50 🛺2.54-3 pitch 6.54-10.50

❱ EHRWALD TIROL

International Dr-Ing E Lauth Zugspitzstr 34
☎ 05673 2666 ▤ 05673 26664
e-mail: camping-ehrwald@tirol.com
On undulating grassland, surrounded by high conifers, below the Wetterstein mountain range. Cars may park by tents in winter.
➲ *To the right of the access road to the Zugspitz funicular.*
All year 1HEC ⅏ ♦🏕️🍴🛠️✕⊙🅿🅰🚿🏧 lau ➧🛠️⚡P

Tiroler Zugspitzcamp Obermoos 1 ☎ 05673 2309 ▤ 230951
e-mail: ferienanlage@zugspitze.com
A well equipped site on several grassy terraces surrounded by woodland. Modern sanitary installations with bathrooms.
➲ *Near the Zugspitz funicular station.*
All year 5HEC ⅏ ♦🏕️🛠️🍴✕⊙🅿🅰🚿⚡ P 🏧🔁

❱ FERNSTEINSEE TIROL

Schloss Fernsteinsee ☎ 05265 5210-157
A shady wooded meadowland site.
➲ *Approx. 3km from Nassereith towards the Fernpass. Signposted.*
Mar-Oct 8HEC ⅏ ♦🏕️🛠️✕⊙🅿🅰🚿⚡ LR 🏧🔁 lau ➧🛠️✕🚿⚡P

❱ FIEBERBRUNN TIROL

Tirol-Camp ☎ 05354 56666 ▤ 05354 52516
e-mail: office@tirol-camp.at
A summer and winter site in pleasant Alpine surroundings.
All year 4.7HEC ⅏ 🏕️🛠️🍴✕⊙🅿🅰🚿⚡ P 🏧🔁➧🔁L

❱ FÜGEN TIROL

Hell Gagering 212b ☎ 05288 62203 ▤ 05288 64615
e-mail: camping.hell@tirol.com
In a meadow surrounding a farm with fine views of the surrounding mountains.
➲ *1km N of Fügen on the B169.*
All year 3HEC ⅏ 🏕️🛠️🍴✕⊙🅿🅰🚿🏪🛒⚡ P 🏧🔁 lau

❱ HAIMING TIROL

Center Oberland Bundestr 9
☎ 05266 88294 ▤ 05266 884589
e-mail: oberland@tirol.com
On a sloping meadow in a picturesque mountain setting. A wide variety of sporting facilities are available.
➲ *Off B171 at Km485.*
All year 4HEC ⅏ 🏕️🛠️🍴✕⊙🅿🅰🚿⚡ P 🏧🔁 lau ➧
⚡R Prices: 🛏️4.36-5.09 🚗3.27-4 🛺3.27-4 🛺3.27-4

❱ HEITERWANG TIROL

Heiterwangersee Hotel Fisher am See
☎ 05674 5116 ▤ 05674 5260
e-mail: fischer.am.see@tirol.com
In a quiet situation in a meadow beside lake behind the hotel.
➲ *By Hotel Fischer am See.*
All year 1HEC ⅏ ♦♦🏕️🍴✕⊙🅿🅰🚿⚡ L 🏧🔁 lau
Prices: 🛏️8 🚗6 🛺6 🛺6 pitch 6

❱ HOPFGARTEN TIROL

Schlossberg Itter 140 ☎ 05335 2181 ▤ 05335 2182
e-mail: camp.itter@netway.at
A family site with good leisure facilities. In terraced meadowland below Schloss Itter on the Brixental Ache.
➲ *2km W on B170.*
Dec-5 November 4HEC ⅏ ⠿ 🏕️🛠️🍴✕⊙🅿🅰🚿⚡ PR 🏧 lau ➧⚡L 🔁

❱ HUBEN TIROL

Ötztaler Naturcamping ☎ 05253 5855 ▤ 05253 5538
e-mail: oetzt-naturcamp@netway.at
A well kept site in a beautiful wooded location beside a mountain stream.
➲ *S of the town. Signposted from Km27 on B186.*
All year 0.5HEC ⅏ 🏕️🛠️✕⊙🅿🅰🚿🏧🔁 lau ➧🛠️✕🅰
Prices: 🛏️4.50-4.65 🚗2.18 🛺4.06-4.06 🛺2.68-4.06

❱ IMST TIROL

Imst-West Langgasse 62
☎ 05412 66293 ▤ 05412 63364
e-mail: fink.franz@aon.at
On open meadowland in the Langgasse area.
➲ *Off the bypass near the turn for the Pitztal.*
All year 1HEC ⅏ 🏕️🛠️🍴⊙🅿🅰🚿🏧 lau ➧✕⚡LPR 🔁
Prices: 🛏️4-4.80 pitch 5.10-6.20

❱ INNSBRUCK TIROL

Innsbruck-Kranebitten Kranebitter Allee 214
☎ 0512 284180 ▤ 0512 284180
e-mail: campinginnsbruck@hotmail.com
In a pleasant location close to the city. An 'Innsbruck Card' giving reductions to many places of interest and some forms of public transport is available at the site.
➲ *Signposted from A12/E60 (Innsbruck-Arlberg).*
All year 3HEC ⅏ 🏕️🛠️🍴✕⊙🅿🅰🚿🏪🅰⚡ R 🏧🔁 lau
➧⚡P Prices: 🛏️4.94 🚗2.91 🛺3.27 🛺2.91

KITZBÜHEL TIROL

Schwarzsee ☎ 05356 62806 ▤ 6447930
In meadowland on the edge of a wood behind a large restaurant.
➲ *2km from town on B170 towards Wörgl turn right, 400m after Schwarzsee railway station.*
All year 6HEC ⟁ ♣ ℝ ⅃ ⅄ ☀ ⊙ ⋤ ∅ ᛤ ⊟ ⅄ L ⌂ ⊞ lau
Prices: ⋔7-7.50 ⇺3.50 ⊞4 ⋏3.50 pitch 7.50

KÖSSEN TIROL

Wilder Kaiser Kranebittau 18 ☎ 05375 6444 ▤ 05375 2113
Situated in a lovely position below Unterberg, this level site is adjoined on three sides by woodland.
➲ *For access follow road to Unterberg Lift, then turn right and continue for 200m.*
All year 5HEC ⟁ ℝ ⅃ ⅄ ⅄ ☀ ⊙ ⋤ ∅ ⋏ ⅄ P ⌂ ⊞ lau

KRAMSACH TIROL

Stadlerhof ☎ 05337 63371 ▤ 05337 65311
e-mail: camping@tirol.com
A pleasant, year-round site on the Reintaler See with well defined pitches and good leisure facilities.
➲ *Access via A12.*
All year 3HEC ⟁ ⟁ ℝ ⅃ ⅄ ⅄ ☀ ⊙ ⋤ ∅ ᛤ ⋤ ⅄ LP ⌂ ⊞ lau ♣ ⅄R Prices: ⋔4.50-5.74 ⇺11.12-13.08

KUFSTEIN TIROL

Hager Au 326 ☎ 05372 64170 ▤ 05332 7296635
Site situated on level meadowland.
All year 0.5HEC ⟁ ♣ ℝ ⅃ ⅄ ⅄ ☀ ⊙ ⋤ ∅ ⅄ ⊟ lau ♣ ⅄LR

Kufstein Salurner Str 36 ☎ 05372 62229
In a pleasant location with a good variety of sporting facilities.
➲ *1km W of Kufstein between River Inn and B171.*
May-Oct 1HEC ⟁ ⟁ ℝ ⅃ ⅄ ⅄ ☀ ⊙ ⋤ ∅ ᛤ ⌂ ⊞ lau ♣ ⅄LPR

LANDECK TIROL

See also Zams

Riffler ☎ 05442 64898 ▤ 05442 648984
e-mail: d.springeth@tirol.com
Site on meadowland between residential housing and the banks of the Sanna.
Closed May 0.3HEC ⟁ ♣ ℝ ⊙ ⋤ ⅄ ⅄ R ⌂ ⊞ lau ♣ ⅃ ⅄
⅄ ∅ ᛤ ⅄P Prices: ⋔4.20 ⇺2.18 ⊞6.90-8 ⋏4.30-6.90

Sport Camp Tirol Mühlkanal 1 ☎ 05442 64636 ▤ 64037
e-mail: info@sportcamptirol.at
Meadowland site with many fruit trees.
➲ *On B316.*
All year 1.5HEC ⟁ ⟁ ℝ ⅃ ⅄ ⅄ ☀ ⊙ ⋤ ∅ ᛤ ⋤ ⅄ R ⌂ ⊞ lau
♣ ⅄P Prices: ⋔5.10 ⇺3.30 ⊞7.60 ⋏3.30-7.60

LÄNGENFELD TIROL

Ötztal ☎ 05253 5348 ▤ 05253 5909
In meadowland with some tall trees on the edge of woodland.
➲ *Turn right off E186 at fire station.*
All year 2.6HEC ⟁ ⟁ ℝ ⅃ ⅄ ⅄ ☀ ⊙ ⋤ ∅ ᛤ ⌂ ⊞ lau ♣ ⅄
⅄P

LERMOOS TIROL

Happy Camp Hofherr Garmischer Str 21 ☎ 05673 2980
▤ 05673 29805
e-mail: info@camping-lermoos.com
Well equipped site in a wooded location with fine views of the surrounding mountains.
➲ *500mtrs from the town, off B187 towards Ehrwald.*
Closed Nov-14 Dec & May 0.8HEC ⟁ ⟁ ℝ ⅄ ⅄ ☀ ⊙ ⋤ ᛤ ⌂
lau ♣ ⅃ ∅ ⅄PR ⊞ Prices: ⋔5.10-6 pitch 6.20-7.70

LEUTASCH TIROL

Caravan Park Leutasch ☎ 05214 65700 ▤ 05214 657030
e-mail: holiday-camping@utanet.at
A modern site on level grassland screened by trees on the Leutascher Ache.
➲ *Turn off B313 (Mittenwald-Scharnitz) towards Leutasch.*
Nov-12 Dec 2.6HEC ⟁ ⟁ ℝ ⅃ ⅄ ⅄ ☀ ⊙ ⋤ ∅ ᛤ ⋤ ⅄ PR ⌂
⊞ lau Prices: ⋔7.50-9 ⇺6-10 ⊞6-10 ⋏4

LIENZ TIROL

Falken Eichholz 7 ☎ 04852 64022 ▤ 04852 640226
e-mail: camping.falken@tirol.com
On open ground on the outskirts of the town with modern sanitary facilities.
➲ *S of Lienz. Signposted from B100.*
20Oct-20Dec 2.5HEC ⟁ ♣ ℝ ⅃ ⅄ ⅄ ☀ ⊙ ⋤ ∅ ᛤ ⌂ lau ♣
⅄LPR ⊞

MAURACH TIROL

Karwendel ☎ 05243 6116 ▤ 05243 20036
e-mail: karwendel-camping@achensee.tirol.at
On a level meadow with fine views of the surrounding mountains.
➲ *In town turn off the B181 and follow the Pertisau road.*
All year 1.8HEC ⟁ ⟁ ℝ ⅃ ⅄ ⅄ ☀ ⊙ ⋤ ∅ ᛤ ⋤ ⌂ lau ♣ ⅃ ⅄LP
⊞ Prices: ⋔4.50 ⇺2.90 ⊞4.40 ⋏2.90-3.70

MAYRHOFEN TIROL

Mayrhofen Laubichl 125 ☎ 05285 6258051 ▤ 05285 6258060
e-mail: kroell.hermann@netwing.at
A modern site with good facilities, a few minutes walk from the centre of the village.
➲ *Near a farm at N entrance to village.*
Nov-mid Dec 2HEC ⟁ ⟁ ℝ ⅃ ⅄ ⅄ ☀ ⊙ ⋤ ∅ ᛤ ⅄ P ⌂ ⊞ lau

NASSEREITH TIROL

Rossbach ☎ 05265 5154
All year 1HEC ⟁ ♣ ℝ ⅃ ⅄ ☀ ⊙ ⋤ ∅ ᛤ ⅄ P ⌂ ⊞

NATTERS TIROL

Natterer See Natterer See 1 ☎ 0512 546732 ▤ 0512 54673216
e-mail: info@natterersee.com
A terraced site beautifully situated amidst woodland and mountains on the shore of Natterersee. A wide variety of leisure facilities are available.
➲ *Approach via Brenner Motorway, exit 'Innsbruck Süd', via Natters, onto B182 and follow signs.*
All year 7.5HEC ⟁ ⟁ ℝ ⅃ ⅄ ⅄ ☀ ⊙ ⋤ ∅ ᛤ ⋤ ⅄ ⅄ L ⌂
⊞ lau Prices: ⋔5.50-7.10 pitch 7.50-9.70

NAUDERS TIROL

Alpencamping Nauders ☎ 0043/5473 87266 ▤ 872682
e-mail: alpencamping@tirol.com
A year-round family site in a delightful Alpine location with good recreational facilities.
➲ *Access via B315.*
Closed Nov-17 Dec 3HEC ⟁ ⟁ ℀ ℝ ⅃ ⅄ ☀ ⊙ ⋤ ∅ ⌂ lau ♣ ⅄
⅄ Prices: ⋔5 ⊞16-18 ⋏12.40-13.40 pitch 16-18 (incl 2 persons)

NEUSTIFT TIROL

Hochstubai ☎ 05226 3484 ▤ 05226 2610
On slightly sloping meadowland.
➲ *Near the Geier Alm approximately 5km S of town on the road towards the Gletscher bahn.*
All year 2.7HEC ⟁ ⟁ ℝ ⅃ ⅄ ☀ ⊙ ⋤ ∅ ᛤ ⅄ R ⌂ ⊞ lau ♣
⅄LP

PFUNDS TIROL

Sonnen ☎ 05474 5232
Site in meadowland with some fruit trees.
➲ *On road B315 between SHELL Garage and Gasthof Sonne.*
All year 1HEC ⸺ � symbols ⮕ ⁀LP

PILL TIROL

Plankenhof ☎ 05242 64195 🖷 72004
e-mail: m.khuen-belais@tirol.com
Site in meadow.
➲ *On B171 near Gasthof Plankenhof.*
May-1 Oct 0.6HEC ⸺ symbols ⁀ P 🖪 lau ⮕ ⁀L
Prices: ⚐3 ▲4.50 pitch 6.50

PRUTZ TIROL

Prutz ☎ 05472 2648 🖷 05472 2652
e-mail: aktiv-camp@netway.at
A pleasant site in a beautiful mountain setting with good, modern facilities.
All year 1.5HEC ⸺ symbols ⁀R 🖪
lau ⮕ ✕ ⁀LP

REUTTE TIROL

Reutte Ehrenbergstr 53 ☎ 05672 62809
Well kept site on a meadow on the edge of a forest near the sports centre. Modern swimming pool in town.
➲ *Turn right towards Waldrast.*
Closed May 2.2HEC ⸺ symbols lau ⮕ ⛾✕
⁀P

Seespitze ☎ 05672 78121
May-15 Oct 2HEC ⸺ symbols ⁀ L 🖪 lau ⮕
✕

Sennalpe ☎ 05672 78115 🖷 05672 63372
In a quiet situation next to the lake.
➲ *On Reutte-Oberammergau road 200m from the Hotel Forelle.*
Closed 16 Oct-14 Dec 4HEC ⸺ symbols ⁀ L 🖪
lau ⮕ ⛾✕

RIED BEI LANDECK TIROL

Dreiländereck ☎ 05472 6025 🖷 05472 60254
e-mail: camping-drellandereck@tirol.com
Level site in centre of village beside a lake with spectacular views.
All year 1HEC ⸺ symbols lau ⮕ ✕
⛪ ⁀LPR

RINN TIROL

Judenstein Judenstein 40 ☎ 05223 78620
In a wooded location with fine views.
➲ *Access via motorway exit Hall.*
Apr-15 Oct 0.6HEC ⸺ symbols lau ⮕ ⛾✕

ST JOHANN TIROL

Michelnhof Weiberndorf 6 ☎ 05352 62584 🖷 05352 625844
e-mail: campingplatz.michelnhof@aou.at
➲ *1.5km S via B161 (St-Johann-Kitzbühel).*
All year 3HEC ⸺ symbols lau ⮕ ⛾ ⁀PR
Prices: ⚐4.72-7 ⮕2.90-3.30 ⮕3.63-4 ▲2.90-3.63

SCHWAZ TIROL
At **WEER**(6km W)

Alpencamping Mark Maholmhof
☎ 05224 68146 🖷 05244 681466
e-mail: alpcamp.mark@aou.at
Situated on meadowland by a farm on the edge of a forest.
➲ *Off B171.*
Apr-Oct 2HEC ⸺ ⮕ symbols ⁀ P 🖪 lau ⮕ ⁀L

SÖLDEN TIROL

Sölden ☎ 05254 26270 🖷 05254 26275
e-mail: camping.soelden@netway.at
Situated on meadowland on left bank of Ötztaler tributary.
Beautiful views of the surrounding mountains.
➲ *By Grauer Bär Inn at Km36 on the B186.*
Closed May-15 Jun 1.3HEC ⸺ symbols lau ⮕
⛾✕ ⁀P Prices: ⚐6.60-8.70 ⮕7.30-11 ⮕7.30-11 pitch 7.30-11

STAMS TIROL

Eichenwald Schiessstand weg 10 ☎ 05263 6159
Well managed terraced site in oak wood.
➲ *Turn off B171 at ESSO filling station in direction of abbey, onto a steep, narrow access road.*
Nov 2HEC ⸺ symbols ⁀ P 🖪 lau ⮕
⁀R Prices: ⚐4 pitch 5.45 (incl 2 persons)

THIERSEE TIROL

Rueppenhof Seebauern 8 ☎ 05376 5694
e-mail: atzl.barbara@tirol.com
Site made up of several meadows surrounding a farm that lies on the banks of the lake.
➲ *Access via A12 exit Kufstein-Nord, then follow signs for Thiersee.*
Apr-Oct 1.5HEC ⸺ symbols ⁀ L 🖪⮕⛾✕
Prices: ⚐4 ⮕1.80 ⮕2.50 ▲1.45-2.18

UMHAUSEN TIROL

Ötztal Arena Camp Krismer ☎ 05255 5390 🖷 05255 5390
e-mail: info@oetztal-camp.com
➲ *Signposted from B186.*
All year 1HEC ⸺ symbols ⁀ R 🖪 lau
Prices: ⚐5.50 pitch 5

UNTERPERFUSS TIROL

Farm ☎ 05232 2209 🖷 22094
Modern site on gently sloping meadow in a beautiful mountain setting.
➲ *W end of village near Amberg railway and main road.*
All year 2HEC ⸺ symbols ⮕⛾✕

VOLDERS TIROL

Schloss ☎ 05224 52333
A pleasant site in the grounds of a castle surrounded by thick woods.
Camping Card Compulsory.
➲ *Access from the B171 by ARAL filling station or from motorway exit Schwaz or Wattens.*
15 May-15 Oct 2.5HEC symbols ⁀ P 🖪 lau

VÖLS TIROL

Völs Bahnhofstr 10 ☎ 0512 303533
➲ *Access via motorway exit Innsbruck-Kranebitten.*
Apr-Nov 0.4HEC ⸺ symbols lau ⮕⛾ ⁀LPR

WAIDRING TIROL

Steinplatte Unterwasser 43 ☎ 05353 5345 🖷 05353 5406
On a level meadow with fine panoramic views of the surrounding mountains.
All year 4HEC ⸺ symbols ⁀ L 🖪⮕
⁀PR

A guide to the Symbols & Abbreviations used in this book can be found on page 5

WALCHSEE TIROL

Seespitz Wassersportzentrum ☎ 05374 5359 ▤ 05374 5845
e-mail: camping.seespitz@netway.at
In pleasant surroundings beside the Walchsee with good
recreational facilities.
➲ *Between B172 and bank of lake.*
All year 3HEC ⣿ ⣿ ⣿ ⚶ ☀ ⌂ ⌇ ✕ ⊙ ⬤ ⊘ ⺸ L ⬛ ⊞ lau

Terrassencamping Süd-See Seestr 76
☎ 05374 5339 ▤ 05374 5529
e-mail: campingwalchsee@aon.at
A lakeside site in wooded surroundings with extensive
terracing and fine mountain views.
➲ *500m W on B172 turn into 'no through road' and continue
for 1500m.*
All year 11HEC ⣿ ⣿ ⚶ ☀ ⌂ ⌇ ✕ ⊙ ⬤ ⊘ ⬛ ⊞ L ⬛
⊞ lau **Prices:** ♠5-5.50 pitch 5.50-6.50

WESTENDORF TIROL

Panorama Mühltal 26 ☎ 05334 6166 ▤ 05334 6843
e-mail: panorama.camping@netway.at
In a beautiful Alpine setting with good modern facilities,
including well furnished studio apartments.
➲ *W towards Wörgl via B170.*
All year 2.2HEC ⣿ ⌂ ⌇ ☀ ✕ ⊙ ⬤ ⊘ ⬛ ⌂ ⬛ ⊞ lau ➜
⺸P **Prices:** ♠5.45-7.27 ➜3.42-5.08 ⚑3.42-5.08 ▲3.42

ZAMS TIROL
See also Landeck

Zams Magdalenaweg 1 ☎ 05442 63289
A comfortable family site in a central location.
➲ *2km NE of Landeck. Access via A12 and B171.*
Jun-20 Sep 0.2HEC ⣿ ⌂ ⌇ ⊙ ⬛ ⊞ ⊞ ➜ ☀ ⌇ ✕ ⊘ ⬛ ⺸LPR

ZELL AM ZILLER TIROL

Hofer Gerlossasstr 33 ☎ 05282 2248 ▤ 05282 2248
e-mail: office@campinghofer.at
On meadowland with some fruit trees.
➲ *Site lies to the end of Zillertal off the road leading to the
Gerlos Pass.*
All year 1.5HEC ⣿ ⌂ ⌇ ☀ ⌇ ✕ ⊙ ⬤ ⊘ ⺸ P ⬛ ⊞ lau
Prices: ♠4.50-7 ▲1.50 pitch 5.50-8

ZIRL TIROL

Alpenfrieden Eigenhofen 11 ☎ 05238 53520
➲ *Terraced site with orchard surroundings.
Near the B171.*
May-Sep 1HEC ⣿ ⌂ ⌇ ☀ ✕ ⊙ ⬤ ⊘ ⚑ ⺸ P ⬛ ⊞ ➜ ⺸R

CARINTHIA

High mountains on all sides tumble down to this sunny,
southern, gentle land of soft light with over a thousand
warm, clear lakes. The climate is kind to holiday-makers as
most of the weather troughs are broken up by the
surrounding mountains, so this province gets many more
sunny days than the rest of the country. The lakes provide a
wealth of water sports in the summer, frequently reaching
temperatures of over 75 degrees F (24 degrees C) - ideal
for swimmers, wind-surfers and sailors. Anglers can fish for
pike, whitefish and carp, and hot springs in the region have
been channelled into waterpark complexes with chutes and
whirling currents, or health spas offering the 'gift of youth'.
But the mild summers are complemented by sharp winters,
making Nassfeld and the Nock district popular areas for
winter sports.
There is a relaxed Mediterranean atmosphere in this region,
and a substantial Slovene minority, dating back to the 6th
century, adds its own distinct character and language to
southern parts.

The capital of Carinthia is Klagenfurt which, according to
legend, was built on a swamp once dominated by a dragon.
The centre of the town now is the Dragon Fountain
(Lindwurmbrunnen), with its huge grim 16th-century
sculpture of the town's heraldic emblem. Now an important
junction and commercial centre, Klagenfurt's old quarter
has many handsome baroque buildings set in attractive
lanes and passageways.

DELLACH KÄRNTEN

Neubauer ☎ 04766 2532 ▤ 04766 25324
A terraced site with direct access to the Millstättersee.
➲ *Access from B100, Leinz-Spittal road. The turn-off is well
signposted in the village.*
May-15 Oct 1.5HEC ⣿ ⌂ ⌇ ✕ ⊙ ⬤ ⊘ ⺸ L ⬛ lau ➜ ☀ ✕ ⊘

DELLACH IM DRAUTAL KÄRNTEN

Waldbad ☎ 04714 288 & 234 ▤ 04714 2343
e-mail: gemeinde.dellach.drautal@netway.at
A small site in a delightful wooded setting with two large
swimming pools.
➲ *Leave A10 at Spittal & turn onto B100.*
May-Sep 2HEC ⣿ ⌂ ⌇ ✕ ⊙ ⬤ ⊘ ⺸ P ⬛ ⊞ lau ➜ ☀ ⺸R

DÖBRIACH KÄRNTEN

Brunner am See Glanzerstr 108 ☎ 04246 7189 ▤ 04246 7837
e-mail: camping.brunner@aon.at
Tidily arranged with poplar trees. Private bathing area.
➲ *The access road is at the E end of Lake Millstatt.*
All year 3.5HEC ⣿ ⣿ ⚶ ⌂ ⌇ ☀ ✕ ⊙ ⬤ ⊘ ⬛ ⺸ L ⬛ ⊞
lau ➜ ⺸P

Burgstaller Seefeldstr 16 ☎ 04246 7774 ▤ 7774-4
e-mail: deiter.burgstaller@campingpark.telecom.at
A quiet site situated 100m from the lake, with good modern
facilities.
➲ *At SE end of lake. From B98 continue towards Lake
Millstatt for 1km.*
All year 7.5HEC ⣿ ⌂ ⌇ ☀ ✕ ⊙ ⬤ ⊘ ⬛ ⌂ ⬛ ⺸ LP ⬛ ⊞ lau

Schwimmbadcamping Ebner Seefeldstr 1 ☎ 04246 7735
▤ 04246 773513
➲ *On either side of the Seefeldstr, beyond Camping
Burgstaller, at E end of Lake Millstatt.*
1HEC ⣿ ⌂ ⌇ ☀ ✕ ⊙ ⬤ ⊘ ⬛ ⺸ P ⬛ ⊞ lau ➜ ⺸L

Winkler Strandweg 26 ☎ 04246 7187 ▤ 04246 7206
Family site on level ground, divided into sections and
surrounded by woodland close to the Millstättersee.
➲ *Approx. 200m E of the lake.*
15 Apr-15 Oct 2HEC ⣿ ⌂ ⌇ ✕ ⊙ ⬤ ⊘ ⚑ ⬛ ⊞ ➜ ☀
⺸LPR

DÖLLACH KÄRNTEN

Zirknitzer ☎ 04825 451 ▤ 04825 45117
e-mail: camping.zirknitzer@utauet.at
Beside the River Möu.
➲ *Between Km8 and Km9 on the Glocknerstr (B107).*
21 Dec-4 Nov 0.6HEC ⣿ ➜ ☀ ⌂ ⌇ ✕ ⊙ ⬤ ⌂ ⚑ ⺸ R ⬛ ⊞
lau ➜ ⊘ ⺸P

DROBOLLACH KÄRNTEN

Mittewald Fuchsbichlweg 9 ☎ 04242 27392 ▤ 04242 373928
In a hollow on slightly rising ground surrounded by trees
and divided into pitches. Large children's playground.
➲ *Off Villach-Faaker See road. Signposted 'Serai'.*
All year 2.5HEC ⣿ ➜ ☀ ⌂ ⌇ ✕ ⊙ ⬤ ⌂ ⺸ P ⬛ lau ➜ ☀

EBERNDORF KÄRNTEN

Rutar Lido ☎ 04236 2262-0 ▤ 04236 2220
On an open meadow at the edge of a forest. A popular family site with good facilities.
All year 15HEC ▦ ♠ ♦ ♚ ✕ ⊙ ☺ ⌀ ☎ ♥ ⚡ LP 🏠 ⊞ lau

FELDKIRCHEN KÄRNTEN

Seewirt-Spiess Maltschach am See 2
☎ 04277 2637 ▤ 04277 2637 - 4
e-mail: office@seewirl-spiess.com
In a pleasant wooded location on the shore of the Maltschacher See.
➲ *Access via B95 towards Klagenfurt.*
May-Sep 1.2HEC ▦ ⊿ ♠ ♥ ✕ ⊙ ☺ ⌀ ☎ ⚡ L 🏠 lau ♦ ⚡
⚡P ⊞ **Prices:** ♟6 pitch 16-22 (incl 2 persons)

HEILIGENBLUT KÄRNTEN

Grossglockner ☎ 04824 2048 ▤ 04824 2048
e-mail: company@heiligenblut.at
In a location on a meadow surrounded by woodland within the National Park.
➲ *Signposted.*
15 May-Oct & Dec-15 Apr 2.5HEC ▦ ⊿ ♠ ♥ ✕ ⊙ ☺ ⌀
♨ ⚡ R 🏠 ⊞ lau ♦ ⚡P

HERMAGOR KÄRNTEN

Schluga Seecamping ☎ 04282 2051 ▤ 288120
e-mail: camping@schluga.com
A well equipped family site approx. 300m N of lake in meadowland with some terraces and fine views.
➲ *6km E of Hermagor.*
20 May-20 Sep 8.8HEC ▦ ♠ ⊿ ♠ ♥ ✕ ⊙ ☺ ⌀ ♨ ♥ ▲ ⚡ L
🏠 ⊞ lau Prices: ♟4.80-6.80 pitch 4.30-7.10

KEUTSCHACH KÄRNTEN

Strandcamping Süd ☎ 04273 2773 ▤ 04273 27734
In a pleasant setting among shrubs and trees on south side of the Keutschachersee.
➲ *Access via motorway exit Valden towards Kreutschacher-Seental.*
20 Apr-Sep 2HEC ▦ ⊿ ♠ ♚ ✕ ⊙ ☺ ⚡ L 🏠 ⊞ lau Prices:
♟5.09-5.81 ♥5.81-6.54

KLAGENFURT KÄRNTEN

Strandbad ☎ 0463 21169 ▤ 0463 21193
e-mail: camping@stw.at
Large site divided into sections by trees and bushes.
➲ *From town centre take B83 towards Velden. Turn left just outside town in direction of bathing area.*
May-Sep 4HEC ▦ ♠ ⊿ ♠ ♚ ♥ ✕ ⊙ ☺ ☎ ⚡ L 🏠 ⊞ lau

KÖTSCHACH-MAUTHEN KÄRNTEN

Alpen ☎ 04715 429 ▤ 04715 429
e-mail: alpencamping@carinthia.com
On level meadowland beside River Gail with good facilities for water sports.
➲ *Turn off B110 in the S part of the village on the road to the Plöcken Pass and drive 800m towards Lesachtal.*
Closed Nov-14 Dec 1.4HEC ▦ ♠ ⊿ ♠ ♥ ✕ ⊙ ☺ ⌀ ♨ ☎ ☎
⊞ lau ♦ ✕ ⚡PR **Prices:** ♟3.20-5 pitch 3.90-6

MALTA KÄRNTEN

Maltatal ☎ 0043 4733 234 ▤ 4733 23416
e-mail: info@maltacamp.at
On a gently rising alpine meadow with breathtaking views of the surrounding mountains.
➲ *In Gmünd turn off B99 and drive 5.5km through Malta valley.*
27 Mar-31 Oct 3.5HEC ▦ ♠ ⊿ ♠ ♚ ♥ ✕ ⊙ ☺ ⌀ ☎ ⚡ PR 🏠
⊞ lau

MÖLLBRÜCKE KÄRNTEN

Rheingold Mölltalstr 65 ☎ 04769 2338
➲ *Site on main road from Spittal to Mallnitz, next to swimming pool.*
All year 2HEC ▦ ⊿ ♠ ✕ ⊙ ☺ ⚡ P 🏠 ♦ ⚡

OBERVELLACH KÄRNTEN

Sport Erlebnis ☎ 04782 2727 ▤ 04782 3183
e-mail: info@sporterlebnis.at
May-Sep 10HEC ▦ ⊿ ♠ ♥ ✕ ⊙ ☺ ⌀ ▲ ⚡ R 🏠 ⊞ ⊞ lau
♦ ⚡ ♨

OSSIACH KÄRNTEN

Ossiach ☎ 04243 436 ▤ 04243 8171
e-mail: martinez@camping.at
Divided into pitches with generally well-situated terraces.
➲ *Off B94 on E bank of Kale Ossiacher.*
May-30 Sep 10HEC ▦ ⊿ ♠ ♚ ♥ ✕ ⊙ ☺ ⌀ ♨ ♥ ▲ ⚡ L 🏠
⊞ ⚡ lau

Parth ☎ 04243 2744
On hilly ground on S shore of the lake. Steep, but there are some terraces.
➲ *Off B94 on S bank of Lake Ossiach.*
Apr-Oct 1.8HEC ▦ ⊿ ♠ ♥ ✕ ⊙ ☺ ⌀ ♨ ☎ ♥ ⚡ L 🏠 ⊞
⚡ lau

At HEILIGEN GESTADE(5km SW)

Seecamping Berghof Ossiachersee-Süduferstr 241
☎ 04242 41133 ▤ 04242 41133-30
e-mail: ertl@camping.at
Terraced meadowland in attractive setting. 800m long promenade with bathing areas. Dogs not allowed Jul-Aug
➲ *E shore of Lake Ossiacher.*
1 Apr-31 Oct 10HEC ▦ ⊿ ♠ ♥ ✕ ⊙ ☺ ⌀ ♨ ☎ ⚡ L 🏠
Prices: ♟5-7.30 pitch 7.50-12.20

SACHSENBURG KÄRNTEN

Markt Sachsenburg Marktpl 12
☎ 04769 292522 ▤ 04769 292520
e-mail: gemeinde.sachsenburg@carinthia.com
A modern family site with good facilities in a delightful mountain setting.
➲ *Access via A10 between Spittal and Lienz.*
May-Sep 1.3HEC ▦ ⊿ ♠ ⊙ ☺ 🏠 ♦ ♚ ♥ ✕ ⌀ ⚡P ⊞

ST PRIMUS KÄRNTEN

Strandcamping Turnersee Breznik
☎ 04239 2350 ▤ 04239 235032
e-mail: info@breznik.at
A quiet site in a picturesque mountain setting with a good variety of recreational facilities.
➲ *Access via B70 Klagenfurt-Graz towards Kopensee.*
30 Mar-05 Oct 6HEC ▦ ♠ ⊿ ♠ ♚ ♥ ✕ ⊙ ☺ ⌀ ♨ ☎ ♥ ⚡ L
🏠 ♦ ⊞ **Prices:** ♟4.14-7.12 pitch 5.81-8.94

SCHIEFLING KÄRNTEN

Weisses Rössl Auenstr 47
☎ 04274 2898 ▤ 04274 28984
e-mail: weisses.roesl@aon.at
In a wooded setting with fine views of the surrounding mountains on the shore of the Wörther See.
May-Sep 2.5HEC ▦ ⊿ ♠ ♥ ✕ ⊙ ☺ ⌀ ☎ ☎ ⚡ L 🏠 ⊞ lau
♦ ⚡L **Prices:** ♟5.50-7 pitch 4.50-5

SEEBODEN KÄRNTEN

Ferienpark Lieseregg Kras 27 ☎ 04762 2723 ▤ 04762 33857
e-mail: info@ferienpark-lieseregg.at
A family site on a large level meadow with terraces and asphalt drives surrounded by woodland.

Cont.

➲ *B99 from Spittal north to B98, then left for 1.5km.*
May-1 Oct 3HEC ▥ ⊶ ⋔ ⛵ ☓ ⊙ ♨ ⌀ ♨ ⚡ P ⊡ ⊞ lau
Prices: ⚓5.85-7.15 pitch 7.30

▶ SPITTAL AN DER DRAU KÄRNTEN

Draufluss ☎ 04762 2466 ▤ 04762 36299
A long, narrow riverside site, partly surrounded by a hedge.
➲ *From town centre follow road to river towards
Goldeckbahn.*
Apr-Oct 0.7HEC ▥ ⊶ ⋔ ⛵ ☓ ⊙ ♨ ⚡ P ⊡ ⊞ lau ➤ ⛴ ⌀

▶ STOCKENBOI KÄRNTEN

Ronacher Möse 6 ☎ 04761 256 ▤ 04761 2564
e-mail: terrassencamping.ronacher@net4you.at
Situated on meadow between forest slopes, gently sloping to
the shore of Lake Weissensee. Shop in high season only.
➲ *Approach for caravans via Weissensee.*
May-10 Oct 1.7HEC ▥ ❀ ⋔ ⛵ ⚡ ☓ ⊙ ♨ ⌀ ⚡ L ⊡ ⊞

▶ TECHENDORF KÄRNTEN

Strandcamping Knaller ☎ 04713 2234
➲ *From B87, drive towards Weissensee.*
May-Oct 1.5HEC ▥ ⊶ ⋔ ☓ ⊙ ♨ ⌀ ⚡ L ⊡ ⊞ ➤ ⛵ ☓

▶ VILLACH KÄRNTEN

Gerli St Georgenerstr 140 ☎ 04242 57402 ▤ 04242 582909
Level, quiet, isolated site, with heated swimming pool
annexed to it which is open to the public.
➲ *From Spittal/Drau turn off B100, turn right just before
Villach and continue for 2km.*
All year 2.3HEC ▥ ⊶ ⋔ ⛴ ☓ ⊙ ♨ ⌀ ⛺ ⚡ P ⊡ ⊞ lau
➤ ⛵

▶ At FAAK AM SEE(10km SE)

Komfortcamping Poglitsch ☎ 04254 2718 ▤ 04254 4144
Mar-Oct 7HEC ▥ ⊶ ⋔ ⛴ ☓ ⊙ ♨ ⌀ ⚡ L ⊡ ⊞ lau

Strandcamping Arneitz ☎ 04254 2137 ▤ 04254 3044
On a wooded peninsula jutting into the Faakersee with good
sporting facilities.
28 Apr-Sep 6HEC ▥ ⋮⋮ ⊶ ⋔ ⛴ ☓ ⊙ ♨ ⌀ ♨ ⚡ L
⊞ lau

Strandcamping Florian Badeweg 3 ☎ 04254 2261
A partially shaded site between the lakeside and the road.
➲ *Access from road by Hotel Fürst.*
May-25 Sep 3.5HEC ▥ ⊶ ⋔ ⛴ ☓ ⊙ ♨ ⌀ ⛺ ⚡ L ⊡ ⊞
lau ➤ ♨

Strandcamping Gruber ☎ 04254 2298 ▤ 04254 2298-7
On level ground beside the lake with fine views of the
surrounding mountains.
May-Sep 2.5HEC ▥ ⋮⋮ ⊶ ⋔ ⛴ ⛵ ☓ ⊙ ♨ ⚡ L ⊡ ⊞ lau ➤
⌀ **Prices:** ⚓85

▶ WERTSCHACH KÄRNTEN

Alpenfreude ☎ 04256 2708 ▤ 04256 27084
e-mail: camping.alpenfreude@aon.at
May-Sep 5HEC ▥ ⊶ ⋔ ⛴ ☓ ⊙ ♨ ⌀ ⛺ ⚡ P ⊡ ⊞ lau
Prices: ⚓3.63-4.36 pitch 5.04-5.81

⬤ ⬤ ⬤ ⬤ STYRIA ⬤ ⬤ ⬤ ⬤

Styria is a mosaic of soft hills in the southern wine-growing
area, wide forest areas which have given the province the
name of the 'green march', and the grand rocky massifs of
the upper Styria. Between the high Alps, crossed by
dramatic mountain passes, and the lowland regions, is a
spectrum of beautiful scenery, with pleasant summer
resorts and winter sports areas. The region is rich in
majestic gorges and waterfalls, the largest and the best
known of which is the Gesause, where the River Enns has

carved its way through the mountains. Caves are a feature
of Styria - the large Lurgrotten at Peggau is well equipped
for visitors - and some caves have revealed evidence of
prehistoric occupation. Austria's second largest city and
Styria's capital, the lively city of Graz is in the south-east
corner of the province. A major industrial and university
town, Graz boasts many interesting historic buildings, and
above the attractive old town, a funicular leads to the
1,552ft (473 metres) Schlossberg which is dominated by the
town's distinctive landmark, a 92ft (28 metre) clock tower
(Uhrturm).

▶ AUSSEE, BAD STEIERMARK

Traun Grundlseer Str 21 ☎ 03622 54565 ▤ 03622 52427
e-mail: gh.staudnwirt@aussee.at
In pleasant wooded surroundings.
➲ *2.5km from Bad Aussee towards Grundlsee.*
All year 0.4HEC ▥ ⊶ ⋔ ⛵ ☓ ⊙ ♨ ♨ ⚡ R ⊡ lau ➤ ⛴ ⌀
⚡ LP ⊞ **Prices:** ⚓5.10 pitch 2.90

▶ GRAZ STEIERMARK

S C Central Martinhofstr 3 ☎ 0316 281831
A site with many lawns separated by asphalt paths and partly
divided into pitches.
➲ *Turn off the B70 in Strassgang S of Graz and continue for
300m.*
Mar-Oct 4HEC ▥ ➤ ⋔ ⛴ ⛵ ☓ ⊙ ♨ ⌀ ♨ ⛺ ⚡ P ⊡ ⊞ lau

▶ HIRSCHEGG STEIERMARK

Hirschegg ☎ 03141 2201
In a delightful Alpine setting.
➲ *Access via A2 towards Klagenfurt, exit Modriach.*
All year 2HEC ▥ ⊶ ⋔ ⊙ ♨ ⌀ ⛺ ⊡ lau ➤ ⛴ ⛵ ☓ ⚡ LR ⊞

▶ LANGENWANG-MÜRTZAL STEIERMARK

Europa Siglstr 5 ☎ 03854 2950
On level meadow with some trees, surrounded by hedges.
The site occupies an attractive alpine setting.
➲ *The B306 (E7) by-passes the town, so be careful not to miss
the exit 6km S of Mürzzuschlag.*
All year 0.6HEC ▥ ⊶ ⋔ ⊙ ♨ ⌀ ♨ ⊡ lau ➤ ⛴ ⛵ ☓ ⚡ R ⊞
Prices: ⚓3.16 ➤2.79 ▲2.79

▶ LEIBNITZ STEIERMARK

Leibnitz R-H-Bartsch-Gasse 33 ☎ 03452 82463 ▤ 84811
e-mail: gde@leibnitz.steiermark.at
A well equipped site in pleasant wooded surroundings with
plenty of leisure facilities.
➲ *W of town. Signposted.*
May-15 Sep 0.7HEC ▥ ➤ ⋔ ☓ ⊙ ♨ ⚡ PR ⊡ ⊞ lau ➤ ⛴ ⛵
☓ ⌀ ⚡ L

▶ LIEBOCH STEIERMARK

Graz-Lieboch ☎ 03136 61797
In a picturesque wooded location with good modern
facilities.
➲ *Access via A2, exit Lieboch.*
May-Oct 0.3HEC ▥ ⊶ ⋔ ☓ ⊙ ♨ ⌀ ⛺ ⚡ P ⊡ ⊞ lau ➤ ⛴ ☓ ⌀
Prices: ⚓5 ➤5 ⛴5 ▲4-5

▶ MARIA LANKOWITZ STEIERMARK

Piberstein Am See 1 ☎ 03144 7095950 ▤ 03144 7095974
e-mail: freizeitinsel_piberstein@aon.at
Large well equipped site surrounding a series of lakes. Plenty
of sporting facilities.
➲ *S of Maria Lankowitz towards Pack.*
May-15 Oct 5.6HEC ▥ ⊶ ⋔ ⛴ ☓ ⊙ ♨ ⛺ ⚡ L ⊡ ⊞ lau ➤
⛵ ⌀ ⌀

MITTERNDORF, BAD STEIERMARK

Grimmingsicht ☎ 03623 2985
e-mail: camping@grimmingsicht.at
A modern site in a picturesque mountain setting with a
variety of sporting facilities.
All year 0.6HEC ⛆ ⚥ ♠ ⚑ ✕ ☉ ⊞ ⛺ ⊞ ⚑ ⚘ ↝ R ☎ ⊞ lau ➧ ⚘
✕ ⚏ ↝P

MÜHLEN STEIERMARK

Badsee Hitzmannsdorf 2 ☎ 03586 2418
Family site with direct access to the lake.
➲ *N via B92. Signposted.*
May-Sep 1.5HEC ⛆ ⚥ ♠ ⚘ ⚑ ✕ ☉ ⊞ ⛺ ⊞ ⚑ ↝ L ☎ lau ➧ ⊘
⚏ ↝P

OBERWÖLZ STEIERMARK

Schloss Rothenfels ☎ 03581 8208 ▤ 03581 82084
e-mail: rothenfels@aon.at
In picturesque Alpine surroundings in the grounds of a
castle, with good recreational facilities.
➲ *On SE outskirts.*
Apr-Oct 8HEC ⛆ ⚥ ♠ ☉ ⊞ ⛺ ⊞ ⚑ ↝ L ☎ lau ➧ ⚘ ⚑ ✕ ⊘
↝PR ⊞

ST GEORGEN STEIERMARK

Olachgut ☎ 03532 2162 ▤ 03532 2162
e-mail: olachgut@murau.at
On a level meadow, surrounded by beautiful mountain
scenery.
➲ *Signposted.*
All year 10HEC ⛆ ⚥ ♠ ☉ ⊞ ⊘ ⚏ ⊞ ⛺ ⚑ ▲ ↝ L ☎ lau
➧ ↝R

ST SEBASTIAN STEIERMARK

Erlaufsee Erlaufseestr 3 ☎ 03882 4937 ▤ 03882 214822
e-mail: sankt.sebastian@aon.at
In a picturesque Alpine setting in woodland, 100mtrs from
the lake.
➲ *Signposted.*
May-15 Sep 1HEC ⛆ ➧ ♠ ☉ ⊞ ⚑ ☎ lau ➧ ✕ ↝L
Prices: ⚑3.60 ⊕2.50 ⊞3 ▲3

SCHLADMING STEIERMARK

Zirngast Linke Ennsau 633 ☎ 0664 4328185 ▤ 03687 23495
e-mail: camping @zirngast.at
Site in meadow on left bank of River Enns next to railway.
➲ *Turn off B308 towards town as far as the MOBIL filling
station.*
All year 1.5HEC ⛆ ⚞ ♠ ⚘ ⚑ ✕ ☉ ⊞ ⊘ ⚏ ↝ R ☎ ⊞ lau ➧
↝P ⊞ Prices: ⚑6 ▲4.50-6

STUBENBERG STEIERMARK

Steinmann ☎ 03176 8390
➲ *5km towards Hirnsdorf towards the lake.*
All year 4HEC ⛆ ➧ ♠ ⚘ ✕ ☉ ⊞ ⊘ ⚏ ↝ L ☎ ⊞

UNGERSDORF BEI FROHNLEITEN STEIERMARK

Lanzmaierhof Ungersdorf 16 ☎ 03126 2360 ▤ 4174
e-mail: tourismus@frohnleiten.at
➲ *Signposted 2km S of Frohnleiten on the Graz road.*
Apr-15 Oct 0.5HEC ⛆ ⚥ ♠ ✕ ☉ ⊞ ⊘ ⚏ ⊞ ⊞ Prices:
⚑3.70 ⊕2.20 ⊞2.20 ▲1.10-2.20 pitch 1.50

WEISSKIRCHEN STEIERMARK

Fisching Fisching 9 ☎ 03577 82284 ▤ 8228440
e-mail: campingpark@fisching.at
A modern site with fine sanitary and sporting facilities, 6km
from the Formula 1 circuit (A1-Ring) in Zeltweg.

➲ *Leave S36 at Zeltweg-Ost exit, head towards Obdach and
follow signs for B78. Site well signposted in centre of Fisching.*
Apr-15 Oct 1.5HEC ⛆ ⚥ ♠ ⚑ ✕ ☉ ⊞ ⊘ ⚏ ⊞ ⚑ ↝ P ⊞ ⊞ ⊘
lau ➧ ⚘

WILDALPEN STEIERMARK

Wildalpen ☎ 03636 342 & 341 ▤ 313
e-mail: tourismus@wildalpen.at
Located in a nature reserve beside the River Salza with good
canoeing facilities.
Apr-Oct 0.8HEC ⛆ ⣿ ⚥ ♠ ☉ ⊞ ⊘ ↝ R ☎ lau ➧ ⚘ ⚑ ✕
↝P ⊞ Prices: ⚑1.90-2.30 ⊕2.30-2.30 ▲1.40-2.50

● ● ● ● **LOWER AUSTRIA** ● ● ● ●

Lower Austria, by far the largest of the nine provinces,
wraps itself around the federal capital of Vienna, itself a
separate province. The Danube divides Lower Austria
roughly in half, and has been central to the development of
the area for centuries: prehistoric and Roman remains have
been found, castles and fortified churches testify to the
Romanesque and Gothic periods, and great monasteries
and pilgrimage churches celebrate the Baroque. North of
the river the countryside, flat in the west, becomes hilly
towards the Czech Republic border; south of the river the
land rises into wooded hills (including the well-known
Vienna Woods - Wienerwald), and climbs to over 6,560ft
(2,000 metres) in the Schneeberg and Rax regions -
popular holiday areas for the Viennese.
Good communications have promoted industrial
development in the Vienna basin and it is now the largest
industrial area in the country. But agriculture is also
important in the province, and vineyards around Krems and
Weinviertel produce excellent wines.
The south of the province, Burgenland the 'land of castles',
has many monuments to a valiant past in what was for
centuries a frontier area, occupied by the Romans and later
vulnerable to attack from the Huns and the Turks. It is now
a peaceful landscape of wooded hills, pastures, fruit
orchards and vineyards.
In dramatic contrast is the impressive expanse of the
'paszta' plain in the north east, and the vast Neusiedler See
- the only steppe lake in central Europe, and well known for
unique flora and fauna - providing good opportunities for
bathing and yachting.
Eisenstadt, the provincial capital is dominated by the
Schloss Esterhazy, where this aristocratic family had its seat
in the 17th and 18th centuries. There is an attractive old
town, a cathedral, and the Haydnhaus (now a museum)
where Haydn lived during the 30 years he was
Kapellmeister here.
....

BREITENBRUNN BURGENLAND

Seebad ☎ 02683 5252 ▤ 02683 5252
May-Sep 1HEC ⛆ ⚥ ♠ ☉ ⚑ ↝ L ⊞ ⊞ ⊘ lau ➧ ⚘ ✕ ↝P
Prices: ⚑3.64 ⊕1.31 ⊞2.91 ▲1.46-1.82

GMÜND NIEDERÖSTERREICH

Assangteich Albrechtser Str 10
☎ 02852 52506 ▤ 02852 54514
e-mail: stadtgemeinde@gmuend.at
In a pleasant location with a good variety of recreational
facilities.
➲ *Signposted from B41.*
5 Apr-6 Oct 0.5HEC ⛆ ➧ ♠ ☉ ✕ ☉ ⊞ ⚑ ☎ lau ➧ ⊘ ⚏
↝LP ⊞ Prices: ⚑4.06 pitch 6.20

HIRTENBERG NIEDERÖSTERREICH

Hirtenberg Leobersdorfefstr
☎ 02256 81111 ▨ 02256 8111117
⮑ *Take exit Leobersdorf on A2/E59 and continue W on B18 for approx. 0.8km.*
15 May-15 Sep 1.5HEC ⸬ ♣ ⋒ ☉ ◲ ▣ ⊘ lau ➧ ⒧ ✕ ⊘ ⭲P ⊞ Prices: ♠4 pitch 5

JENNERSDORF BURGENLAND

Jennersdorf Freizeitzentrum 3
☎ 03329 46133 ▨ 03329 4626121
A pleasant site in wooded surroundings.
⮑ *Access via A2 exit Fürstenfeld.*
16 Mar-Oct 1HEC ⸬ ⒣ ⋒ ☉ ◲ ⭲ P ⊞ lau ➧ ⒧ ✕ ⊘ ⭲R Prices: ♠4.40 pitch 4.80

LAXENBURG NIEDERÖSTERREICH

Schlosspark Laxenburg Münchendorfer Str
☎ 02236 71333 ▨ 02236 73966
e-mail: camping.laxenburg@verkehrsbuero.at
On level meadowland with surfaced roads. The site lies in a recreation centre within the grounds of the historic Laxenburg Castle.
⮑ *Access 600m S on the road leading to the B16.*
Apr-Oct 2.4HEC ⸬ ⒣ ⋒ ☉ ◲ ⊘ ⭲ P ⊞ lau ➧ ✕
Prices: ♠5-5.50 ◧6-6.50 pitch 3-3.50

MARBACH NIEDERÖSTERREICH

Marbach ☎ 0664 5581815 ▨ 07413 703533
e-mail: mfz@wvnet.at
In a pleasant situation beside the River Danube.
⮑ *Access via A1 exit Ybbs.*
Apr-Sep 0.4HEC ⸬ ⒣ ⋒ ✕ ☉ ◲ ⭲ R ⊞ lau ➧ ⭲P

MARKT ST MARTIN BURGENLAND

Markt St Martin Mühlweg 2 ☎ 02618 2239 ▨ 02618 2239
e-mail: post@markt-st-martin.bgld.gv.at
On a level meadow with plenty of trees and bushes.
⮑ *Access via A2 exit Krumbach/Schäffern.*
May-Sep 0.5HEC ⸬ ♣ ⋒ ✕ ☉ ◲ ⭲ PR ▣ ⊞ ⊘ ➧ ⒧ ✕
Prices: ♠4 ◧4 ▲1.50

PODERSDORF BURGENLAND

Strandcamping Podersdorf am See Strandpl ☎ 02177 2279
Directly on the Neusiedler See next to the sportsground.
Apr-Oct 7HEC ⸬ ⸫ ⒣ ⋒ ☉ ◲ ◲ ⭲ L ▣ lau ➧ ⒧ ✕ ⊘ ⊞

RAPPOLTENKIRCHEN NIEDERÖSTERREICH

Rappoltenkirchen Kreuthstr 5 ☎ 02274 8425 ▨ 02274 8422
⮑ *Turn off B1 at Sieghartskirchen and continue S for 3km.*
Closed Jan 2.2HEC ⸬ ⒣ ⋒ ☉ ◲ ⊘ ▣ ⊞ lau ➧ ⒧ ✕

RECHNITZ BURGENLAND

GC Hauptpl 10 ☎ 03363 79202 ▨ 03363 7920222
e-mail: post@rechnitz.bgld.gr.at
On an artificial lake in the heart of the beautiful Faludi Valley.
Jun-Aug 1HEC ⸬ ⸰⸰ ⋒ ✕ ☉ ◲ ⭲ L ▣ ⊞ ➧ ⒧ ✕ ⊘ ⸬

RUST BURGENLAND

Rust ☎ 02685 595 ▨ 5952
e-mail: office@gmeiner.co.at
Situated on level meadowland with young trees.
⮑ *From Rust follow the lake road.*
Apr-Oct 56HEC ⸬ ⒣ ⋒ ⒧ ✕ ☉ ◲ ⊘ ▣ ⊞ lau ➧ ⸬ ⭲LPR

SCHÖNBÜHEL NIEDERÖSTERREICH

Stumpfer ☎ 02752 8510 ▨ 02752 8510
A small site in a wooded location attached to a guesthouse close to the River Donau.
⮑ *SW of town.*
Apr-Oct 1.5HEC ⸬ ⒣ ⋒ ⒧ ▾ ✕ ☉ ◲ ⊘ ◧ ⭲ R ▣ ⊞ lau

TRAISEN NIEDERÖSTERREICH

Terrassen-Camping Traisen Kulmhof 1
☎ 02762 62900 ▨ 02762 629004
e-mail: camping.traisen@netway.at
Set out in a circular formation around the main buildings with plenty of trees around the pitches.
⮑ *0.6km W via B20.*
All year 2.1HEC ⸬ ⒣ ⋒ ☉ ◲ ⊘ ⸬ ◧ ⭲ P ▣ ⊞ lau ➧ ⒧
✕ Prices: ♠4.50-5 pitch 4.50-5

TULLN NIEDERÖSTERREICH

Donaupark-Camping Tulln Hafenstr
☎ 02272 65200 ▨ 02272 65201
e-mail: camptulln@oeamtc.at
A modern site in a peaceful location with good facilities close to the River Danube with a high season bus service to Vienna.
Etr-15 Oct 10HEC ⸬ ⒣ ⋒ ⒧ ✕ ☉ ◲ ⊘ ⸬ ◧ ▲ ⭲ L ▣ ⊞
lau ➧ ⭲PR Prices: ♠5.09 ◧7.99-10.17

WAIDHOFEN AN DER THAYA NIEDERÖSTERREICH

Thayapark Badgasse ☎ 02842 51500 ▨ 02842 51547
e-mail: stadtgem.waidhofenth@wrnet.at
A family site in wooded surroundings close to the River Thaya.
⮑ *Signposted from village.*
May-Sep 10HEC ⸬ ⒣ ☉ ◲ ◲ ⭲ R ▣ ⊞ lau ➧ ⒧ ✕ ⭲P

UPPER AUSTRIA/SALZBURG

The province of Salzburg is wonderfully diverse: in the north mighty massifs fall away to rolling uplands and plains, and to the east the hills of the Salzkammergut merge into the Alpine landscape of Upper Austria. Visitors are drawn to the province by the natural landscape; dozens of attractive summer resorts, smart cosmopolitan spas to picturesque mountain hamlets; and facilities for winter sports in almost every part of the province.

A magnificent setting and a wealth of beautiful buildings and attractive streets have given Salzburg an international reputation as one of the most beautiful cities in the world. It contains a rich heritage of architecture and the arts, and Mozart was born here in 1756. The city is still a major musical centre, and hosts a major music festival every summer.

The scenic facets of Upper Austria (Oberösterreich) stretch from the wooded Mühlviertel area north of the Danube to the lake-studded Salzkammergut and the glacier region of the Dachstein - all dotted with lively holiday centres, peaceful villages and idyllic spas and health resorts.

The provincial capital Linz, Austria's third-largest city, spans both banks of the Danube in the Linz basin. The old town's original market square is flanked by impressive buildings, and the city has many attractive streets and arcaded courtyards.

ABERSEE SALZBURG

Wolfgangblick Seestr 24 ☎ 06227 3475 ▨ 06227 3218
e-mail: camping@wolfgangblickt.at
In a pleasant position directly on the Wolfgangsee.
Camping Card Compulsory.

➲ *Access via B1598 6km from St Gilgen. Signposted from village.*
May-Sep 2HEC ⊞⊞⊞ ⚒ ⋔ ⚓ ⚑ ✕ ⊙ ⚡ ∅ ⟲ LR ⚑ ⊞ lau ♦ ♨ ⊞

⟩ ABTENAU SALZBURG

Oberwötzhof Erlfeld 37 ☎ 06243 2698 ▤ 06243 269855
e-mail: oberwoetzlhof@aon.at
A summer and winter site on a level meadow with panoramic views of the surrounding mountains.
➲ *NW of Abtenau.*
All year 2HEC ⊞⊞⊞ ⚒ ⋔ ⚑ ✕ ⊙ ⚡ ♨ ⚓ ⟲ P ⚑ ⊞ ♦ ⟲R
Prices: ⋔5 ⟲2.50 ⟲5 ▲4-5

⟩ ALTMÜNSTER OBERÖSTERREICH

Schweizerhof Hauptstr 17 ☎ 07612 89313 ▤ 07612 872764
A modern site on the shore of Lake Traunsee with plenty of sporting facilities.
➲ *Signposted from the motorway.*
May-Sep 0.6HEC ⊞⊞⊞ ⚒ ⋔ ⚑ ✕ ⊙ ⚡ ⟲ L ⚑ ⊞ lau ♦ ⚑ ⟲P

⟩ BADGASTEIN SALZBURG

Kurcamping 'Erlengrund' Erlengrundstr 6 ☎ 06434 2790
On meadowland below the road leading to the Tauern railway tunnel.
➲ *From Hofgastein turn left off B167 and descend for 100m.*
All year 4.5HEC ⊞⊞⊞ ⚒ ⋔ ⚑ ⊙ ⚡ ∅ ♨ ⟲ P ⚑ ⊞ lau ♦ ⚑ ✕ ⟲LR

⟩ BRUCK AN DER GROSSGLOCKNERSTRASSE SALZBURG

Woferlgut Kroessenbach 40 ☎ 06545 7303-0 ▤ 7303-3
e-mail: info@sportcamp.at
In a beautiful valley beside a lake with good recreational facilities. Some noise from the main road which bisects the site.
➲ *Access via Bruck-Süd or Grossglockner on B311.*
All year 8HEC ⊞⊞⊞ ⚒ ⋔ ⚑ ✕ ⊙ ⚡ ∅ ♨ ⚓ ⚑ ▲ ⟲ LP ⚑ ⊞ ♦ ⟲R ⚑ Prices: ⋔4.30-5.50 ⟲3.90-5.10 ⟲4.60-5.80 ▲4.60-5.80

⟩ BURGAU SALZBURG

Eitzinger Burgau 4 ☎ 07663 769
In a fine situation directly on the Attersee with good recreational facilities.
➲ *Access from 'Mondsee' exit on Autobahn.*
Apr-Sep ⊞⊞⊞ ⚒ ⋔ ⚑ ✕ ⊙ ⚡ ⟲ L ⚑ ⊞

⟩ ESTERNBERG OBERÖSTERREICH

Pyrawang ☎ 07714 6504 ▤ 6504
➲ *At Km45.5 on B130 (Passau-Linz).*
Apr-Oct 3HEC ⊞⊞⊞ ⚒ ⋔ ⚑ ✕ ⊙ ⚡ ⚑ ⊞ ♦ ⟲R Prices: ⋔3 ⟲2.60 ⟲2.60 ▲1.50

⟩ GLEINKERAU OBERÖSTERREICH

Pyhrn Priel ☎ 07562 7066 ▤ 07562 7192
e-mail: pousek@aon.at
A year-round site with a wide variety of facilities.
➲ *Signposted from Windischgarsten towards Gleinkersee. 2.5km from town.*
All year 1HEC ⊞⊞⊞ ⚒ ⋔ ⚑ ✕ ⊙ ⚡ ⚑ ⚑ ⊞ lau ♦ ⟲LR
Prices: ⋔4.40-5.80 ⟲1.50 pitch 3.65-5.10

⟩ GOLLING SALZBURG

Torrener Hof Torren 24 ☎ 06244 5522
➲ *On the outskirts of the village on the B159.*
All year 2HEC ⊞⊞⊞ ⣿ ⚒ ⋔ ⚑ ✕ ⊙ ⚡ ⚑ ⊞ lau

⟩ KAPRUN SALZBURG

Mühle N-Gassner Str 38 ☎ 06547 8254 ▤ 06547 825489
e-mail: keprun@muchle.at
A pleasant family site on long stretch of meadow by the Kapruner Ache.
➲ *S end of village towards cable lift.*
All year 1.5HEC ⊞⊞⊞ ⚒ ⋔ ⚑ ⚑ ✕ ⊙ ⚡ ∅ ♨ ⟲ P ⚑ ⊞ lau

⟩ MAISHOFEN SALZBURG

Kammerlander Oberreit 18 ☎ 06542 68755
➲ *On B168.*
15 Apr-1 Oct ⊞⊞⊞ ⚒ ⋔ ⚑ ✕ ⊙ ⚡ ⚑ ♦ ⚑ ⟲L

⟩ MITTERSILL SALZBURG

Mittersill Klausgasse 49 ☎ 06562 4811 ▤ 06562 4811-10
A modern, well-equipped site suitable for both summer and winter holidays.
➲ *0.5km from the centre of the town on the shores of the lake.*
All year 1.7HEC ⊞⊞⊞ ⚒ ⋔ ⚑ ⚑ ✕ ⊙ ⚡ ∅ ♨ ⚑ ⊞ lau

⟩ MONDSEE OBERÖSTERREICH

Mond-See-Land Punzau 21
☎ 00436232 2600 ▤ 00436232/27218
e-mail: austria@campmondsee.at
In a picturesque, peaceful location between Lake Mondsee and Lake Irrsee with good facilities.
➲ *From Mondsee exit on A1/E55/E60 take B154 towards Strasswalden for 1.5km, then take Haider-Mühle road for 2km.*
Apr-Oct 3HEC ⊞⊞⊞ ⚒ ⋔ ⚑ ⚑ ✕ ⊙ ⚡ ∅ ♨ ⚓ ⟲ P ⚑ ⊞ lau
Prices: ⋔4.30-4.50 ⟲2.80-3 ⟲2.80-3 ▲2.80-3 pitch 5.60-6

NEUSTIFT OBERÖSTERREICH

Gasthof Weiss Puhret 5 ☎ 07284 8104
⮱ *Leave the motorway at Passau-Nord and take B388.*
Apr-Nov 1HEC ⊞⊞⊞ ⊕ ⋔ ⬤ ✕ ⊙ ⬤ ⋔ ⭑ LPR 🏠 lau
✦ ⬛ 𝑎 ⊞

NUSSDORF OBERÖSTERREICH

See Camping Gruber Dortstr 63
☎ 07666 80450 📠 07666 80456
On fairly long meadow parallel to the promenade.
⮱ *S of village, access is at Km19.7. Turn off B151 towards the lake (Attersee).*
15 Apr-15 Oct 2.6HEC ⊞⊞⊞ ⊕ ⋔ ⬛ ✕ ⊙ ⬤ ⭑ LP 🏠 ⊞ lau
✦ 𝑎

See advertisement on page 77

PERWANG AM GRABENSEE OBERÖSTERREICH

Perwang ☎ 06217 8288 📠 8247-15
e-mail: gemeinde@perwang.ooe.gv.at
Site beside lake.
May-Oct 1.5HEC ⊞⊞⊞ ⊕ ⋔ ⬛ ✕ ⊙ ⬤ ⭑ L ⊞ ⊞ 𝄖 lau ✦ ⬛
Prices: ⭑3.63 ▲3.63 pitch 5.81

PETTENBACH OBERÖSTERREICH

Almtal ☎ 07586 86270
On a level meadow in the grounds of a former castle,with good, modern facilities.
⮱ *Leave A1/E55/E60 at Sattledt exit and continue towards Graz.*
All year 12HEC ⊞⊞⊞ ⊕ ⋔ ⬛ ✕ ⊙ ⬤ 𝑎 ⋔ ⬤ ⭑ P 🏠 ⊞ lau

RADSTADT SALZBURG

Forellencamp Gaismairallee 51 ☎ 06452 7861 📠 06452 5092
e-mail: forellencamp@aon.at
Flat meadowland near town
⮱ *SW via B99.*
All year 1HEC ⊞⊞⊞ ⁘⁘ ⊕ ⋔ ⬛ ✕ ⊙ ⬤ ⋔ 🏠 ⊞ lau ✦ ⭑PR
Prices: ⭑4.40 ⭑2.20 ⭑4.40 ▲2

ST JOHANN IM PONGAU SALZBURG

Hirschenwirt Bundesstr 1 ☎ 06412 6012 📠 06412 60128
e-mail: hirschenwirt@aon.at
A small, pleasant site ideally placed for travelling on the Salzburg-Badgastein road or as a base for exploring this region of mountains and lakes. The flat open site has grass pitches on either side of gravel roads. There is a small pool for summer use. Being on a major road route there is traffic noise.
⮱ *Site is behind Gasthof Hirschenwirt at St Johann im Pongau on B311.*
All year 0.8HEC ⊞⊞⊞ ⋇⋇ ⋔ ⬛ ✕ ⊙ ⬤ 𝑎 ⋔ ⭑ P 🏠 Prices: ⭑4-5 pitch 6-9

Wieshof Wieshofgasse 8 ☎ 06412 8519 📠 06412 82929
On gently sloping meadow behind pension and farmhouse. Modern facilities. Big spa house with sauna, massage facilities and health bars, adjacent to site.
⮱ *Off B311 towards Zell am Zee.*
All year 1.2HEC ⊞⊞⊞ ⊕ ⋔ ⬛ ⊙ ⬤ 𝑎 🏠 lau ✦ ✕ ⭑P ⊞ Prices: ⭑4.80 pitch 4.80

ST LORENZ OBERÖSTERREICH

Austria-Camp St Lorenz 229 ☎ 06232 2927
Level site on grassland bordered by trees and hedges and divided into fields by internal roads. Separate field for young people.
⮱ *4km from Mondsee, beside the lake.*
May-Sep 3.7HEC ⊞⊞⊞ ✦ ⋔ ⬛ ✕ ⊙ ⬤ 𝑎 ▲ ⋔ L 🏠 lau

ST MARTIN BEI LOFER SALZBURG

Park Grubhof ☎ 06588 8237 📠 06588 82377
e-mail: park-grubhof@salzburg.co.at
Situated in meadowland on the banks of the River Saalach. Separate sections for dog owners, families, teenagers and groups.
⮱ *1.5km S of Lofer turn left off B311.*
25 Apr-3 Oct 10HEC ⊞⊞⊞ ✦ ⋔ ⬛ ✕ ⊙ ⬤ 𝑎 ⋔ ⬤ ⬤ ⭑ R 🏠 ⊞ lau ✦ ⭑P Prices: ⭑5.45 ⭑2.18 ⭑3.20-4 ▲2.18-3.20

ST WOLFGANG OBERÖSTERREICH

Appesbach Au 99 ☎ 06138 2206 📠 06138 2206 - 33
e-mail: camping@appesbach.at
On sloping meadow facing lake with no shade at upper end.
⮱ *0.8km E of St Wolfgang between lake and Strobl road.*
Apr-Oct 2HEC ⊞⊞⊞ ⊕ ⋔ ⬛ ✕ ⊙ ⬤ ⋔ L 🏠 lau ✦ ⬤
Prices: ⭑4-5.30 ⭑5.80-10.20 ▲3.60-5.80 pitch 5.80-10.20

Berau Schwarzenbach 16 ☎ 06138 2543 📠 06138 254355
e-mail: camping@berau.at
A family-run site in a picturesque setting on the edge of the Wolfgangsee. Spacious, level pitches and good, modern facilities.
⮱ *From A1 exit 'Talgau' follow signs for Hof and Bad Ischl on N158 through Strobl village towards St Wolfgang and follow signs.*
All year 2HEC ⊞⊞⊞ ⊕ ⋔ ⬛ ✕ ⊙ ⬤ 𝑎 ⋔ L 🏠 lau ✦ ✕
Prices: ⭑4.50-5 ⭑2-3.50 ⭑5.50-6.50 ▲4-5 pitch 7.50-10

SALZBURG SALZBURG

Kasern C-Zuckmayerstr 26 ☎ 0662 450576 📠 450576
e-mail: schwarzkopf@aon.at
⮱ *Access via exit 'Salzburg-Nord' on the A1.*
Apr-Oct 1.1HEC ⊞⊞⊞ ⊕ ⋔ ⬛ ✕ ⊙ ⬤ ⬤ ▲ 🏠 lau ✦ ⬛ ✕ 𝑎

Nord Sam Samstr 22A ☎ 0662 660494 📠 660494
Site divided into pitches.
⮱ *400m from Salzburg Nord Autobahn Exit.*
May-Sep 2HEC ⊞⊞⊞ ⁘⁘ ⊕ ⋔ ⬛ ✕ ⊙ ⬤ 𝑎 ⋔ P 🏠 ⊞ lau ✦ ⋔

Schloss Aigen ☎ 0662 622079
Site divided into pitches in partial clearing on mountain slope.
⮱ *From Salzburg-Süd motorway exit through Anif and Glasenbach.*
May-Sep 25HEC ⊞⊞⊞ ⊕ ⋔ ⬛ ⬛ ✕ ⊙ ⬤ 𝑎 ⋔ 🏠 ⊞ lau

Stadtblick Rauchenbichlerstr 21
☎ 0662 450652 📠 0662 458018
e-mail: panorama.camping@utanet.at
A terraced site affording spectacular views of the surrounding mountains.
⮱ *Leave motorway at exit Salzburg-Nord and follow signs.*
20 Mar-5 Nov 0.8HEC ⊞⊞⊞ ⊕ ⋔ ⬛ ✕ ⊙ ⬤ 𝑎 ⬤ ▲ 🏠 ⊞ lau Prices: ⭑5.45-5.80 ⭑2.90-3.60 ⭑2.90 ▲2-2.90

SCHLÖGEN OBERÖSTERREICH

Terrassencamping Pension Schlögen
☎ 07279 8241 📠 8241-22
e-mail: schloegen.freizeit@netway.at
On level ground beside the River Donau, backed by woods and mountains.
20 Mar-28 Oct 2.8HEC ⊞⊞⊞ ✦ ⋔ ⬛ ✕ ⊙ ⬤ ⭑ PR 🏠 ⊞ lau

SEEKIRCHEN SALZBURG

Strand Seestr 2 ☎ 06212 4088 📠 4088
Beside the Wallersee in beautiful meadow.
15 Apr-15 Oct 2HEC ⊞⊞⊞ ⊕ ⋔ ⬛ ✕ ⊙ ⬤ 𝑎 ⋔ LP 🏠 ⊞ lau ✦ ⬛ Prices: ⭑8.50 pitch 13.80

Zell am Wallersee ☎ 06212 4080
Level meadowland separated from the lake by the Lido.
↪ *Access from A1 exit Wallersee then via Seekirchen to Zell.*
May-Oct 3HEC ⭐ 🅰 🏕 ✕ ☉ 🅿 ⇂ LP 🅰 ⊞ lau **Prices: ⚡4.50**
pitch 9

▶ UNTERACH OBERÖSTERREICH

Insel ☎ 07665 8311 🖹 07665 7255
e-mail: camping@inselcamp.at
Quiet site on shore of Lake Attersee; divided into two
sections by River Seeache. Family site.
↪ *Entrance below B152 towards Steinbach at Km24.5; about
300m from fork with B151.*
15 May-15 Sep 1.8HEC ⭐ 🅰 🏕 🍴 ☉ 🅿 ⇂ LR 🅰 lau ➡ 🍴 ✕
🚿 ⊞

▶ WALD SALZBURG

S.N.P Lahn 65 ☎ 06565 8446-0 🖹 8446-4
e-mail: snp.camping@utaney.at
A small family site in a beautiful Alpine setting.
↪ *W of town.*
All year 0.7HEC ⭐ 🅰 🏕 🍴 🍴 ☉ 🅿 🚿 🅰 ⊞ lau ➡ ✕
⇂LP **Prices: ⚡4.50-5 ➡2-2 ➡2.50-3 ⚡2.50-3**

▶ WESENUFER OBERÖSTERREICH

Nibelungen ☎ 07718 7589 🖹 07718 7589
In a pleasant rural setting beside the River Donau.
↪ *500m from B130.*
Apr-Sep 1.2HEC ⭐ 🅰 🏕 ☉ 🅿 ⇂ R 🅰 ⊞ lau ➡ 🍴 ✕ ⇂P
Prices: ⚡3.20 ➡3.27 ⚡2.18 pitch 4

▶ ZELL AM SEE SALZBURG

Seecamp Zell am See Thumersbacherstr 34
☎ 06542 72115 🖹 06542 72115
e-mail: zell@seecamp.at
In a pleasant wooded location beside the lake with excellent
site and recreational facilities.
↪ *Access via B311, N of lake towards Thumersbach.
Signposted.*
All year 3HEC ⭐ 💧 🅰 🏕 🍴 🍴 ☉ 🅿 🚿 🅰 ⇂ L 🅰 ⊞
lau ➡ ⇂P **Prices: ⚡5.66-7.07 ➡1.78-2.23 ⚡2.98-3.73
pitch 6.38-9.91**

Süedufer Thumersbach, Seeuferstr 196
☎ 06542 56228 🖹 06542 562284
e-mail: zell@camping-suedufer.at
A family site on level ground in a picturesque spot on the
southern bank of the Zeller See.
↪ *S via B311 towards Thumersbach.*
All year 0.6HEC ⭐ ➡ 🅰 🏕 🍴 ✕ ☉ 🅿 🚿 🅰 ⊞ lau ➡ ✕ ⇂LPR
Prices: ⚡4.80-5.60 ➡2-2.30 ⚡4.60-5.30 ⚡3.90-5.30

◉◉◉◉ VORARLBERG ◉◉◉◉

Austria's most western province, Vorarlberg is small but
very beautiful. The gardens and orchards in the Rhine
valley and on the shores of Lake Constance give way to a
forested upland region, and finally to the peaks and glaciers
of the Silvretta, rising to over 9,800ft (3,000 metres). With
its lovely old towns and villages, clear mountain lakes and
rivers, quiet bays on Lake Constance, pastures and
meadowlands, steep-sided valleys and peaks, Vorarlberg is
a province of special charm. Watersports are popular on
Lake Constance, but there is good access to the
mountainous regions, making them popular in the summer
with walkers and climbers, as well as skiers.
The onion-domed St Martin's tower (Martinstrum), dating
back from 1602, distinguishes the skyline of Bregenz, the
provincial capital. The newer districts of the town, on the
shores of Lake Constance, have modern well-equipped
tourist facilities - an open air-pool, lakeside gardens, a
floating stage and a Festspielhaus for festivals and
conferences.
....

▶ BEZAU VORARLBERG

Bezau Ach 206 ☎ 05514 2964
e-mail: camping.bezau@aon.at
Small family-owned site with modern sanitary facilities.
↪ *S via B200 (Dornbirn-Warth).*
All year 0.5HEC ⭐ 🌿 🏕 ☉ 🅿 🅿 ➡ 🍴 🍴 ✕ ⊞

▶ BLUDENZ VORARLBERG

▶ At BRAZ(7km SE)

Traube ☎ 05552 28103-0 🖹 05552 28103-40
e-mail: traube.braz@aon.at
On sloping grassland in the picturesque Klostertal valley with
good, modern facilities.
↪ *7km SE of Bludenz via E17, S16 (Bludenz-Arlberg-
Innsbruck). Signposted. Near railway.*
All year 2HEC ⭐ ➡ 🅰 🏕 ✕ ☉ 🅿 🚿 🅰 ⇂ P 🅰 ⊞ 🍴 lau ➡
⇂R

▶ BREGENZ VORARLBERG

Seecamping Bregenz Bodangasse 7 ☎ 05574 71895
Quiet site on level meadow beside lake.
↪ *From town centre (Bahnhofplatz) follow signs towards
'Seecamping'.*
15 May-15 Sep 8HEC ⭐ 🅰 🏕 🍴 ✕ ☉ 🅿 🅰 ⇂ L 🅰 ⊞ lau
➡ 🚿 ⇂P

▶ DALAAS VORARLBERG

Erne ☎ 05585 7223 🖹 05585 2004
e-mail: angelikaterne@utenet.at
In the town, attached to a guesthouse and next to the
swimming pool.
↪ *Access via S16, exit 'Dalass'.*
All year 0.6HEC ⭐ 🅰 🏕 ☉ 🅿 🚿 ⇂ R 🅰 ➡ 🚿 ✕ ⇂P ⊞
Prices: pitch 16.71-18.17 (incl 2 persons)

▶ DORNBIRN VORARLBERG

In der Enz ☎ 05572 29119
A municipal site beside a public park, in a wooded area some
100m beyond the Karren cable lift.
↪ *Access via autobahn exit Dornbirn-Süd.*
May-Sep 10HEC ⭐ 🅰 🏕 🍴 ✕ ☉ 🅿 🅰 ⊞ lau ➡ ✕ ⇂PR ⊞

▶ LINGENAU VORARLBERG

Feurstein Haidach 185 ☎ 05513 6114 🖹 05513 61144
A small site located in a meadow adjacent to some farm
buildings with sufficient facilities for a pleasant stay.
All year 1HEC ⭐ 🅰 🏕 ☉ 🅿 🚿 🅰 🅿 🅰 ⊞ lau ➡ 🚿 🍴 ✕

▶ NENZING VORARLBERG

Alpencamping Nenzing ☎ 05525 62491 🖹 635676
e-mail: josef.morik@vol.at
A well appointed site in magnificent Alpine scenery. There
are fine sporting facilities and modern sanitary blocks.
↪ *Signposted from B190 from Nenzing-2km towards Gurtis.*
01 Jan-07 Apr 05 May-31 Dec 3HEC ⭐ 🅰 🏕 🍴 ✕ ☉ 🅿 🚿
🅰 🅿 ⇂ P 🅰 ⊞ lau **Prices: pitch 15.99-26.20 (incl 2 persons)**

▶ At NÜZIDERS (2.5km NW)

Sonnenberg Hinteroferst 12 ☎ 05552 33900 🖹 05552 64035
e-mail: camping.sonnenberg@eunet.at
Clean site with modern facilities in gently sloping
meadowland and splendid mountain scenery.

Cont.

➲ *Access from Bludenz-Nüziders road, at first fork follow up hill.*
17 May-3 Nov & 14 Dec-15 Apr 1.9HEC ⟁ ⌂ ⏚ ⊙ ⊡ ⌀
⊡ ⊞ lau ➡ ✗ ⚒ ⟨R Prices: ⋔5 ⊞7-10 ▲7-10 pitch 7-10

RAGGAL-PLAZERA VORARLBERG

Grosswalsertal ☎ 05553 209
A family site in a quiet location on gently sloping terrain, with pleasant views.
➲ *On NE outskirts.*
May-Sep 0.8HEC ⟁ ⚇ ⌂ ⏚ ⊙ ⊡ ⌀ ⊞ ⟨ P ⊡ lau ➡ ⏚ ✗
⊞

TSCHAGGUNS VORARLBERG

Zelfen ☎ 0664 2002326 ▤ 05556 72326
e-mail: dsandrell@sandrell.vol.at
Partly uneven, grassy site in a wooded location beside River Ill. Good recreational facilities.
➲ *Access via A14 to Bludenz, then B188 to Tschagguns.*
All year 2HEC ⟁ ⟁ ⌂ ⏚ ⏚ ✗ ⊙ ⊡ ⌀ ⚒ ⟨ R ⊡ ⊞ lau ➡
⟨P Prices: ⋔4.70 pitch 6.20

VIENNA (WIEN)

For hundreds of years Vienna was the heart of a vast empire and cultural focus of central Europe. Today Vienna is one of the world's great modern tourist cities with a confident and cosmopolitan atmosphere, yet it still keeps a distinctive charm and native flair. The mighty façades of the buildings and palaces of the city have earned it the name 'Vienna gloriosa'. It also builds on its long history of fine music. Many of the world's greatest composers lived and worked here, and the Opera House (Staatsoper) plays a prominent part in the social, cultural and political life of the city. Vienna's cultural district is encircled by the wide boulevard, the Ringstrasse, on which many of the city's main buildings stand: the Opera House, the Burg Theatre, the Hofburg, the Parliament, and the neo-Gothic City Hall (Rathaus), as well as churches, museums and lovely parks, gardens and squares.

There is a full programme of events in the city - everything from operas and concerts to sporting events. For more casual entertainment, though, the Viennese cafés are a famous and historic institution - popular meeting places for the Viennese and a delight for the tourists - with tables outside in the summer, newspapers and magazines always available, and of course, the traditional strong, aromatic Viennese coffee.

....

WIEN (VIENNA) WIEN

Donaupark Klosterneuburg In der Au
☎ 02243 25877 ▤ 02243 25878
e-mail: camp.klosterneuburg@oeamtc.at
A modern site in delightful wooded surroundings with fine recreational facilities and within easy reach of the city centre.
➲ *Signposted from A1.*
All year 2.2HEC ⟁ ⚇ ⌂ ⏚ ✗ ⊙ ⊡ ⌀ ⚒ ⚒ ⊡ ⊞ lau ➡
⟨PR Prices: ⋔5.09 ▲4.36 pitch 7.99-10.17

Neue Donau Am Kaisermühlendamm 119 ☎ 01 2024010
e-mail: camping.neuedonau@verkehrsbuero.at
Situated in a meadow surrounded by trees on the banks of the Danube within a leisure park.
➲ *On E bank of the river with access to the A4 and A22.*
May-Sep 3.2HEC ⟁ ⚇ ⌂ ⏚ ✗ ⊙ ⊡ ⌀ ⊡ lau ➡ ⟨LPR ⊞
Prices: ⋔5-6.50 ▲3-3.50 pitch 6-6.50

Wien-West 2 Hüttelbergstr 80 ☎ 01 9142314 ▤ 9113594
e-mail: camping_wienwest@wigast.com
On slightly rising meadow with asphalt paths.
➲ *From end of A1/E5 (Linz-Wien) to Bräuhausbrücke, then turn left and across road to Linz, continue for approx. 1.8km.*
Closed Feb 2HEC ⟁ ➡ ⌂ ⏚ ⏚ ✗ ⊙ ⊡ ⌀ ⊞ ⊡ lau

At RODAUN(4km SW)

Rodaun An der Au 2 ☎ 01 8884154 ▤ 01 8884154
➲ *Between An der Austr and Leising River dam. Access from Breitenfürter Str N492.*
15 Mar-5 Nov 0.8HEC ⟁ ♦ ➡ ⌂ ⊙ ⊡ ⌀ ⊡ ⊞ lau ➡ ⏚ ✗
⟨P Prices: ⋔5.45 ⊛1.10 ⊞4.36 ▲4.36

BELGIUM

Belgium is a small, densely populated country bordered by France, Germany, Luxembourg and The Netherlands.

FACTS AND FIGURES
Area: 30,528 sq km
(11,787 sq miles)
Population:
10,213,752 (1998)
Capital: Bruxelles (Brussel,
Brussels)
Language: French, Dutch,
German, Flemish
IDD code: 32. To call the
UK dial 00 44
Currency: Euro
Local time: GMT + 1
(summer GMT + 2)
Emergency Services:
Police 101; Fire 100;

Ambulance 100. From a
mobile phone dial 112 and
ask for the service required.
Business hours-
Banks: Mon-Fri 09.00-
12.00, 14.00-16.00
Shops: Mon-Sat 09.00-
18.00. (Supermarkets
20.00)
Average daily temperatures:
Bruxelles (Brussel,
Brussels)

Jan 3°C		Jul 17°C	
Mar 5°C		Sep 14°C	
May 13°C		Nov 5°C	

Tourist Information:
UK Belgian National Tourist
Office (Brussels-Ardennes)
225 Marsh Wall, London
E14 9FW
Tel 0906 3020 245
(premium rate information
line)
Belgian National Tourist
Office (Flanders-Brussels)
31 Pepper Street, London
E14 9RW.
Tel: 09001 887799
(premium rate information
line)

USA
Belgian National Tourist
Office, Suite 1501,
780 Third Ave,
New York,
NY10017
Tel (212) 758 8130
Camping Card
recommended; some
reductions on site fees.
Tourist info website:
www.belgium-tourism.net
www.visitflanders.com

Despite the fact that it is heavily
industrialised, Belgium possesses some
beautiful scenery, notably the great forest of the
Ardennes. The resorts in the Oostende (Ostend)
area offer a selection of wide, safe, sandy
beaches and cover about forty miles of coastline.

The climate is temperate and similar to that of
Britain: the variation between summer and winter
lessened by the effects of the Gulf Stream. Three
main languages are spoken: French, Dutch and
German. There is also a Flemish speaking minority.
(See *language* below.)

Belgium is a varied, charming country in
which to spend a camping holiday - the rivers and
gorges of the Ardennes contrasting sharply with
the rolling plains which make up the rest of the
countryside. There are now over 800 campsites
officially authorised by local authorities. They are
normally open from April to October, but many
are open throughout the year. Coastal sites tend
to be very crowded at the height of the season.

Off-site camping (including sleeping) is
prohibited beside public roads for more than 24
consecutive hours; on seashores; within a 100-
metre radius of a main water point; or on a site
classified for the conservation of monuments.

Elsewhere, camping is permitted free of charge, as
long as the stay does not exceed 24 hours and the
camper has obtained authorisation from the
landowner.

HOW TO GET THERE

There are direct ferry services to Belgium:
To **Oostende** (Ostend) from **Dover** takes 2 hours
by catamaran; to **Zeebrugge** from **Hull** takes 12
hrs 45 mins.

Alternatively, you could use Eurotunnel, or
take a shorter crossing by ferry or catamaran to
Calais, France, and drive along the coast road to
Belgium.

MOTORING & GENERAL INFORMATION

The information given here is specific to
Belgium.
It **must** be read in conjunction with the
Continental ABC at the front of the book, which
covers those regulations which are common to
many countries.

Accidents

The police must be called if an unoccupied,
stationary vehicle is damaged, or if injuries are

caused to persons; in the latter case, the car must not be moved. Please see the recommendations given under *Accidents* and also under *Warning triangle* in the Continental ABC at the front of this guidebook.

British Embassy/Consulates*
The British Embassy is located at 1040 Bruxelles, rue d'Arlon 85 ☎ (02) 2876211. There are British Consulates with Honorary Consuls in Antwerpen (Antwerp) and Liège.

Children in cars
Child under 3 must be in suitable restraint when travelling in the front and, if such a system is fitted, when travelling in the rear. Children over 3 and under 12 seated in front or rear must use seat-belt or child restraint appropriate to their size and weight. See Continental ABC under 'Passengers' and 'Seat Belts'.

Currency*
With the introduction of the Euro, the **Belgian Franc (BEF)** ceased to be legal tender from 28 February 2002. However, BEF coins and notes may still be exchanged at local banks until 30 December 2002, and at the Belgian Central Bank

(**National Bank de België/Banque National de Belgique**) for an unlimited period (banknotes) and until the end of December 2004 (coins).

Dimensions and weight restrictions*
Private **cars** and towed **trailers** or **caravans** are restricted to the following dimensions: height, 4 metres; width, 2.55 metres; length, 12 metres.The maximum permitted overall length of vehicle/ trailer or caravan combination is 18 metres.

Trailers without brakes may have a total maximum weight of 750kg.

Driving Licence*
A valid UK or Republic of Ireland licence is acceptable in Belgium. The minimum age at which visitors from UK or Republic of Ireland may use a temporarily imported car or motorcycle is 18 years.

Foodstuffs*
If the imported foodstuffs are for personal use, there are no limits when travelling between EU countries. Visitors coming from other countries may import up to 1kg of meat for personal consumption. Coffee (500g), coffee extract

A castle high above the town of Durbuy, situated in the Ourthe valley, south of Lieges.

The Brabo Fountain (Jef Lambeaux, 1887) in front of some of the former Guildhouses ('gildehuizen') which border Antwerp's Grote Markt

(200g), tea (100g) and tea extract (40g) are free of customs duties, but visitors under 15 cannot import coffee.

Language

There are *three* official languages in Belgium - *Flemish, French* and *German*. Flemish is spoken in the north, French in the south and, in the eastern provinces, German. Both Flemish and French are spoken in Brussels. These divisions are administrative but act as a rough guide to the areas in which the various languages are spoken.

Some of the town names in the directory are shown in both Flemish and French, and that shown first is the one used locally. However, Brussels (Bruxelles-Brussel) is officially bi-lingual.

Lights*

It is compulsory for motorcyclists to use dipped headlights during the day.

Motoring club

The **Touring Club Royal de Belgique** (TCB) has its head office at 1040 Bruxelles, 44 rue de la Loi ☎(02) 2332211 and branch offices in most towns. The Bruxelles (Brussels) head office is open weekly 08.30-17.30hrs; Saturday 09.00-12.00hrs.

Petrol

See Continental ABC under 'Petrol/Diesel'.

Roads

A good road system is available. However, one international route that has given more cause for complaints than any other is, without doubt, that from Calais (France) through Belgium to Köln/Cologne (Germany). The problem is aggravated by the fact that there are three official languages in Belgium (see *language* above). In the Flemish part of Belgium the destination place

The Belfry in Bruges' Markt, (83m/272ft tall) houses a carillon of 47 bells.

names are in Flemish, in Wallonia they are in French and in the German part of Belgium they are in German and French or just in German. Brussels (Bruxelles-Brussel) seems to be the only neutral ground where the signs show the two alternative spellings of placenames (Antwerpen-

Anvers; Gent-Gand; Liège-Luik; Mons-Bergen; Namur-Namen; Oostend-Ostende; Tournai-Doornik.) From the Flemish part of the country, Dunkirk (Dunkerque) in France is signposted *Duinkerke* and Lille is referred to as *Rijsel*, and even Paris is shown as *Parijs*.

Belgium has a comprehensive system of toll-free motorways linking major towns and adjoining countries. Generally, signposts leading to and on motorways show foreign destination place-names in the language of the country concerned. The exceptions to this are on the E40 and E314 where cities such as Aachen and Köln may be given as Aken (Flemish) and Cologne (French).

Speed limits*
Car/motorcycle/car towning caravan/trailer
Built-up areas 50kph (31mph)
Other roads 90kph (56pmh)
Motorways and 4-lane roads separated by central reservation 120kph (74mph)†. Minimum speed on motorways on straight level stretches is 70kph (43mph).
Vehicles being towed due to accident or breakdown are limited to 25kph (15mph) on all roads and, if on a motorway, must leave at the first exit.
†On dual carriageways separated only by road markings the limit is 90kph (55mph).

Warning triangle*
The use of a warning triangle is compulsory in the event of accident or breakdown. The triangle must be placed 30 metres (33yds) behind the vehicle on ordinary roads and 100 metres (109yds) on motorways to warn following traffic of any obstruction; it must be visible at a distance of 50 metres (55yds). In built-up areas the triangle may be placed close to or even on the vehicle if the 30 metre rule cannot be obeyed.

*Additional information on these topics will be found in the Continental ABC at the front of the book.

TOURIST INFORMATION

SOUTH WEST & COAST
Leaving the ferry from the port and resort of Ostende, many visitors immediately head for the

Decorative mosaics above the archway of Waterloo House in the Zurenborg district of Antwerp's suburbs

Flemish capital of Bruges, which is one of Belgium's most beautiful and elegant cities. Between the 13th and 15th centuries it was also one of the richest in the world.

It offers an explosion of classical architecture decorated in bright colours which are a simply enchanting sight in fair weather, a state of affairs that is notoriously rare in Bruges. There is a local saying, "If you can see the Belfry, it's going to rain. If you can't see the Belfry, it's already raining".

The Belfry is Bruges' most famous landmark, rising high above the town and the famous Markt. It has suffered a calamitous history, to say the least. After the original wooden belfry had been struck by lightning, the first stone belfry was constructed in 1282. In 1486 an octagonal lantern was placed in the tower, only for the belfry to be destroyed by lightning again in 1493. Another one was built in 1501, but burnt

down in 1741. The current structure is now 250 years old. The view from the top justifies the steep climb. American poet, Henry Wadsworth Longfellow thought so much of the Belfrey and its history that he wrote a poem about it in the 1840s.

NORTH & CENTRAL

The Belgian capital, Brussels is a city steeped in historical intrigue and modern day elegance. The civic focus is the 13th-century Grand Place, which in the past had been the site of many of the city's principal events, including public trials and even riots!

Facing onto the square is the imposing Hotel-de-Ville, a Gothic monument to 15th-century civic pride. Elsewhere on the Grand Place there is a positive glut of guild buildings as well as the impressive Maison de Rui, which was constructed as a display of dynastic power by the

A windmill on the banks of a frozen canal near the small Flemish town of Damme, north-east of Bruges

NORTH EAST

The principal town of northern Belgium is Antwerp, which is one of the largest ports in the world, and offers a wealth of history and heritage.

The focal point of the old city, (the largest city in north-western Europe during the Renaissance) is the Grote Markt, which contains a fine Renaissance Town Hall, a giant fountain, and a statue of Silvius Brabo the 'giant killer' who gave the city of Antwerp its name. The fable runs that Silvius cut the hand off a giant and threw it in the River Scheldt; throwing in Flemish is 'werpen', so the city was named Andwerpen, meaning 'hand-throwing'!

The painter Peter Paul Reubens (1577-1640) lived in Antwerp, and his house is now a popular tourist attraction. Reubens also oversaw the first stages of the career of Anthony Van Dyck (1599-1641), one of the greatest portrait painters of the 17th century.

Antwerp is famed for its museums, of which the Royal Museum of Fine Arts is arguably the best; be advised though that the majority of museums in Antwerp are closed on Monday.

SOUTH EAST

Excluding the bilingual city of Brussels, Liège is the largest French-speaking city in Belgium. Sitting on the banks of the River Meuse, the city has much to offer, particularly around the Place St Lambert which is a brisk walk uphill through the city centre from the bustling riverside.

The Place St Lambert is named after Lambert, the Bishop of Tongres-Maastricht who was assassinated in Liège in circa 700 by rival Merovingian clans. The star attraction of the Place is the magnificent Palais des Princes-Évêques, today known as the Palais de Justice (or law courts). Commissioned in 1526 the palace boasts a skilful combination of architectural styles with Gothic ornamentation complimented by an Italian Renaissance-style courtyard with decorative columns and spacious galleries. The South Façade, destroyed by fire in 1734, was replaced with an imposing 18th-century extension, in stark contrast to the Mediterranean elegance of the rest of the palace.

Dukes of Burgundy who once ruled present-day Belgium.

Today the Grand Place is more a centre of national heritage than high politics (the headquarters of NATO and the EC are elsewhere in the city).

SOUTH WEST/COAST

The coastline of Belgium is one of fine sandy beaches backed by dunes, with few openings to the sea. The coast is lined with resorts: De Panne; Niewpoort; Ostende, with its port, is also a fashionable resort; Blankenberge; Zeebrugge; and popular Knokke-Heist. Bruges, once connected to the sea by an inlet, was a great medieval port. When the inlet silted up, the city declined, preserving a city whose architecture and unique atmosphere has survived until today, to the delight of the increasing number of visitors. Ypres is historically an important textile centre. Reduced to rubble in World War I, the town has been almost completely restored, and now has its lovely Cloth Hall and cathedral. There are hundreds of war cemeteries and memorials near by, recalling the massive war casualties suffered in the area. Tournai is one of the oldest cities in Belgium and an important ecclesiastical centre, evidenced by the remarkable Cathedral of Notre Dame, with its rich interior and wealth of treasures.

BELOEIL HAINAUT

Orangerie r du Major 3 ☎ 069 689190
Behind the Château de Beloeil.
Apr-Oct 3HEC ⏛ ⚡ ⏃ ⏃ ▮ ▮ ⏃ ⊙ ▯ ▮ ☎ ⊞ lau ➧ ✗

BLANKENBERGE WEST-VLAANDEREN

Bonanza I Zeebruggelaan 137 ☎ 050 416658 ▤ 050 427349
A family site in wooded surroundings 1km from both the village and the sea.
15 Mar-Sep 4.5HEC ⏛ ⏃ ⏃ ▮ ▮ ✗ ⊙ ▯ ⏃ ⏃ ⏃ P ▯ ⊞
lau ➧ ⏃LS Prices: ⏃1.18 ⏃4.72-7.48 ⏃3.14-5.11

Dallas Ruzettelaan 191 ☎ 050 418157 ▤ 050 429479
Well equipped family site near a large department store 50mtrs from the beach.
15 Mar-28 Sep 3HEC ⏛ ⏃ ⏃ ▮ ⊙ ▯ ⏃ ⏃ ⊞ ⊞ lau ➧ ▮ ✗ ⏃LPS

BRUGELETTE HAINAUT

Parc et Loisirs r de Bolignies 20 ☎ 068 455422
A quiet site in wooded surroundings with well defined pitches and good facilities.
All year 6HEC ⏛ ⏃ ⏃ ⊙ ▯ ⏃ LPR ☎ ⊞ lau ➧ ▮ ✗

KNOKKE-HEIST WEST-VLAANDEREN

De Vuurtoren Heistlaan 168 ☎ 050 511782
e-mail: kampvuurtoren@attglobal.net
On level meadow with tarred roads.
⟳ *Turn S off Knokke-Oostende road 4km from Knokke and follow signposts.*
15 Mar-15 Oct 6.6HEC ⏛ ⏃ ▮ ▮ ✗ ⊙ ▯ ☎ ⊞ lau ➧ ⏃
⏃ ⏃PS Prices: ⏃3.22 ⏃7.44 ⏃6.20 pitch 7.44-15.87

Zilvermeeuw Heistlaan 166 ☎ 050 512726 ▤ 050 512703
e-mail: info@camping-zilvermeeuw.com
Level site in wooded surroundings.
⟳ *SW via N300.*
Mar-15 Nov 7HEC ⏛ ⏃ ▮ ⏃ ✗ ⊙ ▯ ⏃ ⏃ ☎ ⊞ lau ➧ ▮
✗ ⏃LPS

At WESTKAPELLE(3km S)

Holiday Natienlaan 70-72 ☎ 050 601203 ▤ 050 613280
A quiet family site with good modern facilities within easy reach of the sea.
⟳ *On S outskirts near the railway station.*
Apr-Sep 1.5HEC ⏛ ⏃ ▮ ⊙ ▯ ⏃ ⊞ ⊞ ⊗ lau ➧ ▮ ▮ ✗ ⏃PS

KOKSIJDE WEST-VLAANDEREN

Blekker & Blekkerdal Jachtwakerstr 12 ☎ 058 511633
In a peaceful location, surrounded by trees, with good modern facilities.
⟳ *Situated between Dunkerque and Oostende, 5km from the Belgian frontier. Leave motorway and head towards Veurne.*
All year 3HEC ⏛ ⏃ ▮ ✗ ⊙ ▯ ▮ ⊞ lau ➧ ▮ ▮ ✗ ⏃S

LOMBARDSIJDE WEST-VLAANDEREN

Lombarde Elisabethlaan 4 ☎ 058 236839 ▤ 058 239908
e-mail: info@delombarde.be
A well equipped family site 400mtrs from the sea and close to the centre of the village. Some facilities only available March to early November.
⟳ *From E40 exit Nieuwpoort and follow signs.*
All year 8.5HEC ⏛ ⏃ ▮ ▮ ▮ ✗ ⊙ ▯ ▮ ☎ ⏃ L ▯ ⊞ lau ➧
⏃ ⏃PS Prices: pitch 12.50-22.90

Zomerzon Elisabethlaan 1 ☎ 058 237396 ▤ 232817
In a quiet location, 800mtrs from the sand dunes and beach with good facilities.
24 Mar-11 Nov 10HEC ⏛ ⏃ ▮ ▮ ⊙ ▯ ▮ ⊞ ⊗ lau ➧ ▮
✗ ⏃ ⏃PS

LOPPEM WEST-VLAANDEREN

Lac Loppem ☎ 050 824262
Surrounded by fir trees on the edge of a lake.
⟳ *Leave A10/E40 at Torhout exit and turn right by the Esso service station.*
All year 14HEC ⏛ ⏃ ▮ ▮ ✗ ⊙ ▯ ⏃ L ▯ ▯
Prices: ⏃2.50 ⏃2.50 ⏃3

MIDDELKERKE WEST-VLAANDEREN

Myn Plezier Duinenweg 489 ☎ 059 300279 ▤ 059 314503
In wooded surroundings close to the castle. The camp shop only operates during high season.
Apr-10 Sep 3HEC ⏛ ⏃ ▮ ✗ ⊙ ▯ ⏃ ⏃ ⊞ ⊞ lau ➧ ▮ ⏃S
Prices: ⏃3.10 pitch 8.80

MONS HAINAUT

Waux-Hall av St-Pierre 17 ☎ 065 337923 ▤ 065 363848
In a secluded position 1km from the town centre, with direct access to the Parc du Waux-Hall.
⟳ *From town ring road take exit for Beaumont/Binche, Charleroi. Turn right at lights, then take immediate right.*
All year 5HEC ⏛ ⏃ ▮ ⊙ ▯ ▮ ▮ ⊞ lau ➧ ▮ ✗ ⏃ ⏃
Prices: ⏃3.34 ⏃0.86 ⏃1.85 ⏃1.85

NIEUWPOORT WEST-VLAANDEREN

Info Brugsesteenweg 49 ☎ 058 236037 ▤ 058 236037
e-mail: nieuwpoort@ic-camping.be
A family site in pleasant wooded surroundings. Plenty of recreational facilities including watersports.
⟳ *From E40 exit 4 head towards Diksmuide and Nieuwpoort. Signposted from St Joris.*
Apr-12 Nov 24HEC ⏛ ⏃ ▮ ▮ ✗ ⊙ ▯ ⏃ ☎ ▮ ⏃ P ☎ ⊞
lau ➧ ▮ ⏃LRS

OOSTENDE (OSTENDE) WEST-VLAANDEREN

Asterix Duinenstr 200 ☎ 059 331000 ▤ 324202
A family site in wooded surroundings, 500m from the sea.
Camping Card Compulsory.

Cont.

A list of Online Resources can be found on page 12 of this guide.

87

⊃ *From Oostende follow N34 towards Knokke-Heist for 7km then right for Bredene-Dorp.*
All year 3HEC ∷∴ ⊕ ♠ ⛆ ⚡ ✕ ⊙ ⊜ ∅ ⏚ ⊞ ⊞ ⊡ ⊡ ⊞ lau ➤
⁊LPS Prices: ⋔1-2.50 ⊞8-12.50 ▲8-12.50

ST SAUVEUR HAINAUT

Hauts r des Vertes Feuilles 13 ☎ 3269 768672
In a secluded, wooded situation within the Flemish Ardennes with fine facilities.
⊃ *Signposted from Renaix.*
All year 1HEC ⊔⊔⊔ ➤ ♠ ⊙ ⊜ ∅ ⏚ ⊞ ⊞ ⊡ ⊞ lau ➤ ⛆ ⚡ ✕

TOURNAI HAINAUT

Orient Vieux Chemin de Mons 8
☎ 069 222635 ▤ 069 890229
A pleasant site in an area of woodland with good recreational facilities.
⊃ *From motorway exit 'Tournai Est' head towards the town centre. Turn left at first crossroads and follow signs.*
All year 20HEC ⊔⊔⊔ ⊕ ♠ ⚡ ✕ ⊙ ⊜ ⁊ LP ⊡ ⊞ lau ➤ ⛆ ✕

WAREGEM WEST-VLAANDEREN

Gemeentelijk Sportstadion Zuiderlaan 13
☎ 056 609532 ▤ 056 621223
e-mail: info@waregem.be
In a sports and leisure centre SE of the town centre.
⊃ *Access via E17 (Kortrijk-Gent).*
Apr-Sep 1HEC ⊔⊔⊔ ⊕ ♠ ⊙ ⊡ ⊞ ⊞ ➤ ⛆ ⚡ ✕ ∅ ⏚ ⁊P

WAUDREZ HAINAUT

Gloriettes r de la Résistance 92 ☎ 064 368269
Apr-Oct 3HEC ⊔⊔⊔ ⊕ ♠ ⊙ ⊜ ⊡ ⊞ lau

WESTENDE WEST-VLAANDEREN

KACB Bassevillestr 81 ☎ 058 237343 ▤ (058) 233505
e-mail: campingkacbuesten@be.
A well appointed site close to the beach.
Camping Card Compulsory.
⊃ *Situated between Westende and Lombardsijde towards the sea.*
All year 6.5HEC ⊔⊔⊔ ⊕ ♠ ⛆ ⚡ ✕ ⊙ ⊜ ∅ ⊜ ⊡ ⊞ lau ➤ ⏚
⁊LPS Prices: ⋔2.50-3.50 ⊛2-3.50 ⊞14.50-23.30 ▲5.40-6.20

NORTH/CENTRAL

Most of this central region of Belgium is intensely agricultural, vast open plains are covered in crops, with compact villages in the valleys. Gent is the capital of the province of East Flanders, and is a beautiful city with a medieval heart. Rivers and canals dissect the city, which buzzes with commerce and industry, lively shopping streets and markets. Imposing buildings are reminders of a colourful past: the view from St Michael's Bridge takes in the towers of St Nicholas' Church (13th to 15th century), the Belfry (13th to 14th century) and the Cathedral of St Bavo (dating from the 10th century). Also in East Flanders, Oodenaarde is historically a textile centre; its tapestries are still renowned, and the town has many beautiful buildings dating from the late Middle Ages.
In the south of this region is Brussels, capital of Belgium. Although some parts of the old Brussels remain intact, today it is essentially a modern cosmopolitan centre, the cultural and educational capital of Belgium, headquarters of the EU, NATO and many other international organisations. The city exudes vitality and prosperity, in keeping with its position as an international centre.

BACHTE-MARIA-LEERNE OOST-VLAANDEREN

Groeneveld Groenevelddreef ☎ 09 3801014 ▤ 3801760
e-mail: info@campinggroeneveld.be
Well equipped site beside a lake.
⊃ *Approach via E17 or E40.*
24 Mar-12 Nov 1.7HEC ⊔⊔⊔ ⊕ ♠ ⛆ ⚡ ✕ ⊙ ⊜ ∅ ⊜ ⁊ L ⊡ ⊞
➤ ⁊R Prices: pitch 14.80-17.40

BEAUVECHAIN BRABANT

Arpents Verts r Longue 115 ☎ 010 866993 ▤ 010 867457
e-mail: fedfrcampcarbe@belgacom.net
⊃ *Access via E411 exit 8 towards Louvain or E40 exit 23 towards Bevekom.*
May-Aug 1HEC ⊔⊔⊔ ⊕ ♠ ⛆ ⚡ ⊙ ⊙ ⊜ ∅ ⊡ ⊞ ⊞ ⌘ lau Prices:
⋔3.22 ⊛3.35 ⊞11.15 ▲3.35 pitch 11.15-37.19 (incl 2 persons)

BEGYNENDYK BRABANT

Roygaerden Betekomsesteenweg 75
☎ 016 531087 ▤ 016531387
e-mail: immo.vdb@pi.be
Pitches are in wooded surroundings beside a lake.
All year 5HEC ⊔⊔⊔ ⊕ ♠ ⚡ ✕ ⊙ ⊜ ∅ ⏚ ⊜ ⊡ ⊡ ⊞ lau ➤ ⏚
⁊R Prices: ⋔3.72 ⊛2.48 ⊞8.68 ▲3.72

BEVERE OOST-VLAANDEREN

Vlaamse Ardennen Kortrijkstr 342
☎ 055 315473 ▤ 055 300865
A family site with good recreational facilities.
⊃ *Signposted from N453.*
Apr-mid Nov 24HEC ⊔⊔⊔ ➤ ♠ ✕ ⊙ ⊜ ∅ ⏚ ⁊ LP ⊡ ⊞ lau

GENT (GAND) OOST-VLAANDEREN

Blaarmeersen Zuiderlaan 12 ☎ 92215399 ▤ 09 2224184
e-mail: camping.blaarmeersen@gent.be
In pleasant wooded surroundings SW of Gent towards the railway station.
Mar-15 Oct 3HEC ⊔⊔⊔ ⊕ ♠ ⛆ ⚡ ✕ ⊙ ⊜ ∅ ⊜ ⁊ L ⊡ ⊡ ⊞
lau ➤ ⁊P

GRIMBERGEN BRABANT

Grimbergen Veldkanstr 64 ☎ 02 760378 ▤ 02 2701215
⊃ *Access via exit 7 on Bruxelles ringroad.*
15 Mar-Oct 1.5HEC ⊔⊔⊔ ➤ ♠ ⊙ ⊡ ⊞ lau ➤ ⛆ ⚡ ✕ ⁊P
Prices: ⋔3 ⊛1.50 ⊞3 ▲3

HEVERLEE BRABANT

Ter Munck Sint Jansbergsesteenweg 152 ☎ 016 228515
⊃ *Access via E40 or E413.*
18 Jun-9 Sep 1.5HEC ⊔⊔⊔ ⊕ ♠ ⚡ ✕ ⊙ ⊜ ⊡ ⊞ lau ➤ ⛆ ✕ ∅
⏚ ⁊P

JABBEKE OOST-VLAANDEREN

Klein Strand Varsenareweg 29 ☎ 050 811440
e-mail: kleinstrand@online.be
A lakeside site with good modern facilities and offering a wide variety of leisure activities.
⊃ *Off the main Oostende-Brugge road.*
All year 4HEC ⊔⊔⊔ ⊕ ♠ ⛆ ⚡ ✕ ⊙ ⊜ ∅ ⏚ ⊜ ⊜ ⁊ L ⊡ ⊞ lau

LOONBEEK BRABANT

Bergendal Biezen Str 81 ☎ 016 403904 & 470169
Camping Card Compulsory.
⊃ *Access via E411 and RN253.*
15 Mar-15 Nov 9HEC ⊔⊔⊔ ⊕ ♠ ⊙ ⊜ ⊡ ⊞ lau ➤ ∅

ONKERZELE OOST-VLAANDEREN

Gavers Onkerzelestr 280 ☎ 054 416324 ▤ 410388
e-mail: gavers@oost-vlaanderen.be
A quiet, well equipped site beside a lake between the Dendre

Valley and the foothills of the Ardennes. There are good sporting and sanitary facilities.
➲ *NE of town towards the river.*
All year 15HEC ⸺ 🛆 🏕 🛒 🍽 ✕ ☉ 🅟 🏪 ⃨ LPR 🔒 🅿 ⊞ lau

STEKENE OOST-VLAANDEREN

Eurocamping Baudeloo Heirweg 159 ☎ 03 7890663
All year 4.5HEC ⸺ ♠ 🏕 ✕ ☉ 🅟 ⃨ P 🔒 ⊞ lau ➡ 🛒 ✕ ⌀

Reinaert Lunterbergstr 4 ☎ 03 7798525 ▤ 3237798525
Apr-Oct 2HEC ⸺ 🛆 🏕 🛒 ✕ ☉ 🅟 🖴 🔒 ⊞ lau ➡ 🛒 Prices:
⋔1.98 ♠1.74 ⊞1.74 ⋀1.74

WACHTEBEKE OOST-VLAANDEREN

Puyenbroeck Puyenbrug 1A ☎ 09 3424231
Apr-Sep 8HEC ⸺ 🏊 🏕 ☉ 🅟 🏪 ⊞ ⊞ ⊘ lau ➡ 🛒 🛒 ✕ ⃨LP

● ● ● ● ● NORTH EAST ● ● ● ● ●

The natural entrance to this region is Antwerp. One of the great ports of Europe and a fascinating city to visit, it is dominated by the elegant tower of its cathedral. The cathedral's graceful exterior is complemented by a spacious and rich interior, with some fine Rubens masterpieces. Near the cathedral is the Grote Markt, with an impressive town hall, and several guildhalls with wonderful façades. The extensive old city contains many fine old buildings and some fascinating museums, including the Plantin Moretus Museum, and Rubens' House.

Other interesting towns in this region include Turnhout, a commercial centre with a modern town hall and lovely church in the market place; Mechelen - an ecclesiastical centre with a particularly well preserved old town; Tongeren, known as the oldest town in Belgium and containing many interesting reminders of the past; the quiet picturesque town of Zoutleeuw, with its lovely 13th-century church; Lier, with its attractive market place; and the old abbey town of Averbode.

....

ANTWERPEN (ANVERS) ANTWERPEN

De Molen Thonetlaan ☎ 03 2196090
Apr-Sep 1.3HEC ⸺ 🛆 🏕 ☉ 🅟 🏪 🔒 ⊞ lau ➡ 🛒 🛒 ✕ ⃨PR

BRECHT ANTWERPEN

Floreal Het Veen Eekhoornlaan 1, St-Job In't Goor
☎ 03 6361327
A comfortable site in a pleasant wooded setting with residential and touring pitches.
➲ *Leave Autoroute E19 at exit St Job In't Goor.*
Apr-Sep 7.5HEC ⸺ 🛆 🏕 ✕ ☉ 🅟 🏪 ⃨ R 🔒 ⊞ lau ➡ ⌀ 🖴

EKSEL LIMBURG

Lage Kempen Kiefhoeki str 19 ☎ 011 402243 ▤ 011 348812
e-mail: info@lagekempen.net
Situated in the middle of a forest with a variety of recreational facilities.
➲ *From route 67 from Hasselt follow signs 'Lage Kampen' to the left.*
Etr-2 Nov 3.5HEC ⸺ 🏊 🏕 🛒 ✕ ☉ 🅟 ⌀ 🖴 🏪 ⃨ P 🔒 lau
Prices: ⋔3.50 ♠2 ⊞3 ⋀3

GIERLE ANTWERPEN

Lilse Bergen Strandweg 6 ☎ 014 557901 ▤ 014 554454
e-mail: info@lilsebergen.be
A very well equipped family site surrounding a private lake.
➲ *E39 exit 22.*
All year 60HEC ⸺ ♠ 🏕 🛒 ✕ ☉ 🅟 ⌀ 🖴 🏪 🏪 ⃨ L 🔒 🅿 ⊞
lau Prices: pitch 15-19

HOUTHALEN LIMBURG

Hengelhoef Hengelhoefdreef 1 ☎ 089 844583 ▤ 089 386940
e-mail: camp.hengelhoef@belgacom.net
A family site in pleasant wooded surroundings with good, modern facilities.
➲ *Access via E314 exit 30.*
All year 15HEC ⸺ ♠ 🏕 ✕ ☉ 🅟 🔒 ⊞ ⊘ lau ➡ 🛒 ✕
Prices: pitch 15

KASTERLEE ANTWERPEN

Houtum Houtum 51 ☎ 014 852365
An extensive site with well defined pitches shaded by trees and bushes.
➲ *On S outskirts of Kasterlee.*
All year 9HEC ⸺ 🏊 🏕 🛒 ✕ ☉ 🅟 🏪 ⃨ R 🔒 ⊞ ⊘ ➡ 🛒

MOL ANTWERPEN

Zilvermeer Zilvermeerlaan 2 ☎ 014 829500 ▤ 014 829501
e-mail: info@zilvermeer.provant.be
A pleasant lakeside site with good recreational facilities.
Closed 16 Nov-15 Dec 45HEC ⸺ ⁝⁝⁝ ♠ 🏕 🛒 ✕ ☉ 🅟 ⌀
🖴 🏪 ⃨ L 🔒 🅿 ⊞ lau Prices: pitch 7.93-12.89 (incl 4 persons)

OPGLABBEEK LIMBURG

Boseind Speeltuinstr 8 ☎ 089 854347 ▤ 089 854319
e-mail: info@hetlaer.be
A family site adjoining a wood. A wide variety of recreational facilities are available.
➲ *From town centre take N730 towards Bree and follow signs.*
Apr-Sep 8HEC ⸺ 🛆 🏕 🛒 ✕ ☉ 🅟 ⃨ P 🔒 ⊞ ➡ ⌀
Prices: ⋔2.35 ⊞8.18 ⋀1.86

Wilhelm Tell Hoeverweg 87 ☎ 089 854444 ▧ 810010
e-mail: receptie@wilhelmtell.com
A family campsite situated in a vast nature reserve and
offering opportunities for walks in a varied area of
heathland, woodland and marshlands. A large variety of
water attractions on site including a water chute and a
swimming pool with a wave machine. Also an indoor family
pool and bubble bath.
➲ *E313 exit 32 in direction of Opglabbeek*
All year 4HEC ⋘ ⊕ ⋔ ⋉ ✕ ⊙ ▣ ⏀ ⏺ ⏏ ⋜ P ☎ ⊞ lau
Prices: ⋔3.85-5.50 pitch 6.30-9

▷ **RETIE** ANTWERPEN

Berkenstrand Brand 78 ☎ 014 377590 ▧ 014 375139
In wooded surroundings beside a lake.
➲ *3km NE on road to Postel.*
All year 10HEC ⋘ ⊕ ⋔ ⋉ ✕ ⊙ ▣ ⏀ ⏺ ⋜ L ☎ ⊞
lau Prices: ⋔2.98 ⊷2.48 ⊑2.48 ▲2.48

▷ **TURNHOUT** ANTWERPEN

Baalse Hei Roodhuisstr 10 ☎ 014 421931 ▧ 420853
e-mail: info@baalsehei.be
A family site in pleasant wooded surroundings with plenty of
recreational facilities.
All year 30HEC ⋘ ⊕ ⋔ ⋉ ✕ ⊙ ▣ ⏺ ⋜ L ☎ ⊞ lau ⏏ ⋤
Prices: pitch 14-18

▷ **VORST-LAAKDAL** ANTWERPEN

Kasteel Meerlaer Verboekt 115 ☎ 013 661420 ▧ 013 667512
e-mail: campmeerlaer@online.be
➲ *E313 exit 24 towards Hosselt or exit 24 towards Antwerp.*
All year 6HEC ⋘ ⊕ ⋔ ⋉ ✕ ⊙ ▣ ⏀ ⏺ ☎ ⊞ lau ⏏ ⋤ ✕
Prices: ⋔2.24 ⊷2.24 ⊑2.24 ▲2.24

▷ **ZONHOVEN** LIMBURG

Berkenhof Teutseweg 33 ☎ 011 814439 ▧ 011 812736
Apr-Oct 3.5HEC ⋘ ⏏ ⋔ ⋉ ✕ ⊙ ▣ ⏀ ⏺ ⏺ ⏺ ☎ ⊞ ⏏ ⋤

Holsteenbron Hengelhoelseweg 9
☎ 011 817140 ▧ 011 817140
e-mail: camping.holsteenbron@yueom.be
A rural family site in a wooded location.
➲ *Access via E314 exit 29 towards Zondhoven.*
Apr-15 Nov 4HEC ⋘ ⊕ ⏏ ⋔ ⋉ ✕ ⊙ ▣ ⏺ ☎ ⊞ lau
Prices: pitch 11.16-14.87

● ● ● ● **SOUTH EAST** ● ● ● ●

This region is known as the great garden of the Ardennes -
dense forests, hills rising to over 2,000ft, imposing chalk
cliffs, deep, wide valleys and serene reservoirs. Small
villages, ancient monasteries, high fortress citadels and
picturesque towns with imposing civic buildings and half-
timbered dwellings, dot the countryside. The graceful
Meuse flows through the north of this area, historically an
important north-south artery. Today barges frequent its
waters, and the 'castles of Namur' adorn its banks. There
are a number of impressive caves in the region. The most
interesting are the caves at Han-sur-Lesse which stretch for
some miles underground.
Towns set on the River Meuse include Dinant, overlooked
by the mass of its castle; picturesque Namur, between the
banks of the Meuse and the Sambre, also dominated by its
castle; and cosmopolitan Liège, a bustling mix of culture
and industry. La Roche-en-Ardenne is set in a deep valley
on a loop of the Ourthe, and Spa is a traditional resort with
thermal springs.
....

▷ **AISCHE-EN-REFAIL** NAMUR

Manoir de lá Bas rte de Gembloux 180 ☎ 081 655353
In a beautiful situation within the wooded grounds of a
former manor house.
➲ *5km W of Eghezée.*
Apr-Oct 21HEC ⋘ ⊕ ⋔ ⋉ ⋤ ✕ ⊙ ▣ ⏀ ⏺ ⋜ ⋜ P ☎ ⊞ lau ⏏ ⋤

▷ **AMBERLOUP** LUXEMBOURG

Tonny r Tonny 35-36 ☎ 061 688285 ▧ 061 688285
In a pleasant valley beside the River Ourthe with fine
sporting facilities.
➲ *Access via E25 or A4 to Bastogne, then N826.*
15 Feb-15 Nov 3HEC ⋘ ⊕ ⋔ ⋉ ⋤ ✕ ⊙ ▣ ⏀ ⏺ ⏺ ⏺ ⋜ R
▣ ⊞ lau

▷ **AMONINES** LUXEMBOURG

Val de l'Aisne Rue de TTA ☎ 086 470067 ▧ 470043
e-mail: info@levaldelaisne.be
All year 25HEC ⋘ ⊕ ⋔ ⋉ ⋤ ✕ ⊙ ▣ ⏀ ⏺ ⏺ ⏺ ▲ ⋜ LR ☎
⊞ lau

▷ **AVE-ET-AUFFE** NAMUR

Roptai r Roptai 34 ☎ 084 388319 ▧ 084 387327
The site is located in a hilly forest situation in pretty clearings
about 1km from the village.
All year 10HEC ⋘ ⊕ ⋔ ⋤ ⋉ ✕ ⊙ ▣ ⏀ ⏺ ⏺ ⏺ ⋜ P ☎ ⊞
lau ⏏ ✕

▷ **BARVAUX-SUR-OURTHE** LUXEMBOURG

Hazalles Chainrue 77a ☎ 086 211642 ▧ 211642
Situated in an orchard, this site is 600mtrs from the village
and sits beside a stream. Well maintained facilities.
Apr-Sep 0.4HEC ⋘ ⏏ ⋔ ⊙ ▣ ⏺ ☎ ⊞ lau ⏏ ⋤ ⋉ ✕ ⏀ ⋤
⋜PR Prices: ⋔1.75 ▲2.50 pitch 3.75

Rives de l'Ourthe r Inzespres 70 ☎ 086 211730
A large site with plenty of touring pitches beside the River
Ourthe.
➲ *200mtrs from the village towards the river.*
Apr-Sep 2HEC ⋘ ⊕ ⋔ ⋉ ✕ ⊙ ▣ ⋜ R ☎ ⊞ ⏏ ⋤ ✕ ⏀ ⋤
⋜LP

▷ **BERTRIX** LUXEMBOURG

Info rte de Mortehan ☎ 061 412281 ▧ 061 412588
e-mail: bertrix@lc-camping.be
Well equipped family site in a pleasant wooded setting.
➲ *S of town beyond the church. Signposted from N884.*
30 Mar-11 Nov 14HEC ⋘ ⊕ ⋔ ⋉ ⋤ ✕ ⊙ ▣ ⏺ ⏺ ⋜
P ☎ ⊞ lau

▷ **BÜLLINGEN (BULLANGE)** LIÈGE

Hêtraie Rotheck 264 ☎ 80 642413 ▧ 80 642413
This site is situated on a sloping meadow near a fish pond
and is surrounded by groups of beautiful beech trees and
conifers.
➲ *Leave village in direction of Amel then left and continue for
2km. Signposted.*
Apr-15 Nov 3HEC ⋘ ⊕ ⋔ ⊙ ▣ ⏺ ⋜ LP ☎ ⊞ lau
Prices: ⋔1.80 ⊷1.80 ⊑3.60 ▲2.50

▷ **BURE** LUXEMBOURG

Parc la Clusure 30 chemin de la Clusure
☎ 084 366080 ▧ 084 366777
Pleasant site with good facilities in the centre of the
Ardennes.
➲ *Access from E411 and N846 via Tellin.*
All year 13HEC ⋘ ⊕ ⋔ ⋉ ⋤ ✕ ⊙ ▣ ⏀ ⏺ ⏺ ▲
⋜ PR ☎ ⊞ lau

BÜTGENBACH LIÈGE

Worriken Worriken Center 1 ☎ 080 446358 ▤ 080 447089
Situated on the shores of a lake.
Closed 12 Nov-10 Dec 8HEC ⨿⨿⨿ ⇗ ⋔ ⵦ ✕ ⊙ ⬤ ⵦ ⵦ L ☎ ⊞
lau ➡ ⵦ ⵦ ⵦ ⵦPR

CHEVETOGNE NAMUR

Domaine Provincial ☎ 083 687211
Located in the grounds of a castle and surrounded by fine
ornamental gardens. There is a wide variety of leisure
activities.
All year 0.5HEC ⨿⨿⨿ ⇗ ⋔ ⵦ ✕ ⊙ ⬤ ⬛ ⵦ L ☎ ⵦ ⊞ lau ➡ ⵦP

COO-STAVELOT LIÈGE

Cascade Chemin des Faravennes 5 ☎ 080 684312
A small touring and holiday site beside the River Amblève.
⮑ 3km from Trois-Ponts via motorway exit 10 or 11.
Apr-Sep 0.8HEC ⨿⨿⨿ ⇗ ⋔ ⵦ ✕ ⊙ ⬤ ⵦ R ☎ ⊞ lau ➡ ✕ ⵦ
Prices: ⵦ2.25 ⵦ3.25 ⵦ2.50 pitch 5.70

EUPEN LIÈGE

'An der Hill' Hutte 46 ☎ 087 744617 ▤ 087 557232
In wooded surroundings with well defined pitches.
⮑ SW of town via N67 towards Monschau.
All year 0.6HEC ⨿⨿⨿ ⇗ ⋔ ⵦ ✕ ⊙ ⬤ ⵦ ⵦ ☎ ⊞ lau ➡ ⵦ ⵦP

FLORENVILLE LUXEMBOURG

Rosière Rive Gauche de la Semois
☎ 061 311937 ▤ 061 314873
e-mail: larosiere@pi.be
In wooded surroundings close to the town centre.
⮑ Access via E411 exit 26 for Verlaine/Nuefchâteau.
Apr-Oct 10HEC ⨿⨿⨿ ⇗ ⋔ ⵦ ⵦ ✕ ⊙ ⬤ ⵦ ⵦ PR ☎ ⊞ lau
Prices: ⵦ1.90-2.10 ⵦ1-1.30 ⵦ6.20-7.70 ⵦ5.20-5.70

FORRIÈRES LUXEMBOURG

Pré du Blason r de la Ramée 30 ☎ 084 212867 ▤ 084 223650
e-mail: predublason@freegates.be
This well-kept site lies on a meadow surrounded by wooded
hills and is completely divided into pitches and crossed by
rough gravel drives.
⮑ Off N49 Masbourg road.
Apr-Oct 3HEC ⨿⨿⨿ ⇗ ⋔ ⵦ ⵦ ✕ ⊙ ⬤ ⵦ ⵦ ⵦ R ☎ ⊞ lau
Prices: ⵦ1.98 ⵦ6.20 ⵦ4.46

GEMMENICH LIÈGE

Kon Tiki Terstraeten 141 ☎ 087 785973
All year 12HEC ⨿⨿⨿ ⇗ ⋔ ⵦ ⵦ ✕ ⊙ ⬤ ⵦ ⵦ PR ☎ ⊞ lau

GOUVY LUXEMBOURG

Lac de Cherapont Cherapont 2 ☎ 080 517082 ▤ 080 517093
On an extensive lakeside tourist complex with a wide variety
of recreational facilities.
⮑ Access via E25 exit 51 or E42 exit 15.
Mar-Dec 10HEC ⨿⨿⨿ ➡ ⋔ ⵦ ⵦ ✕ ⊙ ⬤ ⵦ ⵦ LR ☎ ⊞
lau ➡ ⵦ Prices: ⵦ1.50 ⵦ1.24 ⵦ1.50

GRAND-HALLEUX LUXEMBOURG

Neuf Prés av de la Résistance ☎ 080 216882
A family site in pleasant wooded surroundings beside a river.
⮑ Access via E42.
Apr-Sep 4HEC ⨿⨿⨿ ⇗ ⋔ ⵦ ✕ ⊙ ⬤ ⵦ PR ☎ lau ➡ ⵦ ✕ ⵦ ⵦ
⊞ Prices: ⵦ2.03 ⵦ1.12 ⵦ2.97 ⵦ2.23

HABAY-LA-NEUVE LUXEMBOURG

Portail de la Forêt r du Bon-Bois 3
☎ 0497 907027 ▤ 063 423410
e-mail: athiry@belgacom.net
Parklike, terraced site on a hill surrounded by woodland.

⮑ Access via E25/E411 exit 29.
16 Mar-14 Oct 2.5HEC ⨿⨿⨿ ⇗ ⋔ ⊙ ⬤ ⵦ ⵦ ➡ ⵦ ⵦ ✕ ⵦ ⵦ ⵦPR
⊞ Prices: pitch 14.80 (incl 4 persons)

HAMOIR-SUR-OURTHE LIÈGE

CM Dessous Hamoir r du Moulin ☎ 086 388925
A municipal site with well equipped pitches and good
facilities for children beside the River Ourthe.
⮑ From the Liège-Luxembourg motorway take exit Werbomont
and continue for 15km.
15 Mar-15 Nov 3.5HEC ⨿⨿⨿ ⇗ ⋔ ⊙ ⬤ ⵦ R ☎ ⊞ lau ➡ ⵦ ⵦ ✕
ⵦ ⵦ

HOGNE NAMUR

Relais 16 r de Serinchamps ☎ 084 311580 ▤ 084 312400
e-mail: bs825815@skynet.be
A pleasant site in a wooded park beside a lake.
⮑ Take N4 from Courrière to Hogne via Marche.
Closed 4 Jan-15 Feb 5HEC ⨿⨿⨿ ⇗ ⋔ ⵦ ✕ ⊙ ⬤ ⵦ ⵦ ⵦ ⵦ
ⵦ L ☎ ⊞ lau Prices: ⵦ2.48 ⵦ7.44 ⵦ3.72

HOUFFALIZE LUXEMBOURG

Chasse et Pêche r de la Roche 63
☎ 061 288314 ▤ 061 289660
A pleasant site attached to a café-restaurant with good
recreational facilities.
⮑ 3km NW off E25.
All year 2HEC ⨿⨿⨿ ➡ ⋔ ⵦ ✕ ⊙ ⬤ ⵦ ⵦ R ☎ ⵦ ⊞ lau

Moulin de Rensiwez Moulin de Rensiwez 1
☎ 061 289027 ▤ 061 289027
A good transit site on a series of terraces beside the River
Ourthe close to an old water-mill.
All year 5HEC ⨿⨿⨿ ⇗ ⋔ ⵦ ⵦ ✕ ⊙ ⬤ ⵦ ⵦ R ☎ ⵦ ⊞ ✕ lau

JAMOIGNE LUXEMBOURG

Faing ☎ 061 330272
A municipal camp on a meadow situated behind a sports
ground which separates the site from the road.
⮑ 400m W on N44.
Jan 3.5HEC ⨿⨿⨿ ⇗ ⋔ ⵦ ✕ ⊙ ⵦ R ☎ lau ➡ ⵦ ⵦ ⵦ ⵦP ⊞

LOUVEIGNÉ LIÈGE

Moulin du Rouge-Thier Rouge-Thier 8
☎ 04 3608341 ▤ 04 3608341
A well equipped site in a pleasant wooded location.
⮑ S of town towards Deigné.
Apr-30 Oct 8HEC ⨿⨿⨿ ⇗ ⋔ ⵦ ✕ ⊙ ⬤ ⵦ ⵦ ⵦ P ☎ ⊞ lau

MALONNE NAMUR

Trieux r des Tris 99 ☎ 081 445583 ▤ 081 /44 5583
Apr-Oct 2HEC ⨿⨿⨿ ⇗ ⋔ ⊙ ⬤ ⵦ ⵦ ⵦ ⊞ lau ➡ ⵦ ✕
Prices: ⵦ2.25 ⵦ2.50 ⵦ3.75 ⵦ3.75

MARCHE-EN-FAMENNE LUXEMBOURG

Euro Camping Paola r du Panorama 10
☎ 084 311704 ▤ 084 314722
A long site on a hill with a beautiful view. The only noise
comes from a railway line, which passes right by the site.
⮑ Take road towards Hotton, turn right after cemetery and
continue 1km.
All year 13HEC ⨿⨿⨿ ⵦ ➡ ⋔ ⊙ ⬤ ⵦ ⵦ ⵦ ⵦ ➡ ⵦ ✕ ⵦP
Prices: ⵦ2.25 ⵦ2.50 ⵦ5 ⵦ2

NEUFCHÂTEAU LUXEMBOURG

International Spineuse rte de Florenville ☎ 061 277320
Camp shop operates July-Aug only.
⮑ Situated 2km from Florenville in the direction of
Neufchâteau.
All year 2.5HEC ⨿⨿⨿ ⇗ ⋔ ⵦ ✕ ⊙ ⬤ ⵦ ⵦ ⵦ LR ☎ ⊞ lau

Camping l'Hirondelle

B-4210 Oteppe
Tel: 00-32/85/711131

Short distance from E40 & E42
Ideal family campsite with all modern
conveniences – Games – swimming –
fishing – walking – relaxing –
bungalows all comforts

OLLOY-SUR-VIROIN NAMUR

Try des Baudets r de la Champagne
☎ 060 390108 ▤ 060 390108
e-mail: masson_p@yahoo.fr
In a peaceful situation on the edge of a forest.
All year 11HEC ⋓ ⊶⋔≿⊻✕⊙⋑⋈⋤⊞ lau ✦≿✕

OTEPPE LIÈGE

Hirondelle r du Château 1 ☎ 085 711131 ▤ 085 711021
e-mail: hirondelle@skynet.be
Ideal family site with modern facilities in the picturesque
Burdinale Valley.
➲ *N of town between E40 and E42. Signposted.*
Etr-Sep 65HEC ⋓ ⊶⋔≿⋤✕⊙⋑⋈⋤⋔≼ P ⊞ lau

POLLEUR LIÈGE

Polleur r de Congrès 90 ☎ 087 541033 ▤ 087 542530
e-mail: info@campingpolleur.be
A family site in a pleasant wooded location.
➲ *Signposted from A27/E42.*
Apr-1 Nov 3.7HEC ⋓ ⋇⋇⋔≿⋤✕⊙⋑⋈⋤≼ PR ⊞
lau Prices: ⋔2.97-3.59 ☛2.97-3.59 ⋑2.97-3.59 ⋀2.97-3.59

PURNODE NAMUR

Camping du Bocq av de la Vallée ☎ 082 612269
In a beautiful wooded location beside the river.
➲ *Leave E411 at exit 19 (Spontin) towards Yvoir, exit
Purnode.*
Apr-Sep 3HEC ⋓ ⊶⋔≿✕⊙⋑⋑≼ R ⊞ lau ✦≿✕
Prices: ⋔3.25 ☛2.50 ⋑2.75 ⋀2.75

REMOUCHAMPS LIÈGE

Eden r de Trois Ponts 92 ☎ 04 3844165 ▤ 3840055
e-mail: edencamping@swing.be
Apr-Oct 3.2HEC ⋓ ⊶⋔≿⋤✕⊙⋑⋈⋤⋔≼ R ⊞ ⊞
✦✕ Prices: ⋔2 pitch 7.50

RENDEUX LUXEMBOURG

Festival rte de la Roche 89 ☎ 084 477371 ▤ 084 477594
In unspoiled surroundings beside the River Ourthe.
15 Mar-Sep 12HEC ⋓ ⊶⋔≿⋤✕⊙⋑⋈⋤⋔≼ R ⊞ P
⊞ lau

ROBERTVILLE LIÈGE

Plage 33 rte des Bains ☎ 080 446658 ▤ 080 446178
All year 1.8HEC ⋓ ⊶⋔≿⋤✕⊙⋑⋈⋤⋔≼ LPR ⊞ ⊞
lau Prices: ⋔3 ☛2.50 ⋑2.75 ⋀2.75

ROCHE-EN-ARDENNE, LA LUXEMBOURG

Grillon r des Echarées ☎ 084 412062 ▤ 084 412128
Well equipped family site in a pleasant wooded setting.
Etr-Oct 3.5HEC ⋓ ⊶⋔≿⋤✕⊙⋑⋈⋤≼ R ⊞ ⊞ lau ✦✕
≼P Prices: ⋔2.23 pitch 6.20

Lohan 20a rte de Houffalize ☎ 084 411545
In a park surrounded by woodland, on N bank of the River
Ourthe.
➲ *3km E of La Roche towards Maboge and Houffalize.*
Apr-1 Nov 4HEC ⋓ ⊶⋔≿⋤✕⊙⋑⋈⋤≼ R ⊞ ⊞ ⊘ lau

Ourthe ☎ 084 411459 ▤ 056 400050
e-mail: samatex@unicall.be
Well kept site, beside the River Ourthe.
➲ *On SW bank of the Ourthe below the N34.*
15 Mar-15 Oct 2HEC ⋓ ✦⋔≿⊙⋑⋈⋤⋔≼ R ⊞ P ⊞
lau ✦≿✕ ⊞

SART-LEZ-SPA LIÈGE

Touring Club Stockay 17 ☎ 087 474400 ▤ 087 475277
e-mail: spador@pophost.elinet.be
➲ *Signposted. The site lies to the E of Spa.*
All year 6HEC ⋓ ⊶⋔≿⋤✕⊙⋑⋈⋤⋔≼ R ⊞ ⊞
lau ✦≼L

SIPPENAEKEN LIÈGE

Vieux Moulin 114 Tebruggen ☎ 087 784255
A family site with good recreational facilities, set in a pleasant
wooded location close to a nature reserve.
➲ *Access via E40 exit Battile towards Aubel-Hombourg-
Sippenaeken.*
Apr-Sep 6HEC ⋓ ⊶⋔≿⋤✕⊙⋑⋈⋤≼ PR ⊞ ⊞ lau
Prices: ⋔3 ⋑3.50 pitch 3.50

SPA LIÈGE

Parc des Sources r de la Sauvenière 141
☎ 087 772311 ▤ 772311
On the outskirts of the town close to the forest.
➲ *S of town centre on N32 towards Malmédy.*
Apr-Oct 2.5HEC ⋓ ⊶⋔≿⊙⋑⋈⋤≼ P ⊞ lau ✦≿✕
⋤ ⊞

SPRIMONT LIÈGE

Tultay r de Tultay 22 ☎ 04 3821162 ▤ 04 3676397
e-mail: sprimont.r3cb@pi.be
A pleasant site in wooded surroundings on the edge of a
nature reserve.
➲ *NE of Sprimont. Access via E9.*
All year 1.5HEC ⋓ ⊶⋔≿✕⊙⋑⋈⊞ lau ✦≿✕⋤
Prices: ⋔2.50 pitch 4

STAVELOT LIÈGE

Domaine de l'Eau Rouge Cheneux 25
☎ 0032-80 863075 ▨ 863075
A pleasant riverside site with good sporting facilities.
➲ *Access via E42 to Francorchamps or Malmedy.*
All year 4HEC ⛺ ⊶ ⌂ ♀ ✕ ⊙ ⊠ ♨ ⊞ ⁊ R ⌸ 🔲 ⊞ lau ➡
⁊P **Prices:** ⊼2.25 ⊞10 ▲10

TENNEVILLE LUXEMBOURG

Pont de Berguème r Berguème 9
☎ 084 455443 ▨ 084 456231
In a peaceful, wooded setting in the beautiful Ardennes area
with good, modern facilities.
➲ *Turn off E40/N4 towards Berguème then turn right.*
All year 3HEC ⛺ ⊶ ⌂ ♀ ⌂ ♀ ✕ ⊙ ⊠ ♨ ⊞ ⁊ R 🔲 ⊞ lau

THOMMEN-REULAND LIÈGE

Hohenbusch Grüfflingen 44 ☎ 080 227523
A well appointed family site on a wooded meadow with
plenty of recreational facilities.
➲ *Off N26 SW of St-Vith.*
Apr-Oct 5HEC ⛺ ⊶ ⊶ ⌂ ✕ ⊙ ⊠ ⁄ ♀ ⁊ P ⌸ lau

VIELSALM LUXEMBOURG

Salm chemin de la Vallée ☎ 080 216241
All year 2.5HEC ⛺ ➡ ⊶ ♀ ✕ ⊙ ⊠ ♨ ♀ ⁊ R ⌸ ⊞ lau ➡ ⊠
✕ ⁄ ⁊LP

VIRTON LUXEMBOURG

Vallée de Rabais r du Bonlieu ☎ 063 570144 ▨ 583342
e-mail: info@campingvalleederabais.be
A secluded family site in the heart of the Gaume region close
to a lake with good recreational facilities.
➲ *NE of Virton between N87 and N82.*
All year 8HEC ⛺ ⊶ ⌂ ⊶ ♀ ✕ ⊙ ⊠ ⁄ ♨ ⊞ ♀ ▲ ⁊ P ⌸ 🔲
⊞ lau ➡ ⁊L **Prices:** pitch 16.50 (incl 2 persons)

WAIMES LIÈGE

Anderegg Bruyères 4 ☎ 080 679393 ▨ 679396
In a peaceful situation beside the Lac de Robertville.
All year 1.5HEC ⛺ ⊶ ⊶ ⌂ ♀ ✕ ⊙ ⊠ ⁄ ♨ ⌸ ⊞ lau
Prices: ⊼2.50 ⊞4.50 ▲4.50

Striking coastline in Flanders

FRANCE

France, rich in history and natural beauty, is bordered by six countries:
Belgium, Germany, Italy, Luxembourg, Spain and Switzerland.

FACTS AND FIGURES
Area: 543,965 sq km
(210,025 sq miles)
Population: 58,416,500
(1998)
Capital: Paris
Language: French
IDD code: 33.
To call the UK dial 00 44
Currency: Euro
Local time: GMT + 1
(summer GMT + 2)
Emergency Services:
Police 17; Fire 18;
Ambulance 15.

Alternatively, dial the
European emergency call
number 112, and request
the service you require.
Business hours-
Banks: 10.00-13.00 &
15.00-17.00 Mon-Fri
(Paris area) and Tue-Sat
elsewhere.
Shops: Mon-Sat 09.00-
18.00 (times may vary for
food shops)
Average daily
temperature: Paris
Jan 3°C   Jul 18°C

Mar 6°C   Sep 15°C
May 13°C   Nov 6°C
Tourist Information:
UK French Government
Tourist Office
178 Piccadilly
London W1V 9AL
Tel 09068 244123
(Premium rate information
line 0830-2000 Mon-Fri)
Monaco Government
Tourist and Convention
Office
The Chambers,
Chelsea Harbour

London SW10 0XF
Tel Freephone 0500 006
114 (Mon-Fri 9.30 - 17.30)
USA French Government
Tourist Office
16th Floor,
444 Madison Ave
New York, NY 10022-6903
Tel (212) 838 7800
Camping Card: advisable
when using *Castels et*
Camping sites and also the
forts domaniales.
Tourist info website:
www.franceguide.com

The country offers a great variety of scenery
from the mountain ranges of the Alps and
the Pyrénées to the attractive river valleys of the
Loire, Rhône and Dordogne. And with some
1,800 miles of coastline, which includes the
golden sands of the Côte-d'Azur, there is a
landscape appealing to everyone's taste.

The climate of France is temperate but varies
considerably. The Mediterranean coast enjoys a
sub-tropical climate with hot summers, while
along the coast of Brittany the climate is very
similar to that of Devon and Cornwall. The
language is, of course, French and this is spoken
throughout the country, although there are many
local dialects and variations, some of which may
be impenetrable even to seasoned French
speakers.

France has an enormous number of
campsites, over 10,000 of them, under the
auspices of the *French Federation of Camping and*
Caravanning. During July and August, however,
thery are heavily booked, specially on the
Mediterranean coast and other popular holiday
destinations.

There are *castels et camping* caravanning sites
in the grounds of châteaux (castles) and many
are included in this guide. On sites in state
forests, *forêts domaniales*, it is necessary to apply to

the *garde forestier* for permission to camp and
evidence of insurance must be produced (such as
the *camping card*). Opening periods vary widely
and some sites are open all year. Local
information offices (see *Tourist information* above)
can supply detailed information about sites in
their locality.

All graded sites must display their official
classification, site regulations, capacity and
current charges at the site entrance. Some sites
have inclusive charges per pitch, others show
basic prices per person, vehicle and space, with
extra facilities like showers, swimming pools and
ironing incurring additional charges. In practice,
most campsites charge from midday to midday,
with each part day being counted as a full day.
Reductions for children are usually allowed up to
7 years of age; there is generally no charge for
children under 3.

Off-site camping in the South of France is
restricted because of the danger of fire; in other
parts, camping is possible, provided that
permission has been obtained, although camping
is seldom allowed near the water's edge, or at a
large seaside resort. Casual camping is prohibited
in state forests, national parks in the Landes and
Gironde *départements* and in the Camargue.
Camping in an unauthorised place renders

offenders liable to prosecution or confiscation of equipment, or both, especially in the South. However, an overnight stop on parking areas of some motorways is tolerated, but make sure you do not contravene local regulations; overnight stops in a lay-by are not permitted. Camping is not permitted in *Monaco*. Caravans in transit are allowed but it is forbidden to park them.

HOW TO GET THERE

Apart from the direct crossing by Eurotunnel (Folkestone-Calais, 35 mins platform to platform), the following services are available:

Short ferry crossings
From **Dover** to **Calais** takes 40 mins (catamaran) or 75-90 mins (ferry).
Longer ferry crossings
From **Dover** to **Dunkerque** takes 2hrs by ferry
From **Newhaven** to **Dieppe** takes 2hrs by catamaran.
From **Portsmouth** to **Le Havre** takes 5hrs 30mins (day) - 7hrs 30mins (night): to **Caen (Ouistreham)** takes 6hrs; to **Cherbourg** takes 5hrs (day) – 7 hrs (night) or 2hrs 45mins (catamaran); to **St Malo** takes 8hrs 45mins (day) – 10hrs 30 mins (night). From **Poole** to **Cherbourg** takes 4hrs 15mins (day) – 5hrs 45mins (night) or 2 hrs 15 mins (catamaran - summer only). From **Plymouth** to **Roscoff** takes 6 hrs; to **St Malo** (winter only) takes 8hrs.

Car sleeper trains
Summer services are available from **Calais** to Avignon, Brive, Narbonne and Toulouse; an all year round service operates to **Nice**.

MOTORING & GENERAL INFORMATION
The information given here is specific to France. It **must** be read in conjunction with the ABC at the front of the book, which covers those regulations which are common to many countries.

British Embassy/Consulates*
The British Embassy is located at 75383 Paris Cedex 08, 35 rue du Faubourg St-Honoré ☎0144513100; consular section 18 bis rue d'Anjou; phone as for Embassy. There are British Consulates in Bordeaux, Lille, Lyon and Marseille.

There are British Consulates with Honorary Consuls in Amiens, Biarritz, Boulogne-sur-Mer, Calais, Cherbourg, Dunkerque (Dunkirk), Le Havre, Lorient, Montpellier, Nantes, Nice, Perpignan, St Malo-Dinard, Saumur, Toulouse and Tours.

Childen in cars
Child under 10 not permitted to travel as front seat passenger, with the exception of baby - up to 9 months and less than 9kg weight - in rear-facing seat. Children under 10 in rear must use restraint system appropriate to age and weight. **Note**: Under no circumstances fit a rearward facing child restraint in a seat with a frontal airbag. See Continental ABC under 'Passengers' and 'Seat Belts'.

Currency*
With the introduction of the Euro, the **French Franc (FRF)** ceased to be legal tender from 17 February 2002. However, FRF coins and notes may still be exchanged at local banks until 30 June 2002 and at the French Central Bank (**Banque de France**) for 10 years (banknotes) and at least 3 years (coins).

Dimensions and weight restrictions*
Private **cars** and towed **trailers** or **caravans** are restricted to the following dimensions - height, no restrictions, but 4 metres is a recommended maximum; width, 2.55 metres; length, 12 metres (excluding tow-bar). The maximum permitted overall length of vehicle/trailer or caravan combination is 18.75 metres.
Trailers without brakes have a maximum authorised weight of 750kg or 50% of unladen weight of the towing vehicle, whichever is lower. If the weight of the trailer exceeds that of the towing vehicle, see also *Speed limits* below.

Driving licence*
(see also *Speed limits* below)
A valid UK or Republic of Ireland licence is acceptable in France. The minimum age at which visitors from UK or Republic of Ireland may use a temporarily imported motorcycle (over 80cc) or car is 18. Visitors may use temporarily imported motorcycles of up to 80cc at 16.

Foodstuffs*

If the imported foodstuffs are for personal use, there are no limits when travelling between EU countries. Visitors entering France from Andorra should ensure that the following are not exceeded – 2.5kg milk powder, 3kg condensed milk, 6kg fresh milk, 1kg butter, 4kg cheese, 5kg sugar/sweets, 5kg meat. Coffee (1kg), coffee extract (400g), tea (200g) and tea extract (80g) are free of customs duties. Visitors coming from other countries may import up to 1kg of meat, but meat and meat products from Africa are prohibited. Coffee (500g), coffee extract (200g), tea (100g) and tea extract (40g) are free of customs duties, but visitors under 15 cannot import coffee.

Lights*

Yellow tinted headlights are no longer necessary in France. It is compulsory for motorcyclists riding machines exceeding 125cc to use dipped headlights during the day.

Motoring club

The AA is affiliated to the **Fédération Française des Automobile-Clubs et des Usagers de la Route (FFAC)** whose office is at 8 place de la Concorde, 75008 Paris. ☎0153308930

Parking*

Parking restrictions are indicated by signs or yellow lines on the kerb. Stopping and parking is prohibited if the yellow line is continuous; parking if it is broken. In Paris parking is forbidden in many city centre streets, and wheelclamps are in use. It is absolutely forbidden to stop or park on a *red route*. The east-west route includes the left bank of the Seine and the Quai de la Megisserie; the north-south route includes the Avenue du Général Leclerc, part of the Boulevard St Michel, the Rue de Rivoli, the Boulevards Sébastopol, Strasbourg, Barbès and Ornano, Rue Lafayette and Avenue Jean Jaurès.

Priority including Roundabouts*

In built-up areas, you must give way to traffic coming from the right - *priorité à droite*. However, at roundabouts with signs bearing the words *"Vous n'avez pas la priorité"* or *"Cédez le passage"* traffic on the roundabout has priority. Where no such sign exists, traffic **entering** the roundabout has priority. Outside built-up areas, all main roads of any importance have right of way. This is indicated by a red-bordered triangle showing a black cross on a white background with the words *"Passage Protégé"* underneath; or a red-bordered triangle showing a pointed black

Mont Blanc

The fortified old town of Briancon, huddled around its ancient citadel, overlooking the rivers Durance and Guisane

upright with horizontal bar on a white background; or a yellow square within a white square with points vertical.

Petrol

See Continental ABC under 'Petrol/Diesel'.

Roads

France has more than 4000 miles of motorway (*autoroute*). With the exception of a few sections into or around large cities, tolls are payable. Emergency telephones which connect the caller to the police are located approximately every 2 kilometres. There is also a very comprehensive

network of other roads, and surfaces are generally good; exceptions are usually signposted *Chauseé déformeé*. The camber is often severe and the edges rough.

During July and August, and especially at weekends, traffic on main roads is likely to be very heavy. Special signs are erected to indicate alternative routes with the least traffic congestion. Wherever they appear, it is usually advantageous to follow them, although you may not save time. The alternative routes are quiet, but they are not as wide as the main roads. They are not suitable for caravans.

A free road map showing the marked

alternative routes, plus information centres and petrol stations open 24 hours, is available from service stations displaying the *Bison Futé* poster (a Red Indian chief in full war bonnet). These maps are also available from *Syndicats d'Initiative* and information offices.

Speed limits*

Built-up areas 50kph (31mph)
Outside built-up areas on normal roads 90kph (55mph); on dual-carriageways separated by a central reservation 110kph (69mph).
On Motorways 130kph (80mph). **Note** The minimum speed in the fast lane on a level stretch of motorway during good daytime visibility is 80kph (49mph), and drivers travelling below this speed are liable to be fined. The maximum speed on the Paris ring road is 80kph (49mph) and, on other urban stretches of motorway, 110kph (69mph).

In fog, when visibility is reduced to 50 metres (55yds), the speed limit on all roads is 50kph (31mph). In wet weather speed limits outside built-up areas are reduced to 80kph (49mph), 100kph (62mph) and 110kph (69mph) on motorways.

The above limits apply to private cars, motorcycles (exceeding 80cc) and private cars towing a trailer or caravan, if the latter's weight does not exceed that of the car and the total weight is less than 3.5 tonnes. However, if the weight of the trailer exceeds that of the car by less than 30%, the speed limit is 65kph (40mph), if more than 30% the speed limit is 45kph (28mph). Additionally these combinations must:

i Display a disc at the rear of the caravan/trailer showing the maximum speed.

ii Not be driven in the fast lane of a 3-lane motorway.

Those motorists who have held a full driving licence for less than two years, must not exceed 80kph (49mph) outside built-up areas, 100kph (62mph) on dual carriageways separated by a central reservation and 110kph (69mph) on motorways.

Warning triangle/Hazard-warning lights*
The use of a warning triangle or hazard-warning lights† is compulsory in the event of accident or breakdown. As hazard-warning lights may be damaged or inoperative, it is recommended that a warning triangle be carried. The triangle must be placed on the road 30 metres (33yds) behind the vehicle and clearly visible from 100 metres (109yds).

†If your vehicle is equipped with hazard warning lights, it is also complusory to use them if you are forced to drive temporarily at a greatly reduced speed. However, when slow moving traffic is established in an uninterrupted lane or lanes, this only applies to the last vehicle in the lane(s).

*Additional information will be found in the Continental ABC at the front of the book.

TOURIST INFORMATION

ALPS & EAST
Europe's highest mountain range reaches its highest point on the French border with Italy at Mont Blanc. However, comparatively few adventurers these days go to the Alps to climb Mont Blanc; during the winter the French Alps

Statue of Joan of Arc, the Archangel Michael, and Saints Catherine and Margaret at Domremy-le-Pucelle, near the basilica of Bois Chene

Part of the formal gardens, designed by Le Notre, at the Chateau de Versailles

provide a playground for skiing, and in summer a completely different, pastoral landscape.

Some of the finest summertime views of the Alps can be enjoyed from the town of l'Alpe d'Huez, 25 kilometres east of the regional centre of Grenoble. The views along the twisty road climbing towards the alpine outpost are impressive enough, but those from the town are even greater. However, l'Alpe d'Huez is famed primarily as a mountain stage in the Tour de France. The world's most famous cycle race has been coming here since the 1950s and has become the blue-riband mountain stage every cyclist wants to win. When 'le Tour' arrives in town in late July or early August, l'Alpe d'Huez comes vibrantly to life. In contrast to most other sporting events, the spectacle is free.

ALSACE & LORRAINE

Directly on the border with Germany, Strasbourg offers a wealth of Franco-German culture, making it a truly unique city.

Strasbourg has a world-famous university, is the seat of the Council of Europe, the International Human Rights, the European Parliament, and the European Science Foundation, and is such has become one of the most important cities in Europe. Among its many sights are the Place Kléber, – named after an 18th-century general – the Cathedral of Notre Dame, – the site of which has been a place of worship since before the 11th century – and the picturesque 'Petite France' area, where half-timbered houses cluster up together in charming narrow streets.

BURGUNDY & CHAMPAGNE

Images of sunny vineyards, cool cellars, and classic wines. Needless to say no trip to this part of France is complete without a wine expedition, and the only problem is knowing where to start.

The village of Aloxe-Corton, just over five kilometres north of Beaune in the Côte d'Or (golden hillside) region of Burgundy is a good place to begin. Aloxe-Corton is world-renowned within the wine trade and has been producing its distinctive wines since the 7th century when the village was owned by Charlemagne, and it is through him (or actually his wife) that Aloxe-Corton produces both red and white wines. The story runs that Charlemagne loved the red wines of the area, but they had an unfortunate habit of staining his white beard, so his wife instructed the local vine growers to produce white wines for her husband to overcome the problem. Not only is Aloxe-Corton connected with Charlemagne, but also Voltaire who had this to say over the village's red wines; "Your good wine is becoming a necessity to me. I keep quite good Beaujolais to give my guests, but I drink Burgundy in secret".

SOUTH WEST & PYRENEES

On the slopes of the Pyrenees stands the small town of Lourdes which has been a centre of pilgrimage for well over a century. In 1858, Bernadette Saubirous saw 18 visions of the Virgin Mary and discovered the 'miraculous' spring of the Massabielle Cave.

Since its discovery, the spring in Massabielle Cave has been celebrated for its supposed healing qualities, and the town of Lourdes has prospered as a result of the massive influx of pilgrims to the shrine and spring. There are three modern basilicas, one of which is underground; the other two are built on top of each other, one with Romanesque architecture, the other in a neo-Gothic style.

LOIRE & CENTRAL

Visitors to this important wine-growing region (Sancerre, Muscadet, Vouvray, Chinon and Bourgueil) are mainly drawn to the impressive series of châteaux. Among the most important are: Amboise, the cradle of French Renaissance architecture; Blois, with its magnificent open spiral staircase; Chambord, a Renaissance masterpiece; Chenonceau, spanning the Cher river, the most romantic of them all; and Villandry, famous for its formal gardens.

The principal city is Tours, home to a quarter of a million people. Although the outskirts are industrial, at the centre you will find one of France's most glorious old towns. Its cathedral took 300 years to build, between the 13th and 16th centuries, and the result is an eclectic mix of architectural designs ranging from the simplicity of the 13th-century chancel

to the exuberance of the Renaissance west façade and ornately decorated twin towers. Inside, the main attraction is the impressive stained glass Rose Window which is over 600 years old.

BRITTANY & NORMANDY

Bayeux is one of the oldest towns in Normandy, even more, one of the oldest in France. In recent history it is noted for being the first town liberated by the Allied forces in 1944. However, a battle of a different era is the subject of Bayeux's primary attraction, *La Tapisserie de la reine Malthilde* (Queen Mathilde's Tapestry). This is known to the English as the Bayeux Tapestry.

It is the most precious medieval document in existence and resides behind bullet-proof glass in the Centre Guillaume le-Conquérant, formerly the Bishop's palace. The 11th-century tapestry depicts the Norman Conquest of England in 58 scenes and took ten years to make. It is not only valuable as a depiction of the conquest, but also as a snap-shot of 11th century life. Expect long queues if you wish to see it at the height of the tourist season.

Bayeux's other attractions include the Cathédrale Notre Dame and the bustling Saturday market on the Place St-Patrice, selling fresh produce along with regional specialities including traditional Bayeux lace.

PARIS & THE NORTH

Northern France may not be the first destination for a camping holiday, but there is no shortage of interesting locations to visit, ranging from First World War battlefields and monuments of the Somme to the capital, Paris.

The perfect combination of history and elegance is captured just outside the capital at the world-famous Palace of Versailles, France's most visited attraction. It is on a gigantic scale, took more than 20 years to build (1661-1682) and guaranteed to require a full day's viewing. The chief attractions include the magnificent palace chapel, and the Kings' Apartments which were home to Louis XIV, Louis XV, and the ill-fated Louis XVI. After catching a glimpse of the French Kings' private lives, relive their social lives in the Grands Apartements. These include the famous Hall of Mirrors where the unfortunate Treaty of Versailles was drawn up in 1919.

Outside the palace, the geometric gardens designed by Le Nôtre are a joy to explore, as are the Grand Trianon, and Petit Trianon, the latter for ever associated with the tragic fate of Queen Marie Antoinette. In this tiny palace she hid from the reality of the French Revolution, and it was from here that she was taken to Paris to be executed in 1793.

AUVERGNE

Dormant volcanoes provide a bizarre character to the Auvergne region of France, home to le Parc Naturel Régional des Volcans d'Auvergne. This national park contains no fewer than 80 extinct volcanoes in a line running under 20 miles, ideal for energetic hikers. The park is still geologically active, with Europe's hottest geothermal springs at Chaudes Aigues, although there is no evidence of a volcanic eruption for 3,500 years.

The highest peak along the Monts Dôme chain to the north is the Puy de Dôme, reaching some 1,464 metres and offering magnificent view, overlooking nearly 100 extinct volcanoes and, allegedly, one eighth of France.

South of the Monts Dôme chain are the remains of two even greater, far more ancient volcanic chains, the Monts Dore and the Monts du Cantal. These have eroded to a shadow of their former selves, and now form a chain of jagged peaks.

SOUTH COAST & RIVIERA

Carcassonne is one of the most beautiful towns in France. Its dual sets of impressive turreted town walls are the largest of their kind in Europe and capture the flavour of a classical citadel.

The citadel was built as the first line of defence against aggressors from Spain. However, when France annexed the Roussillon in 1659 the citadel lost its front-line importance and almost decayed into ruin until a 19th-century architect, Viollet le-Duc stepped in to restore the town to its medieval glory.

The Riveria, a grouping that includes the coastal towns running down from Monte-Carlo to St Tropez, is one of the most exclusive and expensive areas of Europe. This doesn't make it the most camping-caravanning friendly part of France. In fact, camping is not permitted at all in the principality of Monaco. However, a few kilometres inland there are plenty of sites from

A fresh seafood platter in the district of Aquitaine

which to enjoy this colourful and exciting area.

CORSICA

Ajaccio is Corsica's largest town, and contains a bustling port, ancient streets, and a number of beautiful beaches. Ajaccio is also famous as the birth-place of Napoléon Bonaparte, born in 1769. There is no great Bonaparte personality cult in Ajaccio (he is regarded as a mainland Frenchman) but the town has definitely profited from Napoleon's exploits and the legend surrounding the emperor.

The Bonaparte trail begins at the Maison Bonaparte on rue St-Charles where the museum contains a vast array of Napoleonic memorabilia, with some fascinating family insights and items from the Bonaparte dynasty.

Cardinal Joseph Fesch, who was Napoleon's uncle, is also commemorated. A short walk from the Maison Bonaparte, the Palais Fesch contains a wonderful collection of Renaissance art; its fine works include Botticelli's *Virgin and Child*, and Titian's *Man with a Glove*. These, along with countless others, are all on display in the four storey museum.

ALPS/EAST

Within the French Alps is the old Duchy of Savoie, which only became part of France in the middle of the last century, and still retains a distinctive character. The Alps is a region of clear air, majestic mountain peaks, peaceful valleys and meadows. Good roads link the valleys; steep winding mountain roads lead to delightful villages and spectacular viewpoints, but cable cars offer a convenient alternative. A cable car goes up to the 12,000ft Aiguille du Midi, and a funicular railway leads to the spectacular 'Mer de Glace'. Annecy has a delightful, bustling medieval centre, and Lake Annecy, with its backdrop of mountains, provides opportunities for watersports and cruising. There are a number of attractive Alpine resorts - La Clusaz, Morzine, and the sophisticated Chamonix. Savoy's ancient capital, Chambéry, has a fascinating old town and castle. A well-kept secret is the Jura - a land of thickly wooded hills and plateaux with lush meadows grazed by sheep, goats and cattle. The rivers Rhône, Doubs and Ain flow through the region, and the many smaller rivers and lakes make this a fisherman's paradise.

ABRETS, LES ISÈRE

Coin Tranquille ☎ 476321348 ▤ 476374067
e-mail: contact@coin-tranquille.com
Completely divided into pitches with attractive flower beds in rural surroundings.
➲ *2 km E of village, 500m off N6.*
Apr-Oct 6HEC ⸬⸬ ⬥ ↾ ⊙ ▣ ♨ ✕ ⊙ ▣ ⌀ ⬛ ⬛ ↺ P ☎ ⊞ lau

AILLON-LE-JEUNE SAVOIE

Jeanne et Georges Cher ☎ 479546032
On a level meadow with heated sanitary installations. Situated close to the local ski station.
All year 2HEC ⸬⸬ ❆ ↾ ⊙ ▣ ☎ lau ⬥ ♥ ✕

ALBENS SAVOIE

Beauséjour rte de la Rippe ☎ 479541520
In a delightfully peaceful, wooded setting between Aix-les-Bains and Annecy.
➲ *SW via rte de la Chambotte. Signposted*
Jun-20 Sep 2HEC ⸬⸬ ⬥ ↾ ⊙ ▣ ⌀ ☎ lau ⬥ ♥ ✕ ↺R ⊞

ALLEVARD ISÈRE

Clair Matin rte de Pommiers ☎ 476975519 ▤ 476458715
Gently sloping terraced area divided into pitches.
➲ *S of village, 300m off D525.*
May-10 Oct 3.5HEC ⸬⸬ ⬥ ↾ ⊙ ▣ ⌀ ♨ ☎ ⊞ ↺ P ☎ ⊞ lau ⬥ ♥ ✕ ↺LR

ARBOIS JURA

CM Vignes av Gl-Leclerc ☎ 384661412 ▤ 384661412
Terraced site. Shop open Jul-Aug only.
➲ *E on D107 Mesnay road at stadium.*
Apr-Sep 5HEC ⸬⸬ ⸪⸪ ⬥ ↾ ♥ ♥ ⊙ ▣ ⌀ ☎ ⊞ lau ⬥ ✕ ♨ ↺PR

ARGENTIÈRE HAUTE-SAVOIE

Glacier d'Argentière 161 chemin des Chosalets ☎ 450541736 ▤ 450540373
Set on sloping meadowland in a beautiful situation at the foot of the Mont Blanc Massif.
➲ *Access is 1km S of Argentière, turn off N506 towards Cableway Lognan et de Grandes Montets, then a further 200m to site.*
15 May-Sep 1.5HEC ⸬⸬ ❆ ↾ ⊙ ▣ ⌀ ☎ ⊞ lau ⬥ ♥ ✕ ♨
Prices: ♠4 ➍1.50 ➌3 ▲2

ARS-SUR-FORMANS AIN

Bois de la Dame Chemin du Bois de la Dame ☎ 474007723
Compulsory separate car park for arrivals after 22.00hrs.
➲ *Access from A6, exit Villefranche and continue towards Jassans-Riottier.*
Apr-Sep 1.5HEC ⸬⸬ ⬥ ↾ ⊙ ▣ ☎ ▣ ⊞ lau ⬥ ♥ ♥ ✕ ↺P

AUTRANS ISÈRE

Caravaneige du Vercors Les Gaillards
☎ 476953188 ▤ 476953682
Ideal for summer or winter holidays, situated in the heart of the Vercors with easy access to skiing.
➲ *0.6km S via D106 towards Méaudre.*
Closed 2 wks end May & 2 wks end Sep 1HEC ⸬⸬ ❆ ↾ ⊙ ▣ ⌀ ☎ ↺ P ☎ ⊞ lau ⬥ ♥ ✕

Joyeux Réveil ☎ 476953344 ▤ 476957298
e-mail: camping-au-joyeux-reveil@wanadoo.fr
In a beautiful location surrounded by woodland, with fine mountain views.
➲ *NE of town via rte de Montaud.*
Dec-Sep 1.5HEC ⸬⸬ ⬥ ↾ ♥ ✕ ⊙ ▣ ♨ ⬛ ☎ ↺ P ☎ ⊞ lau ⬥ ♥
⦿ Prices: pitch 12.20-13.75 (incl 2 persons)

BARATIER HAUTES-ALPES

Verger ☎ 492431587 ▤ 4924981
e-mail: bresgilbeit@minitel.net
Terraced site in plantation of fruit trees with fine views of Alps. Divided into pitches.
➲ *From N94 drive 2.5km S of Embrun, 1.5km E on D40.*
All year 2.5HEC ⸬⸬ ❆ ↾ ⊙ ▣ ♨ ♨ ⬛ ⬛ ↺ P ☎ ⊞ lau ⬥ ♥ ✕ ↺LR

BELLEGARDE-SUR-VALSERINE AIN

Crêt d'Eau 2 av de Lattre-de-Tassigny ☎ 450566081
In a pleasant mountain setting with good facilities.
➲ *3km N of town, 200m from N84.*
15 May-15 Oct 5HEC ⸬⸬ ⬥ ↾ ✕ ⊙ ▣ ☎ ↺ P ☎ ▣ ⊞ lau ⬥ ♨ ⌀ ♨ ↺R

BOURG-D'OISANS, LE ISÈRE

Caravaneige le Vernis ☎ 476800268 ▤ 476800268
e-mail: camping.vernis@online.fr
Well-kept site at foot of mountain in summer skiing area.
➲ *2.5km of N91, rte de Briançon.*
15 Jan-15 Sep 1.2HEC ⸬⸬ ⬥ ↾ ⊙ ▣ ♨ ↺ P ☎ ⊞ ⊞ ✍ lau ⬥ ♥ ✕ ⌀ ♨

Cascade rte de l'Alpe-d'Huez ☎ 476800242 ▤ 476802263
e-mail: lacascade@wanadoo.fr
Set at the foot of a mountain with a waterfall and modern, very well-kept sanitary arrangements. Television lounge with library, open fireplace. Booking essential.
➲ *From Grenoble follow signs 'Stations de l'Oisans' then from Bourg-d'Oisans continue towards Alpe-d'Huez.*
15 Dec-Sep 2.5HEC ⸬⸬ ⬥ ↾ ♥ ✕ ⊙ ▣ ♨ ♨ ⬛ ↺ PR ☎ lau ⬥ ♥ ✕ ⊞

Rencontre du Soleil rte de l'Alpe-d'Huez ☎ 0476791222 ▤ 0476802637
e-mail: rencontre.soleil@wanadoo.fr
Charming site in a lovely setting in the Dauphiny Alps at the foot of a mountain. Fine rustic common room with open fireplace. TV, playroom for children.
➲ *At the foot of the hairpin road to L'Alp-d'Huez, leave N91 (Grenoble-Briançon road) in Le Bourg d'Oisans.*
11 May-15 Sep 1.6HEC ⸬⸬ ❆ ↾ ✕ ⊙ ▣ ↺ P ☎ lau ⬥ ♥ ✕ ⌀ ♨ ↺R Prices: pitch 14.03-21.98 (incl 2 persons)

At **Venosc**(10km SE on N91 and D530)

Champ de Moulin ☎ 476800738 ▥ 476802444
e-mail: christian.avallet@wanadoo.fr
In a picturesque location with fine views of the surrounding
mountains and a direct cablecar connection to local ski
slopes. Separate car park for late arrivals.
Oct-15 Dec 1HEC ⬛ ⬤ ⬤ ⬤ ⬤ ⬤ ⬤ ⬤ ⬤ ⬤ ⬤ ⬤ R ⬤
lau ➧ ⬤ ⬤ P ⊞ **Prices:** pitch 12-17 (incl 2 persons)

Bourg-en-Bresse Ain

CM de Challes 5 allée du Centre Nautique
☎ 474455995 ▥ 474224032
e-mail: camping_municipal_bourgenbresse@wanadoo.fr
In football ground near swimming pool.
➲ *Well signposted from outskirts of town.*
Apr-15 Oct 2.7HEC ⬛ ⬤⬤ ⬤ ⬤ ⬤ ⬤ ⬤ ⬤ ⬤ ⬤ ⬤ P ⬤ ⬤ ⊞
lau ➧ ⬤ ⬤ **Prices:** ⬤2.64 ⬤5.75 ⬤4.82

Bourget-du-Lac, le Savoie

CM Ile aux Cygnes ☎ 479250176
A family site on the shore of the Lac Bourdeau with plenty of
recreational facilities.
➲ *Access via N514.*
May-24 Sep 4.5HEC ⬛ ⬤ ⬤ ⬤ ⬤ ⬤ ⬤ ⬤ ⬤ LR ⬤ ⊞ lau
➧ ⬤ ⬤

Bourg-st-Maurice Savoie

Versoyen rte des Arcs ☎ 479070345 ▥ 479072541
e-mail: leversoyen@wanadoo.fr
Two communal sanitary blocks - one heated. Skiing facilities.
Many secluded pitches in a wood.
➲ *On S outskirts of town. Access via N90.*
Closed 3 Nov-15 Dec & 3-5 May 4HEC ⬛ ⬤ ⬤ ⬤ ⬤ ⬤ ⬤
⬤ ⬤ ⬤ ⊞ lau ➧ ⬤ ⬤ ⬤ ⬤ ⬤PR **Prices:** ⬤4.57 pitch 3.90

Bout-du-Lac Haute-Savoie

International du Lac Bleu rte d'Albertville
☎ 450443018 ▥ 450448435
e-mail: lac-bleu@nwc.fr
Modern, well-kept site. Overflow area with own sanitary blocks.
➲ *On the southern shores of Lake Annecy via the N508,
opposite ANTAR Garage.*
Apr-25 Sep 3.3HEC ⬛ ⬤ ⬤ ⬤ ⬤ ⬤ ⬤ ⬤ ⬤ LP ⬤ ⊞ lau ➧
⬤ ⬤ ⬤

Nublière ☎ 450443344 ▥ 450443178
e-mail: nubliere@wanadoo.fr
Extensive site divided into pitches in attractive surroundings.
➲ *150m off N508 at S end of Lac d'Annecy.*
May-Sep 9HEC ⬛ ⬤ ⬤ ⬤ ⬤ ⬤ ⬤ ⬤ ⬤ ⬤ ⬤ L ⬤ ⊞ lau
➧ ⬤ ⬤ ⬤ ⬤R

Chalezeule Doubs

Plage 12 rte de Belfort ☎ 381880426
e-mail: f.f.cc@wanadoo.fr
A modern site with good facilities near the main roads and
close to the River Doubs.
➲ *Access via N83 towards Belfort.*
Apr-Sep 1.8HEC ⬛ ⬤⬤ ⬤ ⬤ ⬤ ⬤ ⬤ ⬤ ⬤ PR ⬤ ⊞ lau
➧ ⬤ ⬤ ⬤

Chamonix-mont-blanc Haute-Savoie

Mer de Glace 200 Chemin de la Bagna
☎ 0450 450530863 ▥ 450536083
In a forested setting with pitches divided by hedges. Enjoys
fine mountain views.
➲ *2km NE to Les Praz. On approach to village (from
Chamonix) turn right under railway bridge.*
18 May-29 Sep 2.2HEC ⬛ ⬤⬤ ⬤ ⬤ ⬤ ⬤ ⬤ ⬤ ⬤ ⊞ lau ➧ ⬤
⬤ ⬤ ⬤ ⬤P **Prices:** ⬤4.75-5.50 pitch 4.50-6.30

Rosières 121 Clos des Rosières ☎ 450531042 ▥ 450532955
e-mail: info@campinglesrosieres.com
Picturesque site at the foot of the Mont Blanc range.
➲ *1.2km NE via N506.*
Feb-10 Oct 1.6HEC ⬛ ⬤ ⬤ ⬤ ⬤ ⬤ ⬤ ⬤ ⬤ ⬤ ⬤ ⬤ ⬤ ⊞ lau ➧ ⬤
⬤P **Prices:** ⬤4.75-5.50 pitch 4.20-5.60

At **Bossons, les**(3km W)

Cimes 28 rte des Tissieres ☎ 450535893
In a wooded meadow at the foot of Mont Blanc Massif. Ideal
for hiking and mountain tours.
Jun-Sep 1HEC ⬛ ⬤ ⬤ ⬤ ⬤ ⬤ ⬤ ⬤ ⬤ R ⬤ lau ➧ ⬤ ⬤ ⬤ ⬤
⬤LP ⊞

Deux Glaciers 80 rte des Tissières
☎ 450531584 ▥ 450559081
e-mail: glaciers@clubinternet.fr
A glacial stream runs through the site. Pitches shaded by
trees, very modern, well-kept sanitary installations. Rustic
common room with open fires.
➲ *Leave N506 towards road underpass. 250m to site.*
All year 16HEC ⬛ ⬤ ⬤ ⬤ ⬤ ⬤ ⬤ ⬤ ⬤ ⬤ ⬤ ⬤ ⊞ lau ➧ ⬤ ⬤

Champagnole Jura

CM Boyse r G-Vallery ☎ 384520032 ▥ 384520116
e-mail: boyse@frce.fr
Clean and tidy site with asphalt drives and completely
divided into pitches. In grounds of municipal swimming
pool.
➲ *Turn onto D5 just before town and continue 1.3km to site.*
2 Jun-17 Sep 7HEC ⬛ ⬤ ⬤ ⬤ ⬤ ⬤ ⬤ ⬤ ⬤ ⬤ ⬤ ⬤ PR ⬤ ⊞
lau

Châteauroux-les-alpes Hautes-alpes

Cariamas Font-Molines ☎ 492462263
e-mail: p.tim@free.fr
On a meadow in an attractive mountain setting beside the
River Durance.
➲ *1.5km SE.*
Jul-Aug 5HEC ⬛ ⬤ ⬤ ⬤ ⬤ ⬤ ⬤ ⬤ ⬤ ⬤ ⬤ A ⬤ ⬤ P ⬤ lau ➧ ⬤ ⬤ ⬤
Prices: ⬤4 ⬤5 ⬤5 pitch 5

Choisy Haute-Savoie

Chez Langin ☎ 450774165 ▥ 450774101
In pleasant wooded surroundings.
➲ *1.3km NE via D3.*
14 Apr-14 Oct 3HEC ⬛ ⬤ ⬤ ⬤ ⬤ ⬤ ⬤ ⬤ ⬤ ⬤ ⬤ ⬤ ⬤
P ⬤ ⊞ lau

Clairvaux-les-lacs Jura

Fayolan ☎ 384252619 ▥ 384252620
e-mail: relais.soleil.jura@wanadoo.fr
In a wooded location beside the lake.
➲ *1.2km SE via D118.*
May-22 Sep 17HEC ⬛ ⬤ ⬤ ⬤ ⬤ ⬤ ⬤ ⬤ ⬤ ⬤ ⬤ ⬤ LP ⬤
lau ➧ ⬤R

Grisière et Europe Vacances ☎ 384258048 ▥ 384252234
e-mail: bailly@aricia.fr
Fenced in meadowland with some trees, sloping down to the
Grand Lac. The site is guarded during July and August.
➲ *From village centre turn off N78, follow D118 towards
Châtel-de-Joux for 800m to the site.*
May-Sep 11HEC ⬛ ⬤ ⬤ ⬤ ⬤ ⬤ ⬤ ⬤ ⬤ ⬤ ⬤ ⬤ L ⬤ ⊞ lau

CLUSAZ, LA HAUTE-SAVOIE

Plan du Fernuy route des Confins
☎ 0033 450024475 ▤ 450326702
e-mail: leplan.du.fernuy@wanadoo.fr
Airing rooms. 30 ski-lifts nearby. Several cable cars. Well-situated for skiing or walking.
➲ *At the road fork E of La Clusaz leave N50 the Col des Aravis road, and drive towards Les Confins from road fork 2km to site.*
Jun-9 Sep & 20 Dec-Apr 1.3HEC 🚐 ⬥ ⌾ ⬤ 🍴 ⬛ ⌾ ⬤ ⬛
🔲 ⚡ P 🏠 lau ➡ ✗ ⊘ ⊞ Prices: pitch 15-16.80 (incl 2 persons)

DIVONNE-LES-BAINS AIN

Fleutron Quartier Villard ☎ 450200195 ▤ 450200035
e-mail: info@homair-vacances.fr
In wooded surroundings with large individual pitches.
➲ *3 km N.*
Apr-28 Oct 8HEC 🚐 ⌾ ⬤ 🍴 ⚡ ✗ ⌾ ⬤ ⬛ ⬤ ⬛ ⬤ ⚡ P 🏠 lau
➡ ⊘ ⚡ L ⊞ Prices: ⚡3.66-5.34 pitch 4.27-7.17

DOLE JURA

Pasquier 18 Chelin Theremot ☎ 384720261
Meadow site near River Doubs.
➲ *900m SE of town centre.*
15 Mar-15 Oct 2HEC 🚐 ⬥ ⬤ 🍴 ⚡ ✗ ⌾ ⬤ ⬤ ⬤ ⊞
lau ➡ ✗ ⚡ R

DOUCIER JURA

Domaine de Chalain ☎ 384257878 ▤ 384249407
e-mail: chalain@chalain.com
A large site beside Lake Chalain with a wide variety of recreational facilities.
➲ *3km NE.*
May-21 Sep 20HEC 🚐 ⌾ ⬤ ⚡ ✗ ⌾ ⬤ ⬤ ⬤ ⚡ LP
🏠 ⊞ lau Prices: pitch 18.40-25.50 (incl 3 persons)

DOUSSARD HAUTE-SAVOIE

Ravoire rte de la Ravoire ☎ 450443780 ▤ 45032960
e-mail: info@camping-la-ravoire.fr
A well appointed, modern site on level ground 800mtrs from Lake Annecy. Spectacular mountain views.
➲ *Leave Autoroute at Annecy Sud exit towards Albertville and take N508 as far as Duingt to pick up signs.*
15 May-15 Sep 2HEC 🚐 ⌾ ⬤ ⚡ ✗ ⌾ ⬤ ⊘ ⬤ ⚡ P 🏠
lau ➡ ✗ ⚡ L Prices: pitch 25.92-28.97 (incl 2 persons)

Serraz r de la Poste ☎ 450443068 ▤ 450448107
e-mail: info@campinglaserraz.com
Modern site divided into pitches. Cosy bar in rustic style.
➲ *At E end of village 500m from N508 on D181.*
15 May-20 Sep 4HEC 🚐 ⬥ ⌾ ⚡ ✗ ⌾ ⬤ ⬤ ⚡ P 🏠 ⊞ lau
➡ ⊘ ⚡ L Prices: ⚡3-5 pitch 14-20 (incl 2 persons)

EGATS, LES ISÈRE

Belvédère de l'Obiou ☎ 33 476304080 ▤ 476304080
e-mail: info@camping-obiou.com
Situated in beautiful scenery; modern sanitary installations and good recreational facilities.
➲ *Access via N85 S of Grenoble.*
15 Apr-30 Sep 1HEC 🚐 ⌾ ⚡ ✗ ⌾ ⬤ ⊘ ⬤ ⚡ P 🏠
⊞ lau ➡ ⚡ Prices: ⬤3 pitch 6-13 (incl 2 persons)

EMBRUN HAUTES-ALPES

CM Clapière av du Lac ☎ 492430183
Well-managed site with shaded pitches on stony ground, on N shore of lake. Site shop open during summer only.
➲ *2.5km SW on N94.*
May-Sep 5.3HEC 🚐 ⬥ ⌾ ⌾ ⬤ ⬤ lau ➡ ⚡ ✗ ⊘ ⬤
⚡LPR ⊞

ENTRE-DEUX-GUIERS ISÈRE

Arc en Ciel rue des berges ☎ 476660697 ▤ 476660697
e-mail: camparc@club-internet.fr
In a wooded location on the river bank with well shaded pitches.
➲ *On D520 300m from N6.*
Mar-Oct 1.2HEC 🚐 ⬥ ⚡ ⌾ ⬤ ⊘ ⬤ ⬤ ⚡ R 🏠 ⊞ lau ➡ ⚡ ⚡
✗ ⚡P

ÉVIAN-LES-BAINS HAUTE-SAVOIE

Clos Savoyard Maxilly sur Ciman
☎ 450752584 ▤ 450753019
Attractive site with fine views of the lake and the mountains.
➲ *Turn onto D21 in town 1200m after Hôtel le Maximillien and continue uphill.*
Apr-Sep 2HEC 🚐 ⌾ ⚡ ⌾ ⬤ ⬤ ⬤ ⊞ lau ➡ ⚡ ⚡ ✗ ⊘ ⚡L
Prices: ⚡6.90 ⬤6.90 ⬤6.90 ⚡3.80

At AMPHION-LES-BAINS (3.5km W on N5)

Plage 304 rue de la Garenne, Amphion les Bains
☎ 450700046 ▤ 450700046
e-mail: info@camping-dela-plage.com
A pleasant site with direct access to the lake. There are good recreational facilities and modern, well equipped bungalows and chalets are available for hire.
➲ *NW of town on N5, 150m from lake.*
All year 1HEC 🚐 ⌾ ⚡ ⌾ ✗ ⌾ ⬤ ⬤ ⚡ LP ⊞ ⊞ ⊘ lau ➡ ⚡
✗ ⊘ ⚡ R Prices: ⚡4-6 pitch 13-18 (incl 2 persons)

FERRIÈRE-D'ALLEVARD ISÈRE

CM Neige et Nature chemin de Montarmand ☎ 476451984
e-mail: contact@neige-nature.fr
In a beautiful situation with spectacular mountain views and good, modern facilities.
➲ *In Allevard take D525A towards Le Pleynet.*
Jun-15 Sep 1.2HEC 🚐 ⌾ ⚡ ✗ ⌾ ⬤ ⬤ ⚡ R 🏠 ⊞ lau ➡ ⚡
⊘ ⚡ Prices: ⚡3.90 pitch 3.90

GRESSE-EN-VERCORS ISÈRE

4 Saisons ☎ 476343027 ▤ 476343952
In a picturesque mountain setting with good facilities.
➲ *1.3km SW*
25 May-3 Sep 2.2HEC 🚐 ⬥ ⚡ ⌾ ⬤ ⬤ ⚡ P 🏠 lau
➡ ⚡ ✗ ⚡R ⊞

GUILLESTRE HAUTES-ALPES

Villard Le Villard ☎ 492450654 ▤ 492450052
In a magnificent location between the Ecrins national park and Queyras regional park. Good facilities, but bar and café operate July-Aug only.
➲ *2km W via D902A and N4, rte de Gap.*
All year 3HEC 🚐 ⌾ ⚡ ⌾ ⚡ ✗ ⌾ ⬤ ⊘ ⬤ ⬤ ⚡ PR 🏠 lau
➡ ⊘ ⚡L ⊞

HAUTECOURT-ROMANÈCHE AIN

Ile Chambod ☎ 474372541 ▤ 474372828
e-mail: camping.chambod@free.fr
A well equipped site close to the River Ain where swimming is supervised by lifeguards. Good sanitary and recreational facilities.
➲ *From Bourg-en-Bresse take D979 towards Geneva.*
May-Sep 2.5HEC 🚐 ⌾ ⚡ ⌾ ⬤ ✗ ⌾ ⬤ ⊘ ⬤ ⚡ P 🏠 lau ➡
⚡LR Prices: ⚡3.50 ⬤2 pitch 2.50

HUANNE-MONTMARTIN DOUBS

Étangs du Bois de Reveuge ☎ 381843860 ▤ 381844404
A terraced site in a 20 hectare park surrounded by the Vosges and Jura mountains with good recreational facilities.

⮑ *Access via A36 exit 'Baumes-les-Dames'.*
May-Sep 20HEC ⚑ ∴ ♨ ⚭ ⛵ ⚑ ♥ ✗ ⊙ ⛱ ⌀ ⚟ ⛟ ⁒ LP
⛺ ⊞ lau

ISLE-SUR-LE-DOUBS, L' DOUBS

CM Lumes 10 r des Lumes ☎ 381927305 ▤ 381927305
The site lies close to the town. Common room with TV.
⮑ *Off N83. Entrance near bridge over the Doubs.*
May-Sep 1.5HEC ⚑ ⚭ ⛵ ⊙ ⛱ ⁒ R ⛺ lau ♥ ⚑ ✗ ⌀ ⚟

LANDRY SAVOIE

Eden ☎ 479076181 ▤ 479076217
A modern site with excellent sports and sanitary facilities,
situated in the heart of the Savoie Olympic area.
18 Dec-26 Apr & 21 May-15 Sep 2.7HEC ⚑ ⚭ ⛵ ⚑ ♥ ✗ ⊙
⛱ ⚑ ⚟ ⁒ PR ⛺ ⊞ lau ♥ ✗ ⌀ ⚟

LONS-LE-SAUNIER JURA

Majorie 640 bd de l'Europe ☎ 384242694 ▤ 384240840
e-mail: marjorie@aricia.com
Clean, tidy site with tent and caravan sections separated by a
stream. Caravan pitches (80 sq m) are gravelled and
surrounded by hedges. Heated common room with TV,
reading area, kitchen.
⮑ *Near swimming stadium on outskirts of town.*
Apr-15 Oct 9HEC ⚑ ♨ ⚭ ⛵ ♥ ✗ ⊙ ⛱ ⌀ ⚟ ⛟ ⛺ ⊞
lau ♥ ✗ ⁒P

LUGRIN HAUTE-SAVOIE

Myosotis 28 chemin du Grand Tronc ☎ 450760759
A terraced site with fine views over the lake and of the
surrounding mountains.
⮑ *W of town. Signposted. 1km from Lac Leman*
4May-25 Sep 0.9HEC ⚑ ⚭ ⛵ ⊙ ⛱ ⌀ ⛟ ⛟ ⊞ lau ♥ ⚑ ♥
✗ ⚟ ⁒L Prices: ⚑2.20-2.70 pitch 4.10-4.60

Rys Route le Rys ☎ 450760575 ▤ 450760575
Calm shady site with panoramic views of the lake and
mountains. 10min walk from the beach
⮑ *W of town. Signposted.*
Apr-15 Oct 1.5HEC ⚑ ♥ ⚑ ⊙ ⛱ ⌀ ⚟ ⛟ ⊞ lau ♥ ⚑ ♥ ✗
⁒L Prices: ⚑3 pitch 10 (incl 2 persons)

Vieille Église ☎ 450760195 ▤ 450761312
e-mail: campingvieilleeglise@wanadoo.fr
On rising meadow between lake and mountains with good
views. Close to lake Léman and its beaches.
⮑ *D24 to Neuvecelle, then take D21, 1km after Maxilly on
right.*
Apr-20 Oct 1.5HEC ⚑ ♥ ⚑ ⛵ ✗ ⊙ ⛱ ⌀ ⚟ ⛟ ⛟ ⁒ P ⛺
⊞ lau ♥ ⚑ ⚟ ⁒L Prices: ⚑3.35-4.10 ⛟1.80-1.80 ⛟2.30-3.35
▲2.30-3.35 pitch 3.35

MALBUISSON DOUBS

Fuvettes ☎ 381693150 ▤ 381697046
e-mail: les-fuvettes@wanadoo.fr
Mainly level site with some terraces, gently sloping towards
lake. At an altitude of 900mtrs in the Jura mountains.
⮑ *500m S on D437.*
Apr-Sep 6HEC ⚑ ⚭ ⛵ ⚑ ✗ ⊙ ⛱ ⌀ ⚟ ⛟ ⁒ LP ⛺ ⊞ lau
Prices: pitch 13-17 (incl 2 persons)

MARIGNY JURA

Sunelia la Pergola ☎ 384257003 ▤ 384257596
e-mail: contact@lapergola.fr
A well equipped, terraced site with direct access to the lake.
⮑ *S of Marigny off D27.*
May-Sep 12HEC ⚑ ∴ ⚭ ⛵ ⚑ ♥ ✗ ⊙ ⛱ ⌀ ⛟ ▲ ⁒ LP ⛺
⊞ lau ♥ ⁒R Prices: ⛟2.30 pitch 14-35.50

MÉAUDRE ISÈRE

Buissonnets ☎ 476952104 ▤ 476952614
e-mail: pierre_ravix@yahoo.fr
A quiet, friendly site in the heart of the Vercors Regional Parc
with modern sanitary blocks and a wide range of summer
and winter recreational facilities.
⮑ *200m from village centre.*
All year 2.7HEC ⚑ ⚭ ⛵ ⊙ ⛱ ⌀ ⛟ ⛟ ⁒ P ⛺ ⛺ ⛿ lau ♥ ⚑ ♥
✗ ⊞ Prices: ⚑3.74 pitch 10.60 (incl 2 persons)

MESSERY HAUTE-SAVOIE

Relais du Léman ☎ 0450 450947111 ▤ 0450 947766
Well equipped site in a wooded location on the shore of Lac
Léman.
⮑ *1.5km SW via D25.*
Apr-Sep 3.5HEC ⚑ ♥ ⚑ ✗ ⊙ ⛱ ⌀ ⛟ ⛟ ⁒ P ⛺ lau ♥ ⚑
⁒LP ⊞ Prices: ⚑4.62 pitch 5.38

MEYRIEU-LES-ÉTANGS ISÈRE

Moulin ☎ 474593034
In a quiet, rural setting with good recreational facilities.
⮑ *On D552 between Vienne and Bourgoin-Jallieu.*
Apr-Oct 1.5HEC ⚑ ⚭ ⛵ ⚑ ♥ ✗ ⊙ ⛱ ⛟ ⁒ L ⛺ ⊞ lau

MIRIBEL-LES-ÉCHELLES ISÈRE

Bourdons ☎ 476552853 ▤ 476552582
e-mail: silvestri@met_up.com
A peaceful site in the heart of the Parc Régional de
Chartreuse, with fine views of the surrounding mountains.
⮑ *400m from village centre.*
All year 2HEC ⚑ ⚭ ⛵ ⚑ ♥ ✗ ⊙ ⛱ ⌀ ⛟ ⛟ ⁒ P ⛺ lau ♥
⊞ Prices: ⚑4.20 pitch 12.20 (incl 2 persons)

MONTMAUR HAUTES-ALPES

Mon Repos ☎ 592580314
Generally well-kept site on wooded terrain with shaded
pitches.
⮑ *1km E on D937 and D994.*
May-Oct 7HEC ⚑ ♥ ⚑ ⊙ ⛱ ⌀ ⛟ ⛟ ⁒ L ⛺ ⊞ lau

MONTMÉLIAN SAVOIE

Manoir av du Prés E-Herriot ☎ 0479652238
Situated close to the historical area of the town with 90
pitches divided by hedges.
Closed 25 Oct-Nov 2.8HEC ⚑ ♥ ⚑ ⊙ ⛱ ⛺ ⊞ ♥ ⚑ ♥
✗ ⌀ ⚟

MONTREVEL-EN-BRESSE AIN

Plaine Tonique Base de Plein Air ☎ 474308052
e-mail: plaine.tonique@wanadoo.fr
A well equipped site divided into a series of self contained
sections beside the lake. Entrance closed between 22.00 &
07.00 hrs. Booking advisable in July and August.
⮑ *0.5km E on D28.*
13Apr-27Sep 17HEC ⚑ ♥ ⚑ ♥ ✗ ⊙ ⛱ ⌀ ⚟ ⛟ ⁒ LP ⛺
⊞ lau Prices: ⚑2.50-4 ⛟4.70 pitch 6.50-10

MOUCHARD JURA

Halte Jurassienne Bel Air ☎ 384378392
Camping Card Compulsory.
⮑ *NE, near the service station.*
25 Mar-Oct 0.8HEC ⚑ ⚭ ⊙ ⛱ ⌀ ⚟ ⛺ ⊞ lau ♥ ⚑ ♥ ✗

NEYDENS HAUTE-SAVOIE

Colombière ☎ 450351314 ▤ 450351340
e-mail: la.colombiere@wanadoo.fr
A pleasant, friendly site with good recreational facilities.
Cont.

105

⮩ *Access via A40.*
01 Apr-30 Sep 2.2HEC ▦ ⚓♦♠⛨🛁⚡✕☉☺🅿🚻🔥 ⟨R P
🅿➕lau ➧ 🛒 ⟨R Prices: ♠3.50-4.50 pitch 14-18 (incl 2 persons)

NOVALAISE SAVOIE

Charmilles Lac d'Aiguebelette ☎ 479360467 ▤ 479360467
e-mail: camping.les.charmilles@wanadoo.fr
A terraced site in a beautiful mountain setting, 150m from the lake.
⮩ *On W shore of the lake on D941 towards St-Alban-de-Montbel.*
Jul-Aug 2.3HEC ▦ ∷⚓♠⛨☉☺⚡🗑🅿➕lau ➧ ⚡✕⟨L

ORNANS DOUBS

Chanet rte de Chassagne ☎ 381622344 ▤ 381621397
Comfortable site with good facilities in the peaceful Loue Valley.
⮩ *1.5km SW on D241. Follow green signs.*
Mar-15 Nov 1.5HEC ♦♠🛒☉☺🗑🚭🅿➕lau ➧⚡✕🏐⟨PR Prices: ♠3.20 pitch 11-12.20 (incl 2 persons)

ORPIERRE HAUTES-ALPES

Princes d'Orange ☎ 492662253 ▤ 492663108
e-mail: campingorpierre@wanadoo.fr
The site lies on a meadow with terraces.
⮩ *Exit N75 at Eyguians and take D30.*
Apr-Oct 20HEC ▦ ⚓♠⛨⚡✕☉☺🚭🛁🅿A⟨ P🅿➕lau
➧🛒🗑⟨R Prices: ♠9.50-16.50 ♠14.25-18

OUNANS JURA

Plage Blanche 3 r de la Plage ☎ 384376963 ▤ 384376021
In a pleasant location beside the River Loue with good recreational facilities.
⮩ *1.5km S via D71 (rte de Montbarcy).*
Apr-Sep 5HEC ▦ ⚓♠⛨✕☉☺🚭🛁🔥A⟨ PR🅿lau
➧🛒🗑

PARCEY JURA

Bords de Loue Chemin du Val d'Amour
☎ 384710382 ▤ 384710342
e-mail: contact@jura-camping.com
A quiet site on the River Loue.
⮩ *1.5km from the centre of the village via N5. Signposted.*
20 Apr-15 Sep 18HEC ▦ ⚓♠⛨✕☉☺🚭🗑🔥🚭⟨ PR 🅿➕lau ➧🛒✕ Prices: ♠3.50 pitch 4.10

PATORNAY JURA

Moulin ☎ 384483121 ▤ 384447121
e-mail: feeries@club-internet.fr
A modern site on a level meadow in a peaceful, wooded location on the banks of the River Ain.
⮩ *Access is NE via N78, rte de Clairvaux-les-Lacs.*
31May-17 Sep 5HEC ▦ ∷♦♠🛒⚡✕☉☺🚭🛁🔥A⟨
PR➕lau ➧⟨L➕ Prices: ♠3

PLAGNE-MONTCHAVIN SAVOIE

Montchavin les Coches ☎ 479078323 ▤ 479078018
e-mail: montcahvin@wanadoo.fr
A summer and winter site overlooking the Tarentaise Valley with good, modern facilities.
Nov-Sep 1.3HEC ▦ ♦♠⛨☉😊🗑➕lau ➧🛒⚡✕🚭🛁⟨P
Prices: ♠3.50 pitch 3.50

PONTARLIER DOUBS

Larmont r du Toulombief ☎ 381462333
A mountain site with good facilities in an area associated with winter sports.
All year ▦ 🌊🌿♠🛒⚡✕☉☺🗑🚭🛁🔥🚭➕lau ➧✕
⟨R

PONT-DE-VAUX AIN

Peupliers Port de Fleurville ☎ 385303365 ▤ 385303365
e-mail: camplier@worldonline.fr
A family site beside the River Saône with good facilities.
⮩ *3km from Pont-de-Vaux via N6.*
Etr-1 Oct 7HEC ▦ ⚓♠🛒⚡✕☉☺🗑🚭🛁🔥🚭A⟨ PR🅿
➕lau

PORT-SUR-SAÔNE HAUTE-SAÔNE

CM Maladière ☎ 384915132
A quiet, comfortable site with modern facilities, close to the River Saône.
⮩ *S on the D6, between the River Saône and the Canal*
15 May-15 Sep 2HEC ▦ ⚓♠☉☺🗑🚭➕lau ➧🛒⚡✕🚭🛁
⟨PR

PRESLE SAVOIE

Combe Léat ☎ 479255402
A quiet mountain site.
⮩ *Access via A43 and D207.*
15 Jun-5 Sep 4HEC ▦ ♦♠⛨☉☺🗑🚭➕lau Prices: ♠2.50
♠2.50 pitch 2.50

RENAGE ISÈRE

Verdon 185 av de la Piscine ☎ 476914802
⮩ *5km N of Tullins on D45.*
Apr-15 Oct 1.5HEC ▦ ♦♠⛨☉☺🗑🚭➕lau ➧🛒⚡✕🛁
⟨P

ROCHETTE, LA SAVOIE

Lac St-Clair ☎ 479257355
At the foot of the Belledonne mountains, 1km from a lake with good fishing.
⮩ *Access via D925B Grenoble-Albertville.*
Jun-Aug 3HEC ▦ ⚓♠⛨☉☺🗑🚭A➕lau ➧🛒⚡✕🚭🛁
⟨P

ROSIÈRE-DE-MONTVALEZAN, LA SAVOIE

Forêt ☎ 479068621 ▤ 479401625
A peaceful site in pleasant wooded surroundings, with good, modern facilities.
⮩ *2km S via N90 towards Bourg-St-Maurice.*
15 Jun-15 Sep & 15 Dec-1 May 2.7HEC ▦ ♦♠⚡✕☉☺🗑
🛁🔥🚭A⟨ P🅿➕lau ➧🛒✕🚭⟨R

ROUGEMONT DOUBS

🏕Val de Bonnal Bonnal ☎ 381869087 ▤ 381860392
e-mail: val-de-bonnal@wanadoo.fr
Quiet woodland site beside the River Ognon. Supervised swimming in lake with beach.
12 May-12 Sep 15HEC ▦ ⚓♠🛒⚡✕☉☺🗑🚭🛁⟨ LPR
🅿➕lau

ST-AVRE SAVOIE

Bois Joli St Martin-sur-la-Chambre
☎ 479562128 ▤ 479562995
e-mail: camping-le-bois-joli@wanadoo.fr
Well kept site with pitches and individual washing cabins.
⮩ *1km N of St-Avre, off N6-E70 via La Chambre.*
Apr-15 Sep 4HEC ▦ ♦♠⚡✕☉☺🗑🚭🔥🚭⟨ P🅿➕lau
➧🛒

ST-CLAIR-DU-RHÔNE ISÈRE

Daxia rte du Péage ☎ 474563920 ▤ 0474569346
A riverside site with good sanitary and recreational facilities.
⮩ *Access via N7/A7.*
Apr-Sep 7.5HEC ▦ ⚓♠⚡✕☉☺🗑🚭🔥🚭⟨ PR🅿lau

ST-CLAUDE JURA

Martinet ☎ 384450040
In a wooded location close to the Centre Nautique.
➪ *2km SE, beside the river*
May-Sep 3HEC ⊞ ♦ ⋒ ⅀ ⴼ ✕ ⊙ ⊡ ₹ R 🆙 lau ♦ 🚿 ₹P
Prices: ⋔2.30 ➡1.10 ⊡1.70 ▲1.25

ST-DISDILLE HAUTE-SAVOIE

St-Disdille av de St-Disdille ☎ 450711411 ▤ 450719367
In a peaceful, wooded location in the heart of the Chablais region.
➪ *N of N5. Signposted.*
Apr-Sep 12HEC ⊞ ♦ ⋒ 🅿 ⅀ ✕ ⊙ ⊡ ⊘ ⊞ 🆙 lau ♦ 🚿
₹LPR Prices: ⋔3.50 pitch 13 (incl 2 persons)

ST-GERVAIS-LES-BAINS HAUTE-SAVOIE

Dômes de Miage 197 rte des Contamines
☎ 450934596 ▤ 450781075
e-mail: camping.st-gervais@wanadoo.fr
On a beautiful wooded plateau with fine views of the surrounding mountains.
➪ *2km S on D902.*
Jun-Sep 2.5HEC ⊞ ⊟ ⋒ ⅀ ⴼ ✕ ⊙ ⊡ ⊘ ⊞ 🆙 lau ♦ 🚿 ₹P
Prices: pitch 14-15 (incl 2 persons)

ST-INNOCENT-BRISON SAVOIE

Rolande 24 chemin des Berthets ☎ 479543685
Situated on gently sloping terrain.
➪ *Signposted from village centre.*
May-Sep 1.5HEC ⊞ ⊟ ⋒ ⅀ ✕ ⊙ ⊡ ⊘ 🆙 ⊞ lau ♦ ₹L

ST-JEAN-DE-COUZ SAVOIE

International la Bruyère ☎ 479657911 ▤ 479657427
e-mail: bearob@libertysurf.fr
In wooded surroundings close to the Grande Chartreuse range with a variety of sporting facilities.
➪ *2km S via N6, towards Côte-Barrier*
Apr-Oct 1HEC ⊞ ⊟ ⋒ ⅀ ⴼ ✕ ⊙ ⊡ ⊘ 🚿 ⊡ ⊞ lau ♦ ₹R
Prices: ⋔2.60 pitch 2.60

ST-JEAN-ST-NICOLAS HAUTES-ALPES

CM le Châtelard Pont-du-Fossé ☎ 492559431
15 Jun-15 Sep 4HEC ⊞ ♦ ⋒ ⊙ ⊡ ₹ R 🆙 ⊞ lau ♦ 🚺 ⅀ ✕ ⊘
🚿 ₹LP Prices: ⋔3.05 ⊡4.12 ▲3.35

ST-JORIOZ HAUTE-SAVOIE

Europa 1444 rte d'Albertville ☎ 450685101 ▤ 450685520
e-mail: info@camping-europa.com
Well equipped site in picturesque surroundings close to Lake Annecy.
➪ *1.4km SE*
13 May-20 Sep 3.7HEC ⊞ ⊟ ⋒ ⅀ ⴼ ✕ ⊙ ⊡ 🚿 🚺 ₹ P 🆙 lau ♦ ⊘ 🚿 ₹L ⊞

International du Lac d'Annecy ☎ 450686793 ▤ 456725724
➪ *N508 towards Albertville.*
Jun-15 Sep 2.5HEC ⊞ ♦ ⅀ ✕ ⊙ ⊡ ₹ P 🆙 lau ♦ 🚺 ⊘ ₹L

ST-PIERRE-DE-CHARTREUSE ISÈRE

Martinière rte du Col de Porte ☎ 476886036 ▤ 476886910
e-mail: brice.gaude@wanadoo.fr
In pleasant position surrounded by the Chartreuse mountains and close to the famous monastry.
➪ *2km SW off D512.*
Closed 20 Sep-1 Nov & 30 Apr-16 May 2.5HEC ⊞ ⊟ ⋒ 🚺
⅀ ✕ ⊙ ⊡ ⊘ 🚿 ₹ P ⊞ lau ♦ ✕ Prices: pitch 10.50-12.50 (incl 2 persons)

SALLE-EN-BEAUMONT, LA ISÈRE

Champ-Long ☎ 476304181 ▤ 0476304181
In a beautiful Alpine setting at the entrance to the Ecrins Park at an altitude of 700mtrs.
➪ *1.5km NW off N85.*
Apr-Oct 4HEC ⊞ ⊟ ⋒ 🅿 ⅀ ⴼ ✕ ⊙ ⊡ 🚺 🚿 ₹ P ⊡ 🆙 ⊞ lau ♦ ₹R Prices: ⋔7.93

SÉEZ SAVOIE

Reclus rte de Tignes ☎ 479410105 ▤ 479410479
e-mail: campinglereclus@wanadoo.fr
In a pleasant wooded location within easy reach of the ski slopes.
➪ *NW on N90.*
Dec-Oct 1.8HEC ⊞ ♦ ⋒ ⊙ ⊡ 🚿 ₹ R 🆙 ⊞ lau ♦ 🚺 ⅀ ✕ ⊘
🚿 ₹P Prices: ⋔3.50-3.65 pitch 3.30-3.65

SERRES HAUTES-ALPES

Barillons ☎ 492671735
Well-laid out with terraces.
➪ *1km SE on N75.*
End May- Mid Sep 3HEC ⊞ ♦ ⋒ ⅀ ✕ ⊙ ⊡ ⊘ 🚿 🆙 ⊞ lau ♦ 🚺 ✕ ₹R Prices: ⋔3.20 pitch 12.40 (incl 2 persons)

Domaine des 2 Soleils ☎ 492670133 ▤ 492670802
e-mail: dom.2.soleils@wanadoo.fr
Well-kept terraced site in Buéch Valley.
➪ *S of town off N75. Signposted.*
May-Sep 12HEC ⊞ ⊟ ⊟ ⋒ 🚺 ⅀ ✕ ⊙ ⊡ ⊘ 🚿 🚿 ₹ P 🆙 ⊞ lau ♦ ₹LR

SEYSSEL AIN

International de Seyssel chemin de la Barotte
☎ 450592847 ▤ 450592847
e-mail: camp.inter@wanadoo.fr
A quiet site on steep, terraced meadowland, with individual washbasins and clean sanitary installations.
➪ *1km SW off Culoz road.*
15 Jun-15 Sep 1.5HEC ⊞ ♦ ⅀ ✕ ⊙ ⊡ ⊘ 🚿 🚿 ₹ P 🆙
⊞ lau ♦ 🚺 ₹LR

TALLOIRES HAUTE-SAVOIE

Lanfonnet Angon ☎ 450607212 ▤ 45060712 450233882
A well equipped site 100mtrs from the lake.
➪ *1.5km SE.*
May-Sep 2.5HEC ⊞ ♦ ⋒ 🚺 ⅀ ✕ ⊙ ⊡ ⊘ 🚿 ₹ L ⊡ ⊞ ⊗
lau Prices: ⋔3.96-5.80 pitch 13.70-19.60

THOISSEY AIN

CM ☎ 474040425
e-mail: mairie.thoissey@wanadoo.fr
Situated between two rivers, the Saône and the Chalaronne.
➪ *1km SW on D7.*
Apr-Sep 15HEC ⊞ ⋙ ⊟ ⋒ ⅀ ✕ ⊙ ⊡ 🚿 ₹ PR 🆙 ⊞ lau ♦
🚺 ⊘ 🚿 Prices: pitch 5

THONON-LES-BAINS HAUTE-SAVOIE

Morcy ☎ 450704487
In a quiet location close to Lac Léman and the thermal spa.
➪ *2.5km W of town.*
Apr-Sep 1.2HEC ⊞ ♦ ⋒ 🚺 ✕ ⊙ ⊡ ⊘ 🚿 🚿 ⊡ 🆙 lau ♦ ✕
🚿 ₹LR

TIGNES-LES-BRÉVIÈRES SAVOIE

Escapade rte des Boisses ☎ 479064127
A well equipped site 1km from the centre of the village.
➪ *Signposted from D902.*
15 Jun-Sep 4.5HEC ⊞ ⋙ ⊟ ⋒ 🚺 ⅀ ✕ ⊙ ⊡ ⊘ ₹ P 🆙 ⊞ lau

Camping Caravaneige L'OURSIERE

F-38250 VILLARD-de-LANS

Capital of the VERCORS
Open summer and winter, altitude 1050 m.
Alpine skiing, cross-country skiing,160 km
tracks. Holiday park, ice-skating, swimming
pool with waves open all year. Fully equipped
mobile homes to let in winter season
(4-6 beds). Heated sanitary installations.
TV-room and games.

Tel.: 04 76 95 14 77 - Fax: 04 76 95 58 11
www.camping-oursiere.fr
e-mail:info @camping-oursiere.fr

gentle pastures, fertile plains, enchanting lakes and famous thermal spas. In the summer this region is ablaze with colour - there are brilliant displays of wild flowers in the Vosges, and in the towns and cities, flowers cascade from every available ledge. Gerardmer is at the heart of the Vosges, and La Bresse is also popular with visitors. Nancy, the capital of Lorraine, and Metz, with its lovely old town and fine Gothic cathedral, are great centres for the area, but Strasbourg is a delight to discover. The waterways of the 'Petit France' district are charming, and the splendid soaring spine of the cathedral of Notre Dame is unforgettable.

In the countryside, vineyards surround pretty villages with half-timbered houses and cobbled streets, and produce the fine wines of the area, but hops are also grown in the region, and famous beers are brewed in Strasbourg.

....

TREPT ISÈRE

3 Lac La Plaine ☎ 474929206 ▤ 474929335
e-mail: leslacs@free.fr
Situated at the gateway to the Alps, an undulating woody area with small lakes.
➲ On D517, 2.5km W.
May-10 Sep 4HEC ⊞ ⌷ ⌂ ♻ ♨ ▼ ✕ ⊙ ◘ ☎ ⅌ LP ☎ ⊞ lau
Prices: ☗5 ▲3 pitch 7

VERNIOZ ISÈRE

Bontemps ☎ 474578352 ▤ 474578370
A pleasantly landscaped site beside the River Varèze.
➲ Access via N7 and D131.
Apr-Sep 8HEC ⊞ ♦ ⌂ ♨ ▼ ✕ ⊙ ◘ ⌀ ☴ ☎ ⅌ P ☎ ⊞ lau ♦
⅌R Prices: ☗5 ♦2 ♻6.50 ▲6.50

VILLARD-DE-LANS ISÈRE

L'Oursière ☎ 476951477 ▤ 476955811
e-mail: info@camping-oursiere.fr
Peaceful site in the natural park region of Vercors. Summer and winter facilities.
➲ N off D531 in direction of Grenoble.
Dec-Sep 4.2HEC ⊞ ♨ ⌷ ⌂ ♨ ▼ ⊙ ◘ ⌀ ☴ ☎ ♧ ▲ ☎ ⊞
lau ♦ ⅌P

VILLARS-LES-DOMBES AIN

CM Autières 164 av des Nations ☎ 0474980021
e-mail: campingdesautieres@wanadoo.fr
Clean and tidy park-like site divided into plots and pitches. Part reserved for overnight campers. Clean, modern sanitary installations.
➲ SW off N83.
Apr-26 Sep 4.5HEC ⊞ ⌷ ⌂ ▼ ✕ ⊙ ◘ ☎ ⅌ PR ☎ lau ♦ ⌾
⌀ ☴ ⊞ Prices: ☗3.05 ♦2.13 pitch 3.81

VOIRON ISÈRE

Porte de la Chartreuse 33 ave du 8 Mai 45 ☎ 476051420
On level terrain with some trees, divided into pitches. Much traffic noise from nearby N75. Clean and modern sanitary installations.
➲ Access is NW of town next to the Esso garage.
All year 1.5HEC ⊞ ♨ ♦ ⌂ ▼ ✕ ⊙ ◘ ☎ ☎ ⊞ ♦ ⌾ ⌀ ☴ ⅌P

● ○ ●   **ALSACE/LORRAINE**   ● ○ ●

In its natural border position next to Germany, Alsace enjoys a special identity, neither German nor completely French. And, with Lorraine, it shares some of the most turbulent chapters in French history. They also share the impressive Vosges mountains, with great wooded slopes,

ANOULD VOSGES

Acacias ☎ 329571106 ▤ 329571106
e-mail: contact@occaciascamp.com
In pleasant surroundings with well defined pitches in the heart of the Hautes-Vosges region.
➲ NE of town centre towards the ski slopes.
Dec-10 Oct 2.5HEC ⊞ ♦ ⌷ ⌂ ▼ ✕ ⊙ ◘ ⌀ ☴ ☎ ⅌ P ☎ ⊞
lau ♦ ⌾ ⅌R Prices: ☗3 ♦3.20 ▲1.60 pitch 3.20

AUBURE HAUT-RHIN

CM La Ménère ☎ 389739299
A peaceful site at an altitude of 800mtrs.
➲ Access via N415 or D416, then D11.
15 May-Sep 1.8HEC ⊞ ⋮⋮⋮ ⌷ ⌂ ⊙ ◘ ⌀ ☴ ☎ ⊞ lau ♦ ⌾
▼ ✕

BAERENTHAL MOSELLE

Ramstein Plage Base de Baerenthal, Ramstein Plage
☎ 387065073 ▤ 387066231
The River Zinsel runs through this rural wooded site close to the border with Germany.
➲ W via r du Ramstein.
Apr-Sep 14HEC ⊞ ⋮⋮⋮ ♦ ⌷ ▼ ✕ ⊙ ◘ ☎ ⅌ LP ☎ ⊞ lau ♦
⌾ ✕ ⌀ ⅌R

BIESHEIM HAUT-RHIN

Ile du Rhin Zone Touristique
☎ 389725795 ▤ 389721421
On the Ile du Rhin, between the Canal d'Alsace and the River Rhine in pleasant wooded surroundings.
➲ From Colmar take N415 towards Germany as far as the Rhine bridge.
All year 3HEC ⊞ ⌷ ⌂ ✕ ⊙ ◘ ⌀ ☎ ☎ ⊞ lau
♦ ▼ ✕ ⅌PR

BRESSE, LA Vosges

Belle Hutte Belle Hutte ☎ 329254975 ▤ 329255263
Terraced site beside the River Moselotte.
➲ *Access via D34 towards Col de la Schlucht.*
All year 3.2HEC ⊞⊞⊞ ⊕ ↑ ⛺ ⊙ ☘ ∅ ᴪ ⛱ ⅊ PR 🅿 lau ♦ ⅀ ✕
⅊L ⊞ Prices: ⋔2.20-4.20 ⇐1.30-1.70 ⊕1.40-2.20 ▲1.30-2

BURNHAUPT-LE-HAUT HAUT-RHIN

Le Castor 4 rte de Guewenheim
☎ 389487858 ▤ 0389627466
e-mail: camping.les.castors@wanadoo.fr
A modern site in a rural setting close to a river and
surrounded by woodland.
➲ *E of Burnhaupt towards Guewenheim on D466.*
Apr-Sep 2.5HEC ⊞⊞⊞ ♦ ↑ ⅀ ✕ ⊙ ☘ ∅ ⊕ ⛱ ⅊ R 🅿 lau ♦
⅀ Prices: ⋔3.20 ⊕3.51 ▲3.51 pitch 3.51

BUSSANG Vosges

Domaine de Champé 14 Les Champs Navés
☎ 329858645 ▤ 329615690
e-mail: camping@bussang.com
In pleasant surroundings beside the River Moselle.
➲ *On N57.*
Apr-Oct 1.5HEC ⊞⊞⊞ ᴪ ↑ ⊙ ☘ 🅿 ⊞ lau ♦ ⅀ ⅀ ✕ ∅ ᴪ ⅊L

CELLES-SUR-PLAINE Vosges

Lac Base de Loisirs, Les Lacs de Pierre-Percée
☎ 329411925 ▤ 0329411869
e-mail: camping@sma_lacs_pierre_percee.fr
Set among wooded hills in an extensive natural leisure area
around the Lakes of Pierre-Percée.
➲ *Access via D392A.*
Apr-Sep 3HEC ⊞⊞⊞ ᴪ ↑ ⅀ ✕ ⊙ ☘ ∅ ⊕ ⅊ PR 🅿 ⊞ lau ♦
✕ ᴪ ⅊L Prices: ⋔4-5.15 pitch 4-5.15

CERNAY HAUT-RHIN

CM Acacias 16 rue Ré-Guilbert
☎ 389755697 ▤ 389397229
Clean, quiet site on right bank of the River Thur.
➲ *Off N83 between Colmar and Belfort.*
Apr-Sep 4HEC ⊞⊞⊞ ⊕ ↑ ⅀ ⅀ ✕ ⊙ ☘ ∅ 🅿 lau ♦ ✕ ⅊P ⊞

COLMAR HAUT-RHIN

Intercommunal de l'Ill ☎ 0389411594 ▤ 0389411594
On a meadow beside the river with good, modern facilities.
Separate sections for campers in transit.
➲ *2km E on N415.*
Feb-Nov 2.2HEC ⊞⊞⊞ ⊕ ↑ ⅀ ⅀ ✕ ⊙ ☘ ∅ ⅊ R 🅿 ⊞ lau

CORCIEUX Vosges

⛺Domaine des Bains r J-Wiese ☎ 329516467 ▤ 0329516465
e-mail: les_bans@domaines_des_bans.com
On meadowland divided into pitches with a variety of
recreational facilities.
➲ *E of village off D8.*
All year 30HEC ⊞⊞⊞ ⊕ ↑ ⅀ ⅀ ✕ ⊙ ☘ ∅ ᴪ ⛱ ⊕ ⅊ LP 🅿 ⊞
lau ♦ ✕ Prices: ⋔6.10 pitch 12.20

DABO MOSELLE

Rocher 10 pl de l'Église ☎ 387074751 ▤ 387074773
e-mail: info@ot-dabo.fr
In a beautiful position close to the historic town of Dabo in
the Vosges mountains.
➲ *1.5km SW via D45.*
Etr-Oct 0.5HEC ⦂⦂⦂ ⊕ ↑ ⊙ ☘ 🅿 ⊕ 🅿 lau ♦ ⅀ ⅀ ✕ ∅ ᴪ ⊞

DAMBACH-LA-VILLE BAS-RHIN

CM rte d'Ebersheim ☎ 388924860 ▤ 388926009
e-mail: otdlv@netcourrier.com
In a wooded location close to the town centre. Advance
booking recommended during July and August.
➲ *1km E via D120.*
15 May-Sep 1.8HEC ⊞⊞⊞ ♦ ↑ ⊙ ☘ 🅿 🅿 lau ♦ ⅀ ⅀ ✕ ∅ ᴪ ⊞

EGUISHEIM HAUT-RHIN

CM Aux Trois Châteaux 10 r du Bassin
☎ 389231939 ▤ 389241019
In a peaceful location at an altitude of 210mtrs and
surrounded by vineyards.
➲ *6km S of Colmar on N83.*
Apr-Sep 1.8HEC ⊞⊞⊞ ♦ ⊕ ↑ ⊙ ☘ ∅ 🅿 🅿 lau ♦ ⅀ ⅀ ✕ ⊞
Prices: ⋔3.10 pitch 3.10

FONTENOY-LE-CHÂTEAU Vosges

Fontenoy rte de la Vierge ☎ 329363474 ▤ 329363726
Set on a hill in peaceful, wooded surroundings.
➲ *2.2km S via D40.*
15 Apr-15 Sep 1.2HEC ⊞⊞⊞ ♦ ↑ ⅀ ⅀ ✕ ⊙ ☘ ∅ ⅊ P 🅿 lau
♦ ᴪ ⅊R ⊞

GEMAINGOUTTE Vosges

CM 'Le Violu' ☎ 329577070 ▤ 329517260
➲ *W, beside the river, via N59.*
May-Sep 0.9HEC ⊞⊞⊞ ⊕ ↑ ⊙ ☘ ∅ ⅊ R 🅿 ⊞ lau ♦ ⅀ ⅀ ✕
Prices: ⋔2.35 ⇐1.70 ⊕1.70 ▲1.70 pitch 1.70

GÉRARDMER Vosges

Ramberchamp 21 chemin du Tour du Lac ☎ 329630382
On a level meadow on S side of Lac de Gérardmer.
➲ *2km from the village centre via N417 or 486.*
20 Apr-20 Sep 3.5HEC ⊞⊞⊞ ♦ ↑ ⅀ ⅀ ✕ ⊙ ☘ ⊕ ⛱ ⅊ L 🅿 lau

GRANGES-SUR-VOLOGNE Vosges

Château 2 Les Chappes ☎ 329575083
e-mail: camping-du-chateau@wanadoo.fr
A terraced site with good sports facilities 1km from the
village,
15 Jun-15 Sep 2HEC ⊞⊞⊞ ⊕ ↑ ⅀ ⊙ ☘ ⛱ ⊕ ⊕ ⅊ P 🅿 lau ♦ ⅀
✕ ⅊R ⊞ Prices: ⋔2.90 pitch 3.20

Gina-Park ☎ 0329514195 ▤ 0329575952
In a pleasant park at the foot of a wooded mountain. Streams
cross the site and there is a lake and facilities for a variety of
sports.
➲ *1km SE of town centre.*
All year 4.5HEC ⊞⊞⊞ ♦ ↑ ⅀ ⅀ ⊙ ☘ ∅ ᴪ ⛱ ⊕ ⅊ PR 🅿 lau
♦ ✕ ⊞

HARSKIRCHEN BAS-RHIN

Étang Zone de Loisirs, r du Canal
☎ 388009365 ▤ 388009613
➲ *0.8km NW via D23 beside the lake.*
All year 12HEC ⊞⊞⊞ ⊕ ↑ ⅀ ✕ ⊙ 🅿 ⊞ lau ♦ ⅀ ∅ ᴪ
Prices: ⋔1.83 ⇐1.07 ▲1.52 pitch 2.59

HEIMSBRUNN HAUT-RHIN

Chaumière 62 r de la Galfingue
☎ 389819343 ▤ 389819343
e-mail: accueil@camping-lachaumiere.com
In a pleasant wooded location with good, modern facilities.
➲ *Signposted from village centre.*
All year 1HEC ⊞⊞⊞ ⦂⦂⦂ ♦ ↑ ⅀ ⅀ ⊙ ☘ ∅ ⊕ 🅿 ⊞ ♦ ⅀ ⅀ ✕ ⅊R
Prices: ⋔2.75 pitch 4.25

HOHWALD, LE BAS-RHIN

CM ☎ 388083090
A well equipped terraced site in beautiful wooded surroundings.
➲ *W via D425*
All year 2HEC ⏛ ⚓ ⋔ ☉ ⊙ ⊞ 🗣 lau ➡ 🖪 ⏚ 🍴 ✗ ⌀ ♨ ⊞

KAYSERSBERG HAUT-RHIN

CM r des Acacias ☎ 389471447
Between a sports ground and the River Weiss. Subdivided by low hedges.
Camping Card Recommended.
➲ *200m from N415. Signposted.*
Apr-Sep 1.5HEC ⏛ ⚓ ⋔ ☉ ⊙ ↳ R 🕸 ⊞ lau ➡ 🖪 ⏚ 🍴 ✗ ⌀ ♨
↳P

KRUTH HAUT-RHIN

Schlossberg r du Bourbach ☎ 389822676 ▤ 389822017
e-mail: schlosberg@infonie.fr
In a quiet location in the heart of the Parc des Ballons with good, modern facilities.
➲ *2.3km NW via D13b.*
Etr-Sep 5.2HEC ⏛ ⚓ ⋔ 🖪 ⏚ 🍴 ✗ ☉ ⊙ 🗣 ⌀ 🗣 ↳ R 🕸 ⊞ lau ➡
✗ ♨ ↳L Prices: ⋔3.70 pitch 3.30

LAUTERBOURG BAS-RHIN

CM des Mouettes chemin des Mouettes
☎ 388546860 ▤ 388546860
A level site on the shores of a lake.
➲ *Access via D63 from Haguenau.*
15 Mar-15 Dec 3HEC ⏛ 🔅 ⋔ 🍴 ✗ ☉ ⊙ 🗣 ↳ L 🕸 🅿 ⊞ ✍
lau ➡ ↳R Prices: ⋔3.20 🚗1.70 🗣3.20 ▲2.60

LUTTENBACH HAUT-RHIN

Amis de la Nature 4 r du Château
☎ 389773860 ▤ 389772572
e-mail: camping.an@wanadoo.fr
Situated on a long strip of land, in the heart of Luttenbach countryside. Site is divided into pitches.
➲ *From Munster follow D10 for 1km.*
5 Feb-Nov 7HEC ⏛ ⚓ ⋔ 🖪 ⏚ 🍴 ✗ ☉ ⊙ 🗣 ↳ R 🕸 ⊞ lau ➡ ♨
↳P Prices: ⋔2.30 🚗1.30 pitch 1.75 pp1.52

MASEVAUX HAUT-RHIN

Camping Municipal de Masevaux 3 r du Stade
☎ 389824243 ▤ 389824229
In wooded surroundings beside the River Doller.
➲ *Off the main road to Ballon-d'Alsace.*
Etr-Sep 3.5HEC ⏛ ⚓ ⋔ ☉ ⊙ 🗣 🕸 ⊞ lau ➡ 🖪 ⏚ 🍴 ✗ ⌀ ♨ ↳PR

METZERAL HAUT-RHIN

At MITTLACH (3km SW)

CM ☎ 389776377 ▤ 389776377
Situated in forested area in small village, very quiet.
➲ *From Munster follow signs for Metzeral then Mittlach D10.*
May-Oct ⏛ ⚓ ⋔ 🖪 ⏚ ☉ ⊙ 🗣 ⌀ ↳ R 🕸 lau

MOOSCH HAUT-RHIN

Mine d'Argent r de la Mine d'Argent ☎ 389823066
A well established site in a peaceful wooded setting.
➲ *1.5km SW off N66.*
May-Sep 2HEC ⏛ ⚓ ⋔ ☉ ⊙ 🗣 ⌀ 🕸 ⊞ lau ➡ 🖪 ⏚ 🍴 ✗ ↳R

MULHOUSE HAUT-RHIN

CM Ill av P-de-Coubertin ☎ 89062066
In park between the canal and the River Ill, a few minutes walk from the city centre.
➲ *From town centre follow Signs for 'Fribourg & Allemagne'.
At Ile Napoléon follow campsite signposts.*
Apr-Sep 6HEC ⏛ ⚓ ⋔ 🖪 ☉ ⊙ 🗣 ⌀ ♨ 🕸 ⊞ lau ➡ 🍴 ✗ ↳PR

MUNSTER HAUT-RHIN

CM Parc de la Fecht rte de Gunsbach
☎ 389773108 ▤ 389770455
e-mail: ville.munster@worldonline.fr
Well maintained site close to the town centre within a park-like area surrounded by high walls and trees.
➲ *Access on D417, 200m after entering Munster town centre, near the swimming pool.*
Apr-Sep 4HEC ⏛ ⚓ ⋔ 🖪 ☉ ⊙ 🗣 ⌀ ↳ R 🕸 ⊞ lau ➡ 🍴 ✗ ♨
↳P Prices: ⋔2.43 pitch 4.87

OBERBRONN BAS-RHIN

CM Eichelgarten r de Zinswiller
☎ 388097196 ▤ 388096512
➲ *Follow signpots W from D28 (Oberbronn-Zinswiller).*
18Mar-19Nov 4HEC ⏛ ⚓ ⋔ 🖪 ☉ ⊙ 🗣 ⌀ 🗣 🗣 ↳ 🕸 ⊞ lau ➡
🍴 ✗ ♨ ⊞ Prices: ⋔2.85-3 🚗2.33-2.40 ▲1.71-1.80
pitch 1.90-2

OBERNAI BAS-RHIN

CM rue de Berlin ☎ 388953848 ▤ 388483147
Partly terraced site, situated in park.
➲ *W on D426 towards Ottrott.*
All year 3HEC ⏛ 🔅 ⋔ ☉ ⊙ 🗣 🕸 ⊞ lau ➡ 🍴 ✗ ↳P
Prices: ⋔3 pitch 4

RIBEAUVILLE HAUT-RHIN

Pierre de Coubertin 23 r de Landau
☎ 389736671 ▤ 389736671
e-mail: camping.ribeauville@wanadoo.fr
In a peaceful location. Shop open in summer only.
➲ *Access via D106.*
15 Mar-15 Nov 3.5HEC ⏛ ⚓ ⋔ ☉ ⊙ 🗣 🕸 ⊞ lau ➡ 🍴 ✗
↳P Prices: ⋔3.60 pitch 3.60

RIQUEWIHR HAUT-RHIN

Inter Communal rte des Vins
☎ 389479008 ▤ 389490563
Extensive site overlooking vineyards.
➲ *2km E on D16. Turn W off N83 (Colmar-Strasbourg) at Ostheim.*
Etr-Oct 4HEC ⏛ ⚓ ⋔ 🖪 ☉ ⊙ 🗣 ⌀ ⊞ lau ➡ 🍴 ✗ ♨ ⊞

ST-MAURICE-SUR-MOSELLE VOSGES

Deux Ballons 17 r du Stade ☎ 329251714 ▤ 329252751
e-mail: verocamp@aol.com
Well maintained site beside a stream and surrounded by woodland and mountains.
➲ *1km W on N66.*
30 Mar-30 Sep 4HEC ⏛ ⚓ ⋔ 🍴 ✗ ☉ ⊙ 🗣 ♨ 🗣 ↳ P 🕸 ⊞ lau
➡ 🖪 ✗ ⌀ ↳R Prices: ⋔3.81 🚗2.21 pitch 16.31 (incl 2
persons)

ST-PIERRE BAS-RHIN

Beau Séjour r de l'Église ☎ 388085224 ▤ 388085224
Situated midway between Strasbourg and Colmar with good modern facilities.
15 May-2 Oct 0.6HEC ⏛ ⚓ ⋔ ☉ ⊙ 🗣 ↳ R 🕸 ⊞ lau ➡ 🖪 ⏚ 🍴 ✗
♨ Prices: pitch 9 (incl 2 persons)

STE-CROIX-EN-PLAINE HAUT-RHIN

Clair Vacances rte de Herrlisheim
☎ 389492728 ▤ 389492155
e-mail: clairvacances@wanadoo.fr
In a pleasant woodland setting with good facilities for a family holiday.
➲ *On D1 towards Herrlisheim.*
Etr-Sep 3.5HEC ⏛ ⚓ ⋔ ☉ ⊙ 🗣 ⌀ 🗣 ↳ P 🕸 ⊞ ✍ lau ➡ 🖪 ⏚
✗ Prices: ⋔3-5 pitch 11-15 (incl 2 persons)

SAVERNE BAS-RHIN

CM ☎ 0388913565 ▤ 0388913565
A pleasant tourist site at the foot of the Rocher du Haut Barr.
➲ *1.3km SW via D171*
Apr-Sep 2.5HEC ▦ ♠ ⋔ ⊙ ⬛ ☎ ⊞ lau ♦ ⬛ ✗ ⊘ ⚲

SCHIRMECK BAS-RHIN

Schirmeck 26 rte de Strasbourg ☎ 388970161
➲ *5km NE. Beside Strasbourg road and railway, on level ground.*
Mar-Oct 2.5HEC ▦ ⋔ ⋔ ⊙ ⬛ ⊘ ⋜ R ☎ ⊞ lau ♦ ⬛ ⬛ ✗ ⚲

SÉLESTAT BAS-RHIN

CM Cigognes r de la 1-er DFL ☎ 388920398
In a rural setting at an altitude of 175mtrs.
➲ *900mtrs from the town centre.*
May-15 Oct 0.7HEC ▦ ⋔ ⋔ ⊙ ⬛ ⬛ lau ♦ ⬛ ⬛ ✗ ⊘ ⚲
⋜P ⊞

SEPPOIS-LE-BAS HAUT-RHIN

CM les Lupins r de l'Ancienne Gare ☎ 389256537
Picturesque site close to the German and Swiss borders.
➲ *Access via A36, exit 'Burnhaupt' and continue towards Dannemarie.*
Apr-Oct 4HEC ▦ ⋔ ⋔ ⊙ ⬛ ⊘ ⬛ ⋜ P ☎ ⬛ ⊞ lau ♦ ⬛ ✗ ⚲
⋜R Prices: ⋔3.35 pitch 3.35

SIVRY-SUR-MEUSE MEUSE

Brouzel 26 r du Moulin ☎ 0329858645
Apr-Sep 1.5HEC ▦ ⋔ ⋔ ⊙ ⬛ ☎ ⊞ lau ♦ ⬛ ⬛ ✗ ⊘ ⚲ ⋜R
Prices: ⋔1.83 ♠1.52 ⬛1.83 ▲1.83 pitch 1.83

THOLY, LE VOSGES

Noir Rupt chemin de l'Étang de Noirrupt
☎ 329618127 ▤ 329618305
e-mail: info@jpvacances.com
A peaceful site in a beautiful wooded location. Plenty of facilities.
➲ *2km SE on D417.*
15 Apr-15 Oct 3HEC ▦ ⋔ ⋔ ⬛ ⬛ ✗ ⊙ ⬛ ⊘ ⬛ ⋜ P ☎ ⬛
lau ♦ ✗ ⊞

TONNOY MEURTHE-ET-MOSELLE

Grande Vanné ☎ 383266236
➲ *W via D74, beside the River Moselle*
R 15 Jun-15 Sep 7HEC ▦ ⋔ ⬛ ⬛ ✗ ⊙ ⋜ R ☎ lau ♦ ⬛ ✗

TURCKHEIM HAUT-RHIN

Cigognes 7 quai de la Gare ☎ 389270200
Camping Card Compulsory.
➲ *From Colmar follow N417 to Wintzenheim, then to Turckheim. Before bridge turn left, continue past railway station and stadium.*
15 May-Oct 2.5HEC ▦ ♠ ⋔ ⬛ ⬛ ⊙ ⬛ ⊘ ⋜ R ☎ ⬛ ⊞ lau ♦
✗

URBÈS HAUT-RHIN

CM Benelux Bâle ☎ 389827876
A well maintained site with good facilities.
➲ *W of rte de Bussang.*
Apr-Oct 2.4HEC ▦ ⋔ ⋔ ⊙ ⬛ ☎ ⊞ lau ♦ ⬛ ⊘ ⚲ ⋜R

VAGNEY VOSGES

CM du Mettey ☎ 329248135
➲ *1.3km E on Gérardmer road.*
15 Jun-15 Sep 2HEC ▦ ♠ ⋔ ⊙ ⬛ ☎ ⊞ lau ♦ ⊘ ⚲

VERDUN MEUSE

Breuils allée des Breuils ☎ 329861531 ▤ 329867576
e-mail: camping.les.breuils@wanadoo.fr
A family site in peaceful surroundings. Pitches are divided by trees and bushes and the sanitary facilities are well maintained.
➲ *SW via D34. Signposted.*
Apr-15 Oct 5.5HEC ▦ ♠ ⋔ ⬛ ✗ ⊙ ⬛ ⊘ ⚲ ⬛ ⋜ P ☎ ⊞
lau ♦ ⋜L Prices: ⋔3.66 pitch 3.05

VILLERS-LÈS-NANCY MEURTHE-ET-MOSELLE

Touristique International de Nancy-Brabois av Paul Muller
☎ 383271828 ▤ 383400643
e-mail: campoles.brabois@wanadoo.fr
In beautiful wooded surroundings with well defined pitches and good recreational facilities.
➲ *SW in Brabois park.*
Apr-15 Oct 5HEC ▦ ⋔ ⬛ ✗ ⊙ ⬛ ⊘ ☎ ⊞ lau ♦ ⬛ ✗
⊘ Prices: pitch 9.15-9.90 (incl 2 persons)

WASSELONNE BAS-RHIN

CM rte de Romanswiller ☎ 388870008
On a level meadow adjoining the local sports complex.
➲ *1km W on D224.*
Apr-15 Oct 2.5HEC ▦ ⋔ ⋔ ⬛ ✗ ⊙ ⬛ ⊘ ⋜ P ☎ ⊞ lau ♦
✗ ⚲

WATTWILLER HAUT-RHIN

Sources rte des Crêtes ☎ 389754494 ▤ 389757198
e-mail: camping.les.sources@wanadoo.fr
A family site on the edge of the Vosges forest close to the Route du Vin.
➲ *Approach via N83 exit Cernay Nord.*
Apr-15 Oct 14HEC ▦ ⋮⋮ ⋔ ⋔ ⬛ ✗ ⊙ ⬛ ⊘ ⚲ ⬛ ⬛ ⋜
P ☎ ⬛ ⊞ lau Prices: ⋔5.50 ♠1.90 pitch 7.30

WIHR-AU-VAL HAUT-RHIN

Route Verte 13 r de la Gare ☎ 389711010
e-mail: info@camping-routeverte.com
Near the centre of the village at an altitude of 320mtrs.
➲ *Approach via D10.*
May-Sep 1HEC ▦ ⋔ ⋔ ⬛ ✗ ⊙ ⬛ ⊘ ☎ ⊞ lau ♦ ⋜R
Prices: ⋔2.50 ♠1.30 pitch 3.10

XONRUPT/LONGEMER VOSGES

L'Eau-Vive rte de Colmar ☎ 329630737 ▤ 329630737
On a meadow surrounded by trees, close to the ski slopes.
➲ *2km SE on D67A next to Lac de Longemer.*
All year 1HEC ▦ ⋔ ⋔ ⬛ ✗ ⊙ ⬛ ⊘ ⚲ ⬛ ⬛ ⋜ R ☎ ⊞ lau ♦
⬛ ⋜L Prices: ⋔2.63 pitch 3.20

Jonquilles rte du Lac ☎ 329633401 ▤ 329600928
In a delightful wooded lakeside setting. Advance booking necessary in July and August.
➲ *2km SE on D67A beside Lac de Longemer.*
Apr-10 Oct 4HEC ▦ ⋔ ⋔ ⬛ ✗ ⊙ ⬛ ⊘ ⋜ L ☎ ⊞ lau ♦ ✗
⚲ Prices: pitch 6-10 (incl 2 persons)

● ● ● **BURGUNDY/CHAMPAGNE** ● ● ●

The Champagne region is one of the rich greens and huge landscapes of the Ardennes and the wide meadows of the River Marne. Its former capital, Laon, has a rich medieval heritage and a lovely 12th-century cathedral, while, to the south, Troyes boasts wonderful Renaissance treasures. But the jewel of the area is Reims, with its magnificent Gothic cathedral - an important centre for the region and the whole of France for centuries.

The local wine of Champagne needs no introduction, and pre-arranged visits and regular tours are available from the famous names - Mercier, Moët, Veuve Cliquot - and there is a Champagne Museum (Musée du Champagne) in Épernay.
The representatives of Burgundy also travel the world - names such as Chablis, Mâcon and Nuits St Georges. A wonderful surprise of the area, though, is the network of hundreds of miles of navigable waterways, accessing a wealth of Romanesque churches, abbeys, castles, and medieval fortress towns, exquisite small villages and quiet rolling expanses of rich pastures and vineyards - the quintessential provincial France. Visitors should include a visit to Beaune, famous for its 14th-century hospice.

⟩ **ACCOLAY** YONNE

Moulin Jacquot route de Bazarnes
☎ 386815648 ▦ 386815687
A well equipped site in a pleasant rural setting, close to the village.
➲ *W, beside the Canal du Nivernais.*
Apr-15 Oct 0.8HEC ⟋⟋⟋ ♣ ♠ ⊙ ⊙ ⊡ lau ♦ ⟹ � ✕ ∅ ⟆
⟅R ⊞

⟩ **ANCY-LE-FRANC** YONNE

CM rte de Cusy ☎ 386751321
In a sheltered position just beyond the village.
➲ *Access via Montbard road.*
Jun-15 Sep 0.8HEC ⟋⟋⟋ ♣ ♠ ⊙ ⊡ lau ♦ ⟹ ⟮ ✕ ∅ ⟆
⟅R ⊞

⟩ **ANDRYES** YONNE

Bois Joli ☎ 386817048 ▦ 386817048
A small site in pleasant Burgundian countryside.
➲ *0.6km SW via N151.*
Apr-Sep 5HEC ⟋⟋⟋ ♣ ♠ ⟹ ⟮ ✕ ⊙ ⊙ ⊡ ⊞ ⟅ P ⊡ ⊞ lau ♦ ∅ ⟆
⟅R Prices: ⋔2.30-3.20 ⥡0.60-4.42 ⊞2.30 ▲0.90 pitch 1.70-2.30

⟩ **ARNAY-LE-DUC** CÔTE-D'OR

CM de Fouché ☎ 380900223 ▦ 380901190
e-mail: camparnay@wanadoo.fr
In a quiet location beside a lake with good recreational facilities close to the medieval town of Arnay-le-Duc.
➲ *0.7km E on CD17.*
All year 6HEC ⟋⟋⟋ ♠ ♠ ⊙ ⊙ ∅ ⊞ ⟅ L ⊡ ⊡ ⊞ lau ♦ ⟹ ⟮
✕ ⟆

⟩ **AUXERRE** YONNE

CM 8 rte de Vaux ☎ 386521115
➲ *SE towards Vaux*
Apr-Sep 3HEC ⟋⟋⟋ ♠ ♠ ⊙ ⊙ ⊡ ⊞ lau ♦ ⟮ ✕ ⟅P

⟩ **AUXONNE** CÔTE-D'OR

Arquebuse rte d'Athée ☎ 380373436
Clean, well-equipped site on right bank of River Saône near bathing area.
➲ *From Auxonne travel W on N5 for 3km. Then turn northwards on D24 towards Athée and Pontailler-sur-Saône.*
15 Jun-15 Sep 3HEC ⟋⟋⟋ ♠ ♠ ⟮ ✕ ⊙ ⊙ ⊡ ⊞ lau ♦ ⟹ ✕ ∅
⟆ ⟅PR

⟩ **AVALLON** YONNE

CM Sous Roche 1 r Sous-Roche
☎ 386341039 ▦ 386341039
➲ *2km SE by D944 and D427.*
15 Mar-15 Oct 2HEC ⟋⟋⟋ ♠ ♠ ⟮ ✕ ⊙ ⟅ R ⊡ ⊞ lau
♦ ⟅P

⟩ **BANNES** HAUTE-MARNE

Hautoreille ☎ 325848340 ▦ 325848340
Small grassy site with modern facilities. Separate carpark for late arrivals.
➲ *Access via D74 towards Epinal.*
All year 3.5HEC ⟋⟋⟋ ♠ ♠ ⟮ ✕ ⊙ ⊙ ⊡ ⊡ ⊞ lau ♦ ⟹ ⟅L

⟩ **BAR-SUR-AUBE** AUBE

Gravière av du Parc ☎ 325271294
➲ *0.5km E of D13.*
Apr-15 Oct 2.8HEC ⟋⟋⟋ ♠ ♠ ⊙ ⊙ ⟆ ⟅ PR ⊡ lau ♦ ⟹ ⟮ ✕ ∅
⟆ ⟅P

⟩ **BAZOLLES** NIÈVRE

Baye ☎ 386389033
Apr-Oct 1.5HEC ⟋⟋⟋ ∅ ♠ ♠ ⊙ ⊙ ⊡ ⟆ ⟅ L ⊡ ⊞ lau ♦ ⟹ ⟮ ✕
∅ ⟆

⟩ **BEAUNE** CÔTE-D'OR

CM Cent Vignes 10 rue August Dubois ☎ 380220391
On outskirts of town. Site divided into pitches, clean, well-looked after sanitary installations. From 20 Jun-Aug it is advisable to arrive before 1600 hrs.
➲ *On N74 on Savigny-les-Beaune road.*
15 Mar-Oct 2HEC ⟋⟋⟋ ∅ ♠ ♠ ⟮ ✕ ⊙ ⊙ ⊡ ∅ ⊡ ⊞ lau ♦ ⟆
⟅LP Prices: ⋔2.74 pitch 3.81

⟩ **BOURBON-LANCY** SAÔNE-ET-LOIRE

St-Prix r du St-Prix ☎ 385891485
e-mail: bourbon.loisirs@wanadoo.fr
A well equipped family site close to an extensive water sports centre.
➲ *By the swimming pool off the D979a.*
Apr-Oct 2.5HEC ⟋⟋⟋ ♠ ♠ ⟹ ⟮ ✕ ⊙ ⊙ ⊡ ⟆ ⊡ lau ♦ ✕ ∅ ⟆
⟅LP ⊞

⟩ **BOURBONNE-LES-BAINS** HAUTE-MARNE

Montmorency r du Stade ☎ 325900864
A well equipped site in a pleasant natural setting.
Apr-Oct 2HEC ⟋⟋⟋ ♠ ♠ ⟮ ⟆ ⊙ ∅ ∅ ⟆ ⟅ P ⊡ ⊞ lau

⟩ **BOURG** HAUTE-MARNE

Croix d'Arles ☎ 325882402 ▦ 325882402
e-mail: croix.arles@wanadoo.fr
A peaceful site in wooded surroundings close to Langres.
➲ *Access via N74 or A31.*
15 Mar-31Oct 7HEC ⟋⟋⟋ ♠ ♠ ⟹ ⟮ ✕ ⊙ ⊙ ⟆ ⟆ ⟆ ⟆ ▲ ⟅ P
⊡ ⊞ lau Prices: ⋔3.50 pitch 6

⟩ **BOURG-FIDÈLE** ARDENNES

Murée rte de Rocroi ☎ 324542445
A lakeside site in wooded surroundings.
➲ *1km N via D22.*
All year 1.3HEC ⟋⟋⟋ ♠ ♠ ⟮ ✕ ⊙ ⊙ ⊡ ⟆ lau ♦ ⟹ ∅ ⟆ ⟅P
⊞ Prices: ⋔3 ⥡1.60 pitch 4.60

⟩ **CHAGNY** SAÔNE-ET-LOIRE

CM Pâquier Fané ☎ 385872142
A clean site 600m W of the church.
➲ *Follow the D974 from town centre.*
13 May-4 Sep 1.5HEC ⟋⟋⟋ ♠ ♠ ⟮ ✕ ⊙ ⊙ ∅ ⟆ R ⊡ ⊞ lau
♦ ⟅P

⟩ **CHÂLONS-SUR-MARNE** (**CHÂLONS-EN-CHAMPAGNE**) MARNE

CM r de Plaisance ☎ 326683800 ▦ 0326683800
In a pleasant wooded location with good recreational facilities.
30Mar-31Oct 7.5HEC ⟋⟋⟋ ♠ ♠ ⟮ ✕ ⊙ ⊙ ∅ ⊡ ⊞ lau ♦ ⟹
Prices: ⋔4.15 ▲1.55 pitch 2.75

❯ CHARLEVILLE-MÉZIÈRES ARDENNES

CM Mont Olympe r des Paquis ☎ 324332360
Level meadowland near the town centre and 100m from
municipal indoor swimming pool.
⮕ *Well signed from town centre.*
Etr-15 Oct 2HEC ⸬ ⚃ ᑫ ᴿ ᴸ Ψ ✕ ☉ ◻ ∅ ⨍ ⵏ PR ⸬ ⊞ lau
⮕ ✕

❯ CHAROLLES SAÔNE-ET-LOIRE

CM rte de Viny ☎ 385240490 ▤ 385240820
In pleasant wooded surroundings with good, modern
sanitary facilities.
⮕ *NE of town via D33 towards Viry. Follow signs.*
Apr-5 Oct 0.6HEC ⸬ ᑫ ᴿ Ψ ☉ ◻ ⵏ P ⸬ ⊞ lau ⮕ ⅃ ✕
∅ ⵕ Prices: ⋔2 ⬤1.20 ⬛2 ▲2

❯ CHÂTILLON-SUR-SEINE CÔTE-D'OR

CM espl St-Vorles ☎ 380910305 ▤ 380912146
e-mail: tourism-chatillon-sur-seine@wanadoo.fr
Hilly shaded site near the historic Renaissance church of St
Vorles.
⮕ *SE of town off rte de Langres (D928).*
Apr-Sep 0.8HEC ⸬ ⬥ ᴿ Ψ ☉ ◻ ∅ ⸬ ⊞ lau ⮕ ⅃ ✕ ⵕ ⵏP
Prices: ⋔2.75 ⬤1 pitch 2.25

❯ CHATONRUPT HAUTE-MARNE

CM ☎ 0325948007 ▤ 0325948007
15 Apr-Sep 1.1HEC ⸬ ⵕ ᴿ ☉ ◻ ⵏ R ⸬ lau ⮕ ⅃ Ψ ✕ ⵕ
Prices: ⋔1 ⬤0.90 ⬛0.90 ▲0.90 pitch 0.90

❯ CHEVIGNY NIÈVRE

Hermitage de Chevigny ☎ 386845097
A pleasant site with good facilities in wooded surroundings
within the Morvan Nature Reserve. There is direct access to
the lake and most watersports are available.
Apr-Sep 2.2HEC ⸬ ⬥ ᴿ ᴸ Ψ ✕ ☉ ◻ ∅ ⵕ ⨍ ⨜ ⵏ LR ⸬ ⊞
lau Prices: ⋔4 ⬤2.50 pitch 2.50

❯ CLAMECY NIÈVRE

Pont Picot rte de Chenoches ☎ 0386270597
In a pleasant situation between the River Yonne and the
Canal du Nivernais.
May-Sep 1.2HEC ⸬ ⵕ ᴿ ☉ ◻ ⵏ R ⸬ lau ⮕ ⅃ Ψ ✕ ∅ ⵕ
ⵏP ⊞ Prices: ⋔2.90 ⬤2.40 ⬛2.40 ▲2.40 pitch 2.40

❯ CONFLANS-SUR-SEINE MARNE

Vieille Seine rue du Port ☎ 326426159 ▤ 25882302
On the outskirts of the village, beside the River Seine.
⮕ *3km from Romilly.*
Apr-Sep 6HEC ⸬ ⬥ ᴿ Ψ ✕ ☉ ◻ ⨍ ⨜ ▲ ⵏ R ⸬ ⊞ lau ⮕
⅃ Ψ ∅ ⵕ ⵏR

❯ COSNE-SUR-LOIRE NIÈVRE

Loire & Nohain Ile de Cosne ☎ 386282792 ▤ 386281810
Site borders River Loire.
⮕ *Follow D955 W towards Sancerre.*
Apr-15 Sep 4HEC ⸬ ⚃ ᑫ ᴿ ᴸ Ψ ✕ ☉ ◻ ∅ ⨍ ⨜ ⵏ ⸬ ⊞
lau ⮕ ⵕ ⵏP

❯ CRÊCHES-SUR-SAÔNE SAÔNE-ET-LOIRE

CM Le Port d'Arciat ☎ 385371183 ▤ 385365157
e-mail: camping-creches.sur.saone@wanadoo.fr
In a wooded location beside the River Saône.
⮕ *1.5km E via D31*
May-Sep 6HEC ⸬ ᑫ ᴿ Ψ ✕ ☉ ◻ ⵏ LR ⸬ ⊞ lau ⮕ ⅃ ∅ ⵕ
Prices: ⋔3.05 pitch 6.10

❯ DIGOIN SAÔNE-ET-LOIRE

CM Chevrette r de la Chevrette ☎ 385531149 ▤ 3858166443
⮕ *W of village on N79.*
Apr-Oct 1.5HEC ⸬ ⚃ ᑫ ᴿ ᴸ Ψ ✕ ☉ ◻ ⨍ ⵕ ⵏ PR ⸬ ⊞
lau

❯ DIJON CÔTE-D'OR

Lac 3 bd Chanoine Kir ☎ 0380435472 ▤ 0380435472
e-mail: cparis@ville-dijon.fr
A well maintained site in natural surroundings, an ideal base
for exploring the historic town of Dijon.
⮕ *1.5km W on N5.*
Apr-15 Oct 2.5HEC ⸬ ⸬ ⚃ ᑫ ᴿ ᴸ Ψ ✕ ☉ ◻ ⸬ ⊞ lau ⮕
∅ ⵕ ⵏLPRS Prices: ⬤1.40 pitch 2

❯ DOMPIERRE-LES-ORMES SAÔNE-ET-LOIRE

Village des Meuniers ☎ 385503660 ▤ 385503661
e-mail: levillagedesmeuniers@wanadoo.fr
A well equipped site in the heart of the Southern Burgundy
countryside. Advance booking advisable in July and August.
⮕ *Access via N79. Signposted.*
15 May-15 Sep 4HEC ⸬ ᑫ ᴿ ᴸ Ψ ✕ ☉ ◻ ∅ ⨜ ⨍ ⵏ P ⸬
⊞ lau Prices: ⋔3.50-5.50 pitch 4.50-6

❯ ÉCLARON-BRAUCOURT HAUTE-MARNE

Presqu'île de Champaubert ☎ 325041320 ▤ 325943351
e-mail: lac-du-der@wanadoo.fr
Situated on lake peninsula.
15 Apr-late Sep 3.5HEC ⸬ ᑫ ᴿ ᴸ Ψ ✕ ☉ ◻ ∅ ⸬ ⊞ lau ⮕
ⵏL

❯ EPINAC SAÔNE-ET-LOIRE

Pont Vert ☎ 385820026
In a wooded location on the banks of the river. Modern
facilities and modern toilet within the site area.
⮕ *S via D43 beside the River Drée.*
Jun-Sep 4HEC ⸬ ⬥ ᴿ ᴸ Ψ ✕ ☉ ◻ ⨍ ⵏ R ⸬ ⊞ lau ⮕ ✕ ∅
ⵕ

❯ FRONCLES HAUTE-MARNE

Deux Ponts r des Ponts ☎ 325023121 ▤ 325020980
In a peaceful location beside the River Marne.
Mar-Oct 3HEC ᑫ ᴿ ◻ ⮕ ⅃ Ψ ✕ ⵏR ⊞

❯ GIBLES SAÔNE-ET-LOIRE

Château de Montrouant Montrouant
☎ 385845113 ▤ 385845430
A small site situated in the Charollais hill region with access
to extensive parkland.
⮕ *1.6km NE beside the lake.*
Jun-9 Sep 1HEC ⸬ ⸬ ᑫ ᴿ ᴸ Ψ ✕ ☉ ◻ ∅ ▲ ⵏ LPR ⸬
⊞ lau ⮕ ∅ ⵕ

❯ GIFFAUMONT MARNE

Plage Chemin de la Cachotte, Station Nautique
☎ 326726184
A well maintained site situated at the Station Nautique.
⮕ *2km from the village.*
May-10 Sep 1.5HEC ⸬ ⬥ ᴿ Ψ ☉ ◻ ∅ ⸬ ⊞ lau ⮕ ⅃ ✕ ⵕ
ⵏL

❯ GIGNY-SUR-SAÔNE SAÔNE-ET-LOIRE

⛫Château de l'Épervière ☎ 385441690 ▤ 385941697
e-mail: ffh@wanadoo.fr
Quiet site in park surrounding 16th-century château. Close
to the River Saône for fishing and sailing.
⮕ *N6 to Sennecey-le-Grand, then follow signs.*
Apr-mid Oct 10HEC ⸬ ᑫ ᴿ ᴸ Ψ ✕ ☉ ◻ ∅ ⵏ LP ⸬ ⊞ lau
⮕ ⵏR Prices: ⋔5-6 pitch 6.50-9

GRANDPRÉ ARDENNES

CM ☎ 324305071
A peaceful riverside site.
➔ *150m from village centre on D6.*
Apr-Sep 2HEC ⛭ ♦ ⁂ ⊙ 🞖 🞖 ⌁ R 🞖 ⊞ lau ➔ 🞖 ⁑ ✗ ⌀ 🞖

GUEUGNON SAÔNE-ET-LOIRE

CM rte de Digoin, Chazey ☎ 385855050
A quiet site in wooded surroundings near a lake.
Jun-Sep 3HEC ⛭ ⌁ ⁂ 🞖 ⊙ 🞖 ⌀ 🞖 🞖 ⌁ L 🞖 ⊞ lau ➔ ⁑ ✗

ISSY-L'ÉVÊQUE SAÔNE-ET-LOIRE

CM de l'Étang Neuf ☎ 385249605 ▤ 385249605
e-mail: marc.pille@compaqnet.be
In a fine position beside the lake, overlooking the château.
May-15 Sep 4HEC ⛭ ⌁ ⁂ ⁑ ✗ ⊙ 🞖 ⌀ ▲ ⌁ LP 🞖 ⊞ lau ➔
🞖 🞖 Prices: ♠3.50 ⇦2 pitch 13-16 (incl 2 persons)

LAIVES SAÔNE-ET-LOIRE

Lacs 'La Heronnière' Les Bois de Laives
☎ 385449885 ▤ 385449885
Compulsory separate car park for arrivals after 2200hrs.
➔ *Access via 'Châlon Sud' autoroute exit towards Mâcon.*
15 May-15 Sep 1.5HEC ⛭ ⌁ 🞖 ✗ ⊙ 🞖 ⌀ 🞖 🞖 ⊞ lau ➔
⁑ ✗ ⌁LR Prices: ♠2.75-3.10 ⇦2-2.30

MÂCON SAÔNE-ET-LOIRE

CM ☎ 385381622
Divided into pitches. Water sports centre and pool nearby.
➔ *2km N on N6.*
15 Mar-Oct 5HEC ⛭ ⌁ ⁂ 🞖 ⁑ ✗ ⊙ 🞖 ⌀ ⌁ P 🞖 lau ➔ 🞖
⌁R

MARCENAY CÔTE-D'OR

Grebes Laignes ☎ 380816172 ▤ 380816199
A peaceful site in unspoiled contryside with separate hedged
pitches. Direct access to lake.
Apr-15 Sep 2.4HEC ⛭ ⌁ ⁂ 🞖 ⊙ 🞖 ⌀ 🞖 ⌁ L 🞖 ⊞ lau ➔ ⁑
✗

MATOUR SAÔNE-ET-LOIRE

CM Le Paluet Le Paluet ☎ 385597058 ▤ 0385597454
e-mail: mairie.matour@.fr
In pleasant countryside beside the river.
May-Sep 2HEC ⛭ ⠿ ♦ ⁂ ⁑ ✗ ⊙ 🞖 🞖 ⌁ P 🞖 lau ➔ 🞖 ✗
⌀ 🞖 ⊞ Prices: ♠2.80-3.50 pitch 3.90-4.70

MESNIL-ST PÈRE AUBE

Voie Colette ☎ 325412715 ▤ 325412715
e-mail: voiecolette@yahoo.fr
Grassland, with trees, ornamental shrubs and flower beds.
Slightly sloping, with a man-made lake nearby.
➔ *About 2km from Mesnil-St-Père; signposted from centre.*
Apr-15 Oct 4HEC ⛭ ⌁ ⁂ ⁑ ✗ ⊙ 🞖 ⌀ 🞖 ⊞ lau ➔ 🞖 ⌁L
Prices: ♠2.75-3.05 pitch 9.90-11 (incl 2 persons)

MEURSAULT CÔTE-D'OR

Grappe d'Or 2 rte de Volnay ☎ 380212248
Clean terraced site on an open meadow. Mountain bikes are
available for hire.
➔ *700m NE on D11b.*
28 Mar-15 Oct 5.5HEC ⛭ ⠿ ♦ ⁂ 🞖 ✗ ⊙ 🞖 ⌀ 🞖 ⌁ P 🞖 ⊞
lau ➔ ⁑ Prices: ♠3-3.70 pitch 11-14.50 (incl 2 persons)

MONTAPAS NIÈVRE

CM La Chênaie La Chênaie ☎ 386583432 ▤ 386582905
In a wooded location beside a lake with plenty of recreational
facilities.
➔ *500m from town centre, beside the lake, via D259.*
Apr-Oct 1HEC ⛭ ⌁ ⁂ ✗ ⊙ 🞖 ⌁ L 🞖 ➔ 🞖 ⌀ 🞖

MONTBARD CÔTE-D'OR

CM r M-Servet ☎ 380922160 ▤ 380922160
➔ *NW via rte de Laignes.*
Feb-Oct 2.5HEC ⛭ ♦ ⁂ ✗ ⊙ 🞖 🞖 ⌁ P 🞖 lau ➔ 🞖 ✗ ⌀
🞖 ⌁R ⊞

MONTHERMÉ ARDENNES

Base de Loisirs Départementale ☎ 324328161
In a pleasant wooded situation.
➔ *0.8km NE beside the River Semoy.*
All year 16HEC ⛭ ⌁ ⁂ ⊙ 🞖 🞖 ⌁ R 🞖 lau

MONTSAUCHE NIÈVRE

Mesanges Lac des Settons, Rive Gauche ☎ 0386845577
On the left bank of Lac des Settons.
May-15 Sep 5HEC ⛭ ⌁ ⁂ ⊙ 🞖 🞖 🞖 lau ➔ ⁑ ✗ ⌀ 🞖
⌁LPR

Plage du Midi ☎ 386845197 ▤ 386845731
e-mail: plagedumidi@aol.com
In a wooded setting directly on the Lac des Settons with good
facilities.
➔ *From Salieu (on N6) follow D977. From town centre follow
D193 to Les Sultons, then to site.*
Etr-Sep 4HEC ⛭ ⌁ ⁂ 🞖 ⊙ 🞖 ⌀ 🞖 ⌁ L 🞖 ⊞ lau ➔ ✗
🞖 Prices: ♠4.26 ⇦2.28 ⊞2.28

PARAY-LE-MONIAL SAÔNE-ET-LOIRE

Mambré rte du Gué-Léger ☎ 385888920 ▤ 385888781
On a level meadow with good, modern facilities.
➔ *Well signposted from outskirts of town.*
Apr-Oct 4HEC ⛭ ⌁ ⁂ 🞖 ✗ ⊙ 🞖 🞖 🞖 🞖 ⌁ P 🞖 lau ➔
🞖 ⁑ ✗ ⌀ ⌁R ⊞

POUGUES-LES-EAUX NIÈVRE

CM Chanternes ☎ 386688618
➔ *On N7 approx. 7km N of Nevers.*
Etr-Oct 1.4HEC ⛭ ⌁ ⁂ ⊙ 🞖 🞖 lau ➔ 🞖 ⁑ ✗ ⌁P

PREMEAUX CÔTE-D'OR

Saule Guillaume ☎ 380612799
Pleasant site beside a lake.
➔ *1.5km E via D109G.*
15 Jun-5 Sep 2.1HEC ⛭ ♦ ⁂ ⊙ 🞖 🞖 🞖 ⌁ L 🞖 ⊞ lau
➔ ⁑ ✗ ⌀ ⌁P

RADONVILLIERS AUBE

Garillon Rue des Anciens Combattants ☎ 0325922146
Beside the river, 250m from the lake.
May-30 Sep 1HEC ⛭ ⌁ ⁂ ⊙ 🞖 🞖 lau ➔ ⁑ ✗ ⌁LR ⊞
Prices: ♠2.10 pitch 2.60

RIEL-LES-EAUX CÔTE-D'OR

Riel-les-Eaux ☎ 380937276 ▤ 380937276
A lakeside site with fishing and boating facilities.
➔ *2.2km W via D13.*
Apr-Oct 0.2HEC ⛭ ⌁ ⁂ ⁑ ✗ ⊙ 🞖 ⌀ 🞖 ⌁ L 🞖 lau ➔ 🞖

ST-HILAIRE-SOUS-ROMILLY AUBE

Domaine de La Noue des Rois chemin des Brayes
☎ 325244160 ▤ 325243418
e-mail: michele.desmont@wanadoo.fr
A quiet site in a pine forest on the Basin d'Arcachon.
Booking recommended in July and August.
➔ *2km NE.*
All year 30HEC ⛭ ⌁ ⁂ 🞖 ⁑ ✗ ⊙ 🞖 🞖 🞖 🞖 ⌁ LPR 🞖 🞖
⊞ ⌀ lau Prices: ♠4.50 ⇦2.20 ⊞5.30 ▲4.30

ST-HONORÉ NIÈVRE

Bains 15 av J-Mermoz ☎ 386307344 ▦ 386306188
e-mail: camping-les-bains@wanadoo.fr
A family site with good facilities close to the Morvan
National Park.
➲ *Access via A6 and D985.*
May-5 Oct 4.5HEC ⟱ ⚶ ⌂ ⛟ ⚡ ✕ ⊙ ▣ ∅ ⏚ ⚡ P ⚐ ⊞
lau ➧ ⏚ **Prices:** ⚑2.90-4.20 pitch 10-14.50 (incl 2 persons)

ST-PÉREUSE NIÈVRE

⚑Manoir de Bezolle ☎ 386844255 ▦ 386844377
e-mail: info@bezolle.com
Situated in grounds of a manor house, at the edge of a
National Park. Well-kept site divided by hedges.
➲ *At crossroads of D11 and D978.*
15 Apr-Sep 8HEC ⟱ ➧ ⌂ ⛟ ⚡ ✕ ⊙ ▣ ∅ ⏚ ⚡ ⛏ ⚐ P ⚐ ⊞
lau Prices: pitch 12-20 (incl 2 persons)

STE-MENEHOULD MARNE

CM de la Grelette ☎ 326607389
A well equipped municipal site.
➲ *E of town towards Metz, beside the River Aisne*
May-Sep 1HEC ⟱ ⚶ ⌂ ⊙ ▣ ⚐ lau ➧ ⏚ ✕ ∅ ⚏ ⚐PR ⊞

SAULIEU CÔTE-D'OR

CM Perron ☎ 380641619 ▦ 380641619
e-mail: saulieu.tourisme@wanadoo.fr
On level, open ground with good recreational facilities.
➲ *1 km NW on N6.*
Apr-20 Oct Nov-Mar 4.5HEC ⟱ ⚶ ⌂ ⊙ ▣ ⚡ ⊙ ⏚ ⚐ P ⚐
⊞ lau ➧ ⏚ ✕ ∅ ⚏ ⚐P

SEDAN ARDENNES

CM de la Prairie bd Fabert ☎ 324271305 ▦ 0324271305
A well equipped municipal site on the banks of the River
Meuse, close to the centre of the village.
Etr-15 Oct 1.5HEC ⟱ ⚶ ⌂ ⊙ ▣ ⚐ ⚐ lau ➧ ⚐LP
Prices: ⚑1.52 ▲1.52 pitch 15.24

SELONGEY CÔTE-D'OR

CM Les Courvelles r H-Jevain ☎ 380757074 ▦ 380755665
In a rural location close to the river.
➲ *Access via A31 and N74.*
May-Sep 0.4HEC ⟱ ⚶ ⌂ ⊙ ▣ ⚐ lau ➧ ⏚ ✕ ⚐LPR ⊞

SEURRE CÔTE-D'OR

Piscine ☎ 380204922 ▦ 0380203401
A well equipped municipal site with direct access to the river.
➲ *From town centre follow N73 W for 600m in the direction
of Beaune.*
15 May-15 Sep 15 Sep-15 May ⟱ ⚶ ⌂ ✕ ⊙ ▣ ∅ ⚐ PR ⚐
⊞ lau ➧ ⏚ ✕ ⚐P Prices: ⚑1.52 ⚑1.06 ⚐1.06 ▲1.06

SÉZANNE MARNE

CM rte de Launat ☎ 0326805700
➲ *1.5km W on D239, rte de Launat.*
Apr-15 Oct 1HEC ⟱ ⚶ ⌂ ⊙ ▣ ⚐ P ⚐ lau ➧ ⏚ ✕

SIGNY-LE-PETIT ARDENNES

Pré Hugon Base de Loisirs ☎ 324535101
A pleasant site in wooded surroundings.
➲ *Access via N43.*
May-15 Oct 0.8HEC ⟱ ➧ ⌂ ⊙ ▣ ⚐ lau ➧ ⏚ ✕ ∅ ⚏
⚐LR ⊞

SOULAINES-DHUYS AUBE

CM La Croix Badeau ☎ 325927744
May-Sep 1.5HEC ⟱ ⚶ ⚶ ⌂ ⊙ ▣ ⚐ lau ➧ ⏚ ✕ ∅ ⚏
⚐R ⊞

TAZILLY NIÈVRE

Château de Chigy ☎ 386301080 ▦ 386309022
In a beautiful location within the extensive grounds of a
magnificent chateau. Good sporting facilities and
entertainment programme.
➲ *4km from Luzy on D973 Luzy-Moulins.*
Apr-Sep 7HEC ⟱ ⚶ ⌂ ⛟ ⚡ ✕ ⊙ ▣ ∅ ⏚ ⚐ LP ⚐ ⊞ lau

THONNANCE-LES-MOULINS HAUTE-MARNE

⚑Forge de Ste-Marie ☎ 325944200 ▦ 325944143
e-mail: laforge.de.sainte.mairie@wanadoo.fr
Partially terraced, on the site of an 18th century forge
containing a lake.
➲ *Access via N67 and D427.*
May-Sep 11HEC ⟱ ⚶ ⌂ ⛟ ✕ ⊙ ▣ ∅ ⏚ ⚡ PR ⚐ lau
Prices: ⚑40 pitch 80

TOULON-SUR-ARROUX SAÔNE-ET-LOIRE

CM du Val d'Arroux rte d'Uxeau
☎ 0385795122 ▦ 0385795276
On W outskirts beside the River Arroux.
➲ *Access via D985 then take Uxeau road.*
15 Apr-Oct 0.6HEC ⟱ ➧ ⌂ ⊙ ▣ ⚡ ⚐ R ⚐ ⊞ lau ➧ ⏚ ✕
∅ ⚏

UCHIZY SAÔNE-ET-LOIRE

National 6 ☎ 385405390 ▦ 385405390
Site surrounded by poplar trees on banks of river.
➲ *Turn off N6 towards Saône 6km S of Tournus and continue
0.8km.*
Apr-1 Oct 6HEC ⟱ ➧ ⌂ ⏚ ✕ ⊙ ▣ ∅ ⚏ ⏚ ⚡ ⚐ PR ⚐
⊞ lau Prices: ⚑3.80 pitch 4.60

VAL-DES-PRÉS MARNE

Gentianes La Vachette ☎ 492212141 ▦ 492212412
In a delightful wooded location backed by imposing
mountains and bordered by a river.
➲ *On the edge of the village, 3km SE of Briançon.*
All year 2HEC ⟱ ⚶ ⌂ ⏚ ✕ ⊙ ▣ ∅ ⚏ ⏚ ⚡ ⚐ PR ⚐ ⊞
lau ➧ ∅

VANDENESSE-EN-AUXOIS CÔTE-D'OR

Lac de Panthier ☎ 380492194 ▦ 380492580
e-mail: info@lac-de-panthier.com
In a wooded location beside Lake Panthier with a wide
variety of sporting facilities.
➲ *5km SE from Pouilly-en-Auxois on A6.*
15 Apr-Sep 6HEC ⟱ ⚶ ⌂ ⛟ ✕ ⊙ ▣ ∅ ⏚ ⚐ LP ⚐ ⊞ lau
Prices: ⚑5.34 pitch 6.10

Voiliers ☎ 380492194 ▦ 380492580
e-mail: info@lac-de-panthier.com
In a pleasant situation beside a lake with plenty of facilities
for families.
➲ *2.5km NE via D977.*
15 Apr-Sep 7HEC ⟱ ⠿ ⚶ ⌂ ⛟ ✕ ⊙ ▣ ∅ ⏚ ▲ ⚐
LP ⚐ lau

VENAREY-LES-LAUMES CÔTE-D'OR

Alésia r Dr-Roux ☎ 0380 380960776 ▦ 0380960776
e-mail: mairie.vll@worldonline.fr
A peaceful site close to the lake and river.
1 Apr-15 Oct 2HEC ⟱ ⚶ ⌂ ⊙ ▣ ⚐ L ⚐ lau ➧ ⏚ ✕ ∅
⚐LR ⊞ Prices: ⚑2.30 ⚑2.30 pitch 3.70

VERMENTON YONNE

Coulemières ☎ 386815302
A peaceful site with good facilities set amongst the meadows
of Burgundy.
Cont.

⮕ *On the N6 S of Auxerre.*
10 Apr-10 Oct 1.5HEC ⸺ ⌂ ⌂ ⌂ ⊙ ⌂ ⌀ ⌂ ⤳ R ⊡ ⊞ lau
⮕ ⛺ Prices: ⚹2.90 ⮱1.50 ⌂1.90 ⌂1.90

⧉ **VILLENEUVE-LES-GENÊTS** YONNE

Bois Guillaume ☎ 386454541 ▤ 386454920
e-mail: campingboisguillaume@miritel.net
In wooded surroundings with good, modern facilities.
⮕ *2.7km NE.*
All year 8HEC ⸺ ⌂ ⌂ ⌂ ⌂ ✕ ⊙ ⌂ ⌀ ⌂ ⌂ ⌂ ⤳ P ⊡ ⊞ lau
⮕ ⤳R Prices: ⚹3.20-3.20 ⮱2.20 pitch 2.20

SOUTH WEST/PYRÉNÉES

One of the largest regions of France, Aquitaine stretches
from the lower plateaux of the Massif Central, west to the
Atlantic and south nearly to the foothills of the Pyrénées.
This is a land of sunshine, and the three main rivers - the
Lot, the Garonne and the Dordogne - wind through valleys
and meander through orchards and vineyards, occasionally
flowing between high cliffs with castles perched on rocky
ledges. Along the Vézère valley in the Dordogne are the
impressive caves and grottos with prehistoric remains - the
remarkable Lascaux paintings can be admired in Lascaux II
- a full-scale replica of the original. On the coast in the
south of the region, holidaymakers are attracted by the
sophisticated chic of Biarritz, colourful resorts like St-Jean-
de-Luz, and Atlantic rollers offering some of the best
surfing in Europe. At the foothills of the Pyrénées is Basque
country, with charming white houses and timbered
cottages, colourful cascading flowers, and rich heritage of
festivals and folklore.

Inland, popular centres include Lourdes, which has attracted
pilgrims for over a century, and the fascinating Pyrénées
National Park with its wild flora and fauna. The Renaissance
city of Toulouse has a wonderful heritage, with some of the
finest examples of Romanesque architecture in Europe. The
region is internationally famous for wonderful cuisine. Here
you can find duck liver paté, "fois gras", Armagnac, and the
succulent Toulouse sausage.

....

⧉ **ABZAC** GIRONDE

Paradis rte de Périgueux ☎ 557490510 ▤ 557491888
e-mail: campingleparadis@free.fr
In a centre of gastronomic importance, this site stands on
meadowland near an artificial lake. Pedal boats and fishing
nearby.
⮕ *Drive W on N89 from the direction of Périgueux. After St-
Médard-de-Guizières turn onto D17E and follow signposts.*
Feb-15 Nov 5HEC ⸺ ⌂ ⌂ ⌂ ⌂ ✕ ⊙ ⌂ ⌀ ⌂ ⌂ ⌂ ⤳ LR ⊡
⊞ lau Prices: ⚹3-3.80 pitch 4.50-5.50

⧉ **AIRE-SUR-L'ADOUR** LANDES

Ombrages de l'Adour ☎ 558717510
A clean, tidy site next to a sports stadium beside the river.
Clean sanitary installations.
May-Oct 2HEC ⸺ ⌂ ⌂ ⊙ ⌂ ⌂ ⌂ ⤳ R ⊡ ⊞ lau ⮕ ⌂ ⌂ ✕
⤳P

⧉ **ALBI** TARN

Languedoc allée du Camping Caussels ☎ 563603706
The site is owned by the local automobile club. It lies on
terraced land in a forest next to municipal swimming pools.
Camping Card Compulsory.

CAMPING CARAVANING

FONTAINE VIEILLE

EXTENSION OF WATERPARK

★ ★ ★

4, Boulevard du Colonel Wurtz
F-33510 ANDERNOS-LES-BAINS
Tel. 05 56 82 01 67 - Fax. 05 56 82 09 81

⮑ *From village take N99 towards Millau, then turn left onto D100 and left again into site.*
Apr-Oct 1HEC 〰 ♦ ⋒ ⊙ ⊗ ⊘ ⊘ lau ➧ ⤨ ⵙ ✗ ⵗP

ALLES-SUR-DORDOGNE DORDOGNE

Port de Limeuil ☎ 553632976 ▓ 553630419
e-mail: didierbonvallet@aol.com
Situated in a conservation area at the confluence of the Dordogne and Vézère rivers, with a 400 metre beach.
⮑ *Signed off D51*
May-15 Oct 7HEC ∷∷ ♦ ⋒ ⤨ ⵙ ✗ ⊙ ⊗ ⊘ ⵗ PR ☒ ⊞ lau
Prices: pitch 18.30 (incl 2 persons)

ANDERNOS-LES-BAINS GIRONDE

Fontaine-Vieille 4 bd du Colonel Wurtz
☎ 556820167 ▓ 556820981
On level ground in sparse forest.
⮑ *S of village centre.*
Apr-Sep 12.6HEC 〰 ∷∷ ♦ ⋒ ⤨ ⵙ ✗ ⊙ ⊗ ⊘ ⵗ ⊕ ▲ ⵗ PS ☒ ⊞ lau **Prices:** pitch 12-18 (incl 2 persons)

Pleine Forêt ☎ 556821718
Situated in a quiet location among pines.
⮑ *Off D106E or D106 Andernos-les-Bains-Bordeaux road.*
All year 6HEC 〰 ∷∷ ♦ ⋒ ⵙ ✗ ⊙ ⊗ ⊘ ⊕ ⵗ P ☒ ⊞ lau
➧ ✗ ⊘ ⵗS

ANGLARS-JUILLAC LOT

Floiras ☎ 565362739 ▓ 565214100
e-mail: campingfloiras@aol.com
A quiet, level site beside the River Lot surrounded by vineyards in a hilly landscape dotted with villages, castles and caves. Good facilities for boating etc.
⮑ *SW via D8.*
Apr-15 Oct 1HEC 〰 ♦ ⋒ ⵙ ✗ ⊙ ⊗ ⊘ ▲ ⵗ R ☒ ⊞ lau ➧ ✗
Prices: ⚑3.25-3.50 pitch 4.75-6

ANGLES TARN

▥Manoir de Boutaric rte de Lacabarede ☎ 563709606
e-mail: manoir@boutarie.com
Site lies in the grounds of an old Manor House in the heart of the Haute Languedoc region.
⮑ *S of village, on D52 towards Lacabarède.*
15 May-15 Sep 3.3HEC 〰 ♦ ⋒ ✗ ⊙ ⊗ ⊘ ▲ ⊕ ⵗ P ☒ ⊞ lau ➧ ⤨ ⵗLR

ANGLET PYRÉNÉES-ATLANTIQUES

Parme Quartier Brindos ☎ 559230300 ▓ 559412955
In a wooded area with good facilities on the outskirts of Biarritz.
⮑ *3km SW off N10*
All year 4HEC 〰 ♦ ⋒ ⤨ ⵙ ✗ ⊙ ⊗ ⊘ ▲ ⊕ ⵗ P ☒ ⊞ lau ➧ ⵗL **Prices:** ⚑3.96-6.10 pitch 5.35-6.40

ARCACHON GIRONDE

Camping Club d'Arcachon av de la Galaxie, Les Abatilles
☎ 556832415 ▓ 557522851
e-mail: camparcachon@hotmail.com
In a delightful wooded position 800mtrs from the town and 1km from the beaches.
⮑ *1.5 km S.*
All year 6HEC ∷∷ ♦ ⋒ ⤨ ⵙ ✗ ⊙ ⊗ ⊘ ▲ ⊕ ⵗ P ☒ ▣ ⊞ lau ➧ ⵗS **Prices:** pitch 10-26 (incl 3 persons)

ARCIZANS-AVANT HAUTES-PYRÉNÉES

Lac ☎ 562970188 ▓ 0562970188
e-mail: mylene.peffabes@free.fr
Set in delightful Pyrenean surroundings on outskirts of village. Lakeside site close to a château.

⮑ *S on N21 take D13 through St-Savin.*
Jun-Sep 3HEC 〰 ♦ ⋒ ⤨ ⊙ ⊗ ⊘ ⵗ P ☒ ⊞ lau ➧ ⤨ ✗ ⵗ ⵗL

ARÈS GIRONDE

Canadienne rte de Lège, 82 r du Gl-de-Gaulle
☎ 556602491 ▓ 557704085
e-mail: camping-la-canadienne@wanadoo.fr
A family site surrounded by pine and oak trees with good facilities.
⮑ *1 km N off D106.*
All year 2HEC 〰 ♦ ⋒ ✗ ⊙ ⊗ ⊘ ▲ ⊕ ⵗ P ☒ ⊞ lau ➧ ⊘

Cigale rte de Lège ☎ 556602259 ▓ 557704166
Clean tidy site with good recreational facilities amongst pine trees. Grassy pitches.
⮑ *0.5 km N on D106 between the sea and the Arcachon Basin.*
Apr-10 Oct 2.8HEC 〰 ♦ ⋒ ⤨ ⵙ ✗ ⊙ ⊗ ⊘ ⵗ P ☒ ⊞ lau ➧ ⊘ ▲ ⵗ **Prices:** ⚑4 pitch 16-21 (incl 2 persons)

CM Goëlands av de la Libération ☎ 556825564 ▓ 557760224
Situated among oak trees 200mtrs from the beach with good facilities.
⮑ *1.7km SE*
Apr-Sep 10HEC 〰 ∷∷ ♦ ⋒ ⤨ ⵙ ✗ ⊙ ⊗ ⊘ ▲ ▲ ☒ ⊞ lau ➧ ⵗLP

Pasteur 1 r du Pilote ☎ 556603333 ▓ 556600505
⮑ *S of D3, 300m from the sea.*
Apr-Sep 1HEC 〰 ♦ ⋒ ⵙ ✗ ⊙ ⊗ ⊘ ▲ ⊕ ⵗ P ☒ ⊞ lau ➧ ⤨ ⵗS **Prices:** ⚑3 pitch 11-18 (incl 2 persons)

ARGELÈS-GAZOST HAUTES-PYRÉNÉES
At AGOS-VIDALOS(5km NE)

Soleil du Pibeste ☎ 562975323
e-mail: info@campingpibeste.com
In a beautiful wooded setting in the heart of the Pyrénées.
⮑ *S on N21.*
All year 1.5HEC 〰 ♦ ⋒ ⤨ ⵙ ✗ ⊙ ⊗ ⊘ ⊕ ⵗ P ☒ ⊞ lau ➧ ⵗR

ARREAU HAUTES-PYRÉNÉES

Refuge International rte Internationale
☎ 562986334 ▓ 0562986334
Enclosed terrace site.
⮑ *2km N on D929.*
All year 15HEC 〰 ♦ ⋒ ✗ ⊙ ⊗ ⊘ ▲ ⊕ ⵗ PR ☒ ⊞ lau ➧ ⤨ ✗ ⊘ ▲ ⵗL

ASCAIN PYRÉNÉES-ATLANTIQUES

Nivelle ☎ 559540194 ▓ 559540194
In a picturesque location beside the River Nivelle.
⮑ *2km N of town on D918 to St-Jean-de-Luz.*
15 Jun-15 Sep 2.8HEC 〰 ♦ ⋒ ⤨ ⵙ ✗ ⊙ ⊗ ⊕ ⵗ R ☒ ⊞ lau ➧ ⤨ ⵙ ✗ ⊘ ⵗLPS ⊞

ASCARAT PYRÉNÉES-ATLANTIQUES

Europ' Camping ☎ 559371278 ▓ 559372982
In rustic surroundings of mountains and vineyards, 300m from the River Nive.
⮑ *1km W of St-Jean-Pied-de-Port on D918.*
Etr-Sep 1.8HEC 〰 ♦ ⋒ ⤨ ⵙ ✗ ⊙ ⊗ ⊕ ⵗ P ☒ ⊞ lau ➧ ⵗR

ATUR DORDOGNE

Grand Dague ☎ 553042101 ▓ 553042201
e-mail: info@legranddague.fr
Well equipped family site in the heart of the Dordogne region with pitches divided by bushes and hedges.
⮑ *NE of Atur via D2.*
Etr-Sep 22HEC 〰 ♦ ⋒ ⤨ ⵙ ✗ ⊙ ⊗ ⊘ ▲ ⊕ ⵗ P ☒ ⊞ lau **Prices:** ⚑4-5 pitch 5-7

AUREILHAN LANDES

Aurilandes Camping 1001 promenade de l'Étang
☎ 558091088 ▤ 558093823
e-mail: aurilandes@free.fr
Quiet site separated by a small road on the banks of Lake
Aureilhan.
➲ *D626, 2km before Mimizan, on the right.*
20 May-20 Sep 8HEC ⊞ ♣♠♨♀✕⊙♥∅≞♥⤳L ⬜
⊞ lau ⤳PS Prices: ♦2.13 ♠1.68 ♥1.68

Parc St-James Eurolac Promenade de l'Étang
☎ 558090287 ▤ 558094189
e-mail: info@camping-parcstjames.com
Well tended site under deciduous trees providing shade,
partially on open meadow.
➲ *Turn right at Labouheyre off N10 on D626 to Aureilhan.
Follow signs.*
end Mar-end Sep 13HEC ⊞ ♣♠♨♀✕⊙♥∅≞♥⤳
LP ⬜⊞ lau Prices: ▲4 pitch 8.50-24.50 (incl 2 persons)

AZUR LANDES

CM d'Azur Au bord du lac ☎ 558483072 ▤ 558483072
e-mail: camping-municipal.azur@nanadoo.fr
A family site in wooded surroundings close to the Lac de
Soustons and 8km from the coast.
➲ *2 km S of Azur.*
20 May-15 Sep 7HEC ⊞ ⋮⋰ ♨♠♨♀✕⊙♥∅≞♥⤳
⤳ LPR ⬜⊞ lau

BAGNÈRES-DE-BIGORRE HAUTES-PYRÉNÉES

Bigourdan rte de Tarbes ☎ 0562951357
A level site recommended for caravans in a beautiful
Pyrenean setting.
➲ *2.5km NW at Pouzac.*
Apr-Oct 1HEC ⊞ ♣♠⊙♥♥⤳P⬜⊞ lau ♣♨♀✕∅≞
⤳R⊞

Tilleuls 12 av Maréchal Alan Brooke ☎ 562952604
A well equipped site at an altitude of 500mtrs. There are
good recreational facilities and a bakery operates during July
and August.
May-Sep 2.6HEC ⊞ ♣♠⊙♥♥⬜ lau ♣♨♀✕∅≞⤳P⊞

At TRÉBONS(4km N on D935)

Parc des Oiseaux RD26 ☎ 562953026
Clean, well-kept site with large pitches.
Mar-Nov 2.8HEC ⊞ ♣♠♨⊙♥∅♥⤳R⬜⊞ lau ♣♨✕
⤳P

BASTIDE-DE-SEROU, LA ARIÈGE

Arize rte de Nescus ☎ 561658151 ▤ 561658334
e-mail: camparize@aol.com
A well run site with a wide range of facilities in a peaceful,
wooded location at the foot of the Pyrénées.
Apr-Oct 1.8HEC ⊞ ♣♠♨♀⊙∅♥♥⤳PR⬜⊞
lau ♣✕≞♥Prices: pitch 12.50-18 (incl 2 persons)

BAYONNE PYRÉNÉES-ATLANTIQUES

Airotel la Chêneraie chemin de Cazenare
☎ 559550131 ▤ 559551117
On gently sloping field divided by hedges.
➲ *4km NE off N117 (Pau) road.*
Etr-1 Oct 10HEC ⊞ ♣♨♀✕⊙♥∅♥▲⤳LP⬜ lau
♣⊞

BEAUCENS-LES-BAINS HAUTES-PYRÉNÉES

Viscos ☎ 562970545
In a secluded location at the foot of the Pyrénées.
➲ *1km N on D13, rte de Lourdes.*
15 May-Sep 2HEC ⊞ ♣♠⊙♥∅⬜⊞ lau ♣♀✕⤳R

BELVÈS DORDOGNE

⌂Hauts de Ratebout ☎ 553290210 ▤ 553290828
e-mail: camping@hauts-ratebout.fr
A well equipped site on an old Périgord farm, set in extensive
grounds on top of a hill.
➲ *D710 to Fumel. After Vaurez-de-Belvès, take D54 to Casals.*
27Apr-15Sep 12HEC ⊞ ♣♠♨♀✕⊙♥∅≞♥⤳P⬜
⊞⌥ lau

Moulin de la Pique ☎ 553290115 ▤ 553282909
e-mail: camping@perigord.com
A quiet well equipped site set out around an imposing villa
and a small lake. There are fine entertainment facilities and
modern sanitary installations.
➲ *500m S on D710.*
14 Apr-28 Oct 12HEC ⊞ ♣♠♨♀✕⊙♥∅≞♥▲⤳P
⬜⊞ lau Prices: ♦6 pitch 14

Nauves Bos Rouge ☎ 553291264 ▤ 553291264
e-mail: campinglesnauves@hotmail.com
Located on a site of 40 hectares surrounded by forest
➲ *4.5km SW via D53.*
May-15 Sep 15 Sep-10 May 40HEC ⊞ ♨♠♀✕⊙♥♥♥
⤳P⬜⊞⊞ lau Prices: ♦4 pitch 5.70

BEYNAC-ET-CAZENAC DORDOGNE

Capeyrou ☎ 553295495 ▤ 553283627
Situated beside the River Dordogne close to the gates of the
picturesque medieval town of Beynac.
➲ *Access via D703.*
15 May-15 Sep 5HEC ⊞ ♣♠♀✕⊙♥⤳P⬜ lau ♣♨
✕∅⤳R Prices: ♦4.20 pitch 5.70

BEZ, LE TARN

Plô ☎ 563740082
e-mail: info@leplo.com
A pleasant site in wooded surroundings.
➲ *0.9km W via D30.*
Jun-Aug 3HEC ⊞ ♨♠♨♀✕⊙♥▲⬜⊞ lau ♣✕∅
⤳LPR Prices: ♦12.70 ▲2.80

BIARRITZ PYRÉNÉES-ATLANTIQUES

Biarritz 28 r d'Harcet ☎ 559230012 ▤ 559437467
e-mail: biarritz.camping@wanadoo.fr
A pleasant site with spacious pitches 200m from beach.
➲ *2km from town centre on N10, follow signs 'Espagne'.*
May-25 Sep 2.6HEC ⊞ ♣♠♨♀✕⊙♥∅♥⤳P⬜⊞⌥
lau ♣≞⤳S

At BIDART(4km SW)

Berrua rte d'Arbonne ☎ (33)5 59549666 ▤ 59547830
e-mail: berrua@wanadoo.fr
A well equipped family site 1km from the beach and 500mtrs
from the village.
Apr-5 Oct 5HEC ⊞ ♣♠♨♀✕⊙♥∅♥⤳P⬜⊞ lau ♣
⤳RS Prices: ♦2.50-4.70 pitch 12-22 (incl 2 persons)

Jean Paris Quartier M-Pierre ☎ 559265558
600m from beaches.
➲ *S of town, cross railway line, site on S side of N10.*
Jun-Sep 1.1HEC ⊞ ♣♠♨♀✕⊙♥∅⬜⊞ lau ♣✕⤳S

Oyam Ferme Oyambuerua ☎ 359549161
Level meadow site near farm. Views of the Pyrénées. Simple
but pleasant site.
➲ *Turn off beyond the church in the direction of Arbonne, via
N10, for approx 1km.*
Jun-Sep 6HEC ⊞ ♣♠♀✕⊙♥∅≞♥▲⤳P⬜ lau ♣♨
∅⤳S⊞

Pavillon Royal av Prince de Galles ☎ 559230054
Beautiful, well-kept site, divided into pitches, most of which
have open view of sea. Beside rocky beach.
➲ *2 km N.*
15 May-25 Sep 5HEC ᨈ ⫶⫶⫶ ⌕ ♠ ⛱ ☀ ✕ ⊙ ⬛ ⊘ ⚡
P ☎ ⊞ ⊗ lau

Résidence des Pins rte de Biarritz
☎ 559230029 🗏 559412459
e-mail: contact@campingdespins.com
Terraced site with numbered pitches, 800m from sea.
➲ *2km N on N106 Biarritz road.*
20 May-Sep 10HEC ᨈ ♠ ♠ ⛱ ☀ ✕ ⊙ ⬛ ⊘ ⇱ ⬛ ⚡
P ☎ ⊞ lau ♦ ⚡LS

▟Ruisseau rte d'Arbonne ☎ 559419450 🗏 559419573
e-mail: francoise.dumont3@wanadoo.fr
A well equipped site in wooded surroundings set out around
two lakes.
➲ *2km E on D255.*
19 May-22 Sep 15HEC ᨈ ⌕ ♠ ⛱ ☀ ✕ ⊙ ⬛ ⊘ ⇱ ⬛ ⚡ LP
☎ ⊞ lau

Ur-Onéa r de la Chapelle ☎ 559265361 🗏 559265394
e-mail: uronea@wanadoo.fr
A well equipped site lying at the foot of the Pyrénées with
good recreational facilities.
➲ *0.6km E.*
Apr-25 Sep 5HEC ᨈ ⌕ ♠ ⛱ ☀ ✕ ⊙ ⬛ ⊘ ⇱ ⬛ ⚡ P ☎ ⬛ ⊞
lau ♦ ✕ ⇱ ⚡RS

CM Le Tatiou ☎ 58090476 🗏 558824430
Well equipped family site in a forested setting 4km from the
sea.
➲ *2km W towards Lespecier.*
4 Apr-14 Oct 10HEC ᨈ ⫶⫶⫶ ♠ ♠ ⛱ ☀ ✕ ⊙ ⬛ ⊘ ⇱ ⚡
P ☎ lau

Sunêlia le Moulinal ☎ 33 553408460
e-mail: lemoulinal@perigond.com
In a pleasant situation beside a lake close to the former mill
of Biron Castle. This is a modern holiday village with a wide
variety of recreational facilities.
➲ *2km S on the Lacapelle-Biron road.*
30 Mar-14 Sep 11HEC ᨈ ♠ ♠ ⛱ ☀ ✕ ⊙ ⬛ ⊘ ⇱ ⬛ ▲ ⚡ LP
☎ ⊞ lau Prices: ♠3-7.50 pitch 12-26 (incl 2 persons)

Bimbo 176 chemin de Bimbo ☎ 558098233 🗏 558098014
e-mail: camping.bimbo@free.fr
In delightful wooded surroundings 500mtrs from the lake
and 10 minutes from the sea. Reservations recommended.
➲ *3.5km N towards Sanguinet.*
All year 6HEC ᨈ ♠ ♠ ⛱ ☀ ✕ ⊙ ⬛ ⊘ ⇱ ⬛ ⚡ P ☎ ⊞ lau
♦ ⚡L

Ecureuils Port Navarrosse ☎ 558098000
e-mail: camping.les.ecureuils@wanadoo.fr
In a pleasant wooded location 200mtrs from the lake shore.
Plenty of recreational facilities.
➲ *Access via D652.*
Apr-Sep 7HEC ᨈ ♠ ♠ ✕ ⊙ ⬛ ⬛ ⚡ P ☎ lau ♦ ⛱ ⊘ ⚡L

Rive rte de Bordeaux ☎ 558781233 🗏 558781292
e-mail: larive@wanadoo.fr
Level site in tall pine forest on E side of lake. Private port and
beach.
➲ *N of town off D652 Sanguinet road.*
Apr-Oct 15HEC ᨈ ⫶⫶⫶ ♠ ♠ ⛱ ☀ ✕ ⊙ ⬛ ⊘ ⇱ ⬛ ⚡ LP ☎
⊞ lau

At MAZION(5.5km NE on N937)

Tilleuls ☎ 557421813
➲ *5.5km NE on N937.*
May-Oct 0.5HEC ᨈ ♠ ♠ ⊙ ⬛ ⬛ ⊞ lau ♦ ⛱ ☀ ✕
Prices: ♠3.50 pitch 2.50

Ferme de Bourgade ☎ 553366715
e-mail: bourgade47@libertysurf.fr
A small, tranquil site with good, clean facilities.
➲ *Signposted from N21 between Castillonnès and Villeréal.*
May-15 Oct 1HEC ᨈ ♠ ♠ ⚡ L ☎ ⊞ lau ♦ ☀ ✕ Prices:
♠1.52 ♠1.52 pitch 3.04

Bourgnatelle ☎ 565384407
e-mail: bourgnatel@aol.com
In a pleasant location beside the River Cére. Separate car
park for arrivals after 22.30hrs.
➲ *Access via D940 towards Rocamadour.*
May-Sep 2HEC ᨈ ♠ ⊙ ⬛ ⊘ ⇱ ⬛ ⚡ R ☎ lau ♦ ⛱ ☀ ✕
⇱ P ⊞ Prices: ♠2.50-3.20 pitch 2.50-3.20

Rocher de la Granelle rte du Buisson ☎ 553072432
Surrounded by woodland with pitches set out among trees
and bushes on the banks of the Vézère with a wide variety of
leisure facilities.
➲ *From Le Bugue centre cross the bridge and follow signs.*
Apr-Sep 8HEC ᨈ ⌕ ♠ ⛱ ☀ ✕ ⊙ ⬛ ⊘ ⇱ ⬛ ⚡ PR ☎ ⊞
lau

St-Avit Loisirs St-Avit-de-Vialard
☎ 553026400 🗏 553026439
e-mail: contact@saint-avit.loisirs.com
A pleasant site in natural wooded surroundings.
➲ *W of town via C201.*
Apr-Sep ᨈ ⌕ ♠ ⛱ ☀ ✕ ⊙ ⬛ ⊘ ⇱ ⬛ ⚡ P ☎ ⊞ lau ♦ ⚡R
Prices: ♠3.50-7 pitch 5.50-10.50

Rivière de Cabessut r de la Rivière
☎ 565300630 🗏 565239946
e-mail: camping-riviere-cabessut@wanadoo.fr
➲ *N of town via the Cabessut Bridge over the River Lot.*
Apr-Oct 3HEC ᨈ ♠ ♠ ⛱ ☀ ✕ ⊙ ⬛ ⊘ ⇱ ⚡ PR ☎ ⊞ lau ♦
✕ ⇱ Prices: ♠2.29 pitch 7.62

At ESCLAUZELS(18km SE)

Pompit ☎ 565315340 🗏 565317800
Situated in the heart of a large forest close to the magnificent
Lot Valley.
➲ *5km NW of Esclauzels village.*
All year 4.5HEC ᨈ ♠ ♠ ♠ ⛱ ☀ ✕ ⊙ ⬛ ⊘ ⇱ ⬛ ⚡ P ☎ ⊞
lau Prices: ♠3.40 ♠3.60 ♠3.60 pitch 3.60

Chênes Verts rte de Sarlat, Souillac ☎ 553592107
In a beautiful wooded setting within the Périgord
countryside. A wide variety of recreational facilities are
available.
➲ *On D704A between Sarlat and Calviac.*
May-Sep 6HEC ᨈ ♠ ♠ ⛱ ☀ ✕ ⊙ ⬛ ⊘ ⇱ ⚡ P ☎ ⊞ lau
♦ ⚡LR

CAMPING ★★★AIROTEL LES VIVIERS

Bordering the Arcachon Basin and the Atlantic Ocean

33950 LEGE - CAP FERRET
TEL: 00 33 556 607 004
FAX: 00 33 556 607 614
www.airotel-les-viviers.com
Email: Lesviviers@wanadoo.fr

To let:
Pitches - mobile homes
bungalows - chalets

Trois Sources Le Peyratel ☎ 565330301 ▥ 565330645
e-mail: l3s@wanadoo.fr
Wooded location, family site with plenty of leisure facilities.
➲ *Access via D653, then D25 to Calviac.*
May-Sep 6.4HEC ⬛ ⠂⠂⠂ ♠ ⋔ ⛟ ♐ ✗ ⊙ ⬛ ⬘ ⬛ ⬛ ▲ ⋞
LPR ⬈ ⊞ lau

CAMBO-LES-BAINS PYRÉNÉES-ATLANTIQUES

Bixta Eder rte de St-Jean-de-Luz
☎ 559299423 ▥ 0559297023
e-mail: camping.bixtaeden@wanadoo.fr
Modern site with good sports facilities.
➲ *Near the junction of D932 and D10.*
15 Apr-15 Oct 1HEC ⬛ ♠ ♠ ⋔ ⊙ ⬛ ⊞ lau ➤ ⋞LP ⊞
Prices: ⋔3.20 ♠1.52

CAPBRETON LANDES

Pointe av J-Castigan ☎ 558721498
Family site in a wooded location on the banks of a river,
800mtrs from the sea. Good recreational facilities.
➲ *2km S towards Labenne on N652.*
Jun-Sep 4.5HEC ⠂⠂⠂ ♠ ⋔ ⛟ ✗ ⊙ ⬛ ⬘ ⋞ R ⬈ ⬛ ⊞ lau ➤
⋞S

CAP FERRET GIRONDE

Truc Vert rte Forestière ☎ 556608955 ▥ 556609947
e-mail: camping.trvc-vert@worldonline.fr
In a very pleasant location on a slope in a pine wood close to
the beach.
➲ *On D106 in the direction of Cap Ferret to Petit Piquey.*
Turn right and follow signs.
May-Sep 11HEC ⠂⠂⠂ ♠ ⋔ ⛟ ✗ ⊙ ⬛ ⬘ ⬈ ⊞ lau ➤ ⋞S
Prices: ⋔4.11 ♠9.45 ▲9.45

CARLUCET LOT

Château de Lacomté ☎ 565387546 ▥ 565331768
e-mail: ccl@easynet.fr
In wooded surroundings with good sized pitches and a
variety of recreational facilities.
➲ *Follow signposts from D677/D32.*
May-Oct 12HEC ⬛ ⠂ ♠ ♠ ⋔ ⛟ ♐ ✗ ⊙ ⬛ ⬘ ⬛ ⬛ ▲ ⋞ P ⬈ ⊞
lau Prices: ⋔3.77-5.80 ♠0.99-1.52 pitch 4.77-7.35 pp2.17-
3.35

CASTELJALOUX LOT-ET-GARONNE

Club de Clarens rte de Mont-de-Marsan
☎ 553930745 ▥ 553939309
A large site with direct access to a 17 hectare Lac de Clarens
and good recreational facilities.
Apr-Sep 2HEC ⠂⠂⠂ ♠ ⋔ ⛟ ♐ ✗ ⊙ ⬛ ⬘ ⬛ ⋞ LR ⬈ ⊞ lau ➤ ⛟
✗ ⋞P Prices: ⋔3.81-4.25 pitch 4.25-4.72

CM de la Piscine rte de Marmande
☎ 553935468 ▥ 0553891325
➲ *NW on D933 Marmande road.*
1 Apr-30 Oct 1HEC ⬛ ♠ ♠ ⊙ ⬛ ♐ ⋞ P ⬈ lau ➤ ⛟ ✗ ⊘ ⛏
⋞R ⊞

CASTELNAUD-LA-CHAPELLE DORDOGNE

Maisonneuve ☎ 553295129 ▥ 553302706
e-mail: campmaison@aol.com
In picturesque surroundings, 800mtrs from the village, close
to the River Céou in the heart of the Périgord Noir region.
➲ *10kms S of Sarlat on D57.*
Apr-15 Oct 6HEC ⬛ ♠ ⋔ ⛟ ♐ ✗ ⊙ ⬛ ⬘ ⋞ PR ⬈ ⊞ lau
➤ ⊘ ⛏

CAUTERETS HAUTES-PYRÉNÉES

Mamelon-Vert 32 av du Mamelon-Vert
☎ 562925156 ▥ 562925156
e-mail: mamelon@aol.com
In a beautiful wooded mountain setting close to the local
winter sports facilities.
Closed Oct-10 Nov 2HEC ⬛ ♠ ⋔ ⊙ ⬛ ⊘ ⬛ ♐ ⬈ ⊞ lau ➤
⛟ ✗ ⛏ ⋞PR Prices: ⋔2.30-2.90 ♠0.80-0.95
pitch 2.30-2.90 (incl 2 persons)

CLAOUEY GIRONDE

Airotel les Viviers rte du Cap Ferret
☎ 556607004 ▥ 556607614
e-mail: lesviviers@wanadoo.fr
Beautiful, widespread site in a forest divided by seawater
channels.
➲ *On the D106, 1km S of the town.*
Apr-Sep 33HEC ⠂⠂⠂ ♠ ⋔ ⛟ ♐ ✗ ⊙ ⬛ ⬘ ⬛ ⋞ LPS ⬈ ⊞ lau

CONTIS-PLAGE LANDES

Lous Seurrots ☎ 558428582
Well equipped site in a pine forest on outskirts of village
between road and stream.
➲ *Access via D41.*
Apr-Sep 15HEC ⠂⠂⠂ ♠ ⋔ ⛟ ✗ ⊙ ⬛ ⊘ ⛏ ⬛ ⋞
PRS ⬈ ⊞ lau

CORDES TARN

Moulin de Julien ☎ 563561110 ▥ 0563561110
In a beautiful valley with good pitches for caravans and tents
and plenty of modern facilities.
➲ *900m E on D600 and D922.*
Apr-Sep 6HEC ⬛ ♠ ⋔ ♐ ⊙ ⬛ ⊘ ⬛ ♐ ⋞ LP ⬈ ⊞ lau

27th ANNIVERSARY

In the heart of the Dordogne

A PARADISE FOR CHILDREN

Four heated swimming pool, two
water slides, canoes, entertainment.
All services open from half of May till
half September. Mobile homes to let.

CAMPING LE MOULIN
DE PAULHIAC ★★★★

Patricia and Francis ARMAGNAC
Le Moulin de Paulhiac- 24250 DAGLAN
Tel: 05 53 28 20 88 - Fax: 05 53 29 33 45
www.moulin-de-paulhiac.com • francis.armagnac@wanadoo.fr

COUX-ET-BIGAROQUE DORDOGNE

Clou Meynard Haut ☎ 553316332 ▤ 553316933
e-mail: leclou@perigord.com
Separate section for dog owners.
➲ *Access via D703 (Le Bugue-Delve road).*
Apr-Sep 3.5HEC ⊞⊞⊞ ♣ ₨ ♨ ⚡ ✕ ⊙ ⬛ ⌀ ♨ ⬛ ⬛ 🜨 ✦ P ⊡
⊞ lau Prices: ♠2.50-4.20 pitch 3.80-6.60

Faval ☎ 553316044 ▤ 553283971
e-mail: camping.la.faval@libertysurf.fr
In a wooded location 200m from River Dordogne. A family
site with good recreational facilities.
➲ *1km E of village on D703, near junction with D710.*
Apr-Sep 3HEC ⊞⊞⊞ ♣ ₨ ♨ ⚡ ✕ ⊙ ⬛ ⌀ ⬛ ⬛ 🜨 ✦ P ⊡ ⊞ lau ✦
✕ ⌂ 🜨R

Valades Les Valades ☎ 553291427 ▤ 553281928
e-mail: camping.valades@wanadoo.fr
In wooded surroundings within a pleasant valley. Well
equipped pitches available.
➲ *5km N of village off N703.*
Mar-Nov 11HEC ⊞⊞⊞ ♣ ₨ ♨ ⚡ ✕ ⊙ ⬛ ⬛ 🜨 ✦ LP ⊡ ⊞ lau

DAGLAN DORDOGNE

Moulin de Paulhiac ☎ 553282088 ▤ 553293345
e-mail: francis.armagnac@wanadoo.fr
In picturesque wooded surroundings with wide, well marked
pitches and good, modern facilities.
➲ *4km N via D57 beside the Céou*
20 May-15 Sep 5HEC ⊞⊞⊞ ♣ ₨ ♨ ⚡ ✕ ⊙ ⬛ ⌀ ⌂ ⬛ 🜨 PR ⊡
⊞ lau

DAX LANDES

Chênes Au Bois-de-Boulogne ☎ 558900553 ▤ 558904243
In a wooded park on the edge of the Bois-de-Boulogne with
good facilities.
➲ *1.5km W of town beside River Adour.*
24 Mar-3 Nov 5HEC ⊞⊞⊞ ♣ ₨ ♨ ⊙ ⬛ ⌀ ⬛ ⬛ 🜨 P ⊡ lau ✦ ♨
✕ 🜨R

DURAS LOT-ET-GARONNE

Moulin de Borie Neuve St Sernin de Duras ☎ 553947657
e-mail: info@borieneuve.com
A pleasant site in the Dourdèze valley close to an old mill.
➲ *Access via D244 towards St-Astier-de-Duras.*
Jun-15 Oct 1HEC ⊞⊞⊞ ♣ ₨ ♨ ⊙ ⬛ ⌀ ⌂ ⬛ ♨ 🜨 R ⊡ ⊞ lau ✦
♨ ✕ ⌀ 🜨LP Prices: ♠3.66 ⬛0.76-1.07 pitch 4.27

DURAVEL LOT

Club de Vacances Port de Vire ☎ 565246506
A pleasant site with good facilities beside the River Lot.
Camping Card Compulsory

➲ *2.3km S via D58.*
25 Apr-Sep 7HEC ⊞⊞⊞ ♣ ₨ ♨ ⚡ ✕ ⊙ ⬛ ⌀ ⬛ ⬛ 🜨 PR ⊡
⊞ lau

DURFORT ARIÈGE

Bourdieu ☎ 561673017 ▤ 0561672900
e-mail: lebourdieu@wanadoo.fr
Well equipped site in a picturesque setting with fine views
over the Pyrénées.
➲ *Off D14 Le Fossat-Saverdun.*
All year 20HEC ⊞⊞⊞ ♣ ₨ ♨ ⚡ ✕ ⊙ ⬛ ⌂ ⬛ ⬛ 🜨 LPR ⊡ ⊞
lau Prices: ♠1.71-2.44 ⬛6.08-8.69 pitch 4.48-6.40

ESTAING HAUTES-PYRÉNÉES

🜨Pyrénées Natura rte du Lac ☎ 562974544 ▤ 562974581
e-mail: sarl.ruysschaert@wanadoo.fr
A well run site at an altitude of 1000mtrs, situated on the
edge of the National Park with fine views of the surrounding
mountains.
➲ *From Argèles-Gazost take road towards Arrens, then D13
for Lac d'Estaing.*
May-Sep 2.5HEC ⊞⊞⊞ ♣ ₨ ♨ ⚡ ✕ ⊙ ⬛ ⌀ ⬛ 🜨 R ⊡ ⊞ lau ✦
✕ Prices: pitch 13.50-18.50 (incl 2 persons)

ÉYZIES-DE-TAYAC, LES DORDOGNE

At SIREUIL(7km E off D47)

Mas ☎ 553296806
Forested site on a farm with a direct sales shop selling farm
and local produce.
➲ *N of D47 (Sarlat-Les Éyzies).*
15 May-Sep 5HEC ⊞⊞⊞ ♣ ₨ ♨ ⚡ ✕ ⊙ ⬛ ⌀ ⬛ 🜨 P ⊡ ⊞
lau

FIGEAC LOT

Rives du Célé Domaine du Surgie ☎ 565345900
In a pleasant wooded location on the banks of the River Célé
with plenty of leisure facilities, the site lies within a large
recreation area. Separate carpark for late arrivals.
Apr-Sep 2HEC ⊞⊞⊞ ♣ ₨ ♨ ⚡ ✕ ⊙ ⬛ ⌂ ⬛ 🜨 LPR ⊡ ⊞ lau
✦ ⌀

FOIX ARIÈGE

Lac RN 20 ☎ 561651158 ▤ 561053262
e-mail: camping-du-lac@wanadoo.fr
On well-kept meadow beside the Lac de Labarre.
➲ *3km N on N20.*
May-Sep 5HEC ⊞⊞⊞ ♣ ₨ ⊙ ⬛ ⌀ 🜨 LPR ⊡ lau ✦ ♨ ♨ ✕

GASTES LANDES

Réserve ☎ 0870 242 7777 ▤ 0870 242 9999
A large, popular site situated in one of the largest forests in
Europe. Plenty of sporting and entertainment facilities.
➲ *3km SW via D652*
28 Apr-14 Sep 32HEC ⊞⊞⊞ ♣ ₨ ♨ ⚡ ✕ ⬛ ⌀ ⌂ ⬛ 🜨 LP ⊡
⊞ ⌀ lau

See advertisement on page 122

GAUGEAC DORDOGNE

Moulin de David ☎ 553226525 ▤ 553239976
e-mail: courrier@moulin-de-david.com
Situated in a pleasant valley alongside a small stream with
well defined pitches and good recreational facilities.
➲ *3km from town towards Villeréal.*
18 May-07 Sep 14HEC ⊞⊞⊞ ♣ ₨ ♨ ⚡ ✕ ⊙ ⬛ ⌀ ⬛ ⬛ 🜨
🜨 LP ⊡ ⊞ lau Prices: ♠3.30-5.90 pitch 4.60-8.40

GOURDON LOT

Paradis La Peyrugue ☎ 0565416501 ▤ 0565416501
On a pleasant wooded meadow surrounded by hills.

Cont.

La Réserve ★★★★
Parentis-en-Born

A stunningly beautiful lakeside location, set among scented pines - perfect for lovers of nature, beautiful beaches and watersports.

- Superb touring pitches set close to the beach
- Private lakeside beach on-site
- Heated outdoor pool with new waterslide (open 19 May)
- Extensive programme of sport & leisure, inc. windsurfing & waterskiing†

- Restaurant, takeaway, pool & beach bar
- 3 children's clubs for all ages
- Superb low season prices
- Bilingual staff on parc
- Site open from: 1 May - 28 September

† waterskiing available in July & August only.

La Réserve, Biscarrosse, Gastes, 40160 Parentis-en-Born, France
Tel:00 33 558 09 75 96 Fax:00 33 558 09 78 71

A B T A
V2819

To book from France please call the number above, quoting code FAA03
To book from the UK please call 0870 242 77 77 quoting code FAA03

⮕ *1.6km SW off N673.*
May-1Oct 2HEC �📶 ♀ ♠ ⊙ 🅟 ⌀ 🚿 🏕 🚽 ⁊ LP 🅿 ⊞ lau ♦ 🄻 🍴 ✕ ⁊L Prices: ♠4.50 pitch 2.30

At GROLÉJAC(15km N on D704)

Granges ☎ 553281115 ▥ 553285713
e-mail: lesueur.francine@wanadoo.fr
Beautifully situated terraces on a hill with big pitches. The site has been constructed around a disused railway station, incorporating the old ticket office and the bridge into its modern design. Facilities for sports and entertainment.
⮕ *Turn off D704 in village towards Domme.*
2 May-16 Sep 6.5HEC �📶 ♀ ♠ 🍴 ✕ ⊙ 🅟 🏕 ⁊ PR 🅿 ⊞ lau ♦ 🄻 ⌀ ⁊L

At ST-MARTIAL-DE-NABIRAT(6km W)

Carbonnier ☎ 553284253 ▥ 553285131
Family site in a small, wooded valley with a variety of recreational facilities.
⮕ *Off the D46.*
Etr-15 Sep 8HEC �📶 ♀ ♠ 🄻 🍴 ✕ ⊙ 🅟 ⌀ 🚿 🏕 ⁊ LP 🅿 ⊞ lau Prices: ♠5.49 pitch 7.32

GOURETTE PYRÉNÉES-ATLANTIQUES

Ley ☎ 559051147 ▥ 0559051147
Terraced site with gravel and asphalt caravan pitches. TV, common room.
⮕ *From Laruns drive E to Eaux-Bonnes and drive uphill to Gourette.*
Dec-Apr & Jun-Sep 2HEC �📶 ⚡ ♠ 🍴 ✕ ⊙ 🅟 🏕 🚽 ⁊ R 🅿 ⊞ lau ♦ 🄻 ⌀ Prices: ♠6.10

GRAULGES, LES DORDOGNE

Crozes les Graulges ☎ 553607473
In a picturesque setting in woodland beside a lake.
⮕ *Off D939 between Angoulême and Périgueux.*
Jun-Sep 8HEC 📶 ♦ ♠ 🄻 🍴 ✕ ⊙ 🅟 🚽 ⁊ P 🅿 ⊞ Prices: ♠3.10 🚐4.90 ♠4.90

GRISOLLES TARN-ET-GARONNE

Aquitaine rte Nationale 20 ☎ 563673322
e-mail: campingaquitaine@aol.com
⮕ *1.5km N off crossroads N20/N113.*
(28km N of Toulouse, 22km S of Montauban) All year 3HEC 📶 ♦ ♠ ⊙ 🅟 🏕 🚿 🚽 ⁊ P 🅿 ⊞ lau ♦ 🄻 🍴 ✕ ⌀ 🚿 ⁊R Prices: ♠3 ♠3 pitch 11.50 (incl 2 persons)

HASPARREN PYRÉNÉES-ATLANTIQUES

Chapital rte de Cambo ☎ 0559296294 ▥ 559296971
On level ground, surrounded by woodland. Good facilities for families.
⮕ *0.5km W via D22. Access via A64 towards Hasparren.*
Etr-Oct 2.6HEC 📶 ⚡ ♠ ⊙ 🅟 ⌀ 🏕 🚿 ⊞ lau ♦ 🄻 🚿 ⁊P

HAUTEFORT DORDOGNE

Moulin des Loisirs Le Coucou ☎ 553504655
⮕ *2km SW via D72 & D71, 100m from Coucou lake.*
Etr-Sep 4HEC 📶 ♦ ♠ 🄻 🍴 ✕ ⊙ 🅟 🚿 ⁊ P 🅿 lau ♦ ⌀ 🚿 ⁊L ⊞

HENDAYE PYRÉNÉES-ATLANTIQUES

Acacias ☎ 559207876 ▥ 559207876
A pleasant family site in parkland, 5 minutes from the beach.
⮕ *1.8km E (rte de la Glacière).*
Apr-Sep 5HEC 📶 ♦ ♠ 🍴 ✕ ⊙ 🅟 🚿 🏕 ⁊ L 🅿 🅿 ⊞ lau ♦ 🄻 🍴 ✕ ⁊S

Airotel Eskualduna rte de la Corniche (D-912) ☎ 559200464 ▥ 559200464
On gently sloping meadow.
⮕ *2km from village on N10c.*
15 Jun-Sep 10HEC 📶 ♦ ♠ 🄻 🍴 ✕ ⊙ 🅟 ⌀ 🚿 🏕 🚽 ⁊ PR 🅿 ⊞ lau ♦ ⁊S

HOURTIN GIRONDE

Acacia Ste-Hélène ☎ 556738080
Pleasant, quiet site on the edge of a forest with good sanitary facilities. Compulsory car park for arrivals after 2330hrs.
⮕ *Off D3 towards the lake.*
Jun-Sep 5HEC 📶 ⚡ ♠ 🍴 ⊙ 🅟 🚿 🏕 🅿 🅿 ⊞ lau ♦ ⁊L Prices: ♠3.35 pitch 3.05

Mariflaude ☎ 556091197 ▥ 556092401
Level meadowland, shaded by pines, in rural setting 2km from one of the biggest lakes in the country.
⮕ *Turn onto D4 at the chemist and continue E towards Pauillac.*
May-15 Sep 7HEC 📶 ⚡ ♠ 🄻 🍴 ✕ ⊙ 🅟 ⌀ 🚿 🏕 ⁊ P 🅿 lau ♦ ⁊L

Orée du Bois rte d'Aquitaine ☎ 556091588
In a quiet, wooded location with good facilities.
⮕ *1500m from town centre beside the lake.*
Jun-15 Sep 2HEC ⁙⁙ ⚡ ♠ 🄻 🍴 ✕ ⊙ 🅟 ⌀ 🚿 🏕 ⁊ P 🅿 ⊞ lau ♦ ⁊LR

Ourmes av du Lac ☎ 556091276 ▥ 556092390
e-mail: lesourmes@free.fr
In wooded surroundings close to the beach and 500mtrs from the largest freshwater lake in France.
⮕ *Follow D4 towards lake.*
Apr-Sep 7HEC 📶 ⚡ ♠ 🄻 🍴 ✕ ⊙ 🅟 ⌀ 🏕 ⁊ P 🅿 lau ♦ 🚿 ⁊LS ⊞ Prices: pitch 11-14.70 (incl 2 persons)

HOURTIN-PLAGE GIRONDE

Côte d'Argent ☎ 556091025 ▦ 556092496
e-mail: camping-cote-dargent.com
In a pine and oak forest 500m from beach with good facilities.
➲ *Access via D101 from Hourtin.*
11 May-15 Sep 20HEC ⋮⋮ ♠ ⋔ ⛊ ⛙ ✕ ☉ ⊡ ⬛ ⛐ ⛺ ⛱ S
⛉ ⊞ lau

HUME, LA GIRONDE

At **TESTE, LA** (3km SW)

Village de Loisirs Domaine de la Forge rte Sanguinet
☎ 556660772 ▦ 556667897
e-mail: domainedelaforge@wanadoo.fr
Secluded site in very quiet woodland.
➲ *3km S on D652.*
All year 4HEC ⟱ ⋮⋮ ♠ ⋔ ⛊ ⛙ ✕ ☉ ⬛ ⛺ ⛱ ⛱ P ⛉ ⊡ ⊞
lau ➡ ⛱R

LABENNE LANDES

Savane av de l'Océan ☎ 559454113
➲ *On RN10.*
All year 7HEC ⟱ ♠ ⋔ ⛙ ✕ ☉ ⊡ ⛺ ⛱ ⛼ ⛉ lau ➡ ⛱ ⬛ ⛲
⛱LRS ⊞

LABENNE-OCÉAN LANDES

Boudigau ☎ 559454207 ▦ 559457776
Situated in pine forest.
➲ *Turn right into site after bridge.*
15 May-15 Sep 6HEC ⟱ ⋮⋮ ⛘ ⋔ ⛊ ⛙ ✕ ☉ ⊡ ⬛ ⛺ ⛱ ⛱
P ⛉ ⊞ lau ➡ ⛲ ⛱S

Côte d'Argent av de l'Océan ☎ 559454202 ▦ 559457331
e-mail: info@campingcotedargent.com
Very well-managed modern site attached to holiday village.

➲ *3km W on D126.*
Apr-Oct 4HEC ⟱ ⋮⋮ ♠ ⋔ ⛊ ⛙ ✕ ☉ ⊡ ⬛ ⛺ ⛱ P ⛉ ⊞ lau ➡
⛱ ⬛ ⛱RS

Mer rte de la Plage ☎ 559454209 ▦ 559454307
e-mail: campinglamer@wanadoo.fr
In a pine forest 700mtrs from the beach.
➲ *On D126 (rte de la Plage).*
May-Sep 5.5HEC ⟱ ⋮⋮ ♠ ⋔ ⛊ ⛙ ✕ ☉ ⊡ ⬛ ⛺ ⛱ ⛱ PR ⛉
⊞ lau ➡ ⛱S

Sylvamar av de l'Océan ☎ 559457516
➲ *Access via D126.*
20 May-20 Sep 14.5HEC ⟱ ⋮⋮ ♠ ⋔ ⛊ ⛙ ✕ ☉ ⊡ ⬛ ⛺ ⛱ ⛱ P
⛉ lau ⛱ ⬛ ⛱S

LACANAU-OCÉAN GIRONDE

Airotel de l'Océan 24 r du Répos ☎ 556032445 ▦ 557700187
On rising ground in pine forest. 800m from beach.
May-Sep 9.5HEC ⋮⋮ ♠ ⋔ ⛊ ⛙ ✕ ☉ ⊡ ⬛ ⛺ ⛱ ⛼ ⛱ P ⛱
⛉ ⊞ lau ➡ ⛱S

Grands Pins Plages Nord ☎ 556032077 ▦ 557700389
e-mail: grandspins@wanadoo.fr
On very hilly terrain in woodland. 350m from the beach,
access to which is through dunes.
➲ *Approach via exit 7 on A10, then D6 to Lacanau.*
01May-15 Sep 11HEC ⋮⋮ ♠ ⋔ ⛊ ⛙ ✕ ☉ ⊡ ⬛ ⛺ ⛱ ⛱ P ⛱
⊞ lau ➡ ⛱S Prices: pitch 23-29.50 (incl 2 persons)

At **MEDOC** (8km E)

Talaris rte de l'Océan ☎ 556030415 ▦ 556262156
e-mail: talarisvacances@free.fr
A family site in delightful wooded surroundings 1.2km from
the lake. Separate car park for arrivals after 22.30hrs.

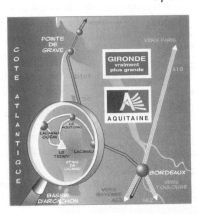

2km E on rte de Lacanau.
May-15 Sep 8.2HEC ⊞ ♦♠☎♋❍⊙🗑⌀❄♨Å٦P🖹
lau ♦ ٦L 🕀 Prices: pitch 15.60-22.50 (incl 2 persons)

At MOUTCHIC(5km E)

Lac ☎ 556030026
On D6 rte de Lacanau, 60m from lake.
Apr-15 Oct 1HEC ⊞ ♦♠☎♋❍⊙🗑⌀🚋🗑🖹🕀 lau ♦
٦L Prices: pitch 11.43-15.24 (incl 2 persons)

Tedey rte de Longarisse ☎ 55603015 ▥ 556030190
e-mail: campingletedey@wanadoo.fr
Quiet site in pine forest, on edge of Lake Lacanau. Private bathing area.
Turn off D6 and continue along narrow track through forest for 0.5km.
29 Apr-16 Sep 14HEC ⫶⫶⫶ ♦♠☎♋❍⊙🗑⌀🗑٦ L🖹🕀
lau Prices: pitch 14-16.50 (incl 2 persons)

See advertisement on page 123

See advertisement on page 123

LACAPELLE-MARIVAL LOT

CM Bois de Sophie Route d'Aymac ☎ 565408259
In a pleasant wooded location with a variety of sporting facilities.
1km NW via D940
15 May-Sep 1HEC ⊞ ♦♠⊙🗑🚋🗑٦ P🖹 lau ♦☎♋✗
⌀❄٦LR🕀

LANTON GIRONDE

Roumingue ☎ 556829748 ▥ 556829609
e-mail: info@roumingue.com
Level terrain under a few deciduous trees partially in open meadow on the Bassin d'Arcachon.
1km NW of village towards sea.
All year 10HEC ⫶⫶⫶ ⊙♋☎♋✗⊙🗑⌀🚋🗑٦PS🖹
🕀 lau ♦ ❄

LARNAGOL LOT

Ruisseau de Treil Le Ruisseau
☎ 565312339 ▥ 565313925
A quiet site situated within a small valley with well defined pitches and good leisure facilities.
0.6km E via D662
Etr-Oct 4.3HEC ⊞ ♦♠☎♋❍⊙🗑🗑٦P🖹 lau ♦ ٦R
Prices: ♦30 pitch 40

LARUNS PYRÉNÉES-ATLANTIQUES

Gaves ☎ 559053237 ▥ 559054714
On the bank of the Gave d'Ossan amid beautiful Pyrenean scenery. Some pitches reserved for caravans.
1km S.
All year 2.5HEC ⊞ ⊙♠♋❍⊙🗑⌀❄🚋🗑٦R🖹 lau ♦❄
✗🕀

LARUSCADE GIRONDE

Relais du Chavan ☎ 557686305
On well-kept meadow edged by a strip of forest. Some traffic noise.
6.5km NW on N10 near Km20.3.
Jun-Aug 3.6HEC ⫶⫶⫶ ⊙♠☎♋❍⊙🗑⌀❄🚋🗑٦P🖹🕀
lau Prices: ♦2.74 pitch 3.05

LECTOURE GERS

▥Lac des Trois Vallées ☎ 562688233 ▥ 562688882
e-mail: lac.des.trois.vallees@wanadoo.com
This rural site is part of a large park and lies next to a lake. It has spacious marked pitches.
3km SE on N21.
05 May-08 Sep 40HEC ⊞ ♦♠☎♋❍✗⊙🗑⌀🗑♋Å٦
LP🖹🕀 lau

LÉON LANDES

Lou Puntaou ☎ 558487430
In oak wood with separate sections for caravans.
Turn off N652 in village and continue towards lake for 1.5km on D142.
15 Apr-Sep 14HEC ⊞ ⫶⫶⫶ ♦♠☎♋❍✗⊙🗑⌀🗑٦P🖹🕀
lau ♦❄٦LR

St-Antoine St-Michel-Escalus ☎ 558487850 ▥ 558487190
A pleasant, well equipped site beside a river in peaceful wooded surroundings.
Mar-Sep 6HEC ⊞ ♦♠☎♋❍✗⊙🗑⌀🚋🗑٦R🖹 lau
Prices: ♦2.60 pitch 4.80

LESCAR PYRÉNÉES-ATLANTIQUES

Terrier av du Vert Galant ☎ 559810182 ▥ 559812683
On meadowland split in two with pitches surrounded by hedges in foreground.
From Pau take N117 towards Bayonne for approx. 6.5km, then turn left onto D501 towards Monein to site towards bridge.
All year 4HEC ⊞ ♋♦♠☎✗⊙🗑⌀❄🗑♋٦PR🖹 lau
♦❄٦L🕀

LINXE LANDES

CM Le Grandjean rte de Mixe ☎ 558429000
A modern site situated on the edge of a forest. Ideal for family holidays.
From the Castets road, take the D42 towards Linxe.
28 Jun-6 Sep 2.7HEC ⊞ ⫶⫶⫶ ♦♠❍⊙🗑🚋🗑 lau ♦❄✗

LIT-ET-MIXE LANDES

Vignes rte du Cap de l'Homy ☎ 558428560 ▥ 558427436
e-mail: camping.vignes@wanadoo.fr
In a pine forest with good sanitary and sports facilities.
3km S via D652 and D89.
Jun-15 Sep 15HEC ⊞ ⫶⫶⫶ ⊙♋☎♋✗⊙🗑⌀❄🚋🗑Å
٦ P🖹 P🕀 lau

LIVERS-CAZELLES TARN

Rédon ☎ 563561464
A quiet site with fine views over the surrounding area and good modern facilities.
4km SE of Cordes on D600.
Apr-Oct 2HEC ⊞ ♦♠❍⊙🗑⌀🗑٦P🖹🕀 lau ♦✗

LOURDES HAUTES-PYRÉNÉES

Arrouach 9 r des Trois Archanges, Quartier Biscaye
☎ 562421143 ▥ 562420507
In pleasant wooded surroundings on N outskirts.
Situated on D947 Soumoulou road.
All year 13HEC ⊞ ♦♠⊙🗑⌀🗑🕀 lau ♦❄✗❄٦LPR

Domec rte de Julos ☎ 0562940879 ▥ 0562940879
Off N21 Tarbes road N of town centre.
Etr-Oct 2.5HEC ⊞ ♦♠❍⌀❍⌀🗑🗑🕀 lau ♦ ❄ ٦PR

LUZ-ST-SAUVEUR HAUTES-PYRÉNÉES

Bergons rte de Barèges ☎ 562929077
In a beautiful setting on a level meadow surrounded by woodland close to the main Pyreneean ski resorts.
600m E on D618 Barèges road.
15 Dec-24 Oct 1HEC ⊞ ♦♠⊙🗑⌀🚋٦R🖹 lau ♦❄♋
✗❄٦P🕀

Pyrénées International rte de Lourdes
☎ 562928202 ▥ 562929687
e-mail: camping.international.luz@wanadoo.fr
In a wooded valley at an altitude of 700mtrs with panoramic views of the surrounding mountains.

⮥ *1.3km NW on N21.*
15 Dec-20 Apr & Jun-Sep 4HEC ⬛ ⚉ 📷 ⛱ ⟈ ✕ ☉ 🗐 🗐 ⛺
⟈ P 🏢 ⊞ lau ➧ ⟈R

Pyrénévasion rte de Luz-Ardiden, Sazos
☎ 562929154 ▤ 562929834
A quiet site in an idyllic mountain setting close to the ski-
runs. The pitches are well defined and all facilities are clean
and modern.
⮥ *2km from town on Luz-Ardiden road.*
All year 2HEC ⬛ ⚉ 📷 ⛱ ✕ ☉ 🗐 🗐 ⛺ 🏢 ⊞ lau ➧ ✕ ⟈R
⊞

▶ MARCILLAC-ST-QUENTIN DORDOGNE

Tailladis ☎ 553591095 ▤ 553294756
e-mail: tailladis@aol.com
Well maintained family site with good recreational facilities.
⮥ *2km N near D48.*
All year 4HEC ⬛ ⚉ 📷 ⛱ ✕ ☉ 🗐 🗐 ⛺ 🏢 ⊞
lau Prices: ⚑4.50 pitch 6.05

▶ MARTRES-TOLOSANE HAUTE-GARONNE

Moulin ☎ 05 561988640 ▤ 561986690
e-mail: info@campinglemoulin.com
In a beautiful wooded location beside the River Garonne at
the foot of the Pyrénées. Well maintained, with a wide variety
of recreational facilities.
⮥ *1.5km SE off N117.*
Etr-Sep 7HEC ⬛ ♠ 📷 ⛱ ☉ 🗐 🗐 ⛺ 🗐 Å ⟈ PR 🏢 🔲 lau
➧ ✕ 🍴 Prices: ⚑3-4 pitch 5-6

▶ MAULÉON-LICHARRE PYRÉNÉES-ATLANTIQUES

Saison rte de Libarrenx ☎ 0559281879 ▤ 559280078
A peaceful site beside the river, near the town centre.
⮥ *1.5km S on D918.*
Apr-Sep 1.1HEC ⬛ ⚉ 📷 ⛱ ✕ ☉ 🗐 🗐 🍴 ⛺ 🗐 ⟈R 🏢 ⊞
lau ➧ ✕ 🍴P Prices: ⚑2.88-3.20 ➧1.09-1.22 pitch 3.31-3.68

▶ MESSANGES LANDES

Côte rte de Vieux Boucau ☎ 558489494 ▤ 558489444
e-mail: lacote@wanadoo.fr
In a picturesque wooded area 1km from the beach.
⮥ *2.3km S via D652.*
Apr-Sep 4HEC ⬛ ⚉ 📷 ⛱ ☉ 🗐 🗐 ⛺ 🏢 ⊞ lau ➧ ✕ ∅
⟈LS Prices: ⚑2.30-2.80

Moïsan rte de la Plage ☎ 558489206 ▤ 558489206
In a pine forest, 800mtrs from the sea with good modern
facilities.
15 May-Sep 7HEC ⬛ ⠿ ♠ 📷 ⛱ ✕ ☉ 🗐 ∅ 🗐 ⛺ 🏢⊞
lau ➧ ⟈PS

Vieux Port Plage Sud ☎ 558482200 ▤ 558480169
e-mail: levieuxport@wanadoo.fr
A family site in the heart of the Landes forest with direct
access to the beach. Good recreational facilities.
⮥ *2.5 km SW via D652.*
Apr-Sep 30HEC ⠿ ♠ 📷 ⛱ ✕ ☉ 🗐 ∅ ⛺ ⟈ PS 🏢 lau
➧ 🍴 ⟈LR ⊞

▶ MÉZOS LANDES

Sen Yan ☎ 558426005 ▤ 558426456
e-mail: reception@sen-yan.com
A pleasant site in exotic tropical gardens, surrounded by a
pine wood.
⮥ *1km E*
15 Jun-15 Sep 8HEC ⬛ ⠿ ⚉ 📷 ⛱ ✕ ☉ 🗐 ∅ 🍴 ⟈ PRS
🏢 🔲 ⊞ lau ➧ 🗐 Prices: pitch 22.56-27.14 (incl 2 persons)

▶ MIERS LOT

Pigeonnier ☎ 05 0565337195 ▤ 0565337195
e-mail: veronique_bouny@wanadoo.fr
Peaceful, shady site close to the River Dordogne amid some
of France's most spectacular scenery.
⮥ *400m E via D91.*
Apr-15 Oct 1HEC ⬛ ♠ 📷 ⛱ ✕ ☉ 🗐 🗐 🍴 ⛺ 🗐 ⟈ P 🏢 lau
➧ ⛱ ✕

▶ MIMIZAN LANDES

At MIMIZAN-PLAGE(6km E by D626)

Marina ☎ 558091266 ▤ 558091640
e-mail: contact@clubmarina.com
In a pinewood. 500m from beach.
⮥ *Take D626 from Mimizan Plage.*
15 May-15 Sep 9HEC ⠿ ⚉ 📷 ⛱ ✕ ☉ 🗐 ∅ 🗐 Å ⟈ P 🏢
lau ➧ ⟈RS
See advertisement in colour section

▶ MIRANDOL TARN

Clots Les Clots ☎ 563769278 ▤ 563769278
e-mail: campclots@wanadoo.fr
In a wooded area within the Viaur Valley with good facilities.
⮥ *5.5km N via D905, rte de Rieupeyroux.*
May-Sep 7HEC ⬛ ♠ 📷 ⛱ ☉ 🗐 ∅ 🗐 ⛺ ⟈ PR 🏢 lau
Prices: ⚑4 ➧1.30

▶ MIREPOIX GERS

Mousquetaires ☎ 562643366 ▤ 562643356
e-mail: camping.des.mousquetaires@wanadoo.fr
Situated on a hill in the heart of Gascony.
⮥ *2km SE.*
Jul-15 Sep 1HEC ⬛ ⚉ 📷 ⛱ ✕ ☉ 🗐 ⛺ Å ⟈ LP 🏢 ⊞ lau

▶ MOLIÈRES DORDOGNE

Grande Veyière ☎ 553632584 ▤ 553631825
e-mail: la_grande_veyiere@wanadoo.fr
Wooded site with good sporting facilities in the heart of
Périgord's Bastides country.
⮥ *2.4km SE.*
Apr-5 Nov 4HEC ⬛ ⚉ ♠ 📷 ⛱ ✕ ☉ 🗐 ∅ ⛺ 🗐
⟈ P 🏢 lau

▶ MOLIÈRES TARN-ET-GARONNE

Les Amis du Lac du Malivert Centre de Loisirs du Malivert
☎ 0563677637 ▤ 05636766217
e-mail: molieres.82@wanadoo.fr
In a pleasant lakeside setting.
⮥ *Approaching Molières from the south, head towards Centre
de Loisirs and Lac Malivert.*
Jul-Aug 0.7HEC ⬛ ⚉ ☉ 🗐 🗐 ⟈ L 🏢 lau ➧ ⛱ ✕ ⊞
Prices: ⚑2 ➧3-4.50 pitch 2.50

▶ MOLIETS-PLAGE LANDES

Airotel St-Martin av de l'Océan ☎ 558485230 ▤ 558485073
e-mail: camping.airotel-saint-martin@wanadoo.fr
Large site on the Atlantic coast with direct access to the
largest sandy beach in the region.
⮥ *Between the village and the beach.*
Etr-mid Oct 18.5HEC ⬛ ⠿ ⚉ 📷 ⛱ ✕ ☉ 🗐 ∅ ⛺ ⟈ P 🏢
lau ➧ 🗐 ⟈S ⊞

Cigales av de l'Océan ☎ 558485118 ▤ 558483527
e-mail: camping-les-cigales@wanadoo.fr
On undulating ground in pine trees.
⮥ *300m from beach.*
Apr-Sep 23HEC ⬛ ♠ 📷 ⛱ ✕ ☉ 🗐 ∅ 🗐 ⛺ 🗐 🏢 ⊞
lau ➧ ⟈LRS

MONCRABEAU LOT-ET-GARONNE

CM Mouliat 'Le Nouliat' ☎ 553654328 ▤ 553652178
A small site in a wooded location on the banks of the River
La Baïse.
➲ *On D219, 200m from D930.*
15Jun-15Sep 1.3HEC ⸗ ♠♟⊙🅟🅟🔄⊞ lau ➡🛁🍽✕
⚡PR

MONTAUBAN-DE-LUCHON HAUTE-GARONNE

Lanette ☎ 561790038
On gently sloping ground surrounded by pastures.
➲ *1.5km E of Luchon. Off D27.*
All year 4.3HEC ⸗ ⚡♟🛁🍽✕⊙🅟⌀🚿🏠🅟🔄⊞ lau ➡
⚡PR

MONTESQUIOU GERS

Château le Haget ☎ 562709580 ▤ 562709483
e-mail: info@lehaget.com
In grounds of Château.
Apr-Oct 12HEC ⸗ ♠♟🛁🍽✕⊙🅟⌀🚿🏠🅟⚡P🔄⊞
lau ➡ ⚡LR

MUSSIDAN DORDOGNE

CM Le Port ☎ 553812009
15 Jun-15 Sep 0.5HEC ⸗ ♠♟⊙🅟🔄⊞ lau ➡🛁🍽✕ ⚡PR
Prices: ⚡2.29 pitch 0.91-1.83

NAGES TARN

Rieu Montagné Lac du Laouzas ☎ 563374052
In a wooded location beside the Laouzas lake with good
recreational facilities.
➲ *4.5km S via D62*
15 Mar-15 Nov 4HEC ⸗ ♠♟🛁🍽✕⊙🅟⌀🚿🏠⚡P🅟
⊞ lau ➡ ⚡L Prices: pitch 21.50-24.50 (incl 2 persons)

OLORON-STE-MARIE PYRÉNÉES-ATLANTIQUES

Val du Gave-d'Aspe rte du Somport, Guermençon
☎ 559360507 ▤ 559360052
e-mail: chalet-aspe@wanadoo.fr
A pleasant site situated in the Aspe Valley amid picturesque
Pyrenean scenery.
All year 0.5HEC ⸗ ♠♟🍽⊙🅟🏠⚡P🅟⊞ lau
➡✕🚿 ⚡R

ONDRES LANDES

Lou Pignada av de la Plage ☎ 559453045
In a forest 3 minutes walk from the sea.
➲ *Turn off the N10 in the village onto rte de la Plage.*
Apr-20 Sep 2HEC ⸗ ☼ ♠♟🛁🍽✕⊙🅟🚿🏠🅟⚡P🔄
⊞ lau ➡⌀ ⚡LRS

ONESSE-ET-LAHARIE LANDES

CM Bienvenu 259 route de Mimizan
☎ 558073049 ▤ 558073078
A family site situated within a forest.
➲ *500m from village centre on D38.*
15 Jun-15 Sep 1.2HEC ⸗ ⚡♟✕⊙🅟🅟🔄⊞ lau ➡🛁
✕ ⚡R

OUSSE PYRÉNÉES-ATLANTIQUES

Sapins ☎ 559817421
➲ *Access via N117, exit 'Pau' or A64, exit Soumoulou.*
All year 1HEC ⸗ ⚡♟🛁🍽✕⊙🅟🅟🔄⊞ lau ➡🛁✕
Prices: ⚡3 pitch 3.50

PADIRAC LOT

Chênes rte du Gouffre ☎ 565336554 ▤ 0565337155
In a fine position in the centre of the Haute-Quercy with
good facilities.
➲ *1.5km NE via D90 towards Gouffre.*
May-Sep 5HEC ⸗ ♠♟🛁🍽✕⊙🅟⌀🚿🏠🅟🏕⚡P🔄⊞
lau

PAMIERS ARIÈGE

Ombrages rte d'Escosse ☎ 561671224
A pleasant site in wooded surroundings beside the River
Ariège, 1.5km from the town centre.
➲ *NW on D119 beside river.*
All year 2.5HEC ⸗ ♠♟🛁🍽✕⊙🅟⌀🚿🅟🔄⊞ lau ➡
⚡PR Prices: ⚡10 ➡6 🅟10 🏕10

PAUILLAC GIRONDE

CM Les Gabarreys rte de la Rivière
☎ 556591003 ▤ 556733068
e-mail: camping.les.gabarreys@wanadoo.fr
A municipal site with good sports facilities.
➲ *S of town. Follow signposts.*
3 Apr-10 Oct 2HEC ⸗ ⌀♠♟⊙🅟🏠 lau ➡🛁🍽✕⌀🚿
⚡P⊞ Prices: ⚡7-7.50 🅟10-11

PAYRAC LOT

Panoramic rte de Loupiac ☎ 565379845 ▤ 565379165
e-mail: camping.panoramic@wanadoo.fr
A peaceful family site 5km from the River Dordogne with
good recreational facilities.
➲ *Off N20 N of Payrac.*
All year 1.5HEC ⸗ ♠♟🍽✕⊙🅟🚿🏠🅟🏕🔄⊞ lau ➡🛁
⌀⚡P Prices: ⚡2.20 pitch 3

Pins rte de Cahors ☎ 565379632 ▤ 0565379108
e-mail: info@les-pins-camping.com
A well-managed site, partly in forest, partly on meadowland.
Sheltered from traffic noise.
➲ *S of village off N20.*
Apr-15 Sep 3.5HEC ⸗ ⚡♟🍽✕⊙🅟⌀🏠🅟⚡
P🔄 lau ➡🛁

PÉRIGUEUX DORDOGNE

Barnabé-Plage 80 r des Bains, Boulazac
☎ 553534145 ▤ 553541662
A well appointed site in a wooded park-like location beside
the river.
➲ *Signposted from N89, 2km E of town centre.*
All year 1.5HEC ⸗ ♠♟🍽✕⊙🅟🔄⊞ lau ➡🛁✕ ⚡P

At BOULAZAC(4km SE)

Isle rte de Brive ☎ 553535775
A family site in wooded surroundings.
➲ *3km from Périgueux in the direction of Brive on D5.*
15 May-15 Sep 3HEC ⸗ ⚡♟🍽✕⊙🅟⌀🏠🅟⚡ PR🔄⊞➡
🛁✕⌀

▶ **PETIT-PALAIS** GIRONDE

Pressoir Queyrai Petit-Palais
☎ 557697325 ▤ 557697736
An old farm in the rolling countryside around St-Emilion.
➲ *On N89 Bordeaux-Périgeux road, exit at St-Médard de Guizières & follow signs.*
Apr-Sep 4HEC ⹀ ♣ ⋔ ᛩ ✕ ⊙ ♨ 🅰 ⋏ P 🅿 ⊞ lau Prices:
⚑5.80 pitch 6.80-9.50

▶ **PEZULS** DORDOGNE

Forêt ☎ 553227169 ▤ 553237779
e-mail: camping.laforet@wanadoo.fr
In extensive grounds on the edge of the forest with modern facilities.
➲ *600m off D703. 3km from the village centre.*
Apr-Oct 9HEC ⹀ ◍ ♣ ⋔ ᛩ ᛩ ⊙ ♨ 🅰 � 🚽 ᛩ ⋏ P 🅿 ⊞
lau Prices: ⚑3.80-4.80 pitch 3.50-4.50

▶ **PONT-ST-MAMET** DORDOGNE

Lestaubière Pont-St-Mamet
☎ 553829815 ▤ 553829017
e-mail: lestaubiere@cs.com
Peaceful and secluded site in attractive part of the Dordogne, occupying the former outbuildings and wooded grounds of the adjacent château. Site commands fine views of the surrounding countryside.
➲ *Off N21.*
May-Sep 8HEC ⹀ 🅰 ⋔ ᛩ ᛩ ✕ ⊙ ♨ ᛩ ⋏ LP 🅿 ⊞ lau

▶ **PUYBRUN** LOT

Sole ☎ 565385237 ▤ 565109109
e-mail: la-sole@wanadoo.fr
A well run site in pleasant wooded surroundings with good facilities.
➲ *On D703 leave village in the direction of Bretenoux and take the first turning after the garage.*
Apr-Sep 3HEC ⹀ ♣ ⋔ ᛩ ✕ ⊙ ♨ ᛩ � 🚽 🚽 ᛩ ⋏ P 🅿 ⊞ lau
➡ ᛩ ᛩLR

▶ **PUY-L'ÉVÊQUE** LOT

▶ At **MONTCABRIER**(7 km NW)

Moulin de Laborde ☎ 565246206 ▤ 565365133
e-mail: moulindelaborde@wanadoo.fr
Well equipped site surrounded by woods and hills, in a picturesque valley on the River Thèze.
➲ *NW off D673.*
May-14 Sep 9HEC ⹀ ♣ ⋔ ᛩ ᛩ ✕ ⊙ ♨ ᛩ ⋏ LPR 🅿 ⊞ ⌇
lau ➡ 🚽 Prices: ⚑5.50 pitch 7

▶ **PYLA-SUR-MER** GIRONDE

Dune rte de Biscarrosse ☎ 556227217 ▤ 556227217
e-mail: campingdeladune@wanadoo.fr
A beautifully situated and quiet site partly on terraced sandy fields. Opposite a dune of over 100m in height, which separates the site from the sea.
➲ *Follow the road between Pilat-Plage.*
May-Sep 6HEC ⹁⹁ ♣ ⋔ ᛩ ᛩ ✕ ⊙ ♨ ᛩ 🚽 🚽 ᛩ ⋏ P 🅿 ⊞ lau ➡
⋏S

Forêt rte de Biscarrosse ☎ 556227328 ▤ 556227050
e-mail: camping.foret@wanadoo.fr
A well equipped site surrounded by pine trees and with direct access to the fine sandy beaches at the mouth of the Arcachon Basin. There are good sporting facilities and evening entertainment is provided on a regular basis.
➲ *Access via N250 then D218.*
Apr-Oct 12HEC ⹀ ♣ ⋔ ᛩ ᛩ ✕ ⊙ ♨ ᛩ 🚽 🚽
⋏ PS 🅿 ⊞ lau

Panorama rte de Biscarrosse ☎ 556221044 ▤ 556221012
e-mail: mail@camping-panorama.com
Partially terraced site amongst dunes, on the edge of the 100m high 'Dune de Pyla'. Views of the sea from some pitches.
➲ *On the D218. Signposted.*
May-Sep 15HEC ⹁⹁ ♣ ⋔ ᛩ ᛩ ✕ ⊙ ♨ ᛩ 🚽 🚽 ᛩ 🅰 ⋏ S 🅿 ⊞
lau

Petit Nice rte de Biscarrosse ☎ 556227403 ▤ 556221431
e-mail: camping.petit.nice@wanadoo.fr
Sandy terraced site, mainly suitable for tents; in parts sloping steeply in pine woodland. Paths and standings are strengthened with timber. 220 steps down to the beach.
➲ *6 km S on D218.*
Apr-Sep 5.5HEC ⹀ 🅰 ⋔ ᛩ ᛩ ✕ ⊙ ♨ ᛩ 🚽 🚽 🚽 🅰 ⋏ PS 🅿 ⊞
lau

Pyla rte de Biscarrosse ☎ 556227456
A well equipped family site with good recreational facilities and direct access to the sea.
May-Sep 8HEC ⹀ ⹁⹁ ♣ ⋔ ᛩ ᛩ ✕ ⊙ ♨ ᛩ 🚽 🚽
⋏ PS 🅿 ⊞ lau

▶ **RAUZAN** GIRONDE

Vieux Château Route de par tementale 123
☎ 557841538 ▤ 557841834
e-mail: hoekstra.camping@wanadoo.fr
A family site situated in a peaceful valley surrounded by vineyards and overlooked by the ruined 12th century Rauzan castle.
➲ *200mtrs N, 1500mtrs from N670.*
Apr-Oct 2.5HEC ⹀ 🅰 ⋔ ᛩ ᛩ ✕ ⊙ ♨ ᛩ 🚽 🚽 🚽 ᛩ ⋏ P 🅿 lau
Prices: ⚑3.66 pitch 4.88

▶ **REYREVIGNES** LOT

Papillon ☎ 565401240 ▤ 565401718
e-mail: domaine.papillon@wanadoo.fr
In a wooded park in the heart of the Haut-Quercy region with good, modern facilities.
➲ *Access via N653.*
Apr-Nov 3HEC ⹀ 🅰 ⋔ ᛩ ᛩ ✕ ⊙ ♨ ᛩ 🚽 🚽 ᛩ ⋏ P 🅿 ⊞ lau ➡
🚽 ᛩLR

▶ **ROCAMADOUR** LOT

Cigales ☎ 565336444 ▤ 565336960
e-mail: camping.cigales@wanadoo.fr
A peaceful, well equipped site with shaded pitches and good, modern facilities. Fine views of Rocamadour.
24 Jun-01Sep 3HEC ⹀ 🅰 ⋔ ᛩ ᛩ ✕ ⊙ ♨ ᛩ 🚽 🚽 ᛩ ⋏ P 🅿 🅿
⊞ lau

Relais du Campeur l'Hospitalet ☎ 565336328
Shady, level site with well marked pitches and good facilities.
Fine views of Rocamadour.
➲ *On D36.*
Apr-Sep 1.7HEC ▩ ⚐♠☏▣☺☺⊘☕ ⚡ P 🏕⊞ lau ➤✕🚿

▶ **ROCHE-CHALAIS, LA** DORDOGNE

Gerbes r de la Dronne ☎ 0553914065 ▤ 0553903201
Well appointed family site on banks of River Dronne.
➲ *Off D674 in village centre. Signposted.*
Apr-Oct 3.5HEC ▩ ♠☏☺☺⚡R🏕⊞ lau ➤☏♥✕⊘🚿
⚡P Prices: 🛏1.98 pitch 2.44 (incl 2 persons)

▶ **ROMIEU, LA** GERS

Camp de Florence ☎ 0562281558 ▤ 0562282004
e-mail: info@campdeflorence.com
Well equipped site in rural surroundings.
➲ *Take D931 in direction Agen-Condom. 3km before Condom turn left to La Romieu.*
Apr-Oct 15HEC ▩ ⚐♠☏♥✕☺☺☕🏠Å⚡ P 🏕⊞ lau ➤☏
Prices: pitch 10.40-20.20 (incl 2 persons)

▶ **ROQUEFORT** LANDES

CM de Nauton Cité Nauton ☎ 558455046 ▤ 558455363
A small municipal site with good facilities.
➲ *1.6km N via D932 towards Bordeaux.*
Jun-Sep 1.4HEC ▩ ♠☏☺☺🏕⊞➤☏♥✕⚡PR
Prices: 🛏12.13 🚐3.05 ▲2.44

▶ **ROQUELAURE** GERS

Talouch ☎ 562655243 ▤ 562655368
e-mail: info@camping-talouch.com
A family site in picturesque wooded surroundings, situated in the heart of Gascony. There are fine sports and entertainment facilities.
➲ *Access via N21 and D148.*
Apr-Sep 9HEC ▩ ♠☏♥☏♥✕☺☺⊘🏠Å⚡ P 🏕⊞ lau

▶ **ROUFFIGNAC** DORDOGNE

Cantegrel ☎ 553054830 ▤ 553054067
In a peaceful location in the heart of the Périgord Noir, with good recreational facilities.
➲ *1.5km N via D31, rte de Thenon.*
Apr-15 Oct 45HEC ▩ ⚐♠☏♥✕☺☺⊘🚿🏠🚐⚡P🏕
⊞ lau

▶ **SADIRAC** GIRONDE

Bel Air ☎ 556230190 ▤ 556230838
e-mail: info@camping-bel-air.com
A well equipped, roomy site on a level meadow shaded by tall trees.
➲ *1 mile W of Créon on D671.*
All year 2HEC ▩ ⚐♠☏♥✕☺☺⊘🚐⚡ P 🏕⊞
Prices: 🛏2.59 🚗1.52 pitch 4.57

▶ **ST-ANTOINE-DE-BREUILH** DORDOGNE

CM St-Aulaye St Aulaye ☎ 553248280 ▤ 553248280
e-mail: info@la-riviere-fleurie.com
➲ *Access via D936. Take a right turn before the village and travel 3kms in the direction of the Dordogne.*
Apr-Sep 2.4HEC ▩ ♠☏♥✕☺☺☕🏠🚐⚡PR🏕⊞
lau Prices: 🛏3.05-20 🚗1.52-10 pitch 10.67-70

▶ **ST-ANTONIN-NOBLE-VAL** TARN-ET-GARONNE

Trois Cantons ☎ 563319857 ▤ 563312593
e-mail: info@3cantons.fr
Divided into pitches, partly on sloping ground within an oak forest. Separate section for teenagers.
➲ *8.5km NW near D926. Signposted.*
15 Apr-Sep 5HEC ▨ ⚐♠☏♥✕☺☺⊘🏠🚐⚡ P 🏕⊞ lau

▶ **ST-BERTRAND-DE-COMMINGES** HAUTE-GARONNE

Es Pibous chemin de St-Just ☎ 561883142 ▤ 561956383
A quiet, shaded site in an elevated position with good facilities.
15 Mar-Oct 1.8HEC ▩ ♠☏☏♥☺☺⊘🏠🚐🏕 lau ➤♥☏✕
🚿 ⚡R Prices: 🛏2.50 pitch 3.50

▶ **ST-CÉRÉ** LOT

CM de Soulhol quai A-Salesse ☎ 565381237
A family site bordered by two rivers with good recreational facilities.
➲ *200m SE on D940.*
Apr-Sep 3.5HEC ▩ ♠☏♥☺☺⊘🏠⚡R🏕⊞ lau ➤☏✕
⊘🚿⚡P

▶ **ST-CIRQ** DORDOGNE

Brin d'Amour Saint Cirq ☎ 553072373 ▤ 553072373
In a fine location overlooking the Vézère Valley with good facilities.
All year 3.8HEC ▩ ♠☏♥☏✕☺☺☕🏠🚐⚡ P 🏕⊞ lau ➤
☏♥✕⊘🚿⚡R Prices: 🛏3.10-3.90 ▲3.10-3.90 pitch 3.90-4.60

▶ **ST-CIRQ-LAPOPIE** LOT

Plage ☎ 565302951 ▤ 565302333
e-mail: camping.laplage@wanadoo.fr
In an ideal location beside the River Lot with well defined pitches and good, modern facilities. Boat and bicycle hire available.
➲ *Access via D41 from N or D42 from S.*
All year 3HEC ▩ ♠☏♥✕☺☺⊘🚿🏠🚐
⚡R🏕⊞ lau ➤☏

▶ **ST-CRICQ** GERS

Lac de Thoux ☎ 562657129 ▤ 562657481
e-mail: lacdethoux@cacg.fr
A family site with good facilities situated on the edge of the lake, 50mtrs from the beach.
➲ *On D654 between Cologne and L'Isle Jourdain.*
Apr-15 Oct 3HEC ▩ ⚐♠☏♥✕☺☺⊘🚿🏠🚐🚐Å
⚡LP🏕⊞ lau

▶ **ST-CYBRANET** DORDOGNE

Bel Ombrage ☎ 553283414 ▤ 553596464
Quiet holiday site in wooded valley.
Jun-5 Sep 6HEC ▩ ♠☏☺☺⚡PR🏕⊞ lau
➤☏♥✕⊘🚿

▶ **ST-CYPRIEN** DORDOGNE

Ferme de Campagnac Castels ☎ 553292603 ▤ 553292603
e-mail: maboureau@libertysurf.fr
A quiet site situated 200mtrs from the farm in a sheltered position.
➲ *Access from town on D25. Signposted*
Apr-Oct 0.8HEC ▩ ♠☏☺☺🏕 lau ➤☏♥☏✕⊘⚡⊞
Prices: 🛏1.50 pitch 5

CM Garrit ☎ 553292056 ▤ 553292056
e-mail: pbecheau@aol.com
In a peaceful location beside the River Dordogne with safe bathing.
➲ *1.5km S on D48.*
Apr-Sep 2HEC ▩ ♠☏♥✕☺☺⊘🏠🚐⚡PR🏕⊞ lau ➤
⊘🚿⚡R

Plage Vezac ☎ 553295083
Modest but attractive site in a pleasant riverside setting.
➲ *Access via D703 beyond La Roque Gageac.*
Apr-Sep 3.5HEC ▩ ⚐♠☏♥☺☺⊘☕⚡R🏕⊞ lau ➤
✕ Prices: 🛏2.74-3.20 🚗1.37-1.52 🚐1 pitch 1.37-1.83

ST-ÉMILION GIRONDE

Barbanne route de Montagne ☎ 557247580 ▤ 57246968
e-mail: barbanne@wanadoo.fr
In a peaceful country setting among vineyards, close to a 12 acre lake.
➲ *3km N via D122.*
Apr-Sep 10HEC ▧ ⌁ ⌂ ⚑ ✕ ⊙ ◘ ⌀ ♨ ⚡ LPR ⌑ ⊞ lau
Prices: ⋔3.50-5.50 pitch 5.50-7

ST-GENIES DORDOGNE

Bouquerie ☎ 553289822 ▤ 553291975
e-mail: labouquerie@wanadoo.fr
A family site in wooded surroundings with a good variety of facilities.
➲ *N of village on D704.*
15 May-15 Sep 8HEC ▧ ⚑ ⌂ ⚑ ⚑ ✕ ⊙ ◘ ⌀ ♨ ⚡ ⚡ P ⌑ ⊞ lau

ST-GIRONS ARIÈGE

Pont du Nert rte de Lacourt (D33) ☎ 561665848
e-mail: dmmadre@aol.com
Grassy site between road and woodland.
➲ *Approx 3km SE at the junction of the D33 and the D3.*
1 Jun-15 Sep 1.5HEC ▧ ⚑ ⌂ ⊙ ◘ ⌑ ⚑ ⌀ ⚡R **Prices:** ⋔13 pitch 2

ST-JEAN-DE-LUZ PYRÉNÉES-ATLANTIQUES

Atlantica Quartier Acotz ☎ 559477244 ▤ 559547227
e-mail: camping@club-internet.fr
A family site with good facilities close to the Spanish border at the foot of the Pyrénées and only 500mtrs from the beach.
➲ *Leave N10 at St-Jean-de-Luz Nord exit and continue towards Biarritz. Site 1km on left.*
15 Mar-15 Oct 3.5HEC ▧ ⌁ ⌂ ⚑ ⚑ ✕ ⊙ ◘ ⌀ ♨ ⚑ ⚡ P ⌑ ⊞ lau ⚡ ⚡S

International d'Erromardie ☎ 559263426 ▤ 559512602
Site is situated by the sea and consists of several sections divided by roads and low hedges. Take away food.
➲ *If approached from N to N10, cross railway bridge and turn immediately right and follow signs.*
15 Mar-15 Oct 2HEC ▧ ⌁ ⌂ ⚑ ✕ ⊙ ◘ ♨ ⚑ ⚡ RS ⌑ ⊞ lau ⚡ ⌀

Iratzia ☎ 559261489
➲ *1km NE off N10. Leave autoroute, signed St-Jean-de-Luz Nord and follow directions for Plage d'Erromardie.*
15 Mar-Sep 4HEC ▧ ⚑ ⌂ ⚑ ⚑ ✕ ⊙ ◘ ⌀ ♨ ⌑ ⊞ lau ⚡ ⚡S

Tamaris Plage quartier d'Acotz ☎ 559265590 ▤ 559477015
e-mail: tamaris@clubinternet.fr
Level family site with good facilities divided into sections by drives and hedges.
➲ *Signposted from N10 towards the sea.*
Apr-Sep 1.2HEC ▧ ⌁ ⌂ ⊙ ◘ ♨ ⚑ ⌑ lau ⚡ ⚑ ⚑ ✕ ⌀ ♨
⚡S ⊞ **Prices:** ⋔3-5 ⚑2.30-2.30 pitch 20-27 (incl 2 persons)

At SOCOA(3km SW)

Juantcho rte de la Corniche ☎ 0559471197 ▤ 0559471197
➲ *2km W on D912.*
10 Apr-30 Sep 6HEC ▧ ⌁ ⌂ ⊙ ◘ ♨ ⌑ ⌑ ⚑ lau ⚡ ⚑ ⚑ ✕ ♨
⚡RS ⊞

ST-JEAN-PIED-DE-PORT PYRÉNÉES-ATLANTIQUES

Narbaïtz rte de Bayonne, Ascarat ☎ 559371013 ▤ 559372142
e-mail: camping-narbaitz@wanadoo.fr
A quiet, comfortable site beside the River Berroua.
➲ *2km NW towards Bayonne.*
15 Mar-30 Sept 2.5HEC ▧ ⚑ ⌂ ✕ ⊙ ◘ ⌀ ♨ ⚡ PR ⌑ lau ⚑ ⚑ ⚑ ♨ **Prices:** pitch 10.37-12.04 (incl 2 persons)

ST-JULIEN-EN-BORN LANDES

Lette Fleurie ☎ 558428008 ▤ 558424151
e-mail: mairie40170@wanadoo.fr
On undulating ground in a pine wood with good facilities, 5 minutes from the beach.
Apr-Sep 18HEC ⸬⸬⸬ ⚑ ⌂ ⚑ ⚑ ✕ ⊙ ◘ ⌀ ♨ ⚑
⚡ P ⌑ ⊞ lau ⚡ ⚡R

ST-JUSTIN LANDES

Pin rte de Roquefort ☎ 558448891 ▤ 358448891
A quiet family site beside the lake. Bar and café open May to 15 September only.
➲ *2.3km N on D626.*
Apr-30 Oct 3HEC ▧ ⸬⸬⸬ ⚑ ⌂ ✕ ⊙ ◘ ⚑ ♨ ⚡ P ⌑ ⊞ lau ⚑ ⚑

ST-LÉON-SUR-VÉZÈRE DORDOGNE

Paradis ☎ 553507264 ▤ 553507590
e-mail: leparadis@perigold.com
Situated on the river bank in the picturesque Vézère valley.
➲ *S of village off D706 Les Éyzies road.*
23 Mar-25 Oct 7HEC ▧ ⌁ ⌂ ⚑ ⚑ ✕ ⊙ ◘ ⌀ ♨ ⚑ ⚡
PR ⌑ ⊞ lau **Prices:** ⋔4.31-6.17 pitch 6.72-9.60

At TURSAC(7km SW)

Pigeonnier ☎ 553069690 ▤ 553069690
A small, peaceful site in the heart of the Dordogne countryside.
➲ *Acces via D706 between Le Moustier and Les Éyzies.*
Jun-Sep 1.1HEC ▧ ⚑ ⌂ ⚑ ⚑ ✕ ⊙ ◘ ⌀ ♨ ⚡ P ⌑ ⊞ lau ⚑
✕ ⚡R **Prices:** ⋔3.51 pitch 3.81

Vézère Périgord ☎ 553069631 ▤ 553067966
A well equipped site in wooded surroundings close to the river.
➲ *0.8km NE on D706.*
Mid Apr-mid Oct 5HEC ▧ ⌁ ⌂ ⚑ ⚑ ✕ ⊙ ◘ ♨ ⚑ ⚡ P ⌑
⊞ lau ⚑ ⌀ ⚡R **Prices:** ⋔3-5 pitch 5

ST-MARTIN-DE-SEIGNANX LANDES

Lou P'tit Poun ☎ 559565579 ▤ 559565371
e-mail: ptitpoun@club-internet.fr
A quiet site with well defined pitches on terraces.
➲ *Access via A63 exit Bayonne Nord towards Pau.*
15 Jun-15 Sep 7HEC ▧ ⌁ ⌂ ⚑ ✕ ⊙ ◘ ♨ ⚑ ⚑ ⚑ ⚑ ⚡ P ⌑
▣ lau

ST-MARTORY HAUTE-GARONNE

CM rte de St-Girons ☎ 561902224
All year ▧ ⌁ ⌂ ⊙ ◘ ⌑ ⊞ lau ⚑ ⚑ ✕ ⌀ ♨ ⚡R

ST-NICOLAS-DE-LA-GRAVE TARN-ET-GARONNE

Plan d'Eau Base de Plein Air, et de Loisirs
☎ 563955002 ▤ 563955001
➲ *2.5km N via D15.*
15 Jun-15 Sep 1.5HEC ▧ ⚑ ⌂ ⊙ ◘ ⚑ ⌑ lau ⚑ ⚑ ✕ ⚡LPR
⊞

ST-PARDOUX-LA-RIVIÈRE DORDOGNE

⌂Château le Verdoyer ☎ 553569464 ▤ 553563870
e-mail: chateau@verdoyer.fr
A small, well equipped site in the grounds of a restored castle.
➲ *3km N via D96.*
May-Sep 17HEC ▧ ⌁ ⌂ ⚑ ⚑ ✕ ⊙ ◘ ⌀ ♨ ⚑ ⚑
⚡ LP ⌑ ⊞ lau

In a wooded and hilly park of 13 ha. with fishing pond, swimming pool, and bordered by a quiet and pleasant river: the Eyre, for family outings in canoe. Numerous animations, familiar atmosphere but also peace, rest and cleanliness assured by our friendly team.

Open from 01/03 till 31/10.

8, route du Minoy - 33770 SALLES
Tel: 05 56 88 47 03
Fax: 05 56 88 47 27

RENTS: Mobil-homes and chalets in the weekend or weekly.

> **ST-PAUL-LES-DAX** LANDES

Pins du Soleil RD459 ☎ 558913791 ▤ 558910024
e-mail: pinsoleil@aol.com
On a hotel complex with good modern facilities.
➲ *SW via D954.*
7 Apr-27 Oct 6HEC ⟡ ♦ ⋔ ☜ ♉ ✕ ⊙ ⛱ ⍟ ⌂ ⛺
⟁ P 🅿 lau ➧ ✕ ⍟ ⛱ ⟁LR

> **ST-PÉE-SUR-NIVELLE** PYRÉNÉES-ATLANTIQUES

Goyetchea ☎ 559541959 ▤ 559541939
e-mail: c.goyetchea@wanadoo.fr
Quiet, peaceful site in a wooded location at the foot of the Pyrénées.
➲ *0.8km N on rte d'Ahetze.*
Jun-25 Sep 3HEC ⟡ ⋔ ☜ ✕ ⊙ ⛱ ⍟ ⛺ ⛽ ⟁ P 🅿 🅷 lau
➧ ♉ ✕ ⛱ ⟁R Prices: ⚑2-3.50 ⛟11.50-16
pitch 7.50-9 (incl 2 persons)

> **At IBARRON**(2km W)

Ibarron ☎ 0559541043
e-mail: campingibarron@wanadoo.fr
In a pleasant wooded location with level pitches and good, modern facilities.
➲ *2km W on D918.*
15 May-20 Sep 2.8HEC ⟡ ⋔ ☜ ⊙ ⛱ ⍟ ⛺ ⛽ 🅿 🅷 lau
➧ ♉ ✕ ⍟ ⛱ ⟁LPR Prices: ⚑3.10-3.50 pitch 4.51-5.19

> **ST-PIERRE-LAFEUILLE** LOT

Graves ☎ 565368312 ▤ 565368312
On a small hill on the northern outskirts of the village providing fine views over the surrounding countryside.
➲ *10km N of Cahors.*
Apr-15 Oct 1HEC ⟡ ⋔ ✕ ⊙ ⛱ ⛽ ⟁ P 🅿 lau ➧ ♉ ✕ ⍟ ⛱

Quercy-Vacances Le Mas de Lacombe
☎ 565368715 ▤ 565368715
A well equipped site in pleasant wooded surroundings.
➲ *On N20. 12km N of Cahors.*
May-Sep 3HEC ⟡ ⋔ ☜ ♉ ✕ ⊙ ⛱ ⍟ ⟁ P 🅿 🅷 lau

> **ST-RÉMY-SUR-LIDOIRE** DORDOGNE

Tuilière ☎ 553824729 ▤ 553824729
e-mail: la-tuiliere@wanadoo.fr
In pleasant wooded surroundings beside a lake. Separate car park for arrivals after 22.00hrs.
➲ *6km from Montpon on D708 towards Ste-Foy-la-Grande.*
Jun-15 Sep 8HEC ⟡ ♦ ⋔ ♉ ✕ ⊙ ⛱ ⍟ ⛺ ⛽ ⟁ LP 🅿
🅷 lau Prices: ⚑2.48-3.10 pitch 3.60-4.50

> **ST-SEURIN-DE-PRATS** DORDOGNE

Plage ☎ 553586107 ▤ 553586267
e-mail: campdelaplage@aol.com
In a peaceful, wooded setting beside the Dordogne with a variety of recreational facilities.
➲ *0.7kms on D11.*
26 May-20 Sep 3.9HEC ⟡ ♦ ⋔ ☜ ♉ ✕ ⊙ ⛱ ⍟ ⟁ PR 🅿 lau
➧ ⍟ ⛱ 🅷

> **STE-EULALIE-EN-BORN** LANDES

Bruyères chemin Laffont ☎ 558097336 ▤ 558097558
e-mail: camping.bruyeres@netclic.fr
In the middle of the Landes forest close to the lakes and the sea.
➲ *2.5km N via D652.*
May-Sep 3HEC ⟡ ♦ ⋔ ☜ ♉ ✕ ⊙ ⛱ ⍟ ⛺ ⛽ ⟁ P 🅿 🅷
lau ➧ ⟁LR

> **SALIGNAC** DORDOGNE

'Les Peneyrals' Le Poujol, St-Crépin Carlucet
☎ 553288571 ▤ 553288099
e-mail: camping.peneyrals@wanadoo.fr
Quiet site among trees between the Vézère and Dordogne rivers.
➲ *10 km N of Sarlat on D60.*
12 May-15 Sep 12HEC ⟡ ♉ ⋔ ♉ ✕ ⊙ ⛱ ⍟ ⛺ ⛽ ⟁ P
🅿 🅷 lau

> **SALLES** GIRONDE

Val de l'Eyre 8 rte de Minoy ☎ 556884703 ▤ 556884727
e-mail: levaldeleyre@free.fr
A well equipped family site in a pleasant wooded location between the Landes forests and the Bordeaux vineyards.
➲ *SW on D108, rte de Lugos.*
Mar-Oct 13HEC ⋮⋮⋮ ⟡ ⋔ ☜ ✕ ⊙ ⛱ ⍟ ⛌ ⟁ LR 🅿 🅷 lau ➧ ♉
⍟ ⟁P

> **SALLES** LOT-ET-GARONNE

Bastides ☎ 553408309 ▤ 553408176
e-mail: bastides@wanadoo.fr
In peaceful wooded surroundings overlooking the Lède Valley with good sporting and entertainment facilities.
➲ *1km N via D150.*
Etr-Sep 6HEC ⟡ ♦ ⋔ ♉ ✕ ⊙ ⛱ ⍟ ⛺ ⛽ ⟁ P 🅿 🅷
lau Prices: ⚑4-5 pitch 2-2.50

> **SARE** PYRÉNÉES-ATLANTIQUES

Goyenetche rte des Grottes ☎ 559542171
In a peaceful location in a wooded valley close to the Caves of Sare.
➲ *3.5km S via D306.*
15 Jun-15 Sep 1HEC ⟡ ⋔ ⊙ ⛱ ⍟ ⟁ R 🅿 🅷 lau ➧ ♉ ✕

> **SARLAT-LA-CANÉDA** DORDOGNE

Maillac Ste-Nathalène ☎ 05553592212
e-mail: campingmaillac@wanadoo.fr
In wooded surroundings in the heart of the Périgord Noir region with good facilities for a family holiday. Separate park for arrivals after 23.00hrs.
➲ *7km NE on D47.*
15 May-Sep 6HEC ⟡ ♦ ⋔ ☜ ♉ ✕ ⊙ ⛱ ⍟ ⛺ ⛽ ⟁ P 🅿
🅷 lau ➧ ⟁LR Prices: ⚑4.50 pitch 5.50

🏔Moulin du Roch rte des Éyzies
☎ 553592027 ▤ 553592095
e-mail: moulin.du.roch@wanadoo.fr
In a picturesque location between the Dordogne and Vézère valleys.
➲ *10km NW via D704-D6-D47.*
11May-15Sep 8HEC ⟡ ♦ ⋔ ☜ ♉ ✕ ⊙ ⛱ ⍟ ⛌ ⛺ ⟁ P 🅿 🅷
⛲ lau Prices: pitch 12-22 (incl 2 persons)

Périères ☎ 05 553590584 ▤ 553285751
e-mail: les-perieres@wanadoo.fr
Very well kept terraced site situated in 12 acres of parkland and woods in the heart of the Périgord Noir with fine views over the Sarlat valley. There are good recreational facilities and modern, well equipped bungalows are available for hire.
↪ *1km N of town on D47.*
Etr-Sep 11HEC ⸗ ✦🏠🛎🍴✕☉🛒⌀🚻 ⟵ P 🏧⊞ lau

At CARSAC-AILLAC(7km SE via D704A)

Aqua Viva ☎ 553314600 ▤ 553293637
e-mail: aqua-viva@perigord.com
Site with numerous terraces in beautiful wooded surroundings in the heart of the Dordogne.
↪ *Along the main road Sarlat/Souillac D704A*
Etr-Sep 11HEC ⸗ ⋯ 🍴✦🏠🛎🍴✕☉🛒⌀🚻
⟵ LP 🏧⊞ lau

Rocher de la Cave ☎ 553281426 ▤ 553282710
e-mail: rocher.de.le-cave@wanadoo.fr
Pleasant family site on a level meadow beside the Dordogne, set in beautiful countryside.
↪ *Access via D703 & D704.*
May-15 Sep 4HEC ⸗ ⋯ ✦🏠🛎🍴✕☉🛒⌀🚻🅰
⟵ R 🏧⊞ lau

At PROISSANS(6km NE)

Val d'Ussel La Fond d'Ussel
☎ 553592873 ▤ 553293825
e-mail: valdussel@online.fr
A well equipped site in woodland in the heart of the Périgord Noir region. Separate car park for late arrivals.
↪ *Off D704 or D56.*
Jun-15 Sep 7.5HEC ⸗ ✦🏠🛎🍴✕☉🛒⌀🚻🚐🅰 ⟵ P 🏧
lau Prices: 🧍3.50-5.75 pitch 4-7.65

SAUVETERRE-DE-BÉARN PYRÉNÉES-ATLANTIQUES

CM Gave av de la Gare ☎ 559385330
↪ *Turn left before bridge on St-Palais road.*
Jun-Sep 1.5HEC ⸗ 🏠🏪☉🛒⟵ R 🏧⊞ lau ⟵🛎🍴✕⌀🚻

SAUVETERRE-LA-LÉMANCE LOT-ET-GARONNE

Moulin du Périé rte de Loubejac ☎ 553406726
In a wooded valley close to an 18th century watermill with good, modern facilities.
↪ *3km E of town off D710. Follow signposts from the entrance to the village and keep to the valley road.*
Apr-Sept 5HEC ⸗ ✦🏠🛎🍴✕☉🛒⌀🚻🚐🅰
⟵ PR 🏧⊞ lau ⟵🛗L

SEIGNOSSE LANDES

Chevreuils rte de Hossegor
☎ 558433280 ▤ 558433280
e-mail: chevreuils@wanadoo.fr
In a pine forest close to the sea with good recreational facilities.
↪ *On CD79 rte de Hossegor.*
Jun-15 Sep 8HEC ⸗ ⋯ ✦🏠🛎🍴✕☉🛒⌀🚻🚐🚐⟵ P
🏧⊞ lau ⟵🛗S Prices: 🧍3.30-4.71 ⟵1.43-2.04 🚐3.62-5.18 🅰3.62-5.18

CM Hourn Naou av des Tucs
☎ 558433030 ▤ 558416421
e-mail: camping.municipal@ville-seignosse.fr
Very clean and tidy site situated in a pine forest 600mtrs from the sea.
↪ *200mtrs from Seignosse town centre.*
6 Apr-Sep 16HEC ⋯ 🏠🛎🍴✕☉🛒⌀🚐🏧🏧⊞ lau ⟵
🚻⟵LPS

Oyats rte de la Plage des Casennes
☎ 558433794 ▤ 0558432329
Level site, subdivided into fields and surrounded by woodland. Separate section for young people. Children's play area.
↪ *Turn off D79 in N outskirts towards Plage des Casernes.*
15 May-Sep 17HEC ⋯ ✦🏠🛎🍴✕☉🛒⌀🚻🚐🅰⟵ P
🏧⊞ lau ⟵🛗S

At SEIGNOSSE-LE-PENON(5km W)

Forêt ☎ 558416850
A pleasant, quiet site 300m from the sea.
10 Jun-2 Sep 11HEC ⋯ ✦🏠🍴✕☉🛒🚐⟵ P 🏧⊞🚿 lau
⟵🛎⌀🚻🛗S

SEIX ARIÈGE

Haut Salat ☎ 561668178 ▤ 561669417
e-mail: camping.le-haut-salat@wanadoo.fr
Very clean, well kept site beside stream. Big gravel pitches for caravans. Common room with TV.
↪ *0.8km NE on D3.*
All year 2.5HEC ⸗ ✦🏠🛎🍴✕☉🛒⌀🚻⟵ PR 🏧⊞
lau ⟵ ✕ Prices: 🅰12.20 pitch 12.20 (incl 2 persons)

SOUILLAC LOT

🏠Domaine de la Paille Basse ☎ 565378548 ▤ 565370958
e-mail: paille.basse@wanadoo.fr
A family site in a picturesque wooded location in the grounds of a former château.
↪ *6.5km NW off D15 Salignac-Eyvignes road.*
15 May-15 Sep 12HEC ⸗ ✦🏠🛎🍴✕☉🛒⌀🚻⟵ P 🏧
⊞ lau Prices: 🧍5.50 🚐10.50 pitch 8.50

SOULAC-SUR-MER GIRONDE

Océan L'Amélie ☎ 556097610 ▤ 556097475
A level site in a pine forest, 300mtrs from the beach.
↪ *3.5km S.*
Jun-15 Sep 6HEC ⸗ ⋯ 🏠🛎🍴✕☉🛒⌀🚻 lau ⟵
🛗S

Sables d'Argent r de l'Amélie ☎ 556098287 ▤ 556099482
e-mail: camping.sables.d.argent@wanadoo.fr
In a pine forest, bordered by sand dunes with direct access to the beach.
↪ *1.5km SW of village.*
Apr-Sep 2.6HEC ⸗ 🏠🛎🍴✕☉🛒⌀🚻🚐🚐⟵ S
🏧⊞ lau ⟵🛗P

At AMÉLIE-SUR-MER, L'(4.5km S)

Amélie-Plage ☎ 556098727 ▤ 56736426
e-mail: camping.amelie.plage@wanadoo.fr
In hilly wooded terrain. Lovely sandy beach.
↪ *3km S on the Soulac road.*
Apr-Oct 8.5HEC ⸗ ⋯ ✦🏠🛎🍴✕☉🛒⌀🚻🚐🚐⟵ S
🏧⊞ lau

At LILIAN(4.5km S)

Pins ☎ 556098252
Situated in beautiful pine forest close to the beach with plenty of sporting facilities.
↪ *S on D101.*
Jun-Sep 3.2HEC ⋯ ✦🏠🛎☉🛒⌀🚐🏧🏧⊞ lau ⟵🛗S

SOUSTONS LANDES

CM Airial ☎ 558411248 ▤ 558415383
e-mail: camping.airial@libertysurf.fr
Situated in a shady park with plenty of recreational facilities and modern installations.
↪ *2km W on D652.*
01 Apr-30 Sep 12HEC ⸗ ✦🏠🛎🍴✕☉🛒🚐🚐⟵ P 🏧
⊞ lau Prices: ⟵1.07 pitch 4.41

TARASCON-SUR-ARIÈGE ARIÈGE

Pré Lombard rte d'Ussat ☎ 561056194 ▤ 561057893
e-mail: contact@camping-leprelombard.com
In beautiful wooded surroundings beside the River Ariège
with good, modern facilities.
➡ *1.5km SE on D23.*
All year 3.5HEC ⊞ ♦♠♈♊✗⊙☕∅⚒♙♨⚛ PR☎⊞
lau ♦☎ Prices: pitch 13-20 (incl 2 persons)

TEILLET TARN

Relais de l'Entre Deux Lacs
☎ 563557445 ▤ 563557565
e-mail: contact@camping-entredeuxlacs.com
Shady terraced site. Various activities arranged. Beautiful
views.
➡ *Off D81 towards Lacaune.*
All year 4HEC ⊞ ♦♠♈✗⊙☕♙♨⚛ P☎⊞ lau ♦☎∅⚒
⚛LR Prices: pitch 12.55

THIVIERS DORDOGNE

CM Le Repaire ☎ 553526975 ▤ 553526975
In a wooded valley, this well appointed family site lies in the
'Périgord Vert' region of the Dordogne some ten minutes
walk from the ancient village of Thiviers.
➡ *1500mtrs along D707 towards Lanouaille.*
May-Sep 11HEC ⊞ ⚥♠♈⊙☕♙⚛ P☎⊞ lau ♦✗
∅⚒⚛L Prices: ♠3.01-3.81 pitch 3.81-5.33

TONNEINS LOT-ET-GARONNE

CM Robinson ☎ 553790228
➡ *500m from town centre on N113 Agen road.*
Jun-Sep 0.7HEC ⊞ ♦♠⊙☕♙⚛R☎ lau ♦☎♊✗∅⚒
⚛P☎

TOUZAC LOT

Ch'Timi ☎ 565365236 ▤ 565365323
e-mail: info.lechtimi@wanadoo.fr
A well equipped site overlooking the River Lot.
Entertainment available in high season.
➡ *800m from Touzac on D8.*
Apr-Sep 3.5HEC ⊞ ♦♠♈♊✗⊙☕∅♙♨⚛ PR☎⊞
lau Prices: ♠4.25 pitch 5.80

Clos Bouyssac ☎ 565365221 ▤ 565246851
e-mail: camping.leclosbouyssac@wanadoo.fr
On the fringe of a wooded hillside by the sandy shore of the
River Lot. Good for walking.
➡ *S of Touzac on D65.*
May-Sep 5HEC ⊞ ♦♠♈♊✗⊙☕∅♙♨⚛ PR☎⊞ lau

URRUGNE PYRÉNÉES-ATLANTIQUES

Larrouleta ☎ 0559473784 ▤ 0559474254
e-mail: larrouleta@free.fr
Hilly meadow with young trees.
➡ *1.5 km N of Urrugne on N1 to Spain.*
All year ⊞ ♦♠♈♊✗⊙☕♙⚛L☎⊞ lau ♦∅
Prices: ♠3.36-4.28 ♠♠1.52-1.75 pitch 3.96-4.44

URT PYRÉNÉES-ATLANTIQUES

Etche Zahar allée de Mesplès
☎ 559562736 ▤ 559562962
e-mail: camping.etche-zahar@wanadoo.fr
A small, privately owned site in a wooded location and
within easy reach of local tourist areas. Separate car parking
for arrivals between 22.00hrs and 7.00hrs.
➡ *Access via exit 8 on A63 or exit 4 on A64.*
Closed 15-31 Jan 2.5HEC ⊞ ⚥♠♈✗⊙☕∅♙♨⚛
P☎⊞ lau ♦♊✗⚛R Prices: ♠3.50 ♠♠2 pitch 6.50

VALEUIL DORDOGNE

Bas Meygnaud D393 Branttme ☎ 553055844
e-mail: camping-du-bas-meygnaud@wanadoo.fr
A quiet, shady site in the Dronne Valley.
➡ *Access via D939, turning off at Lasserre.*
Apr-Sep 1.7HEC ⊞ ♦♠♈♊✗⊙☕♙♨⚛ P☎⊞ lau
♦⚛R

VARILHES ARIÈGE

CM Parc du Château av du 8 Mai 45 ☎ 561674284
On the banks of the river and close to the town.
➡ *N on N20.*
All year 1HEC ⊞ ♦♠♈⊙☕♨⊞ lau ♦☎♊✗∅♙⚛P

VAYRAC LOT

Domaine de Bourzolles Condat ☎ 565321632
➡ *Off D20 between Condat and Vayrac.*
Jun-15 Sep 4HEC ⊞ ♦♠⊙☕⚛ P☎⊞ lau ♦♊✗∅♙
Prices: ♠2.20 pitch 2.30

VENDAYS-MONTALIVET GIRONDE

Mayan 3 route de Mayan ☎ 556417651
A small site situated in a pine wood.
➡ *Access from Bordeaux direction via N215 and D102.*
Jul-Aug 1HEC ⊞ ⚥♠⊙☕♙♨☎⊞ lau

VERDON-SUR-MER, LE GIRONDE

Royannais 88 rte de Soulac
☎ 556096112 ▤ 556737067
e-mail: camping.le.royannais@wanadoo.fr
Level, sandy terrain under high pine and deciduous trees.
➡ *S of Le Verdon-sur-Mer in Le Royannais district on D1.*
15 Jun-15 Sep 2HEC ⊞ ⚙ ♦♠♈♊✗⊙☕∅♙♨⚛☎
⊞ lau ♦⚛RS

VERGT-DE-BIRON DORDOGNE

Patrasses ☎ 553630587 ▤ 6553248895
Situated in the heart of the Périgord Noir region with good
facilities.
➡ *3.6km S via D2E.*
Jun-Sep 4.7HEC ⊞ ⚥♠♈♊✗⊙☕♙♨♠⚛ P☎⊞ lau

VEYRINES-DE-DOMME DORDOGNE

Pastourels Le Brouillet ☎ 553295249
A quiet site in a pleasant rural setting near the Château des
Milandes.
➡ *3.6km N off D53 towards Belvès.*
Apr-Sep 3.5HEC ⊞ ⚙ ♦♠⊙☕♙♨♠⚛ P☎⊞ lau

VÉZAC DORDOGNE

Deux Vallées ☎ 553295355 ▤ 553310981
e-mail: les2v@perigord.com
A level site in a picturesque location in the Dordogne Valley.
Good facilities for families.
➡ *Access via D57 from Sarlat or D703 from Bergerac.*
All year 3.2HEC ⊞ ♦♠♈♊✗⊙☕∅♙♠⚛ P☎ lau ♦
⚛R Prices: ♠3-5 pitch 4-7

VIELLE-ST-GIRONS LANDES

Col Vert Lac de Léon ☎ 558429406 ▤ 558429188
e-mail: contact@colvert.com
Quiet site on lakeside in sparse pine woodland. Small natural
harbour in the mouth of a stream.
➡ *Turn off D652 on N side of village and continue towards
lake.*
Apr-Sep 30HEC ⊞ ⚙♠♈♊✗⊙☕∅♙⚒♨♠⚛ LP☎
⊞ lau Prices: ♠2-4.50 ♠♠1-2.50

Eurosol rte de la Plage ☎ 558479014 ▤ 558477674
e-mail: contact@camping-eurosol.com
Well maintained family site in a pine forest, 700mtrs from
one of the finest beaches in the country.
➲ *Access via A63 exit Castets.*
11 May-21 Sep 18HEC ▥ ⁙ ♠ ⋔ ⅀ ⅄ ✕ ⊙ ⬛ ∅ ⬛ ⁊ P
⬛ ⊞ lau ➧ ⁊S

VIEUX-BOUCAU-LES-BAINS LANDES

CM des Sablères bd du Marensin ☎ 558481229
A family site with modern facilities and direct access to the
beach.
➲ *Access via N10 and D652.*
Apr-15 Oct 11HEC ▥ ⅄ ⋔ ⊙ ⬛ ⬛ ⊞ lau ➧ ⅀ ⅄ ✕ ∅ ⋈
⁊LS

VIGAN, LE LOT

Rêve Revers ☎ 565412520 ▤ 565416852
e-mail: campingalereve@yahoo.fr
A modern family site in wooded surroundings.
➲ *From Payrac take D673 towards Le Vigan and follow signs.*
25 Apr-23 Sep 8HEC ▥ ⅄ ⋔ ⅀ ⅄ ✕ ⊙ ⬛ ∅ ⬛ ⁊ P ⬛ ⊞
lau Prices: ⋔2.66-3.80 pitch 3.50-5

VILLEFRANCHE-DU-QUEYRAN LOT-ET-GARONNE

Moulin de Campech ☎ 553887243 ▤ 553880652
e-mail: campech@fr.packardbell.org
A beautiful site in a peaceful location beside a small lake
stocked with trout.
➲ *Access via D11 towards Casteljaloux.*
25 Mar-01 Nov 4HEC ▥ ♠ ⋔ ⅀ ⅄ ✕ ⊙ ⬛ ⅄ ⁊ LPR ⬛ ⊞
lau Prices: ⋔3.20-4.50 ⬤5 pitch 6.25-7.85

VILLENAVE-D'ORNON GIRONDE

Gravières 35 ave Mirieu de Labarre ☎ 556870036
➲ *2km NE*
All year 3.5HEC ▥ ⁙ ∅ ♠ ⋔ ⅀ ⅄ ✕ ⊙ ⬛ ∅ ⋈ ⬛ ⬛ ⅄ ⁊
L ⬛ ⊞ lau ➧ ∅

VILLERÉAL LOT-ET-GARONNE

⬛Château de Fonrives Rives ☎ 553366338 ▤ 553360998
e-mail: chateau.de.fontives@wanadoo.fr
In a beautiful natural park in the grounds of a château with
good facilities for all ages.
➲ *2.2km NW via D207*
8 May-18 Sep 20HEC ▥ ⁙ ∅ ♠ ⋔ ⅀ ⅄ ✕ ⊙ ⬛ ∅ ⋈ ⬛
⬛ ⅄ ⁊ LP ⬛ ⊞ lau

VITRAC DORDOGNE

Bouysse Caudon ☎ 553283305 ▤ 553303852
e-mail: la-bouysse.24@wanadoo.fr
Well appointed site in a wooded valley beside the Dordogne.
➲ *2km E, near the River Dordogne.*
Etr-Sep 3HEC ▥ ♠ ⋔ ⅀ ⅄ ✕ ⊙ ⬛ ∅ ⬛ ⁊ PR ⬛ ⊞ lau ➧ ✕
⊞ Prices: ⋔4.90 pitch 6.40

Soleil Plage ☎ 553283333 ▤ 553283024
e-mail: soleil.plage@wanadoo.fr
Set out around an old farmhouse bordering the Dordogne
with excellent facilities.
➲ *4km E on D703, turn by 'Camping Clos Bernard'.*
Apr-Sep 8HEC ▥ ♠ ⋔ ⅀ ⅄ ✕ ⊙ ⬛ ∅ ⬛ ⬛ ⁊ PR ⬛ ⊞ lau
Prices: ⋔4.60-6 pitch 7.50-10.05

The undoubted highlight of this area is the Loire, France's
longest river, which winds its unhurried way through green
valleys, vine-covered hills, meadows, and, of course, past
the remarkable châteaux and medieval citadels which are
masterpieces spanning the changing architectural style of
seven centuries. The western Loire region unites a
countryside of soft hills, little farms and vineyards, and
historic châteaux and abbeys with the sea. North of the
river the coastline meets the Atlantic at rocky cliffs; south of
the river great sandy beaches are backed by pine woods.
Still farther south, the province of Charente-Maritime boasts
sunshine totals to rival the Mediterranean, and 150 miles of
coastline with busy ports, family resorts - both on the
mainland and off-lying islands, and harbours bustling with
colourful life. La Rochelle, with its ancient harbour and fine
old houses, is a popular centre. Inland, there are literally
hundreds of interesting churches and abbeys, and vineyards
whose grapes mature into Cognac. Inland still further, the
region of Limousin is a charming backwater of rolling hills,
with Limoges a fascinating porcelain centre.
....

▶ AIGUILLON-SUR-MER, L' VENDÉE

Bel Air ☎ 251564405 ▤ 251971558
e-mail: camping.belair@wanadoo.fr
A long, level stretch of meadowland in rural surroundings.
➲ *1.5 km NW on D44 then turn left.*
Apr-Sep 7HEC ▥ ⅄ ⋔ ⅀ ⅄ ✕ ⊙ ⬛ ∅ ⋈ ⬛ ⬛ ⅄ ⁊ P ⬛ ⊞
lau ➧ ⁊LRS

▶ AIRVAULT DEUX-SÈVRES

Courte Vallée Courte Vallée ☎ 549647065 ▤ 549647065
e-mail: ccv79@aol.com
A modern site, situated in a river valley, with large pitches
and good facilities.
➲ *On the outskirts of the town, 0.5km NW towards Availles.*
May-Sep 3.5HEC ▥ ⅄ ⋔ ⅀ ⊙ ⬛ ∅ ⬛ ⁊ P ⬛ ⊞ lau ➧ ⅀ ⅄
✕ ∅ ⋈ ⁊P Prices: ⋔3.50 pitch 6.50

▶ ALLONNES MAINE-ET-LOIRE

Pô Doré Le Pô Doré ☎ 241387880 ▤ 241387881
A family site in a pleasant rural setting in the heart of the
Anjou region with good recreational facilities. Separate car
park for arrivals 22.00hrs.
➲ *Access via D35 from Tours or N147 from Angers.*
Apr-Oct 2HEC ▥ ⅄ ⋔ ⅀ ⅄ ✕ ⊙ ⬛ ∅ ⁊ P ⬛ lau Prices:
⋔2.43-2.89 pitch 9.90-12.95 (incl 2 persons)

▶ ANDONVILLE LOIRET

Domaine de la Joullière rte de Richerelles
☎ 238395846 ▤ 238396194
Spread over a series of small, wooded valleys with good
sports and leisure facilities.
➲ *1km E on road to Richerelles.*
May-Oct 10HEC ▥ ⅄ ⋔ ⅀ ⅄ ✕ ⊙ ⬛ ⁊ P ⬛ ⊞ lau

▶ ANGERS MAINE-ET-LOIRE

Lac de Maine av du Lac de Maine
☎ 241730503 ▤ 241730220
e-mail: camping@lacdemaine.fr
In pleasant rural surroundings on the shore of the 100
hectares Lac de Maine. There are fine sporting and
entertainment facilities and the historic town of Angers is
within easy reach.
➲ *Access via A11 (Angers/Nantes) at Lac de Maine exit.*
25 Mar-10 Oct 4HEC ▥ ⁙ ⅄ ⋔ ⅀ ✕ ⊙ ⬛ ∅ ⋈ ⬛ ⁊ P ⬛
lau ➧ ⅀ ⁊LR ⊞

ANGLES VENDÉE

Moncalm-Atlantique ☎ 251975550 🗎 251289109
e-mail: camping-apv@wanadoo.fr
Two distinct sites, but sharing the same recreational facilities in a wooded setting close to the beach.
Apr-Sep 10HEC ⚏ ♠♟☎⚡✗⊙☻⊘🚿♨️🐪🅰🔧LP🅿
lau ➡🔧R⊞

ANGOULINS-SUR-MER CHARENTE-MARITIME

Chirats rte de la Platère ☎ 546569416
Modern site with good facilities 100m from a small sandy beach and providing panoramic views over the Bay of Fouras. The more popular, larger beaches of the area are some 3km away. Reservations are strongly recommended.
➲ *7km S of La Rochelle.*
Apr-Sep 4.5HEC ⚏ ⊕♟☎⚡✗⊙☻⊘🚿♨️🔧S🅿🅿
⊞ lau

ARGENTAT CORRÈZE

Gibanel Le Gibanel ☎ 555281011 🗎 555288162
Pleasant site situated in grounds of a château next to a lake. Some facilities are only available in high season.
➲ *S from Tulle on N120.*
Jun-14 Sep 6.5HEC ⚏ ⊕♟☎⚡✗⊙☻⊘♨️🔧LP🅿⊞
lau ➡♨️ Prices: ⚑3.54-4.42 ⚑3.78-4.73

Saulou Vergnolles ☎ 555281233 🗎 555288067
A peaceful site in a wooded location beside the River Dordogne. Ideal for families.
➲ *6km S on D116.*
Apr-Sep 7.5HEC ⚏ ⊕♟☎⚡✗⊙☻⊘🚿♨️🔧PR🅿⊞
lau Prices: pitch 11.04-17.45 (incl 2 persons)

At MONCEAUX-SUR-DORDOGNE(3km SW)

Vaurette ☎ 555280967 🗎 555288114
e-mail: camping.le.vaurette@wanadoo.fr
On the banks of the River Dordogne with a beach, swimming pool & tennis court.
➲ *On D12 between Argentat and Beaulieu.*
May-21 Sep 4HEC ⚏ ⊕♟☎⚡✗⊙☻⊘🚿♨️🔧PR🅿
lau Prices: ⚑4.30 pitch 13-18.50 (incl 2 persons)

ARGENTON-CHÂTEAU DEUX-SÈVRES

CM du Lac d'Hautibus ☎ 0549659508 🗎 0549657084
➲ *0.4km S on D748.*
Apr-Oct 2.6HEC ⚏ ⊕♟☎⊙☻☻🅿 lau ➡⚡✗⊘♨️
🔧PR ⊞ Prices: ⚑1.70 ⚑1.40 pitch 1.55 pp1

AVRILLÉ VENDÉE

Forges Domaine Les Forges ☎ 251223885
In a pleasant position beside a lake, 300m from the town centre. Close to beach, the site has a variety of leisure facilities.
Etr-end Sep 8HEC ⚏ ⊕♟☎⚡✗⊙☻♨️🐪🔧LP🅿⊞
lau ➡⊘

Mancelières rte de Longeville-sur-Mer
☎ 251903597 🗎 251903931
A pleasant site in a wooded park approx. 5km from the fine beaches of South Vendée. Separate car park for arrivals after 23.00hrs.
➲ *1.7km S via D105 towards Longeville*
Easter-15 Sep 2.6HEC ⚏ ⊕♟☎✗⊙☻⊘♨️🐪🅰🔧P🅿
⊞ lau ➡♟✗ Prices: ⚑3.05 pitch 9.82-14.03 (incl 2 persons)

AZAY-LE-RIDEAU INDRE-ET-LOIRE

Parc du Sabot r du Stade ☎ 247454272 🗎 247454911
Site lies in large meadow on bank of River Indre.
➲ *Near château in town centre.*
Etr-Oct 9HEC ⚏ ♟⊙☻🔧R🅿⊞ lau ➡🔧P

BARDÉCILLE CHARENTE-MARITIME

Ferme de Chez Filleux Arces-sur-Gironde
☎ 546908433 🗎 546069284
On a level meadow partly shaded by trees and bushes with good, modern facilities. 10 minutes from the local beaches.
May-15 Sep 3HEC ⚏ ⊕♟☎⚡✗⊙☻⊘🚿♨️🔧P🅿⊞
lau

BARRE-DE-MONTS, LA VENDÉE

Grande Côte ☎ 0251685189 🗎 0251492557
In pine forest behind dunes with direct access to the beach. Plenty of recreational facilities.
➲ *3 km from village beside Noirmoutier toll bridge.*
7Apr-23Sep 22HEC ⚏⚏⚏ ♠♟☎⚡⊙☻☻🐪🅰🔧P🅿 lau ➡✗
⊘♨️🔧S Prices: ⚑3.05 pitch 8.84-15.50 (incl 2 persons)

BATZ-SUR-MER LOIRE-ATLANTIQUE

Govelle rte de la Côte Sauvage ☎ 240239163
Direct access to the sea. Supervised beach and sea-fishing nearby.
➲ *On D45 between Le Pouliguen and Batz.*
15 Jun-15 Sep 6.8HEC ⚏ ♨️♟✗⊙☻☻🐪🔧S🅿🅿⊞
lau Prices: ⚑4.42 ⚑4.57

BAULE, LA LOIRE-ATLANTIQUE

Ajoncs d'Or chemin du Rocher ☎ 240603329 🗎 240244437
e-mail: contact@ajoncs.com
In a large wooded park, close to the beach with well defined pitches.
➲ *Signposted from the entrance to the town.*
Apr-Sep 6HEC ⚏ ♠♟☎⚡✗⊙☻⊘🚿♨️🐪🔧P🅿⊞
lau ➡🔧S

CM av de Diane ☎ 240601740 🗎 240601148
Site consists of two sections, one for caravans, one for tents, each with separate entrance.
➲ *On NE outskirts near the railway.*
Mar-Oct 5HEC ⚏ ⚏⚏⚏ ♠♟☎⚡✗⊙☻☻🐪🐪⊞⊞🚿
lau ➡🔧PS

Eden St-Servais D.99 ☎ 240600323
In pleasant rural surroundings with good sports and sanitary facilities.
➲ *1km NW via N171 exit 'La Baule-Escoublac'.*
8 Apr-Sep 4.7HEC ⚏ ♠♟☎⚡✗⊙☻⊘🚿♨️🔧LP🅿⊞
lau ➡⊘♨️🔧S

Roseraie 20 av J-Sohier ☎ 240604666 🗎 240601184
e-mail: camping@laroserie.com
A well planned site in wooded surroundings with good recreational facilities.
➲ *E of N171 towards the bay.*
Apr-Sep 5HEC ⚏ ⊕♟☎⚡✗⊙☻⊘🚿♨️🔧P🅿⊞ lau ➡
🔧S Prices: ⚑4.50-5.50 ⚑8-10 🅰8-10 pitch 8-10

BAZOUGES-SUR-LE-LOIR SARTHE

CM rte de Cré-sur-Loir ☎ 243459580 🗎 243453826
On the bank of the River Loir with well defined pitches.
➲ *Approach off A11 towards La Flèche.*
15 May-Oct 0.8HEC ⚏ ⊕♟⊙☻☻🐪🅿⊞ lau ➡♟⚡✗⊘
♨️🔧RS

BEAULIEU-SUR-DORDOGNE CORRÈZE

Îles ☎ 555910265 🗎 555910519
e-mail: jycastanet@aol.com
On an island in the River Dordogne, within easy reach of all facilities.
May-Sep 4HEC ⚏ ⚏⚏⚏ ♠♟⊙☻☻🐪🔧R🅿⊞ lau ➡
♟⊘🔧P

▶ **BESSINES-SUR-GARTEMPE** HAUTE-VIENNE
▶ At **MORTEROLLES-SUR-SEMME**(4.5km N on N20)
CM ☎ 555766018
➲ *100m from N20; in town centre.*
All year 8HEC ▦ ⚬ ↑ ⊙ ⚑ ⊞ lau ➡ ♀ ✕ ∅ ₹R ⊞

▶ **BEYNAT** CORRÈZE
Étang de Miel ☎ 555855066 ▤ 0555855796
e-mail: camping.lac.de.miel@wanadoo.fr
A family site in a picturesque wooded setting close to the lake
within the 'Green Valley'.
➲ *4km E on N121 Argentat road.*
Apr-Oct 9HEC ▦ ⚬ ↑ ♀ ♀ ✕ ⊙ ⚑ ∅ ⊞ ⚑
₹ LPR ⊞ lau

▶ **BIGNAC** CHARENTE
Marco de Bignac Lieudit "Les Sablons"
☎ 0545217841 ▤ 0545215237
In a beautiful wooded location set out around the shore of a
5 acre lake with fine entertainment and sporting facilities.
➲ *N of Angoulême off N10. Take D11 W at La Touche
through Vars to Basse then right onto D117 to Bignac. Site well
signposted close to the River Charente.*
Off RN10, take D11 Wat La trouché, through Vaas to Basse
turning R onto D117, follow signs for Camping Bignac. May-
Sep 8HEC ▦ ♠ ↑ ♀ ♀ ✕ ⊙ ⚑ ♀ ₹ P ⊞ ⊞ **Prices:** ↟2-4
pitch 11-15 (incl 2 persons)

▶ **BLÉRÉ** INDRE-ET-LOIRE
CM r de la Gatine ☎ 247579260 ▤ 247579260
e-mail: marie@blere-touraine.com
Well-kept site beside River Cher. Two entrances.
7 Apr-15 Oct 4HEC ▦ ⚬ ↑ ⊙ ⚑ ♀ ⊡ lau ➡ ♀ ♀ ✕
₹P ⊞

▶ **BONNAC-LA-CÔTE** HAUTE-VIENNE
⛪Château de Leychoisier ☎ 0555399343
e-mail: leychoisier@wanadoo.fr
Well-managed site on ground sloping gently towards the
woods. Divided into roomy pitches.
➲ *1km S off N20.*
15 Apr-20 Sep 2HEC ▦ ⚬ ↑ ♀ ♀ ✕ ⊙ ⚑ ∅ ₹ LP ⊞ ⊞ lau
Prices: ↟4.50-5.60 ☞1.50-2.50 pitch 7-8 (incl 2 persons)

▶ **BONNES** VIENNE
CM r de la Varenne ☎ 549564434
A quiet site with plenty of recreational facilities.
➲ *S beside the River Vienne.*
May-Sep 1HEC ▦ ⚬ ↑ ⊙ ⚑ ♀ ₹ R ⊞ lau ➡ ♀ ♀ ✕ ▦ ₹L
⊞

▶ **BONNY-SUR-LOIRE** LOIRET
Val ☎ 238315771 ▤ 238315771
Woodland site situated by the side of the Loire, near the town
centre
➲ *At the junction of N7 and D965.*
mid May-30 Oct 0.8HEC ▦ ⚬ ↑ ⊙ ⚑ ₹ R ⊞ lau
➡ ♀ ♀ ✕ ▦

▶ **BOURGES** CHER
CM de Bourges 26 bd de l'Industrie
☎ 248201685 ▤ 248503239
e-mail: tourisme@wellbourges.fr
In the town near Lake Auron.
➲ *Access via A71, N144 or N76.*
15 Mar-15 Nov 2.2HEC ▦ ⚬ ∴ ↑ ⊙ ⚑ ⊞ ⊞ lau ➡ ♀ ♀
✕ ∅ ▦ ₹LPR

▶ **BOUSSAC-BOURG** CREUSE
⛪Château de Poinsouze rte de La Châtre
☎ 555650221 ▤ 555658649
e-mail: info.camping-de.poinsouze@wanadoo.fr
In a picturesque location in the grounds of a château with
good, modern facilities.
➲ *2km N via D917.*
18 May-16 Sep 22HEC ▦ ⚬ ↑ ♀ ♀ ✕ ⊙ ⚑ ∅ ▦ ⊞ ▲ ⚬
LP ⊞ ⊞ lau ➡ ₹R

▶ **BRACIEUX** LOIR-ET-CHER
CM des Châteaux 11 rue Roger Brun
☎ 254464184 ▤ 254460915
In a pleasant, shady park close to the town centre and
conveniently situated for visiting the castles of Chambord,
Cheverny and Villesavin.
Apr-15 Oct 8HEC ▦ ⚬ ↑ ⊙ ⚑ ⊞ ⊞ ⚑ ₹ PR ⊞ ⊞ lau ➡ ♀ ♀
✕ ∅ ▦

▶ **BRAIN-SUR-L'AUTHION** MAINE-ET-LOIRE
CM Caroline ☎ 241804218
A modern site in a pleasant wooded setting close to the river.
15 Mar-Oct 3.5HEC ▦ ♠ ↑ ⊙ ⚑ ⊞ ⊞ lau
➡ ♀ ♀ ✕ ∅ ▦

▶ **BRÉTIGNOLLES-SUR-MER** VENDÉE
Dunes Plage des Dunes ☎ 251905532 ▤ 251905485
Direct access to the beach. All plots surrounded by hedges.
➲ *2km S turn right off D38 and proceed for 1km across the
dunes. 150m from beach.*
Apr-Oct 12HEC ∴∴∴ ✂ ↑ ♀ ♀ ✕ ⊙ ⚑ ∅ ▦ ⚑ ₹ P ⊞ ⊞ lau
➡ ₹S **Prices:** ↟3.80-5.30 pitch 17.80-29.90 (incl 2 persons)

Motine 4 r des Morinières ☎ 0251900442 ▤ 0251338052
Pleasant site situated 350m from the town centre and 400m
from the beach with good facilities.
Apr-Sep 1.8HEC ▦ ⚬ ↑ ♀ ✕ ⊙ ⚑ ♀ ⚑ ₹ P ⊞ ⊞ lau ➡ ♀
∅ ₹LRS

Trevilliere rte de Bellevue ☎ 0251900965 ▤ 0251900965
e-mail: camping-chadotel@wanadoo.fr
➲ *900mtrs from town centre and 2km from the beach.*
15 Apr-30 Sep 3.5HEC ▦ ♠ ↑ ♀ ♀ ✕ ⊙ ⚑ ∅ ▦ ⚑ ♀ ₹ P
⊞ ⊞ lau ➡ ✕ ₹S **Prices:** pitch 12.20-20.58 (incl 2 persons)
See advertisement in colour section

Vagues 20 bd du Centre ☎ 0251901948 ▤ 0240024988
e-mail: lesvagues@free.fr
A family site situated on the Côte de Lumière in a delightful
rural setting.
➲ *N on D38 towards St-Gilles-Croix-de-Vie.*
Apr-Sep 5HEC ▦ ♠ ↑ ♀ ✕ ⊙ ⚑ ♀ ⚑ ♀ ₹ P ⊞ ⊞ lau ➡ ♀
✕ ∅ ₹LRS **Prices:** pitch 15.24

▶ **BRISSAC-QUINCÉ** MAINE-ET-LOIRE
L'Étang ☎ 241917061 ▤ 241917265
e-mail: camping.etang@wanadoo.fr
A lakeside site in the heart of the Anjou countryside with
good recreational facilities.
➲ *Access via D748 towards Poitiers.*
25 May-7 Sep 3.5HEC ▦ ⚬ ↑ ♀ ✕ ⊙ ⚑ ∅ ⚑ ▲
₹ P ⊞ ⊞ lau ➡ ✕

▶ **BRÛLON** SARTHE
Brûlon-le-Lac ☎ 243956896 ▤ 243926036
In attractive wooded surroundings beside a lake.
➲ *Access via N157 towards Sable-sur-Sarthe.*
15 Apr-Sep 3.5HEC ▦ ♠ ↑ ♀ ✕ ⊙ ⚑ ∅ ▦
₹ LPR ⊞ ⊞ lau

135

▶ **CANDÉ-SUR-BEUVRON** LOIR-ET-CHER

Grande Tortue 3 rte de Pontlevoy
☎ 254441520 ▦ 254441945
e-mail: francois.gonin@valeo.com
A family site in a peaceful wooded setting.
➲ *D751, between Blois and Amboise, on the left bank of the river.*
Etr-Sep 5.8HEC ⟱ ♣ ⋔ ⚊ ⟀ ✕ ⊙ ◙ ∅ ⚌ ⊞
⥾ P ☎ ⊞ lau

▶ **CHALARD, LE** HAUTE-VIENNE

Vigères Les Vigères ☎ 555093722 ▦ 555099339
e-mail: lesvigeres@aol.com
Generally level site in peaceful surroundings in an elevated position with fine views. English management.
➲ *Between Châlus and Le Chalard on D901.*
All year 20HEC ⟱ ⋪ ⋔ ⚊ ⊙ ◙ ⊞ ⥾ LP ☎ ⊞ lau ♦ ✕
Prices: ♠2.50-3 pitch 2.50-3.50

▶ **CHALONNES-SUR-LOIRE** MAINE-ET-LOIRE

CM Candais rte de Rochefort ☎ 241780227
On the banks of the River Loire at its confluence with the River Louet.
➲ *NE off D751 towards Rochefort.*
15 May-Sep 3HEC ⟱ ♣ ⋔ ⊙ ◙ ☎ ⊞ lau
♦ ⚊ ⟀ ✕ ∅ ⚌ ⥾P

▶ **CHARTRES** EURE-ET-LOIR

CM des Bords de l'Eure 9 r de Launay
☎ 237287943 ▦ 237234199
In wooded surroundings beside the river.
➲ *Signposted towards Orléans.*
25 Apr-4 Sep 3.9HEC ⟱ ⋪ ⋔ ⊙ ◙ ⊞ lau ♦ ⚊ ⟀ ✕ ∅ ⚌
⥾PR Prices: pitch 8-11.50 (incl 2 persons)

▶ **CHARTRE-SUR-LE-LOIR, LA** SARTHE

Vieux Moulin av des Déportés ☎ 243444118
e-mail: campingvieuxmoulin@worldonline.fr
15 Apr-Sep 2.4HEC ⟱ ⋪ ⋔ ⊙ ◙ ⥾ PR ☎ ⊞ lau
♦ ⚊ ⟀ ✕ ∅ ⚌ ⥾LP

▶ **CHASSENEUIL-SUR-BONNIEURE** CHARENTE

CM Les Charmilles r des Écoles ☎ 45395536
➲ *W of town via D27, beside the River Bonnieure.*
15 Jun-15 Sep 2HEC ⟱ ⋪ ⋔ ⊙ ◙ ☎ lau
♦ ⚊ ⟀ ✕ ∅ ⥾P ⊞

▶ **CHÂTEAU-DU-LOIR** SARTHE

CM de Coemont ☎ 243794463
Shady site on the bank of the Loir.
15 May-30 Sep 0.6HEC ⟱ ⋪ ⋔ ⊙ ◙ ⥾ R ☎ lau ♦ ⚊ ⟀ ✕ ∅
⥾P ⊞ Prices: ♠5-7 ♠3 pitch 12-21

▶ **CHÂTEAULONG** VENDÉE

Pin Parasol Lac du Jaunay ☎ 251346472
In the heart of the Vendée countryside on the shore of Lac du Jaunay with good, modern facilities.
➲ *Between D6 and D12.*
May-15 Sep 5HEC ⟱ ⋪ ⋔ ⚊ ⟀ ⊙ ◙ ∅ ⚌ ⊡ ◱
⥾ P ☎ ⊞ lau ♦ ⥾L

▶ **CHÂTELAILLON-PLAGE** CHARENTE-MARITIME

Clos des Rivages av des Boucheleurs ☎ 546562609
Level, well-kept site with pitches divided by trees and bushes, 500mtrs from the sea.
➲ *500mtrs from the village. Signposted.*
15 Jun-10 Sep 2.5HEC ⟱ ⋪ ♣ ⋔ ⚊ ⊙ ◙ ∅ ⥾ P ☎ ⊞ lau
♦ ⟀ ✕ ⥾S

Deux Plages ☎ 546562753 ▦ 546435118
e-mail: 2plages@wanadoo.fr
In pleasant wooded surroundings 200mtrs from the beach.
All year 4.5HEC ⟱ ⋙ ⋪ ⋔ ⚊ ⊙ ◙ ☎ ⥾ P ☎ ⊞ ⊘
lau ♦ ⚊ ∅ ⚌ ⥾S Prices: ⊛2.29 ▲3.05 pitch 11.63-16.62 (incl 2 persons)

▶ **CHÂTELLERAULT** VIENNE

Relais du Miel rte d'Antran
☎ 549020627 ▦ 549932576
e-mail: camping@lerelaisdumiel.com
In the grounds of the Château de Valette, beside the River Vienne.
➲ *Access via A10 exit 26 (Châtellerault Nord).*
May-Sep 7HEC ⟱ ♣ ⋔ ⟀ ✕ ⊙ ◙ ⊡ ◱ ⥾ PR ☎ ⊞ lau ♦ ⚊
∅ ⚌ Prices: pitch 2-2.50

▶ **CHÂTRES-SUR-CHER** LOIR-ET-CHER

CM des Saules ☎ 254980455
➲ *On N76 near bridge.*
May-Sep 2HEC ⟱ ⋪ ⊙ ◙ ☎ lau ♦ ⚊ ⟀ ✕ ∅ ⚌ ⊞

▶ **CHAUFFOUR-SUR-VELL** CORRÈZE

Feneyrolles ☎ 555253143
e-mail: feneyrolles@aol.com
In a quiet, wooded location with good facilities. Ideal for exploring the Dordogne Valley and surrounding area.
➲ *2.2km E.*
15 Apr-15 Sep 4HEC ⟱ ♣ ⋔ ⚊ ⟀ ✕ ⊙ ◙ ⊡ ◱ ⥾ P ☎ ⊞
lau Prices: ♠3.50 pitch 4

▶ **CHEF-BOUTONNE** DEUX-SÈVRES

Moulin Treneuillet, rte de Brioux
☎ 549297346 ▦ 549297346
e-mail: campingchef@infonie.fr
Small, secluded family site in a rural setting.
➲ *1km NE via D740.*
All year 2HEC ⟱ ⋪ ⋔ ⚊ ⟀ ✕ ⊙ ◙ ⚌ ⊡
⥾ PR ☎ lau ♦ ∅

▶ **CHÉNIERS** CREUSE

Moulin de Piot ☎ 555621320
In beautiful natural surroundings in the heart of the Creuse region.
➲ *Access via D6. In Chéniers turn left by the bakers in the village square.*
Mar-Oct 1HEC ⟱ ♣ ⋔ ⊙ ◙ ⊡ ▲ ⥾ R ☎ ⊞ lau
♦ ⚊ ⟀ ✕ ∅ ⚌

▶ **CHENONCEAUX** INDRE-ET-LOIRE

Moulin Fort ☎ 247238622
➲ *2km SE*
Apr-Sep 3HEC ⟱ ⋪ ⋔ ⚊ ⟀ ✕ ⊙ ◙ ∅ ⥾ PR ☎ ⊞ lau

▶ **CHÉVERNY** LOIR-ET-CHER

Les Saules rte de Contres ☎ 254799001 ▦ 254792834
e-mail: campsaules@aol.com
In the heart of the Châteaux-du-Val-de-Loire, bordered by a golf course and the Cheverny forest.
➲ *1.5km from town towards Contres on D102.*
Etr-25 Sep 10HEC ⟱ ♣ ⋔ ⚊ ⟀ ✕ ⊙ ◙ ∅ ⚌ ⊡ ▲
⥾ P ☎ ⊞ lau

▶ **CHINON** INDRE-ET-LOIRE

CM ☎ 247930835
On the banks of the river opposite the Château.
➲ *Off D951.*
Apr-Oct 6HEC ⟱ ⋙ ⋪ ⋔ ⊙ ◙ ◱ ⥾ PR ☎ ⊞ lau
♦ ⚊ ⟀ ✕ ⥾S

▶ **CHOLET** MAINE-ET-LOIRE

Lac de Ribou av L-Mandin ☎ 241497430 ▤ 241582122
Well set-out site bordering a lake, with fishing, boating, tennis and volleyball.
➲ *3km from town centre.*
Apr-Oct 5HEC ᛃᛃᛃ ♠ ℝ ⚏ ✕ ⊙ ⬛ ⛺ ⬛ ⟲ P ☎ ⊞ lau
♠ ⚏ ⊘ ⌁ ⟲L

▶ **CHORANCHE** INDRE

Gouffre de la Croix ☎ 476360713 ▤ 476360713
In a quiet location beside the River Bourne with fine views of the surrounding mountains and good, modern facilities.
➲ *Access via A49 exit St-Marcellin or Hostun.*
15 Mar-15 Sep 2.5HEC ᛃᛃᛃ ♠ ℝ ⚏ ⚏ ✕ ⊙ ⬛ ⊘ ⌁ ⛺ ⬛ ⟲ R
☎ ⊞ lau

▶ **CLOYES-SUR-LE-LOIR** EURE-ET-LOIR

Parc des Loisirs rte du Montigny
☎ 237985053 ▤ 237983384
e-mail: info@parc-de-loisirs.com
On the bank of the River Loir. Extensive leisure facilities. Separate section for teenagers. Shop only available in July and August, bar and restaurant only May-September.
➲ *Access from Châteaudun S on N10 towards Cloyes, then right onto Montigny-le-Gamelon road.*
15 Mar-15 Nov 5HEC ᛃᛃᛃ ♁ ℝ ⚏ ⚏ ✕ ⊙ ⬛ ⊘ ⬛
⟲ P ☎ ⊞ lau

▶ **COGNAC** CHARENTE

Cognac rte de Ste-Sévère, bd de Chatenay
☎ 545321332 ▤ 545365529
e-mail: ccdc-camping@wanadoo.fr
In wooded surroundings beside the River Charente with good, modern facilities.
➲ *2km on D24.*
May-15 Oct 1.6HEC ᛃᛃᛃ ♁ ℝ ⚏ ⚏ ✕ ⊙ ⬛ ⬛ ⟲ PR ☎ lau ♠
⚏ ✕ ⟲P ⊞ Prices: pitch 10.70-12.20

▶ **CONTRES** LOIR-ET-CHER

Charmoise Sassay ☎ 02 054795515 ▤ 0254795515
On a level meadow with good facilities.
➲ *N956.*
Apr-Oct 1HEC ᛃᛃᛃ ♁ ℝ ⊙ ⬛ ☎ lau ♠ ⚏ ⚏ ✕ ⊘ ⌁ Prices:
⚓2.30

▶ **COUHÉ-VERAC** VIENNE

Peupliers ☎ 549592116 ▤ 549379209
e-mail: info@camping-les-peupliers.com
A family site in a forested site beside the river.
➲ *N of village on N10 Poitiers road.*
2 May-Sep 16HEC ᛃᛃᛃ ♁ ℝ ⚏ ⚏ ✕ ⊙ ⬛ ⊘ ⛺ ⬛ ⟲ PR ☎ ⊞
lau ♠ ⌁ Prices: ⚓3.50-5 pitch 4.90-7

▶ **COURÇON-D'AUNIS** CHARENTE-MARITIME

Garenne 21 r du Stade ☎ 546016050
Apr-Oct ᛃᛃᛃ ℝ ⊙ ⬛ ☎ lau ♠ ⚏ ⚏ ✕ ⌁ ⟲P ⊞

▶ **COUTURES** MAINE-ET-LOIRE

Européen Montsabert ☎ 241579163 ▤ 241579002
e-mail: anjoucamp@wanadoo.fr
In a picturesque wooded park with mature trees.
➲ *Access via left bank of the River Loire (D751) between Angers and Saumur.*
May-Sep 10HEC ᛃᛃᛃ ♁ ℝ ⚏ ✕ ⊙ ⬛ ⬛ ⟲ P ☎ ⊞ lau ♠ ⚏ ✕
⊘ ⌁ Prices: pitch 13-18.30

▶ **CROISIC, LE** LOIRE-ATLANTIQUE

Océan ☎ 240230769 ▤ 240157063
A quiet, well appointed site situated 150m from the sea.
➲ *1.5km NW via D45*
Apr-Sep 7.5HEC ᛃᛃᛃ ♁ ℝ ⚏ ✕ ⊙ ⬛ ⊘ ⌁ ⛺ ⬛ ⟲ P ☎ ⊞
lau ♠ ⟲S

▶ **DISSAY** VIENNE

Bois de Chaume Chemin des Meuniers ☎ 549623630
Situated on N10 within easy reach of the Futuroscope.
Mar-Oct 1.7HEC ᛃᛃᛃ ♁ ℝ ⊙ ⬛ ⬛ ☎ lau ♠ ✕ ⟲R

CM du Parc ☎ 549628429 ▤ 549625872
Quiet, shady site at the foot of a 15th century castle, with close proximity to Futuroscope, lake of St-Cyr and the Forest of Mouliere.
Jun-15 Sep 1HEC ᛃᛃᛃ ℝ ⊙ ⬛ lau

▶ **DURTAL** MAINE-ET-LOIRE

CM 9 r du Camping ☎ 241763180 ▤ 241763180
e-mail: mairie@ville-durtal.fr
A pleasant site beside the River Loire.
➲ *Near the centre of the town. Access via N23 or A11.*
Etr-Sep 3HEC ᛃᛃᛃ ♁ ℝ ⊙ ⬛ ⊘ ⬛ ⬛ ⟲ ⚏ R ☎ ⊞ lau ♠ ⚏ ⚏
✕ ⌁ ⟲P Prices: pitch 8.38

▶ **EGLETONS** CORRÈZE

Egletons-Lac ☎ 555931475
A lakeside site in wooded surroundings with a fine range of recreational facilities.
➲ *2km from Egletons towards Ussel.*
All year 9HEC ᛃᛃᛃ ♁ ℝ ✕ ⊙ ⬛ ⊘ ⌁ ⬛ ☎ ⊞ lau ♠ ⟲LP

▶ **EYMOUTHIERS** CHARENTE

Gorges du Chambon ☎ 545707170 ▤ 545708002
e-mail: gorges.chambon@wanadoo.fr
In a beautiful location on a wooded hilltop.
➲ *3km N via D163.*
27 Apr-14 Sep 7HEC ᛃᛃᛃ ♠ ℝ ⚏ ✕ ⊙ ⬛ ⊘ ⌁ ⬛ ⬛ ⚓ ⟲ PR
☎ ⊞ ✼ lau Prices: ⚓4.30-5.30 ⚓1.95-1.95 ⚓5.60-6.70
⚓5.60-6.70 pitch 5.60-6.70

▶ **FAUTE-SUR-MER, LA** VENDÉE

Fautais 18 rte de la Tranche ☎ 0251564196
Situated in centre of village. Numbered pitches.
➲ *On D46.*
01 Apr-30 Sep 1HEC ᛃᛃᛃ ♁ ℝ ⊙ ⬛ ⬛ ☎ lau ♠ ⚏ ⚏ ✕ ⊘ ⌁
⟲LS ⊞ Prices: ⚓3.81 ⚓5.81

Flots Bleus aux des Chardons ☎ 251271111 ▤ 251294076
Family site only 100m from the sea.
➲ *In La Faute, cross Pont de l'Aiguillons-sur-Mer and follow Route de la Pointe d'Arçay to site.*
08 May-Sep 1.5HEC ᛃᛃᛃ ⋮⋮⋮ ♁ ℝ ⚏ ✕ ⊙ ⬛ ⊘ ⌁ ⬛ ⬛ ⚏
⊞ lau ♠ ⚏ ✕ ⟲LRS Prices: pitch 10-17 (incl 3 persons)

▶ **FENOUILLER, LE** VENDÉE

Domaine le Pas Opton rte de Nantes
☎ 251551198 ▤ 251554494
e-mail: lepasopton@free.fr
Well equipped family site a few minutes from the beach and close to the "Des Vallées" sailing centre.
➲ *2km N beside the River Vie on D754.*
20 May-10 Sep 6.5HEC ᛃᛃᛃ ♁ ℝ ⚏ ✕ ⊙ ⬛ ⊘ ⬛
⟲ PR ☎ ⊞ ✼ lau

▶ FOURAS CHARENTE-MARITIME

Charmilles St Laurent de la Pree
☎ 546840005 ▤ 0546840287
15 Apr-Sep ⸺ ⌂♠🅿︎⚲🍴✕☉🛒⌀🚿🏕🚐♻︎ ⸏ P ⬚➕✕
Prices: pitch 12.20-20.58 (incl 2 persons)
See advertisement in colour section

▶ FRESNAY-SUR-SARTHE SARTHE

CM Sans Souci r de Haut Ary ☎ 243973287
A family site with good facilities and direct access to the river.
➲ *1km SE on D310.*
Apr-Sep 2HEC ⸺ ⌂♠🅿︎☉🛒⌀ ⸏ PR ⬚ lau ♦ ⚲✕🚿

▶ FRIAUDOUR HAUTE-VIENNE

Freaudour ☎ 555765722
A well equipped site beside Lac de St-Pardoux.
➲ *Access via A20 exit 25.*
Jun-Sep 3.5HEC ⸺ ⌂♠🅿︎⚲🍴✕☉🛒⌀🚿🏕🚐♻︎ ⸏ LP ⬚➕ lau Prices: pitch 11-17 (incl 2 persons)

▶ FROSSAY LOIRE-ATLANTIQUE

Migron Le Square de la Chaussée ☎ 240397783
In a pleasant location beside the canal.
Jun-Sep 2.5HEC ⸺ ♦♠☉🛒⌀🏕🚐♻︎ ⸏ R ⬚➕ lau ♦⚲🅿︎✕

▶ GENNES MAINE-ET-LOIRE

Européen Montsabert ☎ 241579163 ▤ 241579002
e-mail: anjoucamp@wanadoo.fr
In wooded surroundings close to the River Loire with good facilities.
➲ *Access via D751.*
15 May-15 Sep 10HEC ⸺ ♦♠🍴✕☉🛒⌀🚿🏕🚐 ⸏ P ⬚➕ lau ♦⚲⌀

Bord de l'Eau r des Cadets de Saumur ☎ 241380467
In a peaceful location on the river bank.
➲ *N beside the River Loire*
May-Sep 2.5HEC ⸺ ⌂♠🍴✕☉🛒⚲♻︎ ⸏ R ⬚ lau ♦⚲🅿︎✕⌀ ⸏P ➕ Prices: 🅿︎2.50 pitch 2.40

▶ GIEN LOIRET

Bois du Bardelet rte de Bourges, Poilly
☎ 238674739 ▤ 238382716
e-mail: contact@bardelet.com
A family site with a good variety of sporting facilities.
➲ *Access via D940 SW of Gien.*
Apr-Sep 12HEC ⸺ ⌂♠🅿︎⚲🍴✕☉🛒⌀🏕🚐♻︎ ⸏ LP ⬚➕ lau Prices: pitch 12.36-25 (incl 2 persons)

▶ GIVRAND VENDÉE

Europa Le Petit Bois ☎ 251553268 ▤ 251558010
A pleasant family site with a wide variety of recreational facilities and modern sanitary blocks.
➲ *W from St-Gilles-Croix-de-Vie via D6 for 2.5km, then S for 0.2km.*
Apr-Sep 4HEC ⸺ ⌂♠🅿︎⚲✕☉🛒⌀🏕🚐 ⸏ P ⬚➕ lau ♦ ⸏LRS

▶ GRIÈRE VENDÉE

Préveils av Ste-Anne-la-Grière ☎ 251304052
A pleasant site in wooded surroundings 200m from the beach.
15 May-15 Sep 4HEC ⸪⸪ ⌂♠🅿︎⚲🍴✕☉🛒⌀🏕🚐🚐 ⸏ P ⬚➕ lau ♦ ⸏S

▶ GUÉMENÉ-PENFAO LOIRE-ATLANTIQUE

Hermitage 36 av du Paradis ☎ 240792348 ▤ 2405151187
In a beautiful setting overlooking the Don Valley with good, modern facilities.

➲ *1.5km E on rte de Châteaubriant.*
Apr-15 Oct 2.5HEC ⸺ ⌂♠🅿︎☉🛒⚲🍴🚿🏕 ⸏ P ⬚ lau ♦⚲✕ ⌀🚿 ⸏R ➕

▶ GUÉRANDE LOIRE-ATLANTIQUE

Bréhadour ☎ 240249312 ▤ 240621047
e-mail: info@homair-vacances.fr
A well equipped family site with good facilities, a few kilometres from the sea.
➲ *2km NE on D51, rte de St-Lyphard.*
27 Apr-Oct 7HEC ⸺ ⌂♠🅿︎⚲✕☉🛒⌀🏕🚐♻︎A ⸏ P ⬚ lau ♦⌀🚿➕ Prices: 🅿︎3.96-5.18 pitch 4.12-6.86

Parc de Lévéno rte de l'Étang de Sandun
☎ 240247930 ▤ 240620123
e-mail: domaine.leveno@wanadoo.fr
In a pleasant location with good facilities.
➲ *3km E via rte de Sandun.*
28 Apr-Sep 12HEC ⸺ ⌂♠🅿︎⚲🍴✕☉🛒⌀🚿🏕🚐 ⸏ P ⬚➕ lau

🏠Pré du Château de Careil Careil
☎ 33 240602299 ▤ 240602299
e-mail: chateau.careil@free.fr
Divided into pitches. Caravans only. Booking recommended for Jul & Aug.
➲ *2km N of La Baule on D92.*
May-Sep 2HEC ⸺ ⌂♠☉🛒⚲🍴 ⸏ P ⬚➕ lau ♦⚲🍴✕⌀🚿

▶ HÉRIC LOIRE-ATLANTIQUE

Pindière ☎ 240576541 ▤ 0240576541
e-mail: patrick.ara@wanadoo.fr
A family site on a level meadow with good facilities.
➲ *1km from town on D16.*
All year 3HEC ⸺ ⌂♠🅿︎⚲✕☉🛒⌀🚿🏕🚐♻︎ ⸏ P ⬚➕ lau ♦⚲⌀ Prices: 🅿︎2.44 ♦1.22 🚐2.59 🅰︎2.59

▶ HOUMEAU, L' CHARENTE-MARITIME

Trépied au Plomb ☎ 546509082 ▤ 546500133
e-mail: au.petit.port@wanadoo.fr
➲ *NE via D106*
Apr-Sep 2HEC ⸺ ⌂♠🅿︎⚲☉🛒🏕🚐♻︎ ⬚➕ lau ♦⚲✕⌀ ⸏S

▶ INGRANDES VIENNE

At ST-USTRE(2km NE)

🏠Petit Trianon de St-Ustre ☎ 549026147 ▤ 549026881
e-mail: chateau@petit-trianon.fr
In a beautiful park surrounding a small 18th-century castle, the site has good entertainment and recreational facilities.
➲ *Turn off N10 at signpost N of Ingrandes and continue for 1km.*
15 May-20 Sep 7HEC ⸺ ⌂♠🅿︎⚲☉🛒⌀🏕🚐♻︎ ⸏ P ⬚➕ lau ♦⚲🍴✕⌀ Prices: 🅿︎6.30 ♦3.60 🚐3.80-4.20 pitch 3.80

▶ JARD-SUR-MER VENDÉE

Écureuils rte des Goffineaux ☎ 251334274 ▤ 251339114
e-mail: camping-ecureuils@wanadoo.fr
Quiet woodland terrain 500yds from the sea. Large pitches surrounded by hedges.
➲ *Signposted.*
15 May-15 Sep 4.3HEC ⸪⸪ ⌂♠🅿︎⚲🍴✕☉🛒⌀🏕♻︎ ⸏ P ⬚➕♻︎ lau ♦✕ ⸏S Prices: 🅿︎4.95-5.50 pitch 9.90-11

La Mouette Cendrée Les Malecots, St-Vincent-sur-Jard ☎ 251335904
May-15 Sep 1.2HEC ⸺ ♦♠☉🛒⌀🏕🚐♻︎ ⸏ P ⬚➕ lau ♦⚲🍴✕⌀ ⸏S

Océano d'Or r G-Clemenceau
☎ 251336508 🖩 251339404
e-mail: chadotel@wanadoo.fr
A well maintained site 1km from the beach and 500mtrs from the town centre.
⮑ *Access via D19.*
Apr-25 Sep 7.8HEC ⭐ ⬚ ↻ ⬚ ⬚ ⬚ ✕ ☺ ⬚ 🔲 ⬚ ⬚ ⬚ ⬚ ⬚ P
⬚ ⊞ lau ➧ ✕ ⬚S Prices: ⬚5.18-5.18 pitch 12.20-20.58
See advertisement in colour section

Pomme de Pin r Vincent Auriol
☎ 251334385 🖩 0251339404
Situated in a pine forest
⮑ *300mtrs from the town centre and 150mtrs from the beach.*
15 Apr-Sep ⭐ ⬚ ↻ ⬚ ⬚ ⬚ ✕ ☺ ⬚ ⬚ ⬚ ⬚ ⬚ ⬚ LRS ⬚ ⊞ lau
➧ ✕ Prices: pitch 13.72-21.34 (incl 2 persons)
See advertisement in colour section

JARGEAU LOIRET

Isle aux Moulins r du 44ème RI
☎ 238597004 🖩 238591223
e-mail: kas@wanadoo.fr
In a wooded location on the bank of the Loire.
Mar-15 Nov 7HEC ⭐ ⬚ ↻ ⬚ ☺ ⬚ ⬚ ⬚ ⬚ ⬚ ⬚ R ⬚ ⊞ lau ➧
⬚ ✕ ⬚

JAUNAY CLAN VIENNE

Croix du Sud rte de Neuville ☎ 549625814
e-mail: camping@la-croix-du-sud.fr
Within easy reach of 'Futuroscope', the European Park of the Moving Image.
⮑ *Access via A10 and D62.*
24 Mar-15 Oct 4HEC ⭐ ⬚ ↻ ⬚ ⬚ ⬚ ✕ ☺ ⬚ ⬚ ⬚ ⬚ P ⬚
lau Prices: ⬚1.80-3.35 pitch 6.10

LAGORD CHARENTE-MARITIME

CM Parc r du Parc ☎ 546676154
Pleasant municipal site within easy reach of the coast.
⮑ *Access via N137/D735.*
15 May-Sep ⭐ ⬚ ↻ ☺ ⬚ ⬚ ⬚ ⊞ lau ➧ ⬚ ⬚ ✕ ⬚ ⬚

LANDEVIEILLE VENDÉE

Pong r du Stade ☎ 251229263 🖩 251229925
A family site with spacious pitches surrounded by trees and bushes. Good recreational facilities.
Etr-Sep 3HEC ⭐ ⬚ ↻ ⬚ ⬚ ✕ ☺ ⬚ ⬚ ⬚ ⬚ ⬚ ⬚ P ⬚ ⊞ lau
➧ ⊞

LINDOIS, LE CHARENTE

Étang ☎ 545650267 🖩 545650896
Well shaded site with a natural lake, ideal for swimming and fishing with a small beach.
⮑ *From Rochefoucauld take D13 towards Montemboeuf.*
Apr-Oct 10HEC ⭐ ⬚ ↻ ⬚ ✕ ☺ ⬚ ⬚ ⬚ ⬚ L ⬚ ⊞ lau ➧ ⬚ ⬚
⬚

LION D'ANGERS, LE MAINE-ET-LOIRE

CM Frénes ☎ 241953156
A municipal site on the banks of the River Oudon, 300mtrs from the town centre.
⮑ *NE on N162.*
May-Aug 2HEC ⭐ ⬚ ↻ ⬚ ☺ ⬚ ⬚ ⬚ lau ➧ ⬚ ⬚ ✕ ⬚ ⬚ ⬚P ⊞
Prices: ⬚11 ⬚4 pitch 11

LISSAC-SUR-COUZE CORRÈZE

Prairie ☎ 555853797
Jun-13 Sep 3HEC ⭐ ⬚ ⬚ ↻ ⬚ ⬚ ☺ ⬚ ⬚ ⬚ ⊞ lau
➧ ⬚ ✕

LONGEVILLE VENDÉE

Brunelles Le Bouil ☎ 251335075 🖩 251339821
e-mail: camping@les-brunelles.com
A well appointed site in a wooded location 700mtrs from the beach.
⮑ *On the coast between Longeville and Jard-sur-Mer.*
Etr-Sep 4.8HEC ⭐ ⬚ ↻ ⬚ ⬚ ⬚ ✕ ☺ ⬚ ⬚ ⬚ ⬚ ⬚ ⬚ ⬚ P ⬚
⊞ lau ➧ ⬚S

Clos des Pins Les Conches ☎ 251903169 🖩 251903068
e-mail: philip.jones@freesbee.ft
A family run site with good facilities, 250yds from a sandy beach.
⮑ *Between Longeville and La Tranche.*
31 Mar-13 Oct 1.6HEC ⭐ ⬚ ⬚∴ ⬚ ⬚ ↻ ⬚ ⬚ ✕ ☺ ⬚ ⬚ ⬚ ⬚
⬚ P ⬚ ⊞ lau ➧ ⬚ ⬚S

Jarny Océan Le Bouil ☎ 251334221 🖩 251339537
e-mail: jarny-ocean@wanadoo.fr
Subdivided well tended meadow, with a holiday complex of the same name where shopping facilities are provided. 800m to sea via forest path.
⮑ *Turn off D105 about 3km S of Longeville.*
01 May-30 Sep 7.6HEC ⭐ ⬚ ↻ ⬚ ⬚ ⬚ ✕ ☺ ⬚ ⬚ ⬚ ⬚ ⬚ P
⬚ ⊞ lau ➧ ✕ ⬚ ⬚S Prices: pitch 8.38-22.10 (incl 2 persons)

At CONCHES, LES(4km S)

Dunes av de la Plage ☎ 251333293 🖩 251903861
e-mail: contact@camping-lesdunes.com
Well-kept site amongst sand dunes in pine forest.
⮑ *6km S of Longeville on D105.*
May-Sep 5HEC ⬚∴ ⬚ ⬚ ↻ ⬚ ⬚ ✕ ☺ ⬚ ⬚ ⬚ ⬚ P ⬚ ⊞ lau ➧ ✕
⬚PRS

LUCHÉ-PRINGÉ SARTHE

CM de la Chabotière Place des Tilleuls
☎ 243451007 🖩 243451000
e-mail: lachabotiere@ville-luche-pringe.fr
Site by a river just 100 metres from the village and a short drive from several Loire chateaux. Large marked sites are set on terraces above the river and most cars are kept in a private car park to ensure play areas are safe for children.
Apr-15 Oct 1.7HEC ⭐ ⬚ ↻ ☺ ⬚ ⬚ ⬚ ⬚ ⬚ P ⬚ ⊞ lau ➧ ⬚ ⬚
✕ ⬚ ⬚ Prices: ⬚1.50-2.50 ⬚1.20-1.90 ⬚1.70-1.70

LUDE, LE SARTHE

CM rte du Mans ☎ 243946770
Shady site in a rural location with direct access to the River Loir.
⮑ *400m from town centre, direct from N307.*
Apr-Sep 4.5HEC ⭐ ⬚ ↻ ☺ ⬚ ⬚ ⬚ ⬚ PR ⬚ ⊞ lau ➧ ⬚ ⬚ ✕

LUSIGNAN VIENNE

CM Vauchiron Vauchiron ☎ 549433008 🖩 549436119
e-mail: lusignan@cg86.fr
In a quiet wooded location beside the River Vonne with good facilities.
⮑ *500m NE on N11.*
15 Apr-15 Oct 4HEC ⭐ ⬚ ↻ ☺ ⬚ ⬚ ⬚ ⬚ R ⬚ ⊞ lau ➧ ⬚ ⬚
✕ ⬚ ⬚

LUYNES INDRE-ET-LOIRE

CM Granges Les Granges ☎ 247556085
Quiet site close to the village. Ideal for visiting historical sites, fishing, and wine tasting
⮑ *S via D49.*
8 May-15 Sep 0.8HEC ⭐ ⬚ ↻ ☺ ⬚ ⬚ ⬚ ⬚ ⬚ ⊞ lau
➧ ⬚ ⬚ ✕ ⬚P

CAMPING ✱✱

DE MAYENNE △

53100 – ☎ (33) 243 04 57 14 (33) 243 04 19 37

ON SITE

MACHÉ VENDÉE

Val de Vie r du Stade ☎ 251602102 ▤ 251602102
e-mail: campingvaldevie@aol.com
01 May-15 Sep 2.2HEC ⸺ ☆ ♠ ⊙ ◪ ⬛ ⟲ ⥩ P ⊡ lau ♦ ♨
♣ ✕ ⊘ ≋ ⟲LR Prices: pitch 10-12.50 (incl 2 persons)

MAGNAC-BOURG HAUTE-VIENNE

Écureuils rte de Limoges ☎ 555008028 ▤ 555004909
A grassy site close to the historic village
➲ 25 kms S on N20.
Apr-Sep 1.3HEC ⸺ ♨ ♠ ⊙ ◪ ⊡ lau ♦ ♣ ✕ ⊘ ≋ ⊞

MANSIGNÉ SARTHE

CM de la Plage rte du Plessis ☎ 243461417 ▤ 243461665
A holiday complex set in extensive parkland around a 60 acre
lake with good recreational facilities.
➲ On D13, 4km from D307 (Le Mans-Le Lude).
Etr-Oct 3.4HEC ⸺ ♠ ♠ ♣ ✕ ⊙ ◪ ⬛ ⟲ ⥩ LP ⊡ lau ♦
♨ ⊘ ≋

MARANS CHARENTE-MARITIME

CM Le Bois Dinot rte de Nantes ☎ 546011051
Separate car park for arrivals after 22.00hrs.
➲ Access via N137 (Nantes-Bordeaux).
May-Sep 6HEC ⸺ ♨ ♠ ⊙ ◪ ⊡ lau ♦ ♨ ♣ ✕ ⊘ ≋ ⟲PR

MARÇON SARTHE

Lac des Varennes ☎ 243441372 ▤ 243445431
e-mail: camping.des.varennes.marcon@wanadoo.fr
An attractive site bordering the lake in the heart of the Loire
Valley, with spacious pitches and well maintained
installations.
25 Mar-20 Oct 7HEC ⸺ ♨ ♠ ♨ ♣ ✕ ⊙ ◪ ⬛ ⟲ ⥩ LR ⊡ ⊞
lau ♦ ⊘

MATHES, LES CHARENTE-MARITIME

Charmettes av de la Palmyre ☎ 546225096 ▤ 546236970
Large site with plenty of organised activities. 5km from the
beach.
➲ 1km SW via D141.
15 Apr-Sep 34HEC ⸺ ∴ ☆ ♠ ♨ ♣ ✕ ⊙ ◪ ⬛ ⟲ ⥩ PS ⊡
⊡ ⊞ ⊘ lau

Orée du Bois 225 rte de la Bouverie, La Fouasse
☎ 546224243 ▤ 546225476
e-mail: cintact@camping.oree-du-bois.com
A family site situated in a pine and oak forest, 5 minutes
from the beach.
➲ 3.5km NW.
12 May-8 Sep 6HEC ⸺ ∴ ♠ ♠ ♨ ♣ ✕ ⊙ ◪ ⊘ ≋ ⬛ ⟲ ⥩
P ⊡ ⊡ ⊞ lau Prices: pitch 15-28 (incl 2 persons)

Pinède rte de la Fouasse ☎ 546224513 ▤ 546225021
A modern family site in a wooded area around the large
Aquatic Park. Excellent sporting facilities. Entertainment
available in July and August.
➲ 3km NW.
Apr-Sep 7HEC ⸺ ∴ ♠ ♠ ♨ ♣ ✕ ⊙ ◪ ⬛ ⟲ ⥩ P ⊡ lau

MAYENNE MAYENNE

CM Raymond Fauque r St-Léonard ☎ 243045714
In a wooded location on the banks of the River Mayenne.
➲ 800m from town centre near N12.
mid Mar-mid Sep 1.8HEC ⸺ ♠ ♠ ♣ ✕ ⊙ ◪ ⬛ ⟲ ⥩ P ⊡ ⊞
lau ♦ ♨ ♣ ✕ ⊘ ≋ ⊞

MEMBROLLE-SUR-CHOISILLE, LA INDRE-ET-LOIRE

CM rte de Foudettes ☎ 02 0247412040
On level meadow in sports ground beside River Choisille.
➲ N on N138 Le Mans road.
May-Sep 1.3HEC ⸺ ♨ ♠ ⊙ ◪ ⟲ ⥩ R ⊡ ⊞ lau
♦ ♨ ♣ ⟲L

MERVENT VENDÉE

Chêne Tord 34 chemin du Chêne Tord ☎ 251002063
A well appointed site 200mtrs from a large artificial lake in
the heart of the Mervent Forest.
➲ Access via D99.
All year 4HEC ⸺ ♠ ♠ ⊙ ◪ ⊘ ≋ ⬛ ⟲ ⥩ L ⊡ lau
♦ ♨ ♣ ✕ ≋ ⟲R ⊞

MESLAND LOIR-ET-CHER

Parc du Val de Loire rte de Fleuray
☎ 254702718 ▤ 254702171
In a sheltered position in the heart of the Touraine vineyards
with good recreational facilities.
Camping Card Compulsory.
➲ 1.5km W between the A10 and the N152.
28 Apr-15 Sep 13.6HEC ⸺ ♨ ♠ ♨ ♣ ✕ ⊙ ◪ ⊘ ≋ ⬛ ⟲ ⥩ P
⊡ ⊡ ⊞ lau ♦ ⟲L

MESQUER LOIRE-ATLANTIQUE

Au Soir d'Été ☎ 240425726 ▤ 251739776
Apr-15 Sep 1.5HEC ⸺ ♠ ♠ ♣ ✕ ⊙ ◪ ⬛ ⟲ ⥩ P ⊡ ⊞ lau
♦ ♨ ⊘ ⟲S

Beaupré rte de Kervarin, Kercabellec
☎ 240426748 ▤ 2440426672
e-mail: camping.beaupre@wanadoo.fr
Well equipped site 500mtrs from the beach.
➲ On road between Mesquer and Quimiac. Entrance
signposted.
15 Jun-15 Aug 0.6HEC ⸺ ♨ ♠ ⊙ ◪ ⬛ ⟲ ⥩ ⊡ ⊞ lau ♦ ♨ ♣
✕ ⊘ ≋ ⟲S

Château de Petit Bois ☎ 240426877 ▤ 240426558
e-mail: camping_du_petit_bois@wanadoo.fr
In the extensive grounds of an 18th century castle with
shaded, well defined pitches.
Apr-Oct 10HEC ⏚⏚⏚ ♠🛏🛉🏊🍽⊙🚱🎪🛁 ⏚ 🕆 P 🏛 lau ✦ ⌀
🕆S ⊞ Prices: pitch 12.80-16 (incl 2 persons)

Praderoi alleé des Barges, Quimiac
☎ 240426672 ▤ 240426672
e-mail: camping.praderoi@wanadoo.fr
On level ground 70mtrs from Lanseria Beach.
➲ *300mtrs from Quimiac.*
15 Jun-15 Sep 0.5HEC ⏚⏚⏚ ♠🛏⊙🚱🎪🏛 lau ✦🛉🍽🏊⌀
🏖 🕆S

Welcome r de Bel-Air ☎ 240425085 ▤ 251739984
e-mail: lewelcom@club-internet.fre
In pleasant wooded surroundings, 600mtrs from the coast.
Separate car park for arrivals after 22.30 hrs.
➲ *1.8km NW via D352*
Apr-Sep 2HEC ⏚⏚⏚ ♠🛏🛉⊙🚱🏖🎪🚐🕆 P 🏛 lau ✦🍽🏊⌀
🕆S ⊞

) **MISSILLAC** LOIRE-ATLANTIQUE

CM des Platanes 10 r du Château ☎ 240883888
➲ *1km W via D2, 50m from the lake.*
Jul-Aug 2HEC ⏚⏚⏚ 🔧🛏⊙🚱🏛 lau ✦🛏🍽🏊⊞

) **MONTARGIS** LOIRET

CM de la Forêt rte de Paucourt ☎ 238980020
In the Forest of Montargis.
➲ *1.5km NE near the station and the stadium.*
Closed 20 Dec-10 Jan 5.5HEC ⏚⏚⏚ ⋯⋯ 🔧🛏⊙🚱🏛⊞ lau ✦
🛏🍽🏊⌀🏖🕆LPR Prices: ⚑2 ⚑1.50 ⚑2 ▲2

) **MONTGIVRAY** INDRE

CM Solange Sand r du Pont ☎ 254061036 ▤ 254061039
A pleasant, riverside site in the grounds of a château.
15 Mar-15 Oct 1HEC ⏚⏚⏚ 🔧🛏⊙🚱⌀🕆 R 🏛 lau ✦🛏🍽🏊
⌀🏖 Prices: ⚑1.77 pitch 2.52

) **MONTLOUIS-SUR-LOIRE** INDRE-ET-LOIRE

CM Peupliers ☎ 247458585 ▤ 247451574
e-mail: mairie@ville-montlouis-loire.fr
On level meadow.
➲ *1.5km W on N751, next to swimming pool near railway
bridge.*
15 Mar-15 Oct 6HEC ⏚⏚⏚ ♠🛏⊙🚱⌀🕆 P 🏛 lau
✦🍽🏖🕆R

) **MONTMORILLON** VIENNE

CM Allochon av F-Tribot ☎ 549910233 ▤ 549915826
e-mail: montmorillon@cg86.fr
A well equipped municipal site close to the river and 1.5km
from the town centre.
➲ *SE via D54*
Apr-Oct 2HEC ⏚⏚⏚ ♠🛏⊙🚱🏛 lau ✦🛏🍽🏊⌀🏖🕆PR⊞

) **MONTSOREAU** MAINE-ET-LOIRE

Isle Verte av de la Loire ☎ 241517660
e-mail: isleverte@wanadoo.fr
In wooded surroundings beside the River Loire.
➲ *On D947 between road and river.*
Apr-Sep 2HEC ⏚⏚⏚ ♠🛏🍽🏊⊙🚱🏖🛁▲🕆 PR 🏛⊞ lau
✦🛏⌀ Prices: pitch 10-14 (incl 2 persons)

) **MOUSTIERS-EN-RETZ, LES** LOIRE-ATLANTIQUE

Domaine du Collet ☎ 240214092
May-Sep 12HEC ⏚⏚⏚ ♠🛏🛉🏊🍽🏊⊙🚱⌀▲🕆 S 🏛 lau

) **NANTES** LOIRE-ATLANTIQUE

Petit Port bd du Petit Port 21 ☎ 240744794 ▤ 240742306
e-mail: nge@nge-nantes.fr
On modern well kept park by a river.
➲ *In N part of town near Parc du Petit Port. From town
centre follow Rennes road (N137) then signs to camp site.*
All year 6.5HEC ⏚⏚⏚ ♠🛏🛉🚱🎪🏛⊞ lau ✦🛏🍽🏊🕆PR
Prices: ⚑2.20-2.74 pitch 4.51-14.03

) **NEUVILLE-SUR-SARTHE** SARTHE

Vieux Moulin ☎ 243253182 ▤ 243253811
e-mail: vieux.moulin@wanadoo.fr
A pleasant site with good recreational facilities, close to the
village.
➲ *Access via N138 and D197.*
01 Jun-15 Sep 4.8HEC ⏚⏚⏚ ♠🛏🛉⊙🚱🎪🏊🛁 🕆 P 🏛 lau
✦🍽🏊🕆R

) **NIBELLE** LOIRET

Nibelle rte de Boiscommun ☎ 238322355 ▤ 238320387
Level site in the clearing of an oak woodland.
➲ *Access via D921 turning off to Nibelle in an easterly
direction. Signposted.*
Mar-Nov 9HEC ⏚⏚⏚ 🔧🛏🍽🏊⊙🚱🎪🛁🚐🕆 P 🏛 lau ✦🛏🍽🏊
⌀ Prices: ⚑52-65 ⚑10 ⚑10 ▲10

) **NIORT** DEUX-SÈVRES

Niort-Noron 21 bd Salvador-Allendé
☎ 549790506 ▤ 549790506
Shady site by a river.
01 Apr-30 Sep 3HEC ⏚⏚⏚ ♠🛏⊙🚱⌀🕆 R 🏛⊞ lau ✦🛏🍽🏊⌀
🏊🕆P

) **NOIRMOUTIER, ILE DE** VENDÉE

) **BARBÂTRE**

Onchères ☎ 02 251398131 ▤ 251397365
In quiet setting on sand dunes. S of village on D95.
Apr-Sep 10HEC ⋯⋯ 🔧🛏🛉🏊🍽🏊⊙🚱⌀🏖🕆 PS 🏛⊞ lau

) **NOIRMOUTIER-EN-L'ILE**

Vendette rte des Sableaux ☎ 251390624
A well equipped site in a pine wood close to the beach.
➲ *From town centre continue towards Plage des Sableaux.*
27 Mar-Sep 12HEC ⏚⏚⏚ ⋯⋯ ♠🛏🛉🍽🏊⊙🚱🕆 S 🏛 lau ✦
🛏⌀🏖🕆P

) **NOTRE-DAME-DE-MONTS** VENDÉE

Beauséjour ☎ 251588388
➲ *2km NW on D38.*
Etr-Sep 1.3HEC ⏚⏚⏚ 🔧🛏⊙🚱⌀🎪🏛⊞ lau ✦🛏🍽🏊🕆S

Grand Jardin Le Grand Jardin, 50 r de la Barre
☎ 0228112175
A family site in a picturesque location facing the Ile d'Yeu.
Modern sanitary installations and plenty of sporting
facilities. 1km from the beach.
➲ *0.6km N*
All year 2HEC ⏚⏚⏚ ♠🛏🍽🏊⊙🚱🏖🚐🛁🕆 PR 🏛🚱⊞ lau
✦🛏🕆S

) **NOZAY** LOIRE-ATLANTIQUE

CM 'Henri Dubourg' rte de Rennes
☎ 240879433 ▤ 240793564
A small site in a quiet location.
➲ *Access via N137 and N171.*
15 May-15 Sep 1HEC ⏚⏚⏚ 🔧🛏⊙🚱🏛 lau ✦🛏🍽🏊⌀🏖
🕆P ⊞

OLÉRON, ILE D' CHARENTE-MARITIME
BOYARDVILLE

Signol ☎ 546470122
In attractive surroundings within a pine forest, close to the village centre and 800mtrs from the beach.
➲ *W of town, leave D126 by the AVIA service station and follow signs for 0.6km.*
May-Sep 7HEC ⁙ ⚂♠♪♥☗☺☻⛺☎ ⚡ P ☑⊞⍽ lau ♦ 🚐 ☗ ⚡S

CHÂTEAU-D'OLÉRON, LE

Airotel d'Oléron Domaine de Montreavail
☎ 546476182 ▧ 546477967
In a peaceful, parklike setting 1km from the beach and the town centre.
➲ *Signposted from town centre.*
Etr-10 Oct 4HEC ⁙ ♠♪♥☗☺☻⛺☎ ⚡ LPS ☑⊞ lau

Brande rte des Huîtres ☎ 546476237 ▧ 546477170
e-mail: la.brande@wanadoo.fr
A family site with good facilities in beautiful surroundings.
➲ *2.5km NW, 250m from the sea.*
15 Mar-15 Nov 4HEC ⁙ ⚂♠♪♥☗☺☻⛺☎ ⚡ P ☑⊞ lau ♦ ⚡S **Prices:** pitch 11-20 (incl 2 persons)

COTINIÈRE, LA

Tamaris 72 av des Pins ☎ 546471051 ▧ 546472796
About 150m from sea. Level site in pleasant olive grove.
➲ *W side of island. N of town.*
15 Mar-15 Nov 5HEC ⁙ ⚂♪♥☗☺☻⛺🅰⚡ P ☑⊞ lau ♦ 🚐⚡S

DOLUS-D'OLÉRON

Ostréa rte des Huîtres ☎ 546476236 ▧ 546752001
A well equipped site in wooded surroundings close to the beach.
➲ *3.5km NE*
Apr-Sep 2HEC ⁙ ⚂♪♥☗☺☻⛺☎⚡S☑⊞ lau

DOMINO

International Rex Domino ☎ 546765597 ▧ 546766788
Pleasant seaside site with good recreational facilities and access to the beach.
May-14 Sep 0.8HEC ⁙ ⚂♪♥☗☺☻⛺ ⚡ PS ☑⊞ lau ♦ ✕

ST-DENIS-D'OLÉRON

Phare Ouest 7 Impasse des Beaupins
☎ 251975550 ▧ 0251289109
e-mail: camping-apv@wanadoo.fr
On level ground with direct access to the beach.
➲ *1km NW towards the lighthouse.*
Apr-Sep 3.5HEC ⁙ ⚂♪♥☗☺☻⛺⚡S☑ lau ♦⊞

ST-GEORGES-D'OLÉRON

Gautrelle Plage des Saumonards ☎ 546472157
In a pine wood close to the beach.
27 Mar-Sep 6HEC ⁙ ⚂♪☗☺⚡S☑⊞ lau

Quatre Vents La Jousselinière ☎ 546756547 ▧ 546766257
e-mail: 4vents.oleron@wanado.fr
A peaceful site with good facilities.
➲ *3km E via N739.*
Mar-Nov 7.2HEC ⁙ ♠♪♥☗☺☻⛺☎ ⚡ P ☑⊞ lau ♦ ⚡S

Suroît rte Touristique Côte Ouest, l'Ileau
☎ 546470725
On level ground, sheltered by sand dunes with fine, modern facilities.
➲ *5km SW of town.*
Apr-Sep 5HEC ⁙ ⚂♠♪♥☗☺☻⛺ ⚡S☑⊞ lau ♦ ☗

Vérébleu La Jousselinière ☎ 546765770 ▧ 546767056
e-mail: verebleu@wanadoo.fr
➲ *1.7km SE via D273*
3 Apr-20 Sep 7.5HEC ⁙ ⚂♪♥☗☺☻⛺☎⚡ P ☑☑ ⊞ lau ♦ ✕ ☗

Gros Joncs ☎ 546765229 ▧ 546766774
e-mail: camping.gros.joncs@wanadoo.fr
Quiet location on undulating land in the midst of lovely pine woodland.
➲ *On tourist route from La Cotinière about 5km NW in the direction of Domino, 1km SW of St-Georges-d'Oléron.*
All year 5.2HEC ⁙ ⚂♪♥☗☺☻⛺☎ ⚡ PS ☑⊞ lau

ST-PIERRE-D'OLÉRON

Pierrière 18 rte de St-Georges
☎ 546470829 ▧ 546751282
e-mail: camppier@club-internet.fr
A pleasant site in wooded surroundings with well defined pitches.
➲ *NW towards St-Georges-d'Oléron*
3May-21Sep 4HEC ⁙ ♠♪♥☗☺☻⛺ ⚡ P ☑ lau ♦ ⚡⊞ **Prices:** pitch 14-19.50 (incl 2 persons)

Trois Masses Le Marais Doux
☎ 546472396 ▧ 0546751554
A well equipped site in a picturesque location 2.5 km from the beach.
Etr-Sep 3HEC ⁙ ⚂♪♥☗☺☻⛺ ⚡ P ☑⊞ lau ♦ ⚡S

OLIVET LOIRET

CM Olivet r du Pont Bouchet
☎ 238635394 ▧ 238635896
Site lies partly on shaded peninsula, partly on open lawns beside river.
➲ *2km E. Signposted from village.*
Apr-15 Oct 1HEC ⁙ ♪♥☗☺⛺ ⚡ ☑⊞ lau

OLONNE-SUR-MER VENDÉE

Loubine 1 rte de la Mer
☎ 0251331292 ▧ 0251331271
Situated on the edge of a forest bordering the beach.
➲ *N via D87/D80.*
Apr-Sep 8HEC ⁙ ♠♪♥☗☺☻⛺☎ ⚡ P ☑⊞⍽ lau ♦ ⚡S

Moulin de la Salle r.des Moulin de la salle
☎ 251959910 ▧ 251969613
In pleasant surroundings close to the beach with good facilities.
➲ *2.7km W.*
Apr-Oct 3.1HEC ⁙ ♠♪♥☗☺☻⛺☎ ⚡ P ☑⊞ lau ♦ 🚐

Oreé rte des Amis de la Nature
☎ 251331059 ▧ 251331516
➲ *3km N*
Apr-Sep 5.5HEC ⁙ ♠♪♥☗☺☻⛺🅰 ⚡ P ☑⊞ lau ♦ ⚡R

ONZAIN LOIR-ET-CHER

Dugny rte de Chambon-sur-Cisse
☎ 254207066 ▨ 254337169
e-mail: info@camping-de-degny.fr
On a small lake, surrounded by farmland with well marked pitches shaded by poplars.
➲ *From Onzain follow direction Chambon-sur-Cisse (CD45).*
All year 8HEC ⟘ 🖳👫🍴✕⊙🅿🚿🚻🏕🚐🛒⚓ ⚡ P 🅿⊞ lau
Prices: ⭡5-7 pitch 3

PALMYRE, LA CHARENTE-MARITIME

Bonne Anse Plage ☎ 546224090 ▨ 546224230
e-mail: bonne.anse@wanadoo.fr
An extensive, gently undulating site in a pine wood, 400m from the beach.
➲ *1km from La Palmyre roundabout. Follow signs for Ronce-les-Bains.*
18 May-08 Sep 17HEC ⟘ ⁝⁝⁝ ⚓🖳🏕🍴✕⊙🅿🚿🚐🛒⚓
P 🅿⊞🏊 lau ⚓ ⚓🏊⚓S

Palmyre Loisirs 28 des Mathes ☎ 546236766 ▨ 546224881
Well equipped family site with plenty of recreational facilities and well supervised activities for children.
➲ *From Les Mathes take the La Palmyre road.*
16 May-12 Sep 20HEC ⟘ ⁝⁝⁝ ⚓🖳🏕🍴✕⊙🅿🚿🚐🛒🏕🚐
⚓ P 🅿⊞ lau

Palmyr Océana 26 av des Mathes
☎ 0546224035 ▨ 0546236476
e-mail: palmyroceana@wanadoo.fr
A well equipped family site in a delightful wooded setting close to the beach. A wide variety of recreational facilities are available.
Apr-Sep 17HEC ⟘ ⁝⁝⁝ 🖳👫🏕🍴✕⊙🅿🚿🏕🚐🛒⚓P 🅿
⊞🏊 lau ⚓ ⚓RS Prices: pitch 12.19-18.29 (incl 2 persons)

PERRIER, LE VENDÉE

CM de la Maison Blanche ☎ 251493923 ▨ 251493923
A family site on level ground, with pitches divided by trees. 6km from the coast.
15 Jun-15 Sep 3.2HEC ⟘ ⚓🖳⊙🅿🏕🚐⚓ R 🅿 lau ⚓🖳
🍴✕🏕🚻⊞ Prices: ⭡2.55 pitch 7.55-8.40

PEZOU LOIR-ET-CHER

CM "Les Ilots" rte de Renay ☎ 254234069 ▨ 254236240
e-mail: commune.pezou@wanadoo.fr
A well equipped site 400mtrs from the town centre.
➲ *SE via D12, 50m from the River Loir*
03 May-16 Sep 18 Sep-02 May 1HEC ⟘ ⚓🖳⊙🅿🛒lau ⚓
🖳🍴✕⊞ Prices: ⭡1.90 pitch 1.90

PIERREFITTE-SUR-SAULDRE LOIR-ET-CHER

Sologne Parc des Alicourts Domaine des Alicourts
☎ 254886334
In wooded surroundings at the heart of an extensive park, this family site is exceptionally well equipped and provides a wide variety of recreational facilities.
➲ *6km NE via D126 beside the lake.*
May-15 Sep 25HEC ⟘ ⁝⁝⁝ 🏊🖳🏕🍴✕⊙🅿🏕🚐⚓ LP
🅿 lau ⚓ ⚓R

PIRIAC-SUR-MER LOIRE-ATLANTIQUE

Parc du Guibel ☎ 240235267
On level ground in a delightful wooded setting with good recreational facilities.
➲ *3.5km E via D52*
Etr-Sep 10HEC ⟘ ⚓🖳🏕🍴✕⊙🅿🏕🚐🛒⚓ P 🅿⊞
lau ⚓ ⚓PS

In the ♥ of the Castles and vineyards of the Loire

CAMPING CARAVANNING ★★★★
DOMAINE DE DUGNY
41150 ONZAIN
Tel: 33 (0) 254 207 066
Fax: 33 (0) 254 337 169
E-mail: info@camping-de-dugny.fr
www.camping-de-dugny.fr
OPEN ALL YEAR –
CHALETS AND MOBILE HOMES TO LET
Jocelyne and Jean Claude welcome you on a quiet domain bordering a lake of 4 ha.
A PARADISE FOR CHILDREN
Swimming pool, paddling pool, table tennis, entertainment programme in season, trips with the little campsite train, fishing, games for children, sports field. In the old farm: Bar, restaurant, grocery, a hall with a big terrace to spend your evenings. Mountain bikes to let – minigolf. For the lovers of ultra light planes: we have an authorised runway (600m) free of charge, without nuisance for the campsite. Possibilities for beginner lessons.

Pouldroit 247 rte de Mesquer ☎ 240235091
A pleasant site in wooded surroundings 300m from the sea and 600m from the village.
➲ *500m E on D52.*
Apr-15 Sep 12HEC ⟘ ⚓🖳🏕🍴✕⊙🅿🏕🚐
⚓ P 🅿⊞ lau ⚓🏊S

PLAINE-SUR-MER, LA LOIRE-ATLANTIQUE

Tabardière ☎ 603003417 ▨ 240210268
e-mail: info@camping-la-tabardiere
A wooded, terraced site 3km from the sea.
➲ *Situated between Pornic and La Plaine-sur-Mer off D13.*
Apr-Sep 6HEC ⟘ ⚓🖳🏕🍴✕⊙🅿🏕🚐🛒⚓P 🅿⊞ lau ⚓
✕ Prices: ⭡3.10-4.60

POIRÉ-SUR-VELLUIRE, LE VENDÉE

Petits Prés ☎ 251523777
➲ *On S outskirts beside the River Vendée. Well signposted.*
All year 2.6HEC ⟘ ⚓🖳⊙🅿🚐⚓ R 🅿⊞ lau
⚓🖳✕🏕🚻

PONS CHARENTE-MARITIME

Chardon Chardon ☎ 546950125
e-mail: chardon2@wanadoo.fr
Quietly situated on the edge of a small village next to a farm.
➲ *From Pons take D732 westwards towards Royan. The site is 2.5km on the left. Alternatively from exit 36 of the Autoroute A10 and turn towards Pons. Site is 800m on right.*
Apr-Oct 1.6HEC ⟘ ⚓🖳🏕🍴✕⊙🅿🏕🚐🛒⊞ lau
⚓ ⚓R⊞

Washing and drying machines, children's games, tennis. Swimming pool 50m. All shops 300m. Special sanitary installations for babies and handicapped. 30 min. from the sea.

CAMPING MUNICIPAL ★★★
PARC LA GARENNE
17250 Pont-l'Abbé-d'Arnoult
A10-exit 34, follow D18 direction Pont l'Abbé or exit 35, then N137 between Saintes and Rochefort, CD18 direction Pont l'Abbé.
Open from 15th of June til 15th of September
Tel: 05 46 97 01 46 Out of season: 05 46 97 00 19
Fax: 05 46 97 12 31

▶ **PONT-L'ABBÉ-D'ARNOULT** CHARENTE-MARITIME

Parc de la Garenne 1 av Chambenoit
☎ 546970019 ▤ 546971231
➔ *Access via A10, N137 and D18.*
15 Jun-15 Sep 2.8HEC ⛺ ⊞ 🛁 ⊙ 🚻 ⊞ ➤ P ⊞ lau ➤ 🍴 ♥ ✗
Ⓐ Prices: ♠9.76-12.20

▶ **PONTS-DE-CÉ, LES** MAINE-ET-LOIRE

Ile du Château r de la Boire Salée
☎ 241446205 ▤ 241446205
e-mail: ile-du-chateau@wanadoo.fr
Situated on a small island in the River Loire close to the Château des Ponts-de-Cé. Separate car park for arrivals after 9pm.
➔ *SW of Angers towards Cholet.*
01 Apr-30 Sep 2.3HEC ⛺ ♠ 🛁 🍴 ✗ ⊙ 🚻 Ⓐ ⊞ A ➤ PR ⊞ ⊞ lau Prices: pitch 11-11.40 (incl 2 persons)

▶ **PORNIC** LOIRE-ATLANTIQUE

Boutinardière ☎ 240820568 ▤ 240824901
e-mail: boutinardiere@free.fr
The site has three outdoor pools with water slides. Also a heated indoor pool.
Apr-Sep 7.5HEC ⠿ 🛁 ✗ ⚱ ➤ P lau ➤ ⚲S
See advertisement in colour section

Patisseau 29 rue de Patisseau
☎ 240821039 ▤ 240822281
e-mail: contact@lepatisseau.com
In wooded surroundings close to the beach with fine recreational facilities.
➔ *3km E via D751.*
Apr-14 Sep 4HEC ⛺ ⊞ 🛁 🍴 ✗ ⊙ 🚻 Ⓐ ⚱ ⊞ A ➤ PS ⊞ ⊞ lau

▶ **PORNICHET** LOIRE-ATLANTIQUE

Bel Air 150 av de Bonne Source
☎ 33240611078 ▤ 33240612618
In a pleasant, wooded location 50m from the beach.
Apr-Oct 6HEC ⠿ ⊞ 🛁 🍴 ✗ ⊙ 🚻 Ⓐ ⊞ ⊞ lau ➤ ⚱ ⚲S ⊞

Forges 98 rte de Villes Blais
☎ 240611884 ▤ 240601184
In wooded surroundings with well defined pitches and good recreational facilities.
➔ *Access via N171.*
All year 2HEC ⛺ ♠ 🛁 ⊙ 🚻 Ⓐ ⚱ ⊞ ➤ P ⊞ ⊞ lau ➤ ⚲L
Prices: ♠4.50 pitch 7.50

▶ **PORT-DE-PILES** VIENNE

Bec des Deux Eaux rte de Marigny ☎ 247650271
Wooded family site located close to the confluence of the Vienne and Creuse rivers with quite easy access to the Futuroscope.
➔ *E off N10.*
Apr-Sep 3.5HEC ⛺ ♠ 🛁 🍴 ✗ ⊙ 🚻 ⊞ ➤ PR ⊞ lau

▶ **RÉ, ILE DE** CHARENTE-MARITIME
▶ **ARS-EN-RÉ**

Soleil 57 r de la Plage ☎ 546294062
On level, shaded meadow 150mtrs from the beach and 500mtrs from the village.
➔ *Signposted from the N735 shortly before reaching Ars.*
Mar-16 Nov 2HEC ⛺ ♠ 🛁 🍴 ✗ ⊙ 🚻 Ⓐ ⊞ ⊞ lau ➤ ⚲S

▶ **BOIS-PLAGE-EN-RÉ, LE**

Antioche ☎ 546092386 ▤ 546094334
In quiet, wooded area among dunes with direct access to the beach.
➔ *3.5km SE of village towards the beach.*
27 Mar-Sep 2.7HEC ⠿ ⊞ 🛁 🍴 ✗ ⊙ 🚻 Ⓐ ⊞ ⊞ ➤ ⚲S ⊞ lau ➤ Ⓐ

Camping Interlude-Gros-Jonc rte de Gros Jonc
☎ 546091822 ▤ 546092338
e-mail: interlude@ileclere.com
In a pleasant, wooded location 50m from the beach, this site has a fitness centre and can arrange guided tours of the area.
30 Mar-22 Sep 6.5HEC ⛺ ⠿ ⊞ 🛁 🍴 ✗ ⊙ 🚻 ⚱ ⊞ ➤ P ⊞ lau ➤ ⚱ ⚲S ⊞ Prices: ♠4.60-8.90 pitch 6.40-10.10

▶ **COUARDE-SUR-MER, LA**

Océan La Passe ☎ 546298770 ▤ 0546299213
e-mail: campingdelocean@wanadoo.fr
In a fine position facing the sea with good modern facilities.
➔ *3km NW on N735.*
Apr-Sep 7HEC ⛺ ⠿ ♠ 🛁 🍴 ✗ ⊙ 🚻 Ⓐ ⊞ A ➤ P ⊞ ⊞ lau ➤ ⚲S

▶ **FLOTTE, LA**

Blanche Deviation de la Flotte ☎ 546095243 ▤ 546093694
A popular family site in a wooded location.
➔ *N on D735 towards St-Martin.*
Apr-11 Nov 4HEC ⠿ ⊞ 🛁 🍴 ✗ ⊙ 🚻 Ⓐ ⊞ ➤ P ⊞ ⊞ lau ➤ ⚱ ⚲S

Peupliers ☎ 546096235
Siutated in a large, wooded park 800m from the sea with good sporting facilities.
➔ *1.3km SE*
Apr-18 Sep 4.4HEC ⠿ ♠ 🛁 🍴 ✗ ⊙ 🚻 Ⓐ ⚱ ⊞ ➤ P ⊞ ⊞ lau ➤ ⚲S

▶ **LOIX**

Ipares Le Petit Boucheau, rte du Grouin
☎ 546290543 ▤ 546290679
e-mail: ipares@wanadoo.fr
➔ *Access E towards Pointe du Grouin, 500m from the sea.*
Mar-Oct 4.5HEC ⛺ ♥ 🛁 ✗ ⊙ 🚻 ⊞ ➤ P ⊞ ⊞ lau ➤ Ⓐ ⚱

▶ **ST-MARTIN-DE-RÉ**

CM r du Rempart ☎ 546092196 ▤ 546099418
In pleasant wooded surroundings at the foot of the 17th century ramparts.
➔ *N, beyond La Flotte.*
Mar-15 Oct 3HEC ⛺ ♠ 🛁 🍴 ✗ ⊙ 🚻 ⊞ ⊞ lau ➤ 🍴 ⚲S ⊞

RONCE-LES-BAINS CHARENTE-MARITIME

Pignade av des Monards ☎ 0870 2427777 ▤ 0870 2429999
A family site with good recreational facilities.
➲ *1.5km S*
28 Apr-16 Sep 16HEC ⏛ ⠿ ♦ ♠ ⛴ ♀ ✕ ⊟ ⌀ ♨ ⛺ ▲ ⟨
P 🏚 ⊞ ⊗ lau ➡ ⟨S

ROSIERS, LES MAINE-ET-LOIRE

Val de Loire 6 r Ste-Baudruche ☎ 241519433 ▤ 241518913
A comfortable site partly on the banks of the River Loire
with good recreational facilities.
➲ *N via D59*
Etr-15 Sep 4HEC ⏛ ⬡ ♠ ⛴ ✕ ⊙ ⊟ ⛺ ♨ ▲ ⟨ P 🏚 ▣ ⊞
lau ➡ ♀ ✕ ⌀ ♨ ⟨R

ROYAN CHARENTE-MARITIME

At MÉDIS(4km NE)

Chênes La Verdonneric ☎ 546067138
In a wooded location with good facilities. Separate late
arrivals car park after 22.00hrs.
➲ *2km from Royan on the Saintes-Royan road.*
15 Mar-Oct 6.5HEC ⏛ ♦ ♠ ⛴ ♀ ✕ ⊙ ⊟ ⌀ ♨ ⛺ ♨ ⟨ P 🏚
⊞ lau

At PONTAILLAC(2km NE on D25)

Clairfontaine allée des Peupliers ☎ 546390811 ▤ 546381379
e-mail: camping.clairfontaine@wanadoo.fr
A well equipped site in wooded surroundings 300m from the
beach with a variety of recreational facilities.
20 May-15 Sep 5HEC ⏛ ⬡ ♠ ⛴ ♀ ✕ ⊙ ⊟ ⌀ ⟨ PS 🏚 ▣ ⊞
lau

SABLES-D'OLONNE, LES VENDÉE

Dune des Sables La Paracou ☎ 251323121 ▤ 0251323121
In a fine location facing the sea and close to the beach.
15 Apr-Sep 6HEC ⏛ ⥯ ♠ ⛴ ♀ ✕ ⊙ ⊟ ⌀ ♨ ⛺ ♨ ⟨ PS 🏚
⊞ lau ➡ ⟨S
See advertisement in colour section

Roses 1 r des Roses ☎ 251951042 ▤ 251339404
e-mail: camping@chadotel.fr
A level site, shaded by trees and bushes, 500mtrs from the
Remblai beach.
➲ *Close to the town centre off D949.*
Apr-Oct 3.5HEC ⏛ ♦ ♠ ⛴ ♀ ✕ ⊙ ⊟ ⌀ ♨ ⛺ ♨ ⟨ P 🏚 ⊞
lau ➡ ✕ ⟨S
See advertisement in colour section

SABLÉ-SUR-SARTHE SARTHE

Hippodrome allée du Quebec ☎ 243954261 ▤ 243927473
e-mail: camping.sable@dial.oleane.com
In a peaceful wooded setting with a great variety of
recreational facilities.
➲ *Situated 450 yards from the town.*
Apr-Sep 3HEC ⏛ ⬡ ♠ ⛴ ♀ ✕ ⊙ ⊟ ⌀ ♨ ⟨ P 🏚 ⊞ lau ➡ ♀ ✕ ♨
Prices: ⚑1.55-2.06 pitch 2.97-3.96

ST-AIGNAN-SUR-CHER LOIR-ET-CHER

CM Cochards ☎ 0254751559 ▤ 0254754472
e-mail: camping@les_cochards.com
On beautiful meadowland, completely surrounded by
hedges.
➲ *1km from bridge on D17 towards Selles.*
01 Apr-15Oct 4HEC ⏛ ♦ ♠ ⛴ ♀ ✕ ⊙ ⊟ ♨ ⛺ ♨ ▲ ⟨ P 🏚
⊞ lau ➡ ⟨R

ST-AMAND-MONTROND CHER

CM Roche chemin de la Roche ☎ 0248960936 ▤ 0248960591
In a lovely wooded location between the River Cher and the
Berry Canal with good modern facilities.

La Pignade ★★★★
Ronce-les-Bains

**La Pignade is a
typically French parc,
ideal for families.
With swimming pool,
restaurant and
entertainment
facilities at the heart
of the parc.**

- Shaded clusters of
  touring pitches with easy
  access to the central area
- Heated outdoor pools
  with waterslide &
  children's pool
- Wide range of sports
  & leisure activities
- Superb low season prices

- Restaurant, takeaway &
  newly built bar set around
  an attractive piazza
- 3 children's clubs for
  all ages
- Bilingual staff on parc
- Site open from:
  11 May - 21 September

**La Pignade, La Tremblade,
17390 Ronce-les-Bains, France
Tel:00 33 546 36 25 25 Fax:00 33 546 36 34 14** V2819

To book from France please call the number above, quoting code FAA03
To book from the UK please call 0870 242 77 77 quoting code FAA03

➲ *1.5km SW near river and canal.*
Apr-Sep 4HEC ⏛ ♦ ♠ ⊙ ⊟ ♨ ⟨ R 🏚 ⊞ lau ➡ ⛴ ♀ ✕ ♨ ⟨PR
Prices: ⚑2.30 pitch 3.30

ST-ANDRÉ-DES-EAUX LOIRE-ATLANTIQUE

CM Les Chalands Fleuris r du Stade
☎ 240012040 ▤ 240915424
e-mail: chalfleu@club-internet.fr
A peaceful site with good facilities in the middle of a natural
park.
➲ *1km NE.*
Apr-15 Oct 4HEC ⏛ ⥯ ♠ ⛴ ♀ ✕ ⊙ ⊟ ♨ ⛺ ♨ ▲ ⟨ P 🏚
⊞ lau ➡ ⌀

ST-AVERTIN INDRE-ET-LOIRE

CM Rives du Cher 61 r de Rochepinard
☎ 247272760 ▤ 0247258289
e-mail: maqggicc.sarl@wanadoo.fr
Municipal site on the banks of the River Cher. Only caravans
weighing less than 1000kg accepted.
➲ *400mtrs N of the town centre and 4km from Tours.*
Apr-15 Oct 3HEC ⏛ ⬡ ♠ ⊙ ⊟ ⌀ ♨ ⛺ ♨ 🏚 ⊞ lau ➡ ⛴ ♀
✕ ⟨P Prices: ⚑3 ♠2 ⛴5.50-3 ▲5

ST-BRÉVIN-LES-PINS LOIRE-ATLANTIQUE

CM Courance 100/110 av Ml-Foch
☎ 240272291 ▤ 240272459
e-mail: francecamping@wanadoo.fr
In a pine forest with direct access to the beach.
➲ *S off D305.*
All year 4HEC ⏛ ⠿ ♦ ♠ ⛴ ♀ ✕ ⊙ ⊟ ⌀ ♨ ⛺ ▲ ⟨ S 🏚
⊞ lau ➡ ♨ ⟨P Prices: pitch 6.10-6.86 (incl 2 persons)

Clarys Plage av des Epines ☎ 251581024 ▤ 251595196
e-mail: a.rondeou@free.fr
A family site with good facilities including an indoor
swimming pool and an outdoor pool with a water slide.
➲ *S of town 300mtrs from the beach.*
15 May-15 Sep 8HEC ⊞ ⁙⁙ ◆ ♟ ⚏ ❢ ✕ ☉ ☻ ⌀ ☎ ⁝ P ☒
⊞ lau ◆ ⛺ ⁓S **Prices:** pitch 23.17-28.97 (incl 3 persons)

Sirenes av des Demoiselles ☎ 251580131 ▤ 251590367
In a forested location 500m from the beach with good
facilities.
➲ *SE off D38.*
27 Mar-Oct 15HEC ⊞ ⁙⁙ ◆ ♟ ☉ ☻ ☒ P ☒ ⊞ lau ◆ ⚏ ❢ ✕
⌀ ⛺ ⁓PS

Forêt 190 chemin de la Rive ☎ 251588463 ▤ 251588463
A well equipped family site in a pleasant rural setting.
➲ *5.5km NW.*
Apr-Sep 1HEC ⊞ ⁙⁙ ◑ ♟ ⚏ ❢ ☉ ☻ ⌀ ☎ ⁝ P ☒ ⊞ lau ◆ ❢
✕ ⛺ ⁓S **Prices:** ♦3.05-3.84 pitch 15.25-20.58 (incl 2 persons)

At OROUET(6km SE)

Yole chemin des Bosses ☎ 251586717 ▤ 251590535
e-mail: camping.layole@wanadoo.fr
In rural surroundings 1km from a fine sandy beach.
➲ *Signposted from D38 in Orouet.*
May-15 Sep 6HEC ⊞ ⁙⁙ ◑ ♟ ⚏ ❢ ✕ ☉ ☻ ⌀ ☎ ⁝ P ☒ ☒
⁂ lau ◆ ⚏ ⁓S **Prices:** pitch 16.16-25.15 (incl 2 persons)
See advertisement in colour section

ST-JULIEN-DES-LANDES VENDÉE

Fôret ☎ 251466211 ▤ 251466087
e-mail: camping@domainelaforet.com
In a picturesque setting in the grounds of a château with well
defined pitches and modern facilities.
➲ *NE on D55, rte de Martinet.*
15 May-15 Sep 50HEC ⊞ ◑ ♟ ⚏ ❢ ✕ ☉ ☻ ⌀ ☎ ⁝ P ☒
lau **Prices:** pitch 19.65-26.20 (incl 3 persons)

▨Garangeoire ☎ 251466539
Family site set in 200 hectare estate. Pitches separated by
hedges. A good variety of recreational facilities.
➲ *2km N of the village.*
15 May-15 Sep 15HEC ⊞ ◑ ♟ ⚏ ❢ ✕ ☉ ☻ ⌀ ☎ ⁝ LP ☒
⊞ lau

Guyonnière La Guyonnière ☎ 251466259 ▤ 251466289
e-mail: pierre.jaspers@wanadoo.fr
A pleasant site with pitches divided by hedges with good
sanitary and recreational facilities.
➲ *2km from the town centre towards St-Gilles-Croix-de-Vie.*
May-Oct 30HEC ⊞ ◑ ♟ ⚏ ❢ ✕ ☉ ☻ ⌀ ☎ ⛺ ♣ ⁝ LP ☒ ⊞
lau

ST-JUST-LUZAC CHARENTE-MARITIME

▨Séquoia Parc ☎ 546855555 ▤ 546855556
e-mail: sequoia.parc@wanadoo.fr
Situated in a spacious park on the 'La Josephtrie' estate
containing an attractive château some 5km from the coast.
➲ *Access via A10 exit 'Saintes' then D728 towards Ile
d'Oléron and follow signs from St-Just.*
28 Apr-9 Sep 45HEC ⊞ ⁘ ♟ ⚏ ❢ ✕ ☉ ☻ ⌀ ☎ ⁝ P ☒ lau

ST-LAURENT-NOUAN LOIR-ET-CHER

Amitié r du Camping ☎ 54870152 ▤ 0254870973
On the shore of the River Loire between Blois and Orléans.
➲ *On D951.*
All year 2HEC ⊞ ⁘ ♟ ☉ ☻ ⁝ R ☒ lau ◆ ⚏ ❢ ✕ ⌀ ⛺
Prices: ♦1.83-2.13 pitch 3.81-4.57

ST-LÉONARD-DE-NOBLAT HAUTE-VIENNE

CM Beaufort ☎ 05 555560279
In pleasant wooded surroundings with good facilities.
➲ *Access from the D39.*
15 Jun-15 Sep 2HEC ⊞ ◑ ♟ ⚏ ❢ ☉ ☻ ⌀ ☎ ☒ ⊞ lau ◆ ✕
⛺ **Prices:** pitch 6.71-7.93 (incl 2 persons)

ST-MALÔ-DU-BOIS VENDÉE

Plein Air de Poupet ☎ 251923145 ▤ 251923865
In a picturesque location beside the River Sèvre Nantaise,
surrounded by woodland.
➲ *From village take D72 for 1km, then take left fork and
follow signs.*
May-Sep 3HEC ⊞ ◑ ♟ ☉ ☻ ☎ ⁝ R ☒ ⊞ lau ◆ ⚏ ❢ ✕ ⌀

ST-PALAIS-SUR-MER CHARENTE-MARITIME

Ormeaux 44 av de Bernezac ☎ 546390207
Well equipped site in wooded surroundings, 500m from the
beach.
➲ *1km N.*
15 May-15 Sep 3.5HEC ⊞ ◑ ♟ ⚏ ❢ ✕ ☉ ☻ ⌀ ☎ ⛺ ⁝ P ☒
⊞ lau ◆ ⁓LS

Puits de l'Auture La Grande Côte
☎ 546232031 ▤ 546232638
e-mail: camping-lauture@wanadoo.fr
A family site in a picturesque location at the edge of a forest
facing the sea.
➲ *2km NW on D25 La Palmyre road.*
May-Sep 5HEC ⊞ ◆ ♟ ⚏ ❢ ✕ ☉ ☻ ⌀ ☎ ⁝ P ☒ ⊞ ⁂ lau
◆ ⁓S

ST-VINCENT-SUR-JARD VENDÉE

'Bolée d'Air' rte du Bouil ☎ 251903605 ▤ 251339404
e-mail: chadotel@wanadoo.fr
A family site on level ground with pitches divided by hedges.
Good recreational facilities, including a water slide, and
900mtrs from Bouil beach.
➲ *2km E via D21.*
Apr-Sep 6.5HEC ⊞ ◑ ♟ ⚏ ❢ ✕ ☉ ☻ ⌀ ⛺ ☎ ♣ ♠ ⁝ P ☒
⊞ lau ◆ ✕ ⁓S **Prices:** pitch 12.20-20.58 (incl 2 persons)
See advertisement in colour section

STE-CATHERINE-DE-FIERBOIS INDRE-ET-LOIRE

▨Parc de Fierbois ☎ 247654335 ▤ 274655375
e-mail: parc.fierbois@wanadoo.fr
Beside artificial lake; good bathing area.
➲ *Follow D101 off N10, 1.5km SE.*
15 May-15 Sep 20HEC ⊞ ◆ ♟ ⚏ ❢ ✕ ☉ ☻ ☎ ⁝ LP ☒ ⊞
lau

STE-GEMME CHARENTE-MARITIME

Jamica la Sablière Ferme de Magne ☎ 546229099
In a pleasant situation beside a lake within a country park.
➲ *Access via A10 exit 25 (Saintes) and D728 towards Ile
d'Oléron.*
May-15 Oct ⊞ ◆ ♟ ⚏ ❢ ✕ ☉ ☻ ⌀ ⛺ ☎ ⁝ L ☒ ⊞ lau

STE-REINE-DE-BRETAGNE LOIRE-ATLANTIQUE

▨Château du Deffay BP 18 ☎ 240880057 ▤ 240016655
Situated in the beautiful Parc de Brière providing fishing,
walking and horse riding. Games and TV rooms.
➲ *4.5km W on D33 rte de Pontchâteau.*
11May-21Sep 8HEC ⊞ ◑ ♟ ⚏ ❢ ✕ ☉ ☻ ☎ ⁝ LP ☒ ⊞ lau
Prices: ♦2.60-4.20 pitch 6.25-9.45

SANTROP HAUTE-VIENNE

Santrop ☎ 555710808 ▤ 555712393
e-mail: lacsaintpardoux@aol.com
A well equipped family site on the shore of Lac de St-Pardoux with good facilities for water sports.
➲ *Access via A20 exit 25.*
18May-21Sep 4.5HEC ⬛ ♠ ⋔ ⚡ ℡ ⚡ ✕ ⊙ ⚑ ⌀ ♨ ⬛ ⁀ L ▣
⊞ lau **Prices:** pitch 9.50-15.50 (incl 2 persons)

SAUMUR MAINE-ET-LOIRE

Chantepie ☎ 241679534 ▤ 241679585
e-mail: camping.chantepie@wanadoo.fr
A pleasant site with a fine view over the River Loire.
➲ *Access via D751 towards Gennes.*
27 Apr-14 Sep 10HEC ⬛ ⚑ ⋔ ℡ ⚡ ✕ ⊙ ⚑ ⌀ ▲
⁀ P ▣ ⊞ lau

Ile d'Offard av de Verden ☎ 241403000 ▤ 241673781
e-mail: iledoffard@wanadoo.fr
On island in the middle of the Loire near municipal stadium.
Some facilities are only available during the high season.
15 Jan-15 Dec 4.5HEC ⬛ ⚑ ⋔ ℡ ⚡ ✕ ⊙ ⚑ ♨ ⬛ ▲ ⁀ PR
▣ ⊞ lau ➤ ⌀ **Prices:** pitch 13.50-18.50

SELLE CRAONNAISE, LA MAYENNE

Rincerie Base de Loisirs la Rincerie
☎ 243061752 ▤ 243075020
A modern site offering a good selection of sporting facilities.
Separate carpark for arrivals after 22.00hrs.
➲ *N of La Selle-Craonnaise towards Ballots.*
All year 5HEC ⬛ ⚑ ⋔ ⊙ ⚑ ⬛ ▣ ⊞ lau **Prices:** ⋔8.65

SILLÉ-LE-GUILLAUME SARTHE

Privé du Landereau ☎ 0243201269
➲ *1.5km NW via D304*
Etr-15 Oct 15 Oct-01 Apr 2.5HEC ⬛ ⚑ ⋔ ⚡ ✕ ⊙ ⚑ ⌀ ♨
⚑ ▣ ⊞ lau ➤ ✕ ♨ ⁀LR **Prices:** ⋔2.06-2.07 ➡0.84-0.99
⚑1.98-3.05

SILLÉ-LE-PHILIPPE SARTHE

🏰Château de Chanteloup ☎ 243275107 ▤ 243890505
e-mail: chanteloup.souffrot@wanadoo.fr
Set partly in wooded clearings and open ground within the park surrounding an old mansion. Good sanitary installations.
➲ *17km NE of Le Mans on D301.*
Jun-7Sep 20HEC ⬛ ⚑ ⋔ ℡ ⚡ ✕ ⊙ ⚑ ⬛ ⁀ P ▣ ⊞ lau
Prices: ⋔4.50-6 pitch 8-10

SOUTERRAINE, LA CREUSE

Suisse Océan Le Cheix ☎ 555633332
➲ *1.8km E via D912 near the lake.*
All year 2HEC ⬛ ⚑ ⋔ ⚡ ✕ ⊙ ⚑ ⬛ ⚑ ⬛ ⊞ lau ➤ ℡ ⁀L
Prices: ⋔2.51 ➡1.52 ⚑1.52 pitch 1.52

SUÈVRES LOIR-ET-CHER

🏰Château de la Grenouillère ☎ 254878037
Completely divided into pitches. Castle now hotel with common room for campers. Each pitch 150sq m. Separate area for overnight campers.
➲ *3km from village towards Orléans.*
15 May-15 Sep 11HEC ⬛ ⚑ ⋔ ℡ ⚡ ✕ ⊙ ⚑ ⬛
⁀ P ▣ ⊞ lau

SULLY-SUR-LOIRE LOIRET

CM chemin de la Salle Verte ☎ 238362393
Near Château, adjacent to River Loire.
➲ *100m from town.*
Apr-Oct 3.4HEC ⬛ ∵∷ ⚑ ⋔ ⊙ ⚑ ▣ ⊞ lau ➤ ℡ ⚡ ✕ ⁀P

At ST-PÈRE-SUR-LOIRE

St-Père rte d'Orléans ☎ 238363594
On a level meadow on the right bank of the River Loire.
➲ *W on D60 towards St-Benoît-sur-Loire.*
Apr-Oct 2.7HEC ⬛ ♠ ⋔ ⊙ ⚑ ⬛ ⚑ ⁀ P ⊞ lau
➤ ℡ ⚡ ✕ ⁀P

TALMONT-ST-HILAIRE VENDÉE

Littoral Le Porteau
☎ 251220464 ▤ 251220537
Situated near Port Bourgenay, 80m from the sea. Good facilities and entertainment available during the season.
Apr-Sep 8.5HEC ⬛ ⚑ ⋔ ℡ ⚡ ✕ ⊙ ⚑ ⌀ ♨ ⬛ ⁀ P ▣ ⊞ lau
➤ ⁀S **Prices:** ⋔3.80-5.20 pitch 16.80-26.70 (incl 2 persons)

TOURS INDRE-ET-LOIRE

At BALLAN-MIRÉ(8.5km W D751)

Mignardière 22 av des Aubepines
☎ 247733100 ▤ 247733101
e-mail: info@mignardiere.com
A well maintained site with a variety of sporting facilities.
➲ *2.5km NE.*
10 Apr-Sep 3.5HEC ⬛ ⚑ ⋔ ⊙ ⚑ ⌀ ♨ ⬛ ⚑ ⁀ P ▣ ⊞
lau ➤ ⚡ ✕

TRANCHE-SUR-MER, LA VENDÉE

Bale d'Aunis 10 r du Pertuis
☎ 251274736 ▤ 251274454
e-mail: info@camping-baiedaunis.com
On level land on sea-shore, 50mtrs from the beach and 400mtrs from the town centre with a variety of leisure activities.
➲ *300m E on D46.*
Apr-Sep 2.4HEC ∵∷ ♦ ♠ ⋔ ℡ ✕ ⊙ ⚑ ⌀ ⁀ PS ▣ lau
➤ ℡ ♨ ⊞

Bel r du Bottereau
☎ 251304739 ▤ 251277281
A quiet, family-run site 500yds from a magnificent beach and a marine lake. Plenty of sports and entertainment facilities.
➲ *400m from town centre.*
25May-8Sep 3.5HEC ⬛ ∵∷ ♦ ⋔ ℡ ⚡ ✕ ⊙ ⚑ ⁀ PS ▣
⚑ lau ➤ ✕ ⌀ ♨ ⊞ **Prices:** pitch 21.35 (incl 2 persons)

Cottage Fleuri La Grière-Plage
☎ 251303457 ▤ 251277477
A level site with modern facilities.
➲ *2.5km E, 500m from the beach*
Apr-15 Oct 7.5HEC ⬛ ⚑ ⋔ ℡ ✕ ⊙ ⚑ ♨ ⬛ ⁀ P ▣ ⊞ lau
➤ ⁀S

Jard 123 bd de Lattre-de-Tassigny
☎ 251274379 ▤ 251274292
A family site on level ground with clearly defined pitches, 700mtrs from the beach, with plenty of recreational facilities.
➲ *Access via D747.*
25 May-15 Sep 6HEC ⬛ ⚡ ℡ ℡ ⚡ ✕ ⊙ ⚑ ⚑ ⁀ P ▣ ⊞
⚑ lau ➤ ⌀ ♨

Repos du Pêcheur rte de la Roche-sur-Yon
☎ 251303694 ▤ 251303704
Situated on the banks of a canal approx 3km from the sea.
May-Sep 6HEC ⬛ ⚑ ⋔ ℡ ✕ ⊙ ⚑ ⌀ ⬛ ⚑ ⁀ PR ▣ lau

Savinière ☎ 251274270 ▤ 251274048
Set in a beautiful natural park with good, modern facilities.
➲ *1.5km NW via D105.*
Apr-Sep 2.5HEC ⬛ ∵∷ ♦ ⋔ ℡ ⚡ ✕ ⊙ ⚑ ⬛ ⁀ P ▣ ⊞ lau
➤ ⌀ ⁀S

TURBALLE, LA LOIRE-ATLANTIQUE

🏠Parc Ste-Brigitte Domaine de Bréhet
☎ 240248891 🖩 240233042
Site in grounds of old Château. Parkland divided into pitches and surrounded by hedges.
➲ *E of village on D99 Guérande road.*
Apr-Sep 6HEC ▨ ⌂✦🏠🌣🛒⊙💡∅ ⏳ LP 🔳➕ lau
Prices: ♠4.65 ♠2.52 ♠9.53 ▲4.80

VALENÇAY INDRE

CM Chènes rte de Loches ☎ 254000392 🖩 254000392
A quiet site on level ground with well defined pitches.
➲ *1km W on D960*
27 Apr-29 Sep 5HEC ▨ ⌂🏠⊙💡 ⏳ LP 🔳➕ lau ✦🛒🌣✗
∅ 🛏 ⏳R Prices: ♠6.55-6.55 pitch 6.90-6.90

VARENNES-SUR-LOIRE MAINE-ET-LOIRE

🏠Étang de la Brèche 5 Impasse de la Brèche
☎ 241512292 🖩 241512724
e-mail: etang.breche@wanadoo.fr
Relaxing site in the heart of the Loire Valley, ideal base for visiting sites of historical interest.
➲ *4.5km NW via N152.*
19 May-18 Sep 12HEC ▨ ⋙ ✦🏠🛒🌣⊙💡∅🛏⏳ P
🔳➕ lau ✦⏳R Prices: ♠3.50-5 pitch 15-25 (incl 3 persons)

VEILLON, LE VENDÉE

St-Hubert av de la Plage, Bourgenay Le Veillon
☎ 251222230 🖩 0251222230
e-mail: campingsthubert@free.fr
In a wooded location with well defined pitches, 300mtrs from the sea.
➲ *From Talmont-St-Hilaire head towards Bourgenay and Veillon.*
Apr-Sep 1HEC ▨ ✦🏠🌣⊙💡∅🛏🚐🔳➕ lau
✦🛒✗⏳LPS

VELLES INDRE

Grands Pins Les Maisons Neuves
☎ 254366193 🖩 247597675
e-mail: contact@les-grands-pins.fr
The site has individual pitches and has easy access to the countryside. Swimming pool available July-August only.
➲ *7km S of Châteauroux on N20.*
5HEC ▨ ⋙ ✦🏠🌣✗⊙💡🚐⏳ P 🔳 lau

VENDÔME LOIR-ET-CHER

Grand Prés r G-Martel ☎ 254770027 🖩 254834358
e-mail: camping.vendome@free.fr
Site lies on a meadow, next to a sports ground.
➲ *E of town on right bank of Loire.*
Etr-Sep ▨ ⌂🏠⊙💡🚐⏳ P 🔳➕ lau✦🛒🌣✗∅🛏

VINEUIL LOIR-ET-CHER

Châteaux ☎ 254788205 🖩 254786203
Level site on left bank of River Loire with modern buildings. Boating. Bathing not recommended.
➲ *From Blois drive towards St-Dye. After modern bridge continue towards 'Lac de Loire' for 1.5km.*
Apr-15 Oct 30HEC ▨ ⌂🏠🌣✗⊙💡∅🚐
⏳ P 🔳➕ lau

BRITTANY/NORMANDY

France's most westerly province, Brittany's 750 miles of splendid coastline juts proudly out into the Atlantic. This is a wild and rugged coastline, with great rollers crashing into magnificent cliffs and headlands, the unique wooded estuaries, "abers", and sheltered harbour coves and picturesque fine-sand beaches in the south to rival the best in Europe. The sea dominates the province, and the popular and chic coastal resorts, as well as the charming fishing ports, abound in friendly family-run restaurants serving a wonderful variety of fresh seafood. Away from the sea, this is a land of gentle hills, narrow, wooded valleys, wild moors of gorse and heather, and sunken lanes linking sleepy villages and quaint farmhouses.

Behind the Normandy coastline of splendid sandy beaches and sheer chalk cliffs is a lush agricultural countryside which makes a rich contribution to the region's distinctive cuisine. Apple orchards - a splendid sight in spring - result in the ciders and strong Calvados, and from the dairy farms come the famous fine dairy produce and excellent cheeses. But the region is also rich in history - the beaches recalling the Allied landings, feudal castles, elegant châteaux; and the great religious buildings - Mont St Michel, and the cathedrals at Bayeux, Coutances, Evreux, Lisieux, and the great Cathedral of Notre Dame at Rouen.

....

ALENÇON ORNE

CM de Guéramé 65 r de Guéramé ☎ 233263495
Situated in open country near a stream, 500m from town centre.
➲ *Access via the Boulevard Périphérique in the SW part of town.*
All year 1.5HEC ▨ ✦🏠⊙💡 ⏳ R 🔳➕ lau ✦🛒🌣✗∅🛏
⏳P

Jacques Fould av H-Chanteloup ☎ 233292329
➲ *On N12.*
All year 1HEC ▨ ✦🏠⊙💡🚐🔳➕ lau✦🛒🌣✗∅⏳PR

ARRADON MORBIHAN

Penboch 9 chemin de Penboch ☎ 297447129 🖩 297447910
An exceptionally well appointed site in a pleasant wooded location 200mtrs from the beaches of the Gulf of Morbihan.
➲ *Signposted from N165.*
14 Apr-23 Sep 4HEC ▨ ⌂🏠🛒🌣✗⊙💡∅🚐🚐⏳ PS
🔳➕ lau ✦⏳S Prices: pitch 14.50-24.90 (incl 2 persons)

ARZANO FINISTÈRE

🏠Ty Nadan rte d'Arzano ☎ 298717547 🖩 298717731
e-mail: ty-nadan@wanadoo.fr
A quiet riverside site in attractive parkland in the Ellé valley.
➲ *3km W. Leave N165 at Quimperlé exit and drive towards Arzano.*
15May-5Sep 12HEC ▨ ✦🏠🛒🌣✗⊙💡∅🚐🚐▲⏳ PR
🔳➕ lau

AVRANCHES MANCHE
At GENÊTS(10km W on D911)

Coques d'Or 14 rte du Bec d'Andaine
☎ 233708257 ▤ 233708683
A well equipped site 1km from the sea.
Apr-Sep 5HEC ⸺ ᐤ ⌂ ▾ ⊙ ▣ ⊕ ⸗ P ⊡ ⊞ ⊞ lau
⊕ ≋ ✗ ⊘

BADEN MORBIHAN

Mané Guernehué ☎ 297570206 ▤ 297571543
e-mail: mane-guernehue@wanadoo.fr
In a pleasant situation at the head of the Gulf of Morbihan
with good recreational facilities.
➲ 1km SW via Mériadec road.
Apr-Sep 5HEC ⸺ ᐤ ⌂ ▾ ▾ ⊙ ▣ ▣ ⊕ ⸗ P ⊡ ⊞ lau ⊕ ⊘
≋ ⸗S Prices: ᐱ2.75-5.10 pitch 9.60-14.50

BARNEVILLE-CARTERET MANCHE

Bosquets La Plage ☎ 233047362
A quiet site in wooded surroundings, 400mtrs from the
beach with views of the Channel Islands.
Apr-Sep 11HEC ⸺ ⸬ ᐤ ⌂ ▾ ▾ ✗ ⊙ ▣ ≋ ▣ ⸗ P ⊡ ⊞
lau ⊕ ⊘ ⸗S

At BARNEVILLE-PLAGE

Pré Normand St Jean de la Rivière
☎ 233538564 ▤ 233537317
e-mail: camping@pre-normand.fr
On slightly flat meadow away from traffic noise but exposed
to sea winds. Vehicles allowed on beach but beware of tide.
Separate carpark for arrivals after 22.30hrs.
➲ Off D166.
May-15 Sep 2.7HEC ⸺ ⸬ ᐤ ⌂ ▾ ▾ ✗ ⊙ ▣ ≋ ▣ ▣
⸗ P ⊡ ⊞ lau ⊕ ⊘ ⸗S

BAYEUX CALVADOS

CM Calvados bd d'Eindhoven ☎ 231920843 ▤ 231920843
Very clean and tidy site with tarmac drive and hardstanding
for caravans. Adjoins football field.
➲ N side of town on Boulevard Circulaire.
May-Sep 2.9HEC ⸺ ᐤ ⌂ ⊙ ▣ ⊡ ⊞ lau ⊕ ▾ ▾ ✗ ⊘ ≋
⸗P Prices: ᐱ2.85 pitch 3.52

BEG-MEIL FINISTÈRE

Kervastard chemin de Kervastard
☎ 0033 298949152 ▤ 298949983
e-mail: camping.le.kervastard@wanadoo.fr
In a pleasant wooded area close to a fine sandy beach with
plenty of leisure facilities.
➲ Within the village, 250mtrs from the beach.
May-Sep 2HEC ⸺ ᐤ ⌂ ⊙ ▣ ≋ ▣ Å ⸗ P ⊞ lau ⊕ ▾ ▾
✗ ⊘ ⸗S Prices: ᐱ2.83-4.42 pitch 6.71-9

Roche Percée ☎ 298949415 ▤ 298944805
e-mail: info@campingbrittany.com
Wooded family site 400mtrs from the Roche Percée beach.
➲ 1km from Beg Meil towards Fouesnant.
28 Mar-29 Sep 2HEC ⸺ ᐤ ▾ ▾ ✗ ⊙ ▣ ≋ ▣ ⸗ P ⊡
lau ⊕ ✗ ⊘ ⸗S Prices: ᐱ3-4.50 pitch 8.50-11.50

BÉNODET FINISTÈRE

Letty ☎ 298570469 ▤ 298662256
e-mail: reception@campingduletty.com
Site bordering beach, divided into sectors. Good sanitary
installations, ironing rooms and games room. Good beach
for children. Use of car park compulsory after 11pm.
➲ By the sea 1km SE.
15 Jun-6 Sep 10HEC ⸺ ᐤ ⌂ ▾ ▾ ✗ ⊙ ▣ ⊘
⸗ S ⊡ ⊞ ⊞ lau

Pointe St-Gilles r du Poulmic ☎ 298570537 ▤ 298572752
e-mail: information@camping-stgilles.fr
Holiday site south of village, on fields by beach. Divided into
several sectors; individual pitches. Well-equipped sanitary
blocks.
May-Sep 7HEC ⸺ ᐤ ⌂ ▾ ▾ ⊙ ▣ ⊘ ≋ ⸗ PS ⊡ ⊞ ⊗ lau ⊕
✗ Prices: pitch 21-35 (incl 2 persons)

Port de Plaisance 7 rte de Quimper, Prad Puollou
☎ 298570238 ▤ 298572525
e-mail: info@campingbenodet.com
A well equipped family site on the outskirts of the town,
500mtrs from the harbour.
➲ NE off D34 at the entrance to the town.
15 Apr-Sep 10HEC ⸺ ᐤ ⌂ ▾ ▾ ▾ ✗ ⊙ ▣ ≋ ▣ Å ⸗ P ⊡ ⊞
lau ⊕ ⊘ ⸗RS Prices: ᐱ4.27-5.34 pitch 9.15-11.43

BÉNOUVILLE CALVADOS

Hautes Coutures rte de Ouistréham
☎ 231447308 ▤ 231953080
e-mail: camping_hautes_coutures@wanadoo.fr
Pleasant site with good facilities near the Canal Maritime and
within easy reach of the Caen-Portsmouth ferry.
From Caen, driving toward Ouistréham on the dual
carriageway, Camping Les Hautes Coutures has its own exit
shortly after the Pegasus Bridge exit. It can be clearly seen on
the R of the dual carriageway. Apr-Sep 8HEC ⸺ ᐤ ⌂ ▾ ▾
✗ ⊙ ▣ ⊘ ⸗ P ⊡ ⊞ lau ⊕ ⸗S Prices: ᐱ5.80 pitch 6.50

BINIC CÔTES-D'ARMOR

Palmiers Kerviarc'h ☎ 296737259
A well equipped site within the Parc Tropical de Bretagne,
just over one kilometre from the town centre.
➲ Access via N12/D786.
Jun-Sep 2HEC ⸺ ⊙ ᐤ ⌂ ▾ ▾ ✗ ⊙ ▣ ⊘ ▣ ⸗ P ⊡ ⊞ lau
⊕ ✗ ⸗S

Panoramic r Gasselin ☎ 296736043
On a meadow divided into pitches, on a hill above the town.
➲ On S outskirts of village.
All year 5HEC ⸺ ᐤ ⌂ ▾ ▾ ⊙ ▣ ≋ ▣ ▣ Å ⸗ P ⊞ lau
⊕ ✗ ⊘ ⸗S

BLAINVILLE-SUR-MER MANCHE

Senéquet ☎ 233472311
A family site with plenty of recreational facilities.
➲ 2km NW on D651.
Mar-early Dec 13HEC ⸺ ⸬ ⸗ ⌂ ▾ ▾ ✗ ⊙ ▣ ⸗ PS ⊡
⊗ lau ⊕ ⊞

BLANGY-LE-CHÂTEAU CALVADOS

⊞Brévedent ☎ 231647288 ▤ 231643341
e-mail: castelcamp@mageos.com
Situated in the grounds of an 18th century manor house
with good facilities.
➲ 3km SE on D51 beside lake.
11 May-22 Sep 5.5HEC ⸺ ᐤ ⌂ ▾ ▾ ✗ ⊙ ▣ ⊘ ⸗ P ⊡ ⊞ ⊗
lau ⊕ ⸗ Prices: ᐱ4.50-5 pitch 7.20-8

Domaine du Lac ☎ 231646200 ▤ 231641591
Apr-Oct 4HEC ⸺ ⸗ ⌂ ▾ ▾ ✗ ⊙ ▣ ⊘ ≋ ⊡ ⊞ lau
Prices: ᐱ4.60 pitch 4

BLANGY-SUR-BRESLE SEINE-MARITIME

CM r des Étangs ☎ 235945565
In the middle of the local Leisure Park comprising 80
hectares of woodland, lakes and streams.
➲ 300m on N28.
15 Mar-15 Oct 8HEC ⸺ ᐤ ⌂ ⊙ ▣ ⊡ ▣ ⊞ lau ⊕ ⊘ ≋ ⸗R

BLONVILLE-SUR-MER CALVADOS

Village Club le Lieu Bill Le Lieu Bill
☎ 231879727 ▤ 231814715
e-mail: villageclub14@aol.com
A family site in a convenient location for Le Havre and other ferry ports.
➲ *Off D118 Villers-sur-Mer-Pont-l'Évêque*
Apr-Sep 7HEC ⸖ ⌇⌇⌇ ♀ ⋒ ⏚ ❤ ✕ ⊙ ⊙ ➿ ☎ ↻ P ☎ ⊞ lau ➧ ⛺
↻S Prices: ⋔5.50 pitch 24-25.30 (incl 3 persons)

BOURG-ACHARD EURE

Clos Normand 235 rte de Pont-Audemer ☎ 232563484
In a peaceful location within an apple orchard.
➲ *1km from A13 exit Bourg-Achard.*
Apr-Sep 1.5HEC ⸖ ⌇⌇⌇ ♦ ⋒ ⏚ ❤ ✕ ⊙ ⊙ ➿ 🚗 ↻ P ☎ ⊞ lau ➧ ⛺ ⌀
🅿 Prices: ⋔3.20-3.81 ⫴1.37 ⫴2.89 ⛺1.37-2.89

CALLAC CÔTES-D'ARMOR

CM Verte Vallée ☎ 296455850
➲ *W via D28 towards Morlaix*
15 Jun-15 Sep 1HEC ⸖ ⌇⌇⌇ ♀ ⋒ ⊙ ⊙ ➿ 🚗 ☎ lau ➧ ⛺ ⏚ ✕ ⌀ ↻L

CAMARET-SUR-MER FINISTÈRE

Lambézen ☎ 298277733 ▤ 298273838
e-mail: lamorique@club-internet.fr
Situated beside the sea on the edge of the Armorican Natural Park with a wide variety of recreational facilities.
➲ *3km NE on rte de Roscanvel (D355).*
Apr-Sep 2.5HEC ⸖ ⌇⌇⌇ ♀ ⋒ ⏚ ❤ ✕ ⊙ ⊙ ➿ ⌀ 🚗 🚗 ↻ P ☎ ⊞
lau ➧ ↻S Prices: ⋔3.80-4.70 pitch 7-11

Plage de Trez Rouz ☎ 298279396 ▤ 298278454
e-mail: camping-plage-de-trez-rouz@wanadoo.fr
On level ground 50mtrs from the beach.
➲ *3km from Camaret-sur-Mer via D355 towards Pointe-des-Espagnols.*
Etr-Sep 3.1HEC ⸖ ⌇⌇⌇ ♀ ⋒ ⏚ ⊙ ⊙ ➿ ⌀ 🚗 ☎ ⊞ lau ➧ ⛺ ✕ ↻S
Prices: ⋔3.70-4 ⫴1.30-1.60 pitch 3-3.55

CANCALE ILLE-ET-VILAINE

Notre Dame du Verger ☎ 299897284 ▤ 299896011
Terraced site overlooking the sea with direct access to the beach.
➲ *2km from Pointe-du-Grouin on D201.*
Apr-Sep 2.2HEC ⸖ ⌇⌇⌇ ♀ ⋒ ⏚ ❤ ✕ ⊙ ⊙ ➿ ⌀ ☎ ⊞ lau ➧ ↻S
Prices: pitch 12-18 (incl 2 persons)

CARANTEC FINISTÈRE

Mouettes Grande Grève ☎ 298670246 ▤ 298783146
e-mail: camping@lesmouettes.com
Level site divided by low shrubs and trees.

CAMPING LE HAUT DICK
Tel: 02.33.42.16.89
50500 CARENTAN
OPEN ALL YEAR
In the heart of "Parc des Marais", near the historic landing-zones in Normandy, quiet – shady – marked pitches. Free Hot showers. Games hall: table tennis, pinball, table tennis for children, reading material. Curved slide – French boules – Minigolf.
Nearby: Tennis – swimming pool – Harbour: canoe – fishing. 500m. Away from centre of town, with shopping available.

➲ *1.5km SW on rte de St-Pol-de-Léon, towards the sea.*
May-15 Sep 7HEC ⸖ ⌇⌇⌇ ♀ ⋒ ⏚ ❤ ⊙ ⊙ ➿ ⌀ ☎ ⛺ ↻ P ☎ 🅿 ⊞
lau ➧ ↻S Prices: ⋔3.50-5.50 pitch 9.50-16.50

CARENTAN MANCHE

CM le Haut Dyck 30 chemin du Grand-Bas Pays
☎ 0233421689 ▤ 0233421689
e-mail: lehautdick@aol.com
A level site in wooded surroundings with well defined pitches.
➲ *Take village road off N13 towards Le Port.*
All year 2.5HEC ⸖ ⌇⌇⌇ ♀ ⊙ ⊙ ➿ 🚗 🚗 ☎ ⊞ lau ➧ ⛺ ✕ ⌀ ⏚
↻P Prices: ⋔2.29 ⫴1.07 ⫴2.90

CARNAC MORBIHAN

Bruyères Kerogile ☎ 297523057 ▤ 297523057
Partly wooded site with modern facilities close to the local beaches.
➲ *N of Carnac on C4, 2km from Plouharnel.*
Apr-15 Oct 2HEC ⸖ ⌇⌇⌇ ♀ ⋒ ⊙ ⊙ ➿ ⌀ ⏚ 🚗 ☎ ⊞ lau ➧ ⛺ ✕

Étang 67 rte de Kerlann ☎ 297521406
In a rural setting with pitches divided by hedges, 2.5km from the coast.
➲ *2km N at Kerlann on D119.*
Apr-15 Oct 2.5HEC ⸖ ⌇⌇⌇ ♦ ⋒ ⏚ ❤ ✕ ⊙ ⊙ ➿ 🚗 🚗
↻ P ☎ ⊞ lau

🏠Grande Métairie rte des Alignements, de Kermario
☎ 297522401 ▤ 297528358
e-mail: grande.metairie@wanadoo.com
Holiday site with modern amenities, completely divided into pitches.
➲ *2.5km NE on D196.*
30 Mar-14 Sep 15HEC ⸖ ⌇⌇⌇ ♀ ⋒ ⏚ ❤ ✕ ⊙ ⊙ ➿ ⌀ 🚗 🚗 ↻ PS
☎ ⊞ lau Prices: ⋔3.55-5.60 ⛺13.45-22.40 pitch 13.45-25.60

Moulin de Kermaux ☎ 297521590 ▤ 297528385
e-mail: moulin-de-kermaux@wanadoo.fr
In a quiet location, surrounded by trees and bushes, with good facilities. Within easy reach of the coast and the local megaliths.
➲ *2.5km NE.*
Apr-15 Sep 3HEC ⸖ ⌇⌇⌇ ♀ ⋒ ⏚ ❤ ✕ ⊙ ⊙ ➿ 🚗 🚗 ↻ P ☎ ⊞ lau
➧ ✕ ⌀ ↻RS

Moustoir rte du Moustoir ☎ 33 297521618 ▤ 297528837
e-mail: info@lemoustoir.com
Well equipped site in a rural setting close to the sea.
➲ *3 km NE of Carnac.*
May-9 Sep 5HEC ⸖ ⌇⌇⌇ ♦ ⋒ ⏚ ❤ ✕ ⊙ ⊙ ➿ ⌀ 🚗 🚗 ⛺ ↻ P ☎ ⊞
lau ➧ ✕ ↻R Prices: ⋔2.50-4 pitch 7.20-12

Ombrages ☎ 297521652
In a wooded location with shaded pitches divided by hedges.
➲ *Take rte Carnac to Auray and turn left at SHELL filling station.*
15 Jun-Sep 1HEC ⸖ ⌇⌇⌇ ♀ ⋒ ⊙ ⊙ ➿ ⌀ ☎ ⊞ lau ➧ ↻L

Rosnual rte d'Auray ☎ 297521457
A pleasant site in a wooded rural setting with good recreational facilities.
➲ *1.5km from village, 2.5km from the sea.*
Apr-Sep 4HEC ⸖ ⌇⌇⌇ ♦ ⋒ ⏚ ✕ ⊙ ⊙ ➿ ⌀ ⏚ 🚗 🚗
↻ P ☎ ⊞ ⌀ lau ➧

Saules rte de Rosnual ☎ 297521498 ▤ 297526584
Grassland family site with good facilities site between road and deciduous woodland, subdivided by hedges and shrubs.
➲ *2.5km N on D119.*
Apr-Sep 2.5HEC ⸖ ⌇⌇⌇ ♀ ⋒ ⏚ ❤ ⊙ ⊙ ➿ ⌀ 🚗 🚗 🚗 ⛺ ↻ P ☎ ⊞ lau
➧ ⏚ ✕

At CARNAC-PLAGE(1km S)

Druides 55 chemin de Beaumer
☎ 297520818 ▤ 297529613
Family site with well defined pitches, 400m from a fine sandy beach.
➲ SE of town centre. Approach via D781 or D119.
07 May-09 Sep 2.5HEC ⬛ ♠ 🅵 ☉ 🚿 🏪 ⚡ P 🅿 ⊞ lau ➡ 🛒
🍽 ✗ ⌘ 🏊 ⚓S Prices: ♠3.40-4.70 pitch 15.60-25.50 (incl 2 persons)

Men Dû r de Beaumer ☎ 297520423
Peaceful site in a wooded setting close to the beach.
➲ 1km from Carnac Plage via D781 and D186.
Apr-Sep 1.5HEC ⬛ ♠ 🅵 ✗ ☉ 🚿 🏪 🏤 �ⓣ lau ➡ 🛒 🍽 ⌘
⚓PRS ⊞

Menhirs allée St-Michel ☎ 297529467 ▤ 0297522538
e-mail: campinglesmenhirs@free.fr
A family site near the beach and shops with good recreational facilities and modern sanitary blocks, including toilets suitable for the disabled.
May-Sep 6HEC ⬛ ♠ 🅵 🛒 🍽 ✗ ☉ 🚿 🏪 ⚡ P 🅿 ⊞ lau ➡ ✗ ⌘
🏊 ⚓S Prices: ♠3.40-6.80 pitch 13-26

CAUREL CÔTES-D'ARMOR

Nautic International rte de Beau Rivage
☎ 296285794 ▤ 296260200
A terraced site in woodland on the edge of Lake Guerlédan with a variety of recreational facilities.
➲ N164 in the direction of Beau Rivage.
15 May-25 Sep 3.6HEC ⬛ ♠ 🅵 🛒 ☉ 🚿 🏪 ⚡ LP 🅿 ⊞ lau
➡ 🍽 ✗ Prices: ♠3.30-4.60 🚗1.60-1.60 pitch 5.40-6.90

CHAPELLE-AUX-FILZMÉENS, LA ILLE-ET-VILAINE

Camping du Logis ☎ 299452155
A quiet, pleasant site in the wooded grounds of an 18th century château.
➲ NE of town towards Combourg.
All year 20HEC ⬛ ♠ 🅵 🛒 🍽 ✗ ☉ 🚿 🏪 🏤 🏊 🏪 🏤 🅰 ⚡ P 🅿 ⊞
lau ➡ ⚓LR

CHÂTEAULIN FINISTÈRE

La Pointe Superbe rte St-Coulitz
☎ 298865153 ▤ 298865153
In a wooded valley close to the town with good modern facilities. Pitches divided by hedges. British owners.
➲ From centre of Châteaulin take D770 S to Quimper for 1km, then left to St-Coulitz. Site 100mtrs on right.
Mar-Oct 2.5HEC ⬛ 🅶 🅵 ☉ 🚿 🏪 ➡ 🛒 ✗ ⌘ 🏊 ⚓PR ⊞
Prices: ♠2-3 🚗5-5.50 🅰5-5.50

CLÉDER FINISTÈRE

CV Roguennic Roguennic ☎ 298696388
➲ 5km N on coast.
Apr-Sep 8HEC ⬛⬝⬝⬝ 🌿 🅵 🛒 🍽 ✗ ☉ 🚿 🏪 ⌘ 🏊 🏪 ⚓ PS 🅿 ⊞ lau

CLOÎTRE-ST-THEGONNEC, LE FINISTÈRE

Bruyères ☎ 298797176
A small, secluded site in a picturesque setting within the Amorique Nature Park.
➲ 12km S of Morlaix via D769.
Jul-Aug 1HEC ⬛ 🅶 🅵 ⌘ 🅿 ⊞ lau ➡ 🛒 🍽 ✗ 🏊

COMBOURG ILLE-ET-VILAINE

Bois Coudrais Cuguen ☎ 299732745 ▤ 299731308
A small, level site with fine views.
➲ Access via D83 (Combourg-Mont-St-Michel).
Etr-mid Oct 1HEC ⬛ 🌿 🅵 🍽 ✗ ☉ 🚿 🏪 🏤 🅿 ⊞ lau ➡ 🛒

CONCARNEAU FINISTÈRE

Prés Verts Kernous Plage ☎ 298970974 ▤ 298973206
e-mail: pres-verts-camp@wanadoo.fr
A landscaped site with good facilities overlooking Concarneau Bay.
➲ 1.2km NW.
May-10 Sep 3HEC ⬛ 🅶 🅵 🛒 ☉ 🚿 🏪 ⚡ PS 🅿 lau
➡ ⌘ 🏊

COUTERNE ORNE

Clos Normand rte de Bagnoles ☎ 233379243
A pleasant site in rural surroundings in a sheltered position close to the thermal spa of Bagnoles-de-l'Orne.
➲ Approach D916.
May-Sep 1.5HEC ⬛ ♠ 🅵 ✗ ☉ 🚿 🏪 🅿 lau ➡ ⌘ 🏊 ⚓LPR
Prices: ♠2.40 pitch 6.40 (incl 2 persons)

CRACH MORBIHAN

Fort Espagnol rte de Fort Espagnol
☎ 297551488 ▤ 297300104
e-mail: fort-espagnol@wanadoo.fr
In a secluded, wooded location, this is a family site with a wide variety of recreational facilities.
➲ Due E of Crac'h towards the coast.
Apr-15 Sep 4.5HEC ⬛ ♠ 🅵 🛒 🍽 ✗ ☉ 🚿 🏪 ⌘ 🏊 🏪 🅰 ⚡ P 🅿
⊞ lau Prices: ♠3.05-4.20 pitch 5.80-8.20

CRIEL-SUR-MER SEINE-MARITIME

Mouettes r de la Plage ☎ 235867073 ▤ 235867073
Small grassy site overlooking the sea.
Apr-Oct 2HEC ⬛ 🌿 🅵 🛒 🍽 ☉ 🚿 🏪 ⌘ 🏤 🅿 lau ➡ ✗ ⚓RS ⊞

CROZON FINISTÈRE

Pen ar Menez bd de Pralognan ☎ 298271236
On fringe of a pinewood. Water sport facilities 5km away.
Cycles for hire.
All year 2.6HEC ⬛ ♠ 🅵 ✗ ☉ 🚿 🏪 🏪 🏤 lau ➡ 🛒 ✗ ⌘ 🏊
⚓S ⊞

Plage de Goulien Kernaveèno ☎ 0298271710 ▤ 0298272195
e-mail: camping.goulien@presquile-crozon.com
Grassy site in wooded surroundings 150m from the sea.
➲ 5km W on D308.
10 Jun-20 Sep 2.5HEC ⬛ 🅶 🅵 🛒 ☉ 🚿 🏪 ⌘ 🏪 🅿 ⊞ lau ➡
🍽 ✗ ⚓S

At ST-FIACRE(5km NW)

Pieds dans l'Eau ☎ 298276243
Site on several meadows divided by trees. In quiet secluded situation reaching as far as a pebbly beach. Bathing is dependent on tides.
15 Jun-15 Sep 3HEC ⬛ ♠ 🅵 ☉ 🚿 🏪 ⚡ S 🅿 lau ➡ 🛒 🍽 ✗ ⌘

DEAUVILLE CALVADOS

At ST-ARNOULT(3km S)

Vallée route de Beaumont ☎ 231885817 ▤ 0231881157
e-mail: lacca@free.fr
In a pleasant wooded setting with plenty of recreational facilities.
➲ 1km S via D27 and D275
Apr-Oct 19HEC ⬛ 🌿 🅵 🍽 ✗ ☉ 🚿 🏪 🏊 🏪 ⚡ LPR 🅿 lau
➡ 🛒 ⚓S ⊞ Prices: ♠5.72 pitch 6.10

At TOUQUES(3km SE)

Haras chemin du Calvaire ☎ 231884484 ▤ 231889708
e-mail: les.haras@wanadoo.fr
A partially residential site in pleasant surroundings. Ideal for overnight stops, but reservations recommended in July and August.

⮕ *N on D62, to Honfleur.*
Feb-Nov 4HEC ⌂ ❹ ⋔ ♥ ❤ ✕ ⊙ ▣ ⌀ ♨ 🏠 🚐 ☎ ⊞ lau ♦ 🗻
⋜P Prices: ⋔4.60-4.90 pitch 4.60-5.95

DÉVILLE-LÈS-ROUEN SEINE-MARITIME

CM r Jules-Ferry ☎ 235740759
All year 1HEC ⌂ ♠ ☀ ⋔ ⊙ 🚐 ▣ ⊞ lau ♦ 🗻 ♥ ✕ ⋜PR

DIEPPE SEINE-MARITIME

At HAUTOT-SUR-MER(6km SW)

Source Petit Appeville ☎ 235842704
15 Mar-15 Oct 2.5HEC ⌂ ❹ ⋔ ♥ ❤ ✕ ⊙ 🚐 ⌀ ⋜ R ▣ ⊞ lau ♦
🗻 Prices: ⋔3.50 ➍0.92 🚐6.40 ▲4.60

DINAN CÔTES-D'ARMOR

At TADEN(3.5km NE)

CM Hallerais ☎ 296391593
Beautiful clean site with level pitches on gentle slope near a
country estate. Asphalt drives. Good sanitary installations.
Shop, bar and restaurant are only open in July and August.
⮕ *SW of Taden off D12.*
15 Mar-Oct 6HEC ⌂ ➍ ⋔ ♥ ❤ ✕ ⊙ 🚐 ⌀ ☎ 🚐 ⋜ PR ▣
lau ♦ ⊞

DINARD ILLE-ET-VILAINE

See also St-Lunaire

Mauny ☎ 299469473
A family site in pleasant wooded surroundings with a variety
of recreational facilities.
⮕ *Off St-Briac road (CD603).*
3 Mar-25 Sep 5HEC ⌂ ➍ ⋔ 🗻 ♥ ✕ ⊙ 🚐 ⌀ ♨ 🏠 ⋜ P ▣ ⊞
lau ♦ ⋜S

DOL-DE-BRETAGNE ILLE-ET-VILAINE

🏰Château des Ormes ☎ 299735300 ▤ 299735355
e-mail: info@lesormes.com
Site in grounds of château, within a large leisure complex
with excellent facilities.
⮕ *7km S on D795 Rennes road.*
20 May-10 Sep 160HEC ⌂ ➍ ⋔ 🗻 ♥ ❤ ✕ ⊙ 🚐 ⌀ ☎ ⋜ LP ▣
⊞ lau Prices: ⋔6.50 pitch 20

CM r de Dinan ☎ 299481468
On level meadow.
⮕ *SW on rte de Dinan 400m from town centre.*
15 May-15 Sep 1.7HEC ⌂ ❹ ⋔ ⊙ 🚐 ▣ lau ♦ 🗻 ♥ ✕
Prices: ⋔1.96 ➍0.89 🚐0.89 ▲0.89

At BAGUER-PICAN(4km E on N176)

Camping du Vieux Chêne
☎ 299480955 ▤ 299481337
e-mail: vieux.chene@wanadoo.fr
Spacious site in pleasant lakeside situation. Farm produce
available.
⮕ *5km E of Dol-de-Bretagne on D576.*
Apr-Sep 12HEC ⌂ ❹ ⋔ 🗻 ♥ ❤ ✕ ⊙ 🚐 ⌀ ☎ ⋜ P ▣ ⊞ lau
Prices: ⋔4.50 pitch 7-13.50

DOUARNENEZ FINISTÈRE

Kerleyou Tréboul ☎ 33 298741303 ▤ 298740961
e-mail: camp-kerleyou@infonie.fr
Family site in wooded surroundings near the beach. Separate
car park for arrivals after 23.00hrs.
⮕ *1km W on r de Préfet-Collignon towards the sea.*
May-Sep 3HEC ⌂ ❹ ⋔ 🗻 ♥ ❤ ✕ ⊙ 🚐 ☎ 🚐 ⋜ P ▣ ⊞ lau ♦
✕ ⌀ ♨ ⋜S Prices: ⋔3.65 ➍1.70 pitch 6.20

At POULLAN-SUR-MER(5km W on D765)

Pil Koad ☎ 298742639 ▤ 298745597
e-mail: camping.pil.koad@wanadoo.fr
In a natural wooded setting with a variety of recreational
facilities.
⮕ *E via D7 towards Douarnenez.*
Apr-Sep 5.5HEC ⌂ ❹ ⋔ 🗻 ♥ ✕ ⊙ 🚐 ⌀ ♨ 🏠 🚐 ⋜ P ▣ ⊞
lau ♦ ✕ Prices: ⋔3-4.50 🚐6-12

ERDEVEN MORBIHAN

Sept Saints ☎ 297555265 ▤ 297552267
e-mail: campingseptsaints@wanadoo.fr
In wooded surroundings with good recreational facilities.
⮕ *2km NW via D781 rte de Plouhinec.*
15 May-15 Sep 5HEC ⌂ ➍ ⋔ 🗻 ♥ ❤ ⊙ 🚐 ⌀ ♨ 🏠 ⋜ P ▣ ⊞
lau ♦ ✕ ⋜LRS

ERQUY CÔTES-D'ARMOR

Hautes Greés 123 r St-Michel ☎ 296723478 ▤ 296723015
Good family site, 2km from the town centre and 400mtrs
from the beach.
⮕ *500m from the sea.*
15 Apr-15 Sep 3HEC ⌂ ❹ ⋔ 🗻 ♥ ⊙ 🚐 ☎ ▣ ⊞ lau ♦ ♥ ✕ ⌀
♨ ⋜S

Roches Caroual Village ☎ 296723290 ▤ 296723290
e-mail: camping.les.roches@gofornet.com
Rural setting with well marked pitches, 800mtrs from beach.
⮕ *3km SW.*
Apr-15 Sep 3.1HEC ⌂ ❹ ⋔ 🗻 ⊙ 🚐 ♨ 🏠 ▣ ⊞ lau ♦ ⋜S
Prices: ⋔2.70-3 ➍1.80-2 pitch 2.70-3

St-Pabu ☎ 296722465 ▤ 296728717
On big open meadow with several terraces in beautiful,
isolated situation by sea. Divided into pitches.
⮕ *W on D786 then follow signposts from La Coutre.*
Apr-10 Oct 5.5HEC ⌂ ☀ ⋔ 🗻 ♥ ✕ ⊙ 🚐 ⌀ ☎
⋜ S ▣ ⊞ lau

Vieux Moulin r des Moulins ☎ 296723423 ▤ 296723663
e-mail: camp.vieux.moulin@wanadoo.fr
Clean tidy site divided into pitches and surrounded by a pine
forest. Suitable for children.
⮕ *On D783.*
May-15 Sep 4.5HEC ⌂ ❹ ⋔ 🗻 ♥ ✕ ⊙ 🚐 ⌀ ☎ ⋜ P ▣ ⊞
lau ♦ 🗻 ⋜S Prices: ⋔3.90-4.60 ➍3.10-3.80 🚐8.40-10
▲8.40-10

ÉTABLES-SUR-MER CÔTES-D'ARMOR

Abri Côtier ☎ 296706157 ▤ 296706523
e-mail: camping.abricotier@wanadoo.fr
A pleasant family site in a wooded location close to the sea.
⮕ *1km N of town centre on D786.*
4 May-10 Sep 2HEC ⌂ ❹ ⋔ 🗻 ♥ ❤ ✕ ⊙ 🚐 ⌀ ☎ ⋜ P ▣
lau ♦ ✕ ⋜S Prices: ⋔4-4.50 pitch 6-7

ETRÉHAM CALVADOS

Reine Mathilde ☎ 231217655 ▤ 231221833
e-mail: camping.riene_mathilde@wanadoo.fr
In a quiet rural setting 4km from the sea.
⮕ *1km W via D123*
Apr-Sep 6.5HEC ⌂ ❹ ⋔ ♥ ✕ ⊙ 🚐 ⌀ ☎ 🏠 ⋜ P ▣ ⊞ lau
Prices: ⋔4.50 pitch 4.20

FAOUËT, LE MORBIHAN

Beg Er Roch rte de Lorient ☎ 297231511 ▤ 297231166
In pleasant surroundings on the banks of a river. A popular
site with modern sanitary facilities and a wealth of
opportunities for all kinds of sport.
Mar-Sep 3.5HEC ⌂ ❹ ⋔ ⊙ 🚐 🏠 ▲ ⋜ R ▣ lau ♦ 🗻 ♥ ✕ ⌀
♨ ⊞ Prices: ⋔2.44-3.35 ➍1.22-1.83 pitch 1.83-3.05

FORÊT-FOUESNANT, LA FINISTÈRE

Kérantérec ☎ 298569811
Well-kept terraced site, divided into sections by hedges and extending to the sea.
➲ *3km SE.*
3 Apr-26 Sep 6.5HEC ⊞ ⌂ ℝ ♀ ✕ ⊙ ◙ ⌀ ⌲ ⌂ ⊞ ⤴ PS ⊠ 🅿 ⊞ lau ➤ ⅃ ✕

Manoir de Pen Ar Steir ☎ 298569775 ▤ 298568049
e-mail: camping-pen-ar-steir@wanadoo.fr
Well-tended site close to Port La Forêt, a major yachting arena.
➲ *NE off D44.*
Feb-Dec 3HEC ⊞ ⌂ ℝ ⊙ ◙ ⌲ ⌂ ⊞ ⊠ 🅿 ⊞ lau ➤ ⅃ ♀ ✕ ⌀ ⤴PS

Plage Plage de Kerleven, rte de Port la Forêt
☎ 298569625 ▤ 298369625
➲ *2.5km SE on D783.*
Mar-Dec 1HEC ⊞ ⦂⦂ ☀ ⌂ ℝ ⊙ ◙ ⌂ lau ➤ ♀ ✕ ⌀ ⌲ ⤴S ⊞

Pontérec Pontérec ☎ 298569833 ▤ 298569347
A modern site with well defined pitches separated by hedges, 2.5km from the beach.
➲ *0.5km on D44 towards Bénodet.*
Apr-Sep 3HEC ⊞ ⌂ ℝ ⊙ ◙ ⌂ ⌂ ⊞ ⊞ lau ➤ ⅃ ✕ ⌀
Prices: ♠3-3.20 ♠1.50-1.60 pitch 3.20-3.50

St-Laurent Kerleven ☎ 298569765 ▤ 298569251
On rocky coast. Divided into pitches.
➲ *3.5km SE of village.*
May-Sep 5.2HEC ⊞ ♠ ℝ ⅃ ♀ ✕ ⊙ ◙ ⌂ ⤴ PS ⊠ lau ➤ ⌀
⌲ ⊞ Prices: pitch 16.77-25.92 (incl 2 persons)
See advertisement in colour section

FOUESNANT FINISTÈRE

Atlantique rte de Mousterlin ☎ 298561444 ▤ 298561867
e-mail: information@camping-atlantique.fr
Modern site with plenty of amenities 400mtrs from the beach.
➲ *4.5km S on the road to Mousterlin.*
May-15 Sep 9HEC ⊞ ⌂ ℝ ⅃ ✕ ⊙ ◙ ⌀ ⌲ ⌂ ⌂ ⤴ P ⊠ ⊞ ⌀ lau ➤ ✕ ⤴S

Grand Large Pointe de Mousterlin
☎ 298560406 ▤ 298565826
e-mail: info@campingsbretagnesud.com
A family site in a wooded setting with direct access to the beach. Plenty of modern facilities.
➲ *S of Fouesnant via D145.*
4May-8Sep 6HEC ⊞ ⌂ ℝ ⅃ ✕ ⊙ ◙ ⌀ ⌂ ⤴ PR ⊠ ⊞
lau ➤ ⤴S Prices: pitch 17-31 (incl 2 persons)

Piscine Kerleya ☎ 298565606 ▤ 298565764
e-mail: campingdelapiscine@altiea.com
In a beautiful location 1.5km from the beach.
➲ *4km NW towards Kerleya.*
15 May-15 Sep 5HEC ⊞ ⌂ ℝ ⊙ ◙ ⌀ ⌂ ⤴ PS ⊠ ⊞ lau

FOUGÈRES ILLE-ET-VILAINE

CM Paron rte de la Chapelle Janson ☎ 299994081
A well managed site suitable for overnight stays.
➲ *1.5km E via D17*
Mar-Nov 2.5HEC ⊞ ♠ ℝ ⊙ ◙ ⊠ lau ➤ ⅃ ♀ ✕ ⌀ ⤴R ⊞
Prices: pitch 13-14.60

GUILLIGOMARC'H FINISTÈRE

Bois des Ecureuils ☎ 298717098 ▤ 298717098
e-mail: price.reed@wanadoo.fr
Tranquil four acre wooded site set among oak, chestnut and beech trees. An ideal base for walking, cycling, horse-riding and fishing.

➲ *2km W from D769 (Roscoff to Lorient).*
15 May-15 Sep 2.5HEC ⊞ ♠ ℝ ⅃ ⊙ ◙ ⌀ ⊠ ⊞ lau
Prices: ♠2.40 ♠4 ▲4

GUILVINEC FINISTÈRE

Plage rte de Penmarc'h ☎ 298586190 ▤ 298588906
e-mail: info@campingsbretagnesud.com
On level meadow. Divided into pitches. Flat beach suitable for children.
➲ *2km W of village on the Corniche towards Penmarc'h.*
4May-9Sep 14HEC ⦂⦂ ⌂ ℝ ⅃ ♀ ✕ ⊙ ◙ ⌀ ⌲ ⌂ ⤴ PS ⊠
⊞ lau

HAYE-DU-PUITS, LA MANCHE

Étang des Haizes ☎ 233460116 ▤ 233472380
e-mail: etang-des-hiazes@wanadoo.com
A well equipped family site bordering a lake, shaded by apple trees.
➲ *Access via D903 from Carentan.*
15 Apr-15 Oct 5HEC ⊞ ⌂ ℝ ⅃ ✕ ⊙ ◙ ⌂ ⌂ ⤴ LP ⊠ ⊞
lau ➤ ⅃ ✕ Prices: ♠1-4 pitch 13-19

HOULGATE CALVADOS

Vallée 88 r de la Vallée ☎ 0231244069 ▤ 0231280829
e-mail: camping.lavallee@wanadoo.fr
Site with good recreational facilities, 900m from the beach.
➲ *1km N.*
1Apr-30Sep 11HEC ⊞ ⌂ ℝ ⅃ ✕ ⊙ ◙ ⌀ ⌲ ⌂ ⤴ P ⊠ 🅿
⊞ lau ➤ ⤴S Prices: ♠4.57-5.33 pitch 15.24-21.34 (incl 2 persons)

▶ **IFFENDIC** ILLE-ET-VILAINE

Domaine de Trémelin ☎ 299097379 ▦ 299097069
A lakeside site in beautiful wooded surroundings with good sports and entertainment facilities.
⮑ *S of town towards Plélan-le-Grand.*
Apr-Sep 2HEC ⸬ ⌁♠⌂☂⊙☺⊞♨ ⁊ L ⛫⊞

▶ **JULLOUVILLE** MANCHE

Chaussée 1 av de la Libération ☎ 233618018 ▦ 233614526
On large meadow, completely divided into pitches. Separated from beach and coast road by row of houses.
7 Apr-23 Sep 6HEC ⸬ ⌁♠⌂☂♨⊙☺⊘☺☺⛫⊞ lau ➧ ☂♨
✕ ⁊S⊞

▶ **At ST-MICHEL-DES-LOUPS**(4km SE)

Chaumière ☎ 233488293
⮑ *4km SE on D21 via Bouillon.*
2HEC ⸬ ⌁♠⌂✕⊙☺☺☺Å ⁊ LS ⛫ lau

▶ **KERLIN** FINISTÈRE

Étangs de Trévignon Pointe de Trévignon
☎ 298500041 ▦ 298500041
A family site with good, modern facilities 800mtrs from the beach, reached by a short pathway.
Jun-15 Sep 3HEC ⸬ ⌁♠⌂☂♨⊙☺⊘☺☺Å ⁊ P ⛫⊞ lau ➧
⁊S Prices: ☗4.70 ⮡1.30 pitch 5.30

▶ **LANDAUL** MORBIHAN

Pied-à-Terre Branzého ☎ 297246715
In a pleasant, quiet location, 15 minutes from the sea.
⮑ *1km from N165. Signposted from Landaul.*
Jul-Aug 1HEC ⸬ ⌁♠⊙☺☺Å⊞ lau ➧☂♨✕∅⊞
Prices: ☗2.50-3.50 ⮡1.60 ⬛1.60 Å1.60

▶ **LANDÉDA** FINISTÈRE

Abers Dunes de Ste-Marguerite ☎ 298049335 ▦ 298048435
Very quiet beautiful site among dunes. Ideal for children.
⮑ *2.5km NW on a peninsula between bays of Aber-Wrac'h and Aber Benoît.*
14 Apr-22 Sep 4.5HEC ⸬ ⌁♠⌂⊙☺☺ ⁊ S ⛫⊞ lau ➧
☂♨ ⁊R Prices: ☗2.40-3 ⮡1.04-1.30 ⬛3.60-4.50 Å3.60-4.50

▶ **LARMOR-PLAGE** MORBIHAN

Fontaine Kerderff ☎ 297337128
800m from the beach, near the leisure centre.
⮑ *300m from D152.*
2 May-15 Sep 4HEC ⸬ ⌁♠⌂♨⊙☺⛫⊞ lau ➧☂♨✕ ⁊S

▶ **LESCONIL** FINISTÈRE

Dunes 7 r P-Langevin ☎ 298878178 ▦ 298822705
A family site on slightly sloping landscaped ground, 800mtrs from the town centre and the harbour.
⮑ *Access via D53, turning S in Plobannalac. Signposted.*
25 May-15 Sep 2.8HEC ⸬ ⌁♠⊙☺☺☺⊞ lau ➧☂♨✕ ⁊S

Grande Plage 71 r P-Langevin ☎ 298878827 ▦ 298878827
Well equipped site on level ground, surrounded by woodland, 300mtrs from the sea.
Etr-Sep 2.5HEC ⸬ ⌁♠⌂⊙☺∅☺☺⛫⊞ lau ➧☂♨✕
⁊S

▶ **LOUVIERS** EURE

Bel Air Hameau de St-Lubin, rte de la Haye Malherbe
☎ 0232401077 ▦ 0232401077
Small site on the edge of a forest with landscaped pitches and good facilities.
⮑ *3km from the town centre via D81.*
Mar-Nov 2.5HEC ⸬ ⌁♠⌂⊙☺♨☺ ⁊ P ⛫⊞ lau

▶ **LUC-SUR-MER** CALVADOS

Capricieuse 2 r Brummel ☎ 231973443 ▦ 231968278
A large family site 100mtrs from the beach.
⮑ *On W outskirts, access via A13 exit Douvres.*
Apr-Sep 4.5HEC ⸬ ⋇♠⌂⊙☺☺☺⛫⊞ lau ➧☂♨✕∅♨
⁊PS

▶ **MARTIGNY** SEINE-MARITIME

CM ☎ 235856082 ▦ 235859516
On the shore of a lake in pleasant surroundings 8km from Dieppe.
⮑ *Access via D154.*
Apr-15 Oct 6.8HEC ⸬ ⌁♠♨⊙☺☺☺ ⁊ R ⛫⊞ lau ➧
⁊P

▶ **MARTRAGNY** CALVADOS

▥Château de Martragny ☎ 231802140 ▦ 231081491
e-mail: chateau.martragny@wanadoo.fr
Family site in grounds of a château which also offers accommodation.
⮑ *From N13 take exit for Martragny. Drive through St-Léger and campsite is on the right as you leave the village.*
May-15 Sep 15HEC ⸬ ⌁♠♨☂✕⊙☺∅ ⁊ P ⛫⊞ lau ➧
⁊R Prices: ☗3.80-4.43 ⬛0.61-0.76 pitch 7.62-8.84

▶ **MAUPERTUS-SUR-MER** MANCHE

Anse du Brick ☎ 233543357 ▦ 233544966
e-mail: welcome@anse-du-brick.com
Terraced site in a landscaped park between the sea and the forest.
⮑ *200m from beach.*
Apr-15 Sep 17HEC ⸬ ⌁♠♨☂✕⊙☺∅♨☺☺ ⁊ P ⛫
⊞⊞ lau ➧ ⁊S Prices: ☗3.50-4.50 pitch 7.50-13.50

▶ **MERVILLE-FRANCEVILLE** CALVADOS

Peupliers Allée des Pins ☎ 231240507 ▦ 231240507
e-mail: asl.mondeville@wanadoo.fr
Situated in a rural setting, 300 metres from the beach. The sanitary arrangements include a bathroom for babies. Shop, bar and café available high season.
⮑ *Approx 2km E from sign on D514*
Apr-Oct 2HEC ⸬ ⌁♠⌂⊙☺♨☺☺Å ⁊ S ⛫ lau ➧∅
Prices: ☗4.50 pitch 5.40

▶ **MONTERBLANC** MORBIHAN

Haras Aérodrome Vannes-Meucon
☎ 297446606 ▦ 297446606
e-mail: camping-vannes@wanadoo.fr
⮑ *Situated 4kms from Vannes in the direction Aerodrome Vannes-Meucon.*
All year 1HEC ⸬ ⌁♠⌂☂✕⊙☺♨☺☺Å ⁊ P ⛫⊞
lau Prices: ☗3 ⮡1 ⬛3 Å3

▶ **MONT-ST-MICHEL, LE** MANCHE

Gué de Beauvoir 5 rte du Mont-St-Michel, Beauvoir
☎ 233600923
A level site in an orchard close to the River Couesnon.
⮑ *4km S of Abbey on D776 Pontorson road.*
Etr-Sep 0.6HEC ⸬ ⌁♠⌂✕⊙☺☺⛫⊞ lau ➧✕

▶ **MORGAT** FINISTÈRE

Bouis ☎ 298261253
On a meadow surrounded by woodland with pitches divided by hedges on the extremity of the Parc Naturel Régional d'Armorique.
⮑ *From Morgat follow D255 towards Cap de la Chèvre for 1.5km then right towards Bouis.*
Etr-Sep 3HEC ⸬ ⌁♠♨⊙☺∅☺⛫⊞ lau ➧☂✕♨ ⁊S

⟩ **MOYAUX** CALVADOS

🏰Colombier ☎ 231636308 📠 231631597
e-mail: chateau@camping-lecolombier.com
Well-kept site in grounds of manor house.
Camping Card Compulsory.
➲ *3km NE on D143.*
May-15 Sep 10HEC ⸬ ⚒ ⟨ ⚓ ⟁ ✕ ☉ 🛒 ∅ ⟩ P ☎ ⊞ lau

⟩ **NÉVEZ** FINISTÈRE

Deux Fontaine Raguènes ☎ 298068191 📠 2980697180
e-mail: les2fontaines@libertysurf.fr
Mainly level site, subdivided into several fields surrounded by
woodland with good recreational facilities including an
aquaslide.
➲ *700m from Ragunès Beach.*
15 May-15 Sep 7HEC ⸬ ⚒ ⟨ ⚓ ⟁ ✕ ☉ 🛒 🚐 ⟩ P ☎ ⊞ lau
⟩ ⟩S

⟩ **NOYAL-MUZILLAC** MORBIHAN

Moulin de Cadillac Moulin de Cadillac
☎ 297670347 📠 297670002
A well equipped family site in a pleasant wooded location
with good facilities.
➲ *Access via N165, N through Muzillac.*
May-Sep 3HEC ⸬ ⚒ ⟨ ⚓ ⟁ ✕ ☉ 🛒 🚐 ⟩ P ☎ ⊞ lau

⟩ **OUISTREHAM** CALVADOS

Prairies de la Mer rte de Lion, Riva-Bella ☎ 231976161
A camping area attached to a larger static caravan site with
good recreational facilities, 400mtrs from the sea.
➲ *Access via D514.*
13 Mar-17 Oct 80HEC ⸬ ⚒ ⟨ ⚓ ⟁ ✕ ☉ 🛒 ∅ 🚐 ⟩ P ☎
⊞ lau ⟩ ⚓ ✕ ⟩S

⟩ **PÉNESTIN-SUR-MER** MORBIHAN

Airotel-Inly ☎ 299903509 📠 299904093
e-mail: inly-info@wanadoo.fr
Situated in the centre of a nature reserve and close to the
coast, with good recreational facilities.
➲ *2km SE via D201*
Apr-Sep 30HEC ⸬ ⚒ ⟨ ⚓ ⟁ ✕ ☉ 🛒 🚐 ⟩ LP ☎ lau
⟩ ∅ ⛺ ⟩S ⊞

Cénic ☎ 299904565 📠 299904505
In a forested area 2km from the sea. Spacious grassy pitches
ideal for families.
➲ *Access via D34 from La Roche-Bernard.*
Apr-Sep 7HEC ⸬ ⚒ ⟨ ⚓ ⟁ ✕ ☉ 🛒 ∅ 🚐 ⟩ P ☎ ⊞
lau ⟩ ✕ ⟩S

Iles La Pointe du Bile ☎ 299903024
e-mail: accuerl@camping-des-iles.com
A family site with direct access to the beach and a separate
residential section.
➲ *3km S on D201.*
Apr-Sep 4HEC ⸬ ⚒ ⟨ ⚓ ⟁ ✕ ☉ 🛒 ∅ ⟩ PS ☎ lau

⟩ **PENTREZ-PLAGE** FINISTÈRE

Tamaris ☎ 298265395 📠 298265248
Level site divided into pitches 20m from the beach.
➲ *Access via D887.*
May-9 Sep 3HEC ⸬ ⚒ ⟨ ☉ 🛒 ∅ ⛺ 🚐 ☎ ⊞ lau ⟩
⟁ ✕ ⟩S Prices: ⚑2.80-3.50 pitch 4-5

⟩ **PERROS-GUIREC** CÔTES-D'ARMOR

Claire Fontaine Toul ar Lann ☎ 296230355 📠 296490619
Spacious, level site in a rural setting.
➲ *1.2km SW of town centre, 800m from Trestraou beach.*
May-Sep 3HEC ⸬ ⚒ ⟨ ⟁ ☉ 🛒 ∅ 🚐 ☎ ⊞ lau ⟩ ⚓ ⟩S
Prices: pitch 14-17 (incl 2 persons)

⟩ At **LOUANNEC**(3km SE)

CM Ernest Renan-rte de Perros-Guirec
☎ 296231178 📠 293490447
Well situated site next to the sea. Take away food, games
room.
➲ *1km W.*
Jun-Sep 4.5HEC ⸬ ⚒ ⟨ ⚓ ⟁ ✕ ☉ 🛒 🚐 ⟩ LS ☎ lau
⟩ ✕ Prices: ⚑2.80

⟩ At **PLOUMANACH**(2km NW)

🏰Ranolien ☎ 296914358 📠 296914190
e-mail: leranolien@wanadoo.fr
The site is divided into pitches by hedges; separate sections
for caravans.
➲ *500m from the village.*
23 Mar-28 Sep 16HEC ⸬ ⚒ ⟨ ⚓ ⟁ ✕ ☉ 🛒 ∅ ⛺ ⟩ P ☎
⊞ lau ⟩ ⟩S

⟩ **PIEUX, LES** MANCHE

Grand Large ☎ 233524075 📠 233525820
e-mail: le-grand-large@wanadoo.fr
In an unspoilt location with direct access to the beach.
➲ *3km from the town centre on D117.*
6Apr-15Sep 4HEC ⸬ ⚒ ⸬ ⚒ ⟨ ⚓ ⟁ ✕ ☉ 🛒 ∅ 🚐 ⟩ PS
☎ ⊞ lau Prices: pitch 16.80-21 (incl 2 persons)

⟩ **PLÉRIN** CÔTES-D'ARMOR

Mouettes Les Rosaires les Mouettes ☎ 0296745148
Jul-Sep 1HEC ⸬ ⚒ ⟨ ⟁ ☉ 🛒 🚐 ☎ ⊞ lau ⟩ ⚓ ✕ ∅ ⟩PRS
Prices: ⚑2.59 🚐1.22 pitch 1.52

⟩ **PLEUBIAN** CÔTES-D'ARMOR

Port la Chaîne ☎ 296229238 📠 296228792
e-mail: ptchaine@club-internet.fr
A peaceful, terraced site on the 'Wild Peninsula', with direct
access to the sea, with good facilities.
➲ *2km N via D20.*
May-Sep 9HEC ⸬ ⚒ ⟩ ⟨ ⚓ ⟁ ✕ ☉ 🛒 ∅ ⛺ ⟩ PS ☎ ⊞
lau Prices: ⚑4.60 pitch 8

⟩ **PLEUMEUR-BODOU** CÔTES-D'ARMOR

Port Landrellec ☎ 296238779
Beautiful site by the sea with numbered pitches surrounded
by hedges.
➲ *3km from Trégastel turn towards Tréburden.*
Apr-Sep 2HEC ⸬ ⚒ ⚒ ⟨ ✕ ☉ 🛒 ∅ 🚐 ⟩ S ☎ ⊞ lau ⟩ ⚓
⟁ ✕

⟩ **PLOBANNALEC** FINISTÈRE

Manoir de Kerlut ☎ 298822389 📠 298822649
e-mail: info@campingsbretagnesud.com
A peaceful site located in the grounds of a manor house
some 2km from the beach.
➲ *1.6km S via D102.*
4May-15Aug 12HEC ⸬ ⚒ ⟨ ⚓ ⟁ ✕ ☉ 🛒 ∅ ⛺ 🚐 ⟩ PS
☎ ⊞ lau ⟩ ✕ Prices: pitch 17-31

⟩ **PLOËMEL** MORBIHAN

Kergo ☎ 297568066
In pleasant wooded surroundings, close to the neighbouring
beaches.
➲ *2km SE via D186.*
15 May-15 Sep 2.5HEC ⸬ ⚒ ⟨ ⟁ ☉ 🛒 🚐 ☎ ⊞ lau ⟩ ⚓ ⟁ ✕
Prices: ⚑3.30 🚐1.70 🚐3.20 ⚑3.20

⟩ **PLOEMEUR** MORBIHAN

Ajoncs Beg Minio ☎ 297863011
A rural site situated in an orchard.
➲ *From town centre continue towards Fort-Bloqué.*
27 Mar-Sep 2HEC ⸬ ⚒ ⟨ ⟁ ☉ 🛒 🚐 lau ⟩ ⟩P

⟩ **PLOËRMEL** MORBIHAN

Lac Les Belles Rives, Taupont ☎ 297740122
A lakeside family site with plenty of facilities for water sports.
➲ *2km from village centre, beside the lake.*
Apr-Oct 3HEC ⚏ ⌖ ⬥ ⟁ ♨ ⟂ ⊙ ⬤ ⬒ ⏚ ⬛ ⬜ ⟂ L ⬚ ⊞ lau
✦ ⟂P

Vallée du Ninian Le Rocher
☎ 297935301 ⬚ 297935727
Peaceful family site at the heart of Brittany which specialises
in homemade cider beside the River Ninian.
➲ *W of Taupont towards the river.*
May-Sep 2.7HEC ⚏ ⌖ ⬥ ⟁ ⊙ ⬤ ⬒ ⏚ ⬛ ⬜ ⟂ PR ⬚ ⊞
lau ✦ ✗ Prices: ♠2.48-3.10 ⬢4-5 ⬤4-5

⟩ **PLOMEUR** FINISTÈRE

Torche Pointe de la Torche, Roz an Tremen
☎ 298586282 ⬚ 298588969
e-mail: info@campingdelatorche.fr
A family site with pitches surrounded by trees and bushes,
1.5km from the beach.
➲ *3.5km W*
30 Mar-27 Sep 4HEC ⚏ ⌖ ⬥ ⟁ ♨ ⟂ ✗ ⊙ ⬤ ⬒ ⏚ ⬛ ⟂ P ⬚
⊞ lau ✦ ✗ ⟂S Prices: ♠2.10-4.20 ⬢0.90-1.80
pitch 3.40-6.90

⟩ **PLOMODIERN** FINISTÈRE

Iroise Plage de Pors-ar-Vag
☎ 298815272 ⬚ 298812610
e-mail: campingiroise@aol.com
A family site with fine recreational facilities, providing
magnificent views over the Bay of Douarnenez.
➲ *5km SW, 150m from the beach.*
Apr-Sep 2.5HEC ⚏ ⌖ ⬥ ⟁ ♨ ⟂ ✗ ⊙ ⬤ ⬒ ⏚ ⬛ ⟂ P ⬚ ⊞ lau
✦ ✗ ⟂S Prices: ♠3.53-4.70 pitch 7.13-9.50

⟩ **PLONÉVEZ-PORZAY** FINISTÈRE

International de Kervel ☎ 298925154 ⬚ 298925496
e-mail: camping.kervel@wanadoo.fr
Ideal for families. 800m from the sea.
➲ *SW of the village on the D107 Douarnenez road for 3km,*
then towards coast at crossroads.
Apr-12 Sep 7HEC ⚏ ⌖ ⬥ ⟁ ♨ ⟂ ✗ ⊙ ⬤ ⬒ ⏚ ⬛ ⬜ A ⟂ P ⬚
⊞ lau ✦ ⟂S Prices: ♠2.88-4.12 pitch 8.22-11.74

Tréguer-Plage Ste-Anne-la-Palud
☎ 298925352 ⬚ 298925489
A level site with direct access to the beach.
➲ *1.3km N*
15 Jun-15 Sep 6HEC ⚏ ∷ ⬥ ♨ ⟁ ♨ ⟂ ✗ ⊙ ⬤ ⬒ ⏚ ⬛ ⟂ S
⬚ ⊞ lau ✦ ✗ ⊞ Prices: ♠2.50-3.10 ⬢1.85-2.30 pitch 2.50-
3.10

⟩ **PLOUÉZEC** CÔTES-D'ARMOR

Cap Horn Port Lazo ☎ 296206428 ⬚ 296206388
e-mail: lecaphorn@hotmail.com
In an elevated position overlooking the Ile de Bréhat with
direct access to the beach.
➲ *2.3km NE via D77 at Port-Lazo.*
Apr-Sep 5HEC ⚏ ♨ ⬥ ⟁ ♨ ⟂ ✗ ⊙ ⬤ ⬒ ⬛ ⟂ PS ⬚ lau
✦ ⬛ Prices: ♠4.10 ⬢6.80 ⬤6.80

⟩ **PLOUEZOCH** FINISTÈRE

Baie de Térénez ☎ 298672680 ⬚ 298672680
A well equipped site in a pleasant rural setting.
➲ *3.5km NW via D76.*
2 Apr-Sep 3HEC ⚏ ⌖ ⬥ ⟁ ♨ ✗ ⊙ ⬤ ⬒ ⏚ ⬛ ⬜ ⟂ P ⬚ ⊞ lau
✦ ⟂RS

⟩ **PLOUGASNOU** FINISTÈRE

CM Mélin-ar-Mésqueau ☎ 298673745
Large municipal site with good recreational facilities.
➲ *3.5km S via D46*
15 Jun-Aug 15HEC ⚏ ⌖ ⬥ ⟁ ♨ ⟂ ⊙ ⬤ ⬒ ⟂ LR ⬚ ⬛ ⊞ lau

Trégor Kerjean ☎ 298673764
A sheltered site with numbered, grassy pitches. Surrounded
by hedges.
➲ *Off D46 towards Morlaix.*
Jul-Sep 1HEC ⚏ ⌖ ⬥ ⟁ ♨ ⊙ ⬤ ⏚ ⬒ ⬛ lau ✦ ⟁ ♨ ✗ ⊞

⟩ **PLOUHA** CÔTES-D'ARMOR
⟩ At **TRINITÉ, LA**(2km NE)

Domaine de Keravel rte de Port Moguer
☎ 296224913 ⬚ 296224713
e-mail: keravel@wanadoo.fr
Forested site built around an elegant country mansion, 1km
from the sea.
15 May-Sep 5HEC ⚏ ⌖ ⬥ ⟁ ♨ ⊙ ⬤ ⬒ ⏚ ⬛ ⬜ ⟂ P ⬚ ⊞ lau ✦
⟂S Prices: ♠3.92-4.50 pitch 6-7.50

⟩ **PLOUHARNEL** MORBIHAN

Étang de Loperhet ☎ 297523468
➲ *1km NW via D781*
Apr-Oct 6HEC ⚏ ∷ ∷∷ ⬥ ⟁ ♨ ⟂ ✗ ⊙ ⬤ ⬒ ⏚ ⬛ ⬜ ⟂ P ⬚ lau
✦ ✗ ⬒ ⟂S ⊞

Kersily Ste-Barbe ☎ 297523965 ⬚ 297524476
Etr-Oct 3HEC ⚏ ⌖ ⬥ ⟁ ♨ ⟂ ✗ ⊙ ⬤ ⏚ ⬛ ⟂ P ⬚ ⊞ lau ✦
⟂S

Lande Kerzivienne ☎ 02 297523148
On partially shaded terrain, 600mtrs from the beach
Jun-Sep 1HEC ⚏ ⌖ ⬥ ♨ ⊙ ⬤ ⬒ ⏚ ⬛ ⬜ ⊞ lau ✦ ⟁ ♨ ✗ ⟁
⟂S

⟩ **PLOUHINEC** MORBIHAN

Moténo rte du Magouer ☎ 297367663 ⬚ 297858184
On slightly sloping ground, subdivided into several fields in a
wooded area 600mtrs from the beach.
➲ *S beside the Mer d'Etel.*
Apr-Sep 4HEC ⚏ ⌖ ⬥ ⟁ ♨ ⟂ ✗ ⊙ ⬤ ⬒ ⏚ ⬛ ⬜ ⊞ lau ✦
⟂PS

⟩ **PLOZÉVET** FINISTÈRE

Corniche rte de la Corniche ☎ 298913394 ⬚ 0298914153
Peaceful rural site 1.5km from the sea.
15 Jun-15 Sep 2HEC ⚏ ⌖ ⬥ ⟁ ♨ ⟂ ✗ ⊙ ⬤ ⬒ ⬛ ⟂ P ⬚ ⊞
lau ✦ ♨ ✗ ⬛ ⟂LRS

> **PONTAUBAULT** MANCHE

Vallée de la Sélune 7 rue Mal Leclerc ☎ 233603900
This site is in a quiet village near the River Sélune. Ideal base
for exploring the Normandy/Brittany area.
➲ *Access via N175 Portorson-Caen.*
Apr-20 Oct 1.6HEC ⬛ ⚏ 🛉 🆑 🍽 ✕ ⊙ 🏪 🚿 🏕 🚐 🄳 🛟 🏊
🔺R Prices: 🛉15 ➡15 🚐15 ▲10-15

> **PONT-AVEN** FINISTÈRE

Domaine de Kerlann ☎ 0870 242 7777 ▤ 0870 242 9999
A wooded park with shady pitches featuring an indoor pool
complex with waterslide and spa bath.
➲ *Approx 3m E of Pont Aven.*
7 Apr-26 Oct ⬛ 🛉 🆑 🚿 🍽 ✕ ⊙ 🏪 🚿 🚐 ▲ 🔺 PS 🄳 🄲 lau
🛟 🚿 🍽

> **PONT-L'ABBÉ** FINISTÈRE

Écureuil ☎ 298870339
Shady site set in a wooded park with good recreational
facilities.
➲ *3.5km NE onD44.*
15 Jun-15 Sep 3HEC ⬛ 🛉 🆑 🚿 🍽 ✕ ⊙ 🏪 🚿 🏕 🏬 🚐 🄳 🄲 lau

> **PORDIC** CÔTES-D'ARMOR

Madières rte de Vau Madec ☎ 296790248 ▤ 296794667
A quiet coastal site in a well shaded position.
➲ *1500m from village on St-Brieuc road (D786).*
15 May-Sep 2HEC ⬛ ⚏ 🛉 🆑 🚿 🍽 ✕ ⊙ 🏪 🚿 🏕 🏬 🚐 🔺 P 🄳
lau 🛟 🔺S

> **PORT-MANECH** FINISTÈRE

St-Nicolas ☎ 298068975 ▤ 298067461
e-mail: cpsn@club-internet.fr
Divided into hedge-lined pitches in beautiful surroundings
close to the beach.
May-Sep 3.5HEC ⬛ ⚏ 🛉 🆑 ⊙ 🏪 🏕 🚐 🄳 🄲 lau 🛟 🚿 🍽 ✕ 🚿
🏕 🔺S

> **POSES** EURE

Ile Adeline ☎ 232593581 ▤ 232598895
A well equipped site situated close to the Lery-Poses leisure
centre.
➲ *Access via A13 exit 19 towards Val-de-Reuil.*
Apr-Sep 2.5HEC ⬛ ⚏ 🛉 🆑 🚿 🍽 ✕ ⊙ 🏪 🚐 🄳 🄲 lau 🛟 🔺LR

> **POULDU, LE** FINISTÈRE

Embruns r du Philosophe Alain
☎ 298399107 ▤ 298399787
e-mail: camping-les-embruns@wanadoo.fr
A pleasant site with good facilities and easy access to the
beach. Separate car park for arrivals after 22.00hrs.
Apr-15 Sep 4HEC ⬛ ⚏ 🛉 🆑 🚿 🍽 ✕ ⊙ 🏪 🚿 🏕 🏬 🚐 🔺 P 🄳 🄿
🄲 lau 🛟 ✕ 🔺RS Prices: 🛉3.65-4.65 🚐6.50-7.50 pitch 9.50-12

> **QUETTEHOU** MANCHE

Rivage rte de Morsalines ☎ 233541376
Quiet, sheltered site, 400m from the sea.
➲ *Access via D14.*
Apr-Oct 1.6HEC ⬛ 🌿 🆑 ⊙ 🏪 🚿 🏕 🏬 🄳 lau 🛟 🚿 🍽 ✕ 🔺S
🄲

> **QUIBERON** MORBIHAN

Bois d'Amour rue St-Clement ☎ 297504267 ▤ 297501352
e-mail: info@homair-vacances.fr
A family site with plenty of recreational facilities close to the
area's fine beaches.
➲ *1.5 km SE at La Pointe de la Presqu'ile, 100m from beach.*
Apr-Oct 4.5HEC ⬛ ⚏ ⋯⋯ 🌿 🆑 🚿 🍽 ✕ ⊙ 🏪 🏬 🚐 🔺 P 🄳
lau 🛟 🚿 🍽 ✕ 🚿 🏕 🔺S 🄲 Prices: 🛉3.81-6.86 pitch 6.10-12.35

Domaine de Kerlann ★★★★
Pont Aven

Enjoy the relaxed atmosphere at the beautiful Domaine de Kerlann - a lovely wooded parc in a perfect location for making the most of Southern Brittany.

- Good sized pitches grouped together in a grassy area
- Fabulous indoor pool complex with waterslide and spa bath
- Heated outdoor pools & waterslide
- Scattered play areas, multi-sport pitch & tennis courts

- 3 children's clubs for all ages
- Restaurant, takeaway, pub & entertainment's room
- Bilingual staff on parc
- Superb low season prices
- Site open from 23 March - 27 October

Domaine de Kerlann, Land Rosted, 29930 Pont Aven, France
Tel:00 33 298 06 01 77 Fax:00 33 298 06 18 50

ABTA
V2819

To book from France please call the number above, quoting code FAA03
To book from the UK please call 0870 242 77 77 quoting code FAA03

Conguel bd Teignouse ☎ 297501911
Directly on the beach, with fine recreational facilities.
➲ *Near the aerodrome towards Pointe de Conguel.*
Apr-Oct 5HEC ⬛ ⚏ 🛉 🆑 🚿 🍽 ✕ ⊙ 🏪 🚐 🔺 P 🄳 🄲 lau
🛟 🔺S

> **QUIMPER** FINISTÈRE

🏰Orangerie de Lanniron Chateau de Lanniron
☎ 298906202 ▤ 298521556
e-mail: camping@lanniron.com
In the grounds of the former residence of the Bishops of
Quimper, beside the River Odet and surrounded by tropical
vegetation.
➲ *2.5km from town centre via D34.*
15 May-15 Sep 17HEC ⬛ ⚏ 🛉 🆑 🚿 🍽 ✕ ⊙ 🏪 🚿 🏕 🏬 🚐 🔺
PR 🄳 🄲 lau Prices: 🛉4.59-5.40 🚐2.97-3.50

> **RAGUENÈS-PLAGE** FINISTÈRE

Airotel International Raguenès-Plage 19 r des Iles, Raguenel
☎ 298068069 ▤ 298068905
Asphalt drives; 400m from beaches.
➲ *Leave Pont-Aven and take the road to Nevez. At Nevez
follow directions to Raguenès.*
16 Apr-30 Sep 7HEC ⬛ 🛉 🆑 🚿 🍽 ✕ ⊙ 🏪 🚿 🏕 🏬 🚐 🔺 PS
🄳 🄿 🄲 lau Prices: 🛉3.57-4.89 pitch 6-11.59 (incl 2 persons)

> **RAVENOVILLE-PLAGE** MANCHE

Cormoran ☎ 233413394 ▤ 233951680
A pleasant family site with well defined pitches, 20mtrs from
the sea.
➲ *300mtrs from the town towards Utah Beach.*
Apr-Sep 6.5HEC ⬛ ⚏ 🛉 🆑 🚿 🍽 ✕ ⊙ 🏪 🚿 🏕 🏬
🔺 PS 🄳 🄲 lau

RIEC-SUR-BÉLON FINISTÈRE

Château de Bélon Port de Bélon ☎ 298064143
Situated in wooded parkland by the sea with facilities for sailing and fishing.
➲ 3.5km S
Apr-15 Nov 8HEC ⅏ ♣ ⋔ ⅒ ⊙ ⬛ ⌀ ⬛ ⌇ S ⬛ ⊞ lau ➤ ⬛ ✕

ROCHE-BERNARD, LA MORBIHAN

CM Patïs 3 chemin du Patis
☎ 0299906013 ▤ 0299908828
On banks of River Vilaine.
➲ 100m from village centre.
Apr-Sep 1HEC ⅏ ⅍ ⋔ ⊙ ⬛ ⬛ ⬛ ⊞ lau ➤ ⬛ ⬛ ✕ ⌀ ⌇P
Prices: ⭫3.05 ⬥1.06 pitch 20

ROCHEFORT-EN-TERRE MORBIHAN

Moulin Neuf ☎ 297433752 ▤ 297433545
A well equipped site in wooded surroundings. The shop contains only basic items but there is a supermarket nearby.
Camping Card compulsory.
➲ Signposted from D744 in village.
May-Sep 2.5HEC ⅏ ⅍ ⋔ ⬛ ⬛ ⊙ ⬛ ⌇ P ⬛ ⬛ ⊞ lau ➤ ⬛ ✕ ⌀ ⌇LR ⊞ Prices: ⭫3.81-4.57 pitch 6.86-7.62

ROSTRENEN CÔTES-D'ARMOR

Fleur de Bretagne Kerandouaron ☎ 296291645
e-mail: n.eardley@libertysurf.fr
A spacious site in a picturesque, sheltered valley with good, modern facilities.
➲ 1.5km from Rostrenen on D764 towards Pontivy.
Apr-Sep 6HEC ⅏ ⅍ ⋔ ⬛ ⬛ ⊙ ⬛ ⌇ P ⬛ lau ➤ ⬛ ⌀ ⬛ ⊞
Prices: ⭫2.20 ⬥1 pitch 4

ST-ALBAN CÔTES-D'ARMOR

St-Vrêguet St-Vréguet ☎ 0296329021
e-mail: vrguet@wanadoo.fr
A peaceful site in a pleasant park with good sanitary and recreational facilities.
Jun-Sep 1HEC ⅏ ⅍ ⋔ ⬛ ⬛ ⊙ ⬛ ⌀ ⬛ ⬛ ⊞ lau ➤ ⌇R
Prices: ⭫2.75-2.90 ⬥1.50-1.55 pitch 1.65-1.70

ST-AUBIN-SUR-MER CALVADOS

Côte de Nacre 17 r du Major Moulton
☎ 231971445 ▤ 231972211
A pleasant site with good recreational facilities. Reservations recommended in high season. Separate car park for arrivals after 22.00hrs.
Apr-Oct 6HEC ⅏ ⅻ ⋔ ⬛ ⬛ ✕ ⊙ ⬛ ⌀ ⬛ ⌇ P ⬛ ⊞ lau ➤ ⌇S

CM Mesnil ☎ 235830283
A family site attached to a typical Norman farm.
➲ 2 km W on D68.
Apr-Oct 2.3HEC ⅏ ⅍ ⋔ ✕ ⊙ ⬛ ⬛ ⊞ lau ➤ ⬛ ⌇S
Prices: ⭫4.70 ⬥1.81 pitch 2.53

ST-BRIAC ILLE-ET-VILAINE

Emeraude 7 chemin de la Souris ☎ 299883455
e-mail: camping.emeraude@wanadoo.fr
Well-kept site in pleasant quiet situation and divided into pitches.
➲ Turn left off D786 and continue for 0.8 km.
Apr-Sep 2HEC ⅏ ⅍ ⋔ ⬛ ⬛ ⊙ ⬛ ⌀ ⬛ ⬛ ⊞ lau ➤ ✕ ⌇S

ST-BRIEUC CÔTES-D'ARMOR

Vallées Parc de Brézillet ☎ 296940505
e-mail: campingdesvallees@wanadoo.fr
Situated on the edge of the town in a plateau criss-crossed by wooded valleys. Restaurant open July and August only.
Etr-15 Oct 4.8HEC ⅏ ♣ ⋔ ⬛ ⬛ ✕ ⊙ ⬛ ⬛ ⬛ ⌇ R ⬛ ⊞ lau ➤ ⌀ ⌇PS Prices: pitch 7.60-9.50 (incl 1 persons)

ST-CAST-LE-GUILDO CÔTES-D'ARMOR

Château de Galinée ☎ 296411056 ▤ 0296410372
e-mail: chateaudegalinee@wanadoo.fr
A family site in a 5 acre wood incorporating the buildings of an old farm, 3km from the local beaches.
➲ 3km from CD786. Well signposted.
27 May-09 Sep 14HEC ⅏ ⅍ ⋔ ⬛ ⬛ ⊙ ⬛ ⬛ ⬛ ⌇ P ⬛ lau ➤ ⌀ ⌇LS Prices: ⭫3.80-5.30 pitch 8-13

Châtelet r des Nouettes ☎ 296419633
In superb landscaped surroundings overlooking the sea with good sporting facilities.
➲ 1km W, 250m from the beach
6 Jun-10 Sep 8HEC ⅏ ♣ ⋔ ⬛ ⬛ ✕ ⊙ ⬛ ⬛ ⌇ LPS ⬛ ⊞ lau ➤ ⌀ ⬛

ST-EFFLAM CÔTES-D'ARMOR

CM r de Ian-Carré ☎ 296356215 ▤ 296350975
On a level meadow with well defined pitches 100mtrs from a magnificent beach.
Apr-Sep 4HEC ⅏ ⅍ ⋔ ✕ ⊙ ⬛ ⬛ ⊞ lau ➤ ✕ ⌀ ⌇S
Prices: ⭫2.21-2.60 ⬥1.31-1.53 pitch 2.86-3.36

ST-GERMAIN-SUR-AY MANCHE

Aux Grands Espaces ☎ 233071014
On slightly sloping ground among dunes. Children's play area. Lunchtime siesta 12.30-14.30 hrs. 500m from sea.

⮞ *Leave D650 W of town and follow signs 'Plage' on D306.*
May-15 Sep 15HEC ⸿⸿⸿⸿ ⇗⋔⌁⋆⋆✕☉☺⌀☲⇲⋔⇲A⋆P☑ ⊞ lau ➧ ⋆S

ST-GILDAS-DE-RHUYS MORBIHAN

Menhir rte de Port Crouesty ☎ 297452288 ▤ 297453718
A family site with good facilities situated 1km from the beach.
⮞ *3.5km N.*
26 May-12 Sep 3HEC ⸿⸿⸿⸿ ➧⋔⌁⋆⋆✕☉☺⌀⇲
⋆ PS ☑⊞ lau ➧ ⋆S

ST-JOUAN-DES-GUÉRÊTS ILLE-ET-VILAINE

P'tit Bois ☎ 299211430 ▤ 299817414
e-mail: camping.ptitbois@wanadoo.fr
A pleasant family site in quiet wooded surroundings.
⮞ *Access via N137.*
29 Mar-14 Sep 6HEC ⸿⸿⸿⸿ ⇗⋔⌁⋆⋆✕☉☺⌀⇲A⋆P☑
⊞ lau ➧ ⇲ ⋆RS Prices: ⋔6 pitch 10-15

ST-LÉGER-DU-BOURG-DENIS SEINE-MARITIME

Aubette 23 r Vert Buisson ☎ 235084769
In a wooded valley, 3km E of Rouen.
All year 0.8HEC ⸿⸿⸿⸿ ⇗⋔☉☺⌀⇲⇲☑☐⊞ lau ➧⋆⋆✕⌀
⋆R Prices: ⋔15 pitch 16

ST-LUNAIRE ILLE-ET-VILAINE

Longchamp bd de St-Cast ☎ 299463398 ▤ 299460271
In a beautiful wooded setting in the heart of the Emerald coast with a good range of facilities.
⮞ *Turn off D786 towards St-Briac at end of village, site is on left. 100m from the sea.*
15 May-10 Sep 5HEC ⸿⸿⸿⸿ ⇗⋔⌁⋆⋆✕☉☺⌀☑⊞ lau
➧⋆S

Touesse ☎ 299466113 ▤ 299160258
e-mail: camping.la.touesse@wanadoo.fr
A well equipped family site, 300mtrs from the beach.
⮞ *2km E via D786.*
Apr-Sep 2.8HEC ⸿⸿⸿⸿ ⇗⋔⌁⋆⋆✕☉☺⌀⇲⇲☑⊞ lau
➧⋆S

ST-MALO ILLE-ET-VILAINE

CM le Nicet av de la Varde ☎ 299402632 ▤ 0299407137
100m from the beach; direct access via staircase. Water sports and other activities available.
7 Jun-7 Sep 2.9HEC ⸿⸿⸿⸿ ⇗⋔☉☺⋆S☑⊞ lau ➧⋆⋆✕⌀
⇲⋆S

Ville Huchet rte de la Passagère ☎ 299811183 ▤ 299815189
e-mail: domaine-de-la-ville-huchet@wanadoo.fr
⮞ *5km S via N137.*
May-15 Sep 6HEC ⸿⸿⸿⸿ ➧⋔⌁⋆⋆✕☉☺⌀⇲⇲⋆P☑☑
lau ➧ ⋆R Prices: ⋔5.50 pitch 11.50

ST-MARCAN ILLE-ET-VILAINE

Balcon de la Baie ☎ 299802295
In a beautiful location overlooking the bay of Mont-St-Michel.
⮞ *10km NW of Pontorson on D797.*
May-Oct 2.7HEC ⸿⸿⸿⸿ ⇗⋔⌁⋆✕☉☺⌀☑☑ lau ➧✕

ST-MARTIN-DES-BESACES CALVADOS

Puits ☎ 231678002 ▤ 231678002
e-mail: camping.le.puits@wanadoo.fr
A small family run site surrounded by a pleasant garden and lush fields.
⮞ *Access via N175 Caen/Mont-St-Michel.*
Feb-Oct 3.6HEC ⸿⸿⸿⸿ ⚶⋔⌁⋆⋆✕☉☺⌀⇲⇲☑⊞ lau ➧⇲
Prices: ⋔2.30 pitch 4.60

ST-MARTIN-EN-CAMPAGNE SEINE-MARITIME

Goelands r des Grèbes, Saint Martin Plage
☎ 235838290 ▤ 235861799
Site with good recreational facilities in an area of woodland, 100mtrs from a small lake. Shop and bar open in high season only.
⮞ *NE of Dieppe, 2km from D925.*
15 Mar-Oct 4HEC ⸿⸿⸿⸿ ⚶⋔⌁⋆✕☉☺⌀⇲⋆S☑⊞ lau
➧⇲⋆P

ST-MICHEL-EN-GRÈVE CÔTES-D'ARMOR

Capucines Kervourdon ☎ 296357228 ▤ 296357898
e-mail: les.capucines@wanadoo.fr
In a peaceful setting near the beach with a large variety of facilities.
⮞ *On D786 Lannion-Morlaix road.*
4May-8Sep 4HEC ⸿⸿⸿⸿ ⇗⋔⌁⋆⋆✕☉☺⌀⇲⋆P☑☑⊞✍
lau ➧✕⌀⋆S

ST-PAIR-SUR-MER MANCHE

⛫Château de Lez-Eaux St-Aubin-des-Preaux
☎ 233516609 ▤ 233519202
e-mail: lez.eaux@wanadoo.fr
Situated in grounds of an old Château. Bank, TV and reading room. Fishing available.
⮞ *7km SE via D973 rte d'Avranches.*
May-15 Sep 12HEC ⸿⸿⸿⸿ ⇗⋔⌁⋆⋆✕☉☺⌀⇲⋆P☑⊞
lau Prices: pitch 14.50-24 (incl 2 persons)

Ecutot ☎ 233502629 ▤ 233506494
e-mail: camping.ecutot@wanadoo.fr
Situated in an orchard 1km from the sea.
⮞ *On the main road between Granville and Avranches.*
Apr-Sep 4HEC ⸿⸿⸿⸿ ⇗⋔☉☺⌀⋆P☑ lau ➧⋆⋆✕⌀⇲
⋆S ⊞ Prices: ⋔4.60 pitch 4

Mariénée ☎ 0233906005
2km from sea; situated in grounds of old farm.
⮞ *2km S of town on D21.*
Avr-Sep 1.2HEC ⸿⸿⸿⸿ ⇗⋔☉☺⇲⇲☑⊞ lau ➧⋆⋆✕⌀ ⋆PS

ST-PHILIBERT-SUR-MER MORBIHAN

Vieux Logis ☎ 297550117 ▤ 297300391
Beautiful, well-kept site divided by hedges.
⮞ *2km W via D781.*
4 Apr-29 Sep 2.1HEC ⸿⸿⸿⸿ ⇗⋔✕☉☺⌀⇲☑⊞ lau ➧⋆

ST-PIERRE-DU-VAUVRAY EURE

St-Pierre 1 r du Château ☎ 232610155 ▤ 0232610155
In wooded surroundings with pitches divided by hedges, 50mtrs from the River Seine.
⮞ *Access via A13/N15.*
All year 3HEC ⸿⸿⸿⸿ ⇗⋔☉☺⌀⋆P☑ lau ➧⋆⋆✕⇲⋆R⊞
Prices: ⋔3 ⇲5

ST-PIERRE-QUIBERON MORBIHAN

Park-er-Lann ☎ 297502493 ▤ 297502493
⮞ *1.5km W on D768.*
Etr-Sep 2.5HEC ⸿⸿⸿⸿ ⇗⋔⌁✕☉☺⌀⇲⇲☑⊞ lau
➧⋆⌀⋆S

ST-QUAY-PORTRIEUX CÔTES-D'ARMOR

Bellevue 68 bd du Littoral ☎ 296704184 ▤ 269705546
e-mail: campingbellevue@foree.fr
A terraced site adjacent to the sea with numbered pitches.
⮞ *800m from town centre off D786.*
May-15 Sep 4HEC ⸿⸿⸿⸿ ⇗⋔⌁☉☺⌀⇲⋆PS☑⊞ lau
➧⋆⋆✕⌀⇲ Prices: ⋔3.05-3.96 pitch 4.88-5.64

161

St-Vaast-la-Hougue Manche

Gallouette r de la Gallouette ☎ 233542057 ▦ 233541671
e-mail: contact@camping-lagallouette.fr
A well equipped site, 300mtrs from the town centre and with direct access to the beach.
Apr-15 Oct 2.3HEC ⊞⊞⊞ ⊕ ℝ 🏕 ▼ ✕ ⊙ 🕿 ⌀ 🚾 🏕 🚐 ⟲ S 🏧
lau ➡ ✕ Prices: ⋔3.65-4.15 pitch 4.40-4.90

Ste-Marie-du-Mont Manche

Utah Beach La Madeleine ☎ 233715369 ▦ 233710711
On a level meadow 100mtrs from the beach.
↪ 6km NE via D913 and D421.
Apr-Sep 3HEC ⊞⊞⊞ ⠸⠿⠿ ⠜ ℝ 🏕 ▼ ✕ ⊙ 🕿 ⌀ 🚾 🏕
⟲ S 🏧 lau

Ste-Marine Finistère

Hellès ☎ 298563146
↪ 400m from the beach
15 Jun-15 Sep 3HEC ⊞⊞⊞ ⊕ ℝ ⊙ 🕿 ⌀ 🚐 ⊞ lau ➡ ⟲S

Ste-Mère-Église Manche

Cormoran Ravenoville-Plage ☎ 233413394 ▦ 233951608
e-mail: lecormoran@wanadoo.fr
A quiet site with well defined pitches, 20m from the sea.
↪ Drive towards Ravenoville Plage, then take Utah Beach road for 500m.
30 Mar-22 Sep 6.5HEC ⊞⊞⊞ ⊕ ℝ 🏕 ▼ ✕ ⊙ 🕿 ⌀ 🚾 🏕 ⟲ P 🏧
⊞ lau ➡ ⟲S Prices: pitch 14.50-19 (incl 2 persons)

Sarzeau Morbihan

Treste rte de la Plage du Roaliguen
☎ 297417960 ▦ 297413621
e-mail: letreste@campingletreste.com
A family site with good facilities 800mtrs from the Roaliguen beach.
↪ 2.5km S
27 Apr-8 Sep 2.5HEC ⊞⊞⊞ ⠼⠾ ℝ 🏕 ▼ ⊙ 🕿 ⌀ 🚐 ⌀ 🛆 ⟲ P 🏧
lau ➡ ✕ ⟲S Prices: ⋔3.41-4.27 pitch 6.34-7.93

At Penvins(7km SE D198)

Madone ☎ 297673330
Situated 400m from the sea. Extensive sites on edge of village near old country estate. Divided into several sections.
Jun-Sep 6HEC ⊞⊞⊞ ⊕ ℝ 🏕 ▼ ✕ ⊙ 🕿 ⌀ 🚾 🏧 ⊞ lau ➡ ✕ ⌀ 🏕
⟲S

At Pointe-st-Jacques(5.5km S)

CM St-Jacques ☎ 297417929 ▦ 297480445
e-mail: camping.stjacques@wanadoo.fr
On beach protected by dunes. Well kept site with asphalt drives in a pleasant wooded location.
Apr-Sep 7.6HEC ⊞⊞⊞ ⊕ ℝ 🏕 ✕ ⊙ 🕿 ⌀ 🏕 🚾 🛆 ⟲ S 🏧 ⊞
lau ➡ ✕

Sassetot-le-Mauconduit Seine-Maritime

Trois Plages ☎ 235274011 ▦ 235282320
Well equipped site 3km from the coast.
↪ 1.3km S near D925.
25 Apr-15 Sep 4HEC ⊞⊞⊞ ⊕ ℝ 🏕 ⊙ 🕿 ⌀ 🏕 🏧 ⊞ lau ➡ ✕

Subligny Manche

Grand Chemin ☎ 233513096
Small site in a rural setting with well defined pitches within easy reach of the village.
↪ Access via N175 towards Avranches, then D39 and follow signs.
All year ⊞⊞⊞ ⊕ ℝ 🏕 ⊙ 🕿 🚐 🏧 lau

Telgruc-sur-Mer Finistère

Panoramic rte de la Plage ☎ 298277841 ▦ 298273610
Quiet terraced site with views across a wide sandy beach. Secluded pitches.
↪ W on D887 and then S on D208.
15 May-10 Sep 10 Sep-15 Jun 4HEC ⊞⊞⊞ ⠼⠾ ℝ 🏕 ▼ ✕ ⊙ 🕿
⌀ 🏕 🚐 ⟲ P 🏧 ⊞ lau ➡ ⟲S Prices: pitch 10

Theix Morbihan

Rhuys Le Poteau Rouge, Atlantheix
☎ 297541477 ▦ 297759854
Directly on the sea, with good modern facilities.
↪ 3.5km NW via N165
Apr-15 Oct 2HEC ⊞⊞⊞ ⠸⠿⠿ ⊕ ⊙ 🕿 🏕 🚾 🚐 ⟲ P 🏧 🏧 ⊞
lau ➡ 🏕 ▼ ✕

Thury-Harcourt Calvados

Vallée du Traspy ☎ 231796180 ▦ 231525354
Level meadow site near a small reservoir, 250mtrs from Centre Aquatique de la Suisse Normande.
15 Apr-15 Sep 1.5HEC ⊞⊞⊞ ⊕ ℝ ⊙ 🕿 ⟲ LPR 🏧 ⊞ lau ➡ 🏕 ▼
✕ ⌀ ✕

Tinténiac Ille-et-Vilaine

Peupliers La Besnelais ☎ 299454975 ▦ 299455298
e-mail: camping.les.peupliers@wanadoo.fr
A peaceful site in a wooded location with good facilities.
↪ 2km SE via N137.
Mar-Oct 4.5HEC ⊞⊞⊞ ⊕ ℝ 🏕 ▼ ✕ ⊙ 🕿 ⌀ 🏕 🚾 ⟲ P 🏧 ⊞ lau
➡ ✕ Prices: ⋔3.85 pitch 5.50

Tollevast Manche

Pins ☎ 233430078 ▦ 233430338
A peaceful site situated in a pine grove within an extensive park.
↪ From Cherbourg car ferry terminal follow N13 to the Auchan Hypermarket and then continue for 200m for site on left-hand side of the road.
All year 6HEC ⊞⊞⊞ ⊕ ℝ 🏕 ⊙ 🕿 🚾 🚐 🏧 ⊞ ⥊ lau ➡ ▼ ✕ ⌀ 🏕
⟲R

Tourlaville Manche

Espace Loisirs de Collignon ☎ 233201688 ▦ 233205303
A pleasant site with good facilities, 1km from town centre.
23 May-Sep 2HEC ⊞⊞⊞ ⠼⠾ ℝ 🏕 ▼ ✕ ⊙ 🕿 ⌀ 🚾 🏕 🏧 lau
➡ ✕ 🏕 ⟲PS ⊞

Tournières Calvados

Picard Holidays ☎ 0231228244 ▦ 0231517028
e-mail: paul.palmer@wanadoo.fr
A quiet site with pleasant, sheltered pitches conveniently situated between Cherbourg and Caen.
↪ Access via N13 and D15/D5.
All year 2HEC ⊞⊞⊞ ⠼⠾ ℝ 🏕 ▼ ✕ ⊙ 🕿 🚾 🚐 ⟲ LP 🏧 🏧 🏧 ⥊
lau ➡ ⟲R Prices: ⋔4.57 pitch 4.57

Trébeurden Côtes-d'Armor

Armor-Loisirs rue de Kernevez ☎ 296235231 ▦ 296154036
e-mail: armorloisirs@aol.com
Modern site with individual pitches surrounded by hedges. Hardstandings for caravans.
↪ 500m S of the Kernévez road.
Apr-Sep 2.2HEC ⊞⊞⊞ ⊕ ℝ 🏕 ▼ ✕ ⊙ 🕿 ⌀ 🏕 🏕 🚐 🏧 ⊞ lau
➡ ⟲RS

Trégunc Finistère

Pommeraie St-Philibert ☎ 298500273 ▦ 298500791
e-mail: pommeraie@club-internet.fr
A well equipped site with good facilities for children, 1.2km from the beach.

➲ *S via D1.*
Apr-8 Sep 7HEC ▥ ⚅ ♠ ⛟ ⛴ ✕ ⊙ 🖥 ⛺ ⛱ ⚡ P 🏠 ⊞ lau
➡ ∅ ⚡S

TRÉLÉVERN CÔTES-D'ARMOR

Port l'Epine Pors-Garo ☎ 296237194 ▤ 296237783
e-mail: camping-de-port-pepine@wanadoo.fr
Well shaded site directly on the sea.
May-15 Oct 3HEC ▥ ⚁ ♠ ⛟ ⛴ ✕ ⊙ 🖥 ⛺ ∅ ⚍ ⛱ Å ⚡ PS 🏠
⊞ lau Prices: pitch 13-20 (incl 2 persons)

TRÉPORT, LE SEINE-MARITIME

CM les Boucaniers r Mendes-France ☎ 235863547
Well-kept site on flat meadow on E edge of village. Sports
and games nearby.
Etr-Sep 5.5HEC ▥ ⚅ ♠ ⊙ 🖥 ⛺ 🏠 ⊞ lau ➡ ⛟ ⛴ ✕ ⚍
⚡PRS

Parc International du Golf rte de Dieppe
☎ 227280150 ▤ 227280151
In a park on the cliffs.
➲ *1km W on D940.*
Apr-20 Sep 5HEC ▥ ⚁ ♠ ⊙ 🖥 🏠 ⊞ lau ➡ ⛟ ✕ ∅ ⚡PS
Prices: ⚡5-6

At MESNIL-VAL

Parc Val d'Albion 1 r de la Mer ☎ 235862142 ▤ 235867857
Terraced site in wooded parkland next to the sea.
➲ *3km S from Le Tréport on D126.*
Jun-15 Sep 3HEC ▥ ⚁ ♠ ⊙ 🖥 🏠 ⊞ lau ➡ ⛟ ✕ ∅ ⚡S
Prices: ⚡6.85

TRÉVOU-TRÉGUIGNEC CÔTES-D'ARMOR

Mât 38 r de Trestel ☎ 296237152
A family site on level ground, 50m from beach.
➲ *Access via D38.*
15 Apr-15 Sep 1.6HEC ▥ ⚁ ♠ ⊙ 🖥 ∅ ⛺ 🖥 🏠 ⊞ lau
➡ ⛟ ✕ ⚍ ⚡S

TRINITÉ-SUR-MER, LA MORBIHAN

Baie Plage de Kervilen ☎ 297557342 ▤ 297558881
e-mail: camping@camping-la-baie-com
Several strips of land divided by tall trees on the edge of a
fine sandy beach.
➲ *Signposted in the direction of Kerbihan.*
07 May-15 Sep 2.4HEC ▥ ⚁ ♠ ⛟ ⛴ ✕ ⊙ 🖥 ∅ ⚡ P 🏠 ⊞
lau ➡ ⚡S Prices: ⚡2.44-4.88 pitch 9.76-18.29

Kervilor ☎ 297557675 ▤ 297558726
e-mail: ebideau@camping-kervilor.com
In a pleasant wooded location 1.5km from the port. Plenty of
recreational facilities.
➲ *1.6km N*
9 May-15 Sep 4.8HEC ▥ ⚁ ♠ ⛟ ⛴ ⊙ 🖥 ∅ ⛺ ⚡ P 🏠 ⊞ lau
➡ ✕ ⚍ Prices: ⚡4.15 ➡1.70 pitch 10.82

Plage Plage de Kervilen ☎ 297557328 ▤ 297558831
e-mail: laplage@club-internet.fr
A family site divided into pitches and lying behind sand
dunes which give direct access to the beach.
➲ *1km S towards Carnac-Plage.*
8May-15 Sep 3HEC ▥ ⚁ ♠ ⊙ 🖥 ⛺ ⚡ P 🏠 ⊞ lau ➡ ⛟ ⛴
∅ ⚡S Prices: ⚡4 pitch 7.60-19.60

VEULES-LES-ROSES SEINE-MARITIME

Mouettes av J-Moulin ☎ 235976198
15 Feb-Nov 3.6HEC ▥ ⚁ ♠ ⛟ ⊙ 🖥 ∅ 🏠 ⊞ lau
➡ ⛟ ✕ ∅ ⚡S

Paradis chemin de Manneville ☎ 235976142
A municipal site on the southern outskirts of the town.
mid May-mid Sep 0.9HEC ▥ ⚁ ♠ ⊙ 🖥 🏠 ⊞ lau ➡ ⛟ ⛴ ✕
∅ ⚍ ⚡PRS ⊞ Prices: ⚡2.29-2.44 ➡1.53-1.68 pitch 1.68-1.68

VILLERS-SUR-MER CALVADOS

Ammonites rte de la Corniche ☎ 231870606 ▤ 231871800
e-mail: camping.lesammonites@wanadoo.fr
➲ *4km SW on rte de Cabourg and D163 towards Auberville.*
01 Apr-31 Oct 3HEC ▥ ⚅ ⚅ ⛟ ⛴ ✕ ⊙ 🖥 ∅ ⛺ ⚡
P 🏠 ⊞ lau Prices: pitch 6.86-19.82 (incl 2 persons)

● ● ● ● PARIS/NORTH ● ● ●

The chalk cliffs and sands of the northern coast give way to
the two beautiful regions of Picardy and Nord-Pas-de-
Calais. Here quiet country roads meander through green
wooded valleys and rolling farmland. The area has a wealth
of neolithic sites, cathedrals, castles, abbeys, mansions and
museums. Lille is an important centre for northern France,
with its commercial and industrial interests, and has a
bustling cosmopolitan centre. Amiens is the ancient capital
of Picardy, and its remarkable 12th-century Cathedral of
Notre Dame is one of the finest in France.
The Île de France, known as the garden of Paris, is a
delightful region of famous palaces, parklands, forests and
attractive little towns. Visit Fontainbleau, the town of kings
and emperors, with its famous palace, and the dazzling
palace and grounds at Versailles.
Paris has a wealth of things to do and see - rivalling any
other city in the world. Visitors can choose from the
traditional rich treasures of the Louvre or the ultra modern
exhibits and setting of the Pompidou Centre, immerse
themselves in Parisian life along the banks of the Seine or
view it from the giddy heights of Monsieur Eiffel's famous
tower, discover the wonderful wide spaces of the Trocadero,
the Champ de Mars and the Champs Élysées or the
buzzing streets of the city's famous districts - Montmartre
and Marais. And night life, too, is for all tastes, with
everything from the sophisticated entertainment of the
Lido, to a small quiet restaurant on the Left Bank.

ACY-EN-MULTIEN OISE

Ancien Moulin ☎ 344872128
Situated beside a river and a small lake with good sporting
facilities.
All year 5HEC ▥ ⚅ ♠ ⊙ 🖥 🏠 lau ➡ ⛟ ⛴ ✕ ∅ ⚍ ⊞

AMBLETEUSE PAS-DE-CALAIS

Beaucamp 10 r de Ferquent ☎ 321326210
A useful overnight stop between Boulogne and Calais.
All year 9HEC ▥ ⚁ ♠ ⛟ ⛴ ✕ ⊙ 🖥 ∅ ⚍ ⛺ ⛺ ⛺ lau
➡ ⚡RS

AMPLIER PAS-DE-CALAIS

Val d'Authie 93 r du Marais ☎ 321485707 ▤ 321580860
e-mail: a.boulanger@free.fr
In wooded surroundings beside a small lake.
➲ *Access via N25 and D24 or D938.*
16 Apr-14 Oct 2HEC ▥ ♠ ⛟ ⛴ ✕ ⊙ 🖥 ⚡ R 🏠 lau
Prices: ⚡3 ➡3 🖥3 Å3

ARDRES PAS-DE-CALAIS
At AUTINGUES(2km S)

St-Louis 223 r Leulène ☎ 321354683 ▤ 321001978
A well equipped site in pleasant wooded surroundings.

Cont.

⟳ *Turn off N43 approx 1km SE of Ardres onto D224 and follow signs.*
Apr-Oct 1.7HEC ⸺ ⌂ 🝙 🝚 ✕ ⊙ 🝙 🝚 🝚 ⌂ ⊞ lau ➧ 🍴 ✕
⁊L Prices: ⋔2.50 pitch 4

ATTICHY OISE

CM ☎ 344421597
⟳ *On SE outskirts near the swimming pool and the river.*
All year 1.5HEC ⸺ ⌂ 🝙 ⊙ 🝙 ⁊ L ⌂ lau ➧ 🝚 🍴 ✕ ⁊P

AUDRUICQ PAS-DE-CALAIS

CM Les Pyramides ☎ 321355917
A site with good sanitary and sports facilities beside the canal.
Apr-Sep ⸺ ⌂ 🝙 ⊙ 🝙 ⌂ 🄿 ⊞ lau ➧ 🝚 🍴 ✕ 𝄂 ⁊P

BEAUVAIS OISE

Clos Normand 1 r de l'Abbaye, St-Paul ☎ 344822730
A small site on a lake with facilities for fishing.
⟳ *6km W via N31 towards Rouen.*
All year 1.3HEC ⸺ ⌂ 🝙 ⊙ 🝙 ⸺ 🝚 ⁊ L ⌂ lau ➧ 🍴 ✕
Prices: ⋔2.50 ▲6

BERCK-SUR-MER PAS-DE-CALAIS

Orée du Bois chemin Blanc 251, Rang-du-Fliers
☎ 321842851 ▤ 321842856
e-mail: oree.du.bois@wanadoo.fr
A modern site in wooded surroundings with good sports facilities.
⟳ *2km NE.*
Apr-25 Oct 18HEC ⸺ ⌂ 🝙 🍴 ✕ ⊙ 🝙 ⸺ 🝚 ⌂ ⊞ lau ➧ 🝚 ⊘

BERNY-RIVIÈRE AISNE

Croix du Vieux Pont ☎ 323555002 ▤ 0323555002
In wooded surroundings beside the River Aisne with ample facilities.
⟳ *N of N31; cross River Aisne, site is 500m E of Vic-sur-Aisne on D91.*
All year 19HEC ⸺ ⌂ 🝙 🝚 🍴 ✕ ⊙ 🝙 ⊘ ⁊ LPR ⌂ ⊞ lau ➧ ⸺

BERTANGLES SOMME

Château r du Château ☎ 322933773 ▤ 322936836
e-mail: camping.bertangles@wanadoo.fr
Site in old orchard of Château.
⟳ *Signed off Amiens-Doullens road.*
26Apr-9Sep 0.8HEC ⸺ ➧ 🝙 ⊙ 🝙 ⊘ ⌂ lau ➧ 🍴 ✕
Prices: ⋔2.70 🚐1.90 🚗2.85 ▲2.85

BEUVRY PAS-DE-CALAIS

CM r Victor-Dutériez ☎ 321650800
Apr-Oct 1HEC ⸺ ➧ 🝙 ⊙ 🝙 ⌂ lau ➧ 🝚 🍴 ✕ ⊘ ⸺ 𝄂P

BOIRY-NOTRE-DAME PAS-DE-CALAIS

Flandres Artois 1 r Verte ☎ 321481540 ▤ 321220724
On a level meadow with a good variety of recreational facilities.
⟳ *On D34. Access via A1 exit 15 towards Cambrai or A26 exit 8 towards Arras.*
21 Mar-Oct 3.4HEC ⸺ ⌂ 🝙 ✕ ⊙ 🝙 ⌂ lau ➧ 🝚 ⊘ ⸺

BOISSY-LE-CUTTE ESSONNE

Boulinière La Boulinière ☎ 164576523 ▤ 145448516
e-mail: secretariat@campingclub.asso.fr
Situated in a wood 800mtrs from the village.
⟳ *Access via N20 and D148.*
All year 4HEC ⸺ ➧ 🝙 ⊙ 🝙 ⌂ lau ➧ 🝚 🍴 ✕ ⊘ ⸺ 𝄂R ⊞

BOUBERS-SUR-CANCHE PAS-DE-CALAIS

Flore 27 rue de Frevent ☎ 321048520 ▤ 321048520
e-mail: arielle.triart@wanadoo.fr
In a peaceful, rural setting within easy reach of the village.
⟳ *E via D340 towards Frévent.*
Apr-15 Oct 1HEC ⸺ ⌂ 🝙 ⊙ 🝙 ⸺ 🝚 ⌂ ⊞ lau ➧ 𝄂PR
Prices: ⋔3.20 🚐2.50 pitch 2.50

BOULANCOURT SEINE-ET-MARNE

Ile de Boulancourt 6 allée des Marronniers ☎ 164241338
A peaceful site shaded by mature trees in a convenient situation in the Essonne valley.
⟳ *Access via D410.*
All year 5HEC ⸺ ⸻ ⌂ 🝙 ⊙ 🝙 🝚 🝚 ⁊ R ⌂ ⊞ lau ➧ 🝚 ✕ ⊘ 𝄂L Prices: ⋔3.30 pitch 3.70

BRAY-DUNES NORD

Perroquet-Plage ☎ 0033 328583737 ▤ 328583701
e-mail: camping-lezzoquet@wanadoo.fr
An above average site situated among sand dunes with direct access to the beach.
⟳ *3km NE towards La Panne.*
Apr-4 Oct 28HEC ⸺ ⸻ ⌂ 🝙 🝚 🍴 ✕ ⊙ 🝙 ⊘ ⸺ 🝚 ⌂ 𝄂 S ⌂ ⊞ lau Prices: ⋔4.60 🚐1.85 🚗2.55 ▲1.95

CALAIS PAS-DE-CALAIS

Peupliers 394 r du Beau Marais ☎ 321340356
All year 1HEC ⸺ ➧ 🝙 🍴 ✕ ⊙ 🝙 🝚 ⌂ ⊞ lau ➧ 🝚 ✕ ⊘ 𝄂PRS

CAMIERS PAS-DE-CALAIS

Sables d'Or ☎ 321849515
In a wooded location with good recreational facilities.
All year 10HEC ⸺ ⸻ ➧ 🝙 🝚 ⊙ 🝙 🝚 ⁊ P ⌂ ⊞ lau ➧ 𝄂S

CAYEUX-SUR-MER SOMME

Voyeul rte des Canadiens ☎ 322266084 ▤ 322266084
In pleasant surroundings, 400mtrs from the sea, with pitches enclosed by hedges and flowerbeds.
⟳ *1.5km S on D140.*
Apr-15 Oct 1.7HEC ⸺ ⌂ 🝙 🝚 🍴 ✕ ⊙ 🝙 ⸺ ⌂ ⊞ lau ➧ 𝄂S

CHAMOUILLE AISNE

Parc de l'Ailette Parc Nautique de l'Ailette ☎ 323246686
On the shore of a lake within an extensive leisure park and nature reserve.
⟳ *2km SE via D19.*
Apr-Sep 6HEC ⸺ ⌂ 🝙 🝚 🍴 ✕ ⊙ 🝙 ⊘ 🝚 ⁊ L ⌂ ⊞ lau ➧ ✕

CONDETTE PAS-DE-CALAIS

Château 21 r Nouvelle ☎ 321875959 ▤ 321875959
e-mail: campingduchateau@libertysurf.fr
On pleasant parkland, bordered by a forest, 500mtrs from the town centre. Separate car park for arrivals after 23.00hrs.
⟳ *Access via D940 towards Hardelot.*
Apr-Oct 1.2HEC ⸺ ⌂ 🝙 ⊙ 🝙 🝚 ⌂ ⊞ lau ➧ 🝚 🍴 ✕ ⊘ ⸺ 𝄂L

COUDEKERQUE NORD

Bois des Forts ☎ 328610441
⟳ *0.7km NW on D72.*
All year 4HEC ⸺ 🌿 🝙 🍴 ✕ ⊙ 🝙 ⸺ 🝚 🝚 ⌂ lau ➧ 🝚 ⊘

DUNKERQUE (DUNKIRK) NORD

CM bd de l'Europe ☎ 328692668 ▤ 328695621
e-mail: campnglalicorne@wanadoo.fr
Apr-Nov 10HEC ⸺ 🌿 🝙 🍴 ✕ ⊙ 🝙 ⸺ 🝚 ⁊ P ⌂ 🄿 ⊞ lau ➧ 🝚 🍴 ✕ ⊘ ⸺ 𝄂PS ⊞

ÉPERLECQUES PAS-DE-CALAIS

Château de Gandspette ☎ 321934393 ▤ 321957498
e-mail: contact@chateau_gandspette.com
A peaceful site, surrounded by woodland.
➲ 11.5km NW on N43 and D207.
Apr-Sep 11HEC ⊞ 🔼🏕🍴✕⊙🔌🖉⚡ P 🏕🚻 lau ➡🛒
Prices: ⚑4 pitch 7-11

EQUIHEN-PLAGE PAS-DE-CALAIS

CM la Falaise r C-Cazin ☎ 321312261
150mtrs between Boulogne and Le Touquet.
Apr-Oct 8HEC ⊞ ⚕🏕⊙🔌🏕🚻 lau ➡🛒🍴✕🖉🚿
⚡S

ESCALLES PAS-DE-CALAIS

Cap Blanc Nez r de la Mer ☎ 321852738
500m from the beach.
Apr-10 Nov 1.5HEC ⊞ 🔼🏕🛒🍴✕⊙🔌🖉🚻 lau
➡⚡S

ÉTAMPES ESSONNE

Vauvert Ormoy La Rivière
☎ 164942139 ▤ 169927259
In a pleasant woodland situation beside the river.
➲ 2km S via D49.
Closed 15 Dec-15 Jan 11HEC ⊞ 🔼🏕🍴✕⊙🔌🖉🚿⚡ R
🚻➡⚡LP

ÉTAPLES PAS-DE-CALAIS

Pinède ☎ 321943451
A well equipped site situated amongst sand dunes and surrounded by pine trees close to the yacht basin and local shopping facilities.
15Feb-15Dec 3HEC ⊞ 🔼🏕🛒🍴✕⊙🔌🖉🚻 lau ➡🖉🚿
⚡R 🚻

FELLERIES NORD

CM La Boisserellie r de la Place
☎ 327590650 ▤ 327590288
15 Apr-Sep 1HEC ⊞ 🔼🏕⊙🔌🚻➡🛒🍴✕🖉🚿🚻

FERTÉ-SOUS-JOUARRE, LA SEINE-ET-MARNE

Bondons 47/49 r des Bondons
☎ 160220098 ▤ 160229701
Set in a beautiful wooded park. Reserved for caravans.
➲ 2km NE via D402 & D70.
All year 28HEC ⊞ ⚕🏕✕⊙🔌🚻 lau ➡🛒✕⚡PR
Prices: ⚑7 ➡1

FORT-MAHON-PLAGE SOMME

Royon rte de Quend ☎ 322234030 ▤ 322236515
A family site with good facilities and well marked pitches, 2.5km from the beach.
Mar-Oct 4.5HEC ⊞ 🔼🏕🛒🍴✕⊙🔌🖉🚻⚡ P 🚻 lau
➡⚡S Prices: pitch 13-25 (incl 3 persons)

FRIAUCOURT SOMME

CM Au Chant des Oiseaux Ruelle du Grand Patis
☎ 322264954
In pleasant surroundings with good sanitary and sporting facilities 2km from the sea. Separate carpark for arrivals after 22.00hrs.
➲ NE via D63.
Apr-15 Oct 1.4HEC ⊞ 🔼🏕⊙🔌🚻 lau

GOUVIEUX OISE

César rte de Toutevoie 10 ☎ 344571273
On a hill overlooking the River Oise.
➲ Access via A1 to Gouvieux town centre, then towatds Creil.
All year 6HEC ⊞ 🔼🏕⊙🔌🚻 lau ➡🛒🍴✕🚿⚡P

GRAND-FORT-PHILIPPE NORD

CM de la Plage r Ml-Foch ☎ 328653195
On a level meadow separated from the beach (500mtrs away) by sand dunes.
➲ On the seaward extremity of Grand-Fort Philippe.
Apr-Oct 1.5HEC ⊞ 🔼🏕⊙🔌🚻 lau ➡🛒🍴✕🖉
🚿⚡S 🚻

GREZ-SUR-LOING SEINE-ET-MARNE

CM Près chemin des Près
☎ 064457275 ▤ 164457275
➲ NE towards Loing
20 Mar-11 Nov 6HEC ⊞ 🔼🏕🛒⊙🔌🚻 lau ➡🍴✕🖉⚡R
🚻 Prices: ⚑2.30 ➡1.50 ➡2.30 ▲1.80-2.30

GUINES PAS-DE-CALAIS

🏕Bien Assise ☎ 321352077 ▤ 321367920
e-mail: castel@bien-assise.com
A nice site in the country near to a large forest and a charming little town.
➲ Access via D231 towards Marquise.
25 Apr-25 Sep 12HEC ⊞ 🔼🏕🛒🍴✕⊙🔌🖉🚻🏕⚡ P 🚻
🚻 lau

HIRSON AISNE

Cascade ☎ 323580391 ▤ 323582539
In a picturesque woodland setting with good, modern facilities.
➲ 1.8km N via N43 towards La Capelle.
20 Apr-20 Sep 1.6HEC ⊞ 🔼🏕⊙🔌🖉🚗
⚡ P 🚻 lau ➡🚿

HOUDAIN PAS-DE-CALAIS

Parc d'Olhain ☎ 321279179
Situated in an extensive leisure park on the edge of a forest.
➲ 1.5 km S.
Apr-Sep 1HEC ⊞ ⚕🔼🏕⊙🔌⚡ P 🚻🚻➡🍴✕

ISQUES PAS-DE-CALAIS

Cytises r de l'Église ☎ 321311110
In a pleasant rural setting beside the River Liane.
➲ 4km S of Boulogne-sur-Mer towards Abbeville, 100m from N1.
Apr-15 Oct 2.5HEC ⊞ 🔼🍴✕⊙🔌🚗🚻 lau ➡🛒🚿
⚡R Prices: ⚑2.65-3 ➡2.65-3 ▲2.65-3

JABLINES SEINE-ET-MARNE

Base de Loisirs ☎ 160260937 ▤ 160265243
e-mail: mairie.jablines@wanadoo.fr
Only 9km from Disneyland Paris.
➲ Access via A1 or A3 towards Marne-la-Vallée, then N3.
Apr-6 Nov 3.5HEC ⊞ ⚕🛒🍴✕⊙🔌⚡ L 🚻 lau
Prices: 17.50-21 (incl 2 persons)

LAON AISNE

CM La Chênaie allée de la Chênaie
☎ 0323202556 ▤ 0323202556
A peaceful family site with good facilities close to the city centre.
➲ S of the city centre towards N44.
Apr-Oct 3.3HEC ⊞ 🔼🏕⊙🔌🚻 lau ➡🖉🚿⚡LPR
Prices: ⚑2.28 ➡1.45 ➡1.42 ▲1.42

LICQUES PAS-DE-CALAIS

Canchy r de Canchy ☎ 321826341 ▤ 321826341
A quiet site on an open, level meadow well situated for access to the ferries and the Channel Tunnel.
15 Mar-Oct 1HEC ⊞ 🔼🏕🛒🍴✕⊙🔌🖉⚡ R 🚻 lau
Prices: ⚑2.75 pitch 3.10

LYNDE NORD

Becquerel 1396 r du Becquerelle ☎ 328432037
In a rural setting surrounded by woodland and hedges.
Mar-Nov 1.5HEC ⬛ � symbols ⊙ 🔣🔣 ➕ ➤ ⌀ 🏊

MAISONS-LAFFITTE YVELINES

International 1 r Johnson ☎ 139122191 🗎 139127050
e-mail: ci.mlaffitte@fr
A well-kept site in a residential area on the banks of the
Seine. Modern installations, heated in cold weather.
➲ *For access, 8 km N of St-Germain-en-Laye; alternatively
follow N308 from Porte Champerret or from Colombos-Ouest
exit of Autoroute A86.*
17Mar-01Nov/17Dec-07Jan 01Nov-17Dec/07Jan-17Mar
7HEC ⬛ 🔣🔣🔣⊙🔣🏊🔣🔣➕ lau ➤ ⌀ ⌶P

MARNE-LA-VALLÉE SEINE-ET-MARNE

Davy Crockett Ranch Disneyland Paris
☎ 160456900 🗎 160456933
A modern site in wooded surroundings on the Disneyland
Paris complex.
➲ *Access via A4 Serris exit (no 13).*
Apr-Oct 57HEC ⬛ ⠶⠶ ➤🔣🔣🔣🔣⊙🔣🔣🔣➕ ⌶P🔣➕🔣
lau ➤ ✕

MAUBEUGE NORD

Camping Municipal de Clair de Lune rte de Mons
☎ 327622548 🗎 327622548
➲ *1.5km N via N2 (Bruxelles road).*
All year 2.1HEC ⬛ 🔣🔣🔣⊙🔣🔣🔣➕ lau ➤🔣🔣✕⌀🏊
Prices: ⌶3.05 pitch 3.05

MELUN SEINE-ET-MARNE

Belle Étoile Quai Joffre ☎ 164394812 🗎 164372555
e-mail: info@camp-la-belle-etoile.com
Pleasant grassy site with two central blocks.
➲ *At La Rochette, on left bank of River Seine 1km from the
town.*
Apr-Oct 3.5HEC ⬛ 🔣🔣🔣🔣✕⊙🔣🔣⌀🔣🔣⌶P🔣➕🔣➕
lau ➤ ⌀ ⌶LPR Prices: ⌶4.15-4.65 🚗1.30-7.60 pitch 4.20-4.70

MERLIMONT PAS-DE-CALAIS

Parc Résidentiel du Château St-Hubert Bagatelle
☎ 321891010 🗎 321891012
In pleasant wooded surroundings with good recreational
facilities.
➲ *3km S via D940, near Parc de Bagatelle.*
Apr-Oct 16HEC ⬛ 🔣🔣🔣🔣✕⊙🔣🔣🏊⌶P🔣➕ lau

MILLY-LA-FORÊT ESSONNE

Musardière rte des Grandes Vallées
☎ 164989191 🗎 0164989191
In pleasant wooded surroundings.
➲ *4km SE via D948.*
16 Dec-14 Feb 12HEC ⬛ ⠶⠶ 🔣🔣⊙🔣🔣🔣➤⌶P🔣➕
Prices: ⌶5 🚗2.50 🏕5 ⌶2.50

MONNERVILLE ESSONNE

Bois de la Justice ☎ 164950534 🗎 164951731
Pitches separated by trees and hedges in beautiful natural
woodland with good facilities.
➲ *N20 Orléans to Étampes.*
Mar-Nov 5.5HEC ⬛ 🔣🔣🔣✕⊙🔣🏊⌶P🔣➕ lau

MONTIGNY-LE-BRETONNEUX YVELINES

Parc Étang Base de Loisirs-de-St Quentin
☎ 130585620 🗎 134600714
In beautiful rural surroundings within a leisure centre with
easy access to Paris and Versailles.

➲ *SE of town centre towards the Centre de Volle.*
Mar-Oct 12HEC ⬛ 🔣🔣🔣🔣✕⊙🔣🔣⌀🏊🔣🔣➕ lau
➤ ✕ ⌶LP

MONTREUIL-SUR-MER PAS-DE-CALAIS

CM ☎ 321060728
➲ *N of town on N1.*
All year 2HEC ⬛ ➤🔣⊙🔣🔣➤ R🔣➕ lau ➤🔣🔣✕⌀🏊 ⌶P

MOYENNEVILLE SOMME

Val de Trie Bouillancourt-sous-Miannay
☎ 322314888 🗎 322313533
e-mail: raphael@camping-lavaldetrie.fr
A small site in a picturesque wooded location with good
facilities including a lake for fishing.
➲ *1km from the D925 (Abbeville-Le Tréport).*
Apr-Oct 3HEC ⬛ ➤🔣⊙🔣🔣✕⊙🔣🔣➤ P🔣➕ lau ➤🔣
Prices: ⌶2.90-3.70 pitch 4.20-5.60

NEMOURS SEINE-ET-MARNE

ACCCF ☎ 64281062 🗎 64281062
On well-kept meadow. Clean sanitary installations.
➲ *200m from N7.*
15 Mar-11 Nov 4.8HEC ⬛ 🔣🔣⊙🔣🔣➤ R🔣 lau ➤🔣🔣✕
⌀🏊🔣

NESLES-LA-VALLÉE VAL-D'OISE

Parc de Séjour de l'Étang 10 Chemin des Belles Vues
☎ 134706289 🗎 134706289
e-mail: brehinier1@hotmail.com
Level site near a small lake.
➲ *A15 exit 10, then D927 and D79. From N1 take exit for
L'Isle Adam.*
Mar-15 Nov 6HEC ⬛ 🔣🔣⊙🔣🔣🔣➕🔣 lau ➤🔣🔣✕⌀🏊
Prices: ⌶3-4 pitch 3-4

NEUVILLE, LA NORD

Leu Pindu 2 r du Gl-de-Gaulle ☎ 320865087 🗎 320865177
➲ *N on D8.*
All year 1.2HEC ⬛ ➤🔣🔣✕⊙🔣🔣⌀🏊🔣🔣➕ lau ➤🔣🔣
⌶L Prices: pitch 8.55 (incl 2 persons)

ORVILLERS-SOREL OISE

Sorel ☎ 344850274
Divided into pitches. Local tradesmen supply provisions.
➲ *Leave A1 at N17, turn right and continue 400mtrs.*
Feb-15 Dec 3HEC ⬛ 🔣🔣🔣✕⊙🔣🔣🔣➕ lau

OYE-PLAGE PAS-DE-CALAIS

Oyats 272 Digue Vert ☎ 321851540 🗎 328603833
4.5km NW directly on the beach.
May-Sep 5HEC ⬛ 🔣🔣🔣✕⊙🔣🔣➤ PS🔣➕ lau
Prices: ⌶4.60 pitch 6.10

PARIS

Bois de Boulogne 2 allée du Bord de l'Eau
☎ 145243000 🗎 142244295
Much of this site's popularity stems from its location close to
the city centre and it can become crowded during high
season as it is the only site actually in Paris.
All year 7HEC ⬛ ⌀➤🔣🔣🔣✕⊙🔣🔣⌀🔣🔣➕ lau

At CHAMPIGNY-SUR-MARNE(12km SE)

Tremblay bd des Alliés ☎ 143974397 🗎 148890794
Site tends to become full during peak season. Good
transportation into city and well placed for visiting
Disneyland Paris.
Reserved mainly for International Camping Card holders.
➲ *Take N4 and turn left 350m after Joinville bridge.*
All year 8HEC ⬛ 🔣🔣🔣🔣✕⊙🔣🔣⌀🔣🔣➕ lau ➤🏊 ⌶P

At CHOISY-LE-ROI(14km SE)

Paris Sud 125 av de V-St-Georges ☎ 148909230
Located in an attractive sports and leisure park with plenty
of facilities. Popular with student groups on visits to the
Paris area.
⮕ *Signposted from A86 SE of Paris.*
All year 9HEC ⸺ ⚁❀⅃⚑❣⊙◙⌀♨⊞☎⊞ lau ➡
⚡LPR

PLESSIS-FEU-AUSSOUX SEINE-ET-MARNE

Château-de-Chambonnières ☎ 164041585
⮕ *On D231 towards Provins, some 23km from Disneyland
Paris.*
All year 5HEC ⸺ ⚁❀⅃⊙◙⌀☎⊞ lau

POIX-DE-PICARDIE SOMME

Bois des Pêcheurs rte de Forges-les-Eaux ☎ 322901171
In a quiet riverside location with a high standard of sanitary
facilities.
⮕ *W via D919 towards Forges-les-Eaux.*
Apr-Sep 1.5HEC ⸺ ❦❀⊙◙⌀◙☎⊞ lau
➡⅃❣✕♨⚡PR

POTELLE NORD

Pré Vert Chemin du Moulin ☎ 327491987
Apr-20 Sep 2HEC ⸺ ⚁❀❣⊙◙♨◙☎⊞ lau
➡⅃✕⌀⚡LR

PRESLES-VAILLY-SUR-AISNE AISNE

Domaine de la Nature chemin de Boufaud
☎ 323547455 ▤ 323547272
In a pleasant rural setting alongside the canal with well
defined pitches and modern sanitary facilities.
⮕ *4km W via D144 near the canal and lake.*
All year 3HEC ⸺ ⚁❀❣⊙◙◙A☎⊞ lau
➡⅃✕⌀⚡LR

PROYART SOMME

Loisir la Violette rte de Mericourt ☎ 322858136
Mar-Oct 1.8HEC ⸺ ⚁❀⊙◙♨☎ lau ➡⅃❣✕♨⊞

QUEND-PLAGE-LES-PINS SOMME

At MONCHAUX-LES-QUEND(3.5km E via D102E)

Roses ☎ 0322277617 ▤ 0322239306
e-mail: sandrine.bruyelle@wanadoo.fr
Well-kept site with trees and hedges surrounding individual
pitches. Only recommended site in area.
⮕ *Turn off D940 at Quend, site 500m on left of D102.*
15 Mar-Oct 9HEC ⸺ ⚁❀⅃✕⊙◙♨◙◙⚡P☎⊞ lau
➡⅃⌀

RAMBOUILLET YVELINES

CM de l'Étang d'Or r du Château d'Eau
☎ 130410734 ▤ 130410017
e-mail: ramboulllet.tourisme@wanadoo.fr
In a pleasant situation. Shop, bar etc only open Jun-Aug.
⮕ *From railway station follow road SE for 1.3km passing
Camping Pont Hardy.*
All year 4.7HEC ⸺ ❦❀⅃❣✕⊙◙◙☎⊞ lau ➡⚡P
Prices: ♠3.70 pitch 4.10

RUE SOMME

Garenne de Moncourt ☎ 322250693
⮕ *On D85 towards Montreuil-sur-Mer.*
Apr-Oct 8HEC ⸺ ⚁❀⊙◙⌀⚡PR☎⊞ lau ➡♨

ST-AMAND-LES-EAUX NORD

Mont des Bruyères 806 r Basly ☎ 327485687 ▤ 0327485687
⮕ *3.5km SE in the forest of St-Amand*
Mar-Nov 3.5HEC ⸺ ❦❀⅃❣⊙◙♨◙☎⊞ lau ➡✕⌀
⚡LPR

ST-CHÉRON ESSONNE

Parc des Roches La Petite Beauce ☎ 164566550 ▤ 164565450
e-mail: parc.des.roches@free.fr
In a wooded park.
15 Apr-15 Sep 23HEC ⸺ ⚁❀❣✕⊙◙◙⚡P☎⊞ lau
Prices: ♠5.80 ➡2.40 ◙4.40 ▲4.40

ST-CYR-SUR-MORIN SEINE-ET-MARNE

Choisel rte de Rebais ☎ 160238493
In a pleasant situation. Separate carpark for arrivals after
22.00hrs.
⮕ *2km W via D31.*
Mar-Nov 3.5HEC ⸺ ❦❀❣✕⊙◙♨☎⊞ lau ➡⌀⚡PR

ST-JANS-CAPPEL NORD

Domaine de la Sablière Le Mont Noir ☎ 328494634
A pleasant family site in a wooded location with large, well
defined pitches.
⮕ *3.5km NE via D10 and D318.*
Apr-Oct 3HEC ⸺ ⚁❀⊙◙♨☎⊞ lau ➡⅃❣✕⌀⚡LP

ST-LEU-D'ESSERENT OISE

Campix ☎ 44560848
In wooded surroundings, within easy reach of Chantilly.
⮕ *3.5km NE via D12.*
7 Mar-1 Dec 6HEC ⸺ ∷❦⊙◙⌀☎⊞ lau ➡⅃❣✕
⚡L

ST-QUENTIN AISNE

CM bd J-Bouin ☎ 323626866
A good site in pleasant wooded surroundings near the canal.
Mar-Nov 1.9HEC ⸺ ∷⚁❀◙☎➡⌀♨⚡PR⊞

ST-VALÉRY-SUR-SOMME SOMME

▤Domaine du Château de Drancourt ☎ 322269345
In open countryside, surrounded by woods, fields and lakes,
within the grounds of a former hunting lodge.
⮕ *1.5km S via D48.*
Apr-Sep 15HEC ⸺ ⚁❀⅃❣✕⊙◙⌀♨◙⚡P☎⊞ lau
➡✕⚡L

SALENCY OISE

Étang du Moulin 54 r du Moulin ☎ 344099981
A small site opposite a trout fishing lake and recreational
area under the ownership of the site proprietors.
⮕ *3km from Noyon on the N32 towards Chauny.*
All year 0.4HEC ⸺ ⚁❀⅃❣✕⊙◙♨➡⚡PR
Prices: ♠1.83 ➡2.29 ◙3.81 ▲3.81

SERAUCOURT-LE-GRAND AISNE

Pêche du Vivier aux Carpes 10 r Ch-Voyeux
☎ 323605010 ▤ 323605169
e-mail: camping.du.vivier@wanadoo.fr
A peaceful site bordered by lakes. Separate car park for
arrivals after 22.00hrs.
➲ *A26 exit 11-left on D1 exit Essigny-D72.*
Mar-Oct 3HEC ⊞ ⚑ ⟟ ⟈ ⊙ ⚒ ⌀ ⌓ ⚏ ⊞ lau ➡ ⚓ ✕ ᛈ ⟊R
Prices: ⚭2.80 pitch 15 (incl 2 persons)

SERQUES PAS-DE-CALAIS

Frémont rte Nationale 9 ☎ 321930115
A pleasant site near the Éperlecques Forest.
➲ *1.5km SW on N43.*
Apr-15 Oct 2HEC ⊞ ⚑ ⟟ ⟈ ⊙ ⚒ ⚏ ⊞ lau ➡ ✕

SOISSONS AISNE

CM av du Mail ☎ 323745269 ▤ 323596772
e-mail: officedetourisme@ville-soissons.fr
In pleasant surroundings with good, modern facilities.
All year 1.8HEC ⊞ ⚑ ⟟ ⊙ ⚒ ⚏ ⚏ ⌓ lau ➡ ⚓ ⚏ ✕ ᛈ ⟊P
⊞

THIEMBRONNE PAS-DE-CALAIS

Pommiers rte de Desvres ☎ 321395019 ▤ 321957920
A family site in pleasant wooded surroundings
➲ *NW on D132.*
15 Mar-15 Oct 1.8HEC ⊞ ⚑ ⟟ ⊙ ⚒ ⌀ ⚏ ᛈ P ⚏ lau ➡
⚓ ⚏ ✕ ᛈR Prices: ⚭3.05-3.81 ⚓1.52-2.29 pitch 3.05-3.81

TOLLENT PAS-DE-CALAIS

Val d'Authie ☎ 321471427
In a pleasant wooded location with wide, well marked
pitches.
➲ *SE via D119*
Apr-Sep 3.5HEC ⊞ ⚑ ⟟ ⚓ ⚏ ✕ ⊙ ⚒ ᛈ LP ⚏ ⊞ lau ➡ ⌓
ᛈR

TORCY SEINE-ET-MARNE

Parc de la Colline rte de Lagny ☎ 160054232 ▤ 164800517
e-mail: camping.parc.de.la.colline@wanadoo.fr
An ideal base for visiting Paris (30 minutes from the centre
by Metro). Separate car park for arrivals after 22.00 hrs.
➲ *Access via exit 10 on the A104 and D10E.*
All year 10HEC ⊞ ➡ ⟟ ⚓ ⚏ ✕ ⊙ ⚒ ⌀ ⚏ ⌰ ⊞ lau ➡
ᛈLP Prices: ⚭6 pitch 10

TOUQUIN SEINE-ET-MARNE

Étangs Fleuris rte de la Couture ☎ 164041636 ▤ 164041228
In wooded surroundings with well defined pitches and
modern facilities.
➲ *E of town towards Provins.*
Mar-Oct 5.5HEC ⊞ ⚑ ⟟ ⚓ ⚏ ✕ ⊙ ⚒ ᛈ P ⚏ lau ➡ ✕
Prices: ⚭6.60

TOURNEHEM PAS-DE-CALAIS

Bal Parc 500 r du Vieux Château ☎ 321356590 ▤ 321351857
A peaceful site in rural surroundings with good, modern
facilities.
➲ *Access via D218 from village centre.*
All year 1.6HEC ⊞ ⚑ ⟟ ⚓ ⚏ ✕ ⊙ ⚒ ⌓ ⌰ ⚏ ⊞ lau ➡
ᛈR

VILLENNES-SUR-SEINE YVELINES

Club des Renardières rte de Vernouillet ☎ 139587897
Site for caravans only, in beautiful hilly park laid out with
hedges, lawns and flower beds. Fully divided into completely
separated pitches.
➲ *Follow D113 to Maison Blanche turn right, continue 3km.*
All year 7HEC ⊞ ➡ ⟟ ⊙ ⚒ lau ➡ ⚓ ⚏ ✕ ᛈLPR

VILLERS-HÉLON AISNE

Castel des Biches Chateau Alexandre Dumas
☎ 323729393 ▤ 323729333
e-mail: pacal.ginailhac@wanadoo.fr
Attractive site in grounds of an old castle.
➲ *Turn off N2 onto D2 between Soissons and Villers-Cotterêts
and continue for 7km via Longport.*
All year 10HEC ⊞ ⚑ ⟟ ⊙ ⚒ ⚏ ⚏ ⌰ ⚏ ⊞ lau ➡ ⌓ ⌀ ⌓
ᛈLR

VILLERS-SUR-AUTHIE SOMME

Val d'Authie 20 rte de Vercourt ☎ 322299247 ▤ 3222299220
e-mail: camping@valdauthie.fr
A well designed site situated between the Forest of Crécy and
the sea. Bar and café open in high season only.
➲ *Access via N1.*
Apr-Oct 7HEC ⊞ ⚑ ⟟ ⚓ ⚏ ✕ ⊙ ⚒ ⌓ ⚏ ᛈ P ⚏ lau ➡ ᛈR
Prices: ⚭6-6 ⚏4.50 ⚭4.50

VILLEVAUDE SEINE-ET-MARNE

Parc Montjay-la-Tour ☎ 160262079 ▤ 160270275
Bar and restaurant facilities open summer only.
➲ *Access via A104 exit 6B, Marne-la-Vallée.*
All year 10HEC ⊞ ➡ ⟟ ⚏ ✕ ⊙ ⚒ ⚏ ⊞ lau

VIRONCHAUX SOMME

Peupliers 221 r du Cornet ☎ 0322235427 ▤ 0322290519
A peaceful site 3km from the Forest of Crécy.
➲ *Approach via N1 and D938.*
01 Apr-31 Oct 1.5HEC ⊞ ⚑ ⟟ ⚏ ⊙ ⚒ ⌀ ⚏ ⚏ ⚏ ⊞ lau ➡
⚏ ✕ Prices: ⚭2.60 ⚏1.90 pitch 2.50

WACQUINGHEN PAS-DE-CALAIS

Éscale ☎ 321320069 ▤ 0321320069
In a pleasantly landscaped park with modern facilities 5
minutes from the coastal resorts.
➲ *Access via A16 and D231.*
15 Mar-Oct 11HEC ⊞ ⚑ ⟟ ⚓ ⚏ ✕ ⊙ ⚒ ⌓ ⚏ ⚏ ⊞ lau ➡ ⌀
⌓ Prices: ⚭3.50 ⚏1.70 ⚏3.50 ⚭2.50

AUVERGNE

The mountainous Massif Central characterises the
Auvergne, giving an atmosphere of grandeur and
tranquility to this ancient land. The rivers Dordogne and
Allier begin in the region; on the banks of the Allier is the
bustling town of Langeac - especially lively on market days.
The rivers offer good fishing and recreational opportunities,
many of these have been dammed, creating great placid
lakes providing wonderful centres for watersports. A unique
highlight of the area is the remarkable Parc de Volcans,
where 80 extinct volcanos form a majestic line stretching
some 20 miles.
South west of the Auvergne, the département of Aveyron is
a little-known district with a turbulent past, and ancient
abbeys, medieval citadels and fortified towns. Cordes and
Villefranche-de-Rourgue are perfect 15th-century garrison
towns, and Najac stands in a superb position on its 1,200ft
rock. East from Aveyron is Lozère, an arid, rugged
landscape. The highlight here is the well-known Gorges du
Tarn, where the Tarn slices its way through the land for
more than 50 miles, and twisting, narrow roads offer an
unforgettable succession of spectacular views.

ALLANCHE CANTAL

CM Pont Valat ☎ 0471204587
➲ *1km S on D679 towards St-Flour.*
15 Jun-15 Sep 3HEC ⊞ ⚑ ⟟ ⊙ ⚒ ⚏ lau ➡ ⚓ ⚏ ✕ ⌀ ⚏ ⊞

ALLEYRAS HAUTE-LOIRE

CM ☎ 471575686
In pleasant surroundings on level ground beside the River Allier.
➲ *2.5km NW.*
May-Sep 1HEC ⬛ ⭒ ⬕ ⊙ 🚿 ⬀ 🚻 🛒 ⬕⊞ lau ➜ 🛒 ⵏ ✕ 🏖 ⵏR

ANSE RHÔNE

Porte du Beaujolais chemin des Grandes Levées
☎ 474671287 ▤ 474099097
A pleasant, modern site in the heart of the Beaujolais country beside the River Saône.
➲ *Access via A6 or N6 then D39.*
15Mar-27Oct 7HEC ⬛ ⬕ ⭒ 🛒 ⵏ ✕ ⊙ 🚿 ⬀ 🚻 ⵏ PR ⬕⊞
lau ➜ ✕ ⵏ **Prices:** pitch 17.75-20.80 (incl 2 persons)

ARNAC CANTAL

Gineste ☎ 471629190 ▤ 471629272
e-mail: lagineste@mairie-arnac.fr
Situated on a peninsula in Lake Enchanet with good, modern facilities and access to local ski slopes.
➲ *NW of Arnac towards the lake.*
All year 3HEC ⬛ ⬕ ⭒ 🛒 ⵏ ✕ ⊙ 🚿 🚻 ⵏ LP ⬕⊞ lau

ARPAJON-SUR-CÈRE CANTAL

Cère r F-Ramond ☎ 471645507
➲ *S towards Rodez via D920, beside the river.*
Jun-Sep 2HEC ⬛ ⭒ ⬕ ⊙ 🚿 ⵏ R ⬕ lau ➜ 🛒 ⵏ ✕ 🏖 ⊞

AUBIN AVEYRON

CM ☎ 565630386
➲ *100m from the lake.*
15 Apr-Sep 4HEC ⬛ ⵗ ◉ ⭒ ⊙ 🚿 ⬕ lau
➜ 🛒 ⵏ ✕ 🏖 ⵏ ⵏPR

BELMONT-SUR-RANCE AVEYRON

Val Fleuri ☎ 565999513
A peaceful site beside the River Rance with good, modern facilities.
➲ *Access via N9 and D999.*
Jun-Aug 1HEC ⬛ ⬕ ⭒ ⵏ ✕ ⊙ 🚿 ⬀ 🏖 🚻 ⵏ R ⬕⊞ lau
➜ 🛒 ⵏP

BOURBON-L'ARCHAMBAULT ALLIER

CM Parc Bignon Parc Jean Bignon ☎ 0470670883
➲ *1km SW on N153, rte de Montluçon, turn right.*
Mar-Oct 3HEC ⬛ ⭒ ⵏ ⊙ 🚿 ⬕ ⊞ lau ➜ 🛒 ⵏ ✕ 🏖 ⵏ ⵏP
Prices: ⵏ1.98 ◗0.76 pitch 1.14

BOURG-ARGENTAL LOIRE

Astrée 'L'Allier' ☎ 477397297 ▤ 477397297
In pleasant surroundings with good recreational facilities.
➲ *Access via N82.*
15 Mar-15 Oct 2HEC ⬛ ⬕ ⭒ ⊙ 🚿 🚻 🛒 ⵏ R ⬕ lau ➜ 🛒 ⵏ
✕ 🏖 🏖 ⵏP ⊞

BRAIZE ALLIER

Champ de la Chapelle ☎ 470061545 ▤ 470065444
e-mail: ccdlp@aol.com
A family site in the centre of the Tronçais Forest with good recreational facilities.
➲ *7km SE via D28 and D978.*
14 Apr-16 Sep 5.6HEC ⬛ ⬕ ⭒ ✕ ⊙ 🚿 🚻 ⵏ P ⬕⊞ lau
Prices: ⵏ2.44 pitch 7.17 (incl 1 persons)

BRUSQUE AVEYRON

VAL Camping Les Pibouls Domaine de Céras ☎ 565495066
Jul-Aug 1HEC ⬛ ⬕ ⭒ 🛒 ⵏ ✕ ⊙ 🚿 ⵏ L 🏁 lau ➜ 🛒 ⊞

CANET-DE-SALARS AVEYRON

Caussanel Lac de Pareloup ☎ 565468519 ▤ 565468985
e-mail: lecaussanel@wanadoo.fr
Well equipped site on the shore of Lake Pareloup.
➲ *Access via D911.*
All year 10HEC ⬛ ⬕ ⭒ ⵏ 🛒 ⵏ ✕ ⊙ 🚿 🚿 ⬀ 🚻 🚿
ⵏ LP ⬕⊞ lau ➜ 🏖

Soleil Levant Lac de Pareloup ☎ 565460365 ▤ 565460362
A family site set on terraces on the shores of Lac de Pareloup with good recreational facilities.
➲ *S of Canet-de-Salars via D933 towards Salles-Curan.*
Apr-Oct 11HEC ⬛ ➜ ⭒ ⵏ ✕ ⊙ 🚿 🚿 ⬀ 🚻 ⵏ L ⬕⊞ lau

CAPDENAC-GARE AVEYRON

Diège Vallée de la Diège, Sonnac ☎ 565646125
Level, sub-divided terrain located in a narrow valley of La Diège river.
➲ *From Figeac on N140 travel 7km, in the direction of Capdenac-Gare. Turn sharp right after the bridge and continue on D558 for about 7km in the direction of Naussac.*
May-1 Nov 7HEC ⬛ ⬕ ⭒ ⵏ 🛒 ⵏ ✕ ⊙ 🚿 ⬀ 🏖 🚿 🛒
ⵏ R ⬕⊞ lau

CM Rives d'Olt bd Paul-Ramadier ☎ 565808887
A quiet site on level ground with pitches divided by hedges on the bank of a river.
➲ *7km from Figeac via N140 towards Rodez, then D35 to Capendac.*
Etr-Sep 1.3HEC ⬛ ⬕ ⭒ ⵏ ⊙ 🚿 🚿 ⵏ R ⬕⊞ lau ➜ 🛒 ⵏ ✕ ⬀
🏖 ⵏP **Prices:** ⵏ2.44 ◗1.52 🚿2.44 ▲1.68

CHAMPAGNAC-LE-VIEUX HAUTE-LOIRE

Chanterelle Le Plan d'Eau ☎ 471763400 ▤ 471763400
e-mail: camping@es-conseil.fr
Situated in the heart of the Auvergne beside a wooded lake.
➲ *1km N via D5.*
15 Jun-15 Sep 4HEC ⬛ ⭒ ⵏ ⊙ 🚿 🚿 🚻 ▲ ⵏ L ⬕ lau
➜ 🛒 ⵏ ✕ 🏖 ⵏ ⵏR ⊞

CHAMPS-SUR-TARENTAINE CANTAL

Tarentaine ☎ 471787125
In an attractive location surrounded by lakes and woodland.
➲ *1km SW via D679 and D22 beside the River Tarentaine.*
15 Jun-15 Sep 4HEC ⬛ ⵏ ⵏ ⊙ 🚿 ▲ ⬕ lau ➜ 🛒 ⵏ ✕ 🏖 ⵏP ⊞

CHÂTEL-DE-NEUVRE ALLIER

Deneuvre Les Graves ☎ 470420451 ▤ 470420451
e-mail: campingdeneuvre@wanadoo.fr
In pleasant surroundings within a nature reserve beside the River Allier.
➲ *0.5km N via D9.*
Apr-Sep 1HEC ⬛ ⬕ ⭒ ⵏ ✕ ⊙ 🚿 ⬀ ▲ ⵏ R ⬕⊞ lau ➜ 🛒
Prices: ⵏ2.90-3.51 pitch 2.90-3.51

CHÂTEL GUYON PUY-DE-DÔME

Clos de Balanède r de la Piscine ☎ 473860247 ▤ 473860564
e-mail: claude.pougheon@wanadoo.fr
A pleasant site, situated in an orchard.
➲ *Access via A71 and D685.*
14 Apr-30 Sep 4HEC ⬛ ⭒ ⵏ 🛒 ⵏ ✕ ⊙ 🚿 ⬀ 🏖 🚿 🛒 ⵏ P
⬕⊞ lau ➜ ⵏR **Prices:** ⵏ2.59-3.66 ◗0.91-1.22 🚿0.91-1.22
▲0.91-1.22

CHÂTEL-MONTAGNE ALLIER

Croix Cognat ☎ 470593138
Well equipped site at an altitude of 540mtrs.
➲ *0.5km NW via D25 towards Vichy.*
May-Oct 1HEC ⬛ ⵏ ⵏ 🛒 ✕ ⊙ 🚿 ⬀ 🏖 🚿 🛒 ⵏ P ⬕⊞ lau
➜ ⵏR

169

CHAUDES-AIGUES CANTAL

CM du Couffour ☎ 471235708 🖷 471235708
Tastefully sited around the town football pitch in the local leisure area.
➲ *2km S via D921.*
May-20 Oct 2.5HEC ⊞ ⚒ 🏡 ⊙ 🔲 🚱 🕿 ⊞ lau ➧ ⇗R Prices:
⚑2 ♣1 pitch 1

CONDRIEU RHÔNE

Belle Rive La Plaine ☎ 474595108
In wooded surroundings bordering the Rhône.
➲ *11km S of Vienne on N86.*
Apr-Sep 5HEC ⊞ ⚒ 🏡 ⚞ 🏄 ✕ ⊙ 🔲 ⊘ ⇗ PR 🕿 ⊞ lau

CONQUES AVEYRON

Beau Rivage ☎ 0565698223 🖷 0565728929
Peaceful site beside the river with spacious, well marked pitches.
➲ *On D901.*
Apr-Sep 1HEC ⊞ ♠ 🏡 ⚞ ✕ ⊙ 🔲 ⊘ 🕮 🚱 ⇗ PR 🕿 lau ➧
⚏ ⊞ Prices: ⚑3.50-4 ♣2 pitch 3

COURNON-D'AUVERGNE PUY-DE-DÔME

CM Plage r de Laveuses ☎ 473848130 🖷 0473849065
In a rural setting on the shore of a 7 hectare lake, close to the River Allier.
➲ *1.5km E towards Billom.*
All year 5HEC ⊞ ♨ ⚒ 🏡 ⚞ ✕ ⊙ 🔲 🕮 ⇗ LR 🕿 ⊞ lau ➧
⊘ ⚏ ⇗P

DALLET PUY-DE-DÔME

Ombrages rte de Pont-du-Château
☎ 473831097 🖷 473831097
In a wooded location beside the River Allier.
15 May-15 Sep 3.5HEC ⊞ ⚒ 🏡 ✕ ⊙ 🔲 🚱 ⇗ PR 🕿 ⊞ ✕
lau ➧ ⚏

DARDILLY RHÔNE

Ville de Lyon ☎ 478356455 🖷 472170426
e-mail: camping.lyon@mairie_lyon.fr
Generously arranged and equipped site divided into pitches. Ideal for overnight stays near motorway. Concrete platforms for caravans.
➲ *9km N of Lyon La Garde exit off A6.*
All year 6.5HEC ⊞ ♠ 🏡 ✕ ⊙ 🔲 🚱 ⇗ P 🕿 ⊞ lau ➧ ⚏ ⊘
⚏ Prices: ⚑3 🚐8 ⚑6

EBREUIL ALLIER

Filature de la Sioule Ile de Nieres
☎ 470907201 🖷 470907948
e-mail: camping.filature@libertysurf.fr
A peaceful, well equipped site in an orchard beside the River Sioule.
➲ *Access signposted from exit 12 on A71.*
31 Mar-1 Oct 3.6HEC ⊞ ♠ 🏡 ⚞ ✕ ⊙ 🔲 ⊘ 🚱 ⇗ R 🕿 ⊞
lau ➧ ✕ ⚏

FERRIÈRES-ST-MARY CANTAL

Vigeaires ☎ 471206188
A level site surrounded by woodland close to the River Allagnon with good, modern facilities.
➲ *Access via A75 exit Massiac towards Aurillac.*
15 Jun-Aug 0.6HEC ⊞ ♠ 🏡 ⊙ 🔲 🚱 ⇗ R 🕿 ⊞ lau ➧ ⚏ ⚏ ✕
⊘ ⚏

FIRMI AVEYRON

Étang r du Camping ☎ 565634302
In a pleasant situation close to the lake.
➲ *Off the main N140.*
Jul-Aug 1.4HEC ⊞ ⚒ 🏡 ⊙ 🔲 🕿 ✕ lau ➧ ⚏ ⚏ ✕ ⚏ ⇗L ⊞

FLAGNAC AVEYRON

Port de Lacombe ☎ 565601097 🖷 565601688
e-mail: info@campingportdelacombe.com
A shady site in the Lot valley. Water activities including fishing and canoeing on the river and an aquatic area incorporating a large water chute.
➲ *Follow A75 autoroute in the direction of Rodez, turn off for Decazeville/Flagnac.*
15 May-15 Sep 4HEC ⊞ ♠ 🏡 ⚞ ⚏ ✕ ⊙ 🔲 ⊘ ⚏ 🚱 ⇗ R 🕿
⊞ lau Prices: pitch 7.50-12 (incl 2 persons)

FLEURIE RHÔNE

CM la Grappe Fleurie ☎ 474698007
e-mail: info@fleurie.org
A good quality municipal site in a picturesque setting in the heart of the Beaujolais region.
➲ *0.6km SE on D119 E.*
15Mar-26Oct 2.5HEC ⊞ ⚒ 🏡 ⊙ 🔲 ⊘ 🚱 lau ➧ ⚏ ⚏ ✕ ⚏ ⊞

GOUDET HAUTE-LOIRE

Bord de l'Eau Plaine du Chambon
☎ 471571682 🖷 471571288
Well equipped site in wooded surroundings below the ruins of the castle.
➲ *W via D49, beside the River Loire.*
15 Jun-5 Sep 4HEC ⊞ ♠ 🏡 ⚏ ✕ ⊙ 🔲 🚱 🚱 ⇗ PR 🕿 ⊞
lau Prices: ⚑4.12 pitch 4.12

ISLE-ET-BARDAIS ALLIER

Écossais ☎ 470666257 🖷 470066399
In a peaceful location in the heart of the Forest of Tronçais, beside the Pirot Lake.
➲ *Access via A71-E11.*
Apr-Sep 25HEC ⊞ ⚒ 🏡 ⊙ 🔲 ⊘ 🚱 ⇗ L ⊞ lau
Prices: ⚑2.33 ♣1.14 pitch 1.14

JASSAT PUY-DE-DÔME

Ribeyre ☎ 473886429 🖷 473886841
e-mail: laribeyre@free.fr
Situated in the heart of the Auvergne amid lakes and mountains, a flat grassy site with access to a private beach with swimming.
➲ *Autoroute A71 exit 6, then take D978/D996 to Murol, then D5 southwards*
May-15 Sep 10HEC ⊞ ♠ 🏡 ⚏ ✕ ⊙ 🔲 ⊘ 🕮 🚱 ⇗ LPR 🕿
lau ➧ ⚏ ⊞ Prices: pitch 7.60-11

JENZAT ALLIER

Champ de Sioule rte de Chantelle
☎ 470568635 🖷 470568538
4May-29Sep 1HEC ⊞ ⚒ 🏡 ⊙ 🔲 🕿 ⊞ lau ➧ ⚏ ✕ ⊘ ⚏
⇗R Prices: ⚑1.68 🚐0.84 🚐0.84 ⚑0.84

LACAPELLE-VIESCAMP CANTAL

Puech des Ouilhes ☎ 471464238 🖷 0471464738
e-mail: campingpuech@infonie.fr
On a wooded peninsula on Lake St-Étienne-Cantalès.
15 Jun-5 Sep 2HEC ⊞ ♠ 🏡 ⚏ ⊙ 🔲 ⊘ 🚱 ⇗ LP 🕿 ⊞ ✕ lau
➧ ⚏ ✕ Prices: ⚑3.35 pitch 12 (incl 2 persons)

LANGEAC HAUTE-LOIRE

Gorges d'Allier 'Le Pradeau' Domaine du Prad'Eau
☎ 471770501
In wooded surroundings within a natural park, 800mtrs from the river. Good recreational facilities.
➲ *Access via N102.*
Apr-Oct 12HEC ⊞ ⚒ 🏡 ✕ ⊙ 🔲 ⊘ 🚱 🚱 ⚏ ⇗ PR 🕿 lau ➧
⚏ ✕ ⊞

Camping Club A. Tout. Vert.

Route de Chambezon
F-43410 LEMPDES SUR ALLAGNON
Tel: 04 71 76 53 69   Fax: 04 71 76 52 82
80 pitches, Shops and services 300m, Leisure programme, Heated swimming pool (outside of the camping) with entertainment, Tennis, mini-golf, French boules, volleyball. Nearby: horse riding, canoe, rafting, river fishing.
Open 1 March-31 October

LAPEYROUSE PUY-DE-DÔME

CM Les Marins La Loge ☎ 473520273
A modern, lakeside site with good facilities set among the rolling hills of the Combtaille.
➲ *2km E via D998.*
15 Jun-1 Sep 2HEC ⊞ ⌂ ⋔ ⲩ ✕ ☉ ⬤ ⬛ ⌇ L ☒ ⊞ lau ➔ ⧑ ✕

LEMPDES HAUTE-LOIRE

Club A.Tou.Vert ☎ 471765369 ▤ 471765282
All year 2HEC ⌂ ⧑ ⛏ ⌇ R

LOUBEYRAT PUY-DE-DÔME

Colombier ☎ 473866694
➲ *1.5km S via D16.*
15 Apr-15 Oct 1.3HEC ⊞ ⌂ ⌂ ☉ ⬤ ⬛ ⬛ ⌇ P ☒ ⊞ lau ➔ ⛏ ✕ ⋈ Prices: ⛺1.52-2.29 ⟠0.70-1.22 ⬤0.70-1.22 ▲0.76

MARTRES-DE-VEYRE, LES PUY-DE-DÔME

Camping la Font de Bleix r des Roches
☎ 473392649 ▤ 473392011
A pleasant site beside the River Allier. A good centre for touring the surrounding area.
➲ *SE via D225 beside the River Allier.*
All year 1.3HEC ⊞ ⋇ ⌂ ☉ ⬤ ⬛ ⬛ ⌇ R ☒ lau ➔ ⛏ ✕ ⋈ ⊞ Prices: ⛺2.29 ⟠1.52 ▲1.92

MASSIAC CANTAL

CM Allagnon av de Courcelles ☎ 471230393
A riverside site with plenty of facilities.
➲ *0.8km W on N122.*
May-Sep 2.5HEC ⊞ ⌂ ⌂ ☉ ⬤ ⋈ ⌇ R ☒ ⊞ lau ➔ ⧑ ✕ ⋈ ⌇P

MAURS CANTAL

At ST-CONSTANT(4.5Km SE via N663)
Moulin de Chaules rte de Calvinet
☎ 471491102 ▤ 471491363
Terraced site in a valley by the stream of a former watermill with good, modern facilities.
➲ *3km E via D28.*
20 Apr-Oct 3HEC ⊞ ⌂ ⧑ ⛏ ✕ ☉ ⬤ ⬛ ⌇ PR ◻ ⊞ lau

MENDE LOZÈRE

Tivoli av des Gorges-du-Tarn
☎ 466650038 ▤ 466650038
e-mail: tivoli.camping@libertysurf.fr
A level site in wooded surroundings beside the river.
➲ *2km from the town via A75 or N88.*
All year 1.8HEC ⊞ ⌂ ⧑ ⛏ ✕ ☉ ⬤ ⋈ ⬛ ⌇ PR ☒ ⊞ lau

MEYRUEIS LOZÈRE

Ayres rte de la Brêze ☎ 466456051 ▤ 466456051
On a wooded meadow with well defined pitches and modern sanitary installations within easy reach of the picturesque Gorges de la Jonte. Plenty of recreational facilities.
➲ *0.5km E via D57*
Apr-20 Sep 1.5HEC ⊞ ⌂ ⧑ ⛏ ✕ ☉ ⬤ ⋈ ⬛ ⌇ P ☒ ⊞ lau ➔ ⧑ ⋈ ⌇R

Capelan ☎ 33 466456050 ▤ 466456050
e-mail: camping.le.capelan@wanadoo.fr
In picturesque surroundings alongside the Gorges de la Jonte with good sporting facilities.
➲ *Access via D986 from Ste-Enimie.*
30Apr-19Sep 4HEC ⊞ ➔ ⌂ ⧑ ⛏ ✕ ☉ ⬤ ⋈ ⌇ PR ☒ ⊞ lau ➔ ✕ ⋈ Prices: pitch 9.60-14 (incl 2 persons)

MILLAU AVEYRON

Millau Graufesenque av de L'Aigoual
☎ 565611883 ▤ 565611883
➲ *1 km E on D591 next to River Dourbe.*
15 Apr-Sep 3.5HEC ⊞ ➔ ⌂ ⧑ ⛏ ✕ ☉ ⬤ ⋈ ⌇ PR ☒

CM Millau Plage rte de Millau Plage
☎ 565601097 ▤ 565601688
e-mail: info@campingmillauplage.com
Beside the River Tarn, flat shady parkland.
➲ *Access via D187.*
Apr-Sep 5HEC ⊞ ➔ ⌂ ⧑ ⛏ ✕ ☉ ⬤ ⋈ ⋈ ⬛ ⌇ PR ☒ ⊞ lau

Rivages av de l'Aigoual ☎ 565610107 ▤ 565590356
e-mail: campinglesriveages@wanadoo.fr
A family site with good facilities beside the River Dourbie.
➲ *1.7km E via D991.*
May-Sep 7HEC ⊞ ⌂ ⧑ ⛏ ✕ ☉ ⬤ ⋈ ⬛ ▲ ⌇ PR ☒ ⊞ lau ➔ ⋈

MIREMONT PUY-DE-DÔME

Confolant ☎ 473799276
➲ *7km NE via D19 and D19E.*
Jun-10 Sep 2.5HEC ⊞ ➔ ⌂ ⧑ ⛏ ✕ ☉ ⬤ ⋈ ⬛ ⌇ L ☒ ⊞ lau

MONTAIGUT-LE-BLANC PUY-DE-DÔME

CM Le Bourg ☎ 473967507
A quiet, level municipal site with good recreational facilities.
Jun-15 Sep 1.5HEC ⊞ ➔ ⌂ ☉ ⬤ ⬛ ⌇ PR ☒ ⊞ lau ➔ ⧑ ⛏ ✕

MONT-DORE, LE PUY-DE-DÔME

CM du L'Esquiladou rte des Cascades
☎ 473652374 ▤ 473652374
e-mail: camping.esquiladou@wanadoo.fr
Mountainous situation in the heart of a national park region
29Apr-19Oct 2HEC ⸪⸪ ⋇ ⌂ ☉ ⬤ ⊞ ⊞ lau ➔ ⧑ ⛏ ✕ ⋈ ⋈ ⌇R Prices: ⛺2.60 pitch 2.40

MORNANT RHÔNE

CM de la Trillonière bd du Général-de-Gaulle ☎ 478441647
In a rural setting on the southern outskirts of the town at an altitude of 333mtrs.
➲ *Off D30 towards La Condamine.*
May-Sep 1.6HEC ⊞ ⌂ ⧑ ☉ ⬤ ⌇ R ☒ ⊞ ⋇ lau ➔ ⧑ ⛏ ✕ ⋈ ⋈ ⌇P Prices: ⛺2.59-3.66 pitch 2.74

MUROL PUY-DE-DÔME

Europe ☎ 473886046 ▤ 473886957
A family site in rural surroundings on the slopes of a forested valley close to the banks of Lake Chambon.
➲ *Access via A71/75 and D996.*
25 May-9 Sep 5.5HEC ⊞ ➔ ⌂ ⧑ ⛏ ✕ ☉ ⬤ ⋈ ⬛ ⋈ ⌇ P ☒ lau ➔ ⌇LR ⊞

Plage Plage du Lac Chambon
☎ 473886027 ▤ 473888008
Busy site beside lake. Caravan section divided into pitches, terraced area for tents. Asphalt drive.
➲ *1.2km from centre of village. Turn off into allée de Plage before entering village and follow signposts.*
May-Sep 7HEC ⏢ ∷∴ ♦ ↑ ⅏ ⏱ ✕ ⊙ ☺ ∅ 🛖
↺ LR 🏢 ⊞ lau ♦ ⊞

Pré-Bas Lac Chambon ☎ 473886304 ▤ 473886304
e-mail: prebas@lac-chambon.com
On the side of Lake Chambon with direct access to the beach and windsurf beach.
➲ *SW off D996.*
May-30 Sep 3.5HEC ⏢ ⅀ ↑ ⅏ ⏱ ✕ ⊙ ☺ 🛖 ↺ L 🏢 lau
♦⅀✕∅↺LR

Ribeyre Jassat ☎ 473886429 ▤ 473886841
e-mail: laribeyne@free.fr
A modern site in a beautiful mountain location 1km from Lac Chambon.
➲ *1.2km S on rte de Jassat.*
1 May-15 Sep 10HEC ⏢ ♦ ↑ ⅏ ⏱ ✕ ⊙ ☺ 🛖 🚲
↺ LPR 🏢 lau ♦ ⊞ ⊞

▶ **NANT** AVEYRON

🗓Val de Cantobre ☎ 565584300 ▤ 565621036
Beside the river in the picturesque Gorges de la Dourbie with fine views from the terraced pitches.
➲ *4km N of Nant, towards Millau off D591.*
12 May-14 Sep 6.5HEC ⏢ ⊿ ⅀ ↑ ⅏ ⏱ ✕ ⊙ ☺ ∅ 🛖
↺ PR 🏢 ⊞ lau

▶ **NAUCELLE** AVEYRON

Lac de Bonnefon L'etang de Bonnefon
☎ 0565470067 ▤ 0565722082
e-mail: campbonnefon@wanadoo.fr
A peaceful site in a wooded location beside a lake with good modern facilities and well marked pitches.
➲ *NW of N88. Signposted.*
Apr-Oct 2.6HEC ⏢ ⅀ ↑ ⅏ ✕ ⊙ ☺ 🛖 ↺ P 🏢 ⊞ ⍻ lau
♦ ⅀ ✕ ∅ ⊞ Prices: pitch 9-12 (incl 2 persons)

▶ **NAYRAC, LE** AVEYRON

CM La Planque ☎ 565444450
In an ideal situation on the Viadène plateau between the Lot valley and the Aubrac mountains.
➲ *1.4km S via D97 beside the lake.*
Jul-Aug 4.6HEC ⏢ ♦ ↑ ⅏ ⊙ ☺ ↺ LR 🏢 lau ♦ ⅀ ✕ ↺P

▶ **NÉBOUZAT** PUY-DE-DÔME

Domes Les Quatre routes de Neébouzat
☎ 0473 473871406 ▤ 473871881
e-mail: camping.les-domes@wanadoo.fr
A comfortable site with hard-standing for caravans. Advance reservations recommended.
➲ *On D216 towards Orcival.*
15 May-15 Sep 1HEC ⏢ ♦ ↑ ⅏ ⏱ ✕ ⊙ ☺ ∅ 🛖 🛖 🚐 ↺ P 🏢 ⊞
lau ♦ ⅀ ✕ Prices: ⋔8.50 ♠5.50

▶ **NÉRIS-LES-BAINS** ALLIER

du Lac av Marx-Dormoy ☎ 470032470 ▤ 470037999
Situated in a spa town, close to the town centre. Some of the pitches are close to a road with the remainder in the shaded hollow of a valley by the side of a stream.
7 Apr-28 Oct 7HEC ⏢ ⅀ ↑ ⅏ ⏱ ✕ ⊙ ☺ 🛖 🛖 ⊞ P ⊞ lau
♦ ⅀ ↑ ✕ ↺P Prices: ⋔3.20 ⊞8.43 ▲6.78

▶ **NEUVÉGLISE** CANTAL

Belvédère du Pont de Lanau ☎ 471235050 ▤ 0471235893
e-mail: belvedere.cantal@wanadoo.fr
➲ *5km S on D921.*
01 Apr-15 Oct 5HEC ⏢ ♦ ↑ ⅏ ⅀ ✕ ⊙ ☺ ∅ 🛖 🛖 🚐 ▲ ↺
P 🏢 ⊞ lau ♦ ↺LR Prices: pitch 10.70-20.60 (incl 2 persons)

▶ **OLLIERGUES** PUY-DE-DÔME

Chelles ☎ 473955434
A family site in wooded surroundings with good leisure facilities.
➲ *5km from town centre.*
Jan-Nov 3.5HEC ⏢ ♦ ↑ ⅏ ⅀ ✕ ⊙ ☺ 🛖 🚐 ↺ P 🏢 ⊞ lau
Prices: pitch 9 (incl 2 persons)

▶ **ORCET** PUY-DE-DÔME

Clos Auroy r de la Narse ☎ 473842697 ▤ 473842697
e-mail: camping.le.clos.auroy@wanadoo.fr
Terraced site in a green valley next to a small river.
➲ *From Clermont-Ferrand take A75 towards Montpellier, then exit 5 to Orcet (signposted).*
All year 2.5HEC ⏢ ⅀ ↑ ⅏ ⊙ ☺ ∅ 🛖 🚐 ↺ PR 🏢 lau ♦
✕ 🛖 ⊞ Prices: ⋔2.10-3.50 pitch 3.60-6 (incl 2 persons)

▶ **PARAY-SOUS-BRIAILLES** ALLIER

CM Le Moulin du Pré ☎ 470450514 ▤ 470456514
A small municipal site beside the river.
➲ *N via D142.*
Etr-Sep 1.5HEC ⏢ ⅀ ↑ ⊙ ☺ ↺ R 🏢 lau ♦ ⅀ ✕ ∅ 🛖 ⊞

▶ **POLLIONNAY** RHÔNE

Col de la Luère Col de la Luere ☎ 478458111 ▤ 478458947
e-mail: camping-coldelaluere@libertysurf.fr
Situated in the Monts du Lyonnais, 20 minutes from Lyon.
All year 5HEC ⏢ ♦ ↑ ⅏ ⅀ ✕ ⊙ ☺ ∅ 🛖 🛖 🚐 ↺ P 🏢 ⊞ ⍻
lau Prices: ⋔3.05 ♠2.13 ⊞2.44 ▲2.44

▶ **PONT-DE-SALARS** AVEYRON

Lac ☎ 565468486 ▤ 565743310
e-mail: camping.du.lac@wanadoo.fr
A terraced site on the shore of a 200hect lake with good water sports facilities.
➲ *1.5km N via D523.*
Jun-Sep 4.8HEC ⏢ ♦ ↑ ⅏ ⅀ ✕ ⊙ ☺ ∅ 🛖 🛖 🚐 ▲ ↺ LP 🏢
⊞ ⍻ lau Prices: pitch 11-12.50 (incl 2 persons)

Terrasses du Lac rte du Vibal ☎ 565468818 ▤ 565468538
Pleasant lake-side site with terraced pitches overlooking the Pont-de-Salars lake.
➲ *4km N via D523.*
Jun-Sep 6HEC ⏢ ♦ ↑ ⅏ ⅀ ✕ ⊙ ☺ ∅ 🛖 🛖 🚐 ▲ ↺ LP 🏢
lau Prices: pitch 11-17 (incl 2 persons)

Camping Municipal de la Palle ★★★
Route de la Miouze
F-63230 PONTGIBAUD
Tel: 04 73 88 96 99
04 73 88 70 42 (out of season)
Fax: 04 73 88 77 77
Direct access to the river _ Lake 4km – pond 2km – a paradise for fishing – badminton – volleyball – children's games – very quiet.
Reservations recommended in summer.
Open from 15.4 'til 15.10

ROYAT - Thermal Station - Casino
Route de Gravenoire - F-63130 ROYAT - Tel. 04 73 35 97 05
• Fax: 04 73 35 67 69 • Internet: www.camping-royat.com
At the doors of the regional metropolis CLERMOND FERRAND and the Vulcano Park of the Auvergne, 10 mn from the European future park "VULCANIA".

L'OCLEDE ★★★★
7 ha site, quiet and woody • Swimming pool • Camping, caravanning 12 chalets (booking tel: 04 73 19 11 11). Reservations recommended from May to September.
OPEN FROM APRIL TO OCTOBER
FORFAIT 2 persons (without electr.): 10-14.50 € according to period and comfort of pitch.

PONTGIBAUD PUY-DE-DÔME

CM rte de la Miouze
☎ 473889699 ▤ 473887777
In a wooded area beside the River Sioule.
➲ *0.5km SW via D986 towards Rochefort-Montagne.*
15 Apr-15 Oct 4.5HEC � ⚬▯✕⊙◗⊕◘▯ᴿ R ☒⊞ lau
➨≞⤶✕∅♨▯L Prices: ▲2.20 pitch 2.80

PRADEAUX, LES PUY-DE-DÔME

Châteaux la Grange Fort
☎ 473710593 ▤ 473710769
e-mail: chateau@grangefort.com
Parklike area surrounding an old château on the bank of the River Allier.
➲ *From A75 take exit 13 for Parentignat, then take D999. Signposted.*
Mar-Oct 22HEC � ⫶⫶⫶ ⚬▯✕⊙◗∅◘◘Å▯ PR ☒
⊞ lau ➨ ≞

PUY, LE HAUTE-LOIRE

Camping du Puy-en-Velay ☎ 471095509
On a wooded meadow with a section reserved for motor caravans.
➲ *From the town centre follow sign for Clermont-Ferrand; at traffic lights by church of St-Laurent, turn right following 'camping' signpost, site is 500m on left of road.*
Apr-15 Oct 1HEC � ⚬▯⊙◗☒⊞ lau
➨≞≞✕∅♨▯P

At BLAVOZY(9km E)

Moulin de Barette ☎ 471030088
A pleasant site situated in woodland beside a picturesque stream.
➲ *Access via D156 off N88.*
Apr-15 Oct 2HEC � ⚬▯≞≞✕⊙◗♨◘▯ PR ☒ lau

At BRIVES-CHARENSAC(4.5km E)

Audinet Av des Sports
☎ 471091018 ▤ 471091018
A peaceful site in a wooded setting beside the River Loire with good recreational facilities.
➲ *E on N88.*
7 Apr-7 Oct 4.5HEC � ⚬▯≞≞✕⊙◗∅♨◘▯⊞ lau
➨▯R

RIOM-ÈS-MONTAGNES CANTAL

Sédour rte de Condat ☎ 471780571
In a pleasant situation beside the River Véronne.
➲ *Access via D678.*
May-Sep 1.5HEC � ⚬▯⊙◗◘▯ R ☒⊞ lau
➨≞≞✕∅♨▯LP

RIVIÈRE-SUR-TARN AVEYRON

Peyrelade rte des Gorges-du-Tarn
☎ 565626254 ▤ 565626561
In wooded surroundings close to the Gorges du Tarn.
➲ *2km E via D907, beside the River Tarn.*
15 May-15 Sep 4HEC � ➨▯≞≞▯✕⊙◗∅♨Å▯ PR ☒
⊞ lau

RODEZ AVEYRON

CM Layoule ☎ 565670952
Clean, tidy site in valley below town, completely divided into pitches.
➲ *NE of town centre. Well signposted.*
Jun-Sep 3HEC � ⫶⫶⫶ ⚬▯⊙◗◘▯☒⊞ lau ➨≞≞✕∅♨

ROYAT PUY-DE-DÔME

L'Oclède rte de Gravenoire ☎ 473359705 ▤ 473356769
7.5HEC � ⫶⫶⫶ ➨▯≞≞▯✕⊙◗∅♨◘☒ lau ➨✕

RUYNES-EN-MARGERIDE CANTAL

CM Petit Bois ☎ 471234226 ▤ 471234226
A pleasant, well equipped, parklike site on the bank of the River Charente.
➲ *0.5km SW on D13, rte de Garabit. Signposted.*
May-Oct 7HEC � ➨▯⊙◗◘◘☒⊞ lau ➨≞≞✕∅♨▯P
Prices: ▲11 ➡11 ◘11 Å11

SAIGNES CANTAL

Bellevue ☎ 471406840 ▤ 471406165
e-mail: saignes-mairie@wanadoo.fr
A pleasant rural site in the Sumène Valley.
Jul-Aug 0.9HEC � ➨▯✕⊙◗◘☒ lau ➨≞≞✕∅♨▯P

ST-ALBAN-SUR-LIMAGNOLE LOZÈRE

Galier ☎ 466315880 ▤ 466314183
Well equipped site beside the river.
➲ *Access via A75 exit 34.*
01Mar-15 Nov 4HEC � ⚬▯✕⊙◗∅♨◘◘▯ PR ☒
⊞ lau ➨≞✕ Prices: pitch 6.80-8.60 (incl 1 person)

ST-AMANT-ROCHE-SAVINE PUY-DE-DÔME

CM Saviloisirs ☎ 73957360 ▤ 73957360
Run by the local tourist authoriry with plenty of sporting facilities within easy reach.
May-Sep 1.5HEC � ⚬▯⊙◗♨◘☒⊞ lau ➨≞≞✕▯R

ST-BONNET-TRONÇAIS ALLIER

Champ-Fossé ☎ 470061130 ▤ 470061501
In the Forest of Tronçais beside a lake with plenty of recreational facilities.
➲ *Access via A71-E11.*
Apr-Sep 35HEC � ⚬▯≞≞▯⊙◗∅♨▯ L ☒⊞ lau
Prices: ▲2.33 ➡1.14 pitch 1.14

173

ST-CLÉMENT-DE-VALORGUE PUY-DE-DÔME

Narcisses ☎ 473954576
In a beautiful natural setting within the Livradois Forez national park area.
Jun-15 Sep 1.3HEC ⬛ ⌇↑☎♀☉♨⌂☂ ⁀R 🏧⊞ lau
✦✗∅☵ ⁀L Prices: ⋔2.30 ♠1.10 ♨1.70 ▲1.25

ST-GAL-SUR-SIOULE PUY-DE-DÔME

Pont de St-Gal ☎ 473974471
A pleasant site with well defined, shaded pitches and access to the river for boating, fishing etc.
➔ *E via D16 towards Ebreuil, beside the River Sioule.*
May-15 Sep 1HEC ⬛ ♠↑☚✗☉♨∅☵♀▲
⁀R 🏧⊞ lau

ST-GENIEZ-D'OLT AVEYRON

Campéole La Boissière rte de la Cascade
☎ 565704043 ▥ 565475639
A comfortable site in wooded surroundings with good facilities. Entertainment provided in July and August.
➔ *Access via A75 exit 41 towards St-Geniez-d'Olt.*
20 Apr-Sep 4.5HEC ⬛ ⌇↑☚✗☉♨∅☂ ⁀PR 🏧⊞
lau✦✗☵

Marmotel ☎ 565704651 ▥ 565474138
e-mail: marmotel@free.fr
Grassy family site on River Lot with a wide variety of recreational facilities.
➔ *On D19 about 1km NW of St Geniez-d'Olt.*
19 May-10 Sep 4HEC ⬛ ♠↑☚✗☉♨∅☂ ⁀PR 🏧⊞
lau✦☵⁀L

ST-GERMAIN-DE-CALBERTE LOZÈRE

Garde ☎ 466459482 ▥ 466459518
e-mail: camping-lagarde@wanadoo.fr
In a pleasant situation on the edge of the Cevennes National Park.
➔ *Access via A7 or A75.*
15May-Sep 1.5HEC ⬛ ◊♠↑☚✗☉♨ ⁀P 🏧 lau✦▲♀∅
☵ ⁀R ⊞ Prices: ⋔4 pitch 17 (incl 2 persons)

ST-GÉRONS CANTAL

Presqu'île d'Espinet ☎ 471622890
e-mail: camping.despinet@wanadoo.fr
On a wooded peninsula jutting into the lake with fine views of the Cantal mountains.
➔ *8.5km SE, 300m from Lake St-Étienne-Cantalès.*
15 Jun-01 Sep 3HEC ⬛ ⌇↑☚✗☉♨∅♀ ⁀LP 🏧⊞
lau✦☵ Prices: pitch 11 (incl 2 persons)

ST-GERVAIS-D'AUVERGNE PUY-DE-DÔME

CM de l'Étang Philippe rte de St-Eloy-les-Mines
☎ 473857484 ▥ 473858526
e-mail: camping.stgervais-auvergne@wanadoo.com
A small municipal site beside a small lake.
➔ *Access via N987.*
Etr-Sep 5HEC ⬛ ♠↑☉♨♀⁀L 🏧⊞ lau✦✗☵∅

ST-HIPPOLYTE AVEYRON

CM La Rivière ☎ 565661450
A small site in wooded surroundings with good sporting facilities.
➔ *Access via D904.*
15 Jun-15 Sep 0.7HEC ⬛ ♠↑☉♨☂ ⁀PR 🏧⊞ lau✦▲
♀✗∅☵

ST-JACQUES-DES-BLATS CANTAL

CM rte de la Gare ☎ 0471470590
A small site on the banks of the River Cère. A good centre for exploring the surrounding Volcanic Park area.
Jun-Sep 1HEC ⬛ ⌇↑☉♨ ⁀R 🏧⊞ lau✦▲♀✗
Prices: ⋔2.60 pitch 2.60

ST-JODARD LOIRE

CM ☎ 477634242 ▥ 477634001
May-Sep 0.3HEC ⬛ ♠↑☉♨☂ lau✦▲♀✗∅☵⁀P

ST-JUST CANTAL

CM Le Bourg ☎ 471737257 ▥ 471737144
e-mail: commune.stjust@wanadoo.fr
In the centre of the village beside the river.
Easter-Sep 2HEC ⬛ ♠↑☉♨⌂☂ ⁀P 🏧⊞ lau
✦▲♀✗∅☵ ⁀R

ST-MARTIN-VALMEROUX CANTAL

Moulin du Teinturier rte de Loupiac
☎ 471694312 ▥ 4719692452
Wooded valley site close to medieval market town.
➔ *Off D922 Aurillac-Mauriac.*
15 Jun-Sep 2.8HEC ⬛ ☀↑☉♨⌂ ▲⁀R 🏧 lau
✦▲♀✗∅☵ ⁀P ⊞ Prices: ⋔5.79

ST-NECTAIRE PUY-DE-DÔME

Vallée Verte rte des Granges ☎ 0473885268 ▥ 0473885262
e-mail: lavalleeverte@liberty@libertysurf.fr
In wooded surroundings by a river within the Auvergne Natural Volcanic Park.
➔ *On R146, 400 mtrs from R996.*
Apr-Sep 2HEC ⬛ ♠↑♀✗☉♨∅☵ 🏧 lau✦▲✗
⁀R ⊞ Prices: pitch 7.63-9.15 (incl 2 persons)

ST-OURS PUY-DE-DÔME

Bel-Air ☎ 473887214
➔ *1km SW on D941.*
Jun-Aug 2HEC ⬛ ♠↑♀☉♨♀ 🏧⊞ lau✦✗∅

ST-PIERRE-COLAMINE PUY-DE-DÔME

Ombrage ☎ 33 473967787 ▥ 473963040
e-mail: campombrage@infonie.fr
A pleasant site in peaceful wooded surroundings at an altitude of 800 metres on the edge of the Auvergne Volcano Park. All the usual services are provided and there are good recreational facilities.
➔ *300m from D978.*
All year 2HEC ⬛ ♠↑▲☉♨∅☵ ☂♀ ⁀P 🏧 lau
✦♀✗ ⁀R

ST-RÉMY-SUR-DUROLLE PUY-DE-DÔME

CM Chanterelles ☎ 473943171 ▥ 473943171
In pleasant wooded surroundings close to the lake.
➔ *3km NE via D201.*
May-Sep 6HEC ⬛ ♠↑☉♨∅☂⊞ lau✦▲♀✗☵
⁀LP Prices: ⋔2.44 ♠1.25 ♨1.57

ST-ROME-DE-TARN AVEYRON

Cascade ☎ 565625659 ▥ 565625862
e-mail: campingdelacascade@wanadoo.fr
Terraced site beside the River Tarn.
➔ *0.3km N via D993.*
All year 4HEC ⬛ ♠↑▲♀✗☉♨∅☵♨♀
⁀LPR 🏧 lau✦✗⊞

⟩ St-Salvadou Aveyron

Muret ☎ 565818069 ▤ 565818069
A modern site in peaceful, rural surroundings beside the lake.
➲ *3km SE.*
15 Jun-Aug 3HEC ⸺ ♦ ⋔ ⚑ ⚡ ✗ ☉ ⬚ ∅ ⚠
⤳ L ⊞ lau ➤ ⚑

⟩ Ste-Catherine Rhône

CM du Châtelard ☎ 0478818060 ▤ 0478818773
e-mail: ste.catherine@coteaux-lyonnais.com
A quiet, well equipped site providing magnificent views over
the surrounding countryside.
➲ *2km S.*
Mar-Nov 01 Dec-28 Feb 4HEC ⸺ ⚑ ⋔ ☉ ⬚ ⊡ ⊞ lau
➤ ⚑ ⚡ ✗ ∅ ⚠ ⤳R Prices: ↟1.80 pitch 2.10

⟩ Ste-Sigolène Haute-Loire

Vaubarlet Vaubarlet ☎ 471666495 ▤ 471661198
e-mail: vaubarlet@aol.com
In a beautiful wooded valley beside the River Dunières with a
variety of supervised family activities.
➲ *Exit for Ste-Sigolène on D44, then towards Grazac on D43.*
May-Sep 3.5HEC ⸺ ⚑ ⋔ ⚑ ⚡ ✗ ☉ ⬚ ∅ ⚠ ⤳ PR ⊡ lau
➤ ✗

⟩ Salles-Curan Aveyron

Beau Rivage Route des Vernhes, Lac de Pareloup
☎ 565463332 ▤ 565460164
A terraced site located on the shore of Lac de Pareloup. There
are facilities for all kinds of water sports and the site's
popularity makes advance booking advisable.
➲ *3.5km N via D993n and D243.*
Jun-Sep 2HEC ⸺ ⚑ ⋔ ⚑ ⚡ ✗ ☉ ⬚ ∅ ⚑ ⬟ ⬚ ⤳ LP ⊡ ⊞
lau

Genêts ☎ 565463534 ▤ 565780072
e-mail: contact@camping-les-genets.fr
On the edge of the Papeloup lake.
➲ *7 km W via D577.*
Jun-Sep 3HEC ⸺ ⚑ ⋔ ⚑ ⚡ ✗ ☉ ⬚ ∅ ⚑ ⬟ ⚠
⤳ LP ⊡ ⊞ lau Prices: pitch 14-24 (incl 3 persons)

⟩ Sazeret Allier

Petite Valette ☎ 470076457 ▤ 470072548
e-mail: la.petite.valette@wanadoo.fr
A well equipped site attached to a farm with well defined
pitches and organised activities for children.
➲ *Access via A71 exit 11 and follow signs.*
Apr-Oct 4HEC ⸺ ⚑ ⋔ ✗ ☉ ⬚ ⬟ ⚑ ⚠ ⤳ LP ⊡ ⊞ lau

⟩ Sembadel-Gare Haute-Loire

Casses ☎ 471009472
A family site in a rural setting at an altitude of 1000mtrs,
2km from a lake.
➲ *1km W via D22.*
Jul-20 Sep 2.4HEC ⸺ ⚑ ⋔ ☉ ⬚ ⊡ lau ➤ ⚡ ✗ ⚠ ⤳LR

⟩ Sénergues Aveyron

Étang du Camp ☎ 565796225 ▤ 565728158
e-mail: conques@conques.com
Well equipped site in a wooded setting beside the lake.
➲ *6km SW via D242.*
01 Jun-15 sEP 3HEC ⸺ ⚑ ⋔ ☉ ⬚ ∅ ⬚ ⊡ ⊞ lau

⟩ Sévérac-le-Château Aveyron

CM av J-Moulin ☎ 565476482
A quiet, well equipped municipal site close to the town
centre. In a good location for visiting the Gorges du Tarn.
➲ *1.2km S via N9 towards Millau.*
Jun-Sep 1.3HEC ⸺ ⚑ ⋔ ☉ ⬚ ⊡ lau ➤ ⚑ ⚡ ✗ ∅ ⚠ ⤳PR ⊞

⟩ Sévérac-l'Église Aveyron

Grange de Monteillac Monteillac
☎ 565702100 ▤ 565702101
e-mail: info@la-grange-de-monteillac.com
A family site in a quiet wooded location with good
recreational facilities.
➲ *Access via A75 and N88.*
May-15 Sep 4.5HEC ⸺ ⚑ ⋔ ⚑ ⚡ ✗ ☉ ⬚ ⬚ ⚑ ⚠ ⤳ P ⊡
lau ➤ ⚠ ⚑ Prices: ↟3.35 ☎2.74 pitch 18.29 (incl 2 persons)

⟩ Singles Puy-de-Dôme

Moulin de Serre ☎ 473211606 ▤ 473211256
e-mail: moulin-de-serre@wanadoo.fr
A well equipped site beside the River Burande.
➲ *1.7km S of La Guinguette via D73.*
Apr-Oct 6.5HEC ⸺ ⚑ ⋔ ⚑ ⚡ ✗ ☉ ⬚ ∅ ⚠ ⬟ ⬚ ⚠ ⤳ PR
⊡ ⊞ lau

⟩ Thérondels Aveyron

Source Presqu'île de Laussac ☎ 565660562 ▤ 565662100
In a beautiful situation beside Lake Sarrans.
Jul-mid Sep 4.5HEC ⸺ ⚑ ⋔ ⚑ ⚡ ✗ ☉ ⬚ ∅ ⬚ ⤳ LP ⊡ lau

⟩ Trizac Cantal

Pioulat ☎ 471786420 ▤ 471786540
16 Jun-16 Sep 4.7HEC ⸺ ⚹ ⋔ ☉ ⬚ ⬚ ⤳ LR ⊡ lau ➤ ⚑
⚑ ✗ ∅ ⚠ ⊞

⟩ Urçay Allier

CM r de la Gare ☎ 0470069541 ▤ 0470069330
Etr-Sep 0.7HEC ⸺ ⁙ ⚑ ⋔ ☉ ⬚ ⤳ R ⊡ lau
➤ ⚑ ⚡ ✗ ∅ ⚠ ⊞

⟩ Varennes-sur-Allier Allier

⚑Château de Chazeuil ☎ 470450010 ▤ 470450010
On well-kept meadow within the château park.
➲ *3km NW on N7.*
15 Apr-15 Oct 1.5HEC ⸺ ⚑ ⋔ ☉ ⬚ ⤳ P ⊡ ⊞ lau ➤ ⚑ ⚡ ✗
∅ ⤳R Prices: ↟4.27 ☎2.74 pitch 4.27

⟩ Verrières-en-Forez Loire

Ferme Le Soleillant Le Soleillant ☎ 477762273
A small terraced situation within the grounds of a farm.
➲ *Access via A47.*
All year 3.2HEC ⸺ ⚑ ⋔ ✗ ☉ ⬚ ⬚ ⊡ ⊞ lau ➤ ⚑ ⚡ ✗ ⤳
⤳R Prices: ↟1.37-2.74 ☎0.76 pitch 2.13

⟩ Vichy Allier

Les Isles r C-Decloître ☎ 470322685 ▤ 470320394
e-mail: camping-beauzivage@wanadoo.fr
A small site beside the River Allier, connected to Camping
Beau Rivage.
Jul-Aug 1.2HEC ⸺ ♦ ⋔ ☉ ⬚ ∅ ⤳ R ⊡ ⊞ lau ➤ ⚑ ⚡ ✗ ⤳P
Prices: ↟2.50 pitch 2.50

⟩ At Bellerive(3km W)

Acacias r Claude-Decloître ☎ 470323622 ▤ 470598852
e-mail: campingacacias@club-internet.fr
Well-managed site, sub-divided into numbered pitches by
hedges. Clean sanitary installations. Library, billiard room.
Water sports are available nearby on lake.
➲ *From Vichy turn left after bridge beside ESSO garage and
follow river for 500m.*
8 Apr-6 Oct 3HEC ⸺ ♦ ⋔ ⚑ ☉ ⬚ ∅ ⚑ ⚠ ⤳ LPR ⊡ ⊡ ⊞
lau ➤ ⚑ ✗ ⚠ Prices: ↟2.30-4.60 pitch 2.30-4.60

Beau Rivage r Claude Decloitre ☎ 470322685 ▤ 470320394
e-mail: camping-beaurivage@wanadoo.fr
Neat meadowland with marked out pitches. Well kept
sanitary installations. TV.

Cont.

175

⮑ *Watch for turning over bridge onto left bank of River Allier.*
01 May-15 Sep 1.5HEC ▥ ♠ ♠ ♣ ♣ ♀ ✕ ⊙ ♣ ∅ ♣ ♣ ✦ PR
🏢 ⊞ lau **Prices:** ♠2.50-4 pitch 2.50-4

VIC-SUR-CÈRE CANTAL

Pommeraie ☎ 471475418 🖩 471496330
A well equipped family site in a peaceful situation with good
recreational facilities.
⮑ *2km SE.*
May-15 Sep 4HEC ▥ ♠ ♠ ♣ ♣ ♀ ✕ ⊙ ♣ ♣ ♨ ♣ ♣ ▲
✦ P 🏢 ⊞ lau ✦ ∅ ✦R

VIEILLE-BRIOUDE HAUTE-LOIRE

Dintillat ☎ 471509336 🖩 471509336
e-mail: elie.sicard@wanadoo.fr
A terraced site with good modern facilities at an altitude of
500mtrs.
⮑ *Access via N102 and D16.*
May-Sep 1HEC ▥ ♣ ♠ ⊙ ♣ ♣ ♣ ♣ ▲ lau ✦ ✦R
Prices: ♠3.20 ♣2.50 ▲2.50 pitch 2.50

VILLEFORT LOZÈRE

Palhère rte du Mas de la Banque ☎ 466468063
A well equipped, peaceful site on the edge of the Parc
National des Cévennes.
⮑ *4km SW via D66 beside the river.*
May-Sep 2HEC ▥ ♠ ♣ ♠ ♣ ✕ ⊙ ♣ ♣ ✦ PR ☎ ⊞ lau ✦ ♣ ∅
♨ ✦L

VILLEFRANCHE-DE-PANAT AVEYRON

Cantarelles Alrance ☎ 565464035 🖩 565464035
e-mail: cantarelles@wanadoo.fr
On level grassland by Lac de Villefranche-de-Panat.
⮑ *On the D25 about 3km N.*
May-Sep 3.5HEC ▥ ♠ ♠ ♣ ✕ ⊙ ♣ ∅ ♨ ♣ ♣ ✦ L 🏢 ⊞ lau
Prices: pitch 13 (incl 2 persons)

VILLEFRANCHE-DE-ROUERGUE AVEYRON

Rouergue ☎ 565451624 🖩 565455558
e-mail: infos@villefranche.com
A comfortable site in a pleasant, shady situation beside the
River Aveyron.
⮑ *1.5km SW via D47 rte de Monteils.*
Etr-Sep 1.8HEC ▥ ♠ ♠ ♣ ⊙ ♣ ∅ ♣ ▲ 🏢 lau ✦ ♀ ✕ ♨
✦PR ⊞ **Prices:** pitch 10-12 (incl 2 persons)

YSSINGEAUX HAUTE-LOIRE

CM Choumouroux ☎ 471655344
⮑ *800m S of town off the rte de Puy.*
May-Sep 0.8HEC ▥ ♣ ♠ ⊙ ♣ ♣ ⊞ lau
✦ ♣ ♀ ✕ ∅ ♨ ✦P

● ● ● ● **SOUTH COAST/RIVIERA** ● ● ● ●

Stretching along the Golfe du Lion between the Pyrénées
and Provence for 150 miles, the Languedoc-Rousillon
region's vast stretches of beautiful sands are backed by a
gentle countryside covered in vineyards and dotted with
quiet villages. Inland are attractive Roman and medieval
towns - Montpellier, Bézier and the splendid Carcassonne.
High on the crags of the Corbières are the remarkable
medieval castles of the Cathares.
Although away from the sea, the Rhône Valley region is
undoubtedly a Mediterranean land - unparalleled sunshine
warms this unspoilt countryside of vineyards, pastel villages
and cypressus in the valleys, against dramatic backdrops of
the Provençal Alps and Cévennes, with tumbling rivers
running through dramatic spectacular gorges.

South again towards the coast is Provence - a land of blue
clear skies, wonderful wines and superb food. The area's
many rivers begin in the Alpine foothills, and these flow
south and irrigate the rich plains below, filled with fruit and
herbs.
Popular with visitors since the 18th century, the chic coastal
resorts of Nice, Cannes and St Tropez are ablaze with
palatial hotels and celebrated restaurants, and, in the
summer, swarming with holidaymakers - an
acknowledgement of the spectacular coastline where the
Alps meet the sea. But there is still a quieter hinterland,
with ancient villages perched on high peaks, spectacular
deep valleys and canyons, fine lakes, and breathtaking
views from high corniche roads.
The principality of Monaco, which is 350 acres in extent, is
an independent enclave inside France. It consists of three
adjacent towns - Monaco, the capital, la Condamine, along
the harbour and Monte-Carlo, along the coast immediately
to the north. It is a narrow ribbon of coastline backed by
the foothills of the Alps Maritime - a wonderful natural
ampitheatre overlooking the sea.
....

AGAY VAR

Agay Soleil rte de Cannes RN 98 ☎ 494820079 🖩 494828870
A small site in a shady position directly on a sandy beach.
The facilities are good and all kinds of watersports are
available nearby.
⮑ *Between N98 and the sea.*
15 Mar-15 Nov 0.7HEC ▥ ∵∵∵ ♠ ♠ ♀ ✕ ⊙ ♣ ∅ ♣ ✦ S 🏢
⊞ lau ✦ ♣

Estérel rte de Valescure ☎ 494820328 🖩 494828737
e-mail: contact@esterel_caravaning.fr
A pleasant family-site of provincial architecture. There is
plenty to entertain all age groups day and evening. Riding
and cycling can be enjoyed in the surrounding hills and
woods.
⮑ *3km from Agay-Plage towards Valescure. N of Agay near
the golf course.*
Apr-Sep 12.5HEC ▥ ♣ ♣ ♠ ♣ ♀ ✕ ⊙ ♣ ♣ ♣ ✦ P 🏢 ⊞
lau ✦ ✦R **Prices:** pitch 22.11-30 (incl 2 persons)

Rives de l'Agay av du Gratadis
☎ 494820274 🖩 494827414
A level site below a country road.
⮑ *Turn off N98 at Agay beach and continue for 0.5km
towards Valescure.*
15 Feb-4 Nov 1.4HEC ▥ ∵∵∵ ♠ ♠ ♣ ♀ ✕ ⊙ ♣ ∅ ♨ ♣
✦ PR 🏢 ⊞ lau ✦ ✦S

Vallée du Paradis rte du Gratadis
☎ 494821600 🖩 494827221
On a large meadow and a narrow strip of land between the
road and the river.
⮑ *500m inland from N98.*
15 Mar-15 Oct 3HEC ▥ ♠ ♠ ♣ ♀ ✕ ⊙ ♣ ∅ ♨ ♣ ✦ R 🏢
⊞ lau ✦ ✦S

AGDE HÉRAULT

Escale Rte de la Tamarissière ☎ 467212109 🖩 467211024
A riverside site, 900m from the sea, with good recreational
facilities.
1 Apr-30 Sep 3HEC ▥ ♠ ♠ ♣ ♀ ✕ ⊙ ♣ ♣ ✦ PRS 🏢 ⊞ lau
✦ ∅ ✦S

International de l'Hérault rte de la Tamarissière
☎ 467941283
A grassy site on W bank of the River Hérault. There are fine
sporting and recreational facilities and free transport is
provided to the beach 3km away.

⮩ *Take the exit for 'Agde' off autoroute A9, then continue via D13 and D32E.*
Etr-Sep 11HEC ⛺ ⌑♠⛱⛲♨✕☉ΘØ⛺🚐⚡ P lau ♦ ⚍ ⚡RS

Mer et Soliel rte de Rochelongue ☎ 467942114 ▦ 467948194
e-mail: contact@camping-mer-soleil.com
A modern, well equipped family site within easy reach of the beach.
Mar-6 Nov 7.9HEC ⛺ ⠐⠐⠐ ♠⌑⛱⛲♨✕☉ØØ⚍🚐⚡▲ ⚡ P ⟐⊞ lau ♦ ⚡RS Prices: pitch 9-26

At Rochelongue-plage(4km S)

Champs Blancs rte de Rochelongue
☎ 467942342 ▦ 467948781
e-mail: champs.blancs@wanadoo.fr
Quiet shady site with hedged pitches and surrounded by exotic vegetation. Good sporting and entertainment facilities.
⮩ *Situated between Agde and Cap d'Agde on route de Rochelongue.*
Apr-Sep 4HEC ⛺ ⚭♠⌑⛱⛲♨✕☉ΘØ⛺⚡ P ⟐⊞ lau ♦ ✕Ø⚡RS

Aigues mortes Gard

Camping Village La Petite Camargue
☎ 466539898 ▦ 466539880
e-mail: petite.camargue@wanadoo.fr
A grassy site lying amongst vineyards on the D62. 3.5 km from the sea.
⮩ *Access via autoroute exit Gallargues in direction of La Grande Motte.*
27 Apr-22 Sep 13HEC ⛺ ⠐⠐⠐ ⌑♠⌑⛱⛲♨✕☉ΘØ⚍🚐⚡ P ⟐⊞ lau Prices: pitch 15-33 (incl 2 persons)

Aix-en-provence Bouches-du-Rhône

Arc en Ciel Pont de Trois Sautets, rte de Nice ☎ 442261428
A pleasant terraced site on both sides of a stream.
⮩ *Near motorway exit 3 Sautets on N7 towards Toulon. 3km SE near Pont des Trois Sautets.*
Apr-Sep 3HEC ⛺ ⠐⠐⠐ ⚭♠♨☉ØØ⚡ PR ⟐⊞ lau ♦⛱⛲✕⚍

Chanteller Val St-André ☎ 442261298 ▦ 442273353
A well equipped family site set out around an old Provençal country house a short distance from the centre of Aix-en-Provence.
⮩ *Access via A8 exit Val-St-André.*
All year 8HEC ⛺ ♠⌑⛱⛲✕☉ØØ⚍🚐⚡ P ⟐⊞ lau

Alet-les-bains Aude

Val d'Aleth chemin de la Paoulette ☎ 468699040
▦ 468699460
e-mail: camping.valdaleth@wanadoo.fr
In picturesque surroundings beneath the ancient ramparts, on the banks of the River Aude. English owners.
⮩ *From Carcassonne take D118 towards Quillan. Site 8km beyond Limoux.*
All year 0.5HEC ⛺ ⌑♠⛱⛲☉ØØ⚍🚐⚡▲ ⚡ R ⟐⊞ lau ♦⛲✕⚡P Prices: pitch 8.55 (incl 2 persons)

Allègre Gard

Domaine des Fumades ☎ 466248078
On sloping meadow near the river. Extensive leisure facilities. Liable to flooding at certain times.
⮩ *Turn off D7 (Bourgot-les-Allrègre) at TOTAL filling station and follow signs.*
15 May-15 Sep 15HEC ⚭⌑♠⛱⛲♨✕☉ØØ⚍🚐⚡ PR ⟐⊞ lau

Anduze Gard

Arche ☎ 466617408 ▦ 466618894
e-mail: camping.arche@wanadoo.fr
In a beautiful situation on the River Gard with fine views of the surrounding Cevennes scenery.
⮩ *Access via A7 exit Bollène and D907.*
25 Mar-30Sep 10HEC ⛺ ⠐⠐⠐ ♠♨⌑⛱⛲♨✕☉ØØ⚍🚐⚡ R ⟐⊞ lau

Brise des Pins rte de St-Félix de Pallières ☎ 466616339
A terraced site offering fine panoramic views over the surrounding countryside.
⮩ *3km from Anduze.*
Jun-15 Sep ⛺ ♠♨☉ØØ⟐ lau Prices: pitch 7.92 (incl 2 persons)

Castel Rose 610 chemin de Recoulin ☎ 466618015
A well equipped site on the banks of the River Gardon.
⮩ *1 km NW on D907.*
Apr-Sep 7HEC ⛺ ♠♨⛲✕☉ØØ⚍🚐⚡ R ⟐ lau ♦⛱⚍ Prices: ⚡3-4.50 pitch 3-4.50

At Attuech(5km SE on D907)

Fief ☎ 466618171 ▦ 466618171
On level meadow, divided by flowerbeds and shrubs.
⮩ *Turn off D982 E of Attuech and continue for 400m on partially rough track.*
Apr-Sep 4.5HEC ⛺ ⌑♠⛱⛲♨✕☉ØØ⚡ P ⟐⊞ lau ♦⚡LR

At Corbès(5km NW on D907)

Cévennes Provence ☎ 466617310 ▦ 466616074
e-mail: marais@camping-cevennes-provence.com
Situated in a valley bordered by two rivers and offering a choice of pitches in varying levels of shade and terrain.
⮩ *Near railway station.*
20 Mar-Oct 30HEC ⛺ ♠♨⛱⛲♨✕☉ØØ⚍🚐⚡🚐⚡ R ⟐ ⊞ lau Prices: pitch 10.50-15 (incl 2 persons)

Anthéor-plage Var

Azur Rivage RN 98 ☎ 494448312 ▦ 494448439
Well-equipped site only a few metres from the sea and a sandy beach.
Etr-Sep 1HEC ⛺ ♠♨⛱⛲♨✕☉ØØ⚍🚐
⚡ P ⟐⊞ lau ♦⚡S

Viaduc bd des Lucioles ☎ 494448231 ▦ 494448231
A quiet site 150m from a sandy beach, with good facilities.
⮩ *Access via N98.*
Etr-Sep 1.1HEC ⛺ ♠♨☉ØØ⟐⊞ lau ♦⛱⛲✕Ø⚡S Prices: pitch 25 (incl 3 persons)

Antibes Alpes-maritimes

Logis de la Brague 1221 rte de Nice ☎ 493335472
On a level meadow beside a small river.
⮩ *On N7.*
2 May-Sep 1.7HEC ⛺ ♠♨⛱⛲✕☉ØØ
⚡ S ⟐ lau ♦⚍

At Biot(7km N on N7 and A8)

Eden chemin du Val-de-Pome ☎ 493656370 ▦ 493655422
Site on level meadowland, no tents allowed.
⮩ *On D4.*
Apr-30 Oct 2.5HEC ⛺ ⠐⠐⠐ ♠♨⌑⛱⛲♨✕☉ØØ⚍🚐⚡ P ⟐
⊞⚒ lau ♦⚡S

At Brague, la(4km N on N7)

Frênes ☎ 493333652
⮩ *Opposite Biot railway station.*
15 Jun-15 Sep 2.5HEC ⛺ ♠♨⛱⛲♨✕☉ØØ🚐
⚡ S ⟐⊞ lau

Pylône av du Pylone ☎ 493335286 ▤ 493333054
e-mail: @campingpylone.com
In an ideal location between Cannes and Nice, the Pylône is a family site with good facilities.
➲ *From N7 take D4 for Biot. First turning on left.*
All year 16HEC ▥ ♠ ♠ ♠ ♥ ✕ ⊙ ♫ ∅ ♨ 🏕 ♥ ∻ PR 🏚 🖪
⏱ lau ♦ ∻S

《 **ARCS, LES** VAR

Eau Vive Quartier du Pont d'Argens ☎ 494474066
Camping Card Compulsory.
➲ *2km S on N7.*
Mar-Nov 2.5HEC ▥ ♠ ♠ ♥ ✕ ⊙ ♫ 🏕 ♥ ∻ PR 🖪 lau
♦ ♠ ∅ ♨

《 **ARGELÈS-SUR-MER** PYRÉNÉES-ORIENTALES

Criques de Porteils La Corniche de Collioure
☎ 468811273 ▤ 468958576
e-mail: contact@porteils.com
Terraced site with beautiful view of sea.
➲ *4km S on N114 turn left through railway underpass and continue for 0.3km.*
Mar-Oct/Nov 5HEC ⚓ ♠ ♠ ♠ ♥ ✕ ⊙ ♫ ∅ 🏕 ∻ S 🏚 🖪 lau

Dauphin rte de Taxo d'Avall ☎ 468811754 ▤ 468958260
On a long stretch of grassland shaded by poplars, 1500m from sea.
➲ *3km N of town; at Taxo d'Avall turn right onto unclass road.*
25 May-Sep 5.5HEC ▥ ♠ ♠ ♠ ♥ ✕ ⊙ ♫ ∅ ♨ ∻ P 🏚 🖪🖪
lau ♦ ∻LRS Prices: pitch 19-24 (incl 2 persons)

Galets rte de Taxo d'Avall ☎ 468810812 ▤ 468816876
e-mail: lesgalets@wanadoo.fr
A well equipped family site with trees, bushes and exotic plants.
➲ *4km N*
24 Mar-12 Oct 5HEC ▥ ♠ ♠ ♠ ♥ ✕ ⊙ ♫ ∅ ♨ 🏕
∻ P 🏚 🖪 lau ♦ ∅ ∻S

Marsouins chemin du Tamariguer
☎ 468811481 ▤ 468959358
e-mail: marsouin@campmed.com
A large family site with good facilities.
➲ *2km NE towards Plage Nord.*
Apr-Sep 10HEC ▥ ♠ ♠ ♠ ♥ ✕ ⊙ ♫ ∅ ♨ ∻ P 🏚 🖪 lau
♦ ∻S Prices: ♠2.30-5 pitch 11.50-22 (incl 2 persons)

Massane ☎ 468810685 ▤ 468815918
e-mail: camping.massane@infonic.fr
Well laid-out site in shady garden 1km from sea.
➲ *Beside D618 near the municipal sports field.*
15 Mar-15 Oct 3HEC ▥ ∴ ⚓ ♠ ♠ ♠ ♥ ♫ ⊙ ♫ ∅ ♨ 🏕 🏕
∻ P 🏚 🖪 lau ♦ ♠ ♥ ✕ ∻S

Neptune Plage Nord ☎ 468810298 ▤ 468810041
e-mail: neptune@parcpemin.com
Flat site with both sunny and shady pitches 350mtrs from the northern beach. Modern sanitary facilities. Water-slide. Separate car park for arrivals after 23.00 hrs.
May- 15 Sep 4HEC ▥ ✂ ⚓ ♠ ♠ ♠ ♥ ✕ ⊙ ♫ ∅ ♨ ∻ P 🏚
🖪 🖪 lau ♦ ∅ ∻LS

Ombrages av du Général-de-Gaulle
☎ 468812983 ▤ 468812983
In a picturesque wooded setting, 300mtrs from the beach. A well equipped site with good recreational facilities and clearly defined pitches.
Jun-Sep 4HEC ▥ ♠ ♠ ⊙ ♫ ∅ 🏕 🏚 lau ♦ ♠ ♥ ✕ ♨
∻LPRS 🖪

Pujol rte du Tamariguer ☎ 468810025 ▤ 468812121
Set amid rich vegetation with a wide variety of recreational facilities.
➲ *1km from the beach and 500m from the village.*
Jun-Sep 4.5HEC ▥ ♠ ♠ ♠ ♥ ✕ ⊙ ♫ ∅ ♨ ∻ P 🏚 🖪 lau
♦ ∻S

CM Roussillonnais bd de la Mer
☎ 468811042 ▤ 468959611
On a long stretch of sandy terrain adjoining a fine sandy beach.
➲ *In N part of town. Well signposted.*
mid Apr-mid Oct 10HEC ▥ ∴∴ ⚓ ♠ ♠ ♠ ♥ ✕ ⊙ ♫ ∅ 🏕 🏕
∻ S 🏚 🖪 lau

Sirène rte de Taxo d'Avall ☎ 468810461 ▤ 468816974
e-mail: camping.la.sirene@wanadoo.fr
A well appointed family site with good facilities in a delightful wooded setting.
➲ *4km NE.*
23Mar-28Sep 17HEC ▥ ♠ ♠ ♠ ♥ ✕ ⊙ ♫ ∅ ♨ ∻ P 🏚 🖪
lau ♦ ♨ ∻RS Prices: pitch 21-38 (incl 3 persons)

》 At **ARGELÈS-PLAGE**(2.5km E via D618)

Pins av du Tech ☎ 468811046
A peaceful family site situated on a narrow stretch of grassland with some poplar trees.
15 May-21 Sep 4HEC ▥ ♠ ♠ ♥ ✕ ⊙ ♫ 🏚 lau
♦ ♠ ∅ ♨ ∻PS

Soleil rte du Littoral, Plage Nord
☎ 468811448 ▤ 468814434
e-mail: camping.soleil@wanadoo.fr
Peaceful site in wide meadow surrounded by tall trees. Private beach, natural harbour. Pitches must be booked in advance.
➲ *Follow rte du Littoral N out of town then 1.5km towards beach.*
15 May-Sep 16HEC ▥ ♠ ♠ ♠ ♥ ✕ ⊙ ♫ ∅ ♨ ♨ ∻ PRS 🖪
🖪 ⏱ lau Prices: ♠6.50 pitch 5.80-9.20

》 **ARLES** BOUCHES-DU-RHÔNE

Rosiers Pont de Crau ☎ 0490960212 ▤ 0490933672
e-mail: camping-rosiers@wanadoo.fr
On level ground, shaded by bushes.
➲ *Access via autoroute exit 'Arles Sud' or N443.*
15 Mar-30 Oct 3.5HEC ▥ ♠ ♠ ♠ ♥ ✕ ⊙ ♫ ∅ ♨ ♨ ∻ P 🏚 🖪
lau ♦ ♠ ∻R Prices: ♠3.30 ♠1.50 ♠3.42 ♠3.42

》 **ARLES-SUR-TECH** PYRÉNÉES-ORIENTALES

Riuferrer ☎ 468391106 ▤ 468391209
e-mail: campingriuferrer@libertysurf.fr
Quiet holiday site on gently sloping ground in pleasant area. Clean sanitary installations. Separate area reserved for overnight stops. Bar, ice for iceboxes and nearby municipal swimming pool are available in summer only.
➲ *Signposted from N115.*
All year 4.5HEC ∴∴ ⚓ ♠ ♠ ♥ ⊙ ♫ ∅ ♨ ∻ R 🖪 lau ♦
♠ ✕ ∻P Prices: ♠2.75-3.75 pitch 3.05-3.55

》 **ARPAILLARGUES** GARD

Mas de Rey rte d'Anduze ☎ 466221827 ▤ 466221827
In quiet wooded surroundings with pitches divided by trees and bushes. There are good facilities for sports and modern sanitary arrangements.
➲ *3km from Uzès towards Anduze.*
10 Apr-15 Oct 3HEC ▥ ⚓ ♠ ♠ ♠ ♥ ✕ ⊙ ♫ ∅ 🏕 🏕 ∻ P 🏚
🖪 lau ♦ ♨

INTERNATIONAL CAMPING
83630 AUPS (Var)
Route de Fox-Amphoux
Tel: 04.94.70.06.80   Fax: 04.94.70.10.51
www.internationalcamping-aups.com
E-mail: camping-aups@internationalcamping-aups.com

Open: 1/4 – 30/9

Family site, 40,000m², 5 min from the town centre and 15 min from the Lake Ste Croix and the Grand Canyon du Verdon. SWIMMING POOL – TENNIS – SHADED – NICE ATMOSPHERE – SOUNDPROOF DISCOTHEQUE – CARAVAN HIRE AND STORAGE. MOBILE HOMES TO LET. 3 WASHING MACHINES ON THE CAMPSITE. RESERVATIONS POSSIBLE

AUBIGNAN VAUCLUSE

Intercommunal du Brégoux chemin du Vas
☎ 490626250 ▥ 490626521
e-mail: bregoux@lokoce-online.com
A level site with good views of Mt.Ventoux.
➲ *On southern outskirts of town turn off D7 onto D55 and continue towards Caromb for 0.5km.*
Mar-Oct 3.5HEC ▦ ♦ ⋒ ☉ ⊙ ◘ ▣ ⊞ lau ➡ ⋒ ♥ ✕ ∅ ☲ ⋜PR
Prices: ⋔2.60 pitch 2.60

AUPS VAR

International rte de Fox-Amphoux
☎ 494700680 ▥ 494701051
e-mail: camping-aups@internationalcamping-aups.com
In wooded surroundings with well defined pitches and good recreational facilities. An ideal centre for exploring the magnificent Gorges du Verdon.
➲ *0.5km W via D60 towards Fox-Amphoux*
Apr-Sep 4HEC ▦ ⋒ ⋒ ♥ ✕ ☉ ◘ ☲ ⋜ P ▣ lau ➡ ⋒ ✕ ∅ ☲ ⊞

AURIBEAU ALPES-MARITIMES

Parc des Monges 635 Chemin du Gabre
☎ 493609171 ▥ 493609171
In a wooded setting on the banks of a 1st category fishing river, surrounded by mimosa fields.
➲ *Leave A8 at Mandelieu exit and head towards Grasse.*
28 May-1 Oct 1.3HEC ▦ ⋒ ⋒ ♥ ✕ ☉ ◘ ☲ ⋜ PR ▣ lau ➡ ⋒ ∅ ☲ Prices: pitch 13-17 (incl 2 persons)

AVIGNON VAUCLUSE

Bagatelle Ile de la Barthelasse ☎ 490083039 ▥ 490271623
Pleasant site with tall trees on the Isle of Barthelasse. All pitches are numbered; on hard standing and divided by hedges. Separate section for young people.
➲ *Travel alongside the old town wall and the Rhône onto the Rhône bridge (Nîmes road). About halfway along turn right and follow signs.*
All year 4HEC ▦ ♦ ⋒ ♥ ♥ ✕ ☉ ◘ ∅ ☲ ▣ ▣ ⊞ lau ➡ ⋜P
Prices: ⋔3.51-4.12 ♠0.76-0.91 ♣3.20-4.42 ▲1.68-2.59

CM Pont St-Bénézet Ile de la Barthelasse
☎ 490806350 ▥ 490852212
e-mail: info@camping-avignon.com
On island opposite bridge with fine views of town. Several tiled sanitary blocks with individual wash cabins. Individual pitches. Common room with TV, souvenir shop, car wash. Several playing fields for volleyball and basketball. Definite divisions for tents and caravans.
➲ *NW of the town on the right bank of the Rhône, 370m upstream from bridge on right. (N100 leading to Nîmes).*
Mar-Oct 7.5HEC ▦ ♦ ⋒ ♥ ♥ ✕ ☉ ◘ ∅ ☲ ▲ ⋜ P ▣ ⊞ lau
Prices: pitch 11-20 (incl 2 persons)

AXAT AUDE

Crémade ☎ 468205064
A shady, peaceful site, ideal for water sports.
Etr-end Sep 4HEC ▦ ♦ ⋒ ⋒ ✕ ☉ ◘ ∅ ☲ ⋜ P ▣ ⊞ lau ➡ ⋜R Prices: ⋔9.45

Moulin du Pont d'Alies ☎ 468205327 ▥ 468205327
e-mail: contact@alies.fr
In a picturesque location at the entrance to the Gorges de la Pierre.
➲ *Junction of D117 and D118, 800m from Axat.*
10 Mar-11 Nov 2HEC ▦ ♦ ⋒ ♥ ♥ ✕ ☉ ◘ ☲ ⋜ PR ▣ ⊞ lau

BANDOL VAR

Vallongue ☎ 0494294955 ▥ 0494294955
e-mail: camping.vallongue@wanadoo.fr
Terraced site, parts of which have lovely sea views.
Camping Card Compulsory.
Apr-Sep 1.5HEC ◈ ⋒ ⋒ ♥ ✕ ☉ ◘ ☲ ⋜ P ▣ ⊞ lau ➡ ⋒ ☲
Prices: ⋔4 ♠1 ♣14 pitch 12-13

BARCARÈS, LE PYRÉNÉES-ORIENTALES

Bousigues av des Corbières
☎ 468861619 ▥ 468862844
e-mail: lesbousigues@altranet.fr
Well equipped family site approx. 1km from the sea. Bar and café etc open July and August only.
➲ *From D83 take exit 10.*
29 Mar-13 Oct 3HEC ⫶⫶⫶ ♦ ⋒ ♥ ♥ ✕ ☉ ◘ ∅ ☲ ☲ ⋜ P ▣ ⊞ lau ➡ ⋜RS Prices: pitch 11.90-21.50 (incl 2 persons)

California rte de St-Laurent ☎ 468861608
A friendly family site with regular organised entertainment in a pleasant wooded location close to the beach.
➲ *1.5km SW via D90.*
29 Apr-23 Sep 5HEC ▦ ⫶⫶⫶ ♦ ⋒ ♥ ♥ ✕ ☉ ◘ ∅ ☲ ☲ ⋜ P ▣ ⊞ lau ➡ ✕ ⋜RS

Europe rte de St-Laurent ☎ 468861536 ▥ 468869788
e-mail: reception@europe-camping.com
A holiday village type of site with good recreational facilities, 500mtrs from the beach.
➲ *Via D90 2km SW, 200m from Agly.*
All year 6HEC ▦ ⫶⫶⫶ ♦ ⋒ ♥ ♥ ✕ ☉ ◘ ∅ ☲ ☲ ⋜ P ▣ ⊞ lau ➡ ∅ ⋜RS

Presqu'ile ☎ 468861280 ▥ 468862509
e-mail: camppresq@aol.com
A well equipped family site on the edge of the Leucate lake and close to the beach.
➲ *2km on rte de Leucate, turn right. Well-kept family site on strip of land between large inlet and the Mediterranean*
28 Mar-3 Nov 3HEC ▦ ⫶⫶⫶ ♦ ⋒ ♥ ♥ ✕ ☉ ◘ ∅ ☲ ☲ ⋜ LP ▣ ⊞ lau ➡ ✕ ⋜RS Prices: pitch 12-20 (incl 2 persons)

Sable d'Or r des Palombes ☎ 468861841 ▥ 466743730
A wooded site situated between the sea and the Lac Marin.
➲ *From Narbonne leave A9 at exit 40 and head towards Grand Plage.*
All year 4HEC ▦ ⫶⫶⫶ ♦ ⋒ ♥ ♥ ✕ ☉ ◘ ☲ ☲ ⋜ PS ▣ ⊞ lau ➡ ∅ ☲ ⋜L

BAR-SUR-LOUP, LE ALPES-MARITIMES

Gorges du Loup 965 chemin des Vergers ☎ 493345206
Terraced site divided into pitches, in an olive grove. Very steep entrance.
➲ *Access from Grasse on D2085 towards Le Pré du Lac (NE), then turn left on D2210 in the direction of Vence.*
Mar-Sep 2HEC ▦ ♦ ⋒ ♥ ♥ ✕ ☉ ◘ ∅ ☲
⋜ P ⊞ lau ➡ ⋜R

BEAUCHASTEL ARDÈCHE

CM Voiliers ☎ 475622404
In a wooded location beside the River Rhône with good recreational facilities.
⊃ *1km E, 900m S of N86.*
Apr-Oct 1.5HEC �🏠 ♠ ⋔ ⋒ ❌ ⊙ ⋒ ⋔ P ☎ ⊞ lau ♦ ⊘ ⋛R

BEYNES ALPES-DE-HAUTE-PROVENCE

Célestine rte de Moustiers (D907)
☎ 492355254 ▤ 492355007
e-mail: lacelestine@wanadoo.fr
A quiet site on flat ground in the heart of the Haute Provence national park and surrounded by mountains. Facilities for disabled people.
⊃ *Situated on D907, before climb to the village*
Apr-Sep 3HEC �🏠 ⋒ ⋔ ⋛ ⋒ ⊙ ⋒ ⋔ ⋛ PR ☎ Prices: ⋔3.90
⋒3.90 ⋏3.90

BOISSON GARD

⋒Château de Boisson Boisson ☎ 466248221 ▤ 466248014
e-mail: reception@chateau-boisson.com
A peaceful, well equipped site in the beautiful Cevennes region. Painting, bridge and cookery courses are available.
Camping Card Compulsory.
⊃ *D7 in direction Fumades. Boisson is 10km on the right and the campsite is signposted.*
27Apr-14Sep 7HEC �🏠 ♠ ⋒ ⋔ ⋛ ❌ ⊙ ⋒ ⊘ ⋒ ⋔ P ☎ ⊞
⊘ lau Prices: pitch 12.96-35.80

BOLLÈNE VAUCLUSE

Barry Lieu Dit St-Pierre ☎ 490301320 ▤ 490404864
Well-kept site near ruins of Barry village.
⊃ *Signposted from Bollène via D26.*
All year 3HEC �🏠 ♠ ⋔ ⋛ ❌ ⊙ ⋒ ⊘ ⋛ ⋔ P ☎ ⊞ lau ♦
⋛RS

Simioune Quartier Guffiage ☎ 04 490304462
In pleasant wooded surroundings close to the River Rhône
⊃ *From A7 follow signs for Carpentras, at 3rd x-roads turn left towards Lambisque, then follow signposts to site.*
All year 2.5HEC ⋮⋮ ♦ ⋔ ❌ ⊙ ⋒ ⋒ ⋔ ⋛ PR ☎ ⊞ lau

BORMES-LES-MIMOSAS VAR

Clau Mar Jo 895 chemin de Benat ☎ 494715339
A well shaded site 1200mtrs from the sea with good facilities.
⊃ *Access via N98, then D298.*
Apr-Sep 1HEC ⛭ ♠ ⋔ ⊙ ⋒ ⋒ ☎ ⊞ lau ♦ ⋛ ⋛ ❌ ⊘ ⋗
Prices: ⋔4.40 pitch 4.70 (incl 2 persons)

Manjastre 150 Chemin des Girolles
☎ 494710328 ▤ 494716362
e-mail: manjastre@infonie.fr
A peaceful site 6km from the Mediterranean beaches.
⊃ *5km NW via N98 on road to La Môle/Cogolin.*
All year 8HEC ⛭ ♠ ⋔ ⋛ ❌ ⊙ ⋒ ⊘ ⋗ ⋛ P ☎ ⊞ ⊘ lau

At **FAVIÈRE, LA**(3km S)

Domaine ☎ 494710312 ▤ 494151867
e-mail: mail@campdudomaine.com
In a very attractive setting with a long sandy beach and numbered pitches. Fine views of sea. Sport facilities.
⊃ *0.5km E of Bormes-Cap Bénat road.*
6 Apr-Oct 38HEC ⛭ ⋮⋮ ⛭ ♠ ⋔ ⋒ ⋛ ❌ ⊙ ⋒ ⊘ ⋗ ⋒ ⋛ S
☎ ⊞ lau

BOULOU, LE PYRÉNÉES-ORIENTALES

Mas Llinas ☎ 468832546
e-mail: info@camping-mas-llinas.com
A family site in wooded surroundings with a good variety of leisure facilities.

⊃ *3km N via N9.*
Feb-Nov 15HEC ⋮⋮ ♦ ⋒ ⋔ ❌ ⊙ ⋒ ⋒ ⋛ P ☎ lau ♦ ⋛ ❌
⊘ ⋗ ⊞ Prices: ⋔4-4.50 pitch 4.50-5

BOULOURIS-SUR-MER VAR

Ile d'Or ☎ 494955213
In a quiet location, 50mtrs from a private beach with well equipped pitches.
⊃ *E off N98.*
Mar-Oct 10HEC ⛭ ⋒ ⋔ ⋛ ❌ ⊙ ⋒ ⊘ ⋒ ⋗ ⋛ S ☎ ⊞ lau

Val Fleury RN 98 ☎ 494952152 ▤ 494190947
Terraced site with tarred drives set amongst pines and mimosas close to the beach.
⊃ *Off N98 at Km 93.1.*
All year 1HEC ♦ ♠ ⋔ ⋛ ❌ ⊙ ⋒ ⋒ ⋒ ☎ ⊞ lau ♦ ⋛ ⊘ ⋛PS

BOURDEAUX DRÔME

At **POËT-CÉLARD, LE**(3km NW)

Couspeau Quartier Bellevue ☎ 475533014 ▤ 475533723
e-mail: info@couspeau.com
In a beautiful natural setting with well maintained facilities.
⊃ *1.3km SE via D328A.*
May-Sep 3HEC ⛭ ⋒ ⋔ ⋛ ❌ ⊙ ⋒ ⊘ ⋒ ⋒ ⋗ ⋛ P ☎ ⊞
lau Prices: ⋔3.81-5.64 pitch 12.19-19.81 (incl 2 persons)

BOURG-ST-ANDÉOL ARDÈCHE

Lion ☎ 475545320
Large well-shaped park in wooded terrain, beside River Rhône.
⊃ *N86 in direction of Viviers, through the centre of town.*
Apr-15 Sep 8HEC ⛭ ♠ ⋔ ⋛ ❌ ⊙ ⋒ ⋒ ⋏ ⋛ PR ☎ ⊞ lau
♦ ⊘ ⋒

BRISSAC HÉRAULT

Val d'Hérault St-Étienne d'Issensac
☎ 467737229 ▤ 467733081
A terraced site in a quiet location. Bar and restaurant facilities available July and August only.
⊃ *4km S via D4.*
15 Mar-12 Nov 3.4HEC ⋮⋮ ♦ ♠ ⋔ ⋛ ⋛ ❌ ⊙ ⋒ ⊘ ⋒ ⋒
⋛ PR ☎ lau ♦ ⋒

BROUSSES-ET-VILLARET AUDE

Martinet Rouge ☎ 468265198
A pleasant, well equipped site on gently sloping terrain. Terraced, with well marked pitches.
⊃ *Access via D48.*
Apr-Oct 2.8HEC ⛭ ♠ ⋔ ⋛ ⋛ ❌ ⊙ ⋒ ⊘ ⋒ ⋒ ⋛ P ☎ ⊞ lau
♦ ⋛R

CADENET VAUCLUSE

Val de Durance Les Routes ☎ 490683775 ▤ 490681634
e-mail: info@homair-vacances.fr
A well equipped family site on the shore of a lake and close to the River Durance.
Apr-2 Oct 3.5HEC ⛭ ⋒ ⋔ ⋛ ❌ ⊙ ⋒ ⋒ ⋒ ⋏ ⋛ LP ☎ ⊞
lau ♦ ⋛ ⋛ ❌ ⊘ ⋒ ⋛R Prices: ⋔3.96-5.64 pitch 4.27-8.39

CAGNES-SUR-MER ALPES-MARITIMES

Colombier 35 chemin de Ste-Colombe
☎ 0493731277 ▤ 0493731277
Well equipped site in a wooded location 2km from the sea.
Apr-Sep 0.6HEC ⋮⋮ ♦ ♠ ⋔ ⋛ ❌ ⊙ ⋒ ⋒ ⋒ ⋛ P ☎ ⊞
lau ♦ ⋒ ⋛ ⋛S Prices: pitch 10-18 (incl 2 persons)

Green Park 159 Vallon-des-Vaux ☎ 493070996
e-mail: info@greenpark.fr
A modern site with well defined pitches in pleasant wooded surroundings with good recreational facilities.

⮑ *From A8 exit Cagnes-sur-Mer take N7 towards Nice.*
Mar-Oct 3HEC ⸎ ੧ ⋒ ⵣ ⵤ ✕ ⊙ 묘 ⌀ ⍟ ⎙ ⌰ ⸾ P ⊡ ⧫ ⊞ lau

Rivière 168 chemin des Salles ☎ 493206227
In secluded wooded surroundings with good, modern
facilities.
⮑ *4km N beside River Cagne.*
All year 1.2HEC ⸎ ✦ ⋒ ⵣ ⵤ ✕ ⊙ 묘 ⌀ ⌂ ⛺ ⸾ PR ⊡ ⊞
lau **Prices:** pitch 11.74 (incl 2 persons)

Todos 159 Vallon des Vaux ☎ 493312005 ▤ 492128166
In a beautiful Mediterranean setting. Exceptionally shady
with a mixture of flat and terraced sites. Evening
entertainment. Use of car park compulsory after 11pm.
⮑ *Access via N7 towards Nice.*
Feb-Oct 6HEC ⸎ ✦ ⋒ ⵣ ⵤ ✕ ⊙ 묘 ⌀ ⌂ ⛺ ⛺
⸾ P ⊡ ⧫ ⊞ lau

⟩ At **CROS-DE-CAGNES**(2km S)

Panoramer 30 chemin des Gros Buaux
☎ 493311615 ▤ 493311615
Pleasant terraced site with sea view. Separate sections for
tents and caravans.
⮑ *2km N of town.*
Mar-Oct 1.4HEC ⸎ ੧ ⵤ ✕ ⊙ 묘 ⌀ ⊡ ⊞ lau ➧ ⵣ **Prices:**
⚑3.05 ⛺⚑1.83 pitch 10.67-22.87

⟩ **CAMURAC** AUDE

Sapins ☎ 468203811 ▤ 468207475
e-mail: yuan.dabouis@libertysurf.fr
In a picturesque, wooded location on the edge of a forest
with excellent views of the surrounding mountains.
3HEC ⸎ ✦ ⋒ ⵤ ✕ ⊙ 묘 ⌂ ⛺ ⌰ ⸾ P ⊡ ⊞ lau ➧ ⵣ ⌀ ⸾L

⟩ **CANET-PLAGE** PYRÉNÉES-ORIENTALES

Domino r des Palmiers ☎ 468802725 ▤ 468734741
In a wooded location 150mtrs from the sea.
Apr-Sep 0.7HEC ⸎ ✦ ⋒ ⵤ ✕ ⊙ 묘 ⌀ ⊡ ⊞ lau ➧ ⵣ ⌀
⌂ ⸾PRS

Mar Estang 1 rte de St-Cyprien ☎ 468803553 ▤ 468733294
10 Apr-Sep 15HEC ⸎ ⵥ ⋒ ⵣ ⵤ ✕ ⊙ 묘 ⛺ ⌰ ⸾ PS ⊡ ⊞
lau ➧ ✕

⟩ At **CANET-VILLAGE**(2km W)

Brasilia Voie de la Crouste, Zone Technique du Port
☎ 468802382 ▤ 468733297
e-mail: brasilia@mnet.fr
Near beach. Divided into pitches which are surrounded by
bushes and flowerbeds.
⮑ *Turn off main road in village and continue towards beach*
for 2km.
27Apr-5Oct 15HEC ⸎ ✦ ⋒ ⵣ ⵤ ✕ ⊙ 묘 ⌀ ⛺ ⸾ PS ⊡ ⊞
lau ➧ ⵣ **Prices:** pitch 16-30 (incl 2 persons)

Peupliers Voie de la Crouste ☎ 468803587 ▤ 468733875
e-mail: camping.peupliers@little-france.com
Quiet, level site divided into pitches by hedges with a variety
of leisure facilities. Reservations recommended for July and
August.
Jun-Sep 4HEC ⸎ ✦ ⋒ ⵣ ⵤ ✕ ⊙ 묘 ⌀ ⛺ ⸾ PS ⊡ ⧫ ⊞ lau

Ma Prairie rte de St-Nazaire ☎ 468732617 ▤ 468732882
e-mail: ma.prairie@wanadoo.fr
Grassland site in a hollow surrounded by vineyards.
⮑ *Access from D11 in the direction of Elne off N617*
Perpignan-Canet-Plage road.
8 May-20 Sep 4.5HEC ⸎ ✦ ⋒ ⵣ ⵤ ✕ ⊙ 묘 ⌀ ⍟ ⛺ ⸾ P ⊡
⊞ lau **Prices:** pitch 15-24 (incl 2 persons)

⟩ **CANNES** ALPES-MARITIMES

Parc Bellevue 67 av M Chevalier
☎ 493472897 ▤ 493486625
⮑ *leave A41 at the exit for Cannes, at the first set of traffic*
lights turn right.
Apr-Sep 4HEC ⸎ ✦ ⋒ ⵣ ⵤ ✕ ⊙ ⌀ ⛺ ⸾ S

⟩ At **CANNET, LE**

Grand Saule 24 bd J-Moulin
☎ 493905510 ▤ 493472455
e-mail: le-grand.saule@wanadoo.fr
Separate sections for families and groups of young people. 5
mins to beach in peaceful surroundings with fine views and a
variety of sports and leisure activities.
⮑ *Access via A8 towards Ranguin.*
May-Sept 1HEC ⸎ ✦ ⋒ ⵤ ✕ ⊙ 묘 ⛺ ⸾ P ⊡ ⊞ lau
➧ ⵣ ⌀ ⵤ ⸾S

Ranch chemin St-Joseph, L'Aubarède
☎ 493460011 ▤ 493464430
On a wooded hillside 2km from the local beaches with good facilities.
➲ *Access via A8 exit 41 & 42.*
Apr-30 Oct 2HEC ⁘ ⚬⚬⚬ 🛉 🏕 🏪 ☉ 🞓 🖉 🚐 🏪 ⚲ P 🎫 ⊞ lau
➧ 🍴 ✗ ⚲S

▶ CARCASSONNE AUDE

Breil d'Aude Le Breil d'Aude, rte de Limoux
☎ 468268818 ▤ 468268507
e-mail: air-hotel.grand.sud@wanadoo.fr
In a wooded location beside a private lake where free fishing is allowed.
➲ *1.5km N via D118.*
15 May-15 Sep 11HEC ⚬⚬⚬ ➧ 🏕 🏪 ✗ ☉ 🞓 🚐 🏪 🛆
⚲ LP 🎫 lau ➧ 🖉 🚿 ⚲R ⊞

Cité rte de St-Hilaire ☎ 468251177
In wooded surroundings beside the River Aude in a prime position for exploring the surrounding region.
➲ *Access via A61 or A9.*
15May-10Oct 7HEC ⚬⚬⚬ 🏕 🏪 ✗ ☉ 🞓 🖉 🚐
⚲ P 🎫 lau ➧ ⚲R

▶ CARPENTRAS VAUCLUSE

Lou Comtadou 881 av P-de-Coubertin ☎ 490670316
Near the Carpentras swimming pool in pleasant surroundings with good, modern facilities.
➲ *SE of town centre towards St-Didier.*
Apr-6 Nov 2HEC ⚬⚬⚬ 🛉 🏕 🏪 ✗ ☉ 🞓 🖉 🚐 🏪 🛆 🎫 lau
➧ 🚿 ⚲P ⊞

▶ CARQUEIRANNE VAR

🏠Beau-Vezé rte de la Moutonne ☎ 494576530 ▤ 494576530
In a beautiful wooded park with good, modern facilities.
➲ *2.5km NW via N559 and then D76 between Hyères and Toulon.*
Jun-15 Sep 7HEC ⚬⚬⚬ 🛉 🏕 🏪 ✗ ☉ 🞓 🖉 🚿 🚐 🏪
⚲ P 🎫 ⊞ lau

▶ CASTELLANE ALPES-DE-HAUTE-PROVENCE

International rte Napoléon ☎ 492836667
Family site at the foot of the Col des Lèques and close to the Gorges du Verdon.
➲ *1km from the centre of the village. Signposted.*
Apr-Sep 6HEC ⚬⚬⚬ 🏕 🏪 ✗ ☉ 🞓 🚿 🚐 🏪
⚲ P 🎫 lau ➧ 🖉

Nôtre Dame rte des Gorges du Verdon
☎ 492836302 ▤ 492836302
In meadowland with deciduous and fruit trees.
➲ *200m W on D952.*
Apr-14 Oct 0.6HEC ⚬⚬⚬ 🛉 🏕 🏪 ☉ 🞓 🖉 🚐 🎫 ⊞ lau
➧ ✗ 🚿 ⚲PR

🏠Verdon Domain de la Salaou ☎ 492836129 ▤ 492836937
e-mail: contact@camp-du-verdon.com
Well-maintained site on meadowland on banks of River Verdon. Divided into pitches. Rooms in rustic style. Reservations recommended Jul-Aug.
➲ *Below the D952 towards the Gorges du Verdon.*
15 May-15 Sep 14HEC ⚬⚬⚬ 🛉 🏕 🏪 ✗ ☉ 🞓 🖉 🚐
⚲ P 🎫 lau **Prices:** pitch 10-35 (incl 3 persons)

▶ At CHASTEUIL(9km W on D952)

Gorges du Verdon Clos d'Arémus
☎ 492836364 ▤ 492837472
e-mail: aremus@camping-gorgesduverdon.com
Situated on bank of the Verdon, surrounded by mountains

and at an altitude of 660 metres. Fully divided into pitches split into two by road. Bathing in river not advised due to strong current.
➲ *0.5km S of village.*
May-15 Sep 7HEC ⚬⚬⚬ 🛉 🏕 🏪 ✗ ☉ 🞓 🖉 🚐 ⚲ PR 🎫 ⊞ lau

▶ At GARDE-CASTELLANE(7.5km SE)

Clavet rte de Grasse Napoléon
☎ 492836896 ▤ 492837540
e-mail: leclavet@wanadoo.fr
Terraced site on wooded grassland with mountain views and fine recreational facilities.
➲ *On Grasse road beyond La Garde.*
15 May-15 Sep 7HEC ⚬⚬⚬ 🏕 🏪 ✗ ☉ 🞓 🖉 🚿 🚐 🛆 ⚲
P 🎫 lau

▶ CAVAILLON VAUCLUSE

Durance Digue des Grands Jardins
☎ 490711178 ▤ 490719877
Situated in a shaded area with a wide variety of recreational facilities.
➲ *2km S.*
All year 4HEC ⚬⚬⚬ 🛉 🏕 🏪 ☉ 🞓 🖉 🎫 🎫 🎏 ⊞ lau ➧ 🏪 ✗ 🖉

▶ CAVALAIRE-SUR-MER VAR

Cros de Mouton ☎ 494641087
Terraced site with individual pitches, separated for caravans and tents. Good view of sea, 1.5km distance.
➲ *Turn off N559 in town centre and continue inland for 1.5km.*
15 Mar-Oct 5HEC 🛉 🏕 🏪 ✗ ☉ 🞓 🖉 🚐 🏪
⚲ P 🎫 ⊞ lau ➧ ⚲S

Pinède Chemin des Mannes ☎ 494641114 ▤ 494641925
A family site with well defined pitches, 500mtrs from the sea.
➲ *300mtrs from the centre of the village.*
15 Mar-15 Oct 2HEC ⚬⚬⚬ 🏕 🏪 ☉ 🞓 🖉 🎫 ⊞ lau ➧ 🏪 ⚲S

▶ CENDRAS GARD

Croix Clémentine rte de Mende
☎ 466865269 ▤ 466865484
e-mail: clementine@clementine.fr
An extensive, partly terraced site, in wooded surroundings.
➲ *Signposted W of town towards La Baume via D160.*
Apr-20 Sep 12HEC ⚬⚬⚬ 🏕 🏪 ✗ ☉ 🞓 🖉 🚐 🏪 ⚲ P 🎫 ⊞
lau ➧ ⚲R **Prices:** pitch 17.68

▶ CHABEUIL DRÔME

Grand Lierne ☎ 475598314 ▤ 475598795
e-mail: contact@granadlierne.com
On the edge of the Vercors Regional Park.
➲ *Access via A7 exit 'Valence Sud' towards Chabeuil, then follow signs for site.*
27Apr-9Sep 4.8HEC ⚬⚬⚬ 🏕 🏪 ✗ ☉ 🞓 🖉 🚿 🚐 🏪 🛆 ⚲ P
🎫 ⊞ ⊘ lau ➧ ⚲LR **Prices:** ⚽6-7 ➡1-3 🚐1-4 🛆1-4

▶ CHAPELLE-EN-VERCORS, LA DRÔME

Bruyères ☎ 0475482146
e-mail: maine.levercos@wanadoo.fr
A well appointed municipal site in the centre of the Parc Naturel Régional du Vercors.
All year 1HEC ⚬⚬⚬ 🏕 ☉ 🞓 🚐 🏪 🎫 ⊞ lau ➧ 🏪 🍴 ✗ 🖉 🚿 ⚲P
Prices: 🏠305 ➡1.37 🚐1.37 🛆1.37-9

▶ CHARLEVAL BOUCHES-DU-RHÔNE

Orée des Bois av du Bois ☎ 442284175 ▤ 442284748
e-mail: campingclub@wanadoo.fr
Spacious, well shaded pitches. Approx. 500mtrs from the village.

⮩ *Access via A7 exit Sémas. From Charleval follow road towards Cazan.*
All year 5HEC ⭐ ░░░ ♦ ♦ ⊙ ⊙ ∅ ⊞ ☎ ⊞ lau ➡ ♨ ♥ ✗ ♨
⭢P Prices: ♠2.80-4 pitch 3.55-8.10

CHÂTEAU-ARNOUX ALPES-DE-HAUTE-PROVENCE

Salettes ☎ 04 492640240 ▤ 0492640240
e-mail: les.salettes@wanadoo.fr
Some facilities (shop, café etc) available in summer only.
⮩ *1km E beside the river.*
All year 4HEC ⭐ ♦ ♦ ♨ ♥ ✗ ⊙ ⊙ ∅ ☷ ☎ ⭢ P ☎ ⊞ lau

CHÂTEAUNEUF-DU-RHÔNE DRÔME

CM ☎ 475908096
⮩ *N end of village.*
Jun-Sep 0.6HEC ⭐ ♨ ♦ ⊙ ⊙ ⭢ P ☎ ⊞ lau ➡ ♨ ♥ ✗ ∅ ☷

CHAUZON ARDÈCHE

Digue ☎ 475396357 ▤ 475397517
e-mail: bernard@camping-la-digue.fr
In a beautiful wooded location with good recreational facilities.
⮩ *1km E, 100m from the River Ardèche*
20 Mar-Sep 2.5HEC ⭐ ♦ ♦ ♨ ✗ ⊙ ⊙ ∅ ☎
⭢ PR ☎ ⊞ lau

CIOTAT, LA BOUCHES-DU-RHÔNE

Oliviers rte du Bord de Mer ☎ 442831504 ▤ 442839443
A terraced family site between the N559 and the railway line from Nice.
⮩ *Turn inland off the N559 at Km34, some 5km E of the centre of the town and drive for 150m.*
Mar-Sep 10HEC ⭐ ♨ ♨ ♦ ♨ ♥ ✗ ⊙ ⊙ ∅ ☷ ☎ ☎ ⭢ P ☎
⊞ lau ➡ ⭢S Prices: ♠4.88 ⛺5.33 ▲5.33 pitch 5.33

St Jean 30 av de St-Jean ☎ 442831301 ▤ 0442714641
e-mail: stjean@easynet.fr
Site on the right side of the coast road in an excellent position with direct access to the beach.
⮩ *Between D559 and sea behind the motel in NE part of town.*
Apr-Oct 9.9HEC ⭐ ♦ ♦ ♨ ✗ ⊙ ⊙ ∅ ☎ ⭢ S ☎ ⊞ lau
Prices: pitch 19-21

Soleil rte de Cassis ☎ 442715532 ▤ 0442839581
A small site, divided into pitches, 1.5km from the beach.
⮩ *Access via A50 exit 9 (La Ciotat).*
15 Mar-15 Oct 0.5HEC ⭐ ♦ ♦ ✗ ⊙ ⊙ ☎ ☎ ☎ ⊞ lau
➡ ♨ ∅ ☷ ⭢PS

COGOLIN VAR

Argentière chemin de l'Argentière ☎ 494546363
Landscaped, partly terraced site.
⮩ *1500m NW along D48 rte de St-Maur.*
15 Apr-Sep 8HEC ⭐ ♦ ♦ ♨ ♥ ✗ ⊙ ⊙ ∅ ☷ ☎ ☎
⭢ P ☎ ⊞ lau

COLLE-SUR-LOUP, LA ALPES-MARITIMES

Castellas rte de Roquefort ☎ 493329705 ▤ 493587320
In a wooded location with direct access to the river.
All year 1.2HEC ⭐ ♨ ♦ ♦ ♥ ✗ ⊙ ⊙ ∅ ☷ ☎ ☎
⭢ R ☎ ⊞ lau ➡ ⭢P

Pinèdes rte du Pont de Pierre, Departementale No.6
☎ 493329894 ▤ 493325020
e-mail: camplespinedes06@aol.com
Well-kept terraced site on steep slope with woodland providing shade, interesting walks and beautiful views.
⮩ *By the motorway A8 exit 'Cagnes-sur-Mer' turn right off D6 towards La Colle-sur-Loup.*
8 Mar-8 Oct 3.8HEC ⭐ ♦ ♦ ♨ ✗ ⊙ ⊙ ∅ ☎ ☎
⭢ P ☎ ⊞ lau ➡ ☷ ⭢R

Vallon Rouge rte Greolières ☎ 493328612 ▤ 493328009
e-mail: vallonrouge@aol.com
In a picturesque forested location, close to the river, with good facilities.
⮩ *3km W of town, 100m to right of D6 towards Gréolières.*
Apr-Sep 3HEC ⭐ ♦ ♦ ♨ ♥ ✗ ⊙ ⊙ ∅ ☷ ☎ ☎ ⭢ PR ☎ ⊞
lau Prices: ♠2.54-4.12 pitch 8.25-19.02

COURONNE, LA BOUCHES-DU-RHÔNE

Mas Plage de Ste-Croix, La Couronne ☎ 442807034
A well equipped family site on a plateau with a fine view of the bay, and access to a sandy beach.
⮩ *Access from A55, then D49.*
Apr-Sep 6HEC ⭐ ♦ ♦ ♨ ♥ ✗ ⊙ ⊙ ∅ ☷ ☎ ⭢ PS ☎ lau ➡ ⊞

CRAU, LA VAR

Bois de Mont-Redon 480 chemin du Mont-Redon
☎ 494667408 ▤ 494660966
e-mail: mont.redon@wanadoo.fr
Set among oak and pine trees with well defined pitches and plenty of recreational facilities.
⮩ *3km NE via D29*
15 Jun-15 Sep 5HEC ⭐ ♦ ♦ ♨ ✗ ⊙ ⊙ ∅ ☎ ⭢ P ☎ ⊞ lau

CRESPIAN GARD

Mas de Reilhe ☎ 466778212 ▤ 466778212
e-mail: reilhe@wanadoo.fr
In the grounds of a château, surrounded by pine trees with good recreational facilities.
⮩ *On N110.*
Jun-16 Sep 3HEC ⭐ ♦ ♦ ♨ ✗ ⊙ ⊙ ∅ ☎ ▲ ⭢ P ☎ ⊞ lau
➡ ⭢R Prices: pitch 12.20-18.50 (incl 2 persons)

DIE DRÔME

Pinède Quartier du Pont-Neuf ☎ 475221777 ▤ 475222274
e-mail: info@camping-pinede.com
In a picturesque mountain setting beside the River Drôme.
⮩ *W via D93 then cross railway line and the river to site.*
25 Apr-15 Sep 5HEC ⭐ ░░░ ♦ ♦ ♨ ✗ ⊙ ⊙ ∅ ☷ ☎ ▲
⭢ PR ☎ ⊞ lau

DIEULEFIT DRÔME

Source du Jabron Jabron ☎ 04 475906130 ▤ 475906130
A terraced site in a pleasant location beside the River Jabron.
⮩ *N of town on D538.*
May-Sep 5HEC ⭐ ♨ ♦ ♦ ♨ ♥ ✗ ⊙ ⊙ ☎ ☎ ☎ ⭢ P ☎ lau
Prices: ♠2.50-3 ♦1.50-2 ⛺3.50-4.50 ▲3.50-4.50

ENTRECHAUX VAUCLUSE

Bon Crouzet rte de St-Marcelin ☎ 490460162 ▤ 490460162
On level ground with modern facilities beside the river.
⮕ *From Vaison-la-Romaine exit follow road towards St-Marcelin-les-Vaison for 6km.*
Apr-Oct 1.2HEC ⌂⌂⌂ ♦⋔🔥⊑♈✕☉🗘🗗ⵜR 🏧⊞ lau ➡✕
Prices: ⋔3.40-3.50 pitch 3.50-4

ESPARRON-DE-VERDON ALPES-DE-HAUTE-PROVENCE

Soleil rte de la Teillière ☎ 492771378
In wooded surroundings beside Lake Esparron with well defined pitches.
Etr-Sep 1.5HEC ⌂⌂⌂ ⌕♦⋔🔥⊑♈✕☉🗘🗗
ⵜL🅿⊞⌒ lau

FLEURY AUDE

Aux Hamacs Les Cabanes de Fleury
☎ 468332222 ▤ 468332223
e-mail: jhsilberman@wanadoo.fr
A large site beside the River Aude and 1km from the coast.
⮕ *Access via A9 exit Béziers, then 15km W.*
Apr-Sep 10HEC ⌂⌂⌂ ⵘ ⌕⋔🔥⊑♈✕☉🗘🗗🚻🗑
ⵜPR 🏧⊞ lau ➡ⵜS

FONTES HÉRAULT

Clairettes ☎ 467250131 ▤ 0467253864
⮕ *D9 10km N of Pézenas, access via Adissan D128.*
All year 1.8HEC ⌂⌂⌂ ⌕⋔🔥⊑♈✕☉🗘🚻🗗🗑ⵜP 🏧⊞ lau
➡🔥 Prices: pitch 12-16 (incl 2 persons)

FONTVIEILLE BOUCHES-DU-RHÔNE

CM Pins r Michelet ☎ 0490547869 ▤ 0490548125
In a pine wood close to the Moulin d'Alphonse Daudet.
⮕ *1km from village via D17.*
1 Apr-15 Oct 3.5HEC ⌂⌂⌂ ⌕♦⌕🔥☉🗗🏧⊞ lau ➡🔥✕🗑
🚻ⵜP

FOS-SUR-MER BOUCHES-DU-RHÔNE

Estagnon Plage St-Gervais ☎ 442050119
Level, rather dusty site. Public beach on other side of road.
Camping Card Compulsory.
⮕ *Situated S of an industrial zone-Quartier St-Gervais.*
May-Sep 2HEC ⌂⌂⌂ ⌕🔥⊑♈✕☉🗘🗗🗑ⵜS 🏧⊞ lau

FRÉJUS VAR

Dattier rte de Bagnols-en-Forêt ☎ 494408893
Laid out in terraces among typically Mediterranean vegetation this compact family site is well maintained and has good recreational facilities.
⮕ *Access from A8 via RN7, then D4.*
Etr-Sep 4HEC ⌂⌂⌂ ♦⋔🔥⊑♈✕☉🗘🗗🚻ⵜP 🏧⊞ lau

Domaine de Colombier rte de Bagnols
☎ 494515601 ▤ 494515557
e-mail: info@domaine-du-colombier.com
Widespread site on hill on some individual terraces under pine trees. Good recreational facilities.
⮕ *Turn N off N7 onto D4 towards Bagnols and continue for 500m. Access also via A8 exit 38.*
Apr-Sep 10HEC ⌂⌂⌂ ♦⋔🔥⊑♈✕☉🗘🗗
ⵜP 🏧⊞ lau ➡🚻

Fréjus rte de Bagnols ☎ 494199460 ▤ 494199469
e-mail: contact@lefrejus.com
Well equipped site in wooded surroundings.
⮕ *Access via N7 and D4.*
Closed 16 Dec-2 Jan 8HEC ⌂⌂⌂ ⌕⋔🔥⊑♈✕☉🗘🚻🗗
ⵜP 🏧🅿⊞ lau

Holiday Green rte de Bagnols-en-Forêt ☎ 494408820
A family site in a beautiful wooded location, offering fine modern facilities and a wide variety of recreational and entertainment facilities.
⮕ *6km N via D4.*
Apr-Oct 15HEC ⌂⌂⌂ ♦⋔🔥⊑♈✕☉🗘🗗🗑🎪🗗
ⵜPS 🏧⊞ lau

Montourey Quartier Montourey
☎ 494532641 ▤ 494532675
Comfortable, well equipped site within 10 minutes of the beach.
⮕ *2km N.*
Apr-Sep 5HEC ⌂⌂⌂ ⌕⋔🔥⊑♈✕☉🗘🗗🚻🗗🗑ⵜP 🏧⊞ lau
Prices: ⋔5.50 ⮑3.80 pitch 26 (incl 3 persons)

Pierre Verte rte de Bagnols ☎ 494408830 ▤ 494407541
e-mail: camping.lapierre.verte@wanadoo.fr
A large family site in a pine forest 8km from the coast.
⮕ *Access on A8 from Puget-sur-Argens.*
Apr-Sep 28HEC ⌂⌂⌂ ⌕♦⋔🔥⊑♈✕☉🗘🗗🚻🗗🗑
ⵜP 🏧⊞ lau

Pins Parasols rte de Bagnols-en-Forêt
☎ 494408843 ▤ 494408199
e-mail: lespinsparasols@wanadoo.fr
A modern family site shaded by oaks and pines with spacious, well defined pitches and good recreational facilities.
⮕ *4km N via D4.*
Etr-Sep 4.5HEC ⌂⌂⌂ ⌕⋔🔥⊑♈✕☉🗘🗗🗑ⵜP 🏧⊞ lau ➡🚻
Prices: ⋔4.42-5.49 pitch 17.38-21.50 (incl 2 persons)

FRONTIGNAN HÉRAULT

Soleil ☎ 467430202 ▤ 467789002
Family site bordering the beach.
⮕ *NE via D60.*
May-Sep 1.5HEC ⌂⌂⌂ ⌕🔥✕☉🗘🗗🚻🗗🗑
ⵜPS 🏧🅿⊞ lau

Tamaris av d'Ingril ☎ 467434477 ▤ 467189790
e-mail: les-tamaris@wanadoo.fr
A family site on level ground with direct access to the beach. Good recreational facilities.
⮕ *From N112 take D129 and D60/D50 for 6km.*
Apr-Sep 4.5HEC ⸭⸭⸭ ⌕⋔🔥⊑♈✕☉🗘🗗🗑🎪ⵜPS 🏧⊞
lau Prices: pitch 18.50-28 (incl 2 persons)

GALLARGUES-LE-MONTUEUX GARD

Amandiers ☎ 466352802
e-mail: campamandiers@wanadoo.fr
A family site with good facilities in a beautiful wooded situation.
⮕ *Along N113 heading away from Lunel towards Nîmes.*
May-10 Sep 3HEC ⌂⌂⌂ ⌕⋔🔥⊑♈✕☉🗘🗗🚻🎪🗗⛺
ⵜP 🏧⊞ lau ➡✕ⵜR

GALLICIAN GARD

Mourgues Camping des mourgues
☎ 466733088 ▤ 0466733088
e-mail: info@masdemourgues.com
Situated in an old vineyard with some vines retained to separate pitches. Views overlooking the Camargue.
⮕ *On the N572 between St-Gilles and Vauvert at the junction with the road to Gallician.*
Apr-15 Sep 2HEC ⌂⌂⌂ ⌕♦⋔🔥⊑♈☉🗘🗗🎪ⵜP 🏧⊞ lau ➡
✕ Prices: ⋔4 pitch 11 (incl 2 persons)

GASSIN VAR

Moulin de Verdagne ☎ 494797821 ▤ 494542265
Flat grassy site with a family atmosphere 4km from the beach.

➲ *SE of town towards the coast.*
Closed Dec & Jan 5HEC ▦ ⌂♠⛨♠♟✗☉♨∅⛺🏠⚡ P
🏠➕ lau

Parc St-James Gassin rte du Bourrian
☎ 494552020 ▤ 4945634877
Park-like site on slopes of a hill.
➲ *2.5km E of N559. Access from main road at Km84.5 and 84.9 on D89.*
16 Nov-Dec 32HEC ▦ ⠿ ♠♟♠♟✗☉♨∅⛺
⚡ P 🏠➕ lau

▷ **GAUJAC** GARD

Domaine de Gaujac Boisset ☎ 466618065 ▤ 466605390
e-mail: gravieres@clubinternet.fr
A family site in wooded surroundings on the banks of a river.
➲ *Access via D910.*
Apr-Sep 10HEC ▦ ⌂♠♟♠♟✗☉♨∅⛺🏠♨
⚡ PR 🏠➕ lau **Prices:** pitch 15 (incl 2 persons)

▷ **GIENS** VAR

Mediterranée-Les Cigales Quartier du Pousset,
bd Alsace-Lorraine ☎ 494582106 ▤ 494589673
e-mail: aspicq@campinglemed.fr
A well-kept site with numbered pitches. Special places for caravans.
➲ *0.3km E of D97.*
Apr-Sep 1.5HEC ▦ ♠♟♠♟✗☉♨⛺🏠⚡🏠 lau
♠∅⛺⚡S

▷ **GILETTE** ALPES-MARITIMES

Moulin Noù rte de Carros ☎ 493089240
In wooded surroundings between the sea and the mountains with good recreational facilities.
➲ *On the D2209, 1.8km SW of the Pont-Charles-Albert*
6 Apr-25 Sep 3HEC ▦ ⌂♠♟♠♟✗☉♨∅⛺
⚡ PR 🏠➕ lau

▷ **GRANDE-MOTTE, LA** HÉRAULT

Lou Gardian 603 allée de la Petite Motte
☎ 467561414 ▤ 467563103
A well run site with well defined pitches, 0.5km from the beach. Advisable to book in advance in high season.
15 Apr-Sep 2.6HEC ▦ ♠♟♠♟✗☉♨🏠➕ lau ♠∅⛺
⚡LPS

Lous Pibols ☎ 467565008
Well-organised. Divided into level pitches.
➲ *W on D59, 0.4km from sea.*
Apr-Sep 3HEC ⠿ ♠♟♠♟☉♨∅⛺🏠♨Å⚡ P 🏠➕ lau
♠♟✗⚡S

▷ **GRASSE** ALPES-MARITIMES

Paoute 160 rte de Cannes ☎ 493091142 ▤ 493400640
A family site in a wooded location close to the town centre.
➲ *S of town centre, E of the Cannes road just beyond the Centre Commercial.*
Jun-Sep 2.5HEC ▦ ♠♟♠♟✗☉♨∅⛺🏠🏠➕ lau

▷ At **OPIO**(8km E via D2085 & D3)

Caravan Inn 18 rte de Cannes ☎ 493773200 ▤ 493777189
A well equipped site in a wooded location between the sea and the mountains
➲ *1.5km S of Opio on D3.*
Jun-15 Sep 5HEC ▦ ♠♟♠♟✗☉♨∅⛺🏠♨
⚡ P 🏠➕ lau ♠♟

▷ **GRAU-DU-ROI, LE** GARD

Abri de Camargue rte du Phare de l'Espiguette, Port Camargue ☎ 466515483 ▤ 466517642
e-mail: abridecamargue@hotmail.com
A pleasant site near the beach on the edge of the Camargue with well-marked pitches and modern installations.
➲ *2.5km S on L'Espiguette road.*
Apr-Sep 4HEC ▦ ♠♟♠♟✗☉♨∅⛺🏠
⚡ P 🏠➕ lau ♠ ⚡S

Bon Séjour ☎ 466514711
Clean, tidy, well-kept site.
➲ *3km E of village off road to lighthouse.*
Apr-Sep 5HEC ▦ ⌂♠♟♠♟✗☉♨∅⛺🏠♨⚡ L 🏠➕ lau

Boucanet ☎ 466514148 ▤ 466514187
Flat sandy site bordering beach.
➲ *3 km NW on D255.*
26 Apr-20 Sep 7.5HEC ⠿ ♠♟♠♟✗☉♨∅⛺🏠Å
⚡ PS 🏠➕⊘ lau

Eden Port-Camargue ☎ 466514981 ▤ 466531320
e-mail: camping.eden@wanadoo.fr
Quiet site on both sides of access road. 300m from beach.
➲ *On D626 towards Espiguette.*
4 Apr-3 Oct 5.2HEC ▦ ⠿ ♠♟♠♟✗☉♨∅⛺
⚡ P 🏠➕ lau ♠ ⚡LS ➕ **Prices:** pitch 15-31 (incl 2 persons)

Elysée Résidence 980 rte de l'Espiguette
☎ 466535400 ▤ 466518512
e-mail: elysee.residence@elysee-residence.com
Large family site on the edge of the Camargue with a good variety of sporting and entertainment facilities.
➲ *Access via A9.*
13 Apr-Sep 32HEC ⠿ ♠♟♠♟✗☉♨∅⛺🏠
⚡ LP 🏠➕ lau ♠ ⚡S

Jardins de Tivoli rte de l'Éspiquette
☎ 466539700 ▤ 466510981
A modern site with well marked pitches in a wooded setting 600mtrs from the beach. There are good recreational facilities including mountain bike hire.
➲ *Access via A9 continuing SE through Le Grau-du-Roi.*
Apr-Sep 7HEC ▦ ♠♟♠♟✗☉♨∅⛺🏠⚡ P 🏠➕ lau ♠
⚡S **Prices:** pitch 20-45

Mouettes av Jean-Jaurès ☎ 466514400
On level ground, shaded by olive and poplar trees, this site is well equipped and the beach is only 500mtrs away.
➲ *1.2km SE.*
Apr-Sep 1HEC ▦ ♠♟♠✗☉♨∅⛺🏠🏠➕ lau ♠♠✗
⚡S

Petits Camarguais rte du Phare de l'Espiguette
☎ 466511616 ▤ 466211617
e-mail: petite.camargue@wanadoo.fr
A comfortable family site in woodland with a wide range of recreational facilities. Close to the beach.
Apr-23 Sep 4HEC ▦ ⠿ ⌂♠♟♠♟✗☉♨∅⛺🏠⚡ P 🏠
➕ lau ♠ ⚡S

▷ **GRIGNAN** DRÔME

Truffières Lieu-dit Nachony ☎ 475469362
A family site opposite the Château Grignan with good facilities.
➲ *Leave A7 at exit Montélimar Sud and follow N7 E.*
Apr-Sep 3HEC ▦ ♠♟♟✗☉♨∅🏠🏠⚡ P 🏠➕⊘ lau ♠
♟ **Prices:** ♣4.20 pitch 14.50 (incl 2 persons)

GRIMAUD VAR

At **PORT-GRIMAUD**(4km E)

Plage RN 98 ☎ 494563115 ▤ 494564961
e-mail: campingplagegrimaud@wanadoo.fr
Wide area of land on both sides of road beside sea. Partly
terraced and divided into pitches.
➲ N on N98.
Etr-mid Oct 18HEC ⬛ ⠿⠿ ⊕ ⌂ ⚡ ⏚ ⏛ ✗ ⊙ ⬛ ∅ 🚿 ₹ S ⊞
⊞ lau

HYÈRES VAR

At **AYGUADE-CEINTURON**(4km SE)

Ceinturon II ☎ 494663966 ▤ 494664730
e-mail: ceinturon2@provence-campings.com
A popular site on level meadowland divided into pitches.
300yds from the sea. Some individual washing cubicles.
➲ 4km SE of Hyères on D42.
Jun-Aug 4.8HEC ⊕ ⌂ ⏚ ⏛ ✗ ⊙ ⬛ ∅ ⊞ ⊞ lau ♦ 🚿 ₹PS

Ceinturon III L'Ayguade ☎ 494663265 ▤ 494664843
e-mail: ceinturon3@wanadoo.fr
Well-kept site in wooded surroundings divided into
numbered pitches. Individual washing cubicles.
➲ 4km SE of Hyères on D42.
Apr-Sep 3HEC ⬛ ♦ ⌂ ⏚ ⏛ ✗ ⊙ ⬛ ∅ ⏛ ₹ S ⊞ ⊞ lau ♦ ⏛
⊞ Prices: ⋔4.55 ♦4.55 ⬛5.60 ▲5.60

At **HYÈRES-PLAGE**(4km SE)

Pins Maritimes 1633 bd de la Marine ☎ 494663357
Situated in a pine wood close to the beach.
➲ Turn off D42 between Hyères-Plage and L'Ayguade and
continue inland for 200m.
Apr-Sep 37HEC ⬛ ⊕ ⌂ ⏚ ⏛ ✗ ⊙ ⬛ ∅ ⏛ ⊞ ⊞ lau ♦ ₹S

ISLE-SUR-LA-SORGUE, L' VAUCLUSE

CM Sorguette rte d'Apt ☎ 490380571 ▤ 490208461
e-mail: sorguette@wanadoo.fr
In tranquil wooded surroundings beside the River Sorguette
with good sports and entertainment facilities.
➲ Access via N100 towards Apt.
15 Mar-15 Oct 2.5HEC ⬛ ⊕ ⌂ ⏚ ⏛ ✗ ⊙ ⬛ ∅ ⏛ ⏛ ₹
R ⊞ ⊞ lau ♦ ₹P Prices: ⋔4.55-4.90 pitch 4-4.30

ISTRES BOUCHES-DU-RHÔNE

Vitou 31 rte de St-Chamas ☎ 442565157
In a wooded location with a large area for tents.
➲ N of town on D16.
All year 6.5HEC ⬛ ♦ ⌂ ⏚ ⏛ ✗ ⊙ ⬛ ⏛ ₹ L ⊞ ⊞ ♦ ∅

LAGORCE ARDÈCHE

Domaine de Chaussy ☎ 475939966 ▤ 475939056
➲ On D559 near Ruoms.
4 Apr-4 Oct 18.5HEC ⬛ ⊕ ⌂ ⏚ ⏛ ✗ ⊙ ⬛ ∅ ⏛ ⏛ ▲ ₹ P
⊞ ⊞ lau

LAROQUE-DES-ALBÈRES PYRÉNÉES-ORIENTALES

Planes 117 av du Vallespir, rte de Villelongue dels Monts
☎ 468892136 ▤ 468890142
e-mail: francois.camping.las.planes@libertysurf.fr
In a picturesque setting surrounded by trees, bushes and
flowers.
➲ Approach via Laroque towards Villelongue-del-Monts.
15 Jun-Aug 2.5HEC ⬛ ♦ ⌂ ✗ ⊙ ⬛ ∅ ₹ P ⊞ ⊞ lau ♦ ⏚ ⏛
⏛ Prices: ⋔3 ♦1.80-2 pitch 7.80-8

LAURENS HÉRAULT

Oliveraie chemin de Bédarieux ☎ 467902436 ▤ 467901120
Situated in the heart of the Faugères vineyards, this
comfortable family site provides clearly marked pitches and a
wide variety of sporting facilities.

➲ D909 from Bédarieux. 900m from village centre.
All year 7HEC ⬛ ⊕ ⌂ ⏚ ⏛ ✗ ⊙ ⬛ ∅ ⏛ ⏛ ⏛ ₹ P ⊞ ⊞ lau

LÉZIGNAN-CORBIÈRES AUDE

CM Pinède av Gaston-Bonheur ☎ 468270508 ▤ 0468270508
Well-kept terraced site with numbered pitches and tarred
drives, decorated with bushes and flower beds. Shop available
July and August only.
➲ Signposted from N113.
Mar-Oct 3.5HEC ♦ ⌂ ⏚ ⏛ ✗ ⊙ ⬛ ∅ ⏛ ₹ P ⊞ lau ♦ ⏛ ⏛
Prices: ⋔3-4 pitch 5.50-7

LONDE-LES-MAURES, LA VAR

Moulières ☎ 494015321 ▤ 494015322
e-mail: camping.les.moulieres@wanadoo.fr
Well tended level meadowland in quiet location. 1km from
the sea.
Camping Card Compulsory.
➲ On western outskirts towards the coast.
Jun-15 Sep 3HEC ⬛ ♦ ⌂ ⏚ ⏛ ✗ ⊙ ⬛ ∅ ⏛ ⊞ ⊞ lau ♦
₹S Prices: ⋔4.30 ♦2.50 ⬛2

Pansard ☎ 494668322 ▤ 494665612
e-mail: pansardcamping@aol.com
Beautiful, wide piece of land in a pine forest beside the beach.
➲ Turn off N98.
Apr-Sep 6HEC ⬛ ⠿⠿ ♦ ⌂ ⏚ ⏛ ✗ ⊙ ⬛ ∅ ⏛ ⏛ ₹ S ⊞ ⊞ ⊗
lau

Val Rose ☎ 494668136 ▤ 494665267
e-mail: camping-valrose@wanadoo.fr
In a rural setting at the foot of the Maures mountains, close
to a golf course. Well defined pitches and good modern
facilities.
➲ 4km NE on N98.
Mar-Oct 2.5HEC ⬛ ♦ ⌂ ⏚ ⏛ ✗ ⊙ ⬛ ∅ ⏛ ⏛ ₹ P ⊞ ⊞ lau

LUNEL HÉRAULT

Bon Port rte de la Petite Camargue
☎ 467711565 ▤ 467836027
In a pleasant wooded location at the gateway to the
Camargue.
➲ Access via D24.
Mar-Oct 5HEC ⬛ ♦ ⌂ ⏚ ✗ ⊙ ⬛ ∅ ⏛ ⏛
₹ P ⊞ ⊞ lau

Mas de l'Isle 85 chemin du Clapas
☎ 467832652 ▤ 467711388
A pleasant site between the Cévennes mountains and the
Mediterranean.
➲ 1.5km SE via D34 near junction with the D61.
Apr-Sep 4HEC ⬛ ♦ ⌂ ⏛ ✗ ⊙ ⬛ ⏛ ⏛ ₹ P ⊞ ⊞ lau
♦ ⏚ ∅ ₹R ⊞

MALLEMORT BOUCHES-DU-RHÔNE

Durance Luberon Domaine du Vergon
☎ 490591336 ▤ 490574462
e-mail: duranceluberon@aol.com
➲ 2.5 km on D23c, 200m from Canal.
21 Apr-29 Oct 4.4HEC ⬛ ♦ ⌂ ⏚ ⏛ ✗ ⊙ ⬛ ⏛ ₹ P ⊞ lau
♦ ⏚ ✗ ∅ ⏛ ₹R ⊞ Prices: ⋔22-26 pitch 23-38

MANDELIEU-LA-NAPOULE ALPES-MARITIMES

Cigales 505 av de la Mer
☎ 493492353 ▤ 493493045
e-mail: campingcigales@wanadoo.fr
A riverside site with well defined pitches, 800mtrs from the
sea.
➲ S on N7.
All year 2HEC ⬛ ♦ ⌂ ⏚ ✗ ⊙ ⬛ ⏛ ⏛ ₹ P ⊞ ⊞ lau ♦ ⏚ ∅ ⏛
₹S Prices: ⋔4.50 ♦4 ⬛10-20 ▲5-15

Plateau des Chasses r J-Monnet ☎ 493492593
Terraced land, on hill in a park.
➲ *Turn off N7 at Km 4.2 and continue uphill for 1.2km.*
Apr-Sep 4HEC ⊞ ♦ ↿ ❷ ⚓ ✕ ☉ ⊕ ⌂ ⊒ ᕯ P 🆔 ⊞ lau
➟ ⊒ ⌀ ↿RS

▶ **MANOSQUE** ALPES-DE-HAUTE-PROVENCE

Ubacs av de la Repasse ☎ 492722808 ▤ 492877529
A well equipped site in the Durance valley, close to the town
centre.
➲ *1.5 km W off D907, rte d'Apt.*
Apr-Sep 4HEC ⊞ ◊ ⊕ ↿ ✕ ☉ ⊕ ⌀ ᕯ ↿ P 🆔 lau ➟ ⊞
Prices: ₦2.74-3.05 pitch 3.81-3.96

▶ **MARSEILLAN-PLAGE** HÉRAULT

Charlemagne av du Camping ☎ 467219249
200m from the beach in quiet, wooded surroundings with
good sanitary and sporting facilities.
➲ *Access via N112 at Marseillan Plage.*
26 Mar-3 Oct 6.6HEC ⊞ ⁖⁖ ♦ ↿ ❷ ❢ ✕ ☉ ⊕ ⌀ ᕯ ⌂ ⊒
ᕯ PS 🆔 ⊞ lau

Languedoc-Camping 117 chemin du Pairollet
☎ 467219255 ▤ 467016375
A family site in wooded surroundings with direct access to
the beach.
➲ *On the coast road between the Mediterranean and the
Bassin de Thau.*
15 Mar-31 Oct 1.5HEC ⊞ ⁖⁖ ♦ ↿ ❢ ✕ ☉ ⊕ ᕯ ⊒
ᕯ S 🆔 ⊞ lau ➟ ❢ ⌀ ↿R

Plage 69 chemin du Pairollet ☎ 467219254 ▤ 467016357
A family site with direct access to a sandy beach.
15 Mar-Oct 1.3HEC ⁖⁖ ♦ ↿ ❢ ✕ ☉ ⊕ ⌀ ᕯ S 🆔 lau ➟ ⊒ ⊞
Prices: pitch 88-158 (incl 2 persons)

▶ **MAUREILLAS** PYRÉNÉES-ORIENTALES

Val Roma Park Les Thermas du Boulou ☎ 468831972
➲ *2.5km NE on N9.*
All year 3.5HEC ⊞ ♦ ↿ ❷ ❢ ✕ ☉ ⊕ ⌂ ⊒ ᕯ PR 🆔 ⊞ lau

▶ **MENTON** ALPES-MARITIMES

Fleur de Mai 67 rte du Val de Gorbio
☎ 493572236 ▤ 493572236
Terraced site in a peaceful situation by a stream in the heart
of the Côte-d'Azur.
➲ *Exit from D23 at the Parc de la Madone.*
15 Apr-15 Sep 2HEC ⊞ ♦ ↿ ☉ ⊕ 🆔 ⊞ lau ➟ ⊒ ❢ ✕ ⌀
ᕯ ᕯPS Prices: ₦3.50-4.50 ⇔2.50-3.50 ⊒12-13 ▲10-11

▶ **MÉOLANS-REVEL** ALPES-DE-HAUTE-PROVENCE

Domaine de Loisirs de l'Ubaye ☎ 492810196 ▤ 492819253
e-mail: info@loisirsdelubaye.com
A large terraced site in a delightful wooded valley. There is a
small lake and direct access to the river and good sporting
and recreational facilities.
➲ *7km NW of Barcelonnette.*
All year 10HEC ⊞ ♦ ↿ ❢ ✕ ☉ ⊕ ⌀ ⌂ ⊒ ᕯ LPR 🆔
lau Prices: ₦4.20 ⇔1.60 pitch 16.20 (incl 2 persons)

▶ **MIRABEL-ET-BLACONS** DRÔME

Gervanne Camping ☎ 475400020 ▤ 475400397
e-mail: info@gervanne-camping.com
A pleasant site with scattered shade and plenty of facilities
beside the River Drôme.
➲ *Access via D164 Crest-Die.*
Apr-Oct 3.8HEC ⊞ ♦ ↿ ❷ ❢ ✕ ☉ ⊕ ⌀ ᕯ ⌂ ᕯ LPR 🆔 ⊞
lau Prices: ₦3.20-4 ⇔2-2.20 ⊒2.60-3.50 ▲2.60-3.50

▶ **MONTBLANC** HÉRAULT

Rebau ☎ 467985078 ▤ 467986863
e-mail: lerebau@club-internet.fr
Divided into pitches and surrounded by vineyards.
➲ *From Pézenas follow N113; in La Bégude de Jordy turn off
main road and drive 2km on D18 towards Montblanc.*
Apr-Oct 3HEC ⊞ ♦ ↿ ❷ ❢ ✕ ☉ ⊕ ⌀ ⌂ ⊒ ᕯ P 🆔 ⊞ lau
Prices: pitch 16-24

▶ **MONTCLAR** AUDE

Au Pin d'Arnauteille Domaine d'Arnauteille
☎ 468268453 ▤ 468269110
e-mail: arnauteille@mnet.fr
In a natural wooded park with fine views of the surrounding
mountains.
➲ *2.2km SE via D43*
Apr-Sep 7HEC ⊞ ♦ ↿ ❷ ❢ ✕ ☉ ⊕ ⌀ ᕯ ⌂ ▲ ᕯ P 🆔 ⊞ lau
➟ ᕯR Prices: ₦4-5 ⇔2-3 ⊒3-5 ▲3-5

▶ **MONTÉLIMAR** DRÔME

Deux Saisons Chemin des Alexis ☎ 04 75018899
A well equipped site on the bank of River Roubion.
➲ *From town centre follow D540 across Pont de la Libération;
then first turning right into chemin des Alexis.*
Mar-Nov 1.5HEC ⊞ ⁖⁖ ⊕ ↿ ❢ ✕ ☉ ⊕ ⌀ ᕯ R 🆔 ⊞ lau
➟ ᕯ ᕯP

▶ **MONTPELLIER** HÉRAULT

Floréal rte de Palavas ☎ 467929305
On level ground surrounded by vineyards.
➲ *500m off Autoroute A9, exit Montpellier-Sud. From town
centre follow road for Palavas (D986).*
All year 1.6HEC ⊞ ♦ ↿ ❷ ❢ ☉ ⊕ ⌂ ⊒ 🆔 ⊞ lau ➟ ✕ ⌀ ᕯ
ᕯPRS

▶ **MONTPEZAT** ALPES-DE-HAUTE-PROVENCE

Coteau de la Marine ☎ 492775333 ▤ 492775934
A pleasant wooded site, providing easy access to the Verdon
Gorges. There are good facilities, especially for boating.
➲ *Access via D11 and D211.*
May-15 Sep 10HEC ◊ ♦ ↿ ❷ ❢ ✕ ☉ ⊕ ⌀ ᕯ ⌂ ⊒
ᕯ P 🆔 ⊞ lau

▶ **MONTRÉAL** ARDÈCHE

Moulinage rte des Défilés de Ruoms ☎ 475368620
Well-equipped family site with a variety of bungalows,
caravans and timber chalets. Close to the famous Gorges de
l'Ardèche.
Apr-Sep 3.5HEC ⊞ ⊕ ↿ ❢ ✕ ☉ ⊕ ⌂ ▲
ᕯ PR 🆔 ⊞ lau

▶ **MOURIÈS** BOUCHES-DU-RHÔNE

Devenson ☎ 490475201 ▤ 490476309
e-mail: devenson@libertysurf.fr
Terraced site amongst pine and olive trees in Provençal
countryside.
➲ *Turn off N113 at La Samatane and continue N towards
Mouriès. Site is in N part of village.*
Apr-15 Sep 3HEC ⊞ ♦ ↿ ❷ ⚓ ☉ ⊕ ⌀ ⊒ ᕯ P 🆔 lau ➟
❢ ✕ ᕯ Prices: ₦4.50 pitch 5

▶ **MOUSTIERS-STE-MARIE** ALPES-DE-HAUTE-PROVENCE

St-Jean rte de Riez ☎ 492746685 ▤ 492746685
e-mail: camping-st-jean@wanadoo.fr
Quiet and relaxing site located at the gateway to the Gorges
du Verdon, 5 minutes from Ste-Croix Lake.
➲ *Access D952.*
27 Apr-23 Sep 1.6HEC ⊞ ♦ ↿ ❷ ☉ ⊕ ⌀ ⌂ ᕯ R 🆔 ⊞ lau ➟
❢ ✕ ᕯ Prices: ₦3.50 pitch 3.80-25

Camping La Nautique

11100 Narbonne - Languedoc - France
Tel (+33) 04 68 90 48 19 Fax (+33) 04 68 90 73 39
e-mail : info@campinglanautique.com
www.campinglanautique.com

Every plot, 130 m², has a **PRIVATE   SANITARY**
(shower, WC and wash basin) with hot water and
10 amps electricity. Restaurant, bar and snackbar. A pool with waterslide and a paddling pool with
mushroom, children's club and many activities for
all. Tennis, mini-golf etc. Ideal for windsurfing.
Rental of fully equipped mobile-homes. Run by a
Dutch family.
English spoken.

Vieux Colombier Quartier St-Michel
☎ 492746189 ▦ 492746189
e-mail: v.colombier@web.ingenierie.com
A family site near the entrance to the Gorges du Verdon at an
altitude of 630 metres.
⮑ *0.8km S via D952 towards Castellane.*
Apr-Sep 2.7HEC ⸗ 🄰🄵▯🅇⊙🄰◔🄰🄰🄰🄴 lau ➧ 🄰🄰

) **MUY, LE** VAR

Cigales ☎ 494451208 ▦ 494458280
e-mail: contact@les-cigales.com
A family site set among Mediterranean vegetation with
excellent facilities and organised entertainment during the
high season.
⮑ *Exit 'Draguignan' off A8 onto N7. 0.8km to site. Well
signposted.*
Apr-Oct 13.5HEC ⸗ 🅰🄵▯🅇⊙🄰◔🄰 ⸉ P🄴 lau
Prices: ♠3-4.50 ♠2-3 pitch 3-8

Sellig 41 chemin des Valettes ☎ 494451171
A peaceful family site in a wooded location.
⮑ *1.5km W on N7.*
15 Feb-Oct 1.6HEC ⸗ 🅰🄵▯🅇⊙🄰◔🄰🄰
⸉ P🄴 lau

) **NANS-LES-PINS** VAR

Ste-Baume ☎ 494789268
A pleasant, landscaped site in the heart of the local lavender
region. There are modern sanitary installations and varied
recreational facilities.
⮑ *0.9km N via D80*
May-6 Sep 7HEC ◔🅰🄵▯🅇⊙🄰◔🄰🄰🄰
⸉ P🄴 lau

) **NAPOULE, LA** ALPES-MARITIMES

Azur-Vacances bd du Bon Puits
☎ 493499216 ▦ 493499112
Site with many long terraces, on edge of mountain slope in
mixed woodland.
⮑ *Turn inland 200m after fork at railway station and
continue 600m.*
Apr-Sep 6HEC ⸗ 🅰🄵▯🅇⊙🄰◔🄰🄴 lau ➧ ⸉RS

) **NARBONNE** AUDE

Nautique La Nautique ☎ 468904819 ▦ 468907339
e-mail: info@campinglanautique.com
Situated on the salt water lake 'Étang de Bages et de Sigean',
this site is particularly well appointed, each pitch having its
own washing and toilet facilities. There are good recreational
facilities and advance booking is recommended.
⮑ *Access via Narbonne Sud exit on A9.*
Mar-17Nov 16HEC ⸗ ⋮⋮⋮ 🅰🄵▯🅇⊙🄰◔🄰🄰🄰 ⸉ P
🄴 lau Prices: pitch 14.15-24.50 (incl 2 persons)

) At **NARBONNE-PLAGE**(15km E D168)

CM de la Côte des Roses ☎ 468498365 ▦ 468494044
A modern site nestling at the foot of the Massif of the Calpe
close to the sea.
⮑ *3 km SW.*
25 May-01 Sep 16HEC ⸗ 🅰🄵▯🅇⊙🄰◔🄰🄴 lau ➧ 🄰
⸉S Prices: ♠4-5 ♠1.50-2 pitch 11-18 (incl 2 persons)

CM Falaise av des Vacances ☎ 468498077 ▦ 468494044
On level ground at the foot of the Massif of the Calpe with
good modern facilities.
⮑ *W of Narbonne Plage, 400m from beach.*
01 Apr-22 Sep 8HEC ⸗ 🅰🄵▯🅇⊙🄰◔🄰🄴 lau ➧ ⸉S

) **NÉBIAS** AUDE

Fontaulié-Sud ☎ 468201762
In a beautiful setting in the heart of the Cathare region.
⮑ *0.6km S via D117.*
01 May-30 Sep 01 Oct-30 Apr 4HEC ⸗ 🅰🄵▯🅇⊙🄰
◔🄰🄰🄰⸉P🄴 lau ➧ 🅇 Prices: ♠3.40 pitch 5.20

) **NÎMES** GARD

Domaine de la Bastide Rte de Generac
☎ 466380921 ▦ 466380921
In a rural setting with excellent facilities. Shop open summer
only.
⮑ *5km S of town centre on D13. Access via A9 exit 'Nîmes-
Ouest'.*
All year 5HEC ⸗ ◔🅰🄵▯🅇⊙🄰◔🄰🄰🄴 lau ➧
⸉L Prices: ♠4.05 ♠2.35 pitch 7.17-20.12 (incl 4 persons)

) **NIOZELLES** ALPES-DE-HAUTE-PROVENCE

Moulin de Ventre ☎ 492786331 ▦ 492798692
In a rural setting with good facilities.
⮑ *5km E via N100*
25 Mar-Sep 2.8HEC ⸗ 🅰🄵▯🅇⊙🄰◔🄰🅰
⸉ P🄴 lau

) **NYONS** DRÔME

CM Promenade de la Digue ☎ 475262239
Situated on bank of river on level meadow with fruit trees.
Sports ground and golf course in town.
15 Mar-7 Nov 1.6HEC ⸗ 🅰🄵⊙🄰◔🄰🄴 lau ➧ 🅇▯🅇◔🄰
⸉PR

Sagittaire Vinsobres ☎ 475270000 ▦ 475270039
e-mail: camping.sagittaire@wanadoo.fr
Well-kept site divided by hedges in a beautiful Alpine setting.
⮑ *S of town on D538 road to Vaison-la-Romaine.*
All year 14HEC ⸗ 🅰🄵▯🅇⊙🄰◔🄰
⸉ LP🄴 lau ➧ ⸉R

OLLIÈRES-SUR-EYRIEUX, LES ARDÈCHE

🏠Domaine des Plantas ☎ 475662153 ▤ 475662365
e-mail: plantas.ardeche@wanadoo.fr
Games room, discotheque and other leisure activities.
May-20 Sep 7HEC ▦ ♨ ♠ ♠ ⿳ ⵊ ⵏ ✕ ☉ ⬛ ⬢ ⵥ ⵣ ⿳ PR ⬚
⊞ lau

ORANGE VAUCLUSE

Jonquier 1321 r Alexis-Carrel ☎ 0490344948 ▤ 490348654
e-mail: joel.denis@wailea9.com
➲ On the NW outskirts
Apr-Sep 5HEC ▦ ⵖ ♠ ⵊ ✕ ☉ ⬛ ⬢ ⿳ ⵥ P ⬚ ⊞ lau ♦
ⵣR Prices: pitch 16-22.50 (incl 2 persons)

ORGON BOUCHES-DU-RHÔNE

Vallée Heureuse ☎ 490730278 ▤ 490730298
A quiet transit site in a rocky valley.
➲ 1.5km from the village on the N7. Access is past a non-
working quarry.
11 Jun-Aug 8HEC ♨ ♠ ♠ ⵊ ✕ ☉ ⬛ ⬢ ⵥ P ⬚ lau ♦ ⵊ ✕ ⵍ
ⵣL ⊞

PALAVAS-LES-FLOTS HÉRAULT

Roquilles 267 bis av St-Maurice ☎ 467680347
An attractive site 50m from the sea.
15 Apr-25 Sep 15HEC ▦ ⵜⵜ ⵗ ⵖ ♠ ⵊ ⵏ ✕ ☉ ⬛ ⬢ ⬛ ⬢
ⵥ P ⬚ ⊞ ⵞ lau ♦ ✕ ⵍⵣS

PEYREMALE-SUR-CÈZE GARD

Drouilhèdes ☎ 466250480 ▤ 0466251095
In a beautiful location beside the River Cèze surrounded by
pine and chestnut trees.
➲ Access via A6 and D17.
Mar-Sep 2HEC ▦ ♠ ♠ ⵊ ⵏ ✕ ☉ ⬛ ⬢ ⵥ R ⬚ ⊞ lau ♦ ⵎ
Prices: pitch 10-14.50 (incl 2 persons)

PEYRUIS ALPES-DE-HAUTE-PROVENCE

Cigales chemin de la Digue du Bevon
☎ 492681604 ▤ 492681604
A modern site in the heart of the Val de Durance.
➲ Access via A51 and N96.
Apr-Sep ▦ ♠ ⵏ ☉ ⬛ ⵎ ⬚ lau ♦ ⵊ ⵏ ✕ ⵣP ⊞
Prices: pitch 22

PONT-D'HÉRAULT GARD

Magnanarelles Le Rey ☎ 467824013 ▤ 467825061
In a pleasant mountain setting with well defined pitches.
➲ 0.3km W via D999, beside the river.
All year 2HEC ▦ ♠ ♠ ⵏ ☉ ⬛ ⬢ ⬛ ⵥ PR ⬚ ⊞ lau
Prices: ⵏ3.45-3.95 ⬛5.02-5.95 ⵄ17.90

PONT-DU-GARD GARD

International des Gorges du Gardon rte de Uzès
☎ 466228181 ▤ 466229012
e-mail: camping-international@wanadoo.fr
In a peaceful, wooded location beside the River Gardon.
➲ 1km from aqueduct on D981 Uzès road.
15 Mar-15 Oct 4.2HEC ▦ ⵜⵜ ♠ ⵊ ⵏ ✕ ☉ ⬛ ⬢ ⬛ ⬢ ⵥ
PR ⬚ ⊞ lau

PORTIRAGNES-PLAGE HÉRAULT

Mimosas ☎ 467909292 ▤ 467908539
A well equipped family site located in a leisure park on the
banks of the Canal du Midi, 1.3km from the sea.
➲ Leave A9 at exit Béziers Est and continue towards coast via
N112 and D37.
May-15 Sep 7HEC ▦ ⵖ ⵊ ✕ ☉ ⬛ ⬢ ⬛ ⬢ ⵄ ⵥ PR
⬚ ⊞ lau ♦ ⵣS

PRIVAS, CLOSE TO THE RHÔNE VALLEY: A STOPOVER
PRIVAS, IN THE CENTRE OF THE ARDÈCHE: SPEND YOUR
HOLIDAY IN PRIVAS AND **DISCOVER THE ARDÈCHE**

CAMPING MUNICIPAL ESPACE OUVÈZE
★★★ F-07000 PRIVAS

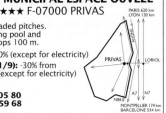

166 marked, shaded pitches.
Heated swimming pool and
tennis 50 m, shops 100 m.
Off season: -30% (except for electricity)
Season (15/6-1/9): -30% from
the 15th night (except for electricity)
RESERVATIONS:
Tel. 04 75 64 05 80
Fax: 04 75 64 59 68

Sablons rte de Portiragnes ☎ 467909055 ▤ 467908291
e-mail: les.sablons@wanadoo.fr
Large site subdivided into fields by fences. Beside beach.
Night club and discothèque.
➲ 0.5km N on D37.
Apr-Sep 15HEC ▦ ⵜⵜⵜ ♠ ⵊ ⵏ ✕ ☉ ⬛ ⬢ ⵎ ⬛ ⬢ ⵥ PS ⬚
⊞ lau

PRADET, LE VAR

Mauvallon chemin de la Gavaresse ☎ 494213173
A well-kept site amidst young trees divided into pitches.
➲ Turn off the N559 in Le Pradet and take the D86 for 2.5km
towards sea.
15 Jun-15 Sep 1.2HEC ▦ ♠ ⵏ ☉ ⬛ ⬢ ⬚ ⊞ lau
♦ ⵊ ⵏ ✕ ⵣS

Pin de Galle Quartier San Peyre ☎ 494212606
In a wooded location 200mtrs from the beach.
➲ On the Toulon road on the outskirts of Pradet.
All year 1HEC ▦ ♠ ⵊ ⵊ ⵏ ✕ ☉ ⬛ ⵎ ⬛ ⬢ ⵄ ⬚ ⊞ lau
♦ ⵏ ⵣS

PRAMOUSQUIER VAR

Pramousquier ☎ 494058395
A terraced site set in a wooded park 400mtrs from a fine
sandy beach. Good recreational facilities.
➲ 2km E via D559
May-Sep 3HEC ⵖ ♠ ⵊ ⵏ ✕ ☉ ⬛ ⬢ ⬛ ⬚ ⊞ lau ♦ ⵣS

PRIVAS ARDÈCHE

CM Espace Ouvèze rte de Montélimar
☎ 475640580 ▤ 475645968
e-mail: marie.privas.@marie-privas.fr
A comfortable municipal site with good facilities in the heart
of the Ardèche region.
Etr-15 Oct 3.5HEC ▦ ♠ ⵏ ☉ ⬛ ⬚ lau ♦ ⵊ ⵏ ✕ ⵏ ⵄ ⵥP ⊞
Prices: ⵏ2.70-3.10 pitch 7.90-10.40 (incl 2 persons)

PUGET-SUR-ARGENS VAR

Aubrèdes 408 chemin des Aubrhdes
☎ 494455146 ▤ 494452892
e-mail: campingaubredes@wanadoo.fr
Situated on undulating meadowland surrounded by pine
trees with good, modern facilities.
➲ Leave autoroute A8 at exit Puget-sur-Argens, then site is
850m. If approaching from Fréjus on N7 turn left before Puget,
cross motorway and follow road towards Lagourin.
31 Mar-25 Sep 3.8HEC ▦ ♠ ⵊ ⵏ ✕ ☉ ⬛ ⬢ ⵎ ⬛ ⵥ P ⬚
⊞ lau Prices: ⵏ3-4.30 ⬛2.19-3.13 ⬛2.19-3.13
pitch 2.19-3.13

Bastiane chemin des Suvières ☎ 494455131 ▤ 494815055
e-mail: bastiane@club-internet.fr
Hilly site divided into numbered pitches in pine and oak wood. Individual washing cubicles. Meals to take away. Separate car park for arrivals after 23.00hrs.
➲ *Access from A8.*
09 Mar-26 Oct 3.1HEC ▥ ⋮⋮⋮ ♠ ♠ ⅃ ⅄ ✕ ⊙ ⊖ ⊞ ₩ ⋜ P
⌂ ⊞ lau ➧ ♨ Prices: ₦6 ⊛5 ▲5 pitch 10-15 (incl 4 persons)

Parc St-James Oasis rte de la Bouverie
☎ 494454464 ▤ 494454499
27 Mar-25 Sep 42HEC ▥ ⅄ ♠ ♨ ⅃ ✕ ⊙ ⊖ ⊞ ⋜ P

〉 **QUILLAN** AUDE

Sapinette 21r René Delpech ☎ 0468201352 ▤ 0468202780
A comfortable site in a forest of fir trees with pitches separated by hedges.
➲ *Access W via D79, rte de Ginoles.*
Apr-Oct 1.8HEC ▥ ⅄ ♠ ⊙ ⊖ ⊞ ⊞ lau ➧ ♨ ⅄ ✕ ⊘ ♨
⋜LPRS

〉 **RACOU, LE** PYRÉNÉES-ORIENTALES

Bois de Valmarie ☎ Central Res 468810461 ▤ 468816974 (Central Res)
e-mail: camping.la.sirene@wanadoo.fr
A family site with plentiful recreational facilities.
➲ *Leave N114 at at Perpignan Sud exit.*
23 Mar-28 Sep 3.5HEC ▥ ⅄ ♠ ♨ ⅃ ✕ ⊙ ⊖ ⊞ ⋜ PS ⌂ lau

〉 **RAMATUELLE** VAR

Croix du Sud rte des Plages ☎ 494798084
Terraced site in beautiful pine forest divided into pitches with view of sea. Minimum stay 3 days.
➲ *3km NE of town, 80m N of D93.*
Apr-Oct 2.5HEC ▥ ♠ ♠ ♨ ⅃ ✕ ⊙ ⊖ ♨ ⊘ ⊞ ⌂ ⊞ P ⊞ lau
➧ ⋜S

Tournels rte de Camarat
☎ 494559090 ▤ 494559099
Lovely views to Pampelonne Bay from part of this site. 1km to beach.
➲ *Access from D93 Croix-Valmer/St-Tropez road, follow the signs to 'Cap Camarat'.*
Closed 10 Jan-10 Feb 20HEC ▥ ♠ ♠ ⅃ ✕ ⊙ ⊖ ♨ ⊘ ⊞ ⌂ ⊞
See advertisement in colour section
lau ➧ ♨ ⋜S

〉 **REMOULINS** GARD

Soubeyranne rte de Beaucaire
☎ 466370321 ▤ 466371465
e-mail: soubeyranne@wanadoo.fr
In a picturesque location close to the River Gard with good, modern facilities.
➲ *S on D986.*
6 Apr-16 Sep 6HEC ▥ ⋮⋮⋮ ♠ ♠ ♨ ⅃ ✕ ⊙ ⊖ ♨ ⊘ ⊞ ⊞
⋜ P ⌂ ⊞ lau ➧ ⋜R Prices: pitch 12-15 (incl 2 persons)

Sousta av du Pont-du-Gard
☎ 466371280 ▤ 466372369
e-mail: info@lasousta.fr
Picturesque forest site a short distance from the Pont du Gard.
➲ *2km NW.*
Mar-Oct 11 Dec-01 Feb 14HEC ⋮⋮⋮ ♠ ♠ ♨ ⅃ ✕ ⊙ ⊖ ♨ ⊘
⊞ ⊞ ⋜ PR ⌂ ⊞ lau ➧ ⋜S Prices: pitch 10.50-18 (incl 2 persons)

〉 **REVENS** GARD

Lou Triadou Le Bourg ☎ 467827358
e-mail: lou.triadou@infonie.fr
A well equipped site in the heart of the Causse Noir.
➲ *Access via D159/D151.*
27 Jun-10 Sep 0.8HEC ▥ ⅊ ♠ ♠ ⅃ ✕ ⊙ ⊖ ♨ ⊘ ⊞ ⊞ ▲ ⌂ ⊞
lau Prices: ₦3 pitch 4 (incl 2 persons)

〉 **RIA** PYRÉNÉES-ORIENTALES

Bellevue 8 r Bellevue ☎ 0468964896
Beautifully situated terraced site. Very well kept. Beside former vineyard.
➲ *2km S on N116, take road to Sirach, turn right and continue 600m up drive which is difficult for caravans.*
Apr-Sep 2.2HEC ♠ ♠ ♨ ⅃ ⊙ ⊖ ♨ ⊘ ♨ ⊞ ⊞ lau ➧ ♨ ✕ ♨
⋜R Prices: ₦2.50 pitch 3.05

〉 **ROQUEBRUNE-SUR-ARGENS** VAR

Domaine de la Bergerie Vallée du Fournel
☎ 494829011 ▤ 498114546
e-mail: info@domainelabergerie.com
A large, well run family site set in pleasant Provençal countryside with fine recreational facilities.
➲ *Access via A8 exit Le Muy N7 and D7.*
Apr-Sep 60HEC ▥ ⅄ ♠ ♨ ⅃ ✕ ⊙ ⊖ ♨ ⊘ ♨ ⊞ ♨ ⋜ P ⊞ ⊞
lau ➧ ⋜L

Domaine J J Bousquet rte de la Bouverie
☎ 494454251 ▤ 494816106
In a quiet, wooded location with good, modern facilities.
➲ *Access via N7 towards Le Muy.*
All year 5HEC ▥ ⅄ ♠ ♨ ⅃ ✕ ⊙ ⊖ ♨ ⊘ ♨ ⊞ ⋜ P ⊞ ⊞ lau

Lei Suves Quartier du Blavet ☎ 494454395 ▤ 494816313
e-mail: camping.lei.suves@wanadoo.fr
In a picturesque forested area with good recreational facilities.
➲ *4km N via N7.*
30 Mar-15 Oct 7.4HEC ▥ ♠ ♠ ♨ ⅃ ✕ ⊙ ⊖ ♨ ⊘ ♨ ⊞ ♨ ⋜ P
⌂ ⊞ lau

Moulin des Iscles Quartier La Valette
☎ 494457074 ▤ 494454609
In a picturesque location beside the River Argens with good, modern facilities.
➲ *Access via D7 towards St-Aygulf.*
Apr-Sep 1.3HEC ▥ ♠ ♠ ♨ ⅃ ✕ ⊙ ⊖ ♨ ⊘ ♨ ⊞ ♨ ⋜ R ⊞ ⊞
lau Prices: ₦3.20 pitch 17.60 (incl 3 persons)

Pêcheurs ☎ 494457125 ▤ 494816513
e-mail: iinfo@camping-les-pecheurs.com
A pleasant site with direct access to the river in a wooded location at the foot of the Roquebrune crag.
➲ *0.5km NW via D7, near the lake*
23 Mar-28 Sep 4HEC ▥ ⋮⋮⋮ ♠ ♠ ♨ ⅃ ✕ ⊙ ⊖ ♨ ⊘ ♨ ⋜ LPR
⌂ ⊞ lau Prices: ₦3.40-5.50 pitch 15-28.50 (incl 2 persons)

〉 **ROQUE-D'ANTHÉRON, LA** BOUCHES-DU-RHÔNE

Domaine les Iscles ☎ 442504425 ▤ 442505629
e-mail: campoclub@wanadoo.com
➲ *1.8km N via D67c.*
Mar-1 Oct 10HEC ▥ ⅄ ♠ ♨ ⅃ ✕ ⊙ ⊖ ♨ ⊘ ♨ ⊞ ⋜ LP ⊞ ⊞
lau Prices: ₦3.40-4.90 pitch 3.80-11.20

Silvacane av de la Libération ☎ 442504054 ▤ 442504375
e-mail: campoclub@wanadoo.fr
Level gravelled ground with 100 sq m pitches. Heated common room with TV. Water sports centre and stables nearby. Site in wood on slopes of hill.
15 Mar-11 Oct 6HEC ▥ ⅊ ♠ ♠ ♨ ⅃ ✕ ⊙ ⊖ ♨ ⊘ ♨ ⊞ ♨ ⋜ PR
⌂ ⊞ lau ➧ ♨ ⋜L

▶ **ROQUETTE-SUR-SIAGNE, LA** ALPES-MARITIMES

Panoramic 1630 av de la République, Quartier St-Jean
☎ 492190777 🖩 0492190777
e-mail: campingpanoramic@wanadoo.fr
A well equipped, modern site in a wooded location affording
magnificent views of the surrounding hills.
➲ *N of village off D9.*
All year 1HEC ⭐ ♣ ♠ ✕ ☉ ❤ ⌀ ☵ 🏠 ❤ ▲ ⊀ P ⊞ ⊞ lau
➡ ☎ ⊀R

St-Louis av de la République ☎ 492192313 🖩 492192314
Well equipped site in a pleasant rural setting, backed by hills.
➲ *On D9, 800m from Pégomas towards La Bocca.*
Apr-1 Oct 5HEC ⭐ ♣ ♠ ☉ ❤ 🏠 ⊀ P ⊞ P ⊞ lau ➡ ☎ ❤ ✕
⌀ ☵ ⊀R ⊞

▶ **RUOMS** ARDÈCHE

🏠Bastide ☎ 475396472 🖩 475397328
e-mail: camping.bastide@wanadoo.fr
Well equipped family site in a pleasant wooded location.
➲ *4km SW on the banks of the Ardèche.*
20 Mar-14 Sep 7HEC ⭐ ♣ ♠ ☎ ✕ ☉ ❤ ⌀ ☵ 🏠 ❤ ▲ ⊀
PR ⊞ ⊞ lau

Ternis rte de Lagorce ☎ 475939315 🖩 475939090
e-mail: campternis@aol.com
A terraced site in a delightful setting in the southern Ardèche
region, with good recreational facilities. Separate car park for
arrivals between 22.00 and 08.00hrs.
➲ *Access via D559 towards Lagorce.*
Etr-20 Sep 6HEC ⭐ ♣ ♠ ☎ ✕ ☉ ❤ ⌀ ☵ 🏠 ❤ ⊀ P ⊞ P
⊞ lau ➡ ⊀R

At **SAMPZON**(6km S)

Aloha-Plage ☎ 475396762 🖩 475891026
In a fine situation beside the River Ardèche, midway between
Ruoms and Vallon-Pont-d'Arc. The site now has two private
swimming pools.
➲ *50m from the river.*
Apr-Sep 3HEC ⭐ ♣ ♠ ✕ ☉ ❤ ⌀ ☵ 🏠 ❤ ⊀ PR ⊞ ⊞ lau
➡ ☎

Soleil Vivarais ☎ 475396756 🖩 475396469
e-mail: camping.soleil.vivarais@wanadoo.fr
An exceptionally well appointed, terraced site surrounded by
the imposing scenery of the Ardèche Gorge. An excellent
canoeing centre with opportunities for all kinds of outdoor/
water activities and regular organised entertainment.
➲ *From Vallon drive towards Ruoms on D579 for 5km and
cross bridge over River Ardèche.*
23Mar-20Sep 12HEC ⭐ ♣ ♠ ☎ ✕ ☉ ❤ ⌀ ☵ 🏠 ❤ ▲ ⊀ PR
⊞ ⊞ lau ➡ ⊀S **Prices:** pitch 19-34

▶ **SAILLAGOUSE** PYRÉNÉES-ORIENTALES

Cerdan 11 r d'Estuar ☎ 468047046 🖩 468040526
e-mail: lecerdan@lecerdan.com
Picturesque setting in meadow with some terraces. Hot meals
served during peak season.
➲ *Access via N116.*
Closed Oct 0.8HEC ⭐ ♣ ♠ ❤ ✕ ☉ ❤ ⌀ ☵ 🏠 ⊞ P lau ➡ ☎ ✕
⊀PR

▶ **ST-ALBAN-AURIOLLES** ARDÈCHE

Ranc Davaine ☎ 475396055 🖩 475393850
e-mail: camping.ranc.davaine@wanadoo.fr
Well equipped, mainly level site with direct access to the
River Chassezac and a variety of entertainment facilities.
➲ *2.3km SW via D58.*
Apr-17 Sep 11HEC ⭐ ⠿ ♣ ♠ ☎ ✕ ☉ ❤ ⌀ 🏠 ❤ ⊀ PR
⊞ ⊞ lau

Ideally located in the heart of the Côte d'Azur,
exceptional site with friendly atmosphere on the
banks of the Argens river with direct access to the
fine sandy beaches (there is one for naturist). Bar,
restaurant, take away food, swimming-pool which
is heated in cool weather.
Entertainment: discotheque, giant barbecues,
cabarets, concerts, excursions and a miniclub for
children.
Mobile home and caravans available for hire.

Camping Caravanning Le Pont d'Argens
RN 98 Fréjus Saint Aygulf – FRANCE
Tél: 04 94 51 14 97 – Fax: 04 94 51 29 44

▶ **ST-AMBROIX** GARD

Beau-Rivage Le Moulinet ☎ 466241017 🖩 466242137
e-mail: mare@camping-beau-rivage.fr
In a fine location between the sea and the Cevennes
mountains beside the River Cèze.
➲ *3.5km SE on D37.*
Apr-Sep 3.5HEC ⭐ ♣ ☉ ❤ ⌀ ⊀ R ⊞ ⊞ lau ➡ ☎ ❤
Prices: ♠4.20 pitch 4.20

Clos ☎ 466241008 🖩 466602562
A quiet site in a pleasant setting beside the River Cèze with
good, modern facilities.
➲ *Access to the right of the church square.*
Apr-Oct 1.8HEC ⭐ ♣ ♠ ❤ ✕ ☉ ❤ ⌀ 🏠 ❤ ⊀ PR ⊞ ⊞
lau ➡ ☎

▶ **ST-ANDIOL** BOUCHES-DU-RHÔNE

St-Andiol ☎ 490950113
Well situated on the edge of the village. Divided into pitches.
➲ *Access via A7.*
All year 1HEC ⭐ ♣ ♠ ☎ ☉ ❤ ⊀ P ⊞ lau ➡ ☎ ✕

▶ **ST-AYGULF** VAR

Étoile d'Argens chemin des Étangs
☎ 494810141 🖩 494812145
e-mail: letoiledargent@wanadoo.fr
In pleasant wooded surroundings 2km from the beach which
can be reached by a private boat service.
➲ *5km NW, beside the River Argens.*
Apr-Sep 11HEC ⭐ ♣ ♠ ☎ ✕ ☉ ❤ ⌀ ☵ 🏠 ❤ ⊀ PR ⊞ ⊞ lau

Paradis des Campeurs La Gaillarde Plage
☎ 494969355 🖩 494496299
A quiet family site in a picturesque location with direct
access to the beach.
➲ *2.5km towards Gaillarde-Plage between St-Aygulf and Ste-
Maxime.*
19 Mar-15 Oct 3.7HEC ⭐ ♣ ♠ ☎ ✕ ☉ ❤ ⌀ ⊀ S ⊞ ⊞
lau

Pont d'Argens RN98 ☎ 494511497 🖩 494512944
A pleasant site with good facilities beside the river.
Apr-15 Oct 7HEC ⭐ ♣ ♠ ☎ ✕ ☉ ❤ ⌀ ☵ 🏠 ❤ ⊀ PRS ⊞
⊞ lau

St-Aygulf 270 av Salvarelli
☎ 494176249 🖩 494810316
e-mail: info@camping-cote-azur.com
A well equipped family site in wooded surroundings with
direct access to the beach.
➲ *Inland from N98 at Km881.3 N of town. Entrance on right
of av Salvarelli.*
Apr-Oct 22HEC ⭐ ⠿ ♣ ♠ ☎ ✕ ☉ ❤ ⌀ ☵ 🏠 ⊀ LS ⊞
⊞ lau

⟩ **St-Chamas** Bouches-du-Rhône

Canet Plage ☎ 490509689 ▒ 490509689
e-mail: canet-plage@wanadoo.fr
A well equipped site beside the Étang de Berre with a wide range of recreational facilities.
➲ *On D10, S of Salon-de-Provence towards La Fare les Oliviers.*
All year 3.7HEC ⬙ ⌂ ♠ ⌐ ⚍ ♀ ✕ ⊙ ☺ ⌷ ⇌ ⊞ ⊡ ⟍ LP ☎ ⊞ lau
✦ ∅ **Prices:** ⋔3.25 ⇐2.29 pitch 3.20

⟩ **St-Cyprien** Pyrénées-Orientales

Roussillon chemin de la Mer
☎ 468216605 ▒ 0468210645
e-mail: chodotel@wanadoo.fr
Close to the Spanish border, flanked on one side by the Mediterranean sea and on the other by the Pyrenees.
15 Apr-Sep 3HEC ⬕ ⚞ ⌐ ⚍ ♀ ✕ ⊙ ☺ ⌷ ⚏ ⇌ ⊞ ⟍ P ☎
⊞ lau ✦ ✕ ⟍S **Prices:** pitch 13.75-21.35 (incl 2 persons)

⟩ **St-Jean-le-Centenier** Ardèche

Arches Patrick Gaschet ☎ 475367545 ▒ 475367545
e-mail: pgaschet@club-internet.fr
A family site in a wooded location with direct access to the river.
➲ *A7 exit Montélimar Nord then follow N102 to exit Mirabel and take D458 for 500mtrs to site on right.*
May-Sep 1.8HEC ⬕ ⌂ ⌐ ⚍ ♀ ✕ ⊙ ☺ ⇌ ⊡ ⟍ R ☎ lau
✦ ⚍ ✕ ∅ ⇌

⟩ **St-Jean-Pla-de-Corts** Pyrénées-Orientales

Casteillets ☎ 468832683 ▒ 468833967
e-mail: casteillets@aol.com
A family site situated between the sea and the mountains close to the River Tech.
➲ *Access via A9 exit Le Boulu.*
All year 5HEC ⬕ ♠ ⌐ ⚍ ♀ ✕ ⊙ ☺ ⌷ ⇌ ⊡ Å ⟍ P ☎ ⊞ lau ✦
∅ ⟍LR **Prices:** ⋔2.50-4 ⇐2 pitch 9-14 (incl 2 persons)

Deux Rivières rte de Maureillas
☎ 468832320 ▒ 468830794
Situated on the banks of the River Tech with large roomy pitches.
➲ *0.5km SE via D13, beside the River Tech*
Apr-15 Oct 11HEC ⬕ ♠ ⌐ ⚍ ♀ ✕ ⊙ ☺ ⌷ ⚏ ⇌ ⊡ ⟍ PR ☎
lau ✦ ⟍L ⊞

⟩ **St-Julien-de-la-Nef** Gard

Isis en Cevennes Domaine de St-Julien
☎ 467738028 ▒ 467738848
e-mail: info@isisencevennes.com
In wooded surroundings with direct access to the River Hérault. Plenty of sporting facilities.
➲ *5km from Ganges towards Le Vigan.*
15 Mar-Oct 4HEC ⬕ ♠ ⌐ ⚍ ♀ ✕ ⊙ ☺ ⇌ ⊡ ⇌
⟍ PR ☎ ⊞ lau

⟩ **St-Laurent-du-Var** Alpes-Maritimes

Magali 1814 rte de la Baronne
☎ 0033 493315700 ▒ 492120133
A family site on level meadowland, surrounded by trees and bushes at the foot of the southern Alps.
➲ *Leave A8 at 'St-Laurent-du-Var' exit, cross industrial zone turn left for 100m, then right and continue for 2km.*
Feb-Oct 1.2HEC ⬕ ⌂ ⌐ ⚍ ✕ ⊙ ☺ ⌷ ⇌ ⇌
⟍ P ☎ ⊞ lau ✦ ♀ ✕

⟩ **St-Laurent-du-Verdon** Alpes-de-Haute-Provence

Farigoulette Lac de St Laurent ☎ 492744162
➲ *1.5km NE near Verdon*
15 May-Sep 14HEC ⬙ ♠ ⌐ ⚍ ♀ ✕ ⊙ ☺ ∅ ⌷ ⇌ ⇌
⟍ LP ☎ ⊞ lau **Prices:** ⋔5.35 ⇐1.55 Å1.55-1.55 pitch 12-16 (incl 2 persons)

⟩ **St-Martin-de-Londres** Hérault

Pic St-Loup rte du Pic St-Loup ☎ 467550053
➲ *E via D122*
Apr-Sep 3HEC ⬕ ⬙ ⌂ ♠ ⌐ ⚍ ♀ ✕ ⊙ ☺ ⌷ ∅ ⇌ ⇌
⟍ P ☎ lau ✦ ⊞

⟩ **St-Maximin-la-Ste-Baume** Var

Provençal rte de Mazaugues ☎ 494781697 ▒ 494780021
e-mail: camping.provencal@wanadoo.fr
A family site in wooded surroundings with plenty of recreational facilties. Bar, café and swimming pool are open Jul-Aug only.
➲ *2.5km S via D64.*
All year 5HEC ⬕ ♠ ⌐ ⚍ ♀ ✕ ⊙ ☺ ∅ ⌷ ⇌
⟍ P ☎ ⊞ lau ✦ ⊞

⟩ **St-Paul-en-Forêt** Var

Parc ☎ 494761535 ▒ 494847184
e-mail: campingleparc@wanadoo.fr
Quiet, fairly isolated site surrounded by woodland.
➲ *3km N on D4.*
Apr-Oct 5HEC ⬕ ♠ ⌐ ⚍ ♀ ✕ ⊙ ☺ ∅ ⌷ ⇌
⟍ P ☎ ⊞ ⊞ lau ✦ ⟍L

⟩ **St-Paul-les-Romans** Drôme

CM de Romans Les Chasses ☎ 475723527
Shady pitches separated by hedges.
May-Sep 1HEC ⬕ ♠ ⌐ ⊙ ☺ ⌷ ⊞ ⊞ lau ✦ ⚍ ✕ ∅ ⇌ ⟍P

⟩ **St-Raphaël** Var

Douce Quiétude bd J-Baudino ☎ 494443000 ▒ 494443030
e-mail: info@douce_quietude.com
Meadowland site in quiet location in attractively hilly countryside with good facilities.
➲ *Approach from Agay Plage past Esterel Camping in direction of Valescure.*
Apr-Sep 10HEC ⬕ ♠ ⌐ ⚍ ♀ ✕ ⊙ ☺ ∅ ⌷ ⇌
⟍ P ☎ ⊞ ⊞ lau

Dramont ☎ 494820768 ▒ 494827530
Located in a pine forest with direct access to the beach and good modern facilities.
➲ *Access via N98 at St-Raphaël. Between Boulouris and Agay.*
15 Mar-15 Oct 6.5HEC ⬕ ♠ ⌐ ⚍ ♀ ✕ ⊙ ☺ ∅ ⌷ ⇌
⟍ S ☎ ⊞ lau

Royal Camp Long ☎ 494820020
Level site divided by walls and hedges. Ideal bathing for children. Bar and hall next to site.
➲ *On N98 towards Cannes.*
20 Jan-30 Oct 0.6HEC ⬕ ⬙ ♠ ⌐ ⚍ ♀ ✕ ⊙ ☺ ∅ ⌷ ⇌
⟍ S ☎ lau ✦ ⚍ ⊞

⟩ **St-Remèze** Ardèche

Domaine de Briange rte de Gras ☎ 475041443
e-mail: briange07@aol.com
In a wooded location close to the Gorges de l'Ardèche.
➲ *1.5km NE.*
May-Sep 4HEC ⬕ ♠ ⌐ ⚍ ♀ ✕ ⊙ ☺ ⌷ ⇌ Å ⟍ P ☎ ⊞ lau
✦ ∅ ⇌ **Prices:** ⋔3-3.50 pitch 10-13 (incl 2 persons)

ST-RÉMY-DE-PROVENCE BOUCHES-DU-RHÔNE

Pégomas ☎ 490920121 ▤ 490925617
Well-tended grassland with trees and bushes. Divided into several fields by high cedars providing shade.
➩ *500m E of village. Well signposted.*
Mar-Oct 2HEC ⬛ ♦ ⋔ ⵢ ⵡ ⊙ ⬛ ⬗ ⬛ ⋔ P ⬛ ⊞ lau ➡ ⵢ ✕
⬛ **Prices:** pitch 7.62-9.50

ST-SAUVEUR-DE-MONTAGUT ARDÈCHE

Ardechois Le Chambon, Gluiras ☎ 475666187 ▤ 475666367
e-mail: ardechois.camping@wanadoo.fr
In the grounds of a restored 18th-century farm set in rolling countryside with fine views of the surrounding hills.
➩ *8.5km W on D102, beside the River Gluèyre.*
29 Mar-31 Oct 5.5HEC ⬛ ♦ ⋔ ⵢ ⵡ ✕ ⊙ ⬛ ⬗ ⬛ ⋔ PR
⬛ ⊞ lau **Prices:** pitch 14.10-19.20 (incl 2 persons)

ST-SORLIN-EN-VALLOIRE DRÔME

Château de la Pérouz ☎ 475317021 ▤ 475316274
e-mail: campingchateaudelaperouz@libertysurf.fr
A well appointed family site with a variety of recreational facilities.
➩ *2.5km SE via D1.*
15 Jun-15 Sep 14HEC ⬛ ⵠ ⋔ ⵢ ✕ ⊙ ⬛ ⬗ ⬛ ⋔ LPR
P ⬛ ⵰ lau

ST-THIBÉRY HÉRAULT

Tane Le Causse ☎ 467778429
In pleasant wooded surroundings, 1km from the River Hérault.
➩ *Access via A9 exit Agde-Pézenas.*
Jun-Sep 2.4HEC ⬛ ⵠ ⋔ ⵢ ✕ ⊙ ⬛ ⬗ ⬛ ⋔ P ⬛ lau ➡ ⵢ ⬗
⬛ ⋔R ⊞

ST-VALLIER-DE-THIEY ALPES-MARITIMES

Parc des Arboins RN85 ☎ 493426389 ▤ 493096154
Pleasantly situated terraced site on hillside with some oak trees.
➩ *Entrance at Km V36 on N85.*
All year 4HEC ⬛ ⵱ ♦ ⋔ ⵢ ⵡ ⵢ ✕ ⊙ ⬛ ⬗ ⬛ ⬛ ⋔ P ⬛ ⊞
lau ➡ ⬛

STE-MARIE PYRÉNÉES-ORIENTALES

At **TORREILLES**(4km NW on D11)

Dunes de Torreilles ☎ 468283829 ▤ 468283257
A well equipped site in wooded surroundings with direct access to the beach.
➩ *E of the village off D81.*
15 Mar-15 Oct 16HEC ⵱ ⬗ ⵠ ⋔ ⵢ ✕ ⊙ ⬛ ⬗ ⬛ ⋔ PS ⬛
⊞ lau ➡ ⋔R

Mar-I-Sol Plage de Torreilles ☎ 468280407 ▤ 468281823
e-mail: marisol@camping-marisol.com
A family site with a wide variety of sports and entertainment facilities in a pleasant park-like setting 350 metres from the beach.
➩ *Off D81 towards the sea.*
All year 9HEC ⬛ ⵱ ⵠ ⋔ ⵢ ✕ ⊙ ⬛ ⬛ ⬛ ⋔ A ⋔ PS
⬛ ⊞ lau ➡ ⋔LR

Trivoly bd des Plages ☎ 468282028 ▤ 0468281648
e-mail: chadotel@wanadoo.fr
A modern site with excellent facilities and well defined pitches, 800mtrs from the beach.
➩ *Access via autoroute exit 'Perpignan Nord' towards Le Barcarès.*
Apr-Sep 4.7HEC ⬛ ♦ ⋔ ⵢ ✕ ⊙ ⬛ ⬗ ⬛ ⬛ ⋔ P ⬛ ⊞
lau ➡ ✕ ⋔RS **Prices:** ⋔5.18 pitch 13.72-21.34 (incl 2 persons)
See advertisement in colour section

STES-MARIES-DE-LA-MER BOUCHES-DU-RHÔNE

CM Brise ☎ 490978467 ▤ 490977201
A well equipped family site with direct access to the beach, situated in the heart of the Camargue. The sanitary blocks are modern and there are facilities for a wide variety of sports.
➩ *NE via D85A, towards the beach*
15 Nov-10 Dec 22HEC ⬛ ⵱ ⵲ ⋔ ⵢ ⊙ ⬛ ⬗ ⬛ A ⋔ P
⬛ ⊞ lau ➡ ✕ ⬛ ⋔S

Clos-du-Rhône BP 74 ☎ 490978599 ▤ 490977885
e-mail: labrise@laforte.net
➩ *2km W via D38, near the beach*
Apr-Sep 7HEC ⬛ ⵲ ⋔ ⵢ ✕ ⊙ ⬛ ⬗ ⬛ ⬛ A ⋔ PRS ⬛
⊞ lau

SALAVAS ARDÈCHE

Chauvieux ☎ 475880537 ▤ 475880537
e-mail: camping.chauvieux@wanadoo.fr
A popular site in a wooded location close to the River Ardèche with plenty of recreational facilities. Advance booking recommended.
➩ *NE off D579.*
Etr-mid Sep 1.8HEC ⬛ ⵱ ♦ ⋔ ⵢ ✕ ⊙ ⬛ ⬛ ⬛ ⋔
PR ⬛ ⊞ lau **Prices:** pitch 12.50-17 (incl 2 persons)

SALERNES VAR

Arnauds Quartier des Arnauds ☎ 494675195 ▤ 494707557
e-mail: lesarnauds@ville-salernes.fr
Level site situated alongside a river and a lake.
➩ *Access via D560. Site entrance just beyond the village.*
May-Sep 3HEC ⬛ ♦ ⋔ ⵢ ✕ ⊙ ⬛ ⬗ ⬛ ⋔ R ⬛ ⊞ lau ➡ ⵢ ✕
⬗ ⬛ **Prices:** ⋔3.50-4.50 pitch 6-8

SALINS-D'HYÈRES, LES VAR

Port Pothuau 101 chemin les Ouriedes
☎ 494664117 ▤ 494663309
A peaceful holiday village, completely divided into pitches with good leisure facilities.
➩ *6km E of Hyères on N98 and D12.*
01 Apr-15 Oct 6HEC ⬛ ⵱ ⵠ ⋔ ⵢ ✕ ⊙ ⬛ ⬗ ⬛ ⬛ ⬛ ⋔ P
⬛ ⊞ lau ➡ ⋔RS

SALON-DE-PROVENCE BOUCHES-DU-RHÔNE

Nostradamus rte d'Eyguières
☎ 490560836 ▤ 490566505
e-mail: gilles.nostra@wanadoo.fr
In pleasant, wooded surroundings with good sporting facilities.
➩ *5km W on D17 towards Eyguières and Arles.*
Mar-Oct 2.2HEC ⬛ ♦ ⋔ ⵢ ✕ ⊙ ⬛ ⬛ ⋔ PR ⬛ ⊞ lau
Prices: pitch 12-13 (incl 2 persons)

SALVETAT, LA HÉRAULT

Goudal rte de Lacaune ☎ 467976044 ▤ 467976044
e-mail: jnf@goudal.com
In a natural mountain setting within the Haut Lanquedoc Park.
➩ *Access via D907.*
May-Sep 5HEC ⬛ ⵱ ⋔ ⵢ ✕ ⊙ ⬛ ⬛ ⬛ ⬛ A
⋔ L ⬛ ⊞ lau ➡ ⋔R **Prices:** ⋔2.15-2.75 pitch 10.70-14.20
(incl 2 persons)

SANARY-SUR-MER VAR

Girelles chemin de Beaucours
☎ 494741318 ▤ 0494796004
A modern family site with good facilities and direct access to the sea.
Camping Card Compulsory.
➩ *3km NW via D539, beside the sea.*
Etr-Sep 2HEC ⬛ ♦ ⋔ ⵢ ✕ ⊙ ⬛ ⬗ ⋔ S ⬛ ⊞ lau

Mogador ☎ 494745316 ▥ 494741058
Situated 800m from the sea. The site, divided into pitches by hedges, is well managed and very well kept.
➔ *2km NW on N559 turn off at Km15 and take next left.*
Etr-5 Oct 2.7HEC ⊞ ♣♠♟♋️☂✗⊙♨️∅⛺️⚡️ॡ P ⚐🄿🅗
⚫️ lau ➧ ॡS

Pierredon r Raoul Coletta ☎ 494742502 ▥ 494746142
e-mail: campasun@free.fr
A well equipped, wooded site providing a variety of family entertainment, 3km from the sea.
➔ *Access via A50 exit Bandol or Sanary.*
15 Mar-15 Oct 4HEC ⊞ ♣♠♟♋️☂✗⊙♨️⛺️⚡️⛺️Å ॡ P ⚐
lau ➧ 🅛∅🅗 **Prices:** ⚓️3.90-5.20 pitch 5-9.30

> **SAUVE** GARD

Domaine de Bagard rte de Nîmes ☎ 466775599
Shady site bordering the River Vidourle, surrounded by hedges.
➔ *1.2km SE via D999.*
Apr-Sep 16HEC ⊞ ♣♠♟♋️☂✗⊙♨️⛺️∅⛺️🚐
ॡ PR ⚐ lau ➧ 🅗

> **SAUVIAN** HÉRAULT

Gabinelle ☎ 467395087
A modern site in pleasant wooded surroundings with good facilities.
➔ *Leave Sauvian in the direction of Valras Plage on D19.*
15 Jun-15 Sep 3HEC ⊞ ◑♟♋️✗⊙♨️🚐ॡ P ⚐🅗 lau
➧🅛✗∅⛺

> **SÉRIGNAN-PLAGE** HÉRAULT

Clos Virgile ☎ 467322064 ▥ 467320542
e-mail: le.clos.virgile@wanadoo.fr
Situated 400m from the beach, the site is on level meadowland with large pitches and has two clean, well kept sanitary blocks.
May-15 Sep 5HEC ⊞ ♣♠♟♋️☂✗⊙♨️∅⛺️🚐ॡ PS ⚐🅗
lau **Prices:** ⚓️2-3 pitch 15-25 (incl 2 persons)

Grand Large ☎ 467397130 ▥ 467325815
e-mail: legrandlarge@wanadoo.fr
Situated by the sea with private access to the beach. Good facilities. Entertainment during high season.
28 Apr-16 Sep 7HEC ⊞ ⫶⫶⫶ ◑♠♟♋️☂✗⊙♨️∅⛺️Å
ॡ PS ⚐🅗 lau

Sérignan-Plage ☎ 467323533 ▥ 467322636
e-mail: info@leserignanplage.com
On a fine sandy beach, this is a family site with good recreational facilities.
➔ *Access via A9 exit Béziers Est.*
25Apr-25Sep 16HEC ⊞ ⫶⫶⫶ ◑♟♋️☂✗⊙♨️∅⛺️🚐Å
ॡ PS ⚐🄿🅗 lau

> **SEYNE-SUR-MER, LA** VAR

Mimosas av M-Paul ☎ 494947315 ▥ 494873613
e-mail: camping_des_mimosas@yahoo.fr
Situated among pine trees facing the fortress of Six-Fours. Bar and café available during high season only.
➔ *Access via A50 exit 13 towards 'La Seyne Centre', then towards 'Sanary-Bandol'.*
All year 1.1HEC ⊞ ◔♠♟☂✗⊙♨️⛺️🚐🚐⚡️🚐⚐ lau ➧🅛∅
ॡP 🅗

> **SILLANS-LA-CASCADE** BOUCHES-DU-RHÔNE

Relais de la Bresque 15 chemin de la Piscine
☎ 494046489
In a beautiful setting among pine trees with good sanitary and recreational facilities.
All year 1.5HEC ⊞ ◔♣♠♟☂✗⊙♨️⛺️🚐⚡️⚐🅗 lau ➧ ॡPR
Prices: ⚓️2.59-4.59 pitch 3.05-3.05

> **SIX-FOURS-LES-PLAGES** VAR

Héliosports La Font de Fillol ☎ 494256276
Between the town centre and the beach.
➔ *1km W*
25 Mar-15 Oct 0.5HEC ⊞ ◔♣♠⊙♨️⚡️⚐ lau
➧🅛☂✗∅ॡPS

International St-Jean av de la Collégiale ☎ 494875151
Site with pitches, separated by hedges and reeds. Well managed, and lies just below the Fort Six-Fours.
➔ *Access from N559 and D63 via chemin de St-Jean.*
All year 3HEC ⊞ ◑♠♟♋️☂✗⊙♨️⚡️⛺️🚐
ॡ P ⚐🅗 lau ➧✗

Playes 419 r Grand ☎ 494255757
Terraced site on north side of town. Trees abound in this excellent location.
➔ *Access from N559 and D63 via chemin de St-Jean.*
Mar-Nov 1.5HEC ⊞ ♣♠♟♋️☂✗⊙♨️∅⛺️Å⚐🅗 lau

> **SORÈDE** PYRÉNÉES-ORIENTALES

Micocouliers rte de Palau del Vidre
☎ 468892027 ▥ 468954525
In a sheltered position 7km from the coast.
➔ *Access via D11 from St-Génis.*
Jun-15 Sep 4HEC ⊞ ◔♠♟♋️✗⊙♨️∅ॡ P

> **SOSPEL** ALPES-MARITIMES

Domaine St-Madeleine rte de Moulinet
☎ 493041048 ▥ 493041837
A peaceful site in beautiful, unspoiled surroundings.
➔ *4.5km NW via D2566.*
Apr-Sept 3.5HEC ⊞ ◔♠♟☂⊙♨️∅⛺️🚐ॡ P ⚐🅗 lau

> **SOUBÈS** HÉRAULT

Les Rials rte de Poujols ☎ 0467441553
A terraced site in wooded surroundings on the banks of the River Lergue.
➔ *4km from Lodève and 10km from Lac du Salagou.*
15 Jun-Aug 3.5HEC ⊞ ♣♠♟⊙♨️ॡ PR ⚐🅗 lau ➧🅛✗
Prices: ⚓️3.81 pitch 4.57

Sources chemin d'Aubaygues ☎ 467443202 ▥ 467443202
A small, friendly site in a quiet location beside a river.
➔ *5km NE. Signposted from N9.*
May-15 Sep 1.2HEC ⊞ ◔♠♟☂✗⊙♨️ॡ PR ⚐⚫️ lau ➧🅛
✗∅🚐ॡL 🅗 **Prices:** pitch 13 (incl 2 persons)

> **TAIN-L'HERMITAGE** DRÔME

CM Lucs 24 av Prés-Roosevelt ☎ 475083282 ▥ 475083282
e-mail: les.lucs@accesinter.com
Good overnight stopping place but some traffic noise.
➔ *S of town near N7. Turn towards River Rhône at ESSO garage.*
15 Mar-Oct 1.5HEC ⊞ ◔♠♟☂✗⊙♨️ॡ P ⚐🅗 lau ➧🅛∅

> **THOR, LE** VAUCLUSE

Jantou Quartier le Bourdis ☎ 490339007 ▥ 490337984
e-mail: lejantou@avignon.pacwan.net
In wooded surroundings beside a river. Separate car park for arrivals after 22.00hrs.

⮑ *Access via N100.*
15 Mar-Oct 6HEC ⸨ᵾ ♠↟⅃ᴎ☒⊙ ☸⌀ᴽ ⊞ 🐂 ⤙ PR ☎
⊞ lau ♦ ⊞ **Prices:** ♠3.60-4.50 pitch 4.32-5.40

TOURNON-SUR-RHÔNE ARDÈCHE

Manoir rte de Lamastre ☎ 475080250 🗏 475085710
e-mail: info@lemanoir-ardeche.com
In picturesque wooded surroundings with good, modern
facilities.
⮑ *From N86 (Lyon-Valence) take Lamastre road for 3km.*
Apr-Sep 2HEC ⸨ᵾ ♠↟⅃ᴎ☒⊙ ☸⌀ᴽ ⊞ 🐂 A ⤙ LPR ☎
lau **Prices:** pitch 10-12 (incl 2 persons)

Tournon 1 Promenade Roche de France
☎ 475080528 🗏 475080528
e-mail: camping.tournon@wanadoo.fr
Well laid-out site in town centre beside River Rhône.
⮑ *NW on N86.*
All year 1HEC ⸨ᵾ ♠↟⊙☸⌀ᴽ ⊞ 🐂 ⤙ R ☎⊞ lau ♦ 🐂⅃
☒ ⤙P **Prices:** pitch 8.90-10.40 (incl 2 persons)

TOURRETTES-SUR-LOUP ALPES-MARITIMES

Camassade 523 rte de Pie Lombard
☎ 493593154 🗏 493593181
e-mail: camassade@aol.com
Quiet site under oak trees and pines with several terraces.
⮑ *From Vence turn left immediately beyond Tourette.*
All year 2HEC ⸨ᵾ ⌀♠↟🐂⊙☸⌀ᴽ ⊞ 🐂 ⤙ P ☎⊞ lau

Rives du Loup rte de la Colle ☎ 493241565 🗏 493241565
e-mail: rdl@netup.com
In a wooded riverside setting with good, modern facilities
adjacent to a small hotel.
⮑ *Between Vence and Grasse, 3km from Pont-du-Loup on the
road to La Colle-sur-Loup.*
Apr-15 Oct 2.2HEC ⸨ᵾ ⸬⸬ ⊣↟🐂⅃ᴎ☒⊙ ☸⌀ᴽ ⊞ 🐂⤙
PR ☎⊞ lau

UCEL ARDÈCHE

Domaine de Gil rte de Vals ☎ 0475946363 🗏 0475940195
e-mail: raf.garcia@wanadoo.fr
Pleasantly situated on the banks of the River Ardèche.
Surrounded by beautiful views of the countryside.
⮑ *N of Aubenas off N104.*
12 Apr-15 Sep 6HEC ⸨ᵾ ⸬⸬ ♠↟🐂⅃ᴎ☒⊙ ☸⌀⊞ ⤙ PR
☎⊞ lau **Prices:** pitch 11.40-19.82 (incl 2 persons)

UR PYRÉNÉES-ORIENTALES

Gare d'Ur rte d'Espagne ☎ 468048095
In a pleasant mountainous setting with well defined pitches.
500mtrs from the village.
Oct 1HEC ⸨ᵾ ♠↟⊙☸⌀⊞ 🐂☎ lau ♦ ☒ ⤙R ⊞

UZÈS GARD
At **ST-QUENTIN-LA-POTERIE**(4km NE)

Moulin Neuf ☎ 466221721 🗏 466229182
e-mail: le.moulin.neuf@wanadoo.fr
Quiet site on extensive meadowland within an estate.
⮑ *4 km NE on D982.*
Etr-Sep 5HEC ⸨ᵾ ⸬⸬ ♠↟🐂⅃ᴎ☒⊙ ☸⌀ᴽ ⤙ P ☎⊞ lau
Prices: ♠3.20-4 pitch 13.50-16.80 (incl 2 persons)

VAISON-LA-ROMAINE VAUCLUSE

International Carpe Diem rte de St-Marcellin
☎ 490360202 🗏 490363690
e-mail: camping.carpe.diem@wanadoo.fr
In wooded surroundings close to Mont Ventoux, with a wide
variety of leisure facilities.
⮑ *S of town towards Malaucène.*
27 Mar-3 Nov 9HEC ⸨ᵾ ⸬⸬ ⊣↟🐂⅃ᴎ☒⊙ ☸ᴽ ⊞ 🐂 A
⤙ P ☎⊞ lau ♦ ⌀ ⤙R

Théâtre Romain Quartier des Arts, chemin du Brusquet
☎ 490287866 🗏 490287876
e-mail: camping.du.theatre.romain@wanadoo.fr
⮑ *500mtrs from the town centre near the Roman Theatre.*
15 Mar-15 Nov 1.5HEC ⸨ᵾ ♠↟⊙ ☸⌀ ⤙ P ☎⊞ lau ♦ 🐂 ⅃
☒⌀ᴽ ⤙R **Prices:** ♠4.30-4.90 ☸4.20-6.80 ▲4.20-6.80

VALENCE DRÔME

CM chemin de l'Epervière ☎ 475423200 🗏 475562067
e-mail: epervier@vacanciel.com
A well equipped site bordering the Rhône.
⮑ *Access via exit Valence Sud off A7.*
All year 3.5HEC ⸨ᵾ ♠↟🐂⅃ᴎ☒⊙ ☸⌀ᴽ ⤙ P lau ♦ 🐂⌀ᴽ ⊞
Prices: ♠3-4.50 pitch 10.20-13.20 (incl 2 persons)

VALLABRÈGUES GARD

Lou Vincen ☎ 466592129 🗏 466590741
In a pleasant shady location in the heart of a Provençal
village.
25 Mar-10 Oct 1.4HEC ⸨ᵾ ♠↟⊙ ☸⌀⊞ ⤙ P ☎⊞ lau ♦
🐂⅃☒⌀ ⤙L ⊞ **Prices:** pitch 10.89-11.89

VALLON-PONT-D'ARC ARDÈCHE

Ardechois ☎ 475880663 🗏 475371497
e-mail: ardecamp@bigfoot.com
In a pleasant situation in the Ardèche Gorge. Good access for
caravans and plentiful sporting facilities.
⮑ *From Vallon take D290 towards St-Martin. Signposted.*
15 Apr-20 Sep 6HEC ⸨ᵾ ♠↟🐂⅃ᴎ☒⊙ ☸⌀⊞ ⤙ PR ☎⊞
lau ♦ ᴽ **Prices:** ♠5-6.50 pitch 21.50-27.50 (incl 2 persons)
See advertisement in colour section

Mondial rte des Gorges de l'Ardèche
☎ 475880044 🗏 475371373
Modernised site on the bank of the Ardèche with good
sanitary arrangements.
⮑ *Access from Vallon-Pont-d'Arc D290. 800m towards Gorge
d'Ardèche.*
15 Mar-10 Oct 4.2HEC ⸨ᵾ ⸬⸬ ♠↟🐂⅃ᴎ☒⊙ ☸⌀ᴽ ⊞ A
⤙ LPR ☎⊞ lau
See advertisement in colour section

Plage Fleurie Les Mazes ☎ 475880115
Holiday site in unspoilt village beside river.
⮑ *Take D579 towards Ruoms, turn left after 2.5km towards
Les Mazes.*
Apr-Sep 12HEC ⸨ᵾ ⸬⸬ ♠↟🐂⅃ᴎ☒⊙ ☸⌀ ⤙ PR ☎⊡ lau

VALRAS-PLAGE HÉRAULT

Lou Village chemin des Montilles
☎ 467373379 🗏 467375356
e-mail: info@louvillage.com
Situated along a sandy beach, bordered by sand-dunes.
⮑ *2km SW, 100m from the beach*
21 Apr-15 Sep 8HEC ⸨ᵾ ♠↟🐂⅃ᴎ☒⊙ ☸⌀ᴽ ⊞ ⤙ PS ☎
⊞ lau

Occitanie ☎ 467395906 🗏 467325820
e-mail: campingoccitanie@wanadoo.fr
Family site on rising ground to the north of town, 1km from
the beach.
⮑ *Access from A9 exit 'Béziers-Est' towards Valras.*
18May-14Sep 6HEC ⸨ᵾ ♠↟🐂⅃ᴎ☒⊙ ☸⌀ A ⤙ P ☎⊞
lau ♦ ⌀ᴽ ⤙RS **Prices:** ♠1.70-2.75 pitch 13.75-21

Vagues Vendres Plage ☎ 467373312
A well-organised family site 400m from the sea with a variety
of sporting and entertainment facilities.
Etr-20 Sep 7HEC ⸬⸬ ⊣↟🐂⅃☒⊙ ☸⌀ᴽ ⊞ 🐂
⤙ P ☎⊞ lau ♦ ⤙S

195

La Carabasse ★★★★
Vias-sur-Mer

An excellently positioned parc on the sunny Mediterranean with two excellent pool complexes & its very own Beach Club.

- Groupings of touring areas, some pitches have their own shower & WC
- Two outdoor pools with new waterslide
- Wide range of sports & leisure activities
- 3 children's clubs for all ages

- Restaurant, bar, pizzeria & takeaway
- Superb low season prices
- Bilingual staff on parc
- Site open from: 15 April - 15 September

La Carabasse, Route de Farinette, 34450 Vias-sur-Mer, France
Tel:00 33 467 21 64 01 Fax:00 33 467 21 76 87 V2819

To book from France please call the number above, quoting code FAA03
To book from the UK please call 0870 242 77 77 quoting code FAA03

Yole ☎ 467373387 ▤ 467374489
e-mail: layole34@aol.com
Very comfortable site divided into pitches. Good sanitary installations with individual washing cubicles. Hot water tap. Sailing boats for hire. Riding stables in village. Reservation recommemded in July and August.
➲ SW of D37E towards Vendres.
27 Apr-21 Sep 20HEC ⬛ ⁝⁝⁝⁝ ♠ ℝ ♨ ♀ ✕ ⊙ ♬ ⊘ ♨ ☎ ♞ ⁌ P ☎ ⊞ lau ♦ ⁌S Prices: pitch 15.55-29.70 (incl 2 persons)
See advertisement in colour section

Tourrades chemin des Canaux ☎ 466888020 ▤ 466883380
A modern family site with a wide range of recreational facilities.
➲ 3km W via N572 and D135.
All year 7.5HEC ⬛ ♠ ℝ ♨ ♀ ✕ ⊙ ♬ ♨ ☎ ♞ ⁌ P ☎ ⊞ lau ♦ ⊘ ⊞

Flory rte d'Entraigues ☎ 490310051 ▤ 490234679
Well-kept site on a pine covered hill with good facilities.
➲ From motorway, do not head for Vedène but follow D942 for 800m.
15 Mar-15 Oct 6.5HEC ⬛ ♠ ℝ ♨ ♀ ✕ ⊙ ♬ ⊘ ♨ ☎ ⁌ P ☎ ⊞ lau Prices: ♠3.40 pitch 3.40

Domaine de la Bergerie rte de la Sine ☎ 493580936 ▤ 0493598044
Well-kept site on hilly land. Pitches near to a wood. Some facilities are only available in high season.
➲ 3km W on D2210.
25 Mar-15 Oct 13HEC ⬛ ♠ ℝ ♨ ♀ ✕ ⊙ ♬ ⊘ ♨ ☎ ⁌ P ☎ ⊞ lau Prices: ♠3.96 pitch 19.66-22.71

Acacias ☎ 475217251 ▤ 475217398
e-mail: lesacacias26@geotour.com
Pleasant site beside the River Drôme.
Camping Card Compulsory.
➲ Access via D93.
Apr-Sep 3HEC ⬛ ♠ ℝ ♨ ♀ ✕ ⊙ ♬ ⊘ ♨ ☎ ♞ ⁌ R ☎ ⊡ ⊞ lau ♦ ✕ Prices: pitch 9.60-10.98 (incl 2 persons)

Sieste ☎ 467237296 ▤ 467237538
In a rural setting on the River Orb.
➲ NE of Bédarieux, 10km from Lodève.
Jun-15 Sep 2HEC ⬛ ♨ ℝ ♨ ♀ ✕ ⊙ ♬ ⊘ ♨ ☎ ♞ ⁌ PR ☎ ⊞ lau Prices: pitch 11.40 (incl 2 persons)

Air Marin ☎ 467216490 ▤ 467217679
A well equipped family site in wooded surroundings 10 minutes walk from the beach.
➲ E of Vias Plage.
19 May-28 Sep 7HEC ⬛ ♠ ℝ ♨ ♀ ✕ ⊙ ♬ ♨ ☎ ♞ ⁌ P ☎ lau ♦ ♨ ⊘ ⁌RS ⊞

Carabasse rte de Farinette
☎ 0870 242 7777 ▤ 0870 242 9999
A lively camping park with a wide range of activites, especially for young families and teenagers, centred around a lagoon pool complex and entertainment terrace.
➲ 1.5m NE of Vias.
15 Apr-14 Sep ♦ ♨ ℝ ♨ ♀ ✕ ⊙ ♬ ⊘ ♨ ♙ ⁌ P ☎ ⊞ ⊗ lau ♦ ⁌S

Farret ☎ 467216445
e-mail: farret@wanadoo.fr
On level meadow beside flat sandy beach, ideal for children.
➲ Access via A9 exit Agde-Vias.
23 Mar-30 Sep 7HEC ⬛ ⁝⁝⁝⁝ ♠ ℝ ♨ ♀ ✕ ⊙ ♬ ⊘ ♨ ☎ ♞ ⁌ PS ☎ ⊞ lau ♦ ⁌R Prices: pitch 20-32 (incl 2 persons)

Cap Soleil Côte Ouest ☎ 467216477 ▤ 467217066
On level land near sea. Divided into pitches.
➲ Cross Canal du Midi, S of town, then turn W.
All year 5HEC ⬛ ♠ ℝ ♨ ♀ ✕ ⊙ ♬ ⊘ ♨ ☎ ♞ ♙ ⁌ P ☎ ⊞ lau ♦ ⁌S Prices: ♠3.05-3.35 pitch 12.20-32.01 (incl 2 persons)

Hélios Vias-Plage ☎ 467216366 ▤ 467216366
On level ground divided into pitches.
➲ On D137 S of village signposted 'Farinette'.
16 May-Sep 3HEC ⁝⁝⁝⁝ ♠ ℝ ♨ ♀ ✕ ⊙ ♬ ⊘ ♨ ☎ ♞ ⁌ ☎ ⊞ lau ♦ ⁌S

Napoléon av de la Mediterranée ☎ 467010780 ▤ 467010785
e-mail: reception@camping-napoleon.fr
A well equipped family site surrounded by tropical vegetation with direct access to the beach.
➲ Access via A9 exit Agde-Vias.
29 Apr-30 Sep 3HEC ⬛ ⁝⁝⁝⁝ ♠ ℝ ♨ ♀ ✕ ⊙ ♬ ⊘ ♨ ☎ ♞ ♙ ⁌ P ☎ ⊞ lau ♦ ⁌RS Prices: ♠3.05 pitch 18-28 (incl 2 persons)

Europe ☎ 467781150 ▤ 467784859
e-mail: campingdeleurope@wanadoo.fr
A pleasant site in peaceful surroundings.
➲ 1.5km W via D114.
Jun-Sep 5HEC ⬛ ♨ ℝ ♨ ♀ ✕ ⊙ ♬ ⊘ ♨ ☎ ♞ ⁌ P ☎ ⊞ lau ♦ ⁌L Prices: pitch 9.50-21.50 (incl 2 persons)

VIGAN, LE GARD

Val de l'Arre rte de Ganges ☎ 467810277 ▤ 467817123
e-mail: valdelarre@wanadoo.fr
In wooded surroundings beside the River Arre. Compulsory separate carpark for late arrivals.
➲ *2.5km E on D999.*
Apr-Sep 4HEC ⟲ ♦ ⋔ ⋤ ⋔ ✗ ☉ ⬛ ⬤ ⬛ ⬛ ⋠ PR ⛺ ⊞ lau ♦ ⛺

VILLARS-COLMARS ALPES-DE-HAUTE-PROVENCE

Haut-Verdon ☎ 492834009 ▤ 492835661
e-mail: sylvie.graziani@wanadoo.fr
A comfortable site in a picturesque wooded location beside the River Verdon.
➲ *N on D908.*
Jul-2 Sep 3.5HEC ⣿ ♦ ♦ ⋔ ⋤ ⋔ ✗ ☉ ⬛ ⬤ ⬛ ⋠ PR ⛺ ⊞ lau ♦ ⛺

VILLEMOUSTAUSSOU AUDE

Pinhiers chemin du Pont Neuf ☎ 468478190 ▤ 468714349
e-mail: campingdaspinhiers@wanadoo.fr
➲ *A61 in the direction of Mazamet.*
Apr-Sep 2HEC ⟲ ⋔ ⋔ ⋤ ⬤ ☉ ⬛ ⬤ ⬛ ⋠ P ⛺ lau ♦ ✗ ⬛ ⛺
Prices: ⚑2.80-3.40 pitch 3.10-3.50

VILLENEUVE-DE-LA-RAHO PYRÉNÉES-ORIENTALES

Rives-du-Lac chemin de la Serre ☎ 468558351 ▤ 468558637
e-mail: camping.villeneuve@worldonline.fr
A quiet family site beside the lake.
➲ *7km from Perpignan.*
Mar-Nov 2.5HEC ⟲ ⍦ ⋔ ⋔ ⋤ ⋔ ✗ ☉ ⬛ ⬤ ⬛ ⛯ ⛺ lau ♦ ⊞ Prices: ⚑9.40-12.40 ⚑8.40-11.40

VILLENEUVE-LÈS-AVIGNON GARD

Île des Papes ☎ 490151590 ▤ 490151591
e-mail: ile.papes@wanadoo.fr
A well equipped site situated on an island between the Rhône Canal and the River Rhône.
➲ *Access via N7 and D228.*
27 Mar-Oct 20HEC ⟲ ⣿ ♦ ⍦ ⋔ ⋤ ⋔ ✗ ☉ ⬛ ⬤ ⬛ ⬛ ⬤
⚑ ⋠ P ⛺ lau

VILLENEUVE-LOUBET-PLAGE ALPES-MARITIMES

Hippodrôme 5 av des Rives ☎ 493200200 ▤ 492132007
e-mail: blsced@aol.com
In a spacious park with pitches divided by hedges with good facilities.
➲ *Turn right off the N7 at ATLAS furniture store.*
All year 7.8HEC ⟲ ♦ ♦ ⋔ ☉ ⬛ ⬤ ⬛ ⛺ ⊞ lau ♦ ⋤ ✗ ⬛ ⛺
⋠S

Panorama ☎ 493209153
Small terraced site mainly for tents 0.8km from the sea.
➲ *About 500m from the Nice-Cannes Autoroute.*
All year 1HEC ⟲ ♦ ⋔ ⬤ ✗ ☉ ⬛ ⬤ ⬛ ⬛ lau ♦ ⋤
⋠RS

Parc des Maurettes 730 av du Dr-Lefebvre
☎ 493209191 ▤ 493737720
Terraced site in a pine forest with good, modern facilities.
➲ *Access via A8: From Cannes take exit 'Villeneuve-Loubet-Plage', then N7 towards Antibes for 1km. From Nice, take Villeneuve exit and A8 for 2km.*
10 Jan-15 Nov 2HEC ⟲ ♦ ⋔ ✗ ☉ ⬛ ⬤ ⬛ ⬛ ⛺ ⊞ lau ♦ ⋤
⛺ ⋠S Prices: ⚑2.40 pitch 17.85-21.50 (incl 2 persons)

┌─────────────────────────────────┐
CAMPING ★★
"LES RIVES DU LAC"
66180 VILLENEUVE DE LA RAHO
Bordering a lake, close to Spain, between the
sea and mountains
★ Peaceful   ★ Windsurfing
★ Family atmosphere   ★ Swimming
★ Fishing (carp,   ★ 15km from the sea
   whitebait)
MOBILE HOMES AND CANVAS
BUNGALOWS TO LET
Open from 1st March to 30th November
Tel: 0468558351 Fax: 0468558637
└─────────────────────────────────┘

Parc St-James Sourire La Tour de la Madone, La Vanade
☎ 493209611 ▤ 493220752
Parkland dominated by an 11th-century monastery.
➲ *2km W on D2085*
end Mar-end Sep 8HEC ⟲ ♦ ⍦ ⋔ ⋤ ⋔ ✗ ☉ ⬛ ⬤ ⛺ ⬛ ⬤
⋠ P ⛺ ⊞ lau ♦ ⋠R

Vieille Ferme 296 bd des Groules ☎ 493334144 ▤ 493333728
e-mail: vieilleferme@bigfoot.com
In a wooded park close to the sea. Shop and café open in summer only.
➲ *Access via A8/N7 from Antibes of Cagnes-sur-Mer.*
All year 2.8HEC ⟲ ♦ ⍦ ⋔ ⋤ ✗ ☉ ⬛ ⬤ ⬛ ⬤ ⋠ P ⛺ ⊞ lau
♦ ⋠S Prices: ⚑3.50-4.50 ⚑2.30-4 pitch 10.50-24 (incl 2 persons)

VILLEROUGE-LA-CRÉMADE AUDE

Pinada ☎ 468436788 ▤ 468436861
e-mail: lepinada@libertysurf.fr
In pleasant rural surroundings on edge of forest.
➲ *600m W on D106.*
All year 4.5HEC ⟲ ⣿ ♦ ♦ ⋔ ✗ ☉ ⬛ ⬛ ⬛ ⬛ ⋠ P ⛺ ⊞
lau Prices: pitch 7.63-16.77 (incl 4 persons)

VILLES-SUR-AUZON VAUCLUSE

Verguettes rte de Carpentras ☎ 490618818 ▤ 490619787
e-mail: info@provence-camping.com
Lying at the foot of Mont Ventoux and Nesque Gorges in a pine forest
➲ *W via D942.*
May-Sep 2HEC ⟲ ♦ ⋔ ✗ ☉ ⬛ ⬤ ⛺ ⋠ P ⛺ ⊞ lau ♦ ⋤ ✗ ⬛
Prices: ⚑4.50 pitch 6.50

VITROLLES BOUCHES-DU-RHÔNE

Marina Plage ☎ 442893146 ▤ 442794990
e-mail: information@marina-plage.com
A family site in pleasant wooded surroundings with good recreational facilities.
➲ *Access via N113 towards Rognac, then turn S at exit after Marignane Airport.*
All year 10HEC ⟲ ♦ ⍦ ⋔ ⋤ ✗ ☉ ⬛ ⬛ ⬛ ⬤ ⋠ L ⛺ ⊞ lau

VIVIERS ARDÈCHE

Centre de Vacances d'Imbours ☎ 475543806 ▤ 475543920
In wooded surroundings with a variety of recreational facilities.
➲ *Access via N86 and D4.*
Jun-Sep 45HEC ⟲ ♦ ⋔ ⋤ ⋔ ✗ ☉ ⬛ ⬤ ⛺ ⋠ P ⛺ ⊞ lau

Rochecondrie Loisirs ☎ 475527466 ▦ 475527466
A level site with good facilities beside the River L'Escoutay.
➲ *N of town on N86.*
Apr-Oct 1.8HEC ⌂⌂⌂ ♣♠♥⊙◍⌂≺ PR 🏠⊞ lau ♦🔦✗ ⌀

VOGÜÉ ARDÈCHE

Domaine du Cros d'Auzon Hotellerie de Plein Air
☎ 475377586 ▦ 475370102
e-mail: cros.d.auzon@wanadoo.fr
In wooded surroundings close to the Gorges de l'Ardèche
with good recreational facilities.
➲ *2.5km via D579 bordering the river.*
15 Apr-15 Sep ⌂⌂⌂ ⛁♣♠♥🔦♥✗⊙◍⌀Ⅲ⌂
≺ PR 🏠⊞ lau Prices: ⋔2.50-5.10 pitch 12.60-20 (incl 2 persons)

VOLONNE ALPES-DE-HAUTE-PROVENCE

Hippocampe rte Napoléon ☎ 492335000 ▦ 492335049
e-mail: l.hippocampe@wanadoo.fr
Several strips of land, interspersed with trees, and running
down the edge of lake. Surrounded by fields and gardens.
➲ *On S edge of town. 2km E of N85.*
Apr-Sep 8HEC ⌂⌂⌂ ⛁♠♥🔦♥✗⊙◍⌀Ⅲ▲≺ P 🏠⊞ lau
Prices: pitch 14.48-23.78 (incl 2 persons)

CORSICA

Corsica is a wonderful blend of green mountains, deep
valleys, and spectacular pink granite peaks where rain and
melting snow merge into torrents that rush down the
hillsides. In the spring the mountains are ablaze with wild
flowers and the maquis - the abundance of which gives the
island its name 'the scented isle'. This southernmost outpost
of France is some 100 miles south of Toulon in the
Mediterranean. Beaches abound, and all kinds of
watersports are available in season, but in this relatively
undiscovered place it is still possible to find a quiet beach
on a summer day.
Corsica's capital is Ajaccio, birthplace of Napoleon, and
today a cosmopolitan centre with its busy harbour and
broad boulevards with smart shops. From Ajaccio there is a
railway to Bastia, in the north. This is a beautiful three-hour
trip, and ideal for drivers reluctant to venture onto more
tortuous minor roads.
....

CORSE (CORSICA)

ALÉRIA HAUTE-CORSE

Marina d'Aléria rte de la Mer
☎ 495570142 ▦ 495570429
e-mail: info@marina-aleria.com
➲ *3km E of Cateraggio via RN200*
Apr-Oct 10HEC ⸭⸭⸭ ♣♠🔦♥✗⊙◍⌀⌂≺ S 🏠 lau
Prices: ⋔4.80-6.40 ♠1.70-12.30 ◫1.80-2.20 ▲1.40-1.70

BONIFACIO CORSE-DU-SUD

Rondinara Suartone ☎ 495704315 ▦ 495705679
In a beautiful situation 300mtrs from the beach with modern
facilities and fine opportunities for water sports.
➲ *Midway between Porto-Vecchio and Bonifacio on N198 in
the direction of Suartone-La Rondinara.*
15 May-Sept 6HEC ⌂⌂⌂ ⛁♠🔦♥✗⊙◍⌀Ⅲ⌂
≺ PS 🏠⊞⌀ lau

CALVI HAUTE-CORSE

Dolce Vita Ponte Bambino ☎ 495650599
In extensive woodland with well defined pitches and good,
modern facilities.
➲ *4km SW of Calvi between N197 to L'Ile Rousse and the sea.*
May-Sep 6HEC ⌂⌂⌂ ♣♠🔦♥♥✗⊙◍⌀⌂≺ RS 🏠⊞ lau

CARGESE CORSE-DU-SUD

Torraccia Bagghiuccia ☎ 495264239 ▦ 495204021
e-mail: contact@camping_torraccia.com
Terraced site close to the Chiuni and Pero beaches and
backed by some fine mountain scenery.
➲ *4km N on N199.*
15May-Sep 3.5HEC ♣♠🔦♥♥✗⊙◍⌀⌂🏠🅿⊞ lau
♦Ⅲ≺S Prices: ⋔4.60-5.30 ♠1.80-2.30 ◫1.80-2.30
▲1.80-2.30

CENTURI HAUTE-CORSE

Isulottu ☎ 495356281
A peaceful, shady site, 200mtrs from the beach.
➲ *1km from Centuri-Port towards Morsiglia.*
21 Dec-21 Jan 3HEC ♣♠🔦♥✗⊙◍⌀⌀🏠⊞ lau ♦≺S

CLOS-DU-MOUFLON HAUTE-CORSE

Mouflon ☎ 495650353
Terraced site, divided into pitches. Very steep access via partly
asphalted, winding road with gradient of 20%. **Tents and
motorised caravans only.**
➲ *15km from Calvi on D81 on the coastal road, in the
direction of Porto.*
6 Jun-25 Sep 2.5HEC ⬙⛁♠🔦♥♥✗⊙⌀≺S 🏠⊞ lau ♦Ⅲ

GALÉRIA HAUTE-CORSE

Deux Torrents ☎ 495620067 ▦ 495620332
e-mail: 2torrents@corsica-net.com
A spacious, well equipped site nestling between two torrents
at the foot of the mountains.
➲ *5km E on D51 towards Calenzana.*
Jun-Sep 6.3HEC ⌂⌂⌂ ⸭⸭⸭ ♣♠🔦♥♥✗⊙◍⌀⌂≺ lau
♦≺R Prices: ⋔4.50 ♠2.50 ◫4 ▲2.50

GHISONACCIA HAUTE-CORSE

Arinella-Bianca Arinella-Bianca
☎ 495560478 ▦ 495561254
e-mail: arinella@arinellabianca.com
In wooded surroundings, directly on the beach with good
recreational facilities.
Etr-Oct 12HEC ⌂⌂⌂ ♣♠🔦♥♥✗⊙◍⌀⌂≺ PRS 🏠⊞ lau

LOZARI HAUTE-CORSE

Clos des Chênes rte de Belgodère
☎ 495601513 ▦ 495602116
In a delightful wooded setting, 1km from a fine sandy beach.
➲ *1.5km S via N197 towards Belgodère*
Etr-Sep 5.5HEC ⌂⌂⌂ ♣♠🔦♥♥✗⊙◍⌀⌂≺ P 🏠⊞ lau
♦≺S

LUMIO HAUTE-CORSE

Panoramic rte de Lavataggio 1 ☎ 495607313
Very clean and tidy site divided into pitches.
➲ *From Calvi, 12km on N197, 200m from main road.*
Jun-15 Sep 6HEC ⸭⸭⸭ ⛁♠🔦♥♥✗⊙◍⌀◫≺ P 🏠⊞ lau ♦
≺S

OLMETO-PLAGE CORSE-DU-SUD

Esplanade ☎ 495760503 ▦ 495761622
In a pleasant natural park, 100mtrs from the sea.
All year 4HEC ⌂⌂⌂ ♣♠🔦♥♥✗⊙◍⌂⌂≺ S 🏠🅿⊞ lau ♦
⌀Ⅲ≺R

PIANOTTOLI CORSE-DU-SUD

Kevano Plage Plage de Kevano ☎ 495718322 ▤ 495718383
In a beautiful setting in the middle of woodland with modern facilities, 400mtrs from the beach.
May-Sep 6HEC ⌂♠♠⌂♣♣⌃✕☉♣☎☎⊞ lau ♦∅⁑S
Prices: ♠5-6.70 ♠1.70-2.30 ♣3-3.80 ♠1.80-2.40

PISCIATELLO CORSE-DU-SUD

Benista ☎ 495251930 ▤ 495259370
In a beautiful wooded setting, 5 minutes from the local beaches. Pitches are divided by hedges and there are good sporting facilities.
Apr-Oct 5HEC ⌂♠♠⌂♣♣⌃✕☉♣∅⌐☎♣⁑ PR☎⊞
lau ♦⁑S Prices: pitch 15.20-19 (incl 2 persons)

PORTO-VECCHIO CORSE-DU-SUD

Pirellu rte de Palombaggia ☎ 495702344 ▤ 495706022
e-mail: v-pirellu@wanadoo.fr
A modern site situated in an oak grove 300mtrs from the beach.
➲ S of Porto-Vecchio, take road for Bonifacio. After Pont du Stabiacco take first road on the left.
Apr-Sep 2.5HEC ⌂♢♠♠⌂♣⌃✕☉♣∅⌐☎⁑P☎⊞
lau

Vetta rte de Bastia ☎ 495700986 ▤ 495704321
e-mail: info@campinglavetta.com
In natural parkland with good, modern facilities 3km from the sea.
➲ 5.5km N on N198.
Jun- Sep 8HEC ⌂♠♠⌂♣⌃✕☉♣∅☎
⁑P☎☐⊞ lau ♦⁑S

ST-FLORENT HAUTE-CORSE

U Pezzo chemin de la Plage ☎ 495370165 ▤ 0495370165
Pleasant site; partly level, partly terraced under eucalyptus trees. Private access to large beach.
➲ S of town on road to beach.
01 Apr-15 Oct 2HEC ⌂♠♠⌂♣⌃✕☉♣∅⁑S☎⊞ lau

SOTTA CORSE-DU-SUD

U Moru ☎ 495712340 ▤ 495712619
A quiet family site 5 minutes from the local beach.
➲ 4km SW via D859.
Jun-Sep 6HEC ⦂♠♠⌂♣⌃✕☉♣∅☎☎⊞ lau

TIUCCIA CORSE-DU-SUD

Couchants rte de Casaglione ☎ 495522660 ▤ 495593177
In a quiet location facing the vast Sagone Bay and close to the Liamone River.
➲ 3km from the sea.
All year 5HEC ⌂♠♠⌃✕☉♣∅⌐☎♣☎⊞ lau ♦
⁑RS Prices: ♠4.57-5.34 ♠1.83-2.29 ♣3.05-3.81 ♠1.83-2.29

U Sommalu rte de Casaglione ☎ 495522421 ▤ 495522085
➲ 2.5km N via D81 and D25.
15 Mar-Sep 6HEC ⌂♠⌂♣⌃✕☉♣∅☎♣☎♠☎ lau ♦
⌐⁑RS ⊞

The main corridor of the Musée d'Orsay, Paris

199

GERMANY

Germany, an economic giant that offers a mix of fairytale castles, ancient towns, enormous forests and bustling modern cities, is a country of contrasts.

Germany is bordered by nine countries: Austria, Belgium, Czech Republic, Denmark, France, Luxembourg, Netherlands, Poland and Switzerland. It is a country of forests, rivers, mountains and history. The Rhine Valley boasts magnificent cliffs and woods whilst the Black Forest has some fine valley scenery with countless waterfalls and gorges.

The climate is temperate and variable but Germany enjoys hotter summers than Britain.

Off-site camping Permission to camp off an official campsite must be obtained from the landowner or local police. Overnight parking at parking places is tolerated for one night, unless otherwise indicated, provided nearby campsites and hotels are fully booked. However, caravans must remain connected to the towing vehicle. Make sure you do not contravene local regulations.

HOW TO GET THERE

For western Germany use the Channel Tunnel, or one of the short Channel crossings and travel via Belgium. For northern Germany take a direct ferry from **Harwich** to **Hamburg** (minimum sailing time 19hrs 30mins) or one of the North Sea crossings to the Netherlands. For southern Germany use Eurotunnel, or one of the short Channel crossings and drive through northern France entering Germany near **Strasbourg**; this is also the route if using one of the longer Channel crossings to Caen (Ouistreham), Cherbourg, Dieppe or Le Havre.

Distance

From the Continental Channel ports, Köln (Cologne) is about 414km (257 miles) and within a comfortable day's drive; routes to southern and eastern Germany usually require one or two overnight stops.

MOTORING & GENERAL INFORMATION

The information given here is specific to Germany. It **must** be read in conjunction with the Continental ABC at the front of the book, which covers those regulations which are common to many countries.

British Embassy/Consulates*

The British Embassy, together with its consular section, is located at 10117 Berlin, Wilhelmstrasse 70 ☎ (030) 20457-0. The British Embassy also has an office at 53115 Bonn, Argelandstrasse 108a ☎ (0228) 9167-0. There are British Consulates in Düsseldorf, Frankfurt am Main, Hamburg, München (Munich) and Stuttgart; there are British Consulates with Honorary Consuls in Bremen, Hanover, Kiel and Nürnberg (Nurenburg).

The cobbled Hauptmarkt in Trier on the Mosel, one of the finest old squares in Germany

Children in cars
Child under 12 and/or 1.5 metres in height are not permitted to travel as front or rear seat passengers unless using suitable restraint system, if fitted. See Continental ABC under 'Passengers' and 'Seat Belts'.

Currency*
With the introduction of the Euro, the Deutsche Mark (DEM) ceased to be legal tender from 28 February 2002. However, DEM coins and notes may still be exchanged at the German Central Bank (Deutsche Bundesbank) for an unlimited period.

Dimensions and weight restrictions*
Private **cars** and **trailers** or **caravans** are restricted to the following dimensions - height, 4 metres; width, 2.55 metres; length, 12 metres. The maximum permitted overall length of

vehicle/trailer or caravan combinations is 18.35 metres. A fully-laden trailer without brakes may have a total maximum weight of 750kg.

Driving licence*
A valid UK or Republic of Ireland licence is acceptable in Germany. The minimum age at which visitors from UK or Republic of Ireland may use a temporarily imported car or motorcycle is 17 years.

First-aid kit*
The German authorities recommend that visiting motorists equip their vehicles with a first-aid kit.

Foodstuffs*
If the imported foodstuff are for personal use, there are no limits when travelling between EU countries. Visitors entering Germany from outside the EU may import up to 1kg of meat

and meat products and up to 30kg of game and poultry. The importation of meat products and sheep and goat's cheese from the CIS, Turkey and all African and Asian countries is prohibited. Coffee (500g) and coffee extract (200g) are free of customs duties, but visitors under 15 cannot import coffee.

Lights*

It is compulsory for motorcyclists to use dipped headlights during the day.

Motoring clubs

The principal motoring club is the **Allgemeiner Deutscher Automobil Club e.V.** (ADAC) based at 81373 München, Am Westpark 8 ☎(089) 7676-0. It has offices in the larger towns, and office hours are 09.00-18.00hrs Mon-Fri. ADAC also has offices at major frontier crossings.

Petrol*

See Continental ABC under 'Petrol/Diesel'.

Roads

Germany has a comprehensive motorway (*Autobahn*) network which takes most of the long-distance traffic. Emergency telephones are sited every 2km, the direction of the nearest telephone is indicated by the point of the black triangle on posts alongside the motorway.

The *Bundesstrassen*, or state roads, vary in

quality. In the north and west, and in the touring areas of the Rhine Valley, Black Forest, and Bavaria, the roads are good and well-graded. Traffic at weekends increases considerably during the school holidays, which are from July to mid September. In order to ease congestion, lorries of more than 7,500kg and lorries towing trailers are subject to restrictions. On all Saturdays from 1 July to 31 August such vehicles are not allowed on state roads or motorways betweeen 0700 and 1800 hours, and generally on all Sundays and public holidays between 0001 and 2200 hours.

Speed limits*

Car/Motorcycle

Built-up areas 50kph (31mph)
Other roads including dual-carriageways 100kph (62mph)
Motorways 130kph (80mph) (recommended maximum)

Car/caravan/trailer

Built-up areas 50kph (31mph)
Other roads 80kph (49mph)
Motorways/dual-carriageways 80kph (49mph)

Note:

Outside special built-up areas, motor vehicles to which a special speed limit applies, as well as vehicles with trailers with a combined length of more than 7 metres (23ft), must keep sufficient distance from the preceding vehicle so that an overtaking vehicle may pull in. Anyone driving so slowly that a line of vehicles has formed behind must permit the following vehicles to pass, by stopping at a suitable place if necessary.

Warning triangle*

The use of a warning triangle is compulsory in the event of accident or breakdown. The triangle must be placed on the road behind the vehicle to warn following traffic of any obstruction: 100 metres (109yds) on ordinary roads and 150 metres (164yds) on motorways.

***Additional information will be found in the Continental ABC at the front of the book.**

TOURIST INFORMATION

SOUTH EAST

Munich is the largest city in southern Germany, and has a vast array of tourist attractions ranging

A Munich resident enjoys one of Germany's finest products

from classical heritage such as the *Alte Pinakothek* (Old Picture Gallery) and *Asamkirche* (Asam Church) to modern diversions such as the B.M.W Car Museum, and the *Forum der Technik* (Technology Forum) which contains Germany's first IMAX cinema screen.

One of the most entertaining times to visit Munich is during the Oktoberfest, for the world famous festival of beer. The festival was uncorked for the first time in 1810 to commemorate the marriage of Crown Prince Ludwig to Princess Therese von Sachsen-Hildburghausen, and instantly became a popular tradition.

The Oktoberfest begins, strangely enough, on the penultimate Saturday of September with a costume carnival and a parade of horse-driven brewing carts. The festival is inaugurated by the Bürgermeister of Munich, who opens the first barrel of beer with the words "Ozapft ist!", meaning "It's open"! The area surrounding Munich produces some of the finest beers in the world. During the duration of the Oktoberfest, around 6 million visitors will consume 200,000 pairs of sausages, and 5 million litres of beer!

SOUTH WEST

This corner of Germany contains the Schwarzwald or Black Forest, one of the prettiest regions in Europe. The centre of the area is Stuttgart, home to no fewer than five castles as a reminder of its historical importance.

One of the best known towns is the famous spa, Baden-Baden (Baden being the German for Bath). The geothermal springs bubble to the surface at a temperature of 69°C, and have brought visitors to the region for the last 2000 years.

The Romans were the first to build spa baths in Baden; the Friedrichsbad is built upon the Roman remains of baths from the first and the third century AD. In the 19th century the crowned heads of Europe were regular visitors, which led to the construction of many fine hotels. and even today there is a distinct air of elegance as you stroll through the town.

BERLIN & EASTERN PROVINCES

Lively Berlin, once again the capital and seat of government of Germany, is famed for the subversive humour and quick-fire repartee of its

The entrance to the Breitscheilzplatz in Berlin, with the Kaiser-Wilhelm-Gedachtniskirche in the background

more than 3.5 million citizens. Among its many attractions are two famous streets, 'Ku 'dam' (Kurfürstendam), the principal shopping street, and *Unter den Linden*, once the heart of Imperial Prussia. Not to be missed are the Bauhaus Museum, the museum of the Berlin Wall at Checkpoint Charlie, Friedrichwerdersche Kirche, and the vast Tiergarten park right in the heart of the city. Close to the city is the massive forest of Grunewald.

South-west is the more tranquil town of Potsdam with, on its western edge, Park Sanssouci, formerly the summer home of the German royal family.

Walkers in Berlin's Tiergarten woods

Europe, and arguably the most impressive building, the Porta Nigra (Black Gate) which was the main entry point to the old city.

Despite its wealth of Roman heritage, Trier is most widely known for its excellent wines, locally produced in the Moselle valley. For a small fee you can go wine-tasting. For further information, visit the Trier tourist office, located next to the Porta Nigra.

NORTH

Hannover was a late developer in European terms, but its rise to eminence in the 18th century brought about the construction of wonderful city parks, the ultimate statement of urban prowess of the time.

The Herrenhäusen Royal Gardens are the star attraction; the others are: Welfengarten, Georgengarten, Grossengarten and Berggarten.

Construction began in 1744 under instruction from Frederick the Great; he wanted a country residence to escape two of his least favourite things - Berlin and his wife - hence the name Sanssouci which means 'without care'. The park stretches for two kilometres and comprises a network of palaces, gardens, and country hideaways woven into the beautiful Rehgarten.

The highlights of Sanssouci are the two palaces, the Neues Palais – at the west end, preserved in its pre-1918 condition, – and at the east end, above the attractive terraced garden, the yellow-and-white-painted Schloss Sanssouci, the perfect summer retreat.

CENTRAL

Trier is the oldest city in Germany having been founded 2,000 years ago. It became the regional capital for the occupying Romans, and then centre of the Christian church in Western Europe. It contains the most impressive collection of Roman monuments in Northern

Berchtesgarten in Bavaria

SOUTH EAST

The highest peak in Germany can be found in the Alps along the southern border of Bavaria. Superb walks and easy climbs bring rewarding views of lush meadows and secluded lakes, and there are some rare and wonderful species of Alpine fauna to be seen.
Bavaria is also a land of spruce, pine, and deciduous forests impressively strewn with massive boulders and rock labyrinths which are perfect for climbing, exploring and caving. Many areas are also excellent for winter sports.
The Octoberfest and the Wagner festival are both held in this region; other attractions include medieval tournaments, Alpine horn-blowing, and Schuhplatter dancing.
To the south of the region, Munich is a most beautiful city famed for art and learning, with an atmosphere and charm of its own. Further north, be sure to visit Passau, which possesses the largest church organ in the world, and the former Imperial city of Regensburg.

AACH BEI OBERSTAUFEN BAYERN

Aach ☎ 08386 363 ▤ 08386 961721
e-mail: camping-aach@t-online.de
A terraced site with beautiful views of the mountains. Sauna, solarium, games room.
➲ *From Oberstaufen follow B308 for 7km towards the Austrian border.*
All year 2.5HEC ▥ ♁♒⚓☎⊙ ◙ ◿ ☵ ⊞ ⚑ ⅋ P ⊡ ♦ ⅋R
Prices: ♦4 ▲4.50-7.50 pitch 4.50-7.50

AITRANG BAYERN

Elbsee 3 Am Elbsee 3 ☎ 08343 248 ▤ 08343 1406
On the E shore of the lake with good bathing facilities. Section reserved for campers with dogs.
➲ *Take B12 from Marktoberdorf travel for 11km then turn N to Aitrang.*
20 Dec-1 Nov 3.5HEC ▥ ♁♒⚓⊙ ◙ ◿ ☵ ⊡ ◲ ⅋ L ⊡⊞ lau ♦ ✗ ⅋P

ARLACHING BAYERN

Kupferschmiede Trostberger Str 4
☎ 086671 446 ▤ 08667 16198
On meadowland. Partially gravel.
➲ *On Seebruck-Traunstein road.*
Apr-Oct 2.5HEC ▥ ♦♒⚓✗⊙ ◙ ◿ ⅋ L ⊡⊞ lau ♦ ⅋PR Prices: ♦4.95-5.50 ♠1.50 ◲4 ▲4

AUGSBURG BAYERN

Augusta Mühlhauser Str 543 ☎ 0821 707575 ▤ 705883
Hard standings for caravans. Separate section for residential caravans.
➲ *Leave E11 by Augsburg-Ost exit. Continue N towards Neuburg and turn right after 400m.*
All year 6.6HEC ▥ ♁♒⚓✗⊙ ◙ ◿ ☵ ◲ ◱ ▲ ⅋ L ⊡ ♦ ⅋

BAMBERG BAYERN
At BUG(5km S)

Insel ☎ 0951 56320 ▤ 56321
The site lies on the bank of the River Regnitz, S of Bamberg.
'Park & Ride' scheme into Bamberg.
➲ *Leave A73 at Bamberg South exit and follow B505/B4 towards Bamberg until you see camping signs leading off left.*
All year 5HEC ▥ ♁♒⅋✗⊙ ◙ ◿ ⅋ R ⊡⊞ lau
Prices: ♦3.90-7.50 ♠3.40-6.80 ◲3.40-6.80 ▲3.40-6.80

BERCHTESGADEN BAYERN

Allwegiehen ☎ 08652 2396 ▤ 08652 63503
A terraced site at the foot of the Untersalzberg Mountain surrounded by bushy woods. There is also a steep and narrow asphalt access road with passing places. A truck is available for towing caravans. The camp is closed between 12.30 and 14.30 hrs and from 21.00 hrs.
➲ *For access, take the B305, and drive approx. 3.5km towards Schellenberg.*
All year 3HEC ▥ ⁝⁝ ♁♒⚓✗⊙ ◙ ◿ ☵ ◱ ⅋ P ⊡⊞ ✣♦ ⅋R

BERGEN BAYERN

Wagnerhof Campingstr 11 ☎ 08662 8557 ▤ 5924
e-mail: info@camping-bergen.de
Level site.
Camping Card Compulsory.
➲ *Access from München-Salzburg motorway, Bergen exit. Turn right at sawmill just before entering town.*
All year 2.8HEC ♦♁♒⚓☎⊙ ◙ ◿ ☵ ♦ ▼✗ ⅋P ⊞
Prices: ♦4-5 ♠2.50-3.25 ▲2.50-3.25 pitch 5-3.50

BERNAU-AM-CHIEMSEE BAYERN
At FELDEN(3km N)

Chiemsee-Süd ☎ 08051 7540 & 7175 ▤ 08051 89403
Level meadowland shaded by trees, on lake shore.
➲ *Leave the A8/E11 (München-Salzburg) at exit Felden, continue W towards lake.*
Apr-15 Oct 2HEC ▥ ⁝⁝ ♁♒⚓✗⊙ ◙ ◿ ☵ ⅋ L ⊡⊞

BRUNNEN FORGGENSEE BAYERN

Brunnen Seestr 81 ☎ 08362 8273 ▤ 08362 8630
e-mail: info@camping-brunnen.de
Situated on E shore of Lake Forggensee.
➲ *From Füssen follow B17 to Schwangau, then continue N on minor road.*
Closed 5 Nov-20 Dec 3.5HEC ▥ ♦♁♒⚓▼✗⊙ ◙ ◿ ☵ ⅋ L ⊡⊞ lau ♦ ⅋P Prices: ♦6-7 pitch 5-6

CHIEMING BAYERN

Chieming Möwenplatz Haupstr 3 ☎ 08664 361 & 653
Small site on shore of lake, with gravelly terrain.
Camping Card Compulsory.
➲ *5km S of Chieming.*
Apr-Sep 0.8HEC ▥ ♒⚓✗⊙ ◙ ⅋ L ⊡⊞ lau ♦ ♒▼✗ ◿ ☵ ⅋P

DIESSEN BAYERN

St-Alban ☎ 08807 7305 ▤ 08807 1057
e-mail: ivan.pavic@t-online.de
Clean site next to St-Alban, lakeside with private bathing beach and reserved section for residential campers.
➲ *From München follow B12 towards Landsberg/Lech. Near Greifenberg turn left, proceed via Utting to St-Alban.*
Apr-Oct 3.8HEC ▥ ♁♒⚓✗⊙ ◙ ◿ ☵ ⅋ L ⊡⊞ ♦ ◿

DINKELSBÜHL BAYERN

Romantische Strasse ☎ 09851 7817 ▤ 09851 7848
Terraced site with some hedges and trees. Separate field for young campers. Good sporting facilities.
➲ *Signposted.*
All year 12HEC ▥ ♁♒⚓✗⊙ ◙ ◿ ⅋ L ⊡ ◲ ⊞ lau ♦ ▼

ENDORF, BAD BAYERN

Stein Hintersee 10 ☎ 08053 9349 ▓ 08053 798745
A family site in wooded surroundings on the shore of the Simsee.
15 May-15 Sep 2.5HEC ⊞ ∷∴ ⩊ 🏕 🛠 ⊙ ▣
⤳ L 🏢 lau ➡ ✗ 📶

ERLANGEN BAYERN

Rangau Campingstr 44 ☎ 091351 8866 ▓ 724743
e-mail: info@camping-rangau.de
Long stretch of land behind the sportsground and next to the Dechsendorfer Weiher Lake in nature reserve.
➲ *Leave motorway (A3/E5 Nürnberg-Würzburg) at exit Erlangen-West.*
Apr-Sep 18HEC ⊞ ⩊ 🏕 ✗ ⊙ ▣ 📶 🏢 ⊞ lau ➡ 🛠 ⤳LP
Prices: ⋔4.10 pitch 4.10

ESCHERNDORF BAYERN

Escherndorf-Main ☎ 09381 2889 ▓ 09381-2889
Site lies on meadowland by the River Main, next to the ferry station (River Ferry Northeim). Lunchtime siesta 13.00-15.00 hrs.
➲ *Site can be reached from motorway A7/E70 via exit Würzburg Estenfeld and follow road E towards 'Volkach'.*
Apr-30 Oct 1.5HEC ⊞ ➡🏕🛠⊙▣🍴⤳ R 🏢🏢
Prices: ⋔5 pitch 5

ESTENFELD BAYERN

Estenfeld Maidbronner Str 38
☎ 09305 228 ▓ 09305 8006
e-mail: cplestenfeld@freenet.de
On meadowland next to sportsground.
➲ *From motorway A7/E70 leave at exit 'Würzburg/Estenfeld' and continue S on B19 for 1km.*
Mar-23 Dec 24 Dec-28 Feb 0.5HEC ⩊🏕🛠🍴✗⊙▣📶🚐
🏢⊞ lau ➡ ✗ ⌀ ⤳P Prices: ⋔4 pitch 3.50-7

FEILNBACH, BAD BAYERN

Tenda Reithof 2 ☎ 08066 533 ▓ 08066 8002
e-mail: info@tenda-camping.de
Well organised site on level grassland with pitches laid out in circles and hardstandings for tourers near the entrance.
Camping Card Compulsory.
➲ *Leave München-Salzburg motorway (A8/E11) at 'Bad Aibling' exit and continue S for 4km on unclass road.*
All year 14HEC ⊞ ⩊🏕✗⊙▣🍴📶⤳P🏢⊞
➡🍴⤳L

FICHTELBERG BAYERN

Fichtelsee ☎ 09272 801 ▓ 09272 909045
e-mail: info@camping-fichtelsee.de
Gently sloping meadow amid pleasant woodland 100m from Lake Fichtelsee.
➲ *From A9/E6 Bad Berneck exit, take B303 to the Fichtelsee Leisure Centre turning.*
6 Nov-15 Dec 2.6HEC ⊞ ⩊🏕⊙▣⌀🏢⊞ lau ➡🍴✗📶
⤳LP

FINSTERAU BAYERN

Nationalpark-Ost ☎ 08557 768 ▓ 08557 1062
e-mail: frank@frg.baynet.de
Terraced site on edge of extensive woodland area at entrance to National Park.
➲ *N of Freyung towards the frontier.*
15 May-30 Oct & 15 Dec-Mar 3HEC ⊞ ⩊🏕✗⊙▣⌀📶
🏢⊞ lau ➡ 🛠🍴 Prices: ⋔4 pitch 4

FISCHBACH AM INN BAYERN

Inntal Mönchbergstr 25 ☎ 08034 2869 ▓ 080342869
On level grassland near a small forest lake.
➲ *Off B15 S of town.*
All year 2.5HEC ⊞ ⩊🏕✗⊙▣⌀⤳L🏢⊞ lau
Prices: ⋔4.50 ➡1.50 🚗4.50 ⋏3.50

FRICKENHAUSEN BAYERN

Knaus Frickenhausen Ochsenfurter Strabe 49
☎ 09331 3171 ▓ 09331 5784
On level meadow in a small poplar wood beside River Main. Lunchtime siesta 13.00-15.00 hrs.
➲ *On N bank of Main 0.5km E of Oshsenfurt.*
Closed Nov 3.4HEC ⊞ ⩊🏕🛠🍴✗⊙▣⌀📶🚐⤳ PR
🏢 lau ➡ ⊞

FÜRTH IM WALD BAYERN

SC Einberg Daberger Str ☎ 09973 1811 ▓ 803220
e-mail: camping@stadtwerke-furth.de
Municipal site in Dabergerstr, near swimming pool.
➲ *NE of Cham on B20.*
Mar-Oct 2HEC ⊞ ⩊🏕⊙▣🍴⤳ R 🏢🏢⊞ lau ➡🛠🍴✗⌀📶
⤳P Prices: ⋔3.60 ➡2.60 🚗3.10 ⋏2

FÜSSING, BAD BAYERN

Max I Falkenstr 12, Egglfing ☎ 08537 96170 ▓ 08537 9617-10
e-mail: info@campingmax.de
On a level meadow with some trees. Good modern facilities.
➲ *Access via B12. Site S of Bad Füssing.*
All year 3HEC ⊞ ➡🏕🛠✗⊙▣🍴📶🏠🚐🏢⊞ lau ➡ ✗
Prices: ⋔4.50 ⋏4 pitch 5.50

GADEN BAYERN

Schwanenplatz Schwanenpl 1 ☎ 08681 281 ▓ 4276
e-mail: info@schwanenplatz.de
Site lies on a meadow, divided into sections beside one of Bavaria's warmest lakes, Waginger See.
➲ *For access drive from Traunstein to Waging, then turn right in direction Freilassing 2km, then left to lake.*
May-25 Sep 4HEC ⊞ ⩊🏕🍴✗⊙▣🍴⤳L🏢⊞🏖➡🛠⌀
Prices: ⋔4.30-5.40 pitch 5-8.70

GARMISCH-PARTENKIRCHEN BAYERN

Zugspitze Griesener Str 4 ☎ 08821 3180 ▓ 947594
In beautiful setting at the foot of the Zugspitze between the road and the Loisach.
➲ *On the B24 towards the Austrian frontier.*
All year 2.9HEC ⊞ ⩊🏕🛠✗⊙▣⌀📶🏠🚐⤳ R 🏢⊞ lau
➡🍴 Prices: ⋔3.20-3.80 pitch 7.50-8.60

GEMÜNDEN AM MAIN BAYERN

Saaleinsel Duivenallee 7 ☎ 09351 8574 ▓ 1093
This municipal site lies a short distance off the main road bordering the River Fränkische Saale. It is in the grounds of a sports field and has a swimming pool. Individual washing cubicles with curtains for the ladies.
➲ *Access signposted off main B26 road.*
Apr-15 Oct 5.1HEC ⊞ ∿🏕✗⊙▣🍴📶🚐⤳ PR 🏢⊞➡
🛠🍴⌀ Prices: ⋔4.50 ➡3 🚗3 ⋏3 pitch 5.60

GEMÜNDEN-HOFSTETTEN BAYERN

Schönrain ☎ 09351 8645 ▓ 8721
e-mail: info@spessart-camping.de
Slightly sloping, partly terraced meadowland E of River Main. Lunchtime siesta 13.00-15.00 hrs.
➲ *From Gemünden/Main along the left bank of the River Main about 3km downstream. Turn left of B26 through Hofstetten to site.*
Oct-Mar 7HEC ⊞ ⩊🏕🛠⊙▣⌀📶⤳ P 🏢⊞ lau
Prices: ⋔5 pitch 4

▶ **GOTTSDORF** BAYERN

AZUR-Ferienzentrum Bayerwald
☎ 08593 880 ▤ 08593 88111
e-mail: gottsdorf@azur-camping.de
Extensive terrain in quiet location.
⮕ *Access via A3 (Regensburg-Passau) and B388.*
All year 12HEC ⛺ ⤶ ⍾ ⌇ ⊙ ⚑ ⤒ ⚏ ⊡ ⊞ lau ➡ ✗ ⳇP
Prices: ⚑4.50-6 ▲3.50-4.50 pitch 5.50-7.50

▶ **GRIESBACH, BAD** BAYERN

Kur-Und Feriencamping Dreiquellenbad
☎ 08532 96130 ▤ 08532 961350
e-mail: info@camping-bad-griesbach.de
In pleasant wooded surroundings with good, modern facilities.
⮕ *1km S of Griesbach Spa, on the Karpfham-Schwaim road.*
All year 2.5HEC ⛺ ♨ ⤶ ⍾ ⌇ ⚊ ✗ ⊙ ⚑ ⚏ ⳇ P ⊡ lau
Prices: ⚑4.50 ▲5.60 pitch 6.90

▶ **HASLACH** BAYERN

Feriencenter Wertacher Hof
☎ 08361 770 ▤ 08361 9344
Well-kept site on Lake Grüntensee.
⮕ *Access road near the Wertach-Haslach railway station.*
All year 3.5HEC ⛺ ♨ ⤶ ⍾ ⌇ ✗ ⊙ ⚑ ⌀ ⳇ L ⊡ lau

▶ **HERSBRUCK** BAYERN

▶ At **HOHENSTADT**(6km E)

Pegnitz Eschenbacher Weg 4
☎ 09154 1500 ▤ 09154-91200
A quiet holiday site in set among wooded hills near the River Pegnitz.
⮕ *About 6km E of Hersbruck.*
Mar-Oct 1.1HEC ⛺ ⮕ ⤶ ✗ ⊙ ⚑ ⌀ ⳇ R ⊡ ⊞ lau ➡ ⍾ ⚊ ✗ ⤒ ⳇLP

▶ **HOFHEIM** BAYERN

Brugger am Riegsee
☎ 08847 728 ▤ 08847 728
e-mail: camping.brugger@t-online.de
A lakeside site in a rural setting with good, modern facilities.
20 Oct-31 Apr 6HEC ⛺ ♨ ⮕ ⤶ ⍾ ⚊ ✗ ⊙ ⚑ ⌀ ⤒ ⚏ ⳇ L ⊡
⊞ lau Prices: ⚑4.90 ⬲1.53 pitch 7.67-12.78

▶ **HOHENWARTH** BAYERN

Fritz-Berger-Comfort ☎ 09946 367 ▤ 477
e-mail: cpl.hohenwarth@fritz-berger.de
Meadowland in the valley of the Weissens Regens with views of the mountain range and town above.
⮕ *Access from Cham on the B85 S to Miltach and continue via Kotzing to Hohenwarth.*
01 Nov-10 Dec 12HEC ⛺ ⤶ ⍾ ✗ ⊙ ⚑ ⌀ ⤒ ⳇ LP ⊡
Prices: ⚑5 ⬲6

▶ **HOPFEN AM SEE** BAYERN

Hopfensee ☎ 08362 917710 ▤ 917720
e-mail: info@camping-hopfensee.com
In quiet situation beside lake. Private beach. Ski-ing lessons.
⮕ *4km N of Füssen.*
4 Nov-16 Dec 8HEC ⛺ ⤶ ⍾ ⚊ ✗ ⊙ ⚑ ⤒ ⳇ LP ⊡ ⊞ lau
Prices: ⚑7-8 pitch 10.50-11.50

▶ **ILLERTISSEN** BAYERN

Illertissen ☎ 07303 7888
Partially terraced site with plenty of trees.
⮕ *Turn off towards Dietenheim at the ARAL filling station and continue along road for 1.5km. Site on left hand side of road.*
Apr-15 Oct 3HEC ⛺ ⤶ ⍾ ⚊ ⚊ ✗ ⊙ ⚑ ⤒ ⚏ ⳇ P ⊡ ⊞ lau

▶ **INGOLSTADT** BAYERN

AZUR Camping Auwaldsee
☎ 0841 9611616 ▤ 0841 9611617
Near to Auwaldsee, this site lies in a beautiful setting beside the München-Ingolstadt motorway.
⮕ *Access via the Ingolstadt-Süd exit off the A9/E6 (Müchen-Nürnberg motorway).*
All year 10HEC ⛺ ⤶ ⍾ ✗ ⊙ ⚑ ⤒
ⳇ L ⊡ ⊞ lau ➡ ⳇP

▶ **ISSIGAU** BAYERN

Schloss Issigau Altes Schloss 3
☎ 09293 7173 ▤ 09293 7050
⮕ *About 5km W off A9/E6 (München-Berlin) road via the Berg/Bad Steben exit.*
15 Mar-Oct 2HEC ⛺ ⤶ ⍾ ✗ ⊙ ⚑ ⤒ ⚏ ⊡ ⊞ lau ➡ ⍾
Prices: ⚑4.20 ⬲5 ▲4-5 pitch 5

▶ **JODITZ** BAYERN

Auensee ☎ 09295 381
Municipal site on partly terraced meadowland above lake.
⮕ *Leave München-Berlin motorway at Berg-Bad Steben exit and drive E for 4km.*
All year 9HEC ⛺ ⤶ ⮕ ⊙ ⚑ ⤒ ⳇ L ⊡ ⊞ lau ➡ ⍾ ✗ ⳇP

▶ **KIPFENBERG** BAYERN

AZUR-Camping Altmühltal Am Festpl 3
☎ 08465 905167 ▤ 08465 3745
e-mail: kipfenberg@azur-camping.de
Well equipped site in an unspoilt wooded location with good canoeing facilities.
All year 5.5HEC ⛺ ⮕ ⤶ ⊙ ⚑ ⚏ ⳇ R ⊡ ⊞ lau ➡ ⍾ ✗ ⳇP
Prices: ⚑4.50-6 ▲3.50-4.50 pitch 5.50-7.50

▶ **KIRCHHAM** BAYERN

Max ☎ 08537 356 ▤ 08537 356
On meadow divided into pitches and 1km from spa baths at Bad Füssing.
⮕ *Turn at Passau end of Tutling on B12 to Kircham then follow signs to site on Egglfinger Strasse, 2km from Bad Füssing.*
All year 1.5HEC ⛺ ⤶ ⍾ ⚊ ✗ ⊙ ⚑ ⤒ ⚏ ⊡ ⊞ lau ➡ ⳇR
Prices: ⚑4.50 ▲4 pitch 5.50

▶ **KIRCHZELL** BAYERN

AZUR-Camping Odenwald
☎ 09373 566 ▤ 09373 7375
e-mail: info@azur-camping.de
In natural terraced meadowland in wooded hilly country. No admission after 21.30 hrs. Lunchtime siesta 13.00-15.00 hrs.
⮕ *From Amorbach follow the Eberbach road for 5km. Site 1km from town.*
All year 7HEC ⛺ ⤶ ⍾ ⚊ ⚊ ✗ ⊙ ⚑ ⤒ ⳇ P ⊡ ⊞ lau
Prices: ⚑4.09-5.87 pitch 5.11-7.41

▶ **KISSINGEN, BAD** BAYERN

Bad Kissingen Euerdorfer Str 1 ☎ 0971 5211
In park beside River Saale. Lunchtime siesta 13.00-15.00 hrs.
⮕ *Access near the southern bridge over the Saale.*
Apr-15 Oct 1.8HEC ⛺ ⤶ ⍾ ✗ ⊙ ⚑ ⌀ ⤒ ⊡ ⊞ lau
➡ ⳇP

▶ **KITZINGEN** BAYERN

Schiefer Turm Marktbreiter Str 20
☎ 09321 33125 ▤ 384795
e-mail: chr.schroeder@t-online.de
⮕ *Access via A3 exit Biebelried/Kitzingen.*
Apr-15 Oct 2.3HEC ⛺ ⤶ ⍾ ⚊ ✗ ⊙ ⚑ ⤒ ⚑
ⳇ R ⊡ lau ➡ ⳇP

207

> **KLINGENBRUNN** BAYERN

NationalPark ☎ 08553 727 ▧ 08553 6930
In pleasant wooded surroundings attractively set out around the restaurant building.
➲ *For access, leave the B85, which turns from Cham to Passau, approx. 12km SE of Regen near Kirchdorf turn off E and drive about 6km towards Klingenbrunn.*
All year 5HEC � ⊕ ✿ ⊙ ☒ ◢ ⚑ ⚐ 🏕 lau ➔ ♛
¿LP Prices: ⭑4 pitch 4

> **KÖNIGSDORF** BAYERN

Königsdorf Am Bibisee ☎ 08171 81580 ▧ 08171 81165
e-mail: mail@camping-koenigsdorf.de
Unspoilt site in natural setting in meadowland.
A number of individual pitches for tourers. Lunchtime siesta 12.30-14.30 hrs.
➲ *Off B11, 2km N of town just beyond the edge of the forest.*
All year 8.6HEC � ⊕ ✿ ⊙ ☒ ◢ ⚑ ¿ L ✆ 🏕 lau
➔ ♛ ¿PRS Prices: ⭑4.50-5 ♠2-2.50 ⚐2.50-3 ▲2.50

> **KÖNIGSSEE** BAYERN

Mühlleiten ☎ 08652 4584 ▧ 08652 69194
e-mail: buchung@camping-muehlleiten.de
A pleasant site in wooded surroundings adjacent to a small guesthouse. Beautiful views of the Berchtesgaden mountains.
➲ *N of Königsee towards Berchtesgaden.*
All year 1.5HEC ⎚ ⊕ ✿ ⊙ ☒ ◢ ¿ R ✆ lau ➔ ♛ ¿LP
Prices: ⭑4.70 ♠2.50 ⚐2.50 ▲2.50 pitch 5

> **KRUN** BAYERN

Tennsee ☎ 08825 170 ▧ 08825 17236
e-mail: info@camping-tennsee.de
A partially terraced site with fine views of the Karwendel and Zugspitz mountains.
➲ *From München-Garmisch-Partenkirchen motorway take B2 to Mittenwald and follow signs "Tennsee".*
11 Nov-15 Dec 5HEC ⎚ ⁝⁝ ✿ ⊕ ✿ ⊙ ☒ ◢ ⚑ 🏕 ✆
🏕 lau ➔ ¿L

> **KÜHNHAUSEN** BAYERN

Stadler Strandbadstr 10 ☎ 08686 8037 ▧ 08685 919555
Level meadow on lake with private beach.
➲ *2m E shore of Lake Waginger.*
Apr-Sep 0.8HEC ⎚ ✿ ⊕ ⊙ ☒ 🏕 ¿ L ✆ lau ➔ ✿ ♛ ✗ ◢
🏕 Prices: ⭑4.50-9 ♠1.50-3 ⚐5-6 ▲2.50-5

> **LACKENHÄUSER** BAYERN

Knaus Lackenhäuser Lackenhauser 127
☎ 08583 311 ▧ 08583 91079
e-mail: knaus-camping-lackenhaeuser@t-online.de
Extensive site with woodland parks, waterfalls.
Siesta 13.00-15.00 hrs. Many health resort facilities.
Garden chess. Curling.
Closed Nov 14.5HEC ⎚ ✿ ⊕ ✿ ✗ ⊙ ☒ ◢ ⚑ 🏕 ⚐ ▲
¿ P ✆ ➔ 🏕

> **LANDSBERG** BAYERN

Romantik am Lech ☎ 08191 47505 ▧ 08191 21406
Level site with some terraces on right bank of the Lech.
Lunchtime siesta 13.00-15.00 hrs.
Camping Card Compulsory.
➲ *S towards Gut Pössing.*
All year 6.5HEC ⎚ ⁝⁝ ✿ ✿ ⊕ ✿ ⊙ ☒ ◢ ✆ 🏕 lau
➔ ♛ ✗ ¿R

> **LANGLAU** BAYERN

Langlau Seestr 30, Kleiner Brombachsee
☎ 09834 96969 ▧ 96968
e-mail: mail@zv-brombachsee.de
On the shores of the Kleiner Brombachsee.

➲ *From Gunzevhausen 10km in the direction of Pleinfield.*
Mar-15 Nov 12.4HEC ⎚ ✿ ⊕ ✿ ☒ ✗ ⊙ ☒ 🏕 ⚐ ✆ lau
➔ ✗ ¿L 🏕 Prices: ⭑5.50 pitch 6.50

> **LECHBRUCK** BAYERN

DCC Stadt Essen Oberer Lechsee
☎ 08862 8426 ▧ 08862 7570
Terraced site, very tidy and well maintained on Oberen Lech lake. Separate section for dog owners. Closed 13.00-15.00 hrs and 22.00-07.00 hrs.
➲ *Signposted from town centre.*
All year 20HEC ⎚ ✿ ⊕ ✿ ✗ ⊙ ☒ ◢ ¿ L ✆ lau ➔ ¿P

> **LENGFURT** BAYERN

Main-Spessart-Park ☎ 09395 1079 ▧ 8295
e-mail: info@camping-main-spessart.de
Site lies partly on terraced meadowland and partly on the E slopes of the Main Valley. Lunchtime siesta 13.00-15.00 hrs, Possibilities for water sports, nearby private mooring on the River Main.
➲ *From Frankfurt-Würzburg motorway A3/E5 leave at exit Markheidenfeld. N to Altfled then E for 6km to Lengfurt. Site lies at NW edge of village.*
All year 10HEC ⎚ ✿ ⊕ ✿ ✗ ⊙ ☒ ◢ ✆ lau ➔ ♛ ¿PR
Prices: ⭑5 ♠2 ⚐3.50 ▲3

> **LINDAU IM BODENSEE** BAYERN

> At **ZECH**(4km SE)

Lindau-Zech Fraunhoferstr 20
☎ 08382 72236 ▧ 08382 976106
e-mail: info@park-camping.de
Site lies on meadowland with trees, reaching down to the lake. Very large sanitary blocks. Common room, reading room, field for ball games and a separate common room for young people.
➲ *From Lindau, take the B31 towards Bregenz and turn right (signposted) just before the level crossing. The site is 500m further down the road.*
All year 5HEC ⎚ ✿ ✿ ✿ ✿ ✗ ⊙ ☒ ⚑ ⚐
¿ L ✆ 🏕 lau ➔ ¿P Prices: ⭑4.50-5.50 ♠2.40-3
▲1.50-2.50 pitch 4.50-5.50

> **MEMMINGEN** BAYERN

> At **BUXHEIM**(5km NW)

See International Am Weiherhaus 7
☎ 08331 71800 ▧ 08331 63554
Terraced site beyond public bathing area.
➲ *Leave Um-Kempten motorway at Memminger Kreuz then right to Buxheim.*
May-Sep 42HEC ⎚ ✿ ✿ ✿ ✿ ✗ ⊙ ☒ ◢ 🏕 ¿ L ✆ 🏕 lau ➔
✗ ◢ Prices: ⭑3.60 ♠2.10 ⚐7.20 ▲3.50

> **MITTENWALD** BAYERN

Isarhorn ☎ 08823 5216
In a loop of the River Isar with many pines. Lunchtime siesta 13.00-15.00 hrs.
➲ *3km N to the W of B2 (Garmisch-Partenkirchen-Mittenwald road).*
All year 7.5HEC ⎚ ✿ ✿ ✿ ✿ ✗ ⊙ ☒ ◢ ¿ R ✆ 🏕 ➔ ♛ ✗
¿LP

> **MÖRSLINGEN** BAYERN

Mörslingen ☎ 09074 4024
Camping Card Compulsory.
➲ *6km N of Dillengen.*
All year 1HEC ⎚ ✿ ✿ ⊙ ☒ 🏕 ⚑ 🏕 ⚐ ¿ L ✆ 🏕 lau
Prices: ⭑4.5 pitch 8

Waldcamping München-Obermenzing

To reach the site from Cross Münich West until the end at Mu-Lochhaüsen.
Set in a large park of 50,000 sq.m 900m from the end of the motorway Stuttgart-München.
350 spaces for caravans and tents, 130 with own electricity supply and separated by hedges. Individual washing cubicles, free hot water for washing, hot showers, washing machine, dryer. heated washrooms, self-service shop. Opportunities for swimming 2.5km from site.
Locked from 22.00 hrs. Good connections to city centre by bus, tram or urban railway. Open from 15.3-31.10.
Farmer: A. Blenck Telephone 089/8 11 22 35 Fax 089/8 14 48 07
www.campingplatz-muenchen.de
email: campingplatz-obermenzing@t-online.de

⏵ **MÜHLHAUSEN BEI AUGSBURG** BAYERN

Lech Seeweg 6 ☎ 08207 2200 ▤ 08207 2202
e-mail: lech-camping-gmbh@t-online.de
On level grassland with own swimming facilities on lakeside.
⮑ *4km N in direction of Neuburg.*
Etr-15 Sep 3HEC ⊞ 🐾 🏕 ✕ ⊙ 🐶 ⌿ 🛆 ⚓ 🕴 L 🏛 ⊞ lau
⮕ 🐾 🕴P Prices: ♦5 ♠1 🚐7 A5-7

Ludwigshof am See Augsburger Str 36
☎ 08027 9617-0 ▤ 961770
e-mail: info@bauer-caravan.de
Clean site with small lake away from motorway, near restaurant of the same name. Separate section for residential pitches.
⮑ *1.5km from Augsburg Ost exit towards Neuberg.*
Apr-Oct 14HEC ⊞ ⮕ 🏕 🛆 ▼ ✕ ⊙ 🐶 ⌿ 🛆 🕴 L 🏛 ⊞ lau
⮕ 🕴P Prices: ♦4 pitch 4-9

⏵ **MÜNCHEN (MUNICH)** BAYERN

⏵ At **OBERMENZING**

München-Obermenzing Lochhausener Str 59
☎ 089 8112235 ▤ 089 8144807
e-mail: campingplatz-obermenzing@t-online.de
Park-like site near motorway. Shop closed in winter and no campers accepted after 31 Oct.
Camping Card or identification papers compulsory.
⮑ *Approx 1km from the end of Stuttgart-München motorway.*
15 Mar-31Oct 5.5HEC ⊞ ⁝⁝⁝ ♠ 🐾 🏕 ✕ ⊙ 🐶 ⌿ 🛆 ⚓ 🏛
⊞ lau ⮕ ▼ ✕ 🕴LPR Prices: ♦4.35 ♠3 🚐4.60 A3.85

⏵ **NEBELBERG** BAYERN

Waldhof ☎ 09922 1024
Partially terraced site on the Schwarzachback.
⮑ *Turn off the B85 to Regen then N to Langdorf and continue NE.*
All year 1HEC ⊞ 🐾 🏕 🛆 ✕ ⊙ 🐶 🛆 ⚓ 🛆 🕴 L 🏛 ⊞ ⮕ 🕴R

⏵ **NEUBÄU** BAYERN

Seecamping Seestr 4 ☎ 09469 331
Meadowland site along lakeshore.
⮑ *Access from Schwandorf on the B85 in direction of Cham.*
Closed Nov 5HEC ⊞ 🐾 🏕 🛆 ▼ ✕ ⊙ 🐶 ⌿ 🛆 🕴 L 🏛 ⊞ lau

⏵ **NEUSTADT** BAYERN

Main-Spessart-Camping-International
☎ 09393 639 ▤ 1607
Beautifully situated site along the River Main. Watersports, including water skiing. Lunchtime siesta 12.00-14.00 hrs.
⮑ *Access from Frankfurt-Würzburg motorway A3/E5, leave at Marktheidenfeld exit, and follow road towards Lohr.*
Apr-Sep 5.6HEC ⊞ 🐾 🏕 ✕ ⊙ 🐶 ⌿ 🛆 🕴 PR 🏛 lau ⮕ ✕
Prices: ♦4.50 pitch 5.50

⏵ **NÜRNBERG (NUREMBERG)** BAYERN

SC Volkspark Dutzendteich Hans-Kalb-Str 56
☎ 0911 9812717 ▤ 9812718
Well-kept municipal site in beautiful situation in a forest between a stadium with a swimming pool and the Trade Fair Centre.
⮑ *Leave A9 München motorway at Nürnberg-Fischbach exit, and continue towards the stadium.*
All year 2.7HEC ⊞ 🐾 🏕 ✕ ⊙ 🐶 ⌿ 🛆 ⚓ 🛆 lau ⮕ 🕴LP
⊞

⏵ **OBERAMMERGAU** BAYERN

Oberammergau Ettaler Str 56
☎ 08822 94105 ▤ 94197
e-mail: campingpark-oberammergau@t-online.de
A year-round site with good, modern facilities providing fine views of the Bavarian Alps.
⮑ *Signposted from the town.*
All year 1.7HEC ⊞ ♠ 🏊 🏕 ✕ ⊙ 🐶 ⌿ 🛆 ⚓ 🛆 🕴 R 🏛 ⊞
lau ⮕ 🕴P Prices: ♦5.50-7.50 🚐1.50-2

⏵ **OBERNDORF** BAYERN

Donau-Lech ☎ 09002 4044 ▤ 09002 4046
A small site beside a lake on the SE outskirts of Donauwörth.
⮑ *From Donauwörth follow B2 towards Augsburg for approx. 5km.*
All year 5HEC ⊞ ♠ 🏕 🛆 ✕ ⊙ 🐶 ⚓ 🕴 L 🏛 lau ⮕ ✕

⏵ **OBERSTDORF** BAYERN

Oberstdorf ☎ 08322 6525 ▤ 809760
e-mail: camping-oberstdorf.de
Level grassland site with fine mountain views.
⮑ *800m N of town centre near railway line.*
All year 16HEC ⊞ ♠ 🐾 🏕 ✕ ⊙ 🐶 ⌿ 🛆 🏛 ⊞ lau ⮕ 🐾 🕴P
Prices: ♦4.60-5.10 🚐2.60 🚐4.60-5.10 A2.60-3.10

⏵ **OBERWÖSSEN** BAYERN

Litzelau ☎ 08640 8704 ▤ 08640 5265
e-mail: camping-litzelau@t-online.de
Almost level meadowland surrounded by forested slopes.
⮑ *Take B305 from Bernau exit on München-Salzburg motorway and continue through Marquartstein and Unterwössen.*
All year 4.5HEC ⊞ ♠ 🐾 🏕 🛆 ✕ ⊙ 🐶 ⌿ 🛆 ⚓ 🕴 R 🏛 ⊞
lau ⮕ 🕴LP

OCHSENFURT BAYERN

Polisina Marktbreiter Str 265 ☎ 09331 8440
Terraced site at edge of wood.
➲ *From town centre follow road towards Markbreit and in 2km turn off under railway and continue uphill.*
All year 2.5HEC ⟁⟁⟁ ♦ ⋔ ⬥ ✕ ⬛ ⊘ ♨ ₹ P 🅿 ⊞ lau ➥ ₹R

PASSAU BAYERN

Dreiflüsse ☎ 08546 633 ⊟ 08546 2686
A well equipped site in pleasant wooded surroundings.
➲ *From A3 exit 'Passau-Nord' follow signposts.*
Apr-Oct 5HEC ⟁⟁⟁ ∴∴ ♦ ⋔ ⬥ ♀ ✕ ⊙ ⬛ ⊘ ♨ ⬛ ⬛ ▲ ₹ P 🅿 🅿 ⊞ lau

PFAFFENHOFEN BAYERN

SC Warmbad Hauptpl 1 ☎ 08441 83543
The municipal site lies on the northern outskirts of the town beside the River Lim.
➲ *Take the München-Nürnberg motorway, and leave at Pfaffenhofen exit, or take the B13 which runs from München to Ingolstadt.*
May-Sep 0.7HEC ⟁⟁⟁ ⚘ ⋔ ✕ ⊙ ⬛ ₹ P 🅿 ⊞ lau ➥ ⬥ ♀ ✕

PFRAUNDORF BAYERN

Kratzmühle ☎ 08461 64170 ⊟ 08461 641717
e-mail: kratzmuehle@t-online.de
Terraced site, divided into pitches, on a wooded hillside overlooking the River Altmühl.
➲ *In village turn off to Kratzmühle.*
All year 9.6HEC ⟁⟁⟁ ⚘ ⋔ ⬥ ✕ ⊙ ⬛ ♨ ⬛ ₹ LR 🅿 ⊞ lau
Prices: ⋔5-6 pitch 6-7

PIDING BAYERN

Staufeneck ☎ 08651 2134 ⊟ 710450
In beautiful and quiet situation beside River Saalach.
➲ *Leave motorway A8/E11 (München-Salzburg) via exit Bad Reichenall road for 2.5km and then turn right.*
Apr-Oct 01Nov-20 Mar 2.7HEC ⟁⟁⟁ ⚙ ⚘ ⋔ ⬥ ⊙ ⬛ ♨ ⊞ lau ➥ ♀ ✕ ⊘ ₹P Prices: ⋔5.10 pitch 5.10

PIELENHOFEN BAYERN

Naabtal ☎ 09409 373 ⊟ 723
e-mail: campingpielenhofen@t-online.de
The site is well-situated beside the River Nab, and has a special section for overnight visitors.
➲ *Access from the Nittendorf turn off from A3/E5 Nürnberg-Regensburg N via Etterzhausen.*
All year 6HEC ⟁⟁⟁ ⚘ ⋔ ⬥ ♀ ✕ ⊙ ⬛ ⊘ ♨ ₹ R 🅿 ⊞ lau
Prices: ⋔4.75 pitch 5.50

POTTENSTEIN BAYERN

Bärenschlucht ☎ 09243 206
The site lies on unspoilt meadowland in the narrow Püttlach valley and is surrounded by the rocky hills of the Fränkische Schweiz range.
➲ *From the München-Berlin motorway leave at the Pegnitz exit and drive W for 10km on the B470 towards Forchheim.*
All year 5HEC ⟁⟁⟁ ⚘ ⋔ ⬥ ✕ ⊙ ⬛ ⊘ ⬛ ⬛ ₹ R 🅿 ⊞ lau

REGENSBURG BAYERN

AZUR-Regensburg Weinweg 40
☎ 0941 270025 ⊟ 0941 299432
The municipal site lies on the western outskirts of the town, and the right bank of the Danube. Has a special section reserved for caravans.
➲ *Access via the western by-pass, and over the Pfaffenstein Bridge.*
All year 2.6HEC ⟁⟁⟁ ⚘ ⋔ ⬥ ✕ ⊙ ⬛ ⊘ 🅿 lau ➥ ₹LPR

ROSSHAUPTEN BAYERN

Warsitzka ☎ 08367 406 ⊟ 08367 1256
e-mail: info@camping-warsitzka.de
A well-kept site with good installations.
➲ *From Füssen follow road B16 for 10km towards Rosshaupten. About 2km before the village and before the bridge turn right.*
All year 4.5HEC ⟁⟁⟁ ⚘ ⋔ ⬥ ♀ ✕ ⊙ ⬛ ⊘ ♨ ₹ LR 🅿 ⊞ lau
Prices: ⋔5-5.20 ⬛6.20-7.70 ▲6.20-7.70

ROTHENBURG OB DER TAUBER BAYERN

Tauber-Idyll Detwang 28A ☎ 09861 3177 ⊟ 09861 92848
e-mail: campingtauber-ldyll@t-online.de
The well-kept site lies on a meadow scattered with trees and bushes, on the outskirts of the N suburb of Detwang and next to the River Tauber.
➲ *Access from all main roads is well signposted. The best route is from Nordinger Str (B25) heading W along the River Tauber in the direction of Bad Mergentheim.*
7 Apr-Oct 0.5HEC ⟁⟁⟁ ⚘ ⋔ ⬥ ⊙ ⬛ ⊘ ⬛ ⊞ lau ➥ ✕ ₹R
Prices: ⋔4 ⬛1.50 ⬛3.50 ▲3 pitch 5

Tauber-Romantik Detwang 39 ☎ 09861 6191 ⊟ 86899
e-mail: info@camping-tauberromantik.de
Apr-Oct 1.2HEC ⟁⟁⟁ ♦ ⋔ ⬥ ♀ ✕ ⊙ ⬛ ⊘ ♨ ⬛ ⬛ ⊞ lau ➥ ₹R Prices: ⋔4.5 ⬛1.5 ⬛5.5 ▲4.5

ROTTENBUCH BAYERN

Terrassen-Camping am Richterbichl
☎ 08867 1500 ⊟ 08867 8300
e-mail: christof.echtler@t-online.de
Several pleasant terraces with good views.
➲ *On S outskirts on B23.*
All year 1.2HEC ⟁⟁⟁ ⚘ ⋔ ⬥ ♀ ⊙ ⬛ ⊘ ♨ ⬛ ₹ L ⊞ lau ➥ ✕ ₹R ⊞ Prices: ⋔4.60 pitch 5.20

RUHPOLDING BAYERN

Ortnerhof Ort 5 ☎ 08663 1764 ⊟ 08663 5073
e-mail: camping-ortnerhof@t-online.de
Well-kept site on a meadow at the foot of the Rauschberg Mountain, opposite the cable-car station.
➲ *Off Deutsche Alpenstr.*
All year 2.4HEC ⟁⟁⟁ ⚘ ⋔ ⬥ ✕ ⊙ ⬛ ⊘ ⬛ ⊞ ⊘ lau ➥ ♀ ♀
Prices: ⋔4.50-4.50 ⬛1.50-1.50 ⬛3-3 ▲3 pitch 4.50

SCHECHEN BAYERN

Erlensee Rosenheimer Str 63 ☎ 08039 1695 ⊟ 08039 9416
The site lies on the shores of an artificial lake.
➲ *If approaching from Rosenheim, take the B15 approx 10km N of Rosenheim towards Wasserburg and turn right upon entering Schechen.*
All year 6HEC ⟁⟁⟁ ⚘ ⋔ ⊙ ⬛ ♨ ₹ L ⊞ ⊞ lau ➥ ♀ ♀ ✕
Prices: ⋔4.50 ⬛2 ⬛5 ▲2.50-6 pitch 7

SCHWANGAU BAYERN

At BANNWALDSEE(4km N)

Bannwaldsee ☎ 08362 81001
Meadow gently sloping towards lake.
➲ *Turn off the B17 about 4km NE of Schwangau, in westerly direction towards lake.*
All year 12HEC ⟁⟁⟁ ∴∴ ⚘ ♦ ⋔ ⬥ ♀ ✕ ⊙ ⬛ ⊘ ♨ ₹ L 🅿 ⊞

SEEFELD BAYERN

Strandbad Pilsensee Graf Toerringstr 11
☎ 08152 7232 ⊟ 78473
e-mail: campingplatzstrandbadpilsensee@t-online.de
➲ *S towards Pilsensee.*
All year 10HEC ⟁⟁⟁ ⚘ ⋔ ⬥ ✕ ⊙ ⬛ ⊘ ♨ ⬛ ₹ L 🅿 ⊞ lau

SOMMERACH AM MAIN BAYERN

Katzenkopf am See ☎ 09381 9215 ▦ 09381 6028
On level ground beside the River Main. Pitches divided by bushes and good recreational facilities.
➡ *Leave A3 (Würzburg-Nürnberg) at exit 'Kitzingen-Schwarzach-Volkach' and continue towards Volkach for 7km.*
6 Apr-21 Oct 4HEC ▥▥▥ ⊞ ⋒ ❡ ⓧ ⊙ ▯ ⌀ ≍ ⋨ LR ⊡⊞ lau
➡ ❡ ⋨P ⊞

SONTHOFEN BAYERN

Iller Sinwagstr 2 ☎ 08321 2350 ▦ 08321 71561
Site lies on the shore of the River Iller (too dangerous for swimming) near a swimming pool.
➡ *1km on the B19 towards Obersdorf, before the bridge over the River Iller.*
Closed Nov-20 Dec 2.1HEC ▥▥▥ ⊞ ⋒ ❡ ⓧ ⊙ ▯ ⌀ ⋨ R ⊡⊞ lau ➡ ⓧ ⋨P

STADTSTEINACH BAYERN

AZUR-Stadtsteinach Badstr 5
☎ 09225 95401 ▦ 09225 95402
Terraced site on SE facing slope with a view over the town and surrounding hills. Lunchtime siesta 13.00-15.00 hrs.
➡ *Access via Badstr.*
All year 5HEC ▥▥▥ ⊞ ⋒ ❡ ⓧ ⊙ ▯ ⌀ ≍ ⊡⊞ lau ➡ ⋨P

TETTENHAUSEN BAYERN

Gut Horn ☎ 08681 227 ▦ 4282
e-mail: info@gut-horn.de
Quiet site, divided into pitches on lake shore, sheltered by forest. Lunchtime siesta 13.00-14.00 hrs.
➡ *SE on Wagingersee.*
Mar-Nov 5HEC ▥▥▥ ⊞ ⋒ ❡ ⓧ ⊙ ▯ ⌀ ⛺ ⋨ L ⓜ lau ➡ ⌀ ⋨PR ⊞ Prices: ⋔4.40-4.90 pitch 4.90-5.40

TITTMONING BAYERN

Seebauer ☎ 08683 541
On meadow with a few terraces. Near a farm, beside a lake.
➡ *3km NW towards Burghausen.*
All year 2.3HEC ▥▥▥ ⊞ ⋒ ❡ ⓧ ⊙ ▯ ⌀ ≍ ⋨ L ⓜ⊞ lau ➡ ❡ ⋨LP

TRAUSNITZ BAYERN

Trausnitz ☎ 09655 1304
In wooded surroundings on the shores of a lake with good, modern facilities.
➡ *Access via A93 exit Pfreimd.*
All year 3.5HEC ▥▥▥ ⊞ ⋒ ❡ ⓧ ⊙ ▯ ⌀ LR ⓜ⊞ lau
Prices: ⋔4 ▲3.50 pitch 5

TÜCHERSFELD BAYERN

Fränkische Schweiz Tüchersfeld
☎ 09242 1788 ▦ 09242 1040
e-mail: spaetling@t-online.de
➡ *Access from motorway A9/E6, leave at exit 'Pegnitz' then 12km W on B470 towards Forchheim.*
Apr-15 Oct 2HEC ▥▥▥ ⊞ ⋒ ❡ ⓧ ⊙ ▯ ⌀ ≍ ⓜ⊞ lau
➡ ⋨P

VELBURG BAYERN

Hauenstein ☎ 09182 454 ▦ 902251
A well-appointed site, lies on several terraces and is completely divided into individual pitches. All with electric points.
➡ *From motorway A3 Nürnberg-Regensburg leave at exit Velberg, then continue through village towards the S following signs Naturbad.*
All year 5HEC ▥▥▥ ⋇ ⋒ ❡ ⓧ ⊙ ▯ ⌀ ≍ ⓜ⊞ lau
➡ ⋨L Prices: ⋔4.50 ⇄2.80 ⇄3.80 ▲3.20

VIECHTACH BAYERN

knaus Viechtach Waldfrieden 22
☎ 09942 1095 ▦ 09942 902222
Site on slightly undulating meadow, divided by rows of trees. The site has modern installations.
➡ *For access, take the B85 which runs from the junction with the road towards Freibad Viechtach, and follow the signposts.*
Closed Nov 5.7HEC ▥▥▥ ⊞ ⋒ ❡ ⓧ ⊙ ▯ ⌀ ≍ ⛺ ▯ ▲
⋨ P ⓜ lau ➡ ⋨R ⊞

WAGING BAYERN

Strandcamping Am See 1 ☎ 08681 552 ▦ 08681 45010
e-mail: strandcamp@aol.com
Extensive, level grassland site divided in two by access road to neighbouring sailing club. The site lies near the Strandbad and Kurhaus bathing area and spa, and the Casino. There is a Kneipp (hydrotherapeutic) pool in the camp.
➡ *Follow the signposts leading to the Strandbad bathing area.*
Apr-Sep 30HEC ▥▥▥ ⊞ ⋒ ❡ ⓧ ⊙ ▯ ⌀ ≍ ⛺ ⋨ L ⓜ⊞ ⊘
lau Prices: ⋔4.90-6.10 pitch 5.70-6.70

WALTENHOFEN BAYERN

Insel-Camping am See ☎ 08379 881 ▦ 08379 7308
e-mail: insel-camping@t-online.de
A well equipped site situated directly on the lake shore with access to neighbouring ski slopes.
➡ *Off B19, S of Memhölz.*
All year 1.5HEC ▥▥▥ ⊞ ⋒ ❡ ⓧ ⊙ ▯ ⌀ ≍ ⋨ L ⓜ⊞ lau ➡ ⌷

WEILER-SIMMERBERG BAYERN

Alpenblick Schreckmanklitz 18 ☎ 08381 3447
Clean facilities on this site belonging to the Deutsche Alpenstrasse.
➡ *Access from the B308 in Weiler. Signposted.*
Etr-4 Nov 2.5HEC ▥▥▥ ⋇ ⋒ ❡ ⓧ ⊙ ▯ ⌀ ≍ ⛺ ⋨ L ⓜ⊞ ⊘
lau ➡ ⌷

WEISSACH BAYERN

Wallberg Rainerweg 10 ☎ 08022 5371 ▦ 670274
e-mail: campingplatz-wallberg@web.de
The well-kept site lies on a level meadow with a few trees beside a stream.
➡ *For access take the B318 from Gmund to Tegernsee, drive through Bad Wiessee, and on to Wiessach, approx 9km further on.*
All year 3HEC ▥▥▥ ⊞ ⋒ ❡ ⓧ ⊙ ▯ ⌀ ≍ ⛺ ⋨ R ⓜ ➡ ⋨L ⊞
Prices: ⋔4.50-5.20 ⇄5.50-6.50 ▲2.30-2.30

WEISSENSTADT BAYERN

Weissenstädter See Badstr 91 ☎ 09253 288 ▦ 8507
e-mail: st.weissenstadt@fichtelgebirge.org
This municipal site is in close proximity to a swimming pool and a lake, so offering numerous sports facilities.
➡ *1km NW of the town.*
All year 1.7HEC ▥▥▥ ⊞ ⋒ ❡ ⓧ ⊙ ▯ ⌀ ⋨ LP ⓜ⊞ ➡ ⌷

WEMDING BAYERN

AZUR Waldsee Wemding ☎ 09092 90101 ▦ 09092 90100
In a wooded lakeside setting with excellent recreational facilities.
15 Mar-15 Nov 9HEC ▥▥▥ ⌀ ⊞ ⋒ ❡ ⓧ ⊙ ▯ ⌀ ⛺ ⋨ L ▯⊞
lau ➡ ⋨P

WERTACH BAYERN

Grüntensee Grüntenseestr 41 ☎ 08365 375 ▦ 08365 1221
e-mail: info@gruentensee.de
A modern site beside Lake Grünten.

Cont.

211

➲ *If approaching from Kempten, turn right entering Nesselwerg, and follow the signposts.*
All year 5HEC ⊞ ⚄ ♠ ♠ ⚓ ⚡ ✕ ⊙ ➒ ⊘ ⚒ ⚓ L 🏕 ⊞ lau ➡ ⚓P
Prices: ♠5.40-6.20 ➟5.20-6.20 ♠3.10-5.20

WINKL BEI BISCHOFSWIESEN BAYERN

Winkllandthal ☎ 08652 8164 ▧ 979831
e-mail: camping-winkl@t-online.de
In meadow between the B20 and edge of woodland.
➲ *From Bad Reichenhall to Berchtesgaden about 8km.*
All year 2.5HEC ⊞ ⁙⁙⁙ ⚄ ⚄ ♠ ♠ ⚓ ⚡ ✕ ⊙ ➒ ⊘ ⚒ ⚓ ♠ ⚓ R
🏕 ⊞ lau Prices: ♠6.03 pitch 5.20

ZWIESEL BAYERN

AZUR-Ferienzentrum Bayerischer Wald Waldesruhweg 34
☎ 09922 802595 ▧ 09922 802594
e-mail: info@azur-camping.de
All year 16HEC ⊞ ⚄ ♠ ⚓ ⚡ ✕ ⊙ ➒ ⊘ ⚒ ⚓ 🏕 ⊞ lau ➡ ⚓P
Prices: ♠4.50-6 ♠3.50-4.50 pitch 5.50-7.50

● ● ● ● **SOUTH WEST** ● ● ● ●

A rich variety of scenery both charming and grandiose, has led this magnificent area of Germany to become one of the most popular holiday regions.
In the far south, Lake Constance is a majestic expanse of water, ideal for watersports, fringed with historic towns and attractive villages.
The Black Forest is a perennial delight with its vast coniferous woodlands, rushing mountain streams, and glacier-cut valleys. Spectacular views are to be had from the popular Black Forest Ridgeway.
The Neckarland-Schwaben covers the rest of the region and is an exciting area to explore. There are castles and palaces, bustling towns and fascinating museums. At its core is Stuttgart, beautifully situated in a basin enclosed by forest-covered hills, orchards and vineyards that extend well into the city.
This undisputed cultural and commercial centre of the state, is a city of technical progress, while five castles remind us of its princely past.
....

ABTSGMÜND BADEN-WÜRTTEMBERG
At POMMERTSWEILER(6km N)

Hammerschmiede-See Hammerschmiede 6
☎ 07963 1205 & 415
e-mail: camping.hammerschmiede@t-online.de
A terraced site in a wooded setting beside the lake. Partly divided into pitches with concrete paths.
➲ *From Abtsgmünd travel for 3km then turn N to Pommertsweiler, site signposted.*
All year 6HEC ⊞ ⚄ ♠ ⚓ ⚡ ⊙ ➒ ⊘ ⚓ L 🏕 ⊞ lau Prices: ♠3.10-6 ➟2.60-5 ➟2.60-5 ♠4.50

ACHERN BADEN-WÜRTTEMBERG

Staedtischer Campingplatz am Achernsee Am Achernsee 8
☎ 07841 25253 ▧ 07841 25253
e-mail: camping@achern.de
All year 6.5HEC ⊞ ⚄ ♠ ⚓ ⚡ ✕ ⊙ ➒ ⊘ ⚒ ⚓ L 🏕 ⊞ lau

ALPIRSBACH BADEN-WÜRTTEMBERG

Wolpert ☎ 07444 6313
On level land beside the River Kinzig.
➲ *1km N of town below B294.*
All year 1.2HEC ⊞ ♠ ⚓ ⚡ ⊙ ➒ ⊘ ⚒ ⚓ R 🏕 ⊞ lau ➡ ⚡✕

ALTENSTEIG BADEN-WÜRTTEMBERG

Schwarzwald ☎ 07453 8415
e-mail: info@schwarzwaldcamping.de
Parkland site of motor sport club Altensteig beside the River Nagold. Separate section for dog owners.
➲ *On road to Garrweiler 1km from Altensteig.*
All year 3.3HEC ⊞ ⚄ ♠ ⚓ ⚡ ✕ ⊙ ➒ ⊘ ⚒ ⚓ ⚓ R 🏕 ⊞ lau ➡ ⚓P

ALTNEUDORF BADEN-WÜRTTEMBERG

Steinachperle ☎ 06228 467 ▧ 06228 8568
The site lies in the narrow shady valley of the River Steinach. Lunchtime siesta 13.00-15.00 hrs.
➲ *The entrance to the camp lies next to the Gasthaus zum Pflug, on the outskirts of Altneudorf.*
Apr-Sep 3.5HEC ⊞ ⚄ ♠ ⚓ ⚡ ✕ ⊙ ➒ ⊘ ⚒ ⚓ R 🏕 ⊞ lau
Prices: ♠4.10-8 pitch 4.60-9

BADENWEILER BADEN-WÜRTTEMBERG

Badenweiler Weilertalstr 73 ☎ 07632 1550 ▧ 07632 5268
e-mail: camping.badenweiler@t-online.de
On a level meadow surrounded by beautiful Black Forest scenery. Good facilities for local walking etc.
➲ *Access via A5 exit Neuenburg.*
16Jan-14Dec 15Dec-15Jan 1.6HEC ⊞ ⚄ ♠ ⚓ ⚡ ✕ ⊙ ➒ ⊘ ⚒ ⚓ P 🏕 ⊞ lau ➡ ✕ Prices: ♠5.90 pitch 8-8.50

BUCHHORN BEI ÖHRINGEN BADEN-WÜRTTEMBERG

Seewiese Seestr 11 ☎ 07941 61568 ▧ 07941 38527
e-mail: campingseewiese@t-online.de
A well equipped site on a meadow beside a lake with fine views of the surrounding mountains. Good recreational facilities.
➲ *7km S of Öhringen via Pfedelbach. Access via A6.*
All year 5.5HEC ⊞ ⚄ ♠ ⚓ ⚡ ✕ ⊙ ➒ ⚒ ⚓ ⚓ L 🏕 ⊞ lau
Prices: ♠4.50 ➟2.60 ➟2.60-3.60 ♠1.60-3.20

BÜHL BADEN-WÜRTTEMBERG

Adam Campingstr 1 ☎ 07223 23194 ▧ 07223 8982
e-mail: webmaster@campingplatz-adam.de
On level grassland, by lake.
➲ *1km from the Bühl exit of the A5/E4-E11 (Karlsruhe-Basel) in direction of Lichtenau.*
All year 15HEC ⊞ ⚄ ♠ ⚓ ⚡ ✕ ⊙ ➒ ⊘ ⚒ ⚓ L 🏕 ⊞ lau ➡ ⚓P Prices: ♠5-6.50 ♠3.50-5 pitch 5-8

CREGLINGEN BADEN-WÜRTTEMBERG

Camping Romantische Strasse
☎ 07933 20289 ▧ 07933 990019
e-mail: camping.hausotter@web.de
A site completely divided into pitches, lying on the S outskirts of Münster. Children's playground. Individual washing cubicles.
➲ *If approaching from Bad Mergentheim or from Rothenburg/Tauber, take the ' Romantic road' up to Creglingen. Then turn S and drive 3km up to Münster.*
15 Mar-15 Nov 6HEC ⊞ ⚄ ♠ ⚓ ⚡ ✕ ⊙ ➒ ⊘ ⚒ ⚓ PR 🏕 ⊞ lau ➡ ⚓L Prices: ♠4.30-5.30 ➟3.10-4.10 ♠2.80-3.50 pitch 5.90-6.90

DINGELSDORF BADEN-WÜRTTEMBERG

Fliesshorn ☎ 07533 5262
At a farm, on meadowland with fine trees.
➲ *In town turn off Stadd-Dettingen road and follow signs to NW for 1.3km.*
Apr-Sep 5HEC ⊞ ⚄ ♠ ⚓ ⚡ ⊙ ➒ ⊘ ⚒ ⊞ ✂ lau ➡ ✕ ⚓LS

DONAUESCHINGEN BADEN-WÜRTTEMBERG

Riedsee ☎ 07711 5511 ▤ 0771 5511
Level meadow on lakeside.
➲ *Turn off A81 exit 'Geisingen' and continue 13km on B31 towards Pfohren, then turn left and continue for 1km.*
All year 8HEC ⊞ ⌁ ⋔ ⛱ ⓧ ⊙ ⬛ ⬚ ⛺ ⌁ L ⛴ lau

DÜRRHEIM, BAD BADEN-WÜRTTEMBERG

Sunthauersee ☎ 07706 712 ▤ 922906
All year 10HEC ⊞ ⌁ ⋔ ⓧ ⊙ ⬛ ⬚ ⛺ ⛴ ▣ ⊞ lau ➡ ⛱ ✗ ⌁P
Prices: ⋔7 pitch 7.50

ELLWANGEN-JAGST BADEN-WÜRTTEMBERG

Azur Ellwangen Rotenbacherstr 45
☎ 07961 7921 ▤ 07961 562330
A modern site with good facilities in a wooded loaction on the banks of the River Jagst.
1 Mar- 17Nov 3.5HEC ⊞ ⌁ ⋔ ⛱ ⓧ ⓧ ⊙ ⬛ ⬚ ⌁ R ⛴ ⊞ lau ➡ ⌁LPR

ERPFINGEN BADEN-WÜRTTEMBERG

Azur Schwäbische Alb (Rosencamping)
☎ 07128 466 ▤ 07128 30137
e-mail: info@azur-camping.de
Extensive site on a hill.
➲ *Access from Reutlingen on B312 in south easterly direction to Grooengstingen, then S on Schwabische Albstr (B313) for 3.5km to Haid , then turn right to Erpfingen. Site on W outskirts.*
All year 9HEC ⊞ ⌁ ⋇ ⋔ ⛱ ⓧ ⓧ ⊙ ⬛ ⬚ ⛺ ⛴ ⌁ P ⛴ ⊞ lau ➡ ⌁L Prices: ⋔4.50-6 ▲3.50-4.50 pitch 5.50-7.50

ETTENHEIM BADEN-WÜRTTEMBERG

Oase ☎ 07822 4459 18 ▤ 07822 445919
e-mail: info@campingpark-oase.de
In a wooded location with good, modern facilities.
➲ *Access via A5 exit Ettenheim.*
23 Mar-26 Oct 6HEC ⊞ ⌁ ⧫ ⌁ ⋔ ⛱ ⓧ ⊙ ⬛ ⬚ ⛺ ⊞ lau ➡ ⌁P
Prices: pitch 6

FREIBURG IM BREISGAU BADEN-WÜRTTEMBERG

Breisgau Seestr 20 ☎ 07665 2346
Extensive level grassland site on outskirts of town. Section reserved for campers with dogs.
➲ *500m E of autobahn exit 'Freiburg Nord'.*
All year 6.5HEC ⊞ ⌁ ⧫ ⋔ ⛱ ⓧ ⊙ ⬛ ⬚ ⛺ ⌁ L ⛴ lau

Ferien & Kurbad Mösle-Park Waldseestr 77
☎ 0761 72938 ▤ 77578
e-mail: campingfreizeit@aol.com
On outskirts of town near 'Busse's Waldschänke' inn.
➲ *Turn right after town hall across railway and follow Waldseestr towards Littenweiler.*
25 Mar-25 Oct 0.7HEC ⊞ ⧫ ⋔ ⛱ ⛱ ⓧ ⊙ ⬛ ⬚ ⛺ ⛴ ⊞ lau ➡ ⌁P Prices: ⋔5 pitch 5

FREUDENSTADT BADEN-WÜRTTEMBERG

Langenwald Strassburgerstr 167 ☎ 07441 2862 ▤ 2893
e-mail: info@camping-langenwald.de
The site consists of several sections and lies next to a former mill beside the River Forbach.
➲ *4km W of Freudenstadt below the B28 (Freudenstadt-Strasbourg).*
Apr-Nov 2HEC ⊞ ⌁ ⋔ ⛱ ⓧ ⊙ ⬛ ⬚ ⛺ ⛺ ⌁ PR ⛴ ⊞ lau
Prices: ⋔4.50 ⬤2.75 ⬛3.25 ▲3.25 pitch 6

HALLWANGEN BADEN-WÜRTTEMBERG

Königskanzel ☎ 07443 6730 ▤ 07443 4574
e-mail: info@camping-koenigskanzel.de
In an elvated position in the centre of the Black Forest.
➲ *Follow B28 from Freudenstadt towards Altensteig past the Hallwangen junction to camping sign on left.*
All year 6HEC ⊞ ⌁ ⋔ ⛱ ⛱ ⓧ ⊙ ⬛ ⬚ ⛺ ⌁ P ⛴ ⊞ lau ➡ ✗ ⌁L Prices: ⋔5.05-5.60 pitch 6.15-6.15

HAUSEN BADEN-WÜRTTEMBERG

Wagenburg ☎ 07579 559 ▤ 07466 1525
On meadowland between the railway bank and the Danube. Site has spectacular view of surrounding landscape. Entrance through subway.
May-Sep 1.2HEC ⊞ ⌁ ⋔ ⛱ ⛱ ⓧ ⊙ ⬛ ⬚ ⛺ ⛺ ⌁ R ⛴ ⊞ lau ➡ ✗

HEIDELBERG BADEN-WÜRTTEMBERG

Heidelberg-Neckartal Schlierbacher Landstr 151
☎ 06221 802506
e-mail: mail@camping-heidelberg.de
15 Mar-15 Oct 3HEC ⊞ ⧫ ⌁ ⋔ ⛱ ⛱ ⓧ ⊙ ⬛ ⬚ ⛺ ⛺ ⛺ ▲ ⌁ R ⛴ ⊞ lau

HERBOLZHEIM BADEN-WÜRTTEMBERG

Herbolzheim Im Laue 1 ☎ 07643 1460 ▤ 913382
e-mail: s.hugoschmidt@t-online.de
In a pleasant rural setting with good facilities, a short distance from the Europa Park Rust amusement park.
➲ *On B3 between Freiburgh and Offenburg.*
Apr-15 Oct 3HEC ⊞ ⌁ ⋔ ⛱ ⛱ ⓧ ⊙ ⬛ ⬚ ⛴ ⊞ lau ➡ ⛺ ⌁P
Prices: ⋔5 pitch 5-8

HÖFEN AN DER ENZ BADEN-WÜRTTEMBERG

Quellgrund ☎ 07081 6984 ▤ 07081 6984
Well maintained municipal site on grassland between the B294 and the River Enz.
➲ *Access from Pforzheim on the B294 in SW direction to the 'Quelle' inn with entrance to ARAL petrol station at entrance to Höfen, then turn right.*
All year 3.6HEC ⊞ ⌁ ⋔ ⛱ ⬛ ⬚ ⌁ R ⛴ lau ➡ ✗ ⌁P ⊞
Prices: ⋔4.10 ⬤1.80 ⬛3.40-3.90 ▲2.60-3.30

HORB BADEN-WÜRTTEMBERG

Schüttehof ☎ 07451 3951 ▤ 07451 1348
Situated on flat mountain top.
➲ *Access from Horb in direction of Freudenstadt. 1.5km beyond the town boundary turn towards stables and site, and onward for 1km.*
All year 6HEC ⊞ ⌁ ⋔ ⓧ ⊙ ⬛ ⬚ ⛺ ⌁ P ⛴ ⊞ lau

HORN BODENSEE BADEN-WÜRTTEMBERG

Horn ☎ 07735 685 ▤ 07735 8806
A large and well-managed municipal site with a pleasant beach.
➲ *In Horn turn off the Radolfszell-Stein am Rhein road and towards the lake.*
Apr-10 Oct 10HEC ⊞ ⌁ ⋔ ⛱ ⓧ ⊙ ⬛ ⬚ ⛺ ▲ ⌁ LP ▣ ⊞ ⫸ lau ➡ ⌁L

ISNY BADEN-WÜRTTEMBERG

Waldbad Isny ☎ 07562 2389 ▤ 07562 2004
In wooded surroundings beside a lake.
➲ *S of town on B12. Signposted.*
Nov 5HEC ⊞ ⌁ ⋔ ⛱ ⓧ ⊙ ⬛ ⬚ ⛺ ⌁ LP ⛴ ⊞ lau
Prices: ⋔5 pitch 7

CAMP SITE SOUTHERN BLACK FORREST

79199 Kirchzarten
Tel. 07661 / 393-75
Fax 07661 / 61624

E-Mail: camping@kirchzarten.de

www.camping-kirchzarten.de

Comfortable holiday site in the
southern Black Forrest near Freiburg.
New toilet facilities, 380 sites for visiting
holiday-makers. Heated outdoor pool 23°C
from 15.5 - 15.9 on the site itself.
Wide range of facilities for sports and games.
Walk in the magnificent
countryside. Trips to the higher parts
of the Black Forest, Switzerland
and France.

KARLSRUHE BADEN-WÜRTTEMBERG

At **DURLACH**(8km SE)

AZUR Türmbergblick Tiegener Str 40
☎ 0721 497236 ▥ 0721 497237
e-mail: info@azur-camping.de
On level ground amongst orchards. Lunchtime siesta 12.30-
15.00 hrs.
➲ *Access via Karlsruhe-Dürlach exit on A5/E4. Signposted.*
15 Mar-15 Nov 3.5HEC ▦ ♁ ♠ ☜ ✕ ⊙ ▣ ⌀ ☎ ⊞ lau ➧ ♥
✕ ♨ ☚LP Prices: ♦4.50-6 ▲3.50-4.50 pitch 5.50-7.50

KEHL BADEN-WÜRTTEMBERG

Kehl-Strassburg ☎ 07851 2603 ▥ 73076
Park-like site divided into separate sections for young
campers, transit and holiday campers. Lunchtime siesta
13.00-15.00 hrs.
➲ *Turn left at the Rhine dam on the outskirts of the town.*
15 Mar-Oct 2.3HEC ▦ ♁ ♠ ☜ ✕ ⊙ ▣ ⌀ ♨ ⊞ lau ➧
☚PR

KIRCHBERG BADEN-WÜRTTEMBERG

Christophorus ☎ 07354 663 ▥ 91314
e-mail: info@camping-christophorus.de
Completely enclosed, clean site.
➲ *Leave motorway A7 (Ulm-Memmingen) at exit Illereichen
Allenstadt to town centre, then towards the railway station.*
All year 9.2HEC ▦ ♁ ♠ ☜ ✕ ⊙ ▣ ⌀ ♨ ☚ LP ☎ ⊞ lau
Prices: ♦4.60 pitch 5.62

KIRCHZARTEN BADEN-WÜRTTEMBERG

Kirchzarten Diefenbacher Str 17
☎ 07661 39375 ▥ 07661 61624
e-mail: camping@kirchzarten.de
Extensive site with trees providing shade.

➲ *About 8km E of Freiburg im Breisgau off the B31.*
All year 5.6HEC ▦ ♦ ♠ ☜ ♥ ✕ ⊙ ▣ ⌀ ♨ ☎ ☚ P ☎ ⊞ ⊞ ✆
lau Prices: ♦5-7.90 ♨5.30-6.60

KRESSBRONN BADEN-WÜRTTEMBERG

Gohren am See ☎ 07543 60590 ▥ 605929
e-mail: info@campingplatz-gohren.de
A large site beside the lake. It has an older section divided by
many hedges reserved for residential campers, and a newer
section with fewer bushes.
➲ *3km from Kressbronn. Well signposted from B31.*
22 Mar-15 Oct 38HEC ▦ ♁ ♠ ☜ ♥ ✕ ⊙ ▣ ⌀ ♨ ☎ ▲ ☚ L
☎ ⊞ lau ➧ ☚P Prices: ♦5 pitch 5

LAICHINGEN BADEN-WÜRTTEMBERG

Heidehof Blaubeurer str 50
☎ 07333 6408 ▥ 07333 21463
e-mail: heidehof.camping@t-online.de
Well-cared for site on hillside with some high firs. Asphalt
roads. Separate section outside enclosure for overnight
campers.
➲ *Leave Ulm-Stuttgart motorway at Merkingen exit, then
continue S via Machtolsheim to camp 2km S.*
All year 25HEC ▦ ♁ ♠ ☜ ✕ ⊙ ▣ ⌀ ♨ ☚ P ☎ ⊞ lau
Prices: ♦5 ♨6

LAUTERBURG BADEN-WÜRTTEMBERG

Hirtenteich ☎ 07365 296 ▥ 07365 251
This site lies on gently sloping terrain, near the Hirtenteich
recreation area.
➲ *Turn off the B29 (Aalen-Schwäbisch Gmünd) in Essingen
and drive S for a pprox. 5km.*
All year 4HEC ▦ ♁ ♠ ☜ ✕ ⊙ ▣ ⌀ ♨ ☎ ☎ ☚ P ☎ ⊞ lau
Prices: ♦3.50 pitch 4.50-5

LENZKIRCH BADEN-WÜRTTEMBERG

Kreuzhof Bonndorfer Str 65 ☎ 07653 700 ▥ 6623
e-mail: info@brauerei-rogg.de
Grassland near former farm below the Rogg Brewery on
the B315.
➲ *Access from Freiburg on the B31 to Titisee, continue on the
B317 towards Schaffhausen junction then take the B315 via
Lenzkirch, site is some 2km from centre.*
All year 2HEC ▦ ♁ ♠ ☜ ♥ ✕ ⊙ ▣ ⌀ ♨ ☚ P ☎ ⊞ lau

LIEBELSBERG BADEN-WÜRTTEMBERG

Erbenwald Neubulach 3
☎ 07053 7382 ▥ 07053 3274
Pleasant site on edge of wood.
➲ *Approach via Calw on the B463 for about 6km travelling S,
then turn right and shortly before Neubulach continue N about
2km.*
All year 7.2HEC ▦ ♁ ♠ ☜ ✕ ⊙ ▣ ⌀ ♨ ☎ ☎ ☎
☚ P ☎ ⊞ lau

LIEBENZELL, BAD BADEN-WÜRTTEMBERG

Bad-Liebenzell Kurhausdamm 2
☎ 07052 935680 ▥ 935681
e-mail: abel-neff@t-online.de
Municipal site with trees near tennis courts. Divided by
hedges and internal aspahlt roads.
➲ *Approach from Pforzheim on the B463 about 19km S. Turn
left 500m before Bad Liebenzell to site on the banks of the
Nagold.*
All year 3HEC ▦ ♁ ♠ ☜ ♥ ✕ ⊙ ▣ ⌀ ♨ ☚ P ☎ ⊞ ✆ lau ➧
✕ Prices: ♦6 ♨6 ♨5.50 ▲4-5.50 pitch 5.50

LÖRRACH BADEN-WÜRTTEMBERG

Grütt Grüttweg 8 ☎ 07621 82588 ▤ 165034
Level, grassy site near frontier.
➲ *From motorway exit Lörrach on B316 then via Freiburger Str and bridge over the Wiesse and turn left after 100m.*
15 Mar-Oct 2.4HEC ⸺ ⌾ ♠ ✕ ⊙ ▣ ∅ 🏛 lau ➧ ⚊ ⍮ ✕ ♨ �ʔPR ⊞

LÖWENSTEIN BADEN-WÜRTTEMBERG

Heilbronn am Breitenauer See ☎ 07130 8558 ▤ 3622
e-mail: camping-breitenauer-see@t-online.de
A large family site surrounded by woodland on the shore of the Breitenauer See.
➲ *Exit at Weinsberg/Elhofen from A81/E41 (Stuttgart-Würzburg) and take B39 to Obersulm.*
All year 10HEC ⸺ ⌾ ♠ ⚊ ✕ ⊙ ▣ ∅ ♨ ʔ L 🏛 lau ➧ ⊞

LUDWIGSHAFEN AM BODENSEE BADEN-WÜRTTEMBERG

See Ende ☎ 07773 5366 ▤ 07773 7375
Meadowland with tall trees W of town, between railway and lake.
➲ *Access via Stuttgart-Singen-Lindau motorway. In Ludwigshafen turn off in direction of Radolfzell.*
May-Sep 2.6HEC ⸺ ⌾ ♠ ⚊ ⍮ ✕ ⊙ ▣ ∅ ♨ ʔ L 🏛 ⊞ ⍣
lau Prices: ⚑5.50 ⇆3.60 ⊞3.50 ▲3.50

MANNHEIM BADEN-WÜRTTEMBERG

At NECKARAU(5.5km S)

Strandbad ☎ 0621 856240
A minicipal site in the grounds of a park beside the Rhine. At high water the site can get flooded.
➲ *From motorway exit 'Mannheim' to Neckarau, via the Freudenheim Bridge, then drive through Morchfeldstr, Friedrichstr, Rheingoldstr, Franzosenweg and Strandbadweg to the camp.*
Mar-Oct 0.9HEC ⸺ ⌾ ♠ ⊙ ▣ ∅ ♨ ʔ R 🏛 ⊞ lau ➧ ⍮ ✕ ʔP

MARKDORF BADEN-WÜRTTEMBERG

Wirthshof ☎ 07544 2325
15 Mar-30 Oct 8HEC ⸺ ⌾ ♠ ⚊ ✕ ⊙ ▣ ∅ ʔ P 🏛 ⊞ lau
➧ ⍮ ✕ ʔL

MERGENTHEIM, BAD BADEN-WÜRTTEMBERG

Willingertal ☎ 07931 2177
Site lies on a meadow between high green bank and wooded hillside.
➲ *From Bad Mergentheim follow B19 S towards Stuttgart, then left towards Wachbach after 2km. then left to Gastätte.*
All year 15HEC ⸺ ⌾ ✂ ♠ ⚊ ✕ ⊙ ▣ ∅ ♨ 🏛 ⊞ ⊞ lau

MÖRTELSTEIN BADEN-WÜRTTEMBERG

Germania Mühlwiese 1 ☎ 06261 1795 ▤ 06261/37455
Site is in Mörtelstein, 5km W of Obrigheim. Site lies between the left bank of the River Neckar and a wooded hillside.
➲ *Follow road B292 W towards 'Sinsheim' to just beyond Oberigheim, then N on a narrow, steep road into the Neckar Valley.*
Apr-Oct 0.8HEC ⸺ ⌾ ♠ ⚊ ✕ ⊙ ▣ ∅ ♨ ⍟ ʔ R 🏛 lau ➧ ✕
⊞ Prices: ⚑6.50 ⇆3 ⊞5 ▲5

MÜNSTERTAL BADEN-WÜRTTEMBERG

Münstertal ☎ 07636 353 ▤ 07636 7448
Level, grassy site in pleasant situation with fine views.
Lunchtime siesta 13.00-15.00 hrs.
➲ *Leave Karlsruhe-Basel motorway at Bad Kroningen exit and continue SE via Stauffen to W outskirts of Untermünstertal.*
All year 3.9HEC ⸺ ⌾ ♠ ⍮ ✕ ⊙ ▣ ∅ ♨ ʔ P 🏛 ⊞ lau

MURRHARDT BADEN-WÜRTTEMBERG

At FORNSBACH(6km E)

Waldsee ☎ 07192 6436 ▤ 5283
e-mail: waldsee@murrhardt.de
The site lies near Lake Waldsee. Asphalt paths and pitches, with gravel surface.
➲ *Drive through Murrhardt towards Fornsbach and the camp, which is on the eastern shore of the lake.*
All year 2HEC ⸺ ⌾ ♠ ⍮ ✕ ⊙ ∅ ♨ ♨ ʔ L 🏛 ⊞ lau
Prices: ⚑3.50-4 ⇆2.50-3.50 ⊞3-3.50 ▲3-3.50 pitch 3-3.50

NECKARGEMÜND BADEN-WÜRTTEMBERG

Friedensbrücke ☎ 06223 2178
Campsite lies on the left bank of the River Neckar below the Frieden's bridge.
Mar-Sep 2.5HEC ⸺ ⌾ ♠ ⍮ ✕ ⊙ ▣ ∅ ♨ ♨ ʔ R 🏛 ⊞ ⊞ lau
➧ ⚊ ✕ ʔP ⊞

Haide ☎ 06223 2111 ▤ 06223 71959
e-mail: camping.haide@t-online.de
A well appointed site in the picturesque Neckar Valley, directly on the river on the outskirts of Heidelberg.
➲ *Follow the river towards the castle and Neckarsteinach.*
Apr-Oct 3.6HEC ⸺ ⌾ ➧ ⍮ ⍮ ✕ ⊙ ▣ ∅ ♨ 🍴 ⊞ ⊞ lau

NECKARZIMMERN BADEN-WÜRTTEMBERG

Cimbria ☎ 06261 2562 ▤ 35716
Site lies on level meadowland on the bank of the River Neckar.
➲ *Access to the site is signposted from road B27.*
Apr-Oct 3HEC ⸺ ⌾ ♠ ⍮ ⍮ ✕ ⊙ ▣ ∅ ♨ ʔ PR 🏛 lau ➧ ⚊ ⊞

NEUENBURG BADEN-WÜRTTEMBERG

Dreiländer Camping und Freizeitpark Oberer Wald
☎ 07631 7719 ▤ 07635 3393
e-mail: info@camping-gugel.de
An excellent site, very extensive, providing many entirely separate pitches.
➲ *Access via Karlsruhe-Basel motorway A5/E4, take the Müllheim/Neuenburg exit, then about 3km to site.*
All year 12.8HEC ⸺ ⌾ ♠ ⍮ ✕ ⊙ ▣ ∅ ♨ ʔ P ⊞ lau ➧
ʔL Prices: ⚑5.75 ⇆4 ⊞5.20 ▲3.50-5.20

NUSSDORF BADEN-WÜRTTEMBERG

Nell Uberlinger See ☎ 07551 4254
e-mail: info@campingplatz-nell.de
Site within orchard between farm of same name and the lakeside promenade. Small private beach.
➲ *Under railway bridge, then turn right.*
Apr-15 Oct 0.6HEC ⸺ ⌾ ♠ ⚊ ⊙ ▣ ∅ ♨ ʔ L 🏛 ⊞ ⍟ lau ➧ ⚊ ⍮ ✕
∅ ♨ ʔP Prices: ⚑4.09 ⇆2.56 ⊞5.11 ▲5.11

OSTRINGEN BADEN-WÜRTTEMBERG

Kraichgau Camping Wackerhof ☎ 07259 361 ▤ 2431
A modern terraced site. Lunchtime siesta 13.00-15.00 hrs (except Saturdays).
➲ *From motorway A5 exit 'Kronau/Bad Schönborn' follow road B292 to Östringen.*
25Mar-15Oct 3HEC ⸺ ⌾ ♠ ⚊ ⊙ ▣ ∅ ♨ 🏛 lau
Prices: ⚑2.80 pitch 2.80

PFORZHEIM BADEN-WÜRTTEMBERG

International Schwarzwald Freibadweg 4
☎ 07234 6517 ▤ 07234 5180
e-mail: fam.frech@t-online.de
Site on edge of wood with southerly aspect. Separate fields for residential, overnight and holiday campers.
➲ *S through Huchenfeld from Pforzheim to Schellbron (15km).*
All year 5HEC ⸺ ⌾ ♠ ⍮ ✕ ⊙ ▣ ∅ ♨ ♨ ʔ P ⊞ ⊞ ⍟ lau
➧ ʔR

RHEINMÜNSTER BADEN-WÜRTTEMBERG

At STOLLHOFEN

Freizeitcenter-Oberrhein ☎ 07227 2500 ▤ 2400
e-mail: info@freizeitcenter-oberrhein.de
Modern leisure complex next to Rhine.
All year 36HEC ⚏ ⚘ ⌂ ⚡ ⚓ ♟ ⊙ ⊞ ⊘ ♨ ⬤ ⚲ L ⊡ ⊞ lau
Prices: ↟5-8 pitch 5-7

ROSENBERG BADEN-WÜRTTEMBERG

Hüttenhof Hüttenhof 1 ☎ 07963 203
Flat meadow on incline in quiet woodland area, next to large farm.
➲ From Ellwangen 3km N towards Crailsheim, turn W towards Adelmannsfelden and continue for 8km to turn off to N at Gaishardt.
All year 4HEC ⚏ ⚘ ⌂ ⚓ ⊙ ⊞ ⊘ ♨ ⚲ LR ⊡ ⊞ lau ➤ ✕
Prices: ↟4 pitch 3.60

ST PETER BADEN-WÜRTTEMBERG

Steingrübenhof ☎ 07660 210 ▤ 1604
e-mail: camp.steingrubenhof@lycosmail.com
On a level plateau, surrounded by delightful mountain scenery.
➲ Access via A5 and B294.
All year 2HEC ⚏ ⚘ ⌂ ⚓ ⊙ ⊞ ⊘ ♨ ⬤ ⊡ lau ➤ ⚲P

SCHAPBACH BADEN-WÜRTTEMBERG

Alisehof ☎ 07839 203 ▤ 07839 1263
The site lies on well-kept ground with several terraces and is separated from the road by the River Wolfach.
➲ In Wolfach turn off the B924 at the Kinzighbrücke and drive N for about 8km to Schapbach. Site is 1km N of village.
All year ⚏ ⚘ ⌂ ⚓ ♟ ⊙ ⊞ ⊘ ♨ ⬤ ⚲ R ⊡ ⊞ lau ➤ ✕ ⚲P Prices: ↟4.50-5.20 ⬤4.70-5.20 ▣4.70-5.20 ▲4.70-5.20 pitch 4.70-5.20

SCHILTACH BADEN-WÜRTTEMBERG

Schiltach ☎ 07836 7289 ▤ 07836 7466
e-mail: info@campingplatz-schittach.de
The site lies on meadowland on the banks of the River Kinzig and is well placed for excursions.
May-Oct 3.6HEC ⚏ ⚘ ⌂ ✕ ⊙ ⊞ ⊘ ♨ ⬤ ⚲ R ⊡ ⊞ ✄ lau

SCHÖMBERG BADEN-WÜRTTEMBERG

Höhen-Camping-Langenbrand ☎ 07084 6131 ▤ 931435
e-mail: eberhardt@hohencamping.de
All year 1.6HEC ⚏ ⚘ ⌂ ⊙ ⊞ ⊘ ⊡ ⊞ lau ➤ ⚡ ⚓ ✕ ⚲P
Prices: ↟4.50-5 ⬤5-6.50 ▣5-6.50 pitch 5-6.50

SCHUSSENRIED, BAD BADEN-WÜRTTEMBERG

Reiterhof von Steinhausen Reiterhof
☎ 07583 3060 ▤ 07583 1004
e-mail: xschmid@t.online.de
In a pleasant rural setting.
➲ Access via B30 Ulm-Bad Waldsee.
All year 1HEC ⚏ ⚘ ⌂ ✕ ⊙ ⊞ ⊘ ♨ ⊡ lau ➤ ⚡ ✕ ⚲LPR

SCHWÄBISCH GMÜND BADEN-WÜRTTEMBERG

At RECHBERG(6km S)

Schurrenhof ☎ 07165 8190 ▤ 07165 1625
The site lies in a beautiful setting on the edge of a forest, and has a lovely view of the surrounding countryside.
➲ Drive S on the B29 from Schwäbisch Gmünd, through Strassdorf and Rechberg, and towards Reichenbach on the B10. Then turn towards Schurrenhof.
All year 3HEC ⚏ ⚘ ⌂ ✕ ⊙ ⊞ ⊘ ♨ ⬤ ⚲ P ⊡ ⊞ lau

SCHWÄBISCH HALL BADEN-WÜRTTEMBERG

Steinbacher See Mühlsteige 26 ☎ 0791 2984 ▤ 0791 2984
e-mail: camping@hohenlohe2000.de
A modern site situated in the beautiful Kocher Valley. There are good sporting facilities and many places of interest nearby in the medieval town.
➲ Access via B14/19 to Steinbach.
All year 1.4HEC ⚏ ⚘ ⌂ ⚡ ⊙ ⊞ ⊘ ♨ ⊡ lau ➤ ⚡ ✕ ⊞ Prices: ↟4.60 pitch 5.10

STAMMHEIM BADEN-WÜRTTEMBERG

Obere Mühle ☎ 07051 4844 ▤ 07051 12485
The site is divided into two sections by the access road, and sub-divided into pitches.
➲ Off B296 almost 3km S of Calw.
All year 2.5HEC ⚏ ⚘ ⌂ ⚡ ⚓ ♟ ⊙ ⊞ ⊘ ♨ ⬤ ⬤ ⚲ P ⊡ ⊞ lau

STAUFEN BADEN-WÜRTTEMBERG

Belchenblick Münstertaler Str 43 ☎ 07633 7045 ▤ 7908
e-mail: camping.belchenbleck@t-online.de
Well kept site on level ground.
➲ Access from motorway exit Bad Krozingen/Staufen and continue 4km SE.
All year 2.5HEC ⚏ ⚘ ⌂ ⚡ ⚓ ♟ ⊙ ⊞ ⊘ ♨ ⚲ PR ⊡ ⊞ lau ➤ ✕ Prices: ↟6-7.50 pitch 7.50-8

STEINACH BADEN-WÜRTTEMBERG

Kinzigtal ☎ 07832 8122 ▤ 07832 6619
Site on level meadowland with tall trees, situated next to the municipal heated swimming pool.
➲ Signposted from Steinach.
All year 2.6HEC ⚏ ⚘ ⌂ ⚡ ⚓ ✕ ⊙ ⊞ ⊘ ♨ ⬤ ⊡ ⊞ lau ➤ ⚲P

STUTTGART BADEN-WÜRTTEMBERG

Canstatter Wasen Mercedesstr 40
☎ 0711 556696 ▤ 0711 557554
Level site with tall poplar trees alongside the River Neckar.
Lunchtime siesta 12.30-14.00 hrs.
➲ Access from Bad Cannstatt near sports stadium.
All year 1.7HEC ⚏ ⚘ ⌂ ⚓ ✕ ⊙ ⊞ ⊘ ⬤ ⊡ ⊞ lau ➤ ⚲P

SULZBURG BADEN-WÜRTTEMBERG

Alte Sägemuhle ☎ 07634 8550
Quiet holiday site in beautiful situation, surrounded by woodland. Partly terraced the site is divided into two sections by the approach road.
➲ From autobahn exit 'Bad Krozingen' and B3 to Heitersheim. Here turn E for site in 6km.
All year 2.5HEC ⚏ ⚘ ⌂ ⊙ ⊞ ⊘ ♨ ⚲ P ⊡ ⊞ ➤ ✕

TITISEE-NEUSTADT BADEN-WÜRTTEMBERG

Bankenhof Bruderhalde 31a ☎ 07652 1351 ▤ 07652 5907
e-mail: info@bankenhof.de
A family site in a wooded location close to the lake.
➲ From Titisee village follow signs 'Camping platz'. Access road to site closed 22.00-06.00 hrs.
All year 3.5HEC ⚏ ❄ ⚘ ⌂ ⚡ ⚓ ✕ ⊙ ⊞ ⊘ ♨ ⬤ ▲ ⚲ R ⊡ ⊞ lau ➤ ⚲L

Bühlhof Bühlhofweg 13 ☎ 07652 1606 ▤ 07652 1827
In pleasant situation on hillside above lake. Lunchtime siesta 13.00-14.30 hrs.
➲ Well signposted.
Closed Nov-15 Dec 10HEC ⚏ ❄ ⚘ ⌂ ⚡ ⚓ ♟ ✕ ⊙ ⊞ ⊘ ♨ ⊡ lau ➤ ⚲LP ⊞

Sandbank ☎ 07651 8243 & 8166 ▦ 8286 & 88444
e-mail: info@camping-sandbank.com
On terrain rising from lakeside, upper part terraced,
landscaped with trees.
⮕ *Access from Titisee, N bank of lake, turn into old
Feldbergstr. At SW end of lake turn left and continue along
narrow private road through Camping 'Bankenhof' (closed
22.00-06.00 hrs) to the site about 700m on SE bank of lake.*
Apr-20 Oct 2HEC ⏚ ⋮⋮ ▲ ⊈ ⋔ ⅀ ✕ ⊙ ▨ ⌀ ⩟ ⥾ L ⌂ ⊞
lau

Wellerhof ☎ 07652 1468 ▦ 1478
Mainly level site with trees, bordering on lake shore for about
400m.
⮕ *Signposted from Titisee.*
15 May-Sep 2HEC ⏚ ⋮⋮ ▲ ⊈ ⋔ ⅀ ✕ ⊙ ▨ ⌀ ⥾ L ⌂ ⊞ lau
Prices: ⚲3.50-4.50 ⊈3.20-3.50 ⊞3.20-3.70 ▲3.20-3.70

TODTNAU BADEN-WÜRTTEMBERG

Hochschwarzwald ☎ 07671 1288 ▦ 07671 95190
e-mail: camping.hochschwarzwald@web.de
Terraced site, partially grassland, by ski-lift.
⮕ *6km NW of Todtnau.*
All year 2.5HEC ⏚ ⋮⋮ ▲ ⊈ ⋔ ⅀ ✕ ⊙ ▨ ⌀ ⥾ R ⌂ ⊞ lau
Prices: ⚲3.80-4.10 ⊈4.60-5.10 ▲3.30-5.10

TÜBINGEN BADEN-WÜRTTEMBERG

Tübingen Fremdenverkehrsgesellschaft, Rappenberghalde 61
☎ 07071 43145 ▦ 43145 & 35070
e-mail: mail@tuebingen-info.de
A quiet site, well situated on the left bank of the River
Neckar.
⮕ *For access from the town centre, cross the Neckar bridge,
then turn right and drive S through Uhlandstr or Bahnhofstr to
next bridge. Cross bridge and drive upstream to the
Rappenberghalde hill.*
Mar-15 Oct 1HEC ⏚ ⋇ ⋔ ⅀ ⋔ ⅀ ✕ ⊙ ▨ ⌀ ⥾ R ⌂ ⊞ lau
⮕ ⥾LP

ÜBERLINGEN BADEN-WÜRTTEMBERG

West Bahnhofstr 57 ☎ 07551 64583 ▦ 07551 1945895
e-mail: info@camping-wolfensperger.de
The site lies on the western outskirts of the town, between
the railway line and the road on one side, and the concrete
shore wall on the other. It is divided into several sections by
low wooden barriers and has a very small beach. No
individual youths under 18.
⮕ *Off B31 towards the lake.*
Apr-5 Oct 3HEC ⏚ ⊈ ⋔ ⅀ ✕ ⊙ ▨ ⌀ ⩟ ⥾ L ⌂ ⊞ lau ⮕ ⅄
⥾P Prices: ⚲4.50-15.80 ▲4

UHLDINGEN BADEN-WÜRTTEMBERG

At SEEFELDEN(1km W)

Seeperle ☎ 07556 5454 ▦ 07556 966221
e-mail: info@camping-seeperle.de
This site has some large trees along the shore of the lake.
50m-long boat landing stage. It is one of the few camps that
does not reserve its best pitches for residential campers.
⮕ *Turn off B31 at Oberuhldingen and head towards
Seefelden. Site 1km.*
Apr-3 Oct 0.7HEC ⏚ ⋮⋮ ⊈ ⋔ ⅀ ⊙ ▨ ⌀ ⥾ L ⌂ ⊞ ⮕ ⅄ ✕
Prices: ⚲10.74 ⊈3.32 ⊞7.41 ▲5.11-7.41

WALDKIRCH BADEN-WÜRTTEMBERG

Elztalblick ☎ 07681 4212 ▦ 07681 4213
e-mail: eltztalblick@t-online.de
A small site with terraced pitches in the heart of the Black
Forest.

⮕ *Leave autobahn at 'Waldkirch/Ost' exit and follow signs for
3km.*
15 Mar-25Oct 2HEC ⏚ ⊈ ⋔ ⅀ ⅀ ✕ ⊙ ▨ ⌀ ⌂ ⊞ lau ⮕
✕ ⥾P Prices: ⚲5 ⊈2.50 ⊞2.50 ▲2.50 pitch 5

WALDSHUT BADEN-WÜRTTEMBERG

Rhein-Camping Jahnweg 22 ☎ 07751 3152 ▦ 07751 3252
e-mail: rheincamping@t-omline.de
In wooded surroundings beside the River Rhein.
⮕ *1km from Waldshut towards the Swiss border.*
All year 8HEC ⏚ ▲ ⊈ ⋔ ⅀ ⅀ ✕ ⊙ ▨ ⌀ ⩟ ⊞ ⥾ R ⌂ ⊞ lau
⮕ ⥾P Prices: ⚲4.50 ⊈8 ▲4.50-5.50 pitch 8

WERTHEIM BADEN-WÜRTTEMBERG

AZUR Wertheim An den Christwiesen 35
☎ 09342 83111 ▦ 09342 83171
e-mail: info@azur-camping.de
Site lies on a level, long stretch of meadowland on the banks
of the River Main next to a swimming pool. Lunchtime siesta
12.00-14.00 hrs.
⮕ *Follow road towards 'Miltenberg', and in 1km turn right at
the ARAL petrol station and head towards the site.*
Apr-Oct 7HEC ⏚ ⊈ ⋔ ⅀ ✕ ⊙ ▨ ⌀ ⩟ ⥾ R ⌂ ⊞ lau ⮕ ⅀ ⥾P
Prices: ⚲4.50-6 ▲3.50-4.50 pitch 5.50-7.50

At BETTINGEN(5km E)

Wertheim-Bettingen Geiselbrunnweg 31
☎ 09342 7077 ▦ 09342-913077
In a peaceful wooded area on the bank of a river.
⮕ *Motorway Frankfurt-Würzburg, exit Wertheim/Lengfurt,
1km.*
Apr-Oct 7.5HEC ⏚ ⊈ ⋔ ⅀ ✕ ⊙ ▨ ⌀ ⩟ ⥾ R ⌂ ⊞ lau

WILDBAD IM SCHWARZWALD BADEN-WÜRTTEMBERG

AZUR-Camping Schwarzwald
☎ 07055 1320 ▦ 07055 929081
e-mail: info@azur-camping.de
Long narrow site with some terraces, set between the River
Enz and the wooded hillside. Separate section for young
campers.
⮕ *Access is from Pforzheim along B294 via Calmbach
southwards.*
All year 2.5HEC ⏚ ⊈ ⋔ ⅀ ✕ ⊙ ▨ ⌀ ⩟ ⥾ R ⌂ ⊞ lau
Prices: ⚲3-5 ▲2.50-3.50 pitch 4-6

Kleinenhof ☎ 07081 3435 ▦ 07081 3770
A family site with good, modern facilities.
⮕ *Access via B294 3km S of Calmbach.*
All year 8HEC ⏚ ⊈ ⋔ ⅀ ✕ ⊙ ▨ ⌀ ⩟ ⊞ ⊈ ⥾ PR ⌂ ⊞ lau

BERLIN AND EASTERN PROVINCES

This unique city is one of the most exciting in Europe. The splendid palaces and monuments are the city's architectural legacies of a rich and colourful history, of many periods and many noble families, of events that have rocked the world and made Berlin a focal point of political and cultural life.

No longer divided, the city offers many contrasts; stroll along the 'Unter den Linden' for an impression of 'old' Berlin; visit the 'Kurfstendamm' which packs no fewer than 1,000 shops, boutiques, restaurants and galleries, into an elegant half-mile; relax in the delightful havens of parks, forests and lakes, which make up one third of the city.

Berlin is alive, bursting with a vibrant energy that never dies down; the nightlife offers everything from grand opera to erotic nightclubs, and stays open longer than you can stay up.

....

ALTENBERG SACHSEN

Kleiner Galgenteich ☎ 035056 31995 ▥ 035056 31993
➲ *Leave E55 at exit Dresden-Nord and continue towards the Czech border via B170/E55.*
All year 4HEC ⚏ ♣ ⋒ ⛟ ✕ ☉ ⬤ ⬗ ⌇ P ⊞ lau ➧ ⚑

ALT SCHWERIN MEKLENBURG-VORPOMMERN

See An der Schaftannen Nr 1
☎ 039932 42073 ▥ 039932 42072
e-mail: info@camping-alt-schwerin.de
A pleasant lakeside site with good, modern facilities.
➲ *Access via B192.*
Apr-Oct 3.6HEC ⚏ ✂ ⋒ ✕ ☉ ⬤ ⬗ ⌁ ⛴ ⌇ S ⊞ lau ➧
⌁LR Prices: ⚑2.50-3 ➧3 ⬛4.50-5.50 ▲3-5

BERLIN

Dreilinden Albrechts-Teerofen ☎ 4930 8051201
A transit site close to the city.
➲ *Access via A115.*
Mar-Oct 1HEC ⚏ ⋒ ✕ ☉ ⬤

Gatow Kladower Damm 213-217
☎ 4930 3654340 ▥ 4930 36808492
A good transit site close to the river.
➲ *Access via B5.*
All year 2.7HEC ⚏ ⋔ ⋒ ⚡ ✕ ☉ ⬤ ⌁ ⛴ ⊞ lau ➧ ⌁R ⊞

At KLADOW

DCC Else-Eckert-Platz Krampnitzer Weg 111-117
☎ 030 3652797 ▥ 030 3651245
Large site in woodland close to the lake. Good, modern facilities.
➲ *Access via B5 and B2 exit Berlin Spandau.*
All year 7HEC ⚏ ⌁⌁ ⋔ ⋒ ✕ ☉ ⬤ ⌁ ⛴ ⊞ lau ➧ ⌁L ⊞

At SCHMÖCKWITZ

Krosssinsee Wernsdorfer Str 45 ☎ 4930 6758687
In pleasant wooded surroundings on the shore of the Krossinsee with plenty of recreational facilities.
➲ *Access via A10 exit Berlin Köpenick.*
All year 7HEC ⚏ ♣ ⋒ ✕ ☉ ⬤ ⌁ ⛴ ⌇ L ⊞ lau

At WANNSEE

Kohlhasenbrück Neue Kreisstr 36 ☎ 4930 8051737
Very pleasantly situated site on shore of Lake Griebnitz, owned by Deutscher Camping Club. Bathing area.
➲ *From Wannsee railway station, drive through Königstr, past Rathaus, through Chausseestr, Kohlhasenbrückerstr, and Kreisstr.*
Mar-Oct 3.6HEC ⚏ ♣ ⋒ ✕ ☉ ⬤ ⊞ lau

BODSTEDT MECKLENBURG-VORPOMMERN

Bodstedt Damm 1 ☎ 038231 4226
A pleasant site on the shore of the Saaler Bodden with good boating facilities.
➲ *Access via B105 exit Zingst/Barth.*
Apr-Sep 3.5HEC ⚏ ♣ ⋒ ☉ ⬤ ⬗ ⬛ ⊞ ⌇ ✕ ⌁LR

CAPUTH BRANDENBURG

Himmelreich Wentorfinsel, Geltow ☎ 033209 70475
All year 6HEC ⚏ ⌁⌁ ⌁ ⋒ ⚡ ✕ ☉ ⬤ ⬗ ⌁ ⌇ LR ⊞ ⊞ lau

COLDITZ SACHSEN

Waldbad ☎ 034381 43122 ▥ 034381 43122
In wooded surroundings with some shaded pitches.
➲ *Access via E176 exit Zschadras.*
28 May-7 Oct 2HEC ⚏ ⋒ ☉ ⬤ ⬗ ⌁ ⛴ ⌇ LPRS ⊞ ⊞ lau
➧ ⚡ ✕ ⌁P

DRESDEN SACHSEN

Wostra Trieskestr 100 ☎ 0351 2013254 ▥ 2013254
Café open May-Sep only.
➲ *Access via B172 towards Heidenau. Signposted.*
Apr-Oct 1.8HEC ⚏ ⌁ ⋒ ☉ ⬤ ⬗ ⊞ ⊞ ➧ ⚡ ✕ ⌁P

FALKENBERG BRANDENBURG

Erholungsgebiet Kiebitz ☎ 035365 2135 ▥ 03536538533
➲ *Access via E55 Duben exit, then B87/B101 towards Herzberg.*
Apr-Oct 5.2HEC ⚏ ⌁ ⋒ ☉ ⬤ ⬗ ⌇ L ⊞ ⊞ lau ➧ ⚡ ✕ ⬗
Prices: ⚑2-3.50 ➧3.50-3.50 ⬛3-4 ▲1.50-5.50

FREEST MECKLENBURG-VORPOMMERN

Waldcamp ☎ 038370 20538 ▥ 20525
A modern site in wooded surroundings with good facilities.
➲ *300mtrs from Freest centre.*
Apr-31 Oct Nov-Mar 30 2HEC ⚏ ⌁⌁ ⌁ ⋒ ⚡ ✕ ☉ ⬤ ⛴ ⬛
⬚ lau ➧ ⚡ ✕ ⬗ ⌁ ⌁S Prices: ⚑4 ➧2 ⬛5-6 ▲4-6

GEORGENTHAL THÜRINGEN

Georgenthal ☎ 036253 41314 ▥ 25207
e-mail: campingplatz70@hotmail.com
Apr-Oct 1HEC ⚏ ⌁⌁ ⌁ ⋒ ⚡ ☉ ⬤ ⬗ ⌁ ⌇ P ⊞ lau ➧ ⚡ ⌁L
⊞ Prices: ⚑3.50 ➧1.50 ⬛4.50 ▲3-6

GROSS-LEUTHEN BRANDENBURG

Spreewaldtor ☎ 035471 303 ▥ 035471 310
e-mail: eurocamp.spreewaldtor@t-online.de
On a level meadow beside the Gorss Leuthener See.
➲ *N off town off B179.*
All year 9HEC ⚏ ⌁⌁ ⌁ ⋒ ✕ ☉ ⬤ ⬗ ⌁ ⛴ ⬛ ⊞ ⊞ lau ➧ ⌁L

GROSS-QUASSOW MECKLENBURG-VORPOMMERN

Havelberge am Wobiltzsee ☎ 03981 24790 ▥ 03981 247999
e-mail: haveltourist@camping.de
In a rural setting beside the lake. Restricted facilities during March.
➲ *1.5km S of town. Signposted.*
Mar-Oct 14HEC ⚏ ⌁⌁ ⌁ ⋒ ⚡ ✕ ☉ ⬤ ⬗ ⌁ ⛴ ⬛ ⬚ ▲ ⌁
L ⊞ ⊞ lau Prices: ⚑2.50-5.20 pitch 3.70-9.80
See advertisement in colour section

KAMENZ SACHSEN

AZUR Waldbad Deutschbaselitz Teichstr 30
☎ 03578 301489 ▥ 03578 308316
e-mail: info@azur.freizeit.de
The site may close for a short time in the winter and the shop and café are only open between May and September.
15 Mar-15 Nov 5HEC ⚏ ⌁ ⋒ ✕ ☉ ⬤ ⌁ ⛴ ⬛ ⌁ L ⊞
Prices: ⚑3.30-5 pitch 4-6

KELBRA THÜRINGEN

Stausee Kelbra Lange Str 150 ☎ 034651 6310 ▤ 034651 6312
All year 6.5HEC ⸺ ⩟ ⋔ ⸚ ✕ ⊙ ◙ ⌀ ⛺ ⋔ ⋟ LP ⊡ ⊞ ➧ ▾
Prices: ⋏3.58 ⚘1.53 ⚑5.11 ▲4.09

KLEINMACHNOW BRANDENBURG

Yacht-Caravan-Club Bäkehang 9a
☎ 033203 79684 ▤ 033203 77913
A riverside site with an hotel SW of town off A115.
All year 2.2HEC ⸺ ⩟ ⋔ ▾ ✕ ⊙ ◙ ⌀ ⋟ R ⊡ ⊞ lau

KLEINRÖHRSDORF SACHSEN

Lux-Oase Arnsdorfer Str 1 ☎ 035952 56666 ▤ 56024
e-mail: camping.luxoase@t-online.de
In beautiful, peaceful surroundings bordering a lake among
meadows and woods.
➲ *Access via A4 (Dresden-Bautzen) exit Pulsnitz towards
Radeberg and continue for 4km through Leppersdorf then 1km
after the village turn right for site.*
Nov 7.2HEC ⸺ ⩟ ⩟ ⋔ ⋔ ▾ ✕ ⊙ ◙ ⌀ ⛺ ⋟ L ⊡ ⊞ lau
Prices: ⋏3.58-4.09 ⚘1.53 ⚑5.11-5.62 ▲4.60-5.11

KLEINSAUBERNITZ SACHSEN

Olbasee Olbaweg 16 ☎ 035932 30232 ▤ 035932 30886
In a rural location on the Olbasee.
➲ *Leave A4 at Bautzen Ost exit and take B156 N to
Kleinsaubernitz.*
May-Sep 10HEC ⸺ ⁛⁛⁛ ⩟ ⋔ ✕ ⊙ ◙ ⋟ L ⊡ ⊞ lau
➧ ⋤ ✕ ⌀ ⛺

KÖNIGSTEIN SACHSEN

Königstein Schandauer Str 25e
☎ 035021 68224 ▤ 035021 60725
e-mail: campingkoenigstein@surfeu.de
On level ground in a wooded location with fine views of the
surrounding mountains.
➲ *Federal road B172 within Königstein near Dresden.*
Apr-Oct 2.4HEC ⸺ ⩟ ⋔ ✕ ⊙ ◙ ⌀ ⛺ ⛺ ⊡ lau ➧ ⋤ ▾ ⋟P
⊞ Prices: ⋏4.50 ⚘3 ⚑3 ▲3

LASSAN MEKLENBURG-VORPOMMERN

Lassan Garthof 5-6 ☎ 038374 80373 ▤ 038374 80373
e-mail: naturcampingplatzlassan@gmx.de
A pleasant site on the Achterwasser.
➲ *Access via B110.*
Etr-Sep 1.4HEC ⸺ ⩟ ⋔ ✕ ⊙ ◙ ◙ ⋟ LRS ⊡ lau ➧ ⋤ ▾ ⌀
⋟P ⊞ Prices: ⋏3-3.60 ⚘2 ⚑3.60-5.20 ▲2.30-4.20

LEHNIN BRANDENBURG

Seeblick am Klostersee ☎ 03382 700274
➲ *50 miles from Berlin on E30.*
1 Apr-15 Oct 16 Oct - 31 Mar 1.5HEC ⸺ ⁛⁛⁛ ⩟ ⋔ ⋤ ⊙ ◙
⋟ L ⊡ ⊞ lau ➧ ⋤ ✕ ⌀ Prices: ⋏4.50 ⚘1.50 ⚑4 ▲2.50

MÜHLBERG THÜRINGEN

Drei Gleichen ☎ 0236256 22715
In pleasant wooded surroundings.
➲ *Access via A4 exit Wandersleben, then follow signs for
Mühlberg.*
Apr-Oct 2.8HEC ⸺ ⩟ ⋔ ✕ ⊙ ◙ ⌀ ⊡ lau ➧ ✕ ⊞

NIESKY SACHSEN

Tonschächte ☎ 03588 205771 ▤ 205771
May-Sep 15HEC ⸺ ⁛⁛⁛ ➧ ⋔ ✕ ⊙ ◙ ⛺ ⛺ ⋟ L ⊡ lau ➧
⋤ ⌀ Prices: pitch 9.50-12 (incl 4 persons)

NIEWISCH BRANDENBURG

Schwielochsee-Camping Uferweg Nord 16
☎ 033676 5186 ▤ 033676 5226
A family site in pleasant wooded surroundings on the banks
of the Schwielochsee.
Est-15 Oct 4.2HEC ⸺ ⁛⁛⁛ ⩟ ⋔ ⋔ ✕ ⊙ ◙ ⌀ ⛺ ⛺ ⋟ L
⊡ ⊞ lau

PLÖTZKY SACHSEN

Waldsee ☎ 039200 50155 ▤ 77120
e-mail: info@ferienpark-ploetsky.de
In a wooded location beside a small lake with well defined
pitches.
➲ *20km S of Magdeburg. Access via A2 and B246.*
All year 8HEC ⸺ ⩟ ⋔ ⋔ ✕ ⊙ ◙ ⌀ ⛺ ⋟ L ⊡ ⊞ lau

POTSDAM BRANDENBURG

Sanssouci-Gaisberg An der Pirscheide, Templiner See 41
☎ 03327 55680 ▤ 55680
e-mail: info@recra.de
In wooded surroundings close to the Templiner See.
➲ *Signposted from the B1.*
Apr-3 Nov 6HEC ⸺ ⁛⁛⁛ ⩟ ⋔ ⋔ ▾ ✕ ⊙ ◙ ⌀ ⛺ ⋟ LR ⊡ ⊞
➧ ⋟P

REICHENBERG SACHSEN

Sonnenland Dresdner Str 115
☎ 0351 8305495 ▤ 0351-8305494
In a pleasant location beside the lake with good, modern
facilities.
➲ *3km S of Moritzburg, access via A4 exit Wilder Mann.*
Apr-30 Oct 18HEC ⸺ ⩟ ⋔ ⋤ ✕ ⊙ ◙ ⌀ ⛺ ⋟ L ⊡ ⊞ lau ➧
▾

SUHRENDORF MECKLENBURG-VORPOMMERN

Suhrendorf ☎ 038305 82234 ▤ 038305 8165
All year 90HEC ⸺ ⩟ ⋔ ⋤ ▾ ✕ ⊙ ◙ ⌀ ⛺ ⛺ ⋟ S ⊡ lau

ZARRENTIN MECKLENBURG-VORPOMMERN

Schaalsee Wittenburger Chaussee ☎ 038851 3110
In a pleasant natural park 600mtrs from the lake.
Apr-Oct 8.5HEC ⸺ ⩟ ⋔ ✕ ⊙ ◙ ⌀ ⊡ lau ➧ ⋟L

ZINNOWITZ MECKLENBURG-VORPOMMERN

Pommerland ☎ 038377 40348 & 40177 ▤ 038377 40349
In wooded surroundings on the north sea coast.
➲ *Access via B111.*
All year 7.7HEC ⸺ ⁛⁛⁛ ➧ ⋔ ⋤ ▾ ✕ ⊙ ◙ ⌀ ⛺ ⛺ ⋟ S ⊡ ⊞
lau ➧ ⋟P

● ● ● ● ● ● **CENTRAL** ● ● ● ● ●

The centre of Germany incorporates an enormous range of
different landscapes - from the heavily-wooded Saarland, to
the gorge-like valleys of the Rhine, to the vine-covered
slopes of the Moselle. There are castles perched above
steeply scarped banks, and ancient but thriving towns
nestling in open valleys, combining scenic beauty with
architectural masterpieces and an historic past.
Contained within this region is Bonn, birthplace of
Beethoven, now a busy commercial and political centre, and
Cologne, a fine modern town centred around a majestic
Gothic cathedral.
Trier is Germany's oldest city and one of the largest wine-
producing communities in the region. Discover the vast

network of cellars extending beneath the streets and passages – a city in itself! One of the most important commercial and economic centres in Germany, by virtue of its central situation, is Frankfurt, birthplace of Goethe, and now home to over 5,000 animals in its famous zoo.

....

AACHEN NORDRHEIN-WESTFALEN

Passtrasse Pass Str.79 ☎ 0241 158502 ▤ 0241 158537
Municipal site in town centre near the Kurplatz. Becomes very full during the peak season.
Apr-Oct 1.2HEC ▥ ⚘ ☂ ☏ ☺ ☓ ⊙ ◪ ▣ ⊞ lau ➧ ☓ ∅ ≞
⚲P

ASBACHERHÜTTE RHEINLAND-PFALZ

Harfenmühle ☎ 06786 7076 ▤ 06786 7570
e-mail: camping-harfenmuehle@t-online.de
A quiet site, beautifully situated in Fischbach Valley. Level grassland, partly terraced.
➲ 3km NW of the B327 towards Kempfeld.
All year 6.2HEC ▥ ⚘ ⚘ ☂ ☏ ☺ ☓ ⊙ ◪ ∅ ≞ ◓ ⚲ L
☎ ⊞ lau Prices: ⚘3.80 ➧1.50 ☗5.50

ATTENDORN NORDRHEIN-WESTFALEN

Biggesee-Waldenburg ☎ 02722 95500 ▤ 955099
e-mail: biggesee@t-online.de
Generously terraced recreational site on the northern shore of the Bigge Reservoir, with adjoining public bathing area. Private sunbathing area. Lunchtime siesta 13.00-15.00 hrs.
➲ From Attendorn follow road towards Heldren. Shortly after the railway turn right and follow the signs to the site, about 1.5km on.
All year 6.5HEC ▥ ⚘ ☂ ☏ ☓ ⊙ ◪ ∅ ≞ ⚲ L ☎ ⊞ lau ➧ ☏
☓ ⚲P Prices: ⚘3.07-3.83 ▲6.65-9.71 pitch 9.46-12.53

Hof Biggen Finnentroper Str 131
☎ 02722 9553-0 ▤ 02722 95563-22
e-mail: info@hof-biggen.de
Well-equipped terraced site, surrounded by woodlands. Lunchtime siesta 13.00-15.00 hrs.
➲ Follow Atterdorn road to Ahauser Reservoir. Entrance near 'Haus am See' inn.
All year 18HEC ▥ ⚘ ⚘ ☂ ☏ ☺ ☓ ⊙ ◪ ∅ ≞ ☎ ⊞ lau ➧ ⚲R

BACHARACH RHEINLAND-PFALZ

Sonnenstrand Strandbadweg 9 ☎ 06743 1752 ▤ 06743 3192
e-mail: info@camping-sonnenstrand.de
On grassland beside the Rhine with some high trees. Close to a main road and two railway lines.
➲ The turn off from B9 into the site can be difficult for caravans coming from the north, due to one way traffic.
15 Mar-Oct 1.4HEC ▥ ⠿ ⚘ ☏ ☺ ☓ ⊙ ◪ ∅ ⚲ R ☎ ⊞ lau

BALHORN HESSEN

Erzeberg ☎ 05625 5274 ▤ 05625 7116
Site lies on meadowland on slightly sloping ground above the village. Lunchtime siesta 13.00-15.00 hrs.
➲ On B450 between Istha and Fritzlar.
All year 5HEC ▥ ➧ ☏ ☓ ☺ ⊙ ◪ ∅ ☗ ◓ ⚲ P ☎ lau ➧ ☂ ≞
⊞

BARNTRUP NORDRHEIN-WESTFALEN

Schwimmbad Fischteiche 4 ☎ 05263 2221 ▤ 2221
This well-kept site lies next to an open-air swimming pool, which is covered over in autumn and winter.
➲ Barntrup lies B66, near to junction with B1. Approach signposted from Barntrup.
All year 2.4HEC ▥ ⚘ ☂ ☺ ⊙ ◪ ∅ ☗ ▲ ◓ ⚲ P ⊞ lau ➧ ☓

BERNKASTEL-KUES RHEINLAND-PFALZ

Kueser Werth Am Hafen 2 ☎ 06531 8200 ▤ 06531-8282
Grassy site near Mosel and boating marina, with view of Castle Landshut.
➲ On S outskirts of town.
Apr-Oct 2.2HEC ▥ ⚘ ☂ ☏ ☓ ⊙ ◪ ∅ ≞ ☎ ⊞ lau

BERNKASTEL-WEHLEN RHEINLAND-PFALZ

Schenk Hauptstr 165 ☎ 06531 8176 ▤ 06531 7681
e-mail: camping.schenk@t-online.de
A site in the Mosel valley, partly set on terraces. The site approach can be difficult for caravans due to the steep gradient. The site has its own vineyard.
➲ From Bernkastel-Kues follow B53 for 4km NW towards 'Koblenz' reaching Wehlen turn right.
28 Mar-Oct 1.5HEC ▥ ⚘ ☂ ⊙ ◪ ≞ ◓ PR ☎ ⊞ lau ➧ ☂
☓ ∅

BIRKENFELD RHEINLAND-PFALZ

Waldwiesen ☎ 06782 5215 ▤ 06782 5219
e-mail: info@waldwiesen.de
In a wooded location close to the lake.
➲ Leave the B41 E of Birkenfeld. Signposted.
15 Apr-15 Oct 4.5HEC ▥ ⚘ ☏ ⊙ ◪ ∅ ☗ ◓ ⚲ L ☎ ⊞
lau ➧ ☂ ☏ ☓ ⚲PR

BÖMIGHAUSEN HESSEN

Barenberg ☎ 05632 1044 ▤ 1044
Beautifully terraced site at Neerdar reservoir.
➲ Access from B251 between Korbach and Brilon.
All year 1HEC ▥ ⠿ ⚘ ☏ ⊙ ◪ ∅ ⚲ LR ☎ lau
Prices: ⚘5 pitch 5

BORLEFZEN NORDRHEIN-WESTFALEN

Borlefzen ☎ 05733 80008
Apr-Oct 40HEC ▥ ⚘ ☂ ☏ ☓ ⊙ ◪ ∅ ☗ ⚲ LR ☎ ⊞ lau

BRAUNFELS HESSEN

Braunfels Am Weiherstieg 2 ☎ 06442 4366 ▤ 06442 6895
A terraced site surrounded by a forest of pine and deciduous trees. Separate meadow for touring campers. Lunchtime siesta 12.30-14.30 hrs.
➲ Access from Köln-Frankfurt motorway, exit 'Limburg', then B49 towards town.
All year 5.2HEC ▥ ⚘ ⚘ ☏ ☓ ⊙ ◪ ∅ ☗ ☎ lau ➧ ☂ ≞
⚲P Prices: ⚘3.58 ➧2.05 ☗7.67 ▲3.07-4.60

BREISIG, BAD RHEINLAND-PFALZ

Rheineck ☎ 02633 95645 ▤ 02633 472008
e-mail: info@camping-rheinek.de
A quiet, well-kept site on a level meadow in Vinxtbach Valley.
➲ From Koblenz follow B9 NW to Bad Breisig, then turn left, cross railway and continue for 400m.
All year 5HEC ▥ ⚘ ☂ ☏ ☺ ⊙ ◪ ∅ ≞ ☎ ⊞ lau ➧ ☓ ⚲PR
Prices: ⚘4-4.50 ➧2-2.50 ☗3-3.50 ▲2.50-4

BULLAY RHEINLAND-PFALZ

Bären-Camp Am Moselüfer 1/3
☎ 06542 900097 ▤ 06542 900098
e-mail: baeren-camp@t-online.de
On level meadow on right bank of the Mosel, next to the football ground. Prices high.
➲ Access via B49 Cochem-Alf, then over the bridge and through the village. Signposted.
15 Mar-5 Nov 1.8HEC ▥ ⚘ ☂ ☏ ☓ ⊙ ◪ ∅ ≞ ◓ ⚲ R ☎ ⊞
lau ➧ ⚲P

BURGEN RHEINLAND-PFALZ

Burgen ☎ 02605 2396 ▤ 02605 4919
A well maintained site with individual pitches set on level meadow with trees by the River Mosel. Site is broken up by shrubs and flower beds.
➲ *On the B49 (Kloblenz-Treis).*
7 Apr-22 Oct 4HEC ⬛ ⌂ ⋔ ⃛ ▼ ☉ ◙ ∅ ㅿ ⌁ PR ☎ ⊞ lau ➡ ✕

COBLENCE

See **KOBLENZ**

COCHEM RHEINLAND-PFALZ

Freizeitzentrum Stadionstr ☎ 02671 4409 ▤ 02671 910719
e-mail: freizeitentram.codiem@rhein-zeitung.de
Site lies on level meadowland with trees. On right bank of the Mosel, downstream from the swimming pool and sports ground.
➲ *From B49 in Cochem, follow 'Freizeitzentrum' signs, crossing the river on the downstream bridge. After swimming pool, turn left for site.*
end Mar-Oct 2.8HEC ⬛ ⌂ ⋔ ⃛ ▼ ✕ ☉ ◙ ∅ ㅿ ◪ ⌁ R ☎ ▣ ⊞ lau ➡ ✕ ⌁P Prices: ⋔3.50 ➡1.80 pitch 3.50-6.20

At **LANDKERN**(7km N)

Altes Forsthaus Haupstr 2 ☎ 02671 8701 ▤ 02671 8722
e-mail: camping.stern@t-online.de
The partly terraced site lies near woodland in the valley below Landkern.
➲ *From motorway A48 (Eifel motorway) leave at exit Kaisersesch, go S to Landkern, then follow signs to site.*
All year 10HEC ⬛ ⌂ ⋔ ▼ ✕ ☉ ◙ ∅ ㅿ ☎ ⊞ lau ➡ ⃛ ✕ ⌁P Prices: ⋔3.25 ➡1.75 ◙4.75-6.25 ▲4.75-6.25

COLOGNE

See **KÖLN**

DAHN RHEINLAND-PFALZ

Büttelwoog ☎ 06391 5622 ▤ 06391 5326
e-mail: buettelwoog-@suedwest-camping.de
Site lies in a magnificent pine forest, partly surrounded by steep hills and rocks. Section reserved for young people with tents. Lunchtime siesta 12.00-14.00 hrs.
➲ *From Pirmasens follow B10 up to Hinterweidenthal then S on B427 to Dahn.*
All year 6HEC ⬛ ⦙⦙⦙ ⌂ ⋔ ⃛ ✕ ☉ ◙ ∅ ㅿ ☎ ⊞ lau ➡ ⌁P Prices: ⋔5 pitch 6

DAUSENAU RHEINLAND-PFALZ

Lahn-Beach Hallgarten 16 ☎ 02603 13084
▤ fpsalthoff@aol.com
A riverside site in a wooded setting.
Apr-Oct 3HEC ⬛ ⌂ ⋔ ⃛ ✕ ☉ ◙ ◙ ⌁ R ☎ lau

DIEMELSEE-HERINGHAUSEN NORDRHEIN-WESTFALEN

AZUR-Camping Hohes Rad ☎ 05633 99099 ▤ 05633 99010
A terraced site in the Sauerland hills overlooking Lake Diemel.
➲ *Access via B251 (Korbach-Beilon).*
All year 2.8HEC ⬛ ⚞ ⋔ ✕ ☉ ◙ ∅ ㅿ lau ➡ ✕ ⌁LP ⊞

DIEZ RHEINLAND-PFALZ

Ochsenwiese ☎ 06432 2122 ▤ 06432 2122
On a meadow on the left bank of the River Lahn, below Schloss Oranienstein.
➲ *From N leave motorway A3 at Diez exit (from S at Limburg-Nord exit) then continue on B54 approx. 7km.*
Apr-Oct 7HEC ⬛ ⚞ ⋔ ⃛ ✕ ☉ ◙ ∅ ㅿ ⌁ R ☎ lau ➡ ⌁L Prices: ⋔3 ➡2.60 ◙3.50 ▲2-3.50

CAMPING HOHENSYBURG

Weitkamp Family
D-44265 Dortmund-Hohensyburg
Tel: 0231/77 43 74 Fax: 0231/774 95 54

– Near the new casino   **Easy access**
– Easy access, road has been widened
Terraced design with all connection facilities – also available to touring vans. Modern washing facilities.
An attractive and quiet location on the Ruhr and Lake Hengstey. Gateway to the Sauerland. Attractive bridleways and footpaths lead to places of historic interest. Ideal centre for touring the new Ruhr tourism area.
Access: Cologne-Bremen motorway (Hansa route) to the Hagen-Nord exit, A1 then to Hohensyburg.
A45 Dortmund-Frankfurt motorway (Sauerland route) to Dortmund-Süd and then the B54 to Hohensyburg.
B1 to Dortmund-Mitte exit and then the B54 to Hohensyburg.

DORSEL AN DER AHR RHEINLAND-PFALZ

Stahlhütte ☎ 02693 438 ▤ 02693 511
Site with individual pitches, on meadowland with trees near River Ahr.
➲ *Off B258 (Aachen-Koblenz) road.*
All year 5HEC ⬛ ⌂ ⋔ ⃛ ▼ ✕ ☉ ◙ ∅ ㅿ ⌁ R ☎ ⊞ lau

DORTMUND NORDRHEIN-WESTFALEN

Hohensyburg Syburger Dorfstr 69
☎ 0231 774374 ▤ 0231 7749554
Terraced site on hilly grassland near Weitkamp inn.
➲ *Access via B54.*
All year 11.5HEC ⬛ ⚞ ⋔ ⃛ ▼ ✕ ☉ ◙ ∅ ⌁ LR ☎ ⊞ lau Prices: ⋔4.50 ➡3 ◙6 ▲4.50

DREIEICH-OFFENTHAL HESSEN

Offenthal Bahnhofstr 77 ☎ 06074 5629 ▤ 06074 5629
e-mail: schoenweitz@t-online.de
A well equipped site in wooded surroundings.
➲ *Exit B486 at Dreieich-Offenthal in direction of Dietzenbach.*
Mar-Oct 3HEC ⬛ ⌂ ⋔ ☉ ◙ ㅿ ⌁ P ☎ ⊞ ⌀ ➡ ✕ Prices: ⋔3.50-3.50 ➡0.50-0.50 ◙4.50

DROLSHAGEN NORDRHEIN-WESTFALEN

Gut Kalberschnacke ☎ 00492763 7501 ▤ 7879
e-mail: camping-kalberschnacke@t-online.de
Terraced site above Bigge-Lister Reservoir in wooded area.
➲ *Turn off A45 (E41) autobahn at Wegringhausen exit and continue NE for approx. 4km.*
All year 13.5HEC ⬛ ⌂ ⋔ ⃛ ✕ ☉ ◙ ∅ ㅿ ☎ lau ➡ ⌁L Prices: ⋔4-5 pitch 4.80-10.50

DÜLMEN NORDRHEIN-WESTFALEN

Tannenwiese Borkenbergestr 217 ☎ 02594 991759
The site lies on meadowland in a well wooded country area, near the gliderdrome. Lunchtime siesta 12.30-14.30 hrs.
➲ *Take the B51 from Recklinghausen towards Münster as far as Hausdülmen, then follow signpost 'Segelflügplatz Borkenberge'.*
Mar-Oct 3.7HEC ⬛ ⌂ ⋔ ⃛ ☉ ◙ ㅿ ☎ ⊞ ➡ ▼ ✕ Prices: ⋔4 ➡1 ◙3.50 ▲2.50-3.10

DÜRKHEIM, BAD RHEINLAND-PFALZ

KNAUS Bad Dürkheim In den Almen 3
☎ 06322 61356 ▤ 06322 8161
e-mail: knaus-camping-duerkheim@t-online.de
Lakeside site on level meadow between vineyards, adjoining a sportsfield. Lunchtime siesta 12.00-15.00 hrs.
➲ *Access from E outskirts of town. Turn N at railway viaduct, near JET petrol station.*
Jan-Oct & Dec 16.3HEC ⬛ ⌂ ⋔ ⃛ ✕ ☉ ◙ ∅ ▲ ⌁ L ☎ ⊞ ⌀ lau

"SPITZER STEIN" campsite

D-35305 Grünberg/Hessen – state-approved health resort

Located in delightful and idyllic countryside at the edge of the "Hoher Vogelsberg" nature reserve and offering rest and relaxation. The spacious campsite (some 40,000 sq.m) is a personal favourite amongst camping enthusiasts. Wide range of sporting facilities in the vicinity and adjacent to family and leisure pool.

Access: 5 minutes from the Kassel-Frankfurt motorway via the B49.

Information from Städt. Fremdenverkehrsamt (tourist office)

Tel. 06401/804-0 or 06401/6553
Postfach 1165, 35301 Grünberg

Campingplatz

„Tiefertswinkel"

at the new swimming pool

Darmstadt
Heppenheim
B 460
A 5   **Fürth**
B 38a
Weinheim
Heidelberg

D-64658 Fürth/Odw.
Tel. 06253-5804
Fax 06253-3717

DÜSSELDORF NORDRHEIN-WESTFALEN

Unterbacher See Kleiner Torfbruch 31
☎ 0049/0211 89-92038 ▦ 0211 8929321
e-mail: service@uunterbachersee.de
Site on sloping grassland.
➲ *From Düsseldorf B326 to 'Erkrath' exit. Turn left by Unterbacher lake.*
28 mar-27 Oct 6.5HEC ⬛ ⌂ ⌂ ✕ ☉ ♨ ⌀ ⌸ ⌇ LP 🅿 ⊞ ⌇
◆ ⌇ ⌇ ✕ Prices: ⋔4 pitch 8

EMS, BAD RHEINLAND-PFALZ

Bad Ems ☎ 02603 4679 ▦ 02603 4487
Level grassy site with isolated trees by the River Lahn.
➲ *On E outskirts on B260.*
Apr-Oct 16HEC ⬛ ⌂ ⌂ ⌇ ⌇ ☉ ♨ ⌀ ⛺ ⌸
⌇ PR 🅿 ⊞ lau

ESSEN NORDRHEIN-WESTFALEN

At WERDEN(10km S)

Essen-Werden Im Löwental 67
☎ 0201 492978 ▦ 0201 8496132
e-mail: stadtcamping@gmx.de
Several fields divided by bushes and surrounded by thick hedges. Lunchtime siesta 13.00-15.00 hrs.
➲ *From centre of Essen towards Werden, then turn towards railway station and follow signposts.*
All year 6HEC ⬛ ⌂ ⌂ ⌇ ⌇ ✕ ☉ ♨ ⌀ ⛐
⌇ R ⊞ ⌇ lau ◆ ⌇P

FULDATAL-KNICKHAGEN HESSEN

Fulda-Freizeitzentrum ☎ 05607 340
On slightly sloping ground surrounded by woodland in a quiet, picturesque location. Lunchtime siesta 13.00-15.00 hrs.
➲ *From B3 Kassel-München turn towards Knickhagen and follow signs.*
All year 3.2HEC ⬛ ⌂ ⌂ ⌇ ✕ ☉ ♨ ⌸ ⛺ ⌇ P 🅿 ⊞ lau

FÜRTH IM ODENWALD HESSEN

Tiefertzwinkel Am Schwimmbad ☎ 06253 5804 ▦ 3717
Pleasantly landscaped site in beautiful setting next to the municipal open-air swimming pool. Lunchtime siesta 13.00-15.00 hrs.
Mar-Nov 4.2HEC ⬛ ⌂ ⌂ ⌇ ☉ ♨ ⌀ ⛐ ⛺ 🅿 ⊞ ⌇ lau ◆
✕ ⌇P Prices: ⋔3.30 ⛐5.50 ▲3.50-4.50

GAMMELSBACH HESSEN

Freienstein Neckarlstr 172 ☎ 06068 1306 ▦ 912121
The site lies just off the B45 in a landscaped preservation area. It is terraced and divided into pitches. Lunchtime siesta 13.00-15.00 hrs.
Apr-Sep 5HEC ⬛ ◆ ⌂ ⌇ ⌇ ✕ ☉ ♨ ⛐ ⛺ 🅿 lau
Prices: ⋔3.50 pitch 4

GERBACH RHEINLAND-PFALZ

AZUR-Camping Pfalz ☎ 06361 8287 ▦ 06361 22523
e-mail: info@azur-camping.de
Lunchtime siesta 13.00-15.00 hrs.
➲ *Access from A8/E12 motorway at junction Enkenbach-Hochspeyer. Then N on B48 via Rockenhausen and at Dielkirchen continue E for 4.5km to Gerbach.*
All year 8.5HEC ⬛ ⌂ ⌇ ✕ ☉ ♨ ⌀ ⌇ P 🅿 ⊞ lau Prices:
⋔4.50-6 ▲3.50-4.50 pitch 5.50-7.50

GILLENFELD RHEINLAND-PFALZ

Feriedorf Pulvermaar ☎ 06573 996500 ▦ 06573 996500
Partly terraced municipal site on a slightly sloping meadow at Pulver Maar, surrounded by woods.
➲ *From motorway A48 (Eifel autobahn) leave at exit Mehren/Daun, continue S on B421 and take the first turning into Gillenfeld. On near side of village turn off towards Pulver Maar.*
All year 3HEC ⬛ ⌂ ⌂ ⌇ ✕ ☉ ♨ ⛐ ⛺ 🅿 ⊞ lau ◆ ⌇ ⌀ ⌇LP
Prices: ⋔2.30-3 ⛐1-2 ⛐5-7 ▲5-15

GRÜNBERG HESSEN

Spitzer Stein Alsfelderstr ☎ 06401 804
Beautifully situated site at a forest swimming pool.
➲ *From the Frankfurt-Kassel motorway (A5) leave at Homberg junction. Campsite is 8km S.*
All year 4HEC ⬛ ⌇ ⌂ ⌇ ☉ ♨ ⌇ P 🅿 ⊞ lau ◆ ⌇ ✕

GRUNDMÜHLE BEI QUENTEL HESSEN

Grundmühle Quentel ☎ 05602 3659 ▦ 05602 915811
A forest camp site with a sunny location. Lunchtime siesta 13.00-15.00 hrs.
➲ *From Melsungen follow road B83 to Röhrenfurth. Here turn right towards 'Furstenhagen' and follow road via Eiterhagen to Quentel.*
All year 1.8HEC ⬛ ◆ ⌂ ⌇ ✕ ☉ ♨ ⌀ ⛐ ⌇ P 🅿 lau ◆ ⌇ ⌇ ✕

GULDENTAL RHEINLAND-PFALZ

Guldental ☎ 06707 633
Site lies in a valley of the Guldenbach Valley. Some terraces are reserved for tourers and there is a lake suitable for bathing.
➲ *From Bad Kreuznach N on road B48 to Langenlonsheim, and on nearside turn left to Guldental.*
All year 8HEC ⬛ ⌂ ⌂ ⌇ ✕ ☉ ♨ ⛐ ⊞

HALDERN NORDRHEIN-WESTFALEN

Strandhaus Sonsfeld ☎ 02857 2247 ▦ 02857 7171
On meadowland at the 'Hagener-Meer' next to B8 and railway line.
All year 15HEC ⬛ ⌂ ⌂ ⌇ ✕ ☉ ♨ ⛐ ⌇ L ⊞ lau
Prices: ⋔3 pitch 6

HAUSBAY RHEINLAND-PFALZ

At PFALZFELD-HAUSBAY

Schinderhannes ☎ 06746 80280 ▤ 06746 802814
e-mail: info@countrycamping.de
Terraced site on S facing slope, broken up by trees and shrubs
beside a small lake. Separate section for young people.
Lunchtime siesta 13.00-15.00 hrs.
➲ E of B327. 29km S of Koblenz.
All year 30HEC ⛺ ♨ ⛽ ♠ ⛱ ✕ ⊙ ◻ ∅ ⛴ ⤳ L 🏛 lau ➜ ⛱ ✕
⤳P Prices: ⚡5 pitch 8

HEIDENBURG RHEINLAND-PFALZ

Moselhöhe ☎ 06509 99016 ▤ 99017
A small, well appointed site on an open meadow.
➲ Access via A1 exit Mehring towards Thalfang am Erbestopf.
15 Nov-15 Dec 3HEC ⛺ ⚡ ♠ ✕ ⊙ ◻ ∅ 🏛 lau ➜ ⛱ ⛴

HEIMBACH NORDRHEIN-WESTFALEN

Rurthal-Burg Blens ☎ 02446 3377 ▤ 911126
Site with individual pitches on meadowland beside the River
Ruhr.
➲ From Düren follow road S via Nideggen and Abenden to
Blens, then cross bridge and turn left.
Oct 7HEC ⛺ ⚡ ♠ ⛱ ✕ ⊙ ◻ ∅ 🏛 ⤳ P 🏛 ⬥ lau ➜ ✕
⤳R Prices: ⚡3.50 ⛘2.80 ⛘3.20 ▲2.65

HEIMERTSHAUSEN HESSEN

Heimertshausen Ehringshauser Str ☎ 06635 206
Near swimming pool in extenisve, grassy, wooded valley.
Lunchtime siesta 13.00-15.00 hrs.
➲ From Kassel-Frankfurt motorway take Alsfeld-West exit,
then continue via Romrod and Zell.
Apr-Sep 3.6HEC ⛺ ⚡ ♠ ⛱ ✕ ⊙ ◻ ∅ 🏛 ⛘ 🏛 ⬥ lau ➜
⤳P Prices: ⚡3.10 ⛘5.20 ▲5.20 pitch 5.20

HELLENTHAL NORDRHEIN-WESTFALEN

Hellenthal Platiss 1 ☎ 02482 1500 ▤ 02482 2171
On extensive meadowland.
➲ 0.5km S of town.
All year 6HEC ⛺ ⚡ ♠ ✕ ✕ ⊙ ◻ ⤳ P 🏛 ⬥ lau ➜ ⛱ ✕ ⤳
Prices: ⚡3.50 pitch 8

HERINGEN HESSEN

Werra ☎ 06624 01708603693 ▤ 06624 915597
Municipal site on slightly sloping ground at the swimming
pool. Lunchtime siesta 13.00-15.00 hrs.
All year 4HEC ⛺ ⬥ ⛱ ⛽ ✕ ⊙ ◻ ∅ 🏛 lau ➜ ⤳PR

HIRSCHHORN AM NECKAR HESSEN

Odenwald Langenthalerstr 80 ☎ 06272 809 ▤ 06272 3658
e-mail: odenwald-camping-park@t-online.de
Extensive site in wooded valley. Divided by River Ülfenbach
and hedges.
➲ Turn off B37 towards Wald-Michelbach and continue for
1.5km.
Apr-Nov 8HEC ⛺ ⚡ ♠ ⛱ ✕ ✕ ⊙ ◻ ∅ 🏛 ⛘ ⤳ PR 🏛 ⬥
lau Prices: ⚡4.50 pitch 6.20

HOFGEISMAR HESSEN

Parkschwimmbad Schöneberger Str 16 ☎ 05671 1215
Municipal site, subdivided by hedges. Next to a swimming
pool. Lunchtime siesta 13.00-15.00 hrs. Mobile shop.
All year 1.5HEC ⛺ ⚡ ♠ ✕ ⊙ ◻ ⛘ ⤳ P 🏛 ⬥ lau ➜ ∅

At LIEBENAU-ZWERGEN(9km W)

Ponyhof Camping Club Warmetal
☎ 05676 1509 ▤ 05676 8880
e-mail: ponyhofcamping@t-online.de
A terraced, south facing site, with magnificent scenery. 300m
from a swimming pool.
➲ Access from B83, at Hofgeismar turn W towards Liebenau,
alternatively from B7 turn N at Obemeiser towards Liebenau.
15 Mar-1 Nov 7HEC ⛺ ⚡ ♠ ⛱ ✕ ⊙ ◻ ∅ 🏛 ⤳ R 🏛 ⬥
⤳LP 🏛 Prices: ⚡5-6 ⛘2 pitch 11-12

HONNEF, BAD NORDRHEIN-WESTFALEN

At HONNEF-HIMBERG, BAD(7km E)

Jillieshof ☎ 02224 972066 ▤ 02224 972067
All year 4HEC ⛺ ⚡ ♠ ⛽ ⊙ ◻ ∅ 🏛 🏛 ⬥ lau ➜ ⛱ ✕
Prices: ⚡4.50 ⛘6

HORN-BAD MEINBERG NORDRHEIN-WESTFALEN

Eggewald Kempener Str 33 ☎ 05255 236 ▤ 05255 1375
Site lies in well wooded countryside.
➲ Access via road B1. In Horn-Bad Meinberg turn off main
road at the Waldschlosschen and follow the 'Altenbeken' road
for about 8km up to Kempen.
All year 2HEC ⛺ ⚡ ♠ ✕ ⊙ ◻ 🏛 ⤳ P 🏛 ⬥ lau

IDSTEIN HESSEN

AZUR-Camping Idstein ☎ 06126 91299 ▤ 06126 990289
In a peaceful rural setting close to the ancient town of
Idstein.
➲ Access via A3 (Frankfurt-Limburg).
All year 2.6HEC ⛺ ⚡ ♠ ⛱ ✕ ⊙ ◻ ∅ ⤳ P 🏛 ⬥ lau ➜ ✕

INGENHEIM RHEINLAND-PFALZ

SC Klingbachtal ☎ 06349 6278
Municipal site lies on level meadowland at the edge of the
village, next to the sports ground.
➲ 8km S of Landau via B38. Final approach well signposted.
Apr-Oct 1.5HEC ⛺ ⚡ ♠ ⊙ ◻ ∅ 🏛 🏛 ⬥ lau ➜ ⛱ ✕ ⤳P

IRREL RHEINLAND-PFALZ

Nimseck ☎ 06525 314 ▤ 1299
e-mail: info@cmaping-nimseck.de
Site on long grassy strip in wooded valley on the bank of
River Nims.
➲ Approach from Bitburg via B257/E42 in SW direction. At
the turn-off from the bypass to Irrel, turn left.
Apr-Nov 7HEC ⛺ ⚡ ♠ ✕ ⊙ ◻ ∅ 🏛 🏛 ⤳ PR 🏛 ⬥ lau ➜ ⛱

KALLETAL-VARENHOLZ NORDRHEIN-WESTFALEN

Ost/Weser/Freizeit-Zentrum ☎ 05755 444
Extensive site in Weser recreation area near River Weser N of
Schloss Varenholz. Separate field and common room for
young campers.
➲ Leave A2/E8 motorway at Exter exit then continue via
Vlotho towards Rintein.
All year 12HEC ⛺ ⚡ ♠ ⛱ ✕ ⊙ ◻ ∅ 🏛 ⤳ L 🏛 ⬥ lau

KELL RHEINLAND-PFALZ

Freibad Hochwald ☎ 06589 1695
On meadow on slightly sloping wooded hillside, near a
public open-air swimming pool. **Advance booking necessary
in high season.**
➲ 2km from B407 towards Trier.
May-Sep 2HEC ⛺ ⚡ ♠ ✕ ⊙ ◻ ⤳ P 🏛 🏛

KIRCHHEIM HESSEN

Seepark Kirchheim ☎ 06628 1525 ▤ 06628 8664
e-mail: info@campseepark.de
This terraced site, with individual pitches, is part of an
extensive and well equipped leisure and recreation centre.
All year 10HEC ⛺ 💧 ⛽ ▬ ▾ ✗ ⊙ ⛽ ⌀ ▥ ⊞ ⤍ LP 🏧 ⊞ lau

KIRN RHEINLAND-PFALZ

Papiermühle Krebsweilererstr 8 ☎ 06752 2267
➲ *Access via B41 exit Meisenheim*
All year 6HEC ⛺ 💧 ⛽ ✗ ⊙ ⛽ ⌀ ▥ ⤍ R 🏧 ⊞
Prices: ⚑3.50 pitch 6

KOBLENZ (COBLENCE) RHEINLAND-PFALZ
At WINNINGEN(9km SW)

Ziehfurt Fährstr 35 ☎ 02606 356 ▤ 2752
Site lies on level wooded meadowland.
➲ *From Koblenz follow road B416 for 11km towards Trièr.*
Access to site at the Schwimmbad (swimming pool).
May-Sep 7HEC ⛺ 💧 ⛽ ▬ ▾ ✗ ⊙ ⛽ ⌀ ⤍ R 🏧 ⊞ lau ⤍ ⤍P
Prices: ⚑5 pitch 5

KÖLN (COLOGNE) NORDRHEIN-WESTFALEN
At RODENKIRCHEN

Berger Ueferstr 71 ☎ 0221 9355240 ▤ 0221 9355246
e-mail: camping.berger@t-online.de
Situated on a meadow beside the River Rhine, the campsite
has fine views of the beautiful surrounding area and good,
modern facilities.
All year 6HEC ⛺ 💧 ⛽ ▬ ▾ ✗ ⊙ ⛽ ⌀ ⤍ R 🏧 lau
Prices: ⚑4.50-4.50 ⛟3-3 ⛟3-3 ⚑3-3 pitch 6-6

KÖNEN RHEINLAND-PFALZ

Horsch Könenerstr 36 ☎ 06501 17571
Apr-Oct ⛺ 💧 ⛽ ▬ ▾ ✗ ⊙ ⛽ ⌀ ⤍ LPR 🏧 ⊞

KÖNIGSTEIN IM TAUNUS HESSEN
At EPPSTEIN(8km SW)

Hubertushof Bezirksstr 2 ☎ 06198 7000 ▤ 7002
e-mail: js@taunuscamp.de
In the Taunus landscape preservation area.
➲ *Follow B455 from Königstein.*
All year 3HEC ⛺ 💧 ⤍ ⛽ ▬ ⊙ ⛽ ⌀ ▥ 🏧 ⊞ ⤍ ▾ ✗ ⤍P

KRÖV RHEINLAND-PFALZ

Kröver-Berg ☎ 06541 70040 ▤ 06541 700444
All year 2HEC ⛺ 💧 ⛽ ▾ ✗ ⊙ ⛽ ⌀ ⛽ ⊞ lau

LADBERGEN NORDRHEIN-WESTFALEN

Waldsee Waldseestr 81 ☎ 05485 1816 ▤ 05485 3560
Site lies at the inn, near the bathing area of the lake.
➲ *2km N. From motorway leave at 'Ladbergen' exit following*
road towards Saerbeck/Emsdetten and after 100m turn right.
All year 7HEC ⛺ 💧 ⛽ ▬ ▾ ✗ ⊙ ⛽ ⌀ ⤍ LP 🏧 ⊞ lau
Prices: ⚑3.07 ⛟6.14 pitch 3.58

LAHNSTEIN RHEINLAND-PFALZ

Burg Lahneck ☎ 02621 2765 ▤ 18290
Level grassland site with sunny aspect and terraces which
provide shade. Situated next to Lahneck Castle. Pleasant view
of the Rhine Valley.
➲ *From Koblenz (8km distance) follow road B42. In*
Lahnstein, leave main road and follow signs (Burg Lahneck),
1.5km to site.
Apr-Oct 1.8HEC ⛺ 💧 ⛽ ▬ ⊙ ⛽ ⌀ 🏧 ⊞ lau ⤍ ✗ ⤍P
Prices: ⚑5.50 ⛟3.50 ⛟5.50 ⚑4.50-5.50

LEIWEN RHEINLAND-PFALZ

AEGON-Ferienpark Sonnenberg
☎ 06507 93690 ▤ 06507 936936
e-mail: info@landal.de
Extensive terraced site in one of the largest wine growing
areas of this district. Lies above the River Mosel.
➲ *Access from main B53 (Mosel Valley road) cross the River*
Mosel at Thornich then via Leiwen to site.
08 Feb-04 Nov 01Jan-07Feb, 04Nov-31Dec 25HEC ⛺ 💧 ⛿
⛽ ▬ ▾ ✗ ⊙ ⛽ ⛽ ⤍ PR 🏧 ⊞ lau ⤍ ▬ ▾ ✗ ⌀ Prices: ⚑2.50
pitch 18-31 (incl 2 persons)

LEMGO NORDRHEIN-WESTFALEN

Alten Hansestadt Regenstorstr
☎ 05261 14858 ▤ 05261-188324
e-mail: info@camping-lemgo.de
The site lies by the swimming pool directly on the river.
All year 15HEC ⛺ 💧 ⛽ ⊙ ⛽ ⌀ ⛽ ⤍ R 🏧 lau ⤍ ▬ ▾ ✗ ⤍P
⊞ Prices: ⚑3.32 ⛟3.32 ⛟3.32 ⚑3-2.30

LIBLAR NORDRHEIN-WESTFALEN

Liblarer See ☎ 02235 3899
This site lies at Lake Liblar, with its own bathing area.
Camping Card Compulsory.
➲ *Access SW from Cologne on the B265 (for approx 15km)*
1km before Liblar turn left towards the lake.
All year 10HEC ⛺ ⛿ ⛺ 💧 ⛽ ▬ ▾ ✗ ⊙ ⛽ ⌀ ▥ ⤍ L 🏧 ⊞ lau

LICHTENBERG HESSEN

Odenwald Idyll Fischbachtal ☎ 06166 8577
In quiet and beautiful setting. Lunchtime siesta
13.00-15.00 hrs.
➲ *Access from Darmstadt amd Gross-Bieberau.*
Apr-15 Oct 3.5HEC ⛺ 💧 ⛽ ▬ ✗ ⊙ ⛽ ⌀ ⤍ P 🏧 ⊞

LINDENFELS HESSEN

Terrassencamping Schlierbach Am Zentbuckel 11
☎ 06255 630 ▤ 3526
Site is fenced and lies on sloping terrain. Lunchtime siesta
13.00-15.00 hrs.
➲ *From Bensheim-Michelstadt road B47, turn off in*
Lindenfels and go SW to Schlierbach.
Apr-Oct 3.2HEC ⛺ ⛿ ⛺ 💧 ⛽ ▬ ⊙ ⛽ ⌀ ▥ 🏧 ⊞ lau ⤍ ▾ ✗
⤍P Prices: ⚑3.50 pitch 5

LINGERHAHN RHEINLAND-PFALZ

Mühlenteich ☎ 067461 533 ▤ 1566
e-mail: info@muehlenteich.de
Site lies on slightly sloping meadowland, divided into
sections by a group of trees. Isolated situation at the edge of
woodland and adjoining the forest swimming pool (free
entry for campers). Lunchtime siesta 13.00-15.00 hrs. Trout
fishing.
➲ *Access is from Koblenz-Bingen motorway A61 via exit*
'Pfalzfeld' - or for caravans, an easier approach would be via
exit 'Laudert'.
All year 15HEC ⛺ ⤍ ⛽ ▬ ▾ ✗ ⊙ ⛽ ⌀ ▥ ⤍ P 🏧 ⊞ ⤍ ⤍R
Prices: ⚑4 ⛟4 ⛟4 ⚑4 pitch 8

LORCH HESSEN

Suleika ☎ 06726 9464 ▤ 06726 9440
Well laid out terraced site in an ideal location for exploring
the historic Rhine Valley. Separate car park for users of the
smaller pitches.
➲ *From Assmannshausen take B42 for 3km towards Lorch*
then turn right into the Bodental - access to site through
railway underpass. Approach for larger caravans - turn right
1km before Lorch.
Apr-Oct 4HEC ⛺ 💧 ⛽ ▬ ▾ ✗ ⊙ ⛽ ⌀ ▥ ⛽ ⛿ ⊞ lau ⤍ ✗
⤍LR Prices: ⚑4.50 ⛟1.50 ⛟4.50 ⚑3-4.50

LOSHEIM SAARLAND

AZUR-Camping Reiterhof Girtenmühle
☎ 06872 9024-0 ▦ 06872 9024-11
e-mail: info@azur-camping.de
⮕ *Access via B268 (Trier-Losheim).*
All year 5HEC ▦ ⌖ ⌂ ✕ ⊙ 🖳 ⌀ 🏥 ⊞ lau ⮕ ⸚LP
Prices: ⭡4-6 ▲3-4 pitch 5-7

MAINZ-KOSTHEIM HESSEN

Mainz-Wiesbaden Maarau ☎ 06134 4383 ▦ 4383
e-mail: info@kakg.de
Shop closed in April.
15 Mar-Oct 2HEC ▦ ⮕ ⌂ ⌖ ✕ ⊙ 🖳 🏥 lau ⮕ ⸚PR

MARBURG AN DER LAHN HESSEN

GC Lahnaue Tro je damm 47 ☎ 06421 21331 ▦ 06421 21331
e-mail: info@lahnaue.de
Municipal site on level meadowland next to the 'Sommerbad'
(swimming pool) in the W part of this 'Town on the River
Lahn'.
Apr-Oct 1HEC ▦ ⌖ ⌂ ✕ ⊙ 🖳 ⌀ ⸚ R 🏥 lau ⮕ ⸚P

MEERBUSCH NORDRHEIN-WESTFALEN

AZUR-Camping Meerbusch Zur Rheinfähre 21
☎ 02150 911817 ▦ 02150 912289
e-mail: info@azur-camping.de
In a peaceful location on the banks of the Rhine within easy
reach of Dusseldorf.
⮕ *Access via A57 (Neuss-Krefeld).*
Apr-Oct 3.8HEC ▦ ⤴ ⌂ ⌖ ✕ ⊙ 🖳 🚌 ⸚ R 🏥 ⊞ lau
Prices: ⭡4-6 ▲3-4 pitch 5-7

MEHLEM NORDRHEIN-WESTFALEN

Genienau ☎ 0228 344949 ▦ 344949
The site lies opposite the Drachenfels.
All year 1.8HEC ▦ ⌖ ⌂ ⌖ ⌀ ⊙ 🖳 ⌀ ⸚ R ⊞ 🏥 lau ⮕ 🖳 ✕ ⌀
🚌 ⸚P Prices: ⭡5.20 ⮕1.60-2.60 🚎2.60-7.70 ▲2.60-5.20

MEINHARD HESSEN

Werra-Meissner-Kreis ☎ 05651 6200 ▦ 22272
e-mail: 0565113805-0001@t-online.de
A lakeside site with facilities for water sports.
⮕ *Access via B27 and B249.*
Apr-Oct 7HEC ▦ ⌖ ⌂ ⌖ ✕ ⊙ 🖳 ⸚ L 🏥 ⊞ ⊘ lau ⮕ 🖳 🚌
⸚P ⊞ Prices: ⭡3.10 🚎6.50 ▲6.50

MESCHEDE NORDRHEIN-WESTFALEN

Sauerland-Camp Hennesee ☎ 0291 99950 ▦ 0291 999515
In pleasant wooded surroundings beside the Hennesee. Shop
and café only open during high season.
⮕ *S via B55.*
All year 13HEC ▦ ⌖ ⌂ ⌖ 🖳 ✕ ⊙ 🖳 ⌀ 🚌
⸚ LP ⊞ 🏥 lau ⮕ ⸚L

MESENICH RHEINLAND-PFALZ

Family Camping Club ☎ 02673 4556 ▦ 02673 1751
A family site with plenty of recreational facilities beside the
River Moselle. Individual pitches are divided by trees and
hedges.
May-Sep 3HEC ▦ ⌖ ⌂ ⌖ 🖳 ✕ ⊙ 🖳 🚌 ▲ ⸚ PR ⊞ lau

MICHELSTADT HESSEN

Odenwaldparadies ☎ 06061 74152/3256
Site is partly fenced in and lies next to the station and
swimming pool in the NE part of town.
⮕ *Site is well signposted from the by-pass road of Michelstadt.*
May-Sep 1.2HEC ▦ ⤴ ⌂ ✕ ⊙ 🖳 ⌀ 🚌 🏥 ⊞ ⊘ ⮕ ⸚P
Prices: ⭡2.60 ⮕1.60 🚎3.60-4.60 ▲3.10-5.20

MITTELHOF RHEINLAND-PFALZ

Eichenwald ☎ 02742 931931/910643 ▦ 9689631/910645
In oakwood, mainly divided into pitches.
Camping Card Compulsory.
⮕ *From Siegen follow B62 towards Wissen. Turning to site
approximately 4km NE of Wissen.*
All year 10HEC ▦ ⌖ ⌂ ⌖ ✕ ⊙ 🖳 ⌀ 🏥 ⊞ lau ⮕ 🖳 ⸚P
Prices: ⭡3.50 ⮕4 🚎4 ▲3 pitch 4

MONSCHAU NORDRHEIN-WESTFALEN

Perlenau Eifel ☎ 02472 4136 ▦ 02472 4493
Apr-Oct 2HEC ▦ ⌖ ⌂ ⌖ 🖳 ⌖ ✕ ⊙ 🖳 ⌀ 🚌 🏠
⸚ PR 🏥 lau ⮕ ⊞

MONTABAUR RHEINLAND-PFALZ

At GIROD(4km E)

Eisenbachtal ☎ 06485 766 ▦ 06485 4938
Situated in the 'Nassau Nature Park'.
⮕ *From motorway exit 40 'Montabaur' turn right, before
Montabaur follow sign 5km towards Limburg. From motorway
exit 41 'Wallmerod/Diez' 5km towards Montabaur.*
All year 3HEC ▦ ⌖ ⌂ ⌖ 🖳 ⌖ ✕ ⊙ 🖳 ⌀ 🏥 ⊞ lau ⮕ ⸚P
Prices: ⭡4 🚎6 pitch 6

MÖRFELDEN-WALLDORF HESSEN

Arndt Mörfelden Am Zeltplatz 5 ☎ 06105 22289 ▦ 277459
Well laid out site in two sections near motorway. Lunchtime
siesta 13.00-15.00 hrs.
⮕ *Well signposted 0.3km from Langen/Mörfelden exit on
A5/E4 Frankfurt-Darmstadt motorway.*
All year 6HEC ▦ ⌖⌖⌖ ⌖ ⌂ ⌖ ✕ ⊙ 🖳 🏥 lau ⮕ 🖳 ✕ ⌀ ⸚LP
⊞ Prices: ⭡4 pitch 8

MÜLHEIM RHEINLAND-PFALZ

AZUR Camping Mülheim ☎ 06534 940157 ▦ 940157
Near Mülheim-Lieser bridge over the Mosel.
⮕ *Access from Bernkastel, 5.5km along B53 towards Trier.*
Est-Oct 1.5HEC ▦ ⌖ ⌂ ⌖ ✕ ⊙ 🖳 ⌀ 🚌 🚎 ⸚ R 🏥 lau ⮕ 🖳
⊞ Prices: ⭡4-5.50 pitch 5-7

MÜLHEIM AN DER RUHR NORDRHEIN-WESTFALEN

Entenfangsee ☎ 0203 760111 ▦ 761030
Extensive site near lake. Touring pitches near railway line.
Adventure playground. Lunchtime siesta 13.00-15.00 hrs.
⮕ *From motorway exit Duisburg-Wedau, continue towards
Bissingheim to lake.*
All year 12.5HEC ▦ ⌖ ⌂ 🖳 ✕ ⊙ 🖳 ⌀ 🚌 ⸚
L 🏥 ⊞ lau ⮕ ⸚P ⊞

MÜLLENBACH RHEINLAND-PFALZ

Nürburgring ☎ 02692 224 ▦ 1020
e-mail: rezeption@camping-am-nuerburgring.de
A large, well equipped site in a wooded location with direct
access to the Nürburgring Grand-Prix circuit.
⮕ *Access via A61/A48 and B412.*
All year 30HEC ▦ ⌖⌖⌖ ⌖ ⌂ ⌖ ✕ ⊙ 🖳 ⌀ 🚌 🏥 ⊞ lau

NEHREN RHEINLAND-PFALZ

Nehren ☎ 02673 4612 ▦ 02671 916170
On level terrain beside the River Moselle. Separate section for
teenagers. Lunchtime siesta 13.00-15.00 hrs. Liable to flood at
certain times of the year.
⮕ *Turn off the B49 Cochem-Alf road in Nehren.*
Apr-14 Oct 5HEC ▦ ⌖ ⌂ ⌖ ✕ ⊙ 🖳 ⸚ R 🏥 ⊞ lau ⮕ 🖳
Prices: ⭡7 🚎13 ▲9

NEUERBURG RHEINLAND-PFALZ

Neuerburg ☎ 06564 2660
Site divided by hedges, close to an open-air pool with a smaller lake for inflatable boats.
⮑ *Access via the B50 (Bitburg-Vianden). At Sinspett turn N and continue to site on N outskirts (7km).*
All year 1.5HEC ⚏ ⊶ ⌂ ♥ ✗ ⊙ ⊟ ∅ ⚓
⌇ PRS 🏕 ♨ lau ♦ 🛁

NIEDEREISENHAUSEN HESSEN

Hinterland Ouotshauser Weg 32, Steffenberg ☎ 06464 7564
Lunchtime siesta 13.00-14.30 hrs.
⮑ *Follow signs to 'Schwimmbad'.*
All year 2HEC ⚏ ♥ ⌂ ✗ ⊙ ⊟ 🖵 ⚓ 🏕 ⊞ lau ♦ 🛁 ⌇P

NIEDERKRÜCHTEN NORDRHEIN-WESTFALEN

Lelefeld Lelefeld 4 ☎ 02163 81203 ▧ 2163/81203
e-mail: gblut@aol.com
In a quiet, wooded, location on the outskirts of the village.
⮑ *Signposted from Elmpt.*
All year 1.5HEC ⚏ ⊶ ⌂ 🛁 ⌀ ⊙ ⊟ ∅ 🖵 🏕 ⊞ lau ♦ ✗
⌇LPR Prices: ⅍3.10 ⚘1.50 ⊕3.10 ▲3.10

NIEDERWÖRRESBACH RHEINLAND-PFALZ

Fischbachtal ☎ 06785 7372
On level grassland in Fischbach valley. Lunchtime siesta 12.00-14.00 hrs.
⮑ *6km N of Fischbach towards Herrsteij.*
All year 1.8HEC ⚏ ⊶ ⌂ 🛁 ✗ ⊙ ⊟ ∅ 🖵 ⌇ R 🏕 ⊞ lau

OBERLAHR RHEINLAND-PFALZ

Lahrer Herrlichkeit In der Huth
☎ 02685 7326 & 8282 ▧ 02687 8672
Holiday site with leisure park in wooded surroundings.
Lunchtime siesta 13.00-15.00 hrs.
⮑ *From motorway A3 (Frankfurt-Köln) leave at exit 'Neuwied/Altenkirchen' then 5km on B256 towards Altenkirchen.*
All year 6.8HEC ⚏ ⊶ ⌂ 🛁 ✗ ⊙ ⊟ ∅ 🖵 🚐 🏕 lau
♦ ⌇ ✗ ⌇PR

OBERSGEGEN RHEINLAND-PFALZ

Reles-Mühle Kapellenstr 3 ☎ 06566 8741 ▧ 931064
e-mail: www.eifelcamping.com
In rural surroundings next to a farmhouse, set on a level meadow at a brook with trees and bushes.
⮑ *From Bitburg on road B50 towards Vianden. Site lies near the Luxembourg frontier.*
All year 2HEC ⚏ ⊶ ⌂ 🛁 ⊙ ⊙ ⊟ 🚐 ⌇ R 🏕 ⊞ lau
♦ ⌇ ✗ ∅ 🖵 ⌇P

OBERWEIS RHEINLAND-PFALZ

Prümtal-Camping In der Klaus 5 ☎ 06527 92920 ▧ 929232
e-mail: pruemtal@t-online.dee
A family site in pleasant wooded surroundings with good sporting facilities.
⮑ *Access from Bitburg on B50 towards Luxembourg border.*
All year 3HEC ⚏ ⊶ ⌂ 🛁 ✗ ⊙ ⊟ ∅ 🖵 🏕 ⌇ PR 🏕 lau ♦
⊞ Prices: ⅍4.20-5.60 ▲2.96-3.95 pitch 5.93-7.90

OLPE NORDRHEIN-WESTFALEN

At KESSENHAMMER

Biggesee-Kessenhammer ☎ 02761 94420 ▧ 944299
e-mail: biggesee@t-online.de
Long, narrow partly terraced site in quiet woodland setting on E shore of Bigge-Reservoir. Lunchtime siesta 13.00-15.00 hrs.
⮑ *A45 exit Olpe continue B54 to Olpe eastwards on B55 and turn off at exit Rhode.*
All year 5.7HEC ⚏ ⊶ ⌂ 🛁 ✗ ⊙ ⊟ ∅ ⌇ L 🏕 ⊞ lau ♦ ✗
Prices: ⅍3.07-73.83 ▲6.65-9.71 pitch 9.46-12.53

At SONDERN

Biggesee-Sondern Sonderner Kopf 3
☎ 02761 944111 ▧ 944122
e-mail: biggesee@t-online.de
A popular site in wooded surroundings on the shore of the Biggersee.
⮑ *Exit Olpe A45 in direction Attendorn. In 6km turn off for Erholungsanlage Biggesee-Sondern.*
All year 6HEC ⚏ ⊶ ♦ ⌂ 🛁 ✗ ⊙ ⊟ ∅ 🖵 ⌇ L 🏕 ⊞ lau ♦ ✗
Prices: ⅍3.07-3.83 pitch 10.23-12.78

PORTA WESTFALICA NORDRHEIN-WESTFALEN

Grosser Weserbogen ☎ 05731 6188 ▧ 6601
e-mail: grosserweserbogen@t-online.de
⮑ *From A2 (travelling towards Dortmund), take exit Porta Westfalica-Minden.*
All year 7HEC ⚏ ⊶ ⋇ ⌂ 🛁 ✗ ⊙ ⊟ ∅ ⌇ L 🏕 ⊞ ♨ lau ♦ ⌇P
Prices: ⅍5.50 ⚘2.50 ⊕7.50 ▲4.50 pitch 4.50

PRÜM RHEINLAND-PFALZ

Waldcampingplatz ☎ 06551 2481 ▧ 06551 6555
e-mail: waldcamping@pruem_web.de
Site lies on both side of the River Prüm and is surrounded by woods. Divided into three sections of level meadowland.
⮑ *Situated at the NW of Prüm.*
All year 3.5HEC ⚏ ⊶ ⌂ 🛁 ✗ ⊙ ⊟ ∅ 🖵 ⌇ R 🏕 ⊞ lau ♦ 🛁
🍴 ✗ ⌇P Prices: ⅍4 pitch 11

REINSFELD RHEINLAND-PFALZ

AZUR Camping Hunsrück
☎ 06503 95123 ▧ 06503 95124
e-mail: info@azur-camping.de
In a peaceful location close to Trier on the Luxembourg border, surrounded by hills.
⮑ *Access via the B52 or B407.*
All year 20HEC ⚏ ⊶ ⌂ 🛁 🍴 ✗ ⊙ ⊟ 🚐 ⌇ P 🏕 ⊞ lau
Prices: ⅍4.50-6 ⚘3.50-4.50 pitch 5.50-7.50

ROTHEMANN HESSEN

Rothemann Maulkuppenstr 17 ☎ 06659 2285
A small, well-kept site surrounded by a hedge, lies next to the main Fulda road.
⮑ *From Fulda follow road B27 for 10km towards Bad Brükenau; can also be reached from the Kassel-Würzburg motorway leaving exit Fulda Süd, then 3km along B27 towards Bad Brükenau.*
Apr-Oct 6.4HEC ⚏ ♥ ⌂ ⊙ ⊟ ∅ 🖵 🏕 ⊞ ♦ ✗

RÜDESHEIM HESSEN

Rhein ☎ 06722 2528 & 2582 ▧ 06722-947046
Near the open-air swimming pool and the River Rhine.
May-3 Oct 3HEC ⚏ ⊶ ⌂ 🛁 🍴 ✗ ⊙ ⊟ ∅ 🏕 lau ♦ ✗ ⌇P
⊞ Prices: ⅍4.10 ⚘3.20 ⊕4.20 ▲4-4.40

RUNKEL AN DER LAHN HESSEN

Runkel Auf der Bleiche ☎ 06482 911022
⮑ *On road from Limburg.*
Apr-Sep 2HEC ⚏ ⊶ ⌂ 🍴 ✗ ⊙ ⊟ ∅ 🖵 ▲ ⌇ R 🏕 ⊞ ♦ 🛁 ✗

SAARBURG RHEINLAND-PFALZ

Landal Greenpark Warsberg
☎ 06581 91460 ▧ 06581 914646
Open site in quiet situation on top of a hill. Chairlift (700m) leads down to the town.
⮑ *At N end of the town leave the B51 'Trier' road and follow signs ' Ferienpark Warsberg' 3km uphill on good road.*
22 Mar-04 Nov 11HEC ⚏ ⊶ ⌂ 🛁 🍴 ✗ ⊙ ⊟ ∅ 🖵 🚐 ⌇ P 🏕
⊞ lau Prices: pitch 8.70

Leukbachtal ☎ 06581 2228 ▧ 06581 2228
Municipal site on level meadows on both sides of the Leuk-Bach (brook).
➲ *Leave Saarburg on road B51 towards Trassen, then after crossroads, turn left off the B51.*
Etr-Oct 3HEC ⊞ ♦ ⋔ ⅄ ✕ ⊙ ⊠ ⌀ ⌷ ⊞ ⊞ lau ♦ ⏚ ⇘P

Waldfrieden Im Fichtenhain 4 ☎ 06581 2255 ▧ 06581 5809
e-mail: camping-waldfrieden@t-online.de
Site lies next to the Café Waldfrieden on unspoilt, slightly rising meadowland in woods.
➲ *S of town leave B51 or B407 and follow road towards Nennig (Luxembourg). 200m to site.*
Mar-Oct 2HEC ⊞ ⌀ ⌷ ⋔ ⅄ ✕ ⊙ ⊠ ⌀ ⌷ ⊞ ⊞ lau ♦ ⏚
⇘PR ⊞ **Prices:** ⚑2.60 ⊷1.60 ⊠5.60 ▲4.50 pitch 7.20

> **SAARLOUIS** SAARLAND

AZUR-Camping Saarlouis St-Nazairer Alle 23
☎ 06831 3691 ▧ 06831 3691
A municipal site, divided into pitches, and set on level meadowland with tall trees. Lunchtime siesta 13.00-14.30 hrs.
➲ *Turn off road B51 in suburb of Roden, cross new bridge over the River Saar and continue to site, beyond sports hall.*
15 Mar-15 Nov 2HEC ⊞ ⥇ ⋔ ✕ ⊙ ⊠ ⌀ ⌷ ⊞ ⊞ lau ♦ ⇘P

> **ST GOAR** RHEINLAND-PFALZ

Friedenau Gruendelbach 103 ☎ 06741 368 ▧ 06741 368
On level, narrow stretch of meadowland at Gasthaus Friedenau.
➲ *Leave B9 in St-Goar and continue through railway underpass towards Emmelshausen for approx 1km.*
15 Mar-Nov 2HEC ⊞ ♦ ⋔ ⏚ ⅄ ✕ ⊙ ⊠ ⌀ ⌷ ⇘ R ⊞ ⊞
lau ♦ ⇘P **Prices:** ⚑4 ⊷2.50 ⊠2.50 ▲2-2.50

> **ST GOARSHAUSEN** RHEINLAND-PFALZ

Loreleystadt ☎ 06771 2592 ▧ 02137 2637
Municipal site on level meadow beside the Rhine. Near a sportsfield and opposite Rheinfels Castle.
➲ *Access via B42.*
15 Mar-Oct 1.5HEC ⊞ ⌀ ⋔ ⏚ ⅄ ⊙ ⊠ ⌀ ⇘ R ⊞ ⊞ lau ♦ ✕

> **SCHACHEN** HESSEN

Hochrhön ☎ 06654 7836 ▧ 7836
e-mail: campinghochrhoen@aol.com
Lies 1.5km from the Kneipp (hydrotherapeutic) Spa area of Gersfeld.
➲ *2km N of Gersfeld.*
All year ⊞ ⌀ ⋔ ⊙ ⊠ ⌀ ⌷ ⊞ lau ♦ ⏚ ✕ ⇘P ⊞
Prices: ⚑3 pitch 4

> **SCHALKENMEHREN** RHEINLAND-PFALZ

Camp am Maar Maarstr 22
☎ 06592 9551-0 ▧ 06592 9551-40
e-mail: hotelschneider@t-online.de
Terraced lakeside site on meadowland at the Schalkenmehrener Maar (water-filled crater). Towing help for caravans.
➲ *From A48 (Eifelautobahn) leave at 'Mehren/Daun' exit and follow B42 to Mehren. Turn off to the SW.*
All year 1HEC ⊞ ♦ ⋔ ⏚ ⅄ ✕ ⊙ ⊠ ⌀ ⌷ ⇘ LP ⊞ lau ♦ ⊞
Prices: ⚑2.60 ⊠8-11 ▲5-11 pitch 8-11

> **SCHLEIDEN** NORDRHEIN-WESTFALEN

Schleiden Im Wiesengrund 39 ☎ 02445 7030
Site lies on hilly, well-wooded country.
➲ *On the B258 to Monschau, 1km to site.*
All year 5HEC ⊞ ⌀ ⋔ ⏚ ✕ ⊙ ⊠ ⌀ ⌷ ⊞ ⊞ ⌾ lau ♦ ⏚ ⅄ ✕
⇘P ⊞ **Prices:** ⚑3.60 ⊷1.60 ⊠4.20 ▲4.60-6.20 pitch 5.20

Landal GreenParks Campsites

Three award-winning campsites with high sanitary standards and privacy are awaiting you in one of the most beautiful areas of Germany. Open year-round in a natural, quiet environment. Satellite-TV and electricity hook-up available. Each park offers indoor-swimming pool, restaurant, snack bar, supermarket, children's playgrounds, tennis, miniature golf, activity-programmes for everyone etc. Panoramic hiking-trails, bicycle-hire, wine tasting and a large variety of things to do and see. Chalet hire and English spoken.

"Wirfttal", distinctively located in a valley of the vulcanic Eifel-hills offers spacious pitches by the Wirft-creek and lake. Rated in 2000 to be one of the best sites of Germany, and Top-Site by the German Automobile Association ADAC.

"Warsberg", overlooking the valley of the river Saar, surrounded by vineyards and forests on top of the hill. Chairlift from the campsite to the romantic town of Saarburg. Near Luxembourg and the Roman Trier. 5-Star Rating and ADAC approved.

"Sonnenberg", Terraced site with a stunning view down the romantic Moselle on top of vineyards edged by forests above the wine-village of Leiwen. Earned the ADAC Camping award for 2000.

For further information or to order our free catalogue write or call:
Landal GreenParks, Postfach 1255, D-54432 Saarburg
Tel: 06581/91 93 93, from GB dial 0049/6581/91 93 93
e-mail: info@landal.de   www.landal.de

> **SCHLÜCHTERN** HESSEN
> At **HUTTEN**(8km E)

Hutten Heiligenborn ☎ 06661 2424 ▥ 917581
Site lies at Heiligenborn and has a pleasant southerly aspect.
Lunchtime siesta 13.00-15.00 hrs.
⮑ *Approach from Fulda on B40 towards Frankfurt to Flieden for 19km, then turn left via Rückers to Hutten (8km).*
All year 3.5HEC ⚏ ⬥ ⋒ ⛐ ✕ ☉ ⊟ ⌀ ㅿ ⊕ lau ⮕ ⟳P
Prices: ⋔4 ▲4 pitch 4.50

> **SCHÖNENBERG** SAARLAND

Ohmbachsee ☎ 06373 4001 ▥ 06373 4002
Terraced site on sloping ground above E bank of the Ohmabachsee. Separate field for young people. Lunchtime siesta 13.00-15.00 hrs.
⮑ *Signposted.*
All year 7.8HEC ⚏ ⬥ ⋒ ⛐ ⟟ ✕ ☉ ⊟ ⌀ ㅿ ⊕ lau ⮕ ⟳L

> **SCHOTTEN** HESSEN

Nidda-Stausee Vogelsbergstr 184
☎ 06044 1418 ▥ 1418 & 6679
e-mail: tourist-info@schotten.de
A pleasant family site on the shore of a lake.
⮑ *Access via B455.*
All year 3.2HEC ⚏ ⬥ ⋒ ✕ ☉ ⊟ ⌀ ⊕ lau ⮕ ✕ ⟳L
Prices: ⋔3.57 ⇔4.09 ▲3.06-4.09 pitch 4.09

> **SCHWEICH** RHEINLAND-PFALZ

Schweich ☎ 06502 91300 ▥ 06502 913050
On level meadowland on the Mosel, next to a marina.
⮑ *Access via A48 (Eifelautobhan) exit 'Schweich' in direction of Trier. Continue through Schweich, turning left just before the Mosel bridge.*
15 Apr-15 Oct 3.5HEC ⚏ ⬥ ⋒ ✕ ☉ ⊟ ⌀ ㅿ ⟳ R ⊞ lau ⮕ ⛐ ⟳P ⊞

> **SECK** RHEINLAND-PFALZ

Weiherhof ☎ 02664 8555 ▥ 02664 6388
Site lies on level meadowland next to a small lake in a wooded nature reserve. Special section reserved for young people. Many bathers at weekends.
⮑ *Take the B255 from Rennerod and drive to Hellenbahn-Schellenberg. Then turn S and continue for approx 2km.*
15 Mar-15 Oct 10HEC ⚏ ⬥ ⋒ ⛐ ✕ ☉ ⊟ ⌀ ㅿ ⟳ L ⊞ lau

> **SENHEIM** RHEINLAND-PFALZ

Internationaler Holländischer Hof
☎ 02673 4660 ▥ 02673 4100
e-mail: holl.hof@t-online.de
On level meadowland, divided into pitches beside the River Mosel which has boatmooring facilities.
⮑ *Access from Cochem on the B49 in direction of Zell as far as Senhals, then over the bridge and turn left.*
15 Apr-Oct 3.5HEC ⚏ ⬥ ⋒ ✕ ☉ ⊟ ⌀ ㅿ ⟳ R ⊞ ⊕ lau Prices: ⋔3.38-3.75 pitch 5.85-6.50

> **SENSWEILER MÜHLE** RHEINLAND-PFALZ

Bauernhof Bundestr 422 ☎ 06786 2395 ▥ 06781 35147
e-mail: info@sensweiler-muehle.de
On extensive grassland beside the Idar, partially terraced, in rural area near a farm. Views of wooded range of hills. Next to Camping Oberes Idartal. Separate section for young groups.
⮑ *From Idar-Oberstein follow road B422 for about 10km to the NW. Site lies between Katzenloch and Allenbach.*
All year 4HEC ⚏ ⬥ ⋒ ✕ ☉ ⊟ ⌀ ⟳ R ⊞ lau ⮕ ⛐ ⛐

Oberes Idartal ☎ 06786 2114 ▥ 2222
Site lies on a farm by the Idar, set on several small meadows and partly on terraced terrain next to Camping Sensweiler Mühel. Blockhouse with facilities for spit-roasting.
⮑ *From Idar-Oberstein follow road B422 for about 10km to the NW. site lies between Katzenloch and Allenbach.*
All year 2.8HEC ⚏ ⬥ ⋒ ⛐ ☉ ⊟ ⌀ ㅿ ⊕ ⛐ ⟳ R ⊞ ⊕ lau ⮕ ⛐ ✕

> **SOLINGEN** NORDRHEIN-WESTFALEN
> At **GLÜDER**

Waldcamping Glüder ☎ 0212 242120 ▥ 24212-34
Site on level terrain surrounded by woodland on banks of the River Wupper.
⮑ *Access via Köln-Kamen Autobahn exit Burscheid, via Hilgen and Witzhelden to Glüder or from Solingen on B299/B224 in direction of Witzhelden via Burg Hohenscheid.*
All year 2HEC ⚏ ⬥ ⋒ ⛐ ⟟ ✕ ☉ ⊟ ⌀ ⊕ ⊞ lau ⮕ ⟳P

> **STADTKYLL** RHEINLAND-PFALZ

Landal Greenparks Wirftt
☎ 06597 92920 ▥ 06597 929250
Extensive, level grassland beside the upper of two small reservoirs, approx 1km outside the town.
⮑ *Access S from Euskirchen on the A1, through Blankenheim and towards Stadtkyll.*
All year 6.4HEC ⚏ ⬥ ⥇ ⋒ ⛐ ⟟ ✕ ☉ ⊟ ⌀ ㅿ ⊕ ⟳ P ⊞ ⊕ lau Prices: pitch 7-13

> **STEINEN** RHEINLAND-PFALZ

Hofgut Schönerlen ☎ 02666 207 ▥ 02666 8429
e-mail: campingkopper@t-online.de
Beautiful and quiet site at Lake Hausweiher, has a special section reserved for residential campers. Young campers under 18 years old not accepted unless with adults.
⮑ *Take the B8 Limburg-Altenkirchen road. In Steinen turn left to the site.*
November 15HEC ⚏ ⬥ ⋒ ☉ ⊟ ⌀ ㅿ ⊞ ⛐ ⟳ L ⊞ ⊕ ⊘ lau ⮕ ⛐ ✕

> **STUKENBROCK** NORDRHEIN-WESTFALEN

Furlbach Am Furlbach 33
☎ 05257 3373 ▥ 05257 940373
Extensive site, partly on level, open meadow and partly in woodland. Separate section for dog owners. Old barn is used as a common room for young campers. Lunchtime siesta 12.30-14.30 hrs.
⮑ *From the Dortmund-Hannover motorway (A2/E73) leave at exit 'Bielefeld/Sennenstadt' then follow B68 for about 12km towards Paderborn. At Km44.2 turn off main road then 400m to site.*
Apr-Oct 9HEC ⚏ ⬥ ⋒ ⛐ ✕ ☉ ⊟ ⌀ ㅿ ⊞ ⊕ lau ⮕ ⛐ ✕
Prices: ⋔4 ⇔2.50 ⇔3.50 ▲3-3.50 pitch 6

> **TANN** HESSEN

Ulstertal Dippach 4 ☎ 06682 8292 ▥ 06682 10086
Terraced site on slightly sloping meadowland.
⮑ *Leave the Bischofsheim-Tann road B278 in Wendershausen and go SE to Dippach.*
All year 2.4HEC ⚏ ⬥ ⋒ ⛐ ✕ ☉ ⊟ ⌀ ㅿ ⊞ ⛐ ⊕ ⊞ lau

> **TREIS-KARDEN** RHEINLAND-PFALZ

Mosel-Islands ☎ 02672 2613 ▥ 912102
An extensive, level site on a grassy island in the Mosel next to a yacht marina.
⮑ *Turn off the B49 in Treis onto the southern coastal road.*
Apr-Oct 4.5HEC ⚏ ⬥ ⋒ ☉ ⊟ ⌀ ㅿ ⟳ R ⊞ lau ⮕ ⛐ ✕ ⟳P ⊞

TRENDELBURG HESSEN

Trendelburg ☎ 05675 301 ▯ 05675 5888
e-mail: conradi-camping@t-online.de
Site located at the foot of the castle, subdivided on the banks
of the River Diemel. Covered tennis court.
⮑ *Access from Kessel N via Hofgeismar (B83) to Trendelburg
cross the bridge and turn sharp left, down to site.*
All year 2.7HEC ⸺ ⌾ ⌂ ⚎ ⚊ ⦿ ✗ ⊙ ☻ ⦰ ⛢ ⚏ ⅀ R ② lau
⬦ ⸰P Prices: ⚏3.10 pitch 4.60

TRIER RHEINLAND-PFALZ

Trier-City Luxemburger Str 81 ☎ 0651 86921 ▯ 0651 83079
Level site owned by the Rowing Club Treviris, on left bank of
the Mosel 1.6km from the city centre.
⮑ *Between the Romer bridge and Adenauer bridge on road
towards Luxembourg.*
Apr-Oct 1.5HEC ⸺ ⬦⌾✗⊙☻⸰R ⅃⬦⚎⚏⦰⚏⸰P

TRIPPSTADT RHEINLAND-PFALZ

Sägmühle Sägmühle 1 ☎ 06306 92190 ▯ 06306 2000
e-mail: info@saegmuehle.de
The site lies in a wooded valley beside the Sagmühle Lake
(Saw Mill Lake). It consists of several unconnected sections,
some of them terraced. Lunchtime siesta 12.30-14.00 hrs.
⮑ *14km S of Kaiserslautern.*
All year 10HEC ⸺ ⌾ ⌂ ⚎ ⚏ ✗ ⊙ ☻ ⦰ ⚏ ⛢ ⸰ L ② ⊞ lau
⬦ ⸰P Prices: ⚏5-6 pitch 5.70-7.20

UTSCHEID RHEINLAND-PFALZ

Michelbach ☎ 06564 2097
A municipal site at the Michelbach, surrounded by meadows
and woods, 50% individual pitches.
⮑ *From the B50 Bittburg-Vianden road turn N in Sinspelt.
Then continue via Niederraden to Utscheid.*
All year 1.5HEC ⌂ ⚏ ✗ ⊙ ☻ ⦰ ② ⊞ lau ⬦ ⚎ ⚏

VINKRATH BEI GREFRATH NORDRHEIN-WESTFALEN

SC Waldfrieden ☎ 02158 3855 ▯ 3685
Site within nature reserve.
⮑ *From Grefrath N towards Wankum after 3km. Turn right.*
Apr-Oct 4.5HEC ⸺ ⌾⌂⊙☻⦰⚏⊞⊞⊞⧆ lau⬦⚎⚏✗
⸰LP Prices: ⚏3.50 pitch 5-8

WARBURG NORDRHEIN-WESTFALEN

Eversburg ☎ 05641 8668
Site lies next to restaurant of the same name on the SE
outskirts of the town.
All year 4.5HEC ⸺ ⌾⌂⚎⚏✗⊙☻⦰⸰R②⊞ lau⬦⸰P
Prices: ⚏8 ⬦3 ⬱12 ⚏6-12

WASSERFALL NORDRHEIN-WESTFALEN

Wasserfall Aurorastr 9 ☎ 02905 332
Terraced site, surrounded by woodland, next to leisure centre
'Fort Fun'. Little room for touring campers during the winter.
⮑ *About 10km E of Meschedes, between Bestwig and Nuttlar,
turn S off the B7. Driver past Gevelinghausen and up to
Wasserfall.*
All year 0.7HEC ⸺ ⌾⌂⚏✗⊙☻⚏⦿⧆⚏A⊞⊞⬦⸰PR

WAXWEILER RHEINLAND-PFALZ

AEGON-Ferienpark Im Prümtal ☎ 06554 92000 ▯ 920029
e-mail: 0655492000-0001@t-online.de
Site lies on level terrain and is divided into pitches, with a
separate field on the opposite side of the River Prüm. Near
swimming pool. Lunchtime siesta between 13.00-15.00 hrs.
⮑ *From N end of Waxweiler, turn off towards the River Prüm.*
31 Mar-5 Nov 3HEC ⸺ ⌾⌂✗⊙☻⦰⚏⦿⸰P②⊞
lau⬦⚏✗⸰P

WEILBURG HESSEN

At ODERSBACH

Odersbach Runkler Str 5A ☎ 06471 7620 ▯ 379603
e-mail: camping-odersbach@t-online.de
In attractive setting beside the River Lahn, next to a public
swimming pool. Lunchtime siesta 12.00-14.00 hrs.
⮑ *On S outskirts of town.*
Apr-Oct 6HEC ⸺ ⌾⌂✗⊙☻⦰⚏⸰PR②⊞ lau⬦⚎⚏
✗ Prices: ⚏3.10-6 ⬦2.30-4.50 ⬱2.60-4.40 ⚏3.50-22

WINTERBERG NORDRHEIN-WESTFALEN

At NIEDERSFELD(8.5km N)

Vossmecke ☎ 02985 8418 ▯ 02985 553
e-mail: camping-rossmeeke@t-online.de
In a pleasant wooded location with facilities for winter
camping.
⮑ *Off B480 towards Winterberg.*
All year 4HEC ⸺ ⬦ ⚺⚏ ⌂⚏✗⊙☻⦰⚏⊞ lau⬦⚎✗⸰L
Prices: pitch 14.27-15.29 (inc 2 persons)

WISSEL NORDRHEIN-WESTFALEN

Wisseler See Am Wisseler See 10 ☎ 02824 96310 ▯ 963131
e-mail: wisseler-see@t-online.de
Well-kept municipal site with modern equipment beside
Lake Wissel. There is a separate car park next to the open-air
swimming pool. The pool belongs to the camp. The
washrooms are closed during lunchtimes and at night.
⮑ *From Kieve, take the B57 towards Xanten. After about 9km,
turn left and drive a further 3km towards Wissel.*
All year 40HEC ⸺ ⌾⌂⚏✗⊙☻⦰⚏⸰L⚏⊞⧆ lau
⬦ ⸰P Prices: ⚏5 ⬦3 ⬱8 ⚏6

WITZENHAUSEN HESSEN

Werratal Am Sande 11 ☎ 05542 1465 ▯ 05542 72418
The site lies on meadow between the outskirts of
Witzenhausen and the banks of the Werra.
⮑ *For access, leave Hannover-Kassel motorway at Werratal.
10km on B80 to Witzenhausen. From market place follow signs.*
All year 30HEC ⸺ ⬦⌾⌂⚏✗⊙☻⦰⚏⛢⦿⚏⸰R②⊞ lau
⬦✗⸰P Prices: ⚏3.60-4 ⬦1.80-2 ⬱3.60-4 ⚏3.60-4 pitch
3.60-6

WOLFSTEIN RHEINLAND-PFALZ

AZUR Camping Königsberg Am schwimmbad 1
☎ 06304 4143 ▯ 06304 7543
e-mail: wolfstein@azur-camping.de
Municipal site, beside small River Lauter next to open air
swimming pool.
⮑ *Site lies at S end of Wolfstein to the right of B270 from
Kaiserslautern.*
All year 1.5HEC ⸺ ⌾⌂⚏✗⊙☻⦰⚏⛢⦿A②⊞ lau⬦⚎
⦰⸰PR

ZERF RHEINLAND-PFALZ

Rübezahl ☎ 06587 814 ▯ 06587 814
e-mail: seyffardt-zerf@t-online.de
Meadows site in natural grounds on wooded hillside.
⮑ *Leave Zerf S on B268 towards Saarbrücken then turn
towards Oberzerf 2.5km to site from turning. From Saarburg,
follow B407 beyond Vierherrenhorn, turn right and follow track
for 60m.*
Apr-Oct 2.5HEC ⸺ ⌾⌂⊙☻⦰⸰P②⊞ Prices: ⚏3.50
pitch 4

ZWESTEN HESSEN

Waldcamping Hinter dem Wasser
☎ 05626 379 ▦ 06695 1320
e-mail: waldcamping@planet-interken.de
Site in bend of River Schwalm. Lunchtime siesta 13.00-15.00
hrs. For touring campers there is also an overflow site outside
the actual campsite.
➲ *Access from Kassel in SW direction via Fritzlar to Zwesten.*
All year 5HEC ▦ ⊕ ⋔ ♀ ✗ ⊙ ♥ ♨ ⌇ PR 🏤 ⊞ lau ♦ ♨ ✗
Prices: ⋔3.60 pitch 4.50

● ● ● ● ● **NORTH** ● ● ● ● ●

The northern finger of Germany has the bracing North Sea
to the west, with a landscape of dykes, green beaches and
pretty offshore islands. The gentle Baltic is to the east, and
its coast is one continuous succession of delightful resorts.
Excellent natural harbours have been formed by "forden"
cut deep into the land between the ridges of wooded hills.
Inland, there are tranquil lakes, stately homes and nature
reserves.
The north of Germany is a land of mountains and plains, of
estuaries and inlets, of forests and heaths. Delightful
undulating landscape is scattered with fascinating towns
and cities; Hamburg, whose beautiful skyline is
characterised by the towers of its principal churches;
Bremen, with its many parks and gardens, its fairytale
streets and passages, and its cosy atmosphere; Hannover,
whose flower-filled Royal Gardens at Herrenhausen have
been a major attraction since 1666.

....

ALTENAU NIEDERSACHSEN

Okertalsperre Kornhardtweg 1 ☎ 05328 702 ▦ 05328 911708
e-mail: okercamping@t.online.de
On a long stretch of grassland at the S end of the Oker
Reservoir. Lunchtime siesta 13.00-15.00 hrs.
➲ *Signposted from B498 (Oker-Altenau road).*
All year 4HEC ▦ ⊕ ⋔ ♨ ✗ ⊙ ♥ ♨ ⌇ ▥ ♥ ⋇ L 🏤 ⊞ ∅
lau

APEN-NORDLOH NIEDERSACHSEN

Nordloh Schanzenweg 4 ☎ 04499 2625
All year 8HEC ▦ ⋇ ⋔ ✗ ⊙ ♥ ∅ ⌇ L 🏤 ⊞ lau ♦ ♨ ♀ ✗

BASSUM NIEDERSACHSEN

At GROSS-RINGMAR

Gross-Ringmar Dorfstr 15 ☎ 04241 5292
On level meadow with trees. Situated approx. 200m from the
edge of the village.
➲ *Turn off B51 approx. 3km SW of Bassum.*
All year 10HEC ▦ ⊕ ⋔ ♨ ✗ ⊙ ♥ ♨ ⌇ LP 🏤 ⊞ lau

BLECKEDE NIEDERSACHSEN

Alt-Garge (ADAC) Am Waldbad 23
☎ 05854 311 ▦ 05854 1640
A modern site surrounded by tall trees, lying at the SE end of
Alt-Garge next to a heated swimming pool in the woods. The
camp has its own gas-filling station. Archery butts.
Lunchtime siesta 13.00-14.30 hrs.
➲ *5km SE of Bleckede.*
All year 6.6HEC ▦ ⋰⋰⋰ ⊕ ⋔ ♨ ⊙ ♥ ♨ ⌇ 🏤 ⊞ ♦ ✗ ∅ ⌇PR
Prices: pitch 15 (incl 2 persons)

BODENWERDER NIEDERSACHSEN

Himmelspforte Ziegeleiweg 1 ☎ 05533 4938 ▦ 05533/4432
Site on grassland, with a fruit orchard, next to River Weser.
Good possibilites for water sport. Separate section and
common room for young campers.

➲ *Cross River Weser and turn right towards Rühle. Site is in
about 2km.*
All year 8HEC ▦ ♦ ⋔ ♨ ♀ ✗ ⊙ ♥ ♨ ⌇ R 🏤 ⊞ ♦ ⌇P

Rühler Schweiz ☎ 05533 2827 ▦ 05533 5882
This site lies on well-kept meadowland by the River Weser.
➲ *From the Weser Bridge in Bodenwerder and follow road for
4km towards Rühle.*
Mar-Oct 50HEC ▦ ⋰ ⋔ ♨ ♀ ✗ ⊙ ♥ ♨ ⌇ ♀ ⌇ PR 🏤 ⊞ lau
♦ ✗ Prices: ⋔3.50 ▲3.50 pitch 4

BOTHEL NIEDERSACHSEN

Hanseat ☎ 04266 355
All year 20HEC ▦ ⊕ ⋔ ✗ ⊙ ♥ ♨ ∅ 🏤 ⊞ lau ♦ ♨ ⌇P

BRAUNLAGE NIEDERSACHSEN

Ferien vom Ich ☎ 05520 413
Quiet site, partly on different levels, near woodland inn.
➲ *2km from town centre on B27 towards Lauterberg.*
All year 5.5HEC ▦ ⊕ ⋔ ♨ ✗ ⊙ ♥ ♨ ∅ ♀ 🏤 ⊞ lau ♦ ⌇P

At ZORGE(14km S)

Waldwinkel ☎ 05586 1048 ▦ 8113
A site on different levels, surrounded by high trees, 200m
from an open-air woodland pool in Kunzen Valley.
All year 1.5HEC ♨ ⊕ ⋔ ♨ ♨ ⊙ ♥ ♨ ∅ ♀ 🏤 ⊞ lau ♦ ♀ ✗ ⌇P
Prices: ⋔7 ♀4 ♀5 ▲5

BREMEN BREMEN

Freie Hansestadt Bremen Am Stadtwaldsee 1 ☎ 0421 212002
▦ 0421 219857
Situated in a Nature Reserve 700m from lake.
➲ *Access from autobahn A27 exit University Bremen.*
All year 5.8HEC ▦ ♦ ⊕ ⋔ ♨ ♀ ✗ ⊙ ♥ ♨ ∅ ♀ 🏤 lau ♦ ⌇LP

BRIETLINGEN-REIHERSEE NIEDERSACHSEN

Reihersee 1 Alte Salzstr 8
☎ 04133 3671 & 3577 ▦ 04133 4391
Divided into pitches by hedges and pine trees. Private
bathing area.
➲ *At car park, 2km beyond Brietlingen, turn E towards
Reihersee and continue for 800m.*
All year 6.2HEC ▦ ⊕ ⋔ ✗ ⊙ ♥ ♨ ♀ ⌇ LR 🏤 ⊞ lau ♦ ♨

BÜCHEN SCHLESWIG-HOLSTEIN

Waldschwimmbad ☎ 04155 5360 ▦ 499140
On gently sloping grassland. Lunchtime siesta 13.00-15.00
hrs.
➲ *From Lauenburg or Mölln follow road to Büchen then
follow signposts to site.*
All year 1.6HEC ▦ ⊕ ⋔ ♨ ♀ ✗ ⊙ ♥ ♨ ∅ ♨ ♀ 🏤 ⊞ lau ♦ ✗
⌇PR

BURG (ISLAND OF FEHMARN) SCHLESWIG-HOLSTEIN

At KLAUSDORF(5km NW)

Klausdorf Strand ☎ 04371 2549
A grassy site with sea views. Divided into pitches. Sandy
beach. Lunchtime siesta 12.30-14.30 hrs.
➲ *From Burg turn off the main road 2.5km before Klausdorf
onto a narrow asphalt road.*
15 Apr-15 Oct 12HEC ▦ ♦ ⋔ ✗ ⊙ ♥ ♨ ♨ ♀ ⌇ S 🏤 ⊞
lau ♦ ⌇L

BURGWEDEL NIEDERSACHSEN

Erholungsgebiet Springhorstsee
☎ 05139 3232 ▦ 05139 27070
e-mail: springhorstsee@aol.com
On level ground on the shores of a lake with well defined
pitches and modern facilities.

⮫ *25km N of Hannover, 2km from Grossburgwedel motorway exit.*
All year 29HEC ⸺ ⚡ ⊕ 🐕 ⚡ ✕ ⊙ 🚽 🏪 🛒 ⚓ ⚑ ⭣ LP ⊠ ⊞
lau ⮕ Ⓓ Prices: ⚡3.50 ⚡0.50 ⚑5 ⚑3.50-5 pitch 15

BUSUM SCHLESWIG-HOLSTEIN

Nordsee Nordseestr 90 ☎ 04834 2515 ▤ 04834 9281
Situated immediately behind the high dyke. The site is
divided into two and surrounded by tall bushes. Lunchtime
siesta 12.30-14.00 hrs.
⮫ *Leave A23 at Heide exit and follow signs.*
Mar-Oct 3.5HEC ⸺ ⚡ 🐕 🛠 ⚡ ✕ ⊙ 🚽 Ⓓ 🏪 ⊠ ⊞ lau ⮕
⭣S

CLAUSTHAL-ZELLERFELD NIEDERSACHSEN

Prahljust ☎ 05323 1300
The site lies on slightly sloping grassland in an area of
woodland and lakes.
⮫ *Follow road B242 SE from outskirts 2km in direction of
Braunlage, then turn right to site in 1.5km.*
All year 13HEC ⸺ ⚡ 🐕 🛠 ⚡ ✕ ⊙ 🚽 Ⓓ ⭣ P ⊠ lau
⮕ 🏪 ⭣L ⊞

Waldweben Spiegelthalerstr 31 ☎ 05323 81712 ▤ 962134
Holiday village with individual pitches in open meadow and
coniferous woodland by three small lakes.
⮫ *Signposted from B241 in direction of Goslar.*
All year 4.5HEC ⸺ ⚡ ⚡ 🐕 🛠 ✕ ⊙ 🚽 🏪 🛒 ⚓ ⮕ ✕ ⭣LP ⊞

DAHRENHORST NIEDERSACHSEN

Irenensee Dahrenhorst ☎ 05173 98120 ▤ 981213
e-mail: info@irenensee.de
A lakeside site on meadowland, partly surrounded by woods,
with separate section for tourers, statics and residentials.
Lunchtime siesta 13.00-15.00 hrs.
⮫ *From Burgdorf follow road B188 for about 15km towards
Uetze.*
All year 120HEC ⸺ ⚡ 🐕 🛠 ⊙ 🚽 Ⓓ 🏪 ⚓ ⚑ ⭣ L ⊠ ⊞ lau

DETERN NIEDERSACHSEN

Jümmesee ☎ 04957 1808
⮫ *Access via B72 (Aurich-Cloppenburg).*
15 Mar-Oct 11.5HEC ⸺ ⚡ 🐕 ✕ ⊙ 🚽 ⚓ ⭣ LR ⊠ ⊞ 🏊 lau
⮕ ⭣S

DORUM SCHLESWIG-HOLSTEIN

AZUR-Camping Dorumer Tief
☎ 04741 5020 ▤ 04741 914061
Next to a small harbour. Separated from the beach by a dyke.
⮫ *Access via A27 (Bremerhaven-Cuxhaven).*
Apr-Sep 7HEC ⸺ ⚡ ⊕ 🐕 🛠 ✕ ⊙ 🚽 🏪 ⭣ PS ⊠ ⊞ lau

DRANSFELD NIEDERSACHSEN

Hohen Hagen ☎ 05502 2147 ▤ 05502 47239
Well laid out municipal site. Lunchtime siesta 13.00-15.00 hrs.
⮫ *S of town off Hohen Hagen road.*
All year 10HEC ⸺ ⚡ ⊕ 🐕 🛠 ⚡ ✕ ⊙ 🚽 Ⓓ 🏪 ⊠ ⊞ lau
⮕ ⭣P

EGESTORF NIEDERSACHSEN

AZUR-Camping Lüneburger Heide
☎ 04175 661 ▤ 04175 8383
e-mail: info@azur-camping.de
Modern site on wooded heathland on the edge of the
Lüneburger Heath Nature Reserve 2km S of town on slightly
sloping terrain with asphalt internal roads.
⮫ *Access via Hamburg-Hannover motorway A7/E4 Egestorf
or Evendorf exits.*
All year 22HEC ⸺ ⁞⁞⁞ ⚡ 🐕 🛠 ✕ ⊙ 🚽 Ⓓ 🏪 ⭣ P ⊠ ⊞
lau ⮕ ⚡ Prices: ⚡4-6 ⚑3-4 pitch 5-7

EIMKE NIEDERSACHSEN

Eimke Im Extertal ☎ 05262 3307 ▤ 05262-992404
Extensive, partly terraced site on slightly sloping meadowland
with two ponds.
Camping Card Compulsory.
⮫ *From Dortmund-Hannover motorway (A2/E8) take 'Bad
Eilsen' exit and follow B238 S. 1km beyond Rinteln, turn left
and continue for 18km along External-Barntrup road.*
All year 20HEC ⸺ ⚡ 🐕 🛠 ⚡ ✕ ⊙ 🚽 Ⓓ 🏪 ⭣ L ⊠ ⊞ lau ⮕
✕ ⭣P

ELISABETH SOPHIENKOOG (ISLAND OF NORDSTRAND)
SCHLESWIG-HOLSTEIN

Elisabeth-Sophienkoog ☎ 04842 8534 ▤ 8306
On meadowland behind the North Sea dyke. Lunchtime
siesta 12.00-14.00 hrs.
⮫ *Access via Husum to Island of Nordstrand.*
Apr-Sep 1.7HEC ⸺ ⚡ ⊕ 🐕 🛠 ⚡ ✕ ⊙ 🚽 Ⓓ ⭣ S ⊠ ⊞ lau

ESENS-BENSERSIEL NIEDERSACHSEN

Bensersiel Am Strand ☎ 04971 917121 ▤ 4988 917190
e-mail: eb-team@t-online.de
Well-managed, extensive leisure centre with harbour, good
fish restaurant and reading room. Swimming pools have sea
water and artificial waves.
⮫ *Take B210 NE from Aurich to Ogenbargenn then via Esens.*
Est-15 Sep 10HEC ⸺ ⁞⁞⁞ ⚡ ⊕ 🐕 🛠 ⚡ ✕ ⊙ 🚽 🏪 🛒 ⚓ ⭣ S ⊠
⊞ 🏊 lau ⮕ Ⓓ ⭣P Prices: ⚡2.4 ⚑1.6 pitch 5

EUTIN-FISSAU SCHLESWIG-HOLSTEIN

Prinzenholz Prinzenholzweg 20 ☎ 04521 5281 ▤ 3601
Terraced lakeside site divided by trees and bushes. Mobile
shop.
⮫ *N of town take Malente road and turn right after 2km.*
Etr-Oct 2HEC ⸺ ⚡ 🐕 🛠 ✕ ⊙ 🚽 Ⓓ 🏪 ⚓ ⭣ L ⊠ lau ⮕ ⚡ ✕
⭣PR ⊞

FALLINGBOSTEL NIEDERSACHSEN

Böhmeschlucht Vierde 22 ☎ 05162 5604 ▤ 05162 5160
Site located in a nature reserve beside the river Böhme.
⮫ *A7/E45, exit 46/47. signed about 3km N*
All year 4HEC ⸺ ⚡ 🐕 🛠 ⚡ ✕ ⊙ 🚽 ⭣ R ⊠ ⊞ ⊡ lau Prices: ⚡2.50
pitch 11

FEHMARN (ISLAND OF)

See **Burg, Dänschendorf, Fehmarnsund, Meeschendorf,
Wulfen**

FEHMARNSUND (ISLAND OF FEHMARN)
SCHLESWIG-HOLSTEIN

Miramar ☎ 04371 3220 & 2221 ▤ 04371 868044
A family site on meadowland situated at the southern end of
the island.
⮫ *Turn off the B207/E4 at the first turning after the
Sundbrücke (bridge) and drive towards Svendorf.*
All year 13HEC ⸺ ⚡ 🐕 🛠 ⚡ ✕ ⊙ 🚽 Ⓓ 🏪 ⭣ LS ⊠ ⊞ lau
Prices: ⚡3.9-5.5 pitch 6.80-10.5

GANDERSHEIM, BAD NIEDERSACHSEN

DCC Kur-Campingpark Braunschweiger Str 12
☎ 05382 1595 ▤ 1599
On level meadow, divided in two by a brook beside a public
park. Good sporting facilities. Separate section for young
people.
⮫ *Access from Hannover-Kassel motorway via exit Soesen.*
All year 9HEC ⸺ ⚡ 🐕 🛠 ✕ ⊙ 🚽 ⊠ ⊞ lau ⮕ ⭣P

GARTOW NIEDERSACHSEN

Gartow am See Am Helk ☎ 05846 2151 ▦ 2151
Situated in woodland with adjoining meadow.
Camping Card Compulsory.
➲ *NE on A493 from Lüchow.*
All year 14HEC ▥ ⌕ ⌂ ▣ ☎ ⟋ P 🅿 lau ➡ 🦺 ✕ ⟋LR ⊞
Prices: ⋔3.20 pitch 7.50-8.60

GIFHORN NIEDERSACHSEN

At RÖTGESBÜTTEL(8km S)

Glockenheide ☎ 05304 1581 ▦ 053041581
Tranquil site in heathland. Lunchtime siesta 13.00-15.00 hrs.
Camping Card Compulsory.
➲ *In Rötgesbüttel turn left, then turn left again after level crossing.*
All year 5HEC ▥ ⌕ ⌂ ⊙ ▣ 🚿 ☎ 🅿 lau ➡ 🦺 ✕ Prices:
⋔3.49 ➡2.55 ▦2.55 ▲2.55

GLÜCKSBURG SCHLESWIG-HOLSTEIN

Schwennau Stoebe ☎ 04631 2670
A watercourse divides the site into two sections which are linked by a bridge.
➲ *In town centre make for Postplatz, then Hindenburgplatz, Collenburger Strasse. Schwennau-Strasse direct onto the site which lies adjacent to the Flensburger Förde.*
All year 1.5HEC ▥ ⌇ ⌂ ✕ ⊙ ▣ 🚿 ⟋ RS 🅿 ⊞ lau
➡ 🦺 ⍭ ⟋PS

GLÜCKSBURG-HOLNIS SCHLESWIG-HOLSTEIN

AZUR Ostseecamp Grenzblick Am Kurstrand 3
☎ 04631 622071 ▦ 04631 622072
e-mail: info@azur-camping.de
Apr-Oct 6HEC ▥ ⍭ ⌇ ⌂ ⊙ ▣ 🚿 ☎ 🅿 ⊞ lau ➡ 🦺 ✕
Prices: ⋔4-6 ▲3-4 pitch 5-7

GRUBE SCHLESWIG-HOLSTEIN

Rosenfelder Strand Textil Segeberger Str 17
☎ 0451 4993015 ▦ 4993691
e-mail: info@rosenfelder-strand.de
Excellently managed family site beside the sea with a 1km long beach. Divided into separate fields by rows of bushes. Children's playground in woodland between site and sea. Strict observance of lunchtime siesta 13.00-15.00 hrs.
➲ *Take the B207/E4 from Lübeck and drive N to Lensahn, then E to Grube.*
Apr-Sep 20HEC ▥ ⌕ ⌇ 🦺 ⍭ ✕ ⊙ ▣ 🚿 🚿 ☎ 🅿 ⊞ ⟋ ➡ ⟋S
Prices: ⋔3.85 pitch 9.20

HADDEBY SCHLESWIG-HOLSTEIN

Haithabu ☎ 04621 32450 ▦ 04621 33122
e-mail: camping@uumail.de
Clean, tidy site beside River Schlei.
➲ *From Schleswig follow B76 towards Eckernförde.*
Apr-Sep 5HEC ▥ ⌕ ⌂ 🦺 ✕ ⊙ ▣ 🚿 ⟋ R 🅿 lau
Prices: ⋔3.50 ➡2 ▦7 ▲5

HADEMSTORF NIEDERSACHSEN

Waldhaus Allertal ☎ 05071 1872 ▦ 1912516
In a picturesque wooded setting with pitches separated by hedges and bushes.
➲ *Access via A27/A7.*
Apr-Sep 4HEC ▥ ➡ ⌇ 🦺 ✕ ⊙ ▣ 🚿 🚿 🅿 lau ➡ ⟋R ⊞

HAHNENKLEE NIEDERSACHSEN

Kreuzeck Goslar 2 ☎ 05325 2570 ▦ 05325 3392
In the forest beside a lake. Terraces and a separate section for dog-owners.

➲ *Beside Café am Kreuzeck at the junction of the B241 and the Hahnenklee road.*
All year 5HEC ▥ ⸬ ⍭ ⌇ ⌂ 🦺 ✕ ⊙ ▣ ☎ ⟋ LP 🅿 ⊞ lau
Prices: ⋔4.05 ➡1.80 ▦4.45 ▲1.30

HAMELN NIEDERSACHSEN

Waldbad Pfedeweg 2 ☎ 05158 2774 ▦ 2774
A grassy terraced site on the edge of woodland beside a public swimming pool.
Camping Card Compulsory.
➲ *Follow 'swimming pool' signs from Havelstorf.*
Apr-Oct 2.8HEC ▥ ⌕ ⌇ ⊙ ▣ 🚿 ☎ 🅿 ⊞ lau ➡ 🦺 ⟋P
Prices: ⋔3 ▦6 ▲4.50

HANNOVER NIEDERSACHSEN

At GARBSEN(10km W)

Blauer See ☎ 05137 8996-0 ▦ 05137 8996-77
e-mail: info@camping-blauer-see.de
On a small lake beside the Garbsen service area on Hannover-Bielefeld motorway A2/E8.
All year 22HEC ▥ ⌕ ⌇ ✕ ⊙ ▣ 🚿 ☎ ⟋ L ⊞ ⊞ lau
Prices: ⋔7 ➡2 ▦4.10 ▲3

At ISERNHAGEN(16km NE)

Parksee Lohne Alter Postweg 12
☎ 05139 88260 ▦ 05139 891665
e-mail: parksee-lohne@t-online.de
Recreation area by a lake. On the flight approach path for Hannover Langenhagen airport. Separate section for tourers.
➲ *From motorway exit 'Kirchorst' follow Altwarmbüchen road to Isernhagen.*
All year 16HEC ▥ ⌕ ⌇ ⍭ ✕ ⊙ ▣ 🚿 ⟋ L ⊞ ⊞ lau

HARDEGSEN NIEDERSACHSEN

Ferienpark Solling ☎ 05505 5585 ▦ 5585
Terraced site in forested area. Separate field for touring pitches. Lunchtime siesta 13.00-15.00 hrs.
➲ *In town take 'Waldgebiet Gladeberg' road.*
All year 2.4HEC ▥ ⌕ ⌂ 🜨 ⌇ ✕ ⊙ ▣ 🚿 🅿 ⊞ lau ➡ 🦺 ✕ ⟋
⟋P Prices: ⋔3.50 pitch 10-12

HASELÜNNE NIEDERSACHSEN

Haseufer Andruper Str 1 ☎ 05961 1331 ▦ 05961 7145
Beside the River Hase in an attractive area E of the town.
Camping Card Compulsory.
➲ *Signposted from Andrup.*
Closed Nov-15 Dec 10HEC ▥ ➡ ⌇ 🦺 ⍭ ✕ ⊙ ▣ 🚿 ☎ ⟋ L
🅿 ⊞ lau ➡ ⟋PRS

HASSENDORF NIEDERSACHSEN

Stürberg ☎ 04264 9124 ▦ 04264 821440
e-mail: campingpark-stuerberg@gmx.net
In pleasant wooded surroundings beside a lake.
➲ *From Ab1 exit Stuckenborstel take B75 towards Rotenburg for 5km.*
Mar-Oct 2HEC ▥ ⌕ ⌇ ⍭ ⊙ ▣ 🚿 🚿 ⟋ L 🅿 ⊞ ➡ ✕ Prices:
⋔3 ▦7 ▲6

HATTEN NIEDERSACHSEN

Freizeitzentrum Hatten Kreyenweg 8 ☎ 04482 677 ▦ 928027
e-mail: info@jzz.hatten.de
All year 2HEC ▥ ⍭ ⌇ 🦺 ✕ ⊙ ▣ 🚿 ⟋ P ▲ ⟋ lau
Prices: ⋔5 ▲2.60 pitch 6

HATTORF NIEDERSACHSEN

Oderbrücke ☎ 05521 4359 ▦ 05521 4360
e-mail: oderbruecke@t-online.de
In a pleasant wooded location with good recreational and sanitary facilities.

⮱ *On the B27 towards Herzberg.*
All year 2.5HEC 🎪 ⊞ Ⴌ 🛁 ¶ ✕ ☉ ◙ ⌀ ᴍ ᴢ R 🅿 lau ➧ ⊞
Prices: ♠3.15-3.50 ⊞5.20-5.20 ▲5.20-5.20

▶ **HEIKENDORF** SCHLESWIG-HOLSTEIN

Möltenort ☎ 0431 241316 ▣ 2379920
e-mail: gronau.heikendorf@freenet.de
Terraced site by the Kieler Förde. 15km NE of Kiel to W of
road B502.
⮱ *Approach to site is via a narrow, winding road.*
Apr-Oct 1 Oct- 1 Apr 2HEC 🎪 ⛄ Ⴌ 🛁 ☉ ◙ ᴢ S 🅿 ⊞ lau
➧ ¶ ✕ ⌀ Prices: ♠4 ⊞6.50-8.50 ▲5.20-6.50

▶ **HELMSTEDT** NIEDERSACHSEN

Waldwinkel Maschweg 46 ☎ 05351 37161
In an orchard next to the Gasthaus Waldwinkel.
⮱ *Signposted from autobahn exit 'Helmstedt'.*
All year 10HEC 🎪 ⊞ Ⴌ 🛁 ✕ ☉ ◙ ⌀ ᴍ 🅿 ⊞ lau ➧ ᴢP

▶ **HEMELN** NIEDERSACHSEN

Hemeln ☎ 05544 1414 ▣ 1414
e-mail: camping-hemeln@gmx.de
Well-kept site on N outskirts of village, beside the River
Weser.
⮱ *From Autobahn A7 take the Gothenburg exit & follow B3 to
Dransfeld then follow signposts.*
All year 20HEC 🎪 ⛄ ⊞ Ⴌ 🛁 ✕ ☉ ◙ ⌀ ᴍ ⊞ 🖣 ᴢ R 🅿 ⊞
lau Prices: ♠3.40 ⊞2.10 ⊞3 ▲2.10

▶ **HERMANNSBURG** NIEDERSACHSEN

Örtzetal ☎ 05052 3072 & 1555
Site lies on meadows on the E bank of the River Örtze, set in
unspoilt woodlands of the Lüneburg Heath. Boat landing
stage. Lunchtime siesta 13.00-15.00 hrs.
⮱ *From the B3 Celle-Soltau road turn off in Bergen and
follow road NE towards Hermannsburg, then continue towards
Eschwege.*
15 Mar-Oct 6HEC 🎪 ∵ ⊞ Ⴌ 🛁 ¶ ✕ ☉ ◙ ⊞ 🖣 ᴢ R 🅿 ⊞
lau ➧ Ⴌ ¶ ᴢP

▶ **HOLLE** NIEDERSACHSEN

At **DERNEBURG**(2km NW on unclass road)

Seecamp-Derneburg ☎ 05062 565 ▣ 8785
A terraced lakeside site on a hill slope with a southerly
aspect. Separate towing field. Useful transit site near
autobahn.
⮱ *From the motorway, leave at exit 'Derneburg' and continue
to road B6.*
Apr-15 Sep 7.8HEC 🎪 ⊞ Ⴌ 🛁 ✕ ☉ ◙ ⌀ ᴍ ᴢ L 🅿 ⊞ lau
Prices: ♠7.50 ⊞3 ⊞8 ▲7-8

▶ **KLEINWAABS** SCHLESWIG-HOLSTEIN

Ostsee Heide ☎ 04352 2530 ▣ 04352 1398
Divided into pitches and pleasantly landscaped. Large games
room for teenagers. Lunchtime siesta 13.00-14.30 hrs.
15 Mar-1 Nov 21.5HEC 🎪 ⊞ Ⴌ 🛁 ¶ ✕ ☉ ◙ ⌀ ᴍ ⊞ 🖣 ᴢ
PS 🅿 lau

▶ **KLINT-BEI-HECHTHAUSEN** NIEDERSACHSEN

Geesthof Am Ferienpark 1 ☎ 04774 512 ▣ 9178
e-mail: ferienpark.geesthof@t-online.de
On dry meadowland next to the River Oste, in quiet setting
with trees. Lunchtime siesta 13.00-15.00 hrs.
⮱ *In Hechthausen leave road B73 and drive W towards
'Lamstedt' for about 3 km.*
All year 15HEC 🎪 ➧ ⊞ Ⴌ 🛁 ¶ ✕ ☉ ◙ ⌀ ᴍ ⊞ ᴢ P 🅿 ⊞ lau
Prices: ♠4-5 ⊞2-3 ⊞7-9 ▲3-5

▶ **LANGHOLZ ÜBER ECKERNFÖRDE**
SCHLESWIG-HOLSTEIN

Langholz Fischerstr 9 ☎ 04352 2542
A holiday site surrounded by a belt of trees situated at a wide
natural beach, at the mouth of the Eckernförde Bay.
Camping Card Compulsory.
⮱ *From the Eckernförde take the B203 towards the NE to the
turn off for Langholz, then right and continue 3km to site.*
Apr-Sep 20HEC 🎪 ⊞ Ⴌ 🛁 ¶ ✕ ☉ ◙ ᴍ ⊞ 🖣 ᴢ S 🅿 ⊞ lau ➧ ⌀

▶ **LAUTERBERG, BAD** NIEDERSACHSEN

Wiesenbeker Teich ☎ 05524 2510 ▣ 932089
e-mail: info@campingwiesen.seh.de
In wooded surroundings on the Wiesenbeker Teich.
⮱ *Approach via B243 SE of Bad Lauterberg.*
All year 10HEC 🎪 ⌀ ⛄ ⊞ ¶ ✕ ☉ ◙ ⌀ ⊞ ᴢ L 🅿 ⊞ lau ➧
Ⴌ ᴢP

▶ **LOOSE** SCHLESWIG-HOLSTEIN

Gut Ludwigsburg ☎ 04358 1068 ▣ 460370
This partly wooded holiday site lies between an inland lake
and the sea. 100m long private beach. It is divided into pitches.
⮱ *From Eckernförde, head towards Klein-Wabbs up to Gut
Ludwigsburg, then follow a dirt track for 2km.*
Apr-Sep 10HEC 🎪 ⊞ Ⴌ 🛁 ¶ ✕ ☉ ◙ ⌀ ᴍ ⊞ 🖣 ᴢ L 🅿 lau ➧
ᴢS Prices: ♠4 pitch 5-11

▶ **LÜNEBURG** NIEDERSACHSEN

Rote Schleuse ☎ 04131 791500
In woodland clearing. Lunchtime siesta 13.00-15.00 hrs.
⮱ *S of town off B4. Signposted.*
Mar-Oct 2HEC 🎪 ⊞ Ⴌ 🛁 ¶ ✕ ☉ ◙ ᴍ ⊞ 🅿 lau ➧ ✕ ᴢR

▶ **MALENTE-GREMSMÜHLEN** SCHLESWIG-HOLSTEIN

Schwentine Wiesenweg 14 ☎ 04523 4327
A park-like setting with trees and bushes, at a river within
the village of Malente.
⮱ *A17 18km NW of Eutin.*
28mar-6 Oct 2.5HEC 🎪 ⊞ Ⴌ 🛁 ¶ ✕ ☉ ◙ ᴍ ᴢ R 🅿 ⊞ lau ➧
⌀ ᴢLP Prices: ♠4.50 ⊞2 ⊞5-6 ▲4-6

▶ **MELBECK** NIEDERSACHSEN

Melbeck ☎ 04134 7311
Extensive site in woodland on the banks of the Ilmenau.
Centre of site free of trees and reserved for tourers.
⮱ *On B4, 9km Lüneburg.*
All year 20HEC 🎪 ⊞ Ⴌ ✕ ☉ ◙ ⌀ ⊞ 🖣 ᴢ R 🅿 lau

▶ **NEUSTADT** SCHLESWIG-HOLSTEIN

Strande Sandbergerweg ☎ 04561 4188 ▣ 04361 7125
e-mail: am.strande@t-online.de
The site is divided into small sections and slopes down to the
sea. Narrow sandy beach.
⮱ *Access from Neustadt towards Pelzerhaken, first site on the
right after leaving Neustadt.*
Apr-Sep 4.5HEC 🎪 ⊞ ⊞ ☉ ◙ ᴍ ⊞ ᴢ S 🅿 ⊞ lau ➧ Ⴌ ¶ ✕
⌀ Prices: ♠4 pitch 6-8.50

▶ **NORDSTRAND (ISLAND OF)**

See **ELISABETH SOPHIENKOOG**

▶ **NORTHEIM** NIEDERSACHSEN

Sultmer Berg Sultmerberg 3 ☎ 05551 51559 ▣ 05551 5656
Grassland site with views of surrounding hills. Lunchtime
siesta 13.00-15.00 hrs.
⮱ *Follow B3 from town centre.*
All year 5HEC 🎪 ⊞ Ⴌ 🛁 ✕ ☉ ◙ ⌀ ᴍ ᴢ P 🅿 ⊞ lau ➧ ¶
✕ ᴢLR Prices: ♠3.80 ⊞4.10 ⊞3.10-5.20 ▲2.30-5.20

Oehe-Draecht Schleswig-Holstein

Oehe-Draecht ☎ 04642 6124 & 6029 ▥ 69159
Grassy site, divided into pitches, on sandy ground behind a sea dyke.
⊃ *From Kappeln follow B199, turn towards Hasselberg and follow signs 'Strand'.*
Apr-Sep 6HEC ⊞ ⁑ ⚡ ⋔ 🅐 ⚍ ♟ ✕ ☉ 🖻 ∅ 🚿 🏪 🗚 ⅀ LS
🅰 ⊞ lau Prices: ⋔3.10 pitch 7

At Orsteil Gottingerode

Freizeit Oase Harz Camp Kreisstr 66, 38667 Bad Harzburg
☎ 05322 81215 ▥ 05322 877533
e-mail: harz-camp@t-online.de
On outskirts of village next to main road. Terraced site with separate touring field. Lunchtime siesta 13.00-15.00 hrs.
⊃ *On the B6 between Bad Harzburg and Goslar.*
All year 6.5HEC ⊞ 🅐 ⋔ ✕ ☉ 🖻 ∅ ⚍ 🗚 ⅀ P 🅰 ⊞ lau
Prices: ⋔4.40 pitch 5

Osnabrück Niedersachsen

Niedersachsenhof Nordstr 109 ☎ 0541 77226 ▥ 0541 70627
e-mail: osnacamp@aol.com
The site lies on a gently sloping meadow bordering a forest, near a converted farmhouse with an inn.
⊃ *On outskirts of town 5km from town centre NW on B51/65 towards Bremen, turn right and continue 300m.*
All year 3HEC ⊞ 🅐 ⋔ ✕ ☉ 🖻 ⚍ 🅰 ⊞ lau ➧ 🗚 ✕ ∅ ⅀PR
⊞ Prices: ⋔3.50 pitch 7

Osterode Niedersachsen

Sösestausee ☎ 05522 3319 ▥ 05522 72378
e-mail: harzcamp@t-online.de
Terraced site on edge of woodland and by reservoir.
⊃ *Follow road B498 from Osterode towards Altenau and after 3km turn right to the site.*
All year 4HEC ⊞ 🅐 ⋔ ✕ ☉ 🖻 ∅ ⚍ ⅀ LR 🅰 ⊞ lau ➧ 🗚 ✕
Prices: pitch 12-15 (incl 2 persons)

Ostrhauderfehn Niedersachsen

AZUR-Camping Idasee ☎ 04952 994297 ▥ 04952 994297
Situated beside a lake between Oldenburg and the Dutch border with good water sports facilities.
⊃ *Access via B27 (Cloppenburg-Aurich).*
15 Mar-15 Nov 5HEC ⊞ 🅐 ⋔ 🅐 ☉ 🖻 ∅ 🏪 ⅀ L 🅰 ⊞ lau

Otterndorf Niedersachsen

See Achtern Diek Deichstr 14 ☎ 04751 2933 ▥ 3016
e-mail: campingplatz@otterndorf.de
A family site with good facilities close to the North Sea coast.
⊃ *Access via B73 Cuxhaven-Hamburg.*
Apr-Oct 13HEC ⊞ 🅐 ⋔ 🅐 ☉ 🖻 ⅀ L 🅰 ⊞ lau ➧ 🗚 ✕ ∅ 🗚
⅀LPRS ⊞ Prices: ⋔4.50-6 🚗2 🚐5-6.5 🗚2-4

Plön Schleswig-Holstein

Spitzenort Ascheberger Str 76 ☎ 04522 2769 ▥ 4574
A pleasantly situated site with hedges on the shore of Lake Plön. Surrounded by the lake on three sides, it is ideal for water sports.
⊃ *Access from Plön on B430 towards Neumünster.*
Apr-15 Oct 4.5HEC ⊞ 🅐 ⋔ 🅐 ⚡ 🗚 ✕ ☉ 🖻 ∅ ⅀ L 🅰 ⊞ lau ➧ ✕
⅀P Prices: ⋔4 🚗3 🚐6.50-8 🗚4.50-5.50

Pyrmont, Bad Niedersachsen

Bad Pyrmont Im Schellental 1-3 ☎ 05281 8772
Site partially flat grassland, partially terraced with large building in the middle. Some tall trees, many bushes and flowers.
⊃ *E from town centre to Dak-Kurcenter, then turn left towards Friedensthal.*
All year 5HEC ⊞ 🅐 ⋔ 🅐 🗚 ✕ ☉ 🖻 ∅ ⚍ 🅰 ⊞ lau ➧ ⅀P

At Lüdge-Elbrinxen(3km S)

Eichwald Obere Dorfstr 80 ☎ 05283 335 ▥ 640
e-mail: campingeichwald@t-online.de
Pleasantly situated grassy site near woodland and pool.
⊃ *S of Lüdge in direction of Rischenau to Elbrinxen.*
All year 10HEC ⊞ 🅐 ⋔ 🅐 🗚 ✕ ☉ 🖻 ∅ ⚍ 🅰 lau ➧ ⅀P
Prices: ⋔4.60 pitch 5.10

Rieste Niedersachsen

Alfsee Am Campingpark 10 ☎ 05464 5166 ▥ 5837
e-mail: info@alfsee.de
All year 15.5HEC ⊞ 🅐 ⋔ 🅐 🗚 ✕ ☉ 🖻 ∅ 🏪 🗚 ⅀ L 🅰 ⊞ lau

Rinteln Niedersachsen

Doktor-See Am Doktor-See8 ☎ 05751 964860 ▥ 964888
e-mail: info@doktorsee.de
In a beautiful situation by a recreation area and beside the Doktor See bathing beach. Section for touring campers.
Lunchtime siesta 13.00-15.00 hrs.
⊃ *In town turn down stream at the River Weser bridge and continue along the left bank for 1.5km.*
All year 15HEC ⊞ 🅐 ⋔ 🅐 🗚 ✕ ☉ 🖻 ∅ ⚍ 🏪 ⅀ L 🅰 ⊞ lau
➧ ⅀PR Prices: ⋔6 pitch 5

St Andreasberg Niedersachsen

Erikabrücke ☎ 05582 1431 ▥ 05582 1431
e-mail: camping@erikabrucke.de
⊃ *Open site next to B27 NE of Oderstausee. Off B27 from Bad Lauterberg towards Braunlage.*
All year 5.5HEC ⊞ ⁑ 🅐 🅐 ⋔ 🅐 🗚 ✕ ☉ 🖻 ∅ ⚍ 🅰 ⅀ LR
🅰 ⊞ lau

Schobüll Schleswig-Holstein

Seeblick ☎ 04841 3321 ▥ 5773
e-mail: info@camping-seeblick.de
Beautifully situated beside the sea and divided into two sections.
⊃ *Turn off the B5 on the northern outskirts of Husum, and drive towards Insel Nordstrand for 4km up to Schobüll.*
Apr-15 Oct 3.4HEC ⊞ ⁑ ⋔ 🅐 🗚 ✕ ☉ 🖻 ∅ ⚍ 🏪 🅰 ⊞ lau
➧ ✕ ⅀P

Schönberg Schleswig-Holstein

At Kalifornien(5km N)

California Deichweg 46-47 ☎ 04344 9591 ▥ 04344 4817
Family site behind the dyke, divided by numerous hedges.
⊃ *Access through Schönberg, follow road to Kalifornien, then left at the dyke. Turn left and continue by rough track for 800m to site.*
Apr-Sep 8HEC ⊞ 🅐 ⋔ 🅐 🗚 ✕ ☉ 🖻 ∅ ⚍ 🏪 ⅀ S 🅰 ⊞ ⊗

Soltau Niedersachsen

Scandinavia-Paradies ☎ 05191 2293 ▥ 05191 18380
Heathland site in pine forest. Useful transit site 1km from motorway (from which there is some noise). Separate section for young campers. Lunchtime siesta 13.00-15.00 hrs.
⊃ *Access from the Soltau Ost (East) motorway exit then 1km on the B209/71 towards Lüneberg.*
All year 25.5HEC ⊞ ⁑ 🅐 ⋔ 🅐 🗚 ✕ ☉ 🖻 ∅ ⚍ ⅀ LP 🅰 🅰
lau

Stelle Niedersachsen

Steller See Zum Steller See 15 ☎ 04206 6490 ▥ 04206 6668
e-mail: steller.see@t-online
⊃ *Delmenhorst-Ost eixt off motorway. Site 300m.*
Apr-Sep 16HEC ⊞ 🅐 ⋔ 🅐 🗚 ✕ ☉ 🖻 ∅ 🏪 ⅀ L 🅰 🅿 🅰 lau
Prices: ⋔4 🚗2 🚐4 🗚4

SUDERBURG NIEDERSACHSEN
At HÖSSERINGEN(5km SW)

Hardausee ☎ 05826 7676 ▤ 8303
e-mail: info@camping-hardausse.de
Grassland site without firm internal roads. Statics have
individual pitches and outbuildings. Separate fields for
tourers.
◐ *Approach from Uelzen S on B4. In 9km turn right, continue
via Suderburg to site on the right just before Hösseringen.*
All year 12HEC ⟱ ⋇ ℝ ⅋ ⅋ ✕ ☉ ⬤ ∅ ᴴ ⚑ lau ✦ ⅃L

TARMSTEDT NIEDERSACHSEN

Rethbergsee ☎ 04283 422 ▤ 980139
e-mail: k.pfleging@rethbergsee-wachfnend-park.de
Level site on a grand scale. Lunchtime siesta 13.00-15.00 hrs.
◐ *About halfway between Bremen-Lilienthal and Zeven.*
All year 10HEC ⟱ ℝ ⅋ ⅋ ✕ ☉ ⬤ ∅ ᴴ ⚑ ⅃ L ⚑ lau ✦
⊞ Prices: ⚲3 ⚘3.50

TELLINGSTEDT SCHLESWIG-HOLSTEIN

Tellingstedt Teichstr ☎ 04838 657
Divided by a row of high shrubs.
◐ *Off B203 towards the swimming pool.*
May-Sep 1.2HEC ⟱ ℝ ⅋ ✕ ☉ ⬤ ⅃ P ⚑ ⊞ lau ✦ ⅃ ⅋ ✕ ∅
⅃RS Prices: ⚲3 ⚘1.50 ⚘3.50 ⚘2.50

TINNUM (ISLAND OF SYLT) SCHLESWIG-HOLSTEIN

Südhörn ☎ 04651 3607 ▤ 3619
Well-kept site divided into pitches.
◐ *Well signposted from railway unloading ramp. No road
connections between the island and the mainland-rail from
Niebüll to Westerland.*
All year 2HEC ⟱ ⋇ ℝ ⅋ ✕ ☉ ⬤ ⚑ ⅃ ⚑
✦ ⅋ ✕ ⅃PS ⊞

TÖNNING SCHLESWIG-HOLSTEIN

Lilienhof Katinger Landstr 5 ☎ 04861 439 ▤ 439
Well-maintained site in the woodland grounds of an old
manor house next to a quiet country road.
◐ *Leave B202 at far end of Tönning, then 2km W towards Welt.*
All year 2HEC ⟱ ℝ ⅋ ☉ ⬤ ᴴ ⚑ ⅃ ⊞ lau ✦ ⅋ ✕ ⅃PR
Prices: ⚲4.50 pitch 7

USLAR NIEDERSACHSEN
At DELLIEHAUSEN SOLLING(8km NE)

Bergsee Bergsee-Camp-Solling
☎ 05573 1217 ▤ 1613
Well-kept site on meadow beside lake, in Solling nature
reserve. Separate section for young campers. Lunchtime
siesta 13.00-15.00 hrs. Mobile shop.
◐ *Access from motorway exit Nörten-Hardenberg, take the
B446 and then the B421 via Hardegsen to Volpriehausen, then
right to Delliehausen (2.5km).*
Etr-Oct 1HEC ⟱ ℝ ⅋ ✕ ☉ ⬤ ⅃ ⅃ L ⅃ ⊞ lau ✦ ⅋ ⅋

WALKENRIED NIEDERSACHSEN

KNAUS Walkenried Ellricher Str 7
☎ 05525 778 ▤ 05525 2332
In an attractive location in the southern Harz area.
◐ *Access via A7 exit 'Seesen' and B243 via Herzberg and Bad
Sachsa.*
Closed Nov 5.4HEC ⟱ ✦ ℝ ⅋ ⅋ ✕ ☉ ⬤ ᴴ ⚑ ⅃ P ⅃
lau ✦ ⅃R ⊞

WEENER NIEDERSACHSEN

Weener Am Erholungsgebiet 4 ☎ 04951 1740 ▤ 8613
e-mail: weener@t-online.de
A municipal site, pleasantly landscaped and set inside a
leisure centre with swimming pool and harbour. Lunchtime
siesta 13.00-15.00 hrs.

◐ *From the main road B75 (E35) from Leer towards the
Dutch frontier and turn off in the centre of Weener and follow
signs to site.*
26 Mar-Oct 3.2HEC ⟱ ℝ ℝ ☉ ⬤ ᴴ ⚑ ⅃ P ⅃ ⊞ lau ✦ ⅋
✕ ∅ ⅃R

WIETZENDORF NIEDERSACHSEN

Südsee Soltau-Süd ☎ 05196 98016
This site is beautifully situated in a forest beside lake.
◐ *Leave the Hannover-Hamburg motorway at the Soltau-Süd
exit, and take the B3 for 2km towards Bergen. At the underpass
in Bokel, turn left and drive on for approx 4km towards
Wietzendorf.*
All year 70HEC ⟱ ℝ ℝ ⅋ ⅋ ✕ ☉ ⬤ ∅ ᴴ ⚑ ⚑ ⅃ LP ⅃ ⊞
lau

WILSUM NIEDERSACHSEN

AZUR-Ferienpark Wilsumer Berge
☎ 05945 1029 ▤ 05945 511
e-mail: wilsum@azur-camping.de
Parts of the site adjoin a large lake. The separate section for
touring campers has its own sanitary building.
◐ *From Nordhorn follow road B403 via Uelsen to Wilsum.
On nearside of Wilsum turn right.*
All year 88HEC ⟱ ⦂⦂⦂ ℝ ℝ ⅋ ⅋ ✕ ☉ ⬤ ∅ ᴴ ⚑ ⅃ L ⅃ ⊞
lau Prices: ⚲4-6 ⚲3-4 pitch 5-7

WINGST NIEDERSACHSEN

Knaus Wingst Schwimmbadallee 13
☎ 04778 7604 ▤ 04778 7608
This modern comfortable site extends over several terraces,
above a small artificial lake on the northern edge of an
extensive forested area. Lunchtime siesta 13.00-15.00 hrs.
Municipal recreation centre across the road.
◐ *Turn off the B73 between Stade and Cuxhaven, about 3km
S of Cadenberge.*
Closed Nov 8.7HEC ⟱ ℝ ℝ ✕ ☉ ⬤ ᴴ ⚑ ⅃ ⅃ P lau
✦ ⅋ ⅃P ⊞

WINSEN-ALLER NIEDERSACHSEN

AZUR Camping Winsen ☎ 05143 93199 ▤ 05143 93144
Site lies on meadowland at the River Aller. Watersports
available. Lunchtime siesta 13.00-15.00 hrs.
◐ *From Celle go NW to Winsen.*
All year 12HEC ⟱ ℝ ℝ ✕ ☉ ⬤ ∅ ⅃ R ⅃ ⊞ lau ✦ ᴴ ⅃P

WITTENBORN SCHLESWIG-HOLSTEIN

Weisser Brunnen ☎ 04554 1757 & 1413 ▤ 4833
e-mail: gert.petzold@t-online.de
A lakeside site consisting of several sections, hilly in parts,
next to Lake Mözen. A public road, leading to the lake, passes
through part of the site.
◐ *Turn off B206 at Km23.6 towards lake.*
Apr-Oct 7HEC ⟱ ℝ ⅋ ⅋ ✕ ☉ ⬤ ∅ ᴴ ⚑ ⅃ L ⅃ ⊞ lau

WULFEN (ISLAND OF FEHMARN)
SCHLESWIG-HOLSTEIN

Wulfener Hals ☎ 04371 8628-0 ▤ 4371 3723
e-mail: camping@wulfenerhals.de
Meadowland site beside the Baltic Sea and an inland lake
(Burger Binnensee). 1700m long private beach.
◐ *Turn off B20/E4 (Vogelfluglinie) after the 'Sundbrücke' and
follow roads towards 'Avendorf', then 'Wulfen' and 'Wulfener
Hals'.*
All year 34HEC ⟱ ℝ ℝ ⅋ ⅋ ✕ ☉ ⬤ ∅ ᴴ ⚑ ⚑ ⅃ PS ⅃ ⊞ lau
Prices: ⚲3.30-6.50 pitch 6.50-17.40

See advertisement in colour section

ITALY

❖

Italy, with its many beautiful cities and rich architectural heritage, is bordered by four countries: from west to east, France, Switzerland, Austria and Slovenia.

❖

FACTS AND FIGURES
Area: 301,323 sq km (116,341 sq miles)
Population: 57,587,985 (1998)
Capital: Roma (Rome)
Language: Italian
IDD code: 39. To call the UK dial 00 44
Currency: Euro.
Local time: GMT + 1 (summer GMT + 2)

Emergency Services: Police 113, Ambulance 113 or 118, Fire 115 (Carabinieri 112)
Banks: Mon-Fri 08.30-13.30 and 15.30-16.30
Shops: Mon-Sat 08.30-13.30 and 15.30-19.30

Average daily temperatures: Roma
Jan 8°C   Jul 25°C
Mar 11°C   Sep 21°C
May 18°C   Nov 12°C
Tourist Information: Italian State Tourist Office (ENIT)
UK 1 Princess Street London W1R 8AY Tel (020) 7408 1254

USA 630 Fifth Avenue, Suite 1565 New York, NY 10111 Tel(212) 245 5618
Camping card: Not generally compulsory, but required on some sites. Reductions available.
Tourist info website: www.enit.it

The approaches to Italy are all dominated by mountains. The lakes of the north present a striking contrast with the sun-parched lands of the south and there is some beautiful countryside in the central Appenines. There are fine, sandy beaches on both the Tyrrhenian and Adriatic coasts. All this and the cities of Rome and Milan. Something for everyone, it seems.

The north has a typically Continental climate whilst the south has a temperate Mediterranean climate with extremely hot summers. The language is Italian, a direct development of Latin. There are several dialect forms such as Sicilian and Sardinian, but the accepted standard derives from the vernacular spoken in Florence 700 years ago. German is spoken, to a small extent, near the Austrian frontier and French in Valle d'Aosta.

The International Reservation Centre in Calenzano (near Florence) *Federcampeggio* provides a campsite information and reservation service ☎ 055-882391.

The *Assessorati Regionali per il Turismo* (ART) and the *Azienda Promozione Turistica* (APT) have regional and local information offices and can provide details of campsites within their locality. In northern Italy, especially by the lakes and along the Adriatic coast, sites tend to become very crowded and it is advisable to book in advance during the season which extends from May to the end of August.

Off-site camping is permitted provided the landowner's permission has been obtained, but is strictly prohibited in State forests and national parks. In built-up areas, if parking is allowed, the towing vehicle must remain connected to the trailer or caravan and the corner steadies must not be used.

HOW TO GET THERE

Although there are several ways of getting to Italy, entry will most probably be by way of France and Switzerland. Some passes, which are closed in winter, are served by road or rail-tunnels. For details of these, please consult the Contents Page.

Distance

From the Channel ports Milano (Milan) is about 1100km (684 miles) requiring one or two overnight stops. Roma (Rome) is about 580km (360 miles) further south.

Car-sleeper trains

Summer services are available from **Denderleeuw** (Belgium) to Bologna, Livorno, Rimini, Roma and Vanezia; an all year round service operates to Milano. Summer services are available from 's-Hertogenbosch (Netherlands) to Bologna and Verona.

MOTORING & GENERAL INFORMATION

The information given here is specific to Italy. It **must** be read in conjunction with the Continental ABC at the front of the book, which covers those regulations which are common to many countries.

British Embassy/Consulates*

The British Embassy together with its consular section is located at 00187 Roma, Via XX Settembre 80A ☎06-4220 0001. There are British Consulates in Firenze (Florence), Milano (Milan), and Napoli (Naples); there are British Consulates with honorary Consuls in Bari, Cagliari, Catania, Genova (Genoa), Palermo, Trieste, Torino (Turin) and Venezia (Venice).

Children in cars

Child under 4 not permitted to travel as front or rear seat passenger unless using suitable restraint system. Child between 4 and 12 travelling in front seat must use suitable restraint system. See the Continental ABC under 'Passengers' and 'Seat Belts'.

Currency

With the introduction of the Euro, the Italian Lira (ITL) ceased to be legal tender from 28 February 2002. However, ITL coins and notes may still be exchanged at local banks until 30 June 2002 (not confirmed), and at the Italian Central Bank (**Banca d'Italia**) for 10 years.

Dimensions and weight restrictions*

Private **cars** and towed **trailers** or **caravans** are restricted to the following dimensions - car height, 4 metres: width, 2.55 metres: length (including tow-bar) 12 metres. Caravan/trailer height, must not exceed 1.8 times the distance between the wheels of the vehicle; width 2.3 metres; length (including tow-bar) with one axle 6.5 metres, with two axles 8 metres. The maximum permitted overall length of vehicle/trailer or caravan combination is 18.75 metres. Trailers with an unladen weight of over 750kg or 50% of the weight of the towing vehicle must have service brakes on all wheels.

A load may only overhang at the rear, and must be indicated by a special reflectorised square panel. The load must not exceed 30% of

The Colosseum in Rome

International Driving Permit (IDP). The minimum age at which visitors from UK or Republic of Ireland may use a temporarily imported car is 18 years. The minimum age for using a temporarily imported motorcycle of up to 125cc, not transporting a passenger, is 16 years; to carry a passenger, or use a motorcycle over 125cc, the minimum age is 18 years.

Fiscal receipt
In Italy, the law provides for a special numbered fiscal receipt (*ricevuta fiscale*) to be issued after paying for a wide range of goods and services including meals and accommodation. This receipt indicates the cost of the various goods and services obtained, and the total charge after adding VAT. Tourists should ensure that this receipt is issued, as spot checks are made by the authorities, and both the proprietor and consumer are liable to an on-the-spot fine if the receipt cannot be produced.

Foodstuffs*
If the imported foodstuffs are for personal use, there are no limits when travelling between EU countries. Visitors entering Italy from outside the EU may import up to 1kg of meat or meat products. Coffee (500g), coffee extract (200g), tea (100g) and tea extract (40g) are free of customs duties, but visitors under 15 cannot import coffee.

Lights
See Continental ABC under 'Lights'.

The picturesque town of Spello, in the Umbrian valley

the length of the vehicle, nor should the combined length of vehicle and overhanging load exceed the length restrictions given above.

Driving Licence*
All valid UK or Republic of Ireland licences should be acceptable in Italy. However, older all-green UK licences (in Northern Ireland any licence issued before 1 Jan 1991) do not conform to the EC model. To update to a photocard licence, apply to DVLA Swansea/DVLNI Coleraine on the appropriate application form available from most post offices. Alternatively, older licences may be accompanied by an

Motoring clubs
There are two motoring organisations in Italy. The **Touring Club Italiano** (TCI) which has its head office at 20122 Milano, 10 Corso Italia ☎02-85261 and the **Automobile Club d'Italia** (ACI) whose head office is at 00185 Roma, 8 Via Marsala ☎06-49981. Both clubs have branch offices in most leading cities and towns.

Roads
Italy has over 4,000 miles of motorway (*autostrada*) with tolls payable on most sections. Emergency telephones are located every 2km on most motorways; there are two call buttons, one to call for technical assistance and one to alert the Red Cross services.

Main and secondary roads are generally good, and there are an exceptional number of by-passes. Mountain roads are usually well engineered; for details of mountain passes, see the contents page.

Speed limits*
The speed limit in *built-up areas* is 50kph (31mph); *outside built-up areas*, 90kph (55mph) on ordinary
roads, 110kph (68mph) on main roads and 130kph (80mph) on motorways. Motorcycles under 150cc are not allowed on motorways, and cannot exceed 90kph (55mph). For cars towing a caravan or trailer the speed limits are 70kph (43mph) outside built-up areas and 80kph (49mph) on motorways.

Warning triangle*
The use of a warning triangle is compulsory outside built-up areas in the event of accident or breakdown. The triangle must be placed 50 metres (55yds) behind the vehicle on ordinary roads and 100 metres (109yds) on motorways. Motorists who fail to do this are liable to an administrative fine of between ITL25,000 and 100,000.

*Additional information will be found in the Continental ABC at the front of the book.

TOURIST INFORMATION

NORTH WEST ALPS & LAKES
One of the prettiest corners of Italy is Lake Como. With its sparkling waters and alpine backdrop on the Swiss border, the region inspired many works by Verdi, Rossini, Bellini, and Liszt. Today the lake is renowned as a playground for the 'beautiful people' of Milan, with a large number of golf courses, and ideal conditions for wind surfing. Surfers will tell you about the bizarre act of nature at Lake Como which makes the wind direction change twice every day, running Breva (north) from noon until sunset, and Tiva (south) for the rest of the time. Boat trips offer a wide choice of vessels ranging from ferries to motor-boats, and hydrofoils to old-fashioned steamers.

From the south, the town of Como, with its elegant shops and cafés is the gateway to the lake and also well worth a visit is Bellagio, with

its wonderful baroque church of San Giovanni and the Villa Serbilloni, which stands on a hill overlooking the lake.

VENICE & THE NORTH
Venice is always packed with visitors and when you think of the richness of the city's architecture and its internationally-known picturesque canals, it is not difficult to understand why. Perhaps its most famous landmark is the Basilica of San Marco. This incredible building traces its history back to the 9th century when it was founded to enshrine the relics of the apostle, Mark. His body still lays there in a white marble tomb.

Inside, the Basilica has a rich mix of architecture and decoration, drawing on Romanesque, Byzantine, and Gothic influences,

A young Roman keeps up to date with world events

with an intricately decorated mosaic ceiling.

The Piazza San Marco (St Mark's Square) is always bustling with visitors and includes the famous astrological clock and the Café Florian with its outdoor orchestra. Also on St Mark's Square is the Palazzo Ducale, house of the Doges, and the famous Bridge of Sighs. The many islands dotted around the city are also fascinating to visit, particularly Murano, famed for its glass, and the Giudecca.

NORTH WEST & MEDITERRANEAN COAST

Firenze (Florence), on the River Arno, is one of Italy's most beautiful cities, and stands in the middle of the enchanting Tuscany region. This is such a popular summer holiday destination for the English, that it is now nicknamed 'Chiantishire'.

The focal point is the Duomo (cathedral) topped by Brunelleschi's celebrated dome. The interior contains many famous works of art. Do not miss the Uffizi Gallery, with its magnificent collection of paintings, or the Academia, where among other treasures Michelangelo's statue of David is housed.

NORTH EAST & ADRIATIC

Urbino is one of the finest towns in the Marche area of Italy, thanks to the rich architectural and artistic legacy left by the Montefeltro family who were prominent in the region between the 12th and 15th centuries, and among the foremost patrons of the Renaissance.

Just outside the town is the Palazzo Ducale, built in the mid-15th century, it is a classic example of Renaissance architecture at its best. During this period it was home to Duke Frederico de Montefeltro, who collected in his court many of the outstanding artistic figure of the time. Today it houses the Galleria Nationale delle Marche.

Inside the city walls is the House of Raphael which is another recommended destination for lovers of fine art.

The Passo Del Bernina stretches from Switzerland to Italy

ROME

Rome encloses the world's smallest nation, Vatican City, home to the Pope and the Roman Catholic Church. The main attractions of Vatican City include St. Peter's Basilica, the Sistine Chapel, and the excellent Vatican museums. The land on which the city stands was contraversially granted to the church by a treaty between Pope Pius XI and Mussolini in 1929.

The Sistine Chapel has recently been restored to its former glory. Its famous ceiling contains no less than nine frescoes by Michaelangelo, the most famous being 'The Last Judgement'. To fully appreciate the Sistine Chapel it is a good idea to bring binoculars as the ceiling frescoes are difficult to see from ground level. If the Sistine Chapel appears large, then St. Peter's Basilica is simply gigantic and one of the most impressive sights in Europe.

SOUTH

The name Pompeii conjures up images of romantic tragedy; its ruins, the site of the world's most famous volcanic catastrophe, are one of southern Italy's premier tourist attractions. The town was destroyed by an eruption from Mount Vesuvius in AD 79, and was not uncovered again until 1750. When excavation began it became clear the ill-fated community of Pompeii had been 'frozen' in time by the dense covering of volcanic ash. The inhabitants of the town had been preserved by the ash and were going about their daily affairs. The town is like a three-dimensional snapshot of life in the 1st century, perfectly preserved from the moment they perished.

SARDINIA

The island offers a chance to escape the bustle of mainland Italy and spend time in several peaceful retreats.

One of its most appealing attractions is the *Santissima Trinità di Saccargia*, the most famous Romanesque church in Sardinia, standing alone in a windswept valley. It acquired its name in the oddest of manners; a passing cow is said to have bowed in the direction of the church, and the name was thereupon changed to *Santissima Trinità di Saccargia*, or the 'Church of the Dappled Cow'.

The 'cow' theme totally dominates the church, with numerous porticoes engraved with cows and other farm mammals.

SICILY

The island of Sicily is home to Europe's largest and highest volcano, Mount Etna, which is still very much active and has erupted several times in the last few decades.

The Etna trail begins with the thought-provoking collection of ruins the volcano has left in its wake. The best is probably the ruin of the *Torre del Filosofo*. After exploring the foothills, take the Etna railway for an impressive view of the volcano and the island of Sicily. Ascending Etna on foot is possible (geological activity permitting) and not especially arduous, but warm clothing is required as the summit is cold, windswept, and usually wet.

Wearing a uniform designed by Michelangelo, the Swiss Guards are the traditional bodyguards of the Pope in that country-within-a-country, Vatican City in Rome.

NORTH WEST/ALPS & LAKES

The Gran Paradiso mountains on the French border, and the Matterhorn and Monte Rosa to the north on the Swiss border, give a dramatic glacier-topped backdrop to the steep-sided valleys and the distinctively Italian Lakes, below which villas and medieval castles border the lakes, and palm trees and magnolias grow. The mountains provide winter skiing, and walking in the summer, and wood and stone chalets contribute to the Alpine landscape. On the lakes, boats take you from harbour to harbour, yet within an hour you can be in Lombardy's capital, Milan. Turin, to the west, is an elegant town with its Piazza San Carlo and many cafés. Nearby, in the Alba region, the vineyards produce the distinguished Barolo red wine and sparkling Asti Spumante.

To the north and eastwards in the Dolomites, roads are good in the summer and the scenery is dramatic with fortresses dominating high peaks. Through wooded countryside is the border town of Bolzano where you will hear German spoken (this was once the South Tyrol) and may be served sausage and sauerkraut and locally produced Reisling wine.

> **ANFO** BRESCIA

Palafitte via Calcaterra ☎ 0365 809051 ▥ 809051
Pleasant site divided into plots, sloping towards the lake where there are some trees.
➲ *Access as for Pilù, then turn right.*
22 Apr-18 Sep 20HEC ⊞ ♦ ♠ ⚑ ⏃ ✕ ☉ ◉ ∅ ⚑ ⟨ LP ⌂
lau ➧ ✕

LAGO AZZURRO CAMPSITE

**VIA E. FERMI, I-28040 DORMELLETTO (NO)
TEL. AND FAX 0039/0322497197 · TEL. 0039/335 5447599
MOBILE. 0039/340 4084035
HTTP://WWW.CAMPINGLAGOAZZURRO.IT
E-MAIL: INFO@CAMPINGLAGOAZZURRO.IT**

Ideal holiday destination at any time of the year, situated right by the lake and with its own sandy beach. The campsite offers quiet and shady pitches surrounded by green and a range of recreation facilities: large swimming pool with chute, mini football pitch on grass, clay and grass tennis courts, beach volleyball, table tennis, refurbished children's play area, entertainment for children and adults, video games. Ideal centre for trips – including by boat – to sites along Lago Maggiore. Fully refurbished restaurant, bar and pizzeria, small shop, hot food stall, satellite television, payphones, Internet and fax service, newsagent and tobacconist.

Fully refurbished toilet **OPEN ALL YEAR ROUND**
and washing facilities,
including hot showers.
Washing machines
and ironing facilities
also available.
Large caravan
sleeps up to 7,
with bath,
air conditioning
and satellite TV.

Pilù via Venturi 4 ☎ 0365 809037 ▥ 0365 809207
e-mail: info@pilu.it
Well-maintained, slightly sloping site subdivided by trees and rows of shrubs on pebble beach from which it is separated by narrow public footpath.
➲ *On southern outskirts; well signed.*
Apr-30 Sep 2HEC ⊞ ♦ ♠ ⚑ ⏃ ✕ ☉ ◉ ∅ ⚍ ⚑ ⟨ LPR ⌂ ⊞
lau ➧ ✕ Prices: ♠4.50-5.50 pitch 7.50-10

> **ANGERA** VARESE

Città di Angera via Bruschera 99
☎ 0331 930736 ▥ 0331 960367
e-mail: info@campingcittadiangera.it
Large family site with plenty of recreational facilities.
➲ *Signposted.*
All year 6.7HEC ⊞ ♦ ♠ ⚑ ⏃ ✕ ☉ ◉ ∅ ⚍ ⟨ LP ⌂ ⊞ lau

> **ARONA** NOVARA

> At **DORMELLETTO**(5km S)

Lago Azzurro via E-Fermi 2 ☎ 0322 497197 ▥ 0322 497197
e-mail: info@campinglagoazzurro.it
A lakeside site in beautiful surroundings with fine sporting facilities.
➲ *S of Arona off SS Sempione 33.*
All year 2.5HEC ⊞ ♦ ♠ ⚑ ⏃ ✕ ☉ ◉ ∅ ⟨ LP ⌂ ⊞ lau

Lago Maggiore via L-da-Vinci 7 ☎ 0322 497193 ▥ 497193
e-mail: maggiore@azzurra.it
Well-maintained site divided into plots, pleasantly landscaped by the lakeside.
➲ *Access from SS33, well signposted.*
Apr-Sep 5HEC ⊞ ♦ ♠ ⚑ ⏃ ✕ ☉ ◉ ∅ ⚑ ⟨ LP ⌂ lau
Prices: ♠3.61-5.16 ♣3.61-3.61 ⚑6.19-10.33

Lido Holiday Inn via M-Polo 1 ☎ 0322 497047 ▥ 497047
e-mail: lido.holidayinn@tin.it
Site on bank of the lake, with some trees.
➲ *Turn off the SS33 at Km60/VII and the IP petrol station.*
Apr-Sep 3.5HEC ⊞ ⚍ ♠ ⚑ ⏃ ✕ ☉ ◉ ⚍ ⚑ ⟨ LP ⌂ P lau
➧ ∅

Smeraldo via Cavour 125 ☎ 0322 497031 ▥ 0322 497031
e-mail: info@camping-smeraldo.com
Well-landscaped site, divided into plots and situated in woodland by lakeside.
➲ *Access from SS33.*
Mar-Oct 24HEC ⊞ ♦ ♠ ⚑ ⏃ ✕ ☉ ◉ ∅ ⚍ ⚑ ⟨ L ⌂ ⊞ lau

> **ARVIER** AOSTA

Arvier via Chaussa 17 ☎ 0165 99088
Wooded quiet site close to mountains and a peaceful village
20 Jun-31 Aug 1HEC ⊞ ♦ ♠ ⚑ ☉ ◉ ⟨ P ⌂ lau ➧ ⏃ ✕ ∅
⚍ ⟨ R ⊞

> **BASTIA MONDOVÌ** CUNEO

Cascina via Pieve 26 ☎ 0174 60181
A peaceful site on level land surrounded by mountains.
➲ *Access via, then head towards Bastia.*
Closed Sep 4HEC ⊞ ♦ ♠ ⚑ ⏃ ✕ ☉ ◉ ⚍ ⟨ PR ⌂ lau
➧ ⚑ ✕

> **BAVENO** NOVARA

Tranquilla via Cave 2 ☎ 0323 923452 ▥ 923452
e-mail: info@tranquilla.it
In a peaceful location with fine panoramic views over the surrounding mountains and Lake Maggiore. Good, modern facilities.
➲ *4 km from Stresa*
Mar-Oct 1.8HEC ⊞ ♦ ♠ ⏃ ✕ ☉ ◉ ⚑ ⟨ P ⌂ lau ➧ ⚑ ∅ ⚍
⟨ LR ⊞ Prices: ♠3.50-4.39 pitch 5.58-7.49

CAMPING ★★★★

Moosbauer

Moritzinger Straße, 83 • BOZEN/Südtirol
Tel. 0039/047191842 • Fax 0039/0471204894
E-mail: moosbauer@dnet.it
Http://www.moosbauer.com

Bolzano: ideal centre for numerous walks and trips, eg to Salten (European long distance footpath) Ritten (earth pillars), Kohlern (Europe's oldest cable car) the Seiser alpine pasture, etc. Day trips to Lake Garda and Verona. The site is set in a delightful landscape in the suburb of Gries on the west of Bolzano. Enjoy a holiday during the spring blossoms or the autumn grape harvest. We offer a friendly atmosphere, a heated swimming pool with sunbathing area. Small shop, grillroom and luxury toilet and washing facilities. Each pitch has its own satellite TV connection, fresh water supply and wastewater connection. Bus into town direct from campsite.

BELLAGIO COMO

Azienda Agricola Clarke via Valassina 170/c ☎ 031 951325
e-mail: elizabethclarke@tin.it
A small, secluded site situated on a horsebreeding farm on the shores of Lake Bellagio.
May-Sep 0.5HEC ⸺ ⟊ ℝ ⟐ ☺ ⊙ 🛒 ⟩ LP 🔳 🔲 ➧ ⟐ ✕ ⟩LP

BOLZANO-BOZEN BOLZANO

Moosbauer Moritzingerweg 83
☎ 0471 918492 ▒ 0471 204894
e-mail: info@moosbauer.com
Small site in attractive valley at the "Gateway to the Dolomites."
All year 1HEC ⸺ ➧ ℝ ⟐ ⟐ ✕ ⊙ 🛒 ⟩ ⟩ P 🔳 lau ➧ ✕ 🔳
Prices: ⟡4.75-5.75 ➧4.50-4.90 🔲10.50-13.50 Δ4.50-4.90

BRÉCCIA COMO

International via Cecilio ☎ 031 521435 ▒ 031 521435
On a level meadow near the motorway. Lunchtime siesta 13.00-15.30 hrs.
➲ Off A9 Como-Milan motorway.
28 Mar-15 Oct 1.8HEC ⸺ ➧ ℝ ⟐ ⟐ ✕ ⊙ 🛒 ⟩ ⟩ P 🔳 🔳 lau

BRENTONICO TRENTO

Polsa Polsa ☎ 0464 867177 ▒ 0464 421003
Situated at 1300mtrs on Mount Baldo with easy access and good, modern facilities.
➲ Access via Brenner Autostrada exit Rovereto Sud and continue through Brentonico and Prada to Polsa.
15 Jun-15 Sep 33HEC ⸺ ☀ ℝ ⟐ ⟐ ✕ ⊙ 🛒 ⟩ ⟐ 🔳 lau ➧ ⟩P

BRESSANONE-BRIXEN BOLZANO

Löwenhof via Brennero 60 ☎ 0472 836216 ▒ 0472 801337
e-mail: info@loewenhof.it
Site offers rafting and canoeing school as well as sauna, pool etc. which are avaliable in the Dolomiti resort 8km away.
➲ Exit Bolzano/Brennero motorway at Varna. Site is just before Brixen.
5 Dec-Oct 0.5HEC ⸺ ⟊ ℝ ⟐ ⟐ ✕ ⊙ 🛒 ⟩ ⟩ PR 🔳 🔳 lau
➧ ⟩L 🔳 Prices: ⟡5.70-7.70 ➧7-12 🔲5-8 Δ3-8

BUISSON AOSTA

Cervino ☎ 0166 545111 ▒ 0166 519882
All year 6HEC ⸺ ⟊ ℝ ⟐ ⟐ ✕ ⊙ 🛒 ⟩ ⟐ ⟩ R lau ➧ 🔳

CALCERANICA TRENTO

Al Pescatore via dei Pescatori 1
☎ 0461 723062 ▒ 0461 724212
e-mail: trentino@campingpescatore.it
The site consists of several sections of meadowland, inland from the lake shore road to Lago di Caldonazzo. Well maintained with private beach.
29 May-15 Sep 3.8HEC ⸺ ⟊ ℝ ⟐ ⟐ ✕ ⊙ 🛒 ⟩ L 🔳 lau ➧ 🔳

Fleiola via Trento 20 ☎ 0461 723153 ▒ 0461 724386
e-mail: info@campingfleiola.it
Site is divided into sectors beside lake.
➲ Exit the Verona/Brennero motorway at Trento, follow signs for Pergine and Caldonazzo.
Apr-5 Oct 1.2HEC ⸺ ⟊ ➧ ℝ ⟐ ⟐ ✕ ⊙ 🛒 ⟩ ⟐ ⟩ L 🔳
lau ➧ ✕ ⟋ 🔳 Prices: ⟡5-6.50 pitch 6-11

Riviera viale Venezia 10 ☎ 0461 724464 ▒ 0461718689
e-mail: riviera@dnet.it
Etr-15 Sep 1.5HEC ⸺ ➧ ℝ ⟐ ⟐ ✕ ⊙ 🛒 ⟩ ⟩ L 🔳 lau ➧ ⟋ 🔳

CAMPITELLO DI FASSA TRENTO

Miravalle vicolo camping 15 ☎ 0462 750502 ▒ 04621 751563
e-mail: info@campingmiravalle.it
In a wooded mountain setting beside the River Avisio and close to the town centre.
➲ Signposted.
Jun-Sep & Dec-Apr Oct-Nov 3HEC ⸺ ⟊ ℝ ⊙ 🛒 ⟩ ⟐ ⟐ ⟩
R 🔳 🔳 🔳 lau ➧ ⟐ ✕ ⟋ ⟩ ⟩P Prices: ⟡6.71-8.26 🔲7.48-8.78 Δ7-7.74

CANAZEI TRENTO

Marmolada via Pareda 60 ☎ 0462 601660 ▒ 0462 601722
Grassland site extending to the river, part of it in spruce woodland.
➲ Located on S outskirts on the right of the road to Alba Penia.
All year 3HEC ⸺ ⠿ ⟊ ℝ ⟐ ⟐ ✕ ⊙ 🛒 ⟩ ⟐ ⟩ R 🔳 lau ➧ ⟐
✕ ⟩P 🔳

CANNOBIO NOVARA

International Paradis via Casali Darbedo 12 ☎ 0323 71227
A level site on the bank of a lake.
➲ Access from the SS34 at Km35/V.
20 Mar-15 Oct 1.2HEC ⸺ ➧ ℝ ⟐ ⟐ ✕ ⊙ 🛒 ⟩ ⟐ ⟩ L 🔳
🔳 lau ➧ ✕ ⟩R

Residence Campagna via Casali Darbedo 20/22
☎ 0323 70100 ▒ 0323 72398
e-mail: campeggio.campagna@cannobio.net
A well equipped site in a pleasant lakeside location.
➲ Turn off SS34 to Locarno at Km35/V on N outskirts of village. W of lake on road 21.
20 Mar-Nov 1.2HEC ⸺ ➧ ℝ ⟐ ⟐ ✕ ⊙ 🛒 ⟩ ⟐ ⟐ ⟩ L 🔳
lau ➧ ⟩R 🔳 Prices: ⟡5.16-5.93 ➧4.13-5.16 🔲4.13-5.16
Δ4.13-5.16

Valle Romantica via Valle Cannobina ☎ 0323 71249 ▤ 71249
e-mail: camping@riviera-valleromantica.com
A pleasant site with trees, shrubs and flowers. Internal roads are asphalted and a mountain stream provides bathing facilities.
➲ *1.5km w off road to Malesco.*
24 Mar-Sep 25HEC ▥ ♠ ⋒ ⅀ ♟ ♥ ✕ ⊙ ⊠ ⌀ ⏢ ⊕ ⃗ PR 🔒 lau ➡ 🚿 ⃗L ⊞

> **CASTELLETTO TICINO** NOVARA

Italia Lido via Cicognola 88 ☎ 0331 923032 ▤ 0331 923032
A large family site with its own private beach on Lake Maggiore. The site is popular with families and there are good recreational facilities.
➲ *From A8 to Milan join A26 is then signposted.*
Mar-Oct 3HEC ▥ ♠ ⋒ ⅀ ♟ ♥ ✕ ⊙ ⊠ 🚿 ⃗ L 🅿 lau ➡ ✕

> **CHIUSA-KLAUSEN** BOLZANO

Gamp Griesbruck 10 ☎ 0472 847425 ▤ 0472 845067
e-mail: info@camping-gamp.com
The site lies next to the Gasthof Gamp, between the Brenner railway line and the motorway bridge, which passes high above the camp.
➲ *Access from the motorway exit and the SS12 is well signposted.*
All year 0.6HEC ▥ ♠ ⋒ ♟ ♥ ✕ ⊙ ⊠ ⃗ P 🔒 lau ➡ ⌀ 🚿 ⃗P
⊞ **Prices:** ♠4.65-5.32 ⇆2.84-3.87 ⊞4.91-5.94 ▲3.62-5.06

> **COLFOSCO** BOLZANO

Colfosco via Sorega 15 ☎ 0471 836515 ▤ 836515
e-mail: camp.colfosco@rolmail.net
In a beautiful setting at the foot of the Sella mountains.
Jun-Sep & Dec-15 Apr 2.5HEC ▥ ⋮⋮⋮ ⋇ ⋒ ⅀ ♟ ♥ ✕ ⊙ ⊠ ⌀ 🚿 ⏢ ⃗ R 🔒 lau ➡ ⃗L ⊞

> **COLOMBARE** BRESCIA

Sirmione via Sirmioncino 9 ☎ 030 919045 ▤ 030 919045
A well equipped site in a beautiful location on the Sirmione peninsula, with direct access to Lake Garda.
➲ *From SS11 drive towards Sirmione and turn right after approx. 6.4km.*
15 Mar-15 Oct 3.5HEC ▥ ⌀ ♠ ⋒ ⅀ ♟ ♥ ✕ ⊙ ⊠ ⏢ ⃗ LP 🔒 ⊞ lau ➡ ⃗ ⌀ 🚿

> **CÚNEO** CUNEO

Turistico Comunale Bisalta San Rocco Castagnaretta
☎ 0171 491334
Large site with well defined pitches and a wide variety of sporting and recreational facilities.
➲ *SW of town towards the French border.*
All year 4HEC ▥ ♠ ⋒ ⅀ ♟ ♥ ✕ ⊙ ⊠ ⏢ ⃗ P 🔒 lau ➡ 🚿 ⊞

> **DESENZANO DEL GARDA** BRESCIA

Vò via Vò 9 ☎ 030 9121325 ▤ 030 9120773
e-mail: vo@voit.it
Situated on Lake Garda, 1500m from Desenzano, surrounded by meadows and woods.
➲ *On the banks of Lake Garda 2km from Desenzano, between Padenghe and Sirmione.*
Apr-Sep 5HEC ▥ ⊿ ⋒ ⅀ ♟ ✕ ⊙ ⊠ ⏢ ⃗ LP 🔒 lau ➡ ⌀
Prices: ♠5.30-7.50 pitch 9-11.50

> **DIMARO** TRENTO

Dolomiti di Brenta via Gole 105
☎ 0463 974332 ▤ 0463 973200
e-mail: dolomitibrenta@camping.it
The campsite has large flat plots which are surrounded by tall pine trees. The facilities for sport are excellent with lessons and tuition for canoeing and white water rafting.
➲ *Turn off SS42, at Km173.5.*
Jun-Sep & 6 Dec-15 Apr 3HEC ▥ ♠ ⋒ ⅀ ♟ ♥ ✕ ⊙ ⊠ ⌀ 🚿 ⏢ ⃗ P 🔒 ⊞ lau ➡ ⃗R

> **DOMASO** COMO

Gardenia via Case Sparse 138
☎ 0344 96262 ▤ 0344 83381
➲ *N at Case Sparse*
Apr-Sep 20HEC ▥ ⊿ ⋒ ⅀ ♟ ♥ ✕ ⊙ ⊠ ⌀ 🚿 ⏢ ⃗ L 🔒 ⊿ lau ➡ ⃗R ⊞

> **EDOLO** BRESCIA

Adamello via Campeggio 10 ☎ 0364 71694
A terraced site in wooded surroundings, 1km from the lake.
➲ *1.5km W of SS39.*
All year 1.2HEC ▥ ♠ ⋒ ⅀ ♟ ♥ ✕ ⊙ ⊠ ⌀ 🚿 ⏢ ⊕ ⊞ lau ➡ ✕ ⃗LPR

> **FERIOLO** NOVARA

Orchidea via Repubblica dell'Ossola
☎ 0323 28257 ▤ 0323 28573
A modern site on the extremity of Lake Maggiore with good sports and entertainment facilities.
➲ *Access via SS33.*
15Mar-13Oct 4HEC ▥ ♠ ⋒ ⅀ ♟ ♥ ✕ ⊙ ⊠ ⌀ 🚿 ⏢ ⊕ ⃗ L 🔒 ⊞ lau

> **FONDOTOCE** NOVARA

Continental Lido via 42 Martiri 156
☎ 0323 496300 ▤ 496218
e-mail: continental@lagomaggior.com
By Lake Mergozzo and 1km from Lake Maggiore.
➲ *On right hand side of road from Verbania Fondotoce to Gravellona.*
23 Mar-22 Sep 8HEC ▥ ⊿ ⋒ ⅀ ♟ ♥ ✕ ⊙ ⊠ ⌀ 🚿 ⏢ ⃗ L 🔒 lau ➡ 🚿 ⃗R **Prices:** ♠3.75-5.55 pitch 15.50-21.95 (incl 2 persons)

Lido Toce via per Feriolo 41
☎ 0323 496298 ▤ 0323 496220
In a beautiful location on the eastern shore of the lake offering spectacular views. Good recreational facilities.
Apr-Sep 2HEC ▥ ⋮⋮⋮ ♠ ⋒ ⅀ ♟ ♥ ✕ ⊙ ⊠ ⃗ LR 🔒 ⊞ lau ➡ ⌀ 🚿

Village Isolino via Per Feriolo 25
☎ 0323 496080 ▤ 496414
e-mail: info@isolino.com
23 Mar-22 Sep 12HEC ▥ ♠ ⋒ ⅀ ♟ ♥ ✕ ⊙ ⊠ ⌀ 🚿 ⏢ ⊕ ⃗ LP 🔒 ⊞ lau ➡ ⃗R **Prices:** ♠3.80-6 ⇆2.90-5.40 pitch 16.50-27 (incl 2 persons)

> **FUCINE DI OSSANA** TRENTO

Cevedale ☎ 0463 751630 ▤ 0463 751630
A well equipped site in a peaceful location at an altitude of 900mtrs, close to the local ski resorts.
➲ *4km W of Savona.*
All year 3HEC ▥ ⊿ ⋒ ⅀ ♟ ♥ ✕ ⊙ ⊠ ⌀ ⏢ ⃗ R 🔒 ⊞ ⊿ lau ➡ ✕

GERMIGNAGA VARESE

Il Boschetto via Mameli ☎ 0332 534740 ▥ 500791
e-mail: boshol@tin.it
In a pleasant location beside Lake Maggiore with a good
variety of facilities and opportunities for water sports.
Apr-Sep 1HEC ▥ ♦ ♠ 𝕃 ♀ ✕ ☉ ▣ ∅ ⊞ ⁀ LPR ⌕ lau ♦ ✕
⏚ ⊞ Prices: ⚹5-6.50 ⇔2.50-3.50 ⇔8-9 ▲4.50-5

IDRO BRESCIA

AZUR Idro Rio Vantone
☎ 0365 83125 ▥ 0365 823663
e-mail: info@azur-freizeit.de
The site lies at the mouth of the river of same name beside
Lake Idro. Subdivided into pitches (separate pitches for
youths) on grass and woodland at the foot of strange rock
formations.
➲ Approach from Idro direction of Vantone, well signed from
there.
15 Mar-15 Nov 4.5HEC ▥ ♠ ♠ 𝕃 ♀ ✕ ☉ ▣ ∅ ⏚ ⊞ ⁀ LP
⌕ ⊞ lau

Vantone Pineta via Capovalle 11 ☎ 0365 823385
On eastern shore of lake. Grassland enclosed by rush and
willow fencing. Part of site in a small wood on the bank of a
stream.
➲ Approach from Idro and follow signs for Camping Idro Rio
Vantone.
Apr-Sep 2HEC ▥ ♦ ♠ 𝕃 ♀ ✕ ☉ ▣ ⊞ ⁀ LP ⌕ lau
♦ ∅ ⏚ ⊞

ISEO BRESCIA

Iseo via Antonioli 57 ☎ 030 980213 ▥ 030 980213
e-mail: campeggioiseo@intelligenza.it
In a picturesque location directly on the lake shore with well
shaded pitches and modern installations.
➲ Access via A4 Brescia-Bergamo.
Apr-Oct 0.7HEC ▥ ♠ ♠ 𝕃 ♀ ✕ ☉ ▣ ∅ ⏚ ⊞ ⁀ L ⌕ lau
♦ ✕ ⁀P ⊞

Punta d'Oro via Antonioli 51/53
☎ 030 980084 ▥ 98008/4
e-mail: punta@franciacorta.it
A well set out campsite with roads and paths reaching every
pitch.
➲ From A4 exit at Rovato and follow signs Iseo.
Apr-Oct 0.6HEC ▥ ♦ ♠ 𝕃 ♀ ✕ ☉ ▣ ⁀ L ⌕ lau ♦ ✕ ∅
⏚ ⁀P ⊞

Quai via Antonioli 73 ☎ 030 981161
Shady site close to the edge of Lake D'Iseo.
➲ W of town. Signposted.
16 Apr-26 Sept 1.3HEC ▥ ♠ ♀ ✕ ☉ ▣ ⊞ ⁀ L ⌕ ▣ ⊗
lau ♦ 𝕃 ✕ ∅ ⁀P ⊞

Sassabanek via Colombera 2 ☎ 030 980300
In a pleasant wooded location on the shore of Lake Iseo with
good recreational facilities.
Apr-Oct 3.5HEC ▥ ♦ ♠ 𝕃 ♀ ✕ ☉ ▣ ∅ ⊞ ⁀ LP ▣ ⊞ ⊗
lau ♦ ⏚

KALTERN BOLZANO

St Josef am Kalterer See Welnstr 75 ☎ 0471 960170
e-mail: camping.st.josef@duet.it
On level ground surrounded by trees close to the lake.
➲ Signposted from the Kalten-Tramin road.
15 Mar-10 Nov 1.4HEC ▥ ∺ ♠ ♠ 𝕃 ♀ ✕ ☉ ▣ ∅ ⁀ L ⌕
⊞ lau

***CAMPING STEINER
I-39055 Laives/Bolzano
Tel. 0039/0471950105 • Fax 0039/0471951572
E-mail: steiner@dnet.it • www.campingsteiner.com
Well-maintained, family-friendly campsite with good facilities.
Located in the South Tyrol on the outskirts of Laives 8km
from Bolzano (towards Trento). Enter by Steiner Hotel. Money
change, safe-deposit boxes, table tennis, lending library,
mini-market, pizza restaurant, cosy wine cellar on site.
Country-style wooden bungalows. Inn (50 rooms),
restaurant and large covered terrace. **Open 23.03 - 3.11**
SouthTyrol - Dolomites - Italy ♿

LAIVES-LEIFERS BOLZANO

Steiner Kennedystr 34 ☎ 0471 950105 ▥ 0471 951572
e-mail: steimer@olnet.it
The site lies behind the Gasthof Steiner, the AGIP petrol
station and a bungalow estate.
➲ Off the SS12 on the northern outskirts of the village.
Apr-5 Nov 2.5HEC ▥ ♦ ♦ ♠ 𝕃 ♀ ✕ ☉ ▣ ∅ ⏚ ⊞ ⁀ P ⌕ ⊞
⊗ lau

LATSCH BOLZANO

Latsch an der Etsch Reichstr 4
☎ 0473 623217 ▥ 0473 622333
e-mail: camping.latsch@dnet.it
A terraced site beside the river.
➲ Campsite is signposted on SS38.
8Nov-20Dec 1.6HEC ▥ ♦ ♠ 𝕃 ♀ ✕ ☉ ▣ ∅ ⊞ ⁀ PR ⌕ ⊞
lau Prices: ⚹4.70-5.20 ▲9.30-10.40 pitch 11.40-12.50

LECCO COMO

Rivabella via Alla Spiaggia 35 ☎ 0341 421143
On a private, guarded beach on the shore of Lake Como.
➲ 3km S towards Bergamo.
May-Sep 2HEC ▥ ♦ ♠ 𝕃 ♀ ✕ ☉ ▣ ∅ ⁀ L ⌕ ⊞ lau ♦ ✕

LEVICO TERME TRENTO

Due Laghi Loc Costa 3 ☎ 0461 512707
Aimed mainly at families this site offers 400 large flat grass
pitches.
➲ From Trento follow signs for Pergine and Lake Caldonazza.
25 May-15 Sep 12HEC ▥ ♦ ♠ 𝕃 ✕ ☉ ▣ ∅ ⏚ ⁀ L ⌕ ⊞
lau

Jolly Loc Pleina ☎ 0461 706934 & 234351 ▥ 707735
The site is divided into plots and lies 200 metres from the
lake with three inside swimming pools.
15 May-15 Sep 2HEC ▥ ♠ ♠ 𝕃 ♀ ✕ ☉ ▣ ∅ ⏚ ⊞ ⁀ P ⌕
⊞ lau ♦ ✕ ⁀LR

Levico ☎ 0461 706491 ▥ 7077635
e-mail: mail@campinglevico.com
Site is beside a lake with a private beach.
➲ Signposted from the Levico/Caldonazzo exit on SS47.
Apr-10 Oct 4HEC ▥ ♦ ♠ 𝕃 ♀ ☉ ▣ ∅ ⏚ ⁀ LR ⌕ ⊞ lau ♦
✕ ⁀P Prices: ⚹5-7 pitch 8.50-14

LILLAZ AOSTA

Salasses ☎ 0165 74252
Pleasant site surrounded by mountains, grassland and
conifers. The site lies at the end of the Val di Cogne.
➲ Entrance to site before Camping al Sole.
All year 1HEC ▥ ∺ ♠ ♠ ✕ ☉ ▣ ⊞ ⁀ R ⌕ ▣ ♦ 𝕃 ✕ ∅
⏚ ⊞

LIMONE PIEMONTE CUNEO

Luis Matlas ☎ 0171 927565
This tidy site offers winter facilities and skiing lessons are provided by the owner. Fishing is also available.
⮑ *It lies to the north of the town, off the Limone-Nice road.*
Closed 1-15 Sep 1.5HEC ⊞ ⌖ ※ ⋔ ♈ ✗ ⊙ ⊕ ∅ ⛺ ↻ R ☒
⊞ lau ➧ ⛺ ✗

LIMONE SUL GARDA BRESCIA

Nanzel via 4 Novembre 3
☎ 0365 954155 ▯ 0365 954468
Well managed site, with low terraces in olive grove.
⮑ *Access from Km101.2 (Hotel Giorgiol).*
Apr-15 Oct 0.7HEC ⊞ ⌖ ⋔ ⛟ ♈ ✗ ⊙ ⊕ ∅ ⛺ ↻ L ☒ lau ➧
✗ ⛺ ⊞ Prices: ⚑4.65-5.62 ⛟2.84-3.36 ⛽5.68-6.20 ⚑5.68-6.20

MACCAGNO VARESE

AZUR-Lago Maggiore ☎ 0332 560203 ▯ 0332 561263
A popular site on the shore of the lake.
⮑ *In village turn off SS394 at Km43/III towards lake and after 500 m turn right.*
15 Mar-15 Nov 1.5HEC ⊞ ⌖ ⋔ ⛟ ✗ ⊙ ⊕ ∅ ⛺ ↻ L ☒ ⊞ lau ➧ ✗

Brancheito via Pietraperzia 13 ☎ 045 6784029
All year 1.6HEC ⊞ ⌖ ※ ⋔ ♈ ⛟ ✗ ⊙ ⊕ ∅ ⛺ ⊞ lau ➧
✗ Prices: ⚑5-6.50 ⛟2.50-63.50 ⛽8-9 ⚑4.50-5

Lido via 6 Pietraperzia ☎ 0332 560250 ▯ 0332 560250
e-mail: boshol@tin.it
Lakeside site with good facilities, 200mtrs from the river.
Apr-Sep 0.8HEC ⊞ ⌖ ⋔ ⛟ ♈ ✗ ⊙ ⊕ ↻ LR ☒ ⊘ lau ➧
⛟ ✗ ∅ ⛺ ↻R ⊞ Prices: ⚑5-6.50 ⛟2.50-3.50 ⛽8-9
⚑4.50-5

MAGGIORE (LAGO)

See **Arona, Baveno, Cannobio, Fondotoce, Maccagno**

MANERBA DEL GARDA BRESCIA

Belvedere via Cavalle 5 ☎ 0365 551175
Terraced site by Lake Garda.
⮑ *Signposted from SS572.*
Etr-13 Oct 2.1HEC ⊞ ⋯ ⌖ ⋔ ⛟ ✗ ⊙ ⊕ ⛺ ↻ L ☒
➧ ⛟ ✗ ⊞

Rio Ferienglück via del Rio 37
☎ 0365 551075 ▯ 0365 551044
⮑ *Follow SS572 Desenzano-Salo road, turn off between Km8 and 9, site 4km N.*
Apr-Sep 5HEC ⊞ ⌖ ⋔ ⛟ ✗ ⊙ ⊕ ∅ ⛺ ⛺ ⛽
↻ LPR ☒ ⊞ lau

Rocca via Cavalle 22 ☎ 0365 551738 ▯ 0365 552045
e-mail: larocca@mtcomputer.it
In a picturesque location with fine views over the Gulf of Manerba.
Apr-Sep 5HEC ⊞ ⌖ ⋔ ⛟ ✗ ⊙ ⊕ ⛺ ↻ LP ☒ ⊞ lau
➧ ✗

Zocco via del Zocco 43
☎ 0365 551605 ▯ 0365 552053
e-mail: info@campingzocco.it
The site consists of several, terraced sections. The section below the maintenance/supply building lies on a sloping olive grove and is somewhat obstructed by bungalows.
⮑ *500m S of Gardonicino di Manerba.*
7 Apr-23 Sep 5HEC ⊞ ⌖ ⋔ ⛟ ✗ ⊙ ⊕ ∅ ⛺ ⛺ ⚑
↻ L ☒ ⊞ lau

MARONE BRESCIA

Riva di San Pietro via Cristini 9 ☎ 030 9827129
A good modern site on the eastern side of Lake Iseo. Plenty of recreational facilities.
⮑ *From Milano-Venezia road exit at Rovato or Palazzolo towards Iseo. Marone 10km N.*
May-Sep 2HEC ⊞ ➧ ⋔ ⛟ ✗ ⊙ ⊕ ∅ ⛺ ↻ LP ☒ lau ➧ ⛺ ⏚

MOLINA DI LEDRO TRENTO

International Camping Al Sole via Maffei
☎ 0464 508496 ▯ 0464-508436
e-mail: info@campingalsole.it
A family site with good, modern facilities situated on the shore of Lake Ledro at an altitude of 655mtrs.
⮑ *W of Molina beside the lake.*
May-Sep 3HEC ⊞ ⌖ ⋔ ⛟ ♈ ✗ ⊙ ⊕ ↻ LP ☒ ⊞ lau ➧ ⚑
Prices: ⚑4.13-5.68 pitch 5.68-7.23

MOLVENO TRENTO

Spiaggia-Lago di Molveno via Lungolago 27
☎ 0461 586978 ▯ 0461 586330
e-mail: camping@molveno.it
In a picturesque setting on the lake shore, at the foot of the Brenta Dolomites.
⮑ *Signposted from SS421.*
All year 4HEC ⊞ ➧ ⋔ ⛟ ♈ ✗ ⊙ ⊕ ∅ ⛺ ↻ LP ☒ ⊞ lau ➧ ⊞
Prices: ⚑4.13-7.23 pitch 5.16-10.33

MONIGA DEL GARDA BRESCIA

Fontanelle via Magone 13 ☎ 0365 502079 ▯ 503324
e-mail: fontanelle@fornella.it
Peaceful site on the shores of Lake Garda shaded by olive trees. All staff speak English.
1 May-22 Sep 45HEC ⊞ ⌖ ⋔ ⛟ ♈ ✗ ⊙ ⊕ ∅ ⛺ ↻ LP ☒ ⊞
lau ➧ ⏚

San Michele via San Michele 8
☎ 0365 502026 ▯ 0365 503443
e-mail: gloriater@tiscalinet.it
A family site with good facilities and direct access to the lake via a private beach.
⮑ *Exit A4 at Desenzano. Site is 8km from Desenzano in direction of Salo.*
Apr-Sep 3HEC ⊞ ➧ ⋔ ⛟ ♈ ✗ ⊙ ⊕ ↻ LP ☒ ⊞ lau ➧ ∅ ⏚

NATURNO-NATURNS BOLZANO

Wald Dornsbergweg 8 ☎ 0473 667298 ▯ 668072
e-mail: info@waldcamping.com
The site lies on gently rising ground, in a forest of pine and deciduous trees.
⮑ *For access, turn off the SS38 near the Gasthof Alderwirt in the village, and drive 0.8km S over the railway line.*
15 Mar-5 Nov 2.3HEC ⊞ ⌖ ⋔ ⛟ ♈ ⊙ ⊕ ⛺ ↻ P ☒ ⊞ lau ➧
⛟ ✗ ∅ ↻R

NOVATE MEZZOLA SONDRIO

El Ranchero via Nazionale 3 ☎ 0343 44169 ▯ 44169
Located on the edge of the Mezzola lake in front of a spectacular view of the mountains.
Apr-Sep 1HEC ⊞ ⌖ ⋔ ♈ ✗ ⊙ ⊕ ⛺ ⛽ ↻ L ☒ ⊘ lau ➧
⛟ ✗ ∅ ⏚ ↻PR ⊞ Prices: ⚑5 ⛟4 ⛽5-10 ⚑5-10

ORTA SAN GIULIO NOVARA

Cusio Lago d'Orta ☎ 0322 90290
In a picturesque alpine valley, surrounded by woodland on the bank of Lake Orta. Good facilities.
⮑ *S of Omegna towards Borgomanero.*
Apr-Nov 2HEC ⊞ ➧ ⋔ ♈ ✗ ⊙ ⊕ ⛺ ↻ P lau ➧ ⛟ ↻L ⊞

246

PADENGHE BRESCIA

Cá via S.Cassiano 12
☎ 030 9907006 ▤ 030 9907693
e-mail: la_ca@ciauweb.it
The site lies in a park-like setting on terraced ground.
➲ *For access, turn off the road along Lake Garda, 1.5km N*
turn for Padenghe, and drive down a very steep road towards
the lake.
Mar-Oct 2HEC ⚏ ♠ ſ ⅀ Ⅰ ✕ ⊙ ◗ ∅ ☎ ♥ ⅂ L 🏠 lau

Campagnola via Marconi 99
☎ 030 9907523 ▤ 030 9908581
In a beautiful position on the shores of Lake Garda with
good, modern facilities.
➲ *4km from Desenzano on the road to Salo.*
May-Sep 5HEC ⚏ ♠ ſ ⅀ Ⅰ ✕ ⊙ ◗ ∅ ∅ ⅂ LP 🏠 🏠 ✕ lau

Villa Garuti via del Porto 5 ☎ 030 9907134 ▤ 030 9907817
A camp site holiday village situated in the garden of the old
Villa Garuti, directly on the lakeside with its own beach.
➲ *A4 from Brescia in direction of Verona, exit for Desenzano*
and follow SS572 to Padenghe.
Mar-Oct 1.5HEC ⚏ ♠ ſ ꙮ Ⅰ ✕ ⊙ ◗ ∅ ☎ ♥
⅂ LP 🏠 🏠 lau ♥ ⅃

PEIO TRENTO

Val di Sole Loc Dossi di Cavia
☎ 0463 753177 ▤ 753176
e-mail: valdisole@camping.it
The site lies on terraced slopes at the foot of the Ortier
mountain range.
➲ *400m off SP87.*
May & Nov 2.3HEC ⚏ ◖ ſ ⅀ Ⅰ ✕ ⊙ ◗ ∅ ᙀ 🏠 lau ♥
✕ ⅂P **Prices:** ♠7 pitch 7

PERA DI FASSA TRENTO

Soal via Dolomiti 32 ☎ 0462 764519 ▤ 764609
e-mail: info@campingsoal.com
Breath-taking location among the Dolomites, ideal for skiing
and walking.
All year 30HEC ⚏ ◖ ſ ⅀ Ⅰ ✕ ⊙ ◗ ∅ ᙀ ⅂ R 🏠 🏠 lau
Prices: ♠5.68-7.75 pitch 6.71-8.26

PÉRGINE TRENTO

Punta Indiani Lago di Caldonazzo
☎ 0461 548062 ▤ 0461 548607
e-mail: info@campingpuntaindiani.it
On level ground surrounded by trees with direct access to
400mtrs of private beach on the banks of the lake.
➲ *From the A22 exit at Trento follow signs for Pergine, S.*
Cristoforo and Caldonazzo.
May-Sep 1.5HEC ⚏ ◖ ſ ꙮ ◗ ⅂ L 🏠 ✕ lau ♥ ⅃ Ⅰ ✕ ∅ ᙀ
🏠 **Prices:** ♠6 pitch 6.50-11.50

San Cristoforo via dei Pescatori
☎ 0461 512707 ▤ 0461 707381
A family-run site in a prime position on the sunniest side of
lake. Owned and run by family Oss with regular guests
helping as staff.
➲ *Follow road 47 from Trento towards Venice for 14km. Site is*
in centre of S. Cristoforo village.
25 May-15 Sept 2.5HEC ⚏ ◖ ſ ⅀ Ⅰ ✕ ⊙ ◗ ∅ ᙀ
⅂ LP 🏠 🏠 lau

PETTENASCO NOVARA

Punta di Crabbia via Crabbia 2/A ☎ 0323 89117
A well equipped site in a pleasant situation providing
panoramic views over the surrounding area.
Apr-Sep 2HEC ⚏ ◖ ſ ꙮ Ⅰ ✕ ⊙ ◗ ⅂ L 🏠 🏠 lau ♥ ⅂L

PIEVE DI MANERBA BRESCIA

Faro via Repubblica 52 ☎ 0365 651704 ▤ 0365 552437
Situated in a peaceful rural area close to the sea.
➲ *Leave A4 at Desenzano and take N572 to Manerba del*
Garda.
15 Apr-15 Sep 1HEC ⚏ ♠ ſ ⊙ ◗ ♥ ⅂ P 🏠 ♥ ⅃ Ⅰ ✕ ∅ ᙀ
⅂L 🏠

PISOGNE BRESCIA

Eden via Piangrande 3 ☎ 0364 880500
The site lies on eastern lake shore with tall trees and a level
beach.
➲ *Turn off SS510 at Km37/VII, over railway line and towards*
lake.
2 Apr-28 Sep 2.5HEC ⚏ ♠ ſ ⅃ Ⅰ ⊙ ◗ ⅂ L 🏠 🏠 lau ♥ ✕
∅ ᙀ ⅂P 🏠

PONTE TRESA VARESE

Trelago via Trelago 20 ☎ 0332 716583 ▤ 0332 719650
Lakeside campsite with grassy pitches shaded by tall trees.
➲ *Follow signs from Milan to Varese and Ghirla. Site is 15km*
from Varese.
Apr-12 Sep 3.3HEC ⚏ ◖ ♠ ſ ꙮ Ⅰ ✕ ⊙ ◗ ∅ ᙀ ☎ ♥ ⅂ LP
🏠 🏠 lau ♥ ✕

PORLEZZA COMO

Paradiso Via Calbiga,30 ☎ 01243220132
The site lies in meadowland on the north eastern lake shore.
➲ *S from SS340.*
15 Mar-15 Nov 5HEC ⚏ ◖ ſ ꙮ Ⅰ ✕ ⊙ ◗ ☎ ⅂ LP 🏠 ♥ ✕

POZZA DI FASSA TRENTO

Rosengarten via Avisio 15, Loc Puccia
☎ 0462 763305 ▤ 0462 763501
In the heart of the Dolomites this well-tended site is an ideal
base for a skiing or walking holiday.
➲ *Signposted from SS48.*
Closed May & Oct 3.5HEC ⚏ ◖ ſ Ⅰ ✕ ⊙ ◗ ∅ ᙀ ☎ ♥
R 🏠 🏠 lau ♥ ⅃ ✕

Vidor via Valle S Nicolo ☎ 0462 763247 ▤ 0462 764780
e-mail: info@campingvidor.it
This traditional family run site is set in a pine forest. Ideal for
skiers, nature lovers and families all year round.
➲ *Signposted from SS48.*
All year 2.5HEC ⚏ ⿻ ſ ⅀ Ⅰ ✕ ⊙ ◗ ∅ ☎ 🏠 🏠 lau ♥
✕ ⅂R **Prices:** ♠5.16-6.71 pitch 6.71-7.75

PRATO ALLO STÉLVIO BOLZANO

Sägomühle via delle Spine ☎ 0473 616078 ▤ 0473 616079
Closed 10 Nov-10 Dec 1.2HEC ⚏ ◖ ſ ⅀ Ⅰ ✕ ⊙ ◗ ᙀ ☎
☎ ⅂ P 🏠 lau ♥ ∅ ⅂LR

RASUN BOLZANO

Corones ☎ 0474 496490 ▤ 0474 498250
e-mail: info@corones.com
A modern site in an ideal mountain location with good
sporting facilities.
➲ *Exit Milan/Brenner motorway at Val Pusteria. Through*
Brunico and Valdaora to Rasun.
All year 2.7HEC ⚏ ◖ ⿻ ſ ⅀ Ⅰ ✕ ⊙ ◗ ∅ ᙀ ☎ ⅂ P 🏠 🏠
lau

RIVA DEL GARDA TRENTO

Bavaria viale Rovereto 100 ☎ 0464 552524 ▤ 0464 559126
e-mail: campingbavaria@yahoo.it
➲ *On SS240 towards Rovereto.*
Apr-Oct 6HEC ⚏ ⁙ ◖ ſ Ⅰ ✕ ⊙ ◗ ⅂ L 🏠 🏠 ♥ ⅃ ∅ ᙀ

Monte Brione via Brione 32 ☎ 0464 520885 ▤ 520890
e-mail: campingbrione@rivadelgarda.com
This site is at the foot of a hill covered with olive trees with good sports facilities.
➲ *250mtrs from San Nicolo' tourist centre.*
Etr-early Oct 3.3HEC ⛺ ♠ ⋔ ⚑ ⚏ ✕ ⊙ ⚑ ⁂ P 🏠 lau
♦ ✕ ⋤L

▶ RIVOLTELLA BRESCIA

San Francesco strada Vicinale San Francesco ☎ 030 9110245 ▤ 030 9119464
e-mail: info@campingsanfrancesco.it
This well-kept site is divided into many sections by drives, vineyards and orchards and has a private gravel beach.
➲ *At Km268 on SSN11.*
Apr-Sep 10.4HEC ⛺ ♠ ⋔ ⚑ ⚏ ✕ ⊙ ⚑ ⊘ ᛙ ⛺ ⋤ LP 🏠 ⊞ lau

▶ SALLE, LA AOSTA

Green Park via dei Romani 4 ☎ 0165 861300
Partly terraced site in a shaded location with good, modern facilities.
➲ *Access via SS26.*
All year 7HEC ⛺ ⊘ ♠ ⋔ ⚑ ⚏ ✕ ⊙ ⚑ ᛙ ⋤ P ▣ lau
♦ ⚑ ⊘ ⋤R ⊞

▶ SAN ANTONIO DI MAVIGNOLA TRENTO

Faé ☎ 0465 507178 ▤ 507178
e-mail: campingfae@campiglio.it
Situated in famous winter skiing region of Madonna di Campiglio. Good base for climbing in Brenta mountain range. On four gravel terraces, and alpine meadow in hollow next to SS239.
Camping Card Compulsory.
15 Jun-Sep & Dec-Apr 2.1HEC ⛺ ⚐ ⋔ ⚏ ✕ ⊙ ⚑ ⊘ ᛙ 🏠 lau ♦ ⚑ ✕

▶ SAN FELICE DEL BENACO BRESCIA

Europa-Silvella via Silvella ☎ 0365 651095 ▤ 0365 654395
One site separated in two parts by the joint approach road. The beach is situated about 80m below.
➲ *Signposted.*
19 Apr-30 Sep 7.4HEC ⛺ ♠ ⋔ ⚑ ⚏ ✕ ⊙ ⚑ ⊘ ⛺ ⚑ ⋤ LP 🏠 ⊞ lau

Fornella via Fornella 1 ☎ 0365 62294 ▤ 0365 559418
e-mail: fornella@fornella.it
A quiet site in an ideal location on the shore of Lake Garda.
➲ *Signposted from SS572 (Salo-Desenzano).*
05 May-22 Sep 7.5HEC ⛺ ⚐ ⋔ ⚑ ⚏ ✕ ⊙ ⚑ ⊘ ⛺ ⚑ ▲ ⋤ LP ▣ ⊞ lau Prices: ⋔4.14-6.72 pitch 8.78-12.40

Gardiola via Gardiola 36 ☎ 0365 559240 ▤ 0365 520690
e-mail: info@lagardiola.com
A terraced site with a wide variety of good facilities on the shore of Lake Garda.
➲ *S of San Felice del Benaco off SS572.*
Apr-Sep 0.4HEC ⛺ ⚐ ⋔ ⚏ ✕ ⊙ ⚑ ⚑ ⋤ L 🏠 lau ♦ ⚑ ✕ ⊘ ᛙ ⋤P

Ideal Molino ☎ 0365 62023 ▤ 0365 559395
e-mail: info@campingmolino.it
Situated right beside Lake Garda amid beautiful scenery. Charming and quiet site 1km from S. Felice. On the beach there is a pier and boat moorings. Pedal boats can be hired for lake trips.
20 Mar-26 Sept 1.7HEC ⛺ ♠ ⋔ ⚑ ⚏ ✕ ⊙ ⚑ ⛺ ⚑ ⋤ L 🏠 ⊞ ⚐ lau ♦ ⊘ ᛙ

... so unique!!

camping ▦ villaggio Via Vallone della Selva. 2
SAN FELICE D/B. (BS)
ITALIA
WEEKEND Tel. 0365 - 43712
Fax 0365 - 42196

Quiet family site, well maintained. Modern toilet facilities. Free hot water in the showers and basins.
Washing machine, bar restaurant, pizzeria, small shop. Very scenic. 2 swimming pools, children's playing area, volleyball, table tennis, music and dancing in the evenings. Send for our brochure. Reservations accepted!
Caravan, tent and bungalow for hire.
http://www.weekend.it • e-mail: cweekend@tin.it

Weekend via Vallone della Selva 2
☎ 0365 43712 ▤ 0365 42196
e-mail: cweekend@tin.it
A quiet family site with modern facilities, situated in a olive grove overlooking Lake Garda.
➲ *Exit A4 at Desenzano following road to Cisano. Signposted S.Felice D/B.*
25 Apr-22 Sept 9HEC ⛺ ⚐ ⋔ ⚑ ⚏ ✕ ⊙ ⚑ ⛺ ⚑ ⚑ ▲ ⋤ P 🏠
⊞ lau ♦ ⊘ ᛙ ⋤L Prices: ⋔4.90-7.05 ⚑10.05-14.10 ▲10.05-14.10

▶ SAN LORENZEN BOLZANO

Wildberg ☎ 0474 474080
All year 1.2HEC ⛺ ⚆ ⋔ ⚏ ⊙ ⚑ ⊘ ᛙ ⛺ ⋤ PR 🏠 ⊞ lau
♦ ⚑ ✕

▶ SAN MARTINO DI CASTROZZA TRENTO

Sass Maor via Laghetto 46 ☎ 0439 68347
A winter sports site in a beautiful mountain setting.
➲ *From Trento travel to Ora, Cavalese and S.Martino di Castrozza.*
All year 0.2HEC ⁞⁞⁞ ⚆ ⋔ ⚑ ⚏ ✕ ⊙ ⚑ ⊘ ᛙ ▣ lau
♦ ⋤LPR ⊞

▶ SAN PIETRO DI CORTENO GOLGI BRESCIA

Villaggio Aprica via Nazionale 507 ☎ 0342 710001 ▤ 710001
e-mail: apricamp@apricaonline.com
A small natural park ideal for winter skiing and summer walking.
➲ *On SS39 (Aprica-Edolo).*
All year 2.4HEC ⛺ ⚐ ⋔ ⚑ ⚏ ✕ ⊙ ⚑ ⊘ ᛙ ⛺ ⚑ ⋤ R 🏠 lau
♦ ⋤LP ⊞

▶ SAN VIGILIO DI MAREBBE BOLZANO

Al Plan ☎ 0474 501694 ▤ 506550
e-mail: camping.alplan@rolmail.net
In a wooded Alpine setting at an altitude of 1200mtrs.
➲ *Access via A22 - Brenner Autostrada.*
Jun-Oct/Dec-Apr Nov & May 1HEC ⛺ ⁞⁞⁞ ⚐ ⋔ ⚑ ⚏ ✕ ⊙ ⚑ ⊘ ⛺ 🏠 lau ♦ ⋤PR ⊞ Prices: ⋔4.50-6.50 ⚑9.50-11.50 ▲4.50-6.50

▶ SARRE AOSTA

International Touring ☎ 0165 257061 ▤ 0165 363907
Flat, wooded site set among the highest mountains in Europe.
➲ *4km W of Aosta on SS26.*
15 May-15 Sep 6HEC ⛺ ♠ ⋔ ⚑ ⚏ ✕ ⊙ ⚑ ⊘ ᛙ ⛺ ⚑
⋤ PR 🏠 ⊞ lau

Monte Bianco Fraz St Maurice 3 ☎ 0165 257523
In wooded surroundings close to the town centre.
➲ *Access via SS26 towards Aosta and Courmayer.*
Apr-Sep 7.5HEC ⊞ ♠ ⋒ ⊙ ⦿ ⅃ R ② ⊞ lau ➡ ⒓ ▼ ✕ ⌀ ᴍ

SEXTEN BOLZANO

Sexten St-Josefstr 54 ☎ 0474 710444 ▤ 710053
e-mail: info@caravanparksexten.it
Closed Nov & Apr 3HEC ⊞ ⌀ ⒢ ⒭ ⒓ ▼ ✕ ⊙ ⦿ ⌀ ᴍ ⅃ PR ② lau

SORICO COMO

Au Lac De Como via C-Battisti 18
☎ 0344 84035 ▤ 0344 84802
The well-kept site lies on the right of the River Mera as it
flows into Lake Como.
➲ *Turn off the SS340d at Km25 near TOTAL petrol station
and drive 200m towards the lake.*
All year 17HEC ⊞ ♠ ⒭ ⒓ ▼ ✕ ⊙ ⦿ ⌀ ᴍ ⬜ ⬛
⅃ LR ⊞ lau

TORBOLE TRENTO

Porto ☎ 0464 505891
e-mail: alporto@torbole.com
A new site with modern facilities, situated in a quiet position
near the lake. Ideal for sports and families.
➲ *At Torbole join SS240 from there it is signposted.*
21Mar-3Nov 1.1HEC ⊞ ♠ ⒭ ▼ ⊙ ⦿ ② lau ➡ ⒓ ✕ ⌀ ⅃LR
Prices: ⚑5.50-6 pitch 7-8.50

TORRE DANIELE TORINO

Mombarone via Nazionale 54 ☎ 0125 757907 ▤ 757396
➲ *13km N of Ivrea on SS26. Very close to River.*
All year 1.2HEC ⊞ ⒢ ⒭ ▼ ✕ ⊙ ⦿ ⬜ ⬛ ⅃ PR ② lau
➡ ⒓ ✕ ⌀ ⊞

TOSCOLANO MADERNO BRESCIA

Chiaro di Luna via Statale 218 ☎ 0365 641179
Apr-Sep 9HEC ⊞ ♠ ⒭ ⒓ ▼ ✕ ⊙ ⦿ ⌀ ᴍ ⬛ ⅃ L 🄿 lau ➡ ✕

VALNONTEY AOSTA

Lo Stambecco ☎ 0165 74152
25 May-20 Sep 1.6HEC ⊞ ⒢ ⒭ ▼ ⊙ ⦿ ⌀ ᴍ ② lau
➡ ⒓ ✕ ⊞

VIPITENO BOLZANO

Sadobre Autoporto ☎ 0472 721793
In a wooded, mountain setting.
➲ *Access via A22.*
All year 1HEC ⌀ ⒢ ⒭ ⒓ ✕ ⊙ ⦿ ②➡ ⅃R ⊞

VIVERONE VERCELLI

Rocca via Lungo Lago 35 ☎ 0161 987479
Apr-Sep 1HEC ⊞ ♠ ⒭ ▼ ✕ ⊙ ⦿ ⬛ ⅃ P ② lau
➡ ⌀ ᴍ ⅃L

VOLS BOLZANO

Seiseralm St Konstantin 16 ☎ 0471 706459
The site is avaliable all year round for skiers and climbers.
Horse riding/trekking is a major activity.
➲ *From Bolzano motorway site is signposted from Fie.*
All year 2.5HEC ⊞ ⌀ ⒢ ⒭ ⒓ ▼ ✕ ⊙ ⦿ ⌀ ᴍ ⬛ ② lau ➡ ⅃L

> A guide to the Symbols &
> Abbreviations used in this book
> can be found on page 5

⬤ ⬤ ⬤ ⬤ VENICE/NORTH ⬤ ⬤ ⬤ ⬤

Venice dominates this region. It is an ancient centre of arts
and trade and is unique in having waterways as roads and
many architectural splendours, as well as producing fine
glass and lace and, due to the revival of the carnival, masks.
Venetian influence is apparent in towns like Udine with its
Piazza della Libertà surrounded by Renaissance buildings or
at Treviso, with its own canal system, and where concerts
and theatre performances are held in the main square.
Echoes of Rome can be found in Palladio's architecture in
Vicenza or in Verona where the amphitheatre is the setting
for the July-September opera season.
Art lovers can enjoy Giotto's frescoes and Donatello's
sculptures in the university town of Padua, and at Rovigo
are paintings by Bellini and Tiepolo.
Trieste is the major port and contains handsome 19th-
century architecture and there are attractive villages like
Bellini on the southern edge of the Dolomites built
overlooking two rivers. Vineyards and wineries (Soave and
Valpolicella) welcome tourists.
....

ARSIE BELLUNO

Gajole Loc Soravigo ☎ 0439 58505 ▤ 58505
In a delightful, peaceful setting on the shore of Lake Corlo.
➲ *Access from SS50 bis.*
Apr-Sep 1.5HEC ⊞ ♠ ⒭ ⒓ ▼ ✕ ⊙ ⦿ ⌀ ⅃ L ② lau

ASIAGO VICENZA

Ekar Loc.Ta' Ekar ☎ 0424 455157
e-mail: campingasiago@keycomm.itg-ekar
On a level meadow in a striking setting among wooded hills
in a popular ski-ing region.
20 May-8 Sep & 15 Nov-15 Apr 3.5HEC ⊞ ♠ ⒭ ⒓ ✕ ⊙ ⦿
⌀ ᴍ ② ⊞ lau

AURISINA TRIESTE

Imperial Aurisina Cave 55 ☎ 040 200459 ▤ 040 200459
e-mail: campimperial@libero.it
A well maintained site in a secluded, wooded location.
➲ *Access via SS14 in Sistiana-Aurisina direction.*
10Apr-15 Sep 1.5HEC ⊞ ♠ ⒭ ⒓ ⊙ ⦿ ⌀ ⅃ P ② ⊞ ➡ ✕
Prices: ⚑3.50-5.15 ⇔3.50-4.75 ⬛3.50-4.75 ⚑3.50-4.75

BARDOLINO VERONA

Continental Localita Reboin ☎ 045 7210192 ▤ 045 7211756
e-mail: continental@campingarda.it
A pleasant site directly on the lake with good, modern
facilities.
Apr-Sep 3.5HEC ⊞ ♠ ⒭ ⒓ ▼ ✕ ⊙ ⦿ ⌀ ⬛ ⅃ L ② ⊞ lau

Rocca S Pietro ☎ 045 7211111 ▤ 045 7211300
Subdivided site in slightly sloping grassland broken up by
rows of trees. Separated from the lake by a public path (no
cars). Part of site on the other side of the main road is
terraced amongst vines and olives with lovely view of lake.
➲ *Below the SS249 at Km40/lV*
7 Apr-Sep 80HEC ⊞ ♠ ⒭ ⒓ ✕ ⊙ ⦿ ⬛ ⅃ LP ② ⊞ lau
➡ ⌀

BIBIONE VENEZIA

Villagio Turistico Internazionale via Colonie 2
☎ 0431 442611 ▤ 0431 43231
e-mail: info@vti.it
Mostly sandy terrain under pine trees. Some meadowland
with a few deciduous trees. Wide sandy beach. Tennis court.
➲ *Access is well signed along approach.*
12 Apr-22 Sep 13HEC ⊞ ⸫⸬ ♠ ⒭ ⒓ ▼ ✕ ⊙ ⦿ ⌀ ᴍ ⬛
⅃ PS ② ⊞ lau

> **BRENZONE** VERONA

Primavera via Benaco 5 ☎ 045 7420421 ▤ 7420421
e-mail: info@camping-primavera.com
Small site on the shore of Lake Garda.
Apr-15 Oct 0.8HEC ⬛ ♦ ⋔ ⅃ ⛱ ✕ ☉ ◲ ∅ ♨ ⌂ ⊠ ⋜ L ⊞ lau
♦ ✕ ⊞

> **CA'NOGHERA** VENEZIA

Alba d'Oro via Triestina 214/B ☎ 041 5415102 ▤ 5475971
e-mail: albadoro@tin.it
On level ground directly on the lagoon with good, modern
facilities including moorings for small boats. Regular bus
service to Venice.
➲ *Access from SS14.*
Apr-Oct 7HEC ⬛ ♦ ⋔ ⅃ ⛱ ✕ ☉ ◲ ∅ ♨ ⌂ ⊠ ▲ ⋜ PR ⊞ lau
♦ ⊞ Prices: ⋔6-7.10 ⊕3.30-4.90 ◲9.90-10.60 ▲8.50-9.50

> **CAORLE** VENEZIA

San Francesco via Selva Rosata ☎ 0421 299333 ▤ 299663
e-mail: vsfrance@alfa.it
This generously laid-out site, on level lawns with shady
poplars, lies in the midst of a holiday village.
➲ *Follow signs from Caorle for access.*
Apr-Sep 32HEC ⬛ ⠿ ♦ ⋔ ⅃ ⛱ ✕ ☉ ◲ ∅ ♨ ⌂ ⊠ ⋜ PS
⊠ ⊞ ⊞ ∅ lau

> **CASSONE** VERONA

Bellavista ☎ 045 7420244
In a fine position in an olive grove overlooking Lake Garda
with modern sanitary installations. Access to the lake is by an
underpass and good watersports facilities are available.
All year 27HEC ⬛ ♦ ⋔ ⅃ ⛱ ✕ ☉ ◲ ∅ ♨ ⌂ ⊠ ⋜ L ⊠ ⊞
∅ lau ♦ ⋜PR

> **CASTELLETTO DI BRENZONE** VERONA

Maior Loc Croce ☎ 045 7430333 ▤ 7430333
A comfortable, modern site in a pleasant, quiet location.
easter-10 Oct 8HEC ⬛ ♦ ⋔ ⅃ ⛱ ✕ ☉ ◲ ∅ ♨ ⌂ ⊠ ⊞ lau
♦ ✕ ⋜L ⊞

San Zeno via A.Vespucci 91 ☎ 045 7430231 ▤ 045 4430171
Situated only a few metres from the lake surrounded by
hundred year old olive groves.
➲ *Exit the southbound motorway from Rovereto at Trento.
The site is 10km S of Malcesine*
May-Sep 1.4HEC ⬛ ♦ ⋔ ⅃ ⛱ ✕ ☉ ◲ ∅ ♨ ⊠ ⊞ ⊞ ♦ ✕ ⋜L

> **CAVALLINO** VENEZIA

Cavallino via delle Batterie 164
☎ 041 966133 ▤ 041 5300827
e-mail: info@campingcavallion.com
In a pinewood close to the sea with plenty of recreational
facilities.
6 Apr-13 Oct 11.4HEC ⬛ ♦ ⋔ ⅃ ⛱ ✕ ☉ ◲ ∅ ⌂ ◲
⋜ PS ⊠ ⊞ ∅ lau

Europa via Fausta 332 ☎ 041 968069 ▤ 041 5370150
e-mail: info@campingeuropa.com
On grassland reaching to the sea, with some poplars.
Lunchtime siesta 13.00-15.00 hrs.
➲ *Well signposted on Punta Sabbioni road.*
Apr-Sep 11HEC ⬛ ⠿ ♦ ⋔ ⅃ ⛱ ✕ ☉ ◲ ∅ ♨ ⌂ ⊠ ⋜ S ⊠
lau ♦ ⊞

Italy via Fausta 272 ☎ 041 968090 ▤ 5370076
e-mail: info@campitaly.it
Small family-type campsite 6km from Lido di Jesolo on a
peninsula. Venice can be reached by public ferry.
➲ *Brennero/Venezia motorway. Then follow signs for Jesolo-
Cavallino.*

Est-22 Sep 3.9HEC ⬛ ♦ ⋔ ⅃ ⛱ ✕ ☉ ◲ ∅ ⌂ ◲ ⋜ PS ⊠
∅ lau ♦ ⊞

Joker via Fausta 318 ☎ 041 5370766 ▤ 041 968216
e-mail: jokercamping@iol.it
Between coastal road and the sandy beach with tall poplars.
Partially subdivided.
May-Sep 4.4HEC ⬛ ♦ ⋔ ⅃ ⛱ ✕ ☉ ◲ ∅ ♨ ⌂ ◲ ◲ ⋜ PS
⊠ ⊞ ∅ lau

Residence via F-Baracca 47 ☎ 041 968027 ▤ 5370164
e-mail: campres@doge.it
Well laid out site on level, wooded grassland, by a sandy
beach, between Jesolo and Cavallino. Lunchtime siesta 13.00-
15.00 hrs.
➲ *Signposted.*
24 Apr-23 Sep 8HEC ⠿ ♦ ⋔ ⅃ ⛱ ✕ ☉ ◲ ∅ ♨ ⌂ ◲ ⋜ PS
⊠ ⊞ ∅ lau ♦ ⋜R

Sant' Angelo via F-Baracca 63 ☎ 041 968882 ▤ 5370242
e-mail: info@santangelo.it
A large beach site decorated by trees and flower beds. Good
entertainment, sports and eating facilities.
➲ *Outside Venice follow signs for Caposile and Jesolo. Crossing
the bridge just after Lido di Jesolo turn right and follow road
round to coast.*
4 May-21 Sep 16HEC ⬛ ♦ ⋔ ⅃ ⛱ ✕ ☉ ◲ ∅ ⌂ ◲ ⋜ PS ⊠
⊞ ∅ lau Prices: ⋔3.72-7.80 ◲7.33-318.59 ▲11300-31500

Silva via F-Baracca 53 ☎ 041 968087 ▤ 968087
The site lies on sand and grassland and is located between
road and beach, divided by a vineyard. The section of site
near the beach is quiet.
15 May-15 Sep 3.3HEC ⬛ ⠿ ♦ ⋔ ⅃ ⛱ ✕ ☉ ◲ ∅ ◲ ⋜ S
⊠ lau

Union-Lido via Fausta 258 ☎ 041 968080 ▤ 041 5370355
e-mail: info@unionlido.com
This large site lies on a long stretch of land next to a 1km-
long beach. Separate section for tents and caravans.
Minimum stay during peak period is one week. Ideal for
families.
➲ *From Tarvisio follow motorway via Udine, San Dona di
Piave then is signposted to Jesolo and Cavallino.*
May-Sep 60HEC ⬛ ♦ ⋔ ⅃ ⛱ ✕ ☉ ◲ ∅ ♨ ⌂ ◲ ◲ ⋜ PS ⊠ ⊞
∅ lau Prices: ⋔5.42-7.85 pitch 9.81-20.14

Villa al Mare via del Faro 12 ☎ 041 968066 ▤ 041 5370576
e-mail: villaalmare@cavallino.net
Level site divided into plots on a peninsula behind the
lighthouse. Direct access to a long, sandy beach.
May-Sep 2HEC ⬛ ♦ ⋔ ⅃ ⛱ ✕ ☉ ◲ ∅ ⌂ ◲ ◲ ⋜ PS ⊠ ⊞ ∅
lau

> **CHIOGGIA** VENEZIA

Miramare via A-Barbarigo 103 ☎ 041 490610 ▤ 490610
e-mail: campmir@tin.it
Longish site reaching as far as the beach, clean and well-
maintained.
➲ *Access from Strada Romeo (SS309) in direction of Chioggia
Sottomarina, turn right on reaching beach and continue 500m.*
May-20 Sep 5HEC ⬛ ⠿ ♦ ⋔ ⅃ ⛱ ✕ ☉ ◲ ∅ ♨ ⋜ PS ⊠ ⊞
∅ lau

Villaggio Turistico Isamar via Isamar 9, Isolaverde
☎ 041 5535811 ▤ 041 490440
e-mail: info@villaggioisamar.com
The site lies on level grassland at the mouth of the River
Etsch. Shade is provided by high poplars. Good beach.
➲ *Access via the SS309. Caravans are advised to approach via
Km84/VII near the Brenta village.*
8 May-19 Sep 33HEC ⬛ ♦ ⋔ ⅃ ⛱ ✕ ☉ ◲ ∅ ⌂ ◲ ⋜ PRS
⊠ ⊞ ∅ lau

CHIOGGIA SOTTOMARINA VENEZIA

Atlanta via Barbarigo 73 ☎ 041 491311
A woodland site directly on the seafront, less than 1km from
Venice.
➔ *W of town centre towards the beach.*
May-14 Sep 7HEC ⚏ ♠ ⋔ ⚑ ⛊ ☍ ✕ ⊙ ⚑ ⌀ 쓰 ⭲ PRS ⛺ ⊘
lau ♦ ⚑ ✕ 쓰 ⭲R ⊞

Oasi via A-Barbarigo 147
☎ 041 490801 ▤ 041 490801
e-mail: info@campingoasi.com
A well equipped site situated on a wooded peninsula near the
mouth of the Brenta River with a wide private beach.
➔ *W of town centre towards the river and the beach.*
1 Apr-30 Sept 1 Oct-31 Mar 3HEC ⚏ ⠿ ♠ ⋔ ⚑ ⛊ ✕ ⊙
⚑ ⌀ 쓰 ⭲ PRS ⛺ lau ♦ ⊞ **Prices:** ⋔4.13-6.20

CISANO VERONA

Cisano via Peschiera ☎ 045 6229098 ▤ 6229059
e-mail: cisano@camping-cisano.it
Quiet, partly terraced site beside Lake Garda with good
watersports facilities and entertainment.
➔ *AFFI exit on Brenner-Verona motorway, access 4km
further.*
20 Mar-4 Oct 14HEC ⚏ ♠ ⋔ ⚑ ⛊ ✕ ⊙ ⚑ ⌀ 쓰 ⛺ ⚏ ⭲ LP
⛺ ⊞ ⊘ lau

San Vito via Pralesi 3
☎ 045 6229026 ▤ 6229059
e-mail: cisano@camping-cisano.it
A tranquil and shady site with many modern facilities.
➔ *Off the Brennero motorway it is signposted to the south of
Cisano.*
20 Mar-5 Oct 5HEC ⚏ ♠ ⋔ ⚑ ⛊ ✕ ⊙ ⚑ ⌀ 쓰 ⭲ LP
⛺ ⊞ ⊘ lau

CORTINA D'AMPEZZO BELLUNO

Cortina via Campo 2 ☎ 0436 867575 ▤ 0436 867917
e-mail: campcortina@tin.it
This site lies amongst pine trees, several hundred metres
away from the edge of town, off the Dolomite road towards
Belluno.
➔ *Turn off road and drive 1km to the campsite which is
situated by a small river.*
All year 45HEC ⚏ ⠿ ♠ ⋔ ⚑ ⛊ ✕ ⊙ ⚑ ⌀ 쓰 ⭲ PR ⛺ lau

Dolomiti via Campo di Sotto
☎ 0436 2485 ▤ 0436 5403
The site is beautifully situated on grassland with pine trees in
a hollow, not far from the Olympic ski-jump.
➔ *For access, follow the directions for Camping Cortina. The
camp is then 500m further on 2.7km S of Cortina.*
15 May-20 Sep 5.4HEC ⚏ ⊙ ♠ ⋔ ⚑ ⛊ ⊙ ⚑ ⌀ 쓰 ⭲ PR ⛺ lau
♦ ✕ ⭲L

Olympia Fiames 1 ☎ 0436 5057 ▤ 5057
A very beautiful site set in the centre of the centre of the
magnificent Dolomite landscape.
➔ *It lies N of town off the SS51.*
5 Dec-5 Nov 4HEC ⚏ ⊙ ♠ ⋔ ⚑ ⛊ ✕ ⊙ ⚑ ⌀ ⛺ ⚏ ⭲R ⛺ ⊞
lau ♦ ⭲LP ⊞

Rocchetta via Campo 1 ☎ 0436 5063 ▤ 5063
e-mail: camping@sunrise.it
In beautiful wooded surroundings.
➔ *Access S from Cortina via SS51.*
Jun-20 Sep & Dec-15 Apr 2.5HEC ⚏ ⊙ ♠ ⋔ ⚑ ⛊ ✕ ⊙ ⚑ ⌀ 쓰
⭲R ⛺ lau ♦ ✕ ⭲LP

DUINO-AURISINA TRIESTE
At SISTIANA

Marepinetà ☎ 040 299264 ▤ 040 299265
A modern site in a pleasant wooded location with a wide
range of recreational facilities. Free bus service to the beach.
➔ *On SS14 near the harbour and beach. Highway A4 Venice-
Trieste, exit Duino 1km on left.*
May-Sep 10.8HEC ♠ ⋔ ⚑ ⛊ ✕ ⊙ ⚑ ⌀ ⛺ ⚏
⭲ P ⛺ ⊞ ⊘ lau ♦ ⭲S

ERACLEA MARE VENEZIA

Portofelice viale dei Fiori 15 ☎ 0421 66021 ▤ 0421 66411
e-mail: info@portofelice.it
A well equipped family village site separated from the beach
by a pinewood. A wide variety of recreational facilities are
available.
➔ *Leave A4 at Venice/Mestre exit and follow signs for Carole
and Eraclea Mare.*
8 May-20 Sep 19HEC ⚏ ♠ ⋔ ⚑ ⛊ ✕ ⊙ ⚑ ⌀ 쓰 ⛺
⭲ PS ⛺ ⊞ ⊞ ⊘ lau

FUSINA VENEZIA VENEZIA

Fusina via Moranzani 79 ☎ 041 5470055 ▤ 5470050
e-mail: info@camping-fusina.com
This well-equipped site is ideal for those visiting Venice and
the Venetian Lagoon.
All year 5.5HEC ⚏ ♠ ⋔ ⚑ ⛊ ✕ ⊙ ⚑ ⌀ 쓰 ⛺ ⚏ ⚑ ⚐ ⭲ S ⛺
⊞ lau **Prices:** ⋔5.68 ♠5.16 pitch 12.91

GEMONA DEL FRIÚLI UDINE

Ai Pioppi via del Bersaglio 44 ☎ 0432 980358 ▤ 980358
e-mail: bar-camping-taxi@aipioppi.it
Quiet, well equipped site in a pleasant mountain setting.
➔ *1km from town centre via N13.*
15 Mar-Oct 11HEC ⚏ ♠ ⋔ ✕ ⊙ ⚑ ⌀ 쓰 ⛺ ⚏ ⚐ ⛺ lau ♦
⚑ ⭲R ⊞ **Prices:** ⋔4.50-4.70 ♠2.10-2.60 ⚐4.60-6 ▲3.10-3.60

GRADO GORIZIA

Europa ☎ 0431 80877 ▧ 0431 82284
e-mail: info@campingeuropa.it
In level terrain under half grown poplars. Partially in shade
in pine forest.
➲ *On road to Monfalcone, 20km from Palmanova via
Aquileia.*
6 Apr-23 Sep 22HEC ⊞ ░ ♠ ♠ ⚲ ⚡ ⚡ ✕ ⊙ ▣ ∅ ♨ ♨ ⊟
⚓ PS ☎ ⊞ lau

Tenuta Primero Loc Primero ☎ 0431 896800 ▧ 896801
e-mail: info@tenuta-primero.com
The site lies in extensive level grassland between the road and
the dam, which is 2m high along the narrow and level beach.
Tennis court.
➲ *Access from Monfalcone road. Signposted.*
6 Apr-Sep 20HEC ⊞ ♠ ♠ ⚲ ⚡ ⚡ ✕ ⊙ ▣ ∅ ⊟ ⚓ PS ☎ ⊞
⊘ lau

IÉSOLO

See Jésolo, Lido di

JÉSOLO, LIDO DI VENEZIA

At JÉSOLO PINETA(6km E)

Malibu Beach viale Oriente 78 ☎ 0421 362212
In a pinewood facing the sea and a fine sandy beach.
➲ *From Venezia via Cavallino on coast road to Cortellazzo.*
15 May-16 Sep 10HEC ░ ♠ ♠ ⚲ ⚡ ⚡ ✕ ⊙ ▣ ∅ ♨ ⊟ ⚓
⚓ PS ☎ ⊞ ⊘ lau

Waikiki viale Oriente 144 ☎ 0421 980186 ▧ 378040
e-mail: info@campingwaikiki.it
A family site in a pine wood with direct access to the beach.
Regular bus service to Venice passes the camp site.
09 May-09 Sep 5.2HEC ⊞ ░ ♠ ♠ ⚲ ⚡ ⚡ ✕ ⊙ ▣ ∅ ⊟ ⚓
⚓ PRS ☎ ⊞ ⊘ lau ♦ ∅ ♨

At PORTO DI PIAVE VECCHIA(8km S)

Jesolo International via a da Giussano 1 ☎ 0421 971826
The site lies on a sandy beach, beside the coast road. It has
modern facilities and is ideal for a relaxing beach holiday.
➲ *Signposted from Cavallino. Opposite lighthouse.*
May-Sep 11HEC ⊞ ░ ♠ ♠ ⚲ ⚡ ✕ ⊙ ▣ ∅ ♨
⚓ PS ☎ ⊞ ⊘ lau

LAZISE VERONA

Ideal Loc Vanon ☎ 045 7580077
On the shore of Lake Garda with asphalt roads and access to
a safe, flat beach.
➲ *1km from the town centre near the Gardaland Amusement
Park.*
Etr-Sep 13HEC ⊞ ♠ ♠ ⚲ ⚡ ⚡ ✕ ⊙ ▣ ∅ ⊟ ⚓ ⚓ LP ☎ ⊞ ⊘
lau ♦ ♨

Parc Loc Sentieri ☎ 045 7580127 ▧ 045 6470150
e-mail: duparc@ifinet.it
Well-kept, lakeside site off main road.
➲ *If approaching from Garda, the site is on S side of Lazise
just after turning for Verona.*
15 Mar-Oct 6HEC ⊞ ♠ ♠ ⚲ ⚡ ⚡ ✕ ⊙ ▣ ⊟ ⚓ L ☎ ⊞ lau
♦ ∅ ♨ ⚓P   see advertisement in colour section

LIDO DI JÉSOLO

See Jésolo, Lido di

LIGNANO SABBIADORO UDINE

Sabbiadoro via Sabbiadoro 8 ☎ 0431 71455 ▧ 721355
e-mail: campsab@dns.netanday.it
A peaceful site situated in a pine grove close to the beach.
13 Mar-29 Sep 13HEC ⊞ ░ ♠ ♠ ⚲ ⚡ ⚡ ✕ ⊙ ▣ ∅ ♨ ⊟ ⚓
⚓ P ☎ ⊞ lau ♦ ⚓S Prices: ⚓3.87-7.23 pitch 6.20-11.36

MALCESINE VERONA

Claudia via Molini 2 ☎ 045 7400786 ▧ 045 7400786
Flat grassy site only 30mtrs from the lake. Excellent facilities
available, especially for water sports.
➲ *From Rome/Brennero motorway, continue via Trento, Arco,
Torbole, and site is on outskirts of Malcesine.*
25 Mar-15 Oct 1HEC ⊞ ░ ♠ ♠ ⚲ ⚡ ⚡ ✕ ⊙ ▣ ☎ ♦ ∅ ♨ ⚓L

MALGA CIAPELA BELLUNO

Malga Ciapela Marmolada ☎ 0437 722064 ▧ 722064
e-mail: camping.mc.marmolada@dolomiti.com
A terraced site in tranquil wooded surroundings at the foot
on Mt. Marmolada.
➲ *Take the Bozen exit off the Brenner/Verona motorway.
Follow signs for Canazei, Malga Ciapela and finally the site,
Marmolada.*
Jun-26 Sep & Dec-25 Apr 3HEC ⊞ ♨ ♠ ♠ ⚲ ⚡ ⚡ ⊙ ▣ ∅ ♨
⚓ R ☎ lau ♦ ✕ Prices: ⚓4.65-5.68 pitch 4.65-6.20

MARGHERA VENEZIA

Jolly delle Querce via A-de-Marchi 7
☎ 041 920312 ▧ 920312
The site lies on meadowland scattered with poplars.
➲ *For access, turn off into the Autostrada in Venezia in the
direction of Chioggia on the SS309 and continue for 200m.*
Apr-Oct 1.2HEC ⊞ ♠ ♠ ⚲ ⚡ ⚡ ✕ ⊙ ▣ ∅ ♨ ⊟ ⚓ ⊞ lau ♦
⚓P

MASARÈ BELLUNO

Alleghe ☎ 0437 723737 ▧ 723874
e-mail: alleghecamp@dolomites.com
Several terraces on a wooded incline below a road.
Jun-Sep & Dec-Apr 2HEC ⊞ ♨ ♠ ♠ ⚲ ✕ ⊙ ▣ ∅ ♨ ▣ lau
♦ ⚲ ✕ ⚓P

MESTRE VENEZIA

Venezia via Orlanda 8 ☎ 041 5312828
A well equipped site on the shore of the Lagoon close to the
causeway with a regular bus service to Venice within easy
reach.
15 Feb-Nov 1.8HEC ⊞ ♠ ♠ ⚲ ⚡ ✕ ⊙ ▣ ∅ ☎ ⊟ lau

MONFALCONE GORIZIA

Isola Panzano Lido via dei Bagni Nuova 171
☎ 0481 411202 ▧ 45958
e-mail: itmargo@yahoo.it
Well equipped family site close to the beach.
➲ *A4 (Venezia-Trieste) exit at Monfalcone/Lisert and follow
signs for the sea. Site is signposted from coast.*
15 May-15 Sep 13HEC ⊞ ♠ ♠ ⚲ ⚡ ⚡ ✕ ⊙ ▣ ∅ ♨ ⊟ ♨ ⚓ S
☎ ⊞ Prices: ⚓4.65-5.68 ▣8.27-9.82 ▲8.27-9.82

MONTEGROTTO TERME PADOVA

Sporting Center ☎ 049 793400 ▧ 049 811152
e-mail: sporting@sportingcenter.it
A peaceful site in a pleasant setting in the Euganean hills
with good facilities including a thermal treatment centre.
5 Mar-10 Nov 6.5HEC ⊞ ♠ ♠ ⚲ ✕ ⊙ ▣ ⚓ P ☎ lau ♦ ⚲ ∅

ORIAGO VENEZIA

Serenissima via Padana 334 ☎ 041 920286 ▧ 920286
e-mail: campingserenissima@shineline.it
A well looked after site with shade provided by the local
woodland. Local bus service every 20 minutes to Venice.
➲ *A4 to Venice, SS11 at Oriago.*
Etr-10 Nov 2HEC ⊞ ♠ ♠ ⚲ ⚡ ⚡ ✕ ⊙ ▣ ∅ ⊟ ♨ ⚓ R ☎ lau

PACENGO VERONA

Camping Lido via Peschiera 2
☎ 045 7590611 ▧ 045 7590030

The Lido campsite is located in Pacengo on the Verona side of Lake Garda between the popular villages of Peschiera and Lazise. It is right by the lake with its clear water and the peace of the lake, the sun and the gentle communion with nature make it an ideal spot for a holiday with direct contact with nature. The site has modern, efficient toilet facilities and amenities for tents, caravans and chalets allowing you to spend a relaxing and enjoyable holiday. Masonry-built chalets furnished with four beds one on top of the other, mattresses and pillows, washbasins with running water, gas stove, fridge, cupboard, 4 chairs and electricity plus terrace and veranda. Blankets, bed linen and crockery/cutlery not provided. Large swimming pool for adults and children. Small harbour for boats. For maximum peace and quiet we recommend early or late season.

CAMPING LIDO • I-Pacengo del Garda (VR) • Tel. 0039/0457590030-0457590611
Fax 0039/0457590030 • Tel./Fax in Winter 0039/0457580334
Http://www.campinglido.it • E-mail info@campinglido.it

e-mail: info@campinglido.it
Apr-Sep 10HEC ⬛ ♣ ♠ 🏊 ⚁ ✕ ⊙ 🔲 ⊘ 🛖 ⚱ LP 🏛 ⊞ lau

▶ PALAFAVERA BELLUNO

Palafavera ☎ 0437 788506 ▮ 0437 788507
In a beautiful location in the heart of the Dolomites at an altitude of 1514mtrs. Good, modern sanitary installations and plenty of recreational facilities.
5HEC ⬛ ♠ ♠ 🏊 ⚁ ✕ ⊙ 🔲 ⊘ ⚱ PR 🏛 ⊞ ⌀ lau

▶ PESCHIERA DEL GARDA VERONA

Bella Italia via Bella Italia 2
☎ 045 6400688 ▮ 6401410
Extensive lakeside site. No animals or motorcycles allowed.
➦ Turn off Brescia road between Km276.2 and Km275.8 and head towards lake.
Apr-Sep 25HEC ⬛ ♣ ♠ 🏊 ⚁ ✕ ⊙ 🔲 ⊘ 🛖 ⛱ 🔲 ▲ ⚱ P 🏛 ⊞ ⌀ lau ♦ ⊘ ⚱LR

Bergamini via Bergamini 51
☎ 045 7550283 ▮ 7550283
Ideal for young families as site has two children's pools and extensive play areas.
➦ Follow signs 'Porto Bergamini'.
May-20 Sep 1.4HEC ⬛ ♣ ♠ 🏊 ⚁ ✕ ⊙ 🔲 🛖 🔲 ⚱ LP 🏛 ⊞ ⌀ lau

Garda via Marzan
☎ 045 7550540 & 7551899 ▮ 045 6400711
A quiet, pleasant site with beach access on the shore of Lake Garda.
➦ Near the town centre, 2km from Milan/Venice motorway exit.
Apr-Sep 20.4HEC ⬛ ♣ ♠ 🏊 ⚁ ✕ ⊙ 🔲 🛖 🔲 ▲ ⚱ LP 🏛 ⌀ lau ♦ ⊘ ⚱ ⚱R ⊞

San Benedetto via Bergamini 14
☎ 045 7550544 ▮ 045 7551512
e-mail: info@campingsanbenedetto.it
A family site in a fine position overlooking the lake.
Apr-Sep 22HEC ⬛ ♣ ♠ 🏊 ⚁ ✕ ⊙ 🔲 🛖 🔲 ▲ ⚱ LP 🏛 lau ♦ ⊘ ⚱ ⊞

▶ PORTO SANTA MARGHERITA VENEZIA

Pra'delle Torri Viale Altanea 201 ☎ 0421 299063 ▮ 299035
e-mail: torri@vacanze-nature.it
Extensive site on flat ground.
➦ 3km W at edge of beach.
20 Apr-28 Sep 53HEC ⬛ ♠ ♠ 🏊 ⚁ ✕ ⊙ 🔲 ⊘ ⚱ 🔲 🔲 ⚱ PS 🏛 ⊞ ⌀ lau

▶ PUNTA SABBIONI VENEZIA

Marina di Venezia via Montello 6

☎ 041 5300955 ▮ 041 966036
Extensive, well-organised and well maintained holiday centre, extremely well appointed, with ample shade by trees. A section of the site is designated for dog owners, caravans and tents.
➦ Access from the coastal road, turn seawards about 500m before the end then continue along narrow asphalt road. Well signposted approach.
15 Apr-Sep 70HEC ⬛ ⠶ ♣ ♠ 🏊 ⚁ ✕ ⊙ 🔲 ⊘ 🛖 🏛 🔲 ▲ ⚱ PS 🏛 ⊞ lau

Miramare Lungomare D-Alighieri 29
☎ 041 966150 ▮ 041 5301150
e-mail: info@camping-miramare.it
In a magnificent location overlooking the lagoon.
Apr-Nov 1.8HEC ⬛ ♣ ♠ 🏊 ⚁ ✕ ⊙ 🔲 ⊘ 🛖 🏛 ⊞ ⌀ lau ♦ ⚱S

▶ ROSOLINA MARE ROVIGO

Margherita via Foci Adige 10 ☎ 0426 68212
A well equipped family site situated between the sea and a pine wood in the Po Delta Park.
May-Sep 6.4HEC ⬛ ⠶ ♣ ♠ 🏊 ⚁ ✕ ⊙ 🔲 ⊘ ⚱ 🔲 ⚱ PRS 🏛 ⊞ lau

Rosapineta Strada Nord 24 ☎ 0426 68033 ▮ 68105
e-mail: info@rosapineta.it
The site lies in the grounds of an extensive holiday camp. Pitches for caravans and tents are separate.
➦ Take Strada Romea towards Ravenna and drive to the bridge over the River Adige. Continue for 800m, then turn off, cross bridge and head towards Rosolina Mare and Rosapineta (approx 8km).
12 May-16 Sep 47HEC ⬛ ⠶ ♣ ♠ 🏊 ⚁ ✕ ⊙ 🔲 ⊘ ⚱ 🔲 🔲 ⚱ PS 🏛 ⊞ lau ♦ ⚱R

▶ TREPORTI VENEZIA

Cá Pasquali via Poerio 33 ☎ 041 966110 ▮ 041 5300797
e-mail: info@capasquali.it
Sandy, meadowland site with poplar and pine trees.
➦ Access from Cavallino-Punta Sabbioni coast road, along an asphalt road for 400m.
20 Apr-22 Sep 9HEC ⠶ ♣ ♠ 🏊 ⚁ ✕ ⊙ 🔲 ⊘ ⚱ 🔲 🔲 ▲ ⚱ PS 🏛 ⊞ ⌀ lau ♦ ⊘ ⚱

Cá Savio via di Ca'Savio 77 ☎ 41 966017 ▮ 5300707
e-mail: info@casavio.it
A level site along the edge of the sea with private, sandy beach. Separate pitches for caravans and tents.
➦ From Cá Savio, at traffic lights, turn towards the sea and continue for 500m to the beach.
01 May-30 Sep 26.8HEC ⠶ ♣ ♠ 🏊 ⚁ ✕ ⊙ 🔲 🛖 🔲 ⚱ PS 🏛 ⊞ ⌀ ♦ ⊘

Fiori via Pisani 52, Ca'vio ☎ 041 966448 ▮ 041 966724
e-mail: fiori@vacanze-natura.it
The site stretches over a wide area of sand dunes and pine trees with separate sections for caravans and tents.
➦ From A4 at Venice follow coast road via Jesolo to Lido del Cavallino.
12 Apr-7 Oct 11HEC ⬛ ⠶ ♣ ♠ 🏊 ⚁ ✕ ⊙ 🔲 🛖 🔲 ⚱ PS 🏛 ⊞ ⌀ ♦ ⊘

Mediterráneo via delle Batterie 38, Ca'Vio
☎ 041 966721 ▮ 041 966944
e-mail: mediterraneo@vacanze-natura.it
Slightly hilly grassland site with trees and sunshade roofs. Lunchtime siesta 13.00-15.00 hrs.
➦ Well signposted from Jesolo.
5 May-24 Sep 17HEC ⠶ ♣ ♠ 🏊 ⚁ ✕ ⊙ 🔲 🛖 🔲 ⚱ PS 🏛 ⊞ ⌀ lau ♦ ⊘ ⚱ ⚱R Prices: ♠3.60-8.05 🚐7.80-19.50 ▲5.60-16.30

Scarpiland via A-Poerio 14 ☎ 041 966488 ▤ 966488
e-mail: info@scarpiland.com
In a beautiful area surrounded by a pinewood with direct
access to the beach and beautiful views of the sea.
28 Apr-22 Sep 4.5HEC ⬛ ⠿ ✦ ℝ ⚡ ⚫ ✕ ⊙ 🖵 ⊘ ☴ ⊞ 🚐
⭐ S ☎ ⊞ lau

VICENZA VICENZA

Vicenza Strada Pelosa 239 ☎ 0444 582311 ▤ 582434
e-mail: camping@ascom.vi.it
A modern, well-equipped site.
➲ *Access via A4 exit 'Vicenza-Est'.*
Apr-Sep 3HEC ⬛ ✦ ℝ ⚡ ✕ ⊙ 🖵 ⊞ 🚐 ☎ lau
✦ ⚡ ✕ ⊘ ⭐R

ZOLDO ALTO BELLUNO

Pala Favera ☎ 0437 788506 & 789161 ▤ 788857
e-mail: palafavera@sunrise.it
Site with some woodland, at the foot of Monte Pelmo.
Dec-Apr & Jun-Sep 5HEC ⬛ ⚴ ⟟ ℝ ⚡ ✕ ⊙ 🖵 ⊘ ☴ ⭐ R
☎ ⊘ lau ✦ ⭐P ⊞

● ● NORTH WEST/MED COAST ● ●

Liguria is known as the Italian Riviera, having many small
harbours and a large and prosperous port, Genoa. Inland,
the slopes of the Alps and Apennines, covered in lavender
and herbs, provide the sheltering warmth in which
carnations and chrysanthemums are grown as a major
industry.
Tuscany stretches down the north western coast with
medieval hill towns, towers and cultural centres such as
Florence and Sienna, a medieval town famous for its fan
shaped square Piazza del Campo and the Palio horse races
run twice a year. Landscapes vary from oak and chestnut
woods near the Apennines, tall cypresses and farmhouses,
vineyards (red Chianti is produced here), olive groves, and
the rugged hills of the Carrara marble. Jousting and archery
competitions take place between rival towns and festivals
are occasions for pageantry.
Elba, off the Tuscan coast, is a thriving holiday island with
resorts around the coast, and inland you can find some
attractive old villages with narrow alleyways or take the
cable car from the village of Marciano to the top of Monte
Capanne.
....

ALBENGA SAVONA

Bella Vista Campochiesa, Reg Campore 23
☎ 0182 540213 ▤ 554925
e-mail: info@campingbellavista.it
A friendly, family orientated site with good facilities. Pitches
are divided by bushes and flowerbeds.
➲ *1km from Km613.5 on SS1.*
All year 0.8HEC ⬛ ⟟ ℝ ⚡ ⚫ ⊙ 🖵 ⊞ 🚐 ☎ ⊞ lau ✦ ✕ ⭐S

Roma Regione Foce ☎ 0182 52317 ▤ 0182 555075
e-mail: info@campingroma.com
The site is divided into pitches and laid out with many flower
beds.
➲ *N of bridge over Centa, turn left.*
Apr-Sep 1HEC ⬛ ✦ ℝ ⚡ ✕ ⊙ 🖵 ⊞ ⭐ RS ☎ ✦ ⊘ ☴ ⭐P
⊞ Prices: ♠4.50-5.50 ▲5.50-8.50 pitch 11-17

ALBINIA GROSSETO

Acapulco via Aurelia Km155 ☎ 0564 870165 ▤ 870165
e-mail: campeggioacapulco@vizgilio.it
Set on hilly terrain in pine woodland.
➲ *Take coast road from via Aurelia at Km155.*
15 May-15 Sep 2HEC ⠿ ✦ ℝ ⚡ ✕ ⊙ 🖵 ⊘ ☴ ⭐ S ⊞
⊘ lau Prices: ♠3.62-7.75 pitch 5.94-11.36

Il Gabbiano ☎ 0564 870202 ▤ 0564 870470
Site in pine woodland and open meadowland with sunshade
roofing.
➲ *Turn off SS at Km155.*
Apr-Sep 2.5HEC ⬛ ⠿ ✦ ℝ ⚡ ✕ ⊙ 🖵 ⊘ ☴ 🚐
⭐ S ⊞ ⊞ lau

Hawaii ☎ 0564 870164 ▤ 872952
The site lies in a pine forest on rather hilly ground.
➲ *Turn off via Aurelia at Km154/V and drive towards the sea.*
23 Apr-Sep 4HEC ⠿ ✦ ℝ ⚡ ✕ ⊙ 🖵 ⊘ ☴
⭐ S ⊞ ⊞ ⊘ lau

BIBBONA, MARINA DI LIVORNO
See also Forte di Bibbona

Capannino via Cavalleggeri Sud 26
☎ 0586 600252 ▤ 0565 600720
e-mail: capannino@capannino.it
Well tended park site in pine woodland with private beach.
➲ *On via Aurelia by Km272/VII turn towards sea.*
May-Sep 3HEC ⬛ ⠿ ✦ ℝ ⚡ ✕ ⊙ 🖵 ⊘ ☴ ⭐ S ⊞ ⊞
⊘ lau Prices: ♠5-19 ☴2-4 pitch 7-11

Casa di Caccia via del Mare 40, La Calafornia
☎ 0586 600000 ▤ 600000
A tranquil site by the sea direct access to a private beach.
➲ *From the A12 exit Rosignano and join SS follow signs for
Cecina. 6km exit "La California" site in a further 3km south.*
Apr-15 Oct 3.5HEC ⠿ ✦ ℝ ⚡ ✕ ⊙ 🖵 ⊘ ☴ 🚐
⭐ S ☎ ⊞ ⊘ lau

Free Beach via Cavalleggeri Nord 88
☎ 0586 600388 ▤ 602984
Situated 300m from the sea through pine woods.
➲ *From the SS206 at Cecina follow signs to S. Guido.*
Etr-Sep 9HEC ⬛ ⠿ ⟟ ℝ ⚡ ✕ ⊙ 🖵 ⊘ ☴ 🚐 ⭐ P ⊞ lau
✦ ⭐S Prices: ♠6-10 ☴4-4 ▲6-8.50 pitch 9-13

Il Gineprino via dei Platani,56a
☎ 0586 600550 ▤ 600550
e-mail: ilgineprino@tiscalinet.it
A modern site situated on the Tuscany coast and shaded by a
pine wood. There are good recreational facilities and the
beach is within 300mtrs.
➲ *Access via motorway exit 'La California' for Marina di
Bibbona.*
Etr-Sep 1.5HEC ⬛ ✦ ℝ ⚡ ✕ ⊙ 🖵 ☴ 🚐 ⭐ P ☎ lau ✦
⊘ ⭐S ⊞ Prices: ♠4.13-9.04 ☴7.75-11.88 ▲7.75-11.88
pitch 7.75-11.88

BOGLIASCO GENOVA

Genova Est via Marconi, Cassa
☎ 010 3472053 ▤ 3472053
e-mail: camping@dada.it
Quiet and shady site 1km from the sea. A free bus service operates from the site to the beaches.
➲ *Exit A12 at Nervi, then 8km east.*
1 Mar-31 Oct 1.2HEC ⊞ ♦ ⋔ ⅀ ⅄ ✕ ⊙ ⬛ ⌀ ⊞ ⬛ lau ♦
⛺ ⌇PS Prices: ⚑5 ♠2.60 ⬛5.40 ▲4.30

BORDIGHERA IMPERIA

Baia La Ruota via Madonna della Ruota 34 ☎ 184 265222
A well equipped holiday village with direct access to a private beach.
➲ *Access via A10.*
Apr-Oct 1.5HEC ⌀ ♦ ⋔ ⅀ ⅄ ✕ ⊙ ⬛ ⊞ ⌇ S ⬛ ⊞ ✍

BOTTAI FIRENZE

Internationale Firenze via S Cristoforo 2
☎ 055 2374704 ▤ 055 2373412
Situated on the welcoming Florentine hills this site offers a restful atmosphere close to many historic places.
Apr-15 Oct 6HEC ⊞ ⊿ ⋔ ⅀ ⅄ ✕ ⊙ ⬛ ⌀ ⊞ ⬛ ⌇ P ⊞ lau
♦ ⛺ ⌇LR ⊞

CALENZANO FIRENZE

Autosole via V-Emanuele 11
☎ 055 8827819 ▤ 8827819
Motorway A1 exit "Calenzano-Sesto Fiorentino" at the traffic light on the L - 200m on L All year 2.2HEC ⊞ ♦ ⋔ ⅀ ⅄ ✕
⊙ ⬛ ⬛ ⌇ P ⊞ lau ♦ ⛺

CAPALBIO GROSSETO

Costa d'Argento Monte Alzato
☎ 0564 893007 ▤ 0564 893107
e-mail: info@costadargento.it
A camping village in the middle of a nature park - 1km from the Maremma coast.
Camping Card Compulsory.
➲ *12km from Orbetello via SS Aurelia.*
Apr-Sep 6HEC ⊞ ♦ ⋔ ⅀ ⅄ ✕ ⊙ ⬛ ⌀ ⊞ ⬛
⌇ P ⬛ ⊞ lau ♦ ⌇S

CAPANNOLE AREZZO

Chiocciola via G-Cesare 14
☎ 055 995776 ▤ 055 995776
A modern site in a rural setting among chestnut trees at an altitude of 250mtrs.
15 Mar-30 Sept 3HEC ⊞ ♦ ⋔ ⅀ ⅄ ✕ ⊙ ⬛ ⌀ ⊞ ⬛ ▲ ⌇ P
⊞ ⊞ lau ♦ ⌇LR Prices: ⚑7 ♠2.50 ⬛9 ▲8

CASALE MARITTIMO PISA

Valle Gaia ☎ 0586 681236 ▤ 0586 683551
e-mail: info@vallegaia.it
Site amongst pines and olive trees in a quiet rural location.
➲ *In Southern Cecina heading south from Livorno take the autostrada/superstrada then take 2nd exit for Cecina (Casale Marittimo - ignore first signpost for Cecina S Pietro). Camp is signposted.*
23Mar-26Oct 4HEC ⊞ ⊿ ⋔ ⅀ ⅄ ✕ ⊙ ⬛ ⌀ ⊞ ⌇ P ⊞ ⊞
lau Prices: ⚑4.65-6.95 pitch 8.50-12.60

CASTAGNETO CARDUCCI LIVORNO

Climatico Le Pianacce via Bolgherese
☎ 0565 763667 ▤ 0565 766085
e-mail: info@campinglepiancce.it
Terraced site on slopes of mountain in typical Tuscany landscape, enhanced by site landscaping. Pleasant climate due to height.

➲ *Turn off via Aurelia at Km344/VIII in direction of Castagneto Carducci/Sassetta. In 3.2km to left in direction of Bolgheri, in 500m turn right towards mountains.*
Apr-Oct 9HEC ⊞ ⋰⋰ ♦ ⋔ ⅀ ⅄ ✕ ⊙ ⬛ ⌀ ⛺ ⬛ ⌇ P ⊞ ⊞
lau

CASTEL DEL PIANO GROSSETO

Amiata via Roma 15 ☎ 0564 955107 ▤ 955107
e-mail: vacanzeamiata@tiscalinet.it
A grassland site with a separate section for dog owners.
➲ *On the outskirts of Castel del Piano, on the national road (SS) 323, towards Arcidosso.*
All year 4.2HEC ⊞ ♦ ⋔ ⅀ ⅄ ✕ ⊙ ⬛ ⌀ ⛺ ⬛ ⬛ lau ♦
⌇P Prices: ⚑4.30-5.90 pitch 4.30-5.90

CASTIGLIONE DELLA PESCAIA GROSSETO

Santa Pomata Strada della Rocchette
☎ 0564 941037 ▤ 0564 941221
Site in hilly woodland terrain with some pitches amongst bushes. Flat clean sandy beach.
➲ *Turn off the SS322 at Km20, then in direction of Le Rocchette 4.5km NW and continue towards the sea for 1km to site on left.*
Apr-20 Oct 6HEC ⊞ ⋰⋰ ♦ ⋔ ⅀ ⅄ ✕ ⊙ ⬛ ⌀ ⛺ ⬛ ⬛
⌇ S ⬛ ⊞ lau

CÉCINA, MARINA DI LIVORNO

Tamerici ☎ 0586 620629 ▤ 0586 622496
Camping Card Compulsory.
All year 8.7HEC ⊞ ♦ ⋔ ⅀ ⅄ ✕ ⊙ ⬛ ⌀ ⛺ ⬛ ⬛ ⊞ lau
♦ ⌇PRS

CERIALE SAVONA

Baciccia via Torino 19
0182 990743 ▤ 0182 993839
e-mail: baciccia@irg.it
An orderly site, lying inland off the via Aurelia, 500mtrs from the sea.
➲ *Entrance 100m W of Km612/V.*
All year 1.2HEC ⊞ ♦ ⋔ ⅀ ⅄ ✕ ⊙ ⬛ ⌀ ⛺ ⬛ ⌇ P ⊞ lau ♦
✕ ⛺ ⌇S ⊞

CERVO IMPERIA

Lino via N Sauro 4
☎ 0183 400087 ▤ 0183 400089
e-mail: info@campinglino.it
A seaside site shaded by grape vines, which is clean and well managed. There is a knee-deep lagoon suitable for children.
➲ *Turn off via Aurelia at Km637/V near the railway underpass and follow via Nazionale Sauro towards sea.*
Apr-20 Oct 1.1HEC ⋰⋰ ♦ ⋔ ⅀ ⅄ ✕ ⊙ ⬛ ⌀ ⛺ ⬛ ⬛ ⊞ ⊞
lau ♦ ⌇S

Camping LA SFINGE
Loc. Gea • 19013 Deiva Marina (SP)
http://www.camping.it/liguria/lasfinge
E-mail: lasfinge@camping.it

The terraced site is located in an enchanting pine wood between the famous "CINQUE TERRE" and Portofino, only 3 km from the sea (free bus service). Entertainment at the weekend in July and August. Ideal for all types of water sports (diving, surfing, fishing, rowing...). Good walking in the delightful woods of Liguria. **Renewed sanitary facilities. For more information: Tel./Fax: 0187 825464**

CUTIGLIANO PISTOIA

Betulle via Cantamaggio 6 ☎ 0573 68004
A pleasant year-round site with good facilities in a central location with access to three popular ski stations.
All year 4HEC ⬛ ♦♠♣♨️♟×⊙☻♨️🏕 ⚑ LR ⚐ lau

DEIVA MARINA LA SPEZIA

Costabella ☎ 0817 825343 ▦ 0817 816433
Etr-Sep 1.5HEC ⬛ ♦♠♣♨️♟×⊙☻♨️🏕P⊘ lau
♦ ⚑S⊞

La Sfinge Gea 5 ☎ 0187 825284 ▦ 0187 825464
e-mail: lasfinge@camping.it
Partly terraced site in pleasant wooded surroundings. Ideal for both nature lovers and families.
➲ *Access via A12 Genova-La Spezia.*
All year 1.8HEC ⬛ ♦♠♣♨️♟×⊙☻♨️🏕⚑ RS ⚐P⊞ lau
♦×Prices: ⚑6 ♠3 ♨️8-18.50 ⚑5.50-9

Villaggio Turistico Arenella Arenella
☎ 0187 825259 ▦ 0187 815861
e-mail: campingarenella@libero.it
In a beautiful, quiet valley 1.5km from the sea with good facilities.
➲ *Access via A12 (Genoa-La Spezia).*
Closed Nov 16.2HEC ⬛ ♦♠♣♨️♟×⊙☻♨️🏕P lau
♦⊘🏕 ⚑S⊞
See advertisement in colour section

ELBA, ISOLA D' LIVORNO
LACONA

Lacona Pineta Lacona CP 186
☎ 0565 964322 ▦ 0565 964087
e-mail: info@campinglaconapineta.com
In a picturesque location on a thickly wooded hillside sloping gently towards a sandy beach with plenty of recreational facilities.
Apr-Oct 4HEC ⬛ ♦♠♣♨️♟×⊙☻♨️⊘🏕 ⚑ S⊞⊞ lau ♦⊘

NISPORTO

Sole e Mare ☎ 0565 934907 ▦ 961180
e-mail: gschezzini@tiscalinet.it
A well equipped, modern site in pleasant wooded surroundings close to the beach. A wide variety of recreational facilities are available.
➲ *From Portoferraio take Porto Azzurro road, then turn towards Rio nell'Elba-Nisporto.*
Apr-Sep 2HEC ⬛ ♦♠♣♨️♟×⊙☻♨️⊘🏕🐾🏕
⚑ S⊞⊞ lau

ORTANO

Canapai Loc Ortano ☎ 0565 939165
Camping Card Compulsory.
Apr-Sep 4HEC ⬛ ⸪♦♠♣♨️♟×⊙☻♨️⊘🏕🐾🏕
⚑ P⊞⊞ ⚑S

OTTONE

Rosselba le Palme Ottone 3 ☎ 0565 933101 ▦ 933041
e-mail: info@rosselbalepalme.it
Pitches are on varying heights up from the beach. Shade is provided by large palm trees.
➲ *8km from Portferraio around bay via Bivo Bagnaia.*
25 Apr-Sep 30HEC ⬛ ♦♠♣♨️♟×⊙☻♨️⊘🏕 ⚑ PS ⚐⊞ lau
Prices: ⚑5.70-12.90 ♠1.60-4.60 ♨️8.80-17.10 ⚑4.90-12.40

PORTO AZZURRO

Reale ☎ 0565 95678 ▦ 0565 920127
e-mail: campingreale@tin.it
A well equipped site in a wooded location with direct access to the beach.
➲ *From Portoferraio take the Porto Azzurro road for 13km, then head towards Rio Marina for 2km and follow signposts.*
5Apr-Sep 2.5HEC ⬛ ♦♠♣♨️♟×⊙☻♨️🏕 ⚑ S lau
♦ ⚑P⊞

PORTOFERRAIO

Acquaviva Acquqviva ☎ 0565 930674 ▦ 0565 915592
e-mail: campingacquaviva@elbalink.it
This seafront site is surrounded by trees and has excellent facilities for scuba diving, watersports etc.
➲ *3km W of town.*
Etr-Oct 1.7HEC ⬛ ♦♠♣♨️♟×⊙☻♨️⊘🏕
⚑ S⊞P lau

Enfola Enfola ☎ 0565 939001 ▦ 0565 918613
Located on the Isle of Elba, ideal for scuba-diving, sailing and sunshine.
Apr-Sep 0.8HEC ⸪♦♠♣♨️♟×⊙☻♨️🐾⚐ lau ♦ ⚑S

Scaglieri via Biodola 1, Casella Postale 158
☎ 0565 969940 ▦ 0565 969834
e-mail: scaglieri@elbalink.it
Sloping terraces 10mtrs from the sea make up this site. Facilities such as tennis and golf are avaliable at the nearby Hotel Hermitage.
➲ *The island is accessible by plane and ferry. The site is on the north coast 7km from Portoferraio.*
Etr-Oct 1.7HEC ⸪♦♠♣♨️♟×⊙☻♨️⊘🏕 ⚑ P⊘ lau ♦ ⚑S

FIÉSOLE FIRENZE

Panoramico via Peramonda 1 ☎ 055 599069 ▦ 055 59186
e-mail: panoramico@florencecamping.com
Site stretches over wide terraces on the Fiesole hillside surrounded by a variety of tall evergreens.
➲ *Exit A1 at Firenze Sud, follow signs through the city to Fiesole. Site is on SS Bolognese.*
All year 5HEC ⬛ ♦♠♣♨️♟×⊙☻♨️⊘🏕🐾 ⚑ P⚐ lau ♦🏕

FIGLINE VALDARNO FIRENZE

Norcenni Girasole via Norcenni 7
☎ 055 959666 ▦ 055 959337
e-mail: girasole@ecvacanze.it
Terraced site on partial slope. Separate section for young people.
➲ *From Florence take Roma A1/E35 autostrada & exit in incisa - Turn L on rd 69 towards Figline, turn R for Greve & look for Camping Girasole signs.*
16Mar-Oct 12HEC ⬛ ⊘♦♠♣♨️♟×⊙☻♨️⊘🏕 ⚑ PR⚐
⊞ lau Prices: ⚑6.45-8.62 ♠3.62-4.80 ♨️5.73-7.54 ⚑5.32-6.92

FIRENZE (FLORENCE) FIRENZE

See also Troghi

Semifonte via Ugo Foscolo 4, Barberino Val d'Elsa
☎ 055 8075454 ▤ 055 8075454
A peaceful, terraced site offering panoramic views over the Chianti Hills. Regular bus services to Firenze and Siena.
➲ *25km S of Firenze and N of Barberino Val d'Elsa.*
10 Apr-20 Oct 1.6HEC ⏛ ⊕ ⋔ ⊙ ⊛ ⅏ ⋔ P ▣ lau ➡ ⊻ ✕ ⊞

At MARCIALLA

Toscana Colliverdi via Marcialla 349, Certaldo
☎ 0571 669334
A sloping, terraced site with good facilities, surrounded by vineyards and olive groves.
➲ *Access via 'Firenze-Certosa' exit on Autostrada del Sole or 'Tavarnelle Valpesa' exit on Autostrada del Palio.*
20 Mar-10 Oct 2.2HEC ⏛ ⊕ ⋔ ⊙ ⊛ ⊘ ⊞ ➡ ⊻ ✕

FLORENCE

See **Firenze**

FORTE DI BIBBONA LIVORNO

See also Bibbona, Marina di

Capanne via Aurelia ☎ 0586 600064 ▤ 0586 600198
e-mail: info@campinglecapanne.it
A pleasant family site situated in a spacious wooded park amid magnificent Tuscan scenery. The pitches are well defined and there is a wide variety of recreational facilities.
➲ *Access from Km273 via Aurelia travelling inland.*
20 Apr-29 Sep 6HEC ⏛ ➡ ⋔ ⊻ ✕ ⊙ ⊛ ⊘ ⊞ ⋔ P ▣ ⊞
lau ➡ ⅏S

Forte via dei Platani 58 ☎ 0586 600155 ▤ 600123
e-mail: campeggiodelforte@campeggiodelforte.it
Level site, grassy, sandy terrain.
4 Apr-20 Sep 8HEC ⏛ ➡ ⋔ ⊻ ✕ ⊙ ⊛ ⊘ ⊞ ⋔ P ▣ ⊞
⊘ lau ➡ ⅏S Prices: ⁂7500-12800 ⊛4000-5500
⊛13000-19500 ▲13000-19500

GROSSETO, MARINA DI GROSSETO

La Marze ☎ 0564 35501 ▤ 0564 35534
➲ *Access via SS322.*
May-15 Oct 20HEC ⁙⁙ ➡ ⋔ ⊻ ✕ ⊙ ⊛ ⊘ ⊞ ⊞
⋔ P ▣ ⊞ lau

Rosmarina via delle Colonie 37 ☎ 0564 36319 ▤ 0564 34758
e-mail: info@campingrosmarina.it
A modern site situated in a pine wood and close to the sea, with beautiful views. Various sports and entertainments for everyone to enjoy.
01 May-30 Sep 1.4HEC ⁙⁙ ➡ ⋔ ⊻ ✕ ⊙ ⊛ ⊘ ⊞ ⊞ ▲ ⊞
⊘ lau ➡ ⅏S Prices: ⁂5.50-10.50 pitch 6.70-13

LERICI LA SPEZIA

Maralunga via Carpanini 61, Maralunga
☎ 0187 966589 ▤ 966589
This terraced site is directly on the seafront and surrounded by olive groves.
➲ *Access from Sarzana-La Spezia motorway.*
Jun-Sep 10HEC ⊛ ➡ ⋔ ⊻ ✕ ⊙ ⊛ ⊘ ⋔ S ▣ ⊞ ➡ ✕

LIMITE FIRENZE

San Giusto via Castra 71 ☎ 055 8712304 ▤ 055 8711856
A useful site on slightly sloping ground within easy reach of Florence by car or public transport.
Etr-Oct 2.5HEC ⏛ ⊕ ⋔ ✕ ⊙ ⊛ ⊘ ⊞ ⊞ ➡ ⋔P

Via Castra, 71
I-50050 Limite sull'Arno
(FLORENCE)
Tel. 0039/0558712304
Fax 0039/0558711856

www.campingsangiusto.it • info@campingsangiusto.it

The nature campsite is located on the verdant slopes of Montalbano in a protected area about to be declared a nature reserve The position of the campsite provides ample opportunity to choose between sun and shade, where you can relax in a quiet atmosphere and family environment. In the heart of Tuscany, not far away from her wonderful cities of art. Mobile homes and bungalows for 4-6 persons for rent. A1 Bologna-Roma, exit Firenze Signa. Follow direction of Livorno-Pisa, exit Montelupo. In town, follow the indications for Limite sull'Arno.

During April, May, June, September and October 7=6 (stay 7 nights and pay for only 6).
Price reductions for groups.

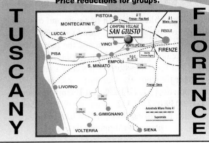

MASSA, MARINA DI MASSA CARRARA

Giardino viale delle Pinete 382
☎ 0585 869291 ▤ 0585 240781
Site in pine woodland and on two meadows, shade provided by roof matting.
➲ *On the island side of the SS328 to Pisa.*
Apr-Sep 3.2HEC ⏛ ➡ ⋔ ⊻ ✕ ⊙ ⊛ ⊞ ⊞ ⅏ lau
➡ ⋔S ⊞

MONÉGLIA GENOVA

Villaggio Smeraldo Preata
☎ 0185 49375 ▤ 0185 490484
A pleasant site in a pine wood overlooking the sea with good, modern facilities and direct access to the beach.
➲ *Access via A12/SS1.*
All year 1.5HEC ⊛ ⊕ ⋔ ⊻ ✕ ⊙ ⊛ ⊞ ⊞
⋔ S ▣ ⅏ lau ➡ ⊘

MONTECATINI TERME PISTOIA

Belsito via delle Vigne 1/A, Vico
☎ 0572 67373 ▤ 0572 67185
e-mail: cbelsito@tin.it
A quiet site at an altitude of 250mtrs with good sized pitches.
16 Feb-Nov 3.5HEC ⏛ ➡ ⋔ ⊻ ✕ ⊙ ⊛ ⊘ ⊞ ⊞ ⊞
⋔ P ▣ ⊞ lau ➡ ⋔L

MONTE DI FO FIRENZE

Sergente ☎ 055 8423018 ▤ 8423907
e-mail: info@campingilsergente.it
The site is at 780m above sea level on a hill. The pitches are flat. Ideal for walkers.
➲ *Exit the SS65 at Barberino Mugollo and follow signs for Monte di Fo.*
All year 3HEC ⏛ ➡ ⋔ ⊻ ✕ ⊙ ⊛ ⊘ ⊞ ⊞ ⊞ ▣ ⊞ lau

In the heart of Tuscany

BARCO REALE

The campsite lies on a hill in a pine and oak wood with a lovely panoramaic view. The house where Leonardo da Vinci was born and the famous towns of Tuscany (Florence, Pisa, Lucca) are not far away, and for the customers it's easy to reach them either by themselves or by the camping bus.
Via Nardini M, I-51030 San Baronto (Pistoia)
Tel: 0039/057388332   Fax: 0039/0573856003
e-mail: barcore@tin.it; info@barcoreale.com
http:www.barcoreale.com

MONTERIGGIONI SIENA

Piscina Luxor Quies Loc. Trasqua ☎ 0577 743047 ▦ 743047
e-mail: info@luxorcamping.com
Lies on a flat-topped hill, partly in an oak wood, partly in meadowland.
➲ *Turn off via Cassia (SS2) at Km239/II or Km238/IX and continue for further 2.5km, crossing railway line. Approach to site via very steep and winding road.*
20 May-10 Sep 1.5HEC ⛺ ∷ ♦ ⋔ ⅀ ⅄ ✕ ⊙ ⨀ ∅ ⯌ P 🕾 ⊞ lau

MONTESCUDÁIO LIVORNO

Montescudáio via del Poggetto
☎ 0586 683477 ▦ 0586 630932
e-mail: info@camping-montescudaio.it
This modern site is situated on a hill and is completely divided into individual pitches, some of which are naturally screened. Children under 2 years are not accepted.
➲ *From Cecinia (on SS1, via Aurelia) follow road to Guardistallo for 2.5km.*
10 May-15 Sep 25HEC ⛺ ♦ ⋔ ⅀ ⅄ ✕ ⊙ ⨀ ∅ ⯌ 🚽 ⯌ S 🕾 ⊁ lau ♦ ⊞ Prices: ⛺4.70-6.50 pitch 10.10-17.90

MONTICELLO AMIATA GROSSETO

Lucherino Lucherino ☎ 0564 992975 ▦ 992975
e-mail: meichu@tiscalinet.it
A peaceful site 735m above sea level on the slopes of Mount Amiata. The shady but sloping site is ideal for walkers and historians.
➲ *Access via SS223 to Paganico then follow signs to Monte Amiata.*
01 May-15 Oct 2HEC ⛺ ♦ ⋔ ⅀ ✕ ⊙ ⨀ ∅ ⯌ 🚽 ⯌ P 🕾 ⊞ lau ♦ 🚽 Prices: ⛺4.13-5.68 ⯌5.68-7.23 ▲5.68-7.23

PEGLI GENOVA

Villa Doria via al Campeggio 15n
☎ 010 6969600 ▦ 6969600
e-mail: villadoria@camping.it
Quiet site in pleasant wooded surroundings.
➲ *Access via SS1. Singposted.*
All year 0.4HEC ⛺ ♦ ⋔ ⅀ ⅄ ✕ ⊙ ⨀ ⯌ 🕾 ⊞ lau ♦ ✕ ∅ ⯌S
Prices: ⛺5.16 ⯌2.58 ⯌6.71 ▲6.71

PISA PISA

Torre Pendente viale della Cascine 86
☎ 050 561704 ▦ 050 561734
e-mail: torrepen@campingtoscana.it
Pleasant, modern site on level ground in a rural setting. 1km walk to the Leaning Tower.
➲ *Situated on the northern outskirts of Pisa.*
2 Apr-15 Oct 2.5HEC ⛺ ♦ ⋔ ⅀ ⅄ ✕ ⊙ ⨀ ∅ ⯌ 🚽 ⯌ 🕾 ⊞ lau ♦ 🚽 ⯌PR ⊞

POPULÓNIA LIVORNO

Sant'Albínia via della Principessa
☎ 0565 29389 ▦ 0565 221310
e-mail: arci.piobino@etruscan.li.it
A good overnight stopping place with plenty of facilities. Ideally placed for the ferry ports.
➲ *10km N of Piombino on the San Vincenzo road.*
May-15 Sep 3HEC ⛺ ♦ ⋔ ⅀ ⅄ ✕ ⊙ ⨀ 🚽 ⯌ ▲ ⯌ S ⊞ ⯌ lau

RIOTORTO LIVORNO

Orizzonte Perelli ☎ 0565 28007 ▦ 0565 28033
In a fine coastal position overlooking the island of Elba.
All year 10HEC ⛺ ♦ ⋔ ⅀ ⅄ ✕ ⊙ ⨀ ∅ ⯌ ⯌ P ⊞ lau ♦ ⯌S

SAN BARONTO FIRENZE

Barco Reale via Nardini 11
☎ 0573 88332 ▦ 0573 856003
e-mail: barcore@tin.it
A well equipped site in a hilly, wooded location.
➲ *Signposted from Lamporecchio.*
Apr-Sep 10HEC ⛺ ♦ ⋔ ⅀ ⅄ ✕ ⊙ ⨀ ∅ ⯌ ⯌ P 🕾 lau

SAN GIMIGNANO SIENA

Boschetto di Piemma Santa Lucia
☎ 0577 940352 ▦ 0577 941982
This small grassy site is well equipped and has many facilities for both families and idividuals.
Apr-15 Oct 1.5HEC ⛺ ♦ ⋔ ⅀ ⅄ ✕ ⊙ ⨀ ∅ 🚽 ⯌ ⯌ P ⊞ ⊞

SAN PIERO A SIEVE FIRENZE

Mugello Verde via Masso Rondinaio 2
☎ 055 848511 ▦ 8486910
Terraced site in wooded surroundings. Lunchtime siesta 14.00-16.00 hrs.
➲ *Leave motorway at exit 18 and follow signs.*
All year 12HEC ⛺ ♦ ⋔ ⅀ ⅄ ✕ ⊙ ⨀ ∅ ⯌ ⯌ P 🕾 ⊞ ♦ 🚽 ⯌R

SAN REMO IMPERIA

Villaggio dei Fiori via Tiro a Volo 3
☎ 0184 660635 ▦ 0184 662377
e-mail: villaggiodeifiori@liberio.it
➲ *1.5km from the town.*
All year 2.6HEC ⛺ ♦ ⋔ ⅀ ✕ ⊙ ⨀ ⯌ ⯌ ⯌ PS 🕾 ⯌ lau ♦ 🚽 ∅ ⊞

SAN VINCENZO LIVORNO

Park Albatros Pineta di Torre Nuova
☎ 0565 701018 ▤ 703589
e-mail: info@parkalbatros.it
The site lies amongst beautiful, tall pine trees. 1km from sea.
➲ *Turn off SP23 beyond San Vincenzo at Km7/III and drive 600m inland.*
25Mar-8Sep 11.4HEC ﹏ ♠ ୮ ≗ ♥ ✗ ⊙ ♨ ⌀ 峇 ⬠ ⊞ ⊡ ⨯ lau ➡ ⸝S ⊞

SARTEANO SIENA

Bagno Santo via del Bagno Santo 29
☎ 0578 26971 ▤ 0578 265889
e-mail: info@bagnosanto.it
23Mar-30Sep 15HEC ﹏ ♠ ୮ ♥ ✗ ⊙ ♨ ⬠ ⸝ P ⊡ ⊞ ⨯ lau ➡ ⸒ Prices: ↟9-11 ⬠3-5 ⸬9-11 ⬠9-11

SARZANA LA SPEZIA

Iron Gate via XXV Aprile 54 ☎ 0187 676370 ▤ 0187 675014
A modern site with good facilities attached to the Iron Gate Marina.
All year 2HEC ﹏ ♠ ୮ ≗ ♥ ✗ ⊙ ♨ ♨ ⸝ PR ⊡ ⊞ ➡ ⌀ 峇

SESTRI LEVANTE GENOVA

Fossa Lupara via Costa 31 ☎ 0185 43992
All year 1.5HEC ﹏ ♠ ୮ ≗ ♥ ✗ ⊙ ♨ ⌀ 峇 ⸬ ⊡ ⊞ lau ➡ ⸝S

SIENA SIENA

Montagnola Sovicille ☎ 0577 314473 ▤ 0577 314473
Quiet site in an oak wood with individual plots separated by hedges. Facilities are modern and extensive.
➲ *From the A1 westbound, exit at Siena, campsite is signposted towards Sovicille.*
Etr-Sep 2.5HEC ﹏ ⁚⁚⁚ ♠ ୮ ≗ ♥ ⊙ ♨ 峇 ⬠ ⸬ ⊡ lau ➡ ⊞

Siena Colleverde Strada di Scacciapensieri 47 ☎ 0577 280044
The site offers both large areas for caravans and mobile homes and a large grassy area for tents. There is a local bus service to the centre of Siena.
➲ *The only campsite in Siena situated just to the north.*
21 Mar-10 Nov 4.5HEC ﹏ ♠ ୮ ≗ ✗ ⊙ ♨ 峇 ⸝ P ⊡ lau ➡ ⸒ ⊞

Soline Casciano di Murlo ☎ 0577 817410 ▤ 0577 817415
e-mail: camping@lesoline.it
Terraced hilly site surrounded by woodland. Offers a wide variety of sports facilities and family entertainment.
➲ *Take the left turning at Fontazzi and ascend hill.*
All year 6HEC ﹏ ⁔ ୮ ≗ ♥ ✗ ⊙ ♨ ⌀ 峇 ⬠ ⸝ P ⊡ ⊞ lau

STELLA SAN GIOVANNI SAVONA

Stella via Rio Basco 62 ☎ 019 703269 ▤ 703269
e-mail: campingdolcevita@libero.it
In wooded surroundings with well defined pitches, 5.5km from the coast.
➲ *Access via SS334.*
Apr-Sep 3.3HEC ﹏ ♠ ୮ ✗ ⊙ ♨ 峇 ⸬ ⸝ PR ⊡ ⊞ lau ➡ ⸒ ⊞

TALAMONE GROSSETO

International Camping Talamone
☎ 0564 887026 ▤ 0564 887170
Some facilities may not be available before April and vehicles must use a separate car park during the high season.
Etr-Sep 5HEC ﹏ ⁔ ⤙ ୮ ≗ ♥ ⊙ ♨ ⸝ P ➡ ⸝S

TORRE DEL LAGO PUCCINI LUCCA

Burlamacco viale G-Marconi Int
☎ 0584 359544 ▤ 0584 359387
In a beautiful wooded location 1km from the sea on the Versilia Riviera and close to the former home of Puccini. A wide variety of facilities are available.
Apr-Sep 4HEC ﹏ ♠ ୮ ≗ ♥ ✗ ⊙ ♨ ⌀ 峇 ⬠ ⸬ ⸝ P ⊡ ⨯ ➡ ⸝LS ⊞

Europa Viale dei Tigli ☎ 0584 350707 ▤ 0584 342592
e-mail: info@europacamp.it
Site in pine and poplar woodland.
➲ *On the land side of the viale dei Tigli, coming from Viareggio.*
Apr-Sep 60HEC ﹏ ⁔ ♠ ୮ ≗ ♥ ✗ ⊙ ♨ ⌀ 峇 ⬠ ⸬ ⊡ ⊞ ⨯ ➡ ⸝S Prices: ↟8000-14000 ⸬12000-19000 ⬠12000-19000

Italia 52 viale dei Tigli ☎ 0584 359828 ▤ 0584 341504
e-mail: info@campingitalia.net
This site is divided into pitches and lies in meadowland planted with poplar trees.
➲ *Inland from the Viareggio road (viale dei Tigli).*
5 Apr-23 Sep 9HEC ﹏ ♠ ୮ ≗ ♥ ✗ ⊙ ♨ ⌀ 峇 ⬠ ⸬ ⊡ ⊞ ⨯ lau ➡ ⸒ ♥ ✗ ⌀ 峇 ⸝LS

Tigli Viale dei Tigli ☎ 0584 341278 ▤ 341278
Shady site close to a Regional Park, Lake Massaciuccoli, and the villa where Puccini wrote much of his music.
Apr-Sep 9HEC ﹏ ⁚⁚⁚ ♠ ୮ ≗ ♥ ✗ ⊙ ♨ 峇 ⬠ ⸬ ⊡ lau ➡ ⸝LS

TROGHI FIRENZE

Il Poggetto via il Poggetto 143 ☎ 055 8307323 ▤ 8307323
e-mail: poggetto@tin.it
A modern site with good facilities. Large, level, grassy pitches.
➲ *5km from exit 'Incisa Valdarno' on the A1.*
All year 4.5HEC ﹏ ⁔ ୮ ≗ ♥ ✗ ⊙ ♨ 峇 ⬠ ⸬ ⬠ ⸝ P ⊡ ⊞ lau Prices: ↟7 pitch 12.50

VADA LIVORNO

Flori ☎ 0586 770096 ▤ 0586 770323
e-mail: campofiori@multinet.it
Level grassland surrounded by fields. Shade provided by roof matting.
➲ *Access from the SS1 S of Vada, after 1.5km turn right and continue for 500m.*
23 Mar-22 Sep 15HEC ﹏ ♠ ୮ ≗ ♥ ✗ ⊙ ♨ ⌀ 峇 ⸝ P ⊡ ⊞ lau ➡ ⸝S Prices: ↟5.16-10.33 ⸬5.16-9.30 ⬠5.16-8.26

VIAREGGIO LUCCA

Pineta via dei Lecci ☎ 0584 383397
A well organised site in a wooded location, 1km from a private beach.
➲ *Access via SSN1 between Km 354 and 355.*
May-20 Sep 3.2HEC ﹏ ♠ ୮ ≗ ♥ ✗ ⊙ ♨ 峇 ⬠ ⸬ ⸝ P ⊡ ⊞ ⨯ lau ➡ ⸝S Prices: ↟4.50-8 ⸬9-15.50 ⬠6-10

Viareggio via Comparini 1 ☎ 0584 391012 ▤ 395462
e-mail: campingviareggio@tin.it
The site lies in a poplar wood 700m from beach.
➲ *1.5km S of town. At Km354/V head towards coast.*
Apr-Sep 2HEC ﹏ ⁚⁚⁚ ♠ ୮ ≗ ♥ ✗ ⊙ ♨ 峇 ⊡ ⊞ lau ➡ ⸝PS

ZINOLA SAVONA

Buggi International via N S del Monte 15 ☎ 019 860120
A well equipped site with plenty of space for tents, approx. 900mtrs from the sea.
All year 2HEC ﹏ ♠ ୮ ≗ ♥ ✗ ⊙ ♨ ♨ ⸬ ⊡ ➡ ⌀ ⸝S ⊞

NORTH EAST/ADRIATIC

This area covers some very dissimilar regions east of the Apennine mountains on whose slopes the glaciers glint for much of the year. Fish from the Adriatic make specialities like the fish soup *brodetto* worth trying. Inland you may like to try Bologna's Mortadella sausage and the Lambrusco Frizzante wine. Emilia Romagna's varied geography - mountains, the River Po and the sea - allows winter skiing, and walking in pine forests in summer. Art lovers can see the mosaics in Ravenna, or Corrigio's paintings in Parma, a town which is famous for its dried ham and cheese. In the rugged Marches you can find the splendid Renaissance palace of Urbino or perhaps visit the hill town of Maceratas which has a Roman arena where concerts and dramas are held, or go to Ascoli Piceno, enclosed by two rivers and with a delightful town centre. The Abruzzo in the centre of Italy is dramatic with high mountains, and a National Park where bears, chamois and wolves live. Attractive towns like L'Aquila dominated by its castle, contrast with the flourishing seaside resorts such as Pescara.

....

▶ **ALBA ADRIATICA** TERAMO
▶ At **TORTORETO, LIDO**(4km S)

Salinello c da Piane a Mare ☎ 0861 786306 ▤ 0861 786451
e-mail: salinello@camping.it
Well-tended meadowland site with numerous rows of poplars. Private beach, siesta 13.30-16.00 hrs.
⊃ *On southern outskirts, signposted from Km405 of the SS16.*
May-Sep 15HEC ⛺ ♣ ♠ ⓩ ⚡ ᵀ ✕ ⊙ 🖫 ∅ � 🛖 ⊀ PS ⌂ ⊞ ✍
lau ♦ ⊰R

▶ **ASSISI** PERUGIA

Internationale Strada San Giovanni In, Campiglione No. 110
☎ 075 813710 ▤ 075 812335
e-mail: info@campingassisi.it
At the foot of the hill on which Assisi stands, this modern campsite is well-equipped and a good touring centre.
⊃ *W via SS147.*
21 Mar-20 Oct 3HEC ⛺ ♣ ♠ ⓩ ⚡ ᵀ ✕ ⊙ 🖫 ∅ ㅗ 🛖 🖙 ☩
⊀ PR ⌂ ⊞ lau Prices: ⚊6-7 ⚊2-3 🚐6-7 ▲5-6

▶ **BARREA** L'AQUILA

Grenziana Parco Nazionale d'Abruzzo, Tre Croci
☎ 0864 88101 ▤ 88101
e-mail: pdsettdnet@tiscdlinet.it
In picturesque wooded surroundings on the shore of a lake.
All year 2HEC ⛺ ⠿⠿ ④ ♠ ⓩ ⚡ ᵀ ✕ ⊙ 🖫 🖙 ▲ ♦ ⓩ ✕ ∅ ㅗ
⊀L ⊞ Prices: ⚊5.20 ⚊2.69 🚐6.70 ▲6.50-6.70

▶ **BELLARIA** FORLI

Happy via Panzini 228 ☎ 0541 346102 ▤ 0541 346102
The campsite is in a quiet position on the sea shore close to the centre of town.
⊃ *A14, SS16, exit for Bellaria Cagnona S. Mauro Mare, and follow signs for Acquabell. Over level crossing and site is on right.*
All year 4HEC ⛺ ⠿⠿ ④ ♠ ⓩ ⚡ ᵀ ✕ ⊙ 🖫 ∅ ㅗ 🛖
⊀ PS ⌂ ⊞ lau ♦ ⓩ ✕ ⊀LR ⊞

▶ **BEVAGNA** PERUGIA

Pian di Boccio Pian di Boccio 10 ☎ 0742 360391 ▤ 360691
e-mail: piandiboccio@tiscaliner.it
In wooded surroundings in the centre of the Umbria region with good modern facilities. Popular with families.
Apr-Sep 8.5HEC ⛺ ♦ ♣ ♠ ⓩ ⚡ ᵀ ✕ ⊙ 🖫 ∅ 🛖 ⊀ LP ⌂
Prices: ⚊9000 ⚊3000 🚐10000 ▲5000-9000

▶ **BOLOGNA** BOLOGNA

Citta di Bologna via Romita 12/IVA
☎ 39051 325016 ▤ 325318
e-mail: info@hotelcamping.com
Located in the northern part of this ancient town this site offers a cheap and convenient alternative to hotels.
All year 6.3HEC ⛺ ♣ ♠ ⓩ ⚡ ᵀ ✕ ⊙ 🖫 🖙 ⌂ ⊞ lau
♦ ✕ ∅ ㅗ ⊀P

▶ **BORGHETTO** PERUGIA

Badiaccia via Trasimenoi, no.91 ☎ 075 9659097
A well equipped site with large grassy pitches and direct access to the lake.
⊃ *From the A1 exit at Valdichiana and join the road to Perugia and follow signs for Lake Trasimeno.*
Apr-Sep 5.5HEC ⛺ ♣ ♠ ⓩ ⚡ ᵀ ✕ ⊙ 🖫 ∅ 🛖 🖙
⊀ LP lau ♦ ㅗ

▶ **CASAL BORSETTI** RAVENNA

Adria via Spallazzi N30 ☎ 0544 445217
The site lies in a field behind the Ristorante Lugo.
⊃ *Turn off the motorway at the Ravenna exit or take the SS309 (Romea) Km13 N of Ravenna.*
May-20 Sep 5.5HEC ⛺ ♣ ♠ ⓩ ⚡ ᵀ ✕ ⊙ 🖫 ∅ ㅗ 🛖
⊀ PS ⌂ ⊞ lau

Reno via Spaccazzi 11 ☎ 0544 445020 ▤ 0544 445020
Meadowland in sparse pine woodland and separated from the sea by dunes.
⊃ *Turn off SS309 at Km8 or 14.*
Apr-Sep 33HEC ⛺ ♣ ♠ ⓩ ⚡ ᵀ ✕ ⊙ 🖫 ∅ ㅗ 🛖 🖙 ⌂ ⊞ lau
♦ ⊀S

▶ **CASTIGLIONE DEL LAGO** PERUGIA

Listro via Lungolago ☎ 075 951193 ▤ 075 951193
Attractive site on a peninsula in Lake Trasimeno.
Apr-Sep 1HEC ⛺ ♣ ♠ ⓩ ⚡ ᵀ ✕ ⊙ 🖫 ㅗ ⊀ L ⌂ lau
♦ ✕ ∅ ⊀P ⊞

▶ **CERVIA** RAVENNA

Adriatico via Pinarella 90 ☎ 0544 71537 ▤ 0544 72346
e-mail: cadriatico@cervia.com
Level meadowland site with plenty of shade, pleasantly landscaped with olives, willows, elms and maples.
⊃ *Located shortly before Pinarella di Cervia. Access by via Cadulti per le Liberta (SS16) 600m from sea.*
27 Apr-15 Sep 3.4HEC ⛺ ♣ ♠ ⓩ ⚡ ᵀ ✕ ⊙ 🖫 ∅ ㅗ ⊀ P ⌂ ⊞
lau ♦ ⓩ ✕ ∅ ㅗ ⊀LS ⊞ Prices: ⚊4.20-5.90 ▲6.90-9.80

▶ **CESENATICO** FORLI

Cesenatico via Mazzini 182 ☎ 0547 81344 ▤ 672452
e-mail: campingcesenatico@gesturist.com
The site stretches over an area of land belonging to the Azienda di Soggiomo e Turismo.
⊃ *1.5km from Km178 turn off the SS16 towards the sea.*
All year 17HEC ⛺ ⠿⠿ ♣ ♠ ⓩ ⚡ ᵀ ✕ ⊙ 🖫 ㅗ 🛖 🖙 ⊀ S ⌂
lau ♦ ⊞

Zadina via Mazzini 184 ☎ 0547 82310 ▤ 0547 672802
Very pleasant terrain in dunes on two sides of a canal.
23 Apr-16 Sep 11HEC ⛺ ♣ ♠ ⓩ ⚡ ᵀ ✕ ⊙ 🖫 ∅ ㅗ ⊀ S ⌂ ⊞
lau Prices: ⚊4-8 🚐10.50-14.50 ▲8-10.50

▶ **CITTA DI CASTELLO** PERUGIA

La Montesca ☎ 075 8521420 ▤ 8520786
e-mail: villamontesca@sogepu.com
In a large, wooded park with excellent facilities. An ideal base for exploring the surrounding area.
⊃ *3km from the town, beside the River Tiber.*
May-Sep 5HEC ⛺ ♣ ♠ ⓩ ⚡ ᵀ ✕ ⊙ 🖫 ∅ ⊀ P 🖙 ⊞ lau

CIVITANOVA MARCHE MACERATA

Nuove Giare via Delle Fosse 46 ☎ 0733 70440
A modern family site with good recreational facilities.
⮕ *Exit A14 at Civitanova Marche, signposted.*
15 May-15 Sep 6HEC ⟱ ♠ ℂ 🆘 ⏰ ✕ ⊙ 🔲 ∅ 💢 🏠 💢 🅰
⮑ PS 🔳 ⊞ lau

CUPRA MARITTIMA ASCOLI PICENO

Calypso via Boccabianca 8 ☎ 0735 778686 ▦ 0735 778106
Apr-Sep 26HEC ⟱ ♠ ℂ 🆘 ⏰ ✕ ⊙ 🔲 ∅ 🏠 ⮑ PS ⊞ lau

DANTE, LIDO DI RAVENNA

Classe viale Catone ☎ 0544 492005 ▦ 0544 492058
Level meadowland in grounds of former farm.
⮕ *Access from the SS16 turning towards the sea at Km154/V and continue 9km to site.*
15 May-Sep 7HEC ⟱ ♠ ℂ 🆘 ⏰ ✕ ⊙ 🔲 🏠 💢 🅰 ⮑ PS 🔳
⊞ lau

ESTENSI, LIDO DEGLI FERRARA

International Mare Pineta via delle Acacie 67
☎ 0533 330110 ▦ 330052
e-mail: info@campingmarepineta.com
Extensive site on slightly hilly ground under pines and decidous trees, providing shade. Near the beach and has numerous mobile homes.
⮕ *2km SE of Port Garibaldi.*
18Apr-21Sep 16HEC ⟱ ⁙⁙⁙ ♠ ℂ 🆘 ⏰ ✕ ⊙ 🔲 ∅ 🏠 🏠
⮑ PS 🔳 lau

See advertisement in colour section

FANO PESARO & URBINO

Mare Blu ☎ 0721 884201 ▦ 0721 884389
The site is surrounded by tall poplars with direct access to a sandy beach. Facilities for most watersports and entertainment for children and families.
⮕ *Exit A14 at Fano and travel south for 3km.*
Apr-Sep 2.5HEC ⟱ ♠ ℂ 🆘 ⏰ ✕ ⊙ 🔲 ∅ 🏠 💢 ⮑ S 🔳 🅿 ⊞
lau ♦ ⮑PR

FERRARA FERRARA

Estense via Gramicia 76 ☎ 0532 752396 ▦ 0532 752396
e-mail: camping.estense@libero.it
A good overnight stop on the way south.
⮕ *NE outskirts of Ferrara*
All year 3.3HEC ⟱ ♠ ℂ ⊙ 🔲 💢 🔳 ♦ 🆘 ⏰ ✕ ∅ 🏠 ⮑P ⊞
Prices: ♠4.50 ♦6.50 🅰6.50 pitch 6.50

FIORENZUOLA DI FOCARA PESARO & URBINO

Panorama Strada Panoramica
☎ 0721 208145 ▦ 0721 208145
e-mail: info@campingpanorama.it
Located in a park 100mtrs above sea level this site welcomes families, animals, cyclists and those wishing to relax.
⮕ *Signposted off the SS16, 10km from Gabicce and 7km from Pesaro.*
May-Sep 2.2HEC ⟱ ♠ ℂ 🆘 ⏰ ✕ ⊙ 🔲 ∅ 🏠 🏠 💢 ⮑ LPS 🔳
⊞ lau Prices: ♠8500-12000 ♦4500-5000 💢10000-14000
🅰10000-14000

GATTEO MARE FORLI

Rose via Adriatica 29 ☎ 0547 86213 ▦ 87583
e-mail: baiocchi@villaggiorose.com
In a peaceful setting close to the sea and the town centre.
⮕ *Turn off SS16, at Km186.*
May-25 Sep 4HEC ⟱ ⁙⁙⁙ ♠ ℂ 🆘 ⏰ ✕ ⊙ 🔲 ∅ 🏠 🏠 💢
⮑ PS 🔳 ⊞ lau ♦ ⮑R Prices: ♠3.72-7.23 🅰3.61-8.78

GIULIANOVA LIDO TERAMO

Baviera Lungomare Zara ☎ 085 8000053 ▦ 085 8004420
A family site in a wooded location with direct access to a private beach. A wide variety of sporting and entertainment facilities are available, particularly in July and August, when all cars must use the designated car park.
⮕ *Access via A14 and SS80.*
31 May-15 Sep 1.8HEC ⟱ ♠ ℂ 🆘 ⏰ ✕ ⊙ 🔲 ∅ 🏠 🏠 ⮑ PS
🔳 lau

GUBBIO PERUGIA

Villa Ortoguidone Ortoguidone 214
☎ 075 9272037 ▦ 9276620
e-mail: gubbiocampings@altec.net
One of two well equipped sites in the same location. Plenty of space for tents.
⮕ *Access via SS298 (Gubbio-Perugia).*
Apr-Sep 2.5HEC ⟱ 🔺 ℂ ✕ ⊙ 🔲 🏠 💢 🔳 lau
♦ 🆘 ✕ ∅ ⮑P

MAGIONE PERUGIA

Polvese via Montivalle ☎ 075 848200 ▦ 075 848050
In a peaceful location beside Lake Trasimeno with plenty of recreational facilities.
Apr-Sep 5HEC ⟱ ♠ ℂ 🆘 ⏰ ✕ ⊙ 🔲 ∅ 🏠 💢 ⮑ LP 🔳 lau

Villaggio Italgest via Martiri di Cefalonia
☎ 075 848238 ▦ 848085
e-mail: camping@italgest.com
Situated by a lake and surrounded by woodland. There are good, modern facilities and all kinds of recreation are available.
Apr-Sep 5.5HEC ⟱ ♠ ℂ 🆘 ⏰ ✕ ⊙ 🔲 ∅ 🏠 🏠 🅰
⮑ LP 🅿 ⊞ lau

MARCELLI DI NUMANA ANCONA

Conero Azzurro via Litoranea ☎ 071 7390507
Well-equipped site situated between the Adriatic and Mount Canero.
Jun-15 Sep 5HEC ⟱ 🔺 ♠ ℂ 🆘 ⏰ ✕ ⊙ 🔲 ∅ 🏠
⮑ PS ⊞ lau ♦ 🏠

MAROTTA PESARO & URBINO

Gabbiano via Faa' di Bruno 95 ☎ 0721 96691 ▦ 0721 96691
Quiet location surrounded by trees overlooking the sea.
⮕ *Exit A14 at Marotta, join SS16 and site is 2.5km in the direction of Fano.*
May-Sep 1.9HEC ⟱ ♠ ℂ 🆘 ⏰ ✕ ⊙ 🔲 ∅ 🏠 🏠
⮑ PS 🔳 ⊞ ⊘ lau

MARTINISCURO TERAMO

Duca Amedeo Lungomare Europa 158
☎ 0861 797376 ▦ 0861 797264
e-mail: ducaamedeo@camping.it
In a pleasant location, surrounded by trees and lush vegetation. Close to the sea.
⮕ *Access via A14 exit Martinsicuro.*
May-20 Sep 1.5HEC ⟱ ♠ ℂ 🆘 ⏰ ✕ ⊙ 🔲 ∅ 🏠 ⮑ PS 🔳 ⊞ lau
♦ 🆘 ✕ Prices: ♠5000-15000 pitch 15000-24000

MILANO MARITTIMA RAVENNA

Romagna viale Matteotti 190 ☎ 0544 949326 ▦ 949345
Level and flat site with young trees.
⮕ *Access via the SS16 (Strada Adriatica) turn off beyond Milano Marittima and follow signs.*
15 Apr-15 Sep 40HEC ⟱ ♠ ℂ 🆘 ⏰ ✕ ⊙ 🔲 ∅ ⮑ S 🔳 ⊘ lau
♦ ⊞

MODENA MODENA

International via Cave di Ramo 111 ☎ 059 332252 ▦ 823235
e-mail: ivanbompani@hotmail.com
All year 2.6HEC ⊞⊞⊞ ♨ ♠ ⋔ ⅀ ⅄ ✕ ⊙ ☺ ∅ ≀ P ⑂ lau ➡ ♨
Prices: ♣6 pitch 10

MONTENERO, MARINA DI CAMPOBASSO

Costa Verde ☎ 0873 803144
e-mail: info@costaverde.it
A level site with good facilities and direct access to the beach
E of San Salvo Marino.
➲ *Leave the coast road, SS16, at Km525/VII and continue by
a farm road for 300m to the site.*
15 May-15 Sep 1HEC ⊞⊞⊞ ⋔ ⋔ ⅀ ⅄ ✕ ⊙ ☺ ∅ ≀ ☺ ☺ ▲ ≀
PRS ⑂ ⊞ ∅ lau ➡ ⊞

NAZIONI, LIDO DELLE FERRARA

Tahiti viale Libia 133 ☎ 0533 379500 ▦ 0533 379700
Pleasantly laid out site 650m from sea. Has own private
beach accessible via a miniature railway. Lunchtime siesta
13.30-15.30 hrs.
➲ *Turn off SS309 near Km32.5 then 2km to site. Signposted.*
10 May-21 Sep 8HEC ⊞⊞⊞ ∷∷ ♠ ⋔ ⅀ ⅄ ✕ ⊙ ☺ ∅ ♨ ☺ ≀ P
⑂ ⊞ ∅ lau ➡ ≀S

OLMO PERUGIA

Rocolo strada Fontana la Trinita ☎ 075 5178550 ▦ 5177538
e-mail: ilrocolo@ilrocolo.it
15 Apr-15 Oct 16 Oct-14 Apr 2.4HEC ⊞⊞⊞ ⋔ ⋔ ⅀ ⅄ ✕ ⊙ ☺
∅ ⑂ ⊞ lau ➡ ♨ ≀P Prices: ♣4-5 ♠2-2.50 ♠4.20-5.50
▲3.20-4

ORVIETO TERNI

Orvieto Lago di Corbara ☎ 0744 950240
A quiet site surrounded by large trees.
➲ *Turn off SS448 at Km3.770.*
All year 1.6HEC ⊞⊞⊞ ♠ ⋔ ⅀ ⅄ ✕ ⊙ ☺ ∅ ≀ LP ⑂

PARMA PARMA

Cittadella parco Cittadella ☎ 0521 961434
Camping Card Compulsory.
Apr-Oct 4HEC ⊞⊞⊞ ♠ ⋔ ⊙ ☺ ⑂ ♠ ⅀ ⅄ ✕ ∅ ♨ ⊞

PASSIGNANO PERUGIA

Europa Loc San Donato ☎ 075 827405 ▦ 827405
e-mail: info@camping-europa.it
Situated by Lake Trasimeno with private beach.
➲ *From the motorway take exit Passignano Est and campsite
is signposted.*
Etr-10 Oct 3HEC ⊞⊞⊞ ♠ ⋔ ⅀ ⅄ ✕ ⊙ ☺ ∅ ☺ ☺ ≀ L ⑂ ⊞ lau

Kursaal viale Europa 24 ☎ 075 828085 ▦ 075 827182
e-mail: kursaalcamp@libero.it
The site is situated between the road and the lake, near the
villa of the same name.
➲ *Access from SS75, Arezzo to Perugia road, from Km35.2.*
1 Apr-15 Oct 1HEC ⊞⊞⊞ ♠ ⋔ ⅀ ⅄ ✕ ⊙ ☺ ∅ ≀ LP ⑂ lau ➡
⊞ Prices: ♣6-7 ♠2 ♠8-9 ▲8-9

PESARO PESARO & URBINO

Marinella via Adriatica 244 ☎ 0721 55795
A flat grassy site with a private beach. Modern and well
maintained facilities.
➲ *Access is through railway underpass from Km244 of SS16.*
Apr-10 Oct 15HEC ⊞⊞⊞ ⋔ ⋔ ⅀ ⅄ ✕ ⊙ ☺ ∅ ♨ ☺ ☺ ≀ S ⑂
⊞ ⊞ lau ➡ ⅀ ✕

PIEVEPELAGO MODENA

Fra Dolcino ☎ 0536 71229
All year 3.6HEC ⊞⊞⊞ ♨ ♠ ⋔ ⅀ ⅄ ✕ ⊙ ☺ ♨ ☺ ⑂ lau ➡ ✕
≀PR ⊞ Prices: ♣5.16 ♠6.20 ▲4.13

RIO VERDE

Rio Verde via M-de-Canossa 34 ☎ 0536 72204
In a wooded mountain setting close to the river with good,
modern facilities.
➲ *Access via A1 from Firenze via Pistoia, La Lima and
Abetone.*
All year 1.8HEC ⊞⊞⊞ ⋔ ⋔ ⅄ ✕ ⊙ ☺ ☺ ☺ ≀ R ⊞ lau ➡ ♨ ♨
≀P ⊞

PINARELLA RAVENNA

Pinarella viale Abruzzi 52 ☎ 0544 987408 ▦ 987408
e-mail: campingpinarella@libero.it
Subdivided terrain surrounded by houses. Partially shaded,
some young poplars. Private beach. Management request
reservations day before arrival.
May-15 Sep 1.8HEC ⊞⊞⊞ ♠ ⋔ ⅀ ✕ ⊙ ☺ ⑂ ⊞ ∅ lau ➡ ♨ ≀
∅ ♨ ≀S Prices: ♣3.62-6.20 ♠7.75-11.37 ▲7.24-10.85

Safari viale Titano 130 ☎ 0544 987356 ▦ 987356
e-mail: csafari@cervia.com
The site is divided into several sections. Only families are
accepted.
28 Apr-9 Sep 3.1HEC ⊞⊞⊞ ♠ ⋔ ⅀ ⅄ ✕ ⊙ ☺ ∅ ⑂ ⊞ ⊞ ∅ lau
➡ ✕ ≀S

PINETO TERAMO

Heliopolis Contrada Villa Fumosa
☎ 085 9492720 ▦ 859492171
e-mail: info@heliopolis.it
Situated near a golden sandy beach. Various activies for all to
enjoy. Idyllic scenery for relaxing walks.
Apr-Sep 12HEC ⊞⊞⊞ ∷∷ ♠ ⋔ ⅀ ⅄ ✕ ⊙ ☺ ∅ ♨ ☺ ≀ PS
⊞ ⊞ lau

International Loc Torre Cerrano ☎ 085 930639 ▦ 930639
e-mail: international.pineto@camping.it
Site on level terrain with young poplars. Sunshade roofing on
the beach.
➲ *Turn off SS16 at Km431.2 and continue under railway
underpass. Adjoining railway line.*
May-Sep 1.5HEC ⊞⊞⊞ ♠ ⋔ ⅀ ⅄ ✕ ⊙ ☺ ∅ ♨ ☺ ≀ S ⑂ ⊞ ⊞
∅ lau

Pineto Beach ☎ 085 9492724 ▦ 9492796
e-mail: pinetobeach@agic.it
A well equipped site in wooded surroundings with direct
access to the beach.
➲ *At Km425 on SS16 'Adriatica'.*
15 May-Sep 3HEC ⊞⊞⊞ ∷∷ ♠ ⋔ ⅀ ⅄ ✕ ⊙ ☺ ∅ ♨ ☺
≀ S ⊞ ⊞ lau

POMPOSA FERRARA

International Tre Moschettieri via Capanno Garibaldi 22
☎ 0533 380376 ▦ 380377
e-mail: info@tremoschettieri.com
Camp site set beneath pine trees next to sea.
➲ *Signposted from SS309.*
23 Apr-9 Sep 11HEC ⊞⊞⊞ ♠ ⋔ ⅀ ⅄ ✕ ⊙ ☺ ∅ ☺ ☺
≀ PS ⑂ ⊞ lau ➡ ♨ ≀L ⊞ Prices: ♣4-7 ♠8-13

PORTO SANT'ELPÍDIO ASCOLI PICENO

Risacca via Gabbie 6 ☎ 0734 991423 ▦ 0734 997276
e-mail: info@larisacca.it
Clean, well-kept site on level meadowland, with some trees
surrounded by fields.
➲ *Turn off main SS16 N of village, follow road seawards
under railway (narrow underpass maximum height 3m), then
1.2km along field paths to site. Caravan access is 400m further
S along SS16, then under railway and along field paths to site.*
19 May-11 Sep 8HEC ⊞⊞⊞ ♠ ⋔ ⅀ ⅄ ✕ ⊙ ☺ ∅ ♨ ☺ ☺
≀ PS ⊞ ⊞ ∅ lau

> **PRECI** PERUGIA

Il Collaccio Castelvecchio di Preci
☎ 0743 939005 ▤ 0743 939094
In beautiful natural surroundings with plenty of roomy pitches and good recreational facilities.
➲ *Access via SS 209.*
Apr-1 Oct 10HEC ⚏ ⊞ ⚑ ⌂ ☎ ⚡ ✕ ☉ ♨ ⌀ ⛺ ⚓ P ⚐ lau

> **PUNTA MARINA** RAVENNA
> At **ADRIANO, LIDO**(4.5km S)

Adriano via dei Campeggi 7 ☎ 0544 437230 ▤ 0544 438510
300m from the sea. A pleasantly landscaped site amidst the dunes of the Punta Marina.
➲ *On SS309 via Lido Adriano to Punta Marina.*
23 Apr-20 Sep 14HEC ⚏ ⁖⁖⁖ ⚑ ⊞ ⚡ ⌂ ✕ ☉ ♨ ⌀ ⚌ ⛺ ⚑
⚓ PS ⚐ lau

Coop 3 via dei Campeggi 8 ☎ 0544 437353 ▤ 438144
e-mail: campingcoop3@libero.it
300m to the sea. Level site under isolated high pines and poplars. Across flat dunes to the beach.
➲ *Signposted.*
25 Apr-16 Sep 7HEC ⚏ ⚑ ⊞ ⚡ ⌂ ✕ ☉ ♨ ⚌ ⚑ ⚐ lau ♦ ⌀
⚓PS ⊞ **Prices:** ⚑6500-11400 pitch 13200-20800

> **RAVENNA, MARINA DI** RAVENNA

International Piomboni via Lungomare 421
☎ 0544 530230 ▤ 0544 538618
e-mail: campingpiomboni.it
Site on slightly undulating mainly grassy terrain with pines and poplars. Separate section for tents. Lunchtime siesta 14.00-15.30 hrs.
➲ *Access is 1km S from town centre off coast road.*
27 Apr-15 Sep 5HEC ⚏ ⚑ ⊞ ⚡ ⌂ ✕ ☉ ♨ ⌀ ⚌ ⛺ ⚑
⚓ S ⚐ ⊞ lau

> **RICCIONE** FORLI

Alberello via Torino 80 ☎ 0541 615402 ▤ 0541 615248
e-mail: direzione@alberello.it
On the seafront connected to the beach by a private subway. Popular with families, with a wide range of recreational facilities.
➲ *Access via A14 and SS16.*
May-20 Sep 4HEC ⚏ ⚑ ⊞ ⚡ ⌂ ✕ ☉ ♨ ⌀ ⚌ ⚐ ⊞ ⚘ lau ♦
⚓RS

Fontanelle via Torino 56 ☎ 0541 615449 ▤ 610193
On southern outskirts separated from beach by coast road. Underpass to public beach.
Camping Card Compulsory.
➲ *Turn off SS16 between Km216 and 217.*
23 Apr-20 Sep 6HEC ⚏ ⚑ ⊞ ⚡ ⌂ ✕ ☉ ♨ ⌀ ⚌ ⚓ S ⚐ ⊞ lau

Riccione via Marsala N10 ☎ 0541 690160 ▤ 0541 690044
e-mail: info@campingriccione.com
About 300m from sea. Extensive flat meadowland, with poplars of medium height.
➲ *From SS16 turn seawards on the S outskirts of the town and continue for 200m. Alternative access from coast road, turn inland on S outskirts at sign and continue for 700m.*
24 Apr-22 Sep 6.5HEC ⚏ ⚑ ⊞ ⚡ ⌂ ✕ ☉ ♨ ⌀ ⚌ ⚑
⚓ P ⚐ lau ♦ ⚓S ⊞

> **ROSETO DEGLI ABRUZZI** TERAMO

Eurcamping-Roseto Lungomare Trieste Sud 90
☎ 085 8993179 ▤ 085 8941493
A meadow site at the S end of the beach road.
➲ *Leave the SS16 within the town, then continue for 500m to the site.*
All year 5HEC ⚏ ⚑ ⊞ ⚡ ⌂ ✕ ☉ ♨ ⌀ ⚌ ⛺ ⚓ PS ⚐ ⊞ lau

Gilda viale Makarska ☎ 085 8941023
In a picturesque wooded setting with direct access to the beach and good, modern facilities.
Jun-Aug 1.5HEC ⚏ ⚑ ⊞ ⚡ ⌂ ✕ ☉ ♨ ⌀ ⛺ ⚑
⚓ S ⚐ ⊞ lau ♦ ⌀ ⚓P

> **SALSOMAGGIORE TERME** PARMA

Arizona via Tabiano 40 ☎ 0524 565648 ▤ 565648
e-mail: info@camping-arizona.com
Family site with plenty of activities, and close to two "thermal cures" establishments.
Apr-15 Oct 13HEC ⚏ ⚑ ⊞ ⚡ ⌂ ✕ ☉ ♨ ⌀ ⚌ ⚑ ⚓ P ⚐ lau
♦ ⚌ ⊞ **Prices:** ⚑5.16-6.71 ⚑7.23-9.81 ⚑4.64-8.26

> **SAN MARINO**

Centro Turistico San Marino Strada San Michele 50
☎ 0549 903964 ▤ 0549 907120
e-mail: camping@sanmarinosite.com
In a quiet, wooded location close to the centre of the Republic of San Marino.
➲ *Access via 'Rimini Sud' exit on the A14.*
All year 100HEC ⚏ ⊞ ⚑ ⊞ ⚡ ⌂ ✕ ☉ ♨ ⌀ ⚌ ⛺ ⚑ ⚑ ⚓
⚓ P ⚐ ⊞ lau

> **SAN PIERO IN BAGNO** FORLI

Altosavio strada per Alfero 37c
☎ 0543 903409 ▤ 903409/917397
e-mail: i48ta@libero.it
On level ground at an altitude of 600mtrs with good facilities.
➲ *Exit E45 at Bagno di Romagna for San Piero in Bagno*
24 Apr-30 Sep 1.3HEC ⚏ ⚑ ⊞ ⚡ ✕ ☉ ♨ ⚐ lau
Prices: ⚑7500-8500 pitch 13000

> **SASSO MARCONI** BOLOGNA

Piccolo Paradiso via Sirano, Marzabotto
☎ 051 842680 ▤ 051 6756581
Pleasant site with plenty of trees. A new sport centre less than 100mtrs from the site provides excellent facilities for sports and recreation.
➲ *Leave A1 autostrada (Milano-Roma) at town exit and continue towards Vado for 2km. Signposted.*
All year 6.5HEC ⚏ ⚑ ⊞ ⚡ ⌂ ✕ ☉ ♨ ⌀ ⚌ ⛺ ⚑ ⚐ lau ♦
⚓LPR **Prices:** ⚑4.13-5.42 ⚑10.85 ⚑8.27

> At **SAVIGNANO SUL RUBICONE**

Rubicone via Matrice Destra 1
☎ 0541 346377 ▤ 0541 346999
e-mail: info@campingrubicone.com
An extensive, level site divided into two sections by a narrow canal. It extends to the beach.
➲ *Situated about 0.8km from the road fork at Km187/0 off SS16 (Strada Adriatica).*
May-25 Sep 13HEC ⚏ ⚑ ⚑ ⊞ ⚡ ⌂ ✕ ☉ ♨ ⌀ ⛺ ⚓ PS ⚐ ⊞
⚘ lau **Prices:** ⚑4.60-8 pitch 9.56-13.94

> **SCACCHI, LIDO DEGLI** FERRARA

Florenz via alpi Centrali 199 ☎ 0533 380193
Site with sand dunes extending to the sea.
➲ *Turn off the Strada Romea in the direction of Lido Degli Scacchi, and continue along an asphalt road to the sandy beach.*
24 Apr-16 Sep 8HEC ⚏ ⁖⁖⁖ ⊞ ⚑ ⊞ ⚡ ⌂ ✕ ☉ ♨ ⌀ ⚌ ⚑
⚓ PS ⚐ ⊞ lau

> **SENIGALLIA** ANCONA

Summerland via Podesti 236 ☎ 071 7926816 ▤ 7926816
A pleasant site with good facilities, 150mtrs from the sea.
➲ *3km from Senigallia exit on SS16.*
Jun-15 Sep 4.5HEC ⚏ ⚑ ⊞ ⚡ ⌂ ✕ ☉ ♨ ⌀ ⛺ ⚑ ⊞ lau ♦
⚓PS

SPINA, LIDO DI FERRARA

Spina via del Campeggio 99 ☎ 0533 330179 ▨ 0533 333566
e-mail: spina@clubdesole.com
Widespread site on level meadowland and on slightly hilly
sand dune terrain. Separate section for owners with dogs.
➲ *Off SS309. Signposted.*
7 Apr-23 Sep 24HEC ⛺ ♠♦♠️♈️♓️✕☉♋♦♨️ ⚓️ PS ⚄ lau
♦ ⊞ Prices: ⚡3.70-7.60 ♠3.70-3.70 pitch 8.20-13.30

SPOLETO PERUGIA

Monteluco S.Pietro ☎ 0743 220358 ▨ 207146
e-mail: primaver@caribusiness.it
A modern site situated on the slopes of Monteluco.
➲ *From the SS75 towards Foligno exit on to the SS3 towards
Spoleto. The Monteluco road leads to the site.*
Apr-Sep 6HEC ⁙ ♦♠️♈️✕☉♋♦♨️⚄♦️♨️⊞

TORINO DI SANGRO MARINA CHIETI

Belvedere ☎ 0873 911381
Jun-15 Sep 1.5HEC ⛺ ♠♦♈️♓️✕☉♋♦♨️⚓️S⚄⊞
lau ♦✕ ⚓P ⊞

VALLICELLA DI MONZUNO BOLOGNA

Le Querce Rioveggio ☎ 051 6770394
A well equipped site in a wooded mountain setting.
➲ *Access via Autostrada del Sole.*
May-Sep 1.2HEC ⛺ ♦♠️♈️♓️✕☉♋♦♨️⚓️♨️A
⚓ LPR ⚄ ⊞ lau

VASTO CHIETI

Europa ☎ 0873 801988
Site on level terrain by the road with poplars.
➲ *At Km522 of road SS16.*
May-Sep 2.3HEC ⛺ ♦♠️♈️♓️✕☉♋♦♨️⚓️ S lau

Grotta del Saraceno via Osca 6, loc Vignola
☎ 0873 310213 ▨ 310295
e-mail: info@grottadelsaraceno.it
Site in olive grove on steep coastal cliffs with lovely views.
Steep path to beach. Siesta 14.00-16.00 hrs.
➲ *Turn off SS16 at Km512.200.*
15 Jun-15 Sep 12HEC ⛺ ♦♠️♈️♓️✕☉♋♦♨️⚓️ S lau
♦♨️♨️

Pioppeto ☎ 0873 801466 ▨ 801466
Camping Card Compulsory.
15 May-15 Sep 1.7HEC ⛺ ♦♠️♈️♓️✕☉♋♦♨️⚓️S⚄
♦ ⊞ Prices: ⚡5.16-6.19 pitch 10.32-12.91

VILLALAGO L'AQUILA

I Lupi ☎ 0864 740100
All year 7HEC ⛺ ♠♠️♈️♓️☉♋♦♨️⚄⊞♦♨️♨️⚓LP

ZOCCA MODENA

Montequestiolo via Montequestiolo 184
☎ 059 985137 ▨ 985137
e-mail: monteq@tin.it
1.8HEC ⛺ ♠♠️♈️♓️✕☉♋♦♨️♨️♦️♨️A⊞⊞ lau ♦ ⚓P

●●●●●● ROME ●●●●●●

Rome has affected western culture and attitudes for more
than 2,000 years. The city is uniquely beautiful; from the
famous Colosseum (a third of which is still intact) to the
elegantly proportioned piazzas and churches, there are
historic buildings which provide dramatic examples of
changing architectural ideals. Of the 22 bridges which span
the Tiber, some date from the first century BC.
Situated on the famous seven hills, the city is the focus of
the province of Latium, which has been described as 'the
cradle of Roman civilization'. Stretching from the Apennines
to the Tyrrhenian sea, it is characterised by magnificent and
beautiful scenery, especially in the volcanic regions, where
long extinct volcanoes form the lakes of Albano, Bracciano,
Bolsena and Vico. Viterbo, in the northern hills, is a large
town with many fine examples of religious architecture,
including the 13th-century Papal Palace. Rieti's Civic
Museum houses an extensive collection of Roman artifacts,
while Frosinone commands breathtaking views of
surrounding countryside. The Latin Lido features sheltered
harbours and sandy beaches.

BOLSENA VITERBO

Blu International via Cassia ☎ 0761 798855 ▨ 798855
e-mail: info@blucamping.it
A modern site with good facilities in a wooded location on
the shore of Lake Bolsena. Compulsory separate car park in
July and August.
➲ *Access via A1 exit Orvieto, then Via Cassia at Km111.650.*
May-Sep 3HEC ⛺ ♦♠️♈️♓️✕☉♋♦♨️A⚓L⚄lau
♦♨️⚄⊞

Lido via Cassia km111 ☎ 0761 799258 ▨ 796105
e-mail: info@atihotels.it
A lakeside family site with good modern facilities.
➲ *Access via motorway exit 'Orvieto'.*
Apr-Sep 10HEC ⛺ ♦♠️♈️♓️✕☉♋♦♨️♨️
⚓ LP ⚄♨️ lau

BRACCIANO ROMA

Porticciolo via Porticciolo ☎ 06 99803060 ▨ 06 998803030
e-mail: romalake@aconet.it
A family site in a pleasant location on the shore of a lake.
➲ *Access via SS493 to Bracciano.*
Apr-Sep 3HEC ⛺ ♦♠️♈️♓️✕☉♋♦♨️♨️A
⚓ L⚄ lau ♦ ⚓P ⊞

FIANO ROMANO ROMA

Bungalow Park I Pini via delle Sassete 1A
☎ 0765 453349 ▨ 0765 453057
e-mail: ipimi@camping.it
A modern, well equipped site within easy reach of the centre
of Rome which makes an excellent base for excursions.
➲ *From A1 Firenze-Roma take exit Fiano Romana.*
15 Mar-15 Nov 5HEC ⛺ ♠♠️♈️♓️✕☉♋♦♨️♨️
⚓ P ⚄⊞ lau

FORMIA LATINA

Gianola via delle Vigne ☎ 0771 720223
Situated in a narrow grassland area near a little stream and
trees amidst agricultural land. Pleasantly sandy beach edged
by rocks.
➲ *Access via Roma-Napoli road, from S Croce 800m.*
Apr-Sep 4HEC ⛺ ⁙ ♦♠️♈️♓️✕☉♋♦♨️♨️⚓ S⚄

MINTURNO, MARINA DI LATINA

Golden Garden via Dunale 74
☎ 0771 681425 ▥ 0771 614059
e-mail: servizio.clienti@goldengarden.it
Secluded, quiet site within agricultural area by the sea.
Camping Card Compulsory.
➲ *Access from the SS7 across river bridge (Garigliano) and continue 4.6km changing direction. Last km sandy field track.*
Etr-20 Oct 2.3HEC ⸬ ♦ ♠ ⅊ ⅄ ✕ ☉ ➈ ⌀ ᴴ ⌂ ⌑ ⅌ S ⊡
⸂ lau ➡ ✕ ⊡

MONTALTO DI CASTRO, MARINA DI VITERBO

California ☎ 0766 802848 ▥ 0766 801210
Situated on the coast below an ancient pine grove with good facilities for sports and leisure.
May-Sep 1.4HEC ⸬ ⸬⸬ ♦ ♠ ⅊ ⅄ ✕ ☉ ➈ ⌀ ⌂ ⌑
⸂ S ⊡ ⊞ lau

Internazionale Pionier Etrusco via Vulsinia
☎ 0766 802199 ▥ 0766 801214
e-mail: meleute@tin
Situated in a pine forest close to the beach. Various leisure and sports activities, also a relaxing atmosphere.
Camping Card Compulsory.
Mar-15 Oct 3HEC ⸬⸬ ♦ ♠ ⅊ ⅄ ✕ ☉ ➈ ⌀ ᴴ ⌂ ⌑ lau
➡ ⸂PRS ⊞ Prices: ⅄4.65-7.75 ⅊3.62-5.68 pitch 19.11-29.18

ROMA (ROME) ROMA

Flaminio via Flaminia 821 ☎ 06 3332604 ▥ 3330653
e-mail: info@villageflainio.com
An extensive site with good facilities, which lies in a quiet valley on narrow terraces on a hill.
➲ *From ring road follow via Flaminia, SS3, for 2.5km towards city centre.*
16 Mar-14 Nov 8.4HEC ⸬ ♦ ♠ ⅊ ⅄ ✕ ☉ ➈ ⌀ ᴴ ⌂ ⌑ ⸂
P ⊡ lau ➡ ⸂R ⊞ Prices: ⅄7.75-8.78 ⅊3.87-4.39 ⌑6.20-6.71
⅄4.39-5.68
See advertisement in colour section

Happy via Prato della Corte 1915
☎ 06 33626401 ▥ 06 33613800
Conveniently placed in northern area of town. Modern installations, electricity and hot water free throughout.
➲ *Exit No.5 "Grande Raccordo Anulare" (ring road).*
15 Mar-Oct 3.6HEC ⸬ ♦ ♠ ⅊ ⅄ ✕ ☉ ➈ ⌀ ⌑
⸂ P ⊡ ⊞ lau
See advertisement in colour section

Roma via Aurelia 831 ☎ 06 6623018 ▥ 06/66418147
The site lies on terraces on a hill near the AGIP Motel. All kinds of excursions can be arranged.
➲ *From ring road follow SS1 (via Aurelia) for 1.5km towards town centre turn off to site at Km8/11.*
All year 3HEC ⸬ ♦ ♠ ⅊ ⅄ ✕ ☉ ➈ ⌀ ᴴ lau ➡ ⊞

Seven Hills via Cassia 1216 ☎ 06 30310826 ▥ 30310039
e-mail: seven-hills@camping.it
A fine, partly terraced site in beautiful rural surroundings yet ideally situated for access to the city by bus or underground.
➲ *2.5km NE of the outer ring road via exit '3'.*
November 5HEC ⸬ ⌀ ♦ ♠ ⅊ ⅄ ✕ ☉ ➈ ⌀ ᴴ ⌂ ⌑
⸂ P ⊡ lau
See advertisement in colour section

Tiber via Tiberina Km1400 ☎ 06 33612314 ▥ 33612314
e-mail: info@campingtiber.com
On level grassland, shaded by poplars beside the Tiber.
➲ *N of city. Signposted from ringroad. Access from N via exit '3' or from S follow signs 'Prima Porta'.*
15 Mar-31 Dec 5HEC ⸬ ♦ ♠ ⅊ ⅄ ✕ ☉ ➈ ⌀ ⌂ ⸂ PR ⊡ ⊞
lau ➡ ᴴ Prices: ⅄8-9 ⅊4-4.50 ⌑6-6.50 ⅄4-5.50
See advertisement in colour section

SALTO DI FONDI LATINA

Fondi Holiday Camp via Flacce Km 6800 ☎ 0771 555009
Well-shaded and well-equipped site only a few metres from the Mediterranean.
1Apr-Sep 4HEC ⸬ ⸬⸬ ♦ ♠ ⅊ ⅄ ✕ ☉ ➈ ⌀ ᴴ ⌂ ⌑ ⸂ PS
⊡ ⊞ ⸂ lau

TERRACINA LATINA

Badino Porto Badino ☎ 0773 764430 ▥ 764430
In wooded surroundings with direct access to the beach.
➲ *From the main Roma-Napoli road head towards the canal (Porto Canale Badino) and the sea.*
Apr-15 Oct 1.8HEC ⸬ ⸬⸬ ♦ ♠ ⅊ ✕ ☉ ➈ ⌀ ᴴ ⌂ ⌑ ⅄
⸂ S ⊡ ➡ ⅊ ✕

● ● ● ● **SOUTH** ● ● ● ●

The area known as the Mezzogiorno, takes in Campania and the 'toe and heel' provinces of Calabria (the toe), Basilicata, and Apulia (the heel).
From Naples, a port set in a beautiful bay with volcanic Vesuvius behind it, you travel south to an area in which you look back in time and where the language is different from northern Italian. Apulia is mountainous but has fertile plains producing olives, wines and tobacco. In the university town of Lecce you can see the exuberant 'Lecce Baroque' ornate stone carving while in Alberobella you find the circular 'trulli' houses made of drystone with cone shaped roofs. Equally intriguing is the abandoned city at Matera where semi-cave dwellings made of tufa used to house hundreds of families.
Baby octopus and other fish are part of a healthy diet of seafood, vegetables and pulses. Travel though the poorest region of Italy, Basilicata, before arriving in Calabria - also mountainous, with skiing in winter, but with 372 miles of coastline. Reggio di Calabria, right on the toe, has a mild climate in which exotic plants like the bergamot orange flourish.

....

ACCIAROLI SALERNO

Ondina ☎ 0974 904040
Delightful seaside site, full of flowers. Lunchtime siesta 14.00-16.00 hrs.
➲ *Turn off towards the sea at Km35/VII.*
Apr-Oct 3HEC ⸬ ♦ ♠ ⅊ ✕ ☉ ➈ ⌀ ᴴ ⌂ ⌑ ⸂ S ⊡ ⊞ ➡
✕

BAIA DOMIZIA CASERTA

Baia Domizia Camping Villaggio Baia Domizia
☎ 0823 930164 ▥ 0823 930375
e-mail: baiadomizia@iol.it
Part of this extensive seaside site is laid out with flower beds. Good sports and leisure facilities. Ideal for families. No radios allowed.
➲ *Turn off the SS7 (qtr) at Km6/V, then 3km seawards.*
28 Apr-23 Sep 30HEC ⸬ ♦ ♠ ⅊ ⅄ ✕ ☉ ➈ ⌀ ᴴ ⌂ ⌑ ⸂ PS
⊡ ⊞ ⸂ lau

BATTIPAGLIA SALERNO

Lido Mediterraneo via Litoranea, Salerno Paestum
☎ 0828 624097 ▦ 624097
e-mail: mediterraneo.campania@camping.it
In a pinewood with direct access to a private beach.
10Mar-22Sept 1.2HEC ⚏ ♠ ⋒ ⚏ ♀ ✕ ⊙ ⚏ ⊘ ♨ ⛺ ☻ ⅞ S
⚎ ➤ ✕ ⅞P ⊞

BRIATICO CATANZARO

Dolomiti ☎ 0963 391355 ▦ 0963 393009
e-mail: dolmar@tin.it
The site is in a delightful setting on two terraces planted with
olive trees. It lies by the road and 150m from the railway.
➲ *Turn off road 522 between Km17 and Km18 and head
towards the sea.*
May-Sep 5HEC ⚏ ♠ ⋒ ⚏ ♀ ✕ ⊙ ⚏ ⊘ ♨ ⛺ ☻ ⅞ PS ▣ lau
➤ ⅞P ⊞

CAMEROTA, MARINA DI SALERNO

Happy Localita Arconte ☎ 0974 932326
The site lies on a park-like hill sloping down to the sea and is
scattered with olive trees.
➲ *1km N of village just off the coast road.*
Jun-Sep 12HEC ⚏ ♠ ⋒ ⚏ ♀ ✕ ⊙ ⚏ ☻ ⅞ S ⊞

Risacca via delle Barche 11, Lentiscella
☎ 0974 932415 ▦ 0974 3290973
On level ground, shaded by olive trees, with direct access to a
sandy beach.
➲ *Approach via SS18.*
20 May-25 Sep 2HEC ⚏ ♠ ⋒ ⚏ ♀ ✕ ⊙ ⚏ ☻
⅞ S ▣ ⊞ ➤ ⊘ ♨

CAPO VATICANO CATANZARO

Gabbiano San Nicolo di Ricadi
☎ 0963 663159 ▦ 0963 663384
Apr-Oct ⚏ ⋮⋮⋮ ♠ ⋒ ⚏ ♀ ✕ ⊙ ⚏ ♨ ☻ ⅞ PS ▣ lau ➤ ⊞

CAROVIGNO BRINDISI

At SPECCHIOLLA, LIDO

Pineta al Mare Lido Specchiolla
☎ 0831 987821 ▦ 0831 397826
e-mail: info@campingpinetamare.com
Site in pine woodland with sandy beach and some rocks.
➲ *E of Bari-Brindisi road at Km21.5.*
All year 5.5HEC ⚏ ♠ ⋒ ⚏ ♀ ✕ ⊙ ⚏ ⊘ ♨ ☻ ⅞ PS ⚎ ⊞
lau Prices: ♠4.90-6.20 ♠1.54-2.58 ⛟5.16-6.19 ▲5.16-6.19

CIRÒ MARINA CATANZARO

Punta Alice ☎ 0962 31160
The site lies on meadowland amidst lush Mediterranean
vegetation and borders a fine gravel beach, some 50m wide.
➲ *2km from town. From SS106 (Strada Ionica) turn off at
Km290 seaward to Cira Marina. Pass through village and
follow beach road for 1.5m towards the lighthouse.*
Apr-Sep 5.5HEC ⋮⋮⋮ ♠ ⋒ ⚏ ♀ ✕ ⊙ ⚏ ⊘ ♨ ⅞ PS ⚎ ⊞ lau

Villaggio Torrenova via Torrenova ☎ 0962 31482
By the sea, with on site facilities to suit all the family.
May-Sep 1.2HEC ⋮⋮⋮ ♠ ⋒ ⚏ ♀ ✕ ⊙ ⚏ ♨ ☻ ⅞ S ⚎ lau

CORIGLIANO CÁLABRO COSENZA

Thurium Contrada Ricota Grande
☎ 0983 851955 ▦ 0983 851955
e-mail: thurium@jonianet.it
The site is close to the beach and has all the facilites needed
for an enjoyable camping break. It is just a walk away from
the woodland and ideal for peaceful walks.
Apr-Dec 16HEC ⋮⋮⋮ ♠ ⋒ ⚏ ♀ ✕ ⊙ ⚏ ⊘ ♨ ☻ ⚏ ⅞ S ⚎ ▣
⊞ lau

EBOLI SALERNO

Paestum Foce Sele ☎ 0828 691003 ▦ 691003
e-mail: info@campingpaestum.com
Sandy, meadowland site in tall poplar wood by river mouth.
Steps and bus service to private beach, 600m from site.
➲ *Access from the Litoranea at Km20 from the road fork to
Santa Cecilia and continue for 0.3km. Signposted.*
15 May-15 Sep 8HEC ⚏ ♠ ⋒ ⚏ ♀ ✕ ⊙ ⚏ ⊘ ♨ ⛺ ☻ ⅞ P ⚎
⊞ lau ➤ ⅞RS Prices: ♠3.87-5.42 ⛟10.45-16.53 ▲8.26-10.45

GALLIPOLI LECCE

Baia di Gallipoli ☎ 0833 273210 ▦ 0833262760
e-mail: info@baiadigallipoli.com
A holiday village set amid pine woods close to the sea with
good facilities. *Camping Card Compulsory.*
➲ *5km SE of Gallipoli.*
Jun-Sep 10HEC ⚏ ♠ ⋒ ⚏ ♀ ✕ ⊙ ⚏ ⊘ ♨ ☻ ⅞ P ⊞ ➤ ⅞S

Vecchia Torre ☎ 0833 209083
This well-kept and clean site lies amidst sand dunes in a pine
wood. Small size pitches.
➲ *5km N of Gallipoli and 200m S of Hotel Rivabella at
seaward side of coast road.*
Jun-Sep 8HEC ⋮⋮⋮ ♠ ⋒ ⚏ ♀ ✕ ⊙ ⚏ ⊘ ♨ ☻ ⅞ S ▣ ⚎ ⊛ lau
Prices: ♠3-5 ⛟6-16 ▲6-16 pitch 6-16

GIOVINAZZO BARI

Campofreddo ☎ 080 3942112 ▦ 080 3942290
Site on level terrain by the sea, mainly under sunshade
roofing. Siesta 14.00-16.00 hrs.
➲ *Turn off the SS16, 20km N of Bari at Km784.300.*
May-Sep 34HEC ⚏ ◷ ⋒ ⚏ ♀ ✕ ⊙ ⚏ ☻ ⚎ ▣ ⊞ ⊛ lau
➤ ✕ ⅞S

GUARDAVALLE, MARINA DI CATANZARO

Dello Ionio via Nazionale ☎ 0967 86002 ▦ 0967 86271
Site is situated on the seafront and along 4km of sandy
beach. All pitches are under the shade of tall trees and have
large grassy areas.
➲ *Situated 2km from Santa Caterina dello Jonio on the
SS106.*
Jun-15 Sep 5HEC ⚏ ♠ ⋒ ⚏ ♀ ✕ ⊙ ⚏ ⊘ ♨ ☻ ⚏ ▲
⅞ P ⚎ ⊞ lau ➤ ⅞S

LÁURA SALERNO

Hera Argiva ☎ 0828 851193
Site in sandy terrain in eucalyptus grove by the sea.
➲ *Signposted from Km88/VII SS18.*
Apr-Sep 40HEC ⋮⋮⋮ ♠ ⋒ ⚏ ♀ ✕ ⊙ ⚏ ⊘ ☻ ⚏ ⅞ S ⚎ lau ➤
⊞

LEPORANO, MARINA DI TARANTO

Porto Pirrone Litoranea Salentina
☎ 099 5334844 ▦ 5334844
e-mail: info@portopirrone.it
Set in a pine wood offering flat large plots for both tents and
caravans. Good sports and entertainment. No Animals.
➲ *From A14 at Massafra towards Taranto and Leporano. Site
is near marina.*
Jun-Sep 3.2HEC ⚏ ⋮⋮⋮ ♠ ⋒ ⚏ ♀ ✕ ⊙ ⚏ ♨ ☻ ⅞ S ⊞
⊛ ➤ ✕ ⊘ ⊞ Prices: ♠4.13-6.20 ♠1.55-2.58 ⛟4.13-6.20
▲3.10-4.13 pitch 4.13-6.20

MÁCCHIA FOGGIA

Monaco ☎ 0884 530280
In a pleasant situation with good facilities and direct access
to the beach.
Jun-Aug 5.3HEC ⬛⬛⬛ ✦ ⌂ ⬛ ▼ ✕ ⊙ ⬛ ⊘ ⬛ ⬛ ⱬ S ⬛ ⊞ ⬚
lau

MANFREDONIA FOGGIA

Ippocampo SS 159 ☎ 0884 571121 ⬛ 571121
e-mail: vitale@clarence.com
In grounds of a holiday village.
15Jun-Sep 8HEC ⠄⠄⠄ ⌴ ⌂ ⬛ ▼ ✕ ⊙ ⬛ ⊘ ⬛ ⬛ ▲
ⱬ S ⬛ ⊞ ✦ ⱬP

MASSA LUBRENSE NAPOLI

Villa Lubrense via Partenope 31 ☎ 081 5339781
All year 2.5HEC ⬛⬛⬛ ✦ ⌂ ⬛ ▼ ✕ ⊙ ⬛ ⊘ ⬛ ⬛ ⱬ PS ⊞
Prices: ⋔6.20-7.23 ⬛3.10-3.62 ⬛6.71-7.75 ▲5.68-6.71

MATTINATA FOGGIA

Villaggio Turistico San Lorenzo ☎ 0884 550152 ⬛ 552042
e-mail: sanlorenzo@tg.hettuno.it
The site is situated above the coast road in direction of
Viesta. Bungalows for hire.
Camping Card Compulsory.
All year 3HEC ⬛⬛⬛ ✦ ⌂ ▼ ✕ ⊙ ⬛ ⬛ ⱬ PS ⬔ ⬛ lau
✦ ⬛ ⊘ ⬛ ⊞

METAPONTO, LIDO DI MATERA

Camel Camping Club viale Magna Grecia ☎ 0835 741926
A modern, well organised site. Sports and entertainment
avaliable all season. Ideal for both relaxing and sightseeing.
Jun-Sep 3.5HEC ⠄⠄⠄ ✦ ⌂ ⬛ ▼ ✕ ⊙ ⬛ ⬛ ⱬ P ✦ ⊘ ⬛ ⱬS ⊞

NICÓTERA MARINA CATANZARO

Sabbia d'Oro ☎ 0963 886395 ⬛ 0966 653312
Lies on level ground amidst farmland 100m from a beautiful
beach.
⮕ *Turn off SS18 at Km453/VII and continue 15km.*
15 Jun-10 Sept 2.7HEC ⠄⠄⠄ ✦ ⌂ ⬛ ▼ ✕ ⊙ ⬛ ⊘ ⬛ ⬛ ⬛
ⱬ S ⬔ ⊞ lau

OTRANTO LECCE

Mulino d'Acqua via S Stefano ☎ 0836 802191 ⬛ 802196
e-mail: mulino.camping@anet.it
Shaded by olive trees, close to the beach and with plenty of
organised activities.
Jun-10 Sep 10HEC ⬛⬛⬛ ✦ ⌂ ⬛ ▼ ✕ ⊙ ⬛ ⬛ ⬛ ⬛ ▲
ⱬ PS ⬛ ⬚ lau

PALMI REGGIO DI CALABRIA

San Fantino via S-Fantino ☎ 0966 479430
Site on several terraces with lovely views of the bay of Lido di
Palmi. 200m to the beach. Siesta 13.00-16.00 hrs.
⮕ *Turn off road SS18 seawards N of Palmi.*
All year 4HEC ⬛⬛⬛ ✦ ⌂ ⬛ ▼ ✕ ⊙ ⬛ ⊘ ⬛ ▲ ⬛ lau
✦ ⱬPS ⊞

PESCHICI FOGGIA

Centro Turistico San Nicola Loc San Nicola ☎ 0884 964024
Terraced site in lovely situation by the sea, in a bay enclosed
by rocks. Can become overcrowded.
⮕ *Turn off coast road Peschici-Vieste, follow signs along
winding road to site in 1km.*
Apr-15 Oct 14HEC ⬛⬛⬛ ✦ ⌂ ⬛ ▼ ✕ ⊙ ⬛ ⊘ ⬛ ⬛
ⱬ S ⬔ ⊞ lau

Internazionale Manacore ☎ 0884 911020 ⬛ 0884 911049
Meadowland with a few terraces in attractive bay, surrounded
by wooded hills.
⮕ *Turn off the coastal road (Peschici-Vieste) towards ths sea
in a wide U bend.*
4 May-20 Oct 20HEC ⬛⬛⬛ ✦ ⌂ ⬛ ▼ ✕ ⊙ ⬛ ⊘ ⬛ ⬛ ⱬ S ⊞

PIZZO CATANZARO

Pinetamare ☎ 0963 534871 ⬛ 534871
A sandy site surrounded by tall pine trees. Most watersports
are avaliable along the private beach and families are
welcomed.
⮕ *From the Salerno/Reggio motorway take the Pizzo exit and
site is north of town.*
Jun-Sep 10HEC ⠄⠄⠄ ✦ ⌂ ⬛ ▼ ✕ ⊙ ⬛ ⊘ ⬛ ⬛ ⬛
ⱬ PS ⬔ ⊞ lau ⱬL

POMPEI NAPOLI

Spartacus via Plinio 127 ☎ 081 5369519 ⬛ 8624078
e-mail: campingspartacus@tin.it
Site is on a level meadow with orange trees.
⮕ *Lies near the motorway exit, Pompei and access is from the
main Napoli road, opposite Scavi di Pompei near an IP petrol
station.*
All year 9HEC ⬛⬛⬛ ✦ ⌂ ⬛ ▼ ✕ ⊙ ⬛ ⊘ ⬛ ⬛ ⬛ ▲ ⬔ ⊞ lau
✦ ⱬP

POZZUOLI NAPOLI

Vulcano Solfatara via Solfatara 161
☎ 081 5267413 ⬛ 081 5263482
e-mail: vulcano.solfatara@iol.it
Clean and orderly site situated in a deciduous forest near the
crater of the extinct Solfatara volcano.
⮕ *Leave Nuova via Domiziana (SS7 qtr) at Km60/1 (at about
6km short of Napoli) and turn inland through stone gate.*
Apr-Oct,24 Dec-8 Jan 3HEC ⬛⬛⬛ ✦ ⌂ ⬛ ▼ ✕ ⊙ ⬛ ⊘ ⬛ ⬛ ⬛
▲ ⱬ P ⬔ ⊞ lau ✦ ⬛ ⱬS

At VARCATURO, MARINA DI(12km N)

Partenope ☎ 081 5091076 ⬛ 5096767
Partially undulating terrain in woodland of medium height.
Camping Card Compulsory.
⮕ *Turn seawards for 300m at Km45/II of the SS7 (via
Domiziana).*
May-15 Sep 6HEC ⬛⬛⬛ ⠄⠄⠄ ✦ ⌂ ⬛ ▼ ✕ ⊙ ⬛ ⊘ ⬛ ⬛
ⱬ LRS ⬔ ⊞ ⬚

PRÁIA A MARE COSENZA

Internazionale sul Mare ☎ 0985 72211 ⬛ 72211
e-mail: info@campinginternational.it
In a beautiful location on the Gulf of Policastro with fine
recreational facilities.
⮕ *Access via A3 to Falerna and then SS18.*
15 Apr-Sep 5.5HEC ⬛⬛⬛ ⬚ ✦ ⌂ ⬛ ▼ ✕ ⊙ ⬛ ⊘ ⬛ ⬛ ⬛
ⱬ PS ⬛ ⊞ lau

RODI GARGANICO FOGGIA

Ripa Contrada Ripa ☎ 0884 965367 ⬛ 0884 965695
e-mail: info@villaggioripa.it
Well-equipped and attractive site close to the beach.
Jun-Sept 6HEC ⬛⬛⬛ ✦ ⌂ ⬛ ▼ ✕ ⊙ ⬛ ⊘ ⬛ ⬛ ⱬ PS ⊞ lau
✦ ⊞

ROSSANO SCALO COSENZA

Marina di Rossano Contrada Leuca
☎ 0983 516054 ⬛ 0983 512069
e-mail: marina.club@tiscalinet.it
In wooded surroundings close to the beach, with good,
modern facilities.

Cont.

⊃ *Access via N106.*
01 may-20 Sep 7HEC ⸺ ♦ ⋔ ⅃ ♨ ⚊ ✕ ⊙ ◘ ⇔
⌇ PS ⊡ ⊞ lau ➧ ⌀

▶ **SAN MENÁIO** FOGGIA

Valle d'Oro via Degli Ulivi ☎ 0884 991580 ▤ 0884 991699
e-mail: campingvalledoro@libero.it
Site in olive grove surrounded by wooded hills with some
terraces.
⊃ *Turn off the SS89 onto SS528 and to site at Km1.800. 2km
from the sea.*
15 Jun-15 Sept 3HEC ⸺ ♦ ⋔ ✕ ⊙ ◘ ⚊ ⇔ ⚑
➧ ⅃ ⌀ ⌇PS ⊞

▶ **SAN NICOLO DI RICADI** CATANZARO

Agrumeto ☎ 0963 663175
The access road leads over a dusty field track, then on to a
steep ramp with large, wide bends. Because the trees are very
close together, the pitches are rather narrow. Lying in a
lemon grove beside the sea, this site looks more like a garden.
Beautiful beach. Excursions by boat can be arranged.
Apr-Sep 3.7HEC ⸺ ♦ ⋔ ⅃ ♨ ✕ ⊙ ◘ ⌀ ⇔ ⌇ S ⚑ ⊞ lau

▶ **SANTA CESÁREA TERME** LECCE

Scogliera ☎ 0836 949802 ▤ 949794
Attractive site close to the sea.
⊃ *1km S on SS173.*
All year 8HEC ⁖⁖⁖ ♦ ⋔ ⅃ ♨ ⚊ ✕ ⊙ ◘ ⌀ ⇔ ⚑ ⌇ P ➧ ⚊
⌇S ⊞

▶ **SANTA MARIA DI CASTELLABATE** SALERNO

Trezene ☎ 0974 965027 ▤ 0974 965013
e-mail: trezene@costacilento
The site is partly divided into pitches and consists of two
sections lying either side of the access road. Pitches between
road and fine sandy beach are reserved for touring campers.
Apr-Oct 2.5HEC ⸺ ♦ ⋔ ⅃ ♨ ✕ ⊙ ◘ ⇔ ⌇ S ⚑ ✕ lau ➧ ⚊
⌀ ⚊ ⊞ Prices: ₳4.65-7.20 pitch 11.30-21.70

▶ **SOLE, LIDO DEL** FOGGIA

Lido del Mare c da Pantanello 27 ☎ 0884 917012
30 May-26 Sep 22HEC ⸺ ♦ ⋔ ♨ ✕ ⊙ ◘ ⚊ ⇔ ⇔ ⌇ S ◪
lau ➧ ⚊ ✕ ⌀ ⌇LPS ⊞

▶ **SORRENTO** NAPOLI

Santa Fortunata Campogaio via Capo 39
☎ 081 8073579 ▤ 081 8073590
e-mail: info@santafortunata.com
A well appointed, terraced site shaded by olive trees and with
direct access to the sea.
⊃ *2km from town centre and 400m beyond the turning from
the SS145 on road towards Massa Lubrense and 50m from sea.*
Apr-15 Oct 20HEC ⸺ ⁖⁖⁖ ♦ ⋔ ⅃ ♨ ✕ ⊙ ◘ ⌀ ⚊ ⇔ ⇔
⌇ PS ⚑ ⊞ lau

Giardino delle Esperidi S.Agnello
☎ 081 8783255 ▤ 081 8785022
e-mail: info@esperidiresort.com
In a pleasant park, surrounded by lemon and orange trees
2km from the centre of Sorrento and 250mtrs from La
Marinella beach. There are good facilities and modern
bungalows are available for hire.
Mar-Oct 3HEC ⸺ ♦ ⋔ ♨ ✕ ⊙ ◘ ⇔ ⚑ ⊞ ⌀
➧ ⚊ ⌀ ⚊ ⌇PS

International Camping Nube d'Argento via Capo 21
☎ 081 8781344 ▤ 081 8073450
e-mail: info@nubedargento.com
The site lies on narrow terraces just off a steep concrete road
between the beach and the outskirts of the town.

⊃ *Access is rather difficult for caravans.*
All year 1.5HEC ⸺ ♦ ⋔ ⅃ ♨ ✕ ⊙ ◘ ⌀ ⚊ ⇔ ⇔ ⌇ PS ⚑ ⊞

Santa Fortunata via Capo ☎ 081 8073579 ▤ 081 8073590
Extensive site lying on terraces in a shady olive grove with
many small secluded pitches.
Camping Card Compulsory
⊃ *1km from town and 50m from sea.*
Apr-Sep 12HEC ⸺ ♦ ⋔ ⅃ ♨ ✕ ⊙ ◘ ⌀ ⚊ ⇔ ⇔ ⚑
⌇ PS ⚑ ⊞ lau

▶ **TORRE RINALDA** LECCE

Torre Rinalda Litoranea Salentina
☎ 0832 652161 ▤ 0832 652165
On an extensive level meadow, separated from the sea by
dunes. Discotheque. Lunchtime siesta 13.30-16.00 hrs.
⊃ *Access via SS613 (Brindisi-Lecce) exit Trepuzzi then coastal
road for 1.5km.*
All year 23HEC ⸺ ♦ ⋔ ⅃ ♨ ✕ ⊙ ◘ ⇔ ⌇ PS ⚑ ⊞ ⌀
➧ ⌀ ⚊

▶ **UGENTO** LECCE

Riva di Ugento Litoranea Gallipoli-SM di Levc
☎ 0833 933600 ▤ 933601
e-mail: rivadiugeunto@puglia.org
A well equipped site in wooded surroundings close to the
beach.
11 May-23 Sep 32HEC ⸺ ⁖⁖⁖ ♦ ⋔ ⅃ ♨ ✕ ⊙ ◘ ⌀ ⚊ ⇔ ⚑
⌇ PS ⚑ ⊞ ⌀ lau Prices: pitch 15-31 (incl 3 persons)

▶ **VICO EQUENSE** NAPOLI

Sant' Antonio Marina d'Equa ☎ 081 8028570 ▤ 8028570
A modern site set among fruit trees, close to the beach with
fine views over the Bay of Naples.
Camping Card Compulsory
15 Mar-15 Oct 1HEC ⸺ ♦ ⋔ ⅃ ♨ ✕ ⊙ ◘ ⌀ ⚊ ⇔
⌇ S ⚑ ⊞ lau ➧ ⌇PS

Seiano Spiaggia Marina Aequa ☎ 081 8028560 ▤ 8028560
e-mail: seianus_village@tin.it
Set in a plantation of evergreen and orange trees only a few
metres from the sea. There are good facilities and the site is
ideally situated for excursions to Pompeii, Naples, Vesuvius etc.
*Motorway A3 (Naples-Pompeii-Salerno) leave m/way at
Castellammare di Stabia-Highway 145 after Seiano tunnel and
bridge turn R to Marina Aequa.* Apr-Sep 1HEC ⸺ ♦ ⋔ ⅃
✕ ⊙ ◘ ⌀ ⚊ lau ➧ ✕ ⌇PS ⊞

▶ **VIESTE** FOGGIA

Baia Turchese 71019 Lungomare Europa ☎ 0884 708587
A family site in wooded surroundings with direct access to
the sea.
⊃ *1km N of Vieste on Strada Panoramica towards Peschici.*
May-Sep 3.6HEC ⸺ ♦ ⋔ ⅃ ♨ ✕ ⊙ ◘ ⌀ ⚊ ⇔ ⌇ S ⚑ ⊞

Capo Vieste ☎ 0884 706326 ▤ 0884 705993
The site lies on a large area of unspoilt land, planted with a
few rows of poplar and pine trees. It is by the sea and has a
large bathing area.
⊃ *Off coastal road to Peschici about 7km beyond Vieste.*
15 Mar-30 Oct 6HEC ⸺ ⁖⁖⁖ ⊿ ♦ ⋔ ⅃ ♨ ✕ ⊙ ◘ ⌀ ⚊ ⇔
⇔ ⌇ S ◪ ⊞ lau

Castello Lungomare E-Mattei 77
☎ 0884 707415 ▤ 0884 708912
Attractive and well-equipped site with access to the beach
and organised entertainment.
Etr-Sep 2HEC ⸺ ♦ ⋔ ⅃ ♨ ✕ ⊙ ◘ ⌀ ⚊ ⇔
⌇ S ◪ ⌀ lau ➧ ⊞

Umbramare Santa Maria di Merino
☎ 0884 706174 ▤ 0884 706174
➲ *On a A14 leave at Poggio Imperiale and take route via Rodi Gargánico and Peschici.*
All year 1.3HEC ▥ ∷ ♦♠♘♡✕⊙Ω∅▥
➴S▣⊞∅♦☶

Vieste Marina Litoranea Viesta ☎ 0884 706471 ▤ 706471
e-mail: eimaglio@viesteonline.it
Tree-lined level site adjacent to the coast road in a quiet situation with good facilities.
➲ *5km N of Vieste, signposted.*
Jun-Sep 5HEC ▥ ♦♠♘♡✕⊙Ω☎Ω➴PS⊞⊞lau♦
∅☶➴S

Village Punta Lunga Defensola, CP 339
☎ 0884 706031 ▤ 706910
e-mail: puntalunga@puntalunga.com
A terraced site in wooded surroundings encompassing two sandy bathing bays and a rocky peninsula.
➲ *2km N of Vieste, signposted from coast road.*
6HEC ▥ ∷ ⚘♦♠♘♡✕⊙Ω∅▥☎➴S▣⊞∅ lau

● ● ● ● **THE ISLANDS** ● ● ● ●

Sardinia and Sicily are virtually the same size but Sardinia's population is 1.5 million compared with Sicily's 5 million. Sardinia's mountains are less dramatic, much of the coast is deserted and the people with their distinctive dialect, clothes and folklore, seem far removed from the 21st century. The Costa Smeralda on the north-east coast is luxuriously developed but elsewhere on the coast tourism is increasing only slowly, and inland, the old town of Nuoro set high on a 1500ft granite hill, remains mysterious. Cagliari is the capital, a modern city, whilst Oristano is the provincial capital with old streets and lively atmosphere. Where Sardinia is an island on which to relax, in Sicily there is much to see: classical sites at Taormina, Syracuse or Agrigento; busy cities like Palermo and Catánia and the dramatic, erupting volcano Etna in whose foothills oranges and lemons grow profusely. There is also poverty and the occasional outburst from the Mafia. The best beaches and clearest waters are around the Aolian islands to the north, but Sicily is not primarily a seaside resort island. Seafood, vegetables and fresh fruit are in abundance, not forgetting of course, the inimitable ice-cream.

··

▶ **SARDEGNA (SARDINIA)**
▶ **AGLIENTU** SASSARI

Baia Blu la Tortuga Pineta di Vignola Mare
☎ 079 602060 ▤ 079 602040
e-mail: info@baiablu.com
Site in pine forest by the sea.
10 Apr-Sep 17HEC ▥ ∷ ♦♠♘♡✕⊙Ω∅☎Ω➴S⊞
⊞ lau

▶ **ARBATAX** NUORO

Telis Porto Frailis ☎ 0782 667261 ▤ 0782 667140
Terraced site by the sea.
➲ *SS125 between Cagliari and Olbia.*
All year 3HEC ∷ ♦♠♘♡✕⊙Ω∅▥☎Ω➴S⊞lau

▶ **BARI SARDO** NUORO

Domus de Janas Torri di Bari ☎ 0782 29361
Well equipped site in a sheltered position with good recreational facilities.
All year 2.5HEC ▥ ♦♠♘♡✕⊙Ω∅▥☎Ω
➴RS▣lau

▶ **CÁGLIARI**
▶ At **SANT'ANTIOCO**

Tonnara Loc Calasapone ☎ 0781 809058 ▤ 0781 809036
Situated in the centre of Calasapone Bay with enclosed plots, good sporting facilities and access to a sandy beach.
➲ *Access is by road, south of Carbonia, to the small island of St Antioco.*
15 Apr-Sep 7HEC ▥ ∷ ⚘♠♘♡✕⊙Ω∅▥☎Ω➴S
▣ lau♦➴P

▶ **CALASETTA** CAGLIARI

Sardi Le Saline Le Saline ☎ 0781 88615 ▤ 0781 88615
In wooded surroundings close to the beach and 500mtrs from the village with good recreational facilities.
All year 6HEC ▥ ♦♠♘♡✕⊙Ω∅☎Ω➴S⊞lau♦∅☶⊞

▶ **CANNIGIONE DI ARZACHENA** SASSARI

Isuledda ☎ 0789 86003 ▤ 0789 86089
e-mail: informazioni@isuledda.it
Near the sea on the beautiful Costa Smeralda with good, modern toilet amenities and plentiful sports and entertainment facilities.
28Mar-15Oct 15HEC ▥ ∷ ♦♠♘♡✕⊙Ω∅☎➴S▣
⊞∅ lau Prices: ♠4.91-9.82 ♠2.07-4.14 ♠5.69-14.47
▲5.69-14.47

▶ **LOTZORAI** NUORO

Cernie via Case Sparse 17 ☎ 0782 669472 ▤ 0782 669612
Close to the beach with beautiful views on all sides. Varied sports and leisure activities.
All year 1.5HEC ∷ ♦♠♘♡✕⊙Ω∅☎Ω
➴S lau♦⊞

▶ **PORTO ROTONDO** SASSARI

Cugnana Loc Cugnana ☎ 0789 33184 ▤ 0789 33398
e-mail: info@campingcugnana.it
A well appointed family site with good recreational facilities and offering free transport to the local beaches.
15 May-Sep 5HEC ▥ ♦♠♘♡✕⊙Ω∅☎➴P▣
♦➴S⊞ Prices: ♠7.23-13.94 ♠2.07-3.10

▶ **SANTA LUCIA** NUORO

Cala-Pineta St Statale Orientale Sarde 125
☎ 0784 819184 ▤ 818128
Well-equipped site 1.5km from a white sand beach.
1 Jun-15 Sep 5HEC ▥ ♦♠♘♡✕⊙Ω∅▲➴S⊞lau
Prices: ♠5.70-9.30 ♠23.30-33.60 ▲8.80-14.50

Selema ☎ 0784 819068 ▤ 819068
e-mail: info@selemacamping.com
Wooded beach site on the island of Sardinia.
May-Oct 7.5HEC ▥ ∷ ♦♠♘♡✕⊙Ω∅▥☎Ω➴RS
⊞▣lau♦☶⊞

▶ **SAN TEODORO** NUORO

San Teodoro la Cinta via del Tirreno
☎ 0784 865777 ▤ 865777
e-mail: info@campingsanteodoro.com
Situated in a large wooded park, the site faces the sea. Ideal for families with small children.
➲ *25km from Olbia.*
15 May-15 Oct 15HEC ▥ ♦♠♘♡✕⊙Ω∅▥☎Ω➴S
⊞⊞∅lau♦✕➴PR

▶ **TEULADA** CAGLIARI

Porto Tramatzu ☎ 070 9283027 ▤ 070 9283028
With extensive facilities and large individual plots. The site is less than 100mtrs from the beautiful Port Tramatzu.
➲ *SS195 from Cagliari.*
Etr-Oct 3.5HEC ▥ ♠♘♡✕⊙Ω∅☎Ω➴S lau

TORRE SALINAS CAGLIARI

Torre Salinas ☎ 070 999032 ▤ 999001
e-mail: information@camping-torre-salinas.de
Apr-15 Oct 1.5HEC ⁙ ♦ ⋔ ⚐ ⲻ ✗ ⊙ ◲ ◲ Å � 〈 S ⊞ lau
Prices: ⋔4.13-8.26 ⇔1.55-3.10 ◲18.59-37.70

VALLEDORIA SASSARI

Foce via Ampurias ☎ 079 582109 ▤ 079 582191
e-mail: info@foce.it
In a delightful wooded setting separated from the main
beach by the River Coghinas which can be crossed by ferry.
Modern toilet amenities and plenty of recreational facilities.
15 May-Sep 30HEC ⤬ ⁙ ♦ ⋔ ⚐ ⲻ ✗ ⊙ ◲ ◲ ⧄ ◲ ◲ 〈
PRS ⊡ lau ♦ ⊞

Valledoria ☎ 079 584070 ▤ 079 584058
Located in a pine wood, this site has both white-sand beaches
and rocky cliffs.
Jun-Sep 10HEC ⁙ ♦ ⋔ ⚐ ⲻ ✗ ⊙ ◲ ⧄ ⧄ ◲ ◲ 〈 S ⊡ ✷
lau Prices: ⋔6.30-10 ⇔1.50-2.60

SICILIA (SICILY)

ACIREALE

At **CARRUBA**(10.2km N)

Praiola ☎ 095 964366 ▤ 095 7124546
In idyllic location, very quiet.
➲ 5km S of Riposto by the sea between orchards. 6km from
A18 exit Giarre.
15 Mar-Sep 22HEC ⧄ ♦ ⋔ ⚐ ⲻ ✗ ⊙ ◲ ⧄ ⧄ ◲ Å 〈 S ⊞ lau

AVOLA SIRACUSA

Pantanello Lungomare di Avola ☎ 0931 823275
All year 7.5HEC ⤬ ♦ ⋔ ⚐ ⲻ ✗ ⊙ ◲ ◲ ◲ ♦ ⚐ ✗ ⧄ 〈S ⊞

Sabbia d'Oro ☎ 0931 822415 ▤ 563311
Situated close to the beach in a picturesque area surrounded
by trees with magnificient views.
All year 2.2HEC ⤬ ♦ ⋔ ⚐ ⲻ ✗ ⊙ ◲ ⧄ ⲻ
〈 RS ⊡ lau
♦ ⊞

CASTEL DI TUSA MESSINA

Scoglio ☎ 0921 334345 ▤ 334405
e-mail: loscoglio@loscoglio.net
A terraced site. No shade on the gravel beach.
➲ Turn off SS113 st Km164, 2km W of Castel di Tusa.
Apr-Sep 1.5HEC ⤬ ♦ ⋔ ⚐ ⲻ ✗ ⊙ ◲ ⧄ ⲻ 〈 S ⊞ ⊞ lau
Prices: ⋔7.75 ⇔2.58 ◲5.16 Å5.16

CATÁNIA CATANIA

Ionio via Villini a Mare 2 ☎ 095 491139 ▤ 095 492277
On a clifftop plateau. Access to beach via steps. Lunchtime
siesta 14.00-17.00 hrs.
➲ Turn off SS14 N of town towards sea.
All year 1.2HEC ⤬ ♦ ⋔ ⚐ ⲻ ✗ ⊙ ◲ ⧄ ⧄ ◲ ◲ 〈 S ⊡
⊞ lau

CEFALÚ PALERMO

Plaja degli Uccelli ☎ 0921 999068 ▤ 0921999068
In wooded surroundings with good, modern equipment
close to a fine sandy beach.
Apr-10 Oct 11 oct- 25mar 1.8HEC ⤬ ⁙ ♦ ⋔ ⚐ ⲻ ✗ ⊙
◲ ⧄ ⲻ ◲ Å 〈 S ⊡ ⊡ ⊞ lau Prices: ⋔4.65-6.20 ⇔2.60-
3.35 ◲10.35-13.40 Å5.95-8.25

FINALE DI POLLINA PALERMO

Rais Gerbi ☎ 0921 426570 ▤ 426577
e-mail: raisgerbi@pn.itnet.it
A well equipped, modern site with its own private beach in
picturesque wooded surroundings.
➲ Take the SS113 Messina-Palermo road to Km172.9.
All year 5HEC ⁙⁙ ⧄ ♦ ⋔ ⚐ ⲻ ✗ ⊙ ◲ ⧄ ◲ ◲ 〈 PS ⊞ lau ♦
ⲻ ⊞ Prices: ⋔4.20-6.70 ⇔3 ◲5.40-8.80 Å4.20-6.30

FONDACHELLO CATANIA

Mokambo ☎ 095 938731
Level terrain, thickly wooded in parts. Not directly next
to the sea.
➲ For access leave A18 (Messina-Catania) at Giarre exit,
through Giarre and via Máscali to Fondachello on coast.
Apr-Sep 2.8HEC ⁙ ♦ ⋔ ⚐ ⲻ ✗ ⊙ ◲ ⧄ ⲻ ◲ ◲ 〈 S ⊞ ⊞
lau

FÚRNARI MARINA MESSINA

Village Bazia Contrada Bazia
☎ 0941 800130 ▤ 81006
e-mail: info@bazia.it
A pleasant seaside site with plenty of recreational facilities.
Jun-Sep 40HEC ⁙ ♦ ⋔ ⚐ ⲻ ✗ ⊙ ◲ ⲻ ◲ 〈 PS ⊞ ⊡

ÍSOLA DELLE FÉMMINE PALERMO

La Playa viale Marino 55 ☎ 091 8677001 ▤ 091 8677001
e-mail: pigiambo@tin.it
A ideal site for a relaxing holiday with beautiful views and
quiet woodland walks. Direct access to the beach.
➲ A29 Palermo to Trapini and SS113.
21 Mar-30 Oct 2HEC ⁙ ♦ ⋔ ⚐ ⲻ ✗ ⊙ ◲ ⧄ ⲻ ◲
〈 S ⊞ lau ♦ ✗ 〈S ⊞

MENFI AGRIGENTO

Palma via delle Palme n 29 ☎ 0925 78392 ▤ 0925 78392
Camping Card Compulsory.
➲ 6km S.
All year 1HEC ⤬ ⁙ ♦ ⋔ ⚐ ⲻ ✗ ⊙ ◲ ⧄ ⲻ ◲ ◲ Å
〈 S ⊞

NICOLOSI CATANIA

Etna via Goethe ☎ 095 914309 ▤ 7915186
e-mail: camping.etna@tiscalimet.it
All year 2.9HEC ⁙ ♦ ⋔ ⚐ ⲻ ✗ ⊙ ◲ ⲻ ◲ ◲ Å 〈 P ⊞ ♦ ⚐ ✗
⧄

OLIVERI MESSINA

Marinello Contrada Marinello
☎ 0941 313000 ▤ 0941 313702
e-mail: marinello@camping.it
Small pitches set in a woodland area 100m from the sea.
Dogs are not allowed during July and August.
➲ On the A20 motorway exiting at Falcone.
Apr-Oct 3.2HEC ⁙ ♦ ⋔ ⚐ ⲻ ✗ ⊙ ◲ ⧄ ◲ 〈 S ⊡ ✷ lau ♦
ⲻ ⊞ Prices: ⋔4.20-6.70 ⇔3-3 Å4.20-6.30 pitch 11-11.40

PACHINO

At **PORTOPALO**(6.6km SE)

Capo Palssero ☎ 0931 842333
Site slightly sloping towards the sea with view of fishing
harbour of Portopalo. Discotheque.
➲ Turn S on 115 in Noto or Iolspica in direction of Pachino.
10 Mar-30 Oct 3.5HEC ⤬ ♦ ⋔ ⚐ ⲻ ✗ ⊙ ◲ ◲ Å ⊞ ⊡ ♦ ✗
⧄ 〈S ⊞

PALAZZOLO ACREIDE SIRACUSA

Torre Torre Tudica ☎ 0931 32694
All year 2HEC ⊞ ♦ ⋔ ⅊ ✕ ⊙ ⋐ ⏏ ⚑ P ⓐ ♦ ⚑ ⊞

PUNTA BRACCETTO RAGUSA

Rocca dei Tramonti ☎ 0932 918054 ▊ 0932 918054
The site lies in a quiet setting on rather barren land near a
beautiful sandy bay surrounded by cliffs.
➲ *From Marina di Ragusa 10km W on coast road to Punta
Braccetto.*
Etr-15 Oct 3HEC ⊞ ∷∴ ♦ ⋔ ⅊ ⅊ ✕ ⊙ ⋐ ⌀ ⏏ ⚑ ⚑ ⚮ S ⓐ
⊞

RAGUSA, MARINA DI RAGUSA

Baia del Sole Lungomare A-Doria ☎ 0932 239844
Well tended level site. Pitches provided with roofs of straw
matting.
All year 3.5HEC ⊞ ♦ ⋔ ⅊ ⅊ ✕ ⊙ ⋐ ⏏ ⚮ PS ⓐ ♦ ⊞

SANT' ALESSIO SICULO MESSINA

Focetta Sicula via Torrente Agrò ☎ 0942 751657 ▊ 756708
e-mail: lafocetta@tin.it
A well equipped site with a private beach in a quiet location.
➲ *From Messina take autostrada to 'Roccalumera' exit, then
SS114 towards Sant' Alessio and follow signs.*
All year 1.2HEC ⊞ ♦ ⋔ ⅊ ⊙ ⋐ ⌀ ⏏ ⚑ ⚮ S ⊞ lau
Prices: ⚘4.13-5.42 ⇜2.84-3.36 ⊞5.68-6.71 ⚑4.65-5.68

SANT' ANTONIO DI BARCELLONA MESSINA

Centro Vacanze Cantoni ☎ 090 9710165
All year 1HEC ⊞ ♦ ⋔ ⅊ ⅊ ✕ ⊙ ⋐ ⚒ ⏏ ⚮ PS ⓐ ⊞

SECCAGRANDE AGRIGENTO

Kameni Camping Village ☎ 0925 69212 ▊ 0925 69212
e-mail: info@kamenicamping.it
In wooded surroundings close to the beach with good
recreational facilities.
All year 5HEC ⊞ ♦ ⋔ ⅊ ⅊ ✕ ⊙ ⋐ ⚑ ⚙ ⚮ PS ⚑ lau ♦ ⌀
⚒ ⊞ **Prices:** ⚘3.61-5.16 ⇜2.58 ⊞5.16-7.23 ⚑3.09-6.71

TAORMINA

At CALATABIANO (5.2km SW)

Castello San Marco via S Marco 40 ☎ 095 641181 ▊ 642635
In lemon grove by an old castle, 9km S of Taormina.
➲ *Turn off SS114 between Calatabiano and Fiumefreddo in
direction of the sea and continue for 1km.*
All year 3.5HEC ⊞ ∷∴ ♦ ⋔ ⅊ ⅊ ✕ ⊙ ⋐ ⚒ ⏏ ⚮ PS ⓐ ℗
⊞ lau ♦ ⚮S

Neptune's horses, designed by Bartolomeo Ammannati, Florence

caravan
AND camping
BRITAIN & IRELAND
2002

All the information you need for a successful camping or caravanning trip.

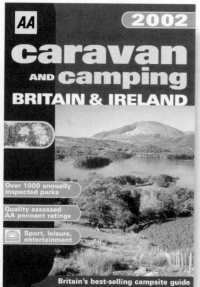

Now with a list of top static caravan parks

- **Opening dates, prices and facilities listed**

- **Colour photographs of sites throughout**

- **Tips for trouble-free touring**

- **AA Campsite of the Year Awards**

- **Premier parks and holiday centres highlighted**

Only £9.99

LUXEMBOURG

Luxembourg, the tiny Grand Duchy only
999 square miles in size, offers a wide range
of facilities to the visitor.

FACTS AND FIGURES

Area: 2,586 sq km (999 sq miles)
Population: 429,000 (1999)
Capital: Luxembourg City
Language: Luxembourgeois, French and German
IDD code: 352. To call the UK dial 00 44

Currency: Euro
Local time: GMT + 1 (summer GMT + 2)
Emergency Services: Fire and ambulance 112; police 113
Banks: Mon-Fri 09.00-12.00 and 13.30-16.30
Shops: Mon-Sat 09.00-18.00

Average daily temperatures:
Luxembourg City
Jan 1°C   Jul 19°C
Mar 6°C   Sep 15°C
May 13°C   Nov 5°C
Tourist Information:
Luxembourg National Tourist Office
UK 122 Regent Street London W1B 5SA

Tel (020) 7434 2800
USA 17 Beekman Place New York, NY 10022
Tel (212) 935 8888
Camping card: Recommended. Few reductions offered.
Tourist info website: www.luxembourg.co.uk

Luxembourg is entirely landlocked by France, Belgium and Germany. One third of the country is occupied by the hills and forests of the Ardennes, while the rest is mostly wooded farmland or the rich wine-growing area around the Moselle. The climate is temperate, with summer often extending from May to late October. Luxembourgeois is the everyday language but the official languages are French and German. English is widely spoken and understood.

There are over 100 officially recognised campsites throughout the country. Most open from April to October, but some function throughout the year. A booklet containing details of campsites is obtainable from the National Tourist Office (PO Box 1001, L-1010 Luxembourg. ☎ 42 82 82 1) or visit website at www.ont.lu. All campsites open to the public must be authorised by the Minister of Tourism.

Off-site camping Caravans may only be parked on campsites. Non-coupled caravans may not be parked on the public highway or used as living accommodation. Casual camping with a tent is permitted, but permission must be obtained
from the landowner. The owner is not allowed to give permission for more than 2 tents to be erected on his/her land. Casual camping is not allowed on the banks of Esch-sur-Sure.

HOW TO GET THERE

Luxembourg is easily approached through either Belgium or France. Apart from crossing by Eurotunnel, the usual Continental Channel ports for this journey are Dunkerque or Calais in France, and Oostende (Ostende) or Zeebrugge in Belgium.

Distance

Luxembourg City is just over 330km (205 miles) from the Belgian ports, or about 420km (260 miles) from the French ports, and is, therefore, within a day's drive of the Channel coast.
See Belgium for location map.

MOTORING & GENERAL INFORMATION

The information given here is specific to Luxembourg. It **must** be read in conjunction with the Continental ABC at the front of the book, which covers those regulations which are common to many countries.

British Embassy/Consulate*

The British Embassy together with its consular section is located at L-2450 Luxembourg, 14 Boulevard Roosevelt ☎229864/65/66

Children in cars
Children under 12 and/or 1.5 metres in height are not permitted to travel as front seat passengers unless using suitable restraint system. Children under 3 in rear must be seated in suitable restraint system. See Continental ABC under 'Passengers' and 'Seat Belts'.

Currency*
With the introduction of the Euro, the Luxembourg Franc (LUF) ceased to be legal tender from 28 February 2002. However, LUF coins and notes may still be exchanged at local banks until June 2002, and at the Luxembourg Central Bank (Banque Central du Luxembourg) for an unlimited period (banknotes) and until the end of 2004 (coins).

Dimensions and weight restrictions*
Private **cars** and towed **trailers** or **caravans** are restricted to the following dimensions - height, 4 metres; width, 2.5 metres; length, 12 metres. The maximum permitted overall length of vehicle/trailer or caravan combination is 25 metres.
The weight of a caravan must not exceed 75% of the weight of the towing vehicle.

Driving licence*
A valid UK or Republic of Ireland licence is acceptable in Luxembourg. The minimum age at which visitors from UK or Republic of Ireland may use a temporarily imported car or motorcycle is 17 years.

Foodstuffs*
The importation of meat is limited to 1kg, but there are no limits on other foodstuffs imported for personal use when travelling between EU countries.

Lights*
It is compulsory for motorcyclists to use dipped headlights during the day.

Motoring club
The **Automobile Club du Grand-Duché de Luxembourg** (ACL) has its head office at 8007 Bertrange, 54 route de Longwy ☎450045-1. ACL office hours are 08.30-12.00hrs and 13.30-18.00hrs from Monday to Friday; closed Saturday and Sunday.

Petrol
See the Continental ABC under "Petrol/Diesel".

Roads
There is a comprehensive system of good main and secondary roads. Luxembourg has 68 miles of toll-free motorway.

Speed limits*
Car/Motorcycle
Built-up areas 50kph (31mph)
Other roads 90kph (55mph)
Motorways 120kph (74mph)
Car/caravan/trailer
Built-up areas 50kph (31mph)
Other roads 75kph (46mph)
Motorways 90kph (56mph)

All motorists who have held a full driving licence for less than one year 75kph (46mph) outside built-up areas, and 90kph (55mph) on motorways.

Warning triangle*
The use of a warning triangle is compulsory in the event of accident or breakdown. The triangle must be placed on the road about 100 metres (109yds) behind the vehicle to on ordinary roads and 200-300 metres (219-328 yds) on motorways to warn following traffic of any obstruction.

*Additional information will be found in the Continental ABC at the front of the book.

Kockelscheuer Campsite Luxembourg
22, route de Bettembourg
L-1899 Kockelscheuer
Tel. 47 18 15 • Fax 40 12 43
www.camp-kockelscheuer.lu

Modern campsite located within the Kockelscheuer leisure centre. Ice rink (artificial surface), tennis, footpaths, boules, bowling alley, sauna, solarium, whirlpool and restaurants. Spacious toilet and washing facilities, large pitches with electricity hook-up. Comfortable lounge with terrace, camp shop.

BERDORF

Parc Martbusch 3 Baim Maartbesch ☎ 79545
A comfortable, modern site in picturesque wooded surroundings.
⮕ *NW of town centre.*
All year 3HEC ⬛ 🛠🏪✕☺🅿🎣🚿🚻🏤 ⭦ P 🏧 lau ✦ 🅿✕

BOULAIDE

Haute-Sûre 34 r J-de-Busleyden ☎ 993061 ▤ 993604
15 Apr-15 Sep 2HEC ⬛ 🏪🚿🍴✕☺🅿🎣🏤 Å
⭦ P 🏧⊞ lau

CLERVAUX

Official de Clervaux 33 r Klatzewee ☎ 352 920042 ▤ 929728
Situated next to the sports stadium, between the La Clervé stream and the railway in a forested area. Trains only run during the day and there is little noise. Separate field for tents.
⮕ *0.5km SW from the village.*
21 Mar-10 Nov 3HEC ⬛ 🛠🏪☺🅿🎣🚿🚻🏤⭦P🏧⊞ lau ✦ 🅿✕ Prices: ♦4 pitch 4

CONSDORF

Bel Air Burgkapp 15 r Burgkapp ☎ 790353
The site is divided into pitches and lies on level meadowland in the forest area of 'Petite Suisse Luxembourgeoise'.
⮕ *On W outskirts of village. Turn right off E42. 6km S of Echternach.*
May-Aug 2HEC ⬛ 🛠🏪☺🅿🎣🏧⊞ lau ✦ 🅿🍴✕

DIEKIRCH

Bleesbruck ☎ 803134
e-mail: info@camping-bleesbruck.lu
A modern site in tranquil wooded surroundings.
Apr-Oct 5HEC ⬛ 🛠🏪🍴✕☺🅿🎣🚿🏤⭦ R 🏧⊞ lau ✦✕⭦P

Op der Sauer rte de Gilsdorf ☎ 00352-808590 ▤ 809470
e-mail: camsauer@pt.lu
⮕ *500m from town centre on Gilsdorf road near the sports stadium.*
All year 5HEC ⬛ 🛠🏪🍴✕☺🅿🎣🏤⭦ P 🏧⊞ lau

DILLINGEN

Benelux 1-3 chemin de la Forêt ☎ 836267
A terraced, grassland site partially in an orchard and divided into pitches.
⮕ *Off N10, turn right before reaching the church.*
15 Apr-11 Nov 1.7HEC ⬛ 🛠🏪☺🅿🎣🏤🏧⊞ lau ✦🅿🍴✕⭦R

Wies-Neu 12 r de la Sûre ☎ 836110
A comfortable family site on the bank of the River Sûre.
⮕ *Between Diekirch and Echternacht.*
Apr-1 Nov 3HEC ⬛ 🛠🏪🏪☺🅿🎣🚿🚻🏤⭦ R 🏧⊞ lau ✦🍴✕

ECHTERNACH

Official 5 rte de Diekirch ☎ 720272 ▤ 720272
⮕ *Take E42 to Echternach.*
25 Mar-25 Oct 7HEC ⬛ 🛠🏪☺🅿🎣🏤🏤⭦ P 🏧⊞ lau ✦🅿
🍴✕🎣⭦LPR Prices: ♦3.72 🚐3.72 ▲3.72 pitch 3.72

ENSCHERANGE

Val d'Or ☎ 920691 ▤ 929725
e-mail: valdor@pt.lu
Quiet family site in a beautiful natural setting beside the River Clerve.
⮕ *8km S of Clervaux between Drauffelt and Wilwerwiltz.*
All year 3HEC ⬛ 🛠🏪🏪🍴✕☺🅿🎣🚿🚻🏤🏤⭦ R 🏧⊞✦🅿🎣
⭦S Prices: ♦4.25 🚐5 ▲5 pitch 5

ESCH-SUR-ALZETTE

Gaalgebierg ☎ 541069 ▤ 549630
e-mail: gaalcamp@pt.lu
A level park-like site with lovely trees on a hillock.
⮕ *SE along N6 from the town centre in the direction of Dudelange as far as the motorway underpass. Then turn right and follow the steep climb uphill.*
All year 2.5HEC ⬛ 🛠🏪🏪🍴✕☺🅿🎣🚿🚻🏤🏧⊞ lau

HEIDERSCHEID

Fuussekaul rte de Bastogne 2 ☎ 352 268888-1 ▤ 268888-28
e-mail: info@fuussekaul.lu
A level grassland family site adjoining a woodland area. Good recreational facilities.
⮕ *Turn off the N15 (Ettelbruck-Wiltz/Bastogne) S of Heiderscheid in a westerly direction.*
All year 12HEC ⬛ 🛠🏪🏪🍴✕☺🅿🎣🚿🚻Å
⭦ P 🏧⊞ lau

INGLEDORF

Gritt r du Pont ☎ 802018 ▤ 802019
On southern bank of River Sûre between Ettelbruck and Diekirch. In beautiful country setting ideal for fishing.
Apr-Oct 5HEC ⬛ 🛠🏪🏪✕☺🅿🎣🚿🚻🏤⭦ R 🏧⊞ lau ✦🅿
⭦LP Prices: ♦3.75 pitch 3.75

KOCKELSCHEUER

Kockelscheuer 22 rte de Bettembourg ☎ 471815 ▤ 401243
A modern site on the edge of a forest.
⮕ *4km from Luxembourg off N31.*
Etr-Oct 3.8HEC ⬛ 🛠🏪☺🅿🎣🚿🏧⊞ lau ✦🅿✕

LAROCHETTE

Kengert ☎ 837186 ▨ 878323
e-mail: info@kengert.lu
On gently sloping meadow in a pleasant, rural location.
➲ *Take the N8 towards Mersch, then the CR119 towards Nommern and turn right after approx 2km.*
Mar-8 Nov 4HEC ⛺ ♣ 🏠 🦽 ⛱ ✕ ⊙ 🍴 🖉 ㅛ 🏕 🚻 ₹ P 🏧 🖽
lau Prices: pitch 10-12

MERSCH

Krounebierg r de la Piscine 12 ☎ 352 329756 ▨ 329756
e-mail: jstraus@internet.lu
A clean, well-kept site on five terraces, split into sections by hedges.
➲ *Approx 0.5km W of village church.*
Apr-Sep 3.5HEC ⛺ ♣ 🏠 🦽 ✕ ⊙ 🍴 🖉 ₹ P 🖽 lau
Prices: pitch 19.83-25.41 (incl 2 persons)

MONDORF-LES-BAINS

Risette 4 rte de Burmerange ☎ 660746 ▨ 660758
e-mail: info@belhorizon.lu
In pleasant wooded surroundings near the French and German borders.
➲ *1km from Mondorf-les-Bains.*
Mar-Oct 5HEC ⛺ 🦽 🏠 🦽 ⛱ ✕ ⊙ 🍴 🖉 ㅛ 🚻 🏧 🖽 lau
♣ ₹LPR

NOMMERN

Belle Vue 3 r Principale ☎ 878068
25 Apr-30 Oct 2HEC ⛺ ♣ 🏠 🦽 ⛱ ✕ ⊙ 🍴 🖉 ㅛ 🏕 ▲ ₹ P 🏧
🖽 lau ♣ ✕

Europe Nommerlayen r Nommerlayen ☎ 878078 ▨ 879678
e-mail: nommerlayen@vo.lu
A terraced site in wooded surroundings with plenty of recreational facilities.
Closed 16 Dec-14 Jan 15HEC ⛺ 🦽 🏠 🦽 ⛱ ✕ ⊙ 🍴 🖉 ㅛ 🏕
🚻 ▲ ₹ P 🏧 🖽 lau Prices: ▲3.25 pitch 17-33 (incl 2 persons)

OBEREISENBACH

Kohnenhof 1 Maison ☎ 929464 ▨ 929690
e-mail: kohnenho@pt.lu
Quiet site in a rural setting in the River Our valley.
Mar-Nov 6HEC ⛺ 🦽 🏠 🦽 ⛱ ✕ ⊙ 🍴 🖉 ㅛ 🏕 🚻
₹ R 🏧 🖽 lau Prices: ▲3-4 pitch 6.75-9

ROSPORT

Barrage rte d'Echternach ☎ 730160 ▨ 735155
e-mail: sit@rosport.citizenet.lu
Situated by Lake Sûre on the German border at the entrance to Luxembourg's 'Little Switzerland'.
➲ *Main road from Echternach to Wasserbillig.*
Mar-Oct 3.2HEC ⛺ 🦽 🏠 ⊙ 🍴 🦽 ₹ LR 🏧 🖽 lau ♣ 🦽 ✕ 🖉 ㅛ

STEINFORT

Steinfort 72 rte de Luxembourg ☎ 398827 ▨ 397410
e-mail: campstei@pt.lu
A small family site with good recreational and entertainment facilities, well situated for exploring the 'Seven Castles' area.
➲ *Access via E25 Steinfort exit.*
All year 3.5HEC ⛺ 🦽 🏠 🦽 ⛱ ✕ ⊙ 🍴 🖉 ㅛ 🚻 🏕 ₹ P 🏧 🖽 lau
Prices: ▲3 ♣3.50 🚐3.50 ▲3.50 pitch 7

VIANDEN

Deich ☎ 84375
Etr-Oct 3HEC ⛺ 🦽 🏠 ⊙ 🍴 🦽 ₹ R 🏧 🖽 lau
♣ 🦽 ⛱ ✕ 🖉 ㅛ ₹P

At WALSDORF (2km SW)

Romantique Tandelerbaach ☎ 834464 ▨ 834440
A terraced grassland site in picturesque wooded surroundings.
➲ *W of Diekirch-Vianden road, access from the N17 and CR354.*
3 Mar-1 Nov 6HEC ⛺ 🦽 🏠 ⛱ ✕ ⊙ 🍴 🖉
₹ R 🏧 🖽 lau ♣ ₹LP

WEILER-LA-TOUR

Ma Campagne 9 rte de Thionville ☎ 00352 369497 ▨ 366912
Camp shop and bar available in August only.
➲ *Access via main road Luxembourg-Thionville.*
All year 0.5HEC ⛺ 🦽 🏠 🦽 ⊙ 🍴 🖉 🚐 🏧 🖽 lau ♣ ✕
Prices: ▲3.72 ♣3.72 🚐3.72 pitch 3.72

NETHERLANDS

The Netherlands is bordered by two countries, Belgium and Germany.

FACTS AND FIGURES
Area: 33,939 sq km (13,104 sq miles)
Population: 15,760,200 (1999)
Capital: Amsterdam
Language: Dutch, English
IDD code: 31. To call the UK dial 00 44
Currency: Euro
Local time: GMT + 1 (summer GMT + 2)
Emergency Services:

Fire, Police and Ambulance 112
Banks: Mon-Fri 09.00-17.00
Shops: Mon-Fri 09.00-18.00, Supermarkets 09.00-20.00, Sat 09.00-17.00, Sun (Amsterdam and Rotterdam) 12.00-17.00.
Average daily temperature: Amsterdam
Jan 2°C   Jul 18°C

Mar 5°C   Sep 15°C
May 13°C   Nov 7°C
Tourist Information:
Netherlands Board of Tourism (postal/telephone enquiries only)
UK PO Box 30783, London WC2B 6DH
Tel: (020) 7539 7950 (Mon-Fri 09.30-17.30) or 09068 717777 (premium rate information line)
USA 355 Lexington

Avenue, 21st Floor, New York, NY 10017
Tel (212) 370 7360
Camping card: Strongly recommended, but few reductions offered.
Tourist info website: www.holland.com/uk

A fifth of this flat, level country lies below sea-level. The areas reclaimed from the sea, the *polders*, are extremely fertile. The landscape is broken up by the forests of Arnhem, the bulbfields in the west, the lakes in the central and northern areas, and the impressive coastal dunes.

The climate is generally mild and tends to be damp. The summers are moderate with changeable weather and are seldom excessively hot. The language, Netherlandish (better known as Dutch!), is fairly guttural and closely allied to the low German dialect. Other dialect forms exist throughout the Netherlands.

There are some 900 officially recognised and classifed campsites throughout the Netherlands. It is not generally possible to book sites in advance. Coastal sites tend to be crowded in June, July and August when the locals take their holidays. Local tourist information offices (VVV) can provide detailed information about sites in their area. The camping season is mainly from April to September, but some sites are open all year. *Off-site camping* is not possible and overnight stops are not permitted.

HOW TO GET THERE

There are direct ferry services to the Netherlands. The services and minimum sailing times are **Harwich to Hoek van Holland**, (3hrs 40mins by catamaran); **Hull to Rotterdam** (Europoort) (12hrs 30mins); **Newcastle to Amsterdam** (terminal at Ijmuiden 29km from Amsterdam) (15hrs). Alternatively, use the Channel Tunnel, or take one of the short Channel crossings and drive through France and Belgium.

Distance

From Calais to Den Haag (The Hague) is just over 340km (211 miles) (within a day's drive).

MOTORING & GENERAL INFORMATION

The information given here is specific to The Netherlands. It **must** be read in conjunction with the Continental ABC at the front of the book, which covers those regulations which are common to many countries.

British Embassy/Consulate*

The British Embassy is located at 2514 ED Den Haag, Lange Voorhout 10 ☎(070) 4270427, but the Embassy has no consular section. The British Consulate is located at 1075 AE Amsterdam, Koningslaan 44 ☎(020) 6764343.

Children in cars

Child under 12 and/or 1.5 metres* in height cannot travel as front seat passenger unless using a suitable restraint. Child under 3 in the rear does not have to wear a seat belt but must use child seat or restraint if fitted; child over 3 and under 12 must wear seat belt in the absence of such equipment. See Continental ABC under 'Passengers' and 'Seat Belts'.

*A child of 10 eg 1.6 metres in height may sit in the front wearing normal seat belts.

Currency*
With the introduction of the Euro, the Netherlands Guilder (NLG) ceased to be legal tender from 18 February 2002. However, NLG coins and notes may still be exchanged at local banks until 31 December 2002 and at the Netherlands Central Bank (**De Nederlandsche Bank**) until 1 January 2032 (banknotes) and 1January 2007 (coins).

Dimensions and weight restrictions*
Private **cars** and towed **trailers** or **caravans** are restricted to the following dimensions - height, 4 metres; width†, 2.55 metres; length, **car** 12 metres, **caravan** 12 metres. The maximum permitted overall length of vehicle/trailer or caravan combination is 18 metres. The maximum weight of caravan/luggage trailers will be determined by the instructions of the manufacturer of the towing vehicle and/or the manufacturer of the caravan/luggage trailer.

†Some very small roads have a maximum width restriction of 2.2 metres.

Driving licence*
A valid UK or Republic of Ireland licence is acceptable in the Netherlands. The minimum age at which visitors from UK or Republic of Ireland may use a temporarily imported car or motorcycle is 18 years.

Firearms
Dutch laws concerning the possession of firearms are the most stringent in Europe. Any person crossing the frontier with any type of firearm will be arrested. The law applies also to any object which, on superficial inspection, shows any resemblance to real firearms (*eg* plastic imitations). If you wish to carry firearms, real or imitation, of any description into the Netherlands, seek the advice of the Netherlands Consulate.

Foodstuffs*
If the imported foodstuffs are for personal use, there are no limits when travelling between EU countries. However, importation of unpreserved meat products is forbidden and any other unpreserved foodstuffs must be declared.

Lights
See Continental ABC under 'Lights'.

Motoring club*
The **Koninklijke Nederlandse Toeristenbond** (ANWB) has its headquarters at 2596 EC 's-Gravenhage, Wassenaarseweg 220, tel (070) 31 47 14 7, and offices in numerous provincial towns. They will assist motoring tourists generally, and supply road and touring information. Offices are usually open 09.00-17.30hrs Mon-Fri and 09.00-14.00hrs on Saturday.

Petrol
See Continental ABC under 'Petrol/Diesel'.

Roads
The Netherlands has a dense network of motorways (*autosnelweg*) carrying most inter-city and long distance traffic. Yellow ANWB emergency telephone pillars are located every 2km along highways.

Main roads usually have only two lanes, but are well-surfaced. The best way to see the countryside is to tour along minor roads, often alongside canals.

Speed limits*
Car/motorcycle
Built-up areas 50kph (31mph)
Other roads 80kph (49mph) or 100kph (62mph)
Motorways 120kph (74mph)

Car/caravan/trailer
Built-up areas 50kph (31mph)
Other roads 80kph (49mph)
Motorways 80kph (49mph)

Warning triangle/Hazard warning lights*
In the event of accident or breakdown a motorist must use either a warning triangle or hazard-warning lights to warn approaching traffic of any obstruction. However, a warning triangle is recommended as hazard-warning lights may be damaged or inoperative. The triangle must be placed 30 metres (33yds) behind the vehicle on ordinary roads and 100 metres 109yds) on motorways: it must be visible at a distance of 100 metres (109yds).

*Additional information will be found in the Continental ABC at the front of the book.

'Riverside buildings in Amsterdam

St John's Cathedral, built between 1380 and 1530 in the southern town of 's-Hertogenbosch

TOURIST INFORMATION

NORTH

The Frisian Islands show another side of the Netherlands, one of spacious beaches and quiet villages that many European travellers are yet to discover.

One of the Waddenzee Islands, Ameland, classified as a bird sanctuary, is a particular gem, that has 16 miles of sandy beach on its north coast. It has four attractive villages which have all been deemed conservation areas in an attempt to preserve the flavour of traditional Frisian life, and the age of navigation, whaling, and fishing. Dairy farming is currently the island's main trade, but even that seems gently archaic until you hear about the ingenious underwater pipeline that pumps all the island's milk to a mainland processing plant.

Hollum, the westernmost village, has a number of 'Commander's Houses' which are worth exploring, including De Ouwe Polle, considered the most beautiful house on the island. The village of Ballum is pleasant to explore. To its north lies Ameland's airfield where the more adventurous can go parachute jumping. The village of Nes offers a small natural history museum and an aquarium and will be the point of arrival for those visiting Ameland by sea. Regular daily ferries run from Holward on the mainland to Nes in summer; the island enjoys a good bus service.

CENTRAL

Amsterdam is one of Europe's finest cities, with a rich and diverse artistic heritage by day and a vibrant and fashionable social outlook by night.

For lovers of fine art there really isn't anywhere in the world quite like the Rijksmuseum. Nowhere else is there such an extensive collection of Dutch masters and their finest works.

By way of introduction, the Rijksmuseum offers free leaflets as guides, and an audio-visual presentation of Holland's 17th-century 'Golden Age'. The Golden Age was a time of great mercantile success for the Netherlands, and led to a thriving art market. Traders would purchase and commission works of art as status symbols; large groups might each contribute six months' wages and hire Rembrandt for the day. This was the case with one of Rembrandt's best known works, *The Nightwatch*.

Van Gogh has an entire museum to himself nearby, the Rijksmuseum Van Gogh which contains 200 paintings and 600 drawings.

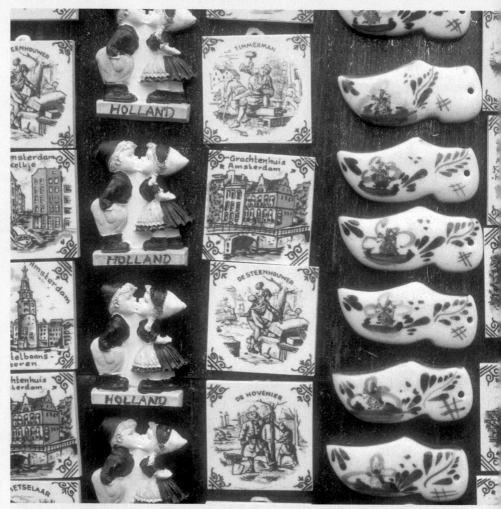

Part of a display of Delftware at the porcelain factory in Delft

SOUTH

Few towns capture the flavour of the Netherlands like Gouda, with its canals, historical heritage, medieval town hall (1450), and famous cheese.

During July and August, Gouda holds a cheese market every Thursday morning at the town weigh-house (the Waag) which has formed part of the town's skyline since 1668, and contains one of the largest pairs of scales in Europe. Market day is always a special occasion; porters dress in traditional costumes to load and unload the local cheeses, known as *Boerenkaas* or 'farmer's cheese'. Some 500 farms bring their cheese to Gouda during the summer so there is always plenty of choice. When the cheese market is not taking place the Waag also houses an exhibition of local handicrafts, including clay tobacco pipes produced by English migrant workers in the 1600s.

Apart from cheese, Gouda is also famed for its rich syrup-filled waffles known as Goudse which are served from open stalls in the town.

Jazz musician in central Amsterdam

An arched bridge across the Brouwersgracht, Amsterdam

NORTH

The Dutch have been doing battle with the sea for centuries. It is part of their history, an essential element in the country's security and prosperity, and a large influence on the people's make-up. It is a battle the people have, for the most part, won. Where there once was nothing but water, we now find one of the most fertile countries in Europe; vast polders with peacefully grazing Frisian cattle, drainage mills along the canals, and drawbridges leading to farmhouses.

The West Frisian islands extend along the coast like a string of pearls, sheltering the mainland from the unpredictable and stormy North Sea, offering visitors long white beaches and many nature parks.

On the mainland, visit Dokkum, the small walled town where St Boniface was murdered in 754; Noordbergum, where clogmakers demonstrate their skills; Hindeloopen, famed for painted furniture; and Leeuwarden, the home of Mata Hari - whose statue stands on the Korfmakerspijp - and of the Princesshof, which houses a unique ceramic museum.

AMEN DRENTHE

Reservaat Diana Heide 53 Amen
☎ 0592 389297 ▓ 0592 389432
e-mail: info@dianaheide.nl
An ideal site for relaxation, which lies away from the traffic amongst forest and heathland.
⮕ *If approaching from Assen along the E35, drive through Amen and on towards Hooghalen.*
1 Apr-1 Oct 30HEC ⸬ ⁙ ⌇ ◑ ⋔ ⚡ ✕ ⊙ ⬤ ⬢ ≡ ⬤ Å
⸰ P ⩊ ⊞ lau ⮕ ⁙L Prices: ⋔2.50 pitch 11.50-15.50

ANNEN DRENTHE

Hondsrug Annerweg 3 ☎ 0592 271292 ▓ 0592 271440
e-mail: info@hondsrug.nl
A family site in a pleasant rural setting with good recreational facilities.
⮕ *Access via N34 to site SE of Annen.*
Apr-1 Oct 18HEC ⸬ ⁙ ⁙ ⌇ ⚡ ✕ ⊙ ⬤ ⬢ ≡ ⬤ Å ⸰ P
⩊ ⊞ lau ⮕ ⁙L Prices: pitch 15-19.50 (incl 2 persons)

ASSEN DRENTHE

Witterzomer Witterzomer 7
☎ 0592 393535 ▓ 0592 393530
e-mail: info@witterzomer.nl
A large site with asphalt internal roads, lying in mixed woodland near nature reserve. Separate sections for dog owners. Individual washing facilities for the disabled.
⮕ *Turn off the E35 at Assen W exit into Europaweg Zuid and continue for 100m, then turn right. Continue through Witten and follow signs.*
All year 75HEC ⸬ ⌇ ⌇ ⚡ ✕ ⊙ ⬤ ⬢ ≡ ⬤ ⬢ Å ⸰ LP ⩊
⬤ lau Prices: pitch 19-22.50 (incl 4 persons)

BERGUM FRIESLAND

Bergumermeer Solcamastr 30
☎ 0511 461385 ▓ 0511 463955
e-mail: info@bergumereer.nl
In pleasant wooded surroundings close to the marina on the Bergumermeer with good recreational facilities.
⮕ *From N355 Groningen-Leeuwarden turn S via Bergum on N356 then exit E to Sumar towards Oostersmeer.*
28 Mar-Oct 29HEC ⸬ ⌇ ⌇ ⚡ ✕ ⊙ ⬤ ⬢ ≡ ⬤ ⬢ ⸰ LP
⬤ ⊞ lau

BORGER DRENTHE

Hunzedal De Drift 3 ☎ 0599 234698 ▓ 0599 235183
e-mail: info@hunzedal.nl
The site is clean, well-kept and lies NE of the village.
⮕ *For access, turn off the road towards Buinen, drive 200m E of the bridge over the Buinen-Schoondoord canal, then head S for a further 1km.*
4 Apr-31 Oct 30HEC ⸬ ⌇ ⌇ ⚡ ✕ ⊙ ⬤ ⬢ ⬤ ⸰ LP ⸰ ⊞
lau ⮕ ▰

DELFZIJL GRONINGEN

Aquariom Delfzijl Hustweg 13
☎ 0596 635453 ▓ 0596 630803
e-mail: info@aquariom.nl
In a wooded setting at the foot of the sea wall, adjoining a mini-golf course and attached to the AquqriOm leisure complex.
Apr-Sep 2HEC ⸬ ⫶ ⁙ ⊙ ⬤ ⬢ ⬤ ⬢ ⸰ S ⸰ ⬤ ⊞ ⮕ ▰ ⚡
✕ ⸰P Prices: ⋔7.50 pitch 10

DIEVER DRENTHE

Hoeve AAn den Weg Bosweg 12
☎ 0521 387269 ▓ 0521 387326
e-mail: camping@hoeveAAndenweg.nl
In pleasant wooded surroundings with good recreational facilities.
Camping Card Compulsory.
Apr-Oct 5HEC ⸬ ⌇ ⌇ ⚡ ✕ ⊙ ⬤ ⬢ ≡ ⬤ ⬢ ⸰ P ⸰ ⊞
lau Prices: ⋔1.75-2.75 pitch 5.75-7.75

DWINGELOO DRENTHE

Noordster Noordster 105 ☎ 0521 597238 ▓ 0521 597589
e-mail: noordster@rcn-centra.nl
A large family site with static and touring pitches, surrounded by woodland.
⮕ *3km S on E35.*
All year 42HEC ⸬ ⌇ ⌇ ⚡ ✕ ⊙ ⬤ ⬢ ≡ ⬤ ⬢ ⸰ P ⸰ ⊞
lau Prices: pitch 17-28 (incl 6 persons)

EMMEN DRENTHE

Emmen Angelsloerdijk 31 ☎ 0591 612080
On several pitches of well-kept meadowland, near an indoor swimming pool.
Camping Card Compulsory.
⮕ *From village drive towards Angelso for 1.5km, then follow signposts.*
All year 6HEC ⸬ ⌇ ⌇ ⚡ ✕ ⊙ ⬤ ⬢ ≡ ⬤ ⬢ ⸰ ⬤ ⊞ lau
⮕ ⁙P

FRANEKER FRIESLAND

Bloemketerp Burg J Dykstraweg 3 ☎ 0517 395099
In a well equipped leisure centre near the historic old city centre of Franeker.
Closed Nov-Mar ⸬ ⌇ ⌇ ⚡ ✕ ⊙ ⬤ ⬢ ⸰ P ⸰ ⊞ lau

GASSELTE DRENTHE

Berken Borgerweg 23 ☎ 0599 564255 ▓ 0599 565315
e-mail: info@campingdeberken.nl
Part of this site lies in wooded surroundings.
⮕ *0.5km SW.*
Apr-25 Oct 3.5HEC ⸬ ⌇ ⌇ ⊙ ⬤ ⬢ ≡ ⬤ ⊞ lau ⮕ ▰ ⚡ ✕

GROLLOO DRENTHE

Berenkuil De Pol 15 ☎ 0592 501242
Partly in a forest and partly on heathland.
⮕ *On the western outskirts of the village towards Hooghalen. Drive a further 0.8km along a road which narrows at the end.*
Apr-Sep 39HEC ⸬ ⌇ ⚡ ✕ ⊙ ⬤ ⬢ ≡ ⸰ LP ⬤ ⊞ lau ⮕ ▰

> **GRONINGEN** GRONINGEN

Stadspark Campinglaan 6 ☎ 050 5251624
A well-kept site on patches of grass between rows of bushes
and groups of pine and deciduous trees. Some of its pitches
are naturally screened.
➲ *For access from the SW outskirts of the town, take the road
towards Peize and Roden.*
15 Mar-15 Oct 6HEC ⊞ ⌷ ⋔ ⅃ ⵣ × ⊙ 🖀 🖉 ⚒ 🅿 ⊞ lau
➜ ⵤLP

> **HARKSTEDE** GRONINGEN

Grunopark Hoofdweg 163 ☎ 050 416371 ▨ 050 424521
Situated within a large waterpark with a great variety of
sporting facilities available.
All year 23HEC ⊞ ⌷ ⋔ ⅃ ⵣ × ⊙ 🖀 🖉 ⚒ A ⵤ L ⚗ ⊞ lau

> **HARLINGEN** FRIESLAND

Zeehoeve ☎ 0517 413465 ▨ 0517 416971
e-mail: info@zeehoeve.nl
A well-kept meadow site which is divided into large sections
by rows of bushes.
➲ *1km S of Harlingen near a dyke.*
Apr-Sep 10HEC ⊞ ⅏ ⋔ ⅃ × ⊙ 🖀 🖉 ⚒ 🖤 ⵤ S ⚗ ⊞ lau ➜
ⵤ Prices: ⋔3.50 ⋒2 ⵤ3.50 ⵙ3.50

> **HEE (ISLAND OF TERSCHELLING)** FRIESLAND

Kooi Hee 9 ☎ 0562 442743 ▨ 0562 442835
➲ *5km from the harbour.*
25 Apr-10 Sep 8.5HEC ⊞ ⌷ ⋔ ⅃ × ⊙ 🖀 🖀 ⊞ lau ➜ ⵤ 🖉
ⵤL Prices: ⋔3.50 ⋒2 ⵤ4 ⵙ2-4

> **HINDELOOPEN** FRIESLAND

Hindeloopen Westerdijk 9 ☎ 0514 521452 ▨ 523221
e-mail: info@campinghindeloopen.nl
A peaceful site on the Ysselmeer with fishing and watersports
facilities.
➲ *1km S.*
Apr-Nov 16HEC ⊞ ⌷ ⋔ ⅃ ⵣ × ⊙ 🖀 🖉 ⚒ ⵤ L ⚗ 🅿 ⊞ lau
Prices: pitch 13.45-14.80 (incl 2 persons)

> **KOUDUM** FRIESLAND

Nautic Park "De Kuilart" Kuilart 1
☎ 0514 522221 ▨ 0514 523010
e-mail: info@kuilart.nl
A camping and watersports centre on the shores of 'De
Fluessen' lake.
➲ *Access via N359.*
All year 30HEC ⊞ ⌷ ⋔ ⅃ ⵣ × ⊙ 🖀 🖉 ⚒ 🖤 ⵤ LP ⚗ 🅿
⊞ lau ➜ ⵤS Prices: ⋔15-19 ⵤ16.50-21.50 pitch 21-30 (incl 2
persons)

> **LAUWERSOOG** GRONINGEN

Lauwersoog Strandweg 5
☎ 0159 349133 ▨ 0519 349195
e-mail: info@lauwersoog.nl
In a pleasant situation on the shores of Lauwersmeer. A good
excursion centre with fine water sports facilities.
Camping Card Compulsory.
All year 11HEC ⊞ ⵦ ⌷ ⋔ ⅃ × ⊙ 🖀 🖉 ⚒ 🖤
ⵤ L 🅿 ⊞ lau ➜ ⵤS

> **MAKKUM** FRIESLAND

Holle Poarte Holle Poarte 2 ☎ 0515 231344 ▨ 0515 231339
A modern site with fine water sports facilities on the
Ijsselmeer.
All year 32HEC ⊞ ⵦ ⌷ ⋔ ⅃ ⵣ × ⊙ 🖀 🖉 ⚒ 🖤 🖀 ⵙ
ⵤ L ⚗ ⊞ lau

> **ONNEN** GRONINGEN

Fruitberg Dorpsweg 67 ☎ 050 4061282
A peaceful site situated in an orchard.
➲ *S of the village, and right of the Haren-Zuidlaren road.*
15 Mar-1 Nov 5.5HEC ⊞ ⌷ ⋔ ⅃ × ⊙ 🖀 🖉 ⚒ 🖤 ⵤ P ⚗ 🅿
⊞ lau ➜ ⵤ × ⵤL

> **OPENDE** FRIESLAND

'T Strandheem Parkweg 2 ☎ 0594 659555 ▨ 658592
e-mail: info@strandheem.nl
A family site with modern sanitary blocks and a wide variety
of recreational facilities.
➲ *Access from A7 (Groningen-Afsluitdijk) exit 31.*
Apr-1 Oct 15HEC ⊞ ⌷ ⋔ ⅃ ⵣ × ⊙ 🖀 🖉 ⚒ 🖤 A ⵤ LP ⚗
🅿 ⊞ lau

> **RUINEN** DRENTHE

Engeland Oude Benderseweg 11 ☎ 0522 471770
A family site in pleasant wooded surroundings with well
sheltered pitches on the edge of a National Park.
➲ *Access via A28 exit Ruinen-Pesse.*
Apr-24 Oct 25HEC ⊞ ⌷ ⋔ ⅃ ⵣ × ⊙ 🖀 🖉 🖤 A
ⵤ P ⚗ ⊞ lau ➜ × ⚒

Wiltzangh Witteveen 2 ☎ 0522 471227 ▨ 0522 472178
e-mail: wiltzangh@dwingelderveld.com
N of the village in the middle of a coniferous and deciduous
forest, and within the grounds of a big holiday village.
Advance booking is necessary for the peak season.
➲ *For access, drive from Ruinen towards Ansen for 3km, then
turn and head N.*
Apr-Oct 13HEC ⊞ ⌷ ⋔ ⅃ × ⊙ 🖀 🖉 ⚒ 🖤 ⵤ P 🅿 ⊞ lau
Prices: pitch 12-17

> **SONDEL** FRIESLAND

Sondel Beuckeswijkstr 26 ☎ 05140 2300
In a dense wood.
➲ *Just off the Sondel-Rijs road.*
Apr-Oct 5HEC ⊞ ⌷ ⋔ ⅃ × ⊙ 🖀 ⵤ LPRS ⚗ 🅿 ⊞ ⋈ lau
➜ ⵤ 🖉 ⚒

> **TERSCHELLING (ISLAND OF)**

See **Hee & West Terschelling**

> **WATEREN** DRENTHE

Olde Lanschap Schurerslaan 4 ☎ 0521 387244
A spacious family site near the outskirts of a National Park.
Apr-Oct 13HEC ⊞ ⌷ ⋔ ⅃ ⵣ × ⊙ 🖀 🖉 ⚒ 🖤 ⵤ LP ⚗ ⊞ lau

> **WEDDE** GRONINGEN

Wedderbergen Molenweg 2 ☎ 0597 561673 ▨ 0597 562595
e-mail: info@wedderbergen.nl
On meadowland divided by deciduous trees and bush
hedges.
➲ *On the E outskirts of the village take a narrow asphalt road,
and drive N for 3.2km. Then take Spanjaardsweg and
Molenweg to the camp.*
Apr-1Nov 40HEC ⊞ ⌷ ⋔ ⅃ × ⊙ 🖀 🖉 ⚒ 🖤 ⵤ LR ⚗ ⊞
lau

> **WEST TERSCHELLING (ISLAND OF TERSCHELLING)**
> FRIESLAND

Cnossen Hoofdweg 8 ☎ 0562 442321
Several patches of meadowland, left of the road towards
Formerum, and right of the forest.
➲ *For access, take the ferry from Harlingen.*
Apr-1 Nov 2.5HEC ⊞ ⌷ ⋔ ⅃ ⵣ × ⊙ 🖀 🖉 ⚒ 🖤 🖀 A 🅿 ⊞
➜ ⵤLP

CENTRAL

In the heart of the Netherlands lies the country's largest nature reserve - the Hogwe Veluwe National Park. In addition to its many rare species, there are numerous museums and galleries, including the National Kröller-Müller Museum which houses a wonderful Van Gogh collection.

The Noord-Holland is *the* flower province of the Netherlands, with fields of daffodils, tulips, hyacinths and crocuses. Beautiful canals run through its capital, Amsterdam, with richly ornamental mansions on their banks. The most attractive and compact shopping centre in Holland, it is said you can buy anything in Amsterdam! In winter, the region of Overijsell is a paradise for those who enjoy long-distance skiing "langlauf". Alternatively, a visit in July to Dedomsvaart during its week-long festival will show you the largest open-air dinner and the largest shovel-board in the world.

Utrecht is truly unique; it combines a rich past and a dynamic present. It is the home of the tallest and finest church tower in Holland - the 'Dom'. Breathtaking views will reward those who climb its 465 steps.

....

AALSMEER NOORD-HOLLAND

Amsterdamse Bos Kleine Noorddijk 1
☎ 020 6416868 ▦ 020 6402378
e-mail: camping@dab.amsterdam.nl
The site is in a park-like setting in the Amsterdam wood. The camp is near the Airport flight path and is subject to noise depending on the wind direction.
⮑ *If approaching from The Hague along the motorway, turn at the northern edge of the airport, and head towards Amstelveen. Then follow directions for Aalsmeer. Alternatively, if approaching from Utrecht, leave the motorway at the Amstelveen exit, and drive towards Aalsmeer, passing through Bovenkerk.*
Apr-14 Oct 6.8HEC ⬛ ⚘ ⟨⟩ 🛁 ⚡ ✗ ⊙ 🚻 ⌂ 🔥 🚽 ⊞ lau ➡ 🚿
⟨⟩LS Prices: ⚑4.09 ➡2.27 ➡3.18 ⚐2.73

ALKMAAR NOORD-HOLLAND

Alkmaar Bergerweg 201 ☎ 072 5116924
The site is well-kept and divided into many sections by rows of trees and bushes.
Camping Card Compulsory.
⮑ *Lies on the NW outskirts of the town, off the Bergen road.*
Apr-Oct 3HEC ⬛ ⚘ ⟨⟩ ⊙ 🚻 ⌂ ⚡ ⊞ lau ➡ 🛁 ⚡ ✗ ⟨⟩ 🚿
⟨⟩LPS Prices: ⚑4.50 ➡2 ⚐4.50 ⚐3.50

AMSTERDAM NOORD-HOLLAND

See also Aalsmeer

Gaasper Camping Amsterdam
Loosdrechtdreef 7,
NL-1108 AZ Amsterdam
Tel: +31 20 696 73 26
Fax: +31 20 696 93 69
www.gaaspercamping-amsterdam.nl
Just 20 minutes from the centre of Amsterdam there is a unique region of natural beauty, the "Gaasperpark" on the Gaasperplas. Within easy reach of a tube-station one of the finest camp sites of the Dutch capital is found: Gaasper Camping Amsterdam, situated on the verge of a park, with many trees and flowers.

Gaasper Loosdrechtdreef 7 ☎ 020 6967326 ▦ 020 6969369
Situated on the edge of the beautiful 'Gaasperpark' within easy reach of Amsterdam.
Camping Card Compulsory.
⮑ *From A9 take Gaasperplas exit before city centre and follow camping signs.*
(Exit A9 J S113 Gaasperplas/Weesp, then follow camping signs) 15 Mar-Dec 5.5HEC ⬛ ⚘ ⟨⟩ 🛁 ⚡ ✗ ⊙ 🚻 ⌂ 🔥 ⊞ ⊞
lau ➡ ✗ ⟨⟩L Prices: ⚑3.63 ➡3.40 ⚐5.22 ▲4.88

Vliegenbos Meeuwenlaan 138 ☎ 0031 20 6368855
This is a tent site for young people.
⮑ *From A9 exit main railway station through tunnel, then right and right again at traffic lights, then follow signposts.*
1 Apr-30 Sep 25HEC ⬛ ⚘ 🌿 ⟨⟩ 🛁 ⚡ ✗ ⊙ 🚻 ⌂ 🔥 ⊞ ⊞
⚙ lau ➡ ⟨⟩P

Zeeburg Zuider Udijk 20
☎ 0031 20-6944430 ▦ 020 6946238
e-mail: info@campingzeeburg.nl
On an island in the Ijmeer, 15 minutes from the city centre, with good facilities. Popular with backpackers and holidaymakers alike.
⮑ *Access via A10 exit S114 by second set of traffic lights.*
All year 3.8HEC ⬛ 🌿 ⟨⟩ 🛁 ⚡ ✗ ⊙ 🚻 ⌂ 🔥 ▲ ⊞ lau
➡ ⟨⟩P Prices: ⚑4 ➡4 ⚐5 ▲3.50 pitch 3.50

ANDIJK NOORD-HOLLAND

Vakantiedorp Het Grootslag Proefpolder 4 ☎ 228 592944
One of the most well equipped sites in the area, situated on the IJsselmeer. Individual bathrooms are allocated to each pitch and a wide range of recreational facilities are available.
⮑ *From A7 exit Hoorn-Noord/Enkhuizen/Lelystad turn left for Andijk, then follow signs for Het Grootslag and Dijkweg.*
Mar-Nov 40HEC ⬛ ⚘ ⟨⟩ 🛁 ⚡ ✗ ⊙ 🚻 ⌂ ⚡ ⟨⟩ LP ⚍ ⊞ lau ➡ ⚙ 🔥

APPELTERN GELDERLAND

Het Groene Eiland Lutenkampstr 2
☎ 0487 562130 ▦ 0487 561540
e-mail: info@hetgroeneeiland.nl
In a 'Water Recreation' park with plenty of sporting facilities.
⮑ *From A15 take Leeuwen turn and follow signs.*
15 Mar-Oct 16HEC ⬛ 🌿 ⟨⟩ 🛁 ⚡ ✗ ⊙ 🚻 ⌂ 🔥 ⟨⟩ LR ⚡
⊞ lau ➡ ✗ Prices: ⚑2.20 ➡1.95 ⚐9.40 ▲9.40

ARNHEM GELDERLAND

Arnhem Kemperbegerweg 771 ☎ 026 4431600 ▦ 4457705
e-mail: arnhem@holiday.nl
The site lies on grassland and is surrounded by trees.
⮑ *NW of town and S of E36.*
Apr-Oct 36HEC ⬛ ⚘ ⟨⟩ 🛁 ⚡ ✗ ⊙ 🚻 ⌂ 🔥 ⟨⟩ P ⚍ ⊞ lau
Prices: pitch 12.10-18.90 (incl 2 persons)

Hooge Veluwe Koningsweg 14
☎ 026 4432272 ▦ 026 4436809
e-mail: hooge.veluwe@vvc.nl
Situated in a pleasant natural park with good facilities.
⮑ *From Apeldoorn exit on E36 drive NW towards Hooge Veluwe.*
31 Mar-28 Oct 18HEC ⬛ ⚘ ⟨⟩ 🛁 ⚡ ✗ ⊙ 🚻 ⌂ 🔥 ⟨⟩ P ⚍ ⊞
⚙ lau

Warnsborn Bakenbergseweg 257
☎ 026 4423469 ▦ 026 4421095
e-mail: info@campingwarnsborn.nl
The site is surrounded by woodland and lies on slightly sloping meadowland. Near zoo and open-air museum.

285

⟳ *Near the E36 motorway NW of town in the direction of Utrecht. 200m S of SHELL filling station, continue in W direction for 0.7km.*
Follow Burgers Zoo-Camping 3km W of Burgers Zoo.
Arnhem-North Apr-Oct 3.5HEC ⚏ ⬢ ⌂ ⚑ ⊙ ⬤ ⧄ ⌗ ⬛
🚐 🏱 🗑 lau ➡ ⚱ ✕ ⟲P Prices: ⋔2.72 ⬤2.27 ⬤3.35 ⚠1.36

▶ BABBERICH GELDERLAND

Rivo Torto Beekseweg 8 ☎ 0316 247332 ▤ 246628
e-mail: rivotorto@hetnet.nl
A riverside site with good recreational facilities.
⟳ *3km W on E36.*
15 Mar-Oct 8.5HEC ⚏ ⬢ ⬛ ⚱ ⚑ ⊙ ⬤ ⌗ ⬛ lau ➡ ✕
⟲L Prices: ⋔1.75 ⬤2.25 ⬤5.75 ⚠3.50

▶ BEEKBERGEN GELDERLAND

Bosgraaf Kanaal Zuid 444 ☎ 055 5051359
Situated on hilly grassland and woodland, but the woodland pitches are mainly used by residential caravans.
⟳ *For access from the N50, Arnhem-Apeldoorn road, turn N in West Hoeve onto the Loenen road, then follow signs for 2km.*
22HEC ⚏ ⬢ ⬛ ⚱ ✕ ⊙ ⬤ ⧄ ⟲ P ⬛ ⚐ lau

▶ BERKHOUT NOORD-HOLLAND

Westerkogge Kerkebuurt 202 ☎ 0229 551208 ▤ 0229 551390
e-mail: info@camping-westerkogge.nl
In a fine situation with well sheltered pitches and a good range of recreational facilities.
⟳ *Access via A7 (Amsterdam-Leeuwarden) exit Hoorn-Berkhout or Berkhout-Avenhorn.*
Apr-Oct 11HEC ⚏ ⬢ ⬛ ⚱ ✕ ⊙ ⬤ ⧄ ⬛ ⚐ ⟲ P 🏱 ⬤
⬛ lau Prices: ⋔2.50-2.75 ⬤2-2.25 ⬤6.75-7.55 ⚠3.75-7.55

▶ BILTHOVEN UTRECHT

Biltse Duinen Burg v.d Borchlaan 7
☎ 030 2286777 ▤ 2293888
e-mail: info@biltseduinen@euroase.nl
Family site in wooded surroundings with asphalt drives.
⟳ *Signposted from town centre.*
Apr-Oct 20HEC ⚏ ⵘ ⬢ ⬛ ⚱ ✕ ⊙ ⬤ ⧄ ⟲ P 🏱 ⬛ lau ➡ ⬛
✕ Prices: ⬤16.55

▶ BLOKZIJL OVERIJSSEL

Tussen de Diepen Duinigermeerweg 1A
☎ 0527 291565 ▤ 0527 292203
e-mail: camping@tussendediepen.nl
Secluded site surrounded by water. Fishing, water-sports and sailing.
Apr-Oct 5.2HEC ⚏ ⬢ ⬛ ⚱ ✕ ⊙ ⬤ ⧄ ⟲ R ⬛ lau ➡
⟲P Prices: ⋔7.25 ⬤2.75 ⬤7.25 ⚠7.25-3.75

▶ BUURSE OVERIJSSEL

't Hazenbos Oude Buurserdijk 1 ☎ 053 5696338
On several meadows, partially surrounded by trees.
⟳ *7km from the German border.*
All year 6HEC ⚏ ⬢ ⬛ ⊙ ⬤ ⧄ ⌗ ⬛ ⬛ ⬛ lau ➡ ⬛ ✕
⟲P Prices: ⋔2.40 ⬤1.70 ⬤2.45 ⚠1.85-2.45

▶ CALLANTSOOG NOORD-HOLLAND

Recreatiecentrum de Nollen Westerweg 8
☎ 0224 581281 ▤ 582098
e-mail: denollen@wxs.nl
A modern family site with plenty of facilities. Less than 1 mile from the beach.
⟳ *E of town towards N9.*
1 Apr-1 Nov 9HEC ⚏ ⬢ ⬛ ⚱ ✕ ⊙ ⬤ ⧄ ⌗ ⬛ ⬛ ⬛ ⬛
lau ➡ ⟲PS

Tempelhof Westerweg 2 ☎ 0224 581522 ▤ 0224 582133
e-mail: tempelhof@wxs.nl
Well equipped site on level meadowland.
All year 12.7HEC ⚏ ⬢ ⬛ ⚱ ✕ ⊙ ⬤ ⧄ ⌗ ⟲ P 🏱 ⬛ lau ➡
⟲LS Prices: ⋔3 pitch 18-25 (incl 2 persons)

▶ COCKSDORP, DE (ISLAND OF TEXEL)
NOORD-HOLLAND

Krim Roggeslootweg 6 ☎ 0222 390111 ▤ 0222 390112
A well kept site with easy access to the nearby beaches.
All year 30HEC ⚏ ⬢ ⬛ ⚱ ✕ ⊙ ⬤ ⧄ ⌗ ⬛ ⬛ ⚠ ⟲ P ⬛ ⬛
lau ➡ ⟲S

Sluftervallei Krimweg 102 ☎ 0222 316214
On sand-dunes. It is advisable to book in advance during the peak season.
⟳ *From the ferry landing stage, drive to the N tip of the island. Just before entering the village, turn left and head towards Vuurtoren (lighthouse). Turn left again after several hundred metres. The road leads directly to the site.*
Etr-Oct 10HEC ⚏ ⵘ ∴ ⵚ ⬢ ⬛ ⚱ ✕ ⊙ ⬤ ⧄ ⟲ P 🏱 ⬛
lau ➡ ⧄ ⌗ ⟲S

▶ DALFSEN OVERIJSSEL

Buitenplaats Gerner Haersolteweg 9-17 ☎ 0529 431181
⟳ *Turn off at Dalfsen and take second road on the left.*
All year 12HEC ⚏ ⬢ ⬛ ⚱ ✕ ⊙ ⬤ ⧄ ⌗ ⬛ ⬛ ⚠ ⟲ LP ⬛ ⬛
lau

▶ DELDEN OVERIJSSEL

Park Camping International De Mors 6 ☎ 074 3763420
On two grassy terraces at the edge of a wood, to the SE of town.
⟳ *Take A1 and exit at Hengelo-Zuid.*
15 Mar-Oct 5HEC ⚏ ⬢ ⬛ ⚱ ✕ ⊙ ⬤ ⧄ ⌗ ⬛ ⬛ ⬛ ⚐ lau ➡ ⬛
⟲P

▶ DENEKAMP OVERIJSSEL

Papillon Kanaalweg 30 ☎ 05413 51670 ▤ 05413 55217
Predominantly a chalet site on meadowland in a tall coniferous and deciduous forest, about 2km N of Denekamp.
It has a few naturally screened pitches.
⟳ *For access, turn off the E72 towards Nordhorn (Germany), about 0.3km N of the signposts for Almelo-Nordhorn canal, and drive NE for 1.5km.*
Apr-1 Oct 11HEC ⚏ ⬢ ⬛ ⚱ ✕ ⊙ ⬤ ⧄ ⌗ ⬛ ⬛ ⚐ ⟲ LP 🏱
⬛ lau Prices: pitch 25 (incl 4 persons)

▶ DIEPENHEIM OVERIJSSEL

Molnhofte Nyhofweg 5 ☎ 0547 351514 ▤ 0547 351641
A family site in a rural setting with modern bungalows for hire.
⟳ *E of town.*
All year 6HEC ⚏ ⬢ ⬛ ⚱ ✕ ⊙ ⬤ ⧄ ⌗ ⬛ ⚐ ⟲ P 🏱 ⬛ ⬛
lau Prices: ⋔2.70 ⬤2.25 ⬤2.70 ⚠2.70

▶ DOESBURG GELDERLAND

Ijsselstrand Eekstr 18 ☎ 313 472797 ▤ 313 473376
On level meadow with trees and hedges beside the River Ijssel. Separate field for young people. Water sports.
⟳ *NE across river. Signposted.*
All year 45HEC ⚏ ⬢ ⬛ ⚱ ✕ ⊙ ⬤ ⧄ ⌗ ⟲ LR 🏱 ⬛ lau

▶ DOETINCHEM GELDERLAND

Wrange Rekhemseweg 144 ☎ 0314 324852 ▤ 0314 324852
e-mail: info@dewrange.nl
On the eastern outskirts of the town. It is set in meadowland and surrounded by bushes and deciduous trees.

⊃ *200m E of link road between roads to Varsseveld and Terborg.*
1 Apr-1 Oct 10HEC 🚙 🚡 ♠ ╲ ╘ ⚑ ✗ ⊙ 🏤 🛇 🚻 🏕 🚐 ⸂ P 🅿 ➕ lau

DOORN UTRECHT

Bonte Vlucht Leersumsestraatweg 23 ☎ 0343 473232
⊃ *3km E.*
Apr-Oct 17HEC 🚙 ⠿ ♠ ╲ ⚑ ✗ ⊙ 🏤 🛇 🅿 🛇 ➤ ⸂P

Het Grote Bos Hydeparklaan 24 ☎ 0343 513644 ▤ 512324
Well layed out site on wooded grassland. Varied leisure activities for children and adults.
⊃ *About 1km NW of Doorn.*
All year 80HEC 🚙 ⠿ ♠ ╲ ⚑ ✗ ⊙ 🏤 🛇 🚻 🚐 ⸂ P ➕ lau

DRONTEN GELDERLAND

At BIDDINGHUIZEN(9km S)

Flevostrand Strandweg 1 ☎ 0320 288480
Plots of grassland separated by close belts of shrubs. Own marina.
⊃ *On the Polder, 5km S of Biddinghuizen turn right near the Veluwemeer.*
Apr-Nov 25HEC 🚙 🚡 ♠ ╲ ╘ ⚑ ✗ ⊙ 🏤 🛇 🚻 🚐
⸂ LP 🅿 ➕ lau

Riviera Park Spijkweg 15 ☎ 0321 331344 ▤ 331402
e-mail: info@riviera.nl
Situated on grassland near a forest of deciduous trees and surrounded by shrubs.
⊃ *On the Polder beside the Veluwemeer, 5km S of Biddinghuizen turn left.*
Closed Nov-Mar 40HEC 🚙 ♠ ╲ ╘ ⚑ ✗ ⊙ 🏤 🛇 🚻 🚐 ▲
⸂ P 🅿 ➕ lau ➤ ⸂L

EDAM NOORD-HOLLAND

Strandbad Zeevangszeedijk 7a
☎ 0299 371994 ▤ 0299 371510
e-mail: www.campingstrandbad.nl
A friendly family site on the Ijssel Lake with plenty of facilities and close to the historical town of Edam.
Apr-Sep 5HEC 🚙 🚡 ♠ ╲ ╘ ✗ ⊙ 🏤 🛇 🚻 🚐 ⸂ L 🏕 ➕ 🛇
lau ➤ ⸂P Prices: ⋔2.60 ⇐2.85 🚐3.85 ▲3.85

EERBEEK GELDERLAND

Landal Greenparks Coldenhove Boshoffweg 6
☎ 0313 659101 ▤ 654776
In woodland.
⊃ *From Apeldoorn-Dieren road, drive 2km SW, then NW for 1km.*
All year 74HEC 🚙 ♠ ╲ ╘ ⚑ ✗ ⊙ 🏤 🛇 🚻 🚐 ⸂ P 🏕 🅿 ➕
🛇 lau ➤ ✗

Robertsoord Doonweg 4 ☎ 0313 651346 ▤ 655751
In a wooded location with good recreational facilities.
⊃ *1km SE.*
All year 2.5HEC 🚙 ♠ ╲ ✗ ⊙ 🏤 🛇 🚻 🚐 🚐 ⸂ ➕ lau ➤ ╘
⸂P Prices: ⋔2 ⇐2 🚐5 ▲5

EGMOND AAN ZEE NOORD-HOLLAND

Camping Egmond ann Zee Nollenweg 1
☎ 072 5061702 ▤ 072 5067147
Part of a chain of family sites with excellent facilities. In a wooded location 1500mtrs from the beach.
Apr-Oct 11HEC 🚙 ♠ ╲ ╘ ⚑ ⊙ 🏤 🛇 🚻 ⸂ PS 🏕 ➕ 🛇
lau ➤ ⸂ ⸂P

EMST GELDERLAND

Wildhoeve Hanendorperweg 102 ☎ 05787 1324
A picturesque, peaceful site within the confines of the Royal Forest with good, modern facilities.

⊃ *3.5km W. Signposted.*
Apr-Oct 11HEC 🚙 🚡 ♠ ╲ ╘ ⚑ ✗ ⊙ 🏤 🛇 🚻 🚐 ⸂ P 🅿 ➕
🛇 lau

ENSCHEDE OVERIJSSEL

De Twentse Es Keppelerdijk 200
☎ 053 4611372 ▤ 053 4618558
e-mail: info@twentse-es.nl
In a wooded location with good recreational facilities.
⊃ *E towards Glanerbrug.*
All year 10HEC 🚙 ♠ ╲ ╘ ✗ ⊙ 🏤 🛇 🚻 ⸂ P 🏕 ➕ lau

EPE GELDERLAND

Euroase Parc Epe Centrumweg 5
☎ 05780 616204 ▤ 05780 627775
On level ground, surrounded by mature woodland, with fine recreational facilities.
⊃ *SW of village.*
Apr-1 Nov 15HEC 🚙 ♠ ╲ ╘ ⚑ ✗ ⊙ 🏤 🛇 🚻 🚐 ⸂ P 🏕 ➕ lau

ERMELO GELDERLAND

Haeghehorst Fazantlaan 4 ☎ 0341 553185 ▤ 562751
e-mail: haeghehorst@vvc.nl
Well equipped site in pleasant wooded surroundings.
Camping Card Compulsory.
⊃ *Access via A28/E35 towards Amersfoort, then N303.*
All year 10HEC 🚙 ♠ ╲ ╘ ⚑ ✗ ⊙ 🏤 🛇 🚻 🚐 🏕 🏕 ➕ 🛇 lau ➤
⸂L Prices: ⋔14-25

GROET NOORD-HOLLAND

Groede Hargerweg 8 ☎ 72 5091555 ▤ 5092862
e-mail: campinggroede@planet.nl
The site consists of a meadow enclosed by hedges.
15 Apr-15 Sep 3HEC 🚙 ♠ ╲ ⊙ 🏤 🛇 🅿 ➕ 🛇 lau ➤ ╘ ✗

GROOTE KEETEN NOORD-HOLLAND

Callassande Voorweg 5A ☎ 0224 581663 ▤ 0224 582588
e-mail: info@callassande.nl
A large tourist site with fine facilities close to the sea.
Apr-Oct 12HEC 🚙 ♠ ╲ ╘ ⊙ 🏤 🛇 🚻 🚐 ⸂ P 🏕 🅿 ➕ lau ➤
🛇 🚻 ⸂S Prices: ⋔3.50 ⇐2.50 🚐6-12.50 ▲6-10

HAAKSBERGEN OVERIJSSEL

't Stien'nboer Scholtenhagenweg 42
☎ 053 5722610 ▤ 5729394
e-mail: info@stien-nboer.nl
A family site with good recreational facilities lying South of the town.
15 Mar-Nov 10.5HEC 🚙 ♠ ╲ ╘ ⚑ ✗ ⊙ 🏤 🛇 🚻 🚐 ▲
⸂ P 🏕 🅿 ➕ lau

HALFWEG NOORD-HOLLAND

Houtrak Zuiderweg 2 ☎ 020 4972796 ▤ 020 4975887
e-mail: info@campinghoutrak.nl
Grassy site on several levels subdivided by trees, hedges and shrubs. Separate section for young campers.
⊃ *Signposted from Spaarwonde exit on A5.*
Apr-Sep 13HEC 🚙 ♠ ╲ ╘ ⚑ ✗ ⊙ 🏤 🛇 🚻 🚐 ⸂ L 🏕 ➕ lau
Prices: ⋔2.90 ⇐2.30 🚐4.10 ▲3.10-4.10

HATTEM GELDERLAND

Leemkule Leemkuilen 6 ☎ 038 4441945 ▤ 038 4446280
e-mail: info@leemkule.nl
A holiday centre situated in one of the largest nature reserves in the country.
⊃ *2.5km SW.*
Apr-Oct 16HEC 🚙 ♣ ♠ ╲ ╘ ✗ ⊙ 🏤 🛇 🚐 ⸂ P 🅿 ➕ 🛇 lau
Prices: pitch 19.29 (incl 2 persons)

HEILOO NOORD-HOLLAND

Heiloo De Omloop 24 ☎ 072 5355555 ▤ 5355551
e-mail: info@campingheiloo.nl
One of the best sites in the area. It is divided into many large squares by hedges.
Apr-Oct 4HEC ⸬ ♁ ⋔ ⛺ ✕ ⊙ ▣ ∅ ≞ ⊞ ▣ ⊞ ⊞ ⊘ lau ➧
⛴ ⸚LP Prices: pitch 11-18.50

Klein Varnebroek De Omloop 22
☎ 072 5331627 ▤ 072 5331620
e-mail: info@kleinvarnebroek.nl
A grassy family campsite surrounded by trees.
➲ Off the Alkmaar road towards the swimming pool.
25 Mar-1 Nov 4.9HEC ⸬ ♁ ⋔ ⛺ ⛴ ✕ ⊙ ▣ ∅ ≞ ▣ ⊞ ⊘
lau ➧ ⸚LPS

HELDER, DEN NOORD-HOLLAND

Donkere Duinen Jan Verfailleweg 616 ☎ 0223 614731
A quiet, pleasant site with good facilities.
➲ 800m towards the beach. Follow signs 'Nieuw-Den Helder' Strand.
1 Apr-15 Sep 7HEC ⸬ ♁ ⋔ ⊙ ▣ ∅ ≞ ⸚ P ⊞ ⊞ lau
➧ ⛴ ✕ ⸚S

Noorder Sandt Noorder Sandt 2, Julianadorp aan Zee
☎ 0223 641266 ▤ 0233 645600
e-mail: info@noordersandt.nl
A flat, well-maintained site on meadowland, with good sanitary blocks.
➲ Access from the Den Helder to Callantsoog coastal road.
Etr-15 Sep 10HEC ⸬ ♁ ⋔ ⛺ ⛴ ✕ ⊙ ▣ ∅ ≞ ⊞ ⊞ ⸚ P ⊞
⊞ lau ➧ ⸚S

HENGELO GELDERLAND

Kom-Es-An Handwijzersdijk 4 ☎ 0575 467242
A family site in wooded surroundings on the outskirts of the village.
➲ NE of village in wooded area in the direction of Ruurlo.
Apr-Oct 10.5HEC ⸬ ♁ ⋔ ⛺ ⛴ ✕ ⊙ ▣ ∅ ≞ ▣
⸚ P ⊞ ▣ ⊞ lau

HENGELO OVERIJSSEL

Zwaaikom Kettingbrugweg 60 ☎ 074 2916560
A family site with good facilities situated on the Twente Canal.
➲ SE towards Enschede between canal and road.
15 Apr-15 Sep 4HEC ⸬ ♁ ⋔ ⛺ ⛴ ✕ ⊙ ▣ ∅ ≞
⸚ P ⊞ ⊞ ⊘

HEUMEN GELDERLAND

Heumens Bos Vosseneindseweg 46
☎ 024 3581481 ▤ 024 3583862
e-mail: info@heumensbos.nl
One of the best sites in the area with good, modern facilities and spacious pitches.
➲ NW of village, 100m N of the Wijchen road.
Apr-Oct 16HEC ⸬ ♁ ⋔ ⛺ ⛴ ✕ ⊙ ▣ ∅ ⊞ ⊞ A ⸚ P ▣ ⊞
lau

HOENDERLOO GELDERLAND

Pampel Woeste Hoefweg 33-35
☎ 055 3781760 ▤ 055 3781992
e-mail: info@pampel.nl
A most attractive site in pleasant wooded surroundings with good facilities for families.
All year 14.5HEC ⸬ ⁙⁙ ♁ ⋔ ⛺ ✕ ⊙ ▣ ∅ ≞
⸚ P ⊞ ⊞ lau Prices: ⊡4.75

't Veluws Hof Krimweg 154 ☎ 055 3781777
Comfortable site with good, modern facilities.
➲ W of N93.
All year 31HEC ⸬ ♁ ⋔ ⛺ ⛴ ✕ ⊙ ▣ ∅ ≞ ⊞ ⊞ ⊞
⸚ P ⊞ ⊞ lau

HOLTEN OVERIJSSEL

Prins Wildweg 2 ☎ 0031 0548 512272 ▤ 0548 522422
A holiday complex operated by the Dutch ENNIA Company, in an area of attraction to the rambler. Swimming pool on edge of site.
➲ Access from the E8 Deventer-Almelo road. Take the Holten/Rijssen exit then turn off.
Apr-Oct 6HEC ⸬ ♁ ➧ ⋔ ⛴ ⛺ ✕ ⊙ ▣ ∅ ∅ ⸚ P ⊞ ▣ ⊞ lau

HOORN, DEN (ISLAND OF TEXEL) NOORD-HOLLAND

Loodsmansduin Rommelpot 19 ☎ 0222 319203
Extensive site, numerous large and small hollows between dunes, connected by paved paths. Several sanitary blocks. On the highest part there is a bungalow village set in a shopping and administrative complex. A section is reserved for naturists and there is a naturists beach 2km away.
➲ From the ferry drive N towards Den Burg, then turn left at crossroads towards Den Hoorn.
1 Apr-25 Oct 38HEC ⸬ ⋇ ⋔ ⛴ ⛺ ✕ ⊙ ▣ ∅ ≞
⸚ PS ⊞ lau

KESTEREN GELDERLAND

Lede en Oudewaard Hogedijkseweg 40
☎ 488 481477 ▤ 488 482599
On level meadowland surrounded by bushy hedges and divided into individual pitches. 100m from private beach and pool.
➲ 2km N of village, turn W off main Rhenen-Kesteren road, and continue for 2.7km.
All year 30HEC ⸬ ♁ ⋔ ⛴ ⛺ ✕ ⊙ ▣ ∅ ≞ ⊞
⸚ L ⊞ ▣ ⊞ lau

KOOG, DE (ISLAND OF TEXEL) NOORD-HOLLAND

Euroase Parc Texel Bosrandweg 395 ☎ 0222 817290
Part of a chain of family sites with excellent facilities.
late Mar-Oct ⸬ ♁ ⋔ ⛺ ✕ ⊙ ▣ ∅ ∅ ⸚ P ⊘ lau ➧ ⛴ ⊞

Shelter Boodtlaan 43 ☎ 0222 317475 ▤ 0222 31745
Small family site a short distance from the sea.
15 Mar-26 Aug 1.1HEC ⸬ ⋇ ⋔ ⊙ ▣ ⊞ ⊞ lau ➧ ⛴ ✕ ∅
≞ ⸚S Prices: ⚡2.20-2.60 ➧1.30 ⊡6-7.15 ▲6-7.15

KOOTWIJK GELDERLAND

Kerkendel Kerkendelweg 49 ☎ 0577 456224 ▤ 0577 456545
e-mail: kerkendel@kerkendel.nl
A family site with good facilities situated in the heart of the Veluwe National Park.
27 Mar-Oct 7.5HEC ⸬ ♁ ⋔ ⛴ ⛺ ✕ ⊙ ▣ ∅ ≞ ⊞ ▲ ⸚ P ▣
⊞ lau ➧ ⸚LR

LAAG-SOEREN GELDERLAND

Jutberg Jutberg 78 ☎ 0313 619220 ▤ 0313 619760
A well equipped site in the woods of the South East Veluwezoom near Arnhem.
➲ Access via A12 (Arnhem) towards Zulfa, then follow signposts.
All year ⸬ ⁙⁙ ♁ ⋔ ⛴ ⛺ ✕ ⊙ ▣ ∅ ≞ ⊞ ⊞ ⊞ ⸚ P ⊞ ⊞ lau

LATHUM GELDERLAND

Mars Marsweg 6 ☎ 0313 631131 ▤ 0313 631435
Divided into pitches on level meadowland beside a dammed tributary of River Ijssel.
➲ Turn off Arnhem-Doesberg road N of village and continue W for 1.7km.
Apr-Oct 10HEC ⸬ ⋇ ⋔ ⛴ ⛺ ✕ ⊙ ▣ ∅ ≞ ⸚ L ⊞ ⊞ lau

LOCHEM GELDERLAND

Ruighenrode Vordenseweg 6 ☎ 0573 289400
Site among mixed woodland with tall spruce.
➲ *2km SW of town. For access, turn off the road to Zutphen at Km10.4 in S direction on the Vorden road for the site.*
All year 58HEC ⬛️ 🛒 🚿🍴✕⊙ 🔾🚽 🚐 🛎
🔦 LP 🔔➕ lau ➡ 🚢

LUTTENBERG OVERIJSSEL

Luttenberg Heuvelweg 9 ☎ 0572 301405 ▥ 0572 301757
e-mail: info@luttenberg.nl
A large holiday park with spacious, well defined pitches separated by bushes. Wide variety of recreational facilities.
Camping Card Compulsory.
Apr-Sep 12HEC ⬛️ ⚡️🛒🚿🍴✕⊙ 🔾🚽 🚢 🛎🔦 P 🔔📅➕
lau Prices: pitch 19.75 (incl 2 persons)

MAARN UTRECHT

Laag-Kanje Laan van Laag-Kanje 1
☎ 0343 441348 ▥ 0343 443295
e-mail: info@laagkanje.nl
Situated 500m from the lake.
➲ *2km NE.*
Apr-Sep 28HEC ⬛️ ⚡️🛒🚿🍴✕⊙ 🔾🚽➕ ➕🔦 lau ➡ 🔦L
Prices: 🚹2.70 🚗1.82 🚐4.83 🅰6.75-5.83

MARKELO OVERIJSSEL

Hessenheem Potdijk 8 ☎ 0547 361200 ▥ 0547 363647
Situated near a swimming pool.
➲ *3km NE.*
All year 30HEC ⬛️ ⋯⋯ ⚡️🛒🚿🍴✕⊙ 🔾🚽 🚢 🚐 🛎🔦 P 🔔
➕ lau

MIJNDEN UTRECHT

Mijnden Bloklaan 22a ☎ 0294 233165 ▥ 0294 233402
e-mail: mijnden@wxs.nl
Situated directly on the Loosdrechtse Plassen lake with good sporting facilities.
Apr-7 Oct 25HEC ⬛️ ⚡️🛒🚿🍴✕⊙ 🔾🚽 🚢 🔦 P 🔔➕ lau

NEEDE GELDERLAND

Eversman Bliksteeg 1 ☎ 0545 291906
Situated in a quiet position, surrounded by trees.
➲ *W of town.*
Apr-Oct 3.8HEC ⬛️ ⚡️🛒🚿⊙ 🔾🚽 🚢 🚐 🔦 P 🔔➕ lau

NOORD SCHARWOUDE NOORD-HOLLAND

Molengroet Molengroet 1 ☎ 0031 226393444 ▥ 226 391426
e-mail: info@molengroet.nl
Site with modern facilities within easy reach of the beach and the 'Geestmerambacht' water park.
➲ *Signposted on N245.*
Apr-Oct 11HEC ⬛️ ⚡️🛒🚿🍴✕⊙ 🔾🚽 🚢 🚐 🔔📅➕ lau ➡
🔦L Prices: 🚹7.50 pitch 9

NUNSPEET GELDERLAND

Vossenberg Groenlaantje 25 ☎ 0341 252458
Apr-1 Nov 3.6HEC ⬛️ ⚡️🛒🚿🍴✕⊙ 🔾🚽 🚢 🚐 🔔📅➕✖
lau ➡ 🚢 ✕ 🔦LP Prices: 🚹3.30 🚗1.30 🚐3.30 🅰3.30

PUTTEN GELDERLAND

Strand Nulde Strandboulevard 27
☎ 341 361304 ▥ 0341 361210
Apr-Oct 8HEC ⬛️ ⚡️🛒🚿🍴✕⊙ 🔾🚽 🅰🔦 L 📅➕✖ lau ➡ 🚢
🚽 🚢 🔦P

REUTUM OVERIJSSEL

De Molenhof Oude Bornsedijk 30
☎ 0541 661165 ▥ 0541 662032
e-mail: molenhof@wxs.nl
A large family site in wooded surroundings with plenty of modern facilities.
➲ *S of Reutum off N343 towards Weerselo.*
Etr-1 Oct 16HEC ⬛️ ⚡️🛒🚿🍴✕⊙ 🔾🚽 🚢 🚐 🔦 P 🔔➕ lau
Prices: pitch 24 (incl 2 persons)

RHENEN UTRECHT

Thymse Berg Nieuwe Veenendaalseweg 229
☎ 317 612384 ▥ 317 618119
e-mail: thymseberg@planet.nl
➲ *N of town.*
Apr-Sep 10HEC ⬛️ ⚡️🛒🚿🍴✕⊙ 🔾🚽 🚢 🚐 🔦 P 📅➕✖
lau ➡ 🚢 🔦LR Prices: 🚹8 🚗2.50 🚐14-19

RUURLO GELDERLAND

't Sikkeler Sikkelerweg 8 ☎ 0573 461221 ▥ 0573 461586
e-mail: info@sikkeler.nl
In a beautiful wooded location with good, modern facilities. Popular with walkers.
➲ *4km SW.*
N315 Ruurlo-Doetinchem.4km from Ruurlo,right. All year
7HEC ⬛️ ⚡️🛒🚿🍴✕⊙ 🔾🚽 🚐 🔔📅➕ lau ➡ 🚢 🔦LP

ST MAARTENSZEE NOORD-HOLLAND

St Maartenszee Westerduinweg 30
☎ 0224 561401 ▥ 0224 561901
e-mail: info@campingsintmaartenszee.nl
Completely surrounded and divided into pitches by hedges, lying on meadowland on the edge of a wide belt of sand dunes.
➲ *For access, turn off the Alkmaar to Den Helder road at St Maartensvlotburg and drive towards the sea. Take the road over the dunes and follow for about 1.5km, then turn right and continue for a further 300m.*
22Mar-22Sep 5HEC ⬛️ ⚡️🛒🚿🍴✕⊙ 🔾🚽 🚢 🚐 🔔📅✖
lau ➡ 🔦LPS Prices: 🚹4 pitch 7.50-11.50

SOEST UTRECHT

King's Home Birkstr 136 ☎ 033 4619118 ▥ 033 4610808
e-mail: camping@kingshome.nl
Well maintained site with modern facilities in a natural setting on the edge of woodland.
➲ *On N221 between Amersfoort and Soest.*
All year 5HEC ⬛️ ⚡️🛒🚿🍴✕⊙ 🔾🚽 🚢 🚐 🚐📅➕ lau ➡ 🚢
✕ 🔦P Prices: 🚹2.40 🚗2.40 🚐9.50 🅰7.20-9.50

STEENWIJK OVERIJSSEL

Kom Bultweg 25 ☎ 521 513736 ▥ 521 518736
e-mail: info@campingdekom.nl
Split into two sections, lying near a country house, and surrounded by a beautiful oak forest.
➲ *The access road off the Steenwijk-Frederiksoord road is easy to miss.*
Apr-Sep 12.5HEC ⬛️ ⋯⋯ ⚡️🛒🛒🚿🍴✕⊙ 🔾🚽 🚢 🚐 🔦
P 🔔📅➕ lau

TEXEL (ISLAND OF)

See **Cocksdorp, de, Hoorn, Den & Koog, de**

UITDAM NOORD-HOLLAND

Uitdam Zeedijk 2 ☎ 020 4031433 ▥ 020 4033692
e-mail: borbv@xs4all.nl
A well maintained site on the Markermeer adjoining the marina.
➲ *Access via N247 Amsterdam-Monnickendam.*
Mar-Oct 21HEC ⬛️ ⚡️🛒🚿🍴✕⊙ 🔾🚽 🚢 🚐 🔦 L 🔔➕
lau Prices: pitch 15-18 (incl 2 persons)

URK FLEVOLAND

Hazevreugd Vormtweg 9 ☎ 0527 681785 ▤ 686298
e-mail: info@hazevreugd.nl
A modern family site in wooded surroundings with a wide variety of recreational facilities.
➲ Access via A6.
Apr-Oct 12HEC ⟱ ⚘ ♠ ⚑ ⚏ ✕ ⊙ 🔄 ⌀ ᴴ ⬛ 🏠
🔀 P ⬚ ⊞ lau ➨ 🔀S

UTRECHT UTRECHT

Berekuil Arienslaan 5 ☎ 030 713870 ▤ 030 721436
In a wooded location beside a lake with well defined pitches and good facilities.
➲ On N outskirts near motorway to Hilversum.
All year 4.5HEC ⟱ ⚘ ♠ ⚑ ⚏ ✕ ⊙ 🔄 ⌀ ᴴ ⬛ 🏠 🔀 P ⬚ ⊞ lau

VAASSEN GELDERLAND

Bosrand Elspeterweg 45 ☎ 0578 571343
In castle grounds surrounded by woods.
➲ Access via A50 Vaassen exit.
All year 3HEC ⟱ ⚘ ♠ ⚑ ✕ ⊙ 🔄 ⌀ ⬛ 🏠 🔀 P ⬚ ⊞ lau ➨ ⚑

VELSEN-ZUID NOORD-HOLLAND

Weltevreden ☎ 023 383726
Camping Card Compulsory.
Apr-Oct 10HEC ⟱ ♠ ♠ ⚑ ⚏ ✕ ⊙ 🔄 ⌀ ᴴ ⬛ 🏠 ⚓ 🔀 LP ⬚ ⊞ lau ➨ ✕ 🔀S

VOGELENZANG NOORD-HOLLAND

Vogelenzang Tweede Doodweg 17
☎ 023 5847014 ▤ 023 5849249
e-mail: camping@vogelenzang.nl
➲ 1km W.
Etr-15 Sep 22HEC ⟱ ⚘ ♠ ⚑ ⚏ ✕ ⊙ 🔄 ⌀ ᴴ 🔀 P ⬚ ⊞ ⊠ lau

WAGENINGEN GELDERLAND

Wielerbaan Zoomweg 7-9 ☎ 0317 413964
A friendly family site on the edge of a forest.
➲ Access via A12, then follow signposts.
All year 7.5HEC ⟱ ⚘ ♠ ⚑ ✕ ⊙ 🔄 ⌀ ᴴ ⬛ 🏠 🔀 P ⬚ ⊞ lau

WEZEP GELDERLAND

Heidehoek Heidehoeksweg 7 ☎ 038 3761382
➲ 0.5km W of railway station.
Apr-Oct 16HEC ⟱ ⚘ ♠ ⚑ ⚏ ✕ ⊙ 🔄 ⌀ 🔀 L ⬚ ⊞ lau

WIJDENES NOORD-HOLLAND

Het Hof Zuideruitweg 64 ☎ 0229 501435 ▤ 0229 503244
A series of fields in a sheltered position on the shore of the Ijsselmeer.
➲ From A7 exit 8 (Hoorn) follow N506 towards Enkhuizen, then right to Wijdenes and follow camping signs.
28 Mar-29 Oct 4.1HEC ⟱ ⚘ ♠ ⚑ ⚏ ✕ ⊙ 🔄 ⌀ ᴴ ⬛ 🏠 🔀 LP 🅿 ⊞ lau Prices: 🏕2.40 ➡7 ⊞7 🅰7 pitch 7

WINTERSWIJK GELDERLAND

Twee Bruggen Meenkmolenweg 11
☎ 0543 565366 ▤ 0543 565222
A family site in pleasant wooded surroundings with good, modern facilities.
All year 34HEC ⟱ ⚘ ♠ ⚑ ⚏ ✕ ⊙ 🔄 ⌀ ᴴ ⬛ 🏠 🔀 LP ⬚ 🅿 ⊞ lau

The south of the Netherlands is the home of the traditional Delft china and Gouda cheese, and is also the location of a project which is the first of its kind in the world: the building of a moveable marine floodgate across the outlet of the Oostenschelde River.
One of the oldest cities in Holland, and the provincial capital of Limburg, is Maastricht. Shaped through the ages by art and culture, the city has a rich heritage and a wealth of historic monuments.
The region also includes two prominent and very different cities. The Hague, with its favourable reputation as the City of Arts, has parliamentary buildings and stately palaces, wide streets and spacious squares, giving an impression of distinction and elegance.
The world's premier harbour has expanded to become the dynamic metropolis of Rotterdam; a city full of vitality and conviviality with a variety of architecture ranging from snug Delfshaven to the futuristic pencil flats and cube houses.
....

AFFERDEN LIMBURG

Klein Canada Dorpsstr 1 ☎ 0485 531223 ▤ 0485 532218
e-mail: info@kleincanada.nl
Situated among heath and woodland close to the River Meuse.
All year 12.5HEC ⟱ ⚘ ♠ ⚑ ⚏ ✕ ⊙ 🔄 ⌀ ᴴ 🔀 P ⊞ lau
Prices: 🏕3.18 ➡5 ⊞8.51-13.61 🅰8.51-13.61 pitch 8.51-13.61 (incl 2 persons)

ARCEN LIMBURG

Maasvallei Dorperheideweg 34 ☎ 077 473 1564
In wooded surroundings near the beach, this family site has varied sporting facilities and play areas for children.
➲ Off the N271.
All year 11HEC ⟱ ⚘ ♠ ⚑ ⚏ ✕ ⊙ 🔄 ⌀ ᴴ ⬛ 🏠 🔀 LP ⬚ ⊞ ⊠ ➨ 🔀R

ARNEMUIDEN ZEELAND

Witte Raaf Muidenweg 3 ☎ 0118 601212 ▤ 0118 603650
A modern well-maintained site in meadowland, divided into sections by rows of shrubs. With a yacht marina, this site is ideal for sailing and motor boat enthusiasts.
➲ Situated on the Veersmeer, N of the Goes-Vlissingen motorway, from Arnemuiden exit follow signs for about 5km.
Apr-Sep 20HEC ⟱ ⚘ ♠ ⚑ ✕ ⊙ 🔄 ⌀ ᴴ 🔀 L ⬚ ⊞ ⊠ lau

BAARLAND ZEELAND

Scheldeoord Landingsweg 1 ☎ 0113 639900 ▤ 0113 639500
e-mail: info@scheldeoord.nl
A popular family site in a beautiful location by the Scheldt River.
➲ S of town on the coast.
Apr-Oct 16HEC ⟱ ⚘ ♠ ⚑ ✕ ⊙ 🔄 ⌀ ᴴ ⬛ 🏠 🔀 PS ⬚ ⊞ lau

BAARLE NASSAU NOORD-BRABANT

Heimolen Heimolen 6 ☎ 0507 9425 ▤ 7885
e-mail: info@deheimolen.nl
In a wooded location with good, modern facilities.
➲ 1.5km SW.
All year 15HEC ⟱ ⚘ ♠ ✕ ⊙ 🔄 ⌀ ᴴ ⬛ 🏠 ⬚ 🅿 ⊞ lau ➨ 🔀P Prices: 🏕2.60 ➡1.13 ⊞3.85 🅰3.85

BAARLO LIMBURG

Euroase Parc Napoleonsbaan Ned 4 ☎ 077 4771547
Part of a chain of family sites with excellent facilities.
➲ *SW of Venlo.*
15 Mar-1 Nov 32HEC ⊞ ⚶ ⌂ ⌇ ☁ ⥙ ✕ ⊙ ⬛ ⌀ ≗ ⌂ ⬛
⟲ P ⊞ ⬛ ⟲ lau

BARENDRECHT ZUID-HOLLAND

Jachthaven de Oude Maas Achterzeedijk 1a
☎ 078 6772445 ▤ 076 773013
e-mail: de.oudemaas@worldonline.nl
On the banks of the Oude Maas, the site is particularly
suitable for families and hikers.
Apr-15 Oct 12HEC ⊞ ⚶ ⌂ ⊙ ⬛ ⌀ ≗ ⌂ ⬛ ⊞ lau ⟳ ⥙ ⌇
✕ ⟲P Prices: ⚑3.18 ⌂3.18 ⬛3.18

BERG EN TERBLIJT LIMBURG

Oriëntal Rijksweg 6 ☎ 043 6040075 ▤ 6042912
e-mail: info@campingoriental.nl
➲ *On Maastricht-Valkenburg road 3km from Maastricht.*
13 Apr-28 Oct 5.5HEC ⊞ ⚶ ⌂ ⌇ ☁ ⥙ ✕ ⊙ ⬛ ⌀ ≗ ⌂ ⟲ P ⌂
⊞ lau ⟳ ✕ Prices: ⚑3.45 pitch 12.50-16.50

BERGEYK NOORD-BRABANT

Paal De Paaldreef 14 ☎ 0497 577164
e-mail: info@depaal.nl
Campsite especially catering for families with children.
Camping Card Compulsory.
➲ *Signposted.*
Etr-Oct 41HEC ⊞ ⚶ ⌂ ⌇ ☁ ⥙ ✕ ⊙ ⬛ ⌀ ≗
⟲ P ⬛ ⊞ lau ⟳ ⟲L

BOXTEL NOORD-BRABANT

Dennenoord Dennendreef 5 ☎ 0411 601280 ▤ 0411 601393
e-mail: info@dennenoord.nl
Level, grassy site with hedging and groups of trees. Leisure
activities organised for adults and young people. Soundproof
disco.
➲ *Turn off the N2 at Esch in direction of Osterwijk. Follow
signs.*
Apr-1 Oct 7HEC ⊞ ⚶ ⌂ ⌇ ☁ ⥙ ✕ ⊙ ⬛ ⌀ ≗ ⟲ P ⬛ ⊞ lau
Prices: pitch 16-18 (incl 2 persons)

BRESKENS ZEELAND

Napoleon Hoeve Zandertje 30
☎ 0117 383838 ▤ 0117 383550
e-mail: camping@napoleonhoeve.nl
A family site with access to the beach.
All year 13HEC ⊞ ⚶ ⌂ ⥙ ✕ ⊙ ⬛ ⌀ ≗ ⌂ ⬛
⟲ PS ⌂ ⬛ ⊞ lau

Schoneveld Schoneveld 1 ☎ 0117 383220
e-mail: schoneveld@zeelandnet.nl
Camping Card Compulsory.
➲ *3km S at the beach.*
All year 14HEC ⊞ ⚶ ⌂ ⌇ ☁ ⥙ ✕ ⊙ ⬛ ⌀ ≗ ⚑ ⟲ PS ⬛ ⊞ lau

BRIELLE ZUID-HOLLAND

Krabbeplaat Oude Veerdam 4
☎ 0181 412363 ▤ 0181 412093
e-mail: info.krabbeplaat@euroase.nl
On level ground scattered with trees and groups of bushes. It
has asphalt drives. Nearest campsite to the coast and ferries.
➲ *Signposted.*
Apr-Oct 18HEC ⊞ ⚶ ⌇ ☁ ⥙ ✕ ⊙ ⬛ ⌀ ⟲ L ⌂ ⊞ ⟲ lau
Prices: pitch 13 (incl 2 persons)

BROEKHUIZENVORST LIMBURG

Kasteel Ooyen Blitterswijkseweg 2
☎ 077 4631307 ▤ 077 4632765
e-mail: info@kasteellouijen.nl
Apr-Oct 16HEC ⊞ ⚶ ⌂ ⌇ ☁ ⥙ ✕ ⊙ ⬛ ⌀ ≗ P ⬛ ⊞ lau

BROUWERSHAVEN ZEELAND

Osse Blankersweg 4 ☎ 0111 691513 ▤ 0111 691058
e-mail: denosse@zeelandnet.nl
An attractive site with good watersports facilities.
Apr-Oct 8.3HEC ⊞ ⚶ ⌂ ⌇ ☁ ⥙ ✕ ⊙ ⬛ ≗ ⌂ ⬛ ⟲ ⟲ P ⌂ ⬛ ⊞
lau ⟳ ⥙ ⌀ ⟲L

BURGH-HAAMSTEDE ZEELAND

Zeelandcamping Duinoord Steenweg 16 ☎ 0111 658888
All year 4.1HEC ⊞ ⚶ ⌂ ⊙ ⬛ ⌀ ≗ ⌂ ⬛ lau ⟳ ⥙ ⌇ ✕ ⟲S

Zeeland Camping Ginsterveld J J Boeijesweg 45
☎ 0111 651590 ▤ 0111 653040
e-mail: ginsterveld@zeelandcamping.nl
A family holiday centre with well defined pitches on level
ground and plenty of recreational facilities.
➲ *NW of town, signposted from R107.*
Apr-Sep 14HEC ⊞ ⚶ ⌂ ⌇ ☁ ⥙ ✕ ⊙ ⬛ ⌀ ≗ ⟲ P ⌂ ⊞ ⟲ lau
Prices: pitch 17-25 (incl 2 persons)

DELFT ZUID-HOLLAND

Delftse Hout Korftlaan 5 ☎ 015 2130040 ▤ 015 2131293
e-mail: info-delftsehout@tours.nl
On a level meadow surrounded by woodland close to the
lake.
Camping Card Compulsory.
➲ *1 mile E of A13. Signposted.*
All year 5.5HEC ⊞ ⚶ ⌂ ⌇ ☁ ⥙ ✕ ⊙ ⬛ ⌀ ≗ ⌂ ⬛ ⟲ P ⌂ ⬛
⊞ lau ⟳ ⟲L Prices: ⚑1.50 ⬛15.50-21.50 ▲15-15
pitch 15.50-21.50 (incl 2 persons)

DOMBURG ZEELAND

Domburg Schelpweg 7 ☎ 0118 588200
On meadowland divided into several sections, with asphalt
drives. It is on the inland side of the road, along the dyke,
with a belt of shrubs dividing it from the road. 2 tennis
courts, small golf course, a children's swimming pool and
play garden.
➲ *500m on main road to Westkapelle.*
All year 8HEC ⊞ ⌇ ⥙ ✕ ⊙ ⬛ ⌀ ≗ ⌂ ⬛ ⚑
⟲ PS ⌂ ⊞ ⟲ lau

ECHT LIMBURG

Marisheem Brugweg 89 ☎ 04754 481458 ▤ 488018
e-mail: info@marisheem.nl
The site is well-kept and lies East of the village.
➲ *From town drive approx 2.2km towards Echterbosch and
the border, then turn left.*
Apr-Oct 12HEC ⊞ ⚶ ⌂ ⌇ ☁ ⥙ ✕ ⊙ ⬛ ⌀ ≗ ⌂
⟲ P ⌂ ⬛ ⊞ ⟲ lau

EERSEL NOORD-BRABANT

Ter Spegelt Postelseweg 88 ☎ 0497 512016 ▤ 0497 514162
e-mail: info@terspegelt.nl
A large family-orientated site with good recreational
facilities.
Mar-Nov 63HEC ⊞ ⚶ ⌂ ⌇ ☁ ⥙ ✕ ⊙ ⬛ ⌀ ≗ ⌂ ⬛
⟲ LP ⬛ ⊞ ⟲ lau

FLUSHING

See **Vlissingen**

'S-GRAVENZANDE ZUID-HOLLAND

Jagtveld Nieuwlandsedijk 41 ☎ 0174 413479 ▤ 0174 422127
e-mail: info@jagtveld.nl
A quiet family site on level meadowland with good facilities.
➲ *Access via N220.*
Apr-Sep 3.3HEC ⬛ ⚫ ⛺ 🅿 🏕 Ⓔ lau
➡ ⤳S Prices: ⚊5.50 ⚊5 ⚊15 ⚊15

GROEDE ZEELAND

Groede Zeeweg 1
☎ 003 (0)117 371384 ▤ 0031 (0) 117 372277
e-mail: info@campinggroede.nl
A large family site with a wide variety of leisure facilities and close to the beach.
Apr-Oct 16HEC ⬛ ⛺ 🏕 🅿 S Ⓔ lau
Prices: ⚊3.90 ⚊10.10 ⚊10.10 pitch 10.10

HAAG, DEN (THE HAGUE) ZUID-HOLLAND

Kijkduinpark Machiel Vrijenhoeklaan 450
☎ 070 4482100 ▤ 3232457
e-mail: info@kijkduinpark.nl
A modern chalet and camping site in an extensive leisure park close to the beach with excellent recreational facilities.
All year 40HEC ⬛ ⛺ 🏕 🅿 P Ⓔ lau ➡ ⤳S
Prices: pitch 17-31 (incl 6 persons)

HELLEVOETSLUIS ZUID-HOLLAND

'T Weergors Zuiddyk 2 ☎ 0181 312430 ▤ 0181 311010
A pleasant, peaceful site on a level meadow close to the beach. A good overnight stopping place or holiday site.
Apr-Oct 9.7HEC ⬛ ⛺ 🏕 PS Ⓔ 🅿 lau

HENGSTDIJK ZEELAND

Vogel Vogelweg 4 ☎ 0114 681625 ▤ 0114 682527
e-mail: info@de-vogel.nl
All year 33HEC ⬛ ⛺ 🏕 L Ⓔ 🅿
lau Prices: pitch 14-24 (incl 5 persons)

HERPEN NOORD-BRABANT

Herperduin Schaykseweg 12 ☎ 0486 411383
Situated in extensive woodland.
➲ *Access from the 'S-Hertogenbosch-Nijmegen motorway. Take the Ravenstein exit and continue towards Herpen, then in direction Bergheim/Oss.*
Apr-20 Oct 45HEC ⬛ ⛺ 🏕 P Ⓔ 🅿
lau

HILVARENBEEK NOORD-BRABANT

Beekse Bergen Beekse Bergen 1
☎ 0031 5360032 ▤ 0031 5366716
e-mail: beeksebergen@libema.nl
Situated in a holiday centre in the Brabant afforestation on the edge of a safari park. Lake suitable for swimming. Various other facilities.
➲ *10km S of Tilburg.*
30 Mar-4 Nov 400HEC ⬛ ⛺ 🏕
⤳ LP 🅿 Ⓔ lau

HOEK ZEELAND

Braakman Holiday Park Middenweg 1
☎ 0115 481730 ▤ 0115 482077
e-mail: holidaypark@braakman.co.uk
A large family site situated on the edge of extensive nature reserves. The pitches are shaded by woodland and there is direct access to the Braakman Lake. Plenty of recreational facilities.
➲ *4km W of town. Signposted from N61.*
All year 80HEC ⬛ ⛺ 🏕
⤳ L Ⓔ 🅿 lau

HOEK VAN HOLLAND ZUID-HOLLAND

Hoek van Holland Wierstraat 101
☎ 0174 382550 ▤ 0174 310210
e-mail: camping.hvh@hetnet.nl
On grass, surrounded by bushes and paved drives.
➲ *If approaching from the N, turn off the E36 and drive to the beach.*
17 Mar-14 Oct 5.5HEC ⬛ ⛺ 🏕 🅿 Ⓔ
lau ➡ ⤳S

HOEVEN NOORD-BRABANT

Bosbad Hoeven Oude Antwerpse Postbaan 81b
☎ 0165 502570 ▤ 0165 504254
e-mail: info@bosbadhoeven.nl
Extensive site with good, modern facilities.
➲ *Between Breda and Roosendaal W of Etten-Leur.*
1 Apr-24 Oct 35HEC ⬛ ⛺ 🏕
⤳ P Ⓔ lau

HOOGERHEIDE NOORD-BRABANT

FamilyLand Groene Papegaai 19
☎ 0164 613155 ▤ 0164 615216
In pleasant wooded surroundings, the site, as its name suggests has fine facilities for both adults and children with all kinds of sports and entertainment available.
➲ *2km from junction of A30 and A58.*
All year 25HEC ⬛ ⛺ 🏕
⤳ P Ⓔ lau

KAMPERLAND ZEELAND

Roompot Beach Resort Mariapolderseweg 1
☎ 0113 374000 ▤ 0113 371095
e-mail: info@roompot.nl
A level, well-maintained site with a private beach.
➲ *Turn off Kamperland-Wissenkerke road and drive N for 0.5km.*
All year 33HEC ⬛ ⛺ 🏕 PS
Ⓔ lau Prices: pitch 17.70-39 (incl 5 persons)

Schotsman Schotsmanweg 1 ☎ 0113 371751
On a large, level meadow beside the Veerse Meer, next to a Nature Reserve. Water sports.
➲ *Signposted.*
27 Mar-1 Nov 30HEC ⬛ ⛺ 🏕
⤳ L Ⓔ lau

KATWIJK AAN ZEE ZUID-HOLLAND

Noordduinen Campingweg 1
☎ 071 4025295 ▤ 071 4033977
Family site set among sand dunes close to the sea.
➲ *Access via Hoorneslaan.*
mid Mar-Oct 11HEC ⬛ ⛺ 🏕
⤳ S Ⓔ lau

KORTGENE ZEELAND

Paardekreek Havenweg 1 ☎ 0113 302051 ▤ 0113 302280
e-mail: paardekreek@zeelandcamping.nl
A municipal site next to the Veerse Meer canal.
➲ *For access, turn off the Zierikzee-Goes trunk road at the Chevron petrol station and drive towards Kortgene, continue through the village and drive SW.*
Apr-Oct 10HEC ⬛ ⛺ 🏕 LP Ⓔ
lau Prices: pitch 15.50-30.40

KOUDEKERKE ZEELAND

Dishoek Dishoek 2 ☎ 118 551348 ▤ 552990
e-mail: info@campingdishoek.nl
➲ *W on Vlissingen-Dihoek road.*
Apr-Oct 4.5HEC ⬛ ⛺ 🏕
⤳ S Ⓔ lau ➡ ✕

292

★★★★★
VAKANTIECENTRUM

de hertenwei
WELLENSEIND 7-9
NL-5094 EG LAGE, MIERDE.
Tel: 013-5091295

Located 2km North of Lage Mierde, on the Tilburg-Reusel road (road No. N.269). Pleasantly wooded site. Ideal starting point for Efteling, Beekse Bergen, Theme Park "Land van Ooit" and Belgium. Modern, heated sanitary blocks with hot water and hot showers. Heated pool and paddling pool. Indoor pool with hot whirlpool, sauna, solarium, bar, supermarket, snackbar, washing machines, tennis-courts, children's play area. Restaurant and disco. Please ask for our brochure.

Duinzicht Strandweg 7 ☎ 0118 551397 ▤ 0118 553222
e-mail: info@campingduinzicht.nl
A small family site with good facilities.
➲ *1.5km SW of Koudekerke.*
Apr-Oct 6.5HEC ⸬ 🏕 📻 🛉 🌭 ⊙ 🍴 ⌀ 🏤 ⊞ lau ➤ 🍴 ✗ ⸗S

LAGE MIERDE NOORD-BRABANT

Vakantiecentrum de Hertenwei Wellenseind 7-9
☎ 013 5091295
Pleasant wooded site with modern facilities.
Camping Card Compulsory.
➲ *2km N on N269 (Tilburg-Reusel).*
All year 20HEC ⸬ 🏕 📻 🛉 🍴 ✗ ⊙ 🍴 ⌀ 🚿 🏤 🏤 ⸗ P ⊞ ⊞
lau

LANDGRAAF LIMBURG

Bousberg Boomweg 10 ☎ 045 5311213 ▤ 045 5323143
➲ *NW towards Kakert.*
Apr-Oct 7.5HEC ⸬ 🏕 📻 🛉 🍴 ✗ ⊙ 🍴 ⌀ 🚿 🏤 🏤 ⸗ P ⊞ ⊞
lau

LUYKSGESTEL NOORD-BRABANT

Zwarte Bergen Zwarte Bergen Dreef 1
☎ 0497 541373 ▤ 0497 542673
e-mail: info@zwartebergen.nl
The site is isolated and very quiet, and lies in a pine forest.
➲ *From Eindhoven through Valkenswaard and Bergiejkl. Signposted.*
All year 25.5HEC ⸬ 🏕 📻 🛉 🍴 ✗ ⊙ 🍴 ⌀ 🚿 🏤 ⊞ P ⊞ 🅿 ⊞
lau ➤ ⸗L Prices: ♠2.50-3.35 pitch 10.70-14.30

MAASBREE LIMBURG

BreeBronne Lange Heide ☎ 77 4652360 ▤ 774652095
e-mail: info@breebronne.nl
A family site in quiet surroundings with good facilities.
➲ *On the E3 just before Venlo, on the border with Germany.*
Apr-Oct 23HEC ⸬ 🌭 🏕 📻 🛉 🍴 ✗ ⊙ 🍴 ⌀ 🚿 🏤 ⸗ LP ⊞ 🅿
⊞ lau Prices: pitch 20-32.50 (incl 4 persons)

MAASTRICHT LIMBURG

Dousberg Dousbergweg 102 ☎ 043 3432171 ▤ 043 3430556
e-mail: dousbergcamping@dousberg.nl
A modern site with good facilities.
➲ *From the Eindhoven-Liège motorway follow sings for Hasselt, then pick up local signs to the site.*
Apr-Oct 10HEC ⸬ 🌭 🏕 📻 🛉 🍴 ✗ ⊙ 🍴 ⌀ 🏤 ⊞ ⊞ lau ➤ ⸗P

MIDDELBURG ZEELAND

Middelburg Koninginnelaan 55 ☎ 118 625395 ▤ 625395
On meadowlands surrounded by trees and bushes.
➲ *On W outskirts of town.*
Etr-15 Oct 3.4HEC ⸬ 🏕 🛉 🍴 ✗ ⊙ 🍴 ⌀ 🚿 🏤 🏤 ⊞ lau ➤
⸗ ⸗PS Prices: ♠3.30 ♦2.95 ♣3.65 ♠2.50-3.40

MIERLO NOORD-BRABANT

Wolfsven Patrijslaan 4 ☎ 0492 661661
Large campsite with wooded areas and several lakes. Asphalt drives.
All year 70HEC ⸬ ⸬⸬ 🌭 🏕 📻 🛉 🍴 ✗ ⊙ 🍴 ⌀ 🏤 ⸗ LP ⊞ ⊞
⊞ lau

NIEUWVLIET ZEELAND

International St-Bavodk 2d ☎ 0117 371233
Well equipped family site close to the beach.
➲ *On N outskirts, near a windmill on the road leading to the dyke.*
Apr-Oct 5.9HEC ⸬ 🏕 📻 🛉 🍴 ✗ ⊙ 🍴 ⌀ 🏤 🏤 ⊞ ⊞ lau ➤ 🍴 ⚑
⸗S

Pannenschuur Zeedijk 19 ☎ 0117 372300 ▤ 0117 371415
e-mail: info@pannenschuur.nl
A modern site with good facilities. Close to the beach.
➲ *NW of town. Signposted.*
All year 14HEC ⸬ 🏕 📻 🛉 🍴 ✗ ⊙ 🍴 ⌀ 🚿 🏤 🏤 ⸗ PS 🅿 ⊞
lau Prices: ♠4 pitch 17.25

NOORDWIJK AAN ZEE ZUID-HOLLAND

Carlton Kraaierslaan 13 ☎ 0253 272783
A good centre for touring the surrounding area and visiting the famous bulb fields.
Camping Card Compulsory.
23 Mar-1 Nov 2HEC ⸬ 🏕 📻 ⊙ 🍴 🏤 ⸗ P 🅿 lau ➤ 🍴 ✗ ⌀ ⸗S

Jan de Wit Kapelleboslaan 10 ☎ 252 372485 ▤ 252 340140
e-mail: camjan@xs4all.nl
A well equipped family site in a wooded location 2km from the beach.
15 Mar-10 Oct 6HEC ⸬ 🏕 📻 🛉 🍴 ✗ ⊙ 🍴 ⌀ 🚿 🏤 ⊞ ⊞ 🞬
lau Prices: ♠4 ♣6 ♠6

At NOORDWIJKERHOUT(5km NE)

Club Soleil Kraaierslaan 7 ☎ 0252 374225 ▤ 0252 376450
e-mail: info@clubsoleil.nl
In a pleasant location near the bulb fields and the sea.
➲ *Signposted.*
Apr-Nov 5.5HEC ⸬ 🏕 📻 🛉 🍴 ✗ ⊙ 🍴 ⌀ 🏤 🏤 ⸗ P 🅿 ⊞
lau ➤ ⸗LS

OISTERWIJK NOORD-BRABANT

Reebok Duinenweg 4 ☎ 013 5282309 ▤ 013 5217592
e-mail: info@dereebok.nl
Situated in a large pine forest, fenced off and impossible to overlook. In attractive surroundings with numerous small lakes.
➲ *SE of town.*
15 Mar-Oct 8HEC ⸬ 🏕 📻 🛉 🍴 ✗ ⊙ 🍴 ⌀ 🚿 🏤 ⊞ lau ➤
⸗LP

OOSTERHOUT NOORD-BRABANT

Katjeskelder Katjeskelder 1 ☎ 0162 453539 ▤ 0162 454090
e-mail: kkinfo@katjeskelder.nl
A large, modern family site with good sanitary and recreational facilities.
➲ *Access via A27 (Breda-Utrecht) exit 17 and follow signs.*
All year 25HEC ⸬ 🏕 📻 🛉 🍴 ✗ ⊙ 🍴 ⌀ 🏤 🏤 ⸗ P ⊞ ⊞ ⊞
lau ➤ 🚿 Prices: pitch 19.50-33 (incl 2 persons)

OOSTKAPELLE ZEELAND

Dennenbos Duinweg 64 ☎ 0118 581310 ▤ 0118 583773
e-mail: dennenbos@zeelandnet.nl
A well maintained family site in a wooded location, 500mtrs from the beach.
Mar-Nov 3HEC ⸬ 🌭 🏕 📻 🛉 🍴 ⌀ 🍴 🚿 🏤 🏤 ⸗ PS ⊞ ⊞ 🞬
lau Prices: pitch 15-18 (incl 2 persons)

In de Bongerd Brouwerijstr 13
☎ 0118 581510 ▤ 0118 581510
e-mail: info@bongerdzeeland.nl
A well-kept family campsite, set in a meadow with hedges and apple trees. There are fine recreational facilities and the beach is within easy reach.
➲ *500m S.*
30Mar-28Oct 7.4HEC ⌂ ⚹ ⚫ ⚫ ✕ ⊙ ⚫ ∅ ⚫ ⚫ ⚫ ⚫ ⚫ PS
⚫ ⊞ lau ➧ ✕ **Prices:** ⚫3.50 pitch 14.50-23 (incl 2 persons)

Ons Buiten Aagtekerkeseweg 2a
☎ 0118 581813 ▤ 0118 583771
e-mail: onsbuiten@zeelandcamping.nl
In a beautiful location with a wide choice of recreational activities.
➲ *From church drive S towards Grijpskerke, turn W and continue 400m.*
22Mar-Oct 11.5HEC ⌂ ⚹ ⚫ ⚫ ⚫ ✕ ⊙ ⚫ ∅ ⚫ ⚫ PS ⚫
⚫ ⊞ ✖ lau **Prices:** pitch 16-26 (incl 2 persons)

Pekelinge Landmetersweg 1 ☎ 0118 582820 ▤ 0118 583782
e-mail: depekelinge@zeelandcamping.nl
The on-site facilities have seasonal opening times.
Apr-Oct 12HEC ⌂ ⚹ ⚫ ⚫ ⚫ ✕ ⊙ ⚫ ∅ ⚫ ⚫ P ⚫ ⊞ ✖ lau
➧ ∅ ⚫L

▶ OOSTVOORNE ZUID-HOLLAND

Kruininger Gors Gorspl 2 ☎ 0181 482711 ▤ 0181 485957
e-mail: info@kruiningergors.nl
A small site, divided by hedges, close to the lake.
➲ *Access via N15.*
Apr-Sep 108HEC ⌂ ⚹ ⚫ ⚫ ⚫ ✕ ⊙ ⚫ ∅ ⚫ ⚫ LPR ⚫ ⊞
✖ lau **Prices:** ⚫2.50 pitch 14.20 (incl 2 persons)

▶ OUDDORP ZUID-HOLLAND

Klepperstee Vrijheidsweg 1 ☎ 0187 681511 ▤ 0187 683060
e-mail: info@klepperstee.nl
On level meadow divided by hedges and trees.
➲ *Access via N57 (Rotterdam-Vlissingen) exit Ouddorp.*
Apr-Oct 40HEC ⌂ ⚹ ⚫ ⚫ ⚫ ✕ ⊙ ⚫ ∅ ⚫ ⚫ P ⚫ ⊞ ✖
lau ➧ ⚫LPS **Prices:** pitch 25-27.50 (incl 4 persons)

▶ PLASMOLEN LIMBURG

Eldorado Witteweg 18 ☎ 024 6961914 ▤ 024 6963017
e-mail: info@eldorado-mook.nl
Well equipped site in wooded surroundings on the Mooker See.
➲ *S of N271.*
Apr-Oct 6HEC ⌂ ⚹ ⚫ ⚫ ⚫ ✕ ⊙ ⚫ ∅ ⚫ ⚫ L ⚫ ⊞ lau
Prices: ⚫3.50 ⚫2 ⚫3.75 ⚫3.75

▶ RENESSE ZEELAND

Brem Hoogenboomlaan 11 ☎ 0111 461403
Well-kept site belonging to a trade union, but also accepting tourists. The last camping site in Hoogenboomlaan with numbered sections. It is advisable to reserve pitches between 21 Jun and 9 Aug.
Apr-25 Oct 12HEC ⌂ ⚹ ⚫ ⚫ ✕ ⊙ ⚫ ⚫ ⚫ ⚫ P ⚫ ⊞ ✖
lau ➧ ⚫ ∅

International Scharendijkseweg 8
☎ 0111 461391 ▤ 0111 462571
e-mail: info@camping-international.net
On grassland, between rows of tall shrubs and trees. Between dyke road and main road to Scharendijk on E outskirts of village.
Mar-Nov 3HEC ⌂ ⚹ ⚫ ⚫ ⚫ ⊙ ⚫ ∅ ⚫ ⚫ ⚫ ⊞ lau ➧ ✕ ⚫S
Prices: ⚫4 ⚫2.40 ⚫3.65 ⚫3.65

Wyde Blick Hagezoom 12 ☎ 0111 468888 ▤ 0111 468889
e-mail: dewijdeblick@zeelandcamping.nl
A family site with good facilities.
➲ *Well signposted.*
All year 10HEC ⌂ ⚹ ⚫ ⚫ ⚫ ✕ ⊙ ⚫ ∅ ⚫ ⚫ ⚫ P ⚫ ⊞ ⚫
lau ➧ ⚫S **Prices:** pitch 15-23.50 (incl 2 persons)

▶ RETRANCHEMENT ZEELAND

De Zwinhoeve Duinweg 1 ☎ 0117 392120 ▤ 0117 392248
In a beautiful position backed by sandunes with easy access to the fine beaches of the Zeeuws-Vlaanderen coast.
All year 9HEC ⌂ ⚹ ⚫ ⚫ ⚫ ✕ ⊙ ⚫ ∅ ⚫ ⚫ ⚫ ⚫ S ⚫ ⚫ ⊞
lau ➧ ⚫P **Prices:** ⚫4.61 ⚫6.35 ⚫6.35

▶ RIJEN NOORD-BRABANT

D'n Mastendol Oosterhoutseweg 7-13
☎ 0161 222664 ▤ 0161 222669
A comfortable site in wooded surroundings.
➲ *SW of town.*
Apr-Oct 10.5HEC ⌂ ⚹ ⚫ ⚫ ⚫ ✕ ⊙ ⚫ ⚫ ⚫ ⚫ ⚫ P ⚫ ⊞
lau ➧ ✕ ∅ ⚫L

▶ RIJNSBURG ZUID-HOLLAND

Koningshof Elsgeesterweg 8 ☎ 071 4026051 ▤ 071 4021336
e-mail: info-koningshof@tours.nl
Modern site on level meadow near the flower fields.
➲ *1km N. Signposted*
All year 7.5HEC ⌂ ⚹ ⚫ ⚫ ⚫ ✕ ⊙ ⚫ ∅ ⚫ ⚫ ⚫ ⚫ P ⚫ ⊞
lau ➧ ⚫S

▶ ROCKANJE ZUID-HOLLAND

Rondeweibos Schapengorsedijk 19
☎ 0181 401944 ▤ 0181 402380
15 Mar-Oct 32HEC ⌂ ⚹ ⚫ ⚫ ⚫ ✕ ⊙ ⚫ ∅ ⚫ ⚫ ⚫ P ⚫ ⊞
lau ➧ ⚫S

Waterboscamping Duinrand 11
☎ 0181 401900 ▤ 0181 404233
e-mail: info@waterboscamping.nl
A small, pleasant site near the beach. **Motor caravans and tents only.**
➲ *Access via N15.*
Apr-Sep 7HEC ⌂ ⚹ ⚫ ⚫ ⚫ ⊙ ⚫ ∅ ⚫ ⚫ ⚫ ⚫ ⊞ ✖ lau ➧ ✕
⚫S **Prices:** ⚫2.05 pitch 14-17 (incl 2 persons)

▶ ROERMOND LIMBURG

Hatenboer Hatenboer 51 ☎ 0475 336727 ▤ 0475 310113
Situated in a 'Waterpark' with access to all watersports.
Camping Card Compulsory
➲ *Leave A68 (Roermond-Eindhoven) at 'Hatenboer' exit.*
Apr-1 Nov 15HEC ⌂ ⚹ ⚫ ⚫ ✕ ⊙ ⚫ ⚫ LR ⚫ ⚫ ⊞ lau ➧
⚫ ∅ ⚫P

Marina Oolderhuuske Oolderhuuske 1
☎ 0475 588686 ▤ 0475 582652
e-mail: oolderhuuske@tref.nl
A well equipped site within the marina area on the Maasplassen.
28 Mar-1 Nov 6HEC ⌂ ⚹ ⚫ ⚫ ⚫ ✕ ⊙ ⚫ ∅ ⚫ ⚫ ⚫ ⚫
LPR ⚫ ⊞ lau

▶ ROOSENDAAL NOORD-BRABANT

Zonneland Tufvaartsestr 6 ☎ 01656 365429
e-mail: info@zonneland.nl
➲ *S of town towards the Belgian border.*
Mar-15 Oct 14HEC ⌂ ➧ ⚫ ⚫ ⚫ ⊙ ⚫ ⚫ ⚫ ⚫ P ⚫ ⊞ ⚫ lau
Prices: ⚫3 ⚫2 ⚫3 ⚫3

ST ANTHONIS NOORD-BRABANT

Ullingse Bergen Bosweg 36 ☎ 0485 388566 ▤ 0485 388569
e-mail: info@ullingsebergen.nl
A family site in natural wooded surroundings with good facilities for children.
⮑ W of town.
Apr-Oct 11HEC ⸺ ⌇ ⌁ ⌇ ✕ ⊙ ⌁ ⌁ ⌁ ⌁ ⌁ P ⌁ P ⊞ ⌁
lau **Prices:** pitch 13.60-18.50 (incl 2 persons)

ST OEDENRODE NOORD-BRABANT

Kienehoef Zwembadweg 35-37
☎ 0413 472877 ▤ 0413 477033
e-mail: info@kienehoef.nl
An exceptionally well appointed site in a peaceful rural setting.
⮑ NW towards Boxtel.
All year 4HEC ⸺ ⌇ ⌁ ⌇ ⌁ ✕ ⊙ ⌁ ⌁ ⌁ ⌁ P ⌁ P ⊞ ⌁
lau ⮕ ✕

SEVENUM LIMBURG

Schatberg Midden Peelweg 5 ☎ 077 4677777 ▤ 077 4677799
e-mail: receptie@schatberg.nl
A well appointed family site in wooded surroundings with plenty of leisure facilities.
⮑ SW towards Eindhoven.
All year 86HEC ⸺ ⌇ ⌁ ⌇ ⌁ ⌇ ✕ ⊙ ⌁ ⌁ ⌁ ⌁ ⌁ LP ⌁ P
⊞ ⌁ lau **Prices:** pitch 14.25-25.50 (incl 2 persons)

SLUIS ZEELAND

Meldoorn Hoogstr 68 ☎ 0117 461662 ▤ 0117 461662
In a meadow surrounded by rows of deciduous trees.
⮑ N on the road to Zuidzande.
All year 6.5HEC ⸺ ⌇ ⌁ ⌇ ✕ ⊙ ⌁ ⌁ ⌁ ⌁ ⌁ ⊞ lau ⮕ ⌁
Prices: ⌁3.30 ⌁2 ⌁3.95 ⌁3

SOERENDONK LIMBURG

Soerendonk Strijperdijk 9 ☎ 0495 591652
A spacious site in wooded surroundings close to the Belgian border. There are good recreational facilities and good fishing is available in the lake.
All year 17.8HEC ⸺ ⌇ ⌁ ⌇ ⌁ ✕ ⊙ ⌁ ⌁ ⌁ ⌁ ⌁ ⌁ P ⌁ ⊞
lau

STRAMPROY LIMBURG

't Vosseven Lochstr 26 ☎ 0495 566023
A family site with adequate facilities.
⮑ Turn right at the church and continue for 5km.
Apr-Oct 11HEC ⸺ ⌇ ⌁ ✕ ⊙ ⌁ ⌁ ⌁ P ⊞ lau ⮕ ⌁ ⌁P

VALKENBURG LIMBURG

Europa Couberg 29 ☎ 043 6013097 ▤ 043 6013525
A quiet family site within easy reach of the town.
⮑ SW of town.
Apr-Oct 10HEC ⸺ ⌁ ⌁ ⌁ ✕ ⊙ ⌁ ⌁ ⌁ ⌁ P ⌁ ⊞ lau

VENLO LIMBURG

Ons Buiten St-Urbansweg 120-122 ☎ 077 3515821
A pleasant family site with plenty of touring pitches in a picturesque wooded location.
⮑ 500mtrs from A67/E34.
All year 12HEC ⸺ ⌇ ⌁ ⌇ ⌁ ✕ ⊙ ⌁ ⌁ ⌁ ⌁ P ⌁ P ⊞ lau ⮕
⌁R

VENRAY LIMBURG

de Oude Barrier Maasheseweg 93 ☎ 0478 582305
A quiet site recommended for young children.
⮑ NE of town.
Apr-Sep 14HEC ⸺ ⌇ ⌁ ⊙ ⌁ ⌁ ⌁ P ⌁ ⊞ lau ⮕ ✕ ⌁
Prices: ⌁6.25 ⌁4 ⌁4 ⌁4

VLISSINGEN (FLUSHING) ZEELAND

Lange Pacht Boksweg 1 ☎ 0118 460447
Apr-Sep 1.2HEC ⸺ ⌇ ⌁ ⊙ ⌁ ⌁ ⮕ ⌁ ✕

VROUWENPOLDER ZEELAND

Oranjezon Koningin Emmaweg 16a
☎ 0118 591549 ▤ 0118 591920
e-mail: oranjezon@oranjezon.nl
Well-kept between tall, thick hedges and bushes. SW of the village.
Camping Card Compulsory.
⮑ For access drive towards Oostkapelle for approx 2.5km, then turn N and continue for 300m.
Apr-Oct 9.8HEC ⸺ ⌇ ⌁ ⌇ ⌁ ✕ ⊙ ⌁ ⌁ ⌁ ⌁ A ⌁ PS ⌁ P
⊞ lau **Prices:** pitch 15-30 (incl 4 persons)

WASSENAAR ZUID-HOLLAND

Duinhorst Buurtweg 135 ☎ 070 3242270 ▤ 070 3246053
A peaceful site in wooded surroundings with modern facilities and good opportunities for sports and entertainment.
Apr-1 Oct 11HEC ⸺ ⌇⌁ ⌇ ⌁ ⌇ ⌁ ✕ ⊙ ⌁ ⌁ ⌁ P ⌁ ⊞
⌁ lau

Duinrell Duinrell 1 ☎ 070 5155255 ▤ 070 5155371
e-mail: info@duinrell.nl
Very well maintained site with additional recreation centre which is free for campers. Some noise from aircraft. Toilets for invalids. Area restricted to cars. Naturist beach nearby.
⮑ Turn off A44 (Den Haag-Leiden) at traffic lights in Wassenaar dorp' and camping signs.
All year 110HEC ⸺ ⌇ ⌁ ⌇ ⌁ ⌇ ✕ ⊙ ⌁ ⌁ ⌁ ⌁ ⌁ A ⌁ P ⌁
P ⊞ lau ⮕ ⌁LS **Prices:** ⌁8.50 ⌁9.50 ⌁8
See advertisement on page 296

WEERT LIMBURG

Ijzeren Man Herenvennenweg 60 ☎ 0495 533202
Well-kept with asphalt drives, in a big nature reserve with zoo, heath and forest.
⮑ Off E9.
1 Apr-1 Oct 11.5HEC ⸺ ⌇⌁ ⌇ ⌁ ⌇ ⌁ ✕ ⊙ ⌁ ⌁ ⌁
⌁ P ⌁ P ⊞ lau

WELL LIMBURG

Leukermeer De Kamp 5 ☎ 0478 502444 ▤ 0478 501260
In beautiful surroundings on Lake Leukermeer with good modern installations and plenty of leisure facilities.
⮑ Signposted from N271.
27 Mar-Oct 9HEC ⸺ ⌁ ⌇ ⌁ ✕ ⊙ ⌁ ⌁ ⌁ ⌁
⌁ LP ⌁ ⊞ lau

WEMELDINGE ZEELAND

Linda Oostkanaalweg 4 ☎ 0113 621259 ▤ 0113 622638
e-mail: info@campinglinda.nl
On meadowland surrounded by rows of tall shrubs.
⮑ Turn opposite bridge in town and continue 100m, over bridge to camp.
Apr-Nov 8HEC ⸺ ⌁ ⌁ ⌇ ⌁ ✕ ⊙ ⌁ ⌁ ⌁ ⌁ ⌁
⌁ S ⌁ lau

WESTKAPELLE ZEELAND

Boomgaard Domineeshofweg 1
☎ 118 571377 ▤ 572383
A flat grassy site.
⮑ For access turn off the Middleburg road on the S outskirts of the town, then follow signs.
27 Mar-24 Oct 8HEC ⸺ ⌇ ⌁ ⌇ ⌁ ✕ ⊙ ⌁ ⌁ ⌁ ⌁ ⌁ P ⌁
⊞ lau ⮕ ⌁S

> **ZEVENHUIZEN** ZUID-HOLLAND

Zevenhuizen Tweemanspolder 8
☎ 0180 631654 ▯ 0180 634471
Situated NW of the village, this site is surrounded by a wide belt of bushes.
➲ *On NW outskirts follow signs . Site on right of the road beyond a car park.*
Apr-Oct 6HEC ⛺ ⊞ 🏠 🛒 🍴 ✕ ⊙ 🚽 🅿 🚿 ⊁ P 🅿 ⊞ lau ➡ ✕ ⊁L

> **ZOUTELANDE** ZEELAND

Meerpaal Duinweg 133 ☎ 118 561300
On meadowland hidden behind bushy hedges at the end of a cul-de-sac.
➲ *1km SE.*
27 Mar-1 Nov 2HEC ⛺ 🌲 🏠 🛒 ⊙ 🚽 🚽 🚙 🚐 ⊁ S 🅿 ⊞ lau ➡ 🛒 ✕

PORTUGAL

This relatively small but once powerful country lies in the south western corner of the Iberian peninsula. Portugal's only land frontier is the Spanish border in the east and north.

FACTS AND FIGURES
Area: 92,345 sq km
Population: 9,979,450 (1998)
Capital: Lisbon
Language: Portuguese
IDD code: 351. To call the UK dial 00 44
Currency: Euro
Local time: GMT(summer GMT+1)

Emergency Services:
Police, Fire and Ambulance 112
Banks: Mon-Fri 08.30-15.00
Shops: Mon-Fri 09.00-13.00; 15.00-19.00, Sat 09.00-13.00;& Dec 15.00-19.00 ; shopping centres Mon-Sun 10.00-24.00
Average daily temperature: Lisbon
Jan 11°C   Jul 21°C

Mar 13°C   Sep 20°C
May 17°C   Nov 14°C
Tourist Information:
ICEP/Portuguese Trade and Tourism Office
UK 22-25A Sackville Street London W1X 2LY
Tel 09063 640610 (premium rate information line)
USA 4th Floor, 590 Fifth Avenue New York, NY 10036-4785

Tel (212) 764 6137
Camping card:
Compulsory at Federaçâo Portuguesa de Campismo parks and camping clubs offering special prices. Recommended elsewhere.
Tourist info website: www.portugal.org/tourism

The country is perhaps, best known for its five hundred miles of coastline. The Algarve in the extreme south is one of the finest stretches of coastline in Europe, with unique caves and a remoteness which has been preserved despite the development of the area. Inland, the cool valleys and pastures of the Tagus contrast sharply with the wooded mountain slopes of the Minho area in the north.

Generally the country enjoys a mild climate with the Algarve being very hot in the summer. The language is Portuguese, which was developed from Latin and closely resembles Spanish, although English is often spoken in the Algarve.

Mainland Portugal has 197 campsites most of which are on the coast. A camping guide is available from Roteiro Campista, Rua do Griestal 5 1ºfte, 1300-274 Lisboa ☎ 213642370 (fax: 213619284 / e-mail: info@roteiro-campista.pt)There are about 23 Orbitur parks in the country which are privately owned and of a high standard, as indeed are the municipal parks. Orbitur parks are open throughout the year and most of them offer fully-equipped bungalows which accommodate four people. A booklet containing details of officially classified parks is produced by the Direcção Geral de Turismo, Palácio Foz, Praça dos Restauradores, Lisboa ☎ 213466307 or 213463624. The Oporto office is

at Praça D João I, 25-4 L 222005805 and the Coimbra office is at Largo da Portagem. Otherwise ask for Comissao Municipal de Turismo, Junta de Turismo or Câmara Municipal.

Off-site camping is prohibited You must stay on an organised site. However, when stopping in a motorway rest or service area with a caravan, it is permissible to cook a meal.

HOW TO GET THERE
You can use one of the direct ferry services to Spain and then travel onwards by road. The services and minimum sailing times are **Plymouth to Santander** (24hrs) and **Portsmouth to Bilbao** (27hrs).

Distance
From Santander to Lisboa (Lisbon) is about 920km (570 miles), normally requiring one or two overnight stops. Using the Channel ports, or the Channel tunnel, driving through France and Spain (enter Spain on the Biarritz to San Sebastian (Donostia) road at the western end of the Pyrénées).

From the Channel ports to Lisboa (Lisbon) is about 2,157km (1,340 miles). This will require 3 or 4 overnight stops.

Car sleeper trains
Summer services are available from **Calais** to Toulouse and **Denderleeuw** (Belgium) to Biarritz. An all-year round service operates from **Denderleeuw** to Toulouse.

See Spain for location map

MOTORING & GENERAL INFORMATION
The information given here is specific to Portugal. It **must** be read in conjunction with the Continental ABC at the front of the book, which covers those regulations which are common to many countries. **Note**: Portuguese law requires that everyone carries photographic proof of identity at all times.

British Embassy/Consulates*
The British Embassy is located at 1249-082 Lisboa, rua de São Bernardo 33 ☎ 213924000; consular section ☎ 213924188. There is a British Consulate in Porto (Oporto) and one with an Honorary Consul in Portimão.

Children in cars
Child under 3 cannot travel as front seat passenger unless seated in approved child seat; child over 3 and under 12 must use approved restraint system unless the car is a two seater. See Continental ABC under 'Passengers' and 'Seat Belts'.

Lisbon

The interior of Braga Cathedral, Braga

Currency

With the introduction of the Euro, the Portuguese Escudo (PTE) ceased to be legal tender from 28 February 2002. However, PTE coins and notes may still be exchanged at local banks until 30 June 2002 and at the Portuguese Central Bank (Banco de Portugal) for 20 years (banknotes) and until 31 December 2002 (coins).

Dimensions and weight restrictions*

Private **cars** and towed **trailers** or **caravans** are restricted to the following dimensions - height, 4 metres; width, 2.55 metres; length, 12 metres. The maximum permitted overall length of vehicle/ trailer or caravan combination is 18.75 metres.

Portuguese traffic regulations stipulate that the total permitted weight of a trailer or caravan may not exceed one and a half times the total permitted weight of the towing vehicle. For example, a car of 1000kg must not tow a trailer or caravan with a total laden weight of more than 1500kg.

Driving licence*

A valid UK or Republic of Ireland licence is acceptable in Portugal. The minimum age at which a visitor may use a temporarily imported motorcycle (over 50cc) or car is 18 years. See also Speed limits below.

Fiscal Receipt

Visiting motorists should ensure that they are able to provide proof of ownership of any goods and electrical equipment carried in the vehicle when entering Portugal. Both the Brigada de Trânsito (traffic police) and the Brigada Fiscal (fiscal police), part of the Guarda Nacional

Dom Sancho I, who founded Guarda in 1199, in front of Guarda Cathedral

Republicana (GNR), have the authority to make spot checks on all roads within Portugal and at the frontier with Spain. Proof of ownership in the form of fiscal receipts may be required for items such as computers, cameras, quantities of wine, cigarettes and groceries, carried in the vehicle.

Foodstuffs*
If the imported foodstuffs are for personal use, there are no limits when travelling between EU countries.

Lights*
It is compulsory for motorcyclists to use dipped headlights during the day.

Motoring club
The **Automóvel Club de Portugal** (ACP) which has its headquarters at Lisboa 1250-195 rua Rosa Araüjo 24 ☎ 213180100 has offices in a number of provincial towns. ACP offices are normally open 09.00-17.00hrs Monday to Friday (to 17.30hrs from 1 April to 30 September); English and French are spoken. Offices are closed on Saturday and Sunday.

Petrol
See Continental ABC under 'Petrol/Diesel'.

Roads
Main roads and most of the important secondary roads are good, as are the mountain roads to the north-east.

Portugal has about 565 miles of motorway (*auto-estrada*) with tolls payable on most sections. Emergency telephones are located every 2km on most motorways.

Speed limits*
Car/motorcycle
Built-up areas 50kph (31mph)
Other roads 90kph (55mph) or 100kph (62mph)
Motorways min† 40kph (24mph)
max 120kph (74mph)
Car/caravan/trailer
Built-up areas 50kph (31mph)
Other roads 70kph (43mph) or 80kph (49mph)
Motorways min† 40kph (24mph)
max 100kph (62mph)
†Minimum speeds on motorways apply, except where otherwise signposted.

Both Portuguese residents and visitors to Portugal, who have held a full driving licence for less than one year, must not exceed 90kph (50mph) when driving on any road or motorway outside built-up areas.

Warning triangle*
The use of a warning triangle or hazard-warning lights is compulsory in the event of accident or breakdown. As hazard warning lights may be damaged or inoperative, it is recommended that a warning triangle be carried. The triangle must be placed on the road 30 metres (33yds) behind the vehicle and must be clearly visible from 100 metres (109yds).

The town of Amarante by River Tamega

*Additional information will be found in the Continental ABC at the front of the book.

TOURIST INFORMATION

SOUTH

The Algarve is one of Europe's favourite holiday destinations, popular for its fine weather, good beaches, and attractive fishing harbours.

One of its most appealing towns is Lagos, a bustling fishing port with an attractive harbour and modern marina, which lies at the western end of the Algarve coastal railway. It has a fascinating history of trade and exploration, and its imposing city walls are still standing, as are the harbour fort, Ponta de Bandeira, and the 18th-century baroque church of Santo António. Among the many coves for sunbathing is the picturesque Praia de Doña Ana, a 30-minute cliff-side walk from Lagos.

NORTH

Northern Portugal is a region of vineyards, coastal castles, and archaeological exploration. Its fascinating provincial centre, Oporto, has given its name to Portugal's most celebrated wine, Port. Its other major centre is the university town of Coimbra, once Portugal's

Similar to the Spanish 'tapas' is the 'petiscos'. This restaurant is in Chaves

capital and headquarters in the 16th century of the dreaded Inquisition. The university buildings formerly housed the Portuguese royal family. In the Sala dos Capelos visitors can view portraits of the early Portuguese Kings, and the University chapel also contains much of interest. The campus library contains nearly 150,000 books.

Outside the university, the Old Cathedral (Sé Velha) and the Igreja de Santa Cruz (Church of the Holy Cross) are worth exploring, the latter holding a large number of royal tombs. One tomb not in the Igreja de Santa Cruz is that of Queen Isabel, who at great cost in the 14th century ordered the construction of the Convento de Santa Clara-a-Velha upon, against usual practice, a swamp. It sank. Today more than half of the building is underground and Queen Isabel's tomb is housed in a 17th-century replacement, the Convento de Santa Clara-a-Nova.

CENTRAL

The Portuguese capital, Lisboa (Lisbon), is one of Europe's more compact capital cities and boasts a number of attractions in its relatively small area. Its historical heritage is impressive, but one of the most interesting places in Lisbon, Expo Urbe, dates from 1998 when the city staged the World Exhibition. The site is five kilometres east of the centre on the banks of the River Tagus and there is a regular bus service. Expo Urbe transformed this formerly derelict area into a gleaming new development, including a marina, a theatre, and also shops, restaurants, and landscaped parks. Its centrepiece, is the Oceanário de Lisboa, which is the largest aquarium in Europe, home to 25,000 fish, mammals, and seabirds.

SOUTH

Bordered by the Atlantic coast on two sides, by mountains in the north and by Spain in the east, the Algarve enjoys one of the most settled climates in the world. Though poorer than the rest of Portugal in art and architecture, the region is rich in subtropical vegetation; almond and orange groves, cotton plantations, and fields of rice and sugar cane. Beyond the mountains in the north, the land is predominantly agricultural, with low rolling hills stretching beyond the horizon. Cork oaks are grown to provide much-needed shade, making an important contribution to the region's economy.

Water is also a major source of income in the south; inland, the salt-pans of the Sado River maintain the pretty towns of narrow twisting lanes and whitewashed houses. On the coast, towns such as Faro, Lagos, and Cape St. Vincent, glory in a history of trade, shipbuilding, sea battles and exploration.

....

ALBUFEIRA ALGARVE

Albufeira ☎ 351289 ▤ 587633
e-mail: campingalbufeira@mail.telepac.pt
A modern, purpose-built site with excellent sanitary blocks and a wide variety of sports and entertainment facilities.
⮑ *1.5km from Albufeira. Signposted from N125*
All year 19HEC ▦ ⬥ ⚓ ♁ 🌿 ♨ ✕ ⊙ 🔲 ⌀ 🏨 ⚡ P ⊞ lau
⮕ ✕ ⌀ 🛁 ⚡S ⊞

ALCANTARILHA ALGARVE

Turismovel - Parque Campismo de Canelas ☎ 082 312612
All year 6.5HEC ⬥ ⚓ ♁ 🌿 ♨ ✕ ⊙ 🔲 ⌀ 🏨 ⚡ P ⊞ lau
⮕ 🛁 🎿 ⚡LRS

ALVITO BAIXO ALENTEJO

Markádia Barragem de Odivelas ☎ 284763141 ▤ 763102
Open savannah terrain beside a lake with good, modern facilities.
⮑ *Leave N121 (Beja-Lisboa) at Ferrera do Alentejo and continue N towards Torrão. From Odivelas follow signposts.*
All year 10HEC ▦ ⬥ ⚓ ♁ 🌿 ♨ ✕ ⊙ 🔲 ⌀ 🏨 ⚡ L ⊞ ⊞
lau ⮕ ⚡P Prices: 🏕2.10-4.20 🚗2.10-4.20 🚐2.10-4.10
🚙2.10-4.20

BEJA BAIXO ALENTEJO

CM de Beja av Vasco da Gama ☎ 284 311911 ▤ 311929
All year 1HEC ⁝⁝⁝ ⬥ ♁ 🌿 ✕ ⊙ 🔲 ⊞ lau ⮕ 🌿 ✕ ⌀ 🎿
⚡LPRS ⊞

PORTIMÃO ALGARVE

Da Dourada Alvor ☎ 282 459178 ▤ 458002
In a park like area close to the beach with good facilities.
⮑ *N off Portimão-Lagos road.*
All year 4HEC ▦ ⁝⁝⁝ ⬥ ♁ 🌿 ✕ ⊙ 🔲 ⌀ 🎿 🏨 ⚡ ♠ 🔺 ⚡
LRS ⊞ lau ⮕ ⚡P Prices: 🏕1.75-3.50 🚗1.38-2.75 🚐2-4
🚙1.75-3.50

PRAIA DA LUZ ALGARVE
At VALVERDE

Orbitur Estrada da Praia da Luz ☎ 082 789211 ▤ 082 789213
Well-equipped site with children's playground and tennis courts.
⮑ *Off N125 Lagos-Cape St Vincent road. 4km from Lagos.*
All year 10HEC ⁝⁝⁝ ⬥ 🌿 🛁 ✕ 🔲 ⌀ 🏨 🚐 ⚡ P ⊞ lau
⮕ 🛁 ✕ ⚡S

QUARTEIRA ALGARVE

Orbitur Estrada da Forte Santa ☎ 089 302826 ▤ 089 302822
A terraced site at the top of a hill.
⮑ *Off M125 in Almoncil and follow signs to Quarteira. About 500m before reaching the sea turn left into the camp.*
All year 10.6HEC ⁝⁝⁝ ⬥ 🌿 🛁 ♨ ✕ 🔲 ⌀ 🏨 ⚡ P ⊞ lau
⮕ 🛁 ✕ ⚡S

SINES BAIXO ALENTEJO

Sines r di Farol ☎ 069 862531
Closed 16 Dec-14 Jan 4.5HEC ▦ ⬥ 🌿 🛁 ♨ ✕ ⊙ 🔲 ⌀ 🎿 🚐
⊞ ⊞ lau ⮕ ⚡S

S. Tonnes S. Tonnes ☎ 269 632105
In a pine wood on the Cabo de Sines peninsula, to the N of the town.
⮑ *Follow signs for Algarve/ S. Tonnes.*
All year 3.5HEC ▦ ⬥ 🌿 ✕ ⊙ 🔲 ⌀ 🎿 🏨 ⊞ ⊞ lau ⮕ ⚡S

VILA DO BISPO ALGARVE
At PRAIA DE SALEMA(7.5km SE)

Quinta dos Carriços Praia da Salema
☎ 282 282695201 ▤ 282 65122
A well equipped site with good facilities. There is a naturist section in a separate valley with its own facilities.
All year 20HEC ▦ ⬥ 🌿 🛁 ♨ ✕ ⊙ 🔲 ⌀ 🎿 🏨 🚐 ⊞ ⊞ lau ⮕
⚡S Prices: 🏕3.60 🚗3.60 🚐5.15

VILA NOVA DE MILFONTES BAIXO ALENTEJO

Parque de Campismo de Milfontes ☎ 283 996104 ▤ 996104
e-mail: parquemilfontes@netc.pt
All year 6.5HEC ⬥ 🌿 🛁 ♨ ✕ ⊙ 🔲 ⌀ 🎿 🏨 🚐 ⊞ lau ⮕ ⚡RS ⊞

NORTH

Northern Portugal offers medieval castles perched on mountain crags, grey stone villages, and purple vineyards whose grapes produce the popular Vinho Verde, Mateus Rosé and Portugal's most famous product - port wine. There are magnificent forests, spectacular lakes, long sandy beaches sheltered by pinewoods, and villages hidden by the springtime blossom of almond and chestnut trees.

A region of ancient human settlement, even the smallest towns are rich in architectural treasures, from palaces of the Renaissance period to prehistoric rock engravings. The region also boasts a wealth of traditional crafts of a variety and colour to match the splendid local costumes worn for the many religious festivals and "romaries" celebrated with enormous enthusiasm and energy throughout the year. The capital of the region, Oporto, is Portugal's second largest city and also is, most untypical - a lively port, a university town and a hub of industry and commerce in one.

....

CAMINHA MINHO

Orbitur Mata do Camarido ☎ 058 921295 ▤ 058 921473
On undulating sandy ground with trees.
⮑ *Turn off N13 at Km89.7 and drive W, along the Rio Minho for about 800m, then turn left.*
16 Jan-Nov 2.8HEC ⁝⁝⁝ ⬥ ♁ 🌿 🛁 ✕ 🔲 ⌀ ⚡ S ⊞ ⊞ lau ⮕ 🛁 ✕

CAMPO DO GERES MINHO

Cerdeira ☎ 253 351005 ▤ 353315
In a picturesque wooded location with mature oak trees surrounding the pitches.
Camping Card Compulsory.
All year 5.1HEC ▦ ⁝⁝⁝ ⬥ 🌿 🛁 ♨ ✕ ⊙ 🔲 ⌀ 🏨 ⊞ ⊞ 🎑 lau
⮕ 🎿 ⚡LR

MATOSINHOS DOURO LITORAL

At **ANGEIRAS**(12km N)

Orbitur Angeiras ☎ 02 9270571 ▨ 02 9271178
A modern, well-kept site in a pine wood on a hill
overlooking the sea.
➲ *W of the N13 at the X-roads at Km12.1, E of Vila do
Pinheiro and towards the sea for 5km.*
All year 9.6HEC ⭡ ✦ ⋔ ⛰ ⵎ ✗ ◉ ᴘ ⌀ ⍰ ⵎ PS ⛌ ⊞ lau
✦ ⵎ ✗ ⵣS

MONDIM DE BASTO MINHO

Mondim de Basto ☎ 055 381650
In wooded surroundings beside the River Olo.
➲ *Signposted.*
Jan-Nov 4HEC ⁚⁚⁚ ⚭ ✦ ⋔ ⛰ ⵎ ✗ ◉ ᴘ ⌀ ⵎ ⛌ ⊞ ⇜ lau ✦ ⵣR

PÓVOA DE VARZIM DOURO LITORAL

Rio Alto Estela-Rio Alto ☎ 052 615699 ▨ 052 615599
Situated near dunes 150m from the sea.
➲ *Off NX111 towards Viana.*
All year 7HEC ⭡ ⁚⁚⁚ ⌕ ⋔ ⛰ ⵎ ✗ ◉ ᴘ ⌀ ⛉
ⵣ PS ⛌ ⊞ lau ✦ ⵣS

VIANA DO CASTELO MINHO

Orbitur Cabedelo ☎ 058 322167 ▨ 058 321946
A well equipped site with direct access to a sandy beach.
➲ *Approach via N13 Porto-Viana do Castelo.*
16 Jan-Nov 3HEC ⁚⁚⁚ ⌕ ⋔ ⛰ ⵎ ✗ ᴘ ⌀ ⛉
ⵣ S ⛌ lau ✦ ✗ ⵣRS

VILA NOVA DE GAIA DOURO LITORAL

Orbitur Madalena ☎ 02 7122520
Well equipped site in a pinewood 500mtrs from Madalena
Beach.
All year 24HEC ⁚⁚⁚ ⌕ ⋔ ⛰ ⵎ ✗ ᴘ ⌀ ⛉
ⵣ P ⛌ ⊞ lau ✦ ✗ ⵣS

VILA REAL TRAS-OS-MONTES ALTO DOURO

Parque Campismo de Vila Real r Dr-Manuel Cardona
☎ 259 324724
➲ *In the E part of town off N2 by GALP petrol station. Site in
300m near new school.*
Closed Jan 4HEC ⁚⁚⁚ ⌕ ⋔ ⛰ ⵎ ✗ ◉ ᴘ ⌀ ⍰ ⊞ lau ✦ ⵣPR

CENTRAL

This is a vast and wonderful region of infinite variety; to the
west, the popular Costa da Prata; the beautiful park-like
landscape in the south; the dramatic mountains in the
north and east; and the cattle-herding country in the centre,
where the fighting bulls graze along the River Tejo,
watched by mounted cattle herders in colourful local
costume.
The highest town in Portugal is Guarda, the ideal base from
which to explore the magnificent Serra da Estrala. Further
west is the romantic town of Coimbra, whose university is
amongst the oldest in the world and until 1911, was the
only one in the country.
Portugal's capital, Lisbon, has the attraction of combining
the charm of the past with the excitement of a progressive
capital city. It is also the heart of the production of the
famous Azulejos - the glazed ornamental tiles which are
Portugal's favourite form of architectural decoration.

ABRANTES RIBATEJO

Castelo do Bode Martinchel ☎ 041 99262
In natural wooded surroundings.
➲ *Signposted.*
Jan-Nov 3HEC ⁚⁚⁚ ✦ ⋔ ⛰ ⵎ ✗ ◉ ᴘ ⌀ ⍰ ⊞ ⇜ lau ✦ ⵣL

ALENQUER ESTREMADURA

Alenquer Estrada Nacional No.9-KM94
☎ 263 710375 ▨ 710375
e-mail: alenquercamping@hotmail.com
A modern well equipped terraced site surrounded by walnut
trees.
**Reductions available to campers presenting this
publication.**
All year 1.5HEC ⚭ ✦ ⋔ ⵎ ✗ ◉ ᴘ ⛉ ⵎ ⌀ Å ⵣ P ⛌ ⊞ lau ✦ ⵎ
⌀ ⛢ ⵣR ⊞ Prices: ⭡2.75-3.30 ⛢4.40-5.30 Å2.75-3.30

ARGANIL BEIRA LITORAL

Orbitur Sarzedo ☎ 035 205706 ▨ 035 25423
In a pleasant situation among pine trees, close to the River
Alva.
➲ *On N342-4.*
All year 2.5HEC ⭡ ⌕ ⋔ ⵎ ✗ ᴘ ⛉ ⵣ R ⛌ ⊞ lau ✦ ⵎ ✗

CASFREIRES BEIRA LITORAL

Quinta Chava Grande ☎ 232 665552 ▨ 665552
A terraced site overlooking a beautiful valley. There are
modern installations and leisure facilities.
Apr-Oct 10HEC ⭡ ⌕ ⋔ ⵎ ✗ ◉ ᴘ ⌀ ⛉ ⵣ P ⛌ ⊞ lau
Prices: ⭡3-3.30 ⛢2-3.08 ⛢3-3.30 Å3-3.30

CASTRO DAIRE BEIRA ALTA

Orbitur Termas do Carvalhal ☎ 032 382803 ▨ 382803
In a beautiful peaceful location, 200mtrs from the sea.
➲ *Access via N2, Km144.2.*
Jun-Sep 1.2HEC ⁚⁚⁚ ⚭ ✦ ⋔ ⵎ ✗ ᴘ ⛌ ⊞ lau ✦ ⵎ ✗

COJA BEIRA LITORAL

Coja ☎ 235 729666
In a wooded location beside the River Alva.
➲ *Signposted.*
17 Jun-13 Oct 3HEC ⭡ ⁚⁚⁚ ✦ ⋔ ⛰ ⵎ ✗ ◉ ᴘ ⌀ ⛉ ⛌ ⊞
⇜ lau ✦ ⵣR

COSTA DA CAPARICA ESTREMADURA

Orbitur ☎ 01 2903894 ▨ 01 2900661
This site has a small touring section and is situated 200mtrs
from a fine sandy beach.
➲ *After crossing the 'Ponte Sul' on the road to Caparica, turn
right at first traffic light. Campsite is 1km on left.*
All year 5.7HEC ⁚⁚⁚ ⌕ ⋔ ⛰ ⵎ ✗ ᴘ ⌀ ⛢ ⛉ ⛌ ⊞ lau ✦ ⵎ ✗
ⵣS

ÉVORA ALTO ALENTEJO

Orbitur Estrada de Alcacovas ☎ 066 705190 ▨ 066 29830
In wooded surroundings with good, modern facilities.
➲ *2km S right of road near Km94.5.*
All year 4HEC ⭡ ⁚⁚⁚ ⌕ ⋔ ⛰ ⵎ ✗ ᴘ ⌀ ⛉ ⵣ P ⛌ ⊞ lau ✦
ⵎ ✗

ÉVORA DE ALCOBAÇA ESTREMADURA

Rural de Silveira Capuchos ☎ 262 509573
e-mail: silveira.capuchos@clix.pt
In a wooded, rural location.
➲ *3km from Alcobaça on N86.*
All year 0.5HEC ⭡ ✦ ⋔ ◉ ᴘ ⛌ ⊞ lau ✦ ⵎ ⵎ ✗ ⌀ ᵚ
Prices: ⭡2.50 ⛢1.50 ⛢3-4 Å2

FIGUEIRA DA FOZ BEIRA LITORAL

Foz do Mondego Cabedelo, Gala ☎ 233 402740 ▤ 402749
13 Jan-11 Nov 4HEC ⁘ ⚡ ⋔ ⌾ ⚑ � ✕ ⊙ ⵎ ⌀ ⵜ S ⬆ ⊞ ⵄ
lau ⬅ ⚡ ✕

Orbitur Gala ☎ 033 431492 ▤ 033 431442
In an enclosed area within a municipal park on top of
Guarda Hill.
➲ *At Km177, on the NW outskirts of the town, turn left off
the N16 Porto road and drive uphill for about 500m.*
All year 6.5HEC ⁘ ⬤ ⋔ ⌾ ⚑ ✕ ⵎ ⌀ ⵐ ⬆ ⊞ lau ⬅ ⌾ ✕ ⵗS

GOUVEIA BEIRA LITORAL

Curral do Negro ☎ 038 491008
In a mountainous setting, surrounded by woodland.
➲ *Signposted.*
Jan-Nov 2HEC ⁘ ⬤ ⋔ ✕ ⊙ ⵎ ⌀ ⵜ P ⬆ ⊞ lau ⬅ ⚡ ✕

GUARDA BEIRA ALTA

Orbitur ☎ 071 211406 ▤ 071 221911
A well equipped site in a pleasant location.
➲ *Access via N18 Guarda-Castelo Branco.*
Mar-Oct 2HEC ⵗ ⬤ ⋔ ⌾ ⵎ ✕ ⵎ ⌀ ⬆ ⊞ lau

GUINCHO ESTREMADURA

Orbitur Areia-Guincho ☎ 01 4870450 ▤ 01 4871014
On hilly ground amidst a pine wood in the Parque du
Guincho, near the Boca do Inferno.
➲ *4km W of Cascais at Km98, turn right and follow road no
247-6 for 1km.*
All year 7HEC ⁘ ⵗ ⬤ ⋔ ⌾ ✕ ⵎ ⌀ ⵐ ⵒ ⬆ ⊞ lau
⬅ ⌾ ✕ ⵗS

LISBOA (LISBON) ESTREMADURA

Lisboa Estrada da Circunvalação
☎ 217 623100 ▤ 01 7609633
On partly level terraced ground. Recently renovated to
become one of the largest sites in the country.
➲ *Access well signposted from the motorway towards Estoril.*
All year 38HEC ⵎ ⬤ ⋔ ⌾ ✕ ⊙ ⵎ ⌀ ⵜ P ⬆ ⊞ lau
See advertisement in colour section

LOURIÇAL BEIRA LITORAL

De Klomp Casas Brancas ☎ 236 952551 ▤ 236 952551
e-mail: campismo.o.tamanco@mail.telepac.pt
In pleasant wooded surroundings.
➲ *Access via N109 or A1.*
Feb-Oct 1.5HEC ⵎ ⵑ ⋔ ⌾ ✕ ⊙ ⵎ ⵒ ⵄ
ⵜ P ⬆ lau ⬅ ⌀ ⊞

LUSO BEIRA LITORAL

Orbitur Bairro Melo Pimenta ☎ 031 930916
All year 2.5HEC ⵎ ⵑ ⋔ ⌾ ✕ ⊙ ⵎ ⌀ ⬆ ⵒ ⊞ lau ⬅ ⵗL

MONTARGIL ALTO ALENTEJO

Orbitur Montargil ☎ 042 901207 ▤ 042 91220
In a beautiful wooded location with good recreational
facilities close to the River Alva.
➲ *N off N2.*
All year 7HEC ⵎ ⁘ ⵑ ⋔ ⌾ ✕ ⵎ ⌀ ⵒ
ⵜ L ⬆ ⊞ lau ⬅ ✕

NAZARÉ ESTREMADURA

Orbitur Valado Valado ☎ 062 561111 ▤ 062 561137
In a pinewood 2km from the village with good facilities.
➲ *300m E of village, S of road 8-4 Nazaré-Alcobaça.*
Feb-Nov 6HEC ⁘ ⬤ ⋔ ⌾ ✕ ⵎ ⌀ ⵎ ⵒ ⬆ ⊞ lau
⬅ ⌾ ✕ ⵗS

Vale Paraiso Estrada Nacional 242
☎ 262 561800 ▤ 262 561900
e-mail: camping.vp.nz@mail.telepac.pt
Situated in a beautiful natural park amid tall pine trees, this
site is exceptionally well appointed with very high standards
of hygiene and varied recreational facilities.
All year 8HEC ⵎ ⬤ ⋔ ⌾ ⚑ ✕ ⊙ ⵎ ⌀ ⵐ ⵒ ⵀ
ⵜ P ⬆ ⊞ lau ⬅ ⵗS

PALHEIROS DE MIRA BEIRA LITORAL

Orbitur ☎ 031 471234 ▤ 031 472047
Site lies in a dense forest.
➲ *N off the N334 at KM2, towards Videira, opposite a road
fork.*
Feb-Nov 3HEC ⁘ ⬤ ⋔ ⌾ ⚑ ✕ ⌀ ⵒ ⵜ LS ⬆ ⊞ lau
⬅ ⌾ ✕ ⵗLS

PENACOVA BEIRA LITORAL

Penacova est da Carvoeira ☎ 039 477464
A pleasant riverside site in wooded surroundings.
➲ *Signposted.*
Jan-Dec 2HEC ⁘ ⬤ ⋔ ⌾ ⚑ ✕ ⊙ ⵎ ⌀ ⬆ ⊞ ⵄ lau ⬅ ⵗR

PENICHE ESTREMADURA

CM ☎ 062 789529 ▤ 062 780111
On a sandy hillock, partly wooded 0.5km from sea.
➲ *2km E.*
All year 12.6HEC ⵎ ⁘ ⚡ ⋔ ⌾ ⚑ ✕ ⊙ ⵎ ⌀ ⬆ ⊞ lau
⬅ ⵐ ⵗPS

Peniche Praia ☎ 062 783460
On level ground 500mtrs from the sea.
➲ *N towards Cabo Carudeiro.*
All year 1.5HEC ⵎ ⁘ ⚡ ⋔ ⌾ ⚑ ✕ ⊙ ⵎ ⌀ ⵐ ⵒ ⬆ ⊞ lau
⬅ ⵗPS ⵎ

PORTALEGRE ALTO ALENTEJO

Orbitur Quinta da Saude ☎ 045 202848
A hilltop site commanding magnificent views.
➲ *Access via N18 Estremoz-Castelo Branco.*
Apr-Sep 2.5HEC ⵎ ⵗ ⬤ ⋔ ⚑ ✕ ⵎ ⌀ ⬆ ⊞ lau ⬅ ✕ ⵗP

SALVATERRA DE MAGOS RIBATEJO

Parque de Campismo de Escaroupim Mata Florestal de
Escaroupim ☎ 263 55484
13 Jan-11 Nov 4HEC ⁘ ⬤ ⋔ ⵑ ⌾ ✕ ⊙ ⵎ ⌀ ⵜ P ⬆ ⊞ ⵄ
lau ⬅ ⵐ ⵗRS

SÃO JACINTO BEIRA LITORAL

Orbitur ☎ 034 838284 ▤ 034 831000
In a dense pine wood site on the sea-side of the uneven,
paved road from Ovar which runs alongside the lagoon.
➲ *1.5km from the sea.*
Feb-Nov 2.5HEC ⵎ ⁘ ⬤ ⋔ ⵑ ⌾ ✕ ⵎ ⵒ
ⵜ R ⬆ ⊞ lau ⬅ ⵗRS

SÃO PEDRO DE MOEL ESTREMADURA

Orbitur ☎ 044 599168 ▤ 044 599148
On a hill amidst pine trees.
➲ *Off road No 242-2 from Marinha Grande at the
roundabout near the SHELL petrol station on the E outskirts of
the village and drive N for 100m.*
All year 7.5HEC ⁘ ⬤ ⋔ ⵑ ⌾ ✕ ⵎ ⌀ ⵒ ⵐ ⵜ P ⬆ ⊞ lau
⬅ ⌾ ✕ ⵗS

VAGOS BEIRA LITORAL

Vagueira ☎ 034 797618 ▤ 034 797093
In pleasant wooded surroundings with good, modern sanitary blocks and a variety of recreational facilities.
All year 10HEC ⋯ ♠ ☂ ☎ ▼ ✕ ⊙ ▣ ∅ ☎ ⊞ lau
➧ ⁀LPRS

VISEU BEIRA ALTA

Orbitur Fontelo ☎ 032 436146
A pleasant, quiet site in a rural location.
➲ *Access via N2.*
Apr-Sep 3HEC ◭ ♠ ☂ ☎ ▼ ✕ ▣ ∅ ☎ ⊞ lau ➧ ☎ ✕

The lighthouse at Casa da Dow

SPAIN

Rich in history and natural beauty, Spain is bordered by Andorra and France in the north and by Portugal in the west.

FACTS AND FIGURES
Capital: Madrid
Area: 504,782 sq km (194,897 sq miles)
Population: 39,371,147
Language: Spanish (Castilian), Catalan, Galician, Basque
IDD code: 34. To call the UK dial 00 44
Currency: Euro

Local time: GMT + 1 (summer GMT + 2)
Emergency Services: Police, Fire and Ambulance 112.
Banks: Mon-Fri 08.30-14.30 (most banks are closed on Sats).
Shops: Mon-Sat 09.00-13.00 and 16.30-19.30.

Average daily temperatures: Madrid
Jan 4°C	Jul 24°C
Mar 9°C	Sep 19°C
May 16°C	Nov 8°C

Tourist Information:
UK Spanish National Tourist Office, 22-23 Manchester Sq., London W1M 5AP
Tel (020) 7486 8077

USA 666 Fifth Avenue, 35th Floor, New York, NY 10103. Tel: (212) 265 8822
Camping card: Not compulsory, but recommended
Tourist info website: www.okspain.org

Central Spain is mountainous and barren while the coastline can be extremely rocky. Some of the most popular holiday areas in Europe are in Spain, the best known being the Costa Brava, the Costa Blanca, the Costa Dorada and the Costa del Sol. More recently, the island of Ibiza has become a very popular destination for young clubbers. All these regions offer fine, sandy and safe beaches. Spain has a varied climate; temperate in the north, dry and hot in the south and in the Balearic Islands. Languages spoken are Spanish, Catalan, Basque and Galician. Spanish has developed from Castilian and there are many local dialects spoken thoughout the provinces.

Sites are numerous on the Costa Brava and elsewhere along the coast, but there are not many inland. They are officially classified according to the facilities and services provided and their classification should be displayed at the site entrance and on any literature. If you intend visiting sites at popular resorts along the coast between late spring and mid-October, it is not generally possible to book in advance. The best advice is to arrive before midday when the new charge begins. Late spring is recommended, as the intense heat of mid-summer is avoided and sites and roads are less congested. Opening dates vary considerably and some sites are open all year. Information about campsites and a detailed guide book are available from the Spanish National Tourist Office (see *Tourist Information*) and local tourist information offices.

Hire of equipment is not generally possible, but some campsites have bungalow accommodation.

Off-site camping is generally prohibited. Permission to camp off an official campsite must be obtained from the landowner or local police. **Camp fires are absolutely forbidden.** Free camping near to beaches, rivers, towns or established campsites is forbidden.

HOW TO GET THERE

There are direct ferry services to Spain. The services and minimum sailing times are **Plymouth** to **Santander** (24hrs) and **Portsmouth** to **Bilbao** (27hrs). Alternatively, using Eurotunnel or the Channel ports, approach Spain by passing either end of the Pyrenean mountains. For **central and southern Spain** take the Biarritz to San Sebastian (Donostia) road or motorway at the western end. For **the Costa Brava and beyond** take the Perpignan to Barcelona road, or motorway, at the eastern end of the mountains. **For Andorra** from France via Pas de la Casa (6860ft) then over the Envalira Pass (7897ft). Nov - Apr roads through the central Pyrénées may sometimes be closed. From Spain, the approach via La Seu d'Urgell is always open.

Distance

From Calais to Madrid is about 1,600km (994 miles), usually requiring two or three overnight stops.

Car sleeper trains

All year round services are available from **Denderleeuw** (Belgium) to **Toulouse**. Summer services are available from **Calais** to **Narbonne** and **Toulouse** and from **Denderleeuw** to **Biarritz** and **Tarbes**.

MOTORING & GENERAL INFORMATION

The information given here is specific to Spain and/or Andorra. It **must** be read in conjunction with the Continental ABC at the front of the book, which covers those regulations which are common to many countries.

British Embassy/Consulates*

The British Embassy is located at Madrid 28010, Calle de Fernando el Santo 16 ☎ 917008200; consular section, 28004 Madrid, Centro Colón Marqués de la Ensenada 16 ☎ 913085201. There are British Consulates in Alicante, Barcelona, Bilbao, Málaga and Palma (Majorca); there are British Consulates with Honorary Consuls in Santander and Vigo. There is a British Vice-Consulate in Ibiza and a British Vice-Consulate with Honorary Vice-Consul in Menorca.

Children in cars

Child under 12 not permitted to travel as front seat passengers unless using suitable restraint system. See Continental ABC under 'Passengers' and 'Seat Belts'.

Currency

With the introduction of the Euro, the **Spanish Peseta** (ESP) ceased to be legal tender from 28 February 2002. However, ESP coins and notes may still be exchanged at local banks until 30 June 2002, and at the Spanish Central Bank (**Banco de España**) for an unlimited period.

Dimensions and weight restrictions*

Private **cars** and towed **trailers** or **caravans** are restricted to the following dimensions - height, 4 metres; width 2.5 metres; length 12 metres. The maximum permitted overall length of private vehicle/trailer or caravan combinations is 18.75 metres.

Trailers with an unladen weight exceeding 750kg must have an independent braking system.

Driving licence*

All valid UK or Republic of Ireland licences should be acceptable in Spain. However, older all green UK licences (in Northern Ireland and licence issued before 1 January 1991) do not conform to the EC model. To update to a photocard licence, apply to DVLA Swansea/DVLNI Coleraine on the appropriate application form available from most post offices. Alternatively, older licences may be accompanied by an International Driving Permit (IDP). The minimum age at which visitors from UK or Republic of Ireland may use a temporarily imported motorcycle (over 75cc) or car is 18 years.

Foodstuffs*

If the imported foodstuffs are for personal use there are no limits when travelling between EU countries.

Lights*

Visitors must equip their vehicle with a spare set of bulbs. It is compulsory for motorcyclists to use dipped headlights during the day.

Motoring club

The **Real Automóvil Club de España** (RACE), which has its headquarters at 28760 Tres Cantos, Isaac Newton 4, Parque Technologico de Madrid ☎ 915947400, is associated with local clubs in a number of provincial towns. The RACE office in Madrid at Calle José Abaseal 10 is open to the public from 08.30-17.30 Mon-Thu and 8.30-14.30 Fri during the summer (June to September) and from 08.30-17.30 Mon-Fri during the winter (Oct to May).

Petrol*

See Continental ABC under 'Petrol/Diesel'.

Roads, including holiday traffic

Spain has an excellent network of motorways (mostly toll) and fast dual carriageways (*autovías*). Emergency telephones are located every 2km on both.

The surfaces of the other main roads vary, but on the whole are good. The roads are winding in many places, and at times it is not advisable to exceed 30-35mph. Secondary roads are often rough and winding. Holiday traffic, particularly on the coast road to Barcelona and

Tarragona and in the San Sebastian-Donostia area, causes congestion which may be severe at weekends.

In the *Basque* and *Catalan* areas some place names appear on signposts as alternative spellings *eg* San Sebastian-Donostia and Gerona-Girona. The current AA directories and maps show both names.

Speed limits*
Car/motorcycle
Built-up areas 50kph (31mph)
Other roads †90kph (55mph)
††100kph (62mph)
Motorways 120kph (74mph)
Car/caravan/trailer
Built-up areas 50kph (31mph)
Other roads †70kph (43mph) or
††80kph (49mph)
Motorways 80kph (49mph)
†On ordinary roads
††On roads with more than one lane in each direction, a special lane for slow-moving vehicles or wide lanes.

Warning triangles*
Non-Spanish registered vehicles entering Spain must be equipped with a warning triangle. The use of a warning triangle is compulsory outside built-up areas when the vehicle (or trailer) is stationary in an area where standing is prohibited.

*Additional information will be found in the Continental ABC at the front of the book.

TOURIST INFORMATION
Spain's coastal resorts stud the entire length of the country's Mediterranean shore, from the Costa Brava in the north, beloved of the cheap package-holiday trade, to the ritzier, glitzier destinations of the extreme south like Marbella. Many tourists content themselves with the sun and sand of a beach holiday, but the country has much more to explore. A long and complex history, a rich and varied culture, and some incredible scenery. Although it is a politically stable nation now, during the 20th century Spain saw revolution, civil war and dictatorship, and the Spanish people can as unpredictable as their history.

Madonna and Child at Iglesia San Sabastian in Estepa

NORTH EAST COAST
Barcelona is Spain's second city and the centre of Catalonia. The city is famed for its lively atmosphere, and impressive Cathedral and flamboyant football team. However, visitors looking to uncover the true Barcelona should head for the Gothic Quarter.

The Barri Gòtic (Gothic Quarter) is built on the site of the original Roman settlement and exudes history from every pore.

The city's political centre is located inside the Barri Gòtic, around Plaça de Sant Jaume which is the area's focal point. The political

A busy main street in Barcelona

buildings include the Palau de la Generalitat, seat of the Catalonia government, and across the Plaça, the Ajuntament which is the seat of the regional Spanish government. The Plaça also contains the world-famous Eglésia Catedral de la Santa Creu, designed by Gaudi, which is defined by its tall, jagged spires. Opposite the Cathedral is the Palau Reial (Royal Palace) which houses two museums: the Museu Frederic Marés which exhibits an unusual collection of sculptures, and the Museu d'Historia de la Ciutat, dedicated to the city's history. Wise travellers acquire a map of the Barri Gòtic from the Tourist Office, as its street-plan is very confusing.

CENTRAL

Central Spain, with its mountains and vineyards , is home to Spain's impressive capital city of Madrid, with its Royal Palace and stunning museums, notably the Prado, the Guernica Museum and the Thyssen Bornemissen collection. The region also contains many other historic sites, such as The Escorial, the awesome and austere palace of Philip II, husband of Mary

Tudor of England and instigator of the ill-fated Armada routed by Sir Francis Drake, and also Toledo, the Spanish capital until 1561. Owing to its position on the River Tagus, which surrounds two-thirds of the town, the old city of Toledo remains a maze of medieval alleys. Its two chief landmarks are the Alcázar, and the Gothic Cathedral with its 100-metre high spire. The religious procession of the Corpus Christi in June, when the entire city is decorated and the streets strewn with evergreens, is well worth a visit, as is the fiesta in late August.

SOUTH EAST COAST

The area in and around the medieval city of Tarragona is home to some of the finest Roman remains in Europe, with a wide range of buildings and exhibits.

A good place to start exploring the Roman remains is the 'Cyclopean Wall', of which the eastern part is the best preserved. Close by is an amphitheatre and remains from two churches, built in the 7th and 12th centuries. To the south of the town lies another group of Roman ruins, including a forum, and also the Cathedral which was a former military centre.

NORTH COAST

Santander is an upmarket coastal resort, and relatively modern, as most of the town was devastated by fire in 1941. It is surrounded by glorious beaches and stands on the Peninsula de la Magdalena, and one of the main attractions is the early 20th-century Palacio, a royal fantasy on the model of the Brighton Pavilion. Santander's Cathedral has been skilfully restored and contains a 13th-century Gothic vault and two museums. The town is also a jumping-off point for the countless fishing villages and mountain hamlets surrounding the city which offer many picture-postcard views.

The primary tourist attraction in the region are the prehistoric paintings in the famous Caves of Altmira, though such is their popularity that bookings to view them have to be made a full twelve months before arrival. There is however, no waiting list to see the caves with no paintings but with impressive stalactites and stalagmites. The Museum of Altmira can also be toured without booking, and offers an impressive range of displays and information. For those who want to see cave paintings without a twelve-month wait, try the nearby smaller caves of El Castillo and la Pasiega.

NORTH EAST

Lying in the lush foothills next to the crags of the Pyrenees, the town of Pamplona is home to one of Europe's most famous festivals, that of *los Sanfermines* or 'The Running of the Bulls', immortalised in Ernest Hemingway's novel *The Sun Also Rises*.

The Running of the Bulls is actually a rather misleading name for the festival, 'The Running of People Being Chased by Bulls' would be far more accurate. Every year competitors journey from all over the world to the steps of Santo Domingo in Pamplona, and on the appropriate morning in July, the bulls are released and chase the hordes of competitors through the streets of this fine old Spanish town.

The origin of this peculiar and sometimes dangerous festival comes from the martyr, San Fermín, who was dragged through streets of bygone Pamplona by a horde of bulls. The festival 're-enacting' this martyrdom is now

roughly 500 years old and continues to draw large crowds. Spectating can be as dangerous as competing, as the bulls charge through the streets, sometimes with fatal consequences. On the big day, narrow alleys and doorways should be avoided at all costs.

The three minutes of early morning mayhem are just one part of a nine day fiesta that runs from the 6th to the 14th of July. The central focus of the fiesta is the Plaza Castillo which has a wide selection of bars and cafés, that are lively throughout the year.

Barcelona's Casa Batllo was transformed by Gaudi in 1904

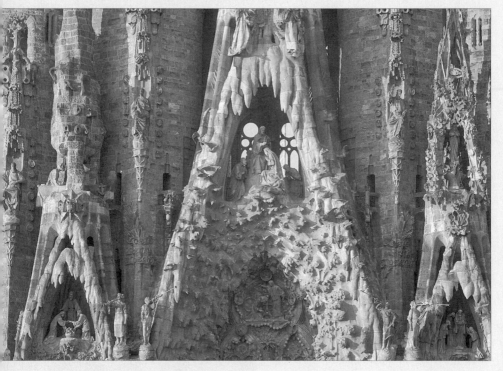

The facade of the Nativitat of La Sagrada Familia in Barcelona, also designed by Gaudi

NORTH WEST

The city of Santiago de Compostela is home to Spain's most famous site of religious pilgrimage, and for centuries has been attracting visitors from all corners of Europe and now the world.

Its awe inspiring twin-towered Cathedral is built on the spot on which in 813 the Bishop of Iria Flavia claimed to have found the remains of the apostle James, who is the patron saint of Spain. It took 151 years, 1060-1211, to build the present structure, which dominates the old quarter of the town. Standing on the Plaza del Obradoiro (also known as the Plaza de España) the Cathedral has magnificent Romanesque architecture and a more recent baroque façade.

SOUTH

Southern Spain is a region of great contrasts, with the energy of the coastal resorts such as Malaga and Marbella, the heritage of Granada, Córdoba, and Seville, and the snow-capped peaks of the Sierra Nevada mountains.

On the banks of the Rio Guadalquivir, Seville is one of Spain's most fascinating cities with its famous landmarks, the Moorish Alcazar and tower of La Giralda, and its magnificent Cathedral, built on the site of a great Mosque and dating from 1401. At the time of the Renaissance it was the world's largest Gothic Cathedral.

Other attractions in Seville include the Puerto de los Naranjos, a gigantic patio lined with orange trees that exude the sweetest aroma in the summer months. In Easter week the city holds a variety festivals and parades, including the famed Procession of the Penitents. It is a local tradition to wear black on Maundy Thursday.

ANDORRA

Andorra is an independent Principality located high in the Pyrenees between France and Spain.

FACTS AND FIGURES
Capital: Andorra la Vella
Area:
468 sq km (180 sq miles)
Population: 65,877 (1998)
Language: Catalan,
Spanish and French
IDD Code: 376. To call the
UK dial 0044

Currency: Euro
Local time: GMT + 1
(summer GMT + 2)
Emergency services: Fire
& Ambulance 118;
Police 110
Business hours: variable
Banks: Mon-Fri 09.00-
13.00/15.00-17.00 Sat

09.00-12.00
Shops: Daily 09.00-20.00
**Average daily
temperatures:**
Jan 3°C   Jul 19°C
Mar 9°C   Sep 16°C
May 11°C   Nov 6°C
Tourist Information:
UK Andorran Delegation

63 Westover Road
London SW18 2RF
Tel (020) 8874 4806 (am if
telephoning; personal visit
by appointment only)
Camping card:
Recommended.
Tourist info website:
www.turisme.ad/index.html

Andorra is administered by its own government and independent Legislative Assembly. The constitutional heads of state are its traditional co-princes, the President of France and the Bishop of Seu d'Urgell. Catalan is the official language, but French and Spanish are widely spoken. General regulations for France and Spain apply to Andorra with the following exceptions.

British Consulate*
The British Consulate with Honorary Consul is located at Casa Jacint Pons 3/2, La Massana, Andorra ☎83 88 39.

Children in cars
Child under 10 not permitted as front-seat passenger. See Continental ABC under 'Passengers' and 'Seat Belts'.

Currency*
Andorra has no currency of its own and has traditionally used the French Franc (FRF) and Spanish Peseta (EPS). With the introduction of the Euro and withdrawal of FRF and EPS, Euro banknotes and coins come into circulation from 1 January 2002.

Dimensions
The maximum height for vehicles going through tunnels is 3.5 metres.

Driving licence*
A valid UK or Republic of Ireland driving licence is acceptable. The minimum age at which a visitor may use a temporarily imported car or motorcycle is 18.

Lights*
Visitors must equip their vehicle with a spare set of bulbs. It is compulsory for motorcyclists to use dipped headlights during the day.

Motoring Club*
The **Automobil Club d'Andorra** (ACA) is the official **Motoring Club**, and has its head office at Andorra, Carrer Babot Camp 13 ☎ 803400.

Petrol*
See Continental ABC under 'Petrol/Diesel'.

Roads
The three main roads in Andorra are prefixed 'N' and numbered; side roads are prefixed 'V'. Andorra has no motorways.

Speed limits*
Car/motorcycle/car towing caravan/trailer
Built-up areas 50kph (31mph)
Other roads 90kph (55mph)
Some villages have a speed limit of 20kph (12mph).

Warning triangle*
The use of a warning triangle is compulsory in the event of an accident or breakdown.

*Additional information will be found in the Continental ABC at the front of the book.

NORTH EAST COAST

The brava, or 'wild' coast, and resorts such as Tossa and Lloret de Mar, have long been a favourite with sun-seekers. Low season can be a perfect time to visit the beautiful coastline, and art lovers are drawn year-long to Figueres' Salvador Dali Museum and historic Girona's impressive cathedral, interesting monuments and medieval Jewish quarter.

On the Mediterranean to the south lies Barcelona, capital of Catalonia. Catalonians are proud of their heritage and language. Host of the 1992 Olympics, this bustling, vital seaport has many faces: literary capital of Spain, shopper's paradise and beach town. Walk along its famous boulevards, the Ramblas, or visit Gaudí's monumental Church of the Holy Family - symbol of the city and its region. The site of the Olympic stadium at Montjuic also boasts several museums and shares spectacular views with its neighbouring hilltop, Tibidabo. The fiesta in September is a colourful carnival famed for its enormous papier-maché figures, its street celebrations and bullfights, and the local sardana dancing.

ARENYS DE MAR BARCELONA

Carlitos Carretera 2 ☎ 93 7921355 ▤ 93 7957342
The slightly sloping site has very friendly family atmosphere and is situated just 150mtrs from the sea on the Costa del Maresme.
May-Sep 3.5HEC ⁙ ♠♠♠♥♥✕⊙♥∅♠ ₹ PS ⚐⊞ lau ♦ ♠ ₹S

BAGUR

See **Begur**

BEGUR GIRONA

Begur ☎ 972 623201 ▤ 972 623201
e-mail: campingbegur@teleline.es
A terraced site in a wooded valley.
➲ *1.4km SE of town and right of the road to Palafrugell, 400m after the turn towards Fornells and Aiguablava.*
7 Apr-2 Sep 4HEC ⧟ ⁙ ♠♠♥✕⊙♥♠⚐⊞ lau ♦ ♠ ∅ ₹S

Maset Playa de sa Riera ☎ 972 623023 ▤ 623901
e-mail: elmaset@jazzfree.com
A well-kept terraced site, divided into pitches in a beautiful valley, 300mtrs from the sea.
➲ *2km N of Begur. If entering from the W, turn left just before reaching the town.*
6 Apr-24 Sep 1.2HEC ⁙ ♠♠♥♥✕⊙♥∅♠ ₹ P ⊡⊞ ✿ lau ♦ ₹S

BLANES GIRONA

Bella Terra av Villa de Madrid ☎ 972 348017 ▤ 972 348275
e-mail: cbellaterra@cbellaterra.com
A large family site in a luxuriant pinewood beside the beach with good, modern facilities.
➲ *Access via main N11.*
Apr-Sep 10.5HEC ⧟ ⁙ ⧓♠♠♥✕⊙♥∅♠♥ ₹ PS ⚐⊞ lau **Prices:** ♠3.61 pitch 10.62-17.70

Blanes ☎ 972 331591 ▤ 337063
e-mail: info@campingblanes.com
In a pine forest bordering the beach, 1km from the town centre.
➲ *On left of the Paseo Villa de Madrid coast road towards town.*
01 Mar-31 Oct 2HEC ⁙ ♠♠♥♥✕⊙♥∅ ₹ PS ⚐⊞ lau ♦ ₹R **Prices:** ♠4.02-5.09 pitch 11.77-14.72

Masia c Colon 44, Los Pinos ☎ 972 331013 ▤ 972 333128
e-mail: info@campinglamasia.com
A pleasant family site on level ground with shady pitches, 150mtrs from the sea.
➲ *50m inland from Paseo Villa de Madrid coast road.*
May-Sep 9HEC ⁙ ♠♠♠♥♥✕⊙♥∅♠ ₹ PRS ⚐⊞ lau **Prices:** ♠3.80-4.80 ♠6-9.50 pitch 12.10-19

Pinar av Villa de Madrid ☎ 972 331083
Divided into two by the coastal road. Partially meadow under poplars.
➲ *1km on Paseo Villa de Madrid coast road.*
Apr-Sep 5HEC ♠♠♠♥♥✕⊙♥∅♠♠♥ ₹ S ⚐⊞ lau

S'Abanell av Villa Madrid 7-9 ☎ 972 331809 ▤ 350506
e-mail: sabanell@grn.es
Within a pine wood, a section of which is inland and open to the public.
➲ *On either side of the Avenida Villa de Madrid road. Off coast road S of Blanes.*
All year 3HEC ⁙ ♠♠♠♥♥✕⊙♥∅♠♠♥ ₹ S ⚐⊞ lau

CALELLA DE LA COSTA BARCELONA

Botanic Bona Vista ☎ 93 7692488 ▤ 93 7695804
e-mail: info@botanic-bonavista.net
Totally subdivided and well tended terraced site on a hillside, beautifully landscaped. Internal roads steep. Access to beach via pedestrian underpass.
Camping Card Compulsory.
➲ *Turn off the N11 at Km665.*
All year 3.4HEC ⁙ ⧓♠♠♠♥♥✕⊙♥∅♠ ₹ S ⚐⊞ lau ♦ ₹P **Prices:** ♠4.01 ♠4.01 ♠4.01 ♠4.01

Far ☎ 93 7690967 ▤ 93 7690967
e-mail: elfar@reset.es
Terraced site on a hillock under deciduous trees with lovely views of Calella and out to sea. Steep internal roads.
➲ *For access, travel S before reaching a major left bend at Km666 to the right of the N11.*
Apr-Sep 2.5HEC ⁙ ♠♠♠♥♥✕⊙♥∅♠⚐⊞ lau ♦ ♠ ₹PS **Prices:** ♠3.95 ♠3.95 ♠3.95 ♠3.95

CASTELL D'ARO GIRONA

Castell d'Aro crta S'Agaro ☎ 972 819699 ▤ 819699
A quiet family site, 2km from the beach, with good recreational facilities.
➲ *Access at Km1 on S'Agaró road.*
Apr-Sep 8HEC ⧟ ⁙ ♠♠♠♥♥✕⊙♥∅♠ ₹ P ⚐⊞ lau ♦ ₹S

CASTELLÓ D'EMPURIES GIRONA

Castell-Mar Platja de la Rubina ☎ 972 450822 ▤ 972 452330
A modern family site close to the beach on the edge of a National Park.
➲ *From A7 exit 3 or 4 (Figueres) follow C260 through Castello d'Empuries towards Roses.*
12 May-23 Oct 4HEC ⧟ ⧓♠♠♠♥♥✕⊙♥∅♠♠♣ ₹ PS ⚐⊞ lau

Mas-Nou ☎ 972 454175 ▤ 972 454358
e-mail: masnou@intercom.es
A family site with good recreational facilities, 2.5km from the coast.
➲ *Exit from the Figueres-Roses road at Km38.*
23Mar-29Sep 9.8HEC ⧟ ⧓♠♥♥✕⊙♥∅♠ ₹ PS ⚐⊞ lau ♦ ♠ ∅ ₹R **Prices:** ♠3.85-5.45 ♠3.85-5.45 ♠3.85-5.45 ♠3.85-5.45

Nautic Almanta ☎ 972 454477 ▤ 972 454686
e-mail: info@almata.com
Level meadowland, no shade, good facilities, reaching as far
as the sea. Alongside the River Fluvia which has been made
into a canal. Boating is possible in the canal which flows into
the sea.
➲ *Turn S at Km11 on C260, approx, halfway along the road
and turn E along the track and continue 2.2km.*
19 May-23 Sep 22HEC ⸤⸥ ♠ ⋔ ⛶ ⓨ ✕ ⊙ ▣ ⊘ ⊞ Å
⚲ PRS ☎ ⊞ lau

CUBELLES BARCELONA

La Rueda ☎ 938 950207 ▤ 938 950347
e-mail: larueda@la-rueda.com
Level terrain between road and railway. Access to beach by
means of an underpass.
➲ *On beach about 1km N of Cunit near C-31, Km 146.2*
12 Sep-6 Apr 6HEC ⸤⸥ ♠ ⋔ ⛶ ⓨ ✕ ⊙ ▣ ⊘ ⊞
⚲ PS ☎ ⊞ lau

ESCALA, L' GIRONA

Escala ☎ 972 770084
Level site, partially under pines and close to the sea.
➲ *Within village on the left of the road towards Riells.*
4 Apr-27 Sep 1.8HEC ⸤⸥ ♠ ⋔ ⛶ ⓨ ✕ ⊙ ▣ ⊘ ⊞ ☎ ⊞
♠ ⛺ ⚲S

Maite Playa Riells ☎ 972 770544
e-mail: maite@campings.net
An extensive site, lying inland, but near the sea, at a small
lake. Partly on a hillock under pine trees.
➲ *The access is well signed from the outskirts of L'Escala on
the road towards Cala Montgo.*
Jun-15 Sep 6HEC ⸤⸥ ♠ ⋔ ⛶ ⓨ ✕ ⊙ ▣ ⊘ ⚲ LS ☎ ⊞
Prices: ♦3.74 ⊞3.74 Å3.74

ESTARTIT, L' GIRONA

Castell Montgri ☎ 972 751630 ▤ 972 750906
e-mail: c.montgri@campingparks.com
On a large terraced meadow in pine woodlands.
➲ *100m N of GE road from Torroella de Montgri and about
0.5km before L'Estartit on a hillock.*
12 May-7 Oct 25HEC ⸤⸥ ♠ ⋔ ⛶ ⓨ ✕ ⊙ ▣ ⊘ ⊞ ⊞ Å ⚲ P
☎ ⊞ lau ♠ ⚲S Prices: ♦3 pitch 7-28

See advertisement in colour section

Estartit Cap Villa Primavera 12 ☎ 972 751909 ▤ 972 750991
In a valley on sloping ground which is rather steep in places.
Some terraces, shaded by pine trees.
➲ *It is located about 200m from the church and the road from
Torroella de Montgri.*
Apr-Sep 2.5HEC ⁑ ♠ ⋔ ⛶ ⓨ ✕ ⊙ ▣ ⊞ Å ⚲ LPRS ☎ ⊞
⊗ lau ♠ ⊘ Prices: ♦4.17 ⊷3.85 ⊞4.50 Å3.70

Medes ☎ 972 751805 ▤ 972 750413
e-mail: campingslesmedes@cambrescat.es
Quiet holiday site in rural surroundings with clearly marked
pitches and good modern facilities.
➲ *Turn right off GE641 from Torroella di Montgri by Km5
and continue for 1.5km .*
Nov 2.6HEC ⸤⸥ ⁑ ⊹ ⋔ ⛶ ⓨ ✕ ⊙ ▣ ⊘ ⊞ ⚲ P ☎ ⊞ ⊗
lau ♠ ⚲S Prices: ♦3.11-4.82 pitch 6.75-10.93

Molino ☎ 972 750629 ▤ 972 750629
e-mail: branders@teleline.es
Divided into several sections of open meadowland near the
beach on grassland with young poplars. The reconstructed
mill is a landmark.
➲ *Approaching from Torroella de Montgri turn right on
entering L'Estartit and follow signs.*
Apr-Sep 10HEC ⸤⸥ ⊹ ⋔ ⛶ ⓨ ✕ ⊙ ▣ ⊘ ⊞ ⚲ S ☎ ⊞ lau ♠
⚲R Prices: ♦3.16-3.20 ⊷3.16-3.20 ⊞3.16-3.20 Å3.16-3.20

Quiet campsite, 100 yards
from a beautiful fine sandy
beach. Flat, well-shaded
completely fenced-in site.
Free hot water, excellent,
varied installations,
swimming-pool. Horseback
riding, tennis, etc... close by.
Close to touristic sites and to PORT AVENTURA
theme park. Access via route C-246, km. 52,1
between Cubellas and Cunit. **Open: 7.4 - 12.9**
Information and reservation:
Apartado de Correos 261 (Post box)
E-08880 CUBELLES (Barcelona)
Acess via route C-31, km. 146,2
Tel. (34) 93 8950207 - Fax (34)93 8950347
www.la-rueda.com • e-mail: larueda@la-rueda.com

FEES - 2002 1 pitch/N + 3 P/N

Dates		EUROS
23.07 - 01.04	10.05 - 05.07	**21,78**
01.04 - 10.05	26.08 - 15.09	**16,33**
05.07 - 26.08		**27,24**

20% Discount P/N for CCI + VAT = 7%

 FIRST CAT.
CATALONIEN TOURISM MERITS MEDAL

GAVÁ BARCELONA

Tortuga Ligera ☎ 93 6580504
Apr-Sep 22HEC ⸤⸥ ⁑ ♠ ⋔ ⛶ ⓨ ✕ ⊙ ▣ ⊘ ⛺ ⊞ ⊞ ⚲ PS
☎ ⊞ lau

GUARDIOLA DE BERGUEDA BARCELONA

El Bergueda ☎ 93 8227432
e-mail: campingbergueda@worldonline.es
A peaceful site in the middle of a forest at an altitude of
900mtrs with a wide variety of sporting facilities.
➲ *On B400.*
All year 3HEC ⸤⸥ ⊹ ♠ ⋔ ⛶ ⓨ ✕ ⊙ ▣ ⊘ ⛺ ⊞ ⊞ ⚲ PR ☎
⊞ lau Prices: ♦3.64 ⊷3.64 ⊞3.64 Å3.64

GUILS DE CERDANYA GIRONA

Pirineus ctra Guils de Cerdanya ☎ 972 881062 ▤ 882471
e-mail: guils@stel.es
In a fine, level location at an altitude of 1200mtrs affording
fine views over the Cerdanya Valley.
➲ *On the main Puigcerda-Guils de Cerdanya road.*
22 Jun-11 Sep 5HEC ⸤⸥ ♠ ⋔ ⛶ ⓨ ✕ ⊙ ▣ ⊘ ⊞ ⚲ P ☎ ⊞
⊗ lau

LLANÇÁ GIRONA

Ombra ☎ 972 380335 ▤ 972 120261
A quiet site, 500mtrs from the sea.
➲ *At Km16.5 on N260.*
All year 1.2HEC ⸤⸥ ⁑ ♠ ⋔ ⛶ ✕ ⊙ ▣ ⊘ ⊞ Å ⚲ P ☎ ⊞
lau ♠ ✕ ⛺ ⚲S

LLORET DE MAR GIRONA

Tucan ☎ 972 369965
A modern family site, close to the sea, with plenty of
recreational facilities.

Cont.

⮕ *Access via A7 exit 9 to Lloret de Mar.*
16 Jun-15 Sep 4HEC ⊞ 🔧 ♠ ⋒ 🗻 🍽 ✕ ☉ 🗨 🔗 🚿 🚑 ⚲ 🄰 ⌇ P 🄿
⊞ lau ➡ 🔥 ⌇S

MALGRAT DE MAR BARCELONA

Naciones ☎ 93 7654153
Level site divided by a small stream. Partially dusty, another part in meadow under high poplars.
⮕ *Approach road passes through Camping Malgrat de Mar.*
Closed 9-31 Dec 9.7HEC ⊞ 🔧 ♠ ⋒ 🗻 🍽 ✕ ☉ 🗨 🔗 🔥 ⚲ ⌇
PS 🄿 ⊞ lau

MASNOU, EL BARCELONA

Masnou ctra Nac 11 ☎ 93 5551503 ▯ 93 5551503
A well equipped site in wooded surroundings, 150mtrs from the beach on the Costa del Maresme.
⮕ *Inland from the N11 at Km633.*
All year 2HEC ⊞ ♠ ⋒ 🗻 🍽 ✕ ☉ 🗨 🔗 ⚲ 🄰 ⌇ PS 🄿 ⊞
lau

PALAFRUGELL GIRONA

At LLAFRANC

Kim's Font d'En Xeco 1 ☎ 972 301156 ▯ 972 610894
e-mail: info@campingkims.com
Terraced site with winding drives, lying on the wooded slopes of a narrow valley leading to the sea.
⮕ *For access, turn right off the Palafrugell-Tamariu road, follow a wide tarred road for 1km, past the El Paranso Hotel and head towards Llafranc. 0.4km from sea.*
17 Jun-Sep 5.8HEC ⊞ ⋮⋮⋮ 🔧 ⋒ 🗻 🍽 ✕ ☉ 🗨 🔗 🚑
⌇ P 🄿 ⊞ 🔌 lau ➡ ⌇S

At MONTRÁS(3km SW)

Relax-Ge ☎ 972 301549
e-mail: campingpal@grn.es
Level meadow under poplars and olive trees.
⮕ *Turn off the C255 at Km38.7. 4km to the sea.*
Jun-Aug 3HEC ⊞ ⋮⋮⋮ ♠ ⋒ 🗻 🍽 ✕ ☉ 🗨 🔗 🚑 ⌇ P 🄿 ⊞ lau
➡ ⌇S

At PLAYA DE ENSUEÑOS

Tamariu ☎ 972 620422 ▯ 620422
e-mail: campingtamariu@teleline.es
Terraced site with mixture of tall, young pines. Direct access to the beach.
⮕ *Turn towards site at beach parking area and continue 300m.*
May-Sep 2HEC ⊞ ♠ ⋒ 🗻 🍽 ✕ ☉ 🗨 🔗 🚑 ⌇ PS 🄿 ⊞ lau
➡ 🗻 🍽 ✕ 🔗 ⊞

PALAMÓS GIRONA

Castell Park ☎ 72 315263 ▯ 72 315263
Level and gently sloping meadow with poplars and pine woodland on a hill.
⮕ *At Km40 about 100m to the right of the C255 to Palamós and 3km S of Montras.*
Apr-Sep 4.5HEC ⊞ ♠ ⋒ 🗻 🍽 ✕ ☉ 🗨 🔗 🚑
⌇ P 🄿 ⊞ lau ➡ ⌇S

Coma Ronda Est ☎ 972 314638 ▯ 972 315470
e-mail: lacoma@campinglacoma.com
Sloping terraced terrain with young deciduous trees and isolated pines. 0.8km from the sea.
⮕ *In N outskirts turn seawards off the C255 near the Renault garage.*
Apr-Sep 5.2HEC ⊞ ♠ ⋒ 🗻 🍽 ✕ ☉ 🗨 🔗 🚑 🄰
⌇ P 🄿 ⊞ lau ➡ ⌇S

Internacional Palamós Playa de la Fosca
☎ 972 314736 ▯ 317626
A family site in a picturesque wooded location close to the beach.
⮕ *Signposted.*
Jun-Sept 5.2HEC ⊞ ♠ ⋒ 🗻 🍽 ✕ ☉ 🗨 🚑 🄰 ⌇ PS 🄿 ⊞
lau ➡ 🔗

Palamós ctra la Fosca 12 ☎ 972 314296 ▯ 972 601100
e-mail: campingpal@grn.es
In a picturesque situation on a wooded headland overlooking the sea.
31 Mar-Sep 5.5HEC ⊞ ⋮⋮⋮ ♠ ⋒ 🗻 🍽 ✕ ☉ 🗨 🔗 🚑 ⌇ PS
🄿 ⊞ lau ➡ 🔥

Vilarromá calle del Mar ☎ 972 314375 ▯ 972 314375
e-mail: vilarroma@eic.ictnet.es
Clean and tidy site, almost completely divided into pitches.
⮕ *Turn off on the eastern outskirts of Palamós near big petrol station.*
Apr-25 Sep 1.8HEC ⊞ ♠ ⋒ 🗻 🍽 ✕ ☉ 🗨 🔗 🚑 🄿 ⊞ lau
➡ ✕ 🔥 ⌇S

At CALONGE(5km W)

Cala Gogo ☎ 972 651564 ▯ 972 650553
e-mail: calagogo@calagogo.es
Terraced site in tall pine woodland and poplars with some good views of the sea. Underpass to section of site with private beach. Some internal dusty roads.
⮕ *Access from Palamós 4 km S on coastal road C253, entrance to site on right shortly after Km47.*
Apr-Sep 16HEC 🔧 ⋒ 🗻 🍽 ✕ ☉ 🗨 🔗 🚑 🄰 ⌇ PS ⊞ 🔌 lau

Internacional de Calonge ☎ 972 651233 ▯ 972 652507
e-mail: intercalonge@intercalonge.com
Set on a pine covered hill overlooking the sea within easy
reach of a sandy beach.
➲ *On the coast road between Platja d'Aro and Palamós.*
All year 11HEC ⁙ ♠♟♈♟✕⊙☻⊘♏♨Å⚡PS 🏤⊞ lau

▶ **PALS** GIRONA

Cypsela ☎ 972 667696 ▯ 972 667300
e-mail: info@cypsela.com
Well-kept grassy site in a pine wood.
➲ *For access, turn towards the sea N of Pals and follow road
towards Playa de Pals, then turn left after Km3.*
11May-22Sep 20HEC ⁙ ♠♟♈♟✕⊙☻⊘♏⚡P🏤📭⊞
⌖ lau ▶ ⚡S

Mas Patoxas ☎ 972 636928 ▯ 972 667349
A family site in a quiet location close to the sea. Good,
modern sanitary blocks and plenty of recreational facilities.
➲ *At Km5 on Palafrugell to Torroella.*
Apr-Sep 5.5HEC ⨆⨆ ♠♟♈♟✕⊙☻⊘Ⳃ♏♨Å⚡P🏤
⊞ lau

▶ At **PLAYA DE PALS**

Playa Brava ☎ 972 636894 ▯ 972636952
e-mail: info@playabrava.com
On level terrain adjoining pine woodlands, golf course, rivers
and sea.
➲ *From N end of village of Pals turn towards sea and Playa de
Pals.*
15 May-19 Sep 11HEC ⨆⨆ ⁙ ♈♟⊙☻⚡S🏤📭⌖ lau ▶
♈♟✕⊘

▶ **PINEDA DE MAR** BARCELONA

Camell Ada de los Naranjos 12 ☎ 93 7671520 ▯ 93 7670270
e-mail: campingcamell@teleline.es
Surrounded by deciduous trees next to a small wood owned
by the Taurus Hotel.
➲ *Turn off the N11 at Km670 and along Ada de los Naranjos
in direction of sea.*
May-Sep 2.2HEC ⁙ ♠♟♈♟✕⊙☻⊘⚡PS🏤⊞ lau ▶ ✕
Prices: ♣3.50 📭10.25 pitch 2.75

▶ **PLATJA D'ARO, LA** GIRONA

Valldaro ctra Santa Cristina 113 ☎ 972 817515 ▯ 972 816662
e-mail: valldaro@valldaro.com
Extensive level meadowland under poplars, pines and
eucalyptus trees. Some large pitches without shade.
➲ *Site lies on the left of the GE662 towards Castell and Santa
Cristinia d 'Aro at Km4.*
15 Mar-06 Oct 20HEC ⨆⨆ ♠♟♈♟✕⊙☻⊘♏♨Ⳃ⚡P🏤
⊞ lau ▶ ⚡S Prices: ♣3-4.50 pitch 14-22.50

▶ **PUIGCERDÀ** GIRONA

Stel ctra Llivia ☎ 972 882361 ▯ 140419
e-mail: puigcerda@stel.es
Modern campsite in the Pyrenees on level land. Has
wonderful views of the mountains and surrounding area.
First class sanitary installations.
➲ *Access via N340 between Comarruga and Tarragona.*
Jun-Sep 7HEC ⁙ ♈♟♈♟✕⊙☻⊘♏⚡P🏤⊞ lau

▶ **RIPOLL** GIRONA

Solana del Ter ☎ 972 701062 ▯ 972 714343
e-mail: hotel@solanadelter.com
In a peaceful location close to the local ski resorts at the foot
of the Pyrenees. Part of a small hotel/restaurant complex.
May-Oct 8.5HEC ⨆⨆ ♈♟♈♟✕⊙☻⚡P🏤⊞ lau ▶ ♈

E-17251 Calonge (Girona)
Tel. (34) 972651095 • Fax (34) 972651671
www.campingtreumal.com
e-mail: info@campingtreumal.com
Beautifully situated, first class site with an old manor,
directly by the beach and well shaded by old pine trees.
Modern sanitary facilities with free hot water in showers
and sinks. Small swimming pool. All facilities of a
modern site. Mobile homes for 4 pers. Access from
the road Platja d'Aro-Palamós, 3 km for Platja d'Aro.

 1.11 - 31.3: Diagonal 477, planta 10, E-08036 Barcelona.
Tel: (34) 93 405 16 70. Fax: (34) 93 405 29 64.
1.4 - 31.10: Ap. de Correos 348, E-17250 Platja d'Aro.

▶ **SALDES** BARCELONA

Repos del Pedraforca ☎ 93 8258044 ▯ 93 8258061
e-mail: pedra@campingpedraforca.com
A well equipped site situated in an area of natural beauty.
All year 4HEC ⨆⨆ ♦♠♟♈♟✕⊙☻⊘♏⚡P🏤⊞ lau
Prices: ♣3.64-4.55 pitch 9.20-11.50

▶ **SANTA CRISTINA D'ARO** GIRONA

Mas St Josep ☎ 972 835081
A family site with plenty of recreational facilities.
➲ *At Km2 on the main Sta. Cristina d'Aro road.*
27 May-1 Oct 20HEC ⨆⨆ ♈♟♈♟✕⊙☻⊘⊘
⚡P🏤⊞ lau ▶ ⚡R

▶ **SANT ANTONI DE CALONGE** GIRONA

Euro Ctra. Palamos-Platja d'Aro
☎ 972 650879 ▯ 661987
e-mail: info@euro-camping.com
A family site in a peaceful location close to the sea with fine
recreational facilities.
➲ *Access via A7 exit 9.*
7 Apr-Sep 13HEC ⨆⨆ ♠♟♈♟✕⊙☻⊘♏
⚡P🏤⊞ lau ▶ ♨ ⚡S

Treumal ☎ 972 651095 ▯ 651674
e-mail: info@campingtreumal.com
A peaceful family site in a beautiful location between a pine
wood and the beach.
➲ *Entrance on Sant Feliú-Platja d'Aro-Palamós road.*
Apr-Sep 7HEC ⨆⨆ ⁙ ♠♟♈♟✕⊙☻⊘♏
⚡PS🏤⊞ lau

SANTA SUSANA BARCELONA

Bon Répos ☎ 93 7678475 ▤ 93 7678526
e-mail: bonrepos@entorno.es
In pine woodland between railway and the beach with some
sunshade roofing.
➲ *Turn off the N11 at Km681 and approach via the
underpass (height 2.5m) just before reaching the beach.*
All year 6HEC ⊞ ⠿ ⚐ ⌂ ☎ 🍴 ✕ ⊙ 🛢 ∅ ♨ ⚡ PS ☎ ⊞ lau
♦ 🛢 ⚡ ⚡S

SANT CEBRIÁ DE VALLALTA BARCELONA

Verneda av Maresme ☎ 93 7631185 ▤ 93 7631185
e-mail: lverneda@teleline.es
Inland and among tall trees.
➲ *Leave the N11 Girona-Barcelona road at the far end of
Sant Pol de Mar, turn inland at Km670. Continue for 2km to
edge of the village and before the bridge over the River Vallala
turn right.*
Apr-Sep 1.6HEC ⠿ ♦ ⌂ 🛢 🍴 ✕ ⊙ 🛢 ∅ ⚡ P ☎ ⊞ lau
Prices: ⚑3.60 ♠3.60 ▣3.60 ▲3.60

SANT FELIU DE GUIXOLS GIRONA

Sant Pol Doctor Fleming ☎ 972 327269 ▤ 972 327211
e-mail: info@campingsantpol.com
In wooded surroundings near the beach with good facilities.
➲ *800m from the town centre towards Palamos.*
15 Mar-Nov 1.2HEC ⊞ ♦ ⌂ 🛢 🍴 ✕ ⊙ 🛢 ♨
⚡ P ⊞ lau ♦ ⚡S

SANT PERE PESCADOR GIRONA

Amfora av J-Terradellas 2 ☎ 972 520540 ▤ 972 520539
e-mail: info@campingamfora.com
A pleasant site, directly on the beach, with good modern
sanitary facilities. There are plentiful leisure facilities and
English is spoken.
6 Apr-Sep 9HEC ⊞ ⚐ ⌂ 🛢 🍴 ✕ ⊙ 🛢 ∅ ♨ ⚡ PRS ☎ ⊞ lau

Aquarius ☎ 972 520003 ▤ 550216
e-mail: camping@aquarius.es
Level meadowland. Partially in shade a quiet, well organised
site by the lovely sandy beach of Bahia de Rosas.
➲ *Travel in direction of L'Escala and turn towards the beach
following signs.*
15 Mar-10 Jan 6HEC ⊞ ⚐ ⌂ 🛢 🍴 ✕ ⊙ 🛢 ∅ ♨
⚡ S ☎ ⊞ lau

Ballena Alegre 2 ☎ 902510520 ▤ 972 520332
e-mail: infb2@ballena-alegre.es
Extensive site near wide sandy beach with dunes. Large
shopping complex. Washing and sanitary facilities have
recently undergone extensive modernisation.
➲ *Access from L'Escala to San Martin de Ampurias, then
onward to site in 2km .*
15 May-24 Sep 24HEC ⊞ ⚐ ⌂ 🛢 🍴 ✕ ⊙ 🛢 ∅ ♨
⚡ PS ☎ ⊞ lau

Dunas ☎ 972 520400
Level extensive grassland site with young poplars, some of
medium height, on the beach, totally subdivided.
➲ *It lies 5km SE of village. If approaching from L'Escala follow
an asphalt road to San Martin, then follow a dusty earth track
for 2.5km.*
9 May-25 Sep 30HEC ⊞ ⚐ ⌂ 🛢 ✕ ⊙ 🛢 ∅ ♨ ▣ ▲
⚡ PS ☎ ⊞ lau

Palmeras ctra de la Platja ☎ 972 520506 ▤ 550285
e-mail: info@campinglaspalmeras.com
On level grassland with plenty of shade. Recently installed
modern sanitary blocks and heated swimming pool.

➲ *Off the road from Sant Pere Pescador to the beach about
200m from the sea.*
Apr-20 Oct 5HEC ⊞ ⚐ ⌂ 🛢 🍴 ✕ ⊙ 🛢 ∅ ♨ ⚡ PS ☎ ⊞ lau
♦ ⚡R

SITGES BARCELONA

Roca av de Ronda ☎ 93 8940043 ▤ 93 8940150
On three terraces with a view of Sitges. Shade is provided by
pines and deciduous trees. Separate section for young people.
1km from the sea.
Camping Card Compulsory.
➲ *Turn off the C246 (Barcelona-Tarragona) in the direction
of Sant Pere de Ribes/San Pedro de Ribas. In 15m turn right to
site.*
Apr-13 Oct 2HEC ⠿ ⚐ ⌂ 🛢 🍴 ✕ ⊙ 🛢 ∅ ♨ ☎ ⊞ lau ♦ ♨
⚡PS Prices: ⚑3.85-4.48 ♠3.85-4.48 ▣3.85-4.48 ▲3.85-4.48

TARADELL BARCELONA

Vall Cami de la Vallmitjana ☎ 93 8126336 ▤ 93 8126027
In the mountains near the Guilleries-Montseny, with good
recreational facilities.
25-26 Dec 8HEC ⊞ ♨ ⚐ ⌂ 🛢 🍴 ✕ ⊙ 🛢 ♨ ♨
⚡ P ☎ ⊞ lau

TORROELLA DE MONTGRI GIRONA

Delfin Verde ☎ 972 758450 ▤ 972 760070
e-mail: eldelfinverde@drac.com
On undulating ground with some pine trees, and an open
meadow beside the long sandy beach.
➲ *Turn left off the road to Begur approx 2km S of Torroella de
Montgri, and head towards Maspinell following a wide asphalt
road 4.8km towards the sea.*
23 Mar-26 Oct 35HEC ⊞ ⚐ ⌂ 🛢 🍴 ✕ ⊙ 🛢 ∅ ♨ ⚡ PRS ☎
⊞ lau Prices: ⚑3.21 pitch 12.04-35.31
See advertisement in colour section

TOSSA DE MAR GIRONA

Cala Llevadó ☎ 972 340314 ▤ 972 341187
e-mail: info@calallevado.com
Magnificent terraced site with hairpin roads overlooking
three bays, all suitable for bathing. Narrow, winding drives
which are quite steep in parts. Separate section for caravans.
➲ *Take the coast road for about 4km towards Lloret de Mar
and turn towards the sea.*
May-Sep 14HEC ⠿ ♨ ♦ ⌂ 🛢 🍴 ✕ ⊙ 🛢 ∅ ♨ ▲ ⚡ PS ☎
▣ ⊞ lau Prices: ⚑4.40-6.60 ♠4.40-6.60 ▣5-7.05 ▲4.40-6.60
See advertisement in colour section

Can Marti ☎ 972 340851 ▤ 972 342461
Pleasant, unspoilt site in a partly wooded location. Good
modern facilities. English spoken.
➲ *1km from the sea.*
12 May-16 Sep 10HEC ⊞ ♦ ⌂ 🛢 🍴 ✕ ⊙ 🛢 ∅
⚡ PRS ☎ ⊞ lau

Tossa ctra Llagostera ☎ 972 340547 ▤ 972 341531
On a meadow in a quiet, isolated valley, in a deciduous
forest. 3km from the sea.
➲ *3km SW near the GE681 (Tossa de Mar-Llagostera), in
600m to site along an unmade road.*
Apr-Sep 9.5HEC ⠿ ♦ ⌂ 🛢 🍴 ✕ ⊙ 🛢 ∅ ♨ ☎ ⚡ PS ⊞ lau

VILADECANS BARCELONA

Ballena Alegre I ☎ 93 6580504 ▤ 93 6580575
e-mail: ballena1@ballena-alegre.es
An exceptionally well run family site with a wide range of
facilities and direct access to a fine, sandy beach.
➲ *Access cia C246. Before entering Barcelona follow signs for
'Airport'.*
Apr-Sep 22HEC ⊞ ⠿ ♦ ⌂ 🛢 🍴 ✕ ⊙ 🛢 ∅ ♨ ♨
⚡ PS ☎ ▣ ⊞ lau

Toro Bravo ☎ 93 6373462
Level site in extensive pine woodland area by the sea. To the left of the access road on the banks of a canal, is a leisure and sports complex with many facilities including evening entertainment in the season.
➲ *Leave the C246 (Barcelona-Castelldeféls), at Km11 and continue towards the sea for 1km.*
All year 30HEC ⊞ ⋮⋮⋮ ♠ ♠ ⚑ ⚑ ✗ ⊙ ⚑ ⊘ ⚏
⭧ PS ⚑ ⊞ lau

VILALLONGA DE TER GIRONA

Conca de Ter ctra Camprodon-Setcases s/n ☎ 972 740629
e-mail: concater@publintur.es
A pleasant family site in wooded surroundings with a variety of recreational facilities.
➲ *Between Camprodón and Setcases, 20km from the French border.*
All year 3.2HEC ⊞ ♠ ♠ ⚑ ⚑ ✗ ⊙ ⚑ ⊘ ☲ ⚏ Å ⭧ PR ⚑ ⊞ lau ➧ ⚑ ⚑ ✗ ⊘ ☲ ⭧R

VILANOVA I LA GELTRÚ BARCELONA

Vilanova Park ☎ 93 8933402 ▤ 93 8935528
e-mail: info@vilanovapark.es
A well equipped family site on the edge of a densely wooded area close to the coast in the heart Catalonian wine-producing area. Modern sanitary block recently added.
➲ *Access via A7 exit 29.*
All year 51HEC ⊞ ⋮⋮⋮ ♠ ♠ ⚑ ⚑ ✗ ⊙ ⚑ ⊘ ☲ ⚏ ⚑ ⭧ P ⚑
⊞ lau Prices: ♠4.12-6.53 ➧4.12-6.53 Å4.12-6.53 pitch 13.30-19.69

See advertisement in colour section

The La Mancha plains and Don Quixote's windmills, massive mountain ranges, pastures, wheatfields, vineyards, and ancient forests are some of the regions's contrasts. Here are St Teresa's walled city of Avila, Cáceres' exceptional old quarter, Guadalajara's outstanding Renaissance palace, Salamanca, with its university and beautiful square and Segovia's dramatic Roman aqueduct and 14th-century palace.
Architectural and artistic riches continue with Cuenca's hanging houses and Teruel, part of which, like Toledo, belongs to the Heritage of Mankind. The framed walled city of Toledo, with its mosque, synagogue and medieval cathedral, has its associations with El Cid and contains El Greco's house and museum.
Spain's vital capital, Madrid, is home to the Prado and numerous other museums, a colourful old town, lovely parks, squares and palaces, while a short drive away lies the Sierra de Guadarrama with its forests, wild animals and birds of prey and the Pedriza del Manzanares' geological wonderland.
....

▶ ALBA DE TORMES SALAMANCA

Tormes av Dehesa Boyal ☎ 923 160998
In a rural setting close to the River Tormes.
Camping Card Compulsory.
➲ *20km from Salamanca.*
All year 2.2HEC ⊞ ⋇ ♠ ⚑ ✗ ⊙ ⚑ Å ⭧ R ⚑ ⊞ lau ➧ ⚑ ✗ ⊘ ☲ ⭧P

ALBARRACIN TERUEL

Ciudad de Albarracin Camino de Gea, Arrabal
☎ 978 710197
A modern site on mainly level ground with good facilities.
➲ *Signposted from A1512.*
Apr-Oct 1.4HEC ▥ ♠ ♠ ☎ ❤ ✕ ⊙ ☺ ∅ ☎ ⊞ lau ➧ ⚓ ✕ ₹PR
Prices: ♠2.40 ➟2.40 ➟2.55 ▲2.40

ARANJUEZ MADRID

Soto del Castillo ctra de Andalucia 1 ☎ 91 8911395
Site developed into two parts with trees and lawns in large
castle park.
➲ *Turn off NIV at Km46. In the village 200m beyond
Firestone petrol station turn sharp NE and continue for 1km.*
All year 33HEC ▥ ♠ ♠ ⚓ ❤ ✕ ⊙ ☺ ∅ ☎ ₹ PR ☎ ⊞ lau

CABRERA, LA MADRID

Pico de la Miel ☎ 91 8688082 ▧ 8688541
e-mail: info@picodelamiel.com
All year 10HEC ▥ ♠ ♠ ⚓ ❤ ✕ ⊙ ☺ ∅ ☎ ₹ P ☎ ⊞ lau ➧
⚏ Prices: ♠4.40 ➟4.40 ➟4.40 ▲4.40

CUENCA CUENCA

Cuenca ☎ 969 231656
A modern site in a peaceful wooded location.
➲ *N towards Mariana.*
15 Mar-13 Oct 23HEC ▥ ⚒ ♠ ⚓ ❤ ✕ ⊙ ☺ ∅ ☎ ₹ P ☎ ⊞
lau ➧ ₹LR Prices: ♠3.50 ➟3 ▲3 pitch 4

ESCORIAL, EL MADRID

El Escorial ctra Guadarrama ☎ 91 8902412 ▧ 91 8961062
e-mail: planeta.azul@retemail.es
In pleasant wooded surroundings with good recreational
facilities.
All year 40HEC ▥ ♠ ♠ ⚓ ❤ ✕ ⊙ ☺ ∅ ⚏ ☎ ₹ P ☎ ⊞ lau

See advertisement on page 319

FUENTE DE SAN ESTEBAN, LA SALAMANCA

Cruce ☎ 923440130
Useful transit site in a quiet location in typically Castillian
countryside.
➲ *50mtrs from N620 at Km291.*
15 Jun-15 Sep 0.5HEC ▥ ⚒ ♠ ⚓ ❤ ⊙ ☺ ∅ ☎ ₹ P ☎ ⊞ lau
➧ ✕ ₹R Prices: ♠2.70 ➟3.31 ▲2.40

GARGANTILLA DE LOZOYA MADRID

Monte Holiday ☎ 91 8695278 ▧ 91 8695278
e-mail: camp.m.holiday@teleline.es
A terraced site with good modern facilities in a beautiful
mountain setting.
➲ *Turn off N1 (Burgos-Madrid) at Km69 towards Cotos and
continue for 10km.*

Visit us, we are in Madrid

Bungalows CAMPING

❋ *Free hot water*
❋ *Regular bus connection to Madrid*

Alpha

E-28906 CTA. N-IV KM. 12,400
GETAFE (MADRID)
Tfn: (34) 916 958 069 Fax: (34) 916 831 659 **Madrid**

All year 30HEC ♠ ⚓ ❤ ✕ ⊙ ☺ ∅ ☺ ☎ ₹ P ☎ ⊞ lau ➧ ₹LR
Prices: ♠4.02 ➟4.02 ▲4.02

GETAFE MADRID

Alpha ☎ 91 6958069 ▧ 91 6831659
Surrounded by pine woods that approximately at the
geographical centre of Spain, with well defined pitches and
modern facilities. Direct bus service to Madrid.
➲ *Access via NIV at Km 12,400.*
All year 4.8HEC ⠿ ♠ ♠ ⚓ ❤ ✕ ⊙ ☺ ∅ ⚏ ☎ ₹ P ☎ ⊞ lau

MADRID MADRID

Arco Iris ☎ 91 6160387 ▧ 91 6160059
e-mail: madrid@bungalowsarcoiris.com
A family site in a peaceful location, yet with easy access to
Madrid.
➲ *From M40 (Madrid ring road) take exit 36 to Boadilla del
Monte and continue towards Villaviciosa to Km12.*
All year 4HEC ▥ ⠿ ♠ ♠ ⚓ ❤ ✕ ⊙ ☺ ∅ ⚏ ☎ ☺ ₹ P ☎
⊞ lau Prices: ♠4.63 ➟4.63 ➟4.63 ▲4.63

Osuna av de Logrono ☎ 91 7410510 ▧ 91 3206365
On long stretch of land, shade being provided by pines,
acacias and maple. Some noise from airfield, road and
railway.
➲ *If approaching from the town centre take N11 road and
drive towards Barajas for about 7.5km. At Km1 in 300m and
after railway underpass turn right.*
All year 23HEC ▥ ♠ ♠ ⚓ ❤ ✕ ⊙ ☺ ∅ ☺ ☎ ☎ ⊞ lau ➧ ✕ ∅
⚏ ₹LP Prices: ♠4.80 ➟4.80 ➟4.80 ▲4.80

MALPARTIDA DE PLASENCIA CÁCERES

Parque Natural de Monfrague Ctra Plasencia-Trujillo
☎ 927 459220 ▧ 927 459233
A modern site with well defined pitches and good facilities.
➲ *10km from Plasencia on C524.*
All year 7HEC ▥ ⚒ ♠ ♠ ⚓ ❤ ✕ ⊙ ☺ ∅ ☎ ₹ P ☎ ⊞ lau ➧ ⛲
Prices: ♠3.20 ➟2.50 ➟3.20 ▲3.20

MÉRIDA BADAJOZ

Lago de Proserpina Apdo 121 ☎ 924 123055 ▧ 924 319710
e-mail: avalverde@interbook.net
Apr-15 Sep 5.5HEC ▥ ⠿ ♠ ♠ ⚓ ❤ ✕ ⊙ ☺ ∅ ☎ ₹ LP ☎
⊞ lau ➧ ₹P Prices: ♠2.65-3 ➟2.65-3 ➟2.65-3 ▲2.65-3

MIRANDA DEL CASTAÑAR SALAMANCA

El Burro Blanco ☎ 923 161100 ▧ 923 161100
e-mail: elbb@infonegocio.com
A well equipped site in an area of woodland overlooking the
village.
➲ *Approx 1km from the village centre.*
Apr-Sep 3.5HEC ▥ ⚒ ♠ ⚓ ❤ ✕ ⊙ ☺ ∅ ☎ ☎ ⊞ lau ➧ ⚓ ✕ ∅
₹PR Prices: ♠4.28 pitch 9.63

NAVALAFUENTE MADRID

Camping Piscis ☎ 91 8432268 ▧ 91 8471341
e-mail: campiscis@campiscis.com
Spacious pitches surrounded by oak trees.
➲ *Turn off N1/E5 (Madrid-Burgos) at exit 50 and continue
towards Guadalix de la Sierra.*
All year 23HEC ⠿ ♠ ♠ ⚓ ❤ ✕ ⊙ ☺ ∅ ☎ ☺ ₹ P ☎ ⊞ lau
Prices: ♠4.15 ➟4.15 ➟4.15 ▲4.15

SALAMANCA SALAMANCA

Don Quijote Cabrerizos ☎ 923 209052 ▧ 923 251066
➲ *NE of the town towards Aldealengua.*
All year 4HEC ▥ ⠿ ⚒ ♠ ⚓ ✕ ⊙ ☺ ∅

SANTA MARTA DE TORMES SALAMANCA

Regio ctra Salamanca/Madrid Km4
☎ 923 138888 ▤ 923 138044
e-mail: recepcion@campingregio.com
A pleasant site, divided into several fields, with good, modern facilities.
➲ *100m from the N501 (Salamanca-Avila) behind Hotel Jardin-Regio.*
All year 3HEC ⏚ 🛇🏕🔌🍴✕☉🟦𝄐🏕🛒 ⚡ PR ⚿✚ lau
Prices: ⚡2.57-3.05 🚗2.57-3.05 ⛺2.57-3.05 pitch 9-10.29

SEGOVIA SEGOVIA

Acueducto ☎ 921 425000 ▤ 425000
e-mail: campingsg@navegalia.com
➲ *SE next to N601 at Km112.*
Apr-Sep 3HEC ⏚ ♠🛇🏕🔌🍴✕☉🟦𝄐🏕🛒🔆🏕 ⚡ P ✚ lau ◆
✕ ⚡L Prices: ⚡3.75-4 🚗4.20-4.50 ⛺3.75-4 pitch 12.62-13

TOLEDO TOLEDO

Greco ☎ 925 220090 ▤ 925 220090
e-mail: elgreco@zetemail.es
Few shady terraces on slope leading down to the River Tajo. On SW outskirts of town.
➲ *Approaching from the town centre take the C401, Carretera Comarcal and drive SW for about 2km. Turn right at Km28 and drive 300m towards Puebla de Montalban.*
All year 2.5HEC ⸬⸬ 🛇🏕🔌🍴✕☉🟦𝄐🏕 ⚡ PR ⚿✚ lau
⸬ Prices: ⚡4.41 🚗4.34 ⛺4.34

VALDEMAQUEDA MADRID

El Canto la Gallina ☎ 091 8984820 ▤ 8984823
In a wooded location at the foot of a mountain.
All year 12HEC ⏚ ⸬⸬ 🛇🏕🔌🍴✕☉🟦𝄐🏖🏕🛒 ⚡ P ⚿✚
lau ◆ ⚡R

VILLAMAYOR SALAMANCA

Ruta de la Plata ctra Villales a Villamayor ☎ 923 289574
e-mail: campingrutadelaplata@turisnet
All year ⏚ 🛇🏕🔌🍴✕☉🟦𝄐 ⚡ P ⚿✚ lau ◆ ✕

● ● ● **SOUTH EAST COAST** ● ● ●

The Costa Blanca is a household name; Benidorm a tourist mecca. South of Alicante, tourism is less developed and, inland, there are lemon and orange groves and picturesque mountain towns.

A busy port and relatively unspoiled, Alicante has a cathedral and museum of 20th-century art, and there are tremendous views from its fascinating castle. Roman remains surround Tarragona, whose medieval walled city has a Gothic cathedral, interesting palace and architectural museum. Journey out to the Monastery of Poblet inside its three perimeter walls and the Abbey of Santa Creus, burial place of the kings of Aragon.
Valencia, home of paella, is Spain's third largest city with a countryside criss-crossed by ancient irrigation channels. Numerous historic buildings include a cathedral with the legendary Holy Grail, beautiful bridges and gardens and many museums. The Fallas - a fortnight of celebrations - take place in mid-March. Inland, Requena has a moorish castle, medieval walls and the house of El Cid.

ALCANAR TARRAGONA

Mare Nostrum ☎ 977 737179
Gently sloping towards the sea with pines, olive and deciduous trees.
➲ *Turn towards the sea off the N340 at Km58.3.*
All year 1.4HEC ⏚ ◆🛇🏕🔌🍴✕☉🟦𝄐🏕 ⚡ S ⚿✚ lau ◆ ✕

ALCOCEBER CASTELLÓN

Playa Tropicana ☎ 964 412463 ▤ 964 412805
e-mail: info@playatropicana.com
On a 500m long sandy beach 3km from the village.
➲ *For access, leave motorway at exit 44, then drive 3km N on the CN340 and turn towards the sea at Km1018.*
15 Mar-Oct 3HEC ⏚ ♠🛇🛟🔌🍴✕☉🟦𝄐🏕🛒 ⚡ PS ⚿✚ 🏊
lau Prices: ⚡6.35 pitch 25

Ribamar Partida Ribamar s/n ☎ 964 761163 ▤ 964 761163
Quiet wooded site between sea and mountains. Individual pitches.
23Mar-29Sep 2.2HEC ◆🛇🏕🔌🍴✕☉🟦𝄐🏕🛒🏕 ⚡ PS ⚿✚
lau Prices: ⚡2.55-3.64 🚗2.58-3.69 🚗3.14-4.49 ⛺3.14-4.49

ALFAZ DEL PI ALICANTE

Excalibur Camino, Viejo del Albir s/n ☎ 96 6867139 ▤ 96 6866928
All year 12HEC ⏚ 🔆🏕🛟✕☉🟦𝄐 ⚡ P ◆ ⚡S
See advertisement in colour section

ALTEA ALICANTE

Cap Blanch Playa del Cap-Blanch
☎ 96 5845946 ▤ 96 5844556
e-mail: capblanch@ctv.es
A well equipped site on Albir beach backed by imposing mountains. Good sporting and recreational facilities.
➲ *Access via A7 exit 65 (Benidorm-Callosa).*
All year 4HEC ◆♠🛇✕☉🟦𝄐🏕 ⚡ S ⚿✚ lau ◆🛟𝄐✚
Prices: ⚡5.50 🚗5.50 🚗7 ⛺5.50

AMETLLA DE MAR, L' TARRAGONA

L'Ametlla Village Platja Paratge Santes Creus
☎ 977 267784 ▤ 977 267868
e-mail: info@campingametlla.com
A modern site with first class equipment. Direct access to two beaches. Substantial improvements have been made to the access road.
➲ *2km W, S of A7.*
Apr-Oct 8HEC ⏚ ⸬⸬ 🛇🏕🛟🔌🍴✕☉🟦𝄐🏖🏕🛒 ⚡ PS ⚿
✚ lau

BENICARLÓ CASTELLÓN

Alegria del Mar Playa Norte ☎ 964 470871 ▤ 964 470871
All year 10HEC ⏚ 🛇🏕🔌🍴✕☉🟦𝄐🏕 ⚡ PS ⚿✚ lau
Prices: ⚡3.55 pitch 14.20 (incl 2 persons)

BENICASIM CASTELLÓN

Bonterra av Barcelona 47 ☎ 964 300007 🖩 300060
e-mail: campingbonterra@ctu.es
Between the railway line and avenida de Barcelona with a
number of deciduous trees.
➲ *300m N towards Las Villas de Benicasim.*
23 Mar-31 Dec 5HEC ⚏ ∴ ♠ ♠ ⚑ ♈ ✕ ⊙ ⊟ ⌀ ⛺ ⫩ P 🖾
🖽 lau ♦ ⌀ ⫩PS Prices: ♠1.95-3.61 pitch 7.21-24.04

BENIDORM ALICANTE

Arena Blanca av Dr Severo Ochoa 44
☎ 96 5861889 🖩 69 5861107
e-mail: arenablanca@ctv.es
A modern site with plenty of good facilities.
➲ *Access via N332 Benidorm-Altea.*
All year 2.2HEC ∴ ♠ ♠ ⚑ ♈ ✕ ⊙ ⊟ ⌀ ⛐ ⫩ PS 🖾🖽 lau
Prices: ♠4.81 ♠4.81 ⛽15.03 ▲4.81

Armanello av Comunidad
☎ 96 5853190 🖩 96 5853190
Divided by bushes with large pitches on terraces under olive
and palm trees next to a small orange grove.
➲ *For access turn off the N332 at Km123.1 N of the town.*
All year 1.6HEC ⚏ ♠ ♠ ⚑ ♈ ✕ ⊙ ⊟ ⌀ ⛐ ⛺ ⫩ PS 🖾🖽 lau
Prices: ♠4.81 ♠4.81 ▲4.81

Benisol av de la Comunidad ☎ 96 5851673 🖩 96 5860895
A modern family site with plenty of facilities. The large
pitches are separated by hedges and the centre of Benidorm
is within easy reach.
➲ *NE of Benidorm off N332 towards Altea.*
All year 7HEC ♦ ♠ ♠ ⚑ ♈ ✕ ⊙ ⊟ ⌀ ⛐ ⛺ ⛊
⫩ P 🖾🖽 lau

BENISA ALICANTE

Fanadix ctra Calpe-Moraira Km 5
☎ 96 5747307 🖩 965747307
e-mail: campingfanadix@campingfanadix.com
Terraced site completely divided into pitches.
➲ *10km E & 400m from the sea. Access off AV-1445.*
Apr-Sep 1.6HEC ⚏ ∴ ♠ ♠ ♈ ✕ ⊙ ⊟ ⌀ ⫩ P 🖾🖽 lau ♦ ⚑ ⌀
⛐ ⫩S Prices: ♠3.47-3.86 pitch 10.43-11.58

CAMBRILS TARRAGONA

Playa Cambrils Auda Diputacion 42
☎ 977 361490 🖩 977 364988
e-mail: camping@playacambrils.com
Divided into pitches, lying on both sides of the coast road in
a wooded location.
➲ *Drive 2km N of the town towards Salou and W of the
bridge over the river.*
15 Mar-12 Oct 11HEC ⚏ ♠ ♠ ⚑ ♈ ✕ ⊙ ⊟ ⌀ ⛺ ⫩ P 🖾🖽
lau ♦ ⫩S

CAMPELLO ALICANTE

Costa Blanca c Convento 143
☎ 0034 965630670 🖩 965630670
e-mail: campingcb@tsc.es
On most level ground scattered with old olive and eucalyptus
trees. The Alicante-Denia railway line runs behind the camp.
➲ *For access turn off the N332 at Km94.2 next to the big
petrol station, and drive along a narrow gravel track towards
the sea for 0.5km.*
All year 1.1HEC ∴ ♦ ♠ ♠ ⚑ ♈ ✕ ⊙ ⊟ ⌀ ⛐ ⛺ ▲ ⫩ P 🖾🖽
lau ♦ ⫩S

CUNIT TARRAGONA

Mar de Cunit Playa Cunit ☎ 977 674058
A friendly site on level ground overlooking the beach.
15 May-Sep 1.2HEC ⠶ ⚲ ⚑ ♨ ♥ ✕ ⊙ ⚑ ∅ ⚓ ⚡ LS ☎ ⊞
lau ➧ ⊞

DAIMUS VALENCIA

Aventura ctra Playa Daimus ☎ 96 2818330
Picturesque setting in wooded surroundings on a safe, sandy
beach.
➲ *Access via N332 Alicante-Valencia.*
Closed 15 Dec-Jan 1.8HEC ⠶ ⠶ ♦ ⚑ ♨ ♥ ✕ ⊙ ⚑ ∅ ⚓
⚡ PS ☎ ⊞ lau

DENIA ALICANTE

Marinas Les Bovetes ☎ 96 5781446
➲ *For access turn off the N332 in Vergel and drive E on the
Denia road for 4km . Turn N, cross the P1324, turn right near
the beach and continue for 200m.*
Apr-Sep 12.7HEC ⠶ ♦ ⚑ ♨ ♥ ✕ ⊙ ⚑ ∅ ⚡ S ☎ ⊞ lau ➧
⚡P

GUARDAMAR DEL SEGURA ALICANTE

Mare Nostrum ☎ 96 5728073 ▤ 965728073
e-mail: diama@cesser.com
Partially terraced meadow with some shade from roofing.
➲ *Turn towards the sea off the N332 Alicante-Cartagena road
at about Km38.5.*
Apr-15 Sep 20HEC ⠸ ⚲ ⚑ ♨ ♥ ✕ ⊙ ⚑ ∅ ⚓ ⚡ PS ☎ ⊞
lau ➧ ✕ ⚡LRS

Marjal Cartagena-Alicante Rd ☎ 966 ▤ 966 726695
e-mail: marjal@futurnet.es
Located in a national park called 'Dunas de Guardamar' next
to the estuary of the Segura River, alongside pine and
eucalyptus forests with access to fine sandy beaches.
All year 3.5HEC ⠶ ⚲ ⚑ ♨ ✕ ⊙ ⚑ ♥ ⚡ PR ☎ lau ➧ ⚡S
See advertisement in colour section

Palm Mar ☎ 96 5728856 ▤ 5728856
Jun-Sep 2HEC ⠶ ♦ ⚑ ♨ ♥ ✕ ⊙ ⚑ ∅ ⚡ S ☎ ⊞ lau ➧ ✕ ⚡P

HOSPITALET DE L'INFANT, L' TARRAGONA

El Templo del Sol Platja del Torn
☎ 977 810486 ▤ 977 811306
A new site with modern sanitary installations and good
recreational facilities on a 1.5km long beach.**This is a
naturist site and only families or holders of an
International Naturism Carnet are allowed.**
➲ *Access via A3 (Barcelona-Valencia), 4km from exit 38
towards the sea.*
1 Jun - 30 Sep 15 Oct - 1 May ⠸ ⚑ ⚑ ♨ ♥ ✕ ⊙ ⚑ ∅ ⚓ ⚡
PS ☎ ⊞ ⚶ lau

JARACO VALENCIA

San Vincente Playa Xeraco ☎ 96 2888188 ▤ 96 2888147
Level subdivided site with some trees.
➲ *On leaving Jaraco at Km332 turn off at Km304 (Valencia-
Alicante) in the direction of Playa to the site in 3.5km.*
All year 5HEC ⠶ ⚑ ♨ ♥ ✕ ⊙ ⚑ ♥ ⚡ S ☎ ⊞ lau ➧ ⚓ ∅ ⚶
⚡PR Prices: ⚡4-4.25 ⚡4-4.25 ⚡5.40-5.95 ⚡4-4.25

MARINA, LA ALICANTE

International la Marina ☎ 96 5419051 ▤ 96 5419110
e-mail: info@campinglamarina.com
A modern site in a wooded setting, 500 metres from a sandy
beach.
➲ *At Km29 on Alicante-Cartagena road.*
All year 6.3HEC ⚑ ⚑ ♨ ♥ ✕ ⊙ ⚑ ∅ ⚶ ⚓ ⚡ P ☎ ⊞ lau ➧ ⚡S
See advertisement in colour section

MIRAMAR PLAYA VALENCIA

Coelius av del Mar ☎ 96 2819574 ▤ 96 2818733
e-mail: coelius@mx3.redestb.es
A fine camp site 500m from the Miramar beach with good,
modern facilities.
➲ *Access via N430.*
All year 2HEC ⚲ ♦ ⚑ ♨ ♥ ✕ ⊙ ⚑ ⚶ ⚓ ⚡ P ☎ ⊞ lau ➧ ∅
⚡S

MONT-ROIG DEL CAMP TARRAGONA

Marius ☎ 977810684 ▤ 977 179658
e-mail: schmid@teleline.es
Pitches are planted with flowers and shrubs. Separate section
for dog owners.
➲ *For access, leave the N340, Tarragona to Valencia road, at
Km1137 and drive through a 4.9m-wide railway underpass
with a clearance of 3.65m, then head towards the beach.*
15 May-Sep 4.5HEC ⠸ ∅ ♦ ⚑ ♨ ♥ ✕ ⊙ ⚑ ∅ ⚡ S ☎ ⊞
lau Prices: ⚡4.50-6 pitch 12-16

Playa Montroig ☎ 977 810637 ▤ 811411
e-mail: info@playamontroig.com
An ideal holiday centre for the whole family with sanitary
installations of the highest quality. Situated on a fine sandy
beach and surrounded by tropical gardens, this award
winning site offers a wide range of sporting and recreational
facilities and is noted for its helpful and friendly staff.
➲ *Turn left off the N340 at Km1136. Use motorway
exit 37 or 38.*
Mar-Oct 35HEC ⠸ ♦ ⚑ ♨ ♥ ✕ ⊙ ⚑ ∅ ⚓
⚡ PS ☎ ⊞ ⚶ lau

Torre Del Sol ☎ 977 810486 ▤ 811306
e-mail: info@latorredelsol.com
A level tidy grassland site on two levels, with young popolars
and some of medium height between a long stretch of beach
and the railway.
➲ *For access, turn off the N340, Tarragona to Valencia road at
Km224.1 then f ollow the road towards the sea.*
15 Mar-15 Oct 24HEC ⠸ ♦ ⚑ ♨ ♥ ✕ ⊙ ⚑ ∅
⚡ S ☎ ⊞ ⚶ lau
See advertisement in colour section

MORAIRA ALICANTE

Moraira Camino Paellero 50
☎ 96 5745249 ▤ 96 5745315
0.3km from the sea in a pine forest. On several terraces and
divided into pitches.
➲ *1km S on AP1347, turn W and continue up a hill for 500m.*
All year 11HEC ⠶ ⚑ ⚑ ♨ ♥ ✕ ⊙ ⚑ ∅ ⚓ ⚡♠
⚡ P ☎ ⊞ lau ➧ ⚡S

OLIVA VALENCIA

Azul Apartado de Correos 96 ☎ 96 2854106
e-mail: campingazul@ctv.es
A well equipped site with direct access to the beach.
All year 2.5HEC ⠶ ♦ ⚑ ♨ ♥ ✕ ⊙ ⚑ ∅ ⚶ ⚓
⚡ S ☎ ⊞ lau ➧ ✕ ⚡R

```
A list of Online Resources can
be found on page 12 of this
guide.
```

Euro Camping ☎ 96 2854098 📠 96 2851753
e-mail: eurocamping@interbook.net
On a wide sandy beach between orange groves and well
shaded with poplar and eucalyptus trees.
➲ *For access turn off the N332 at Km184.9, 600m from Oliva.
Following signs for camp drive towards the sea for 3.3km. The
access road has narrow stretches and some blind corners so
beware of oncoming traffic.*
All year 4.5HEC ⬝⬝⬝ ⬝ ⬝ ⬝ ⬝ ⬝ ⬝ ⬝ ⬝ ⬝ ⬝ ⬝
⬝ S ⬝ ⬝ lau ➡ ⬝R

See advertisement in colour section

Ferienplatz Olé ☎ 96 2857517
An extensive site with some pitches amongst dunes.
➲ *Turn off the N332 at Km209.9 about 5km S of Oliva. In
about 3km continue to site on access road partially asphalt,
through an orchard.*
Apr-Sep 46HEC ⬝⬝⬝ ⬝ ⬝ ⬝ ⬝ ⬝ ⬝ ⬝ ⬝ ⬝
⬝ S ⬝ ⬝ lau ➡ ⬝

Kiko Playa de Oliva ☎ 96 2850905 📠 96 2854320
e-mail: kikooark@interbook.net
Family holiday camp, divided into pitches, lying between
marshland and vineyard. The sea can be reached by crossing
a dyke and there are sunshade roofs.
➲ *Access from motorway A7 exit 61 and continue via CN332
towards Oliva.*
All year 4HEC ⬝ ⬝ ⬝ ⬝ ⬝ ⬝ ⬝ ⬝ ⬝ ⬝
⬝ S ⬝ ⬝ lau ➡ ⬝

◗ OROPESA DEL MAR CASTELLÓN

Didota av de la Didota ☎ 964 319551
Mar-Oct 1.7HEC ⬝ ⬝ ⬝ ⬝ ⬝ ⬝ ⬝ ⬝ ⬝ ⬝ ⬝
⬝ P ⬝ ⬝ lau ➡ ⬝S

◗ PEÑISCOLA CASTELLÓN

Camping Eden ☎ 964 480562 📠 964 489828
A modern, well appointed site on level ground close to the
seafront.
➲ *Access via A7, then head for Peñiscola and turn towards
Benicarlo.*
All year 4HEC ⬝⬝⬝ ⬝ ⬝ ⬝ ⬝ ⬝ ⬝ ⬝ ⬝ ⬝ ⬝ PRS ⬝ ⬝ lau ➡
⬝ ⬝ ⬝

◗ PUEBLA DE FARNALS VALENCIA

Brasa ☎ 96 1460388
Level meadowland site with poplars near village centre.
➲ *For access leave motorway Barcelona-Valencia at exit 3,
towards Playa Puebla de Farnals.*
All year 3.9HEC ⬝⬝⬝ ⬝ ⬝ ⬝ ⬝ ⬝ ⬝ ⬝
⬝ P ⬝ ⬝ lau ➡ ⬝ ⬝S

◗ RODA DE BARÀ TARRAGONA

Playa Bara ☎ 977 802701
Extensive site well kept and laid out in terraces. Separated
from the beautifully situated beach by railway line with an
underpass.
➲ *For accesss turn off the N340 near the Arco de Berá
(triumphant arch) and drive towards the sea for about 1.5 km.*
Apr-Sep 14.5HEC ⬝⬝⬝ ⬝⬝⬝ ⬝ ⬝ ⬝ ⬝ ⬝ ⬝ ⬝ ⬝ ⬝ ⬝ P ⬝
⬝ lau ➡ ⬝S

◗ SALOU TARRAGONA

Cambrils Park Apartado de Correos 123
☎ 977 351031 📠 977 352210
e-mail: mail@cambrilspark.es
A large, well equipped holiday park in a wooded location.
Abundant facilities for all types of recreation.

➲ *Leave main Barcelona/Valencia road at exit 35 Reus/Salou. In Salou head for seafront, then right towards harbour and Cambrils.*
22 Mar-30 Sep 17HEC ⬛⬛ ⬟ ⌂ ▮ ▮ ✕ ☉ ☻ ∅ ♨ ⚓ P 🄿 ⊞ ⊗ lau ➡ ⚓S

Pineda de Salou Playa de la Pineda
☎ 977 373080 ▣ 977 373081
e-mail: info@campingglapineda.com
A well equipped site close to the sea.
➲ *At Km5 on the Tarragona-Salou road.*
All year 4HEC ⬛⬛ ➡ ⌂ ▮ ▮ ✕ ☉ ☻ ∅ ♨ ⚓ P 🄿 ⊞ lau ➡ ▮ ▮ ✕ ⚓ ⚓S Prices: ⚓3.20-4.70 pitch 7.50-14.70

Sanguli-Salou ☎ 977 381641 ▣ 977 384616
e-mail: mail@sanguli.es
A large, family site in pleasant wooded surroundings, 50mtrs from the beach, with extensive sports and entertainment facilities.
➲ *3km from Port Aventura on SW outskirts, 50mtrs inland from coast road to Cambrils*
15 Mar-03 Nov 23HEC ⬛⬛ ⚫⚫ ➡ ⌂ ▮ ▮ ✕ ☉ ☻ ∅ ♨ ⚓ PS 🄿 ⊞ lau Prices: ⚓4.81 pitch 13.91-32.10
See advertisement in colour section

Siesta ☎ 977 380852
Divided into pitches and planted with young deciduous trees and old olive trees. Sunshade roofs.
➲ *If approaching from Tarragona, turn right off the main road on outskirts of Salou and drive a further 150mtrs to the camp. The site is between the railway and road 0.4km from the sea.*
16 Mar-3 Nov 6HEC ⚫⚫ ➡ ⌂ ▮ ▮ ✕ ☉ ☻ ∅ ♨ ⚓ P 🄿 ⊞ lau ➡ ⚓ ⚓S
See advertisement in colour section

Union c Pompeu Fabra 37
☎ 977 384816 ▣ 977 351444
e-mail: launion@campings.net
A well equipped site in wooded surroundings, 350mtrs from the sea.
➲ *On southern outskirts, 1km from the Port Aventura theme park.*
Apr-Sep 3.8HEC ⬛⬛ ➡ ⌂ ▮ ▮ ✕ ☉ ☻ ∅ ♨ ⚓ PS 🄿 ⊞ lau
Prices: ⚓3.60-4.85 ➡3.60-6.45 ♨4.25-7 ▲3.60-4.85

SANTA OLIVA TARRAGONA

Santa Oliva Jaume Balmes 122
☎ 977 679546 ▣ 977 679228
➲ *At Km3 on Vendrell-Santa Oliva road.*
All year 2HEC ⚫⚫ ➡ ⌂ ▮ ▮ ✕ ☉ ☻ ∅ ♨ ⚓ P 🄿 ⊞ lau ➡ ▮ ✕ ⚓S Prices: ⚓3.50 ➡3.50 ♨3.50 ▲3

TAMARIT TARRAGONA

Caledonia ☎ 977 650098 ▣ 77 652867
A well appointed site in wooded surroundings, 800mtrs from the sea.
➲ *At Km1172 on N340.*
18 Jun-20 Sept 3.5HEC ⚫⚫ ∅ ➡ ⌂ ▮ ▮ ✕ ☉ ☻ ∅ ♨ ⚓ P 🄿 ⊞ lau ➡ ⚓S

Trillas Platja Tamarit ☎ 977 650249
About 50mtrs from the sea. On several terraces planted with olive trees next to a farm.
➲ *For access, turn off the N340 at Km1.172, about 8km N of Tarragona. Follow road and cross a narrow railway bridge. (Beware of oncoming traffic).*
Apr-17 Oct 4HEC ⬛⬛ ➡ ⌂ ▮ ▮ ✕ ☉ ☻ ∅ ♨ ♨ ⚓ PRS 🄿 ⊞ lau

TARRAGONA TARRAGONA

Tamarit-Park Platja Tamarit ☎ 977 650128 ▣ 977 650451
e-mail: tamaritpark@tamarit.com
Well-kept site at the sea beneath Tamarit Castle. One section lies under tall shady trees, and a new section lies in a meadow with some trees.
➲ *Turn off N340 at Km1171.5 towards the beach, turn left at end of road.*
All year 16HEC ⬛⬛ ⚫⚫ ➡ ⌂ ▮ ▮ ✕ ☉ ☻ ∅ ♨ ⚓ ▲ ⚓ PRS 🄿
⊞ lau Prices: ⚓4.28-5.90 pitch 18.72-22
See advertisement in colour section

TORREBLANCA CASTELLÓN

Mon Rossi Carrasa Mon Rossi, Torrenostra ☎ 964 425096 ▣ 421147
All year 0.8HEC ∅ ➡ ⌂ ▮ ▮ ✕ ☉ ☻ ∅ ♨ ♨ ⚓ P 🄿 ⊞ lau ➡ ▮ ∅ ♨ ⚓S

VALENCIA VALENCIA

Saler ☎ 96 1830023 ▣ 96 1830024
Amongst pines providing shade with its own entrance to sandy beach in 300mtrs. The site has recently undergone many improvements and has modern sanitary and recreational facilities.
➲ *Access from Valencia via coastal road towards Cullera as far as El Saler, then turn left at SE end of village and turn right.*
All year 80HEC ⚫⚫ ➡ ⌂ ▮ ▮ ✕ ☉ ☻ ∅ ♨ ⚓ P 🄿 ⊞ lau ➡ ▮ ✕ ⚓LS

VENDRELL, EL TARRAGONA

San Salvador av Palfuriana 68 ☎ 977 680804 ▣ 680804
e-mail: campingsantsalvador@trx.com
On two large grassy terraces and has some sunshade roofs. Near the sea in the centre of the town.
➲ *Access via A7 exit 31 (Barcelona-Tarragona). Site in centre of Comarruga-San Salvador.*
6 Apr-Sep 2.9HEC ⚫⚫ ➡ ⌂ ▮ ▮ ✕ ☉ ☻ ∅ ♨ ♨ 🄿 ⊞ lau ➡ ⚓PS

Vendrell Platja ☎ 977 694009 ▣ 977 694106
e-mail: vendrell@camping-vendrellplatja.com
A large family site in a pleasant wooded location close to the beach.
22Mar-Sep 7.3HEC ⚫⚫ ➡ ⌂ ▮ ▮ ✕ ☉ ☻ ∅ ♨ ⚓ P 🄿 ⊞ lau ➡ ⚓S ⊞ Prices: ⚓1.35-5 ➡5 ♨5 ▲5

VILANOVA DE PRADES TARRAGONA

Serra de Prades Sant Antoni ☎ 977 869050
e-mail: serraprades@svt.es
A fine site close to the beach and within easy reach of Barcelona and the Port Aventura theme park.
All year 50HEC ⬛⬛ ➡ ⌂ ▮ ▮ ✕ ☉ ☻ ∅ ♨ ⚓ ▲ ⚓ P 🄿 ⊞ lau ➡ ▮ ✕ ∅ ♨ ⚓R Prices: ⚓4.21-4.50 ➡4.21-4.50 ♨4.21-4.50 ▲4.21-4.50 pitch 13.02-12.85

VILLAJOYOSA ALICANTE

Camping la Cala-Garoa Cala de Finestrat ☎ 96 5851461
On level ground on the seaward side of the N332. Large pitches, asphalt interior roads. Different types of trees provide shade.
➲ *On N332 at Km143.*
All year 3.3HEC ⬛⬛ ➡ ⌂ ▮ ▮ ✕ ☉ ☻ ∅ ♨ ⚓ P 🄿 ⊞ lau ➡ ⚓S

Hércules CN 332 KM 141 ☎ 96 5891343 ▣ 96 5891500
Section near sea is well shaded. Asphalt interior road, separate section for caravans with numbered pitches.
➲ *Turn E off N332 near Km141 then turn S.*
All year 6.3HEC ⚫⚫ ∅ ➡ ⌂ ▮ ▮ ✕ ☉ ☻ ∅ ♨ ♨ ⚓ PS 🄿 ⊞ lau

Sertorium N332.PK 141 ☎ 96 965891599 ▤ 96 6851114
e-mail: sertorium@ctv.es
On level ground on the seaward side of the N332. Small
stony beach, suitable for non-swimmers.
➲ *On N332 at Km141.*
All year 69.7HEC ⚓ ◔ ⋒ ☈ ☎ ✗ ⊙ ◪ ∅ ⌢ ▲ ⋋ PS ☎ ⊞ lau
Prices: ♦4.23 ⬤4.23 ⬤4.23 ▲3.20

VINAROZ CASTELLÓN

Garoa-Sol de Riu Playa ☎ 964 496356 ▤ 964 496356
In wooded surroundings close to the sea with good, modern
facilities.
All year 5.5HEC ⟱ ⚓ ◔ ⋒ ☈ ☎ ✗ ⊙ ◪ ∅ ⋋ PS ☎ ⊞ lau
Prices: ♦3.65-3.65 pitch 10.35-13.60

⬤ ⬤ ⬤ ⬤ NORTH COAST ⬤ ⬤ ⬤ ⬤

The region varies from the beaches of the Cantabrian coast
to mountain gorges, and attracts sun-lovers as well as
hikers, fishermen and outdoor enthusiasts. Of the two
coastal provinces, Cantabria has dairy farms and a huge
hunting reserve; its capital, Santander, has a cathedral and
spectacular beaches, with superb views from the
Magdalene peninsular. The Altamira caves, with wall-
paintings, are nearby. Asturias has a more rugged
countryside. Its capital, Oviedo, is a cathedral city with fine
buildings in the old quarter.
On the Pilgrim Way to Compostela lies Lugo, with its
cathedral and picturesque old quarter of ancient streets and
wrought-iron balconies. Walk around the city's perimeter
on top of encircling walls dating from Roman times.
Famous in both Spanish and British history is Corunna.
Now a bustling seaside resort and good touring centre, this
old town saw the departure of the ill-fated Spanish Armada
and has the tomb of Sir John Moore, killed in the
Napoleonic Wars. There is also a Roman lighthouse. North
east of Corunna is Ferrol, Franco's birthplace.
....

AJO-BAREYO CANTABRIA

Cabo de Ajo ctra al Faro
☎ 942 670624 ▤ 942 630725
e-mail: losmolinos@ceoecant.es
On level ground 2km from the coast.
➲ *Access via A8/E70 exit beranga Km185.*
15 Jun-15 Sep ⟱ ◔ ⋒ ☎ ⊙ ◪ ∅ ⋋ P ☎ lau ♦ ☈ ✗ ⋋S
Prices: ♦3.01 ⬤6.61 ▲3.01

BAREYO CANTABRIA

Los Molinos de Bareyo ctra Bareyo-Güemes
☎ 942 670569 ▤ 942 630725
e-mail: losmolinosdebareyo@ceoecant.es
In a quiet position with fine views.
Jun-Sep 12HEC ⟱ ◔ ⋒ ☈ ☎ ✗ ⊙ ◪ ∅ ⌢ ⋋ P ☎ ⊞ lau
♦ ⋋S Prices: ♦3.22-3.86 pitch 6.43-7.07

BARREIROS LUGO

Gaivota Playa de Barreiros ☎ 982 124451
Site leads down to a sandy beach with windsurfing. The main
buildings have been designed and built by the owner, who is
a painter.
10Jun-20Sep 1HEC ⟱ ♦ ⋒ ☈ ☎ ✗ ⊙ ◪ ∅ ⌢ ⬛ ▲
⋋ S ☎ ⊞ lau ♦ ⋋PR Prices: ♦3 ⬤3 ⬤3.50 ▲3

BERGONDO LA CORUÑA

Santa Marta ☎ 981 795826
Apr-Sept 2.8HEC ⟱ ◔ ⋒ ☈ ☎ ✗ ⊙ ◪ ∅ ⌢ ⬛ ▲
⋋ PS ☎ ⊞ lau

CADAVEDO ASTURIAS

Regalina ctra de la Playa ☎ 98 5645056 ▤ 98 5645014
e-mail: laregalina@la-regalina.com
A modern site with good facilities noted for its mountain
and sea views.
➲ *On N632 between Luarca and Avilés.*
All year 1HEC ⟱ ♦ ⋒ ☈ ☎ ✗ ⊙ ◪ ∅ ⬛ ▲ ⋋ P ☎ ⊞ lau ♦
☈ ☎ ✗ ⌢ ⋋S

CASTRO-URDIALES CANTABRIA

Castro ☎ 942 867423 ▤ 630725
e-mail: losmolinios@ceoecant.es
In a quiet location with terraces.
➲ *Access via A8 exit Castro-Urdiales Km151.*
Nov-Feb 3HEC ⟱ ◔ ⋒ ☈ ☎ ✗ ⊙ ◪ ∅ ⌢ ⋋ P ☎ ⊞ lau ♦
⋋RS Prices: ♦3.86 ▲4.50 pitch 8.36

CÓBRECES CANTABRIA

Cóbreces Playa de Cóbreces ☎ 942 725120
A peaceful site on level ground with modern facilities.
➲ *50m from the Luaña beach.*
15 Jun-15 Sep 1.5HEC ⟱ ⋇ ⋒ ☈ ☎ ⊙ ◪ ∅ ⋋ S ☎ lau

COMILLAS CANTABRIA

Comillas ctra M-Noriga ☎ 942 720074 ▤ 942 720074
Level grassland site to the right of the road to the beach.
➲ *E on C6316 at Km23.*
Jun-Sep 3HEC ⟱ ◔ ⋒ ☈ ☎ ✗ ⊙ ◪ ∅ ⋋ S ☎ ⊞ lau ♦ ✗ ⋋P

CUDILLERO ASTURIAS

Amuravela El Pito ☎ 985 590995 ▤ 985590995
e-mail: amuravela@lamuravela.com
Etr & Jun-15 Sep 2.5HEC ⟱ ◔ ⋒ ☈ ☎ ✗ ⊙ ◪ ∅ ⬛ ⋋ P ☎
⊞ lau ♦ ⌢ ⋋RS Prices: ♦3.69 ⬤3.69 ▲3.54-4.02 pitch 4.34

FOZ LUGO

San Rafael Playa de Peizas ☎ 982 132218
A small site on open, level ground 50mtrs from the beach.
➲ *2km from the town centre.*
Jul-Sep 1.2HEC ⟱ ◔ ⋒ ☈ ☎ ✗ ⊙ ◪ ∅ ⌢ ▲ ☎ ⊞ lau
♦ ⌢ ⋋LPRS

FRANCA, LA ASTURIAS

Las Hortensias Playa de la Franca
☎ 98 5412442 ▤ 98 5412153
e-mail: lashortensias@campinglashortensias.com
A well maintained site with good facilities beside the La
Franca Beach.
Jun-Sep 2.8HEC ⟱ ◔ ⋒ ☈ ☎ ✗ ⊙ ◪ ∅ ⋋ RS ☎ ⊞ lau ♦ ⌢
Prices: ♦4.02 ⬤3.92 ⬤5.34 ▲4.12

ISLARES CANTABRIA

Playa Arenillas ☎ 942 863152 ▤ 942 863152
e-mail: cueva@mundivia.es
Well equipped site in meadowland with some pine trees,
100mtrs from the beach.
➲ *On N634 at Km155.8 turn N and continue 100mtrs. The
entrance is rather steep.*
Apr-Sep 2.5HEC ⟱ ◔ ⋒ ☈ ☎ ✗ ⊙ ◪ ∅ ▲ ⋋ S ☎ ⊞ ∅ lau
Prices: ♦4.02 pitch 10.28

LAREDO CANTABRIA

Carlos V pl de Carlos V ☎ 942 605593
Camp surrounded by walls and buildings on Western
outskirts of Laredo.
➲ *Turn off N634 at Km171.6 into an avenue and drive
towards the sea. Turn left before reaching the beach and drive
around the roundabout on the plaza Carlos V.*
Apr-Oct 10HEC ⟱ ♦ ⋒ ☈ ☎ ✗ ⊙ ◪ ∅ ⬛ ⬜ ▲ ☎ ⊞ lau ♦
✗ ⌢ ⋋LPRS

▶ **LLANES** ASTURIAS

Barcenas Antigua CN 634 ☎ 98 5402887 ▤ 98 5400175
100mtrs from the town centre and beaches beside the
Carrocedo River.
➲ *SW of town beyond the hospital.*
Jun-Sep 2.2HEC ▥ ⊕ ⋒ ▙ ♀ ✕ ⊙ ▨ ⬟ ▲ ☷ ⊞ lau ♦ ✕
▵ ⇲S Prices: ⚲3.22-3.38 ♠2.90-3.22 ♠4.19-4.51 ▲4.19

Brao ☎ 98 5400014
A terraced site surrounded by trees with magnificent
mountain and sea views
➲ *0.5km from the sea. At Km96.2 on N634 turn N for 1.8km
and turn towards Cue for 200m.*
Jun-Sep 27HEC ▥ ♦ ⋒ ▙ ♀ ✕ ⊙ ▨ ⬟ ⇲ PRS ☷ ⊞ lau

Palacio de Garaña ☎ 98 5410075
e-mail: info@campingpalacio.com
Situated in the grounds of the former Palace of the Marquis
of Argüelles, the site is enclosed by stone walls and has good
facilities.
1 May-15 Sept 2.8HEC ▥ ⊕ ⋒ ▙ ♀ ✕ ⊙ ▨ ⬟ ▵ ⬤ ♠ ⇲
PRS ☷ ⊞ lau

▶ **LUARCA** ASTURIAS

Cantiles ☎ 98 5640938 ▤ 985640938
e-mail: cantiles@conectia.net
Meadowland beautifully situated high above the cliffs with
little shade from bushes. Footpath to bay 70mtrs below.
➲ *At Km308.5 turn off the N634 from Oviedo, turn towards
Faro de Luarca beyond the Firestone filling station. In Villar de
Luarca turn right and onwards 1km to site.*
All year 2.3HEC ▥ ⊕ ⋒ ▙ ♀ ✕ ⊙ ▨ ⬟ ▵ ☷ ⊞ lau ♦ ✕
⇲PRS ⊞ Prices: ⚲3.38 ♠3.86 ▲3.54

▶ **MOTRICO (MUTRIKU)** GUIPÚZCOA

Aitzeta ☎ 943 603356
On two sloping meadows, partially terraced. Lovely view of
the sea 1km away.
➲ *0.5km NE on C6212 turn at KmSS56.1.*
All year 1.5HEC ▥ ♦ ⋒ ▙ ♀ ✕ ⊙ ▨ ⬟ ⇲ S ⊞ lau ♦ ✕
Prices: ⚲3.35 pitch 7.21

▶ **NOJA** CANTABRIA

Los Molinos c,la Ria S/N ☎ 942 630426 ▤ 630325
e-mail: losmolinos@ceoecant.es
In pleasant surroundings close to the Esmerald Coast with its
fine beaches. Various leisure and sports activities.
Nov-Feb 18HEC ▥ ⊕ ⋒ ▙ ♀ ✕ ⊙ ▨ ⬟ ⇲ P ☷ ⊞ lau ♦
⇲RS Prices: ⚲3.22-4.18 pitch 6.43-9

Playa Joyel Playa de Ris ☎ 942 630081 ▤ 942 631294
e-mail: campingplayajoyel@yahoo.es
On a level meadow on a peninsula with direct access to the
beach.
➲ *Between Laredo and Solares.*
Jul-Aug Oct-20 Mar 24HEC ▥ ⊕ ⋒ ▙ ♀ ✕ ⊙ ▨ ⬟ ⇲
PS ☷ ⊞ ⊗ lau ♦ ▵ Prices: ⚲3.70-5.50 pitch 9.90-11.70

▶ **ORIO** GUIPÚZCOA

CM Playa de Orio ☎ 943 834801 ▤ 943 133433
e-mail: kanpina@telefonica.net
On two flat terraces along cliffs and surrounded by hedges.
➲ *Turn off the N634 San Sebastian-Bilbao road at about
Km12.5 in Orio. Shortly before the bridge over the River Orio
turn towards the sea and continue for 1.5km.*
Closed 2 Nov-6 Jan 5.4HEC ▥ ⊱ ⋒ ▙ ♀ ✕ ⊙ ▨ ⬟ ⇲ P ☷
⊞ ⊗ lau ♦ ⇲RS Prices: ⚲2.30-3.67 pitch 13.60-22.55

▶ **PECHÓN** CANTABRIA

Arenas ☎ 942 717188
On numerous terraces between rocks, reaching down to the
sea.
➲ *Turn off N634 E of Unquera at Km74 towards sea and take
road towards S.*
Jun-Sep 10HEC ▥ ⋮⋮⋮ ⊕ ⋒ ▙ ♀ ✕ ⊙ ▨ ⬟ ⬤ ⇲ PRS ☷ ⊞
lau

▶ **PERLORA-CANDAS** ASTURIAS

Perlora ☎ 98 5870048
On top of a large hill on a peninsula with a few terraced
pitches.
➲ *Access 7km W of Gijon, turn off N632 in direction Luanco
and continue for 5km.*
All year 1.4HEC ▥ ⊱ ⋒ ▙ ♀ ✕ ⊙ ▨ ⬟ ⇲ S ☷ ⊞ lau ♦ ▵

▶ **REINANTE** LUGO

Reinante ☎ 982 134005
Longish site beyond a range of dunes on lovely sandy beach.
➲ *On N634 at Km391.7.*
All year ▥ ⊱ ⋒ ▙ ♀ ✕ ⊙ ▨ ⬟ ⇲ S ☷ ⊞ lau Prices:
⚲2.55 ♠2.55 ♠2.85 ▲2.85

▶ **SAN SEBASTIÁN (DONOSTIA)** GUIPÚZCOA

▶ At **IGUELDO**

Garoa Camping Igueldo ☎ 943 214502 ▤ 943 280411
Terraced site on Monte Igualdo divided by hedges.
➲ *Follow signs Monte Igualdo from town, and beach road,
about 4.5km.*
All year 5HEC ▥ ⊕ ⋒ ▙ ♀ ✕ ⊙ ▨ ⬟ ☷ ⊞ lau

▶ **SANTIAGO DE COMPOSTELA** LA CORUÑA

As Cancelas r do 25 de Xulls 35 ☎ 981 580266 ▤ 981 575553
All year 1.8HEC ▥ ♦ ⋒ ▙ ♀ ✕ ⊙ ▨ ⬟ ⬤ ▲ ⇲ P ☷ ⊞ lau

▶ **SANTILLANA DEL MAR** CANTABRIA

Santillana ☎ 942 818250 ▤ 942 840183
e-mail: campingsantillana@ceocatnt.es
Slightly sloping meadow with bushes on a hillock set in a
restaurant area adjoining a swimming pool.
➲ *Access from Santander via C6316 turn off shortly after the
Santillana sign and continue up the hill.*
All year 70HEC ▥ ♦ ⋒ ▙ ♀ ✕ ⊙ ▨ ⬟ ⬤ ♠ ▲ ⇲ P ☷ ⊞
lau

▶ **VALDOVIÑO** LA CORUÑA

Valdoviño ctra Ferrol-Cederia ☎ 981 487076 ▤ 981 486131
Six gently sloping fields partly in shade. Located behind
Cafeteria Andy and block of flats with several villas beyond.
➲ *Turn off the C646 towards Cedeira seawards and continue
700m to site.*
All year 2HEC ▥ ♦ ⋒ ▙ ♀ ✕ ⊙ ▨ ⬟ ▵ ⬤ ☷ ⊞ lau ♦
⇲LPRS

▶ **VIVEIRO** LUGO

Vivero ☎ 982 560004
In tall woodland near beach road and sea.
➲ *Turn off the C642 Barreois-Ortueire road at Km443.1 and
follow signs.*
Jun-Sep 1.2HEC ▥ ♦ ⊙ ▨ ⬟ ⬟ ☷ ⊞ lau ♦ ▙ ♀ ✕ ⇲RS
Prices: ⚲3.21 ♠3.21 ♠4.07 ▲3.21

▶ **ZARAUZ (ZARAUTZ)** GUIPÚZCOA

Talai Mendi ☎ 943 830042
In meadowland on hillside divided by interior roads without
shade. 0.5km from the sea.

Cont.

⮕ *On outskirts of town at FIRESTONE filling station at Km17.5 on N634 turn towards the sea and continue for 350m along narrow asphalt road.*
Jul-10 Sep 3.8HEC ⸺ ⚊ ⌂ ⚏ ♕ ✕ ⊙ ☺ ∅ ⤢ S 🅿 ⊞ ➧ ⭍PR

Zarauz Monte "Talai-Mendi" Mountain
☎ 943 831238 ▤ 943 132486
Site with terraces separated by hedges.
⮕ *1.8km from the N634 San Sebastian-Bilbao road. Asphalt access road from Km15.5.*
All year 5HEC ⸺ ⚏ ⌂ ⚏ ♕ ✕ ⊙ ☺ ∅ ⤢ ▲ 🅿 ⊞ lau ➧ ⭍RS
Prices: ⭍3.62 ⭍3.62 ⭍4.26 ▲4.26

● ● ● ● ● NORTH EAST ● ● ● ●

Medieval villages, green valleys, forests, and arid gorges are some of this region's varied attractions.
Tranquil Burgos, with its pleasant river setting and old centre, was Franco's capital during the Civil War. The principal city of Castille has a magnificent Gothic cathedral which reflects its importance on the Pilgrim Way to Compostela and contains the tomb of the legendary El Cid.
The city of Saragossa lies in a fertile pocket. Its basilica contains a national shrine to the Virgin of the Pillar. The province of the same name contains Spain's largest natural inland lake and is a great attraction for ornithologists.
Beautiful scenery surrounds the pleasant cathedral city of Huesca. Nearby Loarre Castle is a wonderful medieval fortress; superb views can be had from its rocky heights and the amazing grotto site of the Monastery of San Juan de la Peña.
Lush valleys and Pyrennean crags are just two faces of Navarre. Its ancient capital, Pamplona, is notorious for the Running of the Bulls each morning during its week-long fiesta celebrations in July. Wine lovers will be attracted to La Rioja - an area renowned for its fine wines.
....

▶ **ARANDA DE DUERO** BURGOS

Costajàn ☎ 947 502070
In a wooded setting with good facilities.
⮕ *Turn off N1 (Burgos-Madrid) at Km162.1 N of town.*
All year 1.8HEC ⸱⸱⸱ ⚏ ⌂ ⚏ ♕ ✕ ⊙ ☺ ∅ ⤢ ⤢ ⭍ P 🅿 ⊞ lau ➧ ⚏ ✕ ⸺ ⭍LR

▶ **BELLVER DE CERDANYA** LLEIDA

Solana del Segre ☎ 973 510310 ▤ 973 510698
e-mail: webmaster@cerdanyne.com
A well equipped site on the River Segre, known for its trout fishing.
⮕ *Off N260.*
All year 6.5HEC ⸺ ♣ ⌂ ⚏ ♕ ✕ ⊙ ☺ ∅ ⤢ ⤢ ⭍ PR 🅿 ⊞ lau ➧ ⭍L

▶ **BIESCAS** HUESCA

Edelweiss ☎ 974 485084
In meadow with deciduous trees on a hill in a pleasant situation.
⮕ *Turn right off C138 at Km97.*
15 Jun-15 Sep 50HEC ⸺ ♣ ⌂ ⚏ ♕ ✕ ⊙ ☺ ∅ 🅿 ⊞ lau ➧ ⭍PR

▶ **BONANSA** HUESCA

Baliera Cruce ctra Castejon Desos ☎ 974 554016 ▤ 554099
e-mail: info@baliera.com
A well equipped site in a beautiful Pyrenean location on the bank of a river.
⮕ *At Km365.5 on N260.*
All year 5HEC ⸺ ♣ ⌂ ⚏ ♕ ✕ ⊙ ☺ ∅ ⤢ ⭍ LPR 🅿 ⊞ lau

▶ **BORDETA, LA** LLEIDA

Prado Verde ☎ 973 647172 ▤ 973 640456
e-mail: euroci@hotmail.com
Level meadowland on River Garona with sparse trees and sheltered by high hedges from traffic noise.
⮕ *On the N230, Puente de Rey (French border)-Lleida road, at Km199 behind Pirelli General filling station.*
All year 1.7HEC ♣ ⌂ ⚏ ♕ ✕ ⊙ ☺ ∅ ⤢ ⭍ LPR 🅿 ⊞ lau
Prices: ⭍3.90 ⭍3.90 ▲3.90

▶ **BOSSOST** LLEIDA

Bedurá-Park ☎ 73 648293 ▤ 73 648293
e-mail: bedurapk@ibercom.com
A terraced site in the Aran Valley offering spectacular views over the surrounding mountains. The site, in wooded surroundings, offers all modern facilities and a wide variety of sporting opportunities.
⮕ *Access via N230 Km174.4.*
Apr-15 Sep 5HEC ⸺ ♣ ⌂ ⚏ ♕ ✕ ⊙ ☺ ∅ ⤢ ⤢ ⭍ PR 🅿 ⊞ ⤢ lau

▶ **CALATAYUD** ZARAGOZA

Calatayud ctra Madrid-Barcelona ☎ 976 880592
15 Mar-15 Oct 1.7HEC ⸺ ⚏ ⌂ ⚏ ♕ ✕ ⊙ ☺ ∅ ⭍ P 🅿 ⊞ lau ➧ ✕

▶ **CASTAÑARES DE RIOJA** LA RIOJA

Rioja ctra Haro a Sto Domingo de la, Calzada ☎ 941 300174
A well appointed site on the banks of the River Oja with a private beach.
21 Jun-21 Sep 10HEC ⸺ ⚏ ♣ ⌂ ⚏ ♕ ✕ ⊙ ☺ ∅ ⭍ PR 🅿 ⊞ lau ➧ ⭍PR

▶ **ESPOT** LLEIDA

Sol I Neu ctra d'Espot ☎ 973 624001 ▤ 973 624001
e-mail: camping@solineu.com
A peaceful site in a beautiful mountain setting with good, modern facilities. Organised Land Rover excursions available.
Jun-Sep 1.5HEC ⸺ ♣ ⌂ ⚏ ♕ ✕ ⊙ ☺ ∅ ⭍ PR 🅿 ⊞ lau ➧ ✕ ⭍L Prices: ⭍3.91 ⭍3.91 ⭍3.91 ▲3.91

▶ **ESTELLA** NAVARRA

Lizarra Paraje de Ordoiz ☎ 948 551733 ▤ 948 554755
All year 40HEC ⸺ ⚏ ⌂ ⚏ ♕ ✕ ⊙ ☺ ∅ ⤢ ▲ ⭍ P 🅿 ⊞ lau

▶ **GUINGUETA, LA** LLEIDA

Vall d'Aneu ☎ 973 626390
In meadowland on rising ground on both sides of the road, partially in shade. No shade on terrace between road and lake.
⮕ *On outskirts of town near the by-pass, C147.*
May-Sep 0.5HEC ⸺ ♣ ⌂ ⚏ ♕ ✕ ⊙ ☺ ⤢ ⭍ P 🅿 ⊞ lau ➧ ⚏ ✕ ∅ ⭍LR Prices: ⭍3-4 ⭍3-4 ⭍3-4 ▲3-4

▶ **HECHO** HUESCA

Selva de Osa Selva de Osa ☎ 974 375168
On meadowland, partly covered with pines and deciduous trees and between a dirt track and a mountain stream.
⮕ *12.5km NE towards Espata.*
15 Jun-15 Sep 2HEC ⸺ ♣ ⌂ ⚏ ♕ ✕ ⊙ ☺ ∅ ⭍ R 🅿 ⊞ lau

▶ **HUESCA** HUESCA

San Jorge Ricardo del Arco ☎ 974 227416
Site with sports field surrounded by high walls. Subdivided by hedges, sparse woodland.
⮕ *From town centre, about 1.5km along M123 towards Zaragoza direction and follow signs.*
Apr-15 Oct 0.7HEC ⸺ ⚏ ⌂ ⚏ ♕ ✕ ⊙ ☺ ∅ ⭍ P 🅿 ⊞ lau ➧ ⚏ ∅
Prices: ⭍3.53 ⭍3.53 ▲3.53

Camping *Caravaning*

ERROTA - EL MOLiNO

Your first class site next to Pamplona!

With a capicity fort 1.500 camper, divided in hedged pitches and free ones; all with conn. for electr., water and waste water. Bungalows and mobile homes for hire. Hostel with bunk beds and pecial prices f. full- and half board. Free hot water. Situated in the centre of Navarra, ideal for excursions to the Pyrenees, the Irati forest (second largest forest of Europe) and the Bardenas Reales (half-desert): all declared protected nature reserves.

MENDIGORRIA . NAVARRA
Tel. (34) 948 34 06 04 . Fax (34) 948 34 00 82
e-mail: molino@cmn.navarra.net
web: www.navarra.net/molino

JACA HUESCA

At GUASA

Peña Oroel ctra Jaca-Sabiñanigo ☎ 974 360215
Grassland site with rows of high poplars.
➲ *At Km13.8 of the C134 Jaca-Sabiñanigo road.*
15 Jun-15 Sep 50HEC ⸜⸜⸜⸜ ♦ ⌂ ⚊ ⚌ ⛱ ✗ ☉ ⚑ ∅
⚡ P ⌦ ⊞ lau

LABUERDA HUESCA

Peña Montañesa ctra Aínsa-Francia,KM2
☎ 974 500032 ▤ 500991
e-mail: info@penamontanesa.com
A well equipped family site in a wooded location near the entrance to the Ordesa and Monte Perdido National Park.
All year 7HEC ⸜⸜⸜⸜ ♦ ⌂ ⚊ ⚌ ⛱ ✗ ☉ ⚑ ∅ ⛺ ⚑ ⚡ P ⌦ ⊞ lau ➤
⚡LR Prices: ⋔5 pitch 14

MENDIGORRIA NAVARRA

El Molino ctra N111 ☎ 948 340604 ▤ 948 340082
e-mail: molino@cmn.navaua.net
All year 15HEC ⸜⸜⸜⸜ ⚊ ♦ ⌂ ⚊ ⚌ ⛱ ✗ ☉ ⚑ ∅ ⛺ ⚑ PR ⌦
⊞ lau ➤ ⚊ ⚡R

NÁJERA LA RIOJA

Ruedo ps San Julian 24 ☎ 941 360102
Amongst poplars and the area of the bullring, almost no shade.
➲ *Turn off the N120 Logroño-Burgos road in Nájera and then continue along the river banks just before the stone bridge across the River Majerilla, then turn left.*
Apr-10 Oct 0.5HEC ⸜⸜⸜⸜ ⚊ ⌂ ⚊ ⚌ ⛱ ✗ ☉ ⚑ ∅ ⌦ ⊞ lau
➤ ⚊ ⚡PR

NUEVALOS ZARAGOZA

Lago Park ctra Alhama de Aragón-Nuevalos ☎ 976 849038
In a pleasant location, 100mtrs from the Laguna de la Tranquera.
➲ *NE towards Alhama de Aragon.*
Apr-Sep 3HEC ⸜⸜⸜⸜ ♦ ♦ ⌂ ⚊ ⚌ ⛱ ✗ ☉ ⚑ ∅ ⚑ ⚊ ⚡ LPR ⌦ ⊞ lau

ORICAIN NAVARRA

Ezcaba ctra Francia-Irun km7 ☎ 948 330315 ▤ 948 331316
Gently sloping meadowland and a few terraces on a flat topped hill.
➲ *N of Pamplona. Turn off N121 at Km7.3 and drive towards Berriosuso. Turn right and drive uphill after crossing the bridge over the River Ulzama.*
May-Sep 2HEC ⸜⸜⸜⸜ ⚊ ⌂ ⚊ ⚌ ⛱ ✗ ☉ ⚑ ∅ ⚌ ⚑ ⚊ ⚡ PR ⌦ ⊞
lau ➤ ⚡R Prices: ⋔3.52 ⚗3.52 ⚑4.33 ⋀3.52

PANCORBO BURGOS

Desfiladero ☎ 947 354027
A well appointed site close to the river.
➲ *Off N1 at Km305.2.*
All year 13HEC ⸜⸜⸜⸜ ♦ ⚊ ⌂ ⚊ ⚌ ⛱ ✗ ☉ ⚑ ⚑ ⚑ ⚡ P ⌦ ⊞ lau
➤ ⚡R

PUEBLA DE CASTRO, LA HUESCA

Lago de Barasona crta Nacional 123
☎ 974 545148 ▤ 974545228
e-mail: info@lagobarasona.com
A well equipped, terraced site in a beautiful setting beside the lake and backed by mountains.
Apr-Sep 3HEC ⸜⸜⸜⸜ ⚊ ⌂ ⚊ ⚌ ⛱ ✗ ☉ ⚑ ∅ ⚑ ⚑ ⚡ P ⌦ ⊞ lau ➤
⚡LR Prices: ⋔5.19 ⚗5.19 ⚑5.19 ⋀5.19

RIBERA DE CARDÓS LLEIDA

Cardós ☎ 973 623112
Long stretch of meadowland divided by four rows of poplars.
Camping Card Compulsory.
➲ *Near the electricity plant in Llavorsi turn NE onto the Ribera road and follow it for 9km. Entrance near hostel Soly Neu.*
Apr-Sep 3HEC ⸜⸜⸜⸜ ⚊ ⌂ ⚊ ⚌ ⛱ ✗ ☉ ⚑ ∅ ⚑ ⚑ ⋀ ⚡ PR ⌦ ⊞
lau Prices: ⋔4.06 ⚑4.06 ⋀4.06

SANTO DOMINGO DE LA CALZADA LA RIOJA

Bañares ☎ 941 342804 ▤ 941 340131
All year 12HEC ⸜⸜⸜⸜ ♦ ⌂ ⚊ ⚌ ⛱ ✗ ☉ ⚑ ∅ ⚌ ⚑ ⚑ ⋀ ⚡ P ⌦ ⊞
lau

SAVIÑAN ZARAGOZA

Saviñan Park ☎ 976 825423 ▤ 976 825423
On meadowland in the Jalón Valley. Plenty of trees for shade.
➲ *Access via NII Zaragoza-Calatayud, exit El Frasno towards Illueca.*
All year 6HEC ⸜⸜⸜⸜ ♦ ⌂ ⚊ ⚌ ⛱ ✗ ☉ ⚑ ∅ ⚡ P

SOLSONA LLEIDA

Solsonès ☎ 973 482861 ▤ 973 481300
e-mail: info@campingsolsones.com
A well equipped site in a picturesque mountain setting with facilities for both summer and winter holidays.
All year 6.3HEC ⸜⸜⸜⸜ ♦ ⌂ ⚊ ⚌ ⛱ ✗ ☉ ⚑ ∅ ⚌ ⚑ ⋀ ⚡ P ⌦ ⊞
⚌ lau ➤ ⚡LR

TIERMAS ZARAGOZA

Mar del Pirineo ☎ 948 398073 ▤ 887177
e-mail: aytosigues@teleline.es
On broad terraces sloping down to the banks of the Embalse de Yese. Roofing provides shade for tents and cars.
➲ *Situated on the N240 Huesca-Pamplona road at Km317.7.*

Cont.

May-Sep 2.9HEC ▥ ∷∷ ✦ ⬢ ⋔ ♨ ♟ ✕ ☉ ♥ ∅ ⬛
⋟ LP ☎ ⊞ lau

▶ TORLA HUESCA

Ordesa ctra de Ordesa ☎ 974 486146 ▤ 974 486381
e-mail: hotelordesa@ibercom.com
On three terraces between well-kept hedges.
⮑ *2km N of the village at Km96 and N of the C138.*
Closed Nov-Xmas 3.5HEC ▥ ✦ ⋔ ♨ ✕ ☉ ♥ ∅
⋟ P ☎ ⊞ lau ✦ ⋟R

▶ VILLOSLADA DE CAMEROS LA RIOJA

Los Cameros ctra La Virgen
☎ 941 468195 ▤ 941 468195
Situated in the National Park of the Sierra Cebollera in the
Iberian mountain range.
⮑ *Access via N111, turn off 50km before Logroño towards
Soria and on to Villoslada.*
All year 4HEC ▥ ✦ ⋔ ♨ ✕ ☉ ♥ ∅ ▲

NORTH WEST

In this region of contrasts are beautiful green valleys,
rugged mountains still inhabited by bears and wolves, a
wealth of historic monuments, fine resorts such as Bayona,
and quiet fishing villages. This is Galicia, a land of mild
climate mostly bordered by the Atlantic - a celtic land with
strong traditions, local costume, bagpipes and drums.
The regional capital, Santiago de Compostela, was once the
most visited city in Europe, ranking alongside Rome and
Jerusalem. The pilgrimage tradition lives on in its cathedral
- one of the finest in the world - and the architecture it
inspired on the Pilgrim Way.
This legacy has left a wealth of historic monuments, such as
the magnificent cathedral at Léon, with its wonderful
stained glass. Mountains form the backdrop to Orense, with
its fine cathedral and interesting museums, while a green
valley is the setting for Pontevedra. Here, in the old town,
lie a fascinating museum and cathedral, and houses bearing
armorial badges and narrow streets, just as they were
hundreds of years ago.
....

▶ BAIONA PONTEVEDRA

Baiona Playa ctra Vigo-Baionna
☎ 986 350035 ▤ 352952
e-mail: campingbayona@bme.es
On a long sandy peninsula on the Galicia coast with direct
access to the beach. The site has good, modern facilities and a
variety of watersports can be enjoyed there.
All year 4HEC ▥ ✦ ⋔ ♨ ✕ ☉ ♥ ∅ ⛺ ⬛ ♥
⋟ PRS ☎ ⊞ lau

▶ CUBILLAS DE SANTA MARTA VALLADOLID

Cubillas ☎ 983 585002 ▤ 983 585016
e-mail: campingcubillas@verial.es
Meadowland with young trees, subdivided by hedges.
⮑ *Entrance on the right of the N620 from Burgos between
Km100 & 101.*
All year 4HEC ▥ ✦ ⬢ ⋔ ♨ ♟ ✕ ☉ ♥ ∅ ⛺ ⬛ ♥
⋟ P ☎ ⊞ lau ✦ ⋟R

▶ LEIRO ORENSE

Leiro ☎ 988 488036
On level meadow in a pine forest in a valley by a stream,
behind the football ground.
Closed Nov 1.8HEC ▥ ♨ ⋔ ♨ ✕ ☉ ♥ ∅ ⬛
⋟ R ☎ ⊞ lau

▶ NIGRÁN PONTEVEDRA

Playa America ☎ 986 365404 ▤ 365404
e-mail: oficina@campingplayaamerica.com
A modern site in a poplar wood, 300mtrs from a magnificent
beach.
⮑ *Access at Km 9.250 on the Vigo-Bayona road.*
15 Jun-15 Sep 4HEC ▥ ✦ ⋔ ♨ ♟ ✕ ☉ ♥ ∅ ∺ ⬛ ⋟ PS ☎
⊞ lau ✦ ⋟R

▶ PORTONOVO PONTEVEDRA

Paxariñas ☎ 986-72 723055
Slightly sloping towards a bay, in amongst dunes, with high
pines and young deciduous trees. Lovely beach.
Camping Card Compulsory.
All year 3HEC ▥ ✦ ⋔ ♨ ♟ ✕ ☉ ♥ ∅ ♥ ▲ ⋟ S ☎ ⊞ lau

▶ SANTA MARINA DE VALDEON LÉON

El Cares ☎ 987 742676
In a wooded mountain setting with good facilities.
⮑ *N off N621 from Portilla de la Reina.*
Jun-Oct 15HEC ▥ ⬢ ⋔ ♨ ♟ ✕ ☉ ∅ ⛺ ⬛ ♥ ▲ ☎ ⊞ lau
✦ ⋟LR

▶ SAN VICENTE DO MAR PONTEVEDRA

Siglo XXI ☎ 986 738100 ▤ 986 738113
e-mail: info@campingsiglo21.com
A popular modern site with individual sanitary facilities
attached to each pitch.
25 Jun- 15 Sep 1.5HEC ▥ ⬢ ⋔ ♨ ♟ ✕ ☉ ♥ ∅ ⋟ PS ☎ ⊞
lau ✦ ⋟S Prices: ♦3.90-4.20 pitch 10.20-15.60

▶ SIMANCAS VALLADOLID

Plantió ☎ 983 590082
In a poplar wood, on the river bank.
⮑ *On outskirts turn off N620 at Km132.2 and continue 500m
on narrow asphalt road and a long single track stone bridge
over the River Pisverga.*
15 Jun-25 Sep 1HEC ▥ ∷∷ ✦ ⋔ ♨ ♟ ✕ ☉ ♥ ∅ ∺ ▲ ⋟ PR
☎ ⊞ lau ✦ ∺

▶ TORDESILLAS VALLADOLID

Astral Camino de Pollos 8 ☎ 983 770953 ▤ 983 770953
e-mail: info@campingelastral.com
A well equipped site in a pleasant rural location close to the
River Duero.
⮑ *Leave motorway at Tordesillas exit and follow signs.*
Apr-Sep 3HEC ▥ ∷∷ ⬢ ⋔ ♨ ♟ ✕ ☉ ♥ ∅ ⬛ ⋟ P ☎ ⊞ lau
✦ ∺ ⋟R Prices: ♦2.89-4.05 ♦2.47-3.48 ♦2.89-4.05
▲2.89-4.05

▶ VALENCIA DE DON JUAN LÉON

Pico Verde c Santas Martas 18 ☎ 987 750525 ▤ 987 750525
e-mail: campingpicoverde@terra.es
⮑ *Turn E off the N630 (Léon-Madrid) at Km32.2 and
continue for 4km.*
15 Jun-13 Sep 2.7HEC ▥ ⬢ ⋔ ♨ ♟ ✕ ☉ ♥ ∅ ⋟ P ☎ ⊞ lau
✦ ⋟R Prices: ♦3 ♦3 ♦3 ▲3

▶ VILLAMEJIL LÉON

Rio Tuerto ☎ 908 226998
Jun-Aug 0.6HEC ▥ ✦ ⋔ ♨ ♟ ✕ ☉ ♥ ∅ ▲ ⋟ R ☎ ⊞ lau

**A Guide to Caravan & Camping
in Great Britain is also available
from The AA**

SOUTH

Forbidding crags, dry river beds, spectacular snow-capped mountains, terraced olive groves, flamenco and some of Spain's finest historic cities, draw the visitor to the Andalusian south , a region with attractions as varied as itself.
The amazing backdrop of the Sierra Nevada towers over lovely Granada and its palace-fortress, the Alhambra. The Moorish heritage of ancient Córdoba is proclaimed by its astonishing mosque-cathedral - one of the glories of Spain. Inside the dazzlingly beautiful mosque's forest of archways and columns, sits a Gothic cathedral. The wonderful gardens of a 14th-century castle are nearby.
Bullfights and carnival are part of the excitement of Cádiz.
In Seville, Easter week sees the procession of penitents while, in May, colourful celebrations drawing vast numbers from throughout Spain, mark the El Rocío pilgrimage.
The isolation of much of Andalusia contrasts with the better- known hectic charms of the coast, which draws sun-seekers and pleasure-lovers to the resorts of Marbella, Málaga and many more.

ADRA ALMERIA

Las Gaviotas ☎ 950 400660 ▦ 400660
A modern site close to the beach with good facilities.
➲ 2km W on N340 (Almeria-Málaga)
All year 2HEC ⊠⊠ ♠♠⌂▒♥✗⊙▣⌀▦♨▲
♦ PS 🏛🕀 lau ♦♦PS

Habana ☎ 950 522127
A quiet site with good facilities and direct access to the sea.
➲ 2km W at Km58.3 on N340 (Almeria-Málaga).
All year 1.5HEC ⊠⊠ ♠♠⌂▒♥✗⊙▣⌀▲♦ S 🏛🕀 lau

AGUILAS MURCIA

Calarreona ctra de Aguilas a Vera
☎ 968 413704 ▦ 968 413704
A quiet site, 50m from the sea.
➲ Near Km4 on N332 (Aguilas-Murcia).
All year 3.6HEC ⊠⊠ ⌂♠⌂▒♥✗⊙▣⌀♦ S 🏛🕀 lau

ALCAZARES, LOS MURCIA

Cartagonova ☎ 968 575100 ▦ 968 575225
➲ On CN332 between Los Alcazares and La Union.
All year 30HEC ⊠⊠ ⌂♠⌂▒♥⊙▣⌀♨▲♦ PS 🏛🕀 lau
♦✗♨

ALMAYATE MÁLAGA

Almayate Costa ☎ 952 556289 ▦ 952 556310
e-mail: almayatecosta@campings.net

CAMPING ALMAYATE COSTA
29749 Almayate (Málaga)
**Autovía del Mediterráneo,
exit nº 258, direction Almería
(old National Road 340, km 267)**

**DIRECT ACCESS TO
THE BEACH and with
SWIMMING POOL**

Tel 952 55 62 89
MÁLAGA

Quiet camping with 234 pitches and family atmosphere. 90% of the camping with shade. Excellent service: bar, with terrace, supermarket, laundry and children's playground. Dogs not allowed in July and August. **Open: 1.4 till 30.9.**

Apr-Sep 2.4HEC ⊞⊞ ⊠⊠ ▒▒♠⌂▒♥✗⊙▣⌀
♦ P 🏛🕀 lau ♦ ♦S

ALMERIMAR ALMERIA

Mar Azul Playa de San Miguel ☎ 950 497505 ▦ 950 497294
e-mail: info@campingmarazul.com
On level ground surrounded by palm trees and tamarins. Sports and recreational facilities available.
➲ 6km from village.
All year 22HEC ▒▒▒ ⊠⊠ ⌂♠⌂▒♥✗⊙▣⌀▣▲♦ PS 🏛
🕀 lau Prices: ♠3.34-4.65 ♠3.34-4.65 ▣3.34-4.65 ▲3.34-4.65

BAÑOS DE FORTUNA MURCIA

Fuente ☎ 968 685125
A camping ground within a hotel complex with individual bathroom facilities attached to each pitch and good recreational facilities.
➲ Take C3223 from Fortuna à Pinoso to Balncario de Fortuna. Signposted.
All year 1.9HEC ⊠⊠ ▒▒♠⌂▒♥✗⊙▣⌀♨♦ LP 🏛🕀 lau

Las Palmeras ☎ 968 685123
Camping Card Compulsory.
All year ⊠⊠ ▒▒⌂♠⌂▒♥✗⊙▣⌀♨♦ P 🏛🕀 lau

BOLNUEVO MURCIA

Garoa Camping Playa de Mazarrón
☎ 968 150660 ▦ 968 150837
On level ground divided by a footpath and partly bordered by palm trees.
➲ Turn W off N332 in Puerto de Mazarrón at approx Km111 and head towards Bolnuevo. Then take the MU road and drive 4.6km to site entrance which is 1km E of Punta Bela.
01 Apr-15 Sep 8.5HEC ⊠⊠ ♦♠⌂▒♥✗⊙▣⌀♦ PS 🏛🕀 lau Prices: ♠3.45 pitch 12.25 (incl 2 persons)

CARCHUNA GRANADA

Don Cactus Carchuna-Motril ☎ 958 623109 ▦ 958 624294
e-mail: camping@doncactus.com
Modern site adjoining the beach. Dogs not allowed in July and August.
➲ At Km343 on N340 (Carchuna-Motril).
All year 4HEC ⊠⊠ ♦♠⌂▒♥✗⊙▣⌀▣♦ PS 🏛🕀 lau

CARLOTA, LA CORDOBA

Carlos III ☎ 957 300697 ▦ 957 3000697
e-mail: campingcarlos@naugalia.com
In wooded surroundings with modern facilities.
➲ Access via 'La Carlota' exit on NIV.
All year 9HEC ⊠⊠ ♦♠⌂▒♥✗⊙▣⌀♨▣♦ LP 🏛🕀 lau
♦♨

CASTILLO DE BAÑOS GRANADA

Castillo de Baños Castillo de Baños, La Mamola
☎ 958 829528 ▦ 958 829768
e-mail: castillo@doucactus.com
Well equipped site next to the beach.
➲ At Km360 on N340 (Castillo de Baños-La Mamola).
All year 3HEC ⊠⊠ ♦♠⌂▒♥✗⊙▣⌀♨♦ PS 🏛🕀 lau

CONIL DE LA FRONTERA CÁDIZ

Fuente del Gallo Fuente del Gallo
☎ 956 440137 ▦ 956 442036
A well equipped site in a wooded location 300m from the beach.
➲ Signposted from N340, Km21.6.
Apr-3 Oct 3HEC ▒▒▒ ⌂♠⌂▒♥✗⊙▣⌀▲♦ P 🏛🕀 lau
♦♦S

Roche Pago del Zorro ☎ 956 442216 ▤ 956 440170
Spread among pine groves with well defined pitches close to the beach.
All year 3.3HEC ▦ ∷ ♦ℝ🏊♀✕⊙🖙𝚊🛏 ᒀ P ☎⊞ lau ➡ ᒀS ⊞

ESTEPONA MÁLAGA

Parque Tropical ☎ 95 2793618 ▤ 95 2793618
A modern site situated at the foot of the Sierra Bermeja mountains, five minutes walk from the sea.
➲ *Access via N340 at Km162.*
All year 12.4HEC ♦🔌ℝ🏊♀✕⊙🖙𝚊🛏🍴 ᒀ P ☎⊞ lau ➡ ᒀRS Prices: ⚑3.50-4.18 ➡3.50-3.83 ⚑4.02-5.46 ▲4.02-5.46

FUENGIROLA MÁLAGA

Calazul Mijas Costa ☎ 95 2493219
A level site in a pleasant rural location with good recreational facilities, 300mtrs from the sea.
➲ *Exit from C340 at Km200.*
All year 5HEC ▦ ∷ 🔌ℝ🏊♀✕⊙🖙𝚊🛏 ᒀ P ☎⊞ lau ➡ ᒀS

GALLARDOS, LOS ALMERIA

Gallardos ☎ 950 528324 ▤ 950 528324
e-mail: questions@almeriaonline.com
Level site with individual pitches, 1km from the sea and 10km from the old Moorish village of Mojacar. English management.
➲ *500m from km 525 on CN340.*
All year 3.5HEC 🔌ℝ🏊♀✕⊙🖙𝚊🍴🛏 ᒀ P ☎⊞ lau
Prices: ⚑3.30 ➡3.30 ⚑3.30 ▲3.30

GRANADA GRANADA

Sierra Nevada ctra de Jaen 107 ☎ 958 150062 ▤ 958 150954
e-mail: campingmotel@terra.es
Almost level grassy site, in numerous sections, within motel complex.
All year 4HEC ▦ ♦ℝ🏊♀✕⊙🖙𝚊🛏 ᒀ P ☎⊞ lau

GUIJAROSSA, LA CORDOBA

Campiña ☎ 957 315303 ▤ 957 315158
e-mail: camping_campina@bch.navegalia.com
In a quiet location in a rural setting surrounded by olive trees and elms with good, modern facilities.
➲ *Access via N4 turn off at Km424 or Km441 and follow signs to Santaella and campsite.*
All year 0.7HEC ∷ 🔌ℝ🏊♀✕⊙🖙𝚊🛏▲ ᒀ P ☎⊞ lau

ISLA CRISTINA HUELVA

Giralda ☎ 959 343318
On level ground dotted with trees within easy reach of the beach. Good, modern facilities and plenty of entertainment.
➲ *On Isla Cristina-La Antilla road.*
All year 15HEC ∷ ♦ℝ🏊♀✕⊙🖙𝚊🛏 ᒀ PR ☎⊞ lau ➡ ᒀS

ISLA PLANA MURCIA

Madrilles ctra de la Azohia Km45 ☎ 968 152151 ▤ 968 152092
Large family site with a wide variety of recreational facilities.
➲ *Access via Mazarron-Cartagena road.*
All year 5.5HEC ▦ 🔌ℝ🏊♀✕⊙🖙𝚊🍴🛏 ᒀ PS ☎⊞ ❀ lau ➡ ✕ Prices: ⚑2.91-3.40 ⚑2.91-3.40 ▲2.70-3.40

MANGA DEL MAR MENOR, LA MURCIA

La Manga ☎ 968 563014 ▤ 563426
e-mail: lamanga@caravaning.com
A large family site on the Mar Menor lagoon. Pitches separated by hedges or trees. Good recreational facilities.
➲ *Off the Cartagena motorway.*
All year 32HEC ♦🔌ℝ🏊♀✕⊙🖙𝚊🍴🛏 ᒀ PS ☎⊞ lau

MARBELLA MÁLAGA

Buganvilla ☎ 95 2831973 ▤ 95 2831974
A well equipped site in a pine forest close to the beach.
Camping Card Compulsory.
➲ *E of Marbella off the N340 coast road towards Mijas.*
All year 4HEC ▦ ∷ 🔌ℝ🏊♀✕⊙🖙𝚊🍴🛏🏍 ᒀ PS ☎⊞ lau

MAZAGÓN HUELVA

Mazagón cuesta de la Barca s/n ☎ 959 376208 ▤ 959 536256
e-mail: info@campingplayamazagon.com
Undulating terrain amongst dunes in sparse pine forest. Long sandy beach.
➲ *Turn off the N431 Sevilla-Huelva road just before San Juan del Puerto in direction of Moguer and continue S via Palso de la Frontera.*
All year 8HEC ∷ 🔌ℝ🏊♀✕⊙🖙𝚊 ᒀ P ☎⊞ lau ➡ ᒀS
Prices: ⚑3.69 ➡3.69 ⚑3.69 ▲3.69

MOJÁCAR ALMERIA

Sopalmo Sopalmo ☎ 950 478413
All year 1.7HEC ∷ 🔌ℝ🏊♀✕⊙🖙🍴☎⊞ lau ➡ ✕ ᒀS

MOLLINA MÁLAGA

Molino de Saydo Molino de Saydo, Tourist Complex
☎ 95 2740475 ▤ 95 2740466
e-mail: saydo@arrakis.es
In an ideal situation with good facilities and English speaking staff.
➲ *Turn off A92 (Málaga-Seville) at junct 142 - Mollina. Continue towards Mollina to site 300yds on right next to hotel.*
All year 3.1HEC ▦ ♦ℝ🏊♀✕⊙🖙𝚊▲ ᒀ P ☎⊞ lau

OTURA GRANADA

Suspiro del Moro ☎ 958 555105 ▤ 555105
A modern site with good facilities, 5 minutes from the town centre.
➲ *10km S of Granada via N323.*
All year 1HEC ∷ ♦ℝ🏊♀✕⊙🖙𝚊🛏 ᒀ P ☎⊞ lau ➡ 🍴 ᒀR

PELIGROS GRANADA

Granada Cerro de la Cruz ☎ 958 340548
In a wooded location with panoramic views.
➲ *Access via N323 Jaen-Granada exit 123 towards Peligros.*
Feb-Nov 2.2HEC ▦ 🔌ℝ🏊♀✕⊙🖙𝚊 ᒀ P ☎⊞ lau
Prices: ⚑3.83 pitch 9

PUERTO DE SANTA MARÍA, EL CÁDIZ

Playa Las Dunas de San Anton ps Maritimo de la Puntilla ☎ 956 872210
Large site with good recreational facilities close to the beach.
All year 13.2HEC ∷ ♦ℝ🏊♀✕⊙🖙𝚊🛏▲ ᒀ P ☎⊞ lau ➡🏊♀✕🍴 ᒀRS ⊞

RONDA MÁLAGA

El Sur ctra de Algeciras ☎ 095 2875939 ▤ 095 2877054
e-mail: camping@camping-elsur.es
In a beautiful location in the heart of the Serrania of Ronda.
All year 4HEC ∷ ♦ℝ🏊♀✕⊙🖙𝚊🛏 ᒀ P ☎⊞ lau
Prices: ⚑3.60 ⚑3.10 ▲3.10

ROQUETAS-DE-MAR ALMERIA

Roquetas Los Parrales ☎ 950 343809 ▤ 950 342525
e-mail: roquetas@campings.net
➲ *Access by road No 340. 1.7km from Km428.6.*
All year 8HEC ∷ 🔌ℝ🏊♀✕⊙🖙𝚊🍴🛏 ᒀ LPS ☎⊞ lau
Prices: ⚑3.45 ⚑3.45 ⚑3.45 ▲3.45

SAN ROQUE CÁDIZ

Motel San Roque ☎ 956 780100
All year 4HEC ⊎⊎⊎⊎ ♠ ╠ ⚑ ♥ ✕ ⊙ ◘ ⊞ ▲ ⁀ P ⓣ ⊞ lau ➡ ⁀S

SANTA ELENA JAÉN

Despeñaperros ☎ 953 664192
A clean, restful site, in a nature reserve with fine views of the surrounding mountains.
➲ *At Km257 on NIV-E5.*
All year ⠅⠅ ⚑ ╠ ⚑ ♥ ✕ ⊙ ◘ ⊘ ⊞ ⁀ P ⓣ ⊞ lau

SEVILLA (SEVILLE) SEVILLA

Sevilla ☎ 954 514379 ▥ 954 514379
Level site near airfield, road and railway.
➲ *About 2km from airfield, 100m from the NIV (Madrid-Sevilla) at Km533.8.*
All year 2HEC ⠅⠅ ⚑ ╠ ⚑ ♥ ✕ ⊙ ◘ ⊘ ⊞ ⁀ P ⓣ ⊞ lau
Prices: ♠3 ♣3-495 ♥3 ▲2.50-3

TARIFA CÁDIZ

Paloma ☎ 956 684203 ▥ 956 681880
A modern site in a secluded situation 400mtrs from the beach and next to the Bronze Age Necrolopis de los Algarbes. Fine views of the African coast across the Straits of Gibraltar.
➲ *Access via N340 Cádiz-Málaga at Km 74.*
All year 4.9HEC ⊎⊎⊎⊎ ⚑ ╠ ⚑ ♥ ✕ ⊙ ◘ ⊘ ⊞ ⁀ P ⓣ ⊞ lau ➡ ⁀RS

Rió Jara ☎ 956 680570
Extensive site on meadowland with good tree coverage. Long sandy beach.
➲ *On the N340 Málaga-Cádiz road at Km79.7 turn towards the sea.*
All year 3HEC ⊎⊎⊎⊎ ♠ ╠ ⚑ ♥ ✕ ⊙ ◘ ⊘ ⁀ RS ⓣ ⊞ lau

Tarifa ☎ 956 684778 ▥ 956 684778
e-mail: camping-tarifa@camping-tarifa.com
A terraced site in wooded surroundings, 100mtrs from the sea.
➲ *At Km78 on Málaga-Cádiz road.*
All year 3.2HEC ⠅⠅ ♠ ╠ ⚑ ♥ ✕ ⊙ ◘ ⊘ ⁀ P ⓣ ⊞ lau ➡ ⁀RS
Prices: ♠5.35 ♣3.32 ▲3.21 pitch 11.77-16.59

▶ At **TORRE DE LA PEÑA**(7km NW)

Torre de la Peña ☎ 956 684903 ▥ 956 681473
e-mail: info@campingtp.com
Terraced, on both sides of through road. Upper terraces are considerably quieter. Roofing provides shade. View of the sea, Tarifa and on clear days N Africa (Tangier).
➲ *Entrance on the N340 Cádiz-Málaga, at Km76.5 turn inland by the old square tower.*
All year 3HEC ⊎⊎⊎⊎ ⠅⠅ ⚑ ╠ ⚑ ♥ ✕ ⊙ ◘ ⊘ ⊞ ⁀ PS ⓣ ⊞ lau

TORRE DEL MAR MÁLAGA

Torre del Mar ☎ 95 2540224
A fine site on a beautiful beach, with good facilities. Shop open June-September only.
➲ *SW of town. Access via N340 (Almeria-Málaga).*
All year 2.4HEC ⊎⊎⊎⊎ ⠅⠅ ♠ ╠ ⚑ ♥ ✕ ⊙ ◘ ⊘ ⁀ P ⓣ ⊞ lau ➡ ⁀S

VEJER DE LA FRONTERA CÁDIZ

Vejer ctra National (N340) ☎ 956 450098 ▥ 956 450098
e-mail: info@campingvejer.com
A quiet family site in a pleasant shady location.
➲ *At Km39.5 on N340 Cádiz-Málaga.*
All year 0.8HEC ⠅⠅ ♠ ╠ ⚑ ♥ ✕ ⊙ ◘ ⊘ ♣ ▲ ⁀ P ⓣ ⊞ lau
Prices: ♠8-10

▶ **ANDORRA**

▶ **SANT JULIÀ DE LÒRIA**

Huguet ctra de Fontaneda ☎ 07376 843718 ▥ 07376 843803
On level strip of meadowland with rows of fruit and deciduous trees.
➲ *Off La Seu d'Urgell road N1, S of village and drive W across river.*
All year 1.5HEC ⊎⊎⊎⊎ ⚑ ♠ ╠ ⊙ ◘ ⁀ R ⓣ ⊞ lau ➡ ⚑ ♥ ⊘ ♨ ⁀LP

SWITZERLAND

❖

Bordered by France in the west, Germany in the north, Austria in the east, and Italy in the south, Switzerland is considered by many to be one of the most beautiful countries in Europe.

❖

FACTS AND FIGURES
Area: 41,285 sq km (15,940 sq miles)
Population: 7,123,537 (1998)
Capital: Bern (Berne)
Language: German, French, Italian, Romansh
IDD code: 41. To call the UK dial 00 44
Currency: Swiss Franc (CHF)

Local time: GMT + 1 (summer GMT + 2)
Emergency Services: Police 117; Fire 118; Ambulance 144.
Business Hours-
Banks: Mon-Fri 08.30-16.30 (in towns)
Shops: Mon-Fri 08.30-12.00 and 14.00-18.30; Sat 08.30-12.00 and 14.00-16.00/17.00 (shops

open all day in cities).
Average daily temperatures: Zurich
Jan 0°C   Jul 19°C
Mar 5°C   Sep 15°C
May 9°C   Nov 5°C
Tourist Information:
Switzerland Travel Centre
UK Swiss Centre, Swiss Court
London W1V 8EE

Tel (020) 7734 1921 (recorded message)
USA 608 Fifth Avenue New York, NY 10020
Tel (212) 757 5944
Camping card:
recommended. Some reductions available.
Tourist info website:
www.myswitzerland.com

It has the highest mountains in Europe and some of the most awe-inspiring waterfalls and lakes, features that are offset by picturesque villages set amid green pastures and an abundance of Alpine flowers covering the valleys and lower mountain slopes during the spring. The highest peaks are Monte Rosa (15,217ft) on the Italian border, the Matterhorn (14,782ft), and the Jungfrau (13,669ft). Some of the most beautiful areas are the Via Mala Gorge, the Falls of the Rhine near Schaffhausen, the Rhône Glacier, and the lakes of Luzern and Thun.

The Alps cause many climatic variations throughout Switzerland, but generally the climate is said to be the healthiest in the world. In the higher Alpine regions temperatures tend to be low, whereas the lower land of the northern area has higher temperatures and hot summers. French is spoken in the western cantons (regions), Swiss-German dialects (although German is understood) in the central and northern cantons and Italian in Ticino. Romansch is spoken in Grisons.

Switzerland has 350 campsites, 74 of them are run by the Touring Club Suisse (TCS) who publish details of classified sites annually. Information can also be obtained from tourist offices, which are to be found in most provincial towns and resorts. The season extends from April or May to September or October, although some sites are open all year, particularly at winter sports resorts.

Off-site camping regulations differ from canton (region) to canton. However, permission to camp off an official campsite must be obtained from the landowner or local police. Overnight parking may be tolerated in rest areas of some motorways, but at all times the high standard of hygiene regulations must be observed. Make sure you do not contravene local laws.

HOW TO GET THERE
From Britain, Switzerland is usually approached via France.

Distance
From the Channel ports to Bern is approximately 810km (503 miles), a distance which will normally require only one overnight stop.

If you intend to use Swiss motorways, you will be liable for a tax of CHF 40 - see 'Motorway tax' below for full details.

Car Sleeper Trains
All year round services are available from **Denderleeuw** (Belgium) to **St Maurice** and summer services from **'s-Hertogenbosch** (Netherlands) to **Bellinzona**.

MOTORING & GENERAL INFORMATION

The information given here is specific to Switzerland. It **must** be read in conjunction with the Continental ABC at the front of the book, which covers those regulations which are common to many countries.

British Embassy/Consulates*

The British Embassy together with its consular section is located at 3005 Berne, Thunstrasse 50 ☎(031) 359 77 00. There are British Consulates and agencies in Basel, Genève (Geneva), Lugano, Montreux/Vevey (St Légier), Valais (Mollens) and Zurich.

Children in cars

Children under seven not permitted to travel as front seat passengers unless using suitable restraint system. Children between 7 and 12 must use seat belts or restraints system appropriate to size when travelling in front or rear. See Continental ABC under 'Passengers' and 'Seat Belts'.

Currency

The currency is the Swiss Franc (CHF), which is divided into 100 centimes. Banknotes have denominations of CHF 10, 20, 50, 100, 200, 500 and 1000; the coins are CHF 1, 2, and 5, and centimes 5, 10, 20 and 50.

There are no restrictions on the import or export of foreign or Swiss currency. In addition to banks there are exchange offices at the border, railway stations in large towns, airports and in travel agencies and hotels which are usually open 08.00-20.00hrs.

Dimensions and weight restrictions*

Private cars and towed trailers or caravans are restricted to the following dimensions - **car** height, 4 metres; width, 2.55 metres; length, 12 metres.

Trailer/caravan height, 4 metres; width, 2.55 metres; length, 12 metres (including tow bar). The maximum permitted overall length of vehicle/trailer or caravan combination is 18.75 metres.

Note: It is dangerous or forbidden to use a vehicle towing a trailer or caravan on some mountain roads; motorists should ensure that roads on which they are about to travel are suitable for the conveyance of vehicle/trailer or caravan combinations.

The fully-laden weight of trailers which do not have an independent braking system should not exceed 50% of the unladen weight of the towing vehicle, but trailers which have an independent braking system can weigh up to 100% of the unladen weight of the towing vehicle.

Driving licence*

A valid UK or Republic of Ireland licence is acceptable in Switzerland. The minimum age at which visitors from UK or Republic of Ireland may use a temporarily imported car is 18 years and a temporarily imported motorcycle of between 50-125cc (not exceeding 40kph) 16 years, exceeding 125cc 18 years.

Foodstuffs*

Visitors may import foodstuffs and non-alcoholic drinks duty-free, provided the quantity does not exceed their daily consumption. Subject to certain prohibitions and restrictions, meat and meat products may be imported duty-free up to a maximum value of CHF100 per person.

Lights*

It is recommended that motorcyclists use dipped headlights during the day.

Motoring club

The **Touring Club Suisse** (TCS) has branch offices in all important towns, and has its head office at 1214 Vernier/Genève, Chemin de Blandonnet 4, ☎(022) 4172727. The TCS will extend a courtesy service to all motorists but their major services will have to be paid for. The opening hours of TCS offices vary according to location and time of year, but generally they are 08.00/09.00-11.45/12.30hrs and 13.30/14.00-17.00/18.30hrs Monday to Friday and 08.00/09.00-11.45/12.00hrs Saturday (summer only).

Motorway tax

The Swiss authorities levy an annual motorway tax and substantial fines are imposed for non-payment (CHF100 plus cost of *vignette*). A vehicle sticker, costing CHF40 for vehicles up to 3.5 tonnes maximum total weight and known locally as a *vignette*, must be displayed by vehicles using Swiss motorways including motorcycles, trailers

The Furka Pass near the Italian border

and caravans. Motorists may purchase the stickers in the UK from the Switzerland Travel Centre, Swiss Centre, Swiss Court, London W1V 8EE, tel (020) 7734 1921; in Switzerland from customs offices, post offices, service stations and garages. Vehicles over 3.5 tonnes maximum total weight are taxed on all roads in Switzerland. For coaches and caravans a licence for one day, 10 days, one month and one year periods can be obtained. For lorries the tax depends on weight and distance. There are no stickers, and the tax must be paid at the Swiss frontier.

Petrol*
See Continental ABC under 'Petrol/Diesel'.

Roads
Switzerland has about 1,000 miles of motorway (*Autobahn* or *autoroute*). Tolls are not payable but see *Motorway Tax* above. Emergency telephones, which connect you to the motorway control police, are located every 2km.

The road surfaces are generally good, but some main roads are narrow in places. Traffic congestion may be severe at the beginning and end of the German school holidays.

On any stretch of mountain road, the driver of a private car may be asked by the driver of a postal bus which is painted yellow, to reverse, or otherwise manoeuvre to allow the postal bus to pass. Postal bus drivers often sound a distinctive three note horn; no other vehicles may use this type of horn in Switzerland.

Speed limits*
Car/motorcycle
Built-up areas 50kph (31mph)
Other roads 80kph (49mph)
semi-motorways 100kph (62mph)
Motorways 120kph (74mph)

Car/caravan/trailer

Built-up areas 50kph (31mph)
Other roads, including semi-motorways 80kph (49mph)
Motorways 80kph (49mph)

These limits do not apply if another limit is indicated by signs, or if the vehicle is subject to a lower general speed limit.

Warning triangle/Hazard warning lights*

The use of a warning triangle is compulsory in the event of accident or breakdown. The triangle must be placed on the road at least 50 metres (55yds) behind the vehicle on ordinary roads, and at least 100 metres (109yds) on high speed roads. If in an emergency lane the triangle must be placed on the right. Hazard warning lights may be used in conjunction with the triangle or when traffic slows due to accident or traffic jam.

*Additional information will be found in the Continental ABC at the front of the book.

TOURIST INFORMATION

NORTH

Basel is often the point of entry for visitors to Switzerland by land, air, and the River Rhine, which ceases to become navigable upstream from the town. It is usually a relatively staid town, but in February it comes alive for the Basel Fasnacht.

Fasnacht translates as 'Carnival', and Basel holds one of the world's finest carnivals, and certainly the one which requires the greatest stamina. It begins on the first Monday after Shrove Tuesday when the clock in Basel's Marktplatz strikes four times at 4am in the morning, and then continues for 72 hours without a pause. The theme is music, and gangs of musicians each with their own band-leader roam around the city giving impromptu concerts and playing noisily at unsuspecting bystanders. The music ranges from military marching music, to contemporary jazz and for the most part performances are remarkably accomplished and always full of energy.

NORTH EAST

Downstream from Zurich and twenty minutes from Schaffhausen is the small town of Neuhausen, close to the impressive Rhine Falls.

The Rheinfall is classed as Europe's largest waterfall in terms of the volume of water:

The Klausen Pass goes from Linthal to Altdorf

somewhere in the region of 25,000 cubic feet plunges over the falls every second and it is a spectacular sight.

NORTH WEST & CENTRAL

Bern is the national capital, but more importantly, it is one of Europe's most beautiful cities.

The old town stands on a peninsula in the River Aare and is one of Europe's most prized

Les Pyramides d' Euseigne, in the Val D'Herens valley, a group of geological formations, formed by the debris of glacial moraines

possessions, and has been designated a "World cultural landmark".

Inside the old town, are medieval arcades which today house high fashion boutiques and make up the oldest covered shopping mall in Europe. There are also many fountains, the best known of which are the Ogre Fountain that depicts a colourful baby-eating beast, and the rather more uplifting Anna Seiler Fountain, which is named after the woman who founded Bern's first hospital. However, Bern's Clock Tower (built in 1218) on the Kramgasse, is probably the city's most immediately recognisable landmark. Its two timepieces were not added until 1530: a conventional clock at the top of the tower and an astrological clock at its base.

EAST

Chur is Switzerland's oldest city, and the provincial centre of its largest canton, Graubünden, renowned for its ski resorts and 3,000 miles of mountain paths. Chur is normally a starting point for hikers and skiers, but it is well worth exploring in its own right. Its old town is a network of ancient streets and squares adorned with fountains. Notable buildings include the medieval Cathedral which houses many treasures, the 15th-century St Martin's Church and the town hall which dates from the same period. To the east of Martinsplatz is the Bischöflicher Hof, of which the main feature is the Bischöfliches Schloss, an early 18th-century baroque palace. Also east of Martinsplatz is the Buol Mansion, housing a museum of Rhaetian life.

SOUTH

Lugano is a town with an Italian flavour, on the shores of the attractive Lake Lugano, and is an excellent base for sightseeing with many local attractions.

The Italian style of Lugano is clearly evident in the piazzas and elegant cafés which make the town so pleasant for relaxing and strolling. Undoubtedly the star attraction is the beautiful lake and the best way to see it is to take a cruise. If you have time, invest in a three-day ticket which covers cruises around the lakes of Lugano, Como, and Maggiore with unlimited ferry and lake access. There is an exciting funicular ride (spring to autumn) from Paradiso up to the heights of Monte San Salvatore where the panoramic views extend over all the region's lakes, and the Swiss and Italian Alps, including Monte Rosa and the magnificent Matterhorn.

SOUTH WEST

Lake Geneva is the largest lake in the Alps, surrounded by the Savoy and Vaad Alps and the Swiss Jura.

Of the wide range of ferries and steamers that criss-cross the lake, offering everything from express shuttles to evening dinner cruises, one of the most characterful is Neptune, a sailing freighter built in 1904.

The north bank of Lake Geneva includes Rolle Castle and the town of Marges which houses the headquarters of the World Wildlife Fund. Attractions on the French south bank include the imposing 16th-century Château de Bloney, and the idyllic town of Meillerie.

The city of Geneva lies on the western edge of the lake and is a bustling centre of European commerce, home to the United Nations and the International Red Cross, both of whose headquarters can be visited.

Sculptured representation of the Last Judgement (1490) composed of 234 carved figures in the main portal of Berne cathedral

NORTH

Basel owes its prosperity to its key geographical position - at the junction of the borders of France, Germany and Switzerland, and at the point on the Rhine where it becomes navigable. It has evolved into an important business and industrial centre. The old town has a great Gothic cathedral - with a fine view from the top of the towers, and a remarkable collection of art in the Fine Arts Museum, "Kunstmuseum". The town also has an extensive Zoological Garden, with an emphasis on breeding threatened species. The countryside of this area is one of medieval castles, quaint villages, thermal spas, dense forests, lush meadows and sparkling lakes. But above the charming Baroque town of Solothurn is the last ridge of the Jura - the giddy crests of the Weissenstein, from where, at over 4,000ft, there is an outstanding view over Berne and the lakes of Neuchâtel, Murten and Biel.

....

KÜNTEN AARGAU

Sulz ☎ 079/076 660 7426 ▤ 056 4964879
e-mail: ivo.kohler@bluewin.ch
Situated by a river.
➲ *From motorway A1 turn off at Baden in the direction of Bremgarten.*
15 Mar-Oct 2.5HEC ⸬⸬⸬⸬ ⚐ ⋔ ⛟ ✕ ⊙ ⬛ ⬤ ⛺ ⬛ ⸜ PR ▣ ⊞ lau

LÄUFELFINGEN BASEL

Läufelfingen ☎ 062 2991189
➲ *On road from Basel to Olten.*
Apr-Oct 0.5HEC ⸬⸬⸬⸬ ⚐ ⋔ ⊙ ⬛ ⬛ ⛺ ⊞ Prices: ⋔4 ⬤3 ⬛5-6 ⬛3-4

MÖHLIN AARGAU

Bachtalen (TCS) ☎ 061 8515095
A pleasant site in a wooded rural setting.
➲ *2km N towards the River Rhine.*
Apr-early Oct 1HEC ⸬⸬⸬⸬ ⸓⸍ ⋔ ⊙ ⬛ ⬤ ⛺ ⊞ lau ➡ ⛟ ⛻ ✕ ⸜PR

REINACH BASEL

Waldhort Heideweg 16 ☎ 061 7139835 ▤ 061 7114833
e-mail: camp.waldhort@gmx.ch
In pleasant wooded surroundings close to the Basle/Delémont road.
Mar-26Oct 3.3HEC ⸬⸬⸬⸬ ⚐ ⋔ ⛟ ✕ ⊙ ⬛ ⬤ ⛺ ⸜ P ⊞ lau ➡ ✕ Prices: ⋔7 ⬛17 ⬛11

ZURZACH AARGAU

Oberfeld ☎ 56 2492575
Apr-Oct 2HEC ⸬⸬⸬⸬ ⬥ ⚐ ⋔ ⛟ ✕ ⊙ ⬛ ⬤ ⬛ ⸜ PR ⬛ ⊞

> **A guide to the Symbols & Abbreviations used in this book can be found on page 5**

NORTH EAST

At the northern gateway to Switzerland, the town of Schaffhausen falls in terraces from the 16th-century Munot Castle, and is the traditional starting point for a visit to the Rhine Falls, "Rheinfall". The most powerfall waterfall in Europe, the Rhine makes a spectacular 70ft drop - one of the most famous sights in Europe. St Gallen is popular with visitors; the twin domed towers of the cathedral overlook the attractive old town. The cathedral's plain exterior belies a wonderfully rich Baroque interior, with mural paintings covering the central dome and nave, and there is a remarkable chancel with a huge high altar.
The largest city in Switzerland, cosmopolitan Zürich hums around the Bahnhofstrasse - a fine, wide, tree-lined boulevard of glittering shops and modern offices and banks. For more sedate pursuits visit the quays along the banks of Lake Zürich - lined with immaculate gardens and lawns, visit the old quarters with their cobbled streets, or take a boat trip on the lake. The Swiss National Museum, "Schweizerisches Landesmuseum" is a treasure-house of Swiss civilisation from prehistoric times to the present. The countryside of the region provides good walking, and the mountains and hills are dotted with attractive farms. Picturesque villages contain traditional colourful houses, and sparkling lakes adorn the valleys.
Between the borders of Switzerland and Austria is the principality of Leichtenstein, with its extensive tourist attractions, but retaining its own individual charm and appeal. The capital and main centre is Vaduz, overlooked by its 14th-century castle.

....

ALTNAU THURGAU

Ruderbaum ☎ 071 6951885 ▤ 071 695 1885
e-mail: office@ruderbaum.ch
A small tourist site with ample facilities.
➲ *Close to the railway station by Lake Bodensee between Constance and Romanshorn.*
Apr-Oct 7.5HEC ⸬⸬⸬⸬ ⚐ ⋔ ✕ ⊙ ⬛ ⬤ ⛺ ⸜ L ⬛ ⊞ lau ➡ ⛟ ⛻

ALT ST JOHANN ST-GALLEN

3 Eidgenossen (TCS) ☎ 071 9991274
All year 0.5HEC ⸬⸬⸬⸬ ⚐ ⋔ ✕ ⊙ ⬛ ⬤ ▣ ⊞ lau ➡ ⸜R

APPENZELL APPENZELL

Kau Appenzell ☎ 071 7875030
A woodland site with good modern installations.
Camping Card Compulsory.
➲ *S of Appenzell towards Wattwil.*
All year 2HEC ⸬⸬⸬⸬ ⸓⸍ ⋔ ⛟ ✕ ⊙ ⬛ ⛺ ⬛ ⊞ ⬚ lau

ESCHENZ THURGAU

Hüttenberg Hüttenberg ☎ 052 7412337 ▤ 052 7415671
e-mail: info@huettenberg.ch
Terraced site lying above village.
➲ *1km SW.*
All year 6HEC ⸬⸬⸬⸬ ⸓⸍ ⋔ ⛟ ⊙ ⬛ ⬤ ⛺ ⬛ ⸜ P ⬛ ⊞ lau ➡ ✕ ⸜LR ⊞

GOLDINGEN ST-GALLEN

Atzmännig ☎ 055 2841235
Suitable for summer and winter holidays, the site is situated close to the main cable car and ski lift stations and the giant mountainside slide.
All year 1.5HEC ⸬⸬⸬⸬ ⸓⸍ ⋔ ✕ ⊙ ⬛ ⛺ ⬛ ⊞ lau

KRUMMENAU ST-GALLEN

Adler ☎ 071 9941030
On edge of village.
All year 0.8HEC 👥 ⚡ ⚤ ℝ ⅄ ✕ ⊙ ⚑ ⊞ lau

LEUTSWIL BEI BISCHOFFZELL THURGAU

Sitterbrücke ☎ 071 4226398
⊃ *Signposted from Bischoffzell on the Konstanz-St Gallen road.*
Apr-15 Oct 1HEC 👥 ⚂ ℝ ⊙ ⚑ ⌀ ⚤ ⅄ R ⊠ ⊞ lau

MAMMERN THURGAU

Guldifuss Guldifusstr 1 ☎ 052 7411320
A terraced site directly on the Untersee.
All year 1.6HEC 👥 ⚡ ℝ ⚤ ✕ ⊙ ⚑ ⌀ ⚤ ⅄ L ℙ lau ◆ ⅄ ⊞

OTTENBACH ZÜRICH

Reussbrücke (TCS) Muristr 32 ☎ 01 7612022
By river of same name.
⊃ *Access from Zürich via road 126 in SW direction, via Affoltern to Ottenbach.*
Apr-Oct 1.5HEC 👥 ⚂ ℝ ⚤ ✕ ⊙ ⚑ ⌀ ⚤ A ⅄ R ⊠ ⊞ lau ◆
⅄ ✕

SCHÖNENGRUND APPENZELL

Schönengrund ☎ 071 3611268 ▤ 3611166
e-mail: hotel.krone.schoenengrund@bluewin.ch
A comfortable, partly residential site with well defined touring pitches.
All year 1HEC 👥 ⚂ ℝ ⊙ ⚑ ⌀ ⚤ ⊠ lau ◆ ⚤ ✕ ⊞

WAGENHAUSEN SCHAFFHAUSEN

Wagenhausen Hauptstr 82 ☎ 052 7414271
In a delightful wooded location beside the River Rhein.
Apr-Oct 4.5HEC 👥 ⚂ ℝ ⚤ ✕ ⊙ ⚑ ⌀ ⚤ ⅄ R ⊠ ⊞ lau

WALENSTADT ST-GALLEN

See-Camping ☎ 081 7351212 ▤ 7351841
A well equipped family site with direct access to the Walensee.
⊃ *Accvess via Zürich-Chur motorway*
15 May-15 Sep 1.2HEC 👥 ⚂ ℝ ⊙ ⚑ ⅄ L ℙ ⋇ lau ◆ ⅄
✕ ⌀ ⚤ ⊞

WILDBERG ZÜRICH

Weid ☎ 052 453388
On a terraced meadow in a very peaceful situation surrounded by woods.
⊃ *In Winterthur, follow Tösstal signs, then turn right after spinning-mill in Turbenthal.*
All year 5.4HEC 👥 ⚂ ℝ ⚤ ⅄ ✕ ⊙ ⚑ ⌀ ⚤ ⚙ ⚑ ⊠ lau ◆
⅄PR

WINTERTHUR ZÜRICH

Winterthur Eichliwaldstr 4 ☎ 052 2125260 ▤ 2125260
⊃ *To the left of the Schaffhausen road, near the Schützenhaus restaurant.*
All year 1HEC 👥 ⚡ ⚂ ℝ ⊙ ⚑ ⌀ ⚤ ⊠ ⊞ ⋇ lau ◆ ⚤ ⅄ ✕
⅄P

● ● ● **NORTH WEST/CENTRAL** ● ● ●

This region extends from the French border in the northwest, to Adermatt in the canton of Uri, in the heart of the St Gothard Massif at the crossroads of the Alps. The Province of Jura makes a lovely transition from the Saône plain to the Germanic 'middle country' - it is a gentle land of peaceful pastures and low houses, and is a favourite with cross-country skiers in winter. Neuchâtel, capital of its own canton, stands in a delightful position between the lake of Neuchâtel and the mountains, and has a picturesque old town. The lake offers good facilities for watersports and cruising, and a nearby funicular railway serves Chaumont, from where there is a vast panorama of the Bernese Alps and the Mont Blanc Massif.
Bern is a delight, with pretty arcaded buildings lining the streets of the old town, and a lovely setting facing the Alps. Lucerne has a superb site at the northwestern end of Lake Lucerne, and cruises on the lake offer breathtaking changing panoramas. The Transport Museum in Lucerne contains a fascinating story of the development of Swiss transport.
But the highlight of the central region must be the Alps, with the Jungfrau Massif reaching heights of over 13,600ft. Of course the winter this is a paradise for winter sports, but during the summer there is good access to the most well-known peaks by road, rail or cable-car, with dizzy heights and spectacular views.

AESCHI BERN

Panorama ☎ 033 2233615 ▤ 22333656
e-mail: postmaster@camping-aeschi.ch
400m SE of Camping Club Bern.
15 May-Sep 1HEC 👥 ⚂ ℝ ⚤ ⊙ ⚑ ⚤ ⊠ ⊞ lau ◆ ⅄ ✕ ⌀
Prices: ⚑5.40 ◆⚑3 ⚑10-12 ▲8-12

ALTDORF URI

Moosbad Flülerstr ☎ 041 8708541
In a delightful mountain setting.
⊃ *Access via Altdorf exit on A2.*
All year 0.9HEC ⋮⋮⋮ ⚡ ⚡ ℝ ⊙ ⚑ ⌀ ⚤ ⚑ ⊠ ⊞ lau

BERN (BERNE) BERN

At **WABERN**

SC Eichholz Strandweg 49 ☎ 031 9612602 ▤ 9613526
e-mail: info@campingeichholz.ch
In municipal parkland. Separate section for caravans.
⊃ *Approach via Gossetstr and track beside river.*
22 Apr-Sep 2HEC 👥 ⚂ ℝ ⅄ ✕ ⊙ ⚑ ⌀ ⚤ ⅄ R ℙ ⊞ lau ◆
⚤ ⅄ ✕ ⌀ ⅄P Prices: ⚑6.90 ◆⚑2-3.20 ⚑9 ▲5-8.50

BRENZIKOFEN BERN

Wydeli (TCS) Wydeli 60 ☎ 031 7711141
⊃ *8km N of Thun.*
May-Sep 1.3HEC 👥 ⚡ ℝ ✕ ⊙ ⚑ ⌀ ⚤ ⚑ ⅄ P ℙ lau ◆ ⚤
⊞

BRUNNEN SCHWYZ

Hopfreben ☎ 041 8201873
On the right bank of the Muotta stream 100m before it flows into the lake.
⊃ *1km W.*
May-29 Sep 1.5HEC 👥 ⚡ ⚂ ℝ ⚤ ⅄ ✕ ⊙ ⚑ ⌀ ⚤ ▲ ⅄ LR ⊠
⊞ lau

BURGDORF BERN

Waldegg (TCS) ☎ 034 4227943
➲ *On Oberburg road, turn left at petrol station.*
Etr-Sep 0.5HEC ⚏ ⬛ ⬛ ⦿ ⬛ ⬛ ➤ ⬛ ⬛ ✕ ⬛ ⛰ ⫟PR ⊞

CHAUX-DE-FONDS, LA NEUCHÂTEL

Bois du Couvent ☎ 079 2405039
Partly on uneven ground.
➲ *Take turning off Neuchâtel road near the Zappella and Moeschier factory and drive for 200m.*
15 Jul-15 Aug 2.5HEC ⚏ ⬛ ⬛ ⬛ ⬛ ✕ ⦿ ⬛ ⬛ ⛰ ⬛ ⬛ ⫟ P
⬛ ⊞ lau

COLOMBIER NEUCHÂTEL

Paradis-Plage ☎ 032 8412446 ▦ 032 8414305
e-mail: paradisplage@freesurf.ch
In a delightful setting beside Lake Neuchâtel with good, modern facilities.
Mar-Oct 4HEC ⚏ ⬛ ⬛ ⬛ ⬛ ✕ ⦿ ⬛ ⬛ ⛰ ⬛ ⫟ L ⊞ Prices:
⚑8-9 ➤1-3 ⬛8-15 ⬛8-15

ENGELBERG OBWALDEN

Eienwäldli Wasserfallstr 108 ☎ 041 6371949
➲ *1.5km SW behind restaurant Eienwäldli.*
Closed Nov 4HEC ⚏ ⬛ ⬛ ⬛ ⬛ ⬛ ✕ ⦿ ⬛ ⬛ ⛰ ⫟ PR ⬛ ⊞
lau

ERLACH BERN

Mon Plaisir ☎ 032 3381358 ▦ 032 3381305
Well equipped site beside the lake.
All year 0.6HEC ⚏ ⬛ ⬛ ⬛ ✕ ⦿ ⬛ ⬛ ⛰ ⬛ ⬛ ⫟ L ⬛ ⊞ lau
➤ ✕ ⫟PR Prices: ⚑10.60-12.60 pitch 25-50

Camping Grassi Frutigen

Located off the road, alongside the Engstligen Stream, this is the location for the quiet and well equipped site in the summer holiday resort of Frutigen, about 15 km from Spiez, Adelboden and Kandersteg

• Inexhaustible choice of excursions
• Free loan of bicycles, guided mountainbike tours

Winter camping: to skiing resorts of Adelboden, Kandersteg, Elsigenalp, Swiss ski-school, only 10–12 km.

Infos: W. Glausen, CH-3714 Frutigen
Tel. 0041-33-671 11 49, Fax 0041-33-671 13 80
E-mail: campinggrassi@bluewin.ch

EUTHAL SCHWYZ

Euthal ☎ 055 4122718 ▦ 055 4127673
e-mail: hotel.post@sihlnet.ch
On the shore of the Sihlsee in a beautiful mountain setting.
The site is reserved for tents only.
Jun-Oct 1HEC ⚏ ⬛ ⬛ ⬛ ✕ ⦿ ⫟ L ⬛ ⬛ ➤ ⬛ ⬛ ⬛ ⊞

FLÜELEN URI

Urnersee ☎ 041 8709222 ▦ 041 8709216
e-mail: info@windsurfing-urnersee.ch
On level ground on the shore of the Vierwaldstättersee with plenty of sporting facilities.
15 Apr-Oct 4.5HEC ⚏ ⬛ ⬛ ⬛ ⬛ ✕ ⦿ ⬛ ⫟ LR ⬛ ⊞ ➤ ⬛
⫟P

FRUTIGEN BERN

Grassi ☎ 033 6711149 ▦ 033 6711380
e-mail: campinggrassi@bluewin.ch
Scattered with fruit trees beside a farm on the right bank of the River Engstilgern.
➲ *From the Haupstr, turn right at the Simplon Hotel.*
All year 1.5HEC ⚏ ⬛ ⬛ ⬛ ⦿ ⬛ ⬛ ⛰ ⬛ ⬛ ⬛ ⊞ lau ➤ ⫟P
Prices: ⚑6.40 pitch 6-12

GAMPELEN BERN

Fanel (TCS) ☎ 032 3132333 ▦ 3131407
e-mail: camping.gampelen@bluewin.ch
A level site on the shore of Lake Neuchâtel protected by trees and bushes.
➲ *Access via A5 towards Gampelen.*
8 Apr-Sep 11.3HEC ⚏ ⬛ ⬛ ✕ ⦿ ⬛ ⬛ ⬛ ⫟ L ⬛ ⊞ lau ➤
⫟R

GISWIL OBWALDEN

Giswil ☎ 041 6752355
Apr-20 Oct 1.9HEC ▦ ░░░ ♦ ♠ ⚡ ✕ ☉ 🍴 ∅ ♨ ⚓ L ☎ ⊞
lau

GOLDAU SCHWYZ

Bernerhöhe ☎ 041 8551887 ▮ 041 8555970
On the edge of a forest with a beautiful view of Lake Lauerz.
Separate field for tents.
➲ *1.5km SE and turn left.*
All year 2.5HEC ▦ ⚘ ☆ ♠ ⚡ ☉ 🍴 ∅ ☎ ⊞ ✗ lau

Buosingen ☎ 041 8553898
All year 1.5HEC ▦ ♁ ♠ ⚡ ✕ ☉ 🍴 ∅ ♨ 🚐 ☎ lau ♦ ▾ ✕
↻LP

GRINDELWALD BERN

Aspen ☎ 033 8531124 ▮ 033 534157
Sunny hill terraces.
Jun-15 Oct 2.5HEC ▦ ☆ ♠ ☉ 🍴 ∅ ☎ lau ♦ ✕ ⊞

GSTAAD BERN

Bellerive ☎ 033 4746330 ▮ 033 7446345
All year 0.8HEC ▦ ♁ ♠ ⚡ ∅ 🍴 🚐 ↻ R ⊞ lau ♦ ↻P
Prices: ♠6.40-7.50 ⬤2.20 ▲13-15

INNERTKIRCHEN BERN

Aareschlucht Hauptstr 6/11 ☎ 033 9715332 ▮ 033 9715344
e-mail: campaareschlucht@bluewin.ch
In a beautiful Alpine location with superb mountain views.
All year 0.5HEC ▦ ♁ ♠ ☉ 🍴 ∅ ♨ ♨ 🚐 ☎ ⊞ lau ♦ ▾ ✕
↻R

Grund ☎ 033 9714409 ▮ 033 9714767
e-mail: camping_grund@bluewin.ch
Next to a farm on southern outskirts of village.
➲ *Turn S off main road in centre of village at hotel Urweider.
Drive for 0.3km, turn right.*
All year 80HEC ▦ ♁ ♠ ☉ 🍴 🚐 ▲ ☎ ⊞ lau ♦ ⚡ ▾ ✕ ∅ ↻R

INTERLAKEN BERN

Alpenblick Seestr 135, Neuhaus ☎ 033 227757
Well equipped family site on the left bank of the River
Lombach upstream from the bridge in a meadow bordering a
forest opposite the Neuhaus Motel and the Strandbad
Restaurant.
➲ *8km N.*
All year 2.3HEC ▦ ♁ ♠ ⚡ ☉ 🍴 ∅ ▲ ☎ ⊞ lau ♦ ▾ ✕ ↻LR

Hobby 3 Lehnweg 16 ☎ 033 8229652 ▮ 033 8229657
e-mail: info@campinghobby.ch
Family site with first class sanitary facilities, quietly situated
with fine views of the surrounding mountains and within
easy walking distance of Interlaken.
➲ *Access via A8 (Spiez-Interlaken) towards
Gunten/Beatenberg.*
Apr-22Sep 1.2HEC ▦ ♦ ♠ ⚡ ✕ ☉ 🍴 ∅ ☎ ⊞ lau ♦ ▾ ✕
↻LPRS

Jungfrau Steindlerstr 50 ☎ 033 8227107 ▮ 033 8225730
Has a beautiful view of the Eiger, the Mönch and the
Jungfrau.
➲ *Turn right at Unterseen, drive through the Schulhaus and
Steiner Str to site.*
May-25Sep 2.5HEC ▦ ♁ ♠ ⚡ ▾ ✕ ☉ 🍴 ∅ ♨ 🚐 ↻ P ☎ lau
♦ ↻LR ⊞

Manor Farm ...	1	033 822 22 64
Alpenblick	2	033 822 77 57
Hobby	3	033 822 96 52
Lazy Rancho ...	4	033 822 87 16
Jungfrau Camp	5	033 822 57 30
Sackgut TCS ...	6	033 822 44 34
Jungfraublick ..	7	033 822 44 14
Oberei	8	033 822 13 35

Jungfraublick Gsteigstr 80 ☎ 033 8224414 ▮ 033 8221619
e-mail: info@jungfraublick.ch
A family site with clean, modern facilities in a fine central
situation.
➲ *Take Autobahn A8 through tunnel, leave at Lauterbrunnen-
Grindelwald exit, site on left, 300m from A8 sliproad.*
May-25 Sep 1.3HEC ▦ ♁ ♠ ⚡ ☉ 🍴 ∅ ↻ P ☎ ⊞ lau ♦ ▾ ✕
↻R

Lazy Rancho 4 ☎ 033 8228716 ▮ 033 8231920
e-mail: info@lazyrancho.ch
A family campsite in a magnificent position with views of the
Eiger, Mönch and Jungfrau with fine facilities.
➲ *Motorway A8: exit Unterseen, turn toward Gunten. After
2km turn right, then at Landhotel Golf turn left.*
15Apr-30Sep 16HEC ▦ ♁ ♠ ⚡ ☉ 🍴 ∅ ↻ P ☎ ⊞ lau ♦ ▾ ✕
↻LR

Manor Farm ☎ 033 8222264 ▮ 8222279
e-mail: manorfarm@swisscamps.ch
A well equipped site in a beautiful mountain setting.
➲ *From motorway A8 (Bern-Speiz-Interlaken-Brienz), exit
Gunten/Beatenberg; follow signposts.*
All year 7.5HEC ▦ ░░░ ♁ ♠ ⚡ ▾ ✕ ☉ 🍴 ∅ ♨ 🚐 ♨ ▲ ↻
LR ☎ ⊞ lau

KANDERSTEG BERN

Rendez-Vous ☎ 033 6751534 ▮ 033 6751737
e-mail: rendez-vous.camping@bluewin.ch
In a delightful mountain setting with good modern facilities.
➲ *750m E of town.*
All year 1HEC ▦ ♁ ♠ ⚡ ✕ ☉ 🍴 ∅ ♨ ☎ ⊞ lau ♦ ↻P

See advertisement on page 344

LANDERON, LE NEUCHÂTEL

Peches ☎ 032 7512900 ▤ 7516354
e-mail: info@camping-lelanderon.ch
A small site at the meeting point of the River Thielle and the Lac de Bienne.
Apr-15 Oct 2.1HEC ⸬⸬⸬ ⩫ ℿ 🛒 ⊙ 🇶 ⌀ ⛲ 🇶 ⸚ LP 🏧 ⊞ lau ➧ 🍴 ✕ ⸚P Prices: ⚤6-7 ⚤4 ⚤9-10.50 ⚤6.50-9.50

LAUTERBRUNNEN BERN

Jungfrau ☎ 036 552010
Widespread site in meadowland crossed by a stream. Partly divided into pitches.
➲ 100m before the church turn right, drive a further 400m.
All year 5HEC ⸬⸬⸬ ⩫ ℿ 🛒 ✕ ⊙ 🇶 ⌀ ⛲ 🏫 🇶 ⚠ 🏧 ⊞ lau ➧ 🍴 ⸚P

Schützenbach (TCS) ☎ 033 8551268 ▤ 0336 8551275
In an fine Alpine location close to the main skiing areas and about 300m from the lake.
➲ S of village to the left of road leading to Stechelberg opposite B50. 0.8km SE towards Stechelberg.
All year 3HEC ⸬⸬⸬ ⩫ ℿ 🛒 🍴 ✕ ⊙ 🇶 ⌀ ⛲ 🏫 🇶 ⚠ 🏧 ⊞ lau ➧ ✕ ⸚P

LIGNIÈRES NEUCHÂTEL

Fraso-Ranch ☎ 032 7514616 ▤ 032 7514614
e-mail: camping.fraso-ranch@bluewin.ch
A modern family site with good recreational facilities and a separate section for tourers.
➲ NE of Lignières on Nods road. Signposted.
All year 8.7HEC ⸬⸬⸬ ⩫ ℿ 🛒 ✕ ⊙ 🇶 ⌀ ⸚ P 🏧
Prices: ⚤6-8 pitch 5.50-15

Modern camping site, especially suitable for families, ideal for walking/biking tours, paragliding and golf, possibilities for horse-riding in the village.
First-class facilities: heated swimming pool, children's paddling pool and large play-ground, 2 tennis courts, volley/soccer-playground, boule-alleys, ping-pong, chess etc.
Shop with restaurant, size of units 100m2.

FRASO RANCH
CH-2523 Lignières
Tel. 0041-32-751 46 16
Fax 0041-32-751 46 14

LOCLE, LE NEUCHÂTEL

Communal (TCS) ☎ 032 9317493 ▤ 9317408
e-mail: camping.lelode@tcs.ch
On a level meadow surrounded by woodland. Good recreational facilities.
➲ S of town off the La Sagne road.
27Apr-20Oct 1.2HEC ⸬⸬⸬ ⩫ ℿ 🛒 🍴 ✕ ⊙ 🇶 ⌀ ⛲ ⸚ P 🏧 ⊞ lau ➧ 🛒 ✕

LUCERNE

See **Luzern**

LUNGERN OBWALDEN

Obsee ☎ 041 6781463 ▤ 6782163
e-mail: camping@obsee.ch
In a beautiful setting between the lake and the mountains with good facilities for watersports.
➲ 1km W.
All year 1.5HEC ⸬⸬⸬ ⩫ ℿ 🛒 🍴 ✕ ⊙ 🇶 ⌀ ⛲ ⸚ LPR 🏧 ⊞ lau ➧ 🛒

LUZERN (LUCERNE) LUZERN

At HORW

Steinibachried (TCS) ☎ 041 3403558
In gently sloping meadow next to the football ground and the beach, separated from the lake by a wide belt of reeds.
➲ 3.2km S of Luzern.
Apr-2 Oct 2HEC ⸬⸬⸬ ⩫ ℿ 🛒 ✕ ⊙ 🇶 ⌀ 🇶 ⊞ lau ➧ 🍴 ⸚L

MAUENSEE LUZERN

Sursee Waldheim ☎ 041 921 11 61
Next to Waldheim Country Estate.
➲ 0.8km W of Sursee, 100m from Sursee-Basel road.
Apr-Sep 1.7HEC ⸬⸬⸬ ⩫ ℿ 🛒 🍴 ✕ ⊙ 🇶 ⌀ ⛲ 🏧 ⊞ lau ➧ ⸚L

MEIRINGEN BERN LUZERN

Balmweid ☎ 033 9715115
e-mail: camping.balmweid@popnet.ch
Mainly flat meadowland site with mountain views.
All year 2.2 HEC ⸬⸬⸬ ⩫ ℿ 🛒 🍴 ✕ ⊙ 🇶 ⛲ lau
See advertisement in colour section

MOSEN LUZERN

Seeblick ☎ 041 9171666 ▤ 041 9171666
e-mail: mptrunz@gmx.ch
In two strips of land on edge of lake, divided by paths into several squares.
➲ N on the A26.
Apr-Oct 3HEC ⸬⸬⸬ ⩫ ℿ 🛒 ⊙ 🇶 ⌀ ⸚ L 🏧 ⊞ lau ➧ ✕

NOTTWIL LUZERN

St Margrethen ☎ 041 9371404 ▤ 9371404
Natural meadowland under fruit trees, with own access to lakeside.
➲ Turn off road to Sursee 400m NW of Nottwil and drive towards lake for 100m.
Apr-Oct 1HEC ⸬⸬⸬ ⩫ ℿ 🛒 ⊙ 🇶 ⌀ ⸚ L 🏧 ⊞ lau ➧ 🛒 ✕ ⸚L

PRÊLES BERN

Prêles ☎ 032 3155160
e-mail: amstad@bluewin.ch
On a wooded plateau overlooking Lake Biel.
➲ Turn off the main Biel-Neuchâtel road at Twann and follow signs for Prêles. Pass through village, site on left.
All year 6HEC ⸬⸬⸬ ⩫ ℿ 🛒 ✕ ⊙ 🇶 ⌀ 🏫 ⸚ P 🏧 ⊞ lau

SAANEN BERN

Beim Kappeli (TCS) ☎ 033 7446191 ▤ 7446184
e-mail: camping.saaren@tcs.ch
In a long meadow between railway and River Saane.
➲ 1km SE.
0.8HEC ⸬⸬⸬ ⚬ ⩫ ℿ ⊙ 🇶 ⛲ ⸚ R 🏧 ⊞ lau ➧ 🛒 🍴 ✕ ⌀ ⸚P

SACHSELN OBWALDEN

Ewil ☎ 041 6663270 ▦ 6663279
e-mail: m.k.berlinger@pop.agri.ch
On a level meadow on the SW shore of the Sarnersee.
➲ W of the main Sachseln-Ewil road towards the lake.
Apr-Sep 1.5HEC ⸗ ⚘ ⟮ 🅻 ⊙ 🗨 𝑎 ⟠ ⟍ L ⟐ ⊞ lau ➧ 𝕐 ✕ ⟍R

SARNER SEE

See **Sachseln**

SEMPACH LUZERN

Seeland (TCS) ☎ 041 4601466 ▦ 4604766
e-mail: camping.sempad@tcs.ch
Rectangular, level site on SW shore of lake.
➲ 700m S on Luzern road by lake.
Apr-Nov 5.2HEC ⸗ ⚘ ➧ ⟮ 🅻 𝕐 ✕ ⊙ 𝑎 𝚫 A ⟍ L ⟐ ⊞ lau

STECHELBERG BERN

Breithorn ☎ 033 8551225 ▦ 8553561
e-mail: breithorn@stechelberg.ch
In a beautiful location in the Lauterbrunnen Valley.
➲ 3km S of Lauterbrunnen.
All year 1HEC ⸗ ⚘ ⟮ 🅻 ⊙ 🗨 𝑎 ⟠ ⟐ ⊞ lau

VITZNAU LUZERN

Vitznau ☎ 041 3971280 ▦ 3972457
e-mail: camping-vitznau@bluewin.ch
Well tended terraced site, in lovely countryside with fine views of lake.
➲ Approaching from N, turn towards mountain at church and follow signs.
Apr-Oct 1.8HEC ⸗ ⚘ ⟮ 🅻 ✕ ⊙ 🗨 𝑎 𝚫 ⟠ ⟍ P ⟐ ⊞ lau ➧ 𝕐 ✕ ⟍L

WILDERSWIL BERN

Oberei ☎ 033 8221335 ▦ 8221335
e-mail: oberei8@swisscamps.ch
A peaceful site in a picturesque village with fine views of the Jungfrau and surrounding mountains. There are good facilities and reservations are recommended during July and August.
Etr-15 Oct 0.6HEC ⸗ ⚘ ⟮ 🅻 ⊙ 🗨 𝑎 𝚫 ⟠ ⟐ ⊞ lau ➧ 𝕐 ✕

ZUG ZUG

Innere Lorzenallmend (TCS) Chamer Fussweg 36 ☎ 041 7418422 ▦ 7418130
e-mail: tcscamping.zug@bluewin.ch
Pleasantly situated with beautiful view of Lake Zug and surrounding mountains. Busy railway which passes the site.
➲ 1km NW by lake.
Apr-Sep 1.1HEC ⸗ ⚘ ⟮ ✕ ⊙ 🗨 𝑎 ⟍ L ⟤ ⊞ lau ➧ 🅻 𝕐 ✕

ZWEISIMMEN BERN

Vermeille ☎ 030 21940 ▦ 030 23625
Well laid-out site along the River Simme.
➲ 1km N towards Lake Thun.
All year 1.3HEC ⬖ ➧ ⟮ 🅻 ⊙ 🗨 𝑎 𝚫 lau ➧ ✕ ⟍P ⊞

● ● ● ● ● **EAST** ● ● ● ● ●

The cantons of Glarus and Grisona make up this region of eastern Switzerland. The town of Glarus still maintains the practice of direct democracy, when every spring all active citizens fill the great Zaunplatz, and in a highly ceremonial meeting decide all issues affecting the community by a show of hands.
Grisons, astride the Alps, is truly Switzerland's holiday corner. Superb road, railway and cable-car networks, run with usual Swiss efficiency, access the wonderful winter sports regions and well-equipped resorts - the elegant Arosa, Davos, Chur, Flims, the famous royal retreat of Klosters and glittering St Moritz. This efficient transport makes the area a summer paradise for walkers and hikers - there are over 3,000 miles of unsignposted cross-country footpaths. Many areas of superb natural beauty are protected by law - the largest is the 65-square-mile Swiss National Park, reached from Zernez, where authorised roads and paths (and guided walks in season), give glimpses of a flora and fauna completely protected from man.
....

ANDEER GRAUBÜNDEN

Sut Baselgia (TCS) ☎ 081 6611453 ▦ 081 6611080
e-mail: camping.andeer@bluewin.ch
In a pleasant, peaceful setting North towards Chur.
Closed Nov 1.2HEC ⸗ ⚘ ⟮ ⊙ 🗨 𝑎 𝚫 ⟐ ⊞ lau ➧ 🅻 𝕐 ✕ ⟍PR Prices: ⚘6.50 ⚗3 ⚑13 A8

AROSA GRAUBÜNDEN

Arosa Tourismus ☎ 081 3771745 ▦ 081 3773005
All year 0.6HEC ⸗ ⚘ ⟮ ⊙ 🗨 𝑎 ⟤ ➧ 🅻 𝕐 ✕ ⟍LP ⊞

CHUR (COIRE) GRAUBÜNDEN

Camp Au Felsenaustr 61 ☎ 081 2842283 ▦ 081 2845683
e-mail: info@camping-chur.ch
A summer and winter site on level ground with fine views of the surrounding mountains. Good recreational facilities.
➲ Take exit Chur-Süd from A13. 2km NW of town centre on bank of Rhein. Access is via outskirts of town.
All year 2.6HEC ⸗ ⚘ ⟮ 🅻 ✕ ⊙ 🗨 𝑎 𝚫 ⟐ ⊞ lau ➧ ⟍P

CHURWALDEN GRAUBÜNDEN

Pradafenz ☎ 081 3821921 ▦ 081 3821921
e-mail: camping@pradafenz.ch
A year round site in a beautiful mountain area close to the local ski slopes.
13Apr-18May & 31Oct-Nov 1.5HEC ⸗ ⚘ ⟮ 🅻 𝕐 ✕ ⊙ 🗨 𝑎 𝚫 ⟐ ⊞ lau ➧ ⟍PR Prices: ⚘6-6.50 ⚑10-13

LENZ GRAUBÜNDEN

St Cassian ☎ 081 3842472 ▦ 3842489
e-mail: camping.st.cassian@bluwin.ch
A level, shady site in a beautiful location at an altitude of 1415mtrs above sea level. There are good facilities and the site is 1km from the town.
➲ Leave motorway at 'Chur-Süd' exit and follow signs for Lenzerheide/St.Moritz up a well constructed mountain road.
All year 25HEC ⸗ ⚡ ⟮ ✕ ⊙ 🗨 𝑎 𝚫 ⟐ ⊞ lau ➧ 🅻 ✕

MÜSTAIR GRAUBÜNDEN

Clenga ☎ 082 85410
Next to small river near the Italian frontier.
15 May-20 Oct 1.5HEC ⸗ ⚘ ⟮ 🅻 𝕐 ⊙ 🗨 𝑎 𝚫 ⚑ ⟍ R ⟐ ⊞ lau

PONTRESINA GRAUBÜNDEN

Plauns (TCS) ☎ 081 8426285
Beautiful situation at foot of Pit Palü.
⤷ *Access from road towards Bernina Pass about 4.5km beyond Pontresina. Turn off main road 29 towards Hotel Morteratsch then 0.5km to site.*
25 May-15 Oct 4HEC ⸿⸿⸿ ⠿⠿⠿ ▲ ⚞ Q ⚭ ⚑ ✕ ⊙ ⚑ ⚊ ⚒ ⚐
⚑ ⊞ lau

POSCHIAVO GRAUBÜNDEN

Boomerang ☎ 081 8440713
In a quiet setting.
⤷ *2km SE.*
All year 1.5HEC ⸿⸿⸿ Q ⚞ ⚭ ⚑ ⊙ ⚑ ⚋ ⚑ ⊞ lau ➧ ⚭LP

SAMEDAN GRAUBÜNDEN

Punt Muragl (TCS) ☎ 081 8428197 ▤ 8428197
e-mail: camping.samedan@tcs.ch
A summer and winter site in a pleasant alpine setting.
⤷ *Near Bernina railway halt, to the right of the fork of the two roads Samedan and Celerina/Schlarigna to Pontresina.*
1 Dec-15 Apr & 1 Jun-30 Sep 2HEC ⸿⸿⸿ Q ⚞ ⚭ ⚑ ✕ ⊙ ⚑ ⚋
⚊ ⚐ ⊞ lau ➧ ✕ ⚭L

SPLÜGEN GRAUBÜNDEN

Sand ☎ 081 6641476 ▤ 6641460
e-mail: camping@splugen.ch
On left bank of River Hinterrhein.
⤷ *Turn off the main trunk road in the village and follow signposts.*
All year 0.8HEC ⸿⸿⸿ ♠ ⚞ ⚭ ⚑ ✕ ⊙ ⚑ ⚋ ⚊ ⚭ R ⚑ ⊞ lau ➧
✕ **Prices:** ♠6.50 ♠3.20 ⚐16 ▲7.20

STRADA IM ENGADIN GRAUBÜNDEN

Arina ☎ 081 8863212
⤷ *At the foot of a mountain, SW of village.*
May-Oct 0.8HEC ⸿⸿⸿ Q ⚞ ⊙ ⚑ ⚭ PR ⚑ ⊞ lau ➧ ⚭ ✕

SUR EN GRAUBÜNDEN

Sur En ☎ 081 8663544
A family site in a beautiful mountain setting surrounded by pine trees with good facilities.
All year 2HEC ⸿⸿⸿ Q ⚞ ⚭ ⚑ ⚑ ✕ ⊙ ⚑ ⚋ ⚊ ⚐ ⚑ ⚭ PR ⚑ ⊞ lau

SUSCH GRAUBÜNDEN

Muglinas ☎ 081 8622744
⤷ *200m W.*
Jun-15 Sep 1HEC ⸿⸿⸿ ⚞ ⊙ ⚑ ⚋ ⚭ R ⚑ ⊞ lau ➧ ⚭ ⚑ ✕

THUSIS GRAUBÜNDEN

Viamala ☎ 081 6512472
In pleasant wooded surroundings near the River Hinterrhein and close to the beautiful Viamala Gorge.
⤷ *NE towards Chur.*
May-Sep 4.5HEC ⸿⸿⸿ ♠ ⚞ ⚭ ⚑ ✕ ⊙ ⚑ ⚋ ⚐ ⚑ ⊞ lau ➧
⚭PR

TSCHIERV GRAUBÜNDEN

Sternen (TCS) Chasa Maruya ☎ 081 8585628
e-mail: maruya@tiscalinet.ch
In village behind the Sternen Hotel.
⤷ *Between Ofen Pass and Santa Maria.*
All year 1HEC ⸿⸿⸿ Q ⚞ ⚭ ⚑ ✕ ⊙ ⚑ ⚋ ⚭ P ⚑ ⊞ lau

VICOSOPRANO GRAUBÜNDEN

Mulina ☎ 081 8221035
May-Oct 1.5HEC ⸿⸿⸿ Q ⚞ ✕ ⊙ ⚑ ⚭ LR ⚑ ➧ ⚭ ⚑ ✕ ⚋ ⊞

ZERNEZ GRAUBÜNDEN

Cul ☎ 081 8561456 ▤ 8561462
e-mail: a.filli@camping-cul.ch
In a delightful mountain setting close to the Swiss National Park.
⤷ *Off road 27 W of Zernez.*
May-15 Oct 3.6HEC ⸿⸿⸿ Q ⚞ ⚭ ⚑ ✕ ⊙ ⚑ ⚋ ⚭ R ⚑ ⊞
lau ➧ ✕ ⚭P

● ● ● ● ● SOUTH ● ● ● ● ●

Here, in the canton of Ticino, the German and Italian cultures mingle in a land where Alpine mountains and valleys fall towards the great lakes and the plain of Lombardy. The province is a climatic oasis: the Alpine chain protects it from strong winds, and even in winter there is a comparatively high number of sunny days. Alpine and Mediterranean plant species flourish side by side, giving Ticino a unique flora.
In this area of outstanding beauty, Lugano remains a favourite with visitors. The town has a traditional atmosphere, with attractive lanes and shopping arcades, spacious parks and lakeside promenades. Excursions from Lugano lead to high mountains and some of the best views in the country - Mount San Salvatore, Mount Bré and Mount Generoso. Locarno, a lovely town on the shores of Lake Maggiore, is also popular, and the exceptionally mild southern climate produces lush vegetation and a wonderfully colourful display of flowers in early spring.
....

ACQUACALDA TICINO

Ai Cembri Lukmanierstr ☎ 091 8722610
In a beautiful mountain location with good hiking facilities.
Apr-Oct 5HEC ⸿⸿⸿ Q ⚞ ⚭ ⚑ ✕ ⊙ ⚑ ⚋ ⚐ ⚐ ⚭ R ⚑ ⊞ ⚑ lau

AGNO TICINO

Eurocampo ☎ 091 6052114 ▤ 091 6053187
Part of site is near its own sandy beach and is divided by groups of trees.
⤷ *600m E on road from Lugano to Ponte Tresa. Entrance opposite Aeroport sign and Alfa Romeo building.*
Apr-Oct 4HEC ⸿⸿⸿ Q ⚞ ⚭ ⚑ ✕ ⊙ ⚑ ⚋ ⚭ LR ⚑ ⊞ lau ➧
✕

Golfo del Sole via Rivera 8 ☎ 091 6054802 ▤ 091 6052319
e-mail: golfo-del-sole@swisscamps.ch
By lake. Separate play area for children.
23 Mar-19 Oct 6HEC ⸿⸿⸿ ♠ Q ⚞ ⚭ ⚑ ✕ ⊙ ⚑ ⚋ ⚭ L ⚑ ⊞
➧ ✕

CHIGGIOGNA TICINO

Gottardo ☎ 091 8661562 ▤ 091 8662113
Open meadowland on mountain slope partly on natural terraces.
⤷ *1km S of Faido, 20m above A2.*
All year 0.8HEC ⸿⸿⸿ Q ⚞ ⚭ ⚑ ✕ ⊙ ⚑ ⚋ ⚭ PR ⚑ ⊞ lau

CLARO TICINO

Censo ☎ 091 8631753
Below a woodland slope.
⤷ *Off the A2 (E9).*
Apr-Sep 2HEC ⸿⸿⸿ ♠ ⚞ ⚭ ⚑ ✕ ⊙ ⚑ ⚋ ⚭ PR ⚑ ⊞ lau

CUGNASCO TICINO

Park-Camping Riarena ☎ 091 8591688 ▤ 091 8592885
e-mail: camping-riarena@bluewin.ch
Beautiful park-like family site in level, natural woodland. All facilities are well maintained and Lake Maggiore is within easy reach.

⮑ *1.5km NW. Turn off road 13 at BP filling station 9km NE of Locarno and continue 0.5km.*
15 Mar-30 Oct 3.2HEC ⚏ ⠿ ♠ ℝ ▙ 𝚼 ✗ ⊙ ☺ ⌀ ▟ ♈ ▲
⚡ P ⊞ lau ♦ ⭍R

GORDEVIO TICINO

Bellariva ☎ 093 871444
In quiet location between the road and the left bank of the River Maggia.
Apr-Oct 2.5HEC ⚏ ⍾ ℝ ▙ ⊙ ☺ ⌀ ⭍ PR ⛫ ⊞ lau ♦ 𝚼 ✗

LOCARNO TICINO

Delta via Respini 7 ☎ 091 7516081 ▤ 7512243
e-mail: info@campingdelta.com
A beautiful, well-equipped and well-organised site at Lake Maggiore.
⮑ *2km away from the city.*
Mar-Oct 60HEC ⚏ ⠿ ⍾ ℝ ▙ 𝚼 ✗ ⊙ ☺ ⌀ ▟ ⭍ LR ⛫
⊞ ⬙ lau ♦ ⭍P

At LOSONE(4km W)

Zandone ☎ 091 7916563 ▤ 091 7910047
In a quiet, picturesque location beside the River Melezza with fine views of the Tessin mountains.
⮑ *Situated between the Losone-Golino road and the river.*
Etr-Oct 2.1HEC ⚏ ⍾ ℝ ▙ ⊙ ☺ ⌀ ▟ ♈ ⭍ R ⛫ ⊞ ♦ 𝚼 ✗

MOLINAZZO DI MONTEGGIO TICINO

Tresiana ☎ 091 6083342 ▤ 091 6083142
e-mail: mail@camping-tresiana
A family site on meadowland with trees on riverbank.
⮑ *Turn right after bridge in Ponte Tresa, then 5km to site.*
27 Mar-20 Oct 1.5HEC ⚏ ⍾ ℝ ▙ ✗ ⊙ ☺ ⌀ ⭍ ♈ ⭍ PR ⛫ ⊞
lau ♦ **Prices:** ⋔6 ♠2.50 ♠10-16.50 ▲5-16.50

ROVEREDO TICINO

Vera ☎ 091 8271857 ▤ 091 8271898
⮑ *10km N of Bellinzona near A13 exit 'Chur-Bellinzona'.*
All year 4HEC ⚏ ⍾ ℝ ✗ ⊙ ☺ ⌀ ⭍ PR ⛫ lau ♦ ▙ ⊞

TENERO TICINO

Campofelice Lago Maggiore
☎ 091 (0041) 745 14 17 ▤ 7451888
e-mail: camping@campofelice.ch
Beautifully situated and extensive site completely divided into pitches, and crossed by asphalt drives.
⮑ *1.9km S. Signposted.*
Apr-17 Oct 15HEC ⚏ ⠿ ♠ ℝ ▙ 𝚼 ✗ ⊙ ☺ ⌀ ▟ ⭍ LR
⛫ ⊞ ⬙ lau

Lido Mappo Via Mappo ☎ 091 7451437 ▤ 7454808
Beautifully situated, well appointed site on lakeside. Teenagers not accepted on their own. Minimum stay, 1 week in Jul-Aug.
⮑ *700m SW. Signposted.*
22 Mar-20 Oct 6.5HEC ⚏ ♠ ℝ ▙ 𝚼 ✗ ⊙ ☺ ⌀ ▟ ⭍ L ⛫ ⊞ ⬙ lau ♦ ⭍PR

Tamaro via Mappo ☎ 091 7452161 ▤ 091 7456636
e-mail: camping.tamaro@tinet.ch
Well equipped site with direct access to the lake. Groups of young persons not admitted unless accompanied by adults.
⮑ *4km from Locano. Signposted from motorway.*
15 Mar-20 Oct 6HEC ⚏ ⍾ ℝ ▙ ✗ ⊙ ☺ ⌀ ♈ ⭍ L ⛫
⊞ ⬙ lau ♦ ⭍P

⬤ ⬤ ⬤ ⬤ **SOUTH WEST** ⬤ ⬤ ⬤ ⬤

Vaud, Fribourg, Valais and Geneva are the cantons in this south-west region. All these provinces have resorts at every altitude to welcome both summer and winter visitors - the mountains and glaciers are easily accessed in winter for skiers, and in summer mountain huts, chalets, and hotels provide facilities for walkers and hikers.
Valais has been a trading crossroads since Roman times, with its passes at St Bernard and Simplon. The Rhône, with its tributaries, cuts a lovely swathe through Valais on its way to the jewel of the south west - Lake Geneva. Resorts dot the lake shores - small towns like Crans, Nyon and Vevey, popular Montreux, cosmopolitan Lausanne, and, of course, the country's great international centre, Geneva. Art, culture and education are great traditions here, and there is a wealth of attractions for tourists - excellent shopping centres, renowned restaurants, an attractive old town, fascinating museums, and miles of attractive promenades along the shores of the lake with wonderful views of the mountains.

....

AGARN VALAIS

Gemmi Briannestr ☎ 027 4731154 ▤ 027 4734295
e-mail: campgemmi@aol.com
In a very pleasant location on the outskirts of the town, providing outstanding views of the surrounding mountains. There are clean, modern facilities and individual bathrooms are available for weekly hire.
⮑ *Exit from A9 at Agarn. Signposted*
12 Apr-13 Oct 0.9HEC ⚏ ⍾ ℝ ▙ ✗ ⊙ ☺ ⌀ ♈ ⛫ ⊞ lau ♦ 𝚼
✗ ⭍P

AIGLE VAUD

Glariers (TCS) ☎ 024 4662660
On level ground with trees and bushes near railway line and the avenue des Glariers. Fine mountain views.
⮑ *800m NE off the A9 near Shell/Migrol petrol station.*
2 Apr-2 Oct 1HEC ⠿ ⭍ ℝ ▙ 𝚼 ✗ ⊙ ☺ ♈ ⭍ PR ⛫ lau ♦
✗ ⌀

AROLLA VALAIS

Petit Praz ☎ 027 2832295
e-mail: camping@arolla.com
In an imposing mountain setting.
Jun-Sep 1HEC ⚏ ⭍ ⭍ ℝ ▙ ⊙ ☺ ⌀ ♈ **Prices:** ⋔6 ♠2
♠6 ▲4-6

BALLENS VAUD

Bois Gentil ☎ 021 8095120
⮑ *200m S of station.*
Apr-Sep 2.5HEC ⚏ ⍾ ℝ ▙ ⊙ ☺ ⌀ ⭍ P ⛫ ⊞

BOURG-ST-PIERRE VALAIS

Grand St-Bernard ☎ 027 7871411 ▤ 027 7871411
e-mail: grand-st-bernard@swisscamps.ch
In beautiful mountain scenery with easy access to winter sports area.
⮑ *Near the Italian border, between Martigny and Aosta.*
May-Sep 1HEC ⚏ ⭍ ℝ ⊙ ☺ ⌀ ⭍ P ⛫ ⊞ lau ♦ ▙ 𝚼 ✗
⭍R

BOUVERET, LE VALAIS

Rive Bleue ☎ 024 4812161
Beside lake with a natural sandy beach and good, modern facilities.
⮑ *Turn off the A37 to Monthey in the SW district of Bouveret and drive NE for about 0.8km.*
Apr-Sep 3HEC ⚏ ⍾ ℝ ▙ ⊙ ☺ ⌀ ♈ ♠ ♈ ▲ ⭍ LP ▣ ⊞ lau
♦ 𝚼 ✗ ⭍R

▶ **BULLET** VAUD

Cluds Camping VD 28 Bullet-les Cluds
☎ 024 4541440 ▤ 024 4263810
e-mail: ccy@bluewin.ch
In beautiful mountain setting among pine trees.
➲ *1.5km NE.*
All year 1.2HEC ⸬ ⚡ ⚌ ⚽ ✕ ⊙ 🗨 ⌀ ⚒ 🄿 ⊞ lau Prices: ⚡7
🚐3 🚐7-14 ▲5.50-14

▶ **CHÂTEAU-D'OEX** VAUD

Berceau (TCS) La Place ☎ 026 9246234 ▤ 026 9242526
e-mail: chateau-doex@bluewin.ch
On level strip of grass between the mountain and river bank.
➲ *1km SE at junction of roads 77 and 76.*
All year 1HEC ⸬ ⚌ ⚡ ⚽ ▲ ✕ ⊙ 🗨 ⌀ ⚒ � PR 🄿 ⊞ lau ➧ 🍽

▶ **CHÂTEL-ST-DENIS** FRIBOURG

Bivouac rte des Paccots ☎ 021 9487849 ▤ 9487849
e-mail: bivouac@swissonline.ch
Beautiful views of the rolling Swiss countryside. Various
sports and leisure activities.
➲ *Turn E in Chatel-St Denis and continue for 2km.*
All year 2HEC ⸬ ⚡ ⚽ ⚡ ✕ ⊙ 🗨 ⌀ ⚒ � PR 🄿 ⊞ lau ➧
✕ Prices: ⚡5-6 pitch 15

▶ **CHESSEL** VAUD

Grands Bois ☎ 024 4814225 ▤ 024 4815113
e-mail: au.grand-bois@bluewin.ch
On a level meadow close to a canal and only a few kilometres
from Lake Geneva.
➲ *N of town towards the lake.*
All year 4HEC ⸬ ⚡ ⚽ ⚡ ⚽ ✕ ⊙ 🗨 ⌀ ⚒ � PR 🄿 lau
Prices: ⚡4.50-6 🚐3 🚐6.50-9 ▲3.50-7

▶ **CUDREFIN** VAUD

Chablais ☎ 037 773277
500mtrs from the town centre, directly on the lake.
15 Mar-Oct 228HEC ⸬ ⚡ ⚽ ⊙ 🗨 � L 🄿 lau ➧ 🍽 ⚡ ✕ ⌀
� R

▶ **DÜDINGEN** FRIBOURG

Schiffenensee ☎ 026 493486
➲ *Leave the A12 (Bern-Fribourg) at Düdingen and proceed
N towards Murten.*
Apr-Oct 9HEC ⸬ ⚡ ⚽ ⚡ ✕ ⊙ 🗨 � LP 🄿 ⊞ lau ➧ ⌀ ▲

▶ **EVOLÈNE** VALAIS

Evolène ☎ 027 2831144 ▤ 027 2833255
e-mail: evolene@swisscamps.ch
On a level meadow with fine views of the surrounding
mountains.
➲ *200m from town*
All year 10HEC ⸬ ⚌ ⚡ ⚽ ⊙ 🗨 ⌀ ⚒ 🄿 ⊞ lau ➧ ⚡ ✕ � R
Prices: ⚡6 🚐3 🚐6 ▲4-6

▶ **FOREL** VAUD

Forel ☎ 021 7811464 ▤ 021 7813126
A family site in a pleasant rural setting with good
recreational facilities.
➲ *Leave the A9 at Chexbres in the direction of Forel and take
left turning to Savigny.*
All year 4HEC ⸬ ⚡ ⚽ ⚡ ✕ ⊙ 🗨 ⌀ ⚒ 🚲 🚐 � P 🄿 ⊞ lau

▶ **FOULY, LA** VALAIS

Glaciers ☎ 027 7831735 ▤ 027 7833605
e-mail: camping.glaciers@st-bernard.ch
At end of village in a beautiful Alpine location with fine
views of the surrounding mountains.
15 May-Sep 8HEC ⸬ ⚡ ⚽ ⊙ 🗨 ⌀ ⚒ 🄿 ⊞ lau ➧ ⚡ ✕
�LPRS Prices: ⚡6.50 pitch 10.16

▶ **GENÈVE (GENEVA)** GENÈVE

At **SATIGNY**(6km SW)

Bois-de-Bay ☎ 022 3410505 ▤ 022 3410606
➲ *Leave A1 at Bernex and follow campsite signs.*
All year 2.8HEC ⸬ ⚡ ⚽ ⚡ ⊙ 🗨 ⌀ ⚒ ⊞ ⊞

At **VÉSENAZ**(6km NE)

Pointe á la Bise (TCS) ☎ 022 7521296 ▤ 022 7523767
e-mail: camping.geneve@tcs.ch
In a pleasant wooded setting on the shore of Lake Léman.
➲ *NE between Vésenaz and Collonge-Bellerive.*
Etr-mid Oct 3.2HEC ⸬ ⚡ ⚽ ⚡ ✕ ⊙ 🗨 ⌀ ⚒ � L ⊞ ⊞
Prices: ⚡5.20-6.20 🚐5.50-7 🚐10.50-12 ▲7.50-9

▶ **GRÄCHEN** VALAIS

Grächbiel ☎ 027 9563202
A modern site with excellent facilities, in a good location for
access to Zermatt.
All year 6HEC ⸬ ⚡ ⚽ ⚡ ✕ ⊙ 🗨 ⌀ ⚒ ⊞ ⊞ lau

▶ **GRANDSON** VAUD

Pécos ☎ 024 4454969 ▤ 024 4462904
e-mail: ccy@bluewin.ch
➲ *400m SW of railway station between railway and lake.*
Apr-Sep 2HEC ⸬ ⚌ ⚡ ⚽ ✕ ⊙ 🗨 ⌀ ⚒ � L ⊞ ⊞ lau
Prices: ⚡6.90 🚐3 🚐7-14 ▲5.50-14

▶ **GUMEFENS** FRIBOURG

Lac ☎ 026 9152162 ▤ 026 9152162
e-mail: campingdulac@planet.ch
On the borders of the lake.
15 May-15 Sep 1.5HEC ⸬ ⚌ ⚡ ⚽ ⊙ 🗨 ⌀ � L ⊞ ⊞
🔒 lau

▶ **LAUSANNE** VAUD

At **OUCHY**

Vidy chemin du Camping 3 ☎ 216225000 ▤ 216225001
e-mail: info@campinglausannevidy.ch
In a delightful location amid trees and flowerbeds
overlooking Lac Léman. Shop and restaurant open May-Sep
only.
All year 4.5HEC ⸬ ⚡ ⚽ ⚡ ✕ ⊙ 🗨 ⌀ ⚒ 🚲 � L ⊞ ⊞ lau

▶ **LEUKERBAD** VALAIS

Sport-Arena Leukerbad ☎ 027 4701037
➲ *On road N of Leuk.*
May-Oct 1HEC ⸬ ⚌ ⚡ ⚽ ✕ ⊙ 🗨 ⊞ ⊞ lau ➧ ⚡ ⌀ �PR

▶ **LEYSIN** VAUD

Sémiramis ☎ 024 4941829 ▤ 024 4942121
e-mail: info@hoteldusoleil
In a picturesque Alpine setting.
➲ *After entering the village turn left at SHELL filling station
and continue for 400mtrs.*
All year 1.1HEC ⸬ ⚌ ⚡ ⚽ ⚡ ✕ ⊙ 🗨 ⌀ ⚒ ⊞ ⊞ lau ➧ ⚡ ✕
�P Prices: ⚡9.05-9.45 🚐4-5.50 🚐7-7.20 ▲3-4

▶ **MORGES** VAUD

Petit Bois (TCS) ☎ 021 8011270
➲ *Follow Geneva road from town. Site by lakeside.*
26 Mar-19 Oct 3.2HEC ⸬ ⚌ ⚡ ⚽ ⚡ ✕ ⊙ 🗨 ⌀ ⚒ ⊞ ⊞ lau
➧ �LP

▶ **MORGINS** VALAIS

Morgins (TCS) ☎ 024 4772361 ▤ 4773708
e-mail: touristoffice@morgins.ch
A terraced site below pine forest.

⮕ *Turn left at end of village towards Pas de Morgins near Swiss Customs.*
All year 1.3HEC ⸽⸽⸽⸽ ⚡ ⌂ ⊙ ⊡ ⚐ ⊞ lau ➧ ⚏ ⚡ ✕ ⊘ ☷
꙼PR Prices: ⊟10

▶ PAYERNE VAUD

Piscine de Payerne ☎ 037 614322
Camping Card compulsory
Apr-Sep 8HEC ⸽⸽⸽⸽ ⚐ ⌂ ✕ ⊙ ⚐ ⊘ ☷ ꙼ P ⊡ ⊞ lau

▶ RARON VALAIS

Santa Monica ☎ 027 9342424
All year 4HEC ⸽⸽⸽⸽ ⚐ ⌂ ⚏ ✕ ⊙ ⚐ ⊘ ⊟ ꙼ P ⊡ lau ➧ ⚡ ꙼LR

Simplonblick ☎ 027 9341274
⮕ *300m W of Turtig.*
Apr-Oct 6HEC ⸽⸽⸽⸽ ⚐ ⌂ ⚏ ⚡ ✕ ⊙ ⚐ ⊘ ☷ ꙼ P ⊡ ⊞ lau ➧ ⚏

▶ RECKINGEN VALAIS

Ellbogen (TCS) ☎ 028 731355
On an alpine meadow close to the River Rhône.
⮕ *400m S on bank of Rhône.*
13 May-13 Oct 1.3HEC ⸽⸽⸽⸽ ⚡ ⌂ ⚏ ✕ ⊙ ⚐ ⊘ ☷ ⊡ ⊞ lau ➧ ꙼P

▶ RIED-BRIG VALAIS

Tropic ☎ 027 9232537
⮕ *To the left of Simplon road near entrance to village. 3km above Brig.*
May-15 Sep 1.5HEC ⸽⸽⸽⸽ ➧ ⌂ ⚏ ⚡ ✕ ⊙ ⚐ ⊘ ⊟ ⚐ ⊡ ⊞ lau ➧ ꙼P Prices: ♦5.50 ➧4 ⊟5-7 ♦4-8

▶ SAAS-GRUND VALAIS

Kapellenweg ☎ 027 9574997 ▤ 027 9573316
e-mail: camping@kapellenweg.ch
On a level meadow in a picturesque mountain setting in the Saas Valley. Good, modern facilities.
⮕ *Turn right over bridge towards Saas-Almagell.*
May-Oct 1.5HEC ⸽⸽⸽⸽ ⚐ ⌂ ⚏ ⊙ ⚐ ⊘ ☷ ꙼ R ⊡ lau ➧ ⚡ ✕

▶ SALGESCH VALAIS

Swiss Plage ☎ 027 4556608 ▤ 027 4813215
Situated beside a small lake and surrounded by vineyards. Good recreational facilities.
Etr-1 Nov 10HEC ⸽⸽⸽⸽ ∷∴ ♦ ⚐ ⌂ ⚏ ⚡ ✕ ⊙ ⚐ ⊘ ☷ ⊟ ⚐ ꙼ L ⊡ ⊞ lau

▶ SEMBRANCHER VALAIS

Prairie (TCS) ☎ 027 7852206 ▤ 027 7852131
⮕ *12km from Martigny and 500m from town.*
All year 50HEC ⸽⸽⸽⸽ ⚡ ⌂ ⚏ ⚡ ✕ ⊙ ⚐ ⊘ ☷ ⊡ lau ➧ ꙼R ⊞

▶ SIERRE (SIDERS) VALAIS

Bois de Finges (TCS) ☎ 027 4550284
Situated in a pine forest with well defined pitches set on terraces.
⮕ *Access via motorway exit Sierre-Ouest towards Sierre.*
Etr-Sep 5HEC ⸽⸽⸽⸽ ∷∴ ⚐ ⌂ ⚏ ⚡ ✕ ⊙ ⚐ ⊘ ☷ ꙼ P ⊡ ⊞ lau ➧ ✕ ꙼LR

▶ SORENS FRIBOURG

Forêt ☎ 026 9151882
e-mail: camping.laforet@caramail.com
A pleasant site on a level meadow surrounded by woodland and with plenty of vegetation.
⮕ *Turn right off the A12 in Gumefens and drive on to the village.*
All year 4HEC ⸽⸽⸽⸽ ⚐ ⌂ ⚏ ✕ ⊙ ⚐ ⊘ ☷ ⚐ ꙼ P ⊡ lau

Rhonetal Simplonblick, Raron
4****-Camping in a park-like situation

Generously equiped site with swimming pool, playgrounds, music , washing machines and tumblers.
Centrally located for excursions to Zermatt, Saas-Fee, etc.

Visit to and free guidance around the Alpine Museum Zermatt (first ascent of the Matterhorn by the English alpinist Edward Whymper).

Phone 0041-27-934 12 74, Fax 0041-27-934 26 00
Phone 0041-27-967 75 75, Fax 0041-27-967 50 12
www.camping-simplonblick.ch
E-Mail: simplonblick@bluewin.ch

▶ SUSTEN VALAIS

Bella Tola (TCS) ☎ 027 4731491 ▤ 4733641
e-mail: bellatola@rhone.ch
A peaceful, terraced site at an altitude of 750mtrs, sheilded by a belt of woodland. Good, clean modern facilities.
⮕ *2km from village.*
8May-29Sep 3.6HEC ⸽⸽⸽⸽ ⚐ ⌂ ⚏ ⚡ ✕ ⊙ ⚐ ⊘ ☷ ꙼ P ⊡ lau

Rhodania Kantonstr ☎ 027 4731312
May-Oct 0.2HEC ⸽⸽⸽⸽ ➧ ⌂ ⚏ ⚡ ✕ ⊙ ⚐ ⊡ ➧ ⚏ ⊘ ꙼PR ⊞
Prices: ♦5 ➧2 ⊟5.50 ♦3.50-5.50

▶ ULRICHEN VALAIS

Nufenen ☎ 027 9731437
e-mail: camping-nufenen@rhone.ch
⮕ *1km SE to right of road to Nufenen Pass.*
Jun-Sep 8HEC ⸽⸽⸽⸽ ⚐ ⌂ ⊙ ⚐ ⊘ ☷ ꙼ R ⊡ ⊞ lau ➧ ⚏ ⚡ ✕

▶ VALLORBE VAUD

Pré sous Ville (TCS) ☎ 021 8432309
In a wooded riverside location. Neighbouring swimming pool available to campers free of charge.
⮕ *On left bank of River Orbe.*
May-Oct 1HEC ⸽⸽⸽⸽ ⚐ ⌂ ⊙ ⚐ ⊘ ꙼ P ⊡ ⊞ lau ➧ ⚏ ⚡ ✕

▶ VERS-L'ÉGLISE VAUD

Murée (TCS) ☎ 021 6345284 ▤ 0216345284
e-mail: dagonch@bluewinich.
Partially terraced site by a stream.
⮕ *Signposted on the right at the entry to the village.*
All year 1.1HEC ⸽⸽⸽⸽ ⚐ ⌂ ⊙ ⚐ ⊘ ☷ ♦ ꙼ R ⊡ lau ➧ ⚡ ✕ ⊞
Prices: ♦4.80-5.30 ⊟9-9 ♦8

VÉTROZ VALAIS

Botza (TCS) ☎ 027 3461940
e-mail: serge@revas.com
On a level meadow with pitches divided by hedges. Fine panoramic views and good leisure facilities.
All year 3HEC ▥ ♠ ⟨⟨ ⟲ ♀ ✕ ☉ 🅾 ⌀ 🎵 🏕 🛖 🔺 ⤳ P ☎ ⊞

YVONAND VAUD

Pointe d'Yvonand ☎ 024 4301655 ▤ 024 4302463
e-mail: ccy@bluewin.ch
6km NE of Yverdon bordering Lake Neuchâtel with private beach 1km away, boat moorings, private jetty and boat hire.
➲ *3km W. Signposted.*
Apr-Sep 5HEC ▥ ∷∷∷ ♠ ⟨⟨ ⟲ ♀ ✕ ☉ 🅾 ⌀ 🎵 🏕 🛖 ⤳ L 🅿
⊞ ⚒ lau **Prices:** ♠6.90 🚗3 ⊞7-14 ▲5.50-14

The 16th-century Astronomical Clock in Kramgrasse, Berne

INDEX

BELGIUM

FRANCE

❖

INDEX

INDEX

INDEX

INDEX

GERMANY

INDEX

INDEX

INDEX

LUXEMBOURG

INDEX

SWITZERLAND

INDEX

PICTURE CREDITS

All the photographs used in this guide are owned and held in the Automobile Association's own Picture Library (AA PHOTOLIBRARY) and were taken by the following photographers:

Adrian Baker Cover and pages 1, 66, 67, 68, 202, 203 and 204
Steve Day pages 51, 60, 240, 310, 311, 312, 350, 336, 337, 338 and 339
Paul Kenward page 101
Alex Kouprianoff pages 82, 83, 84, 85, 86, 93, 237, 239, 241, 280, 300, 302 and 306
Roger Moss page 62
David Noble page 99
Ken Paterson pages 278 and 281, 282
Douglas Robertson pages 98 and 309
Clive Sawyer pages 238 and 271
Tony Souter page 199
Rick Strange pages 96 and 97
Peter Wilson pages 298, 299 and 301

MAJOR ROAD AND RAIL TUNNELS

ROAD TUNNELS

See Lights in the ABC. Minimum and maximum speed limits operate in the road tunnels.

During the winter wheel chains may occasionally be required on the approaches to some tunnels. However, you may not use them in tunnels. Use the laybys provided for removal and refitting. All charges listed below should be used as a guide only.

BIELSA France-Spain

The trans-Pyrenean tunnel is 3km (2 miles) long, and runs nearly 1830 metres (6000ft) above sea level between Aragnouet and Bielsa.

CADI Spain

The tunnel is 5km (3 miles) long and runs about 1220 metres (4000ft) above sea level under the Sierra del Cadi mountain range between the villages of Bellver de Cerdanya and Baga, and to the west of the Toses (Tosas) Pass.

Charges	(in Euros)
Motorcycles	6.10
Cars	7.57
Car/caravan	7.57

FREJUS France-Italy

This tunnel is over 1220 metres (4000ft) above sea level and runs between Modane and Bardonecchia. It is 12.8km (8 miles) long, 4.3 metres (14ft 2in) high, and the single carriageway is 9 metres (29ft 6in) wide. Minimum speed is 60kph (37mph) and the maximum 80kph (49mph).

Charges	(in Euros)
Motorcycles	16.01
Cars wheelbase less than 2.30 metres (7ft 6.5in)	16.01
Wheelbase from 2.30 metres to	
2.63 metres (7ft 6.5in to 8ft 7.5in)	24.24
Wheelbase from 2.63 metres to	
3.30 metres (8ft 7.5in to 10ft 10in)	31.56
Car/caravan	31.56
Wheelbase over 3.30 metres (10ft 10in)	90.86
Vehicles with three axles	138.42
With four or more axles	183.24

MONT BLANC Chamonix (France)- Courmayeur (Italy)

Note: The restoration and modernisation of the Mont Blanc tunnel is expected to be completed by October 2001. Once the services and systems have been tested and trial runs and practice drills completed, the decision as to when the tunnel will reopen rests with the French and Italian governments.

GRAND ST BERNARD Switzerland - Italy

The tunnel is over 1925 metres (7570ft) above sea level. Although there are covered approaches, wheel chains may be needed in winter. Customs, passport control and toll offices are at the entrance. It is 5.9km (3.6 miles) long. Permitted maximum dimensions of vehicles are: height 4 metres (13ft 1in), width 2.5 metres (8ft 2.5in). Minimum speed is 40kph (24mph); maximum 80kph (49mph). Do not stop or overtake. Breakdown bays have telephones.

Charges*	(in Swiss francs)
Motorcycles	15
Cars	27
Car/caravan	40
Minibus, camper van (2 axles)	40
Vehicles with three axles	100
with four or more axles	150

*Motorway tax disc (see Switzerland Country Intro) must be displayed.

ST GOTTHARD Switzerland

This tunnel is 1154 metres (3786 ft) above sea level. It is 16.9km (10.5 miles) long and runs under the St Gotthard Pass from Göschenen, on the northern side in the Alps, to Airolo in the Ticino. The tunnel is 4.5 metres (14ft 9in) high, and the single carriageway is 7.5 metres (25ft) wide. Maximum speed is 80kph (49mph). Forming part of the Swiss motorway network, the tunnel is subject to motorway tax, and the tax disc must be displayed (see Switzerland - Country Intro).

SAN BERNARDINO Switzerland

This tunnel is over 1644 metres (5396ft) above sea level. It is 6.6km (4 miles) long, 4.8 metres (15ft 9in) high; the carriageway is 7 metres (23ft) wide. Do not stop or overtake in the tunnel. Keep 100 metres (110yds) between vehicles. There are breakdown bays with telephones.

As part of the Swiss motorway network, the tunnel is subject to motorway tax (see Switzerland - Country Intro).

ARLBERG Austria

This tunnel is 14km (8.75 miles) long and runs at about 1220 metres (4000ft) above sea level, to the south of and parallel to the Arlberg Pass.

Charges* (in Euros)

Motorcycles	7.27
Cars	9.45
Caravans	4.36

BOSRUCK Austria

This tunnel is 742 metres (2434ft) above sea level. It is 5.5km (3.4 miles) long and runs between Spital am Pyhrn and Selzthal, to the east of the Pyhrn Pass. Maximum speed is 80kph (49mph). Do not overtake. Use of dipped headlights compulsory; occasional emergency laybys with telephones. With the Gleinalm Tunnel (see below) it forms part of the A9 Pyhrn Autobahn between Linz and Graz, being built in stages.

Charges* (in Euros)

Motorcycles	4.36
Cars	5.09
Car/caravan	7.27

*Motorway tax disc (see Austria Country Intro) must be displayed.

FELBERTAUERN Austria

This tunnel, over 1650 metres (5415ft) above sea level, runs between Mittersill and Matrei, west of and parallel to the Grossglockner Pass. The tunnel is 5.2km (3.23 miles) long, 4.5 metres (14ft 9in) high, and the two-lane carriageway is 7 metres (23ft) wide. From November to April, wheel chains may be needed on the approach.

Charges (in Euros)

Motorcycles	7.27
Cars summer rate (May-Oct)	13.81
winter rate (Nov-Apr)	7.99
Car/caravan summer rate (May-Oct)	16.71
winter rate (Nov-Apr)	10.90

GLEINALM Austria

This tunnel, part of the A9 Pyhrn Autobahn, is 817 metres (2680ft) above sea level, 8.3km (5 miles) long and runs between St Michael and Friesach, near Graz.

Charges* (in Euros)

Motorcycles	7.27
Cars	9.45

Car/caravan	11.63

*Motorway tax disc (see Austria Country Intro) must be displayed.

KARAWANKEN Austria-Slovenia

This motorway tunnel under the Karawanken mountains between Rosenbach in Austria and Jesenice in Slovenia is about 610 metres (2000ft) above sea level and nearly 8km (5 miles) long.

Charges* (in Euros)

Motorcycles	xx
Cars	xx
Car/caravan	xxx

*Motorway tax disc (see Austria Country Intro) must be displayed.

TAUERN AUTOBAHN (Katschberg and Radstädter) Austria

Two tunnels, the Katschberg and the Radstädter Tauern, form the key elements of this toll motorway between Salzburg and Carinthia.

The Katschberg tunnel is 1110 metres (3642ft) above sea level. It is 5.4km (3.5 miles) long, 4.5 metres (14ft 9in) high, and the single carriageway is 7.5 metres (25ft) wide.

The Radstädter Tauern tunnel is 1340 metres (4396ft) above sea level and runs east of the Tauern railway tunnel (see below). The tunnel is 6.4km (4 miles) long, 4.5 metres (14ft 9in) high; the single carriageway is 7.5m (25ft) wide.

Charges* (for the whole toll section between Flachau and Rennweg:) (in Euros)

Motorcycles	7.27
Cars	10.17
Car/caravan	13.08

*Motorway tax disc (see Austria Country Intro) must be displayed.

RAIL TUNNELS
EUROTUNNEL See the Continental ABC

LÖTSCHBERG Switzerland

This railway tunnel from Kandersteg to Goppenstein is 14km (8.7miles) in length. Duration of the actual journey is 15 minutes, but loading and unloading formalities can take some time.

Services
Frequent with no advance booking necessary

Charges (in Swiss Francs)

Motorcycles	16
Cars (including passengers)	25
Car/caravan	50

A full timetable and tariff is available from the Swiss National Tourist Office (see Switzerland - Tourist information for address) or at most Swiss frontier crossings.

ALBULA TUNNEL Switzerland

Thusis (723 metres, 2372ft) - Samedan (1722 metres, 5650ft). The railway tunnel is 5.9km (3.5 miles) long. It will accept vehicles, but you must give notice. Thusis telephone 081 811113 and Samedan telephone 082 65404. Journey time 90 minutes.

Services
9 trains daily southbound; 6 trains daily northbound.

Charges (in Swiss franc)

Cars (including driver) & Motorcycles	135
Additional passengers	24
Car/caravan	270

FURKA TUNNEL Switzerland

Oberwald (1367 metres, 4482ft)-Realp (1539 metres, 5046ft). Railway tunnel is 15.4km (9.5 miles) long. Journey time 15 minutes.

Services
Hourly from 06.50-21.00

Charges (in Swiss Francs)

Motorcycles	19
Cars (including passengers)	36
Car/caravan	55

OBERALP RAILWAY Switzerland

Andermatt (1444 metres, 4737ft)-Sedrun (1441 metres, 4728ft). Journey duration 50 minutes.

Booking
Advance booking is necessary;
Andermatt telephone 044 67220, Sedrun tel 086 91137.

Services
2-4 trains daily, winter only (from October-April).

Charges (in Swiss francs)

Cars (including driver)	73
Additional passengers	9
Car/caravan	146

TAUERN TUNNEL Austria

Bockstein (1131 metres, 3711ft)(near Badgastein)-Mallnitz, 8.5km (5.5 miles) long.
Maximum dimensions, caravans and trailers: height 8ft 10.5in, width 8ft 2.5in.

Booking
Advance booking unnecessary (except for request trains), but motorists must report at least 30 minutes before departure. Drivers must drive their vehicles on and off the wagon.

Services
At summer weekends, trains run approximately every half-hour in both directions, 06.30-22.30hrs; and every half-hour at night. For the rest of the year, there is an hourly service from 06.30-22.30hrs (23.30hrs on Fri and Sat from 7 July-9 September). Journey time 12 minutes.

Charges (in Austrian schillings)

Motorcycles (with or without sidecar)	100
Cars (including passengers)	190
Caravans	80

LOCAL AND INTERNATIONAL CALLS

It is no more difficult to use the telephone abroad than it is at home. It only appears to be so because of unfamiliar language and equipment. The following chart may help with elementary principles when making local calls from public callboxes, but try to get help if you encounter language difficulties.

International Direct Dial (IDD) calls can be made from many public callboxes abroad, avoiding surcharges imposed by most hotels.

Types of callboxes from which IDD calls can be made are identified in the chart. You will need to dial the international code, international country code (for the UK it is 44), the telephone dialling code (omitting the initial '0'), followed by the number. Use higher-denomination coins for IDD calls to ensure reasonable periods of conversation before the coin expiry warning. The equivalent of £2 should allow for a reasonable amount of time.

Cardphones are in general use; phonecards may be purchased from a post office or shop in the vicinity.

The introduction of the Euro will make calling from European countries much easier for the traveller.

Country	Insert coin/card before or after lifting receiver	Dialling tone	Making local and national calls
AUSTRIA	After (instructions in English in many callboxes)		
BELGIUM	After	Same as UK	Precede number with relevant area code where necessary
FRANCE	After	Continuous tone	Dial 0 before the 9 digit-number
GERMANY	After	Continuous tone	Precede number with relevant area code when necessary
ITALY	Before		Precede number with relevant area code when necessary
LUXEMBOURG	After	Same as UK	There are no area codes
NETHERLANDS	After (instructions in English in all callboxes)		
PORTUGAL	After	Same as UK	Precede number with relevant area code when necessary
SPAIN	After (instructions in English in many callboxes)		Do not press button to left of the dial or you may lose your money
SWITZERLAND	After	Continuous tone	Precede number with relevant area code when necessary

Some useful premium rate numbers for help and advice on motoring abroad

Hints & Advice

Austria	09003 401 866
Belgium	09003 401 867
France	09003 401 869
Germany	09003 401 870
Italy	09003 401 874
Luxembourg	09003 401 875
Netherlands	09003 401 876
Portugal	09003 401 878

Spain	09003 401 879
Switzerland	09003 401 881

Weather Forecasts

Channel Crossing & Northern France	09003 401 361
World wide City by City 6-day reports	09003 411 212

Other Useful Information

French Motorway Tolls	09003 401 884
European Fuel Prices	09003 401 883

Port Information

Hampshire/Dorset Ports	09003 401 891
Kent Ports	09003 401 890

Calls to 09003 numbers are charged at 60p per minute at all times.

International callbox identification	What to dial for the UK	What to dial for the Irish Republic
All public callboxes	00 44	00 353
Payphones identified with European flags. Cardphones	00 44	00 353
All payphones. Cardphones	00 44	00 353
Payphones and cardphones marked 'International'	00 44	00 353
All public callboxes	00 44	00 353
Roadside callboxes	00 44	00 353
All payphones. Cardphones	00 44	00 353
Payphones with notice in English. Cardphones	00 44	00 353
International calls can be made from all public callboxes	00 44	00 353
All phones including cardphones	00 44	00 353

SAMPLE BOOKING LETTERS FOR RESERVATIONS

Please use block capitals and enclose an International Reply Coupon, obtainable from post offices. Be sure to fill in your own name and address, including the post code and the country.

ENGLISH
Dear Sir,
I intend to stay at your site for ....days, arriving on.............(date and month) and departing on...................(date and month).

We are a party of ....people, including....adults and ....children (aged..........) and would like a pitch for ....tent(s) and/or parking space for our car/caravan/caravan trailer.

We would like to hire a tent/caravan/bungalow.

Please quote full charges when replying and advise on the deposit required, which will be forwarded without delay.

FRENCH
Monsieur,
Je me propose de séjourner à votre terrain de camping pour ....jours, depuis le..... jusqu'au..........

Nous sommes........personnes en tout, y compris ....adultes et ....enfants (âgés de......) et nous aurons besoin d'un emplacement pour ....tente(s), et/ou un parking pour notre voiture/caravane/remorque.

Nous voudrions louer une tente/caravane/bungalow.

Veuillez me donner dans votre réponse une idée de vos prix, m'indiquant en même temps le montant qu'il faut payer en avance, ce qui vous sera envoyé sans délai.

GERMAN
Sehr geehrter Herr!
Ich beabsichtige, mich auf Ihrem Campingplatz ....Tage aufzuhalten, und zwar vom.....bis zum......

Wir sind im ganzen ....Personen, ...Erwachsene und ....Kinder (in Alter von......), und benötigen Platz für Zelt(e) und/oder unseren Wagen/Wohnwagen/Wohnwagenanhänger.

Wir möchten ein Zelt/Wohnwagen/Bungalow mieten.

Bitte, geben Sie mir in Ihrem Antwortschreiben die vollen Preise bekannt, und ebenso die Höhe der von mir zu leistenden Anzahlung, die Ihnen alsdann unverzüglich überwiesen wird.

ITALIAN
Egregio Signore,
Ho intenzione di remanere presso di voi per .....giorni. Arriverò il.....e partirò il......

Siamo un gruppo di.......persone in totale, compreso ......adulti e ......bambini (de età.....) e vorrremo un posto per ......tenda(tende) e/o spazio per parcheggiare la nostra vetture/carovana/roulette.

Desideriamo affittare una tenda/carovana/bungalow.

Vi preghiamo di quotare i prezzi completi quando ci risponderete, e darci informazioni sul deposito richiesto, che vi sarà rimesso senza ritardo.

SPANISH
Muy señor mio,
Desearia me reservara espacio por ......dias, a partir del.......hasta el......

Nuestro grupo comprende .....personas todo comprendido, ...adultos y ....niños (.......de años de edad). Necesitarimos un espacio por......tienda(s) y/o espacio para apacar nuestro choche/caravana/remolque.

Deseariamos alquilar una tienda de campana/caravan/bungalow.

Le ruego nos comunique los precios y nos informe sobre el depósito que debemos remitirle.

COUNTRY MAP SECTION

AUSTRIA

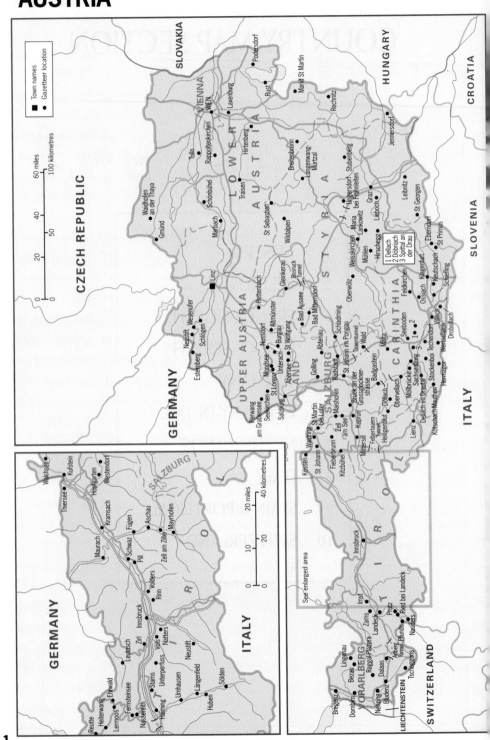

1

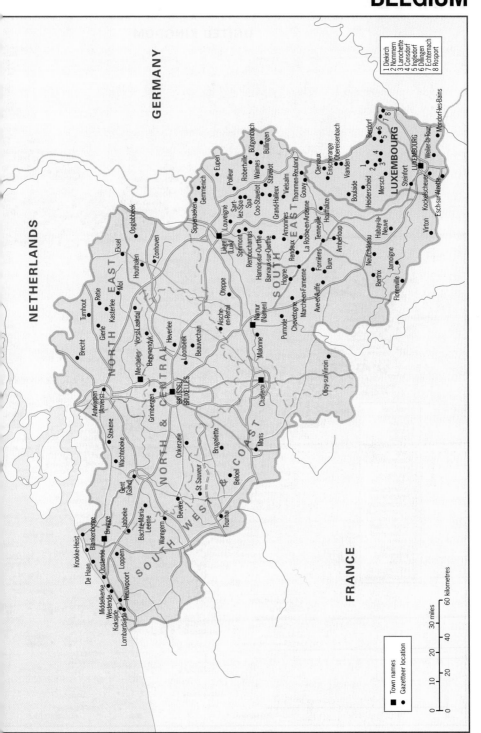

BELGIUM

1 Diekirch
2 Nommern
3 Larochette
4 Consdorf
5 Ingeldorf
6 Dillingen
7 Echternach
8 Rosport

GERMANY

NETHERLANDS

LUXEMBOURG

FRANCE

Mondorf-les-Bains
Esch-sur-Alzette
Weiler-la-Tour
LUXEMBOURG
Kockelscheuer
Virton
Stenfort
Mersch
Oberesenbach
Vianden
Bergdorf
Clervaux
Erscherange
Boulaide
Heiderscheid
Habay-la-Neuve
Neufchâteau
Florenville
Jamoigne
Bertrix
Bure
Amberloup
Tenneville
Houffalize
Hotton
Forrières
Ave-et-Auffe
Marchen-Famenne
La Roche-Ardenne
Rendeux
Hogne
Marche-Famenne
Barvaux-sur-Ourthe
Hamoir-sur-Ourthe
Rembuchamps
Chevetogne
Purnode
Malonne
Namur
(Namen)
Aische-en-Refail
Beauvechain
Loonbeek
Heverlee
Heverlee
Gouvy
Thommen-Reuland
Welsalm
Arnonnes
Grand-Halleux
Coo-Stavelot
Stavelot
Spa
Sart-lez-Spa
Spontin
Spimont
Liège
(Luik)
Louveigne
Louveigne
Spijdenaeken
Gemmenich
Gouvy
Polleur
Robertville
Waimes
Bullingen
Büllingen
Eupen
Bürgenbach
Onglabbeek
Zonhoven
Houthalen
Retie
Gierle
Kasterlee
Mol
Eksel
Turnhout
Brecht
Vorst-Laakdal
Mechelen
Begijnendijk
Antwerpen
(Anvers)
Grimbergen
BRUSSEL
BRUXELLES
Charleroi
Olloy-sur-Viroin
Mons
Brugelette
Onkerzele
St Sauveur
Beloeil
Bevere
Tournai
Waregem
Bachte-Maria-Leerne
Gent
(Gand)
Jabbeke
Loppem
Wachtebeke
Stekene
Brugge
Blankenberge
De Haan
Oostende
Middelkerke
Westende
Koksijde
Lombardsijde
Nieuwpoort
Knokke-Heist

NORTH & CENTRAL
NORTH EAST
SOUTH EAST
SOUTH & COAST
SOUTH WEST

■ Town names
● Gazetteer location

0   10   20   30 miles
0   20   40   60 kilometres

2

FRANCE

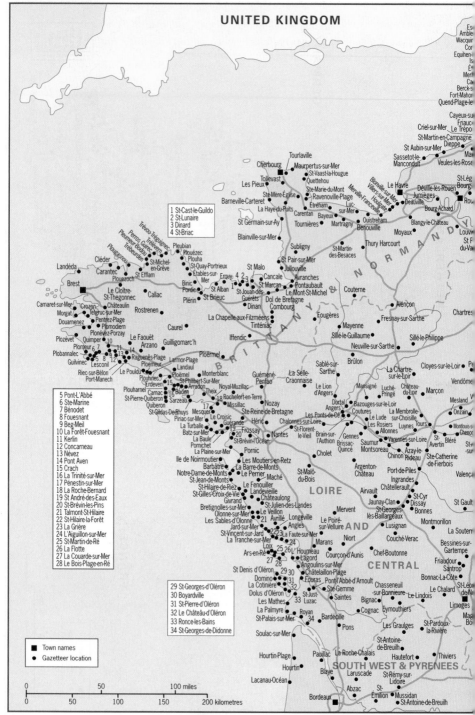

BELGIUM

NETHERLANDS

GERMANY

LUXEMBOURG

ort-Philippe
Oye Dunkerque Bray-Dunes
Plage Coudekerque
Audruicq
Tournehem Éperlecques
unes Serques St-Jans-Cappel
ques Ardres Lynde
Thiembronne Lille
Montreuil-sur-Mer Beuvry La Neuville
Tollent Houdain St-Amand-
les-Eaux
Boubers-sur-
ers-sur-Authie ronchaux Canche Potelle Maubeuge
alery-sur-Somme Boiry-Notre- Felleries
Moyenneville Amplier Dame Signy-le-Petit
Blangy-sur-Bresle
Bertangles Hirson
Proyart Bourg-Fidèle Monthermé
Poix-de-Picardie St-Quentin
P A R I S & Seraucourt-le-Grand Charleville-
Orvilliers-Sorel Mézières Sedan
N O R T H Salency Laon
Beauvais Berny-Rivière Presles-Vailly-sur-Aisne
St-Leu- Attichy Soissons Charnouille
d'Esserent Villers- Grandpré Sivry-sur-
Hélon Meuse
Ste-Menehould Verdun

es-la-Vallée Gouvieux Lauterbourg
aisons-Laffitte Acy-en-Multien La Ferte- Harskirchen Baerenthal
nes- Torcy Jablines sous-Jouarre Oberbronn
eine Villevaude St-Cyr-sur-Morin Châlons-Marne **A L S A C E &** Saverne
uillet PARIS Plessis-Feu Sézanne **L O R R A I N E** Dabo Wasselonne
Marne-la-Vallée Aussoux Conflans- Éclaron- Obernai Strasbourg
Montigny-le- Touquin sur-Seine Braucourt Villers-lès-Nancy Schirmeck St-Pierre
es- Bretonneux Melun Tonnoy Le Hohwald Aubure Dambach-la-Ville
St-Chéron St Hilaire- Giffaumont Chatonrupt Thonnance- Celles-sur-Plaine Sélestat
issy-la-Cutte sous-Romilly les-Moulins Gemaingoutte Anould Ribeauvillé
erville Milly-la-Forêt Grez-sur-Loing Corcieux Turckheim Kaysersberg
Boulancourt Nemours Troyes Radonvilliers Granges-sur-Vologne Colmar Riquewihr
Mesnil-St Père Soulaines-Dhuys Le Tholy 40 39 38 37 Biesheim
ent-Novan Nibelle Froncles La Bresse 44 Ste-Croix-en-Plaine
B U R G U N D Y & Bar-sur-Aube Fontenoy-le- 41 43 Wattwiller
Montargis Bourbonne- Château Metzeral 42 Cernay
C H A M P A G N E Châtillon-sur-Seine les-Bains St-Maurice-sur-Moselle Urbès Mulhouse
Marcenay Rie-les-Eaux Bannes Masevaux Burnhaupt-le-Haut
Olivet Jargeau Auxerre Ancy-le-Franc Selongey Bourg **A L P S &** Rougemont Heimsbrunn
Sully-sur- Gien Villeneuve- Vermenton Montbard Venarey- Port-sur-Saône **E A S T** Seppois-le-Bas
Loire les-Genêts Clamecy les-Laumes Dijon Huanne- L'Isle-sur-le-Doubs 35 Luttenbach
Pierrefitte- Bonny-sur- Accolay Avallon Vandenesse- Montmartin 36 Wihr-au-Val
sur-Sauldre Loire Andryes en-Auxois Besançon Chalezeule 37 Munster
Cosne-sur-Loire Saulieu Premeaux Auxonne Chevigny Ornans 38 Xonrupt/Longemer
Pougues-les-Eaux Montapas Arnay-le- Beaune Seurre Dole Ounans Pontarlier 39 Gérardmer
Bourges Montsauche Duc Meursault Parcey 40 Vagney
Bazolles Epinac Mouchard 41 Kruth
St-Péreuse Chagny Arbois Malbuisson 42 Bussang
St-Amand- St-Honoré Champagnole 43 Moosch
Montrond Toulon-sur- Tazilly Laives Lons-le- Marigny 44 Eguisheim
Boussac- St-Bonnet-Troncais Bourbon-Lancy Arroux Gigny-sur- Saunier Doucier **S W I T Z E R L A N D**
tgivray Bourg Braize Isle-et-Bardais Issy-l'Evêque Saône Patornay
Urçay Bourbon- Gueugnon Uchizy Clairvaux- St-Claude Lugrin
Chéniers Lapeyrouse Sazeret l'Archambault Digoin Charolles Pont- les-Lacs St-Disdille Evian-les-Bains
Châtel- Dompierre-les-Ormes de-Vaux Messery Thonon- Argentière
Néris-les-Bains Jenzat de-Neuvre Varennes-sur-Allier Gibles Matour Mâcon Montrevel- Divonne- les-Bains Chamonix-Mont-Blanc
Vichy Paray-sous-Briailles Crêches-sur-Saône Thoissey en-Bresse Bellegarde-sur- Neydens
St-Gal-sur-Sioule Ebreuil Châtel Fleurie Bourg-en-Bresse Valserine Choisy La Clusaz
St-Gervais-d'Auvergne Loubeyrat Montagne Ars-sur-Formans Villars- Hautecourt Seyssel Argentière
Miremont Châtel Guyon les-Dombes Romanèche St-Gervais-les-Bains
St-Ours St Jodard Dardilly 49 48 Séez Landry
Pontgibaud Royat St-Rémy-sur-Durolle Anse Pollionnay St Innocent-Brison 48 50 Bourg- La Rosière-de-Montvalezan
Nébouzat 52 Dallet **A U V E R G N E** Verrières-en-Forez Mornant Lyon Le Bourget-du-Lac 47 St-Maurice Tignes-les-Brévières
Cournon-d'Auvergne Meyrieu Novalaise 46 La Rochette Plagne-
Le Mont-Dore 53 Murol Orcet St Clément- Les 45 Allevard Montchavin
hamps-sur-Tarentaine Olliergues de-Valorgue Ste- les-Étangs Montmélian La Ferrière
Egletons Jassat St-Pierre- Les Martres-de-Veyre St Amand-Roche-Savine Catherine Les Miribel-les-Échelles St-Avre
Saignes Colamine Pradeaux Champagnac-le-Vieux Verdioz Abrets Presle
Trizac Riom-ès-Montagnes Lempdes Bourg- Voiron 45 Plagne-
St Martin-Valmeroux Massiac Sembadel-Gare Argental St-Clair-du-Rhône St-Pierre-de-Chartreuse
Allanche Langeac St-Sorlin-en- Autrans Grenoble Le Bourg-d'Oisans 45 Entre-deux-Guiers
St-Gérons Ferrières-St-Mary Yssingeaux Tain l'Hermitage Vallorie Méaudre 46 St-Jean-de-Couz
Ruynes-en- St-Paul-lès- Les Egats Val-des-Prés 47 Aillon-le-Jeune
St-Jacques-des-Blats Margeride le Puy Tournon-sur-Rhône Gresse- Romans 48 Bout-du-lac
Arpajon-sur-Cère Vic-sur-Cère St Just Alleyras Goudet en-Vercors La Salle-en-Beaumont 49 Talloires
Arnac Thérondels Neuvéglise St-Alban-sur-Limagnole Valence Choranche 50 Doussard
S O U T H Chabeuil La Chapelle- Guillestre 51 St Jorioz
C O A S T & R I V I E R A en-Vercors 52 Montaigut-le-Blanc
53 St Nectaire

ITALY

3

FRANCE

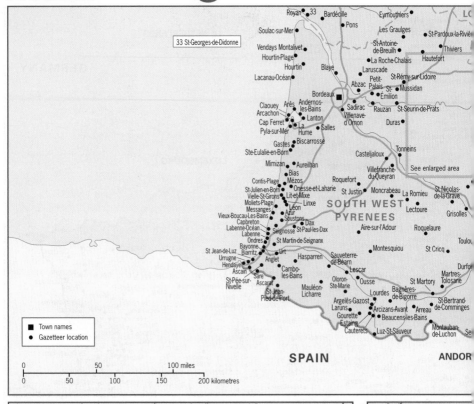

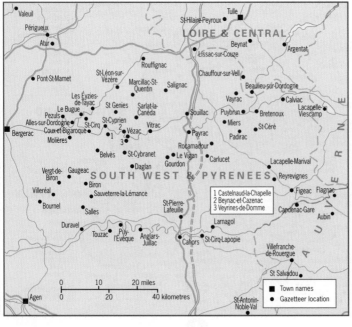

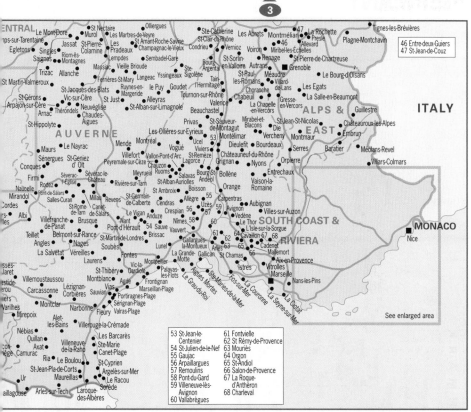

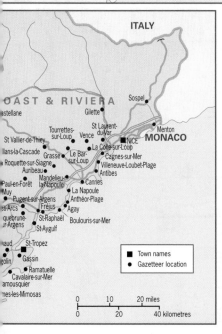

GERMANY

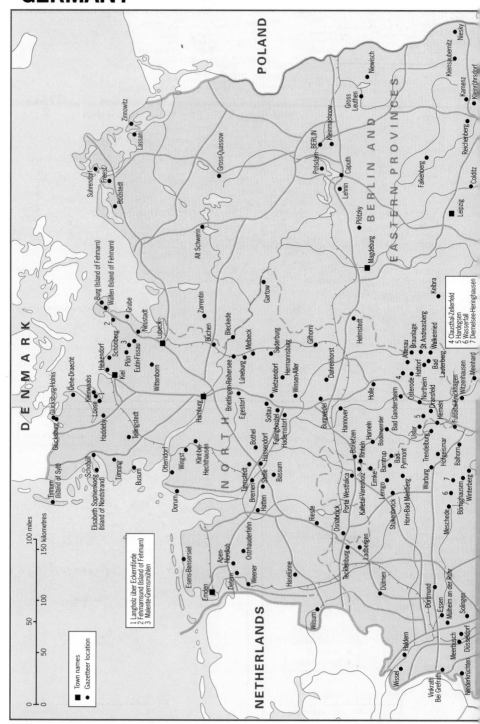

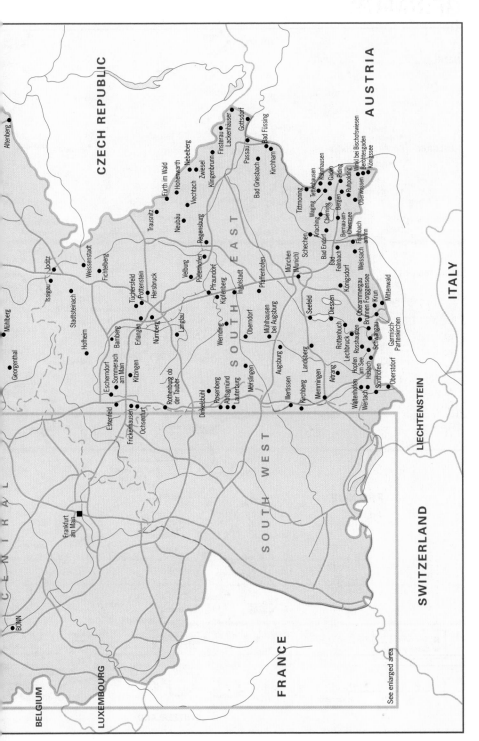

5

GERMANY

NETH

Aachen
Heimbach
Schleiden
Hellenthal
BELGIUM
Monschau
Stadtkyll
Prüm
Waxweiler
Utscheid
Neuerburg
Oberweis
Obersgegen
Irrel
LUXEMBOURG
Schweich
Könen
Trier
Kell
Reinsfeld
Saarburg
Zerf
Losheim
Saarlouis

Drolshagen
KÖLN
Liblar
BONN
Mehlem
Bad Honnef
Bad Breisig
Dorsel an der Ahr
Müllenbach
Schalkenmehren
Gillenfeld
Bernkastel-Wehlen
Kröv
Mülheim
Bernkastel-Kues
Leiwen
Heidenburg
Niederwörresbach
Birkenfeld
Schönenberg
Cochem
Nehren
Bullay
Senheim
Mesenich
Treis-Karden
Burgen
Hausbay
Lingerhahn
Kirn
Asbacherhütte
Sensweiler Mühle
Gerbach
Wolfstein
Trippstadt
Dahn
Ingenheim

Attendorn
Olpe
Niedereisenhausen
Mittelhof
Oberlahr
Steinen
Seck
Montabaur
Weilburg
Runkel
Braunfels
Koblenz
Bad Ems
Diez
Dausenau
Lahnstein
St Goarshausen
St.Goar
Lorch
Bacharach
Rüdesheim
Guldental
Lichtenburg
Bad Dürkheim
MANNHEIM
Heidelberg
Neckargemünd
Mörtelstein
Ostringen
Karlsruhe

CENTRAL

Idstein
Königstein
FRANKFURT AM MAIN
Mainz-Kostheim
Dreieich-Offenthal
Mörfelden-Walldorf
Lindenfels
Fürth im Odenwald
Hirschhorn am Neckar
Neckarzimmern

Zwesten
Heringen
Kirchheim
Heimertshausen
Grünberg
Schotten
Schlüchtern
Tann
Schachen
Rothemann
Bad Kissingen
Gemünden am Main
Gemünden-Hofstetten
Neustadt
SOUTH EAST
Lengfurt
Michelstadt
Wertheim
Kirchzell
Gammelsbach
Altneudorf
Bad Mergentheim
Creglingen
Buchhorn bei Öhringen
Löwenstein
Schwäbisch Ha
Murrhardt
Ellwangen

Grundmühle bei Quentel

FRANCE

Rheinmünster
Kehl
Bühl
Schapbach
Ettenheim
Herbolzheim
Waldkirch
Freiburg im Breisgau
St Peter
Kirchzarten
Staufen
Münstertal
Sulzburg
Neuenburg
Todtnau
Lörrach
Waldshut

Pforzheim
Höfen an der Enz
Achern
Wildbad im Schwarzwald
Altensteig
Hallwangen
Freudenstadt
Steinach
Alpirsbach
Schiltach
Bad Dürrheim
Titisee-Neustadt
Lenzkirch
Badenweiler
Schömberg
Bad Liebenzell
Stammheim
Liebelsberg
Horb
Tübingen
Erpfingen
Donaueschingen
Hausen
Ludwigshafen am Bodensee
STUTTGART
Laichingen
Bad Schussenried
Schwäbisch Gmünd

SOUTH WEST

Überlingen
Markdorf
Dingelsdorf
Nussdorf
Horn Bodensee
Uhldingen
Kressbronn
Lindau im Bodensee
Isn
Weiler-Simmerberg
Aach-Oberstau

SWITZERLAND

AUSTRI

■ Town names
● Gazetteer location

0   10   20   30 miles
0   20   40   60 kilometres

NETHERLANDS

Town names
Gazetteer location

0   20   40   60 miles
0   50   100 kilometres

NORTH

Hee
West
Terschelling
Leeuwarden
Harlingen
Franeker
De Koog
De Cocksdorp
Makkum
Hindeloopen
Den Helder
Groote Keeten
Callantsoog
St Maartenszee
Den Hoorn
Koudum
Sondel
Groet
Andijk
Noord Scharwoude
Egmond aan Zee
Heiloo
Alkmaar
Berkhout
Wijdenes
Velsen-Zuid
Edam
Uitdam
Haarlem
Vogelenzang
Halfweg
Noordwijk aan Zee
Rijnsburg
Aalsmeer
Katwijk aan Zee
Wassenaar
Leiden
Bilthoven
Soest
Utrecht
DEN HAAG
's-Gravenzande
Hoek Van Holland
Delft
Zevenhuizen
Oostvoorne
Brielle
Rockanje
Barendrecht
Ouddorp
Hellevoetsluis
Renesse
Burgh-Haamstede
Brouwershaven
Kamperland
Kortgene
Westkapelle
Zoutelande
Koudekerke
Nieuwvliet
Vlissingen
Arnemuiden
Wemeldinge
Breskens
Groede
Retranchement
Hoek
Baarland
Hengstdijk
Hoogerheide
Sluis

Lauwersoog
Delfzijl
Bergum
Groningen
Harkstede
Opende
Onnen
Wedde
Annen
Assen
Amen
Gasselte
Borger
Wateren
Diever
Grolloo
Steenwijk
Dwingeloo
Emmen
Ruinen
Blokzijl
Urk
Dronten
Hattem
Dalfsen
Reutum
Nunspeet
Wezep
Luttenberg
Denekamp
Ermelo
Ernst
Delden
Putten
Vaassen
Holten
Markelo
Hengelo
Apeldoorn
Diepenheim
Enschede
Kootwijk
Beekbergen
Lochem
Buurse
Hoenderloo
Eerbeek
Hengelo
Neede
Haaksbergen
Maarn
Epe
Ruurlo
Doorn
Laag-Soeren
Lathum
Winterswijk
Rhenen
Arnhem
Doesburg
Doetinchem
Wageningen
Babberich
Kesteren
Nijmegen
Appeltern
Herpen
Heumen
Plasmolen
Hoeven
Breda
Oosterhout
St Anthonis
Afferden
Roosendaal
Rijen
Tilburg
Boxtel
St Oedenrode
Well
Oisterwijk
Eindhoven
Venray
Broekhuizenvorst
Baarle Nassau
Hilvarenbeek
Mierlo
Sevenum
Arden
Lage Mierde
Eersel
Soerendonk
Maasbree
Venlo
Bergeyk
Baarlo
Luyksgestel
Weert
Roermond
Stramproy
Echt
Berg en Terblijt
Landgraaf
Maastricht
Valkenburg

CENTRAL

SOUTH

Rotterdam
AMSTERDAM
Vogelenzang
Mijnden
Soest

1 Domburg
2 Oostkapelle
3 Vrouwenpolder
4 Middelburg

1 2 3
4

BELGIUM

GERMANY

FRANCE

LUX

7

ITALY

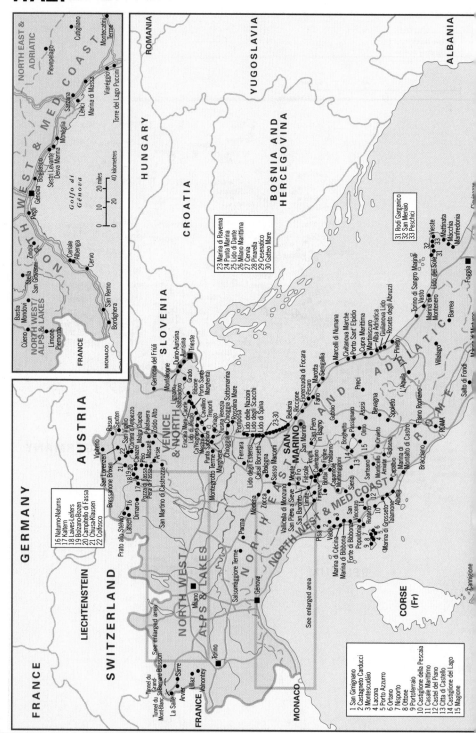

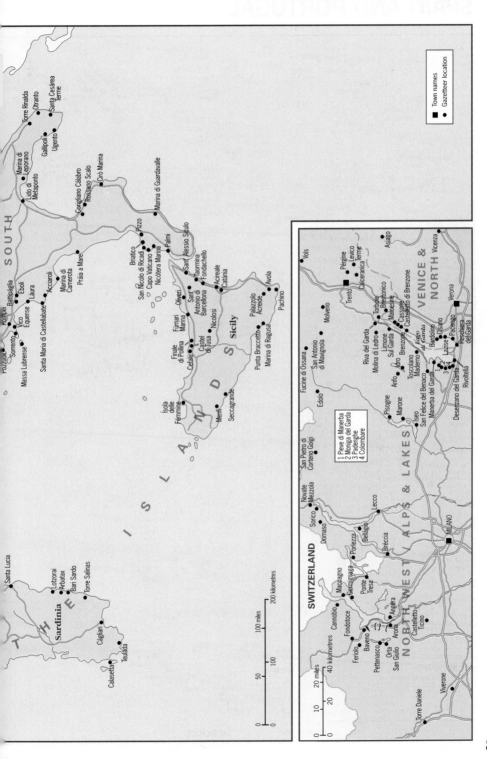

SOUTH

Torre Rinalda
Otranto
Santa Cesarea Terme
Gallipoli
Ugento
Marina di Leporano
Lido di Metaponto
Corigliano Calabro
Rossano Scalo
Ciro Marina
Marina di Guardavalle

Pozzuoli
Pompei
Sorrento
Massa Lubrense
Vico Equense
Santa Maria di Castellabate
Battipaglia
Eboli
Laura
Acciaroli
Marina di Camerota
Praia a Mare
Pizzo
Briatico
San Nicolo di Ricadi
Capo Vaticano
Nicotera Marina
Palmi
Sant' Alessio Siculo
Taormina
Fondachello
Acireale
Catania

Fumari Marina
Olivieri
Sant' Antonio di Barcellona
Nicolosi
Finale di Pollina
Cefalù
Castel di Tusa
Palazzolo Acreide
Avola
Pachino
Punta Braccetto
Marina di Ragusa

Isola delle Femmine
Menfi
Seccagrande

ISLANDS

Sicily

I · S · L · E · S

Sardinia

Santa Lucia
Lotzorai
Arbatax
Bari Sardo
Torre Salinas
Cagliari
Teulada
Calasetta

T · H · E

0   50   100 miles
0   100   200 kilometres

SWITZERLAND

Novate Mezzola
Sorico
Domaso
Maccagno
Germignaga
Porlezza
Bellagio
Breccia
Lecco
Cannobio
Fondotoce
Ponte Tresa
Feriolo
Baveno
Pettenasco
Orta
San Giulio
Arona
Angera
Castelletto Ticino

NORTH WEST

Viverone
Torre Daniele

ALPS & LAKES

MILANO

San Pietro di Corteno Golgi
Fucine di Ossana
Edolo
San Antonio di Mavignola
Molveno
Vols
Pergine
Levico Terme
Asiago
Calceranica Terme
Trento
Riva del Garda
Molina di Ledro
Limone Sul Garda
Torbole
Nago
Arco
Brenzone
Castelletto di Brenzone
Bipentonico
Cassone
Malcesine
Torri del Benaco
Toscolano
Maderno
San Felice del Benaco
Manerba del Garda
Pisogne
Marone
Iseo
Bardolino
Cisano
Lazise
Pacengo
Peschiera del Garda
Rivoltella
Deserzano del Garda
Verona
Vicenza

VENICE & NORTH

Lago di Garda

1 Pieve di Manerba
2 Moniga del Garda
3 Padenghe
4 Colombare

Town names
Gazetteer location

20 miles
0   10   20
0   20   40 kilometres

8

SPAIN AND PORTUGAL

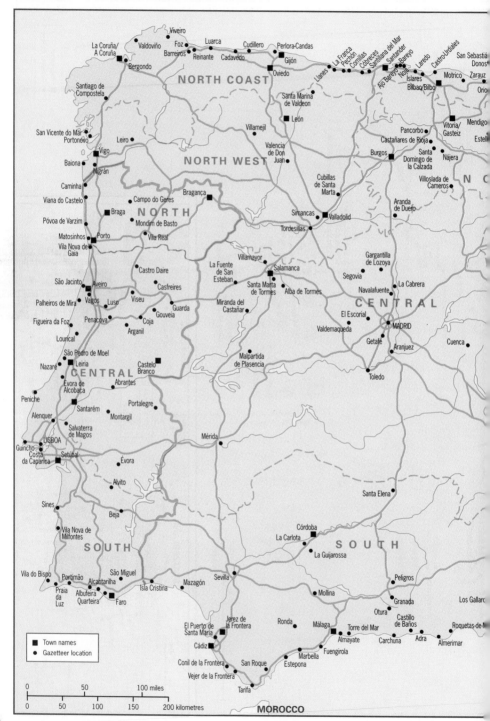

- Town names
- Gazetteer location

| 0 | 50 | 100 miles |

| 0 | 50 | 100 | 150 | 200 kilometres |

FRANCE

Oricain
Pamplona/
Iruñea Tiermas Hecho Torla
Bossost La Bordeta
La Guingueta
Espot ANDORRA
Ribera de Cardós
Biescas
Jaca Bonansa
Labuerda
Huesca La Puebla
de Castro

T H E   E A S T

NORTH EAST
COAST

Saviñan Zaragoza
Calatayud Vilanova
de Prades
Nuevalos BARCELONA

See enlarged area

Salou
Mont-Roig del Camp Cambrils
L'Hospitalet de l'infant
L'Ametlla de Mar

Alcanar
Vinaroz
Peñiscola Benicarló
Alcoceber
Albarracin Torreblanca
Oropesa del Mar
Benicasim
Nules

Puebla de Farnals
Valencia

Islas Baleares

Palma

Jaraco
Miramar Playa
Daimus
Oliva Denia
Benisa Moraira
Alfaz del Pi Altea
Campello Benidorm
Villajoyosa
Baños Alicante/Alacant
de Fortuna
La Marina
Guardamar del Segura
Murcia
Los Alcazares
Isla Plana La Manga del
Mar Menor
Bolnuevo Cartagena
Aguilas
jácar

FRANCE

ANDORRA
Guils de Cerdanya
Santa Juliá Bellver de Puigcerdá
de Lória Cerdanya
Vilallonga de Ter
Túnel Guardiola de
del Cadi Bergueda
NORTH Ripoll
EAST Saldes
NORTH EAST
COAST
Solsona
Taradell
Sabadell

Llançá
Castelló d'Empuries
Sant Pere Pescador
l'Escala l'Estartit
Torroella de Montgri
Pals
Begur
Sant Antoni Palafrugell
de Calonge Pálamós
Castell d'Aro
Santa Cristina d'Aro La Platja d'Aro
Tossa de Mar Sant Feliu de Guixols
Lloret de Mar
Blanes
Santa Susana Malgrat de Mar
Sant Cebriá de Vallalta Pineda de Mar
Arenys de Mar Calella
de la
Costa
El Masnou
Badalona
Viladecans BARCELONA
Gavá
SOUTH
EAST
COAST
Santa Oliva Vilanova
Roda de Bará i la Geltrú Sitges
El Cunit Cubelles
Vendrell
Tamarit
Tarragona

0   20   40 miles
0   20   40   60 kilometres

9

SWITZERLAND

Readers' Report Form

Please send this form to:
   Editor, Caravan & Camping Europe
   AA Lifestyle Guides,
   Fanum House,
   Basingstoke RG21 4EA

or fax: 01256 491647
or e-mail: lifestyleguides@theAA.com

Please use this form to recommend any caravan and camping park where you have stayed, whether it is included in the guide or not. You can also help us to improve the guide by completing the short questionnaire on the reverse.

The AA does not undertake to arbitrate between guide readers and campsites, or to obtain compensation or engage in correspondence.

Date:

Your name (block capitals)

Your address (block capitals)

....

....

....

e-mail address: ....

Name of Park:

Comments

....

....

....

....

....

....

....

(please attach a separate sheet if necessary)

Please tick here if you DO NOT wish to recieve details of AA offers or products ☐

PTO

Readers' Report Form

How often do you visit a caravan park or camp site?

Once a year ☐   Twice a year ☐   3 times a year ☐   More than 3 times ☐

How long do you generally stay at a park or site?

One night ☐   Up to a week ☐   1 week ☐   2 weeks ☐   Over 2 weeks ☐

Do you have a: tent ☐   caravan ☐   motorhome ☐

Which of the following in most important when choosing a site?

☐ Location   ☐ Toilet/Washing facilities
☐ Personal Recommendation   ☐ Leisure facilities
☐ Other

Do you prefer self-contained, cubicled washrooms with WC, shower and washhand basin to open-plan separate facilities?

Yes ☐   No ☐   Don't Mind ☐

Do you buy any other camping guides? If so, which ones?

....

Have you read the introductory pages in this guide? ....

Do you use the location atlas in this guide? ....

Which of the following most influences your choice of park from this guide?

Gazetteer entry information and description ☐

Photograph ☐   Advertisement ☐

Do you have any suggestions to improve the guide?

....

....

....

....

....

Thank you for taking the time to complete this form

Please send this form to:
   Editor, Caravan & Camping Europe
   AA Lifestyle Guides,
   Fanum House,
   Basingstoke RG21 4EA

**Readers'
Report form**

or fax: 01256 491647
or e-mail: lifestyleguides@theAA.com

Please use this form to recommend any caravan and camping park where you have stayed, whether it is included in the guide or not. You can also help us to improve the guide by completing the short questionnaire on the reverse.

The AA does not undertake to arbitrate between guide readers and campsites, or to obtain compensation or engage in correspondence.

Date:

Your name (block capitals)

Your address (block capitals)

....

....

....

e-mail address: ....

Name of Park:

Comments

....

....

....

....

....

....

....

(please attach a separate sheet if necessary)

Please tick here if you DO NOT wish to recieve details of AA offers or products ☐

PTO

Readers' Report Form

How often do you visit a caravan park or camp site?

Once a year ☐   Twice a year ☐   3 times a year ☐   More than 3 times ☐

How long do you generally stay at a park or site?

One night ☐   Up to a week ☐   1 week ☐   2 weeks ☐   Over 2 weeks ☐

Do you have a: tent ☐   caravan ☐   motorhome ☐

Which of the following in most important when choosing a site?

☐ Location   ☐ Toilet/Washing facilities
☐ Personal Recommendation   ☐ Leisure facilities
☐ Other

Do you prefer self-contained, cubicled washrooms with WC, shower and washhand basin to open-plan separate facilities?

Yes ☐   No ☐   Don't Mind ☐

Do you buy any other camping guides? If so, which ones?

....

Have you read the introductory pages in this guide? ....

Do you use the location atlas in this guide? ....

Which of the following most influences your choice of park from this guide?

Gazetteer entry information and description ☐

Photograph ☐   Advertisement ☐

Do you have any suggestions to improve the guide?

....

....

....

....

....

Thank you for taking the time to complete this form